PETERSON'S

HONORS PROGRAMS

The Only Guide to Honors Programs at More Than 350 Colleges and Universities Across the Country

By DR. JOAN DIGBY
Long Island University, C.W. Post Campus

Peterson's
Princeton, New Jersey

About Peterson's

Peterson's is the country's largest educational information/communications company, providing the academic, consumer, and professional communities with books, software, and on-line services in support of lifelong education access and career choice. Well-known references include Peterson's annual guides to private schools, summer programs, colleges and universities, graduate and professional programs, financial aid, international study, adult learning, and career guidance. Peterson's Web site at petersons.com is the only comprehensive—and most heavily traveled—education resource on the Internet. The site carries all of Peterson's fully searchable major databases and includes financial aid sources, test-prep help, job postings, direct inquiry and application features, and specially created Virtual Campuses for every accredited academic institution and summer program in the U.S. and Canada, offering in-depth narratives, announcements, and multimedia features.

Visit Peterson's on the World Wide Web at
http://www.petersons.com

The colleges and universities represented in this book recognize that federal laws, where applicable, require compliance with Title IX (Education Amendments of 1972), Title VII (Civil Rights Act of 1964), and Section 504 of the Rehabilitation Act of 1973 as amended, prohibiting discrimination on the basis of sex, race, color, handicap, or national or ethnic origin in their educational programs and activities, including admissions and employment.

Editorial inquiries concerning this book should be addressed to: Editor, Peterson's, P.O. Box 2123, Princeton, New Jersey 08543-2123

ISBN 1-56079-851-3

Composition and design by Peterson's

Printed in the United States of America

10 9 8 7 6 5 4 3 2 1

To my late secretary, Nancy Jane Meyer, and in her name all honors staff members whose boundless energy and selfless dedication infuse our programs with growth and life.

CONTENTS

▲

ACKNOWLEDGMENTS

▲

I have many people to thank for their assistance in writing this book. First I wish to acknowledge the National Collegiate Honors Council for changing the direction of my own professional life and letting honors education expand my love of college teaching. Within the organization I wish to thank all of the program directors and their staff members for gathering and contributing information. Among the members of NCHC who have brought this book together, I must also credit the Publications Board for their faith in and support of this project and—in alphabetical order—my colleagues Susanna Finnell, John Grady, Herbert Lasky, Ada Long, Bob Spurrier, and Len Zane, for contributions of their personal insight to the introduction. Without students, honors cannot exist, and to those students who gave their testimony and to my own student, Ken Corwin, whose computer skills helped me put together all the bits and bytes of information, my sincere thanks. I must also thank the administration of Long Island University for granting me sabbatical time to write this book. Credit for the final compilation must go to the energetic staff of editors and designers at Peterson's who have brought the work to light.

INTRODUCTION

▲

Dr. Joan Digby, Director of the Honors Program at
Long Island University, C.W. Post Campus

Who Are Honors Program Students?

If you have a strong academic record and think of yourself as a good student, then you should consider gaining admission to an honors program as part of your college education. Honors programs offer some of the finest undergraduate degrees available in American colleges and universities, and they may reward your past academic performance by awarding you scholarships that will contribute to paying for your higher education. This book is designed to help you think seriously and creatively about joining an honors program.

Who are you? You might be a high school junior making out your first college applications. You might be a community college student seeking to transfer to a four-year college. You might already be in a four-year college doing better than you had expected. You might be an international student, or a varsity athlete, or first violin in the campus orchestra. Or are you a returning student, an adult with a grown family striking out on your own to find a new career in the health professions? Honors programs admit students with many different backgrounds. See if you can find glimpses of yourself in the following profiles:

- "I have always kept up a 90 average and I did really well on the SATs. But I'm not just interested in studying. Sure I get A's on exams, but I'm also editor of the school paper and that takes most of my time. I don't know whether to go into journalism or computer graphics, but I'll decide that in college."
- "I'm a varsity baseball player, but I've always done well in academics and my coach wants me to keep up the 3.5 GPA. It's good for me and it's good for the team. I know I probably won't play professional ball, so I want to take my CPA exam in my senior year and get into a good accounting firm."
- "I never did very well in high school, and I won't tell you what I got on my ACTs, but I

loved my first college psychology class, and now I study hard and have a 3.4 GPA. I want to transfer to a four-year school and obtain a B.S. degree so that I can study further to become a clinical psychologist."
- "High school is boring. I'm taking some AP courses along with college English and college accounting. By the time I get to college I'll have a whole semester of credit, so I can start taking the classes I really want—philosophy and astronomy."
- "I always wanted to be a doctor but I hear that the competition for medical school admission gets harder every year. I need to get an edge, and I've heard that doing undergraduate research really helps. I hope I can do research work with my professor in organic chemistry. She's working on some interesting compounds and it would be exciting to get experience in her lab."
- "I don't know what I want to major in. I sort of like everything, and I get A's and B+'s in all my classes, but I can't decide."
- "I'm going to be a TV director. I got into video in high school, but now that I've worked in a college television studio, I know exactly what I want to do. The honors program will support my senior TV project and get me an internship at a station. I'm ready."
- "I'm the first person in my family to go to college. I grew up in a small town that suddenly changed when a big highway came through. As I watched them build that road, I knew I would become a civil engineer."
- "I've always been at the top of my high school class, and I want to go to a good college, but I don't want to go away. My family is very close and I work in my parents' business to help them out. I'd rather stay home."
- "I've come a long distance to study in America. My parents have sacrificed a lot and I know that

I have to concentrate on my studies. There are not many scholarships to help international students, and with a student visa I'm not allowed to work. Maybe honors can help me."

- "I'm a single parent. It's been hard raising two children on my salary. I want to go back to school and get a degree in education so that I can support my family and have a profession that I will really enjoy."

These portraits don't tell the whole story, but they do tell you that honors programs are open to students of all backgrounds and interests. Some are single-minded, others are jacks-of-all-trades. Honors program students often are on the track team, run the student government, and write for the college newspaper. They are everywhere on campus: in plays and concerts, in laboratories and libraries, in sororities and fraternities. Some are clear about their majors and professions; others need direction and advice. One of the great strengths of honors programs is that they are nurturing environments that encourage students to be well rounded and help them make informed life choices.

What Is an Honors Program?

An honors program is a sequence of courses designed specifically to encourage independent and creative learning. Whether you want to attend a large state university or a private one, a small four-year college or your local community college, you can make the decision to join an honors program. For more than three decades "honors" education, given definition by the National Collegiate Honors Council (NCHC), has been an institution on American campuses. Although honors programs have many different designs, there are typical components. In two-year colleges the programs often concentrate on special versions of general education courses and may have individual capstone projects that come out of a student's special interest. In four-year colleges and universities, honors programs are generally designed for students of almost every major in every college on campus. In some cases, they are given additional prominence as honors colleges. Directly below the name of each school you will find a subheading that indicates whether it has a program or a college. The characteristics of both are discussed a little later in the book. Whether a program or a college, honors is most often structured as a general education or "core" component followed by advanced seminars and a thesis or creative project, which may be in the departmental major. Honors curriculum usually is incorporated within whatever number of credits is required for graduation. Students rarely are required to take additional credits. Students who complete an honors program or honors college curriculum frequently receive transcript and diploma notations, as well as certificates, medallions or other citations at graduation ceremonies.

When you read through the various descriptions, you will begin to see typical patterns of academic programming. That is where you must choose the program best suited to your own needs. In every case, catering to the student as an individual plays a central role in honors course design. Most honors classes are small (under 20 students) and discussion oriented— giving students a chance to present their own interpretations of ideas and even teach part of the course. Many classes are interdisciplinary, which means that they are taught by faculty members from two or more departments who provide different perspectives on a theme. All honors classes help students develop and articulate their own perspectives by cultivating verbal and written style. The classes help students mature intellectually and prepare them to engage in their own explorations and research. Some programs even extend the options for self-growth to study abroad and internships in government or industry related to the major. Other programs encourage or require community service. In every case honors is an experiential education that enhances learning and extends far beyond the classroom.

Despite their individual differences, all honors programs and honors colleges rely on faculty who enjoy working with bright, independent students. The ideal honors faculty members are open-minded and encouraging teachers. They want to see their students achieve at their highest capacity, and they are glad to spend time with students in discussions and laboratories, on field trips and at conferences, or on-line in e-mail. They often influence career decisions, provide inspiring models, and remain friends long after they have served as thesis advisers.

Where Are Honors Programs Located?

Because honors programs include students from many different departments or colleges, they usually have their own offices and space on campus. Some have their own buildings. Most programs have honors centers or lounges, where students gather together for informal conversations, luncheons, discussions, lectures, and special projects.

Many honors students have cultivated strong personal interests that have nothing to do with classes; they may be experts at using the Internet. They may be fine artists or poets, musicians or racing car enthusiasts. Some volunteer in hospitals or do landscape gardening to pay for college. Many work in retail stores and catering. Some enjoy exercising and others collect antique watches. When they get together in honors lounges there is always an interesting mixture of ideas.

In general, honors provides an environment in which students feel free to talk about their passionate interests and ideas knowing that they will find good listeners and sometimes arguers. There is no end to conversations among honors students. Like many students in honors, you may feel a great relief in finding a sympathetic group that respects your intelligence and creativity. You can be eccentric. You can be yourself! Some lifelong friendships, even marriages, are the result of relationships developed in honors programs. Of course you will make other friends in classes, clubs, and elsewhere on campus, even through e-mail. But the honors program will build strong bonds, too.

In the honors center or program office, you will find the honors director. In addition to departmental academic advisers, the honors director usually serves as a personal adviser to all of the students in the program. Many programs also have peer counselors and mentors who are upperclass honors students and know the ropes from a student's perspective and experience. The honors office usually is a good place to meet people, ask questions, and solve problems.

Are You Ready for Honors?

Sometimes even the very best students who apply for honors admissions are frightened by the thought of speaking in front of a group, giving seminar papers, or writing a thesis. But if you understand how the programs work, you will see that there is nothing to be frightened about. The basis of honors is confidence in the student and building the student's self confidence. Once you are admitted to an honors program, you have already demonstrated your academic achievement in high school or college classes. You will learn how to formulate and structure ideas so that you can apply critical judgment to sets of facts and opinions. In small seminar classes you practice discussion and arguments. So, by the time you come to the senior thesis or project, the method is second nature. For most honors students the senior thesis, performance, or portfolio presentation is the project that gives them the greatest fulfillment and pride. In many programs, students present their work either to other students in the program or to faculty members in their major departments. Students often present their work at regional and national honors conferences. Some students even publish their work jointly with their faculty mentors. These are great achievements that come with the training. There is nothing to be afraid of. Just do it! Honors will make you ready for life.

Can You Get an Honors Scholarship?

There is no doubt that the reality of life is what pushes some students in the direction of honors programs. One dimension of that reality is money. Let's face it, college is an expensive proposition, and scholarships are tempting solutions. In addition to the federal and state scholarship assistance for which you might be eligible, many honors programs have both need-based (based on your family's income) and merit-based (based on your academic and sometimes extracurricular achievements) scholarships to offer desirable applicants. Some programs have endowed scholarships given by program alumni with a particular interest in supporting honors students. Other honors programs do not have separate scholarship money to offer, yet their applicants may be eligible for general scholarships that are granted by the college or university. There are many different kinds of scholarships related to joining an honors program. They should all be considered carefully.

In general, tuition in state colleges and universities is lower than tuition in private schools, but sometimes honors scholarships narrow the gap. Many private institutions have a great deal of money to spend on honors scholarship assistance, so you might find that going to a private college will not cost much more than attending a state school. How do you make the choice? Look at the program itself and at the departments that you are considering for your major. In the end, you must choose the college or university that seems best for you. As a student, learning will be your primary employment for the duration of your college career. Think of a scholarship as a salary and yourself as a breadwinner.

If you are reading this guide and thinking about honors programs, you are probably just the sort of student who will receive scholarship offers. Both you and your family should feel proud that your academic achievements have earned you the prospect of an honors scholarship that will offset at least part (sometimes all) of your college tuition. But before you accept that scholarship, you must be sure that you want to study at the college or university that has made the scholarship offer, and you must be sure that you want to participate in the honors program. Honors is a commitment to a certain kind of education that demands a great deal of you as an individual. Probably you can accept such demands. You have good grades and many interests. Still, you are a bit frightened and feel the scholarship offer as a kind of pressure. Think it through carefully, remembering that pressure sometimes pushes you to even greater achievement. Remember, too, that in the honors environment there will be many faculty members and advisers to help you, and all of them want to see you succeed. Think through the offer, talk it over with your family, and then have the confidence in yourself to make a sound decision. Most honors students feel the same pressures that you do. When you talk to other students in your orientation group or in the honors lounge, you will be surprised to discover that everyone had the same doubts and anxieties. And when you graduate "with honors" all those doubts will seem part of the distant past.

Can You Lose a Scholarship?

Every scholarship, whether it is attached to honors or not, has academic requirements attached to it. Most scholarships require that students take a certain number of credits per semester and maintain a certain grade point average (GPA). You will need to maintain whatever GPA is required both to stay in an honors program and to keep your scholarship awards. But don't be afraid; you have probably exceeded those standards all along, so maintaining your GPA will not be as big a problem as it sounds. The faculty members and honors director are there to help you achieve and succeed in the program.

Most honors programs have very low attrition rates because students enjoy classes and do well. You have every reason to believe that you can make the grade.

Of course, you must be careful about how you budget your time for studying. Honors encourages well-rounded, diversified students, and you should play a sport if you want to, work at the radio station, join the clubs that interest you, or pledge a sorority or fraternity. You might find a job on campus that will help you pay expenses, and that also is reasonable. But remember, each activity takes time. You must strike a balance that will leave you enough time to do your homework, prepare for seminar discussions, do research, and do well on exams. This guide contains information about extracurricular activities and work opportunities on campus. Choose the ones that attract you, but never let them overshadow your primary purpose—which is to be a student.

How to Use This Guide

As you get ready to use this guide, it is important to look at the key below the name of each institution. This will help you identify the programs that are best suited for your consideration.

- The number **2** or **4** indicates whether the program is part of a two-year or four-year institution
- **Pu** stands for a public or state institution, **Pr** for a private college or university
- **G** tells you that the program is a general honors program, **C** refers to a college program, **D** indicates that it is departmental. Most of the programs listed in the book are general honors.
- Honors programs can also be small (**S**)—under 100 students, midsize (**M**)—100–500 students, or large (**L**)—more than 500 students. You will know what size program best suits your personality. Even large honors programs offer a great deal of individual attention.
- If scholarships are available through the honors program, **Sc** will be listed in the key
- Programs that take transfer students have the designation **Tr**

So a key entry that reads **4 Pr G M Sc Tr** tells you that the program is part of a four-year private college or university that offers general honors to a medium-sized group of students. Scholarships are available and transfer students are admitted. A key entry that reads **2 Pu G S** indicates a two-year public institution (probably a community college) that grants general honors to a small number of students but does not have any money for scholarship assistance.

Now you are ready to read through the program descriptions. Each has been written by the program's own director, so each is an intimate view of the program. Each description tells you what the program is like, how long it has been in existence, how many honors students are enrolled, what kind of courses it usually offers, and what special features constitute student life. Each description includes admissions and participation requirements, so you will know exactly what is expected of you in that particular program.

Under "The Campus Context," you will find a description of the college or university as a whole, including the make-up of the students and faculty. It is important to read this section since it tells you about the geography of the institution, the special facilities that might interest you—such as museums and theaters—as well as the size of its library and range of its computer facilities. In addition, this section will give you information on joining fraternities or sororities, playing varsity sports, studying abroad or working in a laboratory. Make sure that the school can also accommodate any particular needs that you might have.

The final section gives you a look at the cost of tuition and fees as well as room and board. Choosing to live on campus is a very personal and financial matter. Some honors programs have honors dormitories or dorm wings with study areas and computer facilities. Some students find that appealing, while others prefer to live within the general mix of dorm students, in an off-campus apartment, or at home with their families. It is a good idea to confirm all costs when you contact the school since these may have changed since publication. At the same time, you will probably find changes in other figures, like the exact number of students in an honors program or college, the number of books in a library, or the number of computers on campus. Colleges and universities are living institutions and these figures are constantly changing. All of the information in this book was gathered from honors programs and

colleges between March 1996 and January 1997. For the most part, directors responded to a two-page survey, but some schools also contributed information gathered by their offices of institutional research. In most instances, tuition, fee, room and board information was taken from Peterson's database of undergraduate institutions. While every attempt has been made to give you the most current information, you should use this book as a general guide, and then fine-tune your investigation.

Once you have found a college or university that seems to have everything you think you want, you should schedule a visit. You can make a preliminary visit on-line. Most honors programs have established home pages on the World Wide Web, and their addresses are included with their descriptions. Each honors program home page is linked to other on-line information posted by the institution. You can find out a great deal about the schools through the Internet, but that shouldn't replace a personal visit. Before you spend two or four years at a college or university, you should see it with your own eyes and meet the honors director as well as students and faculty members in the program and in your projected major.

All of the honors programs listed in this guide are members of a large national organization, the National Collegiate Honors Council, which has advocated honors education for more than thirty years. NCHC holds meetings every year for honors directors, faculty members, and students. Honors students play a large role in NCHC. They have representatives to cover student issues; they serve on committees and present papers at the national convention. In fact, some years there are as many students as faculty members attending the annual meeting—leading discussions, sharing their research, and shaping the future of American honors education. Many honors programs pay all or part of their students' travel both to the national convention and to regional honors conventions, which also present excellent opportunities for student participation. I hope to meet you there.

In the following pages you will see profiles of honors alumni and hear from some of the officers of the National Collegiate Honors Council, who extend to you their greetings and their experience as honors educators.

ALUMNI PROFILE

▲

Andrea Vogt
Journalism and Mass Communication, 1996 Graduate
Iowa State University Honors Program

The Iowa State University Honors Program offered me many wonderful experiences, but one opportunity in particular stands out among the memories because it truly changed my life. The ISU Freshman Mentor Program presented the chance to challenge myself by performing research with a professor outside of my major department (journalism and mass communication). The research experience was incredible for many reasons: I was introduced to and fell in love with the discipline in which I am now pursuing a doctoral degree (anthropology), it helped me realize that I could challenge myself and succeed in research settings, and I was able to copresent the research with my mentor at a professional meeting for anthropologists. Because of my experience with the Freshman Mentor Program, I realized my own potential and found the courage to tackle a higher degree in a field that fascinates me.

PRESIDENT'S MESSAGE

▲

Dr. Susanna Finnell, Director of the Honors Program at Texas A&M University
President, National Collegiate Honors Council, 1996–97

As a parent or student, you will find in this book a wealth of information that will make choosing your college more fun and rewarding. Successful, confident, and motivated students are always on the lookout for a personally satisfying educational experience. They search for extra academic challenges. From visiting with hundreds of prospective college students over many years, I know that this resource will come in handy because the word is out that it is in honors programs and honors colleges where the excitement of learning can be found. But then again, because there are as many honors programs as there are colleges and universities, how can you begin to compare and make intelligent choices? This guide is the start you have been looking for.

If discussions and ideas undergirded the honors movement at its inception more than thirty years ago, the very idea of honors education still sparks lively and energetic discussion at regional and national honors meetings. The National Collegiate Honors Council, established in 1966, is one of the few professional organizations that does not differentiate between professional and student membership. This is its explicit mission:

NCHC is an organization of institutions (public and private, four-year and two-year), faculty members, students, administrators, and others interested in supporting honors education. The mission of NCHC is to cultivate excellence in American undergraduate education by assisting honors programs to create and enhance opportunities (academic, cultural, and social) for exceptionally able, highly motivated undergraduate students.

Honors programs, although differing in many ways, have in common the offering of rigorous, coherent, and integrative academic experiences and a high degree of student-faculty interchange. Their concern is that honors teaching and learning contribute significantly to the development of the unique capabilities of each student and educator who participates.

The National Collegiate Honors Council promotes honors teaching and learning within higher education by pursuing these goals:

- to encourage the development of new honors programs
- to provide guidelines and expertise for establishing new honors programs and for strengthening developing honors programs
- to assist honors programs in improving intellectual discourse on campuses in ways advantageous to all students and faculty members
- to create and support opportunities that enrich the experience of honors students and educators

All the honors programs and colleges listed in this guide are institutional members of the National Collegiate Honors Council. As institutional members, the programs and colleges are guided by sixteen points that are characteristics of a fully developed honors program (see Basic Characteristics of a Fully Developed Honors Program.) These characteristics are not prescriptions to successful programs, but they do serve as guidelines. These guidelines may even prove useful to you as a "consumer" as you try to understand the nature of the various honors programs and how they differ. Obviously, an honors program at a two-year college will look quite different from that of a four-year college. Each program grows out of the mission and history of its mother institution and each will have strengths and areas of excellence that are unique. The bottom line is that each serves with the philosophy that bright students will be motivated and stretched by participating in the honors experience.

I invite you to read, to compare, and to choose the honors program that best suits your needs and interests. Once your choices are narrowed down, however, nothing will quite convince you until you visit the college or university. Honors advisers and directors will be able to amplify the picture presented in this guide. As you arrive on campus, request to visit with a currently enrolled honors student. No one else will better translate for you what the honors experience means: the assurance that a curious mind has access to resources for growing and testing ideas and beliefs in an environment that encourages active, participatory learning.

As you visit, here are some questions that you might consider asking:

1. Where do graduates of your program go next?
2. How is an honors class different from a regular class?
3. What are the opportunities for independent learning? The opportunities to do undergraduate research?
4. How are honors students recognized on campus? at graduation? on transcripts?
5. What input do honors students have into the running of the honors program?
6. What is this honors program's particular strength?
7. Are there scholarships available for honors students? Does the program offer preparation for national scholarship competitions?

As you visit prospective college campuses, don't forget to visit the honors office. Ask many questions. Seek to understand the culture of each honors program. Catch the excitement of honors learning from other honors students!

You have my best wishes for the expansive and exciting college years that are ahead of you.

ALUMNI PROFILE

▲

Nick Weber
Director of Archives, St. Vincent Medical Center
Alumnus of University of Wisconsin–Milwaukee Honors Program

It is partly due to the honors program that I am where I am now—an archivist and museum curator for the oldest hospital in Los Angeles. The history courses I took as an honors student awoke in me a fascination for the past that I was unaware of throughout my high school history classes, which forced me to memorize dates without any real involvement. The courses in the honors program were a lot of fun, a lot of work (unlike most of my classes), and a good training ground for students wishing to pursue an advanced degree.

HONORS SNAPSHOTS

▲

Happy honors students receive their General Honors Certificate from the honors program at Syracuse University.

Columbia College honors student Melody Johnson applies her training in speech-language pathology.

Well-rounded students are especially encouraged and much sought after. C.W. Post honors student Sheila Verbeck, left, scores on the varsity soccer team.

Brooklyn LIU honors students visit the Metropolitan Museum of Art during the Freshman Sequence.

NATIONAL COLLEGIATE HONORS COUNCIL'S BASIC CHARACTERISTICS OF A FULLY DEVELOPED HONORS PROGRAM

▲

No one model of an honors program can be superimposed on all types of institutions. Listed below are characteristics which are common to successful, fully developed honors programs. Not all characteristics are necessary for an honors program to be considered successful and/or fully developed.

1. A fully developed honors program should be carefully set up to accommodate the special needs and abilities of the undergraduate students it is designed to serve. This entails identifying the targeted student population by some clearly articulated set of criteria (e.g., GPA, SAT scores, a written essay). A program with open admission needs to spell out expectations for retention in the program and for satisfactory completion of program requirements.

2. The program should have a clear mandate from the institutional administration—ideally in the form of a mission statement—clearly stating the objectives and responsibilities of the program and defining its place in both the administrative and academic structure of the institution. This mandate or mission statement should be such as to assure the permanence and stability of the program by guaranteeing an adequate budget and by avoiding the tendency to force the program to depend on temporary or spasmodic dedication of particular faculty members or administrators. In other words, the program should be fully institutionalized, so as to build thereby a genuine tradition of excellence.

3. The honors director should report to the chief academic officer of the institution.

4. There should be an honors curriculum featuring special courses, seminars, colloquia, and independent study established in harmony with the mission statement and in response to the needs of the program.

5. The program requirements themselves should include a substantial portion of the participants' undergraduate work, usually in the vicinity of 20 percent or 25 percent of their total course work and certainly no less than 15 percent.

6. The program should be so formulated that it relates effectively both to all the college work for the degree (e.g., by satisfying general education requirements) and to the area of concentration, departmental specialization, preprofessional, or professional training.

7. The program should be both visible and highly reputed throughout the institution so that it is perceived as providing standards and models of excellence for students and faculty members across the campus.

8. Faculty members participating in the program should be fully identified with the aims of the program. They should be carefully selected on the basis of exceptional teaching skills and the ability to provide intellectual leadership to able students.

9. The program should occupy suitable quarters constituting an honors center with such facilities as an honors library, lounge, reading rooms, personal computers, and other appropriate decor.

10. The director or other administrative officer charged with administering the program should work in close collaboration with a committee or council of faculty members representing the colleges and/or departments served by the program.

11. The program should have in place a committee or honors students to serve as liaison with the honors faculty committee or council who must keep the student group fully informed on the program and elicit their cooperation in evaluation and development. This student group should enjoy as much autonomy as possible conducting the business of the committee in representing the needs and concerns of all honors students to the administration, and it should also be included in governance, serving on the advisory/policy committee as well as constitute the group that governs the student association.

12. There should be provisions for special academic counseling of honors students by uniquely qualified faculty and/or staff personnel.

13. The honors program, in distinguishing itself from the rest of the institution, serves as a kind of laboratory within which faculty members can try things they have always wanted to try, but for which they could find no suitable outlet. When such efforts are demonstrated to be successful, they may well become institutionalized, thereby raising the general level of education within the college or university for all students. In this connection, the honors curriculum should serve as a prototype for educational practices that can work campus-wide in the future.

14. The fully developed honors program must be open to continuous and critical review and be prepared to change in order to maintain its distinctive position of offering distinguished education to the best students in the institution.

15. A fully developed program will emphasize the participatory nature of the honors educational process by adopting such measures as offering opportunities for students to participate in regional and national conferences, honors semesters, international programs, community service, and other forms of experiential education.

16. Fully developed two-year and four-year honors programs should have articulation agreements by which honors graduates from two-year colleges can be accepted into four-year honors programs when they meet previously agreed-upon requirements.

ALUMNI PROFILE

▲

John Knox
The University of Alabama Alumnus

 The University of Alabama Honors Program has been my intellectual and spiritual home-away-from-home for the past thirteen years, from my first moment in college to my current postdoctoral work as a scientist at Columbia University. It's easy to find a college where you can learn with people who all have the same test scores, career objectives, and experiences; in The University of Alabama's Honors Program you learn *from* a community of students who span the spectrum of ages, backgrounds, and majors. In the honors program as a math major, I was encouraged to pursue my passion for English literature—which led to prize-winning essays and a Rhodes Scholarship nomination. Later, as a graduate student in meteorology at the University of Wisconsin, I served the honors program as an occasional lecturer and a mentor for new honors students. The students and faculty, past and present, in the honors program have become like a second family. Two former honors students helped locate an apartment for my family in New York City just on the basis of our University of Alabama connection. The director of the honors program was even a reader at my wedding in Wisconsin, and we still converse via e-mail nearly every day! Lots of people dream about college being like this, but it's been a reality in the University of Alabama Honors Program. Best of all, this "dream education" at a low-cost public university didn't leave me with a penny of student debt!

HONORS SNAPSHOTS

▲

La Salle University students prepare for a seminar in the honors lounge. In most programs the honors lounge is an important gathering place.

Dr. Jim Lacey, Honors Program Director at Eastern Connecticut State University, presents awards at the annual spring picnic in his backyard.

Eastern Illinois University junior and honors business major Kelsey Ballard gains experience working in the honors program office.

Columbia College honors student Traci Gardner, poised mid-air in a dance, captures the creativity of honors students in the performing arts.

HONORS:
PROGRAM OR COLLEGE

▲

Dr. Len Zane, Director of the Honors College at the University of Nevada, Las Vegas
President, National Collegiate Honors Council, 1995–96

As you read through this guide, you will notice that for the most part colleges and universities house honors in one of two distinct units: program or college. Consequently, it is reasonable to ask how an honors college differs from an honors program. Unfortunately, like many questions, the answer you get will depend on who you ask and whether or not they happen to have an honors college or program on their campus.

First it is valuable to describe some of the general characteristics normally associated with a college or program. At universities, colleges are the primary academic units. Colleges typically house a group of academic departments that share some thematic connection. Colleges have faculty, establish requirements for graduation, grant degrees, schedule courses, are led by deans, and operate with a large degree of autonomy. It is more difficult to define a typical program at a college or university because the term "program" has been used to describe a much broader range of units. For example, looking through my campus directory, I can find an Academic Support Program, Asian Studies Program, CCSD/UNLV Cooperative Early Childhood Program, Early Studies Program, and six other programs before reaching honors in the alphabetical listing. Consequently, the distinction between an honors college and an honors program can be expected to be substantial.

However, the differences become much less clear when looked at in detail. Faculty members who teach in honors are almost always part of the regular faculty and are rarely housed in honors. Therefore most honors colleges do not have their own faculty members. Like most honors programs, the vast majority of honors colleges borrow faculty members who are housed in academic departments across campus. I know of no honors college or program that is divided into academic departments. The same lack of consensus is true of the other attributes listed that define a "normal" academic college. Some honors colleges have this particular attribute or that, but there is no characteristic that is uniquely found in honors colleges that is missing in all or most programs.

On average, honors colleges probably have more of the Characteristics of a Fully Developed Honors Program (described in the previous section) than will be found in honors programs. But even this weak statement of the distinction between college and program does not apply to individual institutions. Some of the very largest and best known honors enterprises are programs, and some of the smaller and less well known are colleges. Honors colleges are likely to be more visible on their campuses than honors programs. Although this visibility can help in fundraising and in creating cooperative agreements with people on and off campus, it is primarily a perceptual difference and does not automatically confer substantial advantage to an honors college compared to an honors program.

Each honors program or college approaches its mission differently. Although most honors directors, deans, faculty members, and students, if asked to explain the virtues of their particular program, would find themselves saying things embarrassingly similar to other directors, deans, faculty members, and students; the sounds, sights, taste, smell, and feel of each honors operation is surprisingly unique. In the end, I believe it is less important whether honors is housed in something called a college or a program, than are the distinct opportunities afforded by honors on a particular campus. Much of what happens of value in college takes place in classes, laboratories, and studios across campus and is not substantively affected by the administrative structure of the unit organizing those experiences.

As you face the daunting task of selecting the college or university to which you want to entrust your postsecondary education, I can offer two thoughts that may lessen the stress. First, as you read, ponder, and attempt to use the self-descriptions in this book, know that the information presented empowers you and allows you to make a more informed decision. Second, high-quality, challenging, and inspiring education happens on literally hundreds and hundreds of campuses across the country. Unique opportunities of various kinds are available on most campuses. Part of being a good consumer of higher education is learning how to maximize the value of the collegiate experience. Needless to say, those of us in honors fervently believe that honors, regardless of whether it is housed in a college or program, is the most rewarding educational path on all campuses. In the end, the actual selection of a college or university is substantially less important than the zest, ambition, skill, and study habits brought to the institution selected. Recognizing that each individual student controls, to a surprisingly large degree, the quality of experience that he or she will have for the next four years takes much of the anxiety out of the selection.

Best wishes for a successful conclusion to your search for the right college or university. And more importantly, have a great undergraduate career highlighted by participation in honors at the school of your choice.

ALUMNI PROFILE

▲

Eileen Songer McCarthy
College of New Rochelle, Class of 1991
J.D., Columbia University School of Law, 1995

The honors program at the College of New Rochelle played an integral role in my development as a person and a student. It equipped me with the confidence and critical-thinking skills necessary to be an honors law student and an effective attorney. By offering seminar-type learning experiences, which evoked my critical reflections on assigned readings, it helped me to develop analytical and public-speaking skills which have served me well as an attorney. In addition, being part of the honors community taught me that having a focused and challenging educational experience was not something that could be done alone. A network of faculty and student mentors and my honors peers supported me in the creation of a truly liberal education that I am proud to recommend to others.

HONORS:
A COMMUNITY FOR LIFE

▲

**Dr. Ada Long, Director of the Honors Program at the University of Alabama at Birmingham
President, National Collegiate Honors Council, 1994–95**

Students who join our honors program become members of our academic community not just for the next four years, but in most cases for life. I suspect the same is true for most honors programs. While the larger institutions in which our honors programs are housed provide a series of courses and extracurricular activities that begin with admission and usually end with graduation, we start knowing our students while they're still in high school as we interview them for the program. After they graduate, they serve as mentors to the students who come after them; participate in frequent reunions; help each other find scholarships, jobs, and housing; provide moral support; and visit the honors house whenever they're in town or in the neighborhood. This community provides a sense of belonging and stability that helps each student find his or her bearings in an educational environment dedicated to challenge and change.

Many students entering college today want to remain as inconspicuous as possible, get the degree, and cause minimal change in their "real lives," which they see as life outside of college. Honors programs are designed for the other kind of students: those who see college as real life, as a place and a time in their lives not just to prepare themselves for a career but to learn about themselves and others, to seek wisdom as well as knowledge, to explore the unknown, and to find what most excites them so that they may maintain this excitement for the rest of their lives. Above all, these students want to find a way to make a difference and to leave a mark that is uniquely theirs.

What I think makes honors programs most honorable is their commitment to honoring the distinct gifts of their students within a context of high expectations. And what makes directing an honors program the best

job in academia is watching those gifts develop, deepen, and then go to work in the world. Each student who has entered our program has a story that illustrates this process; I will tell three of them.

Kellie skipped her senior year in high school and started college when she was sixteen. Full of intensity and intelligence but without a direction for them, she tagged along with me one day when I went to the opening of a homeless shelter near the honors house. She immediately started volunteering at the shelter and two years later received the shelter's first Volunteer of the Year Award. For an upper-level honors project, she did a study of homelessness that included two weeks of living on the street and in shelters—scaring the daylights out of me and her parents (we all checked on her constantly)—and leading to an extraordinarily moving and informative analysis of the daily lives of homeless women in Birmingham. She received a Truman Scholarship, which funded her last two years at the University of Alabama and her master's degree at Johns Hopkins University. She now works as a consultant for employment services for the homeless in Washington, D. C., helps our current students who are interested in public service careers, and spends every New Year's Eve at my house catching up on the work she has done in Bulgaria and elsewhere.

I met Cedric when he was a student in my remedial English class. An immensely gifted and original young man, he was struggling to make up for twelve years in a rural Alabama school system. I invited him into the honors program, and he reluctantly agreed to give it a try. He thrived in the program and quickly became a favorite of his classmates. He majored in history because he liked it. When he graduated he took a test for the management training program at State Farm Insurance.

An executive at State Farm called me to say that nobody from Cedric's county had ever performed so well on the test. Cedric married another student in the honors program (about fifteen of us went to the wedding). His wife is now a pediatrician in Panama City. State Farm has transferred Cedric there, and they just had a baby boy.

Katie was an anthropology major at UAB. During the summer, she went to Bali with her adviser to study macaques. She was always a member of the "front porch gang"—part of the way our honors students define themselves is where they hang out in the honors house—and there she met an engineering student whom she married in the honors house two years later. The two of them moved to New York where Katie had a National Science Foundation Fellowship to study for her Ph.D. at the City University of New York (CUNY). Katie now spends much of her time studying chimpanzees in Nigeria, while her husband is currently updating computer hardware for the NOAA at the South Pole. We stay in touch through e-mail, and I see Katie when I go to New York.

Many of our other honors students have become lawyers, doctors, accountants, and virtually any other kind of professional you can think of. When I or any of our students need any kind of service, there's always an alumnus or alumna out there to provide it. Our students past and present—and future—contribute their unique gifts not just to the world at large, but to each other, helping to maintain a community that is always changing but always there as a homebase. It is a community that is now global as well as local and that welcomes each new student as an individual and as a member of this shared community. Surely this is what education is supposed to be, and it is what honors programs throughout the country foster as their special role in higher education.

ALUMNI PROFILE

▲

David Luna, Alumnus
The University of New Mexico General Honors Program

I consider the time I spent in the general honors program (GHP) to be an investment in my future. My experiences in the honors program seminars gave me the opportunity to expand my views on various questions our society now faces. In the process of my undergraduate program of study, the GHP prepared me to raise these questions and gave me some of the tools needed to answer them. This is what I thank the GHP for most.

HONORS SNAPSHOTS

English Professor Hugh Egan leads an honors seminar on the American Frontier at Ithaca College.

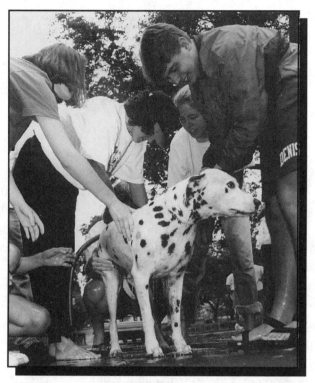

The Community Dog Wash has become an annual tradition for Denison University honors students. Each fall, students volunteer their time to bathe dogs for faculty, staff, and townspeople in exchange for a donation to the Licking County Humane Society. Hoses and water are provided by the college and a local cleaner donates towels. More than $100 has been raised each of the past few years.

College of New Rochelle honors freshman Gloria Romero makes a presentation to the honors class in Cultural Legacies as Dr. Ann Raia looks on.

HONORS:
A GRADUATE'S PERSPECTIVE

▲

Christopher Timura, Denison University, Class of 1996

What struck me most about membership in the honors program was the great degree of openness that characterized it as a group. Being a member never meant sectioning oneself off from the rest of campus life. Rather, membership provided new opportunities for enjoying and taking advantage of additional aspects of the wider intellectual and social life at Denison. My peers included musicians, chemists, political scientists, and actors, and we often shared little else in common than a commitment to scholarship and achievement. It was always exciting to learn about and experience the different ways my peers would make this commitment manifest on stage, in the lab, or in the university literary journal. Interactions with them in class and in other activities inspired me to think of new and different ways I could apply and develop my own efforts and skills.

Characterized succinctly by the title of its major publication, *Arete*, the honors program encouraged each of us to discover and achieve our own personal level of excellence. This encouragement took a concentrated form in highly interactive and creative honors seminars. Time always went too quickly in seminars like "Introduction to Philosophical Thinking" or "Riddles of Human Nature," and I can recall more than a few times leaving class discussions literally feeling elevated by an intellectual discovery.

More inspiration for developing our own interests and skills came during lunch time "Chowder Hours." Faculty and staff members presented us with often humorous descriptions of their own intellectual pursuits and interests. Other honors activities, such as homecoming game tailgate parties, dances, weekend movie marathons, and picnics, reinforced the notion of a balanced social and academic education while giving us opportunities to meet one another and unwind from the more mundane pressures of essays, rehearsals, or problem sets.

In my final two years, the honors program faculty and staff provided me and other interested students invaluable technical advice, program information, and support while making applications for several national scholarships. I received a Fulbright Scholarship to study in the United Kingdom for the 1996–97 year. Indeed, the honors program at Denison University prepared me well for my present graduate work at University College, London.

The tutorial style of my honors seminars, with their small class size and discussion format, gave me practice for the graduate anthropology seminars that I now take part in each week as part of my M.Sc. program, called "Anthropology and Ecology of Development." We are examining communities' struggles for control over natural resources, violence, and conflict resolution. The broad and flexible research skills learned through liberal arts training, coupled with the strong intellectual curiosity nurtured by my honors faculty and peers, have given me the tools and drive necessary to conduct graduate research on these complex themes. Last but not least, the honors program experience more generally allowed me the chance to cultivate manifold and excellent friendships that I continue to maintain (and sometimes host) here in London.

ALUMNI PROFILE

▲

Sasha O'Conner, Class of '96
Long Island University, Brooklyn Campus

I came to honors a shy, timid freshman. I left an assertive, professional young adult. How come? Maybe because every aspect of honors education encouraged me to explore my many interests and to discover some I didn't know were there. Going to NCHC conferences provided a special opportunity to meet students from other schools and different backgrounds. Then when I took my experiences back to class, my presentations improved, my thoughts became sharper, and I learned to think on my feet.

Speaking as
an Honors Parent

▲

Professor John S. Grady, Director of the Honors Program at La Salle University

In addition to providing the most comprehensive collection of honors descriptions ever assembled in one volume, the creators of this project believed I might have some insights to offer that could prove to be of value to you. My contribution to your college search would not be derived as much from my almost three decades as director of an honors program, nor from my experience as one of the first cochairs of the National Collegiate Honors Council's Committee on Honors Evaluation, as it would from my experiences as a parent of five children attempting to make an appropriate college choice. As much as possible then, I write from the same situation in which you now find yourself—a parent attempting to sift through the plethora of college materials in the hope of assisting sons and daughters to make what will obviously be one of the most important decisions of their young lives.

It goes without saying, my experiences as a faculty member for close to four decades and my three decades of honors involvement played roles in the college choice process. However, I believe that the manner in which that experience factored into the discussions and decision-making processes can be of significance for you. All of my children were eligible for tuition grants to La Salle and to numerous other institutions participating in a tuition remission consortium with La Salle, but this did not limit the scope of the investigations. I, like you, wanted the best possible education for each of them—La Salle, or a consortium school, or whatever. Where my experience did become a factor was in the mutually-agreed-upon decision to limit the scope of the search to nationally recognized institutions and those colleges and universities having honors programs with which I had, or could acquire, some familiarity. At

the time of my children's search, I did not have the advantage of a *Peterson's Guide*.

These years of involvement in honors program activity had led me to the awareness that the existence of an honors program on a campus can be taken as strong evidence that my major concerns would be addressed. Those concerns—similar to the ones I'm sure you have—were ones of obtaining a quality educational experience at an affordable cost that would result in outcomes commensurate with what I believed to be the considerable talents of my children. I knew these to be the goals of our honors program at La Salle, and I also knew these same goals were shared by colleagues at numerous institutions nationwide.

If you think about it, a college or university willing to commit significant resources to a quality honors program is making a statement about their philosophy of education. They are saying they recognize the differences among individuals and are willing to do something about these differences. Not all of us were created with the same measure of intellectual gifts. Those who have been blessed with riches of the mind and intellect need an environment that will recognize these gifts, nurture them, and raise them to the next level. The existence of the honors program stands as a testament to an institutional commitment to this goal.

In essence, an honors program has two major components—faculty and students—combining to form a learning community. The honors program faculty is typically drawn from those members of the full faculty who have demonstrated a genuine aptitude and fondness for the teaching enterprise, who have a command of their subject matter that is beyond reproach, and a willingness and facility to engage the student participants in the learning process. They are not fearful of setting high standards and demanding the best from the best. For their part, the students in this community have committed themselves to the pursuit of excellence, to accepting the challenge of similarly talented peers, and to the exercise of a "competitive cooperation" that is the hallmark of the entire community. It is the responsibility of the honors program director to bring these groups together in an environment of mutual support and love of the learning process. It is this environment we call "honors." I can assure you this is the primary objective of the honors directors with whom I have had the pleasure and privilege to work. They will bring this mission to the education of your children.

Realizing this opportunity for excellence must be made affordable to interested and qualified students, I believe you will discover most honors programs are closely associated with the scholarship programs of their colleges. In many cases, as in my own, the honors director will serve as the chair of the scholarship committee. It is obviously in the best interest of the school to use their various scholarship programs, many of them merit-based in these highly competitive times, to enroll the type of student pursuing honors work. Consequently, I discovered the link between honors programs and scholarship programs to be a quite common and natural one. This is all the more important and significant when you realize that many students of this high caliber hope to extend their educations beyond the undergraduate degree. Many are entering their college experience with the goal of professional school to follow the baccalaureate. It is difficult to approach the question of financing the four-year college program in isolation from the resources necessary for postgraduate work. Any easing of the burden through scholarships at the undergraduate level must be considered if ultimate goals are to be realized. Thus it is in your immediate and long-term interest to explore merit-based scholarship opportunities at each school you are considering. I believe you will be pleasantly surprised at the possibility of making this quality educational experience affordable through scholarship assistance.

There is life beyond honors! As wonderful and as rewarding as the undergraduate experience might be, students must move on to the next step. Many of the "gatekeepers" at the next level—be it professional school, graduate school, employment, or other endeavors—are acutely aware of the existence of honors programs. It has been my experience that employers and admissions directors will inquire about the honors experience. Letters of recommendation written by honors directors will detail that experience and address the qualities of students who successfully complete their honors program requirements. This is evidence that such students possess the qualities of self-confidence, accomplishment, scholarship, oral and written communication skills, originality, and analytical ability that are sought after in today's dynamic professional environments. Everyone is looking for that competitive edge in advancing one's career goals, and having experienced an honors community offers this immediate advantage in addition to lifelong rewards.

Having seen more than 1,000 students complete their honors education and move on to successful careers and productive lives has been most rewarding. This has been particularly so in the case of my own children. Each was able to move on from La Salle to quite prestigious graduate and professional schools. Two daughters completed their legal studies and are now attorneys—one with a major law firm as a litigator and one as an in-house counsel with a major medical system, practicing labor and discrimination law. One son is a prosecutor, and his brother completed his M.P.P. degree and works in economic development. My youngest daughter went on to be awarded a Truman Scholarship, which she used to obtain her M.P.P. and is now a budget analyst at the local-government level. There is no doubt in my mind, or in theirs, as to how valuable their honors program experience has been in helping form their values and launch their careers. That same opportunity exists for you in one of the programs described in this volume. My best wishes for a successful conclusion to your search.

ALUMNI PROFILE

▲

Wayne Wright, Alumnus
Long Island University, C.W. Post Campus

Being a member of the honors program not only enhanced my learning experience but contributed substantially to the achievement of my goals in banking. I took advantage of participating in several honors conferences, one of which was held in Salem, Massachusetts, and one in Las Vegas, Nevada. Speaking to my fellow honors program associates from around the nation helped me hone my presentation skills. Not only at conferences but in class, the roundtable format that was employed by most of our honors program professors fostered member participation and allowed us to learn from each other by discussing our ideas. This has helped my productivity in work-related meetings and conferences. The more challenging work load in the honors program ensured that I maintained my focus, managed my time, and as a result, learned more. As a banker, I spend a lot of time traveling, marketing, and attending meetings. I am currently an account officer with a portfolio of approximately $1 billion. I was promoted four times in the last four years as a result of hard work, assertiveness, management's recognition, and a little good luck. My honors experience has proved to be invaluable, as it allowed me to develop the skills that led to my success.

HONORS: A SHARED JOURNEY

▲

Dr. Herbert Lasky, Director of the Honors Programs at Eastern Illinois University
President-Elect, National Collegiate Honors Council

Through honors programs we give academically talented students the attention and guidance they need and deserve. Honors programs are designed to encourage bright students to follow and develop their talents, abilities, and interests. In the course of the average college education, many students, especially bright students, become interested in a wide range of subjects and disciplines, and honors programs encourage diverse interests and studies. Unusual combinations of majors and minors are common among honors students. Not significant or important in themselves, these combinations reflect the qualities of mind that honors programs encourage. Active student participa-

...rs classes is the norm, with undergraduate

...ificant element.

... classes is

... of limited

...pportunity

... course. As

...traordinary

...ith them, so

...ouncil is an

...resent every

... great books

...nars in which

...literature, his-

tory, ...ch focus on a particular discipline, the honors programs represented in the National Collegiate Honors Council bring to education the intellectual and cultural choices we have come to expect from honors education. Honors programs flourish wherever excellence in education is sought. Housed in many different kinds of institutions, honors programs are found in multiversity, private four-year colleges, community colleges and four-year comprehensive institutions.

Honors programs are designed to provide varied educational opportunities to interested and able students. Honors students conform to no particular pattern, and their interests and abilities are as wide ranging as those of any student population. They do, however, share the ability to manage time and are frequently multitalented. Honors students can be, and often are, active in college sports, campus politics, service and fraternal organizations, as well as university and college newspapers and other publications. In short, aside from their collective drive for academic excellence, there is no such thing as a "typical" honors student. Honors programs provide an environment that encourages such students to thrive. It is the school of their dreams. As David Patterson, a noted academic thinker, has observed: "The notion of an honors program remains just that—an idea, a concern for the truth, an embrace of the sacred..." Honors programs are the locus of the highest aspirations in education.

Honors students often inspire their teachers to rise to new heights of accomplishment in their classroom. Something magical occurs or, if you will, something sacred. It is a very special and exciting moment in the classroom, the laboratory, or on the campus when students inspire faculty members and show them new ways of learning and understanding. It is also special when those same students find their minds expanding to assimilate and synthesize what they have helped their teachers to give them. Honors learning is, at its best, a shared journey for students and faculty. It is an exemplary way of going to school. Those of us who have the privilege of working and teaching in honors programs value and treasure the journey with each generation of students and revel in their talents and successes.

ALUMNI PROFILE

▲

Alaina Harrington, Alumna
Oklahoma State University

I took full advantage of the leadership opportunities available through NCHC while earning my honors program degree in accounting at Oklahoma State University. I presented sessions at two national conferences, was elected as a student member of the NCHC Executive Committee, and also served on the Student Concerns Committee, Finance Committee, and 1995 National Conference Planning Committee. In addition to publishing articles in *The National Honors Report,* I also served as Student Editor in 1996 and originated the "Students in Honors" workshop for the national conference. Clearly, I enjoyed being fully involved in honors. As an alumna, I will be using all the leadership skills I learned. I have just completed my master's degree in accounting and passed the CPA exam. In the fall, I will attend law school at Duke University.

COMPUTERS: THE BASIC HONORS TOOLS

▲

Dr. Robert L. Spurrier Jr., Director of the Honors Program at Oklahoma State University
Vice President, National Collegiate Honors Council, 1997 and
Dr. Joan Digby, Director of the Honors Program at Long Island University, C.W. Post Campus

Getting into the Habit of Using Your Computer

It's hard to grow up these days without knowing something about computers. For students in college—and especially in honors programs—computers are essential tools. Mathematics and science as well as statistics, accounting, and graphic design immerse students in the use of computers. In honors programs, the emphasis on writing and critical expression is greatly assisted by computer proficiency. Because essays are important exercises to fine-tune ideas and develop critical-thinking skills, many honors professors allow and encourage students to rewrite papers in order to develop and refine ideas. The best way to do that is on a computer in a word processing program.

In fact, you should get into the habit of doing all of your writing, for political science, management, and philosophy as well as for English, on a computer and saving copies in backup files on disk. That way you can never "lose" a paper and neither can your professor! There will always be a copy available; there can never be a tragedy. Learning to write in a word processing program will save you a great deal of time and enable you to improve your logic and revise your arguments most efficiently. Add and delete. Cut and paste. You are ready to hand in your essay. You might even want to send an e-mail note to say that it's coming.

You will see that many colleges and universities provide e-mail accounts. This will enable you to be in touch with professors and students on campus (as well as family and friends at home). Many faculty members correspond with students in their classes via e-mail. It's easy for a professor to write a helpful note saying, "Your paper is developing nicely, but you really need to refine the introduction." The student who receives that message will know exactly what revisions will improve the paper. Sometimes class schedules make it difficult for students to meet faculty members during their regular office hours. E-mail is a helpful alternative means of discussing your work with your professors. Professors use e-mail to discuss papers, exam questions, thesis chapters, and even keep in touch with students who have gone abroad! Honors directors also use e-mail to network with students in their programs. In some programs, the students themselves have an on-line e-mail newsletter letting students in the program know about upcoming events. E-mail is an important link for students in honors.

You will need all kinds of computer skills as you move toward advanced honors seminars and the thesis. Many honors programs provide students with computer access across the campus, from libraries and academic buildings to dorm rooms. More and more libraries are on-line, meaning that students search for books and periodicals using computers rather than card catalogs. Libraries also offer databases, which allow students to search for information through extensive computer channels. Doing honors research will involve you in using these and other computer tools and programs that are specific to your discipline. Some colleges require "computer literacy" as an essential skill. Whether or not it is required at the college or university of your choice, require it of yourself. Learn how to use the computer programs, databases, and search engines on the Internet that will give you access to the information you need for your courses and your academic growth.

Honors on the World Wide Web

Many of the honors programs described in this book have invited you to learn more about them by providing their URL address, which is the "phone number" of their home page on the World Wide Web. Very often these home pages are written and maintained by students in the program and, therefore, contain information important to students, like current course offerings, events, program guidelines, and faculty profiles. Some pages have interesting graphics and campus photographs, so a visit to a home page might let you see a more intimate view of a prospective school from the inside. It may even give you the names of students active in the program who would welcome a telephone call if you have further questions or want to chat. You might find yourself so enthusiastic that you want to apply right away, and in some cases the home page lets you do it by an on-line application.

But suppose you are at the early stages of looking around for the right honors program. The National Collegiate Honors Council and many of the regional organizations also have home pages. NCHC's home page on the World Wide Web at http://kelp.honors. indiana.edu/nchc/index.html provides information about the national organization as well as links to many other honors-related home pages. The NCHC home page is an excellent starting point in your search for the right educational opportunity in honors.

Some of the regional affiliates of NCHC also have home pages on the World Wide Web at the URLs listed below:

- Great Plains Honors Council (schools in Arkansas, Kansas, Missouri, Nebraska, Oklahoma, and Texas) at http://www.okstate.edu/honors/gphc. html
- Northeast Region of the National Collegiate Honors Council (Connecticut, Delaware, Maine, Maryland, Massachusetts, New Hampshire, New Jersey, New York, Pennsylvania, Rhode Island, Vermont, the District of Columbia, and Puerto Rico) at http://www.bloomu.edu/~honors/
- Southern Regional Honors Council (Alabama, Florida, Georgia, Louisiana, Mississippi, North Carolina, South Carolina, Tennessee) at http://www.utm.edu/srhc
- Western Regional Honors Council (Alaska, Arizona, California, Colorado, Hawaii, Idaho, Montana, Nevada, New Mexico, Oregon, Utah, Washington, and Wyoming) at http://www.honors.unr.edu/wrhc

In addition to what you can learn about specific honors programs, these home pages can tell you all about the organizations themselves, including a directory of all the people who are members. They also provide useful information about conferences that are coming up. In NCHC as well as all the regional honors organizations, students are invited to be presenters at these conferences—to give papers, teach model classes, present their research, act scenes, perform musical pieces, hold committee meetings, lead discussion on critical issues, serve on committees, and run for office. Check out the home pages of NCHC and some of the regional honors organizations to find out what is going on in honors. Being in honors is an invitation to become *involved in issues and ideas.*

Honors on the Web is never a one-way street. Students and faculty members also use the Web to discuss current issues and solve problems within their programs. They do this through LISTSERV, an e-mail contact address to which you can subscribe once you have joined an honors program. As a subscriber, you get all of the messages that are sent out, generally messages that ask questions or invite discussion. Sometimes people are looking for recommendations, like a good reading list for a course on modern religion or guidelines for a creative project. Sometimes they are looking for participants who want to join a roundtable discussion or issues debate at the next conference. Through LISTSERV people often throw out ideas that grow into national honors conversations.

With the idea of building a national honors learning community, one of the most exciting technological developments in communicating ideas is the NCHC Satellite Seminar. This is an interesting cooperative effort among subscribing institutions to make use of live satellite video teleconferencing and (optional) e-mail links among students and faculty to carry on a national dialogue related to a theme that is selected for the fall semester/quarter. The theme of the 1997 fall Satellite Seminar, for example, is "Family: Myth, Metaphor, and Reality," a topic developed in cooperation with the national office of the honors society, Phi Theta Kappa.

In every way, joining the honors community will link you up to what's new and exciting in college education.

ALUMNI PROFILE

▲

Kevin Byrne, B.B.A., Summa Cum Laude, 1990
Mississippi State University

Providing a wealth of learning opportunities and enlightenment, the honors program at Mississippi State University did not influence my educational development—it defined it. The breadth of programs offered in the arts, history, economics, and the humanities continually challenged me to broaden my learning experience, to search beyond textbooks, classrooms, and the requirements of my course of study. The honors program taught me to continually pursue a much higher goal—a lifetime of learning. The program gave me cultural and interpersonal qualities which helped me win a Rotary International Graduate Scholarship to study in Ireland. Its paradigm of a "Renaissance" education has been one of the greatest gifts of my life, and continues to help me achieve my personal, academic, and professional goals.

PROFILES

▲

ABILENE CHRISTIAN UNIVERSITY

4 Pr G M Tr

▼ **Honors Program**

The Honors Program at Abilene Christian University offers academic enrichment and fellowship for highly motivated students in all majors. It requires no extra courses and can be tailored for students with multiple majors or degrees.

Within the program, students pursue either the University Honors track (four years, 30 semester hours) or the Departmental Honors track (two years, 12 semester hours, aimed at transfers with no previous honors credits). Those who finish the requirements and have a cumulative GPA of at least 3.5 receive a gold seal on their diploma, a note on their transcript, and special recognition at Commencement.

Founded in 1984, the program involves an average of 230 students.

Participation Requirements: The University Honors track includes 18 hours of freshman and sophomore Honors classes. These are special versions of core curriculum courses—history, English, Bible, sciences, communications—and their emphasis is on breadth, flexibility, and critical thinking. These classes are kept small (limited to Honors students) and are taught by selected faculty members. Collaborative learning, study abroad, credit by examination, and other options can help meet this requirement.

At the junior and senior level, the University Honors track stresses professional competence, interdisciplinary thinking, and preparation for graduate study or a career. The upper-division requirement (12 hours) includes 6 hours by Honors contract in junior- and senior-level courses and a 3-hour Senior Honors Project, all of which fit into majors' requirements. Also required are three 1-hour interdisciplinary colloquia. Each colloquium lasts six weeks and features discussion and a position paper. Topics have included "Thinking Postmodern," "Science and Religion," "The Human Face of Medical Ethics," "Politics, Art and Society," "China New and Old," and "The Problem of Evil." Course credit fits into elective hours. Requirements for Departmental Honors are the same as the upper-division requirements for University Honors.

In addition to the stimulating classes, Honors Program students enjoy honors social events, visiting speakers, evenings in professors' homes, their own lounge (the HP Commons) for study and Internet-surfing, and their own news server on the campus network. Student representatives attend the Great Plains Honors Council meeting each spring.

Admission Process: Admission to the program is guaranteed for students with a minimum combined SAT score of 1200 or a minimum cumulative ACT score of 27. Applicants whose scores are lower may be granted provisional admission on the basis of high school records or other evidence of high motivation and ability.

Scholarship Availability: The University gives substantial academic scholarships but none through the Honors Program. Small travel awards help Honors Program students attend the University's spring program in Oxford, England.

The Campus Context: Abilene Christian University is a four-year, residential, private university accredited by the Southern Association of Colleges and Schools. Rated a "Best Buy" by *U.S. News & World Report,* the University offers ninety-six bachelor's degree programs. Cooperative programs include nursing, electrical engineering, and criminal justice. Its student population of 4,200 makes it one of the largest universities associated with the Churches of Christ. Abilene, Texas, population 110,000, is located 150 miles west of Fort Worth. It supports three church-related universities, a junior college, an Air Force base, and a lively cultural district downtown.

Student Body Undergraduate enrollment is 3,730: 48 percent men, 52 percent women. Ethnic distribution is 83 percent white, 4 percent African American, 4 percent Hispanic, 3 percent Asian American, 1 percent Native American/Eskimo, 5 percent international. Residential students constitute 43 percent, commuters 57 percent. Eighty-eight percent of first-year students and 75 percent of continuing students receive financial aid. The campus has seven social clubs for men and six for women.

Faculty The total number of faculty is 270 (162 full-time), of whom 79 percent have terminal degrees. The student-faculty ratio is 18:1.

Key Facilities The library houses 1.6 million volumes (446,000 books and government documents, 1.1 million microform, 76,500 other). Computer facilities include fiber-optic network and Internet access nearly complete for all buildings and offices. There are computer labs in each dormitory and network connections in most dorm rooms. Special labs are available for digital media, business, computer science, and English.

Athletics Abilene is in Division II NCAA for women in track and field, softball, volleyball, cross-country, and tennis and for men in football, track and field, basketball, golf, baseball, cross-country, and tennis. There is an active intramural program.

Study Abroad Study-abroad opportunities include annual programs in Oxford, England, (spring semester) and Prague (summer) and a variety of one-time programs (e.g., Japan, China, Switzerland) during May and summer terms.

Support Services Facilities for disabled students are plentiful. The library, Campus Center, coliseum, all dorms, and all but one office building are wheelchair-accessible; accessible restrooms and drinking fountains are numerous.

Job Opportunities Work opportunities on campus and around town are listed in the Campus Placement Office. The Career Services Office assists students nearing graduation.

Tuition: $8640 per year ($274 per semester hour) (1996-97)

Room and board: $2340 minimum

Room only: $1540 minimum

Fees: $440

Contact: Director: Dr. Chris Willerton, ACU Station, Box 8242, Abilene, Texas 79699-8242; Telephone: 915-674-2728; Fax: 915-674-6800; E-mail: willerton@honors.acu.edu; Web site: http://www.acu.edu/academics/honors/

ALCORN STATE UNIVERSITY

4 Pu G M Sc Tr

▼ Honors Curriculum Program

The Honors Curriculum Program is designed to challenge and stimulate the intellectual curiosity of highly motivated students. Courses are taught by senior faculty members and generally have an enrollment of 25 or fewer students. The program is coordinated by the Honors Council, which is chaired by the Director of Honors. A corps of 5 academic advisers is available to participants during the academic year. The Honors Student Organization (HSO) provides a forum for student-initiated social, extracurricular, and academic activities. A special honors workcenter, which contains computers, typewriters, a copy machine, and reference materials, is provided for participants.

The program has been in place for 25 years and currently enrolls 220 students.

Participation Requirements: During freshman year, students are grouped into special honors sections of general education courses. During sophomore year, students enroll in a colloquium designed to encourage and develop lively communication that grows out of enriched reading experiences. Sophomore students may also enroll in special honors sections of multisection courses, which are offered in response to student interest and when departmental personnel resources permit. At the upper level, there is an interdisciplinary honors seminar for juniors, which widens the student's outlook while providing an opportunity for some preliminary investigation in a field of special interest. The senior honors student engages in a program of study related to a single major field that offers the possibility for guided research, a seminar, independent study, or a special project.

Students in the program must enroll in at least 3 hours of honors work each semester. Participants must maintain a cumulative GPA of at least 3.5. Students who complete 28 hours or more of honors credit and maintain at least a 3.5 cumulative average will be recognized as Honors Curriculum Scholars upon graduation. Appropriate citation will be made on the Commencement program and on the degree certificate.

Admission Process: Freshmen are selected on the basis of scores on admissions and placement examinations. Those applying after the first semester of the freshman year are selected on the basis of their cumulative average and upon the recommendation of faculty.

Scholarship Availability: Scholarships are provided to participants through the Admissions Office. Full academic scholarships for incoming freshmen (tuition and room and board) are available on a first-come first-served basis. More than 90 percent of participants hold full academic scholarships. The scholarship is renewable, up to four years, provided the student maintains at least a 3.5 cumulative GPA and remains in good standing with the University.

The Campus Context: Alcorn State University consists of five schools: the School of Arts and Sciences, the School of Business, the School of Education and Psychology, the School of Agriculture and Applied Sciences, and the School of Nursing. Fifty-three degree programs are offered. Special facilities include Oakland Memorial Chapel, 1830 (U.S. Historical Register); Belle Lettre, 1830 (U.S. Historical Register); the Cora S. Balmat School of Nursing (Natchez Campus); and the Science Complex (completed 1996).

Student Body Undergraduate enrollment is 854 men (27 percent) and 2,308 women (73 percent). Ethnic distribution is 92 percent African American, 7.8 percent white, and .2 percent other. There are 20 international students. The residential community of 2,600 students constitutes 82 percent of the student body, while 562 commuters make up 18 percent of the student body. Ninety-three percent of students receive financial aid. There are six fraternities and five sororities.

Faculty Of the 175 total faculty members, 163 are full-time; 60 percent hold terminal degrees. The student-faculty ratio is 18:1.

Key Facilities The library houses 219,271 volumes, 279,003 government documents, 1,000 periodical titles, and 4,770 audiovisual titles. There are ten computer labs campus-wide (PC or Mac-based networks).

Athletics In athletics, Alcorn State is NCAA Division I-AA. Varsity sports are football, basketball (men and women), track, cross-country, baseball, women's softball, golf, and women's volleyball.

Support Services Disabled students will find fully equipped dormitories and classrooms.

Job Opportunities Campus work opportunities include a college work-study program and limited research assistant positions.

Tuition: $2389 for state residents, $4890 for nonresidents, per year (1996-97)

Room and Board: $2229

Contact: Director: Dr. Donzell Lee, 1000 ASU Drive #175, Lorman, Mississippi 39096; Telephone: 601-877-6138; Fax: 601-877-6256; E-mail: dlee@lorman.alcorn.edu; Web site: http://www.academic.alcorn.edu

ALFRED UNIVERSITY

4 Pr G M Sc Tr

▼ University Honors Program

It is the Honors Program's mission to enrich Alfred's best undergraduate students' education by providing seminars—all electives—to add a dimension to their lives. In recent years, these courses have considered things of the spirit. Students have studied T'ai Chi, alternative healing, spirituality and the counterculture, and Zen, and one group even attempted a vision quest. Others have focused on music: the evolution of jazz, the blues, opera, Mozart, musical theater, and music video. There have been seminars on superconductivity and lasers, dream theory, the old order Amish, Claudius Caesar, fairy tales, biotechnology and bioethics, the beauty of chess, and the World Wide Web. There have also been many seminars on film—film noir, Shakespeare and Hollywood, horror films, fiction into film, and the silent screen.

There are currently 175 students in honors comprising less than 10 percent of the student body. In most years there are 50–65 applicants and 75 percent are usually admitted. More than a third of the students in honors are National Merit Scholars, and Alfred has a very generous scholarship offer for them.

Nonacademic activities include the traditional Death by Chocolate reception in the fall; a banquet in the spring, featuring rock Cornish game hens and student entertainment; and each April seniors have dinner at the president's house. There are road trips to Rochester four or five times a year: first dinner out at a Greek, Thai, Chinese, or Indian restaurant, then to the theater or a symphony.

Being in Honors also opens doors to other things. When Trustees visit, for example, and want to have lunch with students, or when Admissions is looking for tour guides, or when Public Relations wants student stringers for the *New York Times,* the expectation is Honors will provide them. In recent years 2 Honors students had their articles printed in the *Times.*

The Honors Program has a motto: Time flies like an arrow; fruit flies like a banana. It is a reminder not to take things too seriously.

Participation Requirements: Honors students are required to take four seminars in their first five semesters. These courses do not substitute for anything else—the idea is to take these classes just for the fun of it; and because they are fun, most students choose to take more than four. The seminars are small (class limit is 15 students), informal (some meet at the Honors House with its comfortable couches and rocking chairs), and in many cases, student-led. Some are the result of student suggestions; others, like the vision quest seminar, are experimental.

To graduate in honors, a student must complete four seminars, write a senior thesis, and finish with a 3.2 GPA. Theses vary widely—students have studied barns, cryptology, vigilantes, and graph theory among other things. While some theses are essentially research papers, many aren't. One student studied traditional quilting techniques and then made a quilt. Other students have built a unicycling robot, created a stained glass window, and wrote and illustrated a children's book. Some have given public performances—a few years ago a premed student wrote and performed his own piano concerto. The common thread is a chance to work closely with 3 faculty member mentors on a project that really matters. Their theses are bound and become a permanent part of Herrick Library's Special Collections. Honors Program graduates have Alfred University Scholar printed on their transcript and handprinted on their diploma.

Admission Process: The single most important consideration for admission is the high school transcript. SAT scores are taken seriously, but they only measure performance on one day's test. A high school transcript shows what was achieved over four years, so it is a major consideration. Students who have done well taking a demanding schedule, including AP or college level courses, are the norm in this program. In fact, the majority of those accepted into Honors graduate in the top 5 percent of their class, and virtually all are in the top 10 percent. An academic recommendation is a must, as is an essay. Excerpts from the best essays are published in the Honors newsletter, Sublunary Life. The deadline for applications is June 1.

The Campus Context: The University is located in a small village 70 miles south of Rochester between the foothills of the Allegheny Mountains and the Finger Lakes Region.

Alfred University is consistently ranked among the top comprehensive universities in the North. It is comprised of five colleges and schools: Liberal Arts and Sciences, Business, Engineering and Professional Studies, and the New York State College of Ceramics (a SUNY statutory unit), which includes the School of Art and Design and the School of Ceramic Engineering and Sciences. Honors is open to students from all colleges.

Student Body There are approximately 1,900 undergraduates and 161 full-time faculty members, about 1 for every 12 students.

Faculty Eighty-eight percent of the faculty members hold the doctorate or the highest degree in their field.

Tuition: $18,498 per year (1996-97)

Room and Board: $6042

Room Only: $3136

Mandatory Fees: $474

Contact: Director: Dr. Paul Strong, Alfred, New York; Telephone: 607-871-2256/2257; Fax: 609-871-2831; E-mail: fstrongp@ bigvax.alfred.edu

---

ALLEGANY COLLEGE OF MARYLAND

2 Pu G S Sc Tr

▼ Honors Program

Graduates of accredited high schools and currently enrolled students who have achieved at least a 3.5 GPA have an exciting and challenging opportunity available to them at Allegany College of Maryland. The ACC Honors Program is a selective set of offerings, which includes special honors sections of specific courses and Honors-by-Contract courses. At least two such courses each semester will be designated as having an honors section, and the student has the opportunity to pursue honors credit through an Honors-by-Contract agreement. The Honors Program is not a separate curriculum; the student may major in any ACC one-year or two-year program.

Special activities such as receptions, conferences, cultural affairs, and travel are also planned for the Honors Program students. The students have access to and use of the Honors Lounge.

Admission Process: Freshmen are selected each summer for the Honors Program on the basis of their high school average and an interview with the Honors Director and/or members of the Honors Committee. Currently enrolled students or transfer students can apply at any time during the academic year. Students in the Honors Program are required to complete 12 hours of honors courses with a grade of A or B and must maintain a 3.5 overall GPA.

Scholarship Availability: All students who enter the Honors Program and are enrolled in one or more honors courses have half of their in-county tuition paid by the Allegany College of Maryland Foundation.

The Campus Context: Allegany Community College was founded in 1961 in Cumberland, Maryland, and has expanded to include three campuses: the Main Campus at Cumberland, Maryland; the Somerset Campus in Somerset, Pennsylvania; and the Bedford Campus in Everett, Pennsylvania. The College is located in scenic western Maryland, about 150 miles from Pittsburgh and about 150 from Washington, D.C.

Student Body The number of undergraduates who are enrolled is 2,551.

Faculty There are 100 full-time faculty members.

Athletics Allegany College of Maryland provides intercollegiate athletics for men and women as well as a wide range of intramural sports.

Job Opportunities Students are offered a range of work opportunities on campus, including work study.

Tuition: $2190 for area residents, $2790 for state residents, $3630 for nonresidents, per year (1996-97)

Mandatory Fees: $100

Contact: Director: Dr. James D. Stickler, 12401 Willowbrook Road, SE, Cumberland, Maryland 21502; Telephone: 301-724-7700 Ext. 256; Fax: 301-724-6892

AMERICAN UNIVERSITY

4 Pr G M Sc Tr

▼ University Honors Program

The University Honors Program provides an extra challenge for especially capable students. Those who participate in the program have the chance to involve themselves in honors work throughout their college years. Honors students broaden their horizons through exposure to a combination of traditional and innovative scholarship in a variety of disciplines. In addition, they are asked to explore challenging aspects of their favored field of study and cultivate the skills required to achieve excellence in this area.

The honors classroom resembles a forum, a place where students can share and debate ideas and opinions. Honors classes consistently allow professors and students to have individual interaction with each other.

The 20-year-old program currently has approximately 500 students.

Participation Requirements: Honors students must complete 30 credit hours of their course work (roughly 10 courses) for honors credit. Students must achieve a grade of B or better in honors courses to attain honors credit. The four-year program of honors options draws from courses in the General Education Program and work in individual departments. Early honors work gives students a broad base of knowledge, skills, and understanding, which serves as a foundation for increasingly specialized and in-depth advanced course work in the major and related areas. Students have the option of completing requirements for either University Honors in the major or University Honors. They differ only in the number of hours that must be completed in the major.

Admission Process: Students are admitted to the University Honors Program in three ways. Approximately 10 percent of the entering freshman class is admitted to the program on the basis of their high school record and SAT scores. Freshmen and sophomores, including transfer students, who have exceptional college grades may be invited to join the program if their cumulative GPA is higher than 3.5. Freshmen and sophomores who are enrolled at American University may also nominate themselves for admission to the program. Students who nominate themselves must have a cumulative GPA of 3.5, complete an application form and personal statement, submit a recommendation from a professor, and be interviewed by the program director. Students who enter the University Honors Program after beginning the freshman year are not required to complete the full 30 hours of honors course work. Exceptions to the number of required hours reduce lower-level course requirements according to an established formula.

Scholarship Availability: Scholarships are not available through the Honors Program but are available from the various colleges in the University.

The Campus Context: American University is composed of five schools and colleges: the College of Arts and Sciences, the School of International Service, the School of Public Affairs, the School of Communication, and the Kogod College of Business. There are fifty-four undergraduate programs on campus.

Student Body Of the 4,498 undergraduates, 60 percent are women. The ethnic distribution of the undergraduate population is 70.4 percent white, 6.3 percent African American, 5.6 percent Hispanic, 4.9 percent Asian, Pacific Island, and .5 percent American Indian. International students comprise 12.5 percent of the student body. Sixty percent of the students receive some kind of financial aid. Students may belong to seventeen sororities and fraternities.

Faculty Of the 526 full-time faculty members, 92 percent have terminal degrees. The student-faculty ratio is 14:1.

Key Facilities The campus library houses more than 618,000 volumes. There are several computing labs on campus, both PC and Mac, linked to Eaglenet, the campus network.

Athletics There are fifteen intercollegiate sports available.

Study Abroad American University's World Capitals Program offers study abroad programs in Beijing, Brussels, Buenos Aires, Copenhagen, London, Madrid, Moscow, Paris, Prague, Rome, Santiago, and Vienna. Other opportunities are also available.

Support Services The Office of Disability Support Services offers assistance to disabled students. The campus is readily accessible to those with disabilities.

Job Opportunities There are numerous work-study positions as well as other job openings.

Tuition: $17,514 per year (1996-97)

Room and Board: $4366 minimum

Mandatory Fees: $230

Contact: Director: Michael Mass, 4400 Massachusetts Avenue, NW, Ward 312, Washington, DC 20016-8119; Telephone: 202-885-6194; Fax: 202-885-7013; E-mail: mmass@american.edu

ANDREWS UNIVERSITY

| 4 Pr G M Sc Tr |

▼ Honors Program

Recognizing its responsibility to challenge its best students, Andrews University established the Honors Program in 1966. Currently it enrolls more than 200 undergraduates. Beyond its underlying purpose of encouraging student scholarship and research, the Honors Program attempts to meet its students' social and spiritual interests as well.

Beginning with the freshman year, honors students—known as Andrews Scholars—enroll in special sections of required courses. Led by devoted faculty members who are respected for their teaching as well as their knowledge, these smaller courses involve wider reading, more writing, and deeper discussion than typical alternatives. In the words of one student, "Honors classes aren't about *more* work; they're about *more interesting* work."

After selecting their majors, Andrews Scholars undertake independent research in their specialized areas and present their senior honors theses. The program encourages students to participate in regional and national honors conventions. All members of the Honors Program are entitled to audit one course per quarter, without tuition.

Thanks to student interest, faculty member initiative, and program development, the honors curriculum changes frequently. However, the University seeks to maintain certain values in every course: a challenge to learn and interaction with peers and instructors.

Given the Andrews University aim to educate the whole person, students in the Honors Program sponsor a variety of social and religious events ranging from banquets and drama performances to retreats and canoe trips. The recently remodeled Forsyth Honors House provides many opportunities for formal and informal student gatherings as well as study.

Participation Requirements: Requirements for graduation with honors include a senior honors thesis, an interdisciplinary senior seminar, 28 quarter credits of honors registration, and a 3.5 GPA in honors and overall. Graduation with honors is noted on the diploma and signified in student regalia. In addition, the honors thesis is listed in the graduation program.

Admission Process: Freshmen are selected each spring from applicants with a minimum high school GPA of 3.5 and high ACT or SAT scores. Transfer students and others may also apply. Continuation in the program requires honors course work and a minimum GPA of 3.33.

Scholarship Availability: There are University tuition awards for National Merit Scholars and individuals earning outstanding scores on the ACT or SAT I. In addition, the Honors Program offers returning honors students modest annual grants based on academic merit.

The Campus Context: Founded as Battle Creek College in 1874, the institution became Emmanuel Missionary College after moving to Berrien Springs in 1901. Following the transfer of several graduate programs to the campus, it was renamed Andrews University in 1960, the first university sponsored by the Seventh-day Adventist Church. Currently Andrews University is ranked nationally by *U.S. News & World Report* and *Peterson's Top Colleges for Science*.

There are two colleges on campus: Arts and Sciences and Technology; two schools: Business and Education; the Division of Architecture; and the Theological Seminary. A total of seventy graduate and undergraduate degree programs are offered. Distinguished facilities include the archaeological and biological museums.

Student Body Undergraduate enrollment is 2,000 (out of 3,100 total students), representing most states and many other countries. Fifty-five percent of the student body are women. The ethnic distribution of U.S. students is 53 percent white, 21 percent African American, 16 percent Asian, 9 percent Hispanic, and 1 percent American Indian. International students make up 18 percent of the student population. Of the 67 percent residential students, 33 percent live in campus apartments and in the local community. Eighty-five percent of the students receive financial aid. There are no fraternities or sororities.

Faculty Of the 234 faculty members, 216 are full-time; 113 hold the doctorate or other terminal degrees. The student-faculty ratio is 13:1.

Key Facilities The library houses 640,000 volumes. There are eight computer labs and nearly 300 personal computers for student use.

Athletics Although Andrews University has no intercollegiate athletics, there are intramural leagues for a variety of sports.

Study Abroad Study abroad opportunities include Newbold College in England and language programs in Spain, France, and Austria. The University also sponsors affiliated programs on campuses in Africa and the Caribbean. University students participate widely in English teaching and other international service programs.

Job Opportunities Students find employment in a wide variety of campus jobs, including work-study and the Community Service Assistantship Program.

Tuition: $11,340 per year (1996-97)

Room and Board: $3510 minimum

Mandatory Fees: $237

Contact: Director: Malcolm Russell, Berrien Springs, Michigan 49104-0075; Telephone: 616-471-3297; Fax: 616-471-6236; E-mail: russell@andrews.edu; Web site: http://www.andrews.edu/honors.html

APPALACHIAN STATE UNIVERSITY

4 Pu D M Sc Tr

▼ **University Honors Program**

Appalachian State University began offering honors work in the late 1960s. Honors at Appalachian is more than a collection of courses; it is an approach to learning designed to stimulate active involvement by students in their own education. Critical thinking and analysis are stimulated by free and structured discussions in and outside the classroom. Independent projects frequently allow the student to probe the depths of a topic, with individual professorial encouragement and direction. In the Honors Program, faculty and students work together to uncover the challenging questions that disciplines pursue.

Approximately 350–375 students enroll in 22–24 honors courses offered each semester. About 25–45 students graduate each year from departmental, college, or General Honors programs.

Participation Requirements: Honors courses are available in several departments. Most departmental honors courses substitute for core curriculum requirements or for popular electives. General Honors offers an interdisciplinary program featuring team-taught topical courses for core curriculum credit in the social sciences and humanities. A unique cross-disciplinary program is available for qualified juniors and seniors in the College of Business. Most programs require that a student maintain a 3.2 GPA (on a 4.0 scale). A generic University Honors Program Graduate designation is awarded to students who take 18 hours of honors classes, complete a senior honors project, and maintain a 3.4 GPA in honors classes.

Beyond the classroom, the Honors Program seeks to maintain a stimulating and supportive atmosphere for serious students. Honors students often take field trips to the facilities the University maintains in New York or Washington, D.C. Some students attend regional, state, or national honors conferences or study abroad for honors credit. Coffey Hall, the coed apartment-style residence hall for up to 105 honors students, provides special facilities for living and learning, including a classroom, word processing lab, and lounge. The Appalachian Honors Association (AHA) is a student-run organization providing social and community service activities for honors students.

Admission Process: The top 10 percent of the incoming freshman class (about 200 students) get an automatic invitation into the Honors Program upon admission or before summer orientation on the basis of their class rank, high school grades, and SAT or ACT scores. Others may request in writing to be considered. Students already enrolled are recommended for honors work by faculty or academic advisers. The number of students admitted is, in part, determined by the number of available seats.

Scholarship Availability: Appalachian's most prestigious merit-based scholarships are the Chancellor's Scholarships. Each year 25 incoming freshmen are selected for these awards (1996–97 stipend: $4000 per year), which are renewable for four years if a 3.4 GPA is maintained. Chancellor's Scholars must take at least one honors course each semester for their first two years. Many scholars go on to graduate from the Honors Program.

The Campus Context: Appalachian State University will celebrate its centennial in 1999. Founded as Watauga Academy to educate teachers for the mountain area, it grew as a teachers' college to become a member institution of the University of North Carolina system in 1971, offering a broad range of academic programs. It offers degrees in ninety-six undergraduate major programs and seventy-nine graduate programs.

With instruction as its primary mission, the University is committed to excellence in teaching and the fostering of scholarship. It continues to serve its region but also draws students from across the state, nation, and from other countries. Its beautiful mountain setting offers many opportunities for outdoor activities, including skiing and hiking. It serves a largely traditional undergraduate population in a residential environment and also offers a wide selection of graduate programs.

Student Body Current enrollment is approximately 12,050; 91 percent undergraduate, 9 percent graduate, and 88 percent from North Carolina.

Faculty The University employs 572 faculty members, 95 percent of whom hold doctoral or terminal degrees. The student-faculty ratio is 16:1.

Key Facilities Approximately $100 million is being spent on new construction projects, which are currently underway on the campus as the University catches up on many needed facilities, including an academic support building, a science building, and a new steam plant. A major addition to the student union opened in summer 1995. Appalachian maintains two campuses away from Boone: the New York Loft in the SoHo district, which began in 1974, and Appalachian House, which opened in 1977, in the heart of the Capitol Hill historic district just a block from the Library of Congress.

Athletics The University's Division I athletic program fields ten men's and nine women's teams. The men's and women's programs are perennial winners of the Commissioner's Cup and the Germann Cup, awarded by the Southern Conference for overall excellence. Appalachian's men's football team went undefeated in the fall 1995 season and its women's basketball team was Southern Conference champion in spring 1996.

Study Abroad Appalachian is one of the top ten master's degree-granting institutions in the United States in the number of students participating in study abroad programs, which can be done for Honors credit.

Tuition: $874 for state residents, $8028 for nonresidents, per year (1996-97)

Room and Board: $2840

Mandatory Fees: $790

Contact: Director: Dr. Donald B. Saunders, Coordinator, Coffey Hall, Boone, North Carolina 28608; Telephone: 704-262-2083 (office); Fax: 704-262-2734; E-mail: saundersdb@appstate.edu

ARIZONA STATE UNIVERSITY

4 Pu C L Sc Tr

▼ University Honors College

The University Honors College has the responsibility of organizing the academic resources of the University for the benefit of talented and motivated undergraduates at all three of Arizona State University's campuses—main, west, and east—and in all majors, minors, and certificate programs offered at those campuses. The College establishes standards for admission, curriculum, and graduation through the Honors College, assuring University-wide transferability and quality for honors education.

The goal of the College's curriculum is to develop habits of mind that enable persons to be lifelong learners, creative problem solvers, and participatory citizens in a democratic society. The College emphasizes small classes, generally limited to 20 students; seminar and other engaged modes of learning; and the development of critical reading, discussion, and writing skills. The College appoints faculty members who are responsible for offering the core honors curriculum, but the College otherwise utilizes the instructional and research resources of the University as a whole.

The University Honors College offers students access to all of the human and physical resources of one of the nation's most rapidly rising research universities. Honors College students have access to honors advisers appointed by the College and to faculty advisers in the colleges and departments. Based in McClintock Hall, a residence hall that accommodates 180 students, the College promotes strong relationships among students, faculty, and the College's administration.

The Honors College's residential space includes classrooms, meeting rooms, a library, a computing lab, and other student services. Arizona State University has more than 1,700 faculty members, most of whom welcome working with strong undergraduates. Honors College students normally fulfill the requirements for their majors and for graduating through the College without having to take additional hours. The College's courses meet a variety of general studies requirements and course work in the major can be adapted to meet college requirements, including the bachelor's honors thesis.

Notable upper division honors programs supporting the College's students are coordinated by the College of Business, which designed one of the first business honors programs in the nation; the College of Nursing; and the College of Public Programs. Other professional colleges are designing similar programs.

Honors students are strongly encouraged to participate in undergraduate research projects and internships. The staff members work closely with colleges and departments to ensure that appropriate programs are available and that honors students have preferential access to them. Many students participate in multiple internships and research projects. These experiences often provide the foundation for an honors theses.

The College offers one of the few study abroad programs—summer study in London, Edinburgh, and Dublin—restricted to honors students and taught exclusively by honors faculty members. The program is open to any college honors student in the nation, and all of its courses carry honors credit.

Students in the University Honors College have established a distinguished record in such scholarship and fellowship competitions as the Rhodes, Marshall, Truman, Goldwater, NSEP, Woodrow Wilson, and Mellon. Since 1990, more than 110 of these fellowships and scholarships have been received by Honors College students.

The University Honors College has been in existence for eight years, superseding a 25-year-old honors program. There are currently 1,750 students enrolled, with an entering freshman class of 450.

Participation Requirements: Graduation through the University Honors College requires students to complete HON 171-172 or HON 394 (for transfer students), a bachelor's honors thesis, 24 additional semester hours of course work for honors credit, the requirements for a bachelor's degree, and maintain a 3.4 GPA (on a 4.0 scale) for work completed at ASU.

All work completed for honors credit is noted as such on the student's transcript. Graduation through the College is acknowledged at the University's Commencement exercises and the College's convocation and is noted on the student's transcript. Students who complete their lower division work (18 hours of honors course work with an overall GPA of 3.4) also have that noted on their transcript.

Admission Process: Students are admitted to the College as freshmen or may transfer into the College either from within the University or from other institutions at any time during their college career as long as time remains to complete the requirements for graduating through the College. Entering freshmen must either graduate in the top 5 percent of their high school class or have scored 1300 on the SAT I or 29 on the ACT. Students not meeting these requirements may petition the Dean for admission. Transfer students are admitted if they are in good standing in the Honors Program at the institution from which they are transferring or if they have established a minimum 3.3 GPA.

Scholarship Availability: Students are eligible for a wide range of scholarships, including in- and out-of-state Regents' partial and full fee and tuition waivers, depending on the student's academic and cocurricular achievements; renewable cash awards for National Merit Semi-Finalists and Finalists and other students whose performance on the SAT or ACT is especially strong; Gammage Scholarships for National Merit Scholars, worth $3500 per year in addition to the National Merit cash award; Leadership Scholar Scholarships, $1500 per year for up to four years; and the Flinn Scholarship, awarded by the Flinn Foundation to Arizona residents attending an Arizona university.

The Campus Context: Arizona State University has several campuses, each with a number of colleges. On the ASU main campus are the Colleges of Architecture and Environmental Design, Business, Education, Engineering and Applied Sciences, Fine Arts, Honors, Law, Liberal Arts and Sciences, Nursing, Public Program, and Social Work. The Graduate School is also located on the main campus. ASU also has a west and an east campus. There are a total of 103 undergraduate degree programs.

Student Body Undergraduate enrollment is 29,181; 46.5 percent men and 53.5 percent women. There is a minority enrollment of 19.4 percent and 1,171 international students. The percentage of students receiving financial aid is 55.3. There are forty-four fraternities and sororities.

Faculty Of the 1,894 faculty members, 1,734 are full-time and 98 percent hold terminal degrees. The student-faculty ratio is 19:1.

Key Facilities Among special and distinguished facilities are the Grady Gammage Auditorium, the Nelson Fine Arts Center, the Computing Commons, the Electron Microscopy Laboratory, the Cancer Research Institute, the Goldwater Center for Engineering Sciences, the Noble Science Library, the Plummer Aquatic Center, and the Student Recreation Complex. The library houses 2,608,775 volumes. The University has thirty-seven computer facilities. In addition to the Computing Commons, computer facilities exist in every college and all residence halls.

Athletics Arizona State University is a member of the NCAA, Division I, and the Pacific Ten Conference. The University has twenty varsity intercollegiate sports and more than 500 participants. Many students in the University Honors College participate in varsity sports as well as club team sports.

Study Abroad The University Honors College offers a summer study abroad program to London, Edinburgh, and Dublin that is restricted to honors students, from either ASU or other universities throughout the nation. The College also sponsors an exchange program with the University of Edinburgh and has an agreement with St. Catherine's College at Cambridge University that allows a restricted number of its students each year to be full matriculants. In addition, the College, in cooperation with the International Programs Office, offers students a full range of overseas study opportunities either as individuals or in groups. For most programs, students can arrange to receive honors credit. Many students use these opportunities to do work that leads to their honors thesis.

Support Services Disability Resources for Students offers a wide range of support services, including academic and career consultation, referral and coordination with other campus programs, the Access Employment Program and Talking Books, nonstandard testing accommodations, an in-class note taking program, assistance with adapting course materials, alternative print formats, Braille production, tutoring, sign language and oral interpreting, and an intracampus cart transport service.

Job Opportunities More than 5,650 students are employed on campus, and jobs are available in every academic, service, and support unit. More than 50 percent of the students in the University Honors College have some kind of campus employment, including paid internships and research laboratory assignments.

Tuition: $1940 for state residents, $8308 for nonresidents, per year (1996-97)

Room and Board: $4287

Mandatory Fees: $69

Contact: Dean: Ted Humphrey, PO Box 873102, Tempe, Arizona 85287-3102; Telephone: 602-965-2359; Fax: 602-965-0760; E-mail: deano@asu.edu; Web site: http://www.asu.edu/honors/

ARIZONA WESTERN COLLEGE

2 Pu G L Sc Tr

▼ **University Honors Program**

The Honors Program at Arizona Western College is eleven years old and has 21 members at the present time. It offers three different courses of study, which provide intellectual challenges and stimulation for academically talented and highly motivated students, encourage students to probe deeply into various subject areas, promote the synthesis of insights they have gained across the curriculum, and facilitate the sharing of their discoveries with faculty members and fellow students. Long-range goals include fostering a lifelong love of scholarly inquiry and independent thinking, building a sense of leadership and responsibility, and evoking an enhanced self-confidence that will result from having met the challenges offered in the program.

Honors courses enrich the regular curriculum with original source material or current research. Honors students have expanded opportunities for discussion and interaction with faculty members and outside experts in a variety of disciplines.

There are currently 600 students enrolled in the program. The deadline for submitting applications is January 15.

Scholarship Availability: Honors grant awards are available to students living on or off campus and to either full- or part-time students. Stipend recipients can receive full tuition, fees, room and board, or partial grant awards. Stipend recipients participate in up to 10 hours per week in service activity to the Honors Program. Students applying for an honors grant must qualify in one of three ways: graduate from high school in the upper 10 percent of their class, receive a composite score of 21 on the American College Test (ACT) or a composite score of 1000 on the Scholastic Assessment Test (SAT I), or complete 12 hours or more of college-level course work with a cumulative GPA of 3.5 or better on a 4.0 scale. All applicants must write a 750-word essay proposing a project to be completed during their time at AWC. Three letters of recommendation are also required.

The Campus Context: Arizona Western is a two-year college offering the A.A., A.A.S., and A.G.S. degrees to 5,754 undergraduates.

Student Body There are 1,688 full-time undergraduates of whom 57.6 percent are women and 4,066 part-time undergraduates of whom 59.2 percent are women. The ethnic distribution of the total undergraduate population is 3.1 percent African American, 2.2 percent American Indian/Alaska Native, 1.6 percent Asian or Pacific Islander, 43.5 percent Hispanic, 48 percent white/non-Hispanic, and 1.4 percent unknown. There are 6 international students.

Faculty Of the 92 full-time faculty members, 98 percent have master's degrees.

Key Facilities The College has a 55,000-volume library and two computer labs.

Athletics The College offers men's and women's intercollegiate athletics. The men's intercollegiate athletics are football, soccer, basketball, and baseball. The women's intercollegiate athletics are volleyball and softball.

Tuition: $810 for state residents, $5130 for nonresidents, per year (1996-97)

Room and Board: $3000

Contact: Director: William R. Gwin, P.O. Box 929, Yuma, Arizona 85366; Telephone: 520-344-7685; Fax: 520-344-7730; E-mail: aw_honors@awc.cc.az.us

ARKANSAS STATE UNIVERSITY

4 Pu G L Sc Tr

▼ **Honors Program**

The Honors Program at Arkansas State University (ASU) offers special opportunities for exceptionally qualified students to develop their abilities to think independently and express their thoughts clearly and forcefully in speech and writing. Students majoring in any department in the University may participate in the program. Honors work supplements regular course work within the student's major field of concentration. It also encourages work that will develop familiarity with the relationships among different academic disciplines.

The honors curriculum includes honors sections of general education courses, honors options (in which an additional component is added to an upper-division course in the major or minor), special-topic honors seminars, honors independent study, and the honors senior thesis. Students in the University Honors Program have additional options for earning honors-caliber credit: they may, with approval, substitute selected upper-level courses for general education courses, claim selected upper-level courses outside the major, and take graduate courses for undergraduate credit as juniors and seniors.

The 16-year-old program currently enrolls 500 people.

Participation Requirements: Students join the Honors Program by enrolling in honors courses; there is no formal application procedure. Aside from Trustees' Scholars and other students who elect to enroll in the University Honors Program, which requires two honors-caliber courses each year, honors students are not required to complete a set number of honors courses each year. To graduate with honors, students must complete at least 18 hours of honors course work, 9 or more of them at the upper level, and earn a minimum cumulative 3.5 GPA. Transfer students may graduate in honors by either meeting these requirements in full or, if entering with 36 or more hours completed, by taking 15 hours of upper-division honors work; they must also have a minimum 3.5 GPA. Diplomas of those fulfilling these requirements bear the designation "Honors Program." Students in the University Honors Program must maintain at least a 3.5 cumulative GPA and complete at least two honors-caliber courses during each academic year, totalling at least 24 credits in all (at least 12 of them at the upper-division level), including an honors senior thesis; diplomas of graduates fulfilling these requirements bear the designation "University Honors Program." All honors courses are indicated as such on the student's transcript. Students graduating with honors and University honors are recognized at Commencement by blue honors cords and by special designation in the Commencement booklet, which also records honors senior theses.

Scholarship Availability: Residents of Arkansas with a composite ACT score of 30 or above who enroll at Arkansas State University in the fall semester immediately following their graduation from an Arkansas high school are eligible to apply for the Board of Trustees Scholarship. This scholarship provides tuition, housing, and a stipend of $1200 per semester for up to eight consecutive semesters as long as the student completes at least 12 hours of course work in the fall and spring semesters and fulfills the requirements of the University Honors Program in which Trustees' Scholars are automatically enrolled. Other honors students may be eligible for the Academic Distinction Scholarship, which provides for full tuition in the fall and spring semesters, or the President's Scholarship, which offers housing and tuition. In addition, two $500 Hazel Deutsch scholarships are awarded each fall to students who have demonstrated outstanding performance in the Honors Program.

The Campus Context: The mission of Arkansas State University is to pursue and share knowledge within a caring community that prepares students in challenging and diverse ways to become more productive global citizens. At its main campus and its partner two-year institutions, ASU provides students with the broad educational foundations that help develop critical analytical and communication skills.

The University's baccalaureate programs, backed by extensive laboratory and library resources and offered by a talented and committed faculty, provide excellent training for graduate and professional school and successful careers. Seventy miles northwest of Memphis and 130 miles northeast of Little Rock, ASU is located in Jonesboro, a thriving city of about 50,000, which serves as the cultural, financial, professional, and retail hub for northeast Arkansas. The ASU campus covers approximately 900 acres. The extensive physical plant, with a replacement value of $300 million, includes sixteen classroom/laboratory facilities, five residence halls, and thirteen administrative and services buildings.

There are seven colleges on campus: Agriculture, Arts and Sciences, Business, Communications, Education, Fine Arts, and Nursing and Health Professions—and the independent Department of Engineering. Students can enroll in eighty-one undergraduate programs and sixty graduate programs.

Student Body Undergraduate enrollment is 8,762, 46 percent men and 54 percent women. The ethnic distribution is 86 percent white, 10 percent African American, and 2 percent Asian. There are 249 international students. Seventeen percent of the students live in residence halls; the remaining 83 percent commute. Fifty-five percent of the students receive financial aid. There are thirteen fraternities and eight sororities.

Faculty Of the 481 faculty members, 405 are full-time and 87 percent hold terminal degrees. The student-faculty ratio is 19:1.

Key Facilities The Dean B. Ellis Library, the expansion of which was dedicated by President Bill Clinton, holds more than 508,000 volumes. The eight-story tower is the principal focus of the campus. Computer facilities include more than 2,000 PCs on campus, about 400 of which are set aside for students in laboratories, the library, and residence halls. The campus is fully networked and all students are given computer accounts, with Internet access, on request.

Athletics ASU is an NCAA Division I institution that fields fourteen teams, including men's and women's basketball, indoor and outdoor track, cross-country, and golf. There are women's teams in tennis and volleyball and men's teams in baseball and football.

Study Abroad In addition to supporting participation in other study-abroad programs, ASU is an active member of the International Student Exchange Program, which allows students to enroll in more than 100 international universities while paying ASU tuition and room and board; the only significant additional expense is airfare.

Support Services The Office of Disability Services coordinates the provision of services to students seeking assistance.

Job Opportunities The Office of Financial Aid assists eligible students with work-study assignments; most campus units also employ part-time student workers through the Office of Human Resources.

Tuition: $1950 for state residents, $5040 for nonresidents, per year (1996-97)

Room and Board: $2620

Mandatory Fees: $20

Contact: Director: Dr. F. David Levenbach; Assistant Director: Dr. Robin Anderson; Post Office Box 2889, State University, Arkansas 72467; Telephone: 501-972-2308; Fax: 501-972-3884; E-mail: honors@quapaw.astate.edu; Web site: http://www.astate.edu

---

Auburn University

4 Pu G L Sc Tr

▼ University Honors Program

The Honors Program at Auburn is part of a long tradition. Swarthmore College established the first honors program in this country in 1922, using as its model the Oxford tutorial system in which small classes of students and faculty members studied the Greek and Latin classics. Other models for honors programs and classes include the Socratic dialogues, the German seminars, and the European guild system.

Drawing on these traditions, the University Honors Program offers gifted Auburn students the advantages of a small school or college in the context of a large university. It is designed for students capable of advanced work and provides a unique opportunity for academic excellence. The Honors Program selects 200 entering freshmen each year. These students may be enrolled in any college or school of the University that has undergraduate programs or offerings. Students already enrolled in Auburn can also qualify for the program. The current composition of honors student's majors is 37.2 percent engineering, 25.7 percent science and math, 16.1 percent liberal arts, 7.6 percent business, 4.3 percent architecture, 3.7 percent education, 2.8 percent agriculture, .9 percent human sciences, .9 percent nursing, .4 percent pharmacy, and .4 percent veterinary medicine.

Participation in the Honors Program exposes students to a wider range of intellectual and academic experience, gives students the opportunity to form lasting friendships with other students committed to academic excellence, and promotes rewarding interaction between students and teachers. As a result of their special college experience, honors students have a distinct advantage in their future pursuits, whether they go on to graduate or professional school or go directly into their chosen professions.

Entering freshmen are introduced to the University Honors Program through Summer Honors Orientation sessions where introductions to faculty members and fellow students are made and friendships begin. Amenities are provided in our Honors Residence Halls to encourage this interaction as well as to encourage individual intellectual growth. The mentor program, organized by upperclass honors students, further assists new students as they adjust to university life. From their second quarter in the program, honors students are given priority at registration to ensure timely progress through their curricula. Most important, honors classes are taught in small sections and are designed to provide in-depth dialogue and interaction between students and faculty members. All honors sections are taught by professorial faculty members. Participation in the Honors Lyceum offers students a unique opportunity to focus on such issues as leadership, career planning, citizenship, creativity, and problem-solving. During their final quarters, honors thesis students are given library carrel privileges. As an ongoing service, honors students are provided with assistance in identifying and applying for scholarships and awards.

The staff of the Honors Program has the responsibility for identifying and developing students to compete for prestigious national and international scholarships (Rhodes, Marshall, Mellon, Fulbright, Rotary, and others). These scholarships have different requirements ranging from a major emphasis on academic achievement to an emphasis on all-around ability. Viable candidates must have a 3.6 GPA and have had leadership positions in many extracurricular activities. Edgar Gentle, an AU graduate and Rhodes scholar, feels that all students who get involved in the process benefit and significantly broaden their understanding. Those who do win one of these scholarships find it to be a life-changing experience.

The University Honors Program provides unique opportunities to excel in academia and to have enriching cultural experiences. The Honors Study Abroad Program is just such an opportunity, enabling Honors students to become more aware of the rich and diverse complexity of the broad world. Students in the program work within their Auburn curriculum and complete honors courses while abroad. There is a year-long program (Honors Junior Year Abroad) as well as possibilities for term or summer study programs. The universities that students may choose from include London, Edinburgh, Cambridge, and Oxford.

The Honors Program has also established an Undergraduate Research Program to provide research opportunities. Currently, students are involved in funded research through the Howard Hughes and Goldwater Scholarship programs, but also in conjunction with Redstone Arsenal and the Colleges of Veterinary Medicine, Science and Mathematics, Architecture, Engineering, and Liberal Arts.

The Honors Center is currently located in the Ralph B. Draughon Library and houses the offices of the director, assistant director, and secretary. Broun and Harper Halls are the Honors Residence Halls and are located in the Quad. They provide a place for the students to live, learn, and relax together. Computers, typewriters, and reference materials are available in the Honors Student Center, located in the basement of Broun Hall.

The 17-year-old program currently enrolls 564 students.

Participation Requirements:
The University Honors Program has two divisions. The curriculum of the lower division was developed to provide students with an opportunity for broad, enriching educational experiences and consists of honors sections of the required University core curriculum courses. Completion of these courses (36 hours) is recognized by a Junior Honors Certificate. The curriculum of the upper division (13-22 credits) consists of upper-level contract courses or reading/thesis courses, which provide opportunities for more focused and in-depth studies in the student's chosen discipline. Completion of these upper-level courses is recognized by a Senior Honors Certificate. Students can participate in either of these programs. Those who complete both programs with a GPA of 3.4 will graduate as University Honors Scholars. This distinction is noted on students' diplomas and transcripts. Other awards associated with the program are the Junior Honors Certificate, the Senior Honors Certificate, the Senior Honors Scholar Award, and the University Honors Scholar Award.

Admission Process:
Entering freshmen and currently enrolled students who demonstrate the potential for outstanding academic achievement are eligible for admission into the University Honors Program. Selection of incoming freshmen is based on ACT/SAT I scores (29/1280 respectively), high school GPA (3.5 minimum), and the candidates' leadership and activities. Selections begin with the highest scores submitted. This selection process is highly competitive; it begins in January/February each year and continues until 200 spaces are filled. Students currently enrolled at Auburn who have a 3.4 cumulative GPA may also be considered for admission.

Scholarship Availability:
The Carolyn Brinson Reed Scholarships in the Arts and Humanities, the Raymond E. Sullivan Scholarships, and the Boshell/Daniel Scholarships are awarded annually to selected upperclassmen.

The Campus Context:
Auburn University is composed of the following thirteen colleges and schools: the College of Agriculture, the College of Business, the College of Education, the College of Engineering, the College of Liberal Arts, the College of Sciences and Mathematics, the College of Veterinary Medicine, the School of Architecture, the School of Forestry, the School of Human Sciences, the School of Nursing, the School of Pharmacy, and the Graduate School. There are 136 baccalaureate degree programs that are offered.

The city of Auburn is a small residential area that is often referred to as the loveliest village of the plains. The University and the local community offer that rare blend of mutual support and cooperation evident only in a true university community. Auburn University, chartered in 1856, retains in its nationally designated Auburn University Historic District much of the ambience and richness of that era.

Student Body Undergraduate enrollment is 21,778: 11,457 men and 10,321 women. The ethnic distribution of minority students is 1 percent Native American, 1 percent Hispanic, 6 percent African American, and 1 percent Asian. There are 591 international students. On-campus housing spaces are available for 3,446 students; off-campus living is permitted. Forty-eight percent of the students receive financial aid. The campus has twenty-eight social fraternities and sixteen sororities.

Faculty Of the 1,259 faculty members, 1,150 are full-time. Ninety-one percent of the full-time faculty members have terminal degrees. The student-faculty ratio is 16:1.

Key Facilities Noteworthy research facilities on campus include the Center for the Arts and Humanities, the Alabama Agricultural Experiment Station, the Material Engineering Lab, the Center for Commercial Development of Space, the Space Power Institute, and the Mises Institute. The RBD Library, plus two branches, house more than 2.4 million books, 2.9 million microform titles, more than 19,000 current serials, and thirteen on-line bibliographic series. There are 600 computers for student use in the computer labs, the library, and the dorms. Access is provided to the campus network, e-mail, the Internet, and the World Wide Web. Computer labs on campus are open 24 hours a day.

Athletics In athletics, Auburn is a member of NCAA Division I in all sports except men's football, which is Division I-A. Intercollegiate sports (some offering scholarships) include baseball and football for men; gymnastics, soccer, softball, and volleyball for women; and basketball, cross-country running, golf, swimming and diving, tennis, and track and field for both men and women. Intramural sports include badminton, basketball, bowling, fencing, football, golf, gymnastics, lacrosse, racquetball, rugby, sailing, soccer, softball, swimming and diving, table tennis, tennis, track and field, volleyball, weight lifting, and wrestling.

Study Abroad Auburn University offers seventy-five study abroad programs in thirty-eight countries. Most major courses are available and many programs do not require prior knowledge of a foreign language. Students may retain official Auburn student status, apply for financial aid, and arrange for a pre-estimation of overseas credits. Study abroad can now be integrated with Auburn University degrees.

Support Services All students being served by the Program for Students with Disabilities have priority registration, use of the Assistive Technology Lab, and appointments with professional staff on request. Other accommodations may include extended time on exams, permission to tape lectures, enlarged print or braille, textbooks on tape, specialized computer equipment, FM system, removal of structural barriers, class note-takers, use of calculator, spellchecker, modified program requirements, alternative evaluation methods, text telephone (TDD), interpreter services, extra time on assignments, special parking, and/or alternative test format. Accommodations are individually determined and must be supported by disability documentation.

Job Opportunities For student employment on campus, work referrals are supplied through Student Employment Services.

Tuition: $2355 for state residents, $7065 for nonresidents, per year (1996-97)

Room: $1650 minimum

Contact: Director: William R. Gwin, RBD Library, Auburn University, Alabama 36849-5360; Telephone: 334-844-5860; Fax: 334-844-4424; E-mail: honors@mail.auburn.edu; Web site: http://www.auburn.edu/academic/other/honors/au_honors.html

AZUSA PACIFIC UNIVERSITY

4 Pr G S Sc

▼ Honors Program

The Azusa Pacific University Honors Program consists of enriched courses developed for 30 talented and motivated students selected from among applicants in each incoming freshman class. These general studies courses are distinguished by their greater depth, intensity, intellectual rigor, and close student-faculty collaboration. The class enrollment is limited to 15 students, and the courses are designed by outstanding professors in their fields. In addition to the honors curriculum, the program offers a variety of extracurricular cultural and social activities and international learning experiences. For qualified students who choose to participate, the Honors Program provides a challenge and opportunity: the challenge to perform at their highest levels of excellence and the opportunity to develop their abilities to the fullest.

Total program enrollment is currently 104. The deadline for applying is April 1.

Participation Requirements: To remain in the program, students must maintain at least a 3.3 cumulative GPA. Those students who complete a minimum of 26 semester units of Honors Program credits will receive an honors certificate and graduate with the Bachelor of Arts (or Science) with Honors degree.

Admission Process: To be considered for admission, potential participants must represent the top 10 percent of incoming freshmen, based on their high school GPA and SAT or ACT scores. Eligible students will be selected for the Honors Program on the basis of academic performance, demonstrated leadership ability, and exemplary character. In addition to completing the usual application and reference forms for admission to Azusa Pacific University, interested students need to complete an Honors Program application and submit one additional reference form from a teacher.

The Honors Program began with the freshman class of 1992. Thirty students are selected from each entering freshman class, which limits the enrollment to a maximum of 120 students.

Scholarship Availability: Trustees', President's, and Dean's scholarships are available to honors students but are granted independently through Admissions.

The Campus Context: Azusa Pacific University was founded in 1899 as an institution of higher education within the Wesleyan evangelical Christian tradition. The University seeks to advance the work of God in the world through academic excellence in liberal arts and professional programs of higher education that encourage students to develop a Christian perspective of truth and life.

The 73-acre campus is located in the San Gabriel Valley community of Azusa, 26 miles northeast of Los Angeles. The surrounding mountains provide a rugged wilderness-like backdrop to the campus. The location affords its residents easy access to the popular mountain and beach resorts of southern California and all of the cultural attractions of Los Angeles County.

The Bachelor of Arts degree is offered with majors in applied environmental technology, art, biblical studies, biology, business administration, chemistry, Christian ministries, communication, English, history, global studies, liberal studies, mathematics, math/physics, music, philosophy, physical education, political science, psychology, social science, social work, sociology, Spanish, and theology. The Bachelor of Science degree is offered with majors in accounting, applied health, biochemistry, biology, chemistry, computer science, life science, management information systems, marketing, mathematics, nursing, and physics.

The University is accredited by the Western Association of Schools and Colleges, the National League for Nursing, the Council on Social Work Education, the Association of Theological Schools, and the California Commission on Teacher Credentialing and Licensing and confers undergraduate and graduate degrees. Lily T. Chou, a December 1995 Honors Program graduate, was selected by *USA Today* (February 8, 1996) from among 1,231 nominees as one of 20 1996 All-USA College Academic First Team members.

Student Body Undergraduate enrollment is 2,463 (2,340 full-time, 123 part-time). The student body is comprised of 63 percent women, 4.2 percent African American/non-Hispanic, .9 percent American Indian, 6.7 percent Asian/Pacific Islanders, 11.6 percent Hispanic, 34.3 percent white, and 2.8 percent unknown. There are 101 international students. Fifty-three percent of the students receive financial aid.

Faculty There are 439 faculty members (179 full-time, 260 part-time). Of the full-time faculty members, 61.5 percent have terminal degrees. The student-faculty ratio is 13:1.

Key Facilities The library contains 130,000 print volumes, plus other media. There are ten computer labs, including IBM and Macintosh computers.

Athletics In athletics, Azusa Pacific University fields a nationally recognized thirteen-team intercollegiate athletic program as a member of the National Association of Intercollegiate

Athletics (NAIA). Men's and women's programs include basketball, cross-country, soccer, and track and field. Men compete in baseball, football, and tennis; women compete in softball and volleyball. In 1994, Azusa Pacific's men's athletic program was recognized as the best in the NAIA. In addition, the Cougar track and field team won its tenth national outdoor championship in the past twelve years.

The men's basketball team, which has been nationally ranked the past four seasons and has won the Golden State Athletic Conference (GSAC) championship the past four years in a row, advanced to the NAIA's Sweet 16 in 1994. The baseball team has been nationally ranked for the past five seasons and is the program with the most wins in GSAC history, averaging more than thirty victories a year in the past ten years.

Azusa Pacific is only one of two Coalition of Christian Colleges and Universities members west of the Rockies to sponsor intercollegiate football, and the team has won more than 55 percent of its gridiron games in the last sixteen years. Men's soccer is ranked sixteenth in the nation.

Study Abroad Several University travel-study programs are offered each year through the Departments of Art, Business, Global Studies, History, Literature, Modern Languages, Religion, and the Honors Program.

Tuition: $13,540 per year (1996-97)

Room and Board: $4200

Mandatory Fees: $56

Contact: Director: Dr. Melvin H. Shoemaker, Azusa, California 91702-7000; Telephone: 818-815-6000 Ext. 3216; Fax: 818-815-3718; E-mail: mshoemak@apu.edu

BALL STATE UNIVERSITY

4 Pu G D L Sc Tr

▼ **Honors College**

...to offer distinctive opportunities for students who show promise of outstanding academic achievement, and to do this so well that our graduates are competitive with the best students of any other college or university.

For nearly forty years, honors education at Ball State University has tried to accomplish the above-stated purpose. While this purpose guides all that happens in the Honors College, it does not explain the attitude behind its operations. Honors education is intended to be interdisciplinary, simply assuming the students' abilities to do rote learning and asking them to do more. Concerns with critical and creative thinking and problem solving tasks form major components of honors education at Ball State.

Classes and other opportunities are not automatically intended to be more difficult than might be experienced in nonhonors situations, but *are* expected to be different. Honors College is as much an attitude as an administrative unit—it is truly a college within a larger university. The excellent instruction and individual attention of the honors programs create many opportunities for students to enrich their educational pursuits and realize the benefits of a first-rate, small-college atmosphere within a progressive university setting.

Honors students take many of their courses in classes of 25 or fewer students, restricted to honors only. All Honors College students are granted extended privileges in the University's libraries. They have scheduling privileges that help ensure enrollment in desired classes at the times preferred. In addition, honors students have their own residence hall, and there is an academic adviser assigned to work exclusively with first-year honors students. Most honors students receive scholarship support.

Honors College and Departmental Honors graduates receive special recognition during graduation ceremonies and are awarded special diplomas. The designations are also part of the final transcript.

There are 1,100 students in the program.

Participation Requirements: The Honors College offers two types of academic programs. The first, designated University Honors, is applicable to all majors. Students must take a core curriculum of six specially designed General Studies courses and at least two upper-level colloquia designed specifically for the Honors College. Furthermore, they must complete senior theses or creative projects and finish their undergraduate work with a cumulative GPA of at least a 3.33 (B+). Students completing this program earn the designation Honors College Graduate on their diplomas.

The second program is called Departmental Honors. Students selecting this option usually begin work in the third year, pursuing specialized study in their majors and completing requirements specifically tailored to those majors. The students must also complete theses or creative projects. Grade point requirements are established individually by each department. A number of students complete both University and Departmental Honors programs.

Admission Process: Students in the top 10 percent of their high school graduating classes with SAT I scores of at least 1180 or ACT composites of 26 or higher are immediately accepted into the Honors College. Other interested students are encouraged to apply. Evaluations are made on the basis of class rank, SAT or ACT scores, academic background, and personal references. Students interested in the Honors College are expected to have had a thorough college-preparatory sequence, including classes in all the basic disciplines. Transfer students are evaluated individually by the Dean of the College.

Scholarship Availability: Ball State University offers many scholarships. Almost all Honors College students can expect to receive a Presidential Scholarship (half tuition and fees) if their application is submitted before the February 1 deadline.

Information about this and other competitive scholarships can be obtained from the Office of Scholarships and Financial Aid.

The Campus Context: Ball State University includes the following colleges: Applied Sciences and Technology; Architecture and Planning; Business; Communication, Information, and Media; Fine Arts; Sciences and Humanities; and Teachers College. There are twenty associate degree programs, twenty-nine endorsement programs, 108 departmental majors, 134 departmental minors, eighty-two master's degree programs, seven specialist programs, and twelve doctoral degree programs.

Student Body Undergraduate enrollment is 17,000 (53 percent women). Ethnic minorities constitute 7.4 percent. There are 152 international students. Thirty-six percent of the students live in residence halls; 64 percent are commuters. Sixty-seven percent of the students receive financial aid. There are eighteen social fraternities and seventeen sororities.

Faculty Of the 1,100 faculty members, 906 are full-time; 68 percent have terminal degrees. The student-faculty ratio is 18:1.

Key Facilities Among its distinguished facilities, Ball State University has an arena that seats more than 11,000 people for basketball, volleyball, concerts, and speakers and excellent performing arts facilities, including a 3,600-seat auditorium for concerts and Broadway shows. The University has well-developed recreational facilities and programs, including an Institute for Wellness.

The telecommunications building has two radio and two television stations. A television, voice, data, and fiber-optic information system is in place throughout the campus, including residence halls. The Honors College has its own residence halls. The campus is also noted for a world-renowned Human Performance Laboratory.

The library contains 1.4 million volumes. There are twenty-six state-of-the-art computer laboratories available to all students as well as an additional fifteen specialized laboratories. The student-computer ratio is 14:1.

Athletics In athletics, Ball State University is a member of the Mid-American Conference, which competes in the NCAA Division I-A in all sports. Ball State has nine women's and nine men's varsity sports: baseball (men) and softball (women), basketball (men and women), swimming and diving (men and women), volleyball (men and women), track and field—indoor and outdoor (men and women), cross-country (men and women), tennis (men and women), golf (men), football (men), field hockey (women), and gymnastics (women). In addition, there are numerous club sports including soccer, lacrosse, hockey, sky-diving, ultimate frisbee, and equestrian sports.

Study Abroad Ball State University participates in the International Student Exchange Program (ISEP), which currently places students in over thirty-five countries. In addition, the University sponsors its own programs in London (2), Keele, and Oxford (3), England, as well as in Gronigen, Holland, and Vienna, and a 5-week program in Korea, China, and Japan. Specific colleges or departments regularly initiate specialized programs or tours in countries throughout the world.

Support Services Ball State University is particularly noted for the facilities and support provided for students with handicaps or disabilities. These include note takers and readers; specialized computer facilities; completely accessible buildings, laboratories, and restroom facilities; shuttle buses; and excellent accommodations for traffic and security throughout campus.

Job Opportunities There are numerous opportunities for employment on campus or within the surrounding community. Although these vary by department, many are career-related. The University encourages experiential education and often awards credit for exceptional undertakings in this area.

Tuition: $3188 for state residents, $8448 for nonresidents, per year (1996-97)

Room and Board: $3952

Contact: Bruce F. Meyer, Acting Dean, Muncie, Indiana 47306; Telephone: 317-285-1024; Fax: 317-285-2072; E-mail: 00bfmeyer@bsuvc.bsu.edu

BARRY UNIVERSITY
4 Pr C S Sc Tr
▼ Undergraduate Honors Program

The Barry University Undergraduate Honors Program, founded in 1982, is designed to add both breadth and depth to the educational experience of students in the Honors Program. The honors curriculum offers the intellectually curious student an opportunity to analyze problems, synthesize theories and actions, evaluate issues facing our complex society, and develop leadership skills. The program gives superior students the opportunity to interact with faculty members whose knowledge and expertise, as well as their own willingness to explore nontraditional academic avenues, will enable these students to challenge the frontiers of their ability.

Qualified first-year students enroll in a year-long seminar in theology and philosophy (THE/PHI 191-192) during both fall and spring semesters. These seminars are team-taught interdisciplinary explorations of the Judeo-Christian tradition that is central to the Adrian Dominican tradition of Barry University. The intellectual environment permits students to focus on the responsibilities and challenges of the program and helps to determine a student's willingness to commit to the entire program.

Second-year students enroll in both fall and spring semesters in a social sciences course sequence focusing on international and multicultural issues, which also form a central part of the mission of Barry University. An interdisciplinary team-taught course called America in the World (HIS/POS 393) examines the role the United States has played and continues to play on the world scene from the perspectives of history and political science. The second half of the sequence, called The World in America (SOC 394), examines the history and present-day reality of the multicultural experience in American society from a sociological perspective.

Junior and senior students enroll for In-Course Honors in regular University classes in which they undertake individualized honors projects relating to those courses under the guidance of the faculty member teaching the course. A thesis, research study, or project, the capstone experience required to graduate from the Honors Program, is expected to emanate from one of these courses.

Currently, there are about 60 students actively pursuing the Honors Program sequence.

Participation Requirements: To graduate from the Honors Program, students must have maintained a minimum 3.25 GPA overall, have completed 24 credit hours in honors classes (including the required THE/PHI 191-192, HIS/POS 393, and SOC 394 sequence), and have submitted an honors thesis or project. Successful completion of the Honors Program requirements is noted at graduation and is recorded on the student's transcript.

Admission Process: First-year students are invited each May to participate in the Honors Program on the basis of their high school average and their SAT I scores (minimum 1100 recentered SAT I combined score). Students who are Trustees Scholarship recipients, with the exception of those majoring in the School of Natural and Health Sciences, are required to participate in the Honors Program. Students with A.A. degrees transferring from nationally recognized honors programs proceed to the junior and senior level honors courses and are exempt from the first- and second-year honors course sequences.

The Campus Context: Barry University is an independent coeducational Catholic institution of higher education in the liberal arts and professional studies within the Judeo-Christian and Dominican traditions. The College, founded in 1940 by the Dominican sisters from Adrian, Michigan, became a University in 1981 and is accredited by the Southern Association of Colleges and Schools. It is located in a beautiful 90-acre suburban campus 14 miles from Ft. Lauderdale and 7 miles from Miami.

The University has six undergraduate college divisions that participate in the Honors Program: the School of Arts and Sciences, the D. Inez Andreas School of Business, the Adrian Dominican School of Education, the School of Human Performance and Leisure Sciences, the School of Natural and Health Sciences, and the School of Nursing. Two divisions (the School of Podiatric Medicine and the School of Social Work) only offer graduate degrees and they, along with the School of Adult and Continuing Education, fall outside the scope of the Undergraduate Honors Program.

The University offers sixty-seven undergraduate majors and academic concentrations leading to the baccalaureate degree.

Student Body Undergraduate enrollment is 1,640 full-time and 2,299 part-time. Student enrollment includes 61 percent Florida residents, 22 percent nonresidents, and 17 percent international. Thirty-five different scholarships are available and 77 percent of undergraduates receive some type of financial assistance, including work-study.

Faculty There are 216 full-time faculty (70 percent hold doctorates or other terminal degrees) and 284 part-time faculty. The student-faculty ratio is 14:1.

Key Facilities Distinguished facilities available for student use include the David Brinkley Studio, with broadcasting equipment comparable to that found in local news stations with satellite capability for live teleconferencing that supports a closed-circuit television/radio station (WBRY). In addition, a state-of-the-art Human Performance Laboratory in a $4.5-million sports complex houses one of two nationally accredited Sports Medicine-Athletic Training programs in the country.

The 656,530 volume library contains 2,300 periodicals, 450,00 microfilms, and 4,200 audiovisual materials. The Academic Computer Center is available to all students, faculty members, and staff. The main lab is equipped with sixty networked microcomputers and a number of minicomputer terminals. The University currently has an inventory of more than 700 microcomputers.

Study Abroad Barry University is a member of the College Consortium for International Studies. Barry students can participate in over fifty programs offered by the member colleges and universities. In addition, Barry University has articulation agreements with a number of universities abroad for student exchanges.

Support Services A fully staffed Office of Disabled Student Services operates under the Division of Academic and Instructional Services. It provides assistance within its resources to students having physical, visual, hearing, speech, learning, psychological, chronic, and temporary disabilities.

Tuition: $12,790 per year (1996-97)

Room and Board: $5680

Mandatory Fees: $260

Contact: Department Chair: Dr. Jesus Mendez; Program Director: Dr. Jung Choi; Department of Interdisciplinary Studies, 11300 NE Second Avenue, Miami Shores, Florida 33161; Telephone: 305-899-3472; Fax: 305-899-3466; E-mail: mendez@ pcsa01.barry.edu or choi@bu4090.barry.edu

BARUCH COLLEGE OF THE CITY UNIVERSITY OF NEW YORK

4 Pu G M Sc Tr

▼ **Baruch College Academic Enrichment Program**

Baruch College is in the process of a significant expansion of opportunities for students to participate in honors programs. There is now a Baruch College Honors Institute that oversees the Baruch College Academic Enrichment Program, consisting of an Academic Honors Program, an Internship and Mentorship Program, a Leadership Program, and a Program on Ethics and Social Responsibility. All aspects of the program are intended to challenge students with outstanding academic ability and the motivation to allow college to provide the foundation for a lifetime of inquiry, analysis, and accomplishment. The activities of the Honors Institute and the Academic Enrichment Program are overseen by a council, which signifies the collegial nature of the program. Members of the council include instructional faculty members, program directors, the Chief Librarian, the Dean of Students, chairs of the school curriculum committees, and representatives from the Students Honors Council and student government.

Best known for its blend of the liberal arts and professional education and for housing the largest collegiate business school in the country, the City University's only School of Public Affairs, and an outstanding School of Liberal Arts and Sciences, Baruch College provides an Academic Enrichment Program that reflects the traditions of an education designed to graduate enlightened leaders. Baruch's alumni are heavily represented in the upper echelons of American business and are prominent leaders in the cultural and social life of New York City.

The Academic Honors Program is designed to combine honors courses in each school with college-wide courses. The classes, which have restricted enrollment to permit lively exchange between faculty members and students, emphasize collaborative learning, communication skills, analytical mastery, and the relationships between the classroom, the workplace, and society. The Program also features seminars with outstanding speakers and capitalizes on the rich cultural milieux of Manhattan and the College's location in the beautiful, historic Gramercy Park region.

The Internship and Mentorship Program seeks meaningful internship placement for all honors students and provides one-on-one mentors from the large cadre of successful Baruch alumni from the business, governmental, and cultural life of New York City. The Leadership Program engages the talent of the Baruch faculty members with special expertise in the theory and practice of leadership. The Program on Ethics and Social Responsibility integrates into the Academic Enrichment Program the philosophical, social, and cultural issues that extend the development of individual potential into a socially conscious, positive force in society.

Students are guided by special faculty advisers in each department and at the school level. There is an Honors Seminar Room outfitted with amenities to enhance the opportunities for interaction among the honors students and between the students and faculty. The Honors Seminar

Room is equipped with advanced computers, study carrels, and a special selection of reading materials relating to the semester's academic work. Baruch's award-winning library offers special services for honors students, coordinated with their honors course work.

The Baruch Scholars Program has existed for many years, and the new Academic Enrichment Program, which is a significant extension of the Scholars Program, was initiated in academic year 1995-1996. There are currently 150 students in the Program.

Participation Requirements: To continue in the Program, students must create and fulfill a contract in consultation with the College Academic Enrichment Council and maintain a minimum GPA of 3.5. Each contract is tailored to the individual student and combines aspects of the comprehensive Enrichment Program.

Students who complete an honors thesis, which is approved by the Honors Committee, are designated for graduation with honors on their diplomas. The College is instituting additional citations that will appear on transcripts showing the completion of other aspects of the new Academic Enrichment Program, including honors in the majors. Honors students are eligible for a number of special awards for outstanding performance in the major. These students are presented with certificates at a public ceremony honoring their performance.

Admission Process: Students may participate in the Honors Program beginning in their freshman year and continue throughout their studies as long as they maintain satisfactory performance. Students who do not participate in their freshman year may join the program in their sophomore year if they meet the eligibility requirements. The College is currently determining standards for direct entry into the Program by transfer students and for their entrance after they have completed course work at Baruch.

All students who qualify for merit-based scholarships (Rosenberg Scholars and Presidential Scholars for freshmen and Provost's Scholars for continuing students) are eligible for the Academic Enrichment Program, and all scholarship students are required to participate in selected aspects of the Program. Other students are eligible for the program after completing 24 credit hours at the College with a cumulative GPA of 3.5. Candidates must write a personal statement and send letters of recommendation from faculty members.

Scholarship Availability: All scholarships are based on merit. For freshmen, merit is based on the high school academic average, SAT scores, an evaluation of essays, and letters of recommendation. Continuation of the scholarship is based on academic performance. For students who do not receive scholarships as freshmen, merit is based on the overall GPA and the evaluation of the essays and recommendations.

Freshman students are required to have a minimum high school academic average of 87 and a combined SAT I score of 1200 in addition to an essay, a personal interview, and letters of recommendation. A special group of scholarships, the Rosenberg Scholars, require a minimum high school academic average of 90 and a combined SAT I score of 1360 as well as an essay, interview, and recommendations. In addition to eligibility for the Honors Program, scholarship students have early registration privileges, a special section of freshman orientation, unique library privileges, and a Scholar Academic Advisor.

The Campus Context: The Bernard M. Baruch College of the City University of New York is composed of three schools: the School of Business, the School of Liberal Arts and Sciences, and the School of Public Affairs. Twenty-six undergraduate and thirty-five graduate programs are offered.

Among distinguished facilities on campus is the newly renovated library, which has received awards from architectural and library organizations; well-appointed offices and recreation spaces for student organizations; and an honors seminar room outfitted with comfortable furniture, study carrels, computers, and seminar tables for the exclusive use of students in the Honors Program.

The special facility for theater use is the Cocteau Theater Company, in residence at Baruch. Baruch also supports the Alexander String Quartet residency and the Mishkin Art Gallery, which exhibits high quality professional artistic work frequently reviewed by major publications. Baruch is located in Manhattan in the Gramercy Park District.

There is a Student Academic Consulting Center, which coordinates supplemental instruction for Baruch students, and Honors Program students have ready access to work as tutors in this Center, providing them with additional funds and experience in serving as instructors. A new 750,000-square-foot Baruch Academic Complex, which will house the School of Business, the School of Liberal Arts and Sciences, the Executive Programs, and extensive recreational facilities, including two theaters, a swimming pool, basketball courts, exercise rooms, and other sports facilities, will be ready for occupancy in the year 2000.

Student Body Undergraduate enrollment is approximately 13,150 (58 percent women). The ethnic distribution of the student body is 31.2 percent white, 23.2 percent African American, 20.6 percent Hispanic, 24.9 percent Asian/Pacific Islander, and .1 percent American Indian/Alaskan. There are 775 undergraduate international students (5.9 percent). All students commute to campus. Seventy-three percent of the students receive financial aid. CUNY does not have fraternities and sororities.

Faculty Of the 757 faculty members, 428 are full-time and 93.5 percent hold terminal degrees. The student-faculty ratio is 23:1.

Key Facilities The 656,530 volume library also contains 2,300 periodicals, 450,00 microfilms, and 4,200 audiovisual materials. The Academic Computer Center is available to all students, faculty members, and staff. The main lab is equipped with sixty networked microcomputers and a number of minicomputer terminals. The University currently has an inventory of more than 700 microcomputers. Modern computer labs are distributed throughout the campus providing ready access to computers on a scheduled and drop-in basis. All students have an e-mail account for electronic access to faculty members.

Athletics There is an Office of Intercollegiate Athletics, which conducts a program of athletic competition with other collegiate institutions in soccer, volleyball, bowling, tennis, basketball, fencing, and baseball for men; volleyball, basketball, bowling, tennis, and fencing for women; and coed archery. It also sponsors a coed cheerleading squad. Membership on these teams and this squad is open to all qualified students. The College is a member of the National Collegiate Athletic Association (NCAA) and the Eastern College Athletic Conference (ECAC) as well as other regional and metropolitan athletic conferences. There is also an Office of Intramurals and Recreation, which offers extensive activities.

Study Abroad Baruch College has study abroad exchange agreements with seven international universities: the Université de Paris, Université Jean Moulin, École Superieure de Commerce de Flouen, Universitat Mannheim, Middlesex University, Universidad Iberoamericana, and Tel-Aviv University.

Support Services The campus has an Office of Services for Students with Disabilities, which oversees compliance with laws and regulations to ensure that students with disabilities receive appropriate assistance. A variety of services and auxiliary aids are provided such as preadmission interviews, liaison with college departments and outside agencies, counseling, alternate testing arrangements, readers, writers, interpreters, library assistants, notetakers, adaptive equipment, priority registration, and classroom changes.

Job Opportunities There are extensive employment opportunities on campus. In addition to student aide work, motivated students with good performance records are assured the opportunity to work as peer assistants for faculty members and as tutors in the College's Student Academic Consulting Center. Students also are employed in technology laboratories.

Tuition: $3200 for state residents, $6800 for nonresidents, per year (1996-97)

Mandatory Fees: $120 per year, full-time. Part-time: $30.85 per semester for day students, $18.85 per semester for evening students.

Contact: Director: Dr. Susan Locke, 17 Lexington Avenue, New York, New York 10010; Telephone: 212-387-1543; Fax: 212-387-1554; Web site: http://www.Baruch.cuny.edu

BAYLOR UNIVERSITY

4 Pr G L Sc Tr

▼ **Honors Program**

Established in 1959, the Honors Program at Baylor enables outstanding students to broaden their intellectual horizons in numerous ways. Through exploring their major fields of study intensely, integrating many areas of knowledge, and through application of independent research techniques, Honors Program students form a community of shared learning with one another and with faculty members from all disciplines within the University.

Honors students enroll in special sections of certain required courses. During their freshman and sophomore years, students take 18 hours of these honors sections. These classes are generally smaller, providing increased class participation and discussion, and are taught by senior members of the faculty.

Sophomores and juniors take two semesters of Colloquium, which consists of small informal groups that meet regularly to discuss something as ancient as Homer's *Iliad* or as contemporary as *Solzhenitsyn: Relic or Prophet*. The wide variety of topics and the creative approaches used within the program make this dimension of the Honors Program one that is often described by students as simply the best course you will take at Baylor. Whether the issue be White House policy, the actions of Dr. Jack Kevorkian, or the writing style of Jane Austen, the sessions are always thought-provoking and filled with lively debates that expand students' viewpoints far beyond the limits of their academic majors.

Juniors participate in two classes in independent readings that help prepare them for their senior essays. Under the mentorship of a professor, the student will focus on readings in one or two fields of study.

Junior and senior honors students produce an original research project. Recent examples include work in genetics, child psychology, economics, French literature, philosophy, and the arts. To design this project, students work closely with a faculty member who serves as a mentor and adviser to the project. Many honors scholars' theses have been published in national journals or have served as the seedbed for books of national significance.

With approximately 500 undergraduates in the program, the Honors Program at Baylor offers its students memorable classes and professors who will smile when they see students knocking on their office doors. In addition, the Student Advisory Council and the Faculty Honors Committee as well as the Honors Program staff are committed to providing rich memories for the students inside and outside the classroom. Therefore, along with the rigorous studies, the Honors Program invites its students to join together in retreats, coffee nights, and countless other gatherings that encourage students to become good friends as well as to develop their individual potential as scholars.

Established in 1959, the program currently enrolls 505 students.

Participation Requirements: To graduate from the Honors Program a student must have at least a 3.2 GPA, both cumulative and in the Honors Program; complete at least 18 hours of honors sections (usually within in the first two years); complete three contracted honors courses, which are designated upper-level courses in the major or related area; and complete 10 hours of Honors Program Courses, including two semesters of Colloquium, 2 contracts for Independent Readings, and 4

hours of course work building toward the completed research essay or significant creative project. Each spring the University holds the Harry and Anna Jeanes Academic Honors Week during which selected honors theses are presented to the community.

Scholarship Availability: Scholarships are granted through the Office of Student Financial Aid.

The Campus Context: Baylor University consists of the following colleges and schools, offering a total of twelve degree programs and 145 majors: College of Arts and Sciences, School of Business, School of Education, School of Engineering and Computer Science, School of Music, and School of Nursing. Baylor University has numerous distinctive qualities, including an extensive full-scale feature known as the Governor Bill and Vera Daniel Historic Village and the Strecker Museum exhibits.

Student Body The undergraduate student body at Baylor is comprised of more than 10,000 students. Approximately 21 percent of these students are minorities and 2 percent are international students. A high percentage of the students live on or near the campus with 33 percent living in the dormitories. Approximately 70 percent of the students receive financial aid. For students interested in fraternities and sororities, many are actively participating at Baylor and sponsor several major events on campus, such as All University Sing. There are eighteen fraternities, fifteen of which are national, and fourteen sororities, twelve of which are national.

Faculty Of the 665 faculty members, 606 are full-time. Eighty percent hold terminal degrees. The student-faculty ratio is 17:1.

Key Facilities Baylor's eight libraries contain 1.5 million bound volumes, 1.3 million microform pieces, and 1.3 million government documents. Among our extensive library holdings, the Armstrong Browning Library in particular houses several unique exhibits relating to Robert and Elizabeth Barrett Browning. As one of our recent graduates said, "Baylor libraries have something else that is even more important—librarians who care."

Computer facilities include extensive Macintosh and IBM facilities available on campus. Terminals are available to students in dorms and in areas such as the Student Union Building. Students have access to e-mail accounts and Internet services as well.

Athletics The following athletic programs are available: baseball, basketball (men and women), football, golf (men and women), softball (women), tennis (men and women), track, and volleyball (women).

Study Abroad Information relating to study abroad opportunities can be obtained through the Office of International Program.

Support Services The Office of Access and Learning Accommodation (OALA) is available to deal with circumstances associated with disabled student facilities.

Job Opportunities The Office of Student Financial Aid is available to answer questions relating to work opportunities on campus.

Tuition: $8640 per year (1997-98)

Room and Board: $4433

Mandatory Fees: $788

Contact: Director: Dr. Wallace Daniel, Dean of the College of Arts and Sciences; Associate Director: Elizabeth Vardaman; Assistant Director: Dr. Steve Sadler, Religion Department; Coordinator: Elaine Harknett; P. O. Box 97122, Waco, Texas 76798-7122; Telephone: 817-755-1119; Fax: 817-755-3639; E-mail: Elaine_Harknett@Baylor.edu; Web site: http://www.baylor.edu/departments/Honors

BELMONT UNIVERSITY

4 Pr G S Tr

▼ Honors Program

The Honors Program at Belmont University was created to provide an enrichment opportunity for students who have a potential for superior academic performance and who seek added challenge and breadth in their studies. The program is designed to allow students to advance as fast as their ability permits and to encourage a range and depth of learning in their study, in keeping with faculty members' expectations of excellence for honors students.

Students are offered a creative curriculum, flexibility and individualization in the formation of their degree plans, the collegiality of like-minded and equally dedicated peers, and academic and personal support from a tutorial relationship with a faculty member in the student's major field.

The honors curriculum is an alternative general education curriculum core that substitutes for the regular general education core for any baccalaureate degree. The 47 hours include 24 hours of interdisciplinary courses arranged around time frames in the development of Western culture, 8 hours of interdisciplinary math and science, 6 hours of courses outside the usual curriculum, 6 hours of tutorial study with a faculty member in the student's major, and a 3-hour thesis.

Successful completion of Belmont's Honors Program gives the student the designation of Belmont Scholar at graduation, which is noted orally, in the bulletin, and on the diploma.

There are approximately 75 students in the program, with the entering class limited to 18 students per year. The deadline for applying is February 15.

Admission Process: Students applying to the Honors Program should have both an outstanding high school record and a composite entrance examination score (ACT or SAT) predic-

tive of their ability to do honors work. In addition, students submit samples of their writing and are interviewed by the director.

Scholarship Availability: Belmont offers many types of financial awards and scholarships to academically superior students. Many students with these awards are also Honors Program students, but no financial aid is linked to participation in the program.

The Campus Context: Belmont University is a student-centered institution dedicated to providing students from diverse backgrounds an academically challenging education in a Christian community. Its vision is to be a premier teaching university, bringing together the best of liberal arts and professional education in a consistently caring Christian environment.

There are six schools on campus: the School of Business, the School of Humanities and Education, the School of Music, the School of Nursing, the School of Religion, and the School of Sciences. The University offers a variety of degree programs: the B.A. (twenty-one majors), the B.B.A. (ten majors), the B.F.A. (three majors), the B.M. (eight majors), the B.S. (twenty majors), and the B.S.N. (one major).

Student Body Undergraduate enrollment is approximately 2,400; 59.9 percent are women, 31 percent Tennessee residents, and 3.8 percent international students.

Faculty There are 154 full-time and 196 part-time faculty, 65 percent with terminal degrees.

Key Facilities The 175,000-volume library also maintains subscriptions to more than 1,200 periodicals. Belmont has a Macintosh computer lab in the library, an IBM PC lab in the business school, and a VAX 4400 computing system available on the campus network. Several of the schools have classrooms equipped with computers and several have student labs.

Athletics Athletics at Belmont are changing. Belmont is in the midst of a shift from the Tennessee Collegiate Athletic Conference of the NAIA to the NCAA. Competition in men's sports includes baseball, basketball, cross-country, golf, soccer, and tennis. Competition in women's sports includes basketball, cross-country, golf, softball, volleyball, and tennis.

Study Abroad Through a wide variety of international study programs, Belmont offers students the opportunity to broaden their education while earning credit hours toward their degrees. These programs, which range in duration from two weeks to a full year, can qualify for financial aid for eligible students, and some scholarship money is available. Currently, programs exist in Great Britain, France, Mexico, the Bahamas, Germany, Russia, and China.

Tuition: $10,050 per year (1997-98)

Room and Board: $3890 minimum

Mandatory Fees: $250

Contact: Director: Devon Boan, Associate Professor, 1900 Belmont Blvd., Nashville, Tennessee 37212; Telephone: 615-460-6000; Web site: http://acklen.belmont.edu/BelmontHome/school.orgs/honors.dept/honors.html

BEMIDJI STATE UNIVERSITY

| 4 Pu D M Sc Tr |

▼ Honors Program

The Honors Program provides an opportunity for academically talented students to meet academic challenges as undergraduates at Bemidji State University. The program includes interdisciplinary honors courses and a rigorous honors thesis or project generally undertaken during the junior year in collaboration with a faculty member and under the supervision of the Honors Council.

Honors scholars have more freedom in planning a program of study and thus assume a greater responsibility for designing their education. Such students also have an opportunity to accelerate study in their major. Participation in honors courses allows students to master interdisciplinary relationships in the social sciences, arts, and natural sciences through coordinated study by students and faculty members. Students who fulfill all Honors Program requirements are exempt from the University's normal liberal education requirements. The program is 27 years old and currently enrolls 200 students.

Participation Requirements: During the freshman and sophomore terms, honors scholars are advised by faculty members on the Honors Council. Freshman and sophomore students are notified by mail about areas of specialization. Honors scholars must maintain a 3.0 GPA in their college work. Honors scholars must also complete five interdisciplinary honors courses and honors core requirements. The Honors Council will consider requests for exemptions on an individual basis. Once honors scholars have declared majors (normally at the end of their sophomore year), honors scholars are advised by the faculty members in their area. They must complete five interdisciplinary honors courses, the honors thesis, and a set of honors core requirements to ensure a broad liberal education. They have the advantage of signing up for courses at the time scheduled for seniors. Students completing the Honors Program receive Honors Program notation on their official transcript and an Honors Program certificate.

Admission Process: High school seniors with superior academic records or college students with a cumulative GPA of 3.25 or above are invited to apply. They must submit a short letter stating their interest in being selected as honors scholars. The number of students admitted each academic year is determined by the number of qualified applications received. Students are appointed to the program on a competitive basis by the Honors Council, the faculty advisers to the Honors Program. Applicants are notified in writing.

The Campus Context: In 1919, Bemidji State Normal School began its first regular school year with 38 students. The school was chartered by the Minnesota State Legislature in response to a growing need for public school teachers, and teacher training was its primary curriculum. Then, in a pattern familiar to American higher education, in 1921 Bemidji Normal became Bemidji State Teachers College, offering a four-year degree. Reflecting ongoing changes in the curriculum, the school was renamed Bemidji State College in 1957. In 1975, in recognition of its growing role as a multipurpose educational institution, it became Bemidji State University. Now, just past its seventy-fifth anniversary, BSU hosts nearly 5,000 undergraduate and graduate students. It offers majors in more than fifty baccalaureate fields of study as well as Master of Arts and Master of Science degrees.

Some of its degree programs and research activities are unique to the state. Bemidji Sate University, located on an 83-acre small town campus, is composed of four colleges and schools: the College of Arts and Letters, the College of Social and Natural Sciences, the College of Professional Studies, and the School of Integrative Studies. The University offers two associate degree programs, forty-four baccalaureate degree programs, and ten graduate degree programs.

Student Body Undergraduate enrollment is 4,310 (54 percent women). The ethnic distribution of the student body is approximately .5 percent African American, .7 percent Asian American, 3 percent Native American, .4 percent Hispanic, 80 percent Caucasian, and 5 percent international. Eighty-eight percent are state residents. Seventy-five percent of students receive financial aid. There are three national fraternities, two national sororities, and one local sorority as well as eighty social organizations on campus.

Faculty Of the 201 undergraduate faculty members, 190 are full-time; 77 percent hold terminal degrees. The student-faculty ratio is 21:1.

Key Facilities The A.C. Clark Library houses 185,000 books, 721,255 microform titles, 1,443 periodicals, and 1,650 records, tapes, and CDs. Computer facilities include more than 280 Macintosh and PC computers that are available to students in the computer center, classrooms, libraries, and dorms. All classrooms, labs, and offices as well as student rooms are linked to the network and have access to e-mail and the Internet.

Athletics Bemidji State is a member of NCAA, Division II in all sports, which include baseball (men), basketball (men and women), cross country (men and women), football (men), golf (men), ice hockey (men), softball (women), tennis (women), track and field (men and women), and volleyball (women). Intramural sports are basketball, football, ice hockey, racquetball, soccer, softball, tennis, track and field, volleyball, and wrestling.

Study Abroad The Office of International Studies coordinates study abroad programs in England/Europe, China, Malaysia, Japan, Sweden, and Ukraine. Students may receive academic credit for participation in international studies programs.

Support Services Students with disabilities are served through the Educational Development Center. Services include notetakers, tutors, academic advising, counseling, testing services, career counseling, study skills, and interpreter services. Most campus buildings are accessible by ramps and tunnels and are equipped with elevators. Handicapped parking is available.

Tuition: $2520 for state residents, $5631 for nonresidents, per year (1996-97); $3780 per year for full-time nonresidents eligible for the Midwest Student Exchange Program, $78.75 per quarter hour for eligible part-time students

Room and Board: $3300

Mandatory Fees: $405

Contact: Director: Dr. Michael Field, Hagg-Sauer Hall 357, 1500 Birchmont Drive NE, Bemidji, Minnesota 56601-2699; Telephone: 218-755-3984; Fax: 218-755-2822; E-mail: mjfield@vax1.bemidji.msus.edu; Web site: http://bsuweb.bemidji.msus.edu/~honors/HonorsPage.html

BENEDICT COLLEGE

2 Pr C S Sc Tr

▼ **Honors Program**

The Benedict College Honors Program is designed to serve the increasing number of academically gifted students who matriculate at Benedict College. Established in 1986, the honors part of this program exists in values. In its commitment to cultivate excellence and nurture the life of the mind, the Honors Program seeks to provide opportunities for honors students to engage in challenging academic experiences through stimulating discussions, critical thinking, free inquiry, and investigation. Students in the program are certain to develop and refine their communication and research skills. Students are also encouraged to develop their leadership skills and engage in active involvement in the wider community. The program provides opportunities for off-campus projects, study abroad, and internships. It also provides opportunities for publishing scholarly papers in honors journals and selected publications and motivates students to continue their academic pursuits in graduate and professional schools. The Honors Program is an environment conducive to effective teaching, studying, and learning. Students who participate in the program receive recognition for superior academic achievement. Honors graduates are recognized during a special capstone graduation ceremony. Their transcripts also indicate that they graduated with honors.

There are currently 89 students in the program.

Participation Requirements: To graduate with honors, a student must maintain a cumulative GPA of 3.2, successfully pass 21 hours of honors courses, complete two community service projects each year, serve as a presenter at one national conference, write and defend an honors research thesis, and sit for at least one graduate or professional school entrance exam.

Additionally, honors students are expected to participate in honors activities, develop a résumé by the end of their

sophomore year, and subscribe to high standards of behavior. Some honors activities include the Honors Lecture Series, the Contract Honors Symposia, Volunteer Service Projects, the Honors Induction Ceremony, the Academic Honors Convocation, and the Capstone Ceremony.

The Campus Context: Benedict College is composed of the School of Arts and Sciences and the School of Professional Programs. The College offers twenty-one degree programs.

Student Body Undergraduate enrollment is 2,138 (53.5 percent women). Of the student body, 99.8 percent are African American. There are 25 international students. South Carolina residents make up 66.5 percent of the population and commuters make up 33.5 percent. Ninety percent of the students receive financial aid. There are four fraternities and four sororities on campus.

Faculty Of the 155 faculty members, 110 are full-time.

Athletics Intercollegiate athletics for men include football, basketball, golf, tennis, and track. Intercollegiate athletics for women include basketball, softball, track, and volleyball. Benedict is governed by the Eastern Intercollegiate Athletic Conference and the National Association of Intercollegiate Athletics (NAIA).

Study Abroad Various opportunities for study abroad are available.

Job Opportunities Students find a variety of work opportunities on campus.

Tuition: $6304 per year (1996-97)

Room and Board: $3620

Mandatory Fees: $516

Contact: Director: Dr. Larry D. Watson, 1600 Harden Street, Columbia, South Carolina 29204; Telephone: 803-253-5413; Fax: 803-253-5184

BERGEN COMMUNITY COLLEGE

2 Pu G M

▼ **Honors Program**

Bergen Community College offers a variety of honors courses in the humanities, social sciences, sciences, and business. The purpose of the program is to challenge and prepare students of superior intellectual ability in smaller-than-average classes taught by university-level faculty members who provide enriched versions of traditional syllabi and stimulating consideration of contemporary issues. The Honors Program seeks faculty members of demonstrated excellence in teaching, often published and involved in current research. It encourages greater student participation in classroom discussion, interdisciplinary and innovative approaches to learning, and individual aspirations. Students benefit not only from a close relationship with honors faculty members and with each other, but also from the recognition of the College and a network of support in seeking transfer to baccalaureate programs.

Founded in 1985, the Honors Program has continued to expand both in size and in the number of courses it offers. In 1996–97, it enrolled students in American literature, art history, biology, composition, cultural anthropology, ethics, marketing principles, music appreciation, philosophy, psychology, sociology, and United States history. In the future, Bergen hopes to add courses in chemistry, computers, mathematics, and physics.

Currently there are 120 students enrolled in the Honors Program.

Participation Requirements: Students who complete at least 21 credits in the Honors Program are awarded a special certificate upon graduation, the designation H appears on their transcripts (enabling them more easily to secure admission to more advanced programs and scholarship aid), and public recognition is accorded them at Commencement.

Admission Process: Students are identified after their first semester upon attainment of a 3.4 GPA. Future plans are to recruit students directly from high school based upon their grades and an interview with an honors officer during their senior year.

The Campus Context: Bergen Community College offers fifty-nine degree programs in addition to twenty-one certificate programs.

Student Body BCC enrolls a student body of 43 percent men and 57 percent women. The ethnic distribution of the student body is 9 percent Asian/Pacific Islander, 5 percent African American, 15 percent Hispanic, 61 percent white, and 10 percent unknown. There are approximately 206 international students. Twenty-four percent of the students receive financial aid. All of the students commute to campus.

Faculty Of the 700 faculty members, 264 are full-time. Nineteen percent of the total faculty members and 29 percent of full-time faculty hold terminal degrees. The student-faculty ratio is approximately 18.6:1.

Key Facilities The library houses 134,883 volumes. The computing facility is a mainframe IBM 4381.

Athletics Bergen provides numerous intramural and intercollegiate activities. Intercollegiate sports include women's volleyball and cross-country; men's soccer, basketball, indoor track, baseball, softball, golf, and track and field; and coed tennis. The College is a member of the Garden State Athletic Conference as well as the national Junior College Athletic Association, Region XIX, which consists of schools from New Jersey, eastern Pennsylvania, and Delaware. The College also competes with schools from neighboring New York State and Connecticut. During the past academic year, intramural sports included soccer, volleyball, and basketball. In addition, students and faculty members join together for occasional softball games. The College also makes its athletic facilities available to area groups such as the New Jersey Wave and the YMCA.

Support Services Disabled students can find assistance from the Office of Specialized Services.

Job Opportunities Limited part-time work (up to 20 hours per week) is available.

Tuition: $1936 for area residents, $4022 for state residents, $7744 for nonresidents, per year (1996-97)

Mandatory Fees: From $291 to $1162

Contact: Directors: Dr. George Skau and Dr. Geoffrey J. Saddock (acting), Humanities Division, 400 Paramus Road, Paramus, New Jersey 07652; Telephone: 201-447-7978 or 201-447-9284

BERRY COLLEGE

4 Pr G S Sc Tr

▼ Honors Program

Berry College offers a stimulating and demanding Honors Program to enhance the academic experience of its top students. The program provides the intellectual challenge of participating in interdisciplinary colloquia, seminars, and honors-designated courses in a student's major field of study, all of which are designed especially for honors students. It also provides the opportunity of engaging in independent research under a scholar of established reputation. Furthermore, there has recently been established an Honors Program Student Association, a recognized organization that sponsors campus-wide activities and offers honors students the opportunity to be represented in various student and select faculty organizations. There is an Honors Program Study/Seminar Room in the College's main library.

Berry's interdisciplinary Honors Program is driven by the notion that there is inherent power in what we do *and* do not know, which allows honors students to follow in the tradition of many individuals who are enshrined in the College's Honors Program curriculum. Students will encounter in their studies the sort of people who, by summoning their courage to defy the certainty and orthodoxy of tradition, inquired into the mystery of things, posed new and probing questions, and offered creative solutions to the problems that they and their fellow human beings have faced and still confront. This was, and is, possible for some people not because they necessarily knew something, but more likely because they did not. Hence, honors students will discover that there is wisdom in doubt and ignorance.

There are currently 82 students in the program.

Participation Requirements: Lower-division course work requirements include satisfactory completion of two 3-credit hour Honors Colloquia (HONORS 201, 202) and at least two Honors Seminars (HONORS 211, 212, 221, 222), for which a student will receive a minimum of 6 credit hours. Honors Seminars vary in content and emphasis and are taught in rotation. Recent offerings include Europe between the Wars, Hindu Religious Texts, Foundations of Modern Biology, and Individual and Society: Economic and Literary Perspectives. Lower-division honors courses may be used to fulfill various general education requirements. Upper-division course work includes the satisfactory completion of at least two 3-credit hour honors-designated courses at the 300 or 400 level in the major or minor to be determined by the student in consultation with his or her adviser and the director of the Honors Program. In addition, the student must complete two honors thesis courses in the major, each of which carries 3 credit hours, and perform satisfactorily in a defense of their Senior Honors Thesis scheduled during the last semester of the student's residence at Berry College.

Admission Process: Students who wish to be admitted into the Honors Program simply complete an application and, upon acceptance, undertake the appropriate course work. Criteria for entering freshmen are scores of 1200 or higher on the SAT I or 27 or higher on the ACT, a 3.5 high school GPA or higher, and a writing sample. Criteria for enrolled Berry students are a 3.5 GPA or higher on college work completed, a writing sample, and names of two Berry College faculty members for reference.

Scholarship Availability: Berry College offers full-tuition Presidential Scholarships as well as partial-tuition Merit and Academic Scholarships. Many students who receive these awards participate in the Honors Program.

The Campus Context: Founded in 1902 by Martha Berry, Berry College is located on 28,000 acres of forests, fields, lakes, and streams, making it the largest campus in the world and one of the most beautiful. It was originally established as a school for mountain children who were willing to work in exchange for an education, and its founder, Miss Berry, is recognized internationally as a pioneer in American education. Berry College is ideally located in the scenic northwest Georgia mountains next to Rome and is situated midway between Atlanta and Chattanooga. There are fifty undergraduate majors leading to the baccalaureate degree, including liberal arts and sciences, business, and education.

Student Body Of the 1,675 undergraduate enrollment, 61.8 percent are women. The ethnic distribution of the total undergraduate population is 1 percent Hispanic, 2 percent African American, and 1 percent Asian American. International students represent 2.5 percent of the total undergraduate population. Seventy-one percent of all undergraduates reside on campus. Ninety-four percent of all new first-year students receive financial aid.

Faculty There are 163 faculty, 89 full-time and 91 percent with a Ph.D. degree. The student-faculty ratio is 16:1.

Key Facilities The library has 145,316 books, 355,573 microform titles, 1,387 periodicals, 75 CD-ROMs, and 1,788 records, tapes, and CDs. There are 100 computers available on campus, with access to the local area network and the Internet. The student-terminal ratio is 18:1. Access to the network will soon be extended into some student dormitories as well.

Athletics Sports teams compete nationally through the National Association of Intercollegiate Athletics (NAIA) in basketball, soccer, tennis, golf, baseball, and cross-country running. Equestrian, rowing, and bicycling teams also compete nationally.

Study Abroad Berry supports an active studies abroad program. Course work completed overseas is applicable for honors credit with the approval of the Honors Program Director.

Support Services Disabled students find that dormitories and academic buildings are totally accessible.

Job Opportunities The Work Program at Berry currently employs 83 percent of the student population, but, according to the Berry tradition, all students are assured a job on campus. The Bonners Scholar Program and the Founders Work Program are other possibilities for students who wish to help finance their education through work and scholarship.

Tuition: $9678 per year (1996-97)

Room and Board: $4380

Contact: Director: Dr. Marc A. Meyer, Mt. Berry, Georgia 30149; Telephone: 706-233-4086; Fax: 706-236-9004; E-mail: mmeyer@odin.berry.edu

BETHEL COLLEGE

4 Pr C S Sc Tr

▼ Honors Program

The Honors Program at Bethel College offers selected students the opportunity to work with other highly motivated scholars during their four years at Bethel. It is a broad-based liberal arts program that combines four all-honors classes, individual work with professors of the student's choice in two additional courses, and an ongoing program of social events, cultural activities, speakers, and forum presentations.

The Honors Program is designed to encourage and serve students desiring a challenging academic program consistent with Bethel's long-standing commitment to the integration of faith and learning. This program provides an educational experience that moves from a generalist emphasis in the first two years to a discipline-specific focus, in the field of the student's choice, in the last two years. The program is designed to provide an enriched educational experience for students with exceptional academic ability, to create a social network for such students, to enhance their preparation for and admission to graduate school as well as to enhance the general academic environment of the College.

There are currently 45 students enrolled in the program.

Participation Requirements: Begun in the 1995–96 academic year, the program goal is to accept 25 new students each year, with an equal number of men and women.

The program consists of two honors courses in the freshman year, one honors course in the sophomore year, and one honors course in the junior year. Students also take any regularly offered course in the sophomore and junior years on an honors basis, in which they develop individual contacts with faculty members for an enriched experience in that class. Students complete an Honors Senior Project in their major during the senior year. In addition to the courses, there are Monday Forums that students are expected to attend in all four years.

As honors students are exempt from several standard curriculum requirements, the honors degree requires no more credits than a regular degree and can be completed within a normal workload. Students who complete the Honors Program will have an Honors Program Graduate designation added to their transcript, along with whatever general academic honors they earn. Such recognition will enhance graduate school applications and employment prospects.

Admission Process: A short essay is required, along with a brief summary of past accomplishments, as described in the application form. Students must commit to two honors courses their freshman year and maintain a GPA of 3.3, rising to 3.4 sophomore year and 3.5 thereafter.

The deadline for applying is March 15.

The Campus Context: Bethel College is a four-year, Christian liberal arts college located on 231 wooded acres on the shores of Lake Valentine in suburban Arden Hills, Minnesota, just 10 minutes from both downtown Minneapolis and St. Paul. It offers the B.A., B.S., B.Mus., and B.Mus.Ed. degrees and fifty-seven different majors.

Student Body Undergraduate enrollment is approximately 2,000. About 60 percent of the students receive financial aid.

Faculty There are 215 faculty; 115 are full-time and 73 percent have terminal degrees. The student-faculty ratio is 15:1.

Key Facilities Bethel's campus is the newest among Minnesota private colleges, providing state-of-the-art computer technology and scientific equipment and modern classrooms, music practice rooms, and residence halls. The Lundquist Community Life Center, completed in 1994, houses the 1,700-seat Benson Great Hall, one of the finest music performance facilities in the Upper Midwest. Bethel's million-dollar Sports and Recreation Center has one of the nation's fastest tracks and is host to national and international meets throughout the year.

Computer facilities include e-mail accounts; access to the Internet; central computer data storage; access to more than 100 PC, Macintosh, NeXT, and Sun systems, all connected to the campus network; high-speed connections to the campus network from on-campus housing; and access to a HELP desk, staffed during regular lab hours.

Athletics Bethel is affiliated with Division III of the National Collegiate Athletic Association (NCAA) and the Minnesota Intercollegiate Athletic Conference (MIAC) for men and women. Bethel offers sixteen intercollegiate sports: baseball (men), basketball (men and women), cross-country (men and women), football (men), golf (men), hockey (men), soccer (men and women), tennis (men and women), track and field (men and women), softball (women), and volleyball (women). A wide variety of recreational and intramural sports are also available.

Study Abroad Bethel provides students with the opportunity to participate in a number of off-campus extension programs such as the Latin America Studies Program in Costa Rica; the Hollywood Film Studies Program in Los Angeles; the American Studies Program in Washington, DC; the AuSable Trails Institute for Environmental Studies in Michigan; the England Term in England studying English Literature and Language; the Institute of Holy Land Studies in Jerusalem; exchange programs through the Christian College Consortium; and study programs through the Upper Midwest Associations for Intercultural Education.

Support Services All of the main campus buildings, along with several residence halls, are accessible to disabled persons.

Job Opportunities Bethel offers many opportunities for on-campus employment in a wide variety of areas. Students usually work 5–12 hours per week.

Tuition: $13,180 per year (1996-97)

Room and Board: $4690

Fees: $20

Contact: Director: Dr. Richard Peterson, 3900 Bethel Drive, St. Paul, Minnesota 55112-6999; Telephone: 612-638-6465; Fax: 612-638-6001; E-mail: petric@bethel.edu; Web site: http://www.bethel.edu

BOISE STATE UNIVERSITY

4 Pu G M Sc Tr

▼ University Honors Program

Featuring small classes, student-taught seminars, and independent study options, the Honors Program at Boise State is designed to enhance a student's academic experience. Along with motivated classmates, students will be challenged by honors courses that require a more thorough and rigorous analysis of the material. In addition, students will have the opportunity to work closely with advisers who will help to identify internship, fellowship, and scholarship options to support a student's educational and career goals.

A fundamental purpose of the program is to encourage and support the efforts of students to assume greater responsibility for their own education. Admission to the Honors Program is an invitation to a lifetime committed to the wonders of the human mind, heart, and spirit. If a student is interested not only in learning the material offered in courses but in learning to learn, they will appreciate the challenges of the BSU Honors Program. Each semester students will choose from a variety of honors courses, including honors seminars, departmental courses, and colloquia. The basic purpose of the seminars is to bring students (especially freshmen and sophomores) together for informal small-group discussions of specific topics. Since each seminar is led by a student, the seminars provide a unique opportunity to meet informally with other students and to explore a topic of mutual interest.

Departmental honors courses are offered regularly in several departments and sometimes may be used to fulfill general University requirements. The honors newsletter, published several times each year, includes a list of courses available each semester. Recommended for juniors and seniors, interdisciplinary honors colloquia feature a personalized and thorough exploration of subject areas. Students will appreciate the small class size and the challenging interaction with faculty members.

The 28-year-old program currently enrolls 250 students.

Participation Requirements: A cumulative GPA of at least 3.5 will be a fixed requirement for retention. Any student whose GPA falls below 3.5 for two consecutive semesters will be automatically dropped from the program. Students who do not complete any honors work for two consecutive semesters will be withdrawn from the program unless they can demonstrate, to the satisfaction of the Director, continuing progress toward the completion of honors graduation requirements. Exceptions may be only to Admission and Retention requirements, and these rare exceptions may be granted by the Honors Program Committee of the Faculty Senate upon express written petition by the student justifying the exceptions on the basis of other evidence of academic potential.

When a student has reached 15 honors credits he or she gets an award. To graduate with honors, a student must have 25 honors credits. To graduate with honors from the program, a student must have a cumulative undergraduate GPA of at least 3.5. Students whose cumulative undergraduate GPA is at least 3.75 and whose records of academic and cocurricular activities indicate outstanding performance in both areas may be considered by the Honors Program Committee of the Faculty Senate for graduation with Distinguished Honors. Cocurricular activities may include publication of undergraduate work, presentations at regional or national conferences, and outstanding service in the Honors Student Association.

Admission Process: Students are required to have a cumulative GPA of at least 3.5 and score in at least the eighty-eighth percentile on the combined portion of the ACT or SAT in order to apply to BSU on the basis of high school graduation. A cumulative GPA of at least 3.5 for a minimum of 15 college credits will be required for all others, including continuing students, transfers, and students whose admission to BSU has not been based upon regular high school graduation and ACT or SAT scores.

Scholarship Availability: Through the generosity of the estate of Dean and Thelma Brown, BSU offers several scholarships. The Brown Scholars receive scholarships ranging from $1000 to full fees plus room and board plus out-of-state tuition worth up to $7500. Moreover, many of these are renewable. Up to five Brown Honors Residential Scholarships are awarded. These cover the cost of room and board and full in-state fees. A limited number of nonresident fee waivers are also available to Brown Honors Residential Scholars. These scholarships are renewable for a second year as residential scholarships, after which they are renewable as Brown Full Fee Honors Scholarships for two additional years.

Also offered are scholarships in two amounts: Brown Full Honors Scholarships, which cover full in-state fees, and Brown Honors Scholarships, which are $1000 per year. Each of these is renewable for up to a total of four years.

The Campus Context: Boise State University is composed of six colleges: the College of Arts and Sciences, the College of Business and Economics, the College of Education, the College of Health Science, the College of Social Sciences and Public Affairs, and the College of Technology. Twenty degree programs are offered.

Student Body Undergraduate enrollment is 3,668 men and 4,402 women full-time; 1,752 men and 2,535 women part-time. The ethnic distribution is 1.1 percent Native American, .9 percent African American, 4.2 percent Hispanic, .7 percent Basque, 85 percent white, 1.2 percent international student, and 2.1 percent Asian/Pacific Islander. There are 170 international students. Approximately 8 percent of the student body lives on campus. Fifty percent of continuing students receive some form of aid; 31 percent of aid is distributed as grants, 64 percent as student loans, and 3 percent as jobs. BSU has six social, five professional, and seven academic/honorary fraternities and sororities.

Faculty Of the 896 faculty members, 586 are full-time; 413 faculty members have terminal degrees.

Key Facilities Some of the distinguishing facilities on campus include the Centennial Amphitheatre, an outdoor venue for lectures, concerts, and plays, and the Morrison Center for the Performing Arts, which houses the music department, the theater arts department, a 2,000-seat performance hall, a 200-seat recital hall, and a 200-seat theater.

The Student Union provides facilities for social, recreational, and cultural activities. In addition to a computer store, a quick-copy center, and three dining areas, the Student Union contains a game room, several lounges, the Outdoor Rental Center, the BSU Bookstore, and the Bronco Shop.

The Intramural/Recreation Office and one of BSU's Children's Centers are located in the BSU Pavilion, Idaho's largest multipurpose arena. When not filled with fans of Bronco basketball, gymnastics, or volleyball, the Pavilion is the site of concerts, professional sporting events, and family entertainment. Nearby is Bronco Stadium, with a seating capacity of 30,000.

The library houses 416,00 monograph volumes, 63,000 bound periodicals, 4,700 current periodicals, 124,000 maps,

153,700 government publications, and over 1 million microfilms. The campus has approximately twenty-two computer labs for student use.

Athletics In the intercollegiate athletic program at Boise State University, students engage in outstanding competition with other universities and colleges of the Big West Conference. This includes the PAC-10 Athletic Conference and the National Collegiate Athletic Association (NCAA). The University fields men's intercollegiate teams in football, basketball, track, wrestling, tennis, cross-country, and golf. The University also fields women's intercollegiate teams in basketball, track, tennis, cross-country, golf, gymnastics, and volleyball.

Study Abroad Boise State University's Honors College and International Programs are dedicated to providing students with the international skills and experiences required by an increasingly interconnected and complex world. Within Idaho alone, over 50,000 jobs are the direct result of international exports. In today's global village, BSU honors graduates will be called upon to utilize firsthand international experiences and knowledge of foreign cultures and second and third languages. International programs provide students with many rich opportunities to gain this highly valued international expertise. Summer, semester, and year-long educational programs are offered in Australia, Chile, Costa Rica, England, France, Germany, Italy, Japan, Mexico, Spain (Basque Country), Thailand, and Quebec, Canada.

Support Services The Student Special Services Office is responsible for providing support services that enable all students with disabilities to participate in BSU's educational programs and activities.

Job Opportunities Included in the many job opportunities available campuswide are both work-study and non-work-study positions.

Tuition: None for state residents, $5346 for nonresidents, per year (1996-97)

Room and Board: $3200 minimum

Fees: $2104

Contact: Director: Dr. William P. Mech, 1910 University Drive, Boise, Idaho 83725-1125; Telephone: 208-385-1122; Fax: 208-385-1247; E-mail: bmech@bsu.idbsu.edu; Web site: http://www.idbsu.edu/honors/

BOWIE STATE UNIVERSITY
4 Pu D M Sc Tr
▼ Honors Program

The Bowie State University Honors Program is designed to both challenge and foster intellectual growth of academically talented students. The program has provided a diverse and stimulating educational experience for its students. Drawing from the rich cultural resources that Bowie State University offers, students are encouraged to confront

contemporary issues facing society. BSU has well-motivated and skilled faculty members who eagerly participate in the program. Honors faculty members are accomplished authorities in their field, proficient at teaching and motivating students to expand their knowledge across disciplines. Students are advised by the program director and by faculty members in the student's field of interest. The relative small size of Bowie State University offers the students close personal attention in their studies.

Students in the Honors Program have access to all BSU facilities. They have the benefits of a small, challenging program and the support of a major university within the Maryland University system. This includes a fully equipped computer laboratory, a fully accredited staff, and a library with nearly a quarter million volumes of information and services.

Honors students must complete the same number of credits required for graduation as all other BSU students. All majors are accepted and honors classes are incorporated into the schedule. Five to six honors classes are offered each semester and center on a wide range of studies and disciplines. Students are encouraged to take two courses per semester or as many as their major will allow. If an Advanced Placement course covers the same material as an honors course, the AP test score, which meets University standards, can be accepted as a substitute.

The Honors Program currently has 103 members and is working toward expanding into an honors college by the 1998 academic year.

Participation Requirements: Honors members must have a 3.0 GPA in order to graduate.

Admission Process: Freshmen and transfer students are selected each fall based upon high school performance and SAT scores. Transfer students must have a 3.0 GPA or higher, 15 completed credit hours, and recommendations from at least two instructors.

The Campus Context: Bowie State University was founded in 1865 by the Baltimore Association for the Moral and Education Improvement of Colored People. For decades, Bowie State College was well known for its education of teachers in high school and secondary education. In 1988 Bowie State College officially became Bowie State University, reflecting the tremendous growth the school had undertaken. Today, BSU resides on a 187-acre campus conveniently located between the major cities of Annapolis, Baltimore, and Washington, D.C. Bowie still holds to a tradition of education in for its racially and culturally diverse student body.

Student Body There are 5,258 undergraduates, 63 percent of whom are women, who are enrolled in sixteen degree programs. The ethnic distribution of the student population is 80 percent African American, 15 percent European American, 1 percent Hispanic, and 1 percent Asian/Pacific Islander. Eighty-five percent of the students are commuters.

Ninety percent of the students receive financial aid. There are four fraternities and two sororities.

Faculty Of the 255 faculty members, 146 are full-time; 42 percent have terminal degrees. The student-faculty ratio is 18:1.

Key Facilities The library houses 190,113 volumes. There are 253 Gateway 2000 computers for instructional and public use in library and academic buildings.

Athletics Bowie State University offers intercollegiate athletic teams in basketball, football, baseball, cross-country, track and field, volleyball, softball, and, soon to be added, golf. Bowie is a member of the NCAA Division II conference and competes in the CIAA. In 1988 the BSU football team, the Bulldogs, were considered one of the top sixteen of that year. Bowie athletes, on average, maintain high academic grades and enter college with higher SAT scores than non-athletes. Over half complete academic programs and graduate.

Job Opportunities Students are offered a range of work opportunities on campus, including assistantships and work study.

Tuition: $2380 for state residents, $6304 for nonresidents, per year (1996-97)

Room and Board: $4410

Mandatory Fees: $722

Contact: Director: Dr. Mary H. McManus, Thurgood Marshall Library, Suite 1700 2nd Floor, 14000 Jericho Park Road, Bowie, Maryland 20715; Telephone: 301-464-7235

BRADFORD COLLEGE

| 4 Pr G S Tr |

▼ **Honors Program**

The four-year Bradford Honors Program offers academically advanced and motivated students the opportunity for substantial challenges during their time at Bradford. The program seeks to create a community of scholars who will invigorate both each other and the College as a whole to higher standards of intellectual and creative activity.

The 12 year-old program currently enrolls approximately 50 students throughout all classes.

Participation Requirements: Students entering with a 3.25 GPA are automatically eligible to enroll in honors courses. In order to remain in the Honors Program, students must maintain a 3.0 GPA or higher in all honors work and a 3.25 GPA or higher in overall college work. Since the College believes that GPAs are not the only measure of honors capability, the program will allow any student to attempt to join the Honors Program in the freshman year regardless of GPA. The above GPA requirements then apply to all students after

one semester of attempted honors work. If a student's GPA falls below the required levels, the student is given a one-semester probationary period to continue honors enrollment and raise their GPA. If they fail to do so, they are dropped from the program. Also, any student with a minimum 2.75 GPA or higher who is not a regular member of the Honors Program may elect to take one honors course during their four years at Bradford if the instructor approves and the topic is of particular interest to the student.

The program is an 18-credit program consisting of a combination of specialized honors seminars, honors sections of core curriculum courses, and the opportunity for Individual Honors Contracts. In the freshman and sophomore years, students must enroll in a specialized honors seminar each year. Students must also choose 6 other credits from sections of Honors English courses or Individual Honors Contracts in selected sections of the core curriculum courses, Human Heritage or Perspective on the Arts. As students become more involved in their major fields in the junior and senior years, the honors requirements ease somewhat, with a topical Junior Honors Seminar and a capstone Senior Honors Seminar, taught interdisciplinarily and cooperatively by honors faculty members. Students completing the required courses and the 18 credit minimum are designated as Honors Scholars at graduation.

The deadline for applying is February 15.

Scholarship Availability: No specific scholarships are available for the Honors Program.

The Campus Context: Bradford College is comprised of a 35-acre campus made up of more than a dozen buildings, a pond, and athletic fields, plus 36 acres of woodland.

Student Body The student population is comprised of 38 percent men and 62 percent women. The ethnic distribution of the student body is 72 percent white, 6 percent African American, 15 percent Asian, 6 percent Hispanic, and 1 percent Native American. There are 115 international students (19 percent). Thirty percent of the students are commuters.

Faculty Of the 67 full-time faculty, 33 have terminal degrees. The student-faculty ratio is 11.75:1.

Key Facilities Among distinguished facilities are the Dorothy Bell Study Center, which houses the college library, art department, art gallery, music department and studios, and Conover Hall, a multipurpose, 225-seat auditorium; Hazeltime Hall, which houses the Writing Center, Media Center, Academic Resource Center, and Computer Center; Denworth Hall, housing the dance studio and two theatres; Bricknell Chapel; and Kimball Tavern, a historic seventeenth century landmark where the College was founded in 1803. The Bradford library houses 60,000 volumes and 250 periodicals. There is a computer center on campus with full Internet access and e-mail with both IBM and Macintosh computers.

Athletics Club sports add an important dimension to student life. The development of sports and recreational clubs fosters intercollegiate competition in such activities as volleyball, soccer, lacrosse, martial arts, basketball, and softball. The number and types of student clubs depend upon student interest and availability of facilities and equipment.

Study Abroad International study or internships during the summer or a semester in the junior year can provide students with the invaluable experience of life in another culture and, in many instances, the opportunity to improve their knowledge of a second or third language. Bradford College's affiliations with the Central College International Studies program, the Council on International Education Exchange, the School for International Training, the American Institute of Foreign Studies, and Boston University's International Internship Programs enables students to study or work in settings around the world while they earn Bradford credit.

Support Services All buildings are accessible to students with disabilities.

Job Opportunities Bradford offers numerous work opportunities through work-study programs.

Tuition: $15,380 per year (1996-97)

Room and Board: $6590

Mandatory Fees: $390

Contact: Director: Dr. Frederik E. Schuetze, 320 South Main Street, Bradford, Massachusetts 01835; Telephone: 508-372-7161 Ext. 5345; Fax: 508-521-0480

BRETHREN COLLEGES ABROAD

4 Pr G S Tr

▼ BCA Honors Program at L'Universite de Strasbourg

Honors students will enjoy an academic program enriched by cross-disciplinary group experiences and extracurricular activities (such as movies, lectures, concerts) chosen for their potential to elicit discussion and reflection. Since honors students have strong academic qualifications, including a high proficiency in French, they are not enrolled in courses for international students at the Institut International d'Études Françaises. Instead, they are fully integrated into the French university and do most of their course work with French students in challenging programs such as those found at the Institut d'Études Politiques, la Faculté de Lettres, or other divisions of the Strasbourg University system.

All honors students take the honors seminar (2 semester hours), a course taught by Dr. Michèle Biermann-Fischer of the Département de Linguistique Française at the Université des Sciences Humaines. Beyond the seminar class hours, Dr. Biermann-Fischer offers honors students tutorial sessions in French academic writing techniques. In addition, the schedules of honors students are supplemented by BCA courses such as French Society Viewed Through Cinema and International Organizations. No diploma is associated with this program; however, honors students do get first priority for internships, and their participation in the Honors Program is noted on their transcript.

The 36-year-old program usually enrolls 10 students per term.

Admission Process: Admission to the Honors Program is based on the quality of the student's application materials, performance in the presemester language intensive, and an oral interview following the language intensive, as well as a commitment to participate fully in the program for the entire year. Decisions are made by Dr. Biermann-Fischer at l'Université de Strasbourg and the BCA-France administration. Year-long students have priority; one-semester students will be accepted only if there are positions available in the group. The deadline for applying is August 10 for the fall term and December 15 for the spring term.

Scholarship Availability: There are no scholarships available.

The Campus Context: L'Université de Strasbourg has three main components: l'Université Robert-Schuman (droit, commerce et gestion, sciences politiques, journalisme, technologie); l'Université des Sciences Humaines (les arts, les langues etrangeres, les sciences et techniques des activites physiques et sportives); l'Université Louis-Pasteur (medicine, chirugie dentaire, pharmacie, sciences de la matiere, sciences de la vie et de la terre, mathematiques et informatique, sciences du comportement et de l'environement, sciences economiques et gestion, geographie, institut universitaire de technologie).

Tuition: $8435 per year (1997-98)

Room and Board: $8255

Mandatory Fees: $640

Contact: U.S. Liaison: Dr. Susan Wennemyr, BCA Headquarters, 605 College Avenue, North Manchester, Indiana 46962; Telephone: 219-982-5244; Fax: 219-982-7755; E-mail: bca@manchester.edu; Web site: http://www.studyabroad.com/bca

BRIGHAM YOUNG UNIVERSITY

4 Pr G L Tr

▼ University Honors Program

The Brigham Young University Honors Program was founded in 1960 and is one of the oldest programs of its kind.

Honors education at BYU provides an unusually rich and challenging experience for capable and motivated undergraduate students. Honors education is not merely a more intensive general education or a more strenuous program in a major; rather, it attempts to link the broad university perspective with the specific concentration associated with a major. Students who pursue honors education at BYU will be offered the challenge of honors courses that form a part of their general education, as well as an intensive experience in their major. Honors education is open to all capable and motivated students and only requires that students have a formal commitment of intent to graduate with University Honors, register for at least one honors course each semester for the first two years in the program, and maintain a 3.5 GPA.

The most important advantage of enrolling in honors is the opportunity to participate in demanding, high-quality courses taught by some of the University's best professors. In addition, honors provides a stimulating learning environment outside formal course settings. Honors offers a curriculum core consisting of two semesters in the History of Civilization and in Intensive Writing. Beyond this core, honors colloquia, seminars, and departmental honors courses provide a variety of experiences for honors students in the historical development of ideas, cultures, arts, letters, and the sciences. Recent colloquia have included Use and Misuse of Human and Natural Resources: Man's Role in Changing the Face of the Earth, The Pen and the Sword: a Study of Writing about How Human Civilization Seeks Peace and Suffers War, The Daedalus Project, Memoir and Imagination, and Shaping the Modern Mind. Recent seminars have included Women's Issues in the Natural Sciences, Wilderness Writing, and Bioethics.

Students in honors benefit most directly from their association with fellow honors students and with honors faculty members. To encourage interaction among students outside the classroom, special noncampus housing for honors students is available. In addition, honors students also have a center in the Karl G. Maeser Memorial Building, which provides them with a quiet study hall, a commons room for informal meetings and discussion, an advisement center, and classrooms. There is also an honors computer lab available to students committed to graduating with University Honors. HSAC, the Honors Student Advisory Council, plans many activities for honors students throughout the semester, including lectures, dances, retreats, and outings. The Honors Program publishes the scholarly work of students in *Insight*, an intellectual journal with an all-student staff. A special series of art exhibitions are sponsored in the Maeser Building.

There are approximately 2,300 honors students.

Participation Requirements: There are certain requirements for students to graduate with University Honors. Students must take the required honors courses (two honors sections of religion courses; two semesters of Honors History of Civilization, Honors Intensive Writing, or Honors Reasoning and Writing; three honors elective courses; two semesters of foreign language; and calculus, principles of statistics, or advanced logic); meet with an Honors Program representative for advisement at least once each year; complete and submit a study contract for The Great Works of Literature, Art, Music and Film before the junior year; demonstrate familiarity with the Great Works during the junior year by turning in a portfolio of one-page responses to the works contracted for study and

also submit a portfolio of work representing each semester of undergraduate study and a one-page description of ongoing service to the community for review by the Honors Deans; submit a proposal for an honors thesis during the junior year; and submit a finished honors thesis and pass a thesis defense with a committee of Honors Deans and faculty members during the senior year.

Scholarship Availability: Though BYU offers a variety of scholarships, the Honors Program itself does not. Most honors students hold, or are eligible for, some kind of scholarship. The Honors Program coordinates information and advisement for many graduate scholarships, grants, and fellowships. Money is available directly from the Honors Program to aid in thesis research.

The Campus Context: There are twelve colleges and schools on campus: the College of Biology and Agriculture; the College of Education; the College of Engineering and Technology; the College of Family, Home, and Social Sciences; the College of Fine Arts and Communications; the College of Humanities; the College of Nursing; the College of Physical and Mathematical Sciences; the College of Physical Education; the J. Rueben Clark Law School; the J. Willard and Alice S. Marriot School of Management; and Graduate Studies. In all, there are 166 degree programs.

Student Body There are approximately 27,000 undergraduates enrolled. The student body is relatively balanced in terms of gender, with approximately 50 percent women and 50 percent men. Ethnic minorities compose 12 percent of the student body, with .4 percent African American, 1 percent Native American, 3 percent Asian and Pacific Islanders, and 3 percent Hispanic. Since BYU is restricted by law from requiring students to provide information about race, these figures are voluntary and may not represent a complete picture. Students whose ethnic background is unknown number 1,392 (5 percent). There were 1,700 daytime international students enrolled at BYU during winter semester 1996. Of all the students, 94.7 percent reside off campus. All BYU students receive tuition subsidization from the LDS Church; 66 percent of these students receive additional financial aid. There are no sororities or fraternities at Brigham Young University.

Faculty There are 1,706 faculty members; 1,385 are full-time. Of the full-time faculty members, 78 percent have doctoral degrees, 40 percent are full professors, 28 percent are associate professors, 23 percent are assistant professors, 4 percent are instructors, and 5 percent have other designations. The student-faculty ratio is 23:1.

Key Facilities The University's 638-acre campus includes 121 buildings for the University's academic programs, 81 for administration and physical plant services, and 281 buildings for student housing. Major campus construction projects include the recently completed Ezra Taft Benson Science Building; expansion of the J. Reuben Clark Law Library, the Harold B. Lee Library, and the Dairy Products Lab (BYU Creamery); and renovations to the Eyring Science Center, the Ernest L. Wilkinson Center, and the bookstore. There are more than 3 million volumes in the library. There are many computer facilities.

Athletics BYU has a well established athletic tradition, repeatedly achieving national rankings and recognition. In 1994, the first annual Sears Directors Cup, sponsored by *USA Today*, and the National Association of Collegiate Directors of Athletics placed BYU's sports programs at twenty-second in the nation. The Cougars have claimed men's national championships in football (1984), outdoor track (1970), and golf (1981) as well as two NIT championships in basketball (1951, 1966). The men's golf team captured twenty WAC titles over the past twenty-six years. BYU's women athletes joined the WAC in 1990–91 and have dominated the league, winning conference championships in six of nine sports (cross country, volleyball, swimming and diving, indoor track, golf, and outdoor track). Seven teams have finished in the top twenty in NCAA championships, five in the top ten. Other athletic teams have also gained national attention. Athletic facilities at BYU include major sports complexes that provide for football, baseball, softball, tennis, and track and field events. In addition, two buildings provide for racquetball, volleyball, basketball, aerobics, dance, and swimming as well as ball courts, weight rooms, indoor track, and facilities for indoor batting practice.

Study Abroad Study abroad programs are open to students from all majors. Students need not be formally admitted to BYU to participate in study abroad, and BYU credit may be transferred to other institutions. Semester and/or term programs are offered in Chile, Jerusalem, London, Moscow, and Vienna. Term programs are also scheduled regularly in many countries in Asia, Europe, South and Central America, and Africa. These programs feature intensive studies in such disciplines as the arts, history, government, and language. Specialized study in other fields may also be offered.

Support Services BYU has established the Services for Students with Disabilities Office. The purpose of this office is to assure that students are provided access to University programs. Mobility impaired students are encouraged to seek help in ensuring the accessibility of classes and other facilities. Hearing impaired students may obtain the services of qualified sign language interpreters and TDD communications by contacting this office. A list of volunteer readers is maintained for visually impaired or learning disabled students. BYU also provides services for students with other forms of disability.

Job Opportunities Students are employed all over campus at jobs ranging from research and cafeteria work to secretarial work and grounds maintenance. Full-time students can work as many as 20 hours a week on campus.

Tuition: $2630 minimum for LDS church members, $3950 for non-members full-time, per year; $200 part-time, per credit (1997-98)

Room and Board: $3805

Contact: Dean: Dr. Paul Alan Cox, Box 22600, Provo, Utah 84602-2600; Telephone: 801-378-3038; Fax: 801-378-5976; E-mail: honors@byu.edu; Web site: http://adm5.byu.edu/ar/dept_gradeval/honors.html

BROWARD COMMUNITY COLLEGE

2 Pu G L Sc Tr

▼ Honors Institute

The Honors Institute is a comprehensive honors program that offers honors classes on three campuses and Phi Theta Kappa chapters on four campuses. The students strive toward excellence in the four hallmarks of scholarship, leadership, service, and fellowship that are promoted in all Phi Theta Kappa chapters. In addition to the honors curriculum, there are honors extracurricular programs that enrich the students' college experiences. For example, the Brain Bowl Team and Mathematics Team provide opportunities for academic competition and teamwork among the participants. Both teams have won numerous state and national honors. The Brain Bowl Team has won the regional championship for eleven years.

Students are encouraged to achieve through a program of recognition, including nominations to the National Dean's List and Who's Who as well as receptions and a convocation where university scholarships are awarded.

The Honors Institute leads the country in the percentage of graduates who receive university scholarships. More than 90 percent of all graduates have continued at universities across the country on scholarship.

The Honors Institute is fifteen years old. College-wide, there are over 650 students enrolled in honors classes.

Participation Requirements: Honors students take a minimum of 18 credits in honors classes, small seminar-type classes that emphasize writing, research, and critical and creative thinking.

Admission Process: Students who graduate in the top 10 percent of their Broward County high school class are eligible for scholarships to the Honors Institute. Other admission criteria include SAT scores, faculty member recommendations, and interviews. The deadline for applying is April 30.

Scholarship Availability: Most students qualifying for the Honors Institute receive scholarships (based on high school performance and/or college record) that cover the two years at Broward Community College and the following two years at universities in Florida. Upon graduation from the Honors Institute, almost all students are awarded continuing scholarships to in-state and out-of-state universities.

The Campus Context: Broward Community College is composed of four campuses, three with honors coordinators and classes and all four with Phi Theta Kappa advisers and chapters. The College offers sixty-four degree programs leading to the A.A. and fifty programs leading to the A.S. as well as twenty certificate programs and six Advanced Technical Certificates.

Student Body There are 25,000 students are enrolled, of whom 60 percent are women. The student body is equally composed of African American, white, and Hispanic students. There are

6,000 international students. About 90 percent of the students commute. Of the students, 13,000 receive financial aid. Broward has no fraternities or sororities.

Faculty There are 350 full-time and 300 part-time faculty members. Twenty-five percent of the faculty members have terminal degrees. The student-faculty ratio is 25:1.

Key Facilities Distinguishing facilities on campus include a planetarium, allied health service, and University Library (combined Florida International University/Florida Atlantic University, BCC). The library houses 650,000 volumes. There are four computer facilities, three IBM and one Macintosh.

Athletics Athletics available are swimming, tennis, baseball, basketball, and soccer.

Study Abroad The study abroad program is extensive with programs located across the globe. Students can spend a semester in Europe or South America. They can go on a 2–4-week seminar study tour to Europe, South America, or the Orient. The College's comprehensive International Program includes study abroad opportunities in England, Spain, Israel, Mexico, and South America. The Honors Institute is offering its first International Study Abroad Program in Ecuador in 1997.

Support Services Students with disabilities are provided with study aids and assistants. All classroom buildings are wheelchair accessible.

Job Opportunities Work opportunities on campus include work study programs on and off campus, job placement, and work community/scholarships.

Tuition: $1176 for state residents, $4288 for nonresidents, per year (1996-97)

Contact: Director: Dr. Mary Jo Henderson, 3501 SW Davie Road, Fort Lauderdale, Florida 33314; Telephone: 954-475-6613; Fax: 954-423-6423

BRYAN COLLEGE

| 4 Pr G S Sc Tr |

▼ **Honors Program**

The Bryan College Honors Program is open to all students in all majors and programs. The program is designed to enhance a student's major area of study by encouraging in-depth independent study and research. To be recognized as an honors graduate of the College, students must complete a minimum of 18 semester hours (approximately 6–7 courses) designated as Honors. Since several sections of general education courses are designed and taught specifically for the Honors Program, most students earn in excess of the minimum number of credit hours. Students are required to complete a sophomore level honors seminar entitled The Contemporary World and a senior level thesis-project.

Approximately 60 students are involved in the program currently. The Honors Program began in 1995 with that year's freshman class.

Admission Process: Students are selected for participation based on high school GPA and ACT scores after their acceptance into the College.

Scholarship Availability: The College makes available several Presidential and Dean's Scholarships for students who will be eligible for the Honors Program.

The Campus Context: Bryan is located in the semirural community of Dayton, location of the world-famous Scopes evolution trial of 1925. The campus is housed on 200 wooded acres. A new Student Life Center is scheduled for occupancy in the summer 1998. The College offers the B.A. and B.S. degrees in twenty academic programs.

Student Body There is an enrollment of 450 students (55 percent women).

Faculty There are 28 full-time and 30 part-time faculty members. Ninety percent of the full-time faculty members have earned the doctorate in their discipline.

Key Facilities The library houses 82,000 volumes and more than 600 CD-ROMs containing full-image periodicals. Computer labs are in every residence hall and academic building. The student-computer ratio is 10:1.

Study Abroad Bryan is a member institution of the Coalition for Christian Colleges and Universities. Its students participate in the Coalition's full range of programs, including international and intercultural study programs.

Tuition: $9700 per year (1997-98 est.)

Room and Board: $3950

Mandatory Fees: $300

Contact: Director: Dr. Dann Brown, Associate Professor, Box 7000, Dayton, Tennessee 37321-7000; Telephone: 423-775-7258; Fax: 423-775-7330; E-mail: brownda@bryannet.bryan.edu

---

BUTTE COLLEGE (BUTTE-GLENN COMMUNITY COLLEGE DISTRICT)

| 2 Pu G S Tr |

▼ **Honors Program**

The Honors Program at Butte College is designed for students who desire an exciting, challenging, and personally rewarding academic experience. All honors classes meet the College's general education requirements and are fully articulated with the transfer general education requirements of the California State University and the University of California.

The Honors Program provides tutorial sessions with faculty members, class projects, field trips, and a variety of cultural and social activities through the Culture of Civilizations Club. Get-togethers at the homes of faculty members and students are a regular occurrence as is the annual trip to the Oregon Shakespeare Festival in Ashland.

The Butte College Honors Program currently consists of six highly interdisciplinary classes, all but one of which are fully team-taught by 2 instructors from contrasting academic disciplines.

Courses are taught as seminars, with no more than 20 students in each. In HON1-4, students read major works, almost always in their entirety, which have influenced the development of Western culture and civilization. Periods covered include the Greco/Roman, Medieval, Renaissance, and Enlightenment. HON 5 is a lab science course and emphasizes Darwin and other seminal thinkers in the biological sciences. Our newest course, HON 6, focuses on contributions of women and people of color, beginning with the twentieth century. Courses are offered during the day, on campus, and at the College's Chico Center in the evening.

Participation Requirements: The Honors Program seeks enthusiastic, imaginative, dedicated students who welcome the challenge of often-difficult readings and who are prepared to express their views. Each honors class requires a minimum of 4,000 words of writing through which students are expected to critically analyze the assigned readings. Students completing HON 5 and at least four other Honors classes with no grade lower than B are awarded a Certificate of Completion in Honors Studies. Those also earning an associate degree receive the Honors Degree of Associate Arts or Sciences.

Admission Process: Prior successful completion of ENGL 2 or its first-year composition course equivalent is strongly encouraged; minimally, ENGL 2 is a corequisite. While a minimum GPA of 3.3 is normally expected, the College is more interested in a student's future potential than in his or her past performance. The application process includes an essay (judged as a writing sample) and at least one letter of recommendation. Those who are eligible for admission to the University of California are assured of acceptance as long as the classes are not yet filled. Once admitted, honors students must maintain a GPA of 3.3 or higher, with no honors grade below B.

The Campus Context: Butte College is a fully accredited two-year college located on a 940-acre campus in the foothills near Chico, California. Bus transportation is offered to campus from all major communities within the College's service region. There are also centers in Chico and Willows. Butte has a wide range of lower-division courses transferable to both the University of California and California State University Systems as well as a variety of highly acclaimed vocational programs. The College offers approximately 1,250 sections in more than seventy areas of study. Associate degrees are awarded in fifty-four vocational areas and twenty-four academic areas.

Butte ranks first among colleges of a similar size when it comes to the number of students who transfer from a community college to a California State University campus, and the Honors Program in particular has been successful in helping students transfer to a variety of prestigious colleges and universities. While most of the students continue their studies at nearby California State University at Chico, they have also been successful in transferring to the most prestigious colleges and universities in the world. Indeed, the opportunity to earn a degree from such a university but at a fraction of the full cost is a primary reason many of our students choose to begin their undergraduate experience at Butte College.

Student Body Butte College has experienced a steady increase in enrollment since its beginning in 1967. There are approximately 6,500 part-time and 3,000 full-time students enrolled. Of the student population, 72 percent are Caucasian, 11 percent are Hispanic, 7 percent are Asian/Pacific Islanders, 2 percent are African American, and 2 percent are American Indian. Of all the students, 53.5 percent are women.

Faculty Approximately 120 full-time faculty members and nearly 400 part-time faculty members are supported by 50 non-teaching faculty members and counselors in providing direct service to students. Although relatively few possess terminal degrees, faculty members are specifically selected for their skill and a commitment to teaching undergraduate students. The average class size at Butte College is 25–35.

Key Facilities The Frederick S. Montgomery Library houses about 50,000 books and also provides on-line access to numerous other libraries. Audiovisual services include 2,500 audio tapes and 4,720 video tapes. In addition to its own holdings, the library recently acquired a 1,000-periodical, full-text database. Butte has about thirty different computer labs on campus and has recently begun offering courses on-line. Both IBM and Macintosh (or their clones) are provided.

Athletics The College is known for its highly competitive athletic teams both for men and women and is a member of the Golden Valley Conference. Intercollegiate competition includes football, basketball, track, golf, cross-country, volleyball, and softball. Tennis competitions are hosted by the Bay Valley Conference for men and women.

Study Abroad Butte College is part of a consortium that provides opportunities for students to spend a semester or more studying abroad. In recent years students have studied in England, Mexico, Spain, and France.

Support Services Various special services are provided for disabled students through Disabled Student Programs and Services.

Job Opportunities Many students are able to find part-time work on campus. The College's Career Center also helps students find job opportunities in our local communities.

Tuition: None for state residents, $3750 for nonresidents, per year (1996-97)

Mandatory Fees: $460

Contact: Director, 3536 Butte Campus Drive, Oroville, California 95965; Telephone: 916-895-2203; Fax: 916-895-2532; E-mail: ekins_r@wiley.butte.cc.ca.us; Web site: http://www.butte.cc.ca.us/

CALIFORNIA STATE UNIVERSITY, LOS ANGELES

4 Pu G M Sc Tr

▼ General Education Honors Program

The University General Education Honors Program at California State University, Los Angeles, provides highly qualified students with diverse, enriched, intellectual activities through a separate General Education curriculum that includes honors classes, seminars, and research. The Honors Program offers special sections of lower division and upper division General Education courses. The University offers at least seven different General Education Honors course sections each quarter and more than twenty-five General Education Honors sections each year. The G.E. Honors Program courses include the following honors courses: English, political science, Spanish, French, geology, anthropology, philosophy, religious studies, history, art, music, dance, speech, critical thinking, mathematics, sociology, psychology, microbiology, geography, and engineering/technology. These sections have lower enrollment (15–25 students), are limited to honors students, and are taught by renowned faculty members. Honors Program faculty members often experiment with innovative teaching techniques, which include expanded and challenging course requirements.

The General Education Honors Program coordinates membership with other honors organizations on campus. For the past five consecutive years, G.E. Honors Program students have been selected as Cal State L.A. Phi Kappa Phi Outstanding Freshmen of the Year. Program students receive priority registration privileges. Augmenting the extensive academic part of the G.E. Honors Program are curriculum-related enrichment opportunities and social events. An annual David Lawrence Memorial Lecture brings creative, cutting-edge faculty members and outside experts to lecture to the Honors Program and campus community. An Annual Honors Preview and Awards Dinner brings honors faculty members, student members (new, returning, and alumni), their families and friends, and campus administrators together for an evening of interaction and networking. It is an opportunity for faculty members to showcase their honors courses for the coming year, for the program to honor the Outstanding Honors Students of the Year, and to present honors faculty members with specially designed awards. Annual receptions are held to recognize the Outstanding Honors Professor of the Year, Graduating Honors Seniors, and Retiring Honors Faculty. These events, along with a quarterly honors newsletter, are planned and sponsored by the G.E. Honors Club Board of Directors.

General Education Honors Program students remain in the program throughout the four years of their baccalaureate degree programs as long as they remain members in good standing. The University's students are as diverse as the program curriculum. They include entering freshmen with outstanding high school academic records; students entering the University through the Early Entrance Program (EEP) who range in age from 11 to 16 and number approximately 20 new admits per year; and returning students who have actively participated in careers, particularly within the arts, and are coming back to Cal State L.A. to complete their bachelor's degree. The University's Honors Program creates opportunities for high-potential students and faculty members to establish closer educational and personal relationships and prepares students for participation in the upper-division Departmental Honors Program.

The Cal State L.A. General Education Honors Program has been in existence since 1978.

There are approximately 350 students retaining active membership in the program each year.

Participation Requirements: To retain active membership in the program, honors students must maintain a minimum cumulative 3.0 GPA, complete a minimum of six General Education courses as honors (two per year), and complete 12 hours per year. General Education Honors scholarship recipients are required to complete eight General Education Honors courses (four per year) within their first two years in residence. Students admitted to General Education Honors with Advanced Placement credit(s) fulfill the General Education course requirement(s) but not the requirement to take a minimum of six/eight General Education courses as honors.

Students who complete all requirements of the Honors Program graduate with a University General Education Honors notation on their transcript. They also receive a special honors certificate of graduation signed by the president of the University. In the year of their entrance to the Honors Program, the General Education Honors students receive special recognition and certificates at the University's annual Honors Convocation.

Admission Process: Freshmen are invited to join the Honors Program based on their high school average (3.0 GPA and above) and their SAT I scores (1000 and above). Sophomores and transfer students who have a minimum of six General Education courses to complete and a minimum 3.0 GPA and above may also apply for admission.

Scholarship Availability: The General Education Honors Program offers $2000 scholarships that carry a stipend of

$500 per year for four years. Entering freshmen with at least a 3.6 high school GPA and a score of at least 1080 on the SAT I are encouraged to apply. Applicants must apply directly through the General Education Honors Program. Recipients of the scholarships are required to join the General Education Honors Program and complete eight General Education Honors courses within their first two years at the University. They must maintain a minimum cumulative 3.0 GPA and complete at least 36 quarter units of course work in each academic year.

The Campus Context: California State University, Los Angeles, is a comprehensive University that was founded in 1947 by action of the California State Legislature. It is one of twenty-three California State University campuses. It is located at the eastern edge of Los Angeles and adjacent to the western San Gabriel Valley cities of Alhambra and Monterey Park. Cal State L.A. occupies nearly 200 acres on a hilltop sight that once housed one of California's thirty-six original adobes, built in 1776 by Franciscan missionaries and destroyed by fire in 1908. Cal State L.A. overlooks mountains to the north, the San Gabriel Valley to the east, metropolitan Los Angeles to the west, and the Palos Verdes Peninsula and Catalina Island to the south.

The Los Angeles Civic Center is 5 miles west of the campus. Cal State L.A. is comprised of six schools: the School of Business and Economics, the School of Arts and Letters, the Charter School Education, the School of Engineering and Technology, the School of Health and Human Services, and the School of Natural and Social Sciences. Cal State L.A. is distinguished by having the largest number of system-wide Outstanding Professors of the Year. Cal State L.A. boasts more alumni in the California Legislature than any other California State University; 5 alumni are members of the United States Congress. More than fifty degree programs are offered.

Student Body Undergraduate enrollment is 14,000 students (59.3 percent women). The ethnic distribution of the student body is .5 percent American Indian, 27.3 percent Asian American/Pacific Islander, 10.2 percent African American, 43.8 percent Latino, and 18.4 percent white. There are more than 1,500 international students who come from 125 countries around the world. Approximately 88 percent of students are commuters. Approximately 49 percent of students receive financial aid. There are six active sororities, three active fraternities, and twenty-three honors societies.

Faculty Of the 1,031 faculty members, 633 are full-time and 98–99 percent hold terminal degrees. The student-faculty ratio is 30:1.

Key Facilities Campus facilities include the Harriet and Charles Luckman Fine Arts Complex that was opened in 1994 and houses a large theater and visual arts gallery; the Royal Center of Applied Gerontology; the Anna Bing Arnold Child Center; and the Edmund G. "Pat" Brown Institute of Public Affairs, a prestigious center that focuses on major issues facing the region and the state. The School of Engineering and Technology is particularly proud of its two world-class solar electric vehicles—the Solar Eagle (I) and the Solar Eagle (II). The Roger Wagner Center for Choral Studies, the Southern California Ocean Studies Institute (SCOSI), and the World Trade Center are also well known.

The library houses 1 million books and periodicals. There are over eight open-access, self-instructional, and specialized computer technology labs on campus that include IBM-compatible and Macintosh computers. Informational services available through these labs include Netscape, the World Wide Web, and on-line educational information resources such as Lexis-Nexis, Legislate, and FEDIX. In addition to these information resources, the University also provides access to on-line card catalogs of various educational sources such as Melvyl (UC libraries card catalog), the Library of Congress, OPAC (in-house library card catalog), and LIBS (U.S./World Libraries).

Athletics More than 300 of the University's undergraduates are enrolled in the intercollegiate athletics program. In athletics, the Cal State L.A. Golden Eagles compete in eleven intercollegiate sports. The University fields six men's teams (cross-country, soccer, basketball, baseball, track, and tennis) and five women's teams (volleyball, cross-country, basketball, track, and tennis). At the national level, the Golden Eagles compete in Division II of the National Collegiate Athletic Association (NCAA). Locally, Cal State L.A. is a member of the California Collegiate Athletic Association (CCAA). Since 1990, Cal State L.A. has produced 18 national champions and 98 All-Americans as part of a total intercollegiate athletics program, which includes 18 Olympians (4 gold medalists, 2 of them in the 1984 Olympic Summer Games).

Study Abroad Cal State L.A. offers numerous opportunities for students through exchange and study abroad programs. These include periods of study from a semester to a full academic year through such programs as the California State University International Programs, the International Student Exchange program, Fulbright and Rotary fellowships, and short-term language and cultural study programs. The University's students are provided opportunities to study at more than 100 universities across the United States. The international programs serve the needs of students in more than 100 designated academic majors. The CSU International Programs are affiliated with thirty-six recognized universities and institutions of higher education in sixteen countries.

Support Services There are a number of support services available at Cal State L.A. through the Office for Students with Disabilities. This office supports and assists students from admissions to graduation. Specific services include disability-related advisement, priority registration, handicapped parking, faculty liaison, and coordination of readers, note takers, sign language interpreters, test proctors, and tutors (disability specific).

Job Opportunities Work study and student assistant positions are available through the campus Center for Career Planning and Placement.

Tuition: None for state residents, $7626 for nonresidents, per year (1996-97)

Mandatory Fees: Full-time, $1742 per year; Part-time, per quarter, $362.75 for first 6 units, $580.75 for next 5 units

Contact: Director: Professor Kathleen M. Costantini, Library South 1040A, 5151 State University Drive, Los Angeles, California 90032-8165; Telephone: 213-343-4960; Fax: 213-343-4772; E-mail: kcostan@calstatela.edu; Web site: http://web.calstatela.edu/academic/gehp/gehome.htm

CALIFORNIA STATE UNIVERSITY, STANISLAUS

4 Pu G S Sc Tr

▼ University Honors Program

The California State University, Stanislaus Honors Program, designed for academically excellent students of unusual curiosity, is open to all undergraduate majors. The University Honors Program is an alternative General Education curriculum. The program believes in taking risks and nurturing students who show exceptional promise, whether they are entering directly from high school or transferring from another institution.

The honors curriculum emphasizes the development of students who can communicate equally well in print, with numbers, electronically, and interpersonally. The heart of the curriculum is a series of small seminars (usually with fewer than 20 students) that are open only to students who are members of the Honors Program, combining information and insights from various fields of study. This interdisciplinary focus is maintained by invited campus faculty members who offer demonstrated excellence in teaching and who draw material and ideas from many fields, addressing concerns common to all disciplines rather than focusing exclusively on their single-subject area of expertise. Some of these seminars are team-taught.

Other faculty members and administrators who are not teaching in the program have a standing invitation to attend and participate in these seminars, thus extending the opportunity for stimulating teacher-student interaction. Students take an active role in the shape and conduct of each honors seminar, allowing them to develop competencies in academic discourse. Teaching faculty members serve as facilitators, catalysts, or models in the exploration of historical antecedents to and intellectual links among contemporary ideas and issues. The University Honors Program maintains a total student population of approximately 100.

Participation Requirements: All students in the program are required to take the first-year sequence of two seminars: Issues and Advocacy, which demands intensive critical reading, writing, and speaking, followed by Advocacy and Society, which considers broader public policy implications and strengthens critical thinking. In addition, all honors students are required to complete a capstone sequence: Honors Research, Honors Individual Study, and Honors Lecture Series. Honors Research provides students with the opportunity to explore, in-depth, a subject of their choice with a faculty member mentor (usually within their major). Honors Individual Study requires them to produce a research document to be jointly evaluated by honors faculty members and the student's faculty member mentor. Students are then required to make a formal presentation of this research to the campus community during Honors Lecture Series, the final course in the sequence.

Students who have already completed the subject matter in these two courses via AP (Advanced Placement) high school course work or through equivalent work taken elsewhere are not required to take this first-year sequence. These students are the only exceptions.

In addition, there are five optional honors seminars in which students may enroll. Each is strongly recommended and satisfies a specific University General Education requirement. These seminars are: Political Polemics; Humanities; Great Thinkers; Science, Technology, and Human Values; and Self and Community. These seminars are guided by the same teaching philosophy and pedagogy as those in the required core.

Continued participation in the Honors Program requires that students maintain an overall GPA of 3.0 and enrollment in the honors core courses. Upon satisfactory completion of all the requirements of the University Honors Program and certification by the co-directors, a student receives an official transcript notation at graduation of University Honors Program membership. During the annual commencement exercises, University Honors Program graduates are designated by the wearing of a special Honors Program cord over their robe and are identified in the Commencement program.

Admission Process: The Honors Program application process (separate from the admission to the University itself) is competitive and based on an assessment of a variety of factors such as grades, test scores, essays, and personal interviews. Students in the program are advised by their major department and by one of the Honors Co-Directors, who also mentor honors students in choosing their career path and provide a myriad of support when students encounter any special difficulties. The co-directors seek to facilitate the development of a learning community among the honors students while placing equal priority on their full and active participation/leadership in campus or community affairs.

Scholarship Availability: The Mary Stuart Rogers Foundation provides eight $3500 Rogers Scholarships, which are awarded annually to Honors Program members who will have completed 56 units by the end of the semester in which application is made. These competitive, non-need-based Rogers Scholarships carry automatic renewal for a second year provided that the student recipient is continuing as a full-time student, has maintained a minimum GPA of 3.0, and remains a member in good standing of the University Honors Program. Support for the student's first postgraduate year is available through a separate competitive application process.

There are special Rogers Scholarship application procedures to be distinguished from those for general scholarships awarded through the University's Financial Aid Office.

Hence, students are urged to contact the co-director via e-mail for the specifics of the Rogers Scholarship competition, its rules, requirements, and deadlines.

The Campus Context: California State University, Stanislaus, one of twenty-two campuses in the California State University system, is located in Turlock, a community of approximately 50,000 people set in the heart of California's great Central Valley. The University offers affordable, high-quality education with all the virtues of a private University (i.e., small classes, faculty member accessibility to students, and faculty member mentors for student research opportunities). The park-like 220-acre campus also offers a variety of recreational and cultural activities and is ideally situated within easy driving distance of San Francisco, Monterey Bay-Carmel, Sacramento, Yosemite National Park, and Lake Tahoe.

Fully accredited by the Western Association of Schools and Colleges (WASC), California State University, Stanislaus, offers over seventy undergraduate majors and concentrations, nine master's programs, and nine credential programs through the College of Arts, Letters, and Sciences; the School of Business Administration; and the School of Education. Master's programs are available in business administration, education, English, history, interdisciplinary studies, marine science, psychology, public administration, and social work. Preprofessional programs are available in law, medicine, dentistry, pharmacy, physical therapy, veterinary medicine, optometry laboratory technology, and medical laboratory technology.

Student Body In fall 1995, there were a total of 5,972 students, 61 percent of whom were women. The ethnic distribution of the student body is 17 percent Hispanic, 4 percent African American, 8 percent Asian American, 1 percent Filipino, 2 percent American Indian, and 58 percent white, with the remaining percentage of unknown or other ethnic origin. There are 59 international students on campus. Fifty-three percent of the students receive financial aid. There are three sororities and fraternities and more than fifty clubs and organizations (social and academic) on campus.

Faculty There are 410 faculty members, 251 full-time and 86 percent having terminal degrees. The student-faculty ratio is 18:1.

Key Facilities Special or distinguishing facilities on campus include the instructional television system that transmits regular courses from two classroom studios on campus and one studio in Stockton, California, to four remote classroom sites in the state and a new third broadcasting channel using compressed video technology, which allows for 2-way audio and 2-way video and reaches reception sites in both Stockton and Merced, California. The CSU Stanislaus Stockton Center on the San Joaquin Delta College campus represents a cooperative arrangement between two segments of California's public higher education system and is now in its twenty-first year of operation. The Stockton Center was selected for national recognition by the American Association of State Colleges and Universities (AASCU) in Washington, D.C., as an innovative educational program in 1984 and was included in 1985 in the Showcase of Excellence awards given for developing innovative teacher preparation curriculum. Degree

and credential programs offered by California State University, Stanislaus, are designed to complement the two-year Associate of Arts work provided by Delta College. Degree programs offered at the Stockton Center are fully accredited by WASC.

The residential-life Village, completed in 1993 with room for 260 students, is a model on-campus coed dorm; completion of Village II in 1996 enables the University to house 356 students in modern and comfortable suites and apartments with a wide variety of amenities including a jacuzzi, pool, computer lab, study areas, and a recreation room.

The library contains 310,000 volumes and includes subscriptions to about 2,200 periodicals. Computerized database searching is available to all students through the use of CD-ROM workstations and on-line access to remote databases. Interlibrary loan service is connected electronically to over 10,000 libraries of all types. Computer facilities include nine computer labs containing about 222 computers (half Macintosh and half DOS) located in dormitories, the library, and academic buildings. The student-computer ratio is 28:1.

Athletics CSU has eleven intercollegiate sports, with men's and women's teams in basketball, track and field, and cross country. There are men's teams in baseball, golf, and soccer and women's teams in softball and volleyball. The University is committed to providing equal athletic opportunities for women. CSU Stanislaus is a member of NCAA Division II with all of its programs operating under NCAA rules, regulations, and bylaws. The University is also a member of the Northern California Athletic Conference (NCAC).

Study Abroad Through its international programs, CSU Stanislaus students in all majors have available the opportunity to study abroad in countries as diverse as France, Mexico, Zimbabwe, and Japan while earning course credit on their home campus.

Support Services Disabled students will find the classroom, science, library, student services, health center, dormitory, gym, drama, music, art, and student union buildings all wheelchair accessible. There is handicapped parking available in all parking lots, and most campus buildings have equipped and accessible restrooms and lowered drinking fountains available. The Disabled Student Services Office offers adaptive equipment such as print enlargers, TDD, tape recorders, manual and electric wheelchairs, talking calculators, one-handed typewriters, volume-controllable telephone receivers, Kurzweil reader, and adaptive computer technology.

Job Opportunities A wide range of work opportunities exist on campus, including assistantships and work study.

Tuition: None for state residents, $7626 for nonresidents, per year (1996-97)

Room and Board: $5500 minimum

Mandatory Fees: $1915

Contact: Co-Directors: Dr. Susan Middleton-Keirn and Prof. Terrie L. Short, 215 Classroom Building, 801 West Monte Vista Avenue, Turlock, California 95382; Telephone: 209-667-3127; Fax: 209-667-3324; E-mail: susan@toto.csustan.edu or tshort@toto.csustan.edu; Web site: http://ctc.csustan.edu/hon/hons.home.html

CALVIN COLLEGE

4 Pr C M Sc Tr

▼ Honors Program

The Calvin College Honors Program, first introduced in 1969 and greatly expanded since 1993, is a four-year program of special courses and opportunities intended to help students of outstanding academic ability and motivation develop their gifts so that they will be equipped for leadership in service to God, their communities, and the world at large.

The curriculum of Calvin's Honors Program annually includes special sections of 10–15 core courses, which are generally taken in the students' first two years at Calvin. In these honors courses, students are encouraged to develop greater than average initiative and independent study skills while working in greater than usual depth and closer collaboration with their professors. At the junior and senior levels, honors work is generally done by contract in each student's major discipline. Honors students receive special advising, orientation, and assistance in scheduling their classes; may contract to take regular courses for honors credit; are offered special opportunities for research and subsidies for participating in academic conferences; and they are invited to various cocurricular activities for honors students, including the Pew Younger Scholars program for students who are considering careers in academic life.

In recent years, approximately 475 students (about 12 percent of the student body) have been involved in the program annually, along with about 20 faculty members in eleven disciplines.

Participation Requirements: To remain in the Honors Program, students must maintain a GPA of at least 3.3 and take at least one honors course per year. To graduate with honors from Calvin College, students must complete at least six honors courses overall (at least two of these in their major), maintain a GPA of at least 3.3, and fulfill any other departmental requirements for honors in their major discipline, which generally means at least a senior-level research project and a thesis or public presentation. Honors graduates are presented with commemorative medallions at the annual Honors Convocation, and they wear their awards at Commencement. Their achievement is also noted on their transcript and diploma.

Admission Process: Calvin's Honors Program is open to students of all majors and class levels. Incoming students are invited to participate in the Honors Program if they have an ACT composite score of 28 or higher or an SAT I combined score of 1240 or higher. Transfer and continuing students who have a college GPA of at least 3.3 are also eligible for the program.

Scholarship Availability: Virtually all of Calvin's honors students receive merit-based scholarships awarded by the College for academic performance in the highest 15–20 percent of their cohorts. While participation in the Honors Program is not a condition for these awards, a high percentage of the top scholarship groups are active in honors work.

The Campus Context: Calvin College is a four-year liberal arts College founded in 1876 and affiliated with the Christian Reformed Church. It occupies a campus of 370 acres in southeast Grand Rapids. Campus facilities include a Service Learning Center, which coordinates academically based service programs in which about 1,500 students participate annually and a 174-acre ecosystem preserve adjacent to campus used for recreation as well as scientific research. Rated ninth among 122 regional (Midwest) universities by *U.S. News & World Report* in 1996, Calvin is also highly ranked in the *Fiske Guide*, *Barron's Best Buys*, and *The Princeton Review*. Students may enroll in eighty academic majors or degree programs.

Student Body Total enrollment for fall 1996 is 3,993 undergraduates and 58 graduate students; 44 percent are men, 56 percent are women. The ethnic distribution of the student body is 93 percent white, 1 percent African American, .8 percent Hispanic, 1.6 percent Asian American, and .2 percent Native American. International students include 236 (5.8 percent) Canadians and 92 (2.3 percent) students from other countries. Fifty-six percent of the students live on campus in fifteen dormitories and eleven apartment complexes; 44 percent commute. Ninety percent receive financial aid (65 percent need-based, 25 percent other).

Faculty There are 263 full-time faculty members, of whom 83 percent have their terminal degrees. There are 261 part-time additional faculty members. The student-faculty ratio is 15:1.

Key Facilities Calvin's main library houses 680,000 books, periodicals, and government documents. Computer facilities include about 1,300 terminals on campus (Sun, Macintosh, and PC), 450 of them in open computer labs. There is e-mail and Net access for all students, faculty members, and staff.

Athletics Calvin College is a member of the Michigan Intercollegiate Athletic Association, with an extensive Division III program of nine women's sports (soccer, cross-country, golf, volleyball, basketball, swimming, softball, tennis, and track) and eight men's sports (soccer, cross-country, golf, basketball, swimming, baseball, tennis, and track). There are also men's club sports in volleyball, ice hockey, and lacrosse and extensive intramurals.

Study Abroad Study abroad includes programs in Britain, Honduras, Hungary, and Spain; affiliated programs in Austria, China, Egypt, France, Germany, the Netherlands, and Russia; and annual 3-week January-term courses in several international locations.

Support Services Disabled students will find all buildings accessible and special housing reserved. The Academic Services Department has a full-time coordinator of services for students with disabilities.

Job Opportunities There are on-campus work opportunities, including about 250 part-time student positions.

Tuition: $11,655 per year (1996-97)

Room and Board: $4160

Mandatory Fees: $25

Contact: Director: Dr. Kenneth Bratt, 359 Hiemenga Hall, 3201 Burton SE, Grand Rapids, Michigan 49546; Telephone: 616-957-6296; Fax: 616-957-8551; E-mail: br_k@calvin.edu; Web site: http://www.calvin.edu

CAMBRIDGE COMMUNITY COLLEGE

2 Pu G S Sc Tr

▼ Honors Program

The Cambridge Community College Honors Program is a curricular, cocurricular, and extracurricular program designed to meet the needs of students who seek a challenge, who are willing to assume part of the responsibility for their own learning experience, and who select courses that provide them with additional intellectual stimulation. The Honors Program is also designed to prepare students to move beyond the two-year college and help meet honors requirements in general education at the four-year institutions to which they transfer.

The Cambridge Community College Honors Program curriculum consists of special honors seminars, core courses with honors designation, honors contracts, and independent study opportunities. Five special honors seminars are offered annually. General Studies 171: Honors Program Orientation is a seminar providing essential information about the collegiate environment that first-time or returning honors students need in order to enhance a successful academic experience. This 1-credit course is required of all students for graduation from the Honors Program. Humanities 171: Honors Seminar is an in-depth study in the humanities with a focus that is interdisciplinary, pertinent to different cultural perspectives, and has ties to economic and sociological concerns. The theme of this seminar utilizes the annual Phi Theta Kappa Honors Study Topic. Humanities 172: Honors Experience is an experiential study and exploration of Minneapolis and St. Paul through a variety of perspectives. Natural Science 171: Honors Seminar is a study of the topic of the annual Nobel Conference held annually at Gustavus Adolphus College in St. Peter, Minnesota. Following attendance at the Conference, the seminar continues further examination of the Conference theme. Social Science 172 is an in-depth study of the changing nature of leadership and leadership patterns. Topics include leadership development, tasks of leadership, uses and abuses of power, motivating others, and sharing leadership responsibilities with constituents and followers.

The special honors seminars involve at least one field trip off campus, which is open to all program students even if they are not enrolled in the seminar. The program also provides students with opportunities to attend the annual conferences of the Upper Midwest Honors Council and the National Collegiate Honors Council.

One literature course is offered annually as a special honors section. Honors Program students may also arrange to convert a non-honors course into an honors course. Honors contracts typically involve extensive use of primary sources, creativity, syntheses, advanced analysis, and/or covering topics in greater depth.

On campus, Honors Program students have the opportunity to interact with scholars, politicians, and other dignitaries. The program sponsors a series of on-campus lectures and programs, and students also present lectures and programs themselves.

Phi Theta Kappa, the International Honors Society for Community Colleges, is the official Honors Program student organization. Alpha Delta Upsilon, the Cambridge Community College chapter, is one of the most active and most distinguished chapters around the world. Phi Theta Kappa involves students in leadership development opportunities, service projects, and social activities. Members travel to conferences, honor seminars, and conventions across the state, region, and nation; work on campus as tutors and guides; and provide service for projects in the community. Membership is extended by invitation to students who complete 15 credits with a cumulative GPA of 3.25.

Four Phi Theta Kappa officers represent students at the monthly Honors Council meetings with 10 faculty members from various academic disciplines.

Established in 1987, the program currently enrolls 34 students.

Participation Requirements: To graduate from the Honors Program, students are required to complete 18 credits in courses designated as honors. Students who complete the program are entitled to an honors notation on their transcript, Certification of Completion presented at the annual Awards Night program in May, medallions presented at graduation, and an opportunity to participate in the Capstone Study Abroad Experience for Honors Program graduates. The Honors Capstone Study Abroad Experience is designed to help Honors Program students learn about and gain appreciation for a culture and country not their own and to reward them for their scholastic achievement. Graduating members of the Honors Program decide what country or part of the world they would like to visit. Upon graduation in June, these students and one or more of the honors professors travel to that part of the world for a study program. This study has been subsidized in part by the Cambridge Community College Foundation. Other honors students may also participate in the Capstone Honors Experience, but they have to pay the full cost for the experience.

Admission Process: Students are admitted to the program on the basis of one or more of the following criteria: high school GPA of 3.5 or higher or college GPA of 3.25 of higher; recommendation by instructors or administrators; high scores on standardized tests such as the ACT, SAT, or PSAT; a 500-word essay; an interview with the Honors Council or Honors Coordinator; demonstration of special abilities or talents through portfolios, projects, papers, awards, or auditions; and a letter of application.

Scholarship Availability: Scholarships are awarded through the Cambridge Community College Foundation.

The Campus Context: Cambridge Community College is a commuter campus of Anoka-Ramsey. The College is located on a 91-square-acre campus on the banks of the Rum River, west of the city of Cambridge. The Instruction Services Building, completed in 1984, has 19,000 square feet; the Humanities Building, completed in 1993, has 11,000 square feet; and the Campus Center, completed in 1996, has 54,000 square feet. There are A.A., A.S., and A.A.S degree programs offered on campus.

Student Body The College enrolls 1,245 students, 66 percent of whom are women. The vast majority of students are of northern European extraction. There are no international students at present. Sixty percent of the students receive financial aid. There are no social fraternities or sororities.

Faculty Of the 40 faculty members, 19 are full-time and 12.5 percent hold the Ph.D. The student-faculty ratio is 23:1. The honors classes student-faculty ratio is often 15:1 or smaller.

Key Facilities The library houses 6,000 volumes. There are two computer labs (including one Pentium lab) with twenty-five stations in the Campus Center, six stations in the Instructional Services Building, and six stations in the Media Center.

Support Services Disabled students will find all buildings and programs accessible.

Job Opportunities Opportunities for employment are available to most students.

Tuition: $1901 for state residents, $3803 for nonresidents, per year (1996-97)

Fees: $20 one-time only application fee, $.17 per credit Student Association fee, $1 per credit parking fee, $2 per credit technology fee

Contact: Director: Dr. Anne S. Levig, 300 Polk Street South, Cambridge, Minnesota 55008; Telephone: 612-689-7019; Fax: 612-689-7004; E-mail: levigan@cc.cc.mn.us

CAMPBELLSVILLE UNIVERSITY

4 Pr G S Sc Tr

▼ **Honors Program**

The Campbellsville University Honors Program offers special curricular and extracurricular opportunities to challenge academically superior students and meet their special needs. The honors curriculum consists of four interdisciplinary classroom courses (Investigations: Creativity and the Arts; Investigations: Civilization and Culture; Investigations: The Sciences; and Investigations: Philosophy and Values), an independent study, and a two-semester thesis. Students who complete the entire 21-hour program are awarded a minor in interdisciplinary studies as well as special recognition at graduation. Classes are small (seldom more than 12 students) and lively, with an emphasis on participatory learning.

The Honors Student Association provides for a variety of extracurricular opportunities designed to confirm and enhance the more formal classroom experiences. Activities include trips to plays, museums, lectures, and concerts; hosting speakers and performers on campus; and a regular HSA Movie Night to see and discuss films. The Academic Team, an auxiliary to the Honors Program, provides opportunity for quick-recall competition.

A close-knit, family-like atmosphere pervades the Honors Program as well as the Campbellsville campus as a whole. Warm and trusting relationships with faculty members and other students provide honors students with a strong base of personal and intellectual support.

First launched in fall 1994, the Honors Program has a membership of 26 students.

Admission Process: To enter the Honors Program, first-time freshmen must have a minimum composite score of 26 on the ACT (or SAT equivalent) plus a minimum high school GPA of 3.5 and/or high school graduation rank within the top 10 percent. To continue in good standing with the Honors Program, honors students must maintain a minimum 3.0 college GPA and take at least one honors course per year.

Scholarship Availability: Academic scholarships are available to students of exceptional ability and are not restricted to honors students. Those with ACT composites (or SAT equivalent) of 25–29 are eligible for half tuition; 30–32 for full tuition; and 33–36 for full tuition plus room and board.

The Campus Context: Campbellsville University is in Campbellsville, a small city (population about 10,000) located in the heart of Kentucky. Only 90 minutes away from Louisville, Lexington, or Bowling Green, Campbellsville enjoys access to big-city opportunities while retaining small-town charm. Affiliated with the Kentucky Baptist Convention, Campbellsville University is open to students of all religions and denominations.

Campbellsville University grants the following degrees: Associate in Arts, Associate in Science, Bachelor of Arts,

Bachelor of Science, Bachelor of Science in Medical Technology, Bachelor of Music, and Master of Arts in Education. These degrees represent approximately thirty-three different disciplines.

Student Body Undergraduate enrollment is approximately 1,240 students of whom 53 percent are women. Fifty-eight percent of the students are commuters and 42 percent are residents. The ethnic distribution of the student body is .2 percent American Indian/Alaskan Native, .2 percent Asian or Pacific Islander, .4 percent Hispanic, 3 percent African American, and 94 percent white. There are 28 international students. Ninety-five percent of the students receive financial aid. The University has no social fraternities or sororities.

Faculty Of the 54 full-time faculty members, 55 percent hold terminal degrees. There are also 62 adjunct faculty members. The student-faculty ratio is 16:1.

Key Facilities The library holds approximately 80,000 volumes. Computer facilities for student use include three large PC labs with a total of about seventy computers, three small dorm labs with about ten computers, one Macintosh lab with four computers, and a 56 kb Internet connection. Computers are provided for each faculty member and administrative office. The University has no social fraternities or sororities.

Athletics Men's intercollegiate athletic teams include basketball, football, golf, tennis, swimming, cross-country, baseball, and soccer. Women's intercollegiate teams include basketball, softball, tennis, swimming, cross-country, soccer, and volleyball. A wide variety of recreational activities are available, including intramural competitions.

Study Abroad Campbellsville participates with a consortium of colleges to offer a semester of study in London, England.

Support Services Many of the University's facilities are wheelchair accessible. Efforts are underway to provide for disabled access to all parts of the campus.

Job Opportunities Work study and workship positions are available for many students on campus.

Tuition: $6800 per year (1996-97)

Room and Board: $3380

Contact: Director: Dr. James W. Moore, 200 West College Street, Campbellsville, Kentucky 42718; Telephone: 502-789-5341 (office), 502-465-8158 (switchboard); Fax: 502-789-5547, 502-789-5050; E-mail: jmoore@campbellsvil.edu; Web site: http://www.campbellsvil.edu

CATAWBA COLLEGE

| 4 Pr C S Tr |

▼ Honors Program

The Catawba College Honors Program offers academically gifted students the opportunity to pursue their interests in company with their intellectual peers and outstanding faculty members. In small classes, often team-taught by 2 or more professors, students explore such topics as Native American Religion and Literature, Man's Place in Nature, and The American Character. The emphasis is interdisciplinary, encouraging creative thinking, productive dialogue, and personal growth. Honors courses frequently carry general education credit so that a student may fulfill general education graduate requirements by taking these courses.

In addition to course work, participation in the Catawba Honors Program brings the opportunity to attend state and national honors conferences and take part in trips to such events as the North Carolina Shakespeare Festival.

Participation Requirements: Students who qualify for the Honors Program may take as few or as many honors courses as they choose. To graduate with College Honors, students must maintain a 3.0 GPA and complete 18 hours of honors courses, including a required freshman-level course and a senior honors seminar. Students who complete the requirements have the designation College Honors added to their diplomas and wear a special honor cord during the Commencement ceremonies.

Admission Process: Approximately 35 of the entering freshmen are invited to be in two honors advisory groups and are thus eligible to take honors courses. In addition, any student with a 3.0 GPA, including transfer students, may apply to the Director for permission to join the program and take honors courses.

The Campus Context: Catawba College, established in 1851, has a beautiful 210-acre campus on the edge of the small historic town of Salisbury, North Carolina. Another 150 acres are devoted to an outstanding ecological preserve.

Student Body Catawba is a four-year liberal arts college with an enrollment of nearly 1,000 students, evenly distributed between men and women. Over twenty-five states and several other countries are represented in the student body. The majority of students reside on campus. Financial aid goes to 93 percent of the students.

Faculty Of the 75 faculty members, 66 are full-time, with 74 percent possessing a terminal degree.

Key Facilities The Corriher-Linn-Black Library resources include over 300,000 volume-equivalents in a wide array of print and nonprint formats. The library is connected to the Internet and thus provides access to library and information resources around the world.

Athletics Intercollegiate athletic competition includes at least a dozen sports.

Tuition: $10,726 per year (1996-97)

Room and Board: $4250

Contact: Director: Dr. Bethany Sinnott, Salisbury, North Carolina 28144-2488; Telephone: 704-637-4452; Fax: 704-637-4444; E-mail: bsinott@catawba.edu

Chadron State College

4 Pu G S Tr

▼ Honors Program

The Chadron State College Honors Program, open to all students, provides 24 hours of honors seminars, which substitute for equivalent hours required in the College's General Studies Program. The seminars are all interdisciplinary, with an emphasis on readings in literature, philosophy, psychology, economics, history, the sciences, myth, and theology. The seminars are arranged and named as follows: Human Understanding of the Psyche, Human Understanding of the Society, Human Understanding of the Natural Order, and Human Understanding of the Cosmos.

Classes are small (no more than 15 students) and conducted in a seminar format to promote a spirited exchange of ideas in the process of discovery. Instructors are chosen from the College's recognized award-winning faculty.

Currently, there are approximately 50 students enrolled in the program.

Admission Process: Entrance to the program for incoming freshmen is competitive, based on a high school transcript, ACT scores, a writing sample, and recommendations. Transfer students may also apply by writing to the Director.

The Campus Context: Located on the Pine Ridge in scenic northwest Nebraska, Chadron State College has evolved from its origins in 1911 as a school for teacher training to a comprehensive four-year institution. The College now has fifty-five undergraduate degree programs and six graduate programs offering the B.A., B.S., M.A., M.S. in Education, and M.B.A. degrees.

Student Body Undergraduate enrollment is 2,500 students, of whom 56 percent are women. The ethnic distribution of the student body is .6 percent African American, 1.7 percent Native American, .7 percent Asian, and 2 percent Hispanic. Eighty-five percent of students receive financial aid.

Faculty There are 101 full-time faculty members, of whom 63 percent have terminal degrees. There are an additional 35 adjunct faculty members.

Key Facilities The College's library houses 190,666 volumes, 891 journal subscriptions, and 285,000 microforms. There are fourteen student computer labs with 141 computers. The Nelson Activity Center and the Student Center provide venues for student social life.

Study Abroad Study abroad includes summer study tours.

Support Services Most of the campus meets ADA guidelines for disabled students.

Job Opportunities Work opportunities via the work study program and the institution are available, as are internships.

Tuition: $1650 for state residents, $3300 for nonresidents, per year (1996-97)

Room and Board: $2926 minimum

Mandatory Fees: $288

Contact: Director: Dr. George V. Griffith, Chadron, Nebraska 69337; Telephone: 308-432-6306; Fax: 308-432-6464; E-mail: ggriffith@csc1.csc.edu

Christian Brothers University

4 Pr G M Tr

▼ Honors Program

The Christian Brothers University Honors Program offers an enriched academic experience to gifted and highly motivated students in all disciplines. Members of the Honors Program take a series of special-topics courses with limited enrollment, usually about 20 students. These courses are offered in a variety of disciplines and fulfill general education requirements for all majors. The program offers students the opportunity to explore challenging topics in small groups led by faculty members chosen for their interest in developing courses especially designed for the Honors Program and for their commitment to teaching honors students. The program offers special-topics courses in English, history, philosophy, political science, psychology, and religion as well as a senior research seminar. The Honors Program Director assists honors students and their academic advisers in planning each student's course of study. Program-sponsored social and cultural events provide opportunities for extracurricular enrichment and create a sense of community among honors students and faculty members.

The CBU Honors Program is now in its eighth year. Currently, there are 120 students in the Honors Program.

Participation Requirements: Students participate in the program at two levels. Some students earn Honors Program Diplomas by taking at least six honors courses, including the senior seminar, and maintaining a 3.2 GPA. Others take fewer honors courses, selecting those most closely related to their academic interests.

Admission Process: First-year students are invited to apply for admission to the Honors Program during the spring before they enroll at CBU. Invitation to the program is based on high school grades and ACT or SAT scores. A personal interview is also part of the selection process. Transfer students and students who are not initially selected for membership may also apply for admission, usually after completing one semester at CBU.

The Campus Context: Christian Brothers University (originally Christian Brothers College) was founded in 1871 by members of the Institute of the Brothers of the Christian Schools, a Roman Catholic religious teaching congregation. The 70-acre campus is located in the Midtown section of Memphis, about 4 miles east of downtown Memphis. Students may enroll in twenty-four undergraduate majors leading to Bachelor of Arts or Bachelor of Science degrees from the schools of business, engineering, liberal arts, and science. Master's degrees are offered in business and engineering.

Student Body The University has an enrollment of 1,800 full-time students representing thirty-five states and nineteen other countries; the men-women ratio is about 1:1. Students may participate in more than thirty clubs, groups, and organizations, including theater, art and musical productions, publications, and academic societies as well as national sororities and fraternities.

Faculty There are 106 full-time faculty members, 75 percent with doctorates or other terminal degrees. The student-faculty ratio is 15:1.

Key Facilities Plough Memorial Library has more than 150,000 volumes, periodicals, and microfilms. Computer facilities include 250 DOS computers for student use, located in the library and in labs across campus.

Athletics CBU began competing in the NCAA's Division II in 1996. Sports include basketball, soccer, tennis, cross-country, softball, and volleyball for women and baseball, basketball, soccer, cross-country, tennis, and golf for men. There are fourteen intramural sports.

Study Abroad Study abroad is coordinated through the CBU Office of Special Programs.

Tuition: Full-time, $10,700 per year; part-time, $300 per semester hour for day classes, $235 for evening classes, $190 for summer classes (1996-97)

Room and Board: $3530

Fees: $330

Contact: Director: Dr. Ann Marie Wranovix, 650 East Parkway South, Memphis, Tennessee 38104-5581; Telephone: 901-321-3352; Fax: 901-321-4340; E-mail: awranovi@odin.cbu.edu

CHRISTOPHER NEWPORT UNIVERSITY

4 Pu G S Sc Tr

▼ **Honors Program**

The Christopher Newport University Honors Program has offered scholarship support and innovative educational opportunities since 1980. Consisting of 100 students, the program encourages intellectual and personal autonomy, scholarship, leadership, and community service. Small class sizes (20 or fewer) permit students to work closely with outstanding faculty members. Honors faculty members also provide advising. Travel to Maine and Washington, D.C., occurs in some courses. The University supports student travel to present research at conferences.

Honors students have a guaranteed registration privilege, except during their first semester.

Participation Requirements: The CNU Honors Program supplements any major on campus. The two-semester Honors English sequence replaces regular freshman writing courses and permits students to study Supreme Court cases and other current issues. Honors students complete community service of their choice during the sophomore year. Junior and senior seminars culminate in a team-taught capstone course entitled Problems in the Modern World. Independent study in the major is required. The total number of credits required in honors is 14.

To graduate from the Honors Program, a student must complete the curricular requirements of the program and maintain a 3.0 GPA overall. Successful completion is noted at graduation and on the student's transcript.

Scholarship Availability: The Honors Council awards forty scholarships each year. Scholarships range from $900 to full-tuition and are renewable as long as students complete 12 credits, meet program requirements, and retain a 3.3 GPA. Top freshmen win Styron Scholarships based on SAT scores, but subsequent awards are based solely on GPA. Transfer students are eligible for scholarships. Greene Scholarships of $2000 go to students with the highest GPA in each class. Full-tuition Beamer Scholarships reward excellence in mathematics and science.

Admission Process: Freshmen are invited to become honors students if they have a high school GPA of 3.0 or higher, rank in the top 20 percent of their classes, and score at least 580 on the SAT I verbal and 520 on the SAT I math. Transfer students and other CNU students are welcome to apply to the program. Approval depends upon a student's GPA and interest.

The Campus Context: Christopher Newport University was founded in 1960 as a branch of the College of William and Mary. Separation from the College of William and Mary occurred 1976, and the Honors Program began in 1980. The University consists of the Colleges of Liberal Arts and of Business, Science, and Technology. Located in southeastern Virginia in midtown Newport News, the attractive 105-acre campus features a recently opened, state-of-the-art, 430-bed residence hall. This small state-supported University has established a reputation for fine teaching, small classes, and a large number of curricular opportunities for students with initiative. Students may enroll in sixty-one undergraduate degree programs in liberal arts, sciences, business, and teaching.

Student Body There are 4,500 undergraduates enrolled, the majority from Virginia, with transfers from every state. Sixty-one percent of the students are women. The ethnic distribution of the student body is 81 percent Caucasian, 16 percent African American, and 2 percent Hispanic. There are 50 international students. Nine percent of the students are residents, 91 percent commute. Of the students, 42 percent receive financial aid. There are five fraternities and five sororities.

Faculty There are 165 full-time faculty members (supplemented by adjunct faculty members), 90 percent with doctorates or terminal degrees. The student-faculty ratio is 16:1.

Key Facilities The 316,000-volume library has several electronic databases and other on-line services available. Computer facilities include more than 100 Macintosh and IBM computers located in residence halls, the library, and all classroom buildings. There are also computerized classrooms and networks. Free student e-mail accounts and on-line classes are available as an option.

Athletics CNU supports men's basketball, baseball, golf, tennis, soccer, cross-country, indoor track, and outdoor track; women's basketball, softball, cross-country, tennis, indoor track, outdoor track, and volleyball; and coed sailing and cheerleading. There have been almost 300 All-American athletes in various sports as well as nine NCAA National team championships (Division III) in women's track. CNU also offers a full program of intramural sports.

Study Abroad CNU belongs to the National Student Exchange and has the following international sister universities: Beijing Polytechnic University (China), Autonomous University of Guadalajara (Mexico), Instituto Nacional de Salud Publica (Cuernavaca, Mexico), Jian Gean University (China), Kansai Gaidai University (Japan), Karlova University (Czech Republic), Keon Yang University (South Korea), Middlesex University (London), Osaka International University (Japan), and Vavilov State Optical Institute (Russia).

Support Services All campus buildings are accessible.

Job Opportunities A work-study program operates campus wide. Academic departments employ assistants. Numerous off-campus working opportunities are conveniently located. Internships are available in many undergraduate majors as are research opportunities at NASA-Langley and the Thomas Jefferson National Accelerator Facility.

Tuition: $3326 for state residents, $7946 for nonresidents, per year (1996-97)

Room and Board: $4650

Mandatory Fees: $40

Contact: Director: Dr. Jay S. Paul, 50 Shoe Lane, Newport News, Virginia 23606; Telephone: 757-594-7072; Fax: 757-594-7577; E-mail: jpaul@cnu.edu

THE CITADEL

| 4 Pr G S Tr |

▼ Honors Program

The Citadel's Honors Program is a specially designed educational experience meeting the needs of students with an outstanding record of academic achievement and a sense of intellectual adventure. While pursuing any one of seventeen degree programs offered by The Citadel, honors students take a series of Core Curriculum Honors Courses—for example, studies based in literature and writing, history, and mathematics—concentrated in their first two years, and an occasional Honors Seminar or Honors Research Project in their third and fourth years.

There are approximately 65 students in the 9-year-old program.

Although The Citadel's Honors Program has many facets, the essential character of our program can be found in three aspects. First, there is a tutorial foundation. All honors courses, from freshman-level courses through senior-level seminars, have attached to them a regularly scheduled, one-on-one meeting between the student and the professor. These are not just check-in meetings to see if the student has any problems; rather, the professor and the student prearrange to work together on one of the assignments of the course.

Second, there is preprofessional counseling. All honors students take a three-semester sequence of courses entitled Personal and Professional Development. Taught entirely in tutorial, it directs students in a three-year period of research, reflection, and writing on the subject of their professional goals, encouraging them to envision their leadership in their future profession and guiding them in exploring, through research and writing, the ideals as well as the facts of that profession.

Finally, there is leadership. The Citadel encourages students to take full advantage of the many leadership opportunities afforded by the military environment of the school. Year after year, the chain of command at The Citadel is heavily populated from top to bottom by Honors Program students. The Citadel has an honors brand of leadership based on the concept of service, which has enabled honors students to consistently earn positions of leadership. The deadline for applying to the program is January 15.

Participation Requirements: Students majoring in one of the sciences or engineering will be required to complete the following honors courses: Honors Personal and Professional Development I, II, and III; Honors English I, II, III, and IV; Honors History I and II; Honors Social Science Project; and one Honors Seminar or Research Project. Students majoring in one of the liberal arts or social sciences will be required to complete the following honors courses: Honors Personal and Professional Development I, II, and III; Honors English I, II,

III, and IV; Honors History I and II; Honors Social Science Project; and two Honors Seminars or Research Projects (or one of each). Students who complete all Honors Program requirements are recognized as Honors Program Graduates in the College Commencement ceremony. They receive an Honors Program certificate as well as a gold honors seal on their diploma. A notation is added to the official College transcript to indicate that they have completed the requirements of the Honors Program and to explain what those requirements are. This note comes at the very beginning of the transcript to assist future employers or graduate/professional school admissions committees in understanding what the Honors Program means at The Citadel.

Scholarship Availability: No scholarships are awarded through the Honors Program, although the Honors Director is a member of the College Scholarships Committee.

The Campus Context: Founded in 1842, The Citadel is a state-assisted, comprehensive, liberal arts college in a military environment. The College has two diverse, but equally important, goals. One is to graduate young men and women with alert minds and sound bodies who have been taught the high ideals of honor, integrity, loyalty, and patriotism; who accept the responsibilities that accompany leadership; and who have sufficient professional knowledge to take their places in the competitive world. The second goal is to serve the citizens of the Lowcountry and the state of South Carolina through its coeducational College of Graduate and Professional Studies and a broad range of noninstructional activities and services. In 1995, the College was ranked in the top 10 percent of regional colleges and universities, eleventh overall in the South.

Characteristic of its unique environment, the Citadel Museum displays military, academic, social, and athletic aspects of life on campus. Handsome exhibits trace the history of the College from 1842 to the present. There are regular Dress Parades: South Carolina Corps of Cadets parade on Friday afternoons during the academic year. Featured in these parades are the world-renowned Citadel Regimental Band and the Pipe band.

There are two colleges at The Citadel: The Corps of Cadets, (the undergraduate College) and the College of Graduate and Professional Studies. There are seventeen degree programs for the undergraduates and ten for the graduates.

Student Body There are 1,847 students (almost all men) in the Corps of Cadets. The ethnic breakdown of the student body is 88 percent Caucasian, 8 percent African American, 2 percent Asian, and 2 percent Hispanic. Currently, there are 43 international students. All cadets are required to live on campus for all four years. Currently, 54 percent of the members of the Corps of Cadets receive financial aid. There are no fraternities or sororities.

Faculty Of the 244 total faculty members, 163 are full-time and 95 percent hold terminal degrees. The student-faculty ratio is 16:1.

Key Facilities The Daniel Library holds 182,000 volumes. Free writing, learning, and word processing strategies are provided to all segments of The Citadel community. The Citadel computer facilities consist of nine labs holding fifty Macintosh computers, seventy IBM-PCs, and twenty DEC terminals.

Athletics Intercollegiate athletics include football, basketball, track, soccer, tennis, golf, and wrestling. The Citadel also offers a wide range of intramural sports.

Study Abroad A summer Study Abroad Program exists for students studying French, German, and Spanish in the countries where the language is spoken.

Job Opportunities Students are offered a range of work opportunities on campus, including assistantships and work study.

Tuition: $3297 for state residents, $7536 for nonresidents, per year (1996-97)

Room and Board: $3679

Fees: $773; a deposit is required to defray the cost of uniforms and supplies: $3574 for freshmen, $1110 for sophomores, $1040 for juniors, $1010 for seniors

Contact: Director: Jack W. Rhodes, 171 Moultrie Street, Charleston, South Carolina 29409; Telephone: 803-953-3708; Fax: 803-953-7084; E-mail: rhodesj@citadel.edu

CLEMSON UNIVERSITY

| 4 Pu G D L Sc Tr |

▼ Calhoun College, Honors Program

Established in 1962, Calhoun College, the Honors Program of Clemson University, strives to enrich the educational experience of highly motivated, academically talented students by providing opportunities for scholarship and research not always available to undergraduates. During the 1995–96 academic year, approximately 850 students were members of the Honors Program. In addition to the intellectual challenge of honors, some of the advantages of membership in Calhoun College are priority course scheduling and registration, the option of honors housing, extended library loan privileges, and special lectures and cultural events.

Participation Requirements: The honors curriculum consists of two components. To earn General Honors, students must demonstrate breadth by completing at least four honors courses totaling a minimum of 14 semester hours with not more than 8 hours or two courses within that minimum in any one subject. Normally undertaken in the junior and senior years, Departmental Honors provides opportunities for honors students to do advanced, in-depth study and research within their major academic disciplines. Specific requirements are set by the department; however, it is expected that all students, regardless of their major, will complete a thesis, a portfolio of creative works, a major research project, or similar capstone achievement.

Recognition for students completing both General Honors and Departmental Honors is at a special awards ceremony on the eve of Commencement at which time they are presented the B.C. Inabinet Honors Medallion. The medallion, as well as the student's diploma, permanent transcript, and Commencement program, recognize Honors Program graduates as Calhoun College Scholars. Students receiving only Departmental Honors receive an honors medallion and certificate of achievement. Those completing General Honors are given a certificate of achievement.

Admission Process:
Entry into the program is by invitation to entering freshmen with SAT I scores of 1300 and above who rank within the top 10 percent of their high school graduating class. To continue membership in Calhoun College, students must maintain a cumulative GPA of 3.4 or higher and must complete one honors course each semester. Transfer and enrolled students may join the program if they have earned a cumulative GPA of 3.4 or better as a full-time student at Clemson University and have earned no more than 75 semester hours or have at least four semesters remaining to complete their degree program requirements.

Scholarship Availability:
Scholarships for Clemson University are administered and/or coordinated through the Office of Student Financial Aid for various types of undergraduate financial aid such as scholarships, loans, grants, and part-time employment. Transfer students applying for student loans will be considered as entering freshmen in determining maximum loan limits. There are no specific scholarships associated with the Honors Program, although many of the honors students receive financial aid because of their academic qualifications.

The Campus Context:
Established in 1889 as Clemson Agricultural College, the College was an all-men military school until 1955, when the change was made to civilian status and the institution became coeducational. In 1964, the College was renamed Clemson University. The 1,400-acre campus is located on the former homestead of statesman John C. Calhoun. Nestled in the foothills of the Blue Ridge Mountains and adjacent to Lake Hartwell, the campus commands an excellent view of the mountains to the north and west. Both Atlanta, Georgia, and Charlotte, North Carolina, are 2 hours' driving time away.

Clemson University's real estate holdings consist of over 32,000 acres of forestry and agricultural lands located throughout South Carolina. The majority of these lands are dedicated to Clemson's research and public-service missions. Fort Hill, the former home of John C. Calhoun and inherited by Thomas Clemson, and the Hanover House are listed on the National Register of Historic Places and are open to the public. The campus also has two recognized Historic Districts: the Strom Thurmond Institute, which houses the institute offices, Senator Thurmond's papers and memorabilia, and the Cooper Library's special collections. The Institute is a part of an instructional and public service district that includes the Brooks Center for the Performing Arts and a continuing education/conference center.

Clemson University offers seventy-four undergraduate degree programs under the Colleges of Agriculture, Forestry, and Life Sciences; Architecture, Arts, and Humanities; Engineering and Science; Business and Public Affairs; and Health, Education, and Human Development.

Student Body The total undergraduate enrollment is 12,260 students, of whom 45 percent are women. The ethnic distribution of the student body is 1 percent international students, 8 percent African American, less than 1 percent Native American, 1 percent Asian American, less than 1 percent Hispanic, and 87 percent Caucasian. All other American ethnic minorities comprise less than 1 percent of the student body. Of all the students, 51.4 percent live on campus and 48.6 percent commute. Fifty-four percent of the undergraduates receive financial aid. There are twenty-five men's general fraternities and fifteen women's general fraternities and sororities.

Faculty The total number of faculty members is 1,746, of whom 1,190 are full-time. Of the full-time faculty members, 948 have the Ph.D./Ed.D. degree. The student-faculty ratio is 18:1.

Key Facilities The Robert Muldrow Cooper Library houses more than 1.5 million books, microforms, periodicals, and other research materials. The Clemson University Division of Computing and Information Technology supports student course work, research, and administrative data processing requirements of the University using a sophisticated network of computers. These include an HDS AS/EX-90 mainframe computer, several VAX computers, and numerous microcomputers. Computer centers are maintained in three main locations, and eleven additional remote sites on campus contain a variety of computers, terminals, and peripheral equipment. Dial-up telephone numbers are available for local as well as national and international network access. Clemson is connected to the Internet, which provides access to the national super-computer centers as well as other network resources.

Athletics Clemson was one of just four schools in the nation to have its football, men's basketball, and baseball teams rank in the top twenty-five of the *USA Today* polls at one time or another during the 1994–95 season. Five programs ended the year ranked in the top twenty in the nation. Nine athletic teams were chosen for NCAA tournaments, including five spring sports. The baseball team was chosen for the ninth straight year, while the men's tennis team was chosen for the fourteenth time in twenty years. The golf team advanced to the NCAA national tournament for the fourteenth consecutive year. The women's soccer and volleyball teams were also chosen for NCAA play. Programs include baseball, football, golf, volleyball, women's and men's soccer, basketball, swimming, tennis, cross-country, and track.

Study Abroad Through the Study Abroad Office, students can choose from of a variety of programs offered. This office can help students choose the opportunity that best complements their major courses of study and career interests. Students in all colleges are eligible to apply. The International Student Exchange Program allows an undergraduate to enroll and pay tuition, fees, and room and board at Clemson, but to study for a semester or a year at one of more than eight institutions worldwide. Not only can students enroll in courses that explore the cultures in which they are interested, but transfer credit often applies within the major.

Support Services The Office of Orientation, Leadership, and Disability Services serves the special needs of students with permanent disabilities. Clemson University recognizes a student with a disability as anyone who has a physical or mental impairment that substantially limits one or more of his/her major life activities.

Job Opportunities Employment opportunities exist in academic departments, the Athletic Department, Career Center, dining halls, Financial Aid Office, Personnel Office, and residence halls.

Tuition: $2922 for state residents, $8126 for nonresidents, per year (1996-97)

Room and Board: $3136 minimum

Fees: $190

Contact: Director: Dr. Stephen H. Wainscott, Clemson, South Carolina 29634; Telephone: 864-656-4762; Fax: 864-656-1472; E-mail: shwns@clemson.edu

---

COASTAL CAROLINA UNIVERSITY

4 Pu G S Sc

▼ Honors Program

The Honors Program at Coastal Carolina University aims to develop the reasoning and articulate student. This significant goal is advanced through a challenging and adventurous curriculum that joins intellectually accomplished and motivated students and faculty members. Honors Program courses provide for enriched study of a carefully focused, often multidisciplinary, subject matter. To ensure participation by students from all disciplines, the Honors Program is designed in accord with the academic requirements of the major areas of study at Coastal Carolina University.

Currently enrolled honors students have major areas of concentration in art studio, biology, business administration, computer science, education, English, finance, marine science, mathematics, physical education, political science, and psychology. The program has approximately 75 students.

Participation Requirements: Course work will be recognized on the students' transcript. Honors Program students are required to maintain a 3.0 GPA to remain in good standing. Students are expected to complete one honors course each semester for a total of eight honors courses. Before graduation, each student is required to complete a thesis in their major and give a public presentation.

All students in the Honors Program are encouraged to be active in the Honors Program Council (HPC), which serves as a representative body for students enrolled in the Coastal Honors Program.

Admission Process: Admission into the Honors Program is by invitation. Students are evaluated on the basis of SAT scores, ACT scores, high school class rank, and their honors program application. Applications are received from January to May.

Scholarship Availability: There are a limited number of $500 scholarships available.

The Campus Context: Coastal Carolina University is located 10 miles from Myrtle Beach. The University offers twenty-two degree programs on campus.

Student Body Undergraduate enrollment is 4,200, of whom 58 percent are women. The ethnic distribution of the student body is 86 percent white, 1 percent Hispanic, 9 percent African American, .5 percent American Indian, and 1 percent Asian. There are 75–80 international students. Fourteen percent of the students are residents and 86 percent are commuters. Fifty-nine percent of the students receive financial aid.

Faculty There are 177 full-time teaching faculty members, 76 with terminal degrees. The student-faculty ratio is 18:1.

Key Facilities The library holds 215,475 volumes. Approximately 700 computers are located in the library and academic buildings.

Athletics Coastal Carolina University fields fourteen intercollegiate teams. The men's program includes cross-country, tennis, basketball, soccer, baseball, golf, and track and field. Women compete in cross-country, tennis, basketball, volleyball, golf, softball, and track and field. The teams are named after the Coastal Carolina University mascot, the Chanticleer. The University is affiliated with the National Collegiate Athletic Association (NCAA) Division I and is a member of the Big South Conference.

Study Abroad Coastal Carolina University provides a number of study-abroad opportunities.

Support Services All of the University's facilities are handicapped-accessible.

Job Opportunities Coastal Carolina University employs approximately 400 students on campus.

Tuition: $2930 for state residents, $7840 for nonresidents, per year (1996-97)

Room and Board: $4265

Contact: Director: Dr. Marios Katsioloudes, P.O. Box 1954, Conway, South Carolina 29528; Telephone: 803-349-2298; Fax: 803-349-2914; E-mail: marios@coastal.edu

COLBY-SAWYER COLLEGE

4Pr G S Tr

▼ **Honors Program**

The Colby-Sawyer College Honors Program is designed to interest and challenge highly motivated and well-prepared students. The program allows students to pursue advanced interdisciplinary study throughout their four years at Colby-Sawyer while providing opportunities for in-depth learning and challenging discussion. Such experiences introduce students to a rich body of knowledge not always available in the regular curriculum. In addition, these experiences provide a means by which students can discover the intellectual stimulation provided by a group of lively thinkers. The College recognizes honors students by permitting them to study in the reading room of the new Colby, Colgate, and Cleveland Archives. Initiated in 1994–95, the program now includes approximately 50 students.

Faculty members who teach honors courses are drawn from across the College and represent a broad range of disciplines. Honors courses for first-year students have included such titles as History of East Asian Art, Environmental Ethics, Native American Literature and Culture, Myth and Folklore, and Cultural Conflict in the United States. For upperclass students, courses have included Gender in Science, Caribbean Oral and Written Literature, Domestic Violence, and Ethics in Literature. Classes are small—a seminar style is adopted whenever possible—and research projects are required.

Participation Requirements: The honors curriculum is based on the completion of elective courses with an honors designation. Each semester, faculty members offer two interdisciplinary courses for those in the Honors Program—one for first-year students and one for upperclass students. These courses may be offered for 1–3 credits. As seniors, honors students are invited to participate in a research colloquium in which they share their senior theses or capstone experiences. These seminars are offered in the spring semester for 1 credit.

Students participate in the Honors Program in addition to their work in the College's Liberal Education Program and their chosen majors, although some honors courses may satisfy part of the College's Liberal Education requirements. On completion of five honors courses, graduating students receive an Honors Certificate and an Honors designation is added to their diploma and transcript.

Admission Process: Incoming students are admitted to the Honors Program based on both superior prior academic performance in high school or at another college and expressed interest in the program. Current students who have earned Dean's List status (3.3 GPA or above) may also apply to the Academic Dean for admission to the program. Because the intention of the program is to be inclusive in providing opportunities for serious students, students who may not yet have earned Dean's List standing may also apply for admission. In order to continue in the program, students must earn and sustain Dean's List status.

The Campus Context: Colby-Sawyer College had its origin in the founding of the New London Academy in 1837. In 1928, after ninety years as a coeducational school, the Academy became Colby Junior College for Women. Baccalaureate programs were introduced in the 1940's, leading to the College's renaming in 1975 as Colby-Sawyer College, a four-year institution. In 1990, Colby-Sawyer once more admitted men, returning the College to its coeducational roots.

Colby-Sawyer College is located on the crest of a hill in New London, New Hampshire, in the heart of the scenic Dartmouth-Lake Sunapee region. A splendid environment for learning is created by the spacious, well-maintained campus and stately buildings that range in style from classic Georgian to the contemporary architecture of the innovative Susan Colgate Cleveland Library/Learning Center. Other special campus facilities include Baker Communications Center, Sawyer Fine Arts Center, Windy Hill Laboratory School (preschool, K-3), and the Hogan Sports Center. Colby-Sawyer is widely recognized as one of the most vital small residential colleges in the Northeast. The College offers eleven undergraduate majors.

Student Body Undergraduate enrollment is 770 students, of whom 65 percent are women. The ethnic distribution of the student body is 96 percent white and 4 percent minority-international. There are 23 international students, which constitutes 3 percent of the student body. Of the total student population, 87 percent are resident and 13 percent commuter. Seventy-seven percent of the students receive financial aid.

Faculty There are 40 full-time faculty members (supplemented by adjunct faculty members), 78 percent with terminal degrees. The student-faculty ratio is 12:1.

Key Facilities The library houses 74,000 volumes. Three computer laboratories contain fifty-five IBM-compatible and fifteen Apple computers.

Athletics In athletics, Colby-Sawyer is NCAA Division III in a variety of team and individual sports. Varsity competition for women is offered in Alpine ski racing, basketball, lacrosse, riding, soccer, tennis, track and field, and volleyball. Varsity competition for men is offered in Alpine ski racing, baseball, basketball, riding, soccer, tennis, and track and field. The Alpine ski racing team is a member of NCAA Division I. Colby-Sawyer College maintains a high-quality program of club, intramural/recreational, and varsity athletics and has a reputation for success in sports throughout the state and region.

Job Opportunities Part-time on-campus employment during the academic year is usually awarded as part of a financial aid package. Campus jobs are assigned by the staff of the Harrington Center for Career Development, and payment is at hourly rates established by state and federal legislation.

Tuition: $16,310 per year (1997-98)

Room and Board: $6240

Contact: Director: Dr. Daniel C. Meerson, Academic Dean, 100 Main Street, New London, New Hampshire 03257; Telephone: 603-526-3761; Fax: 603-526-3452; E-mail: dmeerson@ colby-sawyer.edu; Web site: http://www.colby-sawyer.edu

COLEGIO UNIVERSITARIO DE HUMACAO

4 Pu G S Tr

▼ Programa Académico de Honor

The Programa Académico de Honor (PAH, Academic Honors Program) provides students with the opportunity to take full advantage of the university experience at the Colegio Universitario de Humacao (Humacao University College). Since its inception in 1989, the program has aimed to enrich the educational formation/development of the student within an interdisciplinary context/frame. PAH students benefit from academic offerings unique to the Honors Program, including interdisciplinary seminars, independent studies, a computer room and study area, faculty-level library privileges, and photocopying at no charge. Each student is assigned an academic adviser who helps them plan their program of study and prepare for graduate school. In addition, the program organizes orientation sessions on graduate school admissions requirements, scholarships, and financial aid programs.

There are 58 students in the program.

Participation Requirements: In the first three years of study, students must complete an Independent Study or Introduction to Research course, an honors seminar, and a third language. In their fourth year, students must prepare an honors thesis in their selected area of study under the supervision of a professor. At PAH, there is the belief that the student's learning experience must transcend the classroom. Thus, in order to be considered active members of PAH, students must also participate in cocurricular activities organized by the program. Students who fulfill all the requirements of the program receive a certificate upon graduation and their accomplishment is recorded on their transcript.

Admission Process: Students of all majors with a minimum 3.3 GPA are invited to join the program during their first and second year in college. Admission is contingent upon several factors, including a good GPA, a successful interview, and, most important, the student's willingness to fulfill the requirements of the program. Applications are due in February and March.

Scholarship Availability: Although PAH does not offer any scholarships, students with a high GPA may benefit from tuition exemption offered by the College.

The Campus Context: Thirty-three years ago, the University of Puerto Rico initiated one of the most innovative projects undertaken for many years—to take the University closer to the people by providing access to secondary education to residents of eastern Puerto Rico. The objective was accomplished with the inauguration of the Colegio Regional de Humacao, now the Colegio Universitario de Humacao (CUH, Humacao University College), a state-funded, four-year, coeducational institution, and one of the eleven units that make up the University of Puerto Rico System. The CUH is located in the city of Humacao on the eastern coast of the island of Puerto Rico, 35 miles away from the San Juan metropolitan area. Ten associate degree programs and seventeen bachelor's degree programs are offered on campus.

Student Body The total undergraduate enrollment is 4,228 students, of whom 68 percent are women and 99.9 percent are Hispanic. All students commute to school as there is no college-affiliated student housing. Seventy percent of the students receive financial aid. There are several fraternities and sororities, but only one sorority is officially recognized by the College.

Faculty There are 279 active faculty members, of whom 257 are full-time; 28 percent have doctorates. The student-faculty ratio is 16:1.

Key Facilities The library houses 97,546 volumes and 58,571 microform holdings. There are 152 computer terminals available for student use at various locations throughout the campus.

Athletics Intercollegiate athletics include baseball (men), basketball, cross-country, soccer (men), softball, table tennis, tennis, track and field, volleyball, and wrestling (men). The CUH also offers a wide range of intramural sports for both men and women.

Study Abroad Study-abroad opportunities include participation in the Student Exchange Program and special summer courses that include travel to a different country (e.g., Europe). Students can study in the continental U.S. through the National Collegiate Honors Council Exchange Program.

Support Services Most of the facilities in the College are handicapped-accessible.

Job Opportunities Students who are eligible for financial aid may find employment on campus through the work-study program. Other opportunities for employment are available off campus.

Tuition: $540 for residents, per semester. Nonresident students who are U.S. citizens pay an amount equal to the rate for nonresidents at a state university in their home states. $2400 for international students, per year (1997-98)

Room and Board: $400 per semester

Fees: $35 construction per year, $25 per lab. International students pay an additional $620 per year.

Contact: Coordinator: Dr. Maritza Reyes, Oficina de Asuntos Académicos, CUH Station, Humacao, Puerto Rico 00791; Telephone: 787-850-9417; Fax: 787-850-9416; E-mail: ma_reyes@ cuhac.upr.clu.edu

COLLEGE OF CHARLESTON

| 4 Pu G M Sc Tr |

▼ Honors Program

The Honors Program at the College of Charleston was designed in 1978 to provide a program and a community for talented and motivated students who enjoy active participation in small stimulating classes and like to investigate ideas. At the heart of the program are the Honors Colloquia—small, seminar-style classes that emphasize active student involvement and interdisciplinary learning. Honors Colloquia are taught by teams of professors from different academic disciplines on the following themes: Western Civilization, History and Philosophy of Science, Man in Society, Elements of Human Culture, and Value and Tradition in the Non-Western World. Honors courses in English, the sciences, calculus, and a variety of interdisciplinary special topics are also offered.

Throughout the program, students experience close interaction with faculty members and fellow students and are advised by specially chosen faculty advisers. Students are encouraged to participate in a wide variety of international educational opportunities. Classes, seminars, and student gatherings are held in the Honors Center, the historic William Aiken House built by Governor William Aiken in 1839.

Participation Requirements: All students take Honors English, the Colloquium in Western Civilization, and at least three other honors courses, one of which must be interdisciplinary. They also take one semester of calculus (not necessarily honors) and any math course at the 200-level or above. Each student undertakes a senior research project under the supervision of a faculty tutor, which culminates in a written paper (the Bachelor's Essay). A student must have a GPA of 3.4 or higher to graduate from the program.

Admission Process: About 400 students are in the program. More than 100 entering students are accepted each year by a faculty member/student committee on the basis of applications submitted directly to the program. The successful candidate is typically in the top 10 percent of his/her class, has taken honors and/or AP courses, and is active in extracurricular activities. While there is no minimum SAT score required, the SAT I scores of entering freshmen average about 1300. A student may apply for admission to the program at any time but is encouraged to apply separately to the College of Charleston Admissions Office and the Honors Program before December 15 to maximize the possibility of being accepted to the program and being considered for scholarships. Transfer students and currently enrolled students may also apply to the program.

Scholarship Availability: The Honors Program offers about fifty Presidential Honors Scholarships to students of exceptional ability. A number of other scholarships offered through the admissions office also go to students in the program.

The Campus Context: Situated in the midst of a city that treasures its past while promoting its future, the College of Charleston is one of the nation's most beautiful and historic campuses. Founded in 1770 and chartered in 1785, the College is the oldest institution of higher education in South Carolina and the thirteenth-oldest in the United States. In 1836 it became the nation's first municipal college and in 1970 the College joined the state's higher education system. There are five schools: the Arts, Business, Education, Humanities and Social Sciences, and Science and Mathematics. Forty undergraduate majors and more than a dozen interdisciplinary minors are offered.

The campus consists of more than 100 buildings ranging from historic residences to high-tech classrooms. In addition to the main campus, the College includes a classroom facility in North Charleston, Grice Marine Biological Laboratory on James Island, a 20-acre outdoor sports complex and recreation area in Mt. Pleasant, and a sailing center at the City Marina on the Ashley River.

Student Body There are 8,600 undergraduates, of whom 60 percent are women, 10 percent are African American, 5 percent are other minorities, and 2 percent (181) are international students. Seventy-five percent of the students are South Carolina residents. There are 2,100 students who are housed in six main residence halls and twenty-five houses. Many more rent apartments near campus.

Faculty There are 362 full-time faculty members, 93 percent with terminal degrees. The student-faculty ratio is 19:1.

Key Facilities The library contains 485,174 volumes. The College has two high-end computer centers with more than 100 Mac and DOS computers each, plus smaller centers located in classroom buildings and dorms.

Athletics The College of Charleston is NCAA Division I. Intercollegiate athletic teams include basketball, soccer, sailing, swimming, tennis, golf, equestrian, baseball (men), volleyball (women), and softball (women). The sailing team is ranked in the top five in the nation. The men's soccer team played UCLA in the Final 8 in 1995, and the men's basketball team went to NCAA or NIT post-season play in 1994, 1995, and 1996.

Study Abroad Direct international exchange programs link the College with universities in England, France, the Netherlands, Japan, and the Virgin Islands. Other exchange opportunities exist through the International Student Exchange Program and the National Student Exchange Program. Study-abroad courses are offered in summer.

Tuition: $3190 for state residents, $6380 for nonresidents, per year (1996-97)

Room and Board: $3340

Contact: Director: Dr. Rose Hamm Rowland, Charleston, South Carolina 29424; Telephone: 803-953-7154; Fax: 803-953-7135; E-mail: hammr@cofc.edu; Web site: http://www.cofc.edu

COLLEGE OF DUPAGE

`2 Pu G M Sc Tr`

▼ Honors Program

Honors courses at College of DuPage offer additional challenge and depth to your college experience and more opportunities to use your mind well. If you love to learn, are willing to work, and enjoy bringing your imagination and originality to class, then consider applying yourself to honors.

Honors courses are enriched versions of regular courses, designed to help academically talented and highly motivated students achieve their maximum potential. Each year a range of courses in the liberal arts and sciences are offered, consistent with the emphasis on general education in the first two years of college. Honors classes are characterized by smaller class sizes and a seminar format, which encourages more extensive interaction among students as well as between students and the professor. Many students especially appreciate this opportunity to get to know other students well and to feel more a part of the academic environment of the College.

Each honors course offers an in-depth treatment of course content; emphasizes the development of such intellectual skills as analysis, synthesis, critical inquiry, application and discussion; and contains a significant writing component.

The program began in 1986 and currently has approximately 200 students taking honors courses each quarter. There are currently about 175 students in the Honors Scholar Program.

Participation Requirements: Students may participate in honors in one of two ways: 1) by taking individual honors courses, or 2) by participating in the Honors Scholar Program.

Individual Honors Courses: Students who meet the general eligibility criteria listed below may apply to the honors coordinator for a permit to register for individual honors courses. Entering freshmen may apply after achieving two of these three criteria: (1) a high school GPA of 3.5 (on a 4.0 scale); (2) a composite ACT score of 25 or higher; (3) a ranking in the top 20 percent of the high school graduating class. Current College of DuPage students must meet these two criteria: (1) completion of 12 or more college-level credits; (2) GPA of 3.2.

The Honors Scholar Program: Students who meet the eligibility criteria may apply for admission to the Honors Scholar Program at any time, though first year entrance is preferred. Admissions requirements for freshmen are the same as those listed above for individual courses. Current College of DuPage students must have a 3.5 GPA in addition to having completed 12 credits.

Students who complete the Honors Scholar Program will receive special recognition at commencement and the Celebration of Academic Excellence and on their transcripts and diplomas.

Additional program benefits include the opportunity to select an honors mentor among faculty teaching in the Honors Program, assistance with transfer and scholarship applications, and participation in special, honors-related activities.

Scholarship Availability: Those who are admitted to the program are entitled to a waiver of in-district tuition on all honors courses as long as they maintain a minimum 3.5 GPA and make satisfactory progress toward completing other program requirements (a minimum 22 hours of honors courses from at least three different disciplines, including an honors seminar).

The Campus Context: The College of Dupage is a community college based in the Chicago suburbs. Its enrollment is approximately 33,000. Degrees offered include Associate in Arts, Associate in Science, Associate in Applied Science, and Associate in General Studies. It has an athletic program, study-abroad opportunities, facilities for disabled students, and campus work opportunities. The library contains 142,338 books and 192,021 microfiche.

Tuition: $1392 for area residents, $4368 for state residents, $5616 for nonresidents, per year (1996-97)

Contact: Honors Coordinator: Alice Snelgrove, 22nd Street and Lambert Road, Glen Ellyn, Illinois 60137-6599; Telephone: 708-942-3738; Fax: 708-858-9845; E-mail: snelgrov@cdnet.cod. edu.; Web site: http://www.cod.edu/academic/acadprog/ hon_prog/honors.htm

COLLEGE OF MOUNT SAINT VINCENT

`4 Pr G M Sc Tr`

▼ Honors Program

The College of Mount Saint Vincent Honors Program offers the exceptional, highly motivated student special opportunities for academic enrichment, recognition, and extracurricular activities. The program is part of the College's four-year, eleven-course, multidisciplinary core curriculum, which provides a core of shared learning and a common intellectual experience for all students. During their freshman and sophomore years, honors students are assigned to honors sections of the core courses taught by senior faculty members who have demonstrated particular excellence in and are committed to collaborative teaching. In their junior and senior core courses, honors students are invited to undertake independent honors projects under the guidance of a faculty mentor. These honors projects are outstanding preparation for graduate education and professional leadership roles because they teach students to take extensive responsibility for their own education and to work as collegial partners with other students and with faculty members.

The basic philosophy of the Honors Program at CMSV is that students who have excelled in the College's traditional

3R's of learning deserve another 3R's—recognition, rewards, and recreation—in honor of their accomplishments. The College recognizes honors work with extensive publicity on campus, an honors notation on the academic transcript, awards at graduation, and an annual Showcase Evening, when honors projects are presented to friends and family. The College financially rewards honors students with the preponderance of the College's merit scholarships as well as considerable faculty and administration support for student efforts to obtain outside assistance.

The Honors Program also brings honors students together for social events on campus and for excursions to Manhattan's world famous museums, theaters, and concert and lecture halls. Honors students may enjoy these nearby cultural opportunities for free or at discounted prices because of program funding. Honors at the Mount is meant to be a chance to reach for the very highest goals of a liberal arts education while having an enjoyable time doing it.

There are currently 140 students in the program representing 15 percent of the entering first-year students plus the College Honor Roll.

Admission Process: Incoming freshmen and transfer students with outstanding academic backgrounds and all students on the Academic Honor List for the full year are invited to participate in the Honors Program. The Academic Honor List is comprised of students registered for at least 12 credits a semester who have earned an index of 3.5 in the previous semester.

The Campus Context: The College of Mount Saint Vincent is located on 70 beautiful, wooded acres, directly facing the Hudson River in the Riverdale section of New York City.

Tuition: $13,000 per year (1996-97)

Room and Board: $6240

Contact: Coordinator: Dr. Mary Tait Goldschmid, 6301 Riverdale Avenue, Riverdale, New York 10471-1093; Telephone: 718-405-3372; Fax: 718-405-3374

THE COLLEGE OF NEW JERSEY

4 Pu G M Sc Tr

▼ Honors Program

The College of New Jersey Honors Program, in existence since 1978, provides a high level of challenge and stimulation to talented students seeking a broad educational experience. The program serves students in all majors of the College. Classes, which have a maximum of 22 students, substitute in the general education requirements, and many apply to majors in arts and sciences. The program features interdisciplinary studies, and many courses are team taught. Departmental Honors, available in most majors, double-counts for College Honors. A senior thesis is required in Departmental Honors; a thesis is an option in College Honors. Honors Housing in Brewster Honors House serves 51 students. Through membership in the Honors Advisory Council, students share responsibility for the quality of the academic program and other activities.

The program serves about 360 active members. About 100 first-year students are admitted each year, which is less than 10 percent of the freshman class. Ninety percent of participants are admitted as entering freshmen; another 10 percent, including transfers, enter later. About 50 percent of students who begin the Honors Program complete it satisfactorily upon graduation. Honors Program graduates receive a special medal on graduation day, and the achievement is also indicated on graduates' transcripts and on special diplomas.

Participation Requirements: Graduation with honors requires a minimum of 21 credits in honors courses, including core courses in philosophy, Western culture, and the non-Western world. Third-semester (9 credits) proficiency in a foreign language is also required either by course credit or proficiency exam.

Admission Process: Entrance requirements for high school seniors are either a combined SAT I score of 1270 or placement in the top 5 percent of their class. Transfers and matriculated students must present a 3.4 cumulative GPA or better. All applicants must submit an essay describing personal achievements plus two letters of recommendation.

Applications are received on a rolling basis from January to April.

Scholarship Availability: Most honors students receive merit scholarship support through New Jersey's Bloustein and Garden State Scholarship programs. These scholarships are generously augmented by The College of New Jersey; however, there are no scholarships specifically dedicated to honors students.

The Campus Context: The College of New Jersey consists of five schools: Arts and Sciences, Business, Education, Engineering, and Nursing. Forty degree programs are offered on campus.

Student Body Undergraduate enrollment is 40 percent men and 60 percent women. The ethnic distribution of the student body is 7 percent African American, 5 percent Hispanic, 5 percent Asian, less than 1 percent Native American, and 77 percent Caucasian. There are 32 international students. Fifty-nine percent of the students are residents and 41 percent are commuters. Fifty-one percent of undergraduate students receive financial aid. There are fourteen fraternities and sixteen sororities on campus.

Faculty There are 316 full-time faculty members, 89 percent with doctorate or terminal degrees. The student-faculty ratio is 14.4:1.

Key Facilities Noteworthy facilities include a newly renovated and expanded Kendall Hall Theater with experimental studio theater, radio station, and television studio; a new music building with a 300-seat concert hall; newly renovated and expanded facilities for the School of Engineering; townhouse-style residences with single rooms for 510 students; and a lighted astroturf stadium and aquatic center with a 25-meter pool. The library houses 500,000 volumes. Computer facilities include a fiber-optic campus-wide network providing full access to the Internet, sixteen student labs, and all student residences.

Athletics In the past seventeen years, The College of New Jersey athletes have amassed twenty-eight national championships in NCAA Division III competitions. Men's varsity sports are baseball, basketball, cross-country, football, golf, soccer, swimming, tennis, indoor and outdoor track, and wrestling. Women's sports are basketball, cross-country, field hockey, lacrosse, soccer, softball, swimming, tennis, and indoor and outdoor track. The office of intramurals and recreation services provides the College community with twenty-three intramural sports and a self-governing sports club program.

Study Abroad International exchange opportunities are available through agreements between The College of New Jersey and schools in Australia, Canada, Denmark, England, France, Germany, Greece, Ireland, Israel, Japan, Mexico, and Wales. Exchanges in many other countries can be arranged through the College's membership in the International Student Exchange Program (ISEP) and the College Consortium for International Studies (CCIS).

Support Services Ninety-six percent of the campus buildings and 85 percent of the residence halls are accessible by wheelchair. The Office of Differing Abilities supports students with a variety of disabilities.

Job Opportunities Work opportunities on campus include nearly 200 Federal Work-Study jobs and more than 1,000 part-time jobs (other than FWS).

Tuition: $3465 for state residents, $6051 for nonresidents, per year (1996-97)

Room and Board: $5544 minimum

Mandatory Fees: $981

Contact: Coordinator: Dr. William DeMeritt, Allen Hall 110, Trenton, New Jersey 08650-4700; Telephone: 609-771-2337/2034; Fax: 609-771-3345

COLLEGE OF NEW ROCHELLE

4 Pr G S Sc Tr

▼ School of Arts and Sciences Honors Program

The CNR Honors Program, founded in 1974, is designed to foster intellectual independence and initiative, leader-

ship abilities, and appreciation of the value of collaboration and community involvement. To that end, it offers a variety of challenging interdisciplinary seminars, an annual Honors Colloquium, independent study through contract, and opportunities for leadership and community activity.

Freshmen are enrolled into honors sections of the freshman requirements Cultural Legacies and Critical Research Essay, while seniors conclude their course of study with Senior Symposium. Honors students are closely advised in the selection of appropriate honors learning options, seminars, colloquia, and contract learning, all of which are open to students above the freshman level. Honors faculty members are selected on the basis of their creative student-centered teaching.

Seminars are expressly designed for non-majors as core alternatives or electives. They are interdisciplinary, issue-based, and involve primary-source readings, discussion and presentation, experiential learning environments, and extensive writing. Class size is limited to 15 students.

Honors Colloquia are one-year, 6-credit experiences offered annually to all students above the freshman level and consist of a fall seminar and a spring independent study. Cycled according to student choice, the topics are: New York City: Anatomy of a Metropolis, Democracy in America, Twentieth Century Global Issues, and Science, Technology, and Values.

Students above the freshman level are free to develop independent study contracts with a faculty member mentor as either research projects or internships. On Honors Conference Day they present their honors research before the College community.

There are approximately 60 active full-time student members.

Participation Requirements: Students are required to engage in a minimum of two honors academic studies a year and are strongly encouraged to build honors portfolios by participating in the program, College community, and NCHC governance and committee activity.

The Honors Diploma is awarded to graduating seniors who have a minimum 3.5 GPA; eight honors options, including one Colloquium and Senior Symposium; and a record of leadership. The Honors Certificate is awarded to graduating seniors who have achieved a 3.5 GPA in the Honors Program, completed five honors options, and participated in honors activities.

Admission Process: Academic scholarship recipients who exhibit both promise for academic achievement and leadership potential are invited into the program directly from high school. Enrolled and transfer students below the junior level who have a 3.3 GPA or higher are also invited into the program. Juniors and seniors are required to maintain a minimum 3.5 GPA.

Scholarship Availability: Presidential Scholarships (full tuition), Honors Scholarships ($7500), and Academic Scholarships

($5000) are awarded to academically qualified applicants during the admission process. Students selected for scholarships generally rank in the top 20 percent of their high school graduating class, have SAT I scores above 1000, and have a GPA higher than 90 percent. Applicants must file the Free Application for Federal Student Aid (FAFSA). There is no application deadline for entering freshman and transfer students; all financial aid is renewed annually.

The Campus Context: The College of New Rochelle is located on a beautiful 20-acre campus, 1 mile west of the Long Island Sound and 16 miles north of mid-Manhattan. Additionally, it has six satellite campuses for adult learners in the metropolitan area. One of the oldest colleges in Westchester County, it was founded in 1904 by the Ursuline order as the first Catholic liberal arts college for women in New York State. Today it is an independent institution with a Catholic tradition, consisting of four regionally accredited Schools: Arts and Sciences (for women only), Nursing, New Resources (for adult learners), and Graduate. The College offers twenty-five programs leading to several baccalaureate degrees.

Student Body Approximately 450 undergraduates are enrolled in the School of Arts and Sciences, 80 percent of whom receive financial aid. A majority of students are from the Northeast. Of these, 2 percent hold student visas. The ethnic distribution of the student body is 45 percent Caucasian, 22 percent Hispanic, 28 percent African American, 4 percent Asian, and 1 percent American Indian. The New Rochelle Campus has four residence halls, which house 60 percent of enrolled students.

Faculty There are 81 faculty members; 43 are full-time, 88 percent of whom hold doctorates or terminal degrees. The student-faculty ratio is 11:1.

Key Facilities The College library contains 200,000 volumes. Students have access to IBM and Macintosh computers in the Computer Center, Learning Support Services, and the Honors Center.

Athletics The College has a sports building and tennis courts. It participates in NCAA Division III, offering intercollegiate basketball, volleyball, tennis, softball, and swimming teams for women.

Study Abroad College credit for study abroad is available through the International Studies Program. The Science Division sponsors a math-science course in England. The Modern and Classical Languages Department has offered Bridging Cultures travel-study courses in Italy, Mexico, Puerto Rico, Egypt, and Greece.

Support Services The Learning Support Services provides tutoring for students needing academic assistance in any area of the curriculum. Disabled students find approximately 80 percent of the campus accessible by wheelchair ramps, electronic doors, elevators, special parking, equipped restrooms, and lowered drinking fountains.

Job Opportunities Opportunities for local and New York City internships, co-op work placements, work-study jobs, and career explorations are provided by individual departments and the Center for Counseling, Career Development and Placement.

Tuition: $11,000 minimum per year (1996-97)

Room and Board: $5700

Fees: $100

Contact: Director: Dr. Ann R. Raia, 29 Castle Place, New Rochelle, New York 10805; Telephone: 914-654-5398; Fax: 914-654-5554

COLLEGE OF NOTRE DAME OF MARYLAND

4 Pr C S Sc Tr

▼ The Elizabeth Morrissy Honors Program

Founded in 1981, the Elizabeth Morrissy Honors program, named to honor the memory of an outstanding Notre Dame professor, meets the needs and interests of students with high ability and motivation. Several honors seminars are offered each semester. There are currently 75 students in the program. Students compete for the annual Outstanding Honors Student Award of the Maryland Collegiate Honors Council.

Participation Requirements: Students in the Morrissy Honors program may major in any area that the College offers and take the same number of credits for graduation as every other student. A student must take at least one Morrissy seminar a year and complete a minimum of 18 credits of honors course work to receive an honors diploma.

Scholarship Availability: Morrissy students hold several kinds of scholarships offered by the College as well as outside scholarships.

The Campus Context: The College of Notre Dame of Maryland, founded in 1873 by the School Sisters of Notre Dame, is situated on 58 wooded acres in a residential neighborhood 10 minutes from downtown Baltimore. The College opened as a collegiate institute and in 1895 began offering a four-year college program of study. In 1896 the State of Maryland authorized Notre Dame to grant degrees. The College offers the Bachelor of Arts degree through its day program. The Continuing Education Program is designed for women over 25, and the Weekend College Program is designed for employed women and men. In addition, a coeducational Graduate Studies program offers the M.A. in several fields. There are twenty-two degree programs.

Student Body The undergraduate enrollment is 100 percent women; 6–7 percent are international students. Sixty-five percent of the women are residents. Eighty-six percent of the students receive financial aid. While there are no social sororities, there are many Honors Sororities: Beta Beta Beta, Delta Mu Delta, Eta Sigma Phi, Kappa Mu Epsilon, Phi Alpha Theta, Phi Lambda Upsilon, Psi Chi, Sigma Tau Delta, and Women in Communications, Inc.

Faculty There are 85 faculty members; 74 are full-time, 11 are part-time, and 65 percent have terminal degrees. The student-faculty ratio is 15:1.

Key Facilities The library contains 290,000 bound volumes, 24,000 audiovisual items (many of which are videos and CDs) and 2,000 periodicals. The campus has a Writing Center and an English Language Institute. Computer facilities include a 45-station network that runs DOS, OS/2, and Windows; a 20-station Macintosh network; laser printers; scanners; and CD-ROM. Access to the Loyola/Notre Dame Library CARL system and the Internet is available.

Athletics The Marion Burk Knott Sports and Activities Complex features an NCAA-regulation gymnasium for basketball and volleyball, glass-backed racquetball courts, dance and exercise rooms, and a fully equipped training room. There is also a game room with a pool table, foosball, air hockey, Ping-Pong, and shuffleboard. A walking track overlooks the gym, racquetball courts, and game room. Students also have access to four tennis courts. Two natural grass athletic fields are used for intercollegiate soccer, lacrosse, and field hockey as well as other intercollegiate and intramural athletic activities. Joggers and bikers enjoy the network of paths that crisscross the campus.

Study Abroad The College is committed to providing as much international experience as possible for each student. Through the Office of International Programs, study is offered at international academic institutions during regular semesters or the summer months. In addition, Notre Dame faculty members regularly lead study tours during Winterim and summer terms.

Support Services Dorms and various classrooms are accessible to disabled students.

Job Opportunities Students may work on campus up to 10 hours per week with College approval.

Tuition: $13,125 per year, full-time; $235 per credit, part-time for nursing program (1997-98)

Room and Board: $6130

Mandatory Fees: $240

Contact: Director: Alison Dray-Novey, 4701 N. Charles Street, Baltimore, Maryland 21210-2476; Telephone: 410-532-5372; Fax: 410-532-6287; E-mail: adraynov@ndm.edu

COLLEGE OF ST. CATHERINE

4 Pr G S Sc Tr

▼ Antonian Scholars Honors Program

The objectives of the Antonian Scholars Honors Program are to attract and provide a challenge for women of superior ability; to provide an opportunity for these women to interact with each other and build intellectually supportive relationships with peers and faculty members; to deepen their love of learning, understanding of great

issues, and independent scholarship; and to clarify and emphasize the College's commitment to the liberal arts and academic excellence.

A student will have completed the Honors Program provided she maintains a 3.5 GPA overall and in her major and completes the six components of the program, including a Senior Honors Project. Each student must complete a minimum of two Honors Seminars, which may be team taught, are interdisciplinary, and focus on the liberal arts; a minimum of two Honors Contracts, work that is broader in scope and/or showing greater depth than that required in a course; and a third Honors Seminar, Honors Contract, or foreign study during the regular academic year (not including January term or summer). As a senior, the student undertakes a major piece of research or creative work under the guidance of a faculty member, which is publicly presented.

The privileges of membership include the opportunity to travel to regional and national conferences and the opportunity to register on the first day of registration. Successful completion of the Honors Program is noted at graduation and is recorded on the student's transcript. A special diploma is awarded.

The Honors Program began in 1986 and currently has 67 members.

Participation Requirements: To maintain eligibility, a student must be registered in the Honors Program each year, unless she is away from campus (e.g., abroad). A student must complete at least one Honors Seminar or Honors Contract within the first two semesters after being admitted to the program. She may complete at most three components in her senior year, one of which is the Senior Project. A student must earn a grade of B or higher in the honors courses.

Admission Process: Any student who has completed at least three courses at the College but no more than fifteen courses while enrolled at the College may apply. Admission is determined by student interest as reflected in the application, a faculty member recommendation, and a 3.5 GPA.

Applications are due in December and February.

Scholarship Availability: The College of St. Catherine offers St. Catherine of Alexandria Scholarships to students of exceptional ability. Many students receiving these scholarships are also in the Honors Program.

The Campus Context: The College of St. Catherine is a Catholic college with campuses in St. Paul and Minneapolis. It was founded in 1905 as a women's college by the Sisters of St. Joseph of Carondelet. The St. Paul campus provides undergraduate baccalaureate programs for women in the liberal arts disciplines and several professions. The Honors Program is designed for students on the St. Paul campus. There are thirty-eight undergraduate majors and eight master's programs offered on campus. Thirty additional undergraduate majors are available to College of St. Catherine students through affiliation with the Associated Colleges of the Twin Cities consortium.

Student Body Undergraduate enrollment is 2,257 students, 100 percent women. The ethnic distribution of the student body is 1 percent American Indian, 5.5 percent Asian, 2 percent African American, and 2 percent Hispanic. There are 62 international students. Of the total student population, 65 percent are commuters and 35 percent are resident. Seventy-four percent of all students receive financial aid.

Faculty There are 119 full-time faculty members; 37 are ranked part-time, 93 are adjunct, and 76 percent have terminal degrees. The student-faculty ratio is 14:1.

Key Facilities Among distinguished facilities on campus, Our Lady of Victory Chapel is the embodiment of the College's Catholic nature and its close relationship to the Sisters of St. Joseph of Carondelet. Built in the 1920s, it was placed on the National Register of Historic Places in 1986. The O'Shaughnessy Auditorium is a major Twin Cities professional arts and entertainment stage. The Catherine G. Murphy Gallery focuses on women artists and their work.

The library has a total of 231,453 volumes. There are twenty-five microcomputers in residence halls, forty in department labs, and sixty-nine in public labs. The Honors Lounge provides computer access to students in the program.

Athletics The College of St. Catherine participates in NCAA Division III intercollegiate athletics. The College offers seven varsity sports: basketball, cross-country, softball, swimming/diving, tennis, volleyball, and track and field. In fall 1997 St. Catherine and the University of St. Thomas will co-sponsor a women's ice hockey club program. Also available are intramural and recreational sports opportunities. The Aimee and Patrick Butler Center for Sports and Fitness, which opened in May 1995, is a 56,000-square-foot facility containing training equipment and workout spaces designed with the needs of women athletes in mind. The center includes an eight-lane, 25-yard indoor swimming pool; a sauna and spa; a suspended indoor jogging track; a weight room and cardiovascular workout area; and a gymnasium with courts for volleyball, basketball, and tennis.

Study Abroad The College of St. Catherine actively encourages students to consider incorporating study abroad into their academic curriculum. More than fifty semester and year-long programs, as well as twenty-five January Term programs, are available for 1997. The Honors Program supports this opportunity to study abroad as an option for fulfilling one of the components of the program.

Job Opportunities The Student Employment Program assists students in securing part-time positions on campus to meet a portion of their education expenses. Students with a demonstrated need are offered positions that include computer consultant, library aide, clerical worker, tutor, dining service worker, and receptionist.

Tuition: $13,472 per year (1996-97)

Room and Board: $4582

Mandatory Fees: $230

Contact: Director: Dr. Suzanne M. Molnar, 2004 Randolph Avenue, St. Paul, Minnesota 55105; Telephone: 612-690-6633; Fax: 612-690-6024; Web site: http://www.stkate.edu

COLLEGE OF ST. SCHOLASTICA
4 Pr G S Tr
▼ Honors Program

Begun in 1995, the Honors Program at the College of St. Scholastica was created to provide an environment for honors students to have enriched learning experiences and provide a community of support for learners devoted to vigorous experiences and a vigorous life of the mind. Students who become involved in the Honors Program should strive to love ideas and the discussion of them, not fearing intellectual debate; to be able to listen to the ideas of others with respect, no matter how much those ideas might conflict with personal sentiments; to be willing to risk the analysis of an idea for its improvement and for the individual's greater understanding; and to desire a life of learning.

Approximately 40 students participate in the program each year.

Participation Requirements: The Honors Program consists of lower and upper division honors. Lower division honors consists of four courses taken during the freshman and sophomore years, which are honors sections of the distribution requirements. Upper division honors can be completed in a major or in an interdisciplinary area. Three courses—an upper division honors course or independent study, an honors thesis or project, and an honors senior seminar—are required to complete upper division honors. Students may complete either lower division honors or upper division honors or both.

Admission Process: To be accepted into the program, students must first meet two of the following three guidelines: be in the top 15 percent of their high school class, have a minimum ACT score of 26 or minimum SAT I score of 1100 (PSAT score of approximately 105 is sufficient to apply), and/or a GPA of 3.5 on a 4.0 scale. All applicants must interview with the Honors Director prior to admission to the program. Students who do not meet the criteria stated above may be admitted to the program following a successful interview with the Director. Students must earn a minimum grade of B in all honors courses and have an overall GPA of 3.5 to graduate with honors.

Scholarship Availability: Exceptional students may apply for a Benedictine scholarship through the Admissions Office.

The Campus Context: The campus sits atop a hill overlooking Lake Superior and the cities of Duluth, Minnesota, and Superior, Wisconsin. The facilities include the new Mitchell

Auditorium, a 500-seat music hall, a newly expanded Science Hall, Our Lady Queen of Peace chapel, and a black box Little Theatre as well as the Reif Recreation Center, Somers Residence Hall, the College Library, and a series of apartment complexes for on-campus students. Tower Hall is the center of campus activity. St. Scholastica offers approximately thirty degree programs, six preprofessional programs, and a variety of education and health-care licensure programs as well as a number of free-standing minors.

Student Body The current enrollment is 1,895 students. More than 90 percent of full-time students receive financial aid. The average award is $11,000.

Faculty More than 125 faculty members hold degrees from all over the country. The student-faculty ratio is 12:1, with an average class size of 16. There are no social fraternities or sororities on campus.

Key Facilities The library houses about 120,000 volumes, 9,500 microform titles, and 800 periodicals as well as tapes, records, CDs, and on-line services. On-campus computers include both IBMs and Macs. There are over eighty terminals with access to the Internet.

Athletics Twelve intercollegiate sports teams exist at CSS. Both men and women can participate in cross-country, soccer, basketball, baseball/softball, and tennis. In addition, we offer a women's volleyball team and a men's hockey team. Intramural activities also exist.

Study Abroad There are three study abroad programs. Students can spend the winter quarter in Costa Rica studying at the University of Costa Rica. Spring quarter brings the possibility of studying in Ireland. Every spring, professors from the College of St. Scholastica travel with students to live and study in the cottages at Louisburgh. Through the College's sister college in Petrozavodsk, Kerilia, students can also study the Russian language. This exchange program is one of the most active on campus.

Support Services All buildings are handicapped-accessible. Services are available for special-needs students.

Job Opportunities Several work opportunities exist for students on campus. The College has a very large work-study program for students who meet the financial aid requirements.

Tuition: $13,056 per year (1996-97)

Room and Board: $3807 minimum

Fees: $75

Contact: Director: Dr. Tammy Ostrander, 1200 Kenwood Avenue, Duluth, Minnesota 55811; Telephone: 218-723-6046 (Admissions), 800-447-5444 (toll-free); Fax: 218-723-6290; E-mail: tostrand@facl.css.edu; Web site: http://www.css.edu/admiss/honors.html

COLORADO SCHOOL OF MINES

4 Pu D M Sc Tr

▼ Guy T. McBride Jr. Honors Program

The McBride Honors Program, instituted in 1978 through a grant from the National Endowment for the Humanities, is a 27-semester-hour program of seminars and off-campus activities that has a primary goal: to provide a select number of engineering students the opportunity to cross the boundaries of their technical expertise and gain the sensitivity to prove, project, and test the moral and social implications of their future professional judgments and activities, not only for the organizations with which they will be involved, but also for the nation and the world. To achieve this goal, the program seeks to bring themes from the humanities and the social sciences into the engineering curriculum that will encourage in students the habits of thought necessary for effective management and enlightened leadership.

The curriculum of the McBride Honors Program is unique in the sense that it was designed by teams of faculty members from the humanities, social sciences, sciences, and engineering. It features two educational experiences—the summer practicum and international study. The summer practicum is a central experience in the program that comes during the summer following the junior year. Leadership and management demand an understanding of the accelerating pace of change that marks the social, political, and economic currents of society. While all the seminars in the program are designed to nourish such an understanding, the goal of the practicum is to put students into situations where they can observe firsthand management and decision-making processes of the kind that will challenge them in their professional lives. The international study option is an option in which honors students may choose international study during the summer of the junior year, either through CSM-sponsored trips (if interest warrants) or through individual plans arranged in consultation with the Director. The cost of any international study is the responsibility of the student. The educational experiences in the McBride Honors Program are rigorous and demand a high degree of persistence from the students.

There are two prestigious awards granted by the program. The Leo Borasio Memorial Award, named after a 1950 graduate of the School of Mines, is a plaque and cash award presented each year to the outstanding junior in the McBride Honors Program. The Thomas Philipose Outstanding Senior Award is a plaque and cash award presented to a senior in the McBride Honors Program whose scholarship, character, and personality best exemplify the ideals of the program as determined by a committee of tutors.

CSM graduates who have completed the program have gained positions of their choice in industry more easily than others and have been quite successful in winning admission to high-quality graduate and professional schools.

The 18-year-old program currently enrolls 170 students.

Participation Requirements: Because of the nature of the program, students are expected to do the readings and to prepare interpretations for class discussions. Participation in class projects and discussions is essential and students who do not maintain an appropriate level of such participation may be asked to leave the program.

Academic integrity and honesty are expected of the students in the program. Any infractions in these areas will be handled under the rules of CSM and may result in dismissal from the program.

The program demands a high level of achievement not only in honors courses, but in all academic work. To that end, a student must meet the following requirements: a minimum GPA of 2.7 in all course work at CSM at any given time; a minimum GPA of 2.6 in honors course work by the end of the sophomore year; a minimum GPA of 3.0 in honors course work by the end of the junior year; and a minimum GPA of 3.0 in honors course work at graduation to receive a minor in public affairs. A student who falls below any of the first three minimums will be placed on probation for one semester. If the required minimum GPA has not been met by the end of that semester, the student will be dropped from the program.

Admission Process: The McBride Honors Program seeks to enroll students who can profit most from and contribute most to the learning experiences upon which the program is based—to bring bright young minds into situations where they will be challenged not only by faculty members but also by their colleagues. Whereas many more conventional honors programs admit students almost exclusively on the basis of academic record, in the McBride Honors Program test scores, GPA, and class rank form only part of the criteria used in the admission process. Students must demonstrate their leadership potential, versatility of mind, and writing and speaking abilities through an essay and an interview with 2 faculty members.

Scholarship Availability: Five members of the entering spring class will be awarded $1000 beginning with the students' sophomore year, renewable for two additional years if the recipients meet the criteria listed below. Awards will be based on demonstrated academic excellence and potential contribution to the Honors Program.

Any McBride scholarship recipient who meets the following criteria will be eligible to continue the award for a total of three years: full-time undergraduate at Colorado School of Mines, must complete at least 15 credit-hours each semester for the duration of the scholarship, must remain in the McBride Program for the duration of the scholarship, and must maintain a 2.7 cumulative GPA and a 3.0 GPA in the McBride Program. Students who fall below the standards

will be given one probationary semester in which to return to satisfactory standing or they lose their eligibility; however, they may appeal this decision to the Principal Tutor. If a student leaves Colorado School of Mines and/or the McBride Program, his/her award will be forfeited.

The Campus Context: Colorado School of Mines is a public research university devoted to engineering and applied science related to resources. It has the highest admissions standards of any university in Colorado and among the highest of any public university in the U.S. CSM has dedicated itself to responsible stewardship of the Earth and its resources. It is one of a few institutions in the world having broad expertise in resource exploration, extraction, production, and utilization, which can be brought to bear on the world's pressing resource-related environmental problems. As such, it occupies a unique position among the world's institutions of higher education.

The School offers fourteen degree programs: chemical engineering and petroleum refining, chemistry, geochemistry, economics and business, engineering (civil, electrical, and mechanical options), environmental science and engineering, geology and geological engineering, geophysics, mathematical and computer sciences, mining, metallurgical and materials engineering, material science, petroleum, and physics.

Student Body Of the 2,083 undergraduates, approximately 25 percent are women. The minority ethnic distribution of the student body is 1.4 percent African American, 6.7 percent Hispanic, 1 percent Native American, and 5.1 percent Asian/Pacific Islander. There are 405 international students. Approximately 80 percent of undergraduate students receive some kind of financial aid. There are six national fraternities and two national sororities active on the campus.

Faculty Of the 266 faculty members, 168 are full-time. Ninety-six percent of the full-time faculty members have terminal degrees. The student-faculty ratio is 7.8:1.

Key Facilities The library houses 145,000 volumes. The Computing Center provides computing and networking services to support the academic mission of CSM. It houses central computing equipment and support services to meet the instructional, research, and administrative needs of the CSM community. A staff of professional and student consultants provide guidance and advice to students, faculty members, and staff. Many popular applications are supported, including word processing, spreadsheets, statistics and data analysis, graphics, and others.

Computer accounts and services are available to all registered students and current faculty members and staff. Students and faculty members are provided with access to central computing resources and services for academic use. Centrally managed equipment for academic computing includes a VAX 4500 (VMS operating system) and an IBM RS/6000 Model 930 (AIX/UNIX operating system). These systems are available 24 hours a day, seven days per week. With the exception of the PC and Macintosh servers, most networked resources can be reached via dial-in modem connections.

Computing Center workrooms contain terminals, printers, plotters, and digitizers for general use. Networked PCs,

Macintoshes, and NeXT workstations are also available. Several additional laboratories are open for general use when not reserved for classes. Another general-use computing center cluster is located in the Arthur Lakes Library. Some departments may provide specialized applications or computing laboratories and may allow general access to them.

Athletics Seventeen varsity intercollegiate sports are offered at CSM, the highest number available at any state-supported institution in Colorado. Nearly 20 percent of the student body participates in varsity sports. More than 50 percent are involved in intramurals. Men's sports include football, golf, soccer, cross-country, basketball, swimming and diving, wrestling, lacrosse, tennis, track, and baseball. Women's sports include volleyball, cross-country, basketball, swimming and diving, softball, and track. CSM is a founding member of the Rocky Mountain Athletic Conference (RMAC) and a member of NCAA Division II.

Study Abroad The Office of International Programs fosters and facilitates international education, research, and outreach at Colorado School of Mines. The office works with the departments of the School to help develop and facilitate study abroad opportunities for CSM undergraduates and serves as an informational and advising resource for them.

Support Services Disabled students will find the CSM campus totally handicapped-accessible.

Job Opportunities Work opportunities on campus include work-study and assistantships.

Tuition: $4494 for state residents, $13,980 for nonresidents, per year (1997-98 est.)

Room and Board: $4730

Mandatory Fees: $575

Contact: Director: Dr. Barbara M. Olds, Golden, Colorado 80401-1887; Telephone: 303-273-3990; Fax: 303-384-2129; E-mail: bolds@mines.edu; Web site: http://www.mines.edu/Academic/mcb-honors/

COLORADO STATE UNIVERSITY

4 Pu G L Sc Tr

▼ University Honors Program

The University Honors Program at Colorado State University emphasizes personal advising, an honors academic core of courses, honors residence, and significant cocurricular honors experiences such as undergraduate research, social activities, graduate fellowship preparation, and leadership training. The honors courses are special sections of catalog courses where students have more personal connections with professors and learning. Honors students can major in any area at Colorado State. Honors courses meet University and major requirements, so no extra work is required. Precollege AP, IB, or college work while in high school can be used to satisfy honors requirements.

An important feature of the program is the honors peer adviser program, where upperclassmen learn leadership skills and at the same time work closely with the first-year students. These students are also advised to seek graduate posts and apply for prestigious postgraduate fellowships and scholarships.

Initiated in 1975, the program currently enrolls 950 students.

Participation Requirements: Students who complete the honors core courses and achieve a 3.5 GPA are recognized as University Honors Scholars, a diploma and transcript designation. Students who complete 24 credits of honors work at Colorado State and have a 3.5 GPA are noted as University Honors Participants on their transcripts.

Scholarship Availability: A large number of Honors first-year students are awarded the Colorado State Distinguished Scholar's Award ($2000 per year and $2000 for study abroad). These scholarships are awarded on a merit basis and require acceptance to Colorado State before January 1 of the year of matriculation.

The Campus Context: Colorado State University has eight colleges: Applied Human Sciences, Agricultural Sciences, Business, Engineering, Liberal Arts, Natural Resources, Natural Sciences, and Veterinary Medicine and Biomedical Sciences. Eighty-eight degree programs are offered.

Student Body The undergraduate enrollment is 18,541, almost evenly divided between men and women. About 14 percent of the students come from ethnic minorities. There are 193 international students. Ninety-eight percent of the students are residents.

Faculty Of the 1,423 faculty members, 1,004 are full-time and 88.6 percent hold the Ph.D. or other terminal professional degree. The student-faculty ratio is 13:1.

Key Facilities The library houses approximately 1 million volumes. The campus has extensive computer facilities.

Study Abroad The Study Abroad Office advises students on exchanges and study opportunities. In some cases, scholarships provide support for study abroad.

Tuition: $2224 for state residents, $9160 for nonresidents, per year (1996-97)

Room and Board: $4152 minimum

Mandatory Fees: $631

Contact: Director: Michael B. Histand, Newsom Hall E 204, Fort Collins, Colorado 80523; Telephone: 970-491-5679; Fax: 970-491-1055; E-mail: histand@engr.colostate.edu; Web site: http://www.honors.colostate.edu

COLUMBIA COLLEGE (SOUTH CAROLINA)

4 Pr G M Sc Tr

▼ Honors Program

For more than ten years, the Columbia College Honors Program has provided an enriched academic experience for the outstanding student committed to excellence. The fundamental assumption of honors education is that honors students should continually challenge their intellectual limits, working creatively and seriously to reach their highest potential as a scholar, individual thinker, and leader. The program emphasizes independent learning and a spirited exchange of ideas in a stimulating classroom environment that encourages a student to develop their own ideas in a knowledgeable and reasoned framework.

Seniors are honored with a dinner prior to graduation at which time they are awarded their honors medallions to be worn at graduation. Seniors who complete the honors requirements graduate with cum honore, and their diplomas reflect this achievement.

Approximately 150 students are currently enrolled in the program.

Participation Requirements: Each student must complete 24 hours in honors courses, including the senior seminar and project. A student may enroll in up to 3 hours of honors independent study courses and one honors choice up to 4 hours. Students must maintain at least a B in honors courses in each semester report and in the cumulative average. Failure to maintain a B average results in one semester of academic probation. After two semesters on probation, a student is excluded from the Honors Program.

Admission Process: Students are invited into honors in the freshman year based on their high school GPA, level of courses taken (AP and honors), SAT score, class rank, leadership experience and extracurricular involvement, and application essay. Recently, GPAs have averaged above 3.5 and SAT I scores have averaged above 1200, but any motivated, capable student is encouraged to apply. Students may petition for admission past the freshman year with recommendations from College faculty members.

Scholarship Availability: The outstanding rising senior honors student is awarded the prestigious Tull Scholarship. The 3 or 4 outstanding honors students from each class also receive honors scholarships. These scholarships are based on GPA, involvement in the Honors Program, and leadership in the College and community.

The Campus Context: Since its founding in 1854, Columbia College has emphasized the value of a liberal arts education rooted in a strong commitment to the education of women. Columbia College is a beautiful, 33-acre campus located just minutes from downtown Columbia, South Carolina. Columbia College is affiliated with the United Methodist Church and has been recognized for two consecutive years by *U.S. News & World Report* as being among the top five liberal arts colleges in the South. Only a couple of hours' driving distance from Charleston, Greenville, Myrtle Beach, Charlotte, and Asheville, Columbia College is located in the center of the state. The B.A., B.F.A., B.M., and M.Ed. in elementary education degrees are offered in more than thirty areas.

Student Body The total undergraduate enrollment is 1,229 students. The ethnic distribution of the student body is 29 percent African American, 1 percent Hispanic, less than 1 percent Asian, and less than 1 percent Native American. International students constitute less than 1 percent of the total undergraduate population. Eighty-two percent of students receive financial aid; the average package is $10,060.

Faculty There are 74 full-time faculty members and 6 part-time faculty members. Sixty-two percent hold the Ph.D. or equivalent. The student-faculty ratio is 14:1.

Key Facilities The library houses 163,000 volumes, 650 periodical subscriptions, microfilm, and microfiche. There are a media center and open stacks for easy access. There are four computer labs on campus equipped with e-mail and the Internet. All classrooms and residence hall rooms are wired for computer and Internet access.

The Johnnie Cordell Breed Leadership Center for Women coordinates internal and external leadership programs for women. The Academic Skills Center provides academic assistance in the form of study skills, writing skills, and peer tutoring. The Collaborative Learning Center facilitates collaboration between and among faculty members and students. Our Career Center offers a four-year career planning program, which includes advising, counseling, career planning, and placement.

Athletics Intercollegiate competition exists in tennis and volleyball. Intramural athletics are sponsored by the athletic department and organized by interested students.

Study Abroad Many honors students elect to participate in the study abroad programs in France and Spain.

Support Services All campus buildings are handicapped-accessible.

Job Opportunities The Office of Student Employment coordinates the numerous work opportunities that are available on and off campus.

Tuition: $11,535 per year (1996-97)

Room & Board: $4160

Mandatory Fees: $60

Contact: Director: Dr. John Zubizarreta, E-mail: jzubizarreta@colacoll.edu; Assistant Director: Dr. Vivia Fowler, E-mail: vfowler@colacoll.edu; Columbia, South Carolina 29203; Telephone: 803-786-3014; Fax: 803-786-3054

COPPIN STATE COLLEGE

4 Pu C S Sc Tr

▼ Honors Program

Coppin State College offers an Honors Program for outstanding students who have demonstrated exceptional ability. The primary focus of the Honors Program is to provide academic preparation, character development, and cultural enrichment to the College's high-ability students. Through the offering of honors courses, community-service experiences, and exposure to cultural activities, the program strives to prepare academically outstanding students for progression to graduate and professional schools as well as for employment. In addition, the Honors Program provides students with unique opportunities to hone their analytical and leadership skills.

There are two different categories within the Honors Program to accommodate high-ability students in all majors who desire an honors experience and are at various stages of their college careers. The Four-Year Honors Program is designed for incoming freshmen and the Upper-Division Honors Program is for transfer students.

The first student began in honors in 1981–82. There are 103 students in the program.

Participation Requirements: Students entering the Four-Year Honors Program are required to complete the following courses to earn an honors citation: five honors versions of General Education Requirement courses, HONS 150 (Honors Community-Service Seminar), HONS 380 (Honors Introduction to Research I), and HONS 490 (Honors Thesis). Additionally, students must complete one of the following courses: HONS 381 (Honors Introduction to Research II), HONS 390/391 (Interdisciplinary Honors Seminar), HONS 470 (Honors Field Practicum I), HONS 480 (Honors Research Assistantship), EDUC 460 (Teaching Assistantship Seminar), or MNSC 150 (Computer Literacy). Students who complete the required honors courses and maintain a GPA of at least 3.0 overall and in their honors courses receive honors citations on their academic records. Prior to graduation, these students receive completion certificates from the Four-Year Honors Program.

Students participating in the Upper-Division Honors Program complete HONS 380 (Honors Introduction to Research I) and HONS 490 (Honors Thesis). Additionally, they are required to complete two of the following courses: HONS 381 (Honors Introduction to Research II), HONS 390/391 (Interdisciplinary Honors Seminar), HONS 470 (Honors Field Practicum I), HONS 480 (Honors Research Assistantship), EDUC 460 (Teaching Assistant Seminar), or MNSC 150 (Computer Literacy). Participants in the Upper-Division Honors Program who complete the required honors courses and who maintain a GPA of at least 3.0 overall and in their honors courses receive honors citations on their academic records. Prior to graduation, these students receive completion certificates from the Upper-Division Honors Program.

Admission Process: For the Four-Year Honors Program, a student must have a high school GPA of at least 3.0, a combined Scholastic Assessment Test score of at least 950, and successfully complete the Coppin placement exam. For the Upper-Division Honors Program, a student must have completed at least 45 graduation credits, a transfer GPA of 3.0, successful completion of English Composition I and II or their equivalents, and successfully complete the Coppin English Proficiency Exam.

Scholarship Availability: Participants in the Four-Year Honors Program receive Honors Scholarships (full tuition and fees and a book allowance) for a maximum of eight semesters. Participants in the Upper-Division Honors Program receive Honors Scholarships (full tuition and fees and a book allowance) for a maximum of four semesters. All scholarship recipients are required to maintain a 3.0 GPA overall and in their honors courses and to earn at least 12 graduation credits each semester they receive scholarship support.

The Campus Context: Coppin State College is located on a 38-acre site on West North Avenue in Baltimore, Maryland. There are five divisions on campus: Arts and Sciences, Education, Graduate Studies, Honors, and Nursing. There are fifteen undergraduate degree programs.

Student Body The spring 1996 undergraduate enrollment total was 2,806, 26 percent of whom were men. The ethnic distribution of the student body was 95 percent African American, less than 1 percent Asian, less than 1 percent Hispanic, and less than 1 percent Native American. Two percent of the population was international. There were 287 resident students and 2,519 commuters. Eighty percent of students receive aid. There are four fraternities and five sororities.

Faculty There are a total of 106 full-time faculty members and 85 adjunct faculty members, with 64 percent of all faculty members holding terminal degrees. This gives Coppin State College a 15:1 student-faculty ratio.

Key Facilities The library holds 125,000 volumes and 654 serial subscriptions. The Honors Division at Coppin State College also houses the Ronald E. McNair Post-Baccalaureate Achievement Program, which is designed to prepare low-income, first-generation, and underrepresented undergraduates for the graduate school experience. The program provides all participants with research courses; seminars on graduate education; graduate school visits; workshops on financial support and graduate admissions; academic, career, and personal counseling; tutoring; and mentoring. Additionally, the program provides summer research experiences to selected students. Each McNair Program participant who satisfies program requirements receives a McNair Scholarship equal to the cost of in-state tuition and fees. There are ninety-five DOS computers and five Macintosh computers located in the library, residence hall, classroom building, science building, Division of Education, and Honors Division.

Athletics Coppin State College is a member of the National Association of Intercollegiate Athletics; the National Collegiate Athletic Association, Division I; and the Eastern Collegiate Athletic Association. The College offers a variety of varsity and intramural activities.

Support Services The Disabled Student and Referral Services Coordinator provides a variety of services to students with disabilities, including making referrals and special arrangements for on- and off-campus services such as counseling, academic advisement, and assistance with registration, financial aid, and library acquisitions. Readers, note-takers, interpreters, and other special aids can be provided if requested at least six weeks prior to the beginning of the semester.

Job Opportunities The Federal Work-Study program makes jobs available to undergraduate and graduate students with demonstrated financial need. These jobs are usually assigned as part of the financial aid package.

Tuition: $2867 for state residents, $6872 for nonresidents, per year (1996-97)

Room and Board: $4850

Contact: Dean: Dr. T. J. Bryan, 2500 W. North Avenue, Baltimore, Maryland 21216; Telephone: 410-383-5520; Fax: 410-383-9606; E-mail: tbryan@coe.coppin.umd.edu

CORNING COMMUNITY COLLEGE

2 Pu G S

▼ Honors Program

In 1976, the Council of Full Professors of Corning Community College, under the aegis of the Faculty Association, developed an honors program that would attract and provide an enriched academic experience for high ability and curious students in all academic programs, both technical and transfer, offered by the college. The faculty members, however, were concerned that the honors students should not be segregated from the general student body.

In order to achieve these primary goals, Corning Community College established a unique Honors Program in that there is not a separate honors curriculum or a series of honors courses that a student must take to earn an honors degree. There are no special honors sections that segregate honors students from the general student body. Rather, all academic courses the College offers may be taken at an advanced or honors level by any qualified student in any academic program offered by the College. The program was designed to be interdisciplinary and to give honors students control and responsibility for their own learning and discovery, which very seldom occurs in traditional courses.

An integral part of Corning Community College's Honors Program is the Honors Forum, which is a 3 credit-hour interdisciplinary seminar. The Forum is more similar to a graduate seminar than a community college course. The

average size of the Forum is 12 students and 3 faculty members representing the Social Sciences, Humanities, and the Sciences. The Forum faculty members function as guides as well as participants, learning along with the students. The Honors Forum serves several vital functions. It provides honors students with a venue for the exchange and testing of ideas and theories derived from their honors projects, provides students with the opportunity to analyze and synthesize information from students representing a wide variety of disciplines, and allows the students to develop critical thinking, argumentative, and oral presentation skills usually reserved for upperclassmen or even graduate students.

There are approximately 15–20 students involved in the Honors Program working either in the Honors Forum or independently with their mentor and not enrolled in the Forum.

Corning Community College Honors Program celebrated its twentieth anniversary in 1996, making it the oldest continuous Honors Program in the SUNY College system.

Participation Requirements: A student who has a GPA of 3.5 or better and who is curious as well as highly motivated may take any course at an advanced or honors level by developing an honors project for that course. The honors project or topic to be explored is mutually agreed upon by the student and his/her mentor, who is usually the instructor of that course. The mentor serves as a guide for the honors student, who bears complete responsibility for his/her honors project. The faculty member mentor awards an H (honors designation) for the relevant course.

Honors projects have included the writing of short stories and poems, building and repair of robots, and offering of music recitals as well as the more traditional research projects. Several students have had their honors projects published in professional journals of their chosen field.

Upon successful completion of 12 credit hours of honors level work, which usually entails two or three honors projects as well as Honors Forum and a cumulative GPA of 3.5, the student qualifies for an Honors diploma. Students who successfully complete honors projects also receive individualized letters from faculty member mentors as well as honors faculty members describing their projects and indicating the skills and abilities each student demonstrated throughout the semester. These letters are attached to the student's transcripts and are sent out to potential transfer colleges and/or employers.

The Campus Context: Corning Community College is located on Spencer Hill in Corning, New York. This geographic location is reflected in two distinguished facilities on campus, the Spencer Crest Nature Center and an observatory. Corning is located in upstate New York and is the home of the national and international corporate headquarters of Corning, Inc.

All Honors students are encouraged to participate in a wide range of cultural and civic activities sponsored by the College as well as the local community. Students attend such activities as storytelling festivals, midday concerts, sleeping bag seminars, or an occasional trip to a major metropolitan area for a visit to a museum.

The College offers forty degree programs.

Student Body Undergraduate enrollment is 46 percent men and 54 percent women. Minority students account for about 5 percent of the student population and international students represent less than 7 percent of the student body. All of the students are commuters. Seventy-five percent of all students receive financial aid.

Faculty Of the 187 faculty members, 107 are full-time. Thirty percent of the faculty members have terminal degrees. The student-faculty ratio is 18:1.

Key Facilities The library houses 68,944 volumes. There are approximately 600 PCs on campus linked to a computer network.

Athletics The Athletic Program at Corning Community College is a three-way program of intramurals, recreation, and intercollegiate sports. The College believes that athletics are a part of the total educational thrust of the College. The Intramural Program allows our students to participate in a wide range of competitive/noncompetitive, indoor/outdoor, and day/evening/weekend activities, including badminton, basketball, cross-country, bowling, volleyball, golf, tennis, and wrestling. The Recreation Program is provided for the enjoyment of the community as well as the students. A range of activities, including open gymnasium, open weight rooms, bowling, ice skating, movie discounts, swimming, and table tennis are illustrative examples.

The Intercollegiate Sports Program is offered at the Division III level within the National Junior College Athletic Association (NJCAA). Additionally, the College is a member of the Mid-State Athletic Conference (MSAC) and Region III (NJCAA). Eleven sports are offered: women's soccer, men's soccer, cross-country (coed), volleyball, women's basketball, men's basketball, wrestling, cheerleading, softball, baseball, and lacrosse. The College hosts many conference, regional, and national events highlighted by the Division III Women's National Basketball Championship. The College will host this event through 1999.

Study Abroad Corning Community College belongs to the College Consortium for International Studies and is a member of International Studies Association. Through these affiliations, students at Corning Community College can enroll in summer-long, semester-long, or year-long study abroad programs in some forty different countries around the globe and receive Corning Community College academic credit.

Support Services Disability services are housed with the Student Support Services Office. Adaptive equipment is housed in the library. The campus is equipped with electronic door openers, curb cuts, ramps, and Braille in elevators.

Job Opportunities Student work-study, tutors, and hourly employment are on an as-needed basis in clerical, buildings and grounds, laboratories, and technical area positions.

Tuition: $2400 for state residents, $4800 for nonresidents, per year (1996-97)

Mandatory Fees: $166

Contact: Director: Mr. Joselph J. Hanak, 1 Academic Drive, Corning, New York 14830; Telephone: 607-962-9208; Fax: 607-962-9456 E-mail: hanak@sccvc.corning-cc.edu

DeKalb College

2 Pu G M Sc Tr

▼ Honors Program

The DeKalb College Honors Program is an academic and student services program for students in any area of study who have demonstrated outstanding achievement and motivation. The Honors Program offers intellectually challenging courses taught by dedicated faculty members, interaction with other students, and opportunities for recognition and service. The courses are primarily core courses in the humanities and social sciences. The purpose of the Honors Program is to encourage students to achieve excellence in all aspects of their experience at DeKalb College.

The Honors Program at DeKalb College was founded in 1983 and currently has 350 students.

Participation Requirements: To earn an Honors Certificate, the student must have completed at least 60 quarter-hours of college work with a cumulative GPA of 3.3. Of these 60 quarter-hours, 25 must have been earned in honors courses in which the student received a grade of B or higher. All classes taken through the Honors Program appear on a student's transcript with an honors designation.

Admission Process: Students may join the Honors Program at any point in their academic career at DeKalb College. The following eligibility requirements are considered for acceptance into the Honors Program: a composite SAT I score of 1200 (SAT 1100), a 650 SAT I verbal score (SAT 580), or a 590 SAT I math score (SAT 580); ACT scores of 30 in English or 27 in math; National Merit Semi-Finalist status; eligibility for Phi Theta Kappa, the national honorary society for two-year colleges; 15 or more college-transfer credit hours and a 3.5 GPA from another college; a 3.5 GPA in academic courses taken at DeKalb College; and a recommendation from a DeKalb College faculty member and approval of the Honors Coordinator.

Scholarship Availability: Each campus of DeKalb College has several academic scholarships designated for students in the Honors Program; students who have completed at least two honors courses are eligible to apply. Priority is given to those students who have completed the most honors courses and have the highest cumulative GPA.

The Campus Context: DeKalb College was established in 1964. It is a regional, multicampus, two-year institution in the greater metropolitan Atlanta area. With more than 16,000 students enrolled at its four campuses and one center, DeKalb College comprises the third-largest institution in the University System of Georgia. Thus, DeKalb offers its students the resources of a large state university and the intimacy of a small college because of its multiple campuses. The College is primarily a liberal arts transfer institution preparing students in a variety of areas appropriate to baccalaureate majors at senior institutions. In addition, DeKalb offers degrees in several career programs such as nursing and dental hygiene. There are thirty-five undergraduate majors leading to Associate of Arts and Associate of Science degrees. The College also grants an Associate of Applied Science degree in fourteen business, medical, and technical areas.

DeKalb College offers courses through the Honors Program at its five locations: *Central Campus,* 555 North Indian Creek Drive, Clarkston, Georgia 30021-2396; *Gwinnett Campus,* 5155 Sugarloaf Parkway, Lawrenceville, Georgia 30243-5704; *North Campus,* 2101 Womack Road, Dunwoody, Georgia 30338-4497; *South Campus,* 3251 Panthersville Road, Decatur, Georgia 30034-3897; and *Rockdale Center for Higher Education,* 1115 West Avenue, Conyers, Georgia 30207-9448.

Student Body Undergraduate enrollment is 16,000, of whom 60 percent are women. The minority ethnic distribution of the student body is 6 percent Asian, 30 percent African American, and 2 percent Hispanic. There are 1,830 international students from 117 countries. DeKalb College hosts an extensive list of clubs and organizations ranging from an Adventure Sports Club and African American Association to a Chess Club, Drama Club, and Science Club. Although the College has no sororities and fraternities, it does have chapters of several honors societies including Alpha Beta Gamma, the national business honor society, and Phi Theta Kappa, the national honor society for two-year colleges.

Faculty There are 330 full-time faculty members (supplemented by adjunct faculty members); 95 percent have doctorates or other terminal degrees. The student-faculty ratio is 21:1.

Key Facilities The library houses 220,000 volumes. DeKalb College has five open computer labs housing 130 computers that are 486s or Pentiums. More than thirty-five software packages are available in these labs. Instructional Support Services and its staff of trained tutors maintain four math and writing tutorial facilities that house fifty computers. DeKalb College also has thirteen fully equipped computer classrooms.

Athletics DeKalb College fields teams at the intercollegiate level in men's and women's tennis, men's baseball, women's softball and volleyball, men's basketball, and men's and women's soccer. DeKalb is a member of the National Junior College Athletic Association and the Georgia Junior College Athletic Association. The College also offers an intramural and recreational program for students and faculty members that includes tennis, soccer, softball, basketball, swimming, table tennis, volleyball, and other activities.

Study Abroad DeKalb College's Office of International/ Intercultural Education supplies students with updated information about the study abroad programs in the University System of Georgia as well as programs throughout the country, helps students with applications, and conducts predeparture orientation programs and re-entry programs for those studying abroad. In addition, the University System of Georgia offers a centralized listing of study abroad programs at each of the System's thirty-four colleges and universities, including DeKalb College's own programs. Students register for these programs at their home institution, which facilitates the process of transferring credits and arranging for financial aid.

Support Services The Center for Disability Services coordinates support services provided to students identified as disabled, deaf or hard of hearing, learning disabled, physically disabled, visually impaired, or disabled due to illness. Services include sign language interpreters, tutors, note takers, specialized advisers, and classroom modifications. Specialized equipment, including portable reading machines, TDDs, and assistive listening devices, is also available to students.

Job Opportunities The Federal Work-Study program is available to qualified students. Selection for the program is made on the basis of need as determined by federal guidelines. In addition, DeKalb College provides, through its own resources, a limited number of other student assistantships involving part-time work on campus.

Tuition: $1225 for state residents, $4025 for nonresidents, per year (1996-1997)

Mandatory Fees: $123

Contact: Director, Central Campus: Dr. Susan M. McGrath, 555 North Indian Creek Drive, Clarkston, Georgia 30021-2396; Telephone: 404-299-4154; Fax: 404-298-3834; E-mail: smcgrath@dekalb.dc.peachnet.edu. Director, North Campus: Director: Dr. Jeffrey A. Portnoy, 2101 Womack Road, Dunwoody, Georgia 30338-4497; Telephone: 770-551-3065; Fax: 770-604-3795; E-mail: jportnoy@dekalb.dc.peachnet.edu

DENISON UNIVERSITY

4 Pr G L Sc Tr

▼ Honors Program

The Denison University Honors Program is designed especially for outstanding students in the college. It consists of seminars and courses intended to meet the intellectual aspirations and expectations of highly motivated and academically gifted students. Working closely with the director of the Honors Program and their faculty advisers, honors students may enroll in a select list of course and seminar offerings during the student's Denison career. Special academic events take place each semester for students in the Honors Program. Most honors seminars meet a general education requirement of the college. The honors quarterly newsletter, *Arete,* keeps honors students abreast of current activities in honors work. An Honors Symposium is held annually, and visiting scholars meet regularly with honors students.

The Honors Program is in Gilpatrick House, the Honors Center for the college. This restored Victorian house is centrally located on the Denison campus and serves as the locus for Honors Program activities. The ground level contains a seminar room modeled after Brasenose College, Oxford; a commons for discussion groups and informal seminars; and the administrative offices for the Honors Program. The upstairs serves as a residence area for 10 students in the Honors Program. The Gilpatrick Fellow assists in planning cocurricular events for students in the Honors Program. A popular event is the Gilpatrick Chowder Hour. This faculty-prepared luncheon for 20 students and faculty members, which is followed by discussion on a current topic, takes place five or six times during term.

The program was established in 1965 and revitalized in 1986. As of 1997, 560 students are enrolled in the Honors Program. Upperclass students with a minimum 3.4 GPA are eligible to participate in the program. The number of upperclass students averages between 250 and 300 per semester.

Participation Requirements: Denison students with a 3.4 GPA are eligible to register for seminars in the Honors Program. To be a member of and to graduate from the Honors Program, a student needs to complete the following requirements: achieve and maintain a 3.4 GPA by the end of the sophomore year, declare intention to the director of the program to complete the requirements in the Honors Program no later than preregistration time in the fall of the junior year, complete at least two honors seminars during the first four semesters, complete at least four honors seminars during the Denison career, and complete a senior honors project in the department of the student's major. Students wishing to declare the intention to complete the Honors Program requirements should discuss this option with the director of the Honors Program no later than the end of the sophomore year.

A student may participate in the seminars without completing the specific requirements to become a member of the Honors Program.

Scholarship Availability: Denison University is committed to enrolling academically talented individuals, which is evidenced by our comprehensive scholarship program. More than 500 merit scholarships and awards are offered. Students invited to participate in the Honors Program are awarded half-tuition Heritage Scholarships. For the class of 2000, the college offered twenty-four full-tuition Faculty Scholarships for Achievement and fifty-nine three-quarter tuition Trustee Awards to selected high school valedictorians and salutatorians nationwide. Selection for the valedictorian/salutatorian scholarships is made by the faculty Honors Committee. There is no special application for these awards. To be assured of consideration, the complete Denison application must be received by the admissions office by January 1 of the applicant's senior year.

To receive the Faculty Scholarship for Achievement or the Trustee Award, students must interview with a Denison representative any time prior to March 12 of their senior year and be invited into the Honors Program. Applicants invited to compete for these awards are also contacted in February of their senior year and asked to submit a scholarship essay.

A renewable full-tuition Wells Scholarship in Science is awarded to 1 outstanding science student each year. Interested students must submit a special Wells application by January 1 of their senior year. Another renewable full-tuition award is the Jonathan Everett Dunbar Scholarship in the Humanities, awarded annually to 1 outstanding student in the humanities. Interested students must submit a Dunbar application by January 1 of their senior year.

Information on all awards is available from the Denison Admissions Office. Notification of the Faculty Scholarship for Achievement, Trustee Award, and Wells and Dunbar Scholarship winners takes place in March. The profile for students receiving award offers in recent years has been a class rank in the top decile, strong test scores, and evidence of significant extracurricular achievement and essay writing ability. It is advisable to pay particular attention to the preparation of the Denison essay as well as the scholarship essay.

Students who complete the requirements to graduate as a member of the Honors Program are recognized in several ways. A few days prior to Commencement, the Honors Program sponsors a special graduation ceremony and reception to honor these seniors. Attended by faculty and relatives, the ceremony consists of the presentation of a medal and Latin certificate to each student by the Honors Program director and the president of the college. These students also receive a special designation on their college transcript and in the Commencement program indicating that they have graduated as a member of the Honors Program.

The Campus Context: Denison University is an independently supported coeducational college of liberal arts and sciences that is steeped in tradition and responsive to curricular innovation and creativity in the classroom. Founded in 1831 in Granville, Ohio, Denison has earned a national reputation as an energetic academic community where students participate actively in their education, learn to make informed choices, and develop the skills to become tomorrow's leaders.

Denison offers three undergraduate degrees—the Bachelor of Arts, the Bachelor of Science, and the Bachelor of Fine Arts. Thirty-nine majors and nine preprofessional programs are offered. Special or distinguishing facilities on campus include the Olin Planetarium, a research station in a 350-acre biological reserve, the Swasey Observatory, a high resolution spectrometer lab, a nuclear magnetic resonance spectrometer, and the Burmese art collection.

Student Body Undergraduate enrollment is approximately 1,900, of which women comprise 53 percent. Ninety-seven percent of the students reside on campus. The ethnic distribution is approximately 90 percent Caucasian, 4 percent African American, 2 percent Hispanic, 3 percent Asian American, and 1 percent other. There are also 66 international students enrolled at Denison. Approximately 86 percent of enrolled undergraduates receive some form of aid. There are ten national fraternities and eight national sororities; all are nonresidential.

Faculty Of the 163 faculty members, 150 are full-time, and 97 percent have terminal degrees. The student-faculty ratio is 11:1.

Key Facilities The library houses 325,000 volumes, 290,000 government documents, 1,200 periodical subscriptions, 16,000 sound recordings, and 3,000 videocassettes. Denison also offers a combined catalog to a collection of more than 1 million volumes as a member of the Five Colleges of Ohio consortium and is a member of the OhioLINK state consortium. Computer facilities include 125 PC and Macintosh microcomputers in five student clusters, 150 computers in department labs, and network outlets available to every student living in a residence hall.

Athletics Denison is a member of North Coast Athletic Conference (NCAA Division III). Denison students may also participate in intercollegiate and intramural sports. There are eleven men's and eleven women's intercollegiate sports, and fifteen men's and twelve women's intramural sports.

Study Abroad Study abroad is encouraged as is domestic off-campus study in the Washington Semester, Sea Semester, Arts Program in NYC, Newberry Library Program in Humanities in Illinois, Oak Ridge Science Semester in Tennessee, and Philadelphia Urban Semester.

Job Opportunities Work opportunities on campus are available. Approximately 51 percent of full-time undergraduates work on campus. The average amount undergraduates may expect to earn per year from part-time, on-campus work is $1700.

Tuition: $18,570 per year (1996-97)

Room and Board: $5160

Mandatory Fees: $900

Contact: Director: Dr. Anthony J. Lisska, Granville, Ohio 43023; Telephone: 614-587-6573; Fax: 614-587-6602; E-mail: sunkle@denison.edu; Web site: http://www.denison.edu/honors

DOMINICAN COLLEGE OF SAN RAFAEL

4 Pr G C S Sc Tr

▼ Honors Program

The Dominican College Honors Program is designed to provide enhanced and alternative modes of education for excellent and highly motivated students throughout the college. It encourages the growth of intellectual independence and initiative, offers special opportunities for independent study and research under faculty mentors, and supports the pursuit of scholarly interests in a broad range of disciplines. It aims to bring together enthusiastic students and faculty members to further the Dominican ideal of intellectual excellence. The program is directed toward students who seek the responsibility of determining the pace, organization, and development of their academic experience by electing to take special honors seminars and/or various forms of independent honors work. Students receive academic advisement from both their major adviser and the honors director to help them set and achieve their own educational goals. The Honors Program provides students with the opportunity to enroll in honors seminars or graduate courses and to do an honors course conversion, course expansion, or an honors independent study.

The program began in 1989 and currently enrolls approximately 100 students.

Participation Requirements: Honors students must maintain a minimum 3.3 cumulative index in order to remain active in the program. Honors-related financial awards are in jeopardy if the index slips below 3.1. To become an Honors Program graduate, a student must maintain a 3.5 cumulative index while completing either 21 units of honors work or a combination of honors seminars and honors contracts that totals seven courses/projects. Transfer students are expected to complete a portion of this requirement depending on their academic standing upon entrance to Dominican College. For example, a sophomore transfer student would be expected to complete five courses/projects. The minimum requirement for graduation from the Honors Program by a transfer student is four semesters of residence and four honors projects while maintaining the 3.5 index. For students who successfully complete the Honors Program requirements, the title of the honors thesis and honors program graduation is noted on the official college transcript.

Scholarship Availability: A number of academic scholarships are available at Dominican College. Those of interest to honors students include a Presidential Merit Scholarship and a Dean's Merit Scholarship. These are available for entering freshmen with a strong academic record.

The Campus Context: Dominican College of San Rafael is composed of the following schools: the School of Arts and Sciences, the School of Business and International Studies, the School of Education, the School of Liberal and Professional Studies, and the School of Nursing and Allied Health Professions. There are eighteen undergraduate and five graduate programs offered on campus.

Student Body Undergraduate enrollment is 1,025, of which women comprise 78 percent. The ethnic distribution is approximately 6 percent African American, 20 percent Hispanic, 12 percent Asian, 1 percent Native American, and 2 percent international students. Commuters make up 75 percent of the school's population. Seventy percent of students receive financial aid. Dominican College has no fraternities or sororities.

Faculty Of the 157 faculty members at Dominican College, 46 are full-time. The student-faculty ratio is 13:1.

Key Facilities The library houses 96,487 volumes. The Computer Lab, with twenty-five workstations, is a Windows NT Network, IBM RS6000 Server, campuswide network.

Athletics In athletics, Dominican of San Rafael plays NAIA division men's and women's soccer, cross-country, basketball, and tennis and women's volleyball.

Study Abroad The College currently offers twenty-six study-abroad programs in twenty-two locations in Africa, Australia, Asia, Europe, Central America, and South America. As part of the College's mission to foster an appreciation of cultural diversity and global interdependence, students are encouraged to consider this option. These programs are administered through the International Studies Program.

Support Services There is a disabled-student coordinator on campus. Facilities for disabled students include the Academic Support Department and the Peer Counseling Department.

Job Opportunities Dominican College provides a campuswide work-study program.

Tuition: $14,380 per year (1996-97)

Room and Board: $6370

Mandatory Fees: $290

Contact: Director: Dr. LeeAnn Bartolini, 50 Acacia Avenue, San Rafael, California 94901-8008; Telephone: 415-257-1357; Fax: 415-485-3205; E-mail: bartolin@dominican.edu

DOMINICAN UNIVERSITY

4 Pr C S Sc Tr

▼ Honors Program

The Dominican University Honors Program is designed to stimulate the intellectual growth of academically talented students through small classes featuring group discussion of challenging readings, frequent and varied writing assignments, and close contact between students and instructors. The program consists of a series of interdisciplinary honors seminars, an independent honors project in the major field under the supervision of a faculty adviser, and interaction in and out of the classroom with other honors students and faculty members.

At the heart of the Honors Program are four interdisciplinary seminars, designed by honors faculty members as a sequence and addressing a variety of challenging topics. Recent seminars, for example, have discussed the nature of imagination, varieties of liberty, America at millennium's end, and political economy—conceptions of wealth and power. Most honors students enroll in one seminar in each of the four college years, although students electing to study abroad or participate in an internship program may choose to adapt their selection of seminars to their special curricular needs.

In their junior year, honors students design special projects with professors in their major field of study and present their projects in the spring of their senior year to a college-wide faculty committee, thereby earning a degree with distinction in their field of concentration. Most students do individual research as a part of their honors project; in some cases, the honors project may originate from a challenging internship or reflect outstanding achievement in the arts.

Honors students come together as a community occasionally for program-sponsored theater and museum trips, dinners and receptions with faculty members, and academic conferences. They are also, of course, active as campus leaders in student government, honor societies, and student athletics.

There are approximately 50 students in the program.

Participation Requirements: Students must maintain an overall GPA of 3.3 to remain in the program. Those who complete four honors seminars with a GPA of 3.0 and the honors project, for which a GPA of 3.25 in the major field is required, earn the B.A. Honors Degree with Distinction in their major field.

Admission Process: Entering freshmen are invited to join the Freshman Honors Seminar on the basis of their high school class rank and SAT I and/or ACT scores. Other Dominican students and transfer students may apply to join the program as sophomores.

Scholarship Availability: Scholarships include full-tuition Presidential Scholarships, awarded to winners of a competition held each February; Booth Scholarships, for students who participate in the Presidential Scholarship competition; Honor Scholarships, awarded on the basis of high school class rank; and Phi Theta Kappa Scholarships, for members of the international honor society for two-year colleges.

The Campus Context: A Catholic college of nearly 1,800 men and women, Dominican offers a liberal arts curriculum with a choice of forty major fields of concentration leading to the Bachelor of Arts. Students find a career orientation in a personalized, value-oriented environment. The atmosphere on the 30-acre campus is close-knit. The ivy-covered buildings include a 287,000-volume library, a fine arts building with a recital hall and auditorium, two residence halls, and the recently constructed Student Center, which has an elevated running track, an indoor swimming pool, and a student grill overlooking glass-enclosed racquetball courts. Other important facilities are the O'Connor Art Gallery, Lund Auditorium, and Junior Citizens Center.

The University is located in River Forest, a quiet residential suburb just 10 miles west of Chicago's Loop. Students can take advantage of city offerings by using nearby public transportation, or they can enjoy the surrounding Oak Park-River Forest residential community, which, among other attractions, is home to the largest number of Frank Lloyd Wright houses in the country. These include Wright's first home and studio.

Student Body Undergraduate enrollment is 900, comprised of 25 percent men and 75 percent women. Seventeen percent of students are members of minority groups, and 3 percent are from other countries. Thirty percent of students reside on campus, while the remaining 70 percent commute. Seventy percent of students receive financial aid.

Faculty Of the 62 full-time undergraduate faculty members, 80 percent have terminal degrees. The student-faculty ratio is 12:1.

Key Facilities Computer facilities include computer labs, offices, and classrooms; a language lab; and a distance learning center. The entire campus is scheduled to be networked within two years.

Study Abroad Through the International Studies program, Dominican students in all majors have the opportunity to study overseas in England, France, Spain, Italy, and Germany. Students may study abroad for a summer, semester, or year. Credits earned this way apply to the Dominican University degree requirements.

Support Services Disabled students find all academic buildings, the library, and residence halls handicapped-accessible; special parking, equipped restrooms, and lowered drinking fountains are also available on campus.

Job Opportunities Students are offered a range of work opportunities on campus, including work-study.

Tuition: $12,850 per year (1996-97)

Room and Board: $4880

Mandatory Fees: $100

Contact: Director: Dr. Mary Scott Simpson, 7900 West Division, River Forest, Illinois 60305; Telephone: 708-366-2490; Fax: 708-524-5990

DREXEL UNIVERSITY

4 Pr G M Sc Tr

▼ University Honors Program

The Drexel University Honors Program enriches the university experience for students of superior intellect and demonstrated academic achievement. The Honors Program is in its sixth year of operation. In the Honors Program, students from all majors receive individual attention throughout their academic progress, a variety of courses that engage small groups of students with Drexel's best faculty, special trips and cultural events, and social gatherings. The program offers the advantages of an elite liberal arts college within a major technological university. Incoming students are selected for admission based upon their superior intellectual strengths, accomplishments, and motivation. Current students who meet these criteria are also invited to apply.

The following three types of courses carry honors credits: honors sections of courses offered by various departments; interdisciplinary Honors Colloquia, sponsored by the Honors Program; and Honors Options, the individual enrichment of nonhonors courses for particular students, which must be approved in advance by the instructor and program director.

Currently, there are approximately 400 students in the Honors Program. About 60 entering freshmen are admitted each year, which represents about the top 8 percent of the entering class.

Participation Requirements: Flexibility is the hallmark of the Drexel Honors Program. Students may elect as many courses and events as they wish. To remain in the Honors Program, students must maintain a GPA of 3.0 or higher. Qualified honors students may graduate with distinction from the Honors Program. These students must complete 32 credits of honors courses and projects, maintain an overall GPA of 3.5 or higher, and complete a senior project judged worthy of honors. Students aiming for this distinction will normally meet with the program director in their junior year to ensure that they understand these requirements and are prepared to meet them.

Admission Process: Students apply directly to the director of the program. The application requires standard information and includes a brief essay. The progress of all students in the University is monitored, and accomplished Drexel students not currently in the program are invited to apply.

Scholarship Availability: Need-based and merit scholarships as well as grants, loans, and work-study programs are available. Some co-op positions and faculty research assistant positions are also available to students. The University makes approximately $40 million available annually for scholarship aid. In addition, a six-month co-op typically pays a Drexel student an average of $10,000.

The Campus Context: Drexel University is Philadelphia's second-largest private university. It is also the second-oldest— and largest— university in the nation dedicated to cooperative education. Founded in 1891, the University is comprised of six colleges: Arts and Sciences, Business and Administration, Engineering, Information Science and Technology, Nesbitt College of Design Arts, and Evening College. Forty-six bachelor's, thirty-nine master's, and seventeen doctoral degree programs are offered. Drexel was the first university in the nation to require that each undergraduate have access to a microcomputer, and the campus offers full networking, extensive integration of computers in the instructional program, and access to the Internet across the campus and in the dormitories. Drexel's location in the historic city of Philadelphia also provides diverse cultural sites and activities.

Student Body Of the 7,000 undergraduates, most come from the northeast. The distribution is 40 percent women, 7 percent international undergraduates, and 25 percent commuters. Residents live in one of four residence halls, apartments, or one of four sororities or twelve fraternities on campus. Eighty percent of students receive financial aid; the total aid package equals $40 million annually.

Faculty There are 400 full-time faculty members. Ninety percent hold terminal degrees in their field. The student-faculty ratio is 13:1.

Key Facilities The Hagerty Library contains 400,000 volumes. The 10,000 Apple computers on campus are moving in 1997 to a two-platform environment. Forty-five buildings on campus offer a full range of activities and services.

Athletics The Drexel Dragons compete in NCAA Division I in the following sports: men's and women's basketball, lacrosse, swimming and diving, cross-country, and tennis; men's baseball, crew, golf, soccer, and wrestling; and women's field hockey, softball, and volleyball. Club sports include cheerleading, chess, women's crew, fencing, ice hockey, in-line skating, karate, men's volleyball, riflery, rugby, sailing, skiing and snowboarding, and volleyball. Ten different sports are offered as more informal intramural activities.

Study Abroad Drexel Abroad Programs in Brussels, Bonn, London, Madrid, and Paris combine internships with intensive study of the politics and culture of the host country or, in Brussels, of the European community. Open to students throughout the University; students enroll under Drexel course numbers and receive course credit. Financial aid and merit scholarships travel with the student.

Tuition: $13,680 to $16,298 per year (full-time) or $346 per credit hour for day classes and $185 per credit hour for evening classes (part-time) (1996-97)

Room and Board: $6909

Mandatory Fees: $792

Contact: Director: Mark L. Greenberg, Honors Center, 5016 MacAlister Hall, Philadelphia, Pennsylvania 19104; Telephone: 215-895-1267; Fax: 215-895-6813; E-mail: mcmenaab@duvm. ocs.drexel.edu; Web site: http://www.honors.drexel.edu

DUNDALK COMMUNITY COLLEGE

2 Pu G S Sc Tr

▼ Honors Program

The Honors Program at Dundalk Community College is designed to provide interested, motivated, and high-achieving students with opportunities to enrich their education through specially designed honors courses, learning activities, and extracurricular events. Students benefit from the Honors Program through these courses. There are two types of courses—special sections of regular college courses and seminars—that are interdisciplinary in approach. These seminars include titles such as "Anthropology Through Literature," "The Creative Process," and "Baltimore City as Text," a course modeled on and named for the National Collegiate Honors Council's study and exploration of cities called City as Text.

All honors classes are smaller than regular sections, limited in enrollment to 15 students. The small size presents students with a challenge by promoting active participation. Small class size also enables substantial student-teacher interaction. Students unable to take all of the regularly offered honors courses may still participate in the program by upgrading two courses to the honors level. This is accomplished by writing a contract with a teacher to develop activities to enrich the course. An honors section of cooperative education is also offered.

Honors teachers and courses are carefully selected. Teachers who enjoy working individually with students and who wish to put in the extra effort needed to design a special course for honors students are selected to teach honors courses. All honors courses are designed to promote discussion, interaction, research, and field experiences. There are currently 75 students in the program.

Participation Requirements: Students who complete all of the honors requirements—12 hours of credit, including four regular honors courses and two seminars—are recognized at graduation by special designation on the program, wearing a gold braid, and an announcement of their achievement when graduates' names are called. All students participating in the program gain recognition on their transcripts by special designation for each honors course.

Admission Process: Students complete an honors application, which requires two teacher recommendations and a 500-word essay. They must have a 3.25 GPA.

Scholarship Availability: The Honors Program offers twelve partial-tuition scholarships. All applicants are considered for these scholarships. An effort is made to award half of the available scholarships to newly graduated high school seniors and half to students already attending the college.

The Campus Context: Dundalk Community College is one of three colleges of the Baltimore County Community College System. Dundalk is the smallest of the three and has a reputation for providing individual attention to its students. The 25-year-old campus is located in Dundalk and attracts both full- and part-time students. The college offers fifteen career programs and four transfer programs.

Student Body There are currently 3,000 students enrolled at Dundalk, of whom 82 percent are part-time. African Americans make up 15 percent of the student body.

Faculty There are 55 full-time faculty members and a student-faculty ratio of 16:1.

Athletics Athletics include men's baseball and basketball and women's softball, soccer, volleyball.

Tuition: $1800 for area residents, $3180 for state residents, $4890 for nonresidents, per year (1996-97)

Fees: $80

Contact: Director: Dr. Bernadette Flynn Low, College Community Center, 7200 Sollers Pt. Rd., Baltimore, Maryland 21222; Telephone: 410-285-9886; Fax: 410-285-9903

EAST ARKANSAS COMMUNITY COLLEGE

2 Pu G S Sc Tr

▼ Honors Program

The Honors Program at East Arkansas Community College (EACC) is designed to attract liberal arts students in the three-county service area who wish to complete a two-year course of study before continuing their education at a four-year school. The program emphasizes enriched core courses, engaging teaching styles, low student-teacher ratio, and the nurturing of academic camaraderie among participants. Student admission to the program is based on a competitive application process.

The curriculum of the Honors Program at EACC was designed with the transfer student in mind. The four-semester program includes the core courses required by most four-year colleges and universities in Arkansas. Incoming honors students enroll together in a total of 10 semester hours of honors courses, which includes a one-hour seminar. Each semester, those students who enter the program are enrolled together in the required honors courses. Each student may elect to take an additional course or two outside of the Honors Program to supplement the core curriculum at any time.

While the core courses do not necessarily demand more of honors students in the way of workload, they differ from the College's usual offerings in approach. Each teacher plans his or her course for the student who has demonstrated an unusual tendency to excel academically. Because of this, the teacher is able to offer more suitable strategies for exposing those students to the subject matter at hand. These possibilities are often absent from regular classes.

Another instructional feature of the program is the opportunity for team-teaching. Especially with the Interdisciplinary Seminar (IDS), which is offered each semester, teachers may work together to design a course that bridges different areas of study. For example, a course based on the interplay of musical and theatrical style in history might be taught by faculty members from the music and drama departments. The possibilities for such collaboration are endless, and such interaction can only improve the entire college.

In the same way that student admission to the program is competitive, teachers in the program are also selected on the basis of application. Instructors who wish to teach in the program must submit a completed application, a sample syllabus, and a budget for the intended course. It is anticipated that the existence of such a program on campus will raise teaching standards across the board.

Most honors classes consist of 15 students. A spirited learning atmosphere is further fostered through group field trips. Each semester, faculty members incorporate into their syllabi an outing to a cultural site that augments the course in some way. These trips may be to museums or exhibits in the nearby cities of Memphis and Little Rock, but they are as likely to include a day trip to a university campus or a Civil War battlefield.

Participation Requirements: All students who are admitted to the Honors Program at East Arkansas Community College receive a full two-year scholarship that includes tuition and books. The scholarships are renewable each semester providing the student has maintained a GPA of 3.0 or greater while enrolled in the program. Participation in the program also includes provisions for all program-related travel and field trips.

Admission Process: Admission to the Honors Program at East Arkansas Community College is competitive. Student enrollment in the program is limited to 10–15 in each class. Each spring, applications are accepted from students at area high schools. Qualified applicants must meet at least one of the following criteria: a high school GPA of 3.5 or greater, inclusion among the top ten percent of the graduating class, a minimum ACT composite score of 23 (SAT 1050), or a GPA of 3.5 or greater on 15 transferable college credit hours. Along with the completed application form, the students must submit a 200-word essay and arrange for two letters of recommendation and an official transcript to be sent to the committee. Students may request an application interview as well. Upon acceptance, students are assigned advisers from the Honors Program to help with registration and counseling.

Scholarship Availability: East Arkansas Community College offers full tuition, including books, supplies, and travel, to all students accepted into the Honors Program.

The Campus Context: The 70-acre campus of East Arkansas Community College is located atop Crowley's Ridge just off Highway 284. The campus lies within the limits of Forrest City, which is considered a business and transportation hub of the east central portion of the state. The two-year institution of higher education provides a quality educational experience for individual development and improves the general community. The Associate of Arts (A.A.) and Associate of Applied Science (A.A.S) degrees are offered. Degree programs include emergency medical technical paramedic studies, business administration, information systems management, criminal justice, drafting and design, nursing, and administration office technology.

Student Body There are approximately 1,300 undergraduates, of whom 72 percent are women. The ethnic distribution of undergraduates is approximately 1 percent nonresident alien and American Indian or Alaska Native, 37 percent African American, 1 percent Asian or Pacific Islander, 1 percent Hispanic, and 60 percent Caucasian. There are 4 international students. Sixty-two percent of students receive financial aid.

Faculty Of the 100 faculty members, 32 are full-time and 68 are adjuncts. Seven percent of the faculty members hold terminal degrees. The student-faculty ratio is 13:1.

Key Facilities The library houses 21,942 volumes. Computer facilities include six computer rooms and one large open lab containing sixty-two computers with 486 CPu, fifty-nine computers with 386 CPu, and twenty-eight computers with 8088 CPu.

Support Services All academic buildings, the library, the student center, and the Computer Education Center are completely handicapped-accessible. Handicapped parking is available, and restrooms are specially equipped for the convenience of disabled students.

Job Opportunities East Arkansas Community College cooperates with the Department of Health and Human Services to provide employment to students with financial need.

Tuition: $792 for area residents, $960 for state residents, $1164 for nonresidents, per year (1996-97)

Contact: Director: Jan Haven, Forrest City, Arkansas 72335; Telephone: 501-633-4480 ext. 261; Fax: 501-633-722

EAST CAROLINA UNIVERSITY

4 Pu G L Sc Tr

▼ **Honors Program**

The Honors Program at East Carolina University (ECU) provides special classes with an average size of 18 students and a sense of community for academically superior students. Each semester the program offers four or five honors seminars on different, often interdisciplinary, and frequently controversial topics and some forty honors sections of regular departmental courses. Most of these meet general education requirements and all seminars help satisfy the University requirement for writing-intensive courses. Seminars have covered a wide range of topics in the humanities, fine arts, sciences, and social sciences. Some of these seminars include "The Voices of Generation X," "Gay Literature," "Writing Poems and Making Drawings," "The Music of Latin America," "The Geology of the National Parks," "Chemistry Behind the Headlines," and "Poverty, Discrimination, and Public Policy." Classes emphasize discussion rather than lecture, essay rather than short-answer exams, and active involvement in the education process.

Students who complete 24 semester hours of honors courses with A's or B's and a GPA of 3.3 or higher earn general education honors. Upperclass students with 3.5 GPA are invited to complete a 6-semester-hour senior project, which may take the form of a thesis, field experience, public service, portfolio, coteaching, or creative work and earn University honors in their major or minor.

To foster a sense of community of scholars on the larger campus, the program offers students an honors residence hall, their own state-of-the-art computer lab, an active

student group, a student newsletter, a fall picnic, a spring Honors Recognition Day, representation on the Honors Program Committee, special lectures and trips, occasional teleconferences and seminars, special honors advising and registration assistance, opportunities for exchange and study abroad, and financial assistance in making presentations at regional and national conferences.

Each semester the program sponsors an Honors Recognition Day, at which students make presentations before the honors student body, graduating seniors are presented certificates, and awards are made. The meeting is followed by a reception at the chancellor's house. The names of graduating students are listed in the honors newsletter, the campus newspaper, and the Commencement program. The honors notation becomes a permanent part of the student's transcript as soon as it is earned.

The program is more than thirty years old. In the mid-sixties, the University began offering seminars for selected students by request. In 1978, the current Honors Program was created on a two-year, University-wide format. In 1993, it became a four-year program, with all senior-level departmental honors work being coordinated through the Honors Program. Approximately 550 students are currently enrolled in the program. Fifty-five students graduated from the program in spring 1996. Invitations to participate in the program are issued from November to April.

Participation Requirements: Entering freshmen who present SAT scores of 1300 or higher, a 3.4 GPA, and a top 10 percent high school ranking are invited into the program during their senior year in high school; some freshmen who meet two of these criteria receive provisional invitations. During freshman orientation, students are given academic counseling and are registered for courses. Current ECU students and transfer students with a 3.4 GPA or better also qualify to take honors courses. Students who drop below a 3.0 at the end of the school year are not eligible for courses until they again have a 3.3 GPA.

Scholarship Availability: All merit scholarships are handled by the Office of Admissions, not by the Honors Office, but a large number of honors students hold scholarships. Chancellor's Scholars receive $20,000, University Scholars $12,000, and Alumni Honors Scholars $6000 for the four years. Many special scholarships for in-state, out-of-state, minority, transfer, and other distinct groups of students are available.

The Campus Context: East Carolina University consists of twelve colleges and schools: the College of Arts and Sciences and the Schools of Allied Health Sciences, Art, Business, Education, Health and Human Performance, Human Environmental Sciences, Industry and Technology, Medicine, Music, Nursing, and Social Work. It awards the bachelor's, master's, Ph.D., D.Ed., and M.D. degrees. On campus, there are 102 degree programs. The 109 buildings on the main, medical, and allied health campuses are valued at $308 million and include a newly enlarged library and recreation center.

Student Body ECU enrolls 14,342 undergraduates, of whom 57 percent are women and 13 percent are from minority groups. There are more than 150 international students. Of the student population, 85 percent are residential students. Approximately 35 percent of students receive financial aid. There are twenty-three fraternities and fourteen sororities on the main campus.

Faculty The faculty numbers 1,181, of which 1,122 are full-time and 80 percent hold terminal degrees. The student-faculty ratio is 15:1.

Key Facilities The newly enlarged central campus library contains more than 1 million books, more than 1 million pieces of microform, and holdings in various other media. There are nearly 2,500 microcomputers and 130 special application terminals throughout the campus. Support for education and research is provided through an IBM ED 900/260 mainframe, SunSparc 20, UNIX and DEC Vax 4000, and 3,400 minicomputers. A fiber-optic network installed in 1995 links the computers with other universities, the NC SuperComputer Complex, and the on-line library catalog and bibliographical retrieval system. Computer stations are located across campus and in the residence halls. The honors computer lab is one of the most up-to-date on campus.

Athletics ECU plays Division I intercollegiate sports, including men's football (Conference USA), tennis, track, soccer, basketball, diving and swimming, baseball, and golf and women's volleyball, tennis, track, soccer, basketball, diving and swimming, and softball. Students also participate in an elaborate system of intramural sports. A new recreation center provides up-to-date facilities for minor sports and individual workouts.

Study Abroad The ECU Office of International Affairs is a member of several consortia, which promote the exchange of students in the U.S. and 130 institutions abroad for the modest tuition they pay at home. It also sponsors several study-abroad programs in the summer. Some honors credit is given for study abroad. Financial assistance is available.

Support Services Disability Support Services meets the needs of most individuals by offering academic support, attendant services, barrier-free buildings, and adaptive transportation. Full services for the deaf are available and students may earn a minor in Sign Language Studies. In 1996, the School of Medicine graduated the only profoundly deaf medical student in the nation (a graduate of the Honors Program).

Job Opportunities Work-study and self-help programs assist students with work opportunities on campus. Cooperative education places students in both for-pay and for-credit positions across the country. Other financial aid is available.

Tuition: $874 for state residents, $8028 for nonresidents, per year (1996-97)

Room and Board: $3480

Mandatory Fees: $878

Contact: Director: Dr. Franklin David Sanders, 2026 General Classroom Building, Greenville, North Carolina 27858-4353; Telephone: 919-328-6373; Fax: 919-328-4394; E-mail: hnsander@ecuvm.cis.ecu.edu; Web site: http://ecuvax.cis.ecu/edu/academics/schdept/honors/honors.htm

EASTERN CONNECTICUT STATE UNIVERSITY

4 Pu G S Sc Tr

▼ University Honors Program

The University Honors Program, open to qualified students pursuing any major at Eastern, features an introductory freshman seminar, three interdisciplinary and usually team-taught colloquia, and a three-semester independent project. The colloquia, the heart of the program, are courses especially designed for honors students by faculty members distinguished for teaching and research. They are small classes that encourage active learning and teamwork and often include travel and other off-campus experiences. New England and the Sea, for example, featured seven trips to the shore, including a day on a schooner chartered for the occasion; the Museum and Society will include behind-the-scenes study visits to ten museums, such as Sturbridge Village, Mystic Seaport, and the Wadsworth Atheneum; and Culture Across the African Diaspora, offered last fall, showcased a number of performing artists and concluded with a Caribbean banquet.

Participation Requirements: The honors thesis, the program's capstone experience, is a creative and scholarly or scientific research project undertaken with the help of a student-selected faculty mentor. All honors courses are substitutes for general education requirements. Students who complete the program and maintain a 3.3 GPA are designated University Honors Scholars at graduation and on their official transcripts.

In addition to their academic pursuits, honors scholars become involved in a variety of leadership roles and rewarding activities. Many of these, like the weekend in April when prospective freshmen are invited to visit the campus and stay over in dorms or apartments, are entirely planned and carried out by students. The Honors Club sponsors trips to cultural events, including the NE-NCHC conference each spring, at which 6 to 10 students regularly participate as presenters. The Student Honors Council makes recommendations concerning the honors curriculum and requirements and organizes social and cultural events on campus, including the activities of Honors Week in the spring. Students also publish the Honors Newsletter each month and continue to construct and upgrade our site on the World Wide Web. Everyone connected with the program gets together twice a year at the director's home for a back-to-school party welcoming freshmen in the fall and a picnic-barbecue during Honors Week in the spring. Honors students are encouraged to be venturesome and to take part in exchange programs with universities throughout the United States and abroad.

Admission Process: The Honors Program accepts about 30 entering students, transfers, and continuing students each year, offering full in-state tuition scholarships to most freshmen entering the program. Students in the top 20 percent of their high school graduating class with a minimum SAT combined score of 1150 may be admitted to the University Honors Program. The Honors Council is particularly interested in students who have participated in educational, social, cultural, or other extracurricular projects or activities and whose applications suggest enthusiasm, a willingness to get involved, and leadership.

Scholarship Availability: Instead of a limited number of tuition and fees scholarships, Eastern will be offering tuition scholarships to virtually all freshmen accepted in the Honors Program.

The Campus Context: Eastern is located on a beautiful 175-acre campus on the edge of Willimantic, a New England mill town that produced internationally famous cotton thread and textile products in its heyday.

Student Body Eastern is a largely residential arts and sciences institution with approximately 4,500 full- and part-time students from every region of Connecticut, more than half of the U.S., and twenty other countries. This multicultural community thrives in Eastern's small college atmosphere in which students readily get to know each other and their faculty.

Athletics Eastern has a wide range of sports programs and facilities, and both the men's baseball and women's softball teams have won Division III NCAA national championships.

Tuition: $2062 for state residents, $6674 for nonresidents, $3094 for nonresidents eligible for the New England Regional Student Program, per year (1997-98)

Room and Board: $5048

Mandatory Fees: From $1532 to $2398

Contact: Director: Dr. Jim Lacey, Willimantic, Connecticut 06226; Telephone: 860-465-4317 or 4577; Fax: 860-465-4580; E-mail: lacey@ecsu.ctstateu.edu; Web site: http://www.ecsu.ctstateu.edu

EASTERN ILLINOIS UNIVERSITY

4 Pu G/D M Sc Tr

▼ **Honors Programs**

Eastern Illinois University offers superior students the opportunity to take part in two honors programs—University Honors, a lower division program and Departmental Honors, an upper division program. Both University and Departmental Honors Programs offer students of superior academic ability an unusual opportunity to develop their potential for intellectual achievement. These programs are intended to aid students in developing qualities such as independence of mind by undertaking an enriched curriculum that provides in-depth studies.

The University Honors Program is designed for those who begin as freshmen at Eastern. It provides honors sections of required general education courses and upper division colloquia. Students must take a minimum of 25 hours in honors courses, which will substitute on a one-for-one basis for current general education courses.

The Departmental Honors Program permits all eligible students, including transfer students, to participate in this division of the honors program. All departmental honors programs require a minimum of 12 hours of departmental honors credit. A senior thesis written under the supervision of honors faculty members is required.

The honors faculty members are devoted and experienced professors who enjoy their subjects and care about teaching talented students. Their teaching methods foster inquiry with an emphasis on undergraduate research. Honors faculty members grade students against norms established in regular classes. Students are aware that as a result of this arrangement they will not be penalized for taking classes with other superior students. Further, the intellectual stimulation of excellent teachers and outstanding classmates, together with smaller classes, tends to be reflected in good grades. Honors courses emphasize quality rather than quantity. However, they do cover more material in less time. Assignments are not merely more of the same, but encourage students to think, write, and express themselves with clarity. The excitement of exchanges within smaller classes and the stimulation of intellectual challenge make the question of workload irrelevant.

There are 500 students in the program. Students who join benefit from a centrally located honors residence hall, computer laboratory for use by honors students, study center, priority registration, priority textbook pickup, extensive scholarships, limited class size, active student-driven Association of Honors Students organization, and individualized attention.

Participation Requirements: University and Departmental Honors Programs are open to students who meet at least two of the following criteria: ACT composite of 26 or higher or SAT of 1100 or higher, upper 10 percent of high school graduating class, or 3.5 GPA on a four-point scale for at least 12 hours of course work undertaken at Eastern Illinois University.

The Campus Context: Eastern Illinois University, with a student population of 10,500, is the smallest of the residential state universities. It is situated in Charleston, a town of 20,000 people, and is 180 miles south of Chicago. The location is rural, nestled between glaciated and nonglaciated land.

The University has expanded to more than fifty-five majors and 100 options within those majors. The University is organized into four colleges: the College of Sciences, the College of Arts and Humanities, the College of Education and Professional Studies, and the Lumpkin College of Business and Applied Sciences. Eastern's strength lies in teaching and in professor-student contact. Class size generally runs from 25 to 40 students and, while Eastern does have a Graduate School, rarely do graduate students do the actual teaching of classes. The student-computer ratio is 13:1.

Faculty The faculty members total 659. Sixty-eight percent have doctoral or other terminal degrees. The student-faculty ratio is 17:1.

Key Facilities Student housing consists of modern residence halls, University apartments, and newly-built sorority and fraternity houses. Nearly 6,000 students live in University housing. After the freshman year, on-campus housing is optional. Students who choose to live off-campus do so in nearby private apartments. The campus itself is 360 acres, with buildings arranged in an easy-to-find manner. No classroom building is more than a 5-minute walk from any other.

Athletics Eastern Illinois is NCAA Division I in all sports except football, which is Division I-AA. Men's sports include baseball, basketball, cross-country, football, golf, soccer, swimming, tennis, track and field, and wrestling. Women's sports include basketball, golf, soccer, softball, swimming, tennis, track/cross-country, and volleyball.

Tuition: $2124 for state residents, $6372 for nonresidents, per year (1997-98 est.)

Room and Board: $3362

Mandatory Fees: $792

Contact: Director: Dr. Herbert Lasky, Booth House, Charleston, Illinois 61920; Telephone: 217-581-2017; Fax: 217-581-7222; E-mail: cfhxl@eiu.edu; Web site: http://oldsci.eiu.edu/cos/honors.html

---

EASTERN KENTUCKY UNIVERSITY

| 4 Pu G M Sc Tr |

▼ Honors Program

The Eastern Kentucky University (EKU) Honors Program has been designed especially for those intellectually promising students who seek a strong grounding in the liberal arts along with their more specialized major. Such students may be most at home in an intellectually intense, small-college atmosphere within the context of the larger University. Small class sizes of no more than 20 students per class allows for individualized attention and for one-on-one dialogue with the instructors. A distinctive feature of the Honors Program is that many courses are team-taught by professors from different disciplines. Such an approach contributes to the integration of knowledge,

and the program as a whole provides students with a necessary model of civilized intellectual interaction and allows students to see how ideas become enriched when approached from two different perspectives.

Students share with one another and with the faculty the pleasure and stimulation of outside speakers, films, suppers, trips to historical sites and cultural events, retreats, and state, regional, and national conferences. They have the opportunity of living in an honors hall and making use of an honors common room for study, informal meetings, classes, and programs they plan themselves. A computer network for working on class assignments is also available for students in the program.

The 28-credit-hour program offers courses that emphasize the development of skills in effective communication, critical thinking, and the integration of knowledge from various disciplines. All course work in the EKU Honors Program meets University general education requirements. Therefore, regardless of major, any qualified student can participate in the program.

Fourth-year honors scholars complete a senior-level thesis and seminar. This thesis project can take whatever form suits the subject (e.g., a research paper, a creative composition or art work, a performance or recital). Each student works with a faculty mentor who offers guidance and support throughout the development of the thesis project.

Students who successfully complete the EKU Honors Program curriculum are designated Honors Scholars when they graduate, and the phrase appears on their diplomas and on their official transcripts from the University.

There are currently 120 students in the program.

Admission Process: Students with strong academic backgrounds are invited to apply to the Honors Program. National Merit Finalists and Semi-Finalists are automatically accepted. Beyond these, students with high school GPAs of 3.5 or better on a 4.0 scale and with at least a score of 26 on the American College Test are given priority. Other students demonstrating the potential for outstanding academic performance are considered.

Scholarship Availability: Abundant opportunities for scholarships exist under Eastern's academic scholarship program, and students interested in scholarship aid should apply directly to that program.

The Campus Context: EKU is situated in Richmond, an urban college community of about 25,000 people within a rich farming area. Inter- and intra-state highway systems enhance Richmond's accessibility. Interstate 75 passes within a mile of campus, and Interstate 64 is only 30 minutes away. The Blue Grass and Mountain Parkways are also less than an hour's drive from Richmond. Places of historic and scenic interest surround the University. Richmond, 20 miles south of Lexington on I-75, is within easy driving distance of Boonesborough State Park, Kentucky Horse Park, Herrington

Lake, Cumberland Falls, the State Capitol at Frankfort, Natural Bridge State Park, and My Old Kentucky Home in Bardstown. Students are enrolled in twenty-one associate degree programs, eighty-four baccalaureate programs, and thirty master's degree programs.

Student Body There are 13,657 undergraduates, of whom 57 percent are women. The student body is comprised of 4 percent African American, 1 percent Asian, and less than 1 percent Hispanic and American Indian/Alaskan students. One hundred eighty international students complete this diverse population. Seventy-five percent of students receive financial aid.

Faculty There are 628 full-time faculty members; 68 percent hold doctorates or other terminal degrees.

Key Facilities The library contains 900,000 volumes. Computer labs are available in most academic buildings and PCs are available in dorm lobbies, the library, and the student center.

Athletics Eastern is a member of the Ohio Valley Conference and supports eight varsity sports for men (football in division IAA, basketball, baseball, tennis, golf, cross-country, indoor and outdoor track) and eight varsity sports for women (volleyball, basketball, softball, tennis, golf, cross-country, indoor and outdoor track). A wide range of intramural sports are offered for both men and women.

Study Abroad Students may study in Europe through the Kentucky Institute for International Studies (KIIS), a consortium of Kentucky colleges and universities. KIIS operates a network of summer programs in Munich, Germany; Salzburg and Bregenz, Austria; Nimes and Paris, France; Florence, Italy; Madrid, Spain; and Mexico. Each of these programs offers a variety of academic courses, which students may take for University credit. Students may study in Britain through the Cooperative Center for Study in Britain (CCSB), a consortium of Kentucky colleges and universities. Students may take courses during Christmas vacation in London, a two-week course in May in Ireland, and a five-week course in the summer in England. They may also enroll in a junior-year abroad program or enroll for a semester in Oxford. Costs vary according to program.

Job Opportunities Students are offered a range of work opportunities on campus, including federal and institutional work-study and graduate assistantships.

Tuition and Fees: $1740 for state residents, $5220 for nonresidents, per year (1996-97)

Room and Board: $2706 minimum

Mandatory Fees: $230

Contact: Director: Dr. Bonnie J. Gray, 168 Case Annex, Richmond, Kentucky 40475; Telephone: 606-622-1403; Fax: 606-622-1020; E-mail: hongray@acs.eku.edu; Web site: www.csc.eku.edu/honors

EASTERN WASHINGTON UNIVERSITY

4 Pu G M Sc Tr

▼ **Honors Program**

Honors at Eastern Washington University (EWU) cultivates excellence in undergraduate education by providing enhanced educational opportunities to superior students and special teaching opportunities to outstanding faculty members.

Honors courses and honors activities seek to develop excellent writing, calculation, and critical-thinking skills through knowledge and appreciation of the liberal arts and sciences and inspire an attitude of self-responsibility, lifelong intellectual development, and engagement with the world. Admission to Honors at Eastern is based entirely on demonstrated and potential intellectual and academic qualifications.

There are approximately 275 students in the program, including freshmen, junior-college transfers, and continuing upper-division students. Seventy-five freshmen are admitted each fall.

Participation Requirements: Honors at Eastern has both general and departmental course work components. General honors emphasizes academic excellence in liberal arts curriculum areas. The freshman honors sequence of 24 credits is interdisciplinary in nature. It satisfies 6 of the 9 EWU general education core requirements. University honors seminars encourage students to consider a field of study from a specific perspective and develop research and composition skills. Departmental honors emphasize academic excellence in a student's major. Students enrich selected major courses for honors credit under the direction of departmental faculty members.

Students earning a departmental or university honors designation in conjunction with their degree complete two honors 398 courses and develop an original honors senior project in their major, which is written and presented under faculty direction.

Admission Process: Students complete the honors section on the EWU general scholarship application and/or apply directly with their academic goals statement, recommendation, and transcript. Applicants are encouraged to visit, but an interview is not mandatory. Final selection is made by the third week of May. In general, students invited to participate in freshman honors have a GPA of 3.6 or higher and a combined SAT score of at least 1080 or a comprehensive ACT score of at least 24.

Incoming freshmen should apply to the program by January 15 for priority.

Scholarship Availability: More than 85 percent of the 75 honors freshmen have a scholarship or an assistantship in their academic interest area.

The Campus Context: Eastern's main campus spreads over 300 tree-shaded acres just 18 miles from downtown Spokane, where there are two branch locations for several majors as well as an intercollegiate technology institute. The 1996 edition of *Money Guide: Your Best College Buys Now*, published by *Money Magazine*, ranks EWU fifteenth among colleges and universities in the western states in the "Best Buys in Your Area" category. Eastern recently initiated a four-year guaranteed degree contract for selected majors; freshman honors is an integrated way to satisfy core requirements. Undergraduate majors leading to the baccalaureate include liberal arts and social sciences, business, education, nursing, science, mathematics, and technology.

Student Body The current enrollment is 8,076, comprised of 6,800 undergraduates, 564 postbaccalaureate students, and 712 graduate students; the majority are from Washington state.

Faculty Of the 416 full-time faculty members, 62 percent have doctoral or other terminal degrees. The student-faculty ratio is 18:1.

Key Facilities John F. Kennedy library houses more than 700,000 volumes and maintains more than 5,000 subscriptions to periodicals, newspapers, and serials. There are 375 Macintosh and DOS computers at the library, academic departments, and Spokane academic program and technology sites.

Athletics EWU is a member of the NCAA Division I, Big Sky Conference. Men compete in football, basketball, cross-country, track and field, tennis, and golf. Women compete in volleyball, basketball, cross-country, track and field, tennis, and golf. EWU also offers a wide range of intramural sports as well as an outstanding outdoor recreation program with climbing, kayaking, rafting, canoeing, and backpacking.

Study Abroad Global studies are promoted at Eastern Washington. EWU offers study and internships abroad for all majors. Students may opt for an international experience of a semester, summer, or full year and receive regular credit toward their degree.

Job Opportunities Eastern Washington University offers paid and unpaid internships in the Northwest. Students may work on campus through assistantships and the work-study program.

Tuition: $2430 for state residents, $8610 for nonresidents, per year (1996-97)

Room and Board: $4294

Mandatory Fees: $15

Contact: Director: Dr. Perry Higman, Cheney, Washington 99004; Telephone: 509-359-2822; Fax: 509-359-6044

EDINBORO UNIVERSITY OF PENNSYLVANIA

4 Pu C S Sc Tr

▼ Honors Program

Course contracts, designated honors courses, and independent study are the means by which Edinboro University honors students earn honors credit. When combined, these elements permit the flexibility necessary to accommodate individual student needs in a variety of disciplines. Independent study encourages research and fosters creativity, while course contracts and honors seminars build learning communities.

Program-sponsored trips to places such as Washington, D.C., expand program borders and encourage students to discover larger communities. Honors gives global dimensions to community and widens the scope for significant academic applications.

Begun in 1974, the program currently enrolls 100 students.

Participation Requirements: To earn a University Honors degree, a program participant must successfully complete 21 semester hours of honors credit and maintain a 3.5 overall cumulative GPA. Honors credit hours are taken as part of the student's degree program and are not additional credits earned above the 128 credits required for most degrees at Edinboro. A diploma citation recognizes successful University Honors Program completion as does participation in an Honors Convocation.

Scholarship Availability: Entering freshmen with strong credentials who may be potential honors students may apply for the following scholarships: The Presidential Honors Scholarship, the Freshman Honors Scholarship, the General Telephone Company of Pennsylvania Honors Scholarship, and the Crowe Freshman Honors Scholarship. Upperclassmen in the honors program may apply for Upperclassman Honors Scholarships, which are awarded on a semester-by-semester basis. Money for these awards is provided by the Grace A. Crowe Fund, the Dollars for Honors Fund, and the GTE Honors Fund.

The Campus Context: Offering 122 degree programs, Edinboro University is a 585-acre campus that includes a 5-acre lake, open fields and woods, eight on-campus residence halls for approximately 2,700 students, and a modern seven-story library.

Student Body Edinboro University of Pennsylvania enrolls 7,477 students, 42 percent men and 58 percent women. The ethnic distribution of minority students is 5 percent African American, 1 percent Hispanic, 1 percent Asian, and 2 percent international. Eighty-five percent of students receive financial aid. There are seven national fraternities and five national sororities on campus.

Faculty Of the 313 total faculty members, 287 are full-time, of whom 62 percent have terminal degrees. The student-faculty ratio is 17:1.

Key Facilities The library houses 431,935 books, 1.5 million microfilm titles, and 1,878 periodicals. There are 218 computers for student use in the computer center, computer labs, library, student center, and dorms. They provide access to the main academic computer, off-campus computing facilities, e-mail, and Internet. The staffed computer lab on campus provides training in the use of software. Academic computing expenditure is more than $1 million.

Athletics In athletics, Edinboro is a member of NCAA Division II (except wrestling, which is Division I). Intercollegiate sports are baseball (men's), basketball (men's/women's), cross-country (m/w), football (m), golf (m), soccer (w), softball (w), swimming and diving (m/w), tennis (m/w), track and field (m/w), volleyball (w), and wrestling (m). Intramural sports are badminton, basketball, football, golf, racquetball, soccer, softball, volleyball, and wrestling.

Study Abroad The University Honors Program has offered summer honors study abroad for the past ten years at Oxford University. Study-abroad opportunities remain a feature of the program. Edinboro University offers selected general summer study-abroad opportunities in various countries each year.

Support Services The Office of Disabled Student Services administers a program dedicated to enhancing the University's commitment to equal opportunity for the severely physically disabled. The campus supports the largest residency program of its kind in the commonwealth of Pennsylvania, and the disabled population is one of the largest in the entire United States. Edinboro's disabled students and many visitors benefit from a campus that is almost completely accessible to the handicapped.

Job Opportunities Students who need employment to pay for college expenses are potentially eligible for employment by Edinboro University under the Federal Work-Study Program. Students may work while attending classes full-time. Full-time students average 15 hours per week employment at a minimum wage. Net wages during the academic year are $1700. This amount, through weekly earnings during the school year, could help provide total educational costs, including necessary clothes, transportation, and personal services. Work may be for Edinboro University or for an approved off-campus agency. On-campus jobs may include work in offices, laboratories, the library, maintenance, and the dormitories.

Off-campus jobs are assigned in public or private nonprofit organizations. To work under this program, students must be enrolled or be accepted for enrollment as full-time students at Edinboro University. Eligibility depends upon their need for employment to defray college expenses, with preference given to applicants from low-income families. The Pennsylvania State Grant and Federal Aid Application and the Edinboro University Financial Aid Application are required.

Tuition: $3368 for state residents, $8566 for nonresidents, per year (1996-97)

Room and Board: $3616

Mandatory Fees: $700

Contact: Director: Ted Atkinson, Earp Hall, Edinboro, Pennsylvania 16444; Telephone: 814-732-2981; Fax: 814-732-2982; E-mail: atkinsont@edinboro.edu

EL CAMINO COLLEGE

2 Pu G M Sc

▼ Honors Transfer Program

The El Camino College (ECC) Honors Transfer Program (HTP) offers highly motivated students the opportunity to participate in an academic community where they interact with outstanding faculty members and other students who have the goals to obtain a quality education, be better prepared to transfer to a four-year university, and pursue a bachelor's degree. The HTP is a collegewide program appropriate for all eligible students taking transferable courses.

Twelve to fourteen sections of honors courses are offered each semester. These are primarily general education courses in the fields of art, astronomy, economics, English, history, music, philosophy, and political science. The enrollment in honors classes is limited to about 75 percent of the enrollment for other classes. On rare occasions, honors contract courses are allowed to accommodate special academic needs. The HTP, in conjunction with the Study Abroad Program, allows interested students to do honors work while studying abroad. The College typically runs either two or three study-abroad programs each year.

A cornerstone of the program is the high level of support it receives from several major universities; they offer priority admission guarantees to students who complete the requirements of the HTP. These honors transfer agreements have been established between the HTP and the California State University at Dominguez Hills; Chapman University; Occidental College; Pepperdine University; Pomona College; the University of California at Irvine, Los Angeles, Riverside, and Santa Cruz; and the University of Southern California.

The HTP has an excellent track record for transferring students to the university of their choice. Over the past several years, almost 100 percent of students who completed the program and applied to the universities listed above were accepted.

In addition to the priority admission guarantees offered by the universities listed above, students who complete the HTP have graduation with honors designated on their associate degrees and completion of honors designated on their transcripts. These students have increased chances of receiving scholarships. Some universities offer transfer scholarships designated only for students who have completed community college honors programs while others offer priority consideration for their regular transfer scholarships.

Benefits offered to HTP members prior to their completion of the program include honors membership designated on transcripts each semester and priority registration in all El Camino College classes. Students have opportunities to serve on HTP student committees such as the Newsletter Committee and the Activities Committee. Special privileges are offered by the universities with which ECC has honors transfer agreements. Examples include an organized Honors Transfer Day visit to campuses, use of libraries, priority scholarship consideration, and complimentary opportunities to attend academic, cultural, and athletic events.

The HTP is twelve years old and has a membership of approximately 250 students. Each academic year begins with a welcome reception for new members and their families. A reception at the end of each academic year is held to honor students completing the program and transferring to a university. At this reception students receive a certificate of completion. Special certificates and plaques are given to selected students to recognize outstanding academic achievement in honors and outstanding contributions to the honors program.

Participation Requirements: Each semester students are required to complete at least one honors course, maintain a minimum 3.0 cumulative GPA, and attend at least four honors enrichment seminars. New students must complete English 1A their first semester in the program.

To complete the HTP students must complete at least six honors courses, maintain a minimum 3.0 cumulative GPA, be a member of the HTP for a minimum of three semesters, and complete the requirements necessary to transfer as a junior.

Admission Process: The requirements for admission to the HTP are a minimum 3.0 cumulative GPA from high school or from at least nine academic units in college and eligibility for English 1A Freshman Composition.

The Campus Context: El Camino College is a public two-year community college in the state of California. Founded in 1947, ECC is located in a suburban setting about 15 miles southwest of Los Angeles. In its mission to offer quality, comprehensive educational opportunities to its diverse community, the College offers a wide variety of vocational and academic programs leading to an Associate of Science or an Associate of Arts degree. A certificate of completion or a certificate of competence may be obtained in many vocational areas. El Camino offers the A.S. transfer (twenty-eight majors), A.S. vocational (thirty-five majors), A.A. transfer and/or vocational (thirty-four majors).

El Camino was fully accredited in 1996. The accreditation evaluation team wrote that the College was commended for its demonstrated and continuing commitment to being a College that is "of" and "for" its community, not just "in" the community. The College presents students and citizens with a constellation of cultural, educational, and activity experiences, which are increasingly responsive to a diverse community. Among special facilities, the campus has an excellent planetarium, an Anthropology Museum giving students hands-on curating, and a Child Development Center.

Student Body Undergraduate enrollment is 22,700, of whom 7,300 (26 percent) are full-time-equivalent students. Men comprise 45 percent of the student body. Students have an average age of 27, and all students are commuters. The ethnic distribution at ECC is 28 percent Caucasian, 21 percent African American, 25 percent Hispanic, 15 percent Asian, and 11 percent other. International students comprise 2 percent of the student population. Ten percent of students receive financial aid. While there are no fraternities or sororities on campus, there are more than fifty active academic, service, social, cultural, and religious clubs.

Faculty Of the 805 faculty members, 310 are full-time, and 495 are part-time. Twenty percent of the faculty members hold terminal degrees. The student-faculty ratio is 28:1 or 15:1 if based on full-time-equivalent faculty and students.

Key Facilities The library houses 112,000 volumes. Computer facilities include about thirty labs of varying size that contain a total of about 850 computers.

Athletics El Camino College offers an extremely wide variety of athletic programs, including many adaptive physical education programs and a fully equipped exercise laboratory and wellness center for student, faculty, and staff training and testing. Intercollegiate athletics for men include baseball, basketball, cross-country, football, golf, soccer, swimming, tennis, track and field, volleyball, and water polo. Intercollegiate athletics for women include basketball, cross-country, soccer, softball, swimming, tennis, track and field, volleyball, and water polo.

Support Services The El Camino College campus is totally accessible to disabled students. The Special Resources Center provides comprehensive individual need-based assistance (services, equipment, and/or instruction) for students with any physical or learning disability. The High Tech Center provides alternative input/output devices and instruction enabling students to access computers regardless of their disability.

Job Opportunities Work opportunities on campus range from $5.25 to $20 per hour. The Job Placement Center assists students in finding both on- and off-campus positions.

Tuition: None for state residents, $3510 for nonresidents, per year (1996-97)

Mandatory Fees: $410

Contact: Director: Dr. Robert S. McLeod, 16007 Crenshaw Blvd., Torrance, California 90506; Telephone: 310-660-3815; Fax: 310-660-3818; E-mail: rmcleod@admin.elcamino.cc.ca.us; Web site: http://www.elcamino.cc.ca.us

ELON COLLEGE

4 Pr G M Sc Tr

▼ **Honors Program**

The Elon College Honors Program offers students challenging and unique learning opportunities, small classes, mentor relationships with faculty members, and opportunities for research. Students develop better critical thinking skills, independence, and a sense of community. Established in 1977, the program now has 325 students, which makes up 8–10 percent of the student body.

This program, while open to all qualified students, gains most of its participants through freshman-level scholarships. Monies are retained as long as students remain in good standing in the Honors Program. Nonscholarship lateral-entry students are encouraged to join the program. North Carolina Teaching Fellows are required to participate in the program their first year; Science Fellows are required to remain in the program in order to keep Science Fellow scholarships.

Courses in the program satisfy general degree requirements and are available at all levels and in most disciplines. Approximately seven to ten honors classes are offered each semester and one each winter term. Entering honors students are required to complete 25 hours of honors experiences, including a 1-hour orientation seminar and a 4-hour general studies course entitled "The Global Experience." Other honors experiences are optional and are of the student's choosing. Additional hours come from studies abroad, experiential credit, honors sections of classes, non-honors for honors option, and advanced-level general studies seminars.

Freshmen attend an off-campus retreat to learn more about the honors program. Juniors have the opportunity to attend an off-campus retreat to learn more about graduate school, scholarships, and their senior seminar options. Two honors housing communities exist, and students actively participate in a mentor program for first-year students and other Honors Program activities. Undergraduate research is encouraged, as is participation in national, regional, and state honors conferences. A $500 Intercultural Travel Grant is available to those students studying abroad or participating in intercultural domestic travel.

Participation Requirements: To graduate, students must complete the 25 hours of honors credit and maintain a 3.2 overall GPA. Graduating Honors Fellows are recognized at a pregraduation ceremony. Successful completion of the program is noted at graduation and is recorded on the student's transcript.

Admission Process: Qualified students are invited to participate in Scholarship Day, where they come to campus, participate in an honors seminar, write an essay based on the seminar, and are interviewed by faculty. Honors money is awarded to the majority of this group. Those receiving honors scholarships are admitted into the Honors Program the following fall. General applications are accepted through June.

The Campus Context: Established in 1889, Elon's historic campus, located in the heart of the Central Piedmont, is within an hour's driving distance from Greensboro, Raleigh/ Durham, and Chapel Hill, North Carolina. The College is designed and equipped to serve its learning community with twenty-four academic and administrative buildings and sixteen residence halls. Degree programs at Elon include the Bachelor of Arts (thirty majors), the Bachelor of Fine Arts (one major), the Bachelor of Science (thirteen majors), the Master of Business Administration, and the Master of Education.

Student Body Elon College is a four-year, coeducational liberal arts institution with approximately 3,260 undergraduates and 180 graduate students. Men comprise approximately 40 percent of the student population. There are currently 54 international students enrolled at Elon, and 4 percent of students are from minority groups. There are nineteen fraternities and sororities and eighteen national and departmental honors organizations on campus. Many clubs and organizations, including the newspaper, the literary magazine, campus radio and television stations, and the yearbook are also available to students.

Faculty Elon has 140 full-time and 78 part-time faculty members, of whom 76 percent hold terminal degrees. The student-faculty ratio is 18:1.

Key Facilities The library contains nearly 186,000 books, more than 555,000 microfilms/fiches, and 3,645 film/video and computer files. There are six computer labs containing IBM/PC and Macintosh computers, a Learning Resource Center, a Writing Center, eleven science laboratories, and eight fine arts laboratories on campus.

Athletics Elon College is a member of NCAA Division II. Athletic teams include men's and women's basketball, tennis, soccer, and cross-country; men's football, baseball, golf, and track; and women's volleyball and softball.

Study Abroad Thirty-two percent of Elon students study abroad. Elon offers fall and spring semester programs in London, Spain, Australia, Japan, and South America; winter term travel options to England/Scotland, Ireland, Europe, France, Australia, Mexico, Belize, Costa Rica, Ghana, and Italy; and summer travel to Israel, China, and India.

Support Services All buildings on campus are handicapped-accessible. Help is available for students with learning disabilities through the Academic Advising Center.

Tuition: $10,477 per year (1996-97)

Room and Board: $4170

Mandatory Fees: $190

Contact: Director: Dr. Dan Wright, Elon College, North Carolina 27244; Telephone: 910-584-2296

EMERSON COLLEGE

4 Pr G S Sc Tr

▼ Honors Program

The Emerson College Honors Program is a community of undergraduate scholars who pursue interdisciplinary study in the liberal arts and in the fields of communication and the performing arts. The four-year Honors Program is available to 45 entering students a year and a small number of transfers with outstanding ability. All students in the program receive a Trustee Scholarship. Honors Program students enjoy early registration privileges. Honors Program faculty members excel in teaching and are active researchers, artists, and professionals across the disciplines.

The first two seminars fulfill the College's general education requirements and are team-taught in small discussion-based classes comprised of 15 students and 2 professors. The Freshman Honors Seminar introduces Emerson students to the interdisciplinary study of communication with an emphasis on speaking and writing. The seminar addresses the relationship between communication, power, and social action in various multicultural contexts, including those in Boston. The Sophomore Honors Seminar acquaints students with the methods of scientific reasoning and the philosophy of science and addresses issues of ethics and values in an interdisciplinary manner.

The Junior Seminar represents an opportunity to become acquainted with the theories and methodologies inherent in the student's chosen concentration. It insures that students work closely with a professor in their field in preparation for the senior thesis/project. The Honors Program director and each student's major adviser work with seniors in the completion of their year-long concentrated research or creative project. Seniors meet in workshops where they critique each other's work. Just before graduation, they present their completed work in a Senior Project Showcase before the entire community. Each year one student is granted the Honors Program Senior Project Award.

Participation Requirements: Honors work includes the year-long freshman and sophomore seminars, a one-semester junior seminar in the student's major field of study, and a senior thesis project. Students fulfill six general education requirements upon the completion of four semesters of interdisciplinary work. To graduate from the Honors Program, students must have a 3.3 GPA overall, a 3.0 GPA in Honors Seminars, and complete the senior thesis/project. Successful completion of the Honors Program requirements is noted at graduation and is recorded on the student's transcript.

Admission Process: High school seniors who maintain outstanding academic records and achievement in school and/or community affairs and seek an additional intellectual challenge at the college level may be invited to participate in the Emerson College Honors Program. To be considered, applicants must complete the regular application procedures listed for first-year students by February 1, including the honors essay. Transfer students may enter the program no later than the first term of their sophomore year.

The Campus Context: Founded in 1880 by noted orator Charles Wesley Emerson and located in the urban setting surrounding the Boston Common, Emerson has grown into a comprehensive college offering its more than 2,600 students undergraduate and graduate curricula in the communication arts and sciences and the performing arts. The original concentration on oratory has evolved into specialization in such fields as mass communication (radio and television broadcasting, film, and journalism), theater arts, communication studies, communication disorders, and writing, literature, and publishing.

Student Body Undergraduate enrollment is 2,200. Fifty-eight percent of the students are women. Ethnic minorities, including African American, Hispanic, Asian, and Native American students, constitute 11 percent of the student population. There are also 300 international students currently attending Emerson. The College is comprised of 90 percent resident students. Seventy-five percent of students receive financial aid.

Faculty There are 92 full-time faculty members and 175 adjunct faculty members. Seventy-five percent of all faculty members have terminal degrees. The student-faculty ratio is 16:1.

Key Facilities The library houses 175,000 print and nonprint items and is a member of the Fenway Library Consortium. The Media Center includes 16,300 films, videotapes, phonodiscs, compact disks, phonotapes, and other media. Two academic computer centers contain both Macintosh and IBM PC/compatible microcomputer labs with direct access to a DEC VAX 4500 time-sharing system.

Athletics Varsity and club programs include men's baseball; women's softball and volleyball; men's and women's basketball, soccer, and tennis; and coed golf. Intramural and recreational programs include basketball, tag football, volleyball, aerobics, and weight training.

Study Abroad Students may study overseas at Kasteel Well, located in eastern Holland near the German border. Study is combined with extensive travel and exploring the cultural and historical offerings in several major cities of Europe.

Tuition: $17,376 per year (1997-98)

Room and Board: $8250

Fees: $450

Contact: Director: Dr. Flora M. Gonzàlez, 100 Beacon Street, Boston, Massachusetts 02116; Telephone: 617-824-7872; Fax: 617-824-7857; E-mail: fgonzalez@emerson.edu; Web site: http://www.emerson.edu/admiss/

ERIE COMMUNITY COLLEGE

2 Pu G M

▼ **Honors Program**

Erie Community College is a three-campus SUNY community college. The Honors Program, which has members on each campus, is designed to enhance the education of students showing particular academic ability and interest. It is open to students in all majors but is most accessible to students in the liberal arts and sciences and other programs specifically designed for transfer to four-year institutions since honors courses are liberal arts and science electives.

Honors courses are either selected from general course offerings or represent a special interest topic of a faculty member. Four interdisciplinary honors seminar courses have been developed and are offered on a rotating basis. The Honors Colloquium, which is a 1-credit course and must be taken for three semesters, is really the central focus of the program. Each semester a theme is selected and lectures, tours, and other activities related to the theme are planned. Since there is an honors group at each of the three college campuses, activities that bring the groups together are planned each semester. These include a talent show and The Honors Great Debates, where the campuses debate each other. As part of the colloquium, students are committed to 10 hours of community service per semester.

While all classes at ECC are small, honors courses are limited to 25 students, and faculty members attempt to make the courses more student-oriented. Students are asked to do more writing and to be more self-directed in their studies. Students in the program are required to take a minimum of six honors courses during their time at the College plus three semesters of honors colloquium. The honors coordinator at a student's campus acts as that student's adviser, ensuring that the requirements are met for honors, the student's degree, and transfer. The relationship among the students in the program and between the students and the coordinator is very close. The students feel very much a part of a learning community and report that, rather than a sense of competition, there is a sense of cooperation that helps them succeed.

Graduates receive special recognition at an awards banquet, wear gold braids at Commencement, and have annotated transcripts.

Instituted in 1987, there are currently about 100 students in the program. The Honors Program maintains a maximum of only 35 students per campus.

Participation Requirements: In order to graduate from the Honors Program, students must complete six honors courses, complete three semesters of colloquium, maintain a 3.25 overall GPA and a 3.0 GPA in honors courses, and complete 10 hours per semester of community service.

Admission Process: Students may apply to the program at the time of admission. Placement test scores are used to invite students to apply at admission, and faculty recommendations are used to invite students in their first or second semester. An interview is required.

Scholarships Availability: There are no scholarships specifically designated as honors scholarships.

The Campus Context: Erie Community College is a three-campus community college in the State University of New York system offering sixty-nine registered degree programs. The City Campus is located in downtown Buffalo, New York, and serves the urban population of the city. North Campus is a suburban campus, located north of Buffalo in Williamsville, and South Campus is a suburban/rural campus south of Buffalo in Orchard Park.

Student Body Of the 13,000 students, about half attend the North Campus and one-fourth attend each of the City and South Campuses. Fifty-four percent of the students are women. The ethnic distribution of the student body is 84 percent Caucasian, 11 percent African American, 3 percent Hispanic, 1 percent Asian, less than 1 percent Native American, and less than 1 percent international students. All students are commuters, and 55 percent of students receive financial aid. There are eighty-seven clubs and organizations across the three campuses.

Faculty There are 419 full-time and 989 part-time faculty members. The student-faculty ratio is 22:1.

Key Facilities Three Learning Resource Centers contain a total of 145,000 volumes, 1,100 periodical subscriptions, and 12,000 videocassettes, slides, and computer disks. ECC also has academic computing facilities, computer teaching labs, student tutoring stations, and computer integrated manufacturing.

Athletics Athletics on campus include nationally recognized teams in basketball, softball, hockey and bowling. There are collegiate, extramural, and intramural teams. The City Campus Burt Flickinger Athletic Center, which opened in June 1994, was built to house swimming and other events for the World University Games. It houses an Olympic-size swimming pool with a movable floor, a 25-meter warm-up pool, three regulation basketball courts, a large field house that seats 3,000, an indoor jogging track, and a wellness center. The other campuses also have outstanding athletic facilities.

Support Services There are extensive facilities available for disabled students through the Disabled Students Services Office.

Job Opportunities Work-study opportunities are available through the financial aid office. There are also employment opportunities as student assistants and tutors.

Tuition: $2500 for state residents, $5000 for nonresidents, per year (1996-97)

Mandatory Fees: $100

Contact: Coordinator, South Campus: Dr. Diane R. Schulman, 4041 Southwestern Blvd., Orchard Park, New York 14127; Telephone: 716-851-1795; Fax: 716-851-1629; E-mail: schulmdr@ snybufaa.cs.snybuf.edu; Coordinator, City Campus: William Schuh; Telephone: 716-851-1580; Coordinator, North Campus: Marci Sellers; Telephone: 716-851-1334

FASHION INSTITUTE OF TECHNOLOGY

`2&4 Pu G S`

▼ Presidential Scholars Program

The Presidential Scholars Program at the Fashion Institute of Technology (FIT) is designed to give our highest-achieving students an opportunity to have a dialogue with exceptional students from all majors in the college and to discuss ideas and theories in the liberal arts. The Presidential Scholars Program has two components: specially designed liberal arts courses and a noncredit colloquium. The 10-year-old program enrolls approximately 65 students per semester.

Participation Requirements: Students may participate in the program during their third or fourth semesters and/or in the upper division, which is the third and fourth years. Presidential Scholars courses may be substituted for required liberal arts courses.

Each semester students may choose from among three liberal arts courses. Courses range from an interdisciplinary study of New York City to Greek myths and their transformations to the Bauhaus. In the luncheon colloquium, students from all the honors courses gather to participate in discussion groups and lectures addressing issues related to social, economic, and cultural concerns of the day.

Admission Process: Students invited to be Presidential Scholars must have a cumulative GPA of 3.5 or higher.

The Campus Context: The college occupies a $115-million campus in midtown Manhattan where the worlds of fashion, art, design, communications, and manufacturing converge. There are twenty-five degree programs on campus. The Museum at FIT is the repository of the world's largest collection of costumes, textiles, and accessories of dress. The Office of Special Programs facilitates student access to the professional activities of the "fashion capital of the world" by arranging field trips and inviting prominent guest speakers to the college.

Student Body The number of full-time students is 5,059; the number of part-time students is 7,584. Of the total number, 20 percent of the students are men. Thirty percent of students live on campus, and 64 percent receive financial aid.

Faculty There are 931 faculty members, of whom 181 are full-time. The student-faculty ratio is 14:1.

Key Facilities The library contains more than 115,000 titles, including books, periodicals, and nonprint materials.

Support Services FIT provides support services for learning disabled students.

Job Opportunities The Federal Work-Study Program and institutional employment provide opportunities for work on campus. Off-campus part-time employment opportunities are excellent.

Tuition: $2400 minimum for state residents, $5750 minimum for nonresidents, per year (1996-97)

Room and Board: $5340

Mandatory Fees: $210

Contact: Director: Dr. Irene Buchman, Seventh Avenue at 27th Street, New York, New York 10001; Telephone: 212-760-7994; Fax: 212-760-7965; E-mail: buchmani@sfitva.cc.fitsuny.edu

FELICIAN COLLEGE

`4 Pr G S Sc Tr`

▼ Honors Program

The Felician College Honors Program is open to all academically superior students in all majors who are pursuing associate or baccalaureate degrees regardless of their enrollment status. The Honors Program began in January 1991 and is currently in its sixth year. There are 40 students in the program.

Participation Requirements: Students take the honors sections of the required English courses—Rhetoric and Composition I and II—and honors sections of core courses. All of the core courses are interdisciplinary; focus on content as well as the competencies of critical thinking, written and verbal communication, and social interaction; and center on the theme of "the search for the good life." The honors sections emphasize an extensive use of primary sources and the study of specialized topics. Students take each of the following 3-credit honors sections: "Close Encounters with the Arts" and "Science and the Age of Revolutions" in their freshman year, "The Human Species" in their sophomore year, and "Our Search for Wholeness: An Invitation to Philosophize" in their junior year.

One-credit honors seminars are offered each semester. They are interdisciplinary in nature and are frequently team-taught. Examples include "The French Revolution," "The United States in the 1960s," "Biotechnology," "The Evolution of Language," and "Teleology and Human Existence."

Service learning, consisting of a minimum of 15 hours per semester of relevant, related community involvement, is a part of each honors course. Students complete a reflective paper centering on the relationship of their service to a theme, work, or theory studied in the course.

In their junior or senior year, honors students who have completed 9 or more credits of honors courses may apply to the College's Honors Advisory Board, which meets monthly, to take a nonhonors course for honors credit. The instructor gives a description of how the student's syllabus will reflect the honors-caliber work that would merit the receipt of honors credit.

All graduating seniors in the arts and sciences division complete a senior research project and present it orally before the College community. Honors students may opt to work with a professor and produce an original work of research of honors quality, which will be read before presentation by a faculty member in two disciplines outside of the major.

Each spring, honors students receive certificates at the annual Honors and Service Learning Dinner. All graduating seniors who complete the program are designated as honors scholars and receive a trophy and certificate at the Graduation Dinner, which is held the evening before commencement. They wear a gold medallion inscribed with the word honor and attached to a ribbon with the College's colors. The words honors scholar appear in calligraphy on the diploma near a specially embossed gold College seal.

Admission Process: Newly admitted students to the College are eligible to enter the Honors Program based on their high school averages, SAT scores, and their rank in their graduating class. Transfer students with 40 or fewer credits from other institutions of higher learning may enter the program using the same criteria as well as an evaluation of their other college grades. Current freshmen and first-semester sophomores may be accepted into the program upon application and interview or if placed on the Dean's List for two semesters. Students in the Honors Program are expected to maintain a 3.2 GPA or higher each semester and achieve at least a "B" in all honors courses.

Scholarship Availability: A variety of scholarships are available for students who meet the criteria for each award. Many of the recipients of scholarships offered by the College are in the College's Honors Program.

The Campus Context: Felician College is a four-year, Catholic, coeducational, liberal arts college located in northern New Jersey. There are three academic divisions—arts and sciences, health sciences, and teacher education. The College offers the following degree programs: one master's degree (M.S.) in nursing, thirteen bachelor's degrees (B.A.) in liberal arts and education, three bachelor's degrees (B.S.) in business administration and health sciences, two associate degrees (A.A.S.) in health sciences, and one associate degree (A.A.) in liberal arts.

Felician College is situated in Lodi on the banks of the Saddle River, which winds through the College's beautifully landscaped campus of 27 acres. Located near New York City and other cultural centers in New Jersey and Connecticut, the College is easily accessible and offers students a variety of educational and cultural resources.

Student Body Felician College currently enrolls 1,200 undergraduates. The majority of these students are from northern New Jersey. Eighty-four percent of the students are women. The ethnic distribution of the students is 6 percent Asian/Pacific Islander, 8 percent African American, 14 percent Hispanic, and 72 percent Caucasian. International students comprise 12 percent of the College's population. All students commute, and approximately 50 percent of students receive financial aid. There are one sorority and one fraternity on campus.

Faculty There are 50 full-time faculty members, 68 percent of whom hold doctoral or terminal degrees. There are also approximately 57 adjunct faculty members. The student-faculty ratio is 12:1.

Key Facilities The College library houses 130,000 books and 760 periodical subscriptions. Ninety PC computers are available on campus in three computer labs, the biology lab, the writing lab, the business lab, the psychology lab, the nursing skills lab, the Center for Learning, and the library. There are ten Macintosh computers available in the art room.

Athletics The College participates in the National Association of Intercollegiate Athletics in men's and women's basketball, men's soccer, and women's softball.

Study Abroad The Felician College Honors program offers study abroad opportunities through the Office of Study Abroad or in conjunction with Marymount College. That program offers accredited education opportunities in the United Kingdom or Australia and additional summer trips for credit to Japan, France, or the United Kingdom.

Support Services All campus classrooms, faculty offices, and laboratories and the auditorium and the cafeteria are handicapped-accessible. The library is outfitted with wheelchair ramps.

Job Opportunities The College offers work-study opportunities and part-time staff positions on campus.

Tuition: $9150 per year (1996-97)

Mandatory Fees: $232

Contact: Director: Dr. Maria Vecchio, 262 South Main Street, Lodi, New Jersey 07644; Telephone: 201-778-1190 Ext. 6017

FLORIDA A&M UNIVERSITY

4 Pu G M Sc Tr

▼ Honors Program

The Florida A&M University (FAMU) Honors Program, which is now in its fifth year of operation, offers students a challenging experience. The approaches to learning in the program are stimulating, and the professors are dedicated and hardworking. The program's small classes allow for lively and in-depth discussion of topics. Students in the program also enjoy personalized advising and, when necessary, scheduling priority that allows them access to appropriate professors and courses. There are currently 300 participants in the program.

The Honors Program offers special sections of required courses. These special sections permit students to fulfill requirements in areas such as composition, speech, computer programming, and math in small and exciting classes. The honors seminar encourages students to delve more deeply in specific areas. Honors courses are not necessarily more difficult than other courses, but students assume more responsibility for their performance both in the classroom and in preparation for external experiences. Students may be required to write essays or do individual or group projects as part of their evaluation. The honors students believe that the personal attention they receive in these smaller classes greatly helps them learn.

The program offers a wide variety of experiences for its students. Among its activities are the publication of newsletters, internships to the Washington Center, limited internships at the White House, and attendance and participation in the National African American Honors Conference, Southern Regional Honors Conference, National Collegiate Honors Conference, Florida Honors Conference, and Community Outreach Programs.

Students also plan and participate in the Bernard Hendricks Undergraduate Honors Conference, which is held on the campus during Honors Week. They present research papers and projects and also participate in panel discussions. Successful completion of the program is noted on the students' transcripts. Students who complete the Honors in the Major section of the program are awarded a beautiful plaque. Two separate statements are recorded on their transcripts.

Participation Requirements: To graduate from the Honors Program, students are required to have at least a 3.0 cumulative GPA. They must also have accumulated a total of 17 hours of honors credit for courses taken at the honors level and are required to have completed some type of community service. Juniors and seniors are encouraged to participate in the Honors in the Major section. Students work under the directorship of a major professor on a thesis or project which is begun during the junior year and completed before graduation. To participate, students must have at least a 3.2 GPA. Transfer students are also encouraged to become involved in this aspect of the program. The Honors in the Major section helps to prepare students for graduate or professional school.

Admission Process: The Honors Program recruits capable students who thrive in an atmosphere in which the motto is "excellence with caring." The students are interested in challenging academic activities and intellectual exploration. At the beginning of each school year, new honors students are chosen from among the freshman class. These students meet the following qualifications: a 3.5 high school GPA plus a score of 1000 on the SAT I or 24 on the ACT. In exceptional circumstances, promising students who may not meet the above criteria are given consideration. FAMU's Honors Program welcomes applications from interested students in all disciplines. Students in the Honors Program come from a variety of backgrounds and have diverse academic and social interests. The common thread linking the students in the program is their desire for an innovative and challenging education.

Scholarship Availability: Each semester, six scholarships of $500 each are awarded to participants in the Honors Program who demonstrate a strong need for financial assistance. To qualify for the scholarships, interested students must have at least a 3.2 cumulative GPA and write a 500-word essay explaining their needs. The Honors Program also assists qualified participants in obtaining scholarships and fellowships. The Harry S. Truman Scholarship and the Woodrow Wilson Fellowship are two of the most prestigious awards students have received to date. In addition, some program participants have received scholarships and internships at the Washington Center and the White House.

The Campus Context: There are five colleges and seven schools at FAMU. The colleges are the College of Arts and Sciences, the College of Education, the College of Engineering Sciences Technology and Agriculture (CESTA), the College of Pharmacy and Pharmaceutical Sciences, and the FAMU/FSU College of Engineering. The schools are the School of Allied Health Sciences; the School of Architecture; the School of Business and Industry; the School of General Studies; the School of Graduate Studies, Research, and Continuing Education; the School of Journalism, Media, and Graphic Arts; and the School of Nursing.

Student Body Total undergraduate enrollment at FAMU is currently 10,133. Nearly 58 percent of the students are women. The ethnic distribution of the student population is 68 percent African American, 20 percent Caucasian, 2 percent Hispanic, 3 percent Asian, and 7 percent resident alien. There are 53 international students. Seventy-five percent of the students live off campus, and approximately 75 percent of the students receive some kind of financial aid. There are numerous honorary and religious societies on campus as well as a tremendous diversity of clubs to meet every student's interests. The campus is home to fraternities and sororities.

Faculty The total number of faculty members is 672, of whom 630 are full-time. Fifty-six percent of the faculty members hold doctoral or other professional terminal degrees. The student-faculty ratio is 17:1.

Key Facilities The library has 411,329 bound volumes, 2,735 periodicals, and 72,951 microfilms. Audio/video equipment and facilities include videotape monitors, tape players and recorders, film projectors and screens, overhead projectors, a fully equipped television studio, and a photography laboratory. The Florida Black Archives, Research Center and Museum is located on the campus. This facility, which complements academic studies in history, has become a popular tourist attraction. The University has several computer labs for use by faculty and students. There are approximately fifteen computer sites available to students.

Athletics Athletic competition is available for men in baseball, basketball, tennis, swimming, track, and golf. Women's athletics include basketball, softball, swimming, tennis, track, and volleyball.

Study Abroad Study-abroad opportunities are available to both students and faculty members; opportunities include exchange visits to China by selected students and faculty members. Students majoring in Spanish have the opportunity to spend the summer in a Spanish-speaking country and earn credit for attending classes in that country while learning the language. Students and faculty members also have opportunities for internships and exchange visits to countries such as Sri Lanka, Ireland, Jamaica, Germany, Japan, and several African nations.

Support Services The Learning Development and Evaluation Center (LDEC) provides individualized supportive services to students with learning disabilities. Disabled-student facilities at Florida A&M University cater to the needs of the students who are physically challenged by providing facilities such as ramps, specially designed rest rooms, and vehicles specially designed to transport the students. Students who have special needs because of a physical or mental handicap should contact the Special Programs and Services Office as soon as they arrive on campus. This office has been established to assist handicapped students attending the University. The staff of the Special Programs and Services Office has close contact with federal and state agencies, which provide services to disabled individuals. The office staff works with each student individually in order to develop solutions to meet his or her needs.

Job Opportunities Work-study, other personnel services (OPS), internships, cooperative education, and part-time/summer employment with state agencies and businesses are among the work opportunities on campus for students.

Tuition: $1863 for state residents, $7108 for nonresidents, per year (1996-97)

Room and Board: $3074

Mandatory Fees: $119

Contact: Director: Dr. Ivy A. Mitchell, Modular Unit 1, Orr Drive, Tallahassee, Florida 32307; Interim Director: Dr. Willie T. Williams; Telephone: 904-599-3540; Fax: 904-561-2125; E-mail: imitchel@ns1.famu.edu

FLORIDA ATLANTIC UNIVERSITY

4 Pu G S Sc

▼ Lower Division Honors Program

Since 1992, through its Lower Division Honors Program, Florida Atlantic University (FAU) has offered highly motivated and well-prepared students a unique educational experience that goes well beyond the normal course requirements for freshmen and sophomores.

There are currently 60 students enrolled in the program.

Participation Requirements: The program consists of a minimum of 22 honors course credits. The core of the program is four 3-credit honors seminars taken during the freshman year. These seminars, developed and taught by highly experienced faculty members, are limited to 15 students. They substitute for required core-curriculum courses and topics are drawn from the humanities, social sciences, and the sciences. Because of the small size and individual attention, students typically do as well, if not better, academically in these courses than in the normal core-curriculum courses.

In addition to the core seminars, students are required to take 2 credits of a 1-credit honors colloquium during the fall semester of the freshman and sophomore years. This colloquium includes lectures by distinguished faculty, outside speakers, and performances. Students also take 8 additional credits comprised of honors sections of college writing and of the core curriculum courses, upper division honors equivalences of core courses, elective honors seminars, and a 2- to 3-credit honors-directed independent study.

To successfully complete the program, a student must fulfill all the course requirements and maintain an overall GPA of 3.5 and an honors GPA of 3.0

Admission Process: Minimum requirements for acceptance into the honors program are SAT I scores of 1180 or ACT scores of 26 and a GPA of 3.5. To apply, students must submit an application, a personal statement, and a letter of recommendation. Because of the limited number of spaces in the program, admission is selective; the application deadline is in mid-May. The program accepts 35 entering freshmen each year. Freshmen enrolled in the Lower Division Honors Program are housed in a special dormitory reserved for honors students. A number of classes are conducted in the dorms.

Scholarship Availability: Although the honors program does not award scholarships, a large number of University scholarships are available; many of them are based solely on academic merit. The FAU Presidential Scholarship, for example, awards $2000 per year for four years to students with a high school average of 3.5 on a 4.0 scale and an SAT I score of 1200 or ACT score of 27. It is renewable up to four years based on academic achievement.

The Campus Context: Florida Atlantic University is a doctoral-degree-granting research institution that is one of the ten universities comprising the State University System of Florida. The main campus is located on an 850-acre site in Boca Raton Florida, a coastal residential community located near West Palm Beach, Fort Lauderdale, and Miami. Additional campuses are located in Davie, Ft. Lauderdale, and North Palm Beach.

The University offers fifty-one bachelor's, forty-three master's, and fourteen doctoral degree programs.

Student Body The University has approximately 19,000 students.

Faculty There are 700 full time faculty members, of whom 95 percent hold terminal degrees.

Tuition: $1900 for state residents, $7200 for nonresidents, per year (1996-97)

Room and Board: $4365

Contact: Director: Dr. Fred Fejes, Boca Raton, Florida 33431; Telephone: 407-367-3858; Fax: 407-367-3132; E-mail: fejes@acc.fau.edu; Web site: http://www.fau.edu/academic/freshman/honors.htm

FLORIDA COMMUNITY COLLEGE AT JACKSONVILLE

2 Pu G M Sc Tr

▼ Honors Program

The Honors Program at Florida Community College at Jacksonville (FCCJ) offers gifted students unique learning opportunities in specific sections of the associate degree curriculum. The program philosophy is three-fold and designed to encourage students to become independent learners capable of critical thinking and self-expression, enable students to see connections in learning that allow them to integrate their classroom learning into a common whole, and allow students to explore facets of learning and materials that are not available in traditional curricula.

Students take required core courses, which provide an in-depth study of an international, intercultural, or current affairs topic. Students have the opportunity to examine the culture, history, government, and economics of Asia, Latin America, and Russia. Visiting professors give a first-hand and real-life perspective to the curriculum. Other courses explore medical ethics, constitutional issues, and economic issues. The honors student experiences an expanded curriculum and special speaker symposia. Upon completion of the program students receive a banquet and diploma as recognition. Their transcripts also reflect honors courses and a designated honors seal.

The program began in 1981 and currently has 150 students.

Participation Requirements: Students are required to take 12 hours of honors courses as freshmen and 6 hours as sophomores for a total of 18 credit hours over the two years.

Admission Process: Students wishing to join the honors program must enter as a degree-seeking freshman and have a GPA between 3.25 and 3.4 with corresponding SAT I scores between 1000 and 1100 or corresponding ACT scores between 23 and 26. In addition, students must submit a letter of recommendation from a high school counselor or principal and a 500-word essay. Successful applicants must enroll as full-time students with two honors courses per semester. The application deadline is February 28.

Scholarship Availability: Scholarships are available to students who enroll full-time as degree candidates, complete 12 credit hours with a 3.5 or better GPA, register in one honors course each semester, and submit a 500-word essay. Awards have a financial value of $1600 per year. The application deadline is June 1.

The Campus Context: Florida Community College consists of five campuses (Kent, North, South, Downtown, and the Urban Resource Center) at various locations in the Jacksonville area. FCCJ offers the Associate of Arts and the Associate of Science degrees. The average age of the traditional undergraduate is 29.

Student Body Florida Community College is a two-year community college with an enrollment of 94,601, with 31,649 college-credit students and 62,952 continuing education students. Approximately 58 percent of the students are women. The ethnic distribution of the total undergraduate population is 18.4 percent African American, 72.1 percent Caucasian

and 9.5 percent other. There are also 213 international students. College-credit students who receive financial aid total 8,707.

Faculty There are 397 full-time faculty members and 1,098 adjunct faculty members.

Key Facilities The library contains 193,585 volumes, and there are fifty-nine computer labs collegewide. The student-personal computer ratio is 15:1.

Study Abroad The extended studies-abroad program offers a variety of trips outside the United States. This academic year trips are planned for Spain and England. Scholarships are available for extended studies programs.

Support Services Disabled students will find all academic buildings completely handicapped-accessible. Wheelchair ramps, automatic door openers, and equipped restrooms are available.

Tuition: $1146 for state residents, $4326 for nonresidents, per year (1996-97)

Contact: Co-Director: Dr. Jim Mayes, 3939 Roosevelt Blvd., Jacksonville, Florida 32205; Telephone: 904-381-3451 and 904-646-2415; Fax: 904-381-3462 and 904-646-2209; E-mail: jmayes@ fccjvm.fccj.cc.fl.us

FLORIDA INTERNATIONAL UNIVERSITY

4 Pu G M Sc

▼ Honors College

Talented students are often forced to choose between the exciting opportunities and challenges offered by large, research-oriented universities and the close, personal environment offered by small liberal arts colleges. Florida International University (FIU) offers the best of both worlds. The Honors College is a small community of dedicated scholars consisting of outstanding students and committed teachers who work together in an atmosphere usually associated with small private colleges, but with all of the resources of a major state university.

The college provides an important foundation for students who want to get the most out of their undergraduate years. The transition into higher education is made easier by the student's immediate association with a small group of students and teachers with similar capabilities and aspirations. The undergraduate experience is significantly enhanced by the broad liberal arts focus of the curriculum and the opportunity to work closely with experienced faculty members. The opportunities for graduate and professional study or employment are greatly expanded because of the range of activities and experiences made available to students in the college. The Honors College at FIU offers some of the very best experiences in undergraduate education.

The 6-year-old program currently enrolls 468 students.

Participation Requirements: Students in the college possess dual academic citizenship. They pursue any major available in the University and at the same time complete the honors curriculum. In most cases, participation in the college does not increase the number of credits required for graduation. Each term through the third year, students enroll in one honors seminar that is designed to stimulate thoughtful discussion and creativity and to develop communications skills. Honors seminars are limited to a student-faculty ratio of 20:1 and are taught by some of the best teachers in the University. All classes are interdisciplinary and most are team-taught.

The first three years are structured similarly. All students and faculty members at each level meet in a large group session one day each week for activities such as lectures, panel discussions, case studies, and student presentations; another class meeting each week is spent in small group preceptorials. Professors meet with the same small groups throughout the year. Senior seminars meet as independent classes with an emphasis on synthesizing the students' experiences during the previous three years and introducing them to graduate-level research activities. The curriculum emphasizes critical, integrative, and creative thinking; group and independent research; oral presentation; close contact between students and faculty members; and integration of class work with the broader community.

During the senior year, students may choose to continue the sequence of honors seminars, to complete an honors thesis, or to participate in one of the Honors College study-abroad programs in Florence, Madrid, or Prague.

The unique nature of the college extends far beyond the classroom door. The Honors College Society organizes social and community service activities. The faculty and staff members of the Honors College make every effort to ensure that students are aware of the many opportunities available to them, such as fellowships, internships, and summer-study programs. Every year, as the result of this mentoring, many students win national awards and travel throughout the country for funded activities, and teams of students and faculty members travel to regional and national conferences to make presentations.

Students who complete all graduation requirements receive special recognition at Commencement and a notation on their transcripts indicating that they graduated through the Honors College.

Admission Process: Admission to the Honors College is selective and limited. Students are admitted only at the beginning of each academic year (fall term). Freshmen with a 3.5 overall high school GPA and commensurate scores on the SAT or ACT are eligible for admission to the college. Transfer and continuing FIU students who have maintained a 3.3 GPA in all college-level work and have at least two full academic years remaining in their undergraduate programs are eligible for admission to the college.

Scholarship Availability: Various private and institutional scholarships are available at both the freshman and transfer level.

The Campus Context: Florida International University is composed of the following ten colleges: Arts and Sciences, Business Administration, Computer Science, Education, Engineering and Design, Health, Hospitality Management, Journalism and Mass Communication, Nursing, and Urban and Public Affairs. The campus offers 104 bachelor's, ninety-eight master's, three specialist's, and twenty-eight doctoral degree programs.

Student Body There are 28,000 students, including 1,753 international students. Financial aid is received by 43 percent of the students. Fifty-eight percent of the students are women. The ethnic distribution of the student population is 3.4 percent Asian, 13.8 percent African American, 28 percent Caucasian, 48.5 percent Hispanic. Most students commute. There are nine fraternities and seven sororities on campus.

Faculty The total number of faculty members is 1,400, of whom 1,033 are full-time. Eighty-five percent of the faculty members have terminal degrees. The student-faculty ratio is 27:1.

Key Facilities FIU offers the complete array of student services and activities one would expect at a major state university with several recently constructed facilities, including a performing arts complex, student center, athletic facilities, and library. Volumes in the library total 1,097,300. Students have use of a full range of computer facilities, including mainframe and Internet access, free of charge.

Athletics FIU is a member of the NCAA Division I and the Trans America Athletic Conference (TAAC). In recent years, teams have participated in NCAA tournaments in many sports including baseball and women's and men's soccer and basketball.

Study Abroad The University offers study-abroad programs in many countries, including Costa Rica, the Czech Republic, England, Italy, Spain, and Tibet. Students may also attend one of more than 130 other U.S. institutions for up to one academic year through the National Student Exchange.

Support Services All facilities are fully accessible by students with disabilities, and the Office of Disabled Student Services provides academic support.

Job Opportunities Work opportunities on campus are numerous and include work-study, part-time employment, and assistantships.

Tuition: $1783 for state residents, $7028 for nonresidents, per year (1996-97)

Room: $2400 minimum

Mandatory Fees: $92

Contact: Director: Dr. Joe C. Wisdom, University Park, DM 368, Miami, Florida 33199; Telephone: 305-348-4100; Fax: 305-348-2118; E-mail: wisdom@solix.fiu.edu

FLORIDA STATE UNIVERSITY

4 Pu G L Sc Tr

▼ University Honors Program

The Florida State University (FSU) Honors Program is nourished by deep liberal arts roots planted in the early twentieth century. Florida State University is the home of the first Phi Beta Kappa chapter in Florida, and the University Honors Program supports the University's tradition of academic excellence by offering two intellectually challenging curricula—the Liberal Studies Honors Program and the Honors in the Major Program. The Honors Program is broadly supported by the University. More than 300 Florida State faculty members teach honors courses and serve on honors thesis committees annually. In 1995, the Honors Program was named one of the twenty-six best academic buys in the nation by *Money Magazine*.

Florida State offers the University Honors Colloquium and three types of liberal studies honors courses. The Honors Colloquium is a 1-credit-hour weekly forum designed to introduce honors students to the University's very best faculty members and to the exciting academic fields that they have made their life's work. The colloquium, graded satisfactory or unsatisfactory (S/U) and offered with the ongoing theme "Ideas and Issues in Art and Inquiry," is a required course for entering freshman honors students. Students write responses to the faculty presentations. Honors seminars are special topics courses in the humanities, natural sciences, and social sciences limited to 15 students each and graded S/U. Students can choose among 1,215 honors seminars each fall and spring. Honors sections are special sections of regularly scheduled courses, including American history, chemistry, or Shakespeare, that are offered only to honors students. Enrollment is limited to 25 students. Students have a choice of thirty to forty honors sections each fall and spring. Honors-augmented courses are regularly scheduled classes in which selected faculty members agree to supervise special projects or additional assignments to enable honors students to earn honors credit.

Seventy departments offer Honors in the Major Programs for students pursuing independent research or creative expression thesis writing projects. Guided by an Honors Committee of 3 faculty members, the student carries out the research, creative work, and writing during the late junior or early senior year and defends the honors thesis during the final term at FSU.

The Honors Council is an honors student group that meets monthly to plan activities for fellow honors students. The council is comprised of officers and representatives from the major honors program constituencies.

There are approximately 1,300 students in the program, 90 percent in the Liberal Studies Honors Program and 10 percent in the Honors in the Major Program.

Participation Requirements: Students must maintain at least a 3.2 cumulative GPA and complete 18 credit hours of honors classes in order to finish the program. To participate in the Honors Major Program, juniors or seniors must have completed at least 12 credit hours at FSU, have a cumulative GPA of at least 3.2, and have a project and major professor.

Admission Process: Students must have at least a 4.0 weighted high school GPA and either a 1300 SAT I or a 30 ACT score to be invited into the Liberal Studies Honors Program. Invitations to participate are issued between November 1 and March 1.

Scholarship Availability: All honors students are eligible for a study-abroad scholarship. Other academic scholarships are awarded by the FSU Undergraduate Admissions Office.

The Campus Context: Florida State University is located on 450.5 acres in Tallahassee, the Florida state capital. At FSU, emphasis is placed upon advanced degree programs entailing extensive research activities and preparation for careers in science, the arts, the humanities, the professions, and technological fields. FSU is ranked by the Carnegie Foundation as a Category I research institution and has an established international reputation. It provides for undergraduate students a strong liberal arts-based baccalaureate experience. There are sixteen colleges on the FSU campus, including colleges of engineering, law, film, and theater. The University currently offers degree programs at the following levels: ninety bachelor's degree programs; ninety-seven master's degree programs; twenty-eight advanced master's/specialist degree programs; sixty-eight doctoral degree programs; and one professional degree program.

Student Body Of the undergraduates enrolled at FSU, 54.6 percent are women, 79.1 percent are Caucasian, 10.2 percent are African American, 5.6 percent are Hispanic, and 2.4 percent are Asian.

Key Facilities FSU has several computer labs open to students. These labs house Apple and IBM computers. Individual departments also have separate computer labs for students within those majors.

Landis Hall, the University's honors residence hall, is the focal point for a variety of extracurricular activities sponsored by the Honors Council and provides a living environment that facilitates interaction among honors participants. FSU has twelve residence halls accommodating approximately 4,000 undergraduates. These halls have varied visitation policies and special programs.

Study Abroad Study abroad is encouraged. Each semester, the Honors Program offers $1000 scholarships to honors students engaged in course work at FSU's Study Abroad Programs in London, Florence, and San Jose, Costa Rica.

Tuition: $1882 for state residents, $7127 for nonresidents, per year (1996-97)

Room and Board: $4472

Contact: Director: Dr. R. Bruce Bickley Jr., Suite A5400, University Center, Tallahassee, Florida 32306-4008; Telephone: 904-644-1841; Fax: 904-644-2101; Web site: http://www.fsu.edu/~honors

FOOTHILL COLLEGE

| 2 Pu G M Tr |

▼ Honors Program

The Foothill College Honors Program offers an extensive program designed to prepare academically talented students for transfer to selective colleges and universities. As a two-year California community college, Foothill is close to many students' homes and provides an affordable entree to some of the nation's finest universities.

Honors courses offer students the opportunity to delve deeply into a subject, to be involved in lively discussion groups, and to be stimulated by other highly motivated students. Outstanding members of the Foothill College faculty help students develop and refine their abilities for writing clear, organized prose; reading and thinking analytically; presenting oral arguments cogently; and becoming self-directed learners. All instruction is conducted by experienced, inspiring instructors who hold master's or doctoral degrees in their subject of expertise. Honors students are advised by an Honors Program counselor.

Other benefits offered to honors students include priority registration, complimentary tickets to cultural events, transfer seminars, and guaranteed interviews for NASA/Ames Research Center internships.

Foothill College's Honors Program is 15 years old and currently enrolls 120 students.

Participation Requirements: Honors sections of general education courses are offered each quarter. Students select the honors courses that meet the needs of their major and transfer program. Each course taken in the Honors Program is listed on the student's transcript as honors, and completion of 6 honors courses gives the student's transcript the notation of President's Scholar. President's Scholars are presented recognition at graduation along with a frameable certificate. A minimum GPA of 3.25 must be maintained in order to continue in the program.

Admission Process: Students are invited to apply for the Honors Program based on admission test scores, high school or college scholastic performance of a 3.25 GPA on a 4.0 scale, and a letter of personal recommendation.

Scholarship Availability: Currently, no scholarships are available through the Honors Program.

The Campus Context: The Foothill College campus offers an impressive array of learning facilities, including large and diverse computer instruction centers, a dental hygiene clinic, animal health technology and ornamental horticultural complexes, a student-operated radio station and a state-of-the-art cable television station. The campus also houses the Japanese Cultural Center, a large performance theater, a fitness center, and an Olympic-size swimming pool.

The unique award-winning Pacific-style architecture creates an elegant but energizing setting on 125 picturesque acres in the coastal range foothills. This area, located just an hour south of San Francisco in the heart of Silicon Valley, is rich in cultural, educational, and recreational opportunities. A.A. and A.S. degrees are granted in seventy majors.

Student Body Undergraduate enrollment is 12,653, of whom 54.3 percent of students are women. The ethnic distribution of the student body is 4.3 percent African American, 0.82 percent American Indian, 21.99 percent Asian, 2.52 percent Filipino, 11.31 percent Hispanic, 58 percent Caucasian, and 1 percent other. International students number 450. All students commute to campus, and 12 percent of students receive financial aid. There are no fraternities or sororities. However, a comprehensive student life program is an important element of the educational experience at Foothill College. A broad range of extracurricular activities such as special interest clubs, sports, and student government offer students a chance to expand their education beyond the classroom.

Faculty There are 199 full-time and 333 part-time faculty members. Approximately 26 percent have terminal degrees. The student-faculty ratio is estimated at 29:1.

Key Facilities The library houses 75,000 volumes. Students have access to numerous computer facilities. The library has twenty-two computers linked to the Internet and with full access to libraries nationwide. Other facilities include the Math Computer Lab, the Open Computer Lab, and the Language Arts Writing Computer Lab. The CTIS Division has four computer labs and a Business Computer Lab and the IDEA Lab contains fine arts, multimedia, and five multimedia classrooms.

Athletics A full schedule of athletic programs is available for men and women interested in competitive team sports, including soccer, basketball, golf, track and field, swimming, women's volleyball, and men's football, water polo, and tennis.

Study Abroad Participants in the Campus Abroad Program enjoy a unique opportunity to immerse themselves in international cultures while enrolled in regular Foothill courses for credit. Field trips enhance the classwork taught by Foothill faculty members at the campus sites in England, France, Italy, Germany, Mexico, and Costa Rica.

Support Services The Special Education Division offers courses and services on campus and in the community designed to help physically, communicatively, developmentally, and psychologically disabled adults. A full range of support services is available on campus, including testing, tutoring, counseling, and computer training.

Job Opportunities Work opportunities on campus are available.

Tuition: None for state residents, $3510 for nonresidents, per year (1996-97)

Fees: $447

Contact: Coordinator: Janice Carr, 12345 El Monte Road, Los Altos Hills, California 94022; Telephone: 415-949-7638; Fax: 415-949-7123; E-mail: aca3849@discovery.fhda.edu; Web site: http://www.fhda.edu

FORDHAM UNIVERSITY

4 Pr C S Sc Tr

▼ **Fordham College at Rose Hill Honors Program**

The Fordham College at Rose Hill Honors Program is distinguished by its comprehensive and integrated approach to learning. The heart of the program is a sequence of courses taken during the freshman and sophomore years. These courses work together to provide a comprehensive overview of the intellectual and social forces that have shaped the modern world. Each semester in this sequence is devoted to an integrated study of the art, history, literature, music, philosophy, and religion of a particular period.

In addition, special courses in mathematics and the sciences for nonscience majors help to bring out these disciplines' important role in contemporary society. This sequence is followed by two courses in the junior year that focus on different social and ethical problems of the modern world. The capstone of the honors curriculum is the senior thesis, an extended research project prepared under the individual guidance of a faculty mentor in one's major field.

The Honors Program is not intended for passive students who are satisfied simply to accept and give back the contents of their professors' lectures. Instead, the program offers an environment where students are able to take the initiative in their own education. In order to foster such active learning, most honors classes are seminars of about 12 students that take place around the long wooden table in Alpha House, the program's own building on campus.

A distinctive curriculum and an ideal learning environment are obviously important elements of the Fordham College Honors Program. What really makes the program special, however, is the community of exceptional students who are its members. Such students come from a wide variety of backgrounds and have a number of different majors and career goals. Recent graduates are indicative of this diversity and include students who went on to attend the Johns Hopkins Medical School, the University of Chicago Law School, and Yale Law School. Another recent graduate had to defer her acceptance at Harvard's graduate program in biology in order to study at Oxford on a Fulbright Scholarship. The Honors Program regularly includes among its membership campus leaders in journalism, politics, drama, sports, and community service.

The Honors Program provides an opportunity for such diverse students to get to know each other outside, as well as inside, the classroom. A number of extracurricular activities bring honors students together throughout the year, and these often give students the chance to meet informally with the honors faculty as well. Every honors student has his or her own key to Alpha House, a facility that is available for either private study or meetings with other students 24 hours a day.

The small size of honors classes makes it impossible to invite every qualified student into the program.

Participation Requirements: The honors curriculum takes the place of the regular Fordham College core curriculum, with the exception of the language requirement. Credit is, of course, granted for Advanced Placement courses taken in high school and for college courses taken elsewhere. Successful completion of the program entitles the student to the designation *in cursu honorum* on the diploma and the transcript.

Admission Process: Admission into the program is quite competitive, with usually no more than 25 incoming students entering the program each year. A limited number of first-year students with strong academic records are invited to join the program during their freshman year.

Scholarship Availability: Honors students usually receive Presidential or Dean's Scholarships in addition to their regular financial aid.

The Campus Context: Founded in 1841, Fordham University is New York City's Jesuit university, attracting more than 14,000 students annually to its ten undergraduate, graduate, and professional schools. The campus offers undergraduates thirty-five majors plus the possibility of designing an individualized major. Fordham College at Rose Hill is a four-year liberal arts college for full-time students. Located on 85 acres in the North Bronx, next to the New York Botanical Garden and the Bronx Zoo, Rose Hill is the largest "green campus" in New York.

Student Body There are approximately 3,000 undergraduates at Fordham College at Rose Hill. Fifty-five percent of the students are women. The 2,000 resident students live in two residential colleges offering programs that integrate academic and social life under the guidance of a resident "master."

Faculty Of the 224 full-time faculty members, 98.6 percent have terminal degrees. The student-faculty ratio is 17:1.

Key Facilities The campus has a 1.6-million-volume library.

Athletics Intercollegiate athletics include baseball, basketball, cross country, football, golf, soccer, softball, swimming and diving, tennis, volleyball, and water polo. Fordham participates in the Atlantic 10 Conference for all sports except football, which participates in the Patriot League. A wide range of intramural opportunities is also available.

Study Abroad Study abroad is encouraged for all honors students. Fordham maintains its own study-abroad programs at University College, Dublin; Sogang University in Seoul, South Korea; and Blackfriars College, Oxford.

Tuition: Full-time: $15,800 per year; part-time: $375-$410 per credit (1996-97)

Room and Board: $7125 minimum

Mandatory Fees: $200

Contact: Director: Dr. Harry P. Nasuti, Bronx, New York 10458; Telephone: 718-817-3212; Fax: 718-817-4720; E-mail: ss_nasuti@lars.fordham.edu

---

FRAMINGHAM STATE COLLEGE

4 Pu G S Sc

▼ Honors Program

The Framingham State College Honors Program is designed to provide academically talented students with the opportunity to enrich their college experience. Courses bearing the honors designation are designed to be intensive experiences that are intellectually challenging and emphasize creativity and analytical thinking.

Honors courses are designed for a maximum enrollment of 15 to 20 students to foster in-depth class discussion and a close student-instructor relationship. All honors courses may be applied to the general education requirements specified by the College. Honors courses may be taken by students who are not participating in the program on a space-available basis with the permission of the instructor.

Upon their arrival on campus, honors students receive a special orientation to the College and its Honors Program. Thereafter, these students convene regularly to share information, exchange ideas, and discuss topics of interest. Each honors student has a special Honors Program adviser who assists in course selection. Residents may choose to live in a special dormitory reserved for honors students. Because the program is available to majors from every department on campus, the Academic Vice-President, the Director of the Honors Program, the Honors Program Advisory Committee, and the department chairs make a special effort to develop and offer a wide variety of challenging courses.

In addition, funds are regularly set aside for honors field trips in order to engage guest speakers and performing artists and for other activities intended to enrich learning. In certain courses and in the senior seminar, the team

approach is used so that students receive an extra measure of instruction and mentoring en route to meeting their objectives. In general, the program seeks to expose participants to the best the College has to offer.

Founded in 1990, the program currently enrolls approximately 60 students.

Participation Requirements: Freshmen entering the Framingham State College Honors Program must complete the core courses entitled "Essentials of Writing" and "The Comparative History of World Civilizations." During the remaining three years, participants are required to complete a minimum of four more courses bearing the honors designation, including the honors senior seminar.

Course topics and information about honors courses to be offered can be found in the *Schedule of Classes Bulletin* or through the program administrator's office. During their senior year, participating students must enroll in the honors senior seminar. As a condition of continued enrollment in the Honors Program, a freshman or sophomore must maintain a GPA of at least 3.0 overall and in honors courses. Students falling below these requirements are allowed to continue in the program for a probationary period of one semester. Subsequent continuance is at the discretion of the Honors Program Committee.

Honors students have priority in course registration, special advising, and a customized program of extracurricular enrichment activities. Participation in the Framingham State College Honors Program is noted on the students' transcripts. Students who complete the program also receive a certificate of recognition. The notation of honors student is made on the transcript and the diploma, and students are recognized at graduation.

Admission Process: Entering freshmen are invited to participate in the Framingham State College Honors Program based on a weighted composite of their combined SAT scores, class rank, and demonstrated potential for superior work at the college level. Any student admitted to the College who was not initially invited to participate in the program may apply directly to the Honors Program Committee for admission. Students may also apply for admission to the Framingham State College Honors Program as sophomores. A minimum GPA of 3.25 together with two letters of recommendation from faculty members and a brief statement of intent should be submitted to the Honors Committee for evaluation before October 1 of the student's sophomore year.

Scholarship Availability: Scholarships are awarded annually to the top 5 honors students who have taken at least three honors courses and are in good standing. Scholarship recipients are recognized at the annual awards assembly of the College.

The Campus Context: Framingham State College is a one-college institution offering ninety-two degree programs.

Student Body Framingham State has an undergraduate enrollment that is 63 percent women. The ethnic distribution of students is 81 percent Caucasian, 2.3 percent African American,

1.8 percent Hispanic, 2 percent Asian or Pacific Islander, 0.4 percent Native American, and 12.7 percent other. There are 66 international students. Twenty-eight percent of the students are residents, and 55 percent of students receive financial aid. There are no fraternities or sororities on campus.

Faculty Of the 228 faculty members, 172 are full-time; 77.33 percent have terminal degrees. The student-faculty ratio is 15:1.

Key Facilities The library houses 200,000 print volumes, 16,000 periodical titles and 600,000 units of microfilm. Computer facilities include four general purpose computer labs (130 PCs), four PCs with network access in the Center for Academic Support and Advising, twenty Macs in the Communication Arts Department Lab, fifteen Macs in the Computer Graphics Laboratory in the Art Department, twenty PCs in the Multimedia Laboratory for student and faculty member use in the Media Center of the library. Wiring in the residence halls allows each student to have network access from his or her room.

Athletics Framingham State College offers twelve intercollegiate NCAA Division III sports in addition to coed equestrian and cheerleading. The programs for men include football, basketball, soccer, ice hockey, baseball, and cross-country track. The programs for women are field hockey, soccer, volleyball, basketball, softball, and cross-country track. In addition to the varsity and club offerings, intramural athletics involve more than 2,000 students in seventeen different sports. Through student government, women's and men's rugby are offered at the club level.

In order to ensure that the athletic needs of students are met, an interest survey is administered to each entering class. The commonwealth of Massachusetts has approved $6.2 million to cover half the cost of the proposed human-performance and wellness center. The facility will house varsity, intramural, and recreational sports for men, women, students, and faculty and staff members. It also will accommodate disabled athletes and spectators.

Study Abroad There are many study abroad opportunities available for students. The Modern Languages Department offers study abroad in Spain, Mexico, Latin America, France, and the Province of Quebec. By arrangement, students in other departments may spend as many as two semesters in foreign study.

Support Services Disabled students find that Framingham State College is an institutional member of Recording for the Blind and Dyslexic and a network member of the Massachusetts Radio Reading Service. The campus provides note takers and custom recorded books for its disabled students in addition to a variety of accommodations available at the Center for Academic Support and Advising.

Job Opportunities On-campus student employment falls into the categories of work-study and student payroll. For work-study, a student must be eligible for financial aid. About 1 percent of the financial aid given to students is in the form of compensation for work-study. Among the other employment opportunities for students on campus are employment by the Residence Life Office to staff the desks at the entrances to six of the seven residence halls. Desks are staffed 24 hours per day throughout the academic year in order to ensure that regulations regarding parietal hours are enforced. Desk workers also sort mail.

Food services employs students to work in the three dining facilities on campus. The College Center maintains a large student payroll to help with student activities and college functions. Students are hired as building managers, information booth attendants, gameroom attendants, set-up crews, and pub workers. These students undergo an extensive training program.

The Student Government Association employs students as escorts to accompany students around campus after the college shuttle bus stops operating at 9:30 p.m. This service runs seven days per week until 3 a.m. The College Library employs non-work-study students. Lastly, the athletic department hires students to assist with keeping statistics at home and away games, running the time clocks, refereeing intramural games, and providing additional office support. In fall 1996, the College sponsored a job fair for students interested in on-campus employment for the first time. Both work-study and student-payroll employers attended.

Tuition: $1338 for state residents, $5726 for nonresidents, per year (1996-97)

Room and Board: $3855

Mandatory Fees: Full-time, $1890; part-time per course, $366 for 1 course, $660 for 2 courses

Contact: Director: Dr. Nicholas S. Racheotes, c/o the Dean of Undergraduate Education, P.O. Box 9101, Framingham, Massachusetts 01701-9101; Telephone: 508-626-4816; Fax: 508-626-4022; E-mail: nracheo@frc.mass.edu; Web site: http://www.framingham.edu

FRANCIS MARION UNIVERSITY

4 Pu G M Tr

▼ Honors Program

The Honors Program at Francis Marion University (FMU) exists to give gifted and ambitious students in all majors the opportunity to work with the University's most stimulating faculty in small but challenging classes, to synthesize information gathered from different disciplines into a single and coherent body of knowledge, and to achieve their full academic potential in preparation for careers and/or graduate or professional school.

Most honors courses at FMU are chosen from basic courses, which meet general education requirements, but employ different, more collaborative and interdisciplinary methods and are limited (with the exception of Honors 101) to 15 students. Many honors courses incorporate field trips, dinners, or other special events and the program itself offers periodic receptions.

Honors 101: "Core Concepts Continuum," is strongly recommended for all entering honors freshmen. Besides serving as an orientation course, this course deals with a special topic from three different academic perspectives.

The Honors Student Association fosters a sense of community among honors students by coordinating social and academic activities, including movie nights and research fairs and is currently devising a "Big Siblings" informal advising program between freshman and upperclass honors students.

The Honors Program was founded in 1987. Typically, about 25 percent of the student body (400 students, including some 180 freshmen) are eligible to participate in the program. Students graduating with University honors are awarded an honors cord at Commencement. Each year, the University names a graduating senior its "Outstanding Honors Graduate" and awards him or her a cash prize.

Participation Requirements: To graduate with University honors students must complete 21 semester hours of honors course work with a minimum GPA of 3.25. Nine of these hours must be numbered 300 or above. Also, students must achieve a grade of "B" or higher in the honors colloquium, which deals with a special topic from an interdisciplinary perspective, and successfully complete an honors independent study thesis.

Admission Process: Eligibility for the Honors Program is determined primarily by SAT scores, but also by a predicted GPA formula, which takes into account a student's high school GPA and class rank. A minimum score of 1100 on the SAT I qualifies a student for the Honors Program. The registrar automatically identifies entering freshmen eligible for the program, although anyone curious about his or her eligibility is urged to contact the honors director for more information.

A new Honors Gateway course for all entering freshmen is effective as of fall 1997.

Scholarship Availability: Institutional and Presidential Scholarships are frequently awarded to honors-eligible students.

The Campus Context: Francis Marion University, founded in 1970, occupies 309 beautifully wooded acres just east of Florence, South Carolina, about an hour's drive from Myrtle Beach and 90 minutes from both Charleston and Columbia. FMU is a public, four-year, liberal arts university, including eleven departments and two schools offering twenty-seven majors.

Student Body Undergraduate enrollment is generally around 3,700 students; of these, 1,200 live in on-campus dormitories or apartments. Approximately 54 percent of the students are women. About 60 percent of the students are Caucasian, 25 percent are African American, 8 percent are Asian, and 7 percent are other. Students may participate in a variety of campus activities, including student government, honor and service organizations, and fraternities and sororities.

Faculty Of the 227 full- and part-time faculty members, about 180 hold terminal degrees from universities around the United States and other countries. The student-faculty ratio is 17:1.

Key Facilities The FMU campus consists of sixteen modern buildings, including state-of-the-art science and computer facilities, a student union, and an excellent theater/fine arts center. The James A. Rogers Library, one of the most comprehensive regional libraries in the southeast, has 340,000 volumes and access to a wide variety of electronic databases. The campus is almost completely handicapped-accessible.

Athletics The University participates in NCAA Division II men's and women's basketball, soccer, golf, track, baseball/softball, tennis, and other sports.

Study Abroad Individual departments regularly arrange study-abroad opportunities.

Job Opportunities Students may find work on campus through the Financial Aid Office.

Tuition: $3010 for state residents, $6020 for nonresidents, per year (1996-97)

Room and Board: $3138

Mandatory Fees: $90 for state residents, $180 for nonresidents

Contact: Director: Dr. Jon Tuttle, Florence, South Carolina 29501-0547; Telephone: 803-661-1521; Fax: 803-661-1432; E-mail: jtuttle@fmarion.edu

---

FREED–HARDEMAN UNIVERSITY

4 Pr G S Sc Tr

▼ University Honors Program

The Freed-Hardeman University (FHU) Honors Program seeks to provide the optimum educational experience for the talented student in the setting of a Christian university. In honors, attention is given to oral and written communication skills and to the ability to think and respond quickly under pressure. The program blends a strong emphasis on a liberal arts education with the opportunity to pursue guided, independent study in technical or specialized areas. Graduates of the program have not only the necessary theoretical knowledge for success in their field, but also possess problem-solving and communication skills.

Since 1974, the program has served to enhance the undergraduate experience of Freed-Hardeman's best students. Sixty students have graduated with University honors. More than 700 students, representing every department in the University, have earned H grades (A with honors) in 139 different courses. We currently have 96 members in the Honors Association.

Participation Requirements: Continued participation in the program or association requires that students maintain at least a 3.3 GPA. Freed-Hardeman offers a number of scholarships to students of exceptional ability. Many students receiving these scholarships are also in the Honors Program.

Admission Process:
Entry into the program is by invitation after an application process for incoming freshmen or by invitation based on GPA for students with more than 30 semester hours of completed work at FHU. Students transferring from honors programs at accredited colleges and universities are welcomed into honors at Freed-Hardeman and their prior honors work may count as much as 40 percent of the total requirements for graduation with honors.

The Campus Context:
Freed-Hardeman University traces its origin to the 1869 charter of a private high school and college for Henderson, Tennessee. The University is located in a clean, quiet, west Tennessee county-seat town of approximately 5,200 citizens. The campus consists of about 96 acres with twenty-five main buildings. Supplementing the cultural, entertainment, medical, and shopping facilities of Henderson are those of the regional center of Jackson, which is 17 miles north of campus.

The twelve academic departments at Freed-Hardeman University are grouped into five schools: Arts and Humanities, Biblical Studies, Business, Education, and Sciences and Mathematics. Students may pursue the Bachelor of Arts, Bachelor of Science, Bachelor of Business Administration, or Bachelor of Social Work degrees. Approximately thirty majors with twenty-five different concentrations within those majors are available. Students may earn a Master of Education, Master of Ministry, Master of Arts in New Testament or Master of Science in Counseling degree.

Student Body Undergraduate enrollment is 1,250; 53.5 percent of the students are women. The minority ethnic distribution of the total undergraduate population is 5 percent African American and less than 1 percent for all other minority groups. Eighty-four percent of the students receive financial aid. Social clubs encourage spiritual growth, provide opportunities for social interaction, and present service projects.

Faculty There are 119 faculty members, of whom 96 are full-time and 69 percent have terminal degrees. The student-faculty ratio is 18:1.

Key Facilities The library houses more than 142,000 volumes. Freed-Hardeman University offers a number of computer facilities for student use. The University uses two VAX 4000 Model 200s. One is for the library on-line card catalog and the other for OpenVMS, which is for various on-line uses, including the Internet. Each student on campus is encouraged to have an account on the Internet.

There are also five computer labs with IBM-compatible computers, typically with Windows 3.1 and others with Windows 95 for student use. These computers contain statistical packages that include word processing, spreadsheet, and other programs. A journalism lab includes Macintosh computers with Desktop Publishing. The library includes computers with IBM, Macintosh, and CD-ROM data computers. A home economics lab maintains Macintosh and IBM computers for clothing design.

Athletics Intramural competition between the social clubs includes events in basketball, softball, volleyball, tennis, flag football, and small games such as badminton and raquetball. Intercollegiate sports are played and attract student support. Students compete in basketball, baseball, golf, and tennis for men and basketball, softball, tennis, and volleyball for women. The University is affiliated with the TranSouth Athletic Conference and the National Association of Intercollegiate Athletics.

Study Abroad Freed-Hardeman University sponsors two programs of international studies during the summer semester. The Summer in Italy Program in Florence is offered in cooperation with Harding University and the Studies in Vienna, Austria, Program is offered in cooperation with International Christian University. These programs provide students an opportunity to earn credits while experiencing life in an international setting. This is a highly desirable way for students to earn Global Awareness credits.

Support Services The University is committed to providing equal opportunity in education to qualified students. Disabled students find several buildings totally handicapped-accessible. Modifications or adjustments are made for qualified students with disabilities. Special parking, equipped restrooms, and lowered drinking fountains are also available on campus. The Office of Disability Services assists with the development of an accommodation plan.

Job Opportunities The Federal Work-Study Program is available to students with established financial need. Other campus jobs required by the programs of the University, such as those of teaching assistant or pool lifeguard, may be assigned without regard to the financial need of the student.

Tuition:
$6208 per year (1996-97)

Room and Board:
$3620

Mandatory Fees:
$912

Contact:
Director: Dr. Rolland W. Pack, 158 East Main Street, Henderson, Tennessee 38340; Telephone: 901-989-6057; Fax: 901-989-6065; E-mail: rpack@fhu.edu; Web site: http://www.fhu.edu

---

FROSTBURG STATE UNIVERSITY

4 Pu G M Sc Tr

▼ University Honors Program

Frostburg State University (FSU) prides itself upon blurring boundaries traditionally found in academia. These boundaries include the authority divide between faculty, students, and administrators; the boundaries between academic disciplines; and the boundaries between the classroom and the other arenas.

In FSU's Honors Program, students cofacilitate the freshman orientation course, participate in faculty development workshops, serve on the honors program governing committee, and function as equal partners in the redesign of the program's curriculum and requirements. Administrators from diverse sectors of the University routinely teach honors courses and seminars. There are social activities such as picnics, film discussions, and field trips. Throughout the program, students, faculty members, and administrators operate as collaborators in the learning process.

Honors courses, even if they are housed in a particular discipline, are expected to incorporate material from multiple disciplines and encourage critical thinking. Specially designed interdisciplinary seminars are offered each semester. These seminars are often team taught. Recent topics have included "Women, Science, and Society;" "The Sixties in America;" "Myths of America and the Ecological Dilemma;" "Political Psychology;" "Service Learning;" "Native Peoples of North America;" "Asian Culture;" "Physics and Metaphysics;" "Women in the Arts;" "The African American Experience;" "Self and Other;" and "The Holocaust." Some of the seminars, such as "The Holocaust," are intense, 6-credit experiences.

The Honors Program at Frostburg State offers more than merely a set of traditional courses. Travel/study experiences are offered as honors seminars. Since May 1995, the following honors-sponsored travel/study experiences have been offered: International Politics in Ireland, Mythology as Sacred Geography in Greece, Art and the Social World in New York City, and Discordant Harmonies in Ecuador. Honors/international housing in Cambridge and Westminster Halls offers students the opportunity to live in a learning community with special programming to complement their honors courses. Students and faculty members are active participants in state, regional, and national collegiate honors councils. FSU's Honors Program students are campus leaders active in student government, campus publications, Greek life, and other cocurricular organizations.

Students who complete the 24-credit requirement for graduating with honors in general education receive a certificate and recognition at the University's Honors Convocation. In addition, they are recognized at the Commencement and their transcript notes the distinction of graduated with honors in general education.

The FSU Honors Program is 15 years old and currently enrolls 120 students.

Participation Requirements: Most of the students in the Honors Program are pursuing the distinction of graduating with honors in general education. This requires completion of 24 credits of honors course work, including English 111 or 312; 15 credits of honors variants of GEP courses; 6 credits of Honors seminars; or 3 credits of honors thesis and 3 credits of honors seminars. Students must have a 3.0 GPA in their honors course work and overall. Courses taken for honors credit at a community college or another university may be used to complete these requirements.

Admission Process: Incoming first semester students are invited to join FSU's Honors Program on the basis of their high school GPA and SAT scores (3.5 high school GPA or 1180 combined SAT I score). A minimum verbal SAT I score of 580 is desired. Transfer students and others joining the program after their first semester are expected to have a 3.5 college GPA.

Scholarship Availability: The Nelson Guild Scholarship is available for juniors participating in the Honors Program. Students are nominated by the Honors Program director based upon their GPA, their involvement in the Honors Program, and their leadership activities. The final selection is made by the University's Scholarship Committee.

Meritorious Achievement Awards are available for entering first-year students and transfer students. Eligibility is based upon a combined SAT I score of 1200, a minimum high school GPA of 3.5 and SAT I scores of 1000, a community college A.A. degree with cumulative GPA of 3.5, demonstrated outstanding ability in the visual or performing arts, or academic leadership qualities.

In addition, more than ninety departmental and interest-related scholarships are available for first-year and continuing students.

The Campus Context: Frostburg State University offers thirty-seven degree programs. In addition, FSU has a number of programs in cooperation with other Maryland universities such as the dual degree in engineering offered with the University of Maryland at College Park and the Bachelor's/Juris Doctor program offered with the University of Baltimore. A state-of-the-art Performing Arts Center opened in 1995 with a recital hall, drama theater, studio theater, three rehearsal halls, electronic music and piano labs, teaching studios, and practice labs.

Student Body The student population at FSU is 49 percent women. The ethnic distribution of the student body is 1 percent Asian, 8 percent African American, 1 percent Hispanic, 1 percent Native American, and 89 percent Caucasian. International students constitute 1 percent of the population. Thirty-five percent of the students are residents and 60 percent of the students receive some financial aid. There are seven fraternities and eight sororities on campus.

Faculty Of the 246 faculty members, 220 are full-time and 77 percent have doctoral degrees. The student-faculty ratio is 17:1.

Key Facilities The library contains 522,000 volumes. More than 250 computers are available for student use, including a high-end graphics workstation lab, Macintosh labs, IBM-compatible labs, a robotics and computer interface lab, a Geographic Information Systems/Computer Aided Design lab, writing labs, and residence hall labs.

Athletics FSU's athletic program supplements, but does not overshadow, the academic program. No preferential admission or financial aid is given solely on the basis of athletic talent. FSU is a Division III school, which recruits scholar-athletes and competes in twenty sports. Men compete in basketball, football, soccer, swimming, tennis, baseball, indoor and outdoor track, and cross-country. Women compete in basketball, field hockey, lacrosse, softball, soccer, swimming, tennis, volleyball, outdoor track, and cross-country.

Study Abroad Numerous study-abroad opportunities exist. Frostburg is one of two institutions of higher learning in Maryland participating in the International Student Exchange Program (ISEP). There are more than 100 institutions abroad from which students can make their selections. FSU has official agreements with several universities throughout the world, including Mary Immaculata College, Ireland; Schwabisch Gmund, Germany; and Centro de Estudios Interamericanos, Ecuador, and regularly offers study opportunities at these sites. In addition, individual departments have ties to other universities. As previously mentioned the Honors Program has offered travel/study opportunities to Greece and Ecuador.

Support Services Disabled Student Services provides accommodations to disabled students, which increase their independence in gaining an education. In addition, Student Support Services helps low-income, first-generation, and disabled students achieve their personal and academic goals.

Job Opportunities Work opportunities are available through the Federal Work-Study Program in which paid work is part of the student's financial aid package. Students are also employed by academic and administrative departments on campus, the catering company, and faculty-directed research projects.

Tuition: $3544 for state residents, $7530 for nonresidents, per year (1997-98)

Room and Board: $4786

Contact: Director: Maureen Connelly, Guild Center 028, Frostburg, Maryland 21532; Telephone: 301-687-4998; Fax: 301-687-7964; E-mail: d2pccon@fra00.fsu.umd.edu

FULLERTON COLLEGE

2 Pu G Sc Tr

▼ Honors Program

The program at Fullerton College has just been inaugurated with the first courses to be offered in fall 1997. The College expects to offer a full program of courses so that a student may graduate from the Fullerton Honors Program and qualify for special transfer privileges and financial considerations to area universities. Visiting lecturers and presenters in arts and sciences and other enrichment events will also be part of the program.

Admission Process: Students officially admitted to the Honors Program should have a GPA of at least 3.0 or the equivalent as demonstrated through testing. While the core of the program is academic, students will typically participate in program outreach and recruiting, staffing the honors office and other campus facilities and related activities such as tutoring and other service work.

The Campus Context: Fullerton College offers associate degree programs in approximately 100 majors plus certification in vocational fields. Special facilities include the Transfer Achievement Program and a campus radio station.

Student Body The student body is 52 percent women. The ethnic distribution is approximately 62 percent Caucasian, 20 percent Hispanic, 13 percent Asian, 3 percent African American, 2 percent Native American, and 1 percent international students. All students commute to campus. Twenty-five percent receive college-administered financial aid.

Faculty Of the 678 faculty members, 276 are full-time. The student-faculty ratio is 27:1.

Key Facilities The library houses 113,300 volumes. There are 600 computers for student use in computer labs, academic departments, and the library.

Athletics In athletics, Fullerton offers intercollegiate basketball, cross-country running, football, golf, soccer, swimming and diving, tennis, track and field, volleyball, and water polo.

Study Abroad Study-abroad programs are available in England, France, Germany, and Italy. Some programs are semester-length for full-time credit, others are summer sessions.

Support Services The College has learning resource services for disabled students.

Job Opportunities Federal Work-Study is available on campus, offering 1,000 part-time jobs.

Tuition: None for state residents, $3420 for nonresidents, per year (1996-97)

Mandatory Fees: $410

Contact: Director: Bruce Henderson, 321 E. Chapman Avenue, Fullerton, California 92632; Telephone: 714-992-7370; Fax: 714-447-4097

GALLAUDET UNIVERSITY

4 Pr G S Sc Tr

▼ Honors Program

The Gallaudet University Honors Program, established in 1981, is a program of general study designed to provide an alternative liberal arts curriculum for the motivated and talented learner regardless of major. Course offerings include separate honors sections, honors seminars, and honors options or individual honors contracts in nonhonors sections. Courses are discussion based and encourage student-teacher interaction. Honors students qualify to live in the Academic Community Dormitory, which includes an honors computer lab accessible to honors students 24 hours a day. Approximately 10 percent of entering first-year students are admitted to the Honors Program. There are currently 100 students enrolled in the program.

Participation Requirements: Students in the Honors Program can major in any area and take the same number of credits for graduation as every other Gallaudet University student. Honors Program students must complete a total of 37 credit hours at the honors level with a grade of B or better to qualify for University Honors. Six of these hours are for a senior honors project. Advanced Placement courses fulfill honors course requirements.

Students graduating with University honors are recognized at graduation. Graduation with University honors is recorded on the student's transcript. In addition, the student receives a plaque that is engraved with his or her name, the University Seal, and the signature of the president of the University.

Admission Process: Students enter the program in one of three ways once they have been accepted to or are enrolled in the University. They may be directly admitted based on SAT or ACT scores, they may pass the Honors Qualifying Examination during New Student Orientation, or they may qualify based on a GPA of 3.2 or better and three letters of recommendation from their professors.

The Campus Context: Gallaudet University is located in Washington, D.C. In 1864, President Abraham Lincoln signed the charter establishing what is now Gallaudet University. The Presidents of the United States sign the diplomas of Gallaudet's graduates. The historical front part of the 99-acre campus was designed by Frederick Law Olmsted, who also designed the United States Capitol grounds in Washington and Central Park in New York City.

The mission of Gallaudet University is to serve as a comprehensive, multipurpose institution of higher education for persons who are deaf or hard of hearing. Gallaudet University is the only liberal arts university in the world designed exclusively for deaf and hard of hearing students. Communication among the faculty, the staff, and students, whether in or out of the classroom, is through the use of both sign language and written and spoken English. The University offers twenty-six undergraduate majors.

Gallaudet University is a member of the Consortium of Universities of the Washington Metropolitan Area. Degree-seeking students can enroll in courses through the consortium if those courses are not available at Gallaudet. Other consortium members are American University, the Catholic University of America, George Mason University, the George Washington University, Georgetown University, Howard University, Marymount University, the University of the District of Columbia, the University of Maryland at College Park, Mount Vernon College, and Trinity College.

Student Body There are 1,498 undergraduate students and 594 graduate students at Gallaudet University. Fifty-three percent of undergraduate students are women, 12 percent are African American, 5 percent are Asian American, 6 percent are Hispanic, and 1 percent are Native American. International students from forty-nine countries comprise 10 percent of the total enrollment.

Faculty Gallaudet has 245 full-time teaching faculty members.

Key Facilities The library contains 215,500 book volumes, 371,000 titles on microfilm, and 4,530 audiovisual media and videotape titles. It has an internationally renowned special collection of materials on deafness covering the period from 1546 to the present. There are 164 computers in eight computer labs. All students, faculty members, and staff members have access to e-mail and the Internet.

Study Abroad Since 1974, Gallaudet University has offered study-abroad programs. Participants usually spend three to six weeks studying and traveling in England, France, Costa Rica, Canada, Mexico, Italy, Switzerland, Germany, and Spain. Courses are offered for credit by various academic departments.

Support Services The campus is completely accessible for students with disabilities.

Job Opportunities Students are offered a range of work opportunities on campus, including work-study and internships.

Tuition: $5702 per year (1996-97)

Room and Board: $6708

Mandatory Fees: $480

Contact: Director: Dr. Richard W. Meisegeier, 800 Florida Avenue, NE, Washington, D.C. 20002-3695; Telephone: 202-651-5550; Fax: 202-651-5065; E-mail: rwmeisegeier@gallua. gallaudet.edu

---

GANNON UNIVERSITY

4 Pr G M Tr

▼ University Honors Program

The student-centered and student-governed Gannon University Honors Program is designed to provide a challenging educational experience to talented and highly motivated students willing to accept the challenge. The program is open to students of all majors and consists primarily of honors sections of courses that are required of all students. The honors courses are limited to 15 students, are conducted as seminars, and are highly interactive. The faculty members who teach in the program are encouraged to be creative in the content discussed as well as in the manner in which it is presented. A hallmark of the program is the community that exists, students with students as well as faculty members with students. The program is governed by a 15-member Student Advisory Board that is responsible for suggesting courses and faculty as well as for planning cultural, social, and intellectual outside-the-classroom activities. The Gannon program is a member of the National Collegiate Honors Council, the Northeast Region of the National Collegiate Honors Conference, and the Mid-East Honors Association, and students are encouraged to attend conferences sponsored by each of the associations. The Honors Program at Gannon began in 1989 and is now in its seventh year. There are 140 students in the program.

Participation Requirements: To graduate as honors scholars, students must take 24 credits of honors courses and 6 credits of a foreign language. To graduate as honors associates, they must take 18 credits of honors courses. They must also achieve an overall GPA of 3.25. Honors students complete the same number of credits for graduation as any other Gannon student. Honors students receive special recognition at graduation and their honors courses are documented on their transcripts.

Along with the academic requirements for the program, students are expected to participate in social, cultural, and intellectual activities provided by the program. They are also expected to be involved in some service activity.

Admission Process: Entering freshmen are selected on the basis of their SAT scores, class rank, GPA, and extracurricular activities. Students already attending Gannon and transfer students must have a 3.5 GPA to be considered.

The Campus Context: Gannon University is a private, Roman Catholic, comprehensive university located on the bayfront in Erie, Pennsylvania's third-largest city and one of the busiest ports on the Great Lakes. There are three colleges on campus: the College of Sciences; the College of Engineering and Health Sciences; and the College of Humanities Business and Education. Gannon offers twelve associate degree programs, fifty-eight bachelor's degree programs, ten preprofessional programs, and seventeen graduate degree programs. Gannon's noteworthy facilities include a Computer Integrated Manufacturing Center, the Metalliding Institute, the Schuster Theater, the Schuster Gallery, and WERG Radio.

Student Body There are approximately 3,000 students enrolled, of whom women comprise 56 percent. Resident students make up 41 percent of the student body.

Faculty Out of the 325 faculty members, 189 are full-time and 53 percent hold terminal degrees. The student-faculty ratio is 12:1.

Key Facilities The library holds 248,928 bound volumes. There are 375 computers available through several general use and departmental labs.

Athletics Gannon offers seventeen NCAA Division II sports. Men's sports include baseball, basketball, cross-country, football, golf, soccer, swimming and diving, tennis, and wrestling. Women's sports include basketball, cross-country, lacrosse, soccer, softball, swimming, diving, tennis, and volleyball. Fourteen of the seventeen teams compete in the Great Lakes Intercollegiate Athletic Conference.

Study Abroad The University offers several courses abroad each year. In addition, Gannon cooperates with study-abroad programs offered by other colleges and universities to provide its students with an opportunity to internationalize their education.

Support Services Approximately 85 percent of the campus is accessible to the physically disabled. Wheelchair ramps, elevators, specially equipped restrooms, special drop-off points, lowered drinking fountains and lowered telephones are available, as is a program for students with learning disabilities.

Job Opportunities In addition to the Federal Work-Study Program, approximately 100 part-time job opportunities are available on campus.

Tuition: Full-time: $11,410 (minimum) through $12,100, depending on program, per year (1996-97); part-time: $365–$385 per credit, depending on program

Room and Board: $4710

Mandatory Fees: $284

Contact: Director: Dr. Terry Giles, Erie, Pennsylvania 16541; Telephone: 814-871-7520; Fax: 814-871-5662; E-mail: giles_t@cluster.gannon.edu

GARDNER-WEBB UNIVERSITY

4 Pr G S Sc Tr

▼ **Honors Program**

The Gardner-Webb University (GWU) Honors Program seeks to nurture academically qualified students in all majors by providing a program of enriched learning experiences in courses taught by an honors faculty. Honors students are inquisitive people, excited by the challenge of scholarship and comfortable in an environment that demands the acquisition of knowledge and the need to think critically about what is learned. Regardless of their majors, honors students are interdisciplinary in their approach. They are able to synthesize their studies and learn from varied cultures and from each other. The Honors Program encourages the highest standards in its students who should exert leadership through their academic and cocurricular accomplishments.

The GWU Honors Program has been in existence for eight years. There are 50–70 students in the program each year.

Admission Process: Fifty to 80 students are selected to receive honors program application materials each year. This initial selection is based on SAT scores and class ranking. Applications are reviewed by the Honors Committee. Selection is based on academic achievement, potential for leadership, extracurricular activities, and a written statement of personal goals.

Participation Requirements: The Honors Program requires the completion of a minimum of 24 hours of course work designated as honors. A minimum of 15 hours of course work should be completed in the first two years of study. Honors courses in the first two years may be selected from honors sections (restricted to honors students) of core curriculum offerings or through honors contracts with faculty members teaching regular sections of the college's overall curriculum.

To receive Honors Program recognition during Commencement exercises, a student must meet the following requirements: maintain at least a 3.0 GPA; successfully complete a minimum of 24 hours in honors courses, including HONR 395, 400, and 401; initiate, prepare, present, and defend a senior honors thesis of at least forty pages in length; complete a minimum of 80 hours of community service that contributes to the welfare of the community; and receive the recommendation of the Honors Committee.

Scholarship Availability: Gardner-Webb offers several scholarships, which are available to students in the Honors Program. These include Presidential, University, Honor, and Academic Fellows Scholarships. Some of these provide for full-tuition assistance.

The Campus Context: Gardner-Webb University is a private, coeducational university affiliated with the Baptist State Convention of North Carolina. The University is often referred to as an emerging regional university. The main University campus is situated on 200 rolling, wooded acres in the small town of Boiling Springs in the Piedmont section of western North Carolina. The campus is 60 miles from Asheville and Charlotte. Gardner-Webb students enjoy the lifestyle of a relatively small institution yet have the advantage of being centrally located near major urban resources. Gardner-Webb also offers classes in twelve other regional facilities through its Greater Opportunities for Adult Learners (GOAL) Program. Students and faculty and staff members are part of a community of learning, and Gardner-Webb seeks to prepare and encourage students to make meaningful contributions to the global community in which we live. The University offers thirty-one undergraduate majors leading to the baccalaureate, including liberal arts and sciences, business, education, and nursing.

Student Body Undergraduates enrolled on the main campus total 1,175. Fifty-three percent of the students are women. The ethnic distribution of the student population is 1 percent Asian, 13 percent African American, 1 percent Hispanic, and 1 percent Native American. There are 25 international students. Ninety-three percent of students receive some form of financial aid.

Faculty Of the 99 full-time faculty members (supplemented by 54 adjunct faculty members in the off-campus centers), 64 percent have doctoral or other terminal degrees. The student-faculty ratio is 12:1.

Key Facilities There are 190,000 volumes in Dover Library, plus microforms and other materials for a total item count of more than 724,000. Six computer labs located throughout campus form the core of the campus computer network. Offices and most dorms are to be wired into the campus computer network within the next year.

Athletics Students may participate in fourteen NCAA Division II sports, including football, soccer, cross-country, basketball, wrestling, golf, tennis, and baseball for men and volleyball, soccer, cross-country, basketball, softball, and tennis for women. All of these, with the exception of wrestling, are South Atlantic Conference sports. In addition, men and women can participate in cheerleading and athletic training. Each year the athletic department schedules and participates in more than 275 events.

Study Abroad Study-abroad programs are provided by the Broyhill School of Management and the Departments of Fine Arts, Foreign Languages and Literature, and Religious Studies. Additional travel/study opportunities are available to individual students through a cooperative-study program with CIEE (Council on International Educational Exchange) and AIFS (American Institute for Foreign Study), which permit study in more than thirty countries in Asia, Europe, South and Central America, Africa, and the Caribbean.

Support Services Disabled students find that all campus buildings are accessible. The NOEL Programs for the disabled provide support services to deaf, blind, and other identified disabled students. Reader service as well as a wide variety of equipment, including braillers, adapted tape recorders, talking calculators, and specialized computer technology, is available to blind and visually impaired students. Qualified interpreters, counselors, tutors, and note-takers enable deaf and hard of hearing students to attend fully integrated classes and to participate in extracurricular activities sponsored by the University. Residence halls are equipped with visual fire alarms, doorbell lights, and TTY's.

Job Opportunities Students are offered a range of work opportunities through work-study programs.

Tuition: $8990 per year (1996-97)

Room and Board: $4470

Contact: Director: Dr. Tom Jones, Box 264, Boiling Springs, North Carolina 28017; Telephone: 704-434-9202; Fax: 704-434-4329; E-mail: tjones@gardnerwebb.edu; Web site: http://www.gardner-webb.edu

THE GEORGE WASHINGTON UNIVERSITY

4 Pr G L Sc Tr

▼ University Honors Program

The University Honors Program is designed to enhance the education of undergraduate students at the George Washington University. For entering students, it offers a year-long seminar on the western intellectual tradition. Freshman and sophomore students have access to a series of small seminar courses with some of the top faculty members at the University. For juniors, the program offers the University Symposium, a special weekend seminar with world-renowned authors and scholars. Seniors complete a senior thesis and most do so within a special honors program in their department or major.

The University Honors Program also provides extracurricular activities such as distinguished speakers, visits to museums, and a student service organization. The program offers optional student housing in two residence halls for freshman students.

Established in 1989, the program is now comprised of 600 students. The deadline for applying to the program is January.

Participation Requirements: Students in the University Honors Program must maintain a 3.4 cumulative GPA, take one honors course each semester, and complete a senior thesis. Students who meet these requirements graduate with Latin honors (Cum Laude, Magna Cum Laude, or Summa Cum Laude) and are identified as graduates of the University Honors Program. Students whose cumulative GPA falls below 3.4 may remain in the program as long as it is possible for them to graduate with a 3.4 cumulative GPA at 120 hours.

Scholarship Availability: All students in the University Honors Program receive a Presidential Merit Scholarship of $7500.

The Campus Context: The George Washington University is a private, independent university located in downtown Washington, D.C., immediately adjacent to the White House. There are four other campuses, located in Virginia, for graduate study. There are six schools offering undergraduate degrees. They are the Columbian School of Arts and Sciences, the School of Business and Public Management, the Elliott School of International Affairs, the School of Engineering and Applied Sciences, the School of Medicine and Health Science, and the School of Communication. There are eight schools that offer graduate degrees, including the six previously mentioned plus the School of Education and Human Development and the Law School.

Student Body The undergraduate enrollment is 5,500, of which women comprise 56 percent of the students. There are 600 international students. Ninety-six percent of the undergraduates live on campus. Graduate enrollment is 10,000 students. There are eleven fraternities and four sororities on campus.

Faculty There are 600 full-time faculty members; 92 percent have terminal degrees. The student-faculty ratio is 10:1.

Key Facilities The library houses 1.5 million volumes. The Washington environment offers extensive research facilities. The University is linked to the National Academy of Science, the World Health Organization, and the State Department. Adjacent or close to campus are the Smithsonian, the National Gallery, the Kennedy Center, the Library of Congress, the National Archives, and the Federal Judicial Center.

Athletics The George Washington University is an NCAA Division I School. It is a member of the Atlantic 10 Conference. Varsity men and women's basketball, track, cross-country, crew, and tennis are available, as are men's baseball and golf and women's volleyball and gymnastics. There are also a substantial number of intramural and club athletics.

Support Services The Disabled Student Services Office works to ensure that the special services necessary for disabled students to participate fully in their academic programs and the extracurricular life of the campus are provided through University or community resources.

Tuition: $19,065 per year (1996-97)

Room and Board: $6240 minimum

Mandatory Fees: $915

Contact: Director: Dr. David Alan Grier, Building AF, 2138 G Street NW, Washington, D.C. 20052; Telephone: 202-994-6816; Fax: 202-994-8042; E-mail: uhp@gwis2.gwu.edu; Web site: http://gwis.circ.gwu.edu/~uhpwww

GEORGIA COLLEGE

4 Pu G M Tr

▼ Honors Program

The Honors Program at Georgia College (GC) provides a unique learning opportunity for superior students in an atmosphere that stimulates, challenges, and encourages creative thought and action. The program is divided into four parts, each of which is designed to help students realize their full intellectual potential with individualized instruction and personal guidance. Freshman-level honors section courses are offered as part of the general education program. These sections of regular courses are small, allowing students close contact with some of the best faculty members and providing the opportunity for more than routine lectures.

Honors sections allow students to do different types of work suited to their individual abilities and interests. Students may enroll in interdepartmental seminars offered for 2 credit hours during winter and spring quarters. The seminars consider topics of general interest and help students broaden their horizons by exposure to insights from many fields, thus enabling them to see life's basic problems from multiple viewpoints. Students who have attained junior-level status and have completed at least 20 hours in the upper division major area with a 3.0 overall average and 3.2 average in their major may take upper-level major-area courses for honors credit. Assignments are made in addition to regular work extending to the level of graduate courses.

Seniors who have completed 20 hours with a 3.0 overall average and a 3.2 average in their major have the opportunity to do an independent study, thesis, or other creative research project. For eligibility for an honors internship program, the student should complete 60 hours of his or her general education requirements, in addition to having completed a minimum of 20 hours in the major area. Students should also have a 3.0 overall average and 3.2 average in the major. Upon completion, students present their projects to the Honors Committee and explain the significance of their work.

The 25-year-old program currently enrolls 150 students.

Participation Requirements: Students remain in the program as long as they maintain a 3.0 GPA. If the average falls below the minimum, they are allowed a probationary period of two quarters to return to good standing. Such students may continue to take honors courses but are not eligible for recognition unless their average returns to 3.0. Recognition at graduation is given to those who complete the program. A special certificate is awarded with the diploma. Honors Day recognition is given to all students who take any honors courses during the year.

Admission Process: Entering students who have a high school average of 3.2 and an aggregate SAT I score of at least 1000 (1100 recentered) are invited by letter to join. Transfer students with a cumulative average of 3.2 are also invited. Other students who meet the 3.2 requirement after their first or subsequent quarters are eligible.

Scholarship Availability: Presidential Student Scholarships, available for a limited number of entering students, pay $2100 a year. If the student receives the HOPE Grant, the award amount is adjusted to $600 per quarter. Outstanding Student Scholarships, available for entering students and two-year college transfer students, pay for matriculation and fees of $400 per quarter for students receiving the HOPE Grant.

The Campus Context: Georgia College is composed of four schools—Arts and Sciences, Business, Education, and Nursing—that offer sixty-three degree programs.

Student Body Undergraduate enrollment is 4,523, with 40 percent of the students receiving financial aid. There are five sororities and seven fraternities recognized on campus.

Faculty There are 206 faculty members, and the student-faculty ratio is 22:1.

Key Facilities The library houses 172,386 volumes. The Flannery O'Connor room in the library honors the famous writer who was an alumna. Georgia College has a central Academic Computing Service Lab. Three electronic classrooms are included in the new Arts and Science Building.

Athletics Intercollegiate athletics for men include basketball, baseball, tennis, cross-country, and golf. Intercollegiate athletics for women include basketball, fast-pitch softball, tennis, and cross-country. The Office of Intramural Sports and Recreation provides team and individual sports, including fencing, water skiing, and soccer. GC Centennial Center is a 97,000-square-foot multipurpose center that facilitates a comprehensive health/physical education and intercollegiate athletic program.

Study Abroad Georgia College has developed a program, which enables students to study abroad for one or for part of one academic year while earning academic credit in their major field. An academic year abroad is currently offered at DeMontfort University, Leicester; the United Kingdom; and Universide de Valladolid, Spain. Summer study-abroad programs are available in Western Europe, the Pacific, Canada, and Mexico.

Support Services All buildings are handicapped-accessible.

Job Opportunities The Federal Work-Study Program provides jobs for students who show financial need and who must earn a part of their educational expenses. The Georgia College

Student Employment program provides additional opportunities to secure campus employment. Students are interviewed and hired by the various administrative offices, department offices, and other offices at the college.

Tuition: $1584 for state residents, $5463 for nonresidents, per year (1996-97)

Room and Board: $3345

Mandatory Fees: $339

Contact: Director: John E. Sallstrom, Campus Box 029, Milledgeville, Georgia 31061; Telephone: 912-453-4463; Fax: 912-451-2968; E-mail: jsalstr@mail.gac.peachnet.edu; Assistant Director: Robert J. Wilson; Telephone: 912-454-0956; E-mail: bwilson@mail.gac.peachnet.edu

GEORGIA SOUTHERN UNIVERSITY

4 Pu G S Sc

▼ Orell Bernard Bell and Sue Floyd Bell Honors Program

The Bell Honors Program (BHP) is designed to serve the undergraduate educational needs of exceptionally gifted, well-prepared, highly motivated, and creative students. For BHP scholars, an interdisciplinary and team-taught core curriculum employing seminar methods of instruction replaces the standard core curriculum required of other Georgia Southern University (GSU) students. Classes are small and taught by faculty members chosen from among the University's best professors.

The BHP core emphasizes development of critical-thinking skills, active student participation in their own learning, and extensive use of primary materials rather than conventional textbooks. Weekly seminars and colloquia at the freshman, sophomore, junior, and senior levels offer additional enrichment of the education of BHP scholars. BHP scholars who are undecided as to their majors are advised by the program director; other BHP scholars are advised by faculty members of the Honors Council in the appropriate fields.

BHP scholars enjoy special access to faculty members, including opportunities for undergraduate research in their major fields of study. The special BHP core curriculum is recognized by all programs and majors offered at GSU and BHP scholars may major in any field. The special core curriculum is designed for entry at the first-term freshman level and transfer students normally cannot be accepted into the program. The Bell Honors Program offers the atmosphere of a small and highly selective liberal arts college within the context of a university that is large and diverse enough to offer a wide array of strong major programs. The program reflects the central priority of undergraduate instruction, which lies at the core of Georgia Southern University's mission.

BHP scholars enjoy exclusive 24-hour access to Honors House for study and informal social activity. Honors House contains computers and printers for use of BHP scholars, a reference library, study lounges, and a full kitchen.

The program currently has 70 students enrolled.

Participation Requirements: Graduation with BHP scholar status requires completion of the special Bell Honors Program core curriculum (60 quarter hours), completion of 12 quarter hours of BHP seminars and colloquia, and satisfactory performance in all academic work in the judgment of the faculty members of the Honors Council, which conducts a systematic quarterly review of the academic work of each BHP scholar. BHP scholars completing all requirements are, with their parents, guests of honor at an annual dinner hosted by the University president on the evening prior to the June graduation. At this dinner each BHP scholar graduate is presented with an individually cast and crafted engraved medallion, which is worn at graduation and becomes a permanent memento of the special experience of participation in the program.

BHP scholars are accorded special recognition in graduation ceremonies, graduating first among undergraduate degree recipients. The diploma of each BHP scholar carries a special seal denoting his or her status. The transcripts of BHP scholars include special materials describing the selectivity of the program, the special requirements completed, and descriptions of the special program courses.

Admission Process: The first freshman class entered the BHP in 1982; the first senior class of BHP scholars graduated in 1986. A maximum of 18 new BHP scholars are accepted as entering freshmen annually. The new class is chosen from among high school senior applicants on the basis of SAT and/or ACT scores, high school grades and curricula, extracurricular activities, a required essay, letters of recommendation from teachers, and, for finalists, an individual interview with the Honors Council. Applications from nontraditional students are welcome. The annual deadline for submission of written applications is March 1, and selection decisions are made prior to May 1.

Scholarship Availability: Each BHP scholar is awarded an academic scholarship from the Georgia Southern University Foundation, which covers the cost of tuition and, where applicable, out-of-state fees. This scholarship is renewable for up to four years. BHP scholars who are National Merit Scholars or National Merit Scholarship Finalists qualify for an additional scholarship from the GSU Foundation of $1500 per year.

The Campus Context: Georgia Southern University was founded in 1906 as a district agricultural and mechanical school. It advanced to become a teacher's college, then a senior college, and in 1990 earned its status as one of five state universities in Georgia. Located 60 miles west of the historic city of Savannah, the University is located in Statesboro, a rapidly developing regional trade and manufacturing hub.

Georgia Southern is the most comprehensive university in the southern half of the state. Its more than 600 acres are lush with the traditional oaks, magnolias, pines, and azaleas of the American South. The University is composed of five colleges—Liberal Arts and Social Sciences, Science and Technology, Education, Business Administration, and Health and Professional Studies. One hundred fifty baccalaureate, master's, and doctoral programs are offered.

There are several points of general public interest on the campus, which also contribute to the academic experience of students. The University Museum features permanent and visiting exhibits that highlight the culture and history of south Georgia. It is home to a 40-million-year-old mosasaur fossil and the 80-million-year-old Vogtle whale, the oldest fossil whale skeleton in North America. The University Planetarium offers periodic shows by a nationally renowned astronomer and faculty member affiliated with the Hubble Space Telescope project. The National Tick Collection is a global clearinghouse for the identification and study of ticks and the diseases transmitted by them. The Tools for Life Center provides information, services and equipment for the disabled. Magnolia Gardens, the University's botanical garden, is a haven for plants and wildlife native to the region. It is frequently used by students to further their studies in biology.

Student Body The total enrollment at GSU is 14,157: 12,477 undergraduates and 1,680 graduates. Although 89 percent of the students are Georgia residents, forty-seven states are also represented in the student body. Fifty-six percent of the students are women. The ethnic distribution among students is 73 percent Caucasian, 24 percent African American, and 3 percent Asian, Hispanic, or other ethnic origin. There are 358 international students from sixty-seven nations. Extracurricular activities include twenty-three social fraternities and sororities, academic clubs relating to fields of study, and nationally affiliated political organizations.

Faculty Georgia Southern University has 600 full-time faculty members, and 65 percent have terminal degrees. There are also 70 part-time faculty members. The student-faculty ratio is 24:1.

Key Facilities The library contains 1.9 million volumes and has LEXIS-NEXIS access. The library also houses more than 300 DOS- and MacIntosh-based computers for student use in its Learning Resources Center.

Athletics In athletics, Georgia Southern has NCAA Division I affiliation (I-AA football). Men's sports are football, baseball, basketball, soccer, cross-country, golf, tennis, and swimming. Women's sports include softball, soccer, volleyball, basketball, tennis, swimming, and cross-country. Intramural athletic teams compete in flag football, basketball, softball, volleyball, and other sports. Club intercollegiate teams include rugby, fencing, and horseback riding.

Study Abroad Study-abroad opportunities are sponsored by some academic departments. Other programs are available through shared opportunities at other University System of Georgia schools.

Job Opportunities Many students may supplement their incomes with part-time employment in campus departments or through the Office of Financial Aid as part of an overall assistance package or acquire employment in local retail or service businesses.

Tuition: $1584 for state residents, $5463 for nonresidents, per year (1996-97)

Room and Board: $3675

Fees: $471

Contact: Director: Dr. G. Hewett Joiner, Landrum Box 8036, Statesboro, Georgia 30460; Telephone: 912-681-5773; Fax: 912-681-0377; E-mail: hewjoiner@gsvms2.cc.gasou.edu

GOUCHER COLLEGE

| 4 Pr G S Sc Tr |

▼ General Honors Program

The General Honors Program at Goucher offers students the chance to examine unusual subjects from complex, multicultural perspectives. It seeks to encourage students to cross boundaries and use problem-solving methods from a variety of fields. In most honors classes, students have 2 professors, each from a different academic specialty. Social science and humanities courses are interdisciplinary and team taught. Science courses focus on research in the laboratory.

While team taught, interdisciplinary courses form the core of the General Honors Program. "The Making of the Modern World" is the theme for the program. Honors students participate in the Freshman Honors Colloquium their first semester, which is a companion course to the Common Intellectual Experience (CIE) taken by all freshmen. CIE explores the individual and community in America since 1945, and the Freshman Honors Colloquium investigates coming of age in America from a multicultural perspective. All second-semester freshmen in the General Honors Program take "The Modern Condition," an examination of Western civilization between 1890 and 1945.

From the beginning of the sophomore year through the fall semester of the senior year, honors students choose three interdisciplinary electives. Recent honors offerings include "Philosophy and the Sciences: The Origin of Time," "Shakespeare: Stage and Page," "Vietnam: A Fateful Encounter," "Film and Modern Japan," and "African American Female Voices." In addition, honors sections are offered in biology, chemistry, and physics and honors students may begin taking these freshman year. All honors students must take at least one science honors elective and at least one nonscience honors elective. Students may also pursue independent honors study with individual faculty members.

The capstone experience is the Senior Honors Seminar, which is a course in imaginative problem-solving that offers students the opportunity to investigate a problem and write a research paper combining two disciplinary approaches. The most recent seminar explored the boundaries between nature and culture.

Besides taking honors courses, students attend plays, concerts, lectures, and other cultural events on and off campus. Each semester the Honors Program holds dinners to allow the faculty and students to exchange ideas and enjoy each other's company. General honors is noted on the student's diploma and transcript.

The 8-year-old program currently enrolls 83 students.

Participation Requirements: General honors students must maintain a 3.25 GPA in honors work. An overall GPA of 3.5, with at least 80 percent of the credits taken in residence on a graded basis, and no fewer than 60 total graded credits are also required for general honors.

Admission Process: Incoming freshmen must have a combined SAT I score of at least 1200 (with neither math nor verbal score below 550) and a ranking in the upper 10 percent of their high school class. There is also an on-campus interview during Scholar's Day. Other students who excel during their first year at Goucher and outstanding transfer students are also invited at the beginning of their sophomore year.

Applications must be received by March.

Scholarship Availability: Numerous merit awards are available to honors and nonhonors students, including Trustee Scholarships (full tuition, room, and board for four years); Dean's Scholarships (full tuition for four years); Marvin Perry Scholarships (partial tuition for four years); and Rosenberg Scholarships in the Arts ($5000 one-year scholarships).

Scholars must maintain full-time status and remain in good academic and disciplinary standing with the College. The awards fund 33 credits per year. Scholars must complete a minimum of 24 graded credits and a total of 30 credits per year and maintain the following GPAs throughout their matriculation at Goucher: Trustee Scholars, 3.0 GPA each semester freshman year, 3.25 GPA each semester sophomore year, and 3.5 GPA each semester during junior and senior years; Dean's Scholars, 3.0 cumulative GPA throughout freshman year and 3.25 cumulative GPA in subsequent years; Marvin Perry Scholars, 3.0 semester GPA throughout the four years.

The Campus Context: Goucher College offers eighteen majors for the Bachelor of Arts degree and five degrees in interdisciplinary areas. On the graduate level, Goucher offers the Master of Arts in Teaching degree, the Master of Arts in Historic Preservation degree, and the Master of Arts in Education degree. Among the distinguished facilities on campus are the Robert and Jane Meyerhoff Arts Center, the Thormann International Technology and Media Center, the Kraushaar Auditorium (seats 1,000), the Mildred Dunnock Theatre (black-box theater), the Todd Dance Studio, the Computer Music Studio, and the Huges Center for Public Affairs.

Student Body The student body at Goucher is 70.7 percent women. The ethnic distribution of the students is 7.8 percent African American, 4 percent Asian, 2.8 percent Hispanic, 4 percent nonresident, 73.1 percent Caucasian, and 8.3 percent other. There are 41 international students currently attending Goucher. Residents constitute 68 percent of the student body. Nearly 79 percent of students receive financial aid. There are no fraternities or sororities at Goucher.

Faculty Of the 147 total faculty members, 78 are full-time and 72 percent have a terminal degree. The student-faculty ratio is 10:1.

Key Facilities The Julia Rogers Library houses 282,531 volumes. There are a number of computer facilities on campus, including the Thormann International Technology and Media Center, which has approximately thirty computers; the Hoffberger 117, which has approximately fifteen computers; the Advanced Technology Lab, which has approximately fifteen computers; the Julia Rogers Library, which has approximately ten computers; and various terminals in areas such as the student center and dormitories

Athletics Goucher is an NCAA Division III competitor and a member of the Capital Athletic Conference. The Gophers, as the teams are called, compete in eight varsity sports for women (cross-country, field hockey, basketball, volleyball, lacrosse, swimming, tennis, and soccer) and six for men (cross-country, tennis, soccer, swimming, basketball, and lacrosse), as well as an equestrian intercollegiate program for both men and women.

Study Abroad Goucher's study-abroad programs include a junior year in Exeter, England; the Goucher College-Roehampton Institute Dance Exchange in London; a semester abroad in Salamanca, Spain; study-abroad in France (a semester or a year at the Sorbonne); The Politics of Great Britain (January); British Literary Study Tour (January or May); Tropical Marine Biology in Honduras (January); a Summer at London/Cambridge Institute; the Odessa Exchange Program; Summer Study in Greece; European Community Tour (January or summer); a semester/year in Tubingen, Germany; a semester/year in Jerusalem, Israel; a semester/year in Mexico; and the Instep Summer Internship Program (various locations).

Support Services Disabled students find that all programs are handicapped-accessible. Students with special needs can be accommodated. Handicapped-accessible parking is available in all lots and near most buildings. Equipped bathrooms and lowered drinking fountains are available in nearly all campus buildings.

While Goucher does not have a separate program for students with learning disabilities, the College does offer a variety of academic support services to all students through the Writing Center and the Academic Center for Excellence (ACE). Services offered through ACE include a mathematics lab, supervised study groups, academic skills peer tutoring, and content area peer tutoring for most courses.

Job Opportunities Eligible Goucher students may work on campus in federally funded work-study positions; non-work-study jobs are also available. In addition, students may receive payment through the Federal Work-Study Program for community service work. For those choosing employment outside of the campus community, many job opportunities are available in and around the Towson and Baltimore areas.

Tuition: $17,510 per year (1996-97)

Room and Board: $6570

Mandatory Fees: $250

Contact: Director: Dr. Julie Roy Jeffrey, 1021 Dulaney Valley Road, Baltimore, Maryland 21204-2794; Telephone: 410-337-6253; Fax: 410-337-6405; E-mail: jjeffrey@goucher.edu; Web site: http://www.goucher.edu

GRAMBLING STATE UNIVERSITY

4 Pu G M Sc

▼ Earl Lester Cole Honors College

The Earl Lester Cole Honors College is another dimension of excellence at Grambling State University designed to strengthen the development of scholars for service. The Honors College, a unit within the academic structure, began in 1990. The program enables academically talented students to take greater responsibility for their own education. Bright, determined students who wish to focus and broaden their horizons while earning a degree have the support of coadvisers and special faculty members, including those in the Honors College. All freshman students in the honors sequence are guided in the selection of required courses in liberal arts from the designated listing of honors sections. Students admitted to the Honors College after the freshman year are advised in their choice of interdisciplinary seminars and a variety of unique, challenging experiences, which lead to the achievement of their goals as effective leaders and workers. Honors College students are free to make choices that enrich their chosen degree-granting programs and that enhance sociocultural understandings and relationships.

Highly motivated students in the Honors College pursue a degree in a selected major in any one of the six colleges and schools. The Honors College does not offer a degree. Students are involved in diverse interdisciplinary seminars and academic and creative experiences. Along with a variety of unique academic courses and challenging seminars, students have the option of earning honors points of service (HPOS) through University and community outreach endeavors. HPOS are considered in determining the three levels of recognition/distinction in the Honors College at graduation.

The curriculum of the Honors College focuses on intellectually challenging learning activities, including general education courses, interdisciplinary seminars, colloquia, lecture series, independent study, research, and community service. The goal of the Honors College is to provide greater breadth, depth, diversity, creativity, skill in speaking, research, writing, and opportunities for intensive discourse. The college is designed to develop a national perspective and to empower students as responsible leaders for now and the twenty-first century.

There are currently 160 members of the Honors College. In the freshman honors sequence, there are approximately 110 students enrolled. To date, 252 members of the Honors College have graduated with recognition. The annual formal induction into the Honors College is held each fall during the last week in October. Parents attend the ceremony. Parents, teachers, and friends pin the inductees. During the fall ceremony, honorary members are presented.

Participation Requirements: Once admitted, students enroll in interdisciplinary seminars and other nontraditional curriculum offerings. Plans are underway for an honors student to make arrangements with a professor and receive honors credit, with the attendant notation on the transcript, for any course offered within the University curriculum. The honors student and the professor must agree on additional study, which exceeds the regular course requirements. Approval is granted by the Honors College director, the deans, and the professor with consent of the registrar.

The Honors College Program provides for extended academic challenges, various points of admission, and three levels of distinction in honors. Students begin as freshmen or enter as upperclassmen. They may choose to customize their honors plan of study. Members of the Honors College graduate with honors from the University and from the Honors College in keeping with the number and quality of hours earned in honors general education, the number of interdisciplinary seminars pursued and hours earned, and the number of general education honors hours plus the number of interdisciplinary seminar honors hours completed.

Incentives and recognition are provided. Membership in the Honors College is recognition in itself. To the extent possible, Honors College participants are housed in the honors dorms. At graduation, students in the Honors College wear bronze, silver, or gold medallions that represent their levels of distinction in honors. Other incentives include a symbol that identifies the graduate as a member of the Honors College, which is printed opposite each name on the Commencement program; verbal recognition that is given to each Honors College graduate by the deans during the awarding of diplomas; notations on the program referring to the quality of performance in honors, and printed symbols that indicate the level of academic honors achieved in the Honors College by the respective graduate.

The Commencement program shows the three levels of distinction in honors, which are based on the courses completed in the freshman honors sequence, hours earned in interdisciplinary seminars and related experiences, and a combination of foundation and interdisciplinary hours. Those who earn 24–26 semester hours in general education in honors with a minimum CGPA of 3.3 receive foundation honors. Students who participate in the Honors College after their freshman year and who complete 9–12 semester hours in the nontraditional honors sequence, with a minimum CGPA of 3.5 receive interdisciplinary honors. Those who graduate with combined honors hours in foundation and interdisciplinary

honors with a CGPA of 3.8, are awarded distinction in University honors. Honors College students are further recognized by a listing on the Commencement program with their names indicated according to the level of Honors Achieved.

Admission Process: Freshman students with the required ACT/SAT scores are permitted to enroll in the freshman honors sequence (FHS), which is the first level of participation in the Honors College. They take the required general education courses in English, history, mathematics, and the sciences designated as honors. The honors courses are taught by professors in the respective departments. Students admitted to the Honors College as sophomores and above must have an earned CGPA of 3.5 or better. An application and letters of recommendation are evaluated for approval.

Scholarship Availability: Funds are not available from the state and other sources for scholarships for the Honors College. Most of the students have been awarded Presidential Scholarships from other sources. However, a number of the participants do not have scholarships. The Honors College is considering a plan to secure funds for future scholarships and other needs through the establishment of a National Honors Board.

Tuition: $2088 for state residents, $4038 for nonresidents, per year (1996-97)

Room and Board: $2636

Contact: Director: Helen Richards-Smith, Adams Hall, Grambling, Louisiana 71245; Telephone: 318-274-2286; Fax: 318-274-6037; E-mail: honorsc@medgar.gram.edu

GUILFORD COLLEGE

4 Pr G M Sc Tr

▼ Honors Program

The Guilford College Honors Program provides a sequence of classes and independent study options designed to reward and intellectually challenge students seeking superior educational opportunities. Honors classes are small and usually taught as discussion-style seminars, which allow intensive learning in a close and supportive instructional relationship.

Students must take a minimum of six courses during their academic career. Students choose from a variety of team-taught, codisciplinary courses, and specially designed departmental offerings. Under the individual supervision of a faculty adviser, each student completes a senior thesis or project. The program is open to students majoring in all departments of the College. Successful completion of the Honors Program requirements is noted at graduation and on the student's transcript.

In addition to classwork and independent study, students in the Honors Program are invited to participate in a variety of social, cultural, and educational events. These include dinners with faculty members, informal discussions with other honors students and faculty members, visits to museums and concerts, and sponsored lectures and receptions with distinguished visitors.

In keeping with the College's Quaker heritage, honors students at Guilford participate fully in the larger campus community. They live in residence halls and take most of their courses with the full student body. Honors students are active in a full range of campus activities, including athletics, student government, campus publications, choir, theater, community service projects, and special interest clubs.

Guilford College, a founding member of the North Carolina Honors Association, participates in the National Collegiate Honors Council and Southern Regional Honors Council. Students, faculty members, and administrators from the College attend the conferences of all three organizations.

There are currently 140 students in the Honors Program.

Admission Process: Most students are admitted to the Honors Program as entering first-year students, and approximately 15–20 percent of the freshman class is accepted into honors. Based on standardized test scores, high school achievement, writing samples, and recommendations, students are invited to attend Spring Interview Day. On that day, prospective honors students are interviewed by faculty members and current students. In addition, first-year and sophomore students who have earned a cumulative GPA of 3.5 or higher are invited to join the program.

Scholarship Availability: Guilford College has allocated substantial funds for honors scholarships, which are awarded without regard to financial need and are currently held by two-thirds of the students in the program. Scholarships are normally awarded when students are admitted to the College.

The Campus Context: Guilford College is a private liberal arts college founded by the Religious Society of Friends (Quakers) in 1837. It is located in Greensboro, North Carolina, on a wooded 300-acre campus that contributes to a serene and friendly atmosphere. Its outstanding faculty is dedicated to undergraduate teaching and views learning as a collaborative venture between students and faculty members. The College offers twenty-nine academic majors plus five cooperative preprofessional programs and eight concentrations. There is also a domestic program in Washington, D.C.

Student Body The undergraduate enrollment at Guilford is 1,500 students. Women comprise 52 percent of the student body. Students are drawn from thirty-eight states and thirty-five other nations.

Faculty There are 88 full-time faculty members supplemented by a number of qualified part-time lecturers. Eighty-six percent of the full-time faculty members have terminal degrees. The student-faculty ratio is 14:1.

Key Facilities The library houses more than 220,000 volumes, and there are 700,000 volumes in the consortium libraries data base. The DEC ALPHA 2100 computing facilities have terminals in ten campus buildings and eight residence halls. There are three student computer labs on campus.

Athletics Athletic activities include seven men's varsity sports and five women's varsity sports as well as an intramural program and club sports. The campus has a Physical Education Center.

Study Abroad Study abroad is available in semester or year programs in Africa, China, England, France, Germany, Italy, Japan, and Mexico.

Tuition: $14,180 per year (1996-97)

Room and Board: $5270

Mandatory Fees: $270

Contact: Director: Dr. Robert B. Williams, 5800 W. Friendly Ave., Greensboro, North Carolina 27410; Telephone: 910-316-2218; Fax: 910-316-2950; E-mail: williams@rascal.guilford.edu

HAMPTON UNIVERSITY

4 Pr G M Sc Tr

▼ Honors College

Honors College (HC), the primary component of Hampton University's Honors Program, is a special honors track for motivated, high-achieving students who are willing to seek success rather than avoid failure, who have the courage to take intellectual risks, and who are able to see the world in a "grain of sand." Honors College, established on Hampton University's campus in fall 1986, is designed to promote the development of intellectual, ethical leadership skills while fostering excellence in education, commitment to the learning process, experimentation, and a sense of a learning community. Honors College involves all academic units of the University and includes experiences from the freshman through the senior years. It includes an innovative curriculum; individualized advising and support services; special options, opportunities, and financial incentives; and extracurricular activities.

The honors faculty is made up of teachers who have demonstrated excellence in teaching, who are interested in interdisciplinary applications, who are committed to working with students to facilitate learning and discovery, and who are willing to work with other faculty members to improve the academic environment of the University as a whole.

In addition to participating in enriched courses with others of a similar scholastic aptitude, the student may receive or take advantage of Honors College perquisites, which include the HC pin; priority in course selection at each semester's registration; individualized advising; eligibility for scholarships and internships; participation in special events, field trips, and social activities; a fee waiver for transcripts; individualized assistance in preparing resumes and/or applications for fellowships and postgraduate study; special recognition during Honors Day Convocation; the honors designation on transcripts, Commencement certificates, and the Commencement programs; special honors cords to be worn with graduation regalia; subsidized honors program and honors conference expenses; and the honors newsletter, *Word of Honor.* There are currently 150 students are enrolled in Honors College.

Participation Requirements: The Honors College requires students to complete 12 hours of honors credit in the general education courses and 12 hours of honors credit in the major, usually by contract. In addition, the Honors College student must take Argumentation and Debate or Logic and Ethics plus four University honors seminars, including UNV 200 Honors Service Learning Seminar, UNV 290 and 390 University Honors Seminar I and II, and UNV 400 Honors Independent Study Capstone Seminar. For the independent study, students are encouraged to choose a topic of interest that is not directly related to their major.

Admission Process: Entering freshmen, transfer students, and other students who are interested in pursuing an honors experience must apply for admission to Honors College after completing at least 15 hours of course work at the University. A student in Honors College is required to maintain a minimum GPA of 3.2. Other additional requirements are to perform at least 150 hours of community service, serve on an HC Committee for at least one semester, participate in a conference experience, and take the appropriate exam for graduate study.

Scholarship Availability: Hampton University offers a number of Presidential and Merit Scholarships. Many students who receive these scholarships are in the Honors College program.

The Campus Context: Hampton University is a privately endowed, coeducational, nonsectarian, comprehensive institution of higher learning with accreditation by the Southern Association of Colleges and Schools and the Department of Education of the Commonwealth of Virginia. A historically black institution, the University serves students from diverse national, cultural, educational, and economic backgrounds. Its curricula emphasis is scientific and professional with a strong liberal arts undergird. The University offers the bachelor's degree in forty-seven areas, the master's degree in eighteen areas, and a Ph.D in physics.

A picturesque campus, surrounded on three sides by water, comprises fifty main buildings and seventy-five auxiliary structures spread out over 204 acres. Five buildings on campus are registered as National Historic Landmarks. The Emancipation Oak, 95 feet in diameter, is designated by the National Geographic Society as one of the ten great trees in the world. This live oak earned its name because the Emancipation Proclamation was read to Hampton residents there in 1863. The shade of the oak served as the first classroom for a newly freed people seeking the blessings of education.

Student Body There are 4,741 undergraduate students, of whom 61 percent are women. There are six fraternities and sororities and eleven active honor societies on campus.

Faculty A faculty of 300 members plus adjunct faculty members afford a student-teacher ratio of 16:1.

Key Facilities The William R. and Norma B. Harvey Library is a major focal point of the academic and intellectual environment of Hampton University. This 125,000-square-foot, five-story facility has the capacity for more than 600,000 volumes. The fifth floor houses the Academic Technology Mall, which features state-of-the-art technology for student and faculty use.

Athletics Athletics play an important role in college life at Hampton. These activities offer every student a chance to take part in a sport of his or her choice. There is a program of intramural and recreational activities and intercollegiate athletic sports (NCAA Division I). Teams are fielded in football, basketball, tennis, track, volleyball, softball, golf, and sailing.

Study Abroad Hampton encourages study abroad. The Office of International Programs coordinates activities in fulfillment of the University's special emphasis in international affairs, culture, and global education. This office administers and oversees the development of cooperative agreements and exchange programs that provide mutually beneficial exchanges of scholars, students, and staff members as well as collaborative research projects.

Tuition: $8198 per year (1996-97)

Room and Board: $3878

Mandatory Fees: $750

Contact: Director: Dr. Freddye Davy, Box 6174, Hampton, Virginia 23668; Telephone: 804-727-5076; Fax: 804-727-5084

HARDING UNIVERSITY

4 Pr G M Tr

▼ Honors Program

The Harding University Honors Program was created in 1989 to better serve some of the University's many talented students. It provides opportunities for these students to enrich and broaden their academic experiences. Honors courses stimulate and challenge promising students to develop their scholarship and leadership skills as fully as possible. In particular, this program encourages students to develop high intellectual standards, independent thought, logical analysis, and insight into the nature of knowledge while building their faith in God.

Harding University's Honors Program features a three-tier approach to honors education. The Honors Scholar

Program serves 40 of Harding's top incoming students each year. Recruited from National Merit Finalists and Trustee Scholars in the freshman class, these students earn some of their general education credits in five honors classes that are limited to 20 students each and are based on discussion and student participation rather than lecture. The classes involve more written and oral work from the students, but they also allow an exceptionally close relationship with the teachers. Honors 201 deals with communication and critical thinking skills. Honors 202 replaces the New Testament survey for freshmen. Honors 203 fits in the humanities area of general education, focusing on the big questions that man has always asked. Honors 204 deals with man and society, covering issues that range from twin studies to chaos theory. Honors 205 addresses the issues of man and his environment.

The Honors Student Program offers students the opportunity to take one or more honors sections of general education classes such as speech, English, art, music, and Bible. To qualify, students must score 27 or above on the ACT or 1200 or above on the SAT I. The courses emphasize student responsibility and participation more than rote memorization. Some classes have more limited enrollment than the "regular" sections, and all are taught by faculty members selected and trained especially for honors education. Great care is taken that the courses are neither more difficult nor easier than the other general education offerings; instead, the focus is on different teaching styles and critical thinking. By following an honors track, students are preparing for their future careers in courses geared more to their academic preparation and ability.

Upper-level students who have completed the general education curriculum in either tier and upper-level and transfer students who qualify can participate in honors contract courses. In these courses students and teachers rewrite the syllabus of a course in the student's major, thereby turning it into an honors course. By changing some course requirements for other options that fit more with the ideals of honors education, the students can enhance the benefits they receive from courses that they take to complete their majors. The flexible nature of these contracts allows students to go into greater depth in some classes, to explore some supplementary topics in others, and to fine tune their educational experiences within the limitations of their major and the honors program.

The Honors Program is administered by a director and the Honors Council, which is comprised of faculty members, administrators, and students. The students elect an executive council that participates on the Honors Council and organizes various activities including speakers, retreats, picnics, and other social and cultural events. There are currently 450 students enrolled in the Honors Program.

Participation Requirements: To remain eligible for the Honors Program, students must maintain a 3.25 GPA. Transfers and other students may petition for acceptance by submitting an application and two letters of recommendation from faculty members. To complete the Honors Program, students must take a minimum of four courses in either the honors scholars tier or the honors student tier and then earn 15 hours (five courses) through upper-level contracts. Those who fulfill these requirements are identified at graduation as Honors Program graduates with distinction.

Scholarship Availability: Although many honors students receive University scholarships, the Honors Program itself does not award scholarships. Eighty percent of Harding University students receive some type of financial aid.

The Campus Context: Harding University is a private Christian institution of higher education committed to the tradition of the liberal arts and sciences. It is composed of the following academic units: a College of Arts and Sciences; a College of Bible and Religion; a School of Business, Education, and Nursing; and graduate programs in religion and education. Harding University has seventy-five undergraduate and three graduate degree programs on campus.

Student Body Women comprise 53 percent of the student body. The ethnic distribution of students is 3 percent African American, 1 percent American Indian, 1 percent Hispanic American, 1 percent Asian American, 5 percent foreign national, 88 percent Caucasian, and 1 percent other. There are 169 international students. Sixty-four percent of the students are residents. Social clubs involve a large majority of Harding students. Fourteen women's clubs and fifteen men's clubs provide students with a variety of club interests and sizes.

Faculty There is a total of 226 faculty members, of whom 178 are full-time. Seventy percent of the faculty members have terminal degrees. The student-faculty ratio is 17:1.

Key Facilities The library's collections include 407,000 volumes and other media, including records, videos, kits, and maps. Harding's Ethernet local area network interconnects campus computer and information resources and also provides access to global facilities via the Internet. Digital Equipment Corporation VAXs and Sun Microsystems UNIX machines support centralized computing services. Campus labs, which are open to all students, provide access to DOS/Windows applications and Macintosh applications. These public facilities are complemented by a diverse collection of departmental equipment, which addresses the unique needs of the various disciplines.

Athletics Athletics play an important role in Harding's educational and recreational life. Men's teams are fielded in football, baseball, basketball, track, cross-country, tennis, and golf. Women's teams include basketball, cross-country, tennis, track, and volleyball. Harding's outstanding intramural program involves about 70 percent of men and 55 percent of women. The program includes both team and individual sports, with competition among social clubs and teams organized by the program directors.

Study Abroad The Harding University International Programs, academic programs based in Florence, Italy (HUF); London, England (HUE); Brisbane, Australia (HUA); and Athens, Greece (HUG), provide unique opportunities for study and travel in Europe. No attempt is made to provide a broad curriculum but rather to offer courses that may be studied with profit in a European setting. Serious involvement in classes combined with the experience of international living furnish students with insights and perspectives that can be gained in no other way. Applications are accepted from students of Harding University and other institutions. Only students with a GPA of 2.0 on at least 27 semester hours are considered. Formal acceptance occurs the last full semester prior to the semester chosen for attendance.

Support Services Harding complies with the Americans with Disabilities Act of 1990. Most campus buildings are equipped for and accessible to handicapped persons. Class schedules are arranged and other measures taken to provide reasonable accommodations when necessary. New construction is in full compliance with the act.

Job Opportunities Work on campus is a source of financial aid to students, some of whom work up to 20 hours a week and earn more than $1400 per semester. Many, of course, work fewer hours and earn less. There are two work programs: the Federal Work-Study Program, funded by the federal government, and the Harding Program. To qualify for either program, students must complete an approved need-analysis application and the Harding Student Data Form. Students are paid minimum wage on the Federal Work-Study Program and are switched to the Harding Program when work-study funds are expended. The Harding Program rate of pay is 85 percent of minimum wage.

Tuition: $5775 per year (1996-97)

Room and Board: $3797

Mandatory Fees: $1050

Contact: Director: Dr. Larry R. Long, Box 898, Searcy, Arkansas 72149-0001; Telephone: 501-279-4617; E-mail: llong@harding.edu; Web site: http://www.harding.edu/

HENDERSON STATE UNIVERSITY

| 4 Pu G M Sc Tr |

▼ **Honors College**

The Honors College provides special attention, support, and opportunities for those students of the highest academic achievement and potential. The curriculum, which is planned and delivered primarily by a select honors faculty, comprises honors general education courses, upper-level interdisciplinary honors seminars and colloquia, independent- and directed-study opportunities, and honors work in each student's major field of study. The curriculum is arranged

so that Honors College students do not need to earn more credits for graduation than their contemporaries who are not in the Honors College.

As a complement to its academic program, the Honors College promotes a strong sense of community among students through an emphasis on University service, as well as on cultural and social activities. The Honors College Center and the Honors College residence hall are important hubs of community for students. Honors students also have their own organization, the Areté Society, which is administered by the Honors College Council and composed of 8 students, 2 from each academic classification. The Council members are representatives for, and leaders among, their honors classmates. Among its many accomplishments, the Areté Society numbers the establishment and staffing of an award-winning journal, which includes some of the best scholarly and creative work submitted by Henderson students.

The seed of Henderson's Honors College was a single course, the Honors Colloquium, first offered in the spring of 1979. From that course, the honors effort developed into a program by 1982 and a college by 1992.

Currently, 125 students are members of the Honors College.

Participation Requirements: Once admitted to the Honors College, a student remains in good standing by taking at least one honors class each fall and spring, and by maintaining a cumulative GPA of 3.25. To graduate as Honors College scholars, students must complete at least 24 hours of honors-designated work and earn a cumulative GPA of 3.25. In order to satisfy the 24-hour requirement, each Honors College scholar must complete 12 hours of honors general education courses and 12 hours of upper-division credit, which includes 6 hours designated by the student's major department. At Commencement, Honors College scholars lead the procession of graduates, are the first to receive their diplomas, and are presented with commemorative medallions. The designation Honors College Scholar is recorded on the diploma and the official transcript of each Honors College graduate, as well as in the Commencement program.

Admission Process: High school students are invited to apply for admission to the Honors College based on their ACT scores. They are selected on the basis of these scores, high school GPA, rank in class, a brief essay, and recommendations.

Scholarship Availability: A limited number of Honors College stipends are available on a competitive basis and are renewable as long as students remain in good standing. Any freshman who is accepted into the Honors College without a stipend may be eligible for one at the beginning of the sophomore year. Freshmen eligible for the Honors College are also eligible to compete for University scholarships, which are awarded on the basis of ACT composite scores at three levels, covering either tuition alone, room and tuition, or room, board, and tuition.

The Campus Context: Henderson State University's overarching mission is to serve as "Arkansas's public liberal arts university." Founded in 1890 as a private liberal arts institution, Henderson remains dedicated to providing excellent undergraduate education in the arts and sciences. Through a common core of courses in the liberal arts, as well as through more specialized curricula in a variety of major disciplines, the University fosters the maximum growth and development of each student. Henderson State University offers forty-nine degree programs on campus.

Henderson State is in Arkadelphia, a progressive city of 10,000 people set among forested hills, lakes, and rivers. The University is 67 miles southwest of Little Rock, the state's capital and largest city, and about 35 miles south of Hot Springs, home of America's oldest state park.

Student Body Undergraduate enrollment is 3,288; 1,828 of the students are women. The ethnic distribution of the student body is 80.9 percent Caucasian, 15.9 percent African American, and 3.2 percent other. There are 23 international students. Thirty-three percent of the students are residents, while the remaining 67 percent commute to campus. Sixty-six percent of students receive financial aid. There are seventeen sororities and fraternities at Henderson.

Faculty Of the 231 total faculty members, 163 are full-time and 68 are adjunct. Terminal degrees are held by 64.4 percent of the faculty. The student-faculty ratio is 19:1.

Key Facilities Among its special buildings and facilities are the Martin Garrison Activity and Conference Center, which serves as the student center and houses the Reddie Café; the student gymnasium; the game room; racquetball courts; a weight room; and student organization offices, as well as the radio station, the *Oracle* newspaper, and the *Star* yearbook. Foster Hall houses the Honors College Student Center, classrooms, administrative offices, and the *Arete* magazine office.

Henderson's Huie Library is one of the foremost research libraries in Arkansas, housing a collection of nearly half a million items. The library subscribes to more than 1,500 periodicals as well as more than fifty periodical indexes, including several computerized indexes. The library is a member of AMIGOS, a regional bibliographic network, and OCLC, an international bibliographic network, which give patrons access to more than 25 million items from more than 13,000 libraries worldwide.

Athletics Henderson belongs to NCAA Division II. Women's athletics are basketball, cross-country, swimming, tennis, and volleyball; men's athletics are baseball, basketball, cross-country, football, golf, swimming, and tennis.

Study Abroad Honors College students may take advantage of the British Studies Program, a residential summer session conducted annually at the University of London. The five-week sessions offer study for transfer credit in a variety of disciplines.

Tuition: $1860 for state residents, $3720 for nonresidents, per year (1996-97)

Room and Board: $2720

Mandatory Fees: $174

Contact: Director: Dr. David Thomson, 1100 Henderson Street, Arkadelphia, Arkansas 71999-0001; Telephone: 501-230-5192; Fax: 501-230-5144; E-mail: thomson@oaks.hsu.edu

HENRY FORD COMMUNITY COLLEGE

2 Pu G S Sc Tr

▼ **Honors Program**

The Honors Program at Henry Ford Community College is currently undergoing a major reorganization. Since its inception in 1978, the program has been largely unstructured; the only requirements were that students enroll in the Honors Colloquium, a 2-credit-hour humanities course, in their first semester and then sign-up for an honors option or directed study in the three subsequent semesters. The Honors Colloquium is organized by a member of the honors faculty around a humanities theme. Typically, the convener enlists the participation of other faculty members from across the College to present guest lectures on an overarching theme. Students are exposed to a wide variety of faculty members and diverse topics as well as teaching styles.

Students and faculty members alike praise the one-on-one contact they experience in the honors options and directed studies. In the honors options, faculty members agree to meet with an honors student enrolled in their regular course for 1 hour per week outside the classroom to explore course topics at greater depth.

With the appointment of a new director, the Honors Program at Henry Ford is currently discussing adding greater structure to its program with the addition of core courses aimed at strengthening the writing and research skills of its students. In addition to the Honors Colloquium and options/directed studies, the program would also require students to take a series of core courses in English, speech, computer literacy, social science research methods, foreign language, and math statistics. Nonscience majors would also be required to take two semesters of lab science in their second year, while science majors would be required to take two courses in literature, social science, or humanities to qualify for a new honors concentration on their degree.

Participation Requirements: Honors students must maintain a minimum 3.3 GPA. Students receive an honors designation on their transcripts denoting courses taken as honors options or directed studies.

Admission Process: Currently, successful high school applicants to the Honors Program must have a 3.0 GPA and have scored in the 80th percentile (composite) or above in the ACT or SAT. Internal applicants must have a 3.5 GPA.

Scholarship Availability: Henry Ford's Honors Program provides full tuition scholarships for its 50 students. The new program envisages expanding enrollment to 100–150 students, some paying their own way. It hopes to achieve this by aiding students in gaining admission to top-tier four-year institutions of their choice and increasing the students' likelihood of obtaining transfer scholarships. The new program, as currently envisaged, will offer a faculty mentoring program for students.

The Campus Context: Henry Ford Community College was established in 1938 as the Fordson Junior College. Classes were suspended for two years during World War II. In 1952, the College adopted its current name. In 1956, the Ford Motor Company donated 75 acres for use by the College not far from the company's world headquarters. Among distinguished facilities are a state-of-the-art robotics lab and the Ford-UAW national training institute on campus. The College offers three degree programs, including the Associate in Arts, the Associate in Business, and the Associate in Science.

Student Body There are about 16,000 full- and part-time students on two campuses (a main campus in Dearborn and another in nearby Dearborn Heights). The College currently enrolls 82 international students (F-1 visa holders) from thirty-three countries in Europe, the Middle East, Africa, Asia, and Latin America. All students commute to campus. While there are no fraternities or sororities on campus, there is an active Phi Theta Kappa chapter.

Faculty The faculty consists of approximately 220 full-time and 530 adjunct faculty members; 19 percent hold doctorates, 78 percent have a master's degree or higher, and 3 percent hold bachelor's degrees. The student-faculty ratio 22:1.

Key Facilities The library houses 89,000 volumes. There are approximately twelve computer labs, and additional labs are being planned.

Athletics Athletics include four women's sports (volleyball, softball, basketball, and tennis) and four men's sports (golf, baseball, basketball, and tennis). The athletic program is in the top five annually in the MCCAA competition for the All-Sports Trophy. Henry Ford has fielded a number of state, regional, and national championship teams, as well as several Academic All-Americans. Last year, 2 student athletes were named Distinguished Academic All-Americans with GPAs of 3.9 or better, and another student was named to the Academic All-American Team with a GPA of 3.6 or better.

Study Abroad The College offers a European Study Abroad program in the summer semester. Students may arrange part of their study abroad by registering for study courses under the direction of faculty members in various departments. The work is planned and evaluated on campus but carried out overseas.

Support Services The College maintains an Office of Special Needs, a comprehensive facility serving students with physical and mental needs and learning handicaps. The Office of Special Needs assists about 300 students a semester. The College also provides special computer labs to assist visual- and learning-impaired students.

Job Opportunities Three types of work opportunities for students are available. They are co-op education programs, college work-study, and employment by individual department.

Tuition: $1470 for area residents, $2310 for state residents, $2610 for nonresidents, per year (1997-98)

Mandatory Fees: $240

Contact: Director: Dr. Nabeel Abraham, L-109E Liberal Arts Building, 5101 Evergreen Road, Dearborn, Michigan 48128; Telephone: 313-845-6460; Fax: 313-845-9778; E-mail: nabraham@mail.henryford.cc.mi.us

HILLSBOROUGH COMMUNITY COLLEGE

2 Pu G S Sc Tr

▼ Honors Program

Hillsborough Community College's (HCC) Honors Program is designed to provide an intellectually stimulating academic program for exceptionally talented and motivated students. The overall goal of the program is to provide an academic atmosphere in which students learn to think critically, to grow intellectually, and to mature as responsible citizens and leaders. Academic emphasis is on encouraging students to present scholarly papers and projects, to use primary sources, to participate in alternative learning strategies, and to experience related cultural and social activities.

The HCC honors faculty is dedicated to inspiring students to participate actively in their own educational experience so that together the students and faculty members achieve the following goals: create an atmosphere of scholarly research resulting in a major documented paper or project; cultivate the higher levels of the cognitive domain, including application, analysis, synthesis, and evaluation; experiment with alternative learning strategies to foster an environment of creative interaction and intellectual flexibility; and explore personal attitudes and values to form an ethical canon with which to meet the challenge of a world of extreme transitions.

In addition to enhanced educational opportunities, honors students may have the following advantages: additional scholarship opportunities, honors counseling and priority registration, small classes, an honors study lounge, cultural and social activities, advanced university preparation, extended library privileges, travel opportunities, special recognition at graduation, and an honors designation on diploma and transcripts.

The program began in fall 1996 and currently enrolls 70 students.

Participation Requirements:
Students must take a minimum of 6 honors courses selected from at least four of five discipline areas, including communications, humanities, mathematics, natural science, and social science. Students are introduced to the Honors Program and college work in a 1-credit orientation seminar. They must also perform 12 hours of community service during each honors semester. At graduation, HCC formally recognizes students who complete their honors work with a minimum GPA of 3.0 by awarding them diplomas denoting distinction in honors. Students who do not fulfill all Honors Program requirements but complete at least four honors courses with a minimum overall GPA of 3.0 earn the HCC Honors Certificate.

Admission Process:
Students must complete the HCC application forms for admission and the HCC Honors Program application forms, which include an essay writing sample, high school or college transcripts, and a written recommendation from a high school or college faculty member. Applicants must meet a least one of the following criteria to qualify for the Honors Program: a minimum high school GPA of 3.5 on a 4.0 scale (unweighted); a minimum of 12 semester hours of college credit with a minimum GPA of 3.3; a minimum SAT I score of 1160 or ACT composite score of 26; or a minimum of 12 semester hours of dual enrollment credit with a minimum GPA of 3.3. For the fall term, the application deadline is April 9. Students should apply by December 1 for the spring term.

Scholarship Availability:
There are forty-eight tuition scholarships available on a competitive basis.

The Campus Context:
Hillsborough Community College has four campuses: the Dale Mabry Campus, the Ybor Campus, the Brandon Campus, and Plant City. The College offers thirty-five associate degree programs.

Student Body Undergraduate enrollment is 20,738, and 58 percent of the students are women. The ethnic distribution for the student body is 2 percent international students and resident aliens, 3 percent Asian, 1 percent Indian, 12 percent African American, 13 percent Hispanic, and 69 percent Caucasian. All students commute to campus, and 29 percent of the students receive financial aid. While there are no fraternities or sororities, students will find at least fifteen student organizations on the several campuses.

Faculty Of the 708 faculty members, 253 are full-time. The student-faculty ratio is 21:1.

Key Facilities The library houses 94,977 volumes. There are fourteen computer labs on campus, including a Developmental English Lab, an ESL Lab, a Graphics Lab, a Word Processing Lab, and a Project Literacy Lab.

Athletics The varsity sports program consists of volleyball, basketball, and softball (fastpitch) for women and basketball and baseball for men. The Hawks are members of the Florida Community College Activities Association, Suncoast Conference (Division III), and Region VIII of the National Junior College Athletic Association. Tennis and racquetball courts are available for educational and recreational use by HCC students and the community. The gymnasium, which serves as the home court of the Hawks basketball and volleyball teams, also houses faculty offices and classrooms. The weight training room and gymnasium are open for student use free of charge at designated times. The HCC cheerleading squad performs at many athletic events and represents HCC at parades and other community events.

The Athletic Division sponsors intramural programs in the fall and spring semesters. The program includes club activities, league and tournament play, open recreation, and special events.

Support Services Disabled-student accommodations include tutors/notetakers/readers, an LD specialist, adjustable tables and chairs, Braille writers and printers, wheelchairs on every campus, tape recorders, talking scientific calculators on each campus, and visual techs.

Job Opportunities Work opportunities include college work-study and student assistantships.

Tuition:
$34.47 for state residents, $131.50 for nonresidents, per credit hour (1997-98)

Contact:
Director: Dr. Lydia Daniel, HCC Honors Office, 10414 E. Columbus Drive, Tampa, Florida 33619; Telephone: 813-253-7894; Fax: 813-253-7850; Web site: http://www.hcc.cc.fl.us

HILLSDALE COLLEGE

4 Pr G S Sc Tr

▼ Honors Program

Founded in 1975, the Hillsdale College Honors Program exists to encourage and support exceptionally gifted students in becoming broadly and deeply versed in the contents and methods of inquiry of the liberal arts, especially as conveyed by the great thinkers of the Western tradition, to the full measure of their capacity. Its interdisciplinary nature encourages students to explore the common threads that link fields of intellectual inquiry.

The core curriculum represents the College's vision of what a liberal arts education should be. Since the Honors Program aims to promote academic excellence in the Western tradition of the liberal arts and great books, it is based firmly on that common vision. To that end, the honors curriculum consists of two complementary components: a more rigorous version of the core curriculum and a sequence of honors seminars designed to emphasize the connections between the various parts of the core.

The first tier of the core curriculum requires students to take two semesters of English, history, and science. Students in the Honors Program satisfy this part of the core by taking honors sections of freshman English and heritage, differential calculus, and two introductory science courses chosen from college or university physics, general chemistry, evolution and ecology, and molecular genetics and cellular function. Appropriate Advanced Placement credit may be accepted in fulfillment of the science and mathematics requirements. In the second tier, the core curriculum requires students to choose one course in literature, one in the fine arts, one in philosophy or religion, and two in the social sciences. Students in the Honors Program take honors sections of at least three of their five second-tier core courses, including at least one in the social sciences. The humanities and social science divisions each offer at least one honors core course every semester, to be rotated among the disciplines offering second-tier core courses.

Each semester, students in the Honors Program participate in 1-credit seminars, which are broadly interdisciplinary in focus. These seminars emphasize the common themes that link the liberal arts, thereby encouraging students in the program to integrate the insights they have gained from their core courses. Each seminar or sequence of seminars requires students to write and present one or more essays. Seniors present their papers at the Honors Colloquium each spring. The senior paper represents the culmination of the honors experience. A journal for the publication of each year's best seminar papers is currently being planned.

Acropolis, the extracurricular wing of the Honors Program, provides opportunities for interaction among honors students in different classes, thereby contributing to the formation of an intellectual community among students in the program. It meets regularly during the academic year for social interaction, discussion, and occasional special speakers and field trips.

The Honors Lounge, which the program shares with English majors, provides study facilities, including a Power Macintosh 7100 computer with Internet access.

Participation Requirements:
All honors students must maintain a cumulative GPA of 3.4 and exhibit character consistent with the program's purposes. Students whose averages fall below 3.4 are placed on probation and given one semester to attain the required standard. Failure to do so normally results in dismissal from the Honors Program. Failure in any course is grounds for dismissal from the program at the discretion of the Honors Committee.

Honors Program graduates receive specially designated diplomas, and their permanent transcripts note their successful completion of the Honors Program curriculum.

Admission Process:
Freshmen admitted to the Honors Program generally have a high school GPA of 3.5 or better and a combined SAT I score of 1300 or better or a composite ACT of 30 or better. Invitations to apply for the program by submitting essays on topics set by the Honors Committee are sent out in late January; prospective students interested in the program should apply for admission to the College by January 15. A maximum of 36 freshmen and transfer students are admitted annually to the honors program. Students may seek admission after enrolling at Hillsdale; however, they are only rarely admitted following the beginning of their sophomore year.

Scholarship Availability:
The College maintains a comprehensive scholarship program for students with outstanding high school records, without regard to financial need. These scholarships are renewable each semester for four years, provided the holder has maintained a 3.0 cumulative scholastic average. A limited number of full tuition scholarships are awarded to incoming freshmen who graduate in the top 5 percent of their high school classes, place in the top 5 percent of national SAT or ACT norms, present two strong letters of recommendation from high school officials, and have a superior interview with the Scholarship Selection Committee. Several half-tuition awards assist incoming freshmen who graduate in the top 10 percent of their high school classes, rank in the top 10 percent of national SAT or ACT norms, have a strong leadership record and extracurricular involvement, obtain two supportive recommendations from high school officials, and have a favorable interview with the Scholarship Selection Committee.

The Campus Context:
Hillsdale College is an independent, nonsectarian institution of higher learning founded in 1844 by men and women "grateful to God for the inestimable blessings" resulting from civil and religious liberty and "believing that the diffusion of learning is essential to the perpetuity of these blessings." It pursues the stated objectives of the founders: "to furnish all persons who wish, irrespective of nation, color, or sex, a literary and scientific education" outstanding among American colleges and to combine with this such moral "and social instruction as will best develop the minds and improve the hearts of its pupils."

The College considers itself a trustee of modern man's intellectual and spiritual inheritance from the Judeo-Christian faith and Greco-Roman culture, a heritage finding its clearest expression in the American experiment of self-government under law. By training the young in the liberal arts, Hillsdale College prepares students to become leaders worthy of that legacy. By encouraging the scholarship of its faculty, it contributes to the preservation of the legacy for future generations. By publicly defending that legacy, it enlists the aid of other friends of free civilization and thus secures the conditions of its own survival and independence. Hillsdale offers forty-two degree programs.

Student Body Approximately 1,150 students, of whom 52 percent are women, are enrolled full time, and more than 90 percent of them are residents. The College values the unique merit of each individual and so keeps no record of students' racial or ethnic backgrounds. There are approximately 15 international students. More than 80 percent of Hillsdale students receive tuition assistance, largely from the College's privately funded scholarships. Students are not permitted to receive federal grants or loans. Michigan residents may be eligible for merit- and need-based awards from the state. There are four national fraternities and four national sororities that have chartered chapters at Hillsdale.

Faculty There are a total of 124 faculty members, 89 of whom are full-time and 83 percent of whom earned terminal degrees. The student-faculty ratio is 12:1.

Key Facilities There are a number of exceptional facilities on campus. Hillsdale Academy, a K–8 model school established by the College in 1990, and the Mary Proctor Randall Preschool, an innovative structure praised by experts as "a model for the nation," provide students in Hillsdale's state-certified Teacher Education Program with extensive, practical classroom experience. The Dow Leadership Development Center allows students to earn academic credit in professional seminars attended by representatives of major corporations and successful family businesses. Slayton Arboretum, a 48-acre outdoor laboratory, strengthens the botany curriculum and enhances the atmosphere of the campus with its well-tended rare tree and shrub collections, ponds, bridges, and hand-built fieldstone walls, gazebos, and walkways. Athletes benefit from the state-of-the-art Prescription Athletic Turf installed on Waters Field just as Division I and professional teams began to adopt the technology.

The College's library houses 201,137 volumes. The Place for Information Technology, a networked lab, offers high-use word-processing, spreadsheet and statistical software and worldwide electronic mail and Internet access on Apple Macintosh computers. The facility also has two IBM-compatibles. The Wiegand Lab is an interactive classroom equipped with nearly two dozen more powerful Macintosh machines for interactive computerized instruction across the disciplines. A graphics lab in the Sage Center for the Arts features high-end Macintosh models, numerous graphic-design software packages, and state-of-the-art peripherals. In the Mathematics/Computer Science Lab, twenty-four Power Macintosh 8500 computers and two Gateway 2000 computers are available for student use. Various software packages are available on these units, including word processing, spreadsheet, database, graphics, and statistical and mathematical applications. Also, a DEC Micro VAX II minicomputer is available in the lab. This system utilizes several computer languages and the UNIX operating system. A number of individual departments, both in the sciences and in the humanities, maintain individual computer minilabs for students in those disciplines.

Athletics Hillsdale is a member of the National Collegiate Athletic Association (Division II) and the National Association of Intercollegiate Athletics (Division I). Regionally, the College is affiliated with the Midwestern Intercollegiate Football Conference and the Great Lakes Intercollegiate Athletic Conference. Women compete in cross-country, indoor and outdoor track, volleyball, basketball, softball, tennis, and swimming while men's teams are fielded in baseball, basketball, cross-country, football, golf, tennis, and indoor and outdoor track. Intramural teams compete actively in football, basketball, and other sports and club teams have formed to play hockey, lacrosse, and soccer.

Study Abroad Hillsdale allows 3 highly qualified juniors or seniors to study abroad each semester at Oxford University, where they participate in all academic and social programs of Oxford's Keble College and Center for Medieval and Renaissance Studies. Students may also apply for Oxford summer school, a six-week program held from early July through mid-August. Economics, business, and accounting students may study at Regent's College, London, a British-American center of international education. Qualified students may spend a semester in Seville, Spain, studying the Spanish language and culture and may also attend courses at the University of Seville. Students may enroll in language courses taught each summer at Universität Wuerzburg, Germany, by Hillsdale College faculty members and other American German professors.

Support Services All of the College's academic buildings are handicapped-accessible, barrier-free facilities.

Job Opportunities After being accepted for admission, a prospective freshman may request a part-time job application from the Office of Student Financial Aid. An average student job requires a commitment of at least 10 hours per week. Marriott Corporation Food Service employs many students each semester to work during mealtimes and to help in catering and serving special dinners and luncheons on campus. Other students work in the library, bookstore, student union, or as part-time office help for professors or College departments. Some are employed by the maintenance department to help with grounds work, while others work as chauffeurs and escorts for campus guests. Students are paid an hourly wage. Through its Service Opportunities and Rewards program, the College places mature, responsible students with local community service agencies and, in many cases, pays some or all of their wages. Transportation for program participants is provided.

Tuition: $12,110 per year (1996-97)

Room and Board: $5180

Mandatory Fees: $210 full-time; $105 part-time

Contact: Director: Dr. Christopher Busch, 33 East College Street, Hillsdale, Michigan 49242; Telephone: 517-439-1524 ext. 2386; Fax: 517-437-3923; E-mail: christopher.busch@ac. hillsdale.edu; Web site: http://www.hillsdale.edu/ honorsprogram/catalogue.html

HINDS COMMUNITY COLLEGE

2 Pu G M Sc

▼ **Honors Program**

The mission of Hinds Community College Honors Program (HCCH) is to provide an enhanced and supportive learning environment for outstanding students. The honors program curriculum features designated core-curriculum honors course sections, seminars, interdisciplinary studies, independent study, research opportunities, international study, and leadership development. Special cocurricular activities and field trips are also part of the honors program. Individual and group counseling are provided through the College Counseling Offices and the HCCH Center. HCCH students are given priority in scheduling courses at HCC. The program also helps honors students locate and apply for scholarships at four-year institutions and schedules campus visits and introductions to honors programs at four-year institutions. The HCCH program works closely with Phi Theta Kappa and other honorary scholastic societies with HCC chapters to encourage and reward academic excellence.

Honors courses are offered in the core curriculum areas of art, biology, education, English, history, humanities, math, psychology, and speech. In addition, courses are offered in career exploration, leadership development, and improvement of study. Classes typically have 15–20 students. This allows for collaborative and experiential learning, an assortment of hands-on activities, and more opportunities to read and write at advanced levels. Students are encouraged to become outstanding, independent learners capable of critical thinking and self-expression. Honors courses are taught by experienced members of the Hinds teaching faculty who are known for excellence in the classroom as well as in their academic fields. Students have frequent interaction with other honors students and faculty members help to build a community spirit. The HCCH Center provides a location for students to gather and visit or study. The center has a library, computer lab, group study area, and lounge for both faculty member and student use. The Honors Forum, a weekly seminar for all honors students, provides an opportunity for intellectual discussion on the issues facing society today. Honors advisers in the HCC counseling offices and HCCH Center provide students with personalized attention. Students' individual needs and interests are given priority in all advising.

Students also enjoy picnics, lectures, special presentations, workshops, and field trips. Special events are also scheduled for those students living in Main Hall and Virden Hall on the Raymond Campus.

The first year of a comprehensive program was 1995. Courses have been taught on the Raymond Campus for 20 years. There are now 150 students enrolled in the program. For priority, students should apply no later than March 1.

Participation Requirements: Students are eligible to receive all of the HCCH benefits and fringe benefits as long as they are registered participants. A registered participant of the Honors Program must undertake at least 3 hours of honors work during a semester. Honors scholarship students must undertake at least 7 hours of honors work during a semester and must enroll in the Honors Humanities Forum each semester (1 semester-hour credit). To graduate from Hinds Community College Honors Program with honors, the HCCH student must complete 30 hours of honors study and maintain

a minimum overall GPA of 3.0. Students who accomplish this receive an Honors Program medallion at the graduation ceremonies and an honors seal on the diploma. Honors certificates are given to those graduating students who complete 18–29 honors credits with an overall GPA of 3.0.

Scholarship Availability: The following scholarships are contingent on criteria in parenthesis: Faculty Scholarships (ACT 21–24); Dean's Scholarships (ACT 25–28); Residential Scholarship (ACT 29+); and Development Foundation Scholarships (criteria vary). HCCH scholarships are available for a maximum of four consecutive fall and spring semesters. Applicants must be Mississippi residents and must be enrolled in 12 or more semester hours, 7 of which must be in honors studies. Scholarship recipients must maintain full-time student status and a minimum 3.0 GPA. Applicants must complete an HCC Financial Aid /Scholarship Application and an HCCH Application and must submit both forms to the HCCH Center. Recipients must be registered with the HCCH Program. The deadline for application is March 1 of each year for the following school year.

The Campus Context: Hinds Community College is composed of six campuses, including the Academic/Technical Center, the Nursing and Allied Health Campus, the Rankin Campus, the Raymond Campus, the Utica Campus, and the Vicksburg Campus. The Raymond Campus offers twenty-eight degree programs.

Student Body On the Raymond Campus, the chief location of the Honors Program, undergraduate enrollment is almost equally divided between men and women. The ethnic distribution of students on campus is 34.5 percent African American, 60.9 percent Caucasian, and about 4.5 percent representing other groups. There are 2 international students. Residents make up 23.7 percent of the Raymond population. Approximately 52 percent of students on campus receive financial aid. There are thirty-four student clubs and social organizations on the Raymond Campus.

Faculty Of the 237 faculty members teaching on the Raymond campus, 178 are full-time. The student-faculty ratio is 16:1.

Key Facilities Noteworthy facilities on campus include the One-Stop Career Center, the Learning Assistance Center, the Resource and Coordinating Unit for Economic Development, the Video Production Studio, the Interactive Classroom, the Deaf and Hard of Hearing Services, the Eagle Ridge Conference Center, the Eagle Ridge Challenge Course, and the Eagle Ridge Golf Course.

The Raymond Library houses 92,325 volumes. The existing library system is currently an on-line catalog only and interconnects each of the libraries on all six campuses, which contain a composite collection of 164,084 volumes.

Computer facilities include the state-wide Community College Network (CNN) that is available at Hinds only on the Raymond campus. Eighteen other universities and schools of higher education are connected to this network, which provides two-way audio and video for conferences, and/or distance learning as may be required.

There are 1,127 PCs available for student use, including 880 modem units (IBM 386s and 486s and Macs), which attach to the collegewide network. The largest and latest computer facility on the Raymond Campus is Moss Hall and there are plans to open further facilities in the Media Center. The Raymond Campus currently has a total of fifteen instructional networks.

Athletics Hinds Community College is a member of the Mississippi Junior College Athletic Association and National Junior College Athletic Association. Varsity athletics at the Raymond Campus include football, baseball, golf, softball, track, and soccer.

Study Abroad Hinds Community College is a member of an academic consortium of several colleges and universities in the southern and southwestern United States, supporting an international study program entitled The British Studies Program. This program is a residential summer session offered annually during July and August in London, England. While allowing participants ample free time for independent travel, the session offers upper-division undergraduate and graduate course work. Students can earn up to 8 semester hours in on-site lecturing coordinated by local British scholars who are experts in their fields.

Three- and five-week courses in a wide range of academic disciplines, including humanities, business, education, and fine arts, are offered through the British Studies Program. A minibreak is also scheduled to allow time for personal travel outside of London, along with low-cost optional day tours to general places of interest. Paris, Scotland, Cambridge, Dover, Canterbury, Bath, and Stonehenge are often included.

Support Services Facilities include wheelchair ramps, elevators, and restrooms in instructional buildings, libraries, and residence halls; telecommunications devices (TDD); decoders for closed captioned TV viewing; and flashing fire alarms and doorbells. Interpreters are provided for the deaf and hard of hearing students. Special assistance is given to the visually impaired by the provision of readers, part-time guides, and library visual aid interpreting equipment, including Braille textbooks, tape textbooks, visual tech and Braille typewriters. The Disability Support Services Department provides tutorial and other support services for students who qualify through federal guidelines for Student Support Services for Disadvantaged Students.

Job Opportunities Work opportunities on campus include student worker and work-study positions.

Tuition: $1020 for state residents, $3226 for nonresidents, per year (1996-97)

Room and Board: $1070

Mandatory Fees: $50

Contact: Director: Kristi Sather-Smith or Associate Director: Dr. Lura Scales, P.O. Box 1292, HCCH, 212 Administration Building, Raymond, Mississippi 39154; Telephone: 601-857-3531 or 800-HINDSCC Ext. 3531; Fax: 601-857-3392

HOLYOKE COMMUNITY COLLEGE

2 Pu G S Sc Tr

▼ Honors Program

The Honors Program at Holyoke Community College (HCC) offers a challenging and rigorous program of study that can be individually designed to fit a student's interests and curriculum. The Honors Program provides a chance to obtain an excellent education at a very low cost with unequaled opportunities for transfer.

The Honors Program consists of five different components. During the freshman year, the program offers an honors learning community that is team taught, integrating the arts and sciences. Students have the opportunity to work closely with faculty members, a reference librarian, and with each other. Learning communities promote multidisciplinary learning experiences that emphasize student seminars, collaborative research projects, and an introduction to scientific and humanistic intellectual history while completing required courses. Learning communities at HCC have been supported by grants from the National Endowment for the Humanities, the National Science Foundation, the Fund for the Improvement of Post-Secondary Education, and the National Collegiate Honors Council.

Honors colloquia are designed to bring students from all academic disciplines together to confront a theme or issue of current concern from the variety of perspectives that the different disciplines represent. Honors colloquia are multidisciplinary courses (e.g. Infinity, Visions of Nature, Monsters, The Evolution of Reality) that are competitively enrolled and limited to 15 students who are selected each semester by the Honors Committee. The Honors Program awards a colloquium textbook scholarship to all colloquium students. Colloquia generally offer field trips and a series of expert guest speakers. An Honors Colloquium is strongly recommended to those students who wish to transfer to more selective colleges and universities.

An honors project consists of additional, independent work that a student chooses to undertake in conjunction with a professor in most HCC courses. Such work may consist of an extra paper, a paper of greater length or complexity, a research project in a practical setting such as a lab or darkroom, or creative work such as painting, sculpture, writing, or performance. Project topics are limited only by the student's imagination or ability, the professor's course guidelines, and a regard for the degree of academic rigor that is expected by the HCC Honors Program.

The Honors Program was founded in 1984 by Dr. Marion Copeland. The program averages about 100 students per year who are generally expected to maintain a GPA of at least 3.5.

Participation Requirements: Entrance into the program is flexible. Usually, a student must either enter the College as an honors student or achieve a GPA of at least 3.5 after earning at least 12 credit hours. All courses within the program emphasize writing, critical and creative thinking across disciplines, and analysis. Upon successful completion of an honors project, the student receives an additional credit for the course and the student's transcript shows that the course was taken with honors. Projects must receive initial and final approval from the Honors Committee.

Students may elect to fulfill the honors curriculum option, which amounts to choosing honors as a major. This option is similar to the arts and science transfer option, but requires completion of an honors learning community, an honors colloquium, and a foreign language.

Students who achieve a GPA of at least 3.5 after 30 hours earned at HCC are invited to be inducted into the international honor society of Phi Theta Kappa. Members are eligible for scholarships and other benefits.

Scholarship Availability: Several scholarships are awarded each year to entering students. Three Honors Program scholarships of $500 each are given annually to graduating students, and the College offers several larger scholarships that are frequently awarded to Honors Program students. Additional scholarship opportunities are also available.

The Campus Context: Holyoke Community College was founded in 1946 but moved into its modern, 135-acre facility in 1974. HCC is located in the Connecticut River Valley of western Massachusetts, close to the Massachusetts Turnpike (I-90) and just off I-91. HCC is located in the region of Springfield, Northampton, and Amherst and is in the heart of the Five College Area (Amherst College, the University of Massachusetts at Amherst, Hampshire College, Mount Holyoke College, and Smith College). A.A. and A.S. degrees and certificates are offered.

Student Body There are 3,300 Day Division students and 2,900 Division of Continuing Education students.

Faculty The student-faculty ratio is 17:1.

Athletics Intercollegiate soccer, baseball, tennis, basketball, softball, and golf are available. There are twenty-nine clubs and student organizations.

Support Services Facilities for disabled students are excellent.

Tuition: $2460 for state residents, $7590 for nonresidents, per year (1996-97)

Mandatory Fees: $796

Contact: Director: Dr. James M. Dutcher, 303 Homestead Avenue, Holyoke, Massachusetts 01040; Telephone: 413-552-2357; Fax: 413-534-8975; E-mail: jdutcher@mecn.mass.edu; Web site: http://www.hcc.mass.edu/home.html

HOOD COLLEGE

4 Pr G S Sc Tr

▼ Honors Program

The Hood College Honors Program, open to students of all majors, offers challenging and rewarding opportunities for academically exceptional students. All courses in the Honors Program have been specifically designed for honors—all are interdisciplinary and many are team-taught. The program provides an exciting learning experience for students who like the challenge of small, discussion-based classes and look forward to the stimulation of teacher-student interaction.

Students take one course a semester designated as honors in their first and second years at Hood (12 hours) and then take two electives and a senior seminar in the final two years at Hood (9 hours). Students in the program may substitute these courses for some requirements in the College's Core Curriculum. In the first year, the Honors Colloquia are designed to refine skills in critical thinking, writing, and speaking. In the fall semester, students study Social Justice and Ethical Judgment and in the spring semester continue with Science and Knowledge. In the second year, honors students have a seminar and external community service project devoted to the common good.

Transfer students from a recognized community college honors program may transfer with ease into Hood's program. Transfer students who have not completed a community college honors program may, if invited, join the Hood program in the sophomore year.

Participation in the Hood College Honors Program means becoming part of a learning community. Students in the program often room with other participating students. The program offers monthly dinners, trips to Washington, D.C., and Baltimore, and other social events. Honors students have specially selected faculty advisers.

There are 100 students currently enrolled in the program.

Participation Requirements: To graduate from the Honors Program, students must maintain a 3.25 overall GPA. Successful completion of the Honors Program requirements is recorded on the student's transcript and recognized at Commencement.

Admission Process: Students are selected for the Honors Program on the basis of their GPA, SAT I scores, and extracurricular activity experience. Interested students should contact the Program Director or the Admissions Office. The last date for consideration of applications is April 15.

Scholarship Availability: Hood College offers a number of Beneficial Hodson Scholarships to students of exceptional ability. Many students receiving these scholarships are also in the Honors Program. In addition, the College offers Trustee Scholarships to students with excellent academic records.

The Campus Context: Hood College is a beautiful 50-acre Georgian campus located in the tree-filled residential section of Frederick, Maryland, and is only an hour from either Baltimore or Washington. Degree programs offered are the Bachelor of Arts (twenty-five majors), Bachelor of Science (one major), Bachelor of Business Administration, Master of Business Administration, Master of Science (six programs), and the Master of Arts in human sciences (two concentrations).

Student Body Hood is a four-year liberal arts college and has 1,036 undergraduates: 13 percent men and 87 percent women. The ethnic distribution of the total undergraduate population includes 9 percent African American and 3 percent Hispanic. International students comprise 3 percent of the total population. Seventy-seven percent of the students receive financial aid.

Faculty There are 77 full-time faculty members, 21 full-time-equivalent faculty members, and approximately 55 adjunct faculty members. Eighty-four percent of full-time faculty members have terminal degrees.

Key Facilities The library houses 170,000 volumes. There are fourteen computer labs; the undergraduate student/PC ratio is 6:1.

Study Abroad Study abroad is encouraged by eliminating one elective requirement in the Honors Program if an honors student studies abroad. Hood runs an excellent Junior-Year Abroad program in Strasbourg, France.

Support Services Disabled students find that several of the academic buildings, the library, the dining hall, and one of the residence halls are totally handicapped-accessible. Other buildings on campus will be outfitted with wheelchair ramps within the year. Special parking, equipped restrooms, and lowered drinking fountains are also available on campus. The Learning Assessment and Resource Center provides learning support for any student on campus.

Tuition: $16,218 per year (1997-98)

Room and Board: $6592

Mandatory Fees: $200

Contact: Director: Dr. Shannon E. Griffiths, 401 Rosemont Avenue, Frederick, Maryland 21701; Telephone: 301-696-3742; Fax: 301-696-3819; E-mail: griffiths@nimue.hood.edu

HUTCHINSON COMMUNITY COLLEGE AND AREA VOCATIONAL SCHOOL

2 Pu C S Sc Tr

▼ Honors Program

The Hutchinson Community College (HCC) Honors Program was developed in conjunction with a Presidential Scholarship program. The Presidential Scholars are on scholarships provided by donors from the Hutchinson community. These scholars, and other students who qualify, are offered honors sections of general education courses. Currently, honors students at HCC may enroll in calculus, chemistry, American history, principles of speech, music appreciation, and art appreciation. The program also offers a few courses as honors courses by contract.

The 4-year-old program currently enrolls approximately 70 students.

Participation Requirements: Students who complete 18 hours in the program graduate with an Honors Graduate designation at Commencement.

Admission Process: An ACT score of 26 or higher automatically qualifies a student for the HCC Honors Program. A 3.25 college GPA also qualifies a student for admission. Special applications may be submitted for enrollment in a particular honors class on the consent of the instructor.

Scholarship Availability: Students with an ACT score of 26 or higher may be considered for an HCC Presidential Scholarship. Applicants are screened. HCC currently maintains 60 scholars on campus.

The Campus Context: Hutchinson Community College and Area Vocational School offers sixty-two Associate in Arts programs, thirty-nine Associate in Applied Arts programs, and eighteen certificate programs.

Student Body The College has an undergraduate enrollment of 4,171. On a three-year average, the gender division is 41 percent men and 58 percent women. The ethnic distribution (using the same three-year average) is 88.5 percent Caucasian, 2.9 percent black, 2.67 percent Hispanic, .9 percent American Indian, .6 percent Asian-American, and .3 percent other, with 3.7 percent not recorded. There are fewer than 10 international students. Of the total student population, 91.3 percent are commuters and 8.7 percent are dorm residents. Thirty-two percent of students receive federal financial aid, and 24.8 percent receive some form of scholarship. There are no fraternities or sororities.

Faculty Of the 280 faculty members, 105 are full time. Nine percent have doctoral degrees and another 3 percent specialized terminal degree. Seventy-seven percent hold the master's degree and 11 percent the bachelor's. The student-faculty ratio is 17:1.

Key Facilities Among the special facilities on campus are the new addition to the Student Union, the Kansas Cosmosphere and Space Center, Hutchinson Sports Arena, and Stringer Fine Arts Center. The library houses 44,127 volumes. The central computer facility is networked together with the entire campus by either fiber-optic cable or microwave connections. Each staff member and full-time faculty member in each office and department throughout campus has a desktop computer (approximately half of which are PCs). There are thirteen computer labs throughout campus that are dedicated to providing instruction to students.

Athletics In athletics, HCC is a member of the Kansas Jayhawk Community College Conference and the National Junior College Athletic Association. HCC's men's teams participate in football, basketball, baseball, cross-country, track and field, golf, and tennis. Women's teams participate in basketball, volleyball, tennis, track and field, cross-country, and softball.

Study Abroad There are no programs for study abroad.

Support Services Disabled students find all facilities accessible. Special academic services are available upon request for the hearing impaired, physically impaired, or otherwise disabled.

Job Opportunities Work-study programs are available in most offices or departments.

Tuition: $960 for state residents, $2880 for nonresidents, per year (1996-97)

Room and Board: $2590

Mandatory Fees: $320

Contact: Director: Sharon Stephenson, 1300 North Plum, Hutchinson, Kansas 67502; Telephone: 316-665-3314; Fax: 316-665-3310; E-mail: stephenson@hutchcc.edu; Web site: http://www.hutchcc.edu

---

ILLINOIS STATE UNIVERSITY

| 4 Pu G L Sc Tr |

▼ Honors Program

The principal objective of the Honors Program is to enrich the academic experience of those students who wish to participate in it. The Honors Program offers these students opportunities to engage in a wide variety of formal and informal learning experiences and encourages interaction among students and faculty members in and out of the classroom. Students are able to get to know faculty members and discuss ideas with them in honors classes, especially Honors Colloquia. In addition, there are several major-based learning communities specific to the Honors Program. Honors students also collaborate with faculty members through in-course honors projects, undergraduate research participation, independent honors study, and honors mentorship projects. The Presidential Scholars Program, a competitive four-year scholarship program with a special curriculum, is part of the Honors Program. Presidential scholars have both a required public service requirement and an international component as part of their curriculum.

There are a variety of services provided by the program to the students. First and foremost, the program advises all entering honors students. After the freshman year, students have the option to continue being advised by the program or going to their major for advisement or to do both. The program serves as a clearinghouse for faculty members and students seeking to work on various projects, both paid mentorships and undergraduate research.

The Honors Program has pioneered in making available new opportunities for students on campus. One of the most popular of these opportunities is priority registration. The program was one of the leaders in providing undergraduate research participation opportunities on campus. Its Senior Professional Mentorship Program pairs honors students with retired professionals in the community. The Honors Residential Program (Honors House) shares residence hall space with both the International House and the Minority Professional Opportunities Programs. In addition to its programmatic emphases, the program encourages social interaction among its students through a variety of activities, including student-planned dances, programs, and study breaks at the Honors House and off-campus events and community service activities coordinated by the Honors Student Organization (HSO).

The program formally recognizes its students' accomplishments through several means. All honors course work and designations are placed on the student's transcript. After four semesters, students may earn the Certificate in University Honors. Students meeting requirements in their major are eligible for Departmental Honors. Finally, students graduating cum laude or better and meeting other requirements in the program graduate as University Honors Scholars.

The program was founded in 1964 to meet the needs of those students who wished to get more out of their education. It currently enrolls 1,000 students. That is slightly more than 5 percent of the undergraduate student enrollment.

Participation Requirements: Students in the program are expected to complete a minimum of 3 credit hours of honors course work per semester. Students taking more than 3 credits of honors work can have these hours banked against future semesters. Students in the residential program and those applying for special designations are expected to take an honors colloquium. Once students have accumulated 24 credit hours, they have met the participation requirements.

Admission Process: There are two ways students enter the Honors Program. The first is for high school seniors with a minimum ACT score of 27 who are in the 90th percentile of their graduating class and have a 3.3 GPA (A = 4.0). The second point of entry is through the college GPA—any student, either native or transfer, who has a 3.3 GPA average (A = 4.0) may join the program.

Scholarship Availability: There are several opportunities for financial support other than the Presidential Scholars Program. All financial support given through the Honors Program is on a competitive non-need base. Students in the Honors Program are eligible for two different awards: there are a limited number of tuition waivers available each year and there are paid mentorships in which students are remunerated for their work with a faculty mentor.

The Campus Context: Illinois State University was founded in 1857 as the first public institution of higher learning in Illinois. It is a multipurpose institution committed to providing undergraduate and selected graduate programs of the highest quality in the state of Illinois. There are fifty-eight undergraduate programs in 161 fields of study that are offered through the Colleges of Applied Science and Technology, Arts and Sciences, Business, Education, and Fine Arts. There are thirty-four departments housed in the five colleges. The University's academic programs are supported by the services and collections of the Milner Library, which contains more than 3 million holdings and special collections. Illinois State University is fully accredited by the Commission on Institutions of Higher Education of the North Central Association of Colleges and Schools. The teacher preparation programs are accredited by the National Council for Accreditation of Teacher Education.

Student Body The University currently enrolls 19,600 students, of whom 16,663 are undergraduates. The undergraduate population is 56 percent women and 44 percent men. The ethnic composition of the undergraduate enrollment is as follows: white/non-Hispanic, 86.7 percent; African American/non-Hispanic, 8.5 percent; Hispanic, 2.3 percent; Asian/Pacific Islander, 1.6 percent; American Indian/Alaska Native, 0.3 percent; and not reported/nonresident alien, 0.6 percent. Included in this number are 257 international students, of whom 95 are undergraduates. Seventy percent of all students receive some form of financial aid. There are twenty-five fraternities and seventeen sororities on campus.

Faculty There are 950 instructional faculty members.

Key Facilities The campus has a fiber-optic network, and all classroom buildings and residence halls are on ISU Net, the campus network. There are computer laboratories in all of the classroom buildings and the library.

There are 8,000 spaces on campus in twelve residence halls. University apartment housing is also available. In addition, a relatively large number of upperclassmen live in apartments in Bloomington/Normal. The actual number of commuter students is fewer than one third of the total enrollment.

Athletics The University competes at the I-A level in fifteen sports (men's and women's) and I-AA in football.

Study Abroad The University offers both study abroad and exchange programs through its Office of International Studies and Programs. Honors students play a prominent part in its activities.

Support Services The University is committed to providing access to students with disabilities. It has a very active Office of Disability Concerns.

Job Opportunities There are many work opportunities in virtually all areas of the campus.

Tuition and Fees: $2846 for state residents, $8537 for nonresidents, per year (1996-97)

Room and Board: $3765

Mandatory Fees: $874

Contact: Director: Dr. Ira Cohen, Normal, Illinois 61790-6100; Telephone: 309-438-2559; Fax: 309-439-8196; E-mail: honcohen@rs6000.cmp.ilstu.edu; Web site: http://www.ilstu.edu/depts/honors/

ILLINOIS VALLEY COMMUNITY COLLEGE

2 Pu C G S Sc Tr

▼ **Honors Program**

Illinois Valley Community College (IVCC) has established the Honors Program to recognize those students who have demonstrated or who evidence the potential for demonstrating consistent academic excellence. The program is limited to 50 participants selected by a faculty/staff/student committee from among currently enrolled full-time or part-time Illinois Valley Community College students who apply. Honors students are eligible to apply for designated scholarships, honors courses appear on student transcripts, and the honors degree is clearly indicated on transcripts, diplomas, and certificates.

The Honors Program offers three distinct choices to students: at least a three-semester commitment to honors across the general education curriculum, honors in a specific discipline or "major" (to include A.A., A.S., A.A.S., and certificate program areas), and honors experiences limited to specific courses. Opportunities exist for participation in colloquia and special projects.

Begun in fall 1991, the program is limited to 50 students.

Participation Requirements: A degree with honors involves required enrollment and participation each semester in the honors colloquium for 1 semester hour of credit and recommended enrollment in no more than two honors courses per semester. The required honors project is a one-time separate course (1–3 semester hours of credit), to be completed by the end of the final semester of study and to be designed by the student under advice of and consultation with an instructor and approved by the honors committee. Such projects include (but are not limited to) a research essay/report, exhibition, or recital. Students must have a required minimum of 18 semester hours (including the colloquium and honors project) and have completed at least four honors courses. The term "Degree with Honors" appears on the student's transcript and diploma (or certificate).

Honors in the discipline introduces the possibility of honors work in a specific area of study (e.g., art, history, music, biology, economics, or physics) as determined by the faculty of the particular academic discipline. This involves recommended enrollment in no more than two honors courses per semester from among those designated by the faculty of the particular academic discipline; recommended participation in the honors colloquium as determined by consultation among the student, faculty, and counselor; and a required honors project as a one-time separate course (1–3 semester hours of credit), to be completed by the end of the final semester of study and to be designed by the student under advice of and consultation with an instructor and approved by the honors committee. Such projects include (but are not limited to) a research essay/report, exhibition, or recital. There is a required minimum of 12 semester hours (including the colloquium and honors project), and students must have completed at least three honors courses. The term "Honors in the Discipline" appears on the student's transcript and diploma (or certificate).

Honors Courses Only: Students may enroll in individual honors courses (as many or as few as they desire) without necessarily participating in the Degree with Honors or Honors in the Discipline programs.

In the most general sense, an honors course allows students to explore new ideas suggested by a recognized area or discipline of study; expand their knowledge on topics not considered (or merely alluded to) in their regular classes; attempt skills learned in a class, but for which there appears little or no time for application; and enjoy opportunities to originate and develop talents in a recognized area or discipline.

One type of available honors course is that developed by a faculty member, in which the substance, methodology, and form extend beyond a course offered within the regular curriculum. To facilitate articulation and transfer, this course is offered (and appears on the student's transcript) under the prefix, number, and title of a regular course but designated as "Honors." There are also regular courses offered with an honors contract, in which the student pursues the requirements of the course content under advice and guidance from the instructor and completes such enrichment activities and exercises as (but not limited to) additional essays, experiments, fieldwork, readings, discussions, research, presentations to the class, production of work for publication and performance, research into original sources or reviews of current literature, or group projects with other honors students. The designation "Honors" identifies each appropriate course on the student's transcript.

The Honors Colloquium is a requirement for all students pursuing the Degree with Honors and is recommended to students pursuing Honors in the Discipline. It is also available to students pursuing honors courses only. In the colloquium, enrolled students meet regularly, as determined by the structure and content for discussion among themselves and with those faculty members involved with the various honors options. Invited guest specialists may attend, which includes participation of the general public and members of the College community. The content and structure of the colloquium are determined by the Honors Committee and the faculty.

To remain in the program, the honors student must maintain a minimum GPA of 3.5 for all courses in which he or she is enrolled. A student dismissed from the program may petition the Honors Committee for readmission. All honors work is listed as such on transcripts. Students receive a certificate upon completion of the program and recognition at Commencement.

Admission Process: To be considered for admission to any aspect of the Honors Program, students must meet all of the criteria of the category into which they qualify: high school students must have an ACT score of 26 or above (an equivalent SAT I score) or be in the upper 10 percent of their high school graduating class. A high school transcript and letters of recommendation from 2 members of the high school faculty must be presented, along with results of IVCC placement tests demonstrating that the student reads, writes, and reasons at levels appropriate for honors work.

Currently enrolled IVCC students must have a minimum GPA of 3.5 at Illinois Valley Community College and present an IVCC transcript for review, along with letters of recommendation from at least 2 members of the College faculty. Transfer students must have a GPA of 3.5 at the institution(s) from which they transfer. In addition to the review of college transcripts, letters of recommendation are required from at least 2 members of the faculty at the institution(s) from which the student transfers. Students who do not fall into the above categories may also be reviewed for admission.

The Campus Context: The Illinois Valley Community College offers thirty-two baccalaureate transfer degree programs, thirteen vocational programs, and twenty-four certificate programs.

Student Body IVCC has an undergraduate enrollment of 4,200: 45 percent men and 55 percent women. The ethnic distribution is 95 percent Caucasian and 5 percent members of minority groups. There are 15 international students on this 100-percent commuter campus. Seventy-five percent of all students receive financial aid.

Faculty There are 210 faculty members, of whom 73 are part-time. Five percent of the faculty members have terminal degrees. The student-faculty ratio is 26:1.

Key Facilities The library contains 85,000 volumes. There are four computer labs with 300 stations on campus. There is also an automated manufacturing center.

Athletics Athletics include men's football, basketball, baseball, and tennis and women's volleyball, tennis, and softball.

Study Abroad Illinois Valley Community College is a member of the Illinois Consortium for International Studies and Programs, offering students opportunities to spend a semester in England (Canterbury) or Austria (Salzburg) or a summer session at Costa Rica (San Jose).

Support Services The College offers full academic support for all special-needs students, including an assessment center, peer and professional tutoring, extended testing, and notetaking. In addition, the College is in complete compliance with the Americans with Disabilities Act.

Job Opportunities IVCC employs more than 300 students in clerical, tutorial, and custodial positions.

Tuition: $1152 for area residents, $3504 for state residents, $4512 for nonresidents, per year (1996-97)

Mandatory Fees: $62

Contact: Director: Samuel J. Rogal, Division of Humanities and Fine Arts, 815 North Orlando Smith Avenue, Oglesby,

Illinois 61348; Telephone: 815-224-2720 Ext. 491; Fax: 815-224-3033

INDIANA STATE UNIVERSITY

4 Pu G M Sc Tr

▼ University Honors Program

The University Honors Program of Indiana State University (ISU) seeks to meet the educational needs of its most highly motivated students. To complete the program's 18 credit hours, students take 12 hours of honors core classes from among nineteen core courses offered on rotation. For the remaining 6 hours, upperclass students are given the option of independent study, the honors senior thesis, or the opportunity to earn honors credit in their major area by special arrangement with the professor and Director of Honors.

Advantages of the Honors Program include small class sizes (about 20 students), close contact with faculty members, and challenging interdisciplinary courses that also provide increased skill and confidence in writing. Special academic advising is regularly offered, as are extracurricular activities such as field trips, lectures, social events, and honors housing.

An important factor in the success of the program is the honors faculty. It is a group of recognized scholars and highly regarded teachers who devote time to teaching and meeting informally with honors students and to teaching and conducting research in their own departments.

Upon satisfactory completion of the honors requirements, a student's transcript bears the inscription "Graduate of the University Honors Program." The student also receives special recognition at the Honors Senior Banquet, the University Honors Day Convocation, and graduation ceremonies by wearing a special stole.

There are currently 320 students enrolled in the program.

Participation Requirements: A minimum of 18 credit hours in honors of the 124 needed for graduation is required in order to complete the program, and a minimum 3.0 overall GPA must be maintained.

Admission Process: The program is open to entering freshmen who, by reason of their high SAT I or ACT scores and high school graduation rank, have demonstrated outstanding academic aptitude and achievement. ISU students already enrolled or transfer students who have demonstrated superior scholastic ability are also eligible.

The Campus Context: Indiana Sate University in Terre Haute, Indiana, was created by an Indiana statute on December 20, 1865. Formally named Indiana State Normal, its primary purpose was defined to be "the preparation of teachers for teaching in the common schools of Indiana." The main campus adjoins the north side of Terre Haute's downtown business district and covers about 91 acres in the heart of the city. It serves as the cultural center for western Indiana and eastern Illinois. The University offers 155 degree programs.

Student Body Of the 8,857 undergraduates enrolled, the majority are from the Midwest; 48 percent are men and 52 percent are women. There are approximately 270 international students. Residents make up 47 percent of the student population, commuters the remaining 53 percent. Fifty-eight percent of the students receive financial aid. There are twenty-one national fraternities and thirteen national sororities and a number of scholastic honorary societies open to students.

Faculty Of the 641 total faculty members, 561 are full-time, 78 percent of whom have terminal degrees. The student-faculty ratio is 19:1.

Athletics Intercollegiate athletics for men include baseball, basketball, cross-country, football, and tennis; sports available for women include basketball, cross-country, softball, tennis, indoor and outdoor track, and volleyball.

Study Abroad Through the study-abroad programs in the Office of International Studies, ISU students in all majors have the opportunity to study overseas, particularly in England, France, Spain, Mexico, Italy, Germany, and Japan. Students may study abroad for a semester, summer, or year. Credits earned apply to the student's degree requirements.

Support Services Services for disabled persons include assistance in accessing recorded textbooks or readers for the blind and learning disabled. Arrangements are made for note takers or signers for hearing-impaired students. Alternate testing procedures may be arranged as needed.

Job Opportunities Students are offered work opportunities on campus, including assistantships and work-study. Various offices on campus hire student workers.

Tuition: $3072 for state residents, $7604 for nonresidents, per year (1996-97)

Room and Board: $3995

Contact: Director: Dr. Donald L. Jennermann, A-137 Root Hall, Terre Haute, Indiana 47809; Telephone: 812-237-3225; Fax: 812-237-3062; E-mail: hujenn@root.indstate.edu; Web site: http://web.indstate.edu:80/honors/

INDIANA UNIVERSITY BLOOMINGTON

4 Pu G L Sc Tr

▼ University Honors Division

The Honors Division represents a commitment made by Indiana University (IU) to broaden and enrich the college experience of bright, highly motivated, and creative students. For the University, the Honors Division is a way to coordinate honors programs on campus and provide special services for honors students. For faculty members serving in the Honors Division, the program means the opportunity to teach bright students in inventive, interdisciplinary, and small-class settings and advanced or intensive classes devoted to particular disciplines. For the prospective honors student, participation in the Honors Division can mean opportunities for scholarships, additional housing options, access to special extracurricular programs, study abroad, opportunities to participate in faculty research projects, or a chance to spend a semester or summer pursuing research interests or gaining teaching or other professional experience through internships.

Begun in 1965, the 32-year-old Honors Division Program currently enrolls 2,400 students. Special opportunities include the Liberal Arts and Management Program (LAMP), which combines the study of arts and sciences with a solid grounding in business. Initiated in 1988, LAMP is a unique interdisciplinary offering of the College of Arts and Sciences in partnership with the School of Business that integrates practical training in business management with a liberal arts and sciences degree.

Participation Requirements: Honors students normally take one honors course each semester. It's a challenging experience, but it's also fun. Right from the start, students get to know their fellow students in a small-class environment as they begin the process of expanding each other's minds under the tutelage of an outstanding teacher.

Admission Process: Students interested in the Honors Division Program should obtain and file the freshman application for admission with the IU Office of Admissions. Freshman applicants with combined SAT I scores of 1270 or above (recentered) or an ACT composite score of 30 or above and who rank in the top 10 percent of their graduating class automatically receive an invitation to join the Honors Division Program.

The program encourages other highly motivated students interested in the academic opportunities provided by the Honors Division to apply directly after they have been accepted to IU. Students who do not meet initial criteria may have their high school English teacher send a letter of recommendation attesting to their ability to do honors work. Applicants should also send a copy of their high school transcript and write a brief letter explaining why they wish to join the program. The program is especially interested in candidates who have taken either Advanced Placement, accelerated, or honors courses in high school.

Students who do not enter the Honors Division Program as incoming freshmen but show outstanding academic performance in the first semester or year of college may ask to participate in the program at the end of the first or second semester.

Scholarship Availability: The Honors Division gives more than 200 scholarships each year to entering freshmen. Honors Division Scholarships are competitive merit scholarships that range in value from $500 to $5000 per year and are awarded solely on the basis of high school achievement. The application requires information about test scores (SAT I and ACT), class rank, and academic and extracurricular involvement; a short essay; and a brief personal statement. Honors Division faculty members carefully read each application and select the award recipients.

The Wells Scholars Program offers a unique educational opportunity to a select group of young scholars. The program emphasizes closer interaction with faculty members, an individually tailored curriculum, and special opportunities for internships and study abroad. The full four-year Wells merit scholarships include tuition and room and board. They may also be used to pursue any course of undergraduate study at Indiana University. Applicants must be nominated by their high school to compete for a Wells scholarship.

The Campus Context: Indiana University at Bloomington is composed of the following colleges and schools: College of Arts and Sciences, Herron School of Arts, School of Business, School of Continuing Studies, School of Fine Arts, School of Education, School of Library and Information Science, School of Journalism. School of Music, School of Nursing, School of Allied and Health Sciences, School of Social Work, School of Optometry, School of Law, School of Medicine, School of Dentistry, School of Physical Education, and School of Health, Physical Education, and Recreation. There are ninety-six degree programs offered on campus.

Student Body Of the 25,451 students in attendance, 42 percent are men and 58 percent are women. Members of ethnic minority groups constitute 11.4 percent of the student population. Sixty-four percent of students are residents. Forty percent of students receive financial aid.

Faculty There are 1,576 full-time and 223 part-time faculty members. Eighty-nine percent of faculty members hold terminal degrees. The student-faculty ratio is 21:1.

Key Facilities The Lilly Library houses 5 million books and 7 million other materials. It has a collection of rare books and special collections of film and television scripts, sheet music, and children's books.

Throughout the campus, including the main library and student union building, there are twenty-six staffed computer labs. All schools have both staffed and unstaffed computer facilities. All dormitories have computer labs and computer access.

Other distinguished campus facilities are the Mathers Museum of World Cultures, Indiana University Art Museum, Indiana University Musical Arts Center, Elizabeth Sage Historic Costume Collection, Cyclotron, Glenn A. Black Laboratory of Archaeology, Kinsey Institute, and many laboratory facilities.

Athletics In athletics, Indiana University has consistently been one of the nation's premier programs, participating in the NCAA and the Big Ten Conference. In addition to winning twenty NCAA team championships in men's basketball (five), men's swimming and diving (six), men's soccer (three), men's cross-country (three), wrestling (one), men's outdoor track and field (one), and women's tennis (one), Hoosier student-athletes have won a total of 122 individual NCAA crowns. The Athletics Department at IU is committed to academic integrity and compliance with NCAA regulations.

155

Study Abroad At Indiana University, students can make overseas study part of the regular degree program, whatever the major. Students have the opportunity to spend a full academic year, semester, or summer abroad earning IU credit while enrolled in outstanding international universities or classes specially designed for international students. IU's programs abroad are intensive educational experiences that combine academic excellence with cross-cultural learning. IU offers more than sixty overseas programs in sixteen languages (including English) in twenty-seven countries and nearly every field of study. For example, students can study Renaissance Art in Florence, French media in Strasbourg, the European Union in Maastricht, international marketing in Finland, tropical biology in Costa Rica, intensive Russian in St. Petersburg, Japanese in Nagoya, aboriginal culture in Wollongong, or African history in Ghana.

Support Services Disabled students find the campus accessible and special facilities available.

Job Opportunities Work opportunities on campus are available.

Tuition: $3320 for state residents, $10,868 for nonresidents, per year (1996-97)

Room and Board: $4220

Mandatory Fees: $431

Contact: Director: Lewis H. Miller Jr., 324 North Jordan Avenue, Bloomington, Indiana 47405; Telephone: 812-855-3550; Fax: 812-855-5416; E-mail: miller@indiana.edu; Web site: http://www.honors.indiana.edu/

INDIANA UNIVERSITY-PURDUE UNIVERSITY INDIANAPOLIS

4 Pu G S Sc Tr

▼ Honors Program

The Honors Program was developed in 1979 to enhance the evolvement of Indiana University-Purdue University, Indianapolis (IUPUI) as a national leader among urban institutions, with its mission to promote excellence in research, teaching, and service. In emphasizing honors programming, IUPUI demonstrates its conviction that the creation of knowledge through research, the dissemination of knowledge through teaching, and the cultivation of knowledge through student learning are its principal values. Students are not required to pursue their degree with honors in order to participate in honors courses. To optimize opportunities for academic achievement, the Honors Program offers courses designed specifically for honors students, departmental courses for honors and highly motivated students in their majors, and honors independent research papers or projects. Students are also encouraged to participate in international study, field study, and the National Collegiate Honors Council (NCHC)

Honors Semesters. Outstanding undergraduates, with the permission of their department, may earn honors credit by enrolling and successfully completing graduate course work.

In addition to academic enrichment, honors students, through their Honors Lounge, can access their personal e-mail and all of the research opportunities available in the University library. The lounge is equipped with an electronic scanner and software, enabling honors students to enhance their papers and presentations. It is also the meeting area for members of the Honors Club, who use it as a base for campus/club activities and personal socialization. Because the campus is located only six blocks from downtown Indianapolis, students have excellent opportunities for internships and partnerships with the city. The Honors Club annually cosponsors two campus blood drives with the Central Indiana Regional Blood Bank for the benefit of central Indiana citizens.

Upon completion of the honors requirements, Honors Program participants are awarded with the following: mention at graduation, a medallion on a neck ribbon that is worn during graduation ceremonies, honors notations placed on the transcript and diploma, certificates for outstanding service to Honors Club members, and a certificate for completing the Honors Fellows Program.

The 17-year-old program enrolls about 200 students per year.

Participation Requirements: All students graduating with general honors degrees must earn a minimum of 24 honors credit hours, an overall GPA of 3.3, and a 3.5 GPA in all honors work. The overall requirement is reduced to 21 honors credit hours for those completing a 6-credit–hour Honors Senior Thesis. Students earning Departmental Honors must meet the additional requirements prescribed by their department and earn a 3.5 GPA in their major. A third option, graduation with honors from one's school, is available to students in the Schools of Business, Nursing, and Public and Environmental Affairs.

Admission Process: Acceptance into the Honors Program is based on meeting one of the following qualifications: 1200 SAT I scores and rank in the top 10 percent of one's high school class; a 3.3 GPA earned in the first year of college course work; or transferring from another university with a 3.3 GPA or from another university's Honors Program. Application to enroll in specific honors courses or independent study is also available to students with a strong interest or demonstrably high ability in a specific area or study. Academically gifted high school students who are admitted to IUPUI through the SPAN Program (based on high SAT I scores and part-time non-degree-student status) may apply to the director for permission to enroll in honors courses.

Scholarship Availability: The Honors Program administers three University scholarship and grant programs that are open to all eligible students and one grant program for honors students only. All honors students are encouraged to apply for them. They include the Honors Fellows Program, which offers $1000 for students entering their first year in the Honors Program. Each must meet SAT and class rank requirements for entering freshmen and agree to complete four honors courses within three years. Second-year students may apply with a 3.5 GPA and a record of campus service. The Outstanding Upperclass Scholarship offers $2500 for students demonstrating outstanding academic achievement and campus/community service. The SUR (Support for Undergraduate Research) scholarship offers $1500 to encourage working students to participate in research with an instructor for one semester. They must submit an application form and a five-page research proposal. The research may be either student- or faculty-initiated, but the student must be involved in numerous facets of the research process. The SUMA (Support for Undergraduate Meeting Attendance) scholarship offers a variable stipend to help defray costs involved when students are invited to present their research or participate in a panel discussion or poster session at a local, state, or national conference.

The Campus Context: IUPUI is an urban campus that offers students the dynamic spirit that characterizes a metropolitan city. As a twenty-first-century model for American public higher education, the campus thrives on a fast pace and connections with Indianapolis and its people. It serves 27,000 students who may earn degrees from either Indiana or Purdue University. Twenty schools offer a total of 180 degree programs. Although a growing number of its students enter IUPUI immediately following high school graduation, 53 percent return to or start college after working and beginning a family. To better accommodate the student body, IUPUI offers flexible scheduling options, including night, weekend, and televised courses.

The University comprises twenty colleges on campus, including Allied Health Sciences, Art, Business, Continuing Studies, Dentistry, Education, Engineering and Technology, Journalism, Law, Liberal Arts, Library and Information Science, Medicine, Music, Nursing, Physical Education, Public and Environmental Affairs, Science, Social Work, and IU and Purdue Graduate Schools.

Student Body Of the undergraduates, 44.5 percent are men and 55.5 percent are women. Of the ethnic population, 9.9 percent of the students are African American, 1.6 percent are Asian, 1.4 percent are Hispanic, and .02 percent are American Indian. Nine percent of the students are residents; 91 percent commute. Ninety-six percent receive financial aid.

Faculty Of the 2,440 total faculty members, 1,600 are full-time. The student-faculty ratio is 17:1.

Key Facilities Some of the distinguishing features on campus are a Child Care Center, a Counseling Center, the Indiana University Medical School, the Natatorium (Olympic-size swimming facility), the National Institute for Fitness and Health, a state-of-the-art lecture hall, the Undergraduate Education Center, and an excellent library. The library holds 570,000 volumes and 4,500 current periodicals and 120 computer workstations. There are thirteen computer learning centers.

Athletics In athletics, IUPUI is NCAA Division II; men's sports include baseball, basketball, golf, soccer, and tennis and women's sports include basketball, softball, tennis, and volleyball.

Support Services Disabled-student facilities include the Office of Adaptive Education, sign-language interpreters, note-takers, readers, exam proctors, classroom aides, an active Disabled Students Organization, a special registration process that includes information about campus facilities and parking privileges, computer reading systems, large-print video, and voice character generators.

Job Opportunities Work-study and part-time employment are available.

Tuition: $3065 for state residents, $9405 for nonresidents, per year (1996-97)

Room and Board: $3000 minimum

Mandatory Fees: $500

Contact: Interim Director: Sally Cone, ES2126, Indianapolis, Indiana 46202-5154; Telephone: 317-274-2314; Fax: 317-274-2365; E-mail: scone@indyvax.iupui.edu; Web site: http://www.iupui.edu/it/honors

---

INDIANA UNIVERSITY SOUTH BEND

4 Pu G M Sc Tr

▼ Honors Program

Through its Honors Program, Indiana University South Bend (IUSB) provides a special intellectual challenge for its keenest and most highly motivated undergraduates. Drawing upon the full range of resources that a large university can offer, this program encompasses a broad variety of classes, tutorials, and independent study opportunities. The program expects most talented students to respond by engaging in academic pursuits that encourage them to strive for individual excellence in their University course of study.

Approximately 85 incoming freshmen annually and approximately 75–100 students participate in the program.

Participation Requirements: Classes in the arts and humanities, business and economics, education, nursing, social and behavioral sciences, and science are offered. An Honors Program certificate is granted to students who have taken 15 hours of credit in at least four honors-eligible courses and have completed an honors-qualified project under the individual mentoring of an IUSB faculty member.

Offered for the first time in fall 1996, the Freshman Honors Colloquium consists of lectures by distinguished faculty members from across the University and a weekend symposium spearheaded by a noted scholar. The faculty members chosen to make these ten presentations include the best teachers and scholars on the campus. Each honors student then prepares a 250–500 word response to the lecture/discussion and turns in a paper at the next lecture. Graduate students grade the papers and return them to the students on a weekly basis.

A weekend symposium led by a well-known scholar serves as the capstone event of the Colloquium. One week before the symposium, each honors student turns in a five-page opinion paper based on materials written by the scholar. After the weekend of presentations by the scholar, each honors student submits a twelve- to twenty-page research paper that examines a topic or issue generated by the symposium. All incoming freshman honors students are required to take this class. Although the 2 credit hours earned count toward the student's completion of the honors certificate, the course ordinarily does not fulfill the requirement that all students who receive an Honors Scholarship take at least one honors class during the year.

Admission Process: Admission to the Honors Program and its classes is open to all qualified students (those with an overall GPA of 3.3 or higher), including part-time students and those who enter the University several years after leaving high school, without restriction with regard to division, major, or class standing.

Scholarship Availability: Several scholarships available only to Honors Program participants are awarded each year. These scholarships are extended to a few particularly promising undergraduates regardless of financial need. Freshman Honors Scholarships are awarded by the Honors Program to entering freshmen who fulfill at least two of the following three criteria: a score of 1100 or above on the SAT I, a class rank in the top 10 percent of their high school graduating class, and the attainment of an overall high school GPA of at least 3.5. These scholarships also are available to transfer students who enter with a cumulative 3.5 GPA. Annual continuation of these scholarships is based on students' attaining a cumulative GPA of 3.5 or above (on a 4.0 scale) and the completion of at least one honors course during the academic year. To remain in the program, non-scholarship recipients must maintain a 3.3 cumulative GPA.

The Campus Context: Indiana University South Bend, one of the eight campuses of Indiana University, offers an exceptional education to students of north central Indiana and southwestern Michigan. Overlooking a picturesque stretch of the St. Joseph River and east of downtown South Bend, IUSB is centrally located in the Michiana area. IUSB's buildings contain modern classrooms and science laboratories, spacious auditoriums and studios for the fine arts and the performing arts, a library, extensive audiovisual facilities, and links to computer and instructional-television networks serving the entire IU system. The University offers 100 majors leading to the associate, baccalaureate, or master's degree.

Student Body There are 6,032 undergraduates and 1,508 graduate students. Of the undergraduates, 63.7 percent are women and 36.3 percent are men. Minority ethnic distribution is 5.6 percent African American, 1.4 percent Hispanic, and .9 percent Asian. International students constitute 2.4 percent.

Most students commute to campus; however, nearby housing can be arranged. Fifty-one percent of students (defined as full-time undergraduates receiving need-based aid) receive financial aid. The campus has one national sorority and one local fraternity.

Faculty There are 228 full-time faculty members, 90 percent of whom have earned the highest degrees within their discipline. Another 268 associate (i.e., adjunct) faculty members teach on campus. The student-faculty ratio is 14:1.

Key Facilities The 476,000-volume library houses several special collections. The seven computer labs located in classroom buildings and the library are available for student use.

Athletics IUSB offers opportunities in men and women's basketball, men's baseball, and several intramural sports.

Study Abroad Many opportunities for study-abroad programs are available through IUSB and through the IU system.

Support Services By coordinating such services as providing texts for students with vision impairments and students with hearing impairments, the Office of Disabled Student Services, which acts as a liaison between the students, instructors, and other University resources, supports disabled students in achieving their academic potential to the greatest extent possible. Other commonly offered services include assistance in scheduling and registering for classes, obtaining books and handicapped parking permits, and arranging for alternative testing and referral to and from Vocational Rehabilitation and other community agencies.

Job Opportunities Work opportunities vary on campus. The World Wide Web (at http://www.iusb.edu/~human/) contains a list of current job postings.

Tuition: $2658 for state residents, $7271 for nonresidents, per year (1996-97)

Mandatory Fees: Full-time: $180 to $210, according to course load and class level; part-time: $27 to $97 per semester, according to course load and class level.

Contact: Director: Dr. Brenda E. Knowles, 1700 Mishawaka Avenue, P.O. Box 7111, Administration Building 206(a), South Bend, Indiana 46634-7111; Telephone: 219-237-4355; Fax: 219-237-4866; E-mail: bknowles@vines.iusb.edu

IONA COLLEGE

4 Pr G S Sc Tr

▼ Honors Degree Program

The Iona College Honors Degree Program is designed to meet the educational needs of the ablest and most highly motivated students at Iona. To accomplish this goal, the program provides academic opportunities that challenge students to perform at their peak and stimulate them to become independent learners. The course of study is designed to develop curiosity, analytical abilities, and awareness of ethical and civic responsibilities. The program fosters a sense of dignity and self-esteem in students, encouraging them to stretch their abilities in pursuit of lifelong learning and personal fulfillment.

The curriculum promotes an appreciation and understanding of the interrelatedness of knowledge and culture, particularly through its interdisciplinary courses and its study-abroad program. Small class sizes of approximately 15 encourage student participation and promote a close student-faculty relationship. Students are offered two tuition-free courses each academic year. These courses may be taken in the Intersession, summer, or as extra courses during the fall and spring semesters. These free courses can facilitate double majors, accelerate graduation, or broaden the educational experience with no financial burden. Honors students also enjoy priority registration.

The program, which has been in existence for more than twenty years, admits 30 freshmen each year. There are approximately 100 students currently enrolled in the program.

Participation Requirements: In their freshman year, students take two honors communications courses and a freshman seminar designed to integrate them into the academic life of the College. In their sophomore year, students take two 6-credit interdisciplinary humanities courses. In the spring of their sophomore year, students are encouraged to study in Ireland and Belgium. In their junior year, students take a lecture and seminar course centered around a specific topic. The curriculum culminates with an independent research project undertaken with a faculty mentor. Seniors present the results of their research in a conference setting open to the College community.

To remain in the program, students must maintain a 3.5 cumulative GPA. Successful completion of the program is recognized at Commencement and is also noted on the official transcript and diploma.

Admission Process: High school students are recruited on the basis of their high school average, SAT I or ACT scores, an application and an essay, and a personal interview. Students may apply for admission after the first or second semester of freshman year. Students may major in any discipline in the School of Arts and Science or the Hagan School of Business. The deadline for applying to the program is March 1.

Scholarship Availability: Scholarships of various amounts are awarded through the Office of Admissions based on academic performance. Scholarships are not offered through the Honors Degree Program. Most honors students are recipients of academic scholarships.

The Campus Context: Iona College is located in the gracious Beechmont section of New Rochelle. A city of 72,000 people on the Long Island Sound in Westchester County, New Rochelle offers the sophistication of an established suburb and easy access to New York City by automobile or public transportation. Founded by the Christian Brothers in 1940, Iona has grown to be an institution recognized for innovative scholarship, distinguished faculty, and successful alumni. The College offers forty-four baccalaureate degree programs. There are three schools on campus: the School of Arts and Science, the Hagan School of Business, and the Columba School.

Student Body The undergraduate enrollment is 43 percent men and 57 percent women. The ethnic distribution is 66 percent white, 19 percent black, 13 percent Hispanic, and 2 percent Asian/Pacific Islander. Ninety-four percent of the students receive financial aid.

Faculty The total number of faculty members is 359, of whom 175 are full-time. Seventy-eight percent of the full-time faculty members have terminal degrees. The student-faculty ratio is 19:1.

Key Facilities The library contains more than 235,000 volumes. The Helen Arrigoni Library/Technology Center houses all materials for the disciplines of mass communications, computer science, education, and management information sciences. In addition to Internet access, the center is equipped with CD-ROM capabilities and headphone and speaker connections that allow for small-group projects on the multimedia systems. About 300 microcomputers (Pentium 486 systems and 386 systems) are available for student use at the New Rochelle, Rockland, and New York City campuses.

Athletics The Athletic Department offers a wide variety of sports and intramural programs for all members of the Iona community to enjoy. Iona competes in the Metro Atlantic Conference and fields twenty-one Division I teams. Iona supports a Division I-AA non-scholarship football team and plays traditional rivals St. John's, Georgetown, and Wagner. An extensive intramural program allows up to 1,200 students per year to engage in athletic activities. The John A. Mulcahy Center houses the athletic staff and provides recreational swimming in an Olympic-size pool, a full Nautilus fitness center, men's and women's saunas, and a gymnasium for basketball and volleyball. The Mazella multisports field is also available for recreational use.

Study Abroad Iona College encourages students to broaden their educational experiences and gain cultural perspectives through study and travel abroad, especially in areas less affluent than the United States. Iona College has sponsored summer and intercession programs in Ireland, Belgium, France, England, Spain, Italy, Mexico, and Morocco. Full-time students may enroll for a semester-long program in Dublin, Ireland, at St. Mary's College, a constituent part of the famed Trinity College, and at the Irish Institute in Louvain, Belgium. Students enrolled in this program may take Iona courses in Irish history and culture, philosophy, the industrial revolution, peace and justice, and literature. Arrangements can also be made for students to pursue a selected major and foreign language courses. Students may also spend a semester or a year studying independently at an international university. Earned credits may be transferred to Iona College with prior approval.

Support Services The Samuel Rudin Academic Resource Center, which is wheelchair-accessible, provides reasonable auxiliary aids and services to students with disabilities. In addition to providing legally mandated services for persons with disabilities who voluntarily seek additional services, the College Assistance Program provides professional tutoring, academic advisement, and other support services.

Job Opportunities A limited number of part-time positions on campus are available to students who demonstrate financial need. The wage rate varies depending upon skills required and experience.

Tuition: $12,200 per year (1996-97)

Room and Board: $7520

Mandatory Fees: $320

Contact: Director: Dr. Frances K. Bailie, 715 North Avenue, New Rochelle, New York 10801; Telephone: 914-633-2335; Fax: 914-633-2144; E-mail: fbailie@iona.edu; Web site: http://www.iona.edu

---

IOWA STATE UNIVERSITY OF SCIENCE AND TECHNOLOGY

| 4 Pu G L Tr |

▼ University Honors Program

The Iowa State University (ISU) Honors Program is a University-wide program that provides opportunities for students who want to achieve academic excellence, get ahead of the competition, and have a great time in college. It allows students the option of taking introductory courses with smaller enrollments and top-notch instruction. It also assists honors students in creating their own degree programs and working closely with faculty members through a mentor program and honors project.

Honors courses offer small class sizes and stress more student interaction than lecture. Most students find that taking honors courses does not hurt their GPAs. In fact, students often do their best work in these classes.

Honors seminars give students the opportunity to explore topics not offered to the larger University population. Seminars are offered for 1–2 credits on a pass/fail basis. Students are encouraged to take seminars outside of their major field. Recent popular seminar topics have included virtual reality, alternative medicine, the works of J.R.R. Tolkien, tropical ecology, the Holocaust, and dinosaurs.

Honors projects give students the opportunity to choose a topic for in-depth study. Many times, students decide to do projects completely outside of their major. Research grants are awarded to students to help defray the cost of their projects.

The Freshman Honors Program introduces a limited number of qualified and motivated students to the advantages of an honors education, emphasizes learning in small groups, and fosters a sense of community among students with similar abilities and interests.

An Honors English composition class, a special Freshman Honors seminar, and an honors section of the required University library course form the academic core of the program during the fall semester. During spring semester, students may opt to participate in the Mentor Program, a program that places the freshmen with faculty members in a research environment.

Iowa State has offered University Honors since 1960 and Freshman Honors since 1973. There are approximately 820 students in the seven-college Honors Program and 250 students in the Freshman Honors Program. The notation "Graduated in the University Honors Program" is entered on the permanent record, diploma, and in the Commencement program. A certificate is also awarded at the College convocations preceding the University Commencement ceremony.

Participation Requirements: Students must submit a program of study approved by the College Honors Committee. Graduation in the University Honors Program requires a minimum GPA of 3.35, completion of the required number of honors courses and honors seminars, and completion of the Honors Project.

Admission Process: For the Freshman Honors Program, invitations are sent to students who meet one of the following categories: upper 5 percent of high school class; ACT composite score of 30 or above; or National Merit or National Achievement Finalist. Admission is competitive, and the program size is limited to 250 students.

Scholarship Availability: There are five competitive scholarships based on the activity level of Honors Program membership.

The Campus Context: Iowa State University is composed of nine colleges: Agriculture, Business, Design, Education, Engineering, Family and Consumer Sciences, Liberal Arts and Sciences, Veterinary Medicine, and Graduate. The University offers 100 bachelor's degree programs, 1 veterinary medicine program (professional), 105 master's programs, 1 specialist program, and 82 Ph.D. programs.

The parklike campus of 1,170 acres includes the $12-million Durham Computation Center, the $30-million molecular biology building, and the $13-million Leid Recreation Athletic Center. Cultural and athletic facilities include a 2,600-seat symphony hall, a 13,000-seat coliseum (filled to capacity for basketball games and major rock/country concerts), and a 48,000-seat football stadium (also filled to capacity with outdoor rock concerts).

Student Body The undergraduate enrollment is 19,806: 57 percent men and 43 percent women. The ethnic distribution is as follows: African American, 553 (2.8 percent); American Indian/Alaskan Indian, 47 (0.2 percent); Asian/Pacific Islander, 445 (2.2 percent); Hispanic 321, (1.6 percent); and international students, 1,164 (5.9 percent). Forty-two percent of the students are residents; the remaining 58 percent commute. Sixty-five percent of the students receive financial aid. This includes 5,000 merit-based scholarships and outside sources of funding (excluding parental support). Thirty-three percent receive Iowa State need-based aid. There are thirty-six fraternities and sixteen sororities.

Faculty The total number of faculty members is 1,781, of whom 1,560 are full-time. Almost 80 percent have terminal degrees. This figure does not include faculty members with terminal degrees such as the M.F.A. and M.B.A. The student-faculty ratio is 18:1.

Key Facilities The library houses more than 2 million volumes and bound serials. A campus telecommunications system allows students to use their personal computers to connect with the University system, Project Vincent. In addition to personal computers, Vincent provides more than 900 workstations located throughout campus, including academic building and residence halls that serve 23,000 people. All ISU students, faculty members, and staff members have access to the Web through Vincent. Vincent not only connects the people on campus to each other, it also connects people on campus to people around the world.

Iowa State has sixteen large classrooms and auditoriums outfitted with high-tech teaching equipment. There are thirty classrooms in which faculty members project information stored in their own computers onto large screens.

Athletics Iowa State's Division I intercollegiate athletic teams compete in the Big Eight (changing to Big 12) Conference. There are nine competitive sports for men (baseball, basketball, cross-country, football, golf, indoor track, outdoor track, swimming, and wrestling) and eleven for women (basketball, cross-country, golf, gymnastics, indoor track, outdoor track, soccer, softball, swimming, tennis, and volleyball). In sports, men's basketball is king—Iowa State is the 1996 Big Eight Champion. The men's cross-country team won the NCAA championship in 1989 and 1994, and both the men's and women's squads have won recent Big Eight titles. A new cross-country course was opened in 1995. An astounding 80 percent of the students participate in one of the largest intramural sports program in the nation.

Study Abroad For students who wish to study abroad, there are fifty programs involving study or internships in forty countries.

Support Services The University employs a program coordinator for disabled student services. Academic services and support are provided as required by the Americans with Disabilities Act. Residences halls can accommodate wheelchairs, and there is a residence apartment for a quadraplegic. There are hearing-impaired accommodations as needed and accommodations for guide dogs.

Job Opportunities ISU has more than 1,500 college work-study jobs available each year. An Undergraduate Research Assistant Program places 150 upperclass students with high GPAs and financial need with faculty researchers. ISU has a central location for the listing of on- and off-campus jobs. Numerous students who are not work-study-eligible are employed in campus offices and laboratories, ranging from office clerks and computer lab monitors to tutors to undergraduate teaching assistants and laboratory assistants.

Tuition: $2470 for state residents, $8284 for nonresidents per year (1996-97)

Room and Board: $3508

Mandatory Fees: $196 minimum

Contact: Coordinator: Elizabeth C. Beck, Osborn Cottage, Ames, Iowa 50011-1150; Telephone: 515-294-4371; Fax: 515-294-2970; E-mail: lcbeck@iastate.edu; Web site: http://www.public.iastate.edu/~honors/homepage.html

ITHACA COLLEGE

4 Pr G S Tr

▼ Honors Program

Based upon a spirit of inquiry, the Ithaca College Honors Program in Humanities and Sciences seeks to build an interdisciplinary academic community both in and out of the classroom. Each year, exceptionally qualified applicants to the College's School of Humanities and Sciences will be invited to apply to the honors program. Accepted students will be eligible for a series of special seminar courses and an array of program-financed, out-of-class activities.

Honors courses are imaginative, intensive seminars in which students accept a great degree of responsibility for their own learning. The courses center on a problem or theme that can be looked at from multiple or even conflicting perspectives: current topics include the American frontier, the "cultural brain," and the concept of nationhood in the twenty-first century. In the process of exploring this subject, honors students read important and original texts, test time-honored theories, and engage in an active and ongoing exchange of ideas. Dedicated to interdisciplinary education and designed to help students fulfill the general education requirements in the School, the honors program provides the Ithaca College student with the very best the campus has to offer.

Coordinated with the required honors seminars are various out-of-class activities, including pre-semester honors orientation, an honors film series, honors-financed trips to cultural events, and informal get-togethers with fellow students and faculty members. Incoming students are sent two books over the summer, compliments of the program, and encouraged to read them before the first honors gathering in fall.

All honors students are encouraged to partake in the administration of the honors program itself. A student advisory committee will provide crucial input on the current needs of the program, and students are invited to play a major role in matters of publicity, recruitment, and cocurricular activities.

Participation Requirements: There are four levels of honors seminars. An entering student will take an honors first-year seminar in the fall semester. Over the next three semesters, the student will take a total of five intermediate honors seminars. Next comes a junior year cultural themes honors seminar, followed by a senior year contemporary issues honors seminar.

Honors students of nearly any major in humanities and sciences can complete the program. Honors requirements are designed not to conflict with departmental requirements, including departmental honors requirements. Qualified students can complete both the school-wide honors program as well as honors within a specific major.

Students successfully completing the full sequence of course work will graduate with Honors in Humanities and Sciences on the official college transcript.

Admission Process: The honors program enrolled its first class of 40 students in fall 1996, currently has 75 students, and plans to build toward a full complement of 160 students by fall 1999. Based on information from the Admissions Office, the honors program invites exceptional applicants to the School of Humanities and Sciences to apply to the program. The application process involves a writing sample, such as a graded high school essay, and a letter of recommendation from a high school teacher. Qualified students not originally invited into the program can apply after they have completed a semester of work at Ithaca College. Transfer students can apply and will be considered on a case by case basis. Transfer students with associate honors degrees will, if admitted, have a slightly different set of requirements to complete.

Scholarship Availability: Ithaca College offers different levels of merit-based scholarships to qualified applicants. Many students in the honors program are recipients of these merit scholarships.

The Campus Context: Ithaca College is a fully accredited, coeducational, private institution in upstate New York offering a broadly diversified program of professional and liberal arts studies. Founded as a music conservatory in 1892, Ithaca now has four professional schools (Music, Business, Communications, and Health Science and Human Performance) in addition to the School of Humanities and Sciences. Enrolling an undergraduate population of 5,500 and a graduate population of 200, Ithaca College occupies the natural beauty of a hillside location overlooking the city of Ithaca, Cayuga Lake, and Cornell University. Ithaca College offers more than 100 different courses of study across its five schools, including fifty possible B.A., B.S., and B.F.A. majors in humanities and sciences. The new Science Building, with state-of-the-art undergraduate research facilities, attracts future science majors from all over the country. The Dillingham Center, with its modern architectural design and spacious stage, houses the nationally renowned Theatre Arts program.

Student Body The student population is 53 percent women, 47 percent men. The ethnic distribution is 92 percent white or Caucasian, 2 percent black or African American, 2 percent Hispanic or Latino, 2 percent Asian or Asian American, 2 percent nonresidential alien, and less than 1 percent Native American. There are 96 international students. Sixty-eight percent of students reside on campus. There are no nation-ally affiliated social fraternities on campus; there are 4 professional music fraternities and one social service sorority.

Faculty There are 539 faculty members, 440 full-time. Eighty-nine percent of faculty members have terminal degrees. The student-faculty ratio is 13:1.

Key Facilities The Ithaca College library holds 340,000 volumes. There are thirteen computer laboratories across campus, with more than 350 computers available for student use. Macintosh and DOS capabilities are regularly updated.

Athletics Ithaca College is a Division III school, offering eleven varsity athletic programs for men and twelve varsity programs for women. Its athletic teams have enjoyed great success, with national championships in women's soccer, football, baseball, and wrestling within the last decade. In addition to varsity athletics, there is an active intramural program.

Study Abroad The Office on International Programs offers a number of study opportunities throughout the world, and provides advice on both affiliated and nonaffiliated study abroad programs. The College also administers its own program in London, England, where students may take courses in the liberal arts, business, communications, music, and theater arts for a semester or for a year.

Support Services Ithaca College seeks to ensure that all students, including students with disabilities, have equal access to its programs and activities. The Office of Academic Support for Students with Disabilities assists students in making reasonable classroom accommodations.

Job Opportunities Ithaca College provides a wide variety of work opportunities—ranging from employment in the dining halls to the college library—as part of its financial aid support. In addition, the Dana Internship Program provides educationally relevant opportunities for highly qualified students with financial need. As Dana interns, students may work during the academic year with faculty on special projects or in the local community in not-for-profit organizations.

Tuition: $16,130 per year (1996-97)

Room and Board: $6990

Contact: Director: Hugh Egan, School of Humanities and Sciences, Ithaca, New York 14850-7270; Telephone: 607-274-1375; Fax: 607-274-3474; E-mail: eganh@ithaca.edu; Web site: http://www.ithaca.edu/hs/honors/honors1

JACKSON STATE UNIVERSITY

4 Pu G L Sc Tr

▼ W.E.B. DuBois Honors College

The W.E.B. DuBois Honors College at Jackson State University has graduated more than 1,000 students since its inception in 1980. Graduates of the Honors College have a 100 percent admission rate to graduate and professional schools and an equally successful record of employment.

Designed to provide its participants with an enriched, rigorous, and challenging curriculum, the W.E.B. DuBois Honors College aims to foster the intellectual development of students; to encourage creative and analytical thinking, critical inquiry, and scholarship; to nurture intellectual independence; and to prepare students well for graduate and professional schools.

Assistance in securing admission to research programs and graduate and professional schools is available. Smaller classes, honors floors for freshmen in two of the dorms, and honors dorms for upperclassmen are offered. Scholarships are available.

Current enrollment is 500 students. All majors at the University are represented in the enrollment.

Participation Requirements: Honors sections of the University's general education core curriculum constitute the basis of the Honors College requirements at Jackson State University. In addition, students may take honors courses offered by their departments or by other departments. Weekly meetings for freshmen, special lectures, and individualized advice and guidance throughout the students' tenure are aspects of the program.

Certificates of participation are awarded to students after graduation, and all honors classes taken are recorded on student transcripts as such.

Admission Process: Selection of incoming freshmen to the Honors College is based on ACT/SAT I scores, high school GPA, and rank in class. Transfer students may join the Honors College during their freshman or sophomore year.

The Campus Context: Located in Jackson, capital city of the state of Mississippi, Jackson State University is a public, historically black, multiracial, multiethnic, multicultural, coeducational institution that offers forty bachelor's degree, thirty-four master's degree, five educational specialist degree, and nine doctoral degree programs.

Founded in 1877, Jackson State University has a distinguished history, rich in the tradition of educating young men and women for positions of leadership.

Student Body The University has an overall enrollment of 6,118 students.

Tuition: $2380 for state residents, $4974 for nonresidents, per year (1996-97)

Room and Board: $2988

Contact: Dean: Maria Luisa Alvarez Harvey, P.O. Box 17004, Jackson, Mississippi 39217-0104; Telephone: 601-968-2107; Fax: 601-968-2299

JACKSONVILLE UNIVERSITY

4 Pr G S Tr

▼ University Honors Program

The Jacksonville University Honors Program is entering its thirteenth year and incorporates a variety of special courses. Some of these courses are honors sections of the core courses. Core courses are courses required of all students graduating from Jacksonville University. The Honors Colloquium is a 1-credit course designed to take advantage of the many scholarly and cultural activities that happen at Jacksonville University and in the surrounding communities. Other honors courses are primarily upper-level and often interdisciplinary in nature. The honors sections of core courses and some of the other honors courses are offered on a regular basis. The course offering varies from time to time, depending upon student demand and faculty interests. There is at least one upper-level honors seminar course offered each semester.

Approximately 80 students are participating in the Honors Program at Jacksonville University this year.

Participation Requirements: Students in the University Honors Program can major in any area the University offers. They may take as many or as few honors courses as they desire. However, to graduate with University Honors, a student must complete at least 25 credits of honors courses, including the Honors Colloquium and at least one upper-level honors seminar. Moreover, students must maintain an overall GPA of 3.5 or better and have a 3.5 or better GPA in the honors courses as well. AP credit for a course may be included as an honors course if the AP score is greater than the minimum score needed for credit at Jacksonville University. Many honors students also achieve departmental honors by completing significant research theses or creative productions as evidence of advanced attainment in addition to maintaining a GPA of 3.5 or better in their major fields.

Admission Process: To be eligible for honors, an entering freshman must have a GPA of 3.2 or better and a combined SAT I score of 1200 or ACT score of 27. Returning students and transfer students must have earned a cumulative GPA of 3.2 or better.

The Campus Context: Jacksonville University, located amid magnificent oak trees on the banks of the St. John's River in northeastern Florida, was founded in 1934 as a junior college and became a four-year university in 1956. Currently, Jacksonville University is composed of three colleges: the College of Arts and Sciences, the College of Fine Arts, and the College of Business. There are fifty-seven different undergraduate majors in eight undergraduate degree programs.

Student Body Of the 2,050 undergraduates enrolled, 54.7 percent are women and 45.3 percent men. Thirty-eight percent are housed in the eight residence halls and 62 percent commute. The ethnic distribution is .6 percent Native American/Alaskan, 9.7 percent black, 2.5 percent Asian/ Pacific Islander, 4.8 percent Hispanic, 75.2 percent white, 4.5 percent international (92 international students representing forty-eight countries), and 2.6 percent unknown. Seventy-seven percent of undergraduates receive financial aid. Jacksonville University hosts six fraternities and five sororities.

Faculty Of the 247 faculty members (175 full-time-equivalent faculty members), 110 are full-time faculty members and 137 are adjunct faculty members. Seventy-one percent of the full-time faculty members have terminal degrees. The student-faculty ratio is 14:1.

Key Facilities The University Library contains more than 500,000 volumes. There are more than 200 personal computers on campus for student use located in the dormitories, the library, and in classrooms throughout the campus.

Athletics Intercollegiate athletics for men include baseball, basketball, crew, cross-country, golf, soccer, and tennis. Intercollegiate athletics for women include crew, cross-country, golf, soccer, tennis, indoor and outdoor track, and volleyball. Active intramural and club sport programs are available to all interested students.

Study Abroad Jacksonville University recognizes the general educational value of travel and study abroad and cooperates in enabling students to take advantage of such opportunities. JU is affiliated with the American Institute of Foreign Study and will accept courses in the French language offered at the Ecole Superieure de Commerce in Nantes, France. In recent years JU students have studied in Mexico, Spain, Syria, France, England, Australia, Guatemala, and Costa Rica.

Job Opportunities Students are offered a wide variety of work opportunities on campus. All work programs originate in the Financial Aid Office.

Tuition: $13,360 per year (1997-98)

Room and Board: $4900

Mandatory Fees: $540

Contact: Director: Dr. Robert A. Hollister, 2800 University Boulevard North, Jacksonville, Florida 32211; Telephone: 904-744-3950 Ext. 7310; Fax: 904-745-7573; E-mail: bhollis@ju.junix.edu

JAMES MADISON UNIVERSITY

| 4 Pu G L Sc Tr |

▼ Honors Program

The James Madison University Honors Program enhances the intellectual, cultural, social, and career opportunities for JMU's most motivated, enthusiastic, and curious students. It offers rigorous and creative courses and interdisciplinary seminars taught by outstanding professors in small classes to facilitate discussion and critical thinking; organizes outside lectures, field trips to galleries, concerts and theater, and other special events to stimulate and challenge intellectual and social development; and provides opportunities for significant independent research and creative work with faculty mentors. First- and second-year honors students enjoy priority registration.

The Honors Program began in 1961 as 6 hours of independent study culminating in a senior thesis. In 1975

it offered honors sections and seminars to highly qualified first- and second-year students. The first program director was named in 1982, and 50 honors scholars were admitted. The current three-mode structure was instituted in 1986. Today, academically talented JMU students may participate in one of three honors programs: the Honors Scholars, Subject-Area Honors, or Senior Honors Project.

There are 443 students in the program (4 percent of undergraduates), including 103 freshmen, 140 sophomores, 75 juniors, and 125 seniors. There are 298 honors scholars, 104 subject-area honors students, and 41 senior honors project students.

Participation Requirements: Honors scholars participate in four years of honors study in a bachelor's degree program in any major. They complete 30 hours of honors work—a combination of honors courses, seminars, and independent study—and maintain a 3.25 cumulative GPA. Subject-area honors students enter the program in their second, third, or fourth semesters at JMU. They complete 24 hours of honors work—a combination of honors courses, seminars, and independent study—and maintain a 3.25 cumulative GPA. Senior honors project students enter the program in the second semester of their junior year and complete 6 hours of independent study over three semesters, culminating in documents of significant research or creative work. Each program is designed to prepare students for graduate or professional schools, enhance their opportunities for a rewarding career, and expand their knowledge of themselves, others, and the world.

Honors organizations provide activities and support. The Honors Student Advisory Council advises the staff on program, policies, and student needs. The Honors Scholars Society plans social activities building community and providing a support network. Honors Ambassadors, an outreach group, greet prospective students and their parents on campus visits and at admissions receptions, providing information on the honors curriculum and activities. Honors students are also among the most active in a wide range of campus organizations and in service to the community through programs such as Habitat for Humanity, ESL tutoring and adult literacy, and Camp Heartland for children with HIV.

Junior and senior honors students in good standing receive honors pins at an annual awards ceremony. Seniors completing the honors scholars or subject-area honors programs receive a medallion to wear at Commencement. All seniors completing a senior honors project and, thus, graduating with distinction, receive a certificate and have their names, project titles, and project directors listed in the Commencement program. The two most coveted awards are the Phi Beta Kappa Award for the most outstanding honors project and the Service Award for exceptional service to the program.

Admission Process: To participate in the Honors Scholars program, a student must apply and be invited to join the program during the senior year in high school. Applicants are evaluated on SAT I scores (the minimum combined score is 1200); class rank, GPA, and strength of high school program; participation in school and community activities; two letters of recommendation; and a personal statement. Admission is competitive; approximately 125 entering freshmen are admitted as Honors Scholars.

To apply for Subject-Area Honors, a student must have earned a 3.25 GPA at JMU and must submit an application, including a personal statement. All qualified applicants are accepted. To qualify for participation in the Senior Honors Project, a student must have a cumulative GPA of at least 3.25 and submit a project proposal with the approval of a project director; two readers; the department head, dean, or provost; and the director of the Honors Program. Transfer students from recognized honors programs are admitted as subject-area or senior honors project students.

Scholarship Availability:
Honors students are eligible to apply for all scholarships and grants offered by the University. Most of these are need-based (FAFSA required). A limited number of merit-based awards are available. These include departmental awards and the James Madison Scholar Awards, which are three four-year awards to National Merit finalists. The Honors Program has very limited scholarship funds. Honors Scholarships, typically $250, are awarded to returning students to assist in foreign study. Edythe Rowley scholarships, typically $1000, are awarded to returning students to meet unanticipated financial needs.

The Campus Context:
Founded in 1908, James Madison University has grown from a state normal and industrial school for women to a coeducational comprehensive university. The 472-acre campus is located in Harrisonburg, a progressive city of 30,000 people, in the heart of Virginia's historic Shenandoah Valley. Flanked by the Blue Ridge Mountains on the east and the Alleghenies on the west, Harrisonburg is at the intersection of three major highways: Interstate 81, U.S. 33, and U.S. 11, and is only a 2-hour drive from Washington, D.C.

The University offers small-college friendliness in a large-campus setting. It includes five undergraduate colleges: Arts and Letters, Business, Education and Psychology, Integrated Science and Technology, and Science and Mathematics. Undergraduate degree programs include B.A., B.B.A., B.F.A., B.G.S., B.M., B.S., B.S.N., and B.S.W. degrees.

Student Body The undergraduate student body numbers 10,503; 46 percent are men, 54 percent are women. Twelve percent of the student body are members of minority groups, including 6 percent African-American students. There are 323 international students. Residence halls house 49 percent of undergraduates; 51 percent commute, a majority of those from non-University-sponsored, off-campus student housing apartment complexes. City bus service is convenient and free to JMU students. Fifty-nine percent of students receive scholarships and grants; 43 percent receive loans. There are more than 200 student organizations, including twenty fraternities and twelve sororities (about 19 percent of undergraduates pledge).

Faculty There are 528 full-time faculty members and 188 part-time; 83 percent hold terminal degrees. The student-faculty ratio is 19:1.

Key Facilities The library houses 600,000 volumes, 3,000 subscriptions to current periodicals, and more than 30 CD-ROM databases; the library also provides access to the Virtual Library of Virginia (VIVA) and to additional resources worldwide through the Internet.

Computer facilities include twelve computer labs (including two 24-hour labs) with 262 computers (a mix of PCs and Macs) and seventy-six terminals are open to all students. In addition, some academic departments such as Art and Art History, Computer Science, English, Foreign Languages and Literatures, and Music have specialized labs for majors. All residence hall rooms are wired for campuswide network access. Students have access to the library's on-line computer, e-mail, and the Internet from labs and from their own personal computers in residence hall rooms or off-campus housing.

Athletics More than 500 student athletes compete in NCAA Division I sports in the Colonial Athletic Association, except in football, which competes in the Yankee Conference. Women's teams include archery, basketball, cheerleading, cross-country, fencing, field hockey, golf, gymnastics, track and field, lacrosse, soccer, swimming and diving, tennis, and volleyball. Men's teams include archery, baseball, basketball, cheerleading, cross-country, football, golf, gymnastics, track and field, soccer, swimming, diving, tennis, and wrestling.

Study Abroad JMU offers students the opportunity to study for a semester or year anywhere in the world. The University oversees semester-abroad programs in Florence, London, Martinique, Paris, and Salamanca. Students may participate in international exchange or consortium programs in Africa, Asia, the Caribbean, Europe, Latin America, and the Middle East. Travel programs are also available during the summer.

Support Services The Office of Disability Services assists a comprehensive population of students with disabilities. Documentation of the disability is required for those with nonvisible disabilities, so that appropriate accommodations may be negotiated. Services include priority registration, course scheduling information, and advising in relation to the disability; interpreters for the deaf; support lab providing equipment for students with visual impairments and learning disabilities; assistance in procuring auxiliary aids and equipment such as taped books; classroom accommodations; and other assistance as needed.

Job Opportunities Work opportunities on campus include Federal Work-Study in administrative and academic offices (FAFSA required), institutional employment by individual departments and service agencies, dining services, campus cadet program, and residence hall advisers and directors. Most on-campus jobs average 10–15 hours per week. Many students also find part-time jobs off campus in Harrisonburg.

Tuition: $4104 for state residents, $8580 for nonresidents, per year (1996-97)

Room and Board: $4666

Contact: Director: Dr. Joanne V. Gabbin, Hillcrest House, Harrisonburg, Virginia 22807; Telephone: 540-568-6953; Fax: 540-568-6240; E-mail: kimmelbl@jmu.edu; Web site: http://www.jmu.edu/honorsprog

JEFFERSON DAVIS COMMUNITY COLLEGE

2 Pu C S Sc Tr

▼ **Honors Program**

A major thrust of the Honors Program is not only to offer expanded and enriched courses, but to require off-campus trips that will broaden students culturally, socially, and aesthetically. Each professor is required to submit a course syllabus that includes the proposed enrichment activity or trip. The college president fully funds the student travel, which costs approximately $8000 per year. At least one trip is an overnight trip to a major city, including a play and tours of historic and artistic points.

There is an outstanding honors student named annually. Students diplomas include the designation Honors Graduate. Students' transcripts list honors courses.

The 6-year-old program currently enrolls 43 students. The deadline for applying is May 1.

Participation Requirements: Participation in the honors program is limited to 20 new students each year for a total of approximately 40 in the freshman and sophomore classes. The freshmen take two honors classes each quarter, and the sophomores take one honors course each quarter. Due to differing majors, it was felt by the Honors Council that one honors course in the sophomore year would fit well into students' curriculums. In addition, all honors students are required to take a 1-hour interdisciplinary course each quarter.

Scholarship Availability: Thirty scholarships are awarded per year. Program participants are selected from applicants who rank in the top 10 percent of their high school graduating class, have a high school GPA of 3.5 or higher, or score 25 or higher on the ACT. When program slots are available, previously enrolled college students who have maintained a 3.5 GPA on 30 or more college credits may be considered.

Approximately 90 percent of students receive some form of academic scholarship.

The Campus Context: *Student Body* The student body at Jefferson Community College is 58 percent men and 42 percent women. The ethnic distribution is 63 percent white, 33.6 percent black, .5 percent Asian, .5 percent Hispanic, 2.3 percent Native American, and 1 percent other. There is one international student. Thirty percent of students receive financial aid, excluding scholarships.

Faculty There are 82 faculty members: 47 full-time and 35 part-time. The student-faculty ratio is 19:1.

Key Facilities The campus library houses 31,056 volumes. There are IBM computers available in a computer lab and four in the library for student use. The campus also has teleconferencing facilities. There are no fraternities or sororities.

Athletics Athletics include men's and women's tennis, men's basketball, women's volleyball, women's softball, and men's baseball.

Study Abroad Study abroad is available through a formal link with UNO–Innsbruck International Summer School.

Special Services Disabled students will find excellent parking, ramps, and special desks.

Job Opportunities Work-study employment is available.

Tuition: $1350 per year (1997-98)

Mandatory Fees: $261

Contact: Director: Rosemary C. Jernigan, 220 Alco Drive, Brewton, Alabama 36426; Telephone: 334-809-1614; Fax: 334-867-7399

JOHN BROWN UNIVERSITY

4 Pr G S Sc Tr

▼ **University Honors Program**

The John Brown University (JBU) Honors Program, begun in 1987, includes a core of enriched courses that have been developed for gifted, highly motivated students. Participants must complete at least 18 honors hours to receive a University Honors degree. Courses emphasize the development of analytical skills, scholarly growth, and intellectual curiosity. The classes replace regular general education courses. Perhaps more important, the program is the impetus for continued development of JBU as a community of scholars. Many of the courses are experiential, with collaborative and integrative elements that cross disciplinary lines and narrow the gap between school and community by way of projects, field trips, guest speakers, and multimedia experiences. Some courses are modeled on NCHC's Honors Semesters, highlighting Native American and Ozark Mountain cultures, local businesses, and regional arts. The Honors Program emphasizes the exchange of ideas in a variety of settings: in the classroom, in the Honors Center, on field trips, and in the homes of professors.

The Honors Program attempts to recruit successful, innovative professors and serves as a laboratory for the development of pedagogical techniques and courses for the non-honors curriculum.

JBU honors students are strongly encouraged to model Judeo-Christian principles and good stewardship of their academic gifts through serving in leadership positions on campus and participating in service activities both on and off campus. The Student Honors Organization promotes scholarly presentations and service by the student body as a whole and serves as a peer support group for honors students. The Honors Center, available to honors students 24 hours a day, provides an attractive location for studying, cooking, watching television, and tutoring. Some classes are held in the center.

The total program has approximately 100 students.

Participation Requirements: To continue in the program, a student must maintain an overall cumulative GPA of 3.2 for the freshman and sophomore years, 3.3 by the end of the junior year, and 3.4 by the end of the senior year. Successful completion of the program is highlighted at an Honors Convocation and by the presentation of a special Honors Degree diploma at graduation. Courses are designated as "Honors" on the transcript.

Admission Process: In addition to 8 Presidential Scholars who are admitted to the program as a result of their scholarship, 17–22 entering freshmen are selected by application each June from a rather large and very well qualified pool of applicants. Transfer students and currently enrolled JBU students who have enough general education courses remaining to be taken for the honors degree may also apply. Eligibility for admission is based on high school GPA and class rank, SAT I/ACT scores, letter of application, and interview by the Honors Committee.

Scholarship Availability: Each year JBU awards eight 4-year, full-tuition scholarships to incoming freshmen who have met the following requirements: scored in the 95th national percentile or above on the ACT or SAT I, graduated with a 3.9 cumulative high school GPA or above (on 4.0 scale), ranked in the top 5 percent in the high school class, demonstrated leadership abilities, written an outstanding letter of application, and successfully completed an interview process. Presidential scholars may also receive other scholarships to cover room and board.

A large number of JBU honors participants come from the remaining scholarship pool. The institution awards ten $3000 divisional scholarships, numerous academic achievement scholarships ranging from $800 to $2000 per year, named scholarships donated by individuals and organizations, scholarships in the majors, and various leadership scholarships.

The Campus Context: Founded in 1919 as a nondenominational Christian liberal arts university, John Brown University is located in the foothills of the Ozark Mountains on the Arkansas-Oklahoma border. The campus is surrounded by rural and small-town scenic beauty. Major libraries, theaters, and museums are available with a short drive to Tulsa, Oklahoma.

Recent awards indicate JBU's growing reputation for excellence. For example, John Brown University has been ranked as one of the top 10 regional liberal arts colleges in the south by *U.S. News & World Report's America's Best Colleges* for the past few years and by the Templeton Foundation's "Honor Roll for Character Building Colleges" since that award's inception in 1988. Cancer and DNA research conducted by JBU science faculty members and students has been supported and recognized by the NSF, the National Cancer Institute, and the Radiation Research Institute. JBU is the only undergraduate institution in Arkansas approved to use human cadavers. JBU is beginning a major capital campaign, the first stage of which is to endow faculty chairs, increase programs, and add a new state-of-the-art computer and science facility and a living-learning campus center. John Brown offers forty-nine majors leading to five baccalaureate degrees in the liberal arts, science, engineering, communications, business, and education.

Student Body JBU has an undergraduate population of approximately 1,300: 56 percent women and 44 percent men. Two hundred are nontraditional students already in the workplace who are seeking degrees through the University's Advanced Degree Completion Program. The remaining 1,100 traditional students come from forty-one states and thirty other countries; 20–25 percent are either international or foreign-born U.S. students. Seventy percent of students live on campus. Eighty percent receive financial aid either by scholarship or work-study.

Faculty Students are taught by 89 faculty members (64 full-time). Seventy percent have doctorates or other terminal degrees. The student-faculty ratio is 16:1.

Key Facilities There are four public computer labs (seventy computers) and several departmental labs. All have Internet and network capacity. All students have network accounts. The library has 100,000 volumes.

Athletics Varsity teams include basketball, swimming, soccer, tennis, and volleyball. The University also offers a wide range of intramural sports.

Study Abroad There are several opportunities for study abroad through affiliated programs such as Latin American Studies, Holy Land Studies, Russian Studies, Medieval and Renaissance Studies (Oxford), and Cambridge Semester. An Irish semester as a part of JBU's regular curriculum is in the planning stage. JBU honors students regularly participate in NCHC's Semesters Program.

Support Services The Office of the Advocate for Students with Disabilities meets the needs of disabled students on an individual basis.

Tuition: $8860 per year (1997-98)

Room and Board: $4390

Mandatory Fees: $260

Contact: Director: Dr. Shirley Forbes Thomas, Honors Center Box 3074, Siloam Springs, Arkansas 72761; Telephone: 501-524-7426 or 7459; Fax: 501-524-9548; E-mail: sthomas@acc.jbu.edu; Web site: http://www.jbu.edu

JOHN CARROLL UNIVERSITY

4 Pr C S Tr

▼ **Honors Program**

The Honors Program at John Carroll University provides exceptional students the opportunity to expand and amplify their educational experience during college. The Honors Program, in conjunction with the Liberal Arts Core, seeks not only to prepare students for a lifetime of learning and to provide them with specific academic content, but also to foster in students a love of learning and the problem-solving and critical-thinking abilities essential for excellence.

The John Carroll University Honors Program is a University-based honors program, rather than a departmentally based honors program or a separate honors college. Thus, students take honors courses as part of the basic Liberal Arts Core. The University, as well as the Honors Program, believes a strong liberal arts background is essential for all bachelor degrees, so students take a selection of courses from different discipline areas designed to provide such a broad base to the undergraduate educational experience. The Honors Program is integrated into the University Core Curriculum and allows Honors Students to satisfy the Core Curriculum in ways consistent with their academic abilities and preparation.

In concert with the tradition of Jesuit education, the goal of the Honors Program is to pursue excellence in an environment that promotes the development and understanding of values and emphasizes freedom of inquiry, integration of knowledge, and social responsibility. These themes manifest themselves not just in the academic arena, but also in the development of the whole person.

Through small classes and close contact with faculty members, the Honors Program provides opportunities for greater depth and mastery in a student's education. Through interdisciplinary classes and the cross-disciplinary study of topics and issues, the Honors Program builds a broader perspective out of which a student can reflect on the world and its needs. Through the latitude to construct self-designed majors, the program encourages students to be creative in their college program. Through foreign language study and honors seminars, the Honors Program fosters a better understanding of a global society. Finally, through the community of honors students, who meet together and share social, cultural, and artistic events and have continual contact in classes, the Honors Program develops a camaraderie that strengthens students' ability to participate in the world.

The Honors Program endeavors to prepare a person to be a constructive, thoughtful, and active participant in the local and world communities. An honors graduate is one who values learning, service, and excellence, and thus will continue to learn, serve, and excel in whatever he or she does in life. The modern Honors Program at John Carroll was instituted in 1989–90. The first Honors Program began in 1963. There are approximately 200 students participating in the program.

Participation Requirements: Requirements include competency in English composition, demonstrated by one year of English Composition, or, if a student is exempt through AP credit or testing, one additional course in English that emphasizes writing; competency in oral communication as demonstrated by a one semester course specially designed for honors students or by testing out; competency in foreign language or calculus, demonstrated by two years of a language or by one year of calculus; six H or HP courses that fulfill portions of University Core Curriculum (H courses are honors sections of regularly taught courses; HP courses are special interdisciplinary or team-taught courses designed for honors students); participation in the First-Year Honors Seminar, which uses an interdisciplinary approach to explore a general topic (this seminar is team-taught by 3 faculty members, with each faculty member bringing his or her expertise to bear on the topic); and participation in a Senior Honors Seminar or Senior Honors Project. The seminar uses an interdisciplinary approach to explore a specific topic. This course is jointly taught and usually continues the topic from the First-Year Honors Seminar taken by these students. The Senior Honors Project requires at least 3 hours of independent research under the direction of an adviser.

Honors participants must maintain a 3.5 GPA, and must have a 3.5 GPA at graduation. Students who graduate from the Honors Program are identified by the words Honors Scholar on their transcripts and by a special gold seal on their diplomas. In addition, at graduation, Honors Students are recognized by a gold cord worn with their academic gown.

Admission Process: Entering freshmen seeking admission to the Honors Program should normally have a minimum combined score of at least 1270 on the SAT I or at least a 28 composite score on the ACT, rank in the top 10 percent of their high school class, and have at least a 3.5 GPA in their high school college-preparatory courses. In short, the program is seeking students who rank above the 90th percentile of freshmen throughout the nation. Students in their sophomore and junior years, transfer students, and nontraditional students are also welcome to apply to the program. Currently enrolled students should have a 3.5 GPA in college prior to applying to the Honors Program.

Scholarship Availability: The Honors Program does not administer any scholarships or financial aid. However, the University provides solid financial assistance to Honors Students. As an indication of that support, all First-Year Honors Students who entered between 1990 and 1995 and who requested financial assistance received merit scholarships. These grants included such awards as American Values Scholarships ($1000–$3000 per year, renewable, based on merit), President's Honor Awards (amounts vary, renewable, merit- and need-based), Mastin Scholarships in the sciences ($10,000 per year, renewable, merit-based), John Carroll grants (amount varies, renewable, merit- and need-based), and National Merit Scholarships (sponsored by John Carroll, merit-based).

The Campus Context: John Carroll University is characterized by several distinguished facilities, including the Breen Learning Center, a recent $6.8-million addition to the Grasselli Library, which has doubled the capacity of the building and has enhanced accessibility of electronic databases; the O'Malley

Center for Communications and Language Arts, which features a television studio and newsroom, computer-assisted and audio language laboratories, and a center for writing instruction; and the Boler School of Business' Bruening Hall, which houses high-tech presentation classrooms featuring computerized audio/visual technology. The University offers twenty-seven bachelor's degrees.

Student Body There are 2,871 full-time and 156 part-time students in the College of Arts and Sciences, plus 139 full- and part-time nondegree students. The School of Business enrolls 332 students full-time and 31 part-time. The total enrollment is about 3,600 students. Forty-nine percent of the population are men, and 51 percent are women. The ethnic distribution is 4.4 percent African American, .9 percent Hispanic, 2.8 percent members of other minority groups, 90.5 percent white, and 1.5 percent other. There are 25 international students, and 56.8 percent of students reside on campus. Sixty-five percent of students receive financial aid. There are nine fraternities and six sororities.

Faculty The total number of faculty members is 419, of whom 285 are full-time. Eighty-eight percent of faculty members hold terminal degrees. The student-faculty ratio is 14:1.

Key Facilities The library holds 564,640 volumes. Two hundred microcomputers are available for student use, and students have access to the Internet.

Athletics The University is a member of the National Collegiate Athletic Association Division III and the Ohio Athletic Conference. Men compete in baseball, basketball, cross-country, football, golf, soccer, swimming, tennis, track, and wrestling. Women compete in basketball, cross-country, soccer, softball, swimming, tennis, track, and volleyball. The Don Shula Sports Center, natatorium, tennis courts, weight-training room, handball and racquetball courts, and gymnasium are available for student use.

Study Abroad John Carroll University, through the Office of International Studies, has organized six geographic areas of concentration: European, East Asian, Hispanic, African, Russian, and Middle Eastern. Each of these areas is represented by a coordinator. Study-abroad and international exchange programs are administered through the College of Arts and Sciences.

Support Services Ninety-six percent of the campus is accessible to physically disabled people.

Job Opportunities The University participates in the Federal Work-Study Program.

Tuition: $13,883 per year (1997-98)

Room and Board: $5662

Contact: Director: Dr. John R. Spencer, 20700 North Park Boulevard, University Heights, Ohio 44118; Telephone: 216-397-4677; Fax: 216-397-4256; E-mail: honors@jcvaxa.jcu.edu; Web site: http://www.jcu.edu

JOHNSON COUNTY COMMUNITY COLLEGE

2 Pu D S Sc

▼ Honors Program

The Honors Program curriculum at Johnson County Community College is designed to stimulate and challenge academically talented students. Enrolling in the Honors Program will help students develop their intellectual potential as college students and as members of the academic community. While a part of the Honors Program, students receive a newsletter every three weeks, keeping them informed of campus activities, scholarships, and study-abroad programs. Students are also offered tickets to selected cultural events on campus and invited to participate in the National Collegiate Honors Council conferences. Graduates are recognized at graduation and at a special ceremony.

The number of students in the program varies each semester from approximately 80 in the fall semester to approximately 100 students in the spring.

Participation Requirements: Students may elect to participate in any part of the Honors Program, but to graduate from the program students must take an interdisciplinary course that emphasizes inquiry, discovery, and critical thinking and discussion methods that stress student participation; the Honors Forum class, which focuses on a current issue that affects the local, national, and global communities; four honors contracts, which are 1 hour of additional credit extensions to the regularly scheduled courses throughout the curriculum; and perform some volunteer community service.

Admission Process: Students wanting to take an honors contract must have a high school or college cumulative GPA of 3.5 or higher.

Scholarship Availability: Johnson County Community College offers a number of scholarships to students who plan to graduate from the Honors Program and the College. Students submit an application form and are interviewed.

The Campus Context: There are thirteen buildings on campus, including the Cultural Education Center, housing Yardley Hall, which seats 1,300; the Theatre, which seats 400; the Black Box Theatre for academic productions; and the Recital Hall. The College offers more than forty career and certificate programs, eight selective admission programs, and eight selective admission cooperative programs with the Metropolitan Community College District.

Student Body Student enrollment is 15,477; of these, 44.2 percent are men and 55.8 percent are women. Members of minority groups account for 8.7 percent of the enrollment. Almost 78 percent of students are Johnson County residents, 16.8 percent are other Kansas residents, and 5.9 percent are out-of-state residents.

Faculty There are 270 full-time and 498 part-time faculty members.

Key Facilities The library houses 85,000 bound volumes; 600 periodical subscriptions; 400,000 titles on microfilm; 4,000 records, tapes, and CDs; and nine on-line bibliographic sources.

Study Abroad Through the College Consortium for International studies, JCCC students have an opportunity to study in any one of nineteen countries for a semester or a year. Programs that focus on liberal arts, language and culture, business, and performing and visual arts are available in countries in Europe, Latin America, the Middle East, and Asia.

Support Services Students with disabilities have access to a variety of support services, including reading, notetaking, tutoring, and other services that allow equal access to courses. Assistive computer equipment especially designed for students with disabilities (such as speech synthesizers, screen readers, scanners, adjustable tables, and Braille printers) are also available. Campus buildings are equipped with ramps, elevators, and restrooms designed to accommodate wheelchairs. Parking areas convenient to the buildings are reserved for students with disabilities. In addition, an orientation for students with disabilities is held at the beginning of the fall and spring semesters.

Tuition: $1216 for state residents, $3904 for nonresidents, per year (1996-97)

Mandatory Fees: $256

Contact: Director: Matt Campbell, 12345 College Boulevard, Overland Park, Kansas 66210-1299; Telephone: 913-469-2512; Fax: 913-469-4409

JOLIET JUNIOR COLLEGE

2 Pu G S Tr

▼ Honors Program

The Joliet Junior College Honors Program, currently in its tenth year, is designed to intellectually stimulate and challenge students striving for the utmost in their college education. It consists of a select group of students and faculty members from all disciplines and a core of courses in which the material is covered in greater depth and breadth than in regular courses. Writing and critical thinking are stressed, and because honors classes are small (15 students maximum), many teaching and learning approaches are used.

As their adviser, the coordinator of the Honors Program assists all honors students during their careers at Joliet Junior College and thereafter in, among other things, transferring, seeking scholarships, and gaining employment.

There are currently 60 students in the program.

Participation Requirements: To graduate from the Honors Program students must satisfy all college requirements for graduation, complete 15 credit hours of honors course work, participate in at least one half of all honors colloquia (lecture-discussion sessions run by guest scholars) and honors forums (biweekly discussion sessions run by honors students), and earn a 3.5 or better GPA. All honors courses are designated as such on student transcripts, as is successful completion of the program.

Admission Process: Entering freshmen must satisfy one of the following requirements: graduation in the top 10 percent of the high school class, an ACT composite score of 25 or better, or membership in the National Honor Society. Joliet Junior College students must have a 3.5 GPA for 15 or more credit hours or two letters of recommendation from college faculty members. An interview with the Honors Program Coordinator is required of all applicants.

Scholarship Availability: Joliet Junior College offers a number of endowed scholarships to qualified applicants. In some cases, participation in the Honors Program may be a factor.

The Campus Context: Joliet Junior College, America's oldest public community college, began with 6 students in 1901 as an experimental postgraduate high school program. Today, JJC serves more than 10,000 students in credit classes and another 5,000 students in noncredit courses. JJC is a comprehensive community college that offers prebaccalaureate programs for students planning to transfer to a four-year university, occupational and technical education programs leading directly to employment, adult education and literacy programs, work force and workplace development programs, and academic support services to help students succeed. A total of thirty-four two-year transfer degree programs and thirty-three two-year terminal degree programs are offered.

Student Body Undergraduate enrollment is 10,400. The student population is 40 percent men, 60 percent women. Ethnic distribution is .5 percent Native American/Alaska Native, 8 percent black/African American, 7 percent Hispanic, .5 percent Asian/Pacific Islander, and 83 percent white. There are 7 international students. All students are commuters. Fifty percent of students receive financial aid.

Faculty Of the 500 total faculty members, 150 are full-time. Seventy-five percent have an M.A. or the equivalent, 20 percent hold a Ph.D., and 5 percent hold other degrees. The student-faculty ratio is 20:1.

Key Facilities The library has 70,000 volumes and is a member of ILCSO (Illinois Library Computer Systems Organization). Computer facilities include 1,000 computers on campus (800 are IBM-compatible), fourteen labs—most are networked, Internet access, and the Technology Planning Committee, which has an annual budget of nearly $1 million for upgrades and expansion.

Athletics Joliet Junior College has the following intercollegiate athletic teams: men's football and women's volleyball and tennis, men's and women's basketball, and men's baseball and tennis and women's softball. These teams are nonscholarship and compete in Divisions II and III of the NJCAA.

Study Abroad A member of the Illinois Consortium for International Studies and Programs (ICISP), Joliet Junior College currently offers students opportunities to study in England, Austria, the Netherlands, Costa Rica, Mexico, and France. In addition, College staff participate in the ICISP faculty exchange program.

Support Services The Joliet Junior College Special Needs Department provides qualified students with assistance ranging from adaptive testing to notetaking assistance, signers, and a special learning resources room.

Job Opportunities Numerous part-time jobs are available on campus to qualified students.

Tuition: $1248 for area residents, $4479 for state residents, $5482 for nonresidents, per year (1996-97)

Mandatory Fees: $77

Contact: Coordinator: Peter L. Neff, 1215 Houbolt Road, Joliet, Illinois 60431-8938; Telephone: 815-729-9020 Ext. 2384; E-mail: pneff@jjc.cc.il.us

KALAMAZOO VALLEY COMMUNITY COLLEGE

2 Pu G S Sc Tr

▼ **Honors Program**

The goals of the Kalamazoo Valley Community College Honors Program are to provide an enriched academic environment that is both supportive and challenging, to encourage and reward high academic achievement, to inspire leadership, to stimulate the creative energies of faculty members and students, to foster community service, and to help academically superior students transfer to baccalaureate institutions.

KVCC honors scholars may be admitted as full-time or part-time students, and enroll in day, evening, or weekend classes, at either of the two campuses. They may enroll in any associate degree program, and may choose the associate degree as their final academic step or transfer credits to a four-year institution.

The program emphasizes studies that stimulate and broaden student knowledge in and across disciplines, with small, specially structured courses, along with honors options designed to challenge and motivate. The Honors Program encourages a variety of on- and off-campus educational and social experiences, subsidizing student costs of plays, lectures, and musical and other cultural events. Through conferences and shared activities with other college and university students, KVCC Honors Scholars meet and interact with honor students from four-year college campuses. Students in the program are matched with a faculty mentor of their choosing, who can help plan for a most successful college career.

Honors Program students are recognized in a variety of ways, beginning with local news releases. The director and other college officials host receptions for honor students, and the College sponsors an Honors Convocation annually to laud honor students. Each month a certificate is awarded to the Community Service Leader of the Month. At graduation, Honors Program graduates are recognized in the Commencement program and with honors cords. Membership in the Honors Program is indicated on official diplomas and transcripts.

The program was established in 1988. There are currently 50 students enrolled.

Participation Requirements: Students designated as Honors Program graduates will be those who have successfully completed all course work necessary for graduation, who have a GPA of 3.25 or better, and who have at least 25 percent of their credits designated honors, either through honors courses or honors options. They will also have taken part in initial and concluding common experiences developed for the program; HUM 120HC and HUM 121HC; and honors seminars, including community/volunteer service.

Admission Process: Honors Scholars are selected during the summer for fall enrollment on the basis of academic achievement, letters of recommendation, a writing sample, community involvement, personal interview with the director, and final selection by the Honors Advisory Committee comprised of the director, faculty representatives, and other designated College staff. Students must have at least 20 credit hours remaining for degree requirements at KVCC.

Scholarship Availability: Full-tuition scholarships are awarded to all students in the program, subject to funding by the KVCC Foundation Board. This scholarship will be used for courses counting toward graduation, for a maximum of 70 credit hours, allowing for required honors courses and a possible change in major. Honors Program students are also eligible to apply for any other collegewide scholarships offered through the Financial Aid Office at KVCC.

The Campus Context: Kalamazoo Valley Community College was established in 1966 and opened its Texas Township Campus doors in September 1968 as a commuter college for the pioneer class of 1,518 students. The educational program included vocational, technical, health service, social service, general education, liberal arts, and community services. There are a total of forty-one degree programs. The history of the College has been characterized by continual growth, with a current enrollment of approximately 11,000 students each semester. The Texas Township Campus is located on 187 acres of natural landscape 8 miles west of the city of Kalamazoo, Michigan. The campus is accessible from two major highways (Interstate I-94 and U.S. 131). For students using public transportation, the Kalamazoo Metro Bus system makes daily stops on campus.

In September 1994, the College opened the Arcadia Commons Campus, located in the heart of downtown

Kalamazoo. This 55,000-square-foot campus is designed to meet the education and training needs of business and industry.

The fall of 1994 also saw the opening of the Technology Applications Center on the Texas Township Campus, where enterprise, education, and technology fuse to introduce innovative manufacturing and management techniques. The TAC encompasses 26,500 square feet of classroom, lab, office, meeting, and demonstration space. Services include customized training; consulting; assessments; meeting and conference space; space for equipment demonstrations, receptions, and dining; trade show capability; and vendor equipment demonstrations.

KVCC assumed governance of the Kalamazoo Public Museum in July 1991, and through generous contributions of its community raised $20 million to build a new museum. In February 1996 the Kalamazoo Valley Museum opened its doors. The new museum houses a Digistar Theater, lecture hall, Challenger Learning Center, Children's Landscape, planetarium, Discovery Center, and exhibits.

Student Body Undergraduate enrollment is 45 percent men and 55 percent women. The ethnic distribution is 87 percent white, 9 percent black, 2 percent Hispanic, 1 percent Native American/Alaska Native, 1 percent Asian/Pacific Islander, and 2 percent international students. All students at KVCC commute. Among students, 17.4 percent receive financial aid. There are two fraternities and sororities.

Faculty The total number of faculty is 349. Full-time faculty members number 103. Ten percent of the faculty have terminal degrees.

Key Facilities The library houses 88,900 volumes. The campus has microcomputer classrooms and a lab for student use.

Athletics The college is a member of the Michigan Community College Athletic Association and the National Junior College Athletic Association. Intercollegiate sports include volleyball, basketball, softball, and tennis for women and basketball, baseball, tennis, and golf for men. The intramural program at KVCC provides a variety of activities in both athletic and nonathletic areas. The program is structured to encourage student participation and to play a part in the total development of students during their educational experience. An Olympic-size swimming pool is open to students and the public.

Study Abroad The International Studies Program offers an associate degree and a certificate in international studies. The program also functions as an information and resource center on international matters through such activities as lectures, seminars, workshops, networks, festivals, and a substantial collection of printed and audiovisual material. The IS program offers and participates in a variety of direct international experiences through student and faculty member overseas travel, study, research, and exchange opportunities. Through the business department, the College also offers an international marketing degree.

Support Services There are comprehensive support services for disabled students.

Job Opportunities Work opportunities for students include Federal Work-Study, part-time jobs, and local opportunities.

Tuition: $1178 for area residents, $2201 for state residents, $3224 for nonresidents, per year (1996-97)

Contact: Director: William H. Lay, 6767 West O Avenue, P.O. Box 4070, Kalamazoo, Michigan 49003-4070; Telephone: 616-372-5286; Fax: 616-372-5458; E-mail: lay01@vax.kvcc.edu; Web site: www.kvcc.edu

KENNESAW STATE UNIVERSITY

4 Pu G M Tr

▼ Honors Program

In its inaugural year (1996–97), the Honors Program at Kennesaw State University is serving two student groups: a group of 20 students who have taken between 45 and 90 quarter hours of course work at Kennesaw and are earning a GPA of at least 3.8, and a group of almost 130 high school students who are satisfying both senior-year high school requirements and college requirements in freshman-level courses at the University.

Participation Requirements: To remain in good standing, students must maintain a cumulative GPA of 3.8 or better in their course work. For the students in the first group, the Honors Program is organized around three fundamental principles: honors faculty mentorship, formal honors experiences, and the honors colloquium. As soon as they are notified of their acceptance to the Honors Program, these students are assigned individual faculty mentors (members of the honors faculty) who share their academic interests and professional objectives. Such mentorship has two distinct objectives: to help honors students create a balanced and academically rigorous curriculum consistent with their goals and to foster active intellectual exchange between honors students and faculty members in a long-standing peer relationship.

The second fundamental principle of the program, the completion of four honors experiences, is designed to tailor the honors curriculum to the needs of traditional and nontraditional students. These honors experiences must include at least one experience based exclusively in course work and conducted in a traditional academic setting. These are designated on student transcripts with the suffix H for Honors. Such honors experiences can be satisfied through stand-alone honors courses such as the honors seminar or through honors contracting in non-honors courses taught by honors faculty members. The honors experiences must also include at least one experience based in a context where honors students can apply their knowledge to general practice, primarily (though not exclusively) outside the traditional classroom. These are designated with the suffix AH for Applied Honors. Such honors experiences may be satisfied through activities such as teaching, research assistantships, or through carefully selected and challenging internships. Finally, the honors experiences must include a senior capstone honors experience.

The Honors Program's third fundamental principle, the honors colloquium, is a 2-quarter-hour course designed to help honors students develop a sense of community with other honors students and with honors faculty members. In addition to meeting regularly to discuss interdisciplinary themes, the students participate in a prearranged number of discipline-specific experiences, including at least three off-campus cultural activities. They are required to complete two colloquia before they graduate, documenting the details of their participation in an honors portfolio.

Whether attending Kennesaw full- or part-time, the joint-enrollment honors students in the program's second charter group have the option of taking special honors sections of core courses designed exclusively for the joint-enrollment honors program. They are also assigned mentors from the ranks of the honors faculty, and they can receive special honors recognition (including automatic admission to Kennesaw's regular Honors Program their freshman year) for participating in a series of enrichment activities and maintaining a 3.5 GPA (or better) in 30 hours of course work at Kennesaw. They are not required to complete a specific number of honors experiences or to take one or more honors colloquia.

Admission Process: In the inaugural year, students admitted to the regular Honors Program at Kennesaw were required to have a cumulative or adjusted GPA of 3.8 or higher in no fewer than 45 and no more than 90 hours of course work taken at Kennesaw. Students admitted to the joint-enrollment honors program needed to be rising high school seniors and have at least a 3.0 academic GPA in their high school courses, and SAT I scores (or ACT equivalents) of at least 530 verbal, 470 math, and 1100 combined. Entering freshmen and transfer students with fewer than 45 hours of college-earned transfer credit are considered for admission in their second year.

The Campus Context: Kennesaw State University, one of the fastest-growing members of the University System of Georgia, has served students throughout metropolitan Atlanta and northwest Georgia for more than three decades, offering day, evening, and weekend classes to a variety of traditional and nontraditional students. The University has five schools of instruction, including the School of Arts, Humanities, and Social Sciences; the School of Business; the School of Education; the School of Nursing; and the School of Science and Mathematics. These schools support forty-one undergraduate degree programs, seven preprofessional programs of study, and nine graduate degree programs.

Student Body Kennesaw enrolls about 12,000 undergraduates; of these, 39 percent are men and 61 percent are women. An analysis of the ethnic distribution reveals that 88 percent are white, 7 percent are black, 2.8 percent are Asian, 1.8 percent are Latino, and .4 percent are Native American. Almost 600 international students attend Kennesaw, and almost 41 percent of the undergraduates receive some form of financial aid. All students commute to campus. Students who wish to pursue extracurricular activities at Kennesaw may enjoy a variety of

cultural arts programs, including the Premier Music Series, the Cobb Symphony Orchestra (in residence at the University), and three prominent lecture series. In addition, they may rush one of five social fraternities or three social sororities.

Faculty Kennesaw has 528 faculty members, 364 of whom are full-time. Eighty percent of faculty members have terminal degrees. The student-faculty ratio is 23:1.

Key Facilities The University's library has 550,000 volumes. Kennesaw has four open computer labs (all networked), fourteen electronic classrooms, 500 student work stations, and special-purpose advanced computer labs for majors in accounting, computer science, education, and information systems. Other special or distinguishing facilities on campus include the Georgia Department of Education Technology Center, the Teacher Resource and Activity Center, and the Bentley Special Collections, which are showcased in the Rare Book Room of the Horace W. Sturgis Library.

Athletics Students may participate in women's basketball, cross-country, softball, and tennis or men's baseball, basketball, cross-country, and golf. A member of Division II of the National Collegiate Athletic Association, Kennesaw's intercollegiate sports program includes the 1995 NCAA Division II National Softball Champions, as well as the 1994 NAIA National Champion baseball team.

Study Abroad Through its Office of International Programs, Kennesaw operates two summer study-abroad programs, one in Mexico and a second in Belize, Central America. Participants in the Mexico program may study Mexican history, culture, and the visual arts, as well as the Spanish language. The Tropical Ecology in Belize program gives its participants the opportunity to earn upper-level biology credits while experiencing an array of tropical ecosystems and living with Belizean families. The Office of International Programs also coordinates the participation of Kennesaw students in any of several thousand study-abroad programs run by other fully accredited academic institutions.

Support Services Kennesaw's Disabled Student Support Services provides eligible students with handicapped-accessible parking spaces; special test administration; classroom accessibility; sign language interpreters; note takers; readers; tutors; tape recording; personal, academic, and career counseling; library or laboratory assistance; adaptive computer equipment (configured, for example, with screen magnification and voice synthesis); and referral to community resources.

Job Opportunities A limited number of part-time jobs are available in each division of the University for Kennesaw students who wish to earn part of their college expenses by working on campus.

Tuition: $1584 for state residents, $5463 for nonresidents, per year (1996-97)

Mandatory Fees: $240

Contact: Director: Dr. Liza Davis, 1000 Chastain Road, Kennesaw, Georgia 30144; Telephone: 770-423-6116; Fax: 770-423-6748; E-mail: ldavis@ksumail.kennesaw.edu

KENT STATE UNIVERSITY

4 Pu G L Sc Tr

▼ Honors College

Honors at Kent State University began in 1934 when the first senior honors thesis was written. In 1960 the program attained University-wide status and in 1965 became a collegial unit headed by a dean.

The Honors College, open to students of all majors, is at the center of Kent State University's long tradition of providing special attention to undergraduates with outstanding intellectual and creative ability. Within the framework of the larger University, with its diverse academic programs and excellent research and library facilities, the Honors College offers students enriched and challenging courses and programs, opportunities for close relationships with peers and faculty members, and careful advising to meet their interests and goals.

The Honors College is guided by two basic principles. The first is a responsibility to provide academic work that offers intellectual challenge to the best students in the University and demands of them the best effort of which they are capable. To this end courses are designed to stretch the mind, sharpen skills, and encourage high standards of performance.

The second is the belief that regardless of degree program, students should be liberally educated. That is, they should understand and appreciate the language, literature, and history of cultures; the social, political, and economic structure of societies; the creative achievements that enrich lives; and the basic assumptions and substance of the natural sciences. In keeping with this belief, the College provides honors sections of many of the University's Liberal Education Requirement courses. Honors students are also encouraged to enrich their major programs by enrolling in related courses across disciplinary boundaries, e.g., studying foreign languages to complement degree programs in business. In addition, honors students pursue double majors in unusual combinations such as mathematics and theater, art and French, and elementary education and dance.

Honors courses are available throughout the undergraduate years and can be used to meet requirements in all the degree-granting colleges and schools of the University.

All honors freshmen are enrolled in the year-long Freshman Honors Colloquium. The colloquium is a rigorous course in reading, thinking, and writing about literature and ideas. The goal of the course is to develop habits of inquiry, understanding, and communication that will serve the student through the college years and beyond.

In addition to the Freshman Colloquium, many honors courses are taught each semester by distinguished faculty members throughout the University. Although these courses differ in content from art to zoology, they share a common form. Class enrollments are small (no more than 20), and students get to know each other and their professors in an environment that encourages learning through discussion, reading, individual work, and writing.

Honors students are also encouraged to study on a one-to-one basis with members of the faculty. The Individual Honors Work course is available from the freshman through senior years and can take many forms. For example, it has been used by students to "create" a course not available in the regular curriculum, intern off campus, or undertake a specialized scholarly or creative project. Seniors are strongly encouraged to complete the Senior Honors Thesis/Project.

Honors students are advised by the dean and a professional advising staff and by collegial and faculty advisers in their majors. Honors students must meet with their honors adviser at least once each semester in order to register for the following term.

There are currently 940 students enrolled; in addition, 50–60 are registered at two regional campuses.

Participation Requirements: There are three general categories of graduation with honors at Kent State. University Honors requires students to complete seven honors classes and have a cumulative GPA of 3.8. Students in this category must take 10 hours of independent study, at least 6 of which must be the thesis but all of which can be. The thesis must be of outstanding quality. General Honors requires seven honors classes, a cumulative GPA of 3.2 or higher, a major GPA of 3.4 or higher, and an honors GPA of 3.4 or higher. In this category, students complete 10 hours of independent study, at least 6 of which must be the thesis but all of which can be. The thesis must be of "A" or "B" quality. For Departmental Honors, students must have a minimum of 10 upper division honors hours in the major, 6 of which must be the thesis but all of which can be. (Note: This minimum set of requirements is available only to those who come in late in their college career just to do the senior thesis. Those who come in earlier must complete some course work as well since students cannot go more than one semester without engaging in honors work of some kind.) Students seeking Departmental Honors must have a cumulative GPA of 3.2 or higher, a major GPA of 3.4 or higher, and an Honors GPA of 3.4 or higher. The thesis must be of "A" or "B" quality.

All of the above represent minimum requirements. Students may take more courses, and GPAs may be higher. A student with twelve honors courses, for example, and a cumulative GPA of 3.7 receives General Honors. Likewise, a student who completes five honors courses with a GPA of 3.8 receives Departmental Honors. General and University Honors were designed to recognize breadth in honors work; Departmental Honors was designed to indicate less broad participation in the Honors Program. "Breadth" was defined as having completed at least seven honors courses.

Graduation as a member in good standing (course work only) requires eight honors courses/experiences and at least a 3.0 GPA. Two categories of graduation recognition are possible: one with a thesis (graduation with honors) and one with course work only (graduation as a member in good standing of the Honors College). Graduation with honors exists in three categories and includes a certificate announcing "Distinction" in the student's major. Students graduating from the Honors College are recognized at Commencement; in addition, thesis students are recognized at the annual University-wide Honors Day Convocation.

Admission Process: Students apply directly to the Honors College by having guidance counselors send a copy of their high school transcript (showing class rank, GPA, ACT/SAT scores, and senior courses). Admission and scholarship decisions are made on an ongoing basis. Students who apply after the freshman year are evaluated on the basis of actual college performance. Students may apply as late as the end of the junior year.

Scholarship Availability: The Honors College directly distributes renewable merit scholarships ranging from $1200 to full in-state tuition to approximately 65 percent of the freshman honors class. Also included are some discipline-specific awards. Minimum requirements are usually the top 10 percent in both class rank and national test scores.

The Campus Context: Located in Kent, Ohio (population 30,000), Kent State University was founded in 1910 as Kent Normal School and became a university in 1935. It is an eight-campus system serving the needs of the northeast Ohio region. Regional campuses include Ashtabula, East Liverpool, Geauga, Salem, Stark, Trumbull, and Tuscarawas. The centrally located Kent campus lies approximately 35 miles south of Cleveland and 11 miles east of Akron. There are 109 buildings on the 824-acre Kent campus. These include a twelve-story research library with almost 2 million volumes, which also houses the executive offices; a student center, which includes a bookstore, food court, cafeteria, rathskeller, restaurant, ballroom, music listening center, governance chambers, bowling alley, and auditorium; an ice arena, athletic and convocation center, stadium, and field house; and numerous classroom buildings and residence halls. There is a campus bus service.

The Kent campus provides baccalaureate, master's, and doctoral degrees.

In addition to traditional collegial and departmental areas, the campus has institutes for liquid crystals, applied linguistics, bibliography and editing, computational mathematics, and water resources and centers for applied psychology, Conrad studies, counseling and human development, employee ownership, international and comparative studies, literature and psychoanalysis, world musics, Pan-African culture, NATO and European community studies, and urban design.

Student Body Of the 15,958 undergraduate and 4,642 graduate students enrolled on the Kent campus, the majority are from northeast Ohio.

Key Facilities The library houses 1.8 million volumes. There is active chapter of Phi Beta Kappa.

Job Opportunities Students are offered a range of work opportunities on campus, including work-study, assistantships and fellowships, and University-funded employment.

Tuition: $4288 for state residents, $8576 for nonresidents, per year (1996-97)

Room and Board: $4030

Contact: Dean: Dr. Larry R. Andrews, P.O. Box 5190, Kent, Ohio 44242; Telephone: 330-672-2312; Fax: 330-672-3327; E-mail: landrews@kentvm.kent.edu; Web site: http://orion.kent.edu/front.htm

KINGSBOROUGH COMMUNITY COLLEGE OF THE CITY UNIVERSITY OF NEW YORK

2 Pu G M Sc Tr

▼ Honors Option Program

The Honors Option Program at Kingsborough Community College of the City University of New York was designed to offer a select group of able and motivated students the opportunity for a more challenging and stimulating education. To achieve this purpose, the College offers each semester a series of courses open only to students in this program. Thus, eligible students are given the option with other students of similar ability and motivation, designed to stimulate thinking, creative endeavor, and intellectual curiosity. Some of the courses are interdisciplinary in nature and are team taught by professors from various academic disciplines. All classes are small enough to facilitate faculty-student interchange and to encourage discussion. The students are also encouraged to become actively involved in the initiation and development of courses and in the evaluation of the program.

In addition to being provided with the option of taking the enriched and horizon-broadening courses scheduled specifically for the program, students are also provided with the opportunity of designing independent study courses or research projects with the assistance and under the supervision of a faculty mentor. In this manner, students may explore topics in a given discipline, or of an interdisciplinary nature, from a variety of perspectives, with creative initiative and in greater depth. The close relationship usually established between students in this program and members of its faculty greatly facilitate such arrangements for the highly motivated and intellectually curious student. The completion of at least 12 honors credits is so noted on the students' transcripts and on the annual graduation program.

Kingsborough encourages its students to participate in student government and a large variety of cocurricular activities, to enrich the students' total college experience, enhance interpersonal relationships, and develop leadership skills. Students in the Honors Option Program are eligible to join the Corporate Career Honors Club, which offers them the opportunity to meet other students of similar interests and abilities, to conduct stimulating programs, and to promote their educational and vocational objectives. The club sponsors lectures, discussions, workshops, social and recreational functions, and various modalities for career exploration and ongoing career development assistance, based on the needs and interests of its members. There are 175 students currently enrolled in the program.

Admission Process: Students admitted to the College and completing 12–28 credits with a cumulative index of 3.20 (on a scale of 4.0) or better, are eligible to apply for acceptance to the program. A special screening committee reviews and acts on these applications.

Applications must be submitted in January and June.

The Campus Context: Kingsborough Community College, a unit of the City University of New York and accredited by the Middle States Association of Colleges and Schools, is located in Manhattan Beach and has a beautiful 67-acre campus bordered on three sides of the waters of Sheepshead Bay, Jamaica Bay, and the Atlantic Ocean. The ultramodern campus of interconnected buildings is situated in a setting that is convenient to public transportation and provides supervised on-campus or nearby free municipal parking.

Within the framework of the liberal arts curriculum leading to the Associate in Arts (A.A.) degree, students may choose to take the appropriate foundation courses in preparation for professional careers such as medicine, dentistry, pharmacy, law, and education. They receive specific guidance from counselors and faculty advisers concerning the course of studies most suitable for transfer and the achievement of professional objectives. Students may also opt to work toward the Associate in Science (A.S.) degree in the areas of mathematics, computer science, the biological and physical sciences, fine arts, music, and theater arts.

They may also choose from a large variety of career programs, leading to Associate in Applied Science (A.A.S.) degrees. These programs enable students to commence a career upon the completion of the two-year sequence, while leaving open the option of continuing their education toward a higher degree at a senior college.

The College offers high-quality educational programs with a unique and exclusive academic calendar that alternates required twelve-week fall and spring semesters with two optional winter and summer six-week modules at no additional tuition for full-time students. To accomplish its goals, Kingsborough Community College offers a wide range of personalized services such as freshman orientation, academic advisement, free tutoring, career counseling, job placement, and supervised field experience within one's major concentration. The College facilities include an art gallery, a performing arts center, and Olympic-size swimming pool, a private beach, library, and computer and media centers.

Student Body Enrollment is 14,553 students; 63 percent are women. The ethnic distribution is 28 percent black/African American, .1 percent Native American, 51 percent white, and 13 percent Hispanic. There are 334 nonresident aliens.

Faculty Of the 726 faculty members, 211 are full-time. Eighty-two percent of full-time faculty members have terminal degrees.

Key Facilities The library houses 133,242 volumes. Computers number more than 1,000 PCs in thirteen labs and at other sites.

Athletics Major intercollegiate athletics include baseball, basketball, and tennis for men and volleyball, softball, and basketball for women. Intramural sports include football, basketball, softball, soccer, volleyball, and Ping-Pong.

Support Services The College buildings are equipped to be accessible to disabled students. Mathematics and English Skills Laboratories and a Speech, Language and Hearing Center offer support to students in need of remediation or special assistance. The College is also equipped with a Center for the Learning Disabled.

Tuition: $2500 for area residents, $3076 for state residents, $3076 for nonresidents, per year (1996-97)

Mandatory Fees: $100

Contact: Director: Dr. Eric Willner, 2001 Oriental Boulevard, Brooklyn, New York 11235; Telephone: 718-368-5365; Fax: 718-368-4836

KUTZTOWN UNIVERSITY OF PENNSYLVANIA

4 Pu G S Sc Tr

▼ Honors Program

Founded in 1986, the Kutztown University Honors Program is designed to provide academic and leadership opportunities for the University's most proficient and highly motivated students. The undergraduate program is open to full-time students. It requires a minimum of 21 credits in honors courses that stress in-depth study, research, and challenging exploration of various areas of study. The 21 honors credits also count toward the 128 credits for graduation. Students may earn these honors credits through a variety of methods, including honors courses, internships, course by contract, and by independent study (thesis).

In addition to honors course work, students in the Honors Program also complete two units of service, which do not carry academic credit allocation (one for the community and one for the University). Service opportunities in the community will be offered through a variety of official University sources (under the auspices of the Off-Campus Student Life Center), and an agreement to serve a minimum of 30 hours of service, approved by the Honors Director and the Honors Council, will be established between the student and the community agency in advance of the term in which the service is to be completed. For the second unit, students may select from a variety of services to the University, approved by the Director and Honors Council in advance of student participation. The service component of the Honors Program should begin in the student's sophomore year at Kutztown University.

There are currently 97 students enrolled in the program.

Participation Requirements: An Honors Diploma is awarded to those students in the program who have met all college requirements, completed at least 21 credits in honors course work through any variety of the methods described above, have attained a minimum cumulative quality point average of 3.25, and have completed a two-unit service component.

Admission Process: Freshmen who have been identified as potential honors students based on their high school record and SAT I scores, transfer students from other honors programs, and incumbent students who have earned a cumulative QPA of 3.25 or higher are invited to join the Honors Program. Undergraduate students who are not members of the Honors Program may take an honors course if they have a quality point average of 3.0 or higher in 15 credits taken at the University. These students will not receive honors credits for the course. Permission of the Honors Program Director is required.

Applications must be submitted in the spring semester.

Scholarship Availability: Scholarships based upon merit are available to entering freshmen and to upperclassmen who participate in the Honors Program.

The Campus Context: Kutztown University, a member of the Pennsylvania State System of Higher Education, was founded in 1866 as Keystone Normal School, became Kutztown State Teachers College in 1926, Kutztown State College in 1960, and achieved university status in 1983. Kutztown University is a picturesque 325-acre campus located in Pennsylvania Dutch community mid-way between Allentown and Reading with easy access to Philadelphia and New York City. There are twelve undergraduate and twenty-one graduate degree programs offered.

The University consists of five colleges: the College of Business, the College of Education, College of Liberal Arts and Sciences, the College of Visual and Performing Arts, and the College of Graduate Studies. Special facilities on campus include an art gallery, planetarium, observatory, weather station, full TV production studios, state-of the-art computer labs, cartography lab, day-care center, and the Pennsylvania Heritage Center. Students also have access to the Wallops Island Marine Science consortium facility in Virginia.

Student Body Undergraduate enrollment is 43 percent men, 57 percent women. The ethnic distribution is 92.5 percent white, 4 percent African American, 2 percent Latino, 1 percent Asian, and .5 percent Native American. There are 72 international students. Forty-two percent of students are residents,

58 percent commute. Eighty percent of students receive financial aid. There are six fraternities and six sororities.

Faculty There are 455 faculty members, 349 are full-time and 58.2 percent hold doctoral degrees. The student-faculty ratio is 17:1.

Key Facilities The library holds 406,094 volumes. The University supports well over 1,000 micros, terminals, and printers for students, faculty members, and administrators. Additionally, there are two terminal rooms and seven microcomputer labs on campus.

Athletics Athletics include ten men's intercollegiate sports and ten women's sports and an extensive intramural program. Modern athletic facilities include a football stadium, a field house, a gymnasium, playing fields, a track, and a cross-country course.

Study Abroad There are twelve international exchange and study-abroad programs.

Support Services Disabled students will find handicapped parking, curb cuts, ramps, electronic doors, and specialized equipment such as Skurzweil Reading Edge, CCTV, and voice-activated computers.

Job Opportunities Work opportunities are available in most departments.

Tuition: $3368 for state residents, $8566 for nonresidents, per year (1996-97)

Room and Board: $3258

Mandatory Fees: $730

Contact: Director: Dr. Judith E. Kennedy, P.O. Box 730, Kutztown, Pennsylvania 19530; Telephone: 610-683-1391; Fax: 610-683-1393; E-mail: vigoda@kutztown.edu

---

LaGuardia Community College

2 Pu G M Tr

▼ The Honors Experience

The LaGuardia Honors Experience is dedicated to providing an enriched education to highly motivated students interested in transferring to four-year institutions. The ultimate aim is to equip honors students with the academic competencies and personal confidence needed for success at demanding public and private four-year colleges and universities. Honors students enroll in special sections of regular courses. These sections provide additional instruction in reading complex texts, thinking critically, and writing gracefully and analytically. Students are guided in independent research, oral debate, and the creative examination of ideas. Class sizes are kept small to emphasize discussion and active learning.

Approximately 130 students enroll in honors courses each fall and spring semester.

Participation Requirements: Each semester, approximately eight honors courses are offered in a variety of disciplines. In past semesters, they have included The Novel, American History, Pre-Calculus and Calculus, Sociology, Introduction to Poetry, Principles of Management, and Exploring the Humanities. Students are free to take one or several honors courses in any semester as long as they meet the course prerequisites and honors student prerequisites.

Honors students receive an honors designation on their transcripts and they are invited to attend special transfer information sessions, honors receptions, and guest lectures.

Admission Process: Students are not chosen on the basis of SAT I scores or high school grades, but are recruited from enrolled students who have completed a minimum of 12 credits with a cumulative GPA of at least 3.2. Students are sought for honors who are strong in potential and ambition and who have a desire to engage in challenging academic work.

The Campus Context: Fiorello H. LaGuardia Community College, one of the seventeen undergraduate colleges of the City University of New York, is a vibrant community of teachers and learners. Founded in 1970 and admitting its first class of 540 students in 1971, the College has continually supported the principles of open access and equal opportunity for all. The College serves almost 11,000 students in growing neighborhoods of western Queens as well as the larger New York metropolitan area. It ranks fourth in the nation in the number of degrees granted to minority students and offers the following degree programs: A.A.S. (twenty majors), A.A. (six majors), and A.S. (seven majors).

Student Body There are 10,695 students enrolled in degree programs; 28,000 are enrolled in nondegree programs. Sixty-seven percent are women and 33 percent are men. The ethnic distribution is 38 percent Hispanic, 22 percent black, 14 percent white, and 13 percent Asian. Students are drawn from more than 100 countries. Fifty percent of students are eligible for federal or state financial aid.

Faculty Of the 238 full-time faculty members, the majority possess terminal degrees. An additional 408 adjunct faculty members are employed.

Key Facilities The library houses 65,000 books and 800 journals. Through an electronic network connected to the entire collection of the City University of New York, students have access to 5 million books and 25,000 journals.

Job Opportunities LaGuardia, the only community college with a required co-op ed program for day students, is the second-largest cooperative education college in the country. Each year, 2,200 full-time students are placed in internships at 400 companies, including many of the larger corporations in New York City.

Tuition: $2500 for area residents, $3076 for state residents, $3076 for nonresidents, per year (1996-97)

Mandatory Fees: $110

Contact: Coordinator: Dr. Lawrence Rushing, 31-10 Thomson Avenue, Long Island City, New York 11101; Telephone: 718-482-5792; Fax: 718-482-5599; E-mail: lhrushing@aol.com

LAKE LAND COLLEGE

| 2 Pu G S Sc Tr |

▼ **Honors Program**

In 1978, Lake Land College began its Honors Program. Since that time, 104 students have completed the requirements and have graduated as Lake Land College honors students. The purpose of the program is to provide enriched learning opportunities for superior students through special honors classes and through optional honors independent study in specialized areas. The focus in on the students' academic talents and career goals.

There are currently 35 students enrolled in the program.

Participation Requirements: Program requirements include a 3.5 overall GPA, graduation from a transfer program, and completion of four honors courses (specific classes or independent study—two of the four required honors courses may be independent study) for full-status graduation.

The Honors Program has many advantages, including attending class with other academically talented students. In addition to enriched learning opportunities, honors students may receive special scholarship aid (monetary awards have been made to approximately 15 students per term in this program, in which scholarship is the primary basis for the award); may be recognized by the *National Dean's List, Who's Who In American Junior Colleges,* or *All American Scholars;* will carry an honors designation on their transcripts for each honors course or honors independent study successfully completed; are guests at the annual honors banquet; and receive honors recognition at Commencement.

Admission Process: Students who apply must plan to pursue a college-transfer major at Lake Land College and they must have graduated in the top 10 percent of their high school class or have a composite ACT of 25 or more or have a GPA of 3.5 or above in transfer classes after the completion of at least 12 semester hours of transfer classes.

The Campus Context: Lake Land College is a public community college. Lake Land is located near Mattoon, Illinois, about 45 miles south of Urbana-Champaign and 180 miles south of Chicago. It was founded in 1966. The 308-acre campus hosts seven major buildings plus seven supportive buildings, two campus ponds, a 160-acre agriculture land laboratory, the 30,000-volume Virgil H. Judge Learning Resource Center, computer labs, a CAD lab, a child-care lab, a cosmetology clinic, and a dental clinic.

Student Body Lake Land has 5,000 students from across east central Illinois; 54 percent are women and 46 percent are men.

Faculty Seventy-eight percent of full-time faculty members hold master's degrees or terminal degrees in their teaching fields. The student-faculty ratio is 21:1.

Athletics Lake Land is a member of the National Junior College Athletic Association. Men's sports include baseball, basketball, and tennis. Women's sports include basketball, softball, and volleyball.

Support Services Lake Land College employs a Special Needs Counselor and a Vocational Special Needs Coordinator to provide support services to students with a variety of special needs. The architectural design of the campus and buildings is such that Lake Land College has been deemed very accessible by the Illinois Department of Rehabilitation Services.

Tuition: $1248 for area residents, $3262 for state residents, $6354 for nonresidents, per year (1996-97)

Mandatory Fees: $250

Contact: Director: Harold Strangeman, 5001 Lake Land Boulevard, Mattoon, Illinois 61938; Telephone: 217-234-5279; Fax: 217-258-6459

LAKE SUPERIOR STATE UNIVERSITY

| 4 Pu G M Sc Tr |

▼ University Honors Program

The LSSU University Honors Program provides an important dimension of the University's commitment to excellence in teaching and learning. The Honors Program seeks to create a community of scholars characterized by strong student and faculty interaction around the world of ideas. This community fosters an approach to education that incorporates the qualities of self-directed learning, a positive response to demanding work, and an appreciation of knowledge for its own sake.

Classes are limited to 15–18 students and active participation of students is considered essential to the development of a scholarly community. In addition, an interdisciplinary focus is promoted by the inclusion of students and faculty members from all majors as well as in the course design of the honors core curriculum. Excellence in teaching is emphasized in the selection of faculty members, as is a commitment to work with students in and out of the classroom setting.

Honors students are advised by the Honors Director and by faculty members in their major course of study. They are eligible for advanced scheduling and extended library privileges, opportunities for supportive living and learning arrangements, and an enriched educational experience.

Participation Requirements: The Honors Program student completes 21 credit hours of honors designated courses. About half of these designated credits may satisfy requirements for General Education and the student's major. The remaining 10 credits meet core requirements for the Honors Program, namely a sophomore- and junior-year seminar as well as the completion of a senior project for honors credit. To remain eligible for participation the Honors Program, students must achieve at least a 3.3 GPA at the end of the sophomore year and a 3.4 GPA at the end of the junior year. Only those students who achieve a 3.5 overall GPA and are active participants in the Honors Program receive an honors degree upon graduation.

Admission Process: Students are invited to become honors candidates as freshmen, based on a combination of ACT scores, high school GPA, essay, and/or an interview. Honors candidates and other full-time students who achieve a GPA of 3.5 for their first two semesters at LSSU are then invited to apply for full admission to the Honors Program.

The Campus Context: Lake Superior State University is composed of five schools: the School of Arts, Letters, and Social Sciences; the School of Business and Economics; the School of Engineering Technology and Mathematical Sciences; the School of Health and Human Services; and the School of Science and Natural Resources. There are sixty-five degree programs offered. Special facilities on campus include a planetarium and a physical education complex with an ice arena, pool, and aquatics laboratory.

Student Body Undergraduate enrollment is 3,400: 52 percent men and 48 percent women. The minority ethnic distribution is .5 percent black, 5.4 percent Native American, .6 percent Asian, and .5 percent Hispanic. International students number 553. The student population is 27 percent resident and 73 percent commuter. Seventy percent of students receive financial aid. There are six fraternities/sororities.

Faculty Of the 175 faculty members, 110 are full-time and 65 percent have terminal degrees. The student-faculty ratio is 19:1.

Key Facilities The library houses 155,000 volumes. Computer facilities include 250 PC stations with Internet and LAN access.

Athletics Lake Superior State offers NCAA Division I men's hockey. All other sports are Division II. Sports offered include men's and women's basketball, men's and women's golf, women's volleyball, men's and women's track, women's softball, men's and women's tennis, and men's and women's cross-country.

Support Services Disabled-student facilities are available.

Job Opportunities Students will find many work opportunities on campus.

Tuition: $3534 for state residents, $6948 for nonresidents, per year (1996-97)

Room and Board: $4464

Contact: Director: Dr. Diana R. Pingatore, Erie Hall N4, Sault Ste. Marie, Michigan 49783; Telephone: 906-635-2101; Fax:

906-635-6678; E-mail: dpingatore@lakers.lssu.edu; Web site: http://www.lssu.edu

LA SALLE UNIVERSITY

4 Pr G M Sc Tr

▼ University Honors Program

The pedagogical philosophy of La Salle University emphasizes the need for a strong basis in the humanities for all undergraduates and, for this reason, requires everyone to complete a set of courses that focus on these humanities. Individual academic departments offer students a more intensive study in a specific discipline, but only after the majority of the requirements in this humanistically based core have been completed.

The curricular structure of the Honors Program follows this general University model, but with modifications that recognize the needs and abilities of the highly motivated and intellectually gifted student. These modifications are primarily in the manner in which the Honors Program student satisfies these essential University-wide requirements.

In the first year of studies, the Honors Program student will normally complete three honors courses each term. These courses will be in the disciplines of history, literature, and philosophy and will, over the course of the year, take the student from the early Greco-Roman period to the contemporary period. The professors teaching in this first-year program make every attempt to coordinate their readings and assignments so that, at any particular time during the academic year, the students will be viewing the same period of civilization through the perspective of three different disciplines.

A typical week would have the student spending 3 hours of class time in each of the three disciplines and 3 hours of time in a special situation in which an attempt is made to integrate the three seemingly distinct disciplines. This last 3-hour period of time brings together all of the students in the program and their professors in a variety of experiences. Some of the sessions will be held on campus and others will make use of the many museums and resources of the Philadelphia area. In recent years this has meant afternoons or evenings spent at the Academy of Music with the Philadelphia Orchestra, at the Philadelphia Museum of Art with the curator of the medieval collection, at the Arden Theater with the artistic director, or at the Franklin Institute. Each activity is designed to complement and supplement the work of the classroom—a humanities lab, in effect.

Total enrollment in the Honors Program is approximately 210 students over the four class years.

Participation Requirements: The total number of courses required in honors is a minimum of fourteen, including the independent project. One of the courses must be an ethical issues seminar in the student's major. In addition to the curricular requirements, students are required to maintain a cumulative GPA of 3.0 and a 3.0 GPA in Honors Program courses to remain active in the Honors Program.

Having successfully completed the first year of studies, the Honors Program student is then offered a wide variety of seminars in honors. These seminars allow the student to study topics, time periods, and areas of interest in considerably more depth, using the broad overview of the first year as a solid foundation upon which to build. Serving as the substitutes for the regular core requirements of the University, these seminars are often cross-disciplinary. They can be single course offerings or multiple course offerings (i.e., with 2 teachers team teaching a course). In addition, each Honors Program student will be required to complete an independent study project that will be the equivalent of one 3-credit course. This will be done on a topic of the student's choosing (not necessarily in the major) and will be directed by a faculty member.

Students who complete all of the requirements of the Honors Program are graduated from La Salle with the special distinction of General University Honors. This distinction is noted on their official transcript, on their diploma, and in a special listing in the Commencement program.

Admission Process: Each year approximately 60 students are admitted to the Honors Program (from a freshman class of approximately 700 students). Invitations are extended to students who have been accepted for admission by the University, who have combined SAT I scores of approximately 1250, and who rank in the first quintile of their graduating class.

The application deadline is May 1.

Scholarship Availability: Each year La Salle awards approximately 45 full-tuition scholarships to high school seniors. The Scholarship Selection Committee looks for students with a combined SAT I score of approximately 1300 or higher and rank in the top 10 percent of the graduating class. A separate application for a scholarship must be submitted in addition to the application for admission to the University. Scholarship applications may be obtained by contacting the office of the Director of the Honors Program or through the Office of Admissions.

The Campus Context: La Salle University is a private institution under the auspices of the Brothers of the Christian Schools. Located on a 100-acre campus in the historic Germantown section of Philadelphia, the University is composed of a School of Arts and Sciences, a School of Nursing, and a School of Business Administration. Current undergraduate enrollment is approximately 2,800 full-time students with a faculty of just over 200 full-time professors. Average class size is 20 students. The graduate division offers advanced degrees in nine areas and currently enrolls approximately 2,500 students.

Tuition: $13,770 per year (1996-97)

Room and Board: $5950

Mandatory Fees: $170

Contact: Director: John S. Grady, 1900 West Olney Avenue, Philadelphia, Pennsylvania 19141-1199; Telephone: 215-951-1360; Fax: 215-951-1488 E-mail: grady@lasalle.edu

LEWIS-CLARK STATE COLLEGE

4 Pu G S Tr

▼ LCSC Honors Program

The Honors Program systematically offers integrated course work and supportive interaction among honors students and faculty mentors to provide students with the skills and experiences necessary to produce meaningful research and scholarship within their disciplines. The introductory course is ID289—Knowledge and Values. This experiential course challenges students to apply and to react to the views about knowledge and values examined by such thinkers as Plato, Descartes, Hume, Mead, Kuhn, Gilligan, and Perry. Following the successful completion of ID289, students work with a faculty mentor to develop a course plan for one of the three curricular paths tailored to their specific major and interests. The remaining courses in the program reside largely within the specific academic majors. Honors students receive special recognition at the graduation ceremony, special notation as an honors student on their final transcripts, and a special honors seal on their diploma.

The LCSC Honors Program is now in its fourth year. A total of 54 students are in the Honors Program.

Admission Process: If students are seriously interested in developing their capacities for critical thinking and research within their major, they enroll in the introductory course (ID289) in the Honors Program. While most honors students have a strong history of excellent academic performance, there is no minimum test score or GPA requirement to enroll in honors. The completion of ID289 with an A or B is the entrance into the Honors Program.

Scholarship Availability: No special scholarships are available for honors students. Most receive financial aid through the campus financial aid office.

The Campus Context: Lewis-Clark State College is a regional undergraduate institution offering an alternative learning environment. It offers programs in the liberal arts and sciences; professional programs in education, nursing, business, and criminal justice; and technical programs. The College is located in an attractive residential area of Lewiston, Idaho, a city of approximately 30,000 located at the confluence of the Snake and Clearwater Rivers. Across the Snake River in Washington is Clarkson, estimated population of 12,000. Within a 50-mile radius is the point at which Idaho, Oregon, and Washington join. The new library and the Centennial

Mall provide a positive focal point to the center of campus with statues depicting the travels of Lewis and Clark through the region. The College offers thirty-nine majors for the baccalaureate degree.

Student Body There are 3,000 undergraduate students from two thirds of the United States and approximately twenty-five other countries. Fifty-six percent of students are women and 44 percent are men. The ethnic distribution is 90 percent white American, 3 percent Native American, 2 percent members of American minority groups, and 5 percent international students. Ninety percent of students are commuters; 10 percent are residential. More than 70 percent of students receive financial aid.

Faculty The College employs more than 118 full-time faculty members and a similar number of adjunct members. More than 80 percent of the academic faculty have doctorates or other terminal degrees in their disciplines. The student-faculty ratio is 16:1.

Key Facilities The campus has a 255,000-volume library. There are three computer labs (Mac and DOS platforms) and three computer classrooms.

Athletics Lewis-Clark State College, home of the Warriors, will compete in the National Association of Intercollegiate Athletics' Pacific Northwest Division until 1998 and then move to NCAA Division II status. The College fields nationally competitive teams in baseball, men's and women's basketball, men's and women's cross-country, men's and women's golf, men's and women's tennis, and men's and women's rodeo.

Study Abroad Study-abroad programs are offered throughout the world.

Support Services Disabled students will find classrooms, faculty offices, the student union building, and other campus buildings accessible.

Job Opportunities Students are offered a range of work-study, assistantships, and other employment possibilities on campus.

Tuition: None for state residents, $4726 for nonresidents, per year (1996-97)

Room and Board: $3130

Mandatory Fees: $1626

Contact: Director: Dan Mayton, 500 8th Avenue, Lewiston, Idaho 83501; Telephone: 208-799-2280; Fax: 208-799-2820; E-mail: dmayton@lcsc.edu

LINCOLN LAND COMMUNITY COLLEGE

2 Pu G S Sc Tr

▼ Honors Program

The Lincoln Land Community College Honors Program provides unique educational experiences for academically superior students in order to challenge, educate, and reward them at a level consistent with their intellectual needs and abilities. The Honors Program, initiated fall 1996, offers opportunities for critical thinking, greater student/teacher interaction, in-depth reading and discussion, smaller classes, and contact with other high-ability students.

Each honors student is assigned an administrator or faculty person as a mentor. The mentor advises the student on such matters as Honors Program requirements, scheduling, transferability, and career opportunities.

There are currently 35 students enrolled in the program.

Participation Requirements: To complete the program and receive special recognition at Commencement, students must have successfully completed 15 credit hours of honors course work maintaining a minimum cumulative GPA of 3.25. Successful course completion is defined as receiving a grade of C or higher in all honors courses. Honors courses include enhanced sections of current courses, interdisciplinary courses designed specifically for the Honors Program, and special honors courses. Honors students must register for Leadership (SOC 299). This course is an interdisciplinary course based on the PTK leadership model. Students are also strongly encouraged to attend an orientation program. Monthly student meetings are an integral part of the program.

Students who complete the program are awarded a medallion to wear at graduation. Nominated on the basis of high scholarship, evidence of leadership and Honors Program participation, one student, upon program completion, is selected as the outstanding honors student. Students who serve on committees are given certificates of appreciation.

Admission Process: Students may be admitted to the Honors Program at any time. However, the deadline for scholarship applications is March 1. Transfer students can be admitted to the program; however, as most honors classes offered are general education courses, the student may have already completed some of these courses. Therefore, it is more difficult for transfer students to complete the program.

An LLCC Honors Escrow Program was implemented fall 1996. Selection is based upon ACT scores, class rank, and GPA. Beginning the fall of students' junior years and continuing through the spring of students' senior years, students progress together through the five classes on the LLCC campus. The program includes one summer class between the students' junior and senior years. Credits earned in the Honors Escrow Program fulfill a substantial part of the general education requirements for the degree. The credits earned in the program are held in escrow for the student until he or she graduates from high school. At that time, the credits can be applied toward an LLCC degree if the student continues his or her education at Lincoln Land Community College or will be transferred to the four-year institution at which the student enrolls.

Scholarship Availability: The LLCC Foundation has established ten $800 renewable Honors Program scholarships. Scholarships are available to entering freshmen or LLCC students who have earned fewer than 12 semester hours of college

credit. Applications must be sent to the Honors Program Director by March 1. Applicants should return the application form and submit high school and college transcripts, two letters of recommendation, and an essay before the applicant can be considered for a scholarship. The Committee meets in mid-March to review applications for scholarships and admission to the program.

The Campus Context: Established in 1967 as a community college district, LLCC formally opened its doors September 23, 1968. The college district has grown steadily and serves more than 16,000 students annually from a 4,007-square-mile district, the largest geographical community college district in Illinois, serving all or parts of fifteen counties. In addition to offering courses during days, evenings, and Saturdays on the 441-acre main campus on the south edge of Springfield, LLCC offers courses at more than ninety-five locations in thirty-one off-campus communities throughout the district. Degree programs include Associate in Arts, Associate in Science, Associate in Applied Science, Associate in General Education, Associate in Engineering Science, and Associate in Fine Arts.

LLCC strives to provide, at an affordable cost, educational, cultural, social, and economic development opportunities for all citizens of District 526. The College guarantees open access, quality education, and the opportunity for success to the student who invests effort, demonstrates ability, and achieves competency. The College recognizes the worth of all individuals and is committed to providing opportunities for them to learn and develop as contributing members of society.

Student Body Undergraduate enrollment is 8,556 students. Forty-five percent are men and 55 percent are women. The ethnic distribution is 1 percent Asian/Pacific, .1 percent Native American, 7 percent black, 1 percent Hispanic, and 90 percent white. There are 17 international students, 1 percent of the student population. All of the students are commuters. Twenty percent of all students receive financial aid. There are twenty-nine clubs and organizations at LLCC. These include Phi Theta Kappa and Alpha Beta Gamma.

Faculty The total number of faculty members is 428; 125 are full-time and 303 are adjunct. Thirty percent of the faculty have terminal degrees.

Key Facilities The library houses 55,000–60,000 volumes. There are six classroom computer labs plus an open lab in the library.

Athletics Athletics is one part of the many faceted experiences a student may enjoy in receiving a total education at LLCC. A wide variety of intercollegiate athletic team offerings is available for the aspiring student athlete. Highly competitive schedules are arranged for each team, enabling the athletes to test their athletic skills against other community college athletes. In addition to regular season play, each team plays in post-season tournaments leading to the NJCAA championships. LLCC is a member in good standing with the National Junior College Athletic Association and abides by its rules of eligibility for student participation.

Study Abroad In 1996, LLCC students had the opportunity for the first time to earn 14 hours of college transfer credit in an oversees immersion study program in London, England, which featured four fully articulated courses in history, humanities, and political science. The curriculum is innovative and interdisciplinary and features the study of British and American cultures. A second program in Ireland was provided during the spring break period. Emphasis was on Irish social justice with particular focus on similarities and differences between the American and Irish social justice systems. Students earned 4 college credits in SOC 299 for this experience. Similar programs will be offered in the future.

Job Opportunities Funds are provided by the federal government and matched partially with College funds to provide part-time jobs for students who have financial need. Jobs are available in almost every campus department. The program is open to students enrolled in a minimum of 6 credit hours.

Tuition: $1170 for area residents, $2434 for state residents, $3998 for nonresidents, per year (1996-97)

Mandatory Fees: $5

Contact: Director: Dr. Patricia Eggers, Shepherd Road, Springfield, Illinois 62794-9256; Telephone: 217-786-2276; Fax: 217-786-2468; E-mail: peggers@cabin.llcc.il.us

LOCK HAVEN UNIVERSITY OF PENNSYLVANIA

4 Pu G S Sc Tr

▼ Honors Program

The Honors Program expresses Lock Haven University's commitment to academic excellence by providing faculty members and students alike with challenging opportunities for creative intellectual growth. The honors curriculum combines a rigorous subject matter grounded in the broad sweep of human civilization and an integrated four-year program for the development of sophisticated intellectual abilities. A spirit of inquiry in the tradition of the liberal arts inspires the program and fosters in each student the capacity for independent learning. Honors courses share an interdisciplinary approach, heavy reliance on classic sources, intensive writing, small size (usually 15–20 students), and active student involvement.

The Honors Program began in 1988 with an entering freshman class of 20 students. The program's growing reputation made possible an expansion to 40 freshmen for fall 1996. Total enrollment is expected to increase gradually from 50 to 100. This expansion has been carefully designed to ensure that the small learning communities of 20 freshmen will remain intact. With the expansion will come a greater variety of honors courses and cocurricular activities.

Participation Requirements: The heart of the Honors Program is a 30-hour program of studies providing students with a

uniquely challenging and rewarding educational experience while meeting University requirements both in general education and in the student's major. The particular strength of the honors curriculum lies in its integration of these courses into a cohesive and developmentally sequenced program of study culminating in a senior project and the oral presentation of that project in the honors colloquium.

Honors freshmen form learning communities of 18–20 students and take two classes together each semester: honors composition and literature I/II and honors historical and philosophical studies I/II. Navigating the sometimes difficult transition from high school to university is made easier by 4 hours per week of cocurricular activities that provide the supportive mentoring of upperclass honors students and faculty mentoring, which shows freshmen the way to success and helps them develop their own unique voices as adult learners.

After the freshman year, students take one course for honors credit each semester, either an honors course that satisfies a general education requirement or an honors augmentation of a non-honors course, usually in the student's major. Augmentation projects are planned to build a foundation for the honors senior project, the culmination of the student's academic program. These projects provide excellent preparation and credentials for graduate and professional schools. Honors students are also encouraged to take advantage of the University's many study-abroad and internship opportunities.

Cocurricular activities are an important part of the honors experience throughout the four years although the minimum requirement drops to 2 hours per week after the first year. However, many honors students decide to work more hours, assuming responsibility for programs such as freshmen study groups, weekly faculty member and student discussion groups, and service programs such as tutoring in the local schools.

Honors students may earn official recognition in one of three categories: honors in general education (completed in the sophomore year), university honors (completed in four years), and upper-division honors (completed in five to six semesters by students entering the program as sophomores or second-semester freshmen). Honors graduation in each of the three categories requires completion of honors curricular requirements with a minimum GPA of 3.2 in honors courses and overall as well as active participation in honors cocurricular activities.

Admission Process: Entering freshmen are selected on the basis of high school grades, SAT I scores, essays, recommendations, and high school activities. Continuation in the Honors Program requires a 3.0 GPA (overall and in honors) at the end of the first year and a 3.2 GPA thereafter. Lock Haven University students may also enter upper-division honors after one to three semesters of study; a 3.2 GPA is required.

Scholarship Availability: Three forms of merit-based financial aid are available to honors students. The Lock Haven University Foundation awards five Presidential Scholarships of $2000 and fifteen Academic Honors Scholarships of $1000 to entering freshmen enrolling in the Honors Program. The Presidential Scholarships are renewable for up to three years.

A limited number of Academic Honors Scholarships are awarded to continuing students on a competitive basis. All scholarship renewals and awards after the first year require a minimum GPA of 3.2, continuation in the Honors Program is optional. In addition to these scholarships, many honors students are employed in the Honors Center for 2–5 hours per week.

The Campus Context: Located in beautiful central Pennsylvania on the banks of the Susquehanna River, Lock Haven University is one of fourteen institutions that make up the commonwealth's State System of Higher Education. This central location combines the benefits of a rural area and bountiful outdoor activities with quick access to Philadelphia, Pittsburgh, and New York City in about 4 hours. Lock Haven University is primarily an undergraduate institution with Colleges of Arts and Sciences and Education and Human Services. The Lock Haven University faculty concentrates on teaching and working closely with students even while finding time to publish bestselling textbooks and conduct groundbreaking research. Classes are never taught by graduate assistants or lab assistants.

The University offers sixty-two degree programs, including nineteen teacher certification programs and pre-professional preparation for law, dentistry, medicine, veterinary science, and physical therapy. Degrees include Bachelor of Arts; Bachelor of Fine Arts (in music); Bachelor of Science; Bachelor of Science in Education; Bachelor of Science in Health and Physical Education, Health Sciences, and Recreation; an associate degree in nursing (at the Clearfield Campus); a cooperative five-year, dual-degree engineering program leading to a B.A. and a B.S.; Master of Liberal Arts; Master of Education in Curriculum and Instruction; and Master in Health Science/Physician Assistant. General education requirements provide a liberal arts background for every undergraduate degree.

Student Body There are 3,244 undergraduates at the main campus and 271 at the Clearfield campus. Forty-five percent are men and 55 percent are women. The student body includes 128 international students, primarily residential, and 5 percent of students are members of minority groups. Forty percent of students are residential; 80 percent of students receive financial aid. Students are offered nine honorary societies and six nationally affiliated fraternities and five nationally affiliated sororities.

Faculty There are 211 faculty members; 208 are full-time. Fifty-eight percent of tenure-track faculty members have doctorates. The student-faculty ratio is 16:1.

Key Facilities The Stevenson Library collection contains 356,206 volumes. Student computer laboratories located in all residence halls and most classroom buildings are connected via a high-speed fiber-optic network to the University's full-range of information resources and applications and to electronic services worldwide.

Athletics In athletics, Lock Haven fields Division I men's wrestling and fifteen men's and women's Division II sports.

Study Abroad The study-abroad program offers twenty-six low-cost programs in eighteen countries.

Tuition: $3368 for state residents, $8566 for nonresidents, per year (1996-97)

Room and Board: $3784

Mandatory Fees: $620

Contact: Director: Dr. James T. Knauer, Lock Haven, Pennsylvania 17745; Telephone: 717-893-2491; Fax: 717-893-2201; E-mail: jknauer@eagle.lhup.edu; Web site: http://www.lhup.edu/academics/department/honr/

LONG ISLAND UNIVERSITY, BROOKLYN CAMPUS

4 Pr G M Sc Tr

▼ University Honors Program

The University Honors Program at the Brooklyn Campus is a liberal arts program for students in all disciplines at the University, designed to assist them to become critical and independent thinkers. This is accomplished through an enriched core curriculum in the liberal arts, with courses usually interdisciplinary in nature, limited to 16 students, stressing student participation and independent study. The Honors Program also gives students freedom to design their own majors. The honors student body reflects the rich cultural and ethnic diversity of New York City, and the cultural advantages offered by New York are incorporated both formally and informally into every facet of the honors experience. Within the University, the Honors Program develops an active community of learners, providing opportunities for intellectual support and social interaction. Most University Honors Program students go on to graduate school or take advanced professional degrees.

The Honors curriculum is divided into three components: the freshman sequence, the sophomore sequence, and advanced electives. The freshman sequence is taken by all freshmen and newcomers to honors who have not fulfilled their core requirements. It is a year-long course cluster of history, English, and philosophy in which students study a selected theme that allows the work of each discipline to be interrelated. The sophomore sequence enables students to complete their requirements in speech, psychology, and foreign languages in an honors environment. The advanced electives are interdisciplinary courses designed specifically for honors students. Offered in seminar format, the electives encourage student involvement through an emphasis on field experience, the development of original research or arts projects, and other experiential activities. In order to graduate with honors, students must complete the freshman sequence and three advanced electives.

Transfer students who have completed their core requirements can graduate with honors by completing four advanced electives.

Distinction in honors is granted to students who complete an advanced project expanded from a paper or project originally written for an advanced honors elective. These expanded projects are developed under the guidance of a faculty mentor and a two-member committee. Distinction in honors projects that meet with the approval of the committee and faculty mentor are presented prior to graduation in the annual distinction in honors forum, open to the campus community.

Participation in the Honors Program gives students membership in two governance boards: The Honors Advisory Board and the Student Activities Board. The Honors Advisory Board determines the Honors Program curriculum, its instructors, electives, and other Honors activities. It draws its members from the faculty and students in all disciplines across the University. The Student Activities Board, a student club, sponsors activities such as poetry readings, faculty and student presentations, as well as sponsoring honors students' attendance to the National Collegiate Honors Council national and regional conferences and other NCHC events.

Students in the Honors Program can also participate in *Spectrum*, the literary journal of the Honors Program. Edited by honors students, it accepts fiction, poetry, essays, photographs, and art work from students, faculty members, and administrators across the campus.

There are 340 students in the program.

Participation Requirements: Students are required to have a minimum 88 percent high school average and a minimum combined score of 1050 on the SAT I. Students meeting these criteria may apply for admission and are interviewed after submitting an application. A minimum GPA of 3.0 is required for participation in honors events.

Scholarship Availability: The University Honors Scholar Award is granted, in addition to any University or departmental scholarships, to new Honors students who have exhibited extraordinary merit. Honors also grants some book voucher awards for incoming freshmen and some residence hall awards for those who wish to live on campus. Long Island University also offers generous academic scholarships to incoming students who have already distinguished themselves in the classroom—in high school or at another college. There is also a competitive Continuing Student Study Grant for students who have exhibited extraordinary academic performance while at the University. Student Activity Grants are available for those with outstanding records who wish to work on campus to earn up to 6 tuition credits free each semester.

The Campus Context: The 22-acre urban campus, founded in 1926, is 10 minutes from Manhattan, on Flatbush and Dekalb Avenues. Long Island University is a four-year private coeducational campus with regional accreditation. University Honors students come from all seven schools and colleges of the University: the College of Liberal Arts and Sciences; the School of Business, Public Administration, and Information Sciences; the School of Education; the School of Nursing; the School of Health Professions; and the College of Pharmacy and Health Sciences. The campus has fifty programs leading to the baccalaureate, including liberal arts and sciences, accounting, business, education, pharmacy, nursing, physician's assistant, media arts, and art.

Student Body There are 6,279 undergraduates enrolled; 33 percent are men and 67 percent are women. The majority come from New York City and surrounding areas. The campus has an average of 300 international students (international students are required to have a minimum score of 500 on the TOEFL). Ninety-five percent of students receive financial aid. There are four fraternities and four sororities with no chapter houses.

Faculty Of the 741 total faculty members (241 full-time), 85 percent have doctorates or other terminal degrees. The student-faculty ratio is 8.5:1.

Key Facilities There are 300,000 volumes in the campus library, which is also connected to the 2.1-million-volume University system.

Athletics Intercollegiate sports for men include baseball, basketball, cross-country, soccer, track (indoor and outdoor), and golf. Intercollegiate sports for women are basketball, tennis, softball, volleyball, cross-country, and track (indoor and outdoor). The University offers NCAA Division I sports.

Study Abroad Study abroad is available through LIU's Friends World Program in England, Kenya, India, China, Japan, Israel, and Costa Rica. Other opportunities exist by department.

Support Services Disabled students will find 95 percent of the campus accessible. Features include wheelchair ramps, electronic doors, elevators, special parking, and specially equipped restrooms.

Job Opportunities Internships, co-op work placements, work-study jobs and career placement services are provided through the University's Career Planning and Placement Center.

Tuition: $13,056 per year (1996-97)

Room and Board: $5090

Mandatory Fees: Full-time: $540; part-time: $50 to $140 per semester

Contact: Director: Dr. Bernice Braid, Brooklyn Campus, 1 University Plaza, LLC 240, Brooklyn, New York 11201; Telephone: 718-488-1657; Fax: 718-488-1370; E-mail: rwheeler@ aurora.liunet.edu

LONG ISLAND UNIVERSITY, C.W. POST CAMPUS

4 Pr G M Sc Tr

▼ Honors Program and Merit Fellowship

The C.W. Post Honors Program is open to students of all majors. It offers a 30-credit course of study designed to cultivate enrichment and critical thinking. Focused on the individual honors student as a distinct intellectual personality, the discussion-style classes encourage writing and oral presentation. Class size is limited to 20, and the curriculum emphasizes a balance between traditional and innovative studies. There are 410 students in the program (8 percent of undergraduate students).

Participation Requirements: Students take approximately 18 credits of Honors Program core courses (available in anthropology, art/music, biology, cinema, communications, dance, economics, English, geology, geography, history, math, philosophy, physics, political science, psychology, sociology) and 6 credits of advanced electives. These are invented specifically for the program and are chosen by a student-faculty advisory board. Advanced electives reflect current issues or faculty research and expertise. Recent courses to attract an enthusiastic following include The Great Pharaohs of Egypt; The Worlds of Impressionism; Feminist Ethics; Japan, China and the Economics of Southeast Asia; Fractals; and Gender and Language in the Classroom. At the most advanced level, students work privately with professors in their major on a 6-credit tutorial and thesis project of their own creation. Honors credits are generally completed *within* the 128-credit bachelor's degree. To remain in the program students must maintain a 3.2 GPA in the freshman year and a 3.4 GPA every year thereafter. Completion of the 30 credit Honors Program is indicated on the diploma.

Transfer students may become junior/senior participants by maintaining an 3.4 GPA and completing 12 credits in the Honors Program, consisting of two courses, tutorial and thesis. These members receive an Honors Program certificate at graduation.

All Honors Program participants are recognized at Commencement. Each year the top scholars receive the Charles M. Garrett Honors Award at Recognition Day. Other awards for service to the program, for outstanding thesis and for junior-senior participation, are also given.

Participation in the Honors Program means membership in a decision-making community that is both academic and social. The diverse group of students, from all disciplines and many countries, joins with faculty to choose Honors Program curriculum, instructors, and extracurricular activities. They hold luncheons and Broadway theater parties as well as an annual evening of creativity in which students sing everything from arias to jazz and read from their own poetry and stories.

Students in Honors also have the advantage of enriched advisement. In addition to a freshman Honors adviser and special orientation sections of College 101, the Honors Program Director serves as a general mentor to students in the program.

Students in the Honors Program also participate in the extracurricular *Merit Fellowship*, which offers several different noncredit series of lectures and cultural events. At the beginning of each year, students elect an area of investigation: Visual and Performing Arts, Media Arts, Education, Humanities, Aspects of Business, Natural and Social Sciences, Community Service and Advocacy. These often include concerts, theater, and trips to New York museums and business and research environments.

Admission Process: Entering freshmen with a high school average of 90 and combined SAT scores of 1200 (minimum 550 verbal) or above are advised to apply for admission to the Honors Program. Admission is based on high school credentials, including extracurricular activities and other evidence of particular talents and interests, which are discussed in an interview with the director.

Transfer students and continuing C.W. Post students with a GPA of at least 3.4 (freshmen 3.2) are also eligible to apply and request an interview.

Scholarship Availability: There are three important categories of scholarship awards for students in the Honors Program: *University Scholar Award* ($10,000—24 available) requires a 92 HS average and 1300 SAT. Students must maintain 3.5 GPA all years to retain the scholarship. *Academic Excellence Award* ($5000—24 available) requires an 88 HS average and 1200 SAT. Students must maintain 3.2 GPA as freshmen, 3.4 GPA as upperclassmen. *Transfer Excellence Award* ($5000) is based on a 3.5 GPA transfer credits and maintenance all years. The *Post Outstanding Scholars Award* ($6000) is based on an essay contest and may be held in conjunction with other awards (not to exceed full tuition).

Students receiving other university aid or currently attending C.W. Post without aid may apply for admission to the Honors Program and be considered for scholarships up to $2000/year from the Honors Program and Merit Fellowship. Students must file a Free Application for Federal Student Aid (FAFSA) by May 15. Scholarships are renewed for the length of student participation in the Honors Program/Merit Fellowship (up to four years).

Students who do not wish scholarship consideration are also eligible for the Honors Program with a 90 HS average and 1200 SAT (550 minimum verbal score) or 3.2 college transfer credit.

The Campus Context: Founded In 1954, the C.W. Post Campus of Long Island University is a wooded, 305-acre campus 25 miles from New York City on Route 25A. The four-year, private, coed campus, with regional accreditation, includes the College of Liberal Arts and Sciences, College of Management, School of Education, School of Visual and Performing Arts, and the School of Health Professions. There are seventy-eight programs leading to the baccalaureate, including liberal arts and sciences, accounting, business, education, and media and performing arts. The Tillis Center offers concerts (with inexpensive students tickets) by international symphonies and ballet and opera companies touring the New York area. A student-run radio station, WCWP, state-of-the-art television studio, and computer graphics laboratory are among the facilities that attract students.

Student Body There are 4,991 undergraduates enrolled: 45 percent men, 55 percent women, the majority from the Northeast. The ethnic distribution is 79.9 percent white, 8.6 percent African American, 6.5 percent Hispanic, 3.7 percent Asian-Pacific, 1.3 percent Native American. There are about 250 international students. Seventy-five percent of the students receive financial aid. There are ten fraternities and twelve sororities with no chapter houses. There are seventy student clubs on campus as well as academic honorary societies.

Faculty Of the 675 total faculty (339 full-time), 80 percent hold doctorates or other terminal degrees. The student-faculty ratio is 12:1.

Key Facilities The University library houses 2.1 million volumes as well as an extensive academic computing center. There are 350 microcomputers for student use located in dormitories, classroom buildings, and the computer center. Students may also be linked to the VAX system, with Internet usage.

Athletics Intercollegiate sports for men include baseball, basketball, cross-country, football, lacrosse, soccer, track (indoor), and track and field. Intercollegiate sports for women are basketball, cross-country, field hockey, softball, tennis, track and field, and volleyball. C.W. Post won the 1996 National Championship in men's lacrosse. CWP is NCAA, Division III football. Club sports and intramurals are widely available. The North Shore Equestrian Center housed on the campus presents an opportunity for students interested in boarding their own horses or riding and jumping to participate in Equestrian Team competitions.

Study Abroad Unique study-abroad opportunities exist through LIU's Friends World Program in England, Kenya, India, China, Japan, Israel, Costa Rica. Students who go abroad with Friend's World design their own independent study programs and participate in active community field work in the host country. Comparative world religions, alternative medicine, global ecology, and the status of women are some of the threads of study that students develop through Friend's World. Exchange programs also exist with Keimyung University in South Korea and Meiji Gakuin University in Japan. Other opportunities are available by department.

Support Services Disabled students will find 75 percent of the campus accessible by wheelchair ramps, electronic doors, elevators, special parking, equipped rest rooms, and lowered drinking fountains. The Academic Resource Center provides support for learning-disabled students.

Job Opportunities Internships, co-op work placements, work-study jobs, and career placement services are provided through the University's Center for Professional Experience and Placement (PEP).

Tuition: $14,345 per year (1997-98)

Room and Board: $6285 per year

Fees: $280

Contact: Director: Dr. Joan Digby, C.W. Post Campus, 311 Humanities Hall, Brookville, NY 11548; Telephone: (516) 299-2840; Fax: (516) 299-4180; E-mail: digby@aurora.liunet. edu; Web site: www.cwpost.liunet.edu/cwis/honors/main. htm

LONG ISLAND UNIVERSITY, SOUTHAMPTON COLLEGE

4 Pr C M Sc Tr

▼ Southampton College Honors Society

The goal of the Southampton College Honors Program is to form a community of the most intellectually motivated students in all academic disciplines in attendance at the College. It offers an exciting and challenging supplement to the undergraduate curriculum, serves as the focus for both traditional and innovative studies, and enables students to engage in an expanded spectrum of creative as well as social activities, independent research, seminars, and greater interaction with honors faculty members.

The Honors Program began in 1984 and there are approximately 350 students currently in the program.

Participation Requirements: There are four basic components of the Honors Program: participation in a total of seven honors courses (21 credits) for incoming freshmen, proportionally less for upperclassmen and transfer students; maintenance of a 3.0 GPA (3.25 to receive an honors diploma); attendance at the Merit Fellows Lecture Series (involves registering for LECT 201H each semester); attendance at five of the nine lectures each semester; and participation in the honors thesis (for students seeking an Honors Diploma), which can be satisfied either through an internship (490) in conjunction with honors research (492H) or an independent study/research (minimum 3 credit course) with a faculty member.

All students in the Honors Program are expected to participate in the Merit Fellows Lecture Series, attending five of the nine lectures per semester. There is an honors society which sponsors a variety of social and cultural activities during each semester. In the fall semester there is an honors banquet, held in conjunction with one of the Merit Fellows Lectures.

Admission Process: Students are invited to join the Honors Program either as freshmen, on the basis of combined SAT I scores (minimum of 1230) or high school averages (minimum of 88 percent), or as transfer students (3.25 GPA or better). Students who do not enter the Honors Program upon entry to the College, may, upon completion of at least 15 credits with a 3.25 GPA, enter the program at a later date.

Scholarship Availability: Honor students are offered merit-based scholarships, ranging from $1000 to $10,000 per year, based on the high school or transfer record, in addition to need-based financial aid.

The Campus Context: Southampton College is the smallest of the three main campuses of Long Island University, situated in a rural setting on the East End of Long Island. The others are C.W. Post campus (approximately 65 miles west—a suburban campus) and Brooklyn campus (another 20 miles west—an urban campus). The Southamptom Campus offers thirty-five degree programs. Among these is an internationally known program in marine biology with facilities that include a Marine Station, with five outboard boats and two larger vessels.

Student Body The undergraduate enrollment of about 1,350 full-time students is approximately 60 percent women, with student members of minority groups comprising between 10 and 15 percent of the population. Approximately half the students live on campus, with the remainder commuting or living in plentiful off-campus housing during the academic year (Labor Day through Memorial Day). Southampton is a popular resort community, with a large summer population, and students taking summer courses generally live on campus. About 85 percent of students are traditional students (i.e., between the ages of 17 and 23). Approximately 75 percent of the students receive some kind of scholarship and/or need-based financial aid. There are no fraternities or sororities.

Faculty The total number of faculty members is 200. There are 65 full-time members and 134 adjunct members. Ninety-three percent have terminal degrees. The student-faculty ratio is: 11.8:1.

Key Facilities The campus library houses 150,000 volumes, but students may access more than 1 million volumes through the University collection. Computer facilities include six laboratories and 180 IBM-compatible (486) and Macintosh computers.

Study Abroad Study-abroad opportunities include internships, co-op placements, and the Friends World Program (housed at the Southampton Campus) with programs around the world.

Support Services Disabled-student facilities are minimally compliant.

Job Opportunities Work opportunities on campus include tutoring, lab assistants, college work-study, and campus cafeteria employment.

Tuition: $13,120 per year (1996-97)

Room and Board: $6550

Mandatory Fees: $640

Contact: Director: Dr. Robert M. Danziger, 139 Montauk Highway, Southampton, New York 11968; Telephone: 516-287-8410, -8306, or -8302; Fax: 516-287-8419; E-mail: danziger@sunburn.liunet.edu; Web site: http://www.liunet.edu

LONGVIEW COMMUNITY COLLEGE

2 Pu G S Sc Tr

▼ Honors Program

The Honors Program at Longview provides an enriched experience for the exceptional student. The programs, courses, and activities promote creative and analytical thinking and aim to foster the development of intellectual skills and interests. The program features small classes, an emphasis on participatory classroom experiences, regular contact with highly stimulating faculty members, an interdisciplinary approach to learning, and elements of independent study.

Honors seminars are restricted to no more than 12 students, while honors sections are typically small but may have as many as 20 students enrolled. The program is small, usually including about 30–40 students each semester, 20 of whom will be eligible to receive honors scholarships. The program was started in 1991.

Participation Requirements: The program requires students to complete at least 15 credit hours of honors course work as part of their associate degree program. Each semester, three to five honors sections of regular courses are offered. These courses are restricted to students eligible for honors work. In addition, three to five one-credit-hour honors seminars are offered. The honors seminars are topical with new topics appearing each semester. Finally, students may take almost any regularly scheduled course for honors credit by contract. In order to be eligible for honors scholarships, a student must be enrolled at least half-time and take at least 4 credit hours of honors courses each semester, chosen from either special sections or by contract, but always including a seminar.

Admission Process: Students may qualify for enrollment in honors courses by submitting composite ACT scores at the 85th percentile, documenting a high school GPA of at least 3.5 (on a 4.0 scale), earning qualifying scores on the reading portion of the new student placement test, or by submitting writing samples along with recommendations from other teachers.

Scholarship Availability: Twenty honors scholarships in the amount of at least $500 are awarded in the fall semester of each year. Successful recipients will have earned a cumulative 3.5 GPA, be at least a half-time student, and be enrolled in at least 4 credit hours of honors course work, including a seminar. Scholarships are renewable for up to two years.

The Campus Context: Longview Community College is the southernmost member of a four-campus community college district that serves a seven-county area near Kansas City, Missouri. The campus is located on 146 acres of rolling hills in the suburban community of Lee's Summit. The College awards the Associate in Arts degree, the Associate in Applied Science degree, the Associate in Computer Science degree, the Associate in Science degree, and a number of certificate programs in business and technology.

Student Body There are approximately 6,000 students, two thirds attending day classes and the rest enrolled in evening and weekend classes. The student body is about 55 percent women, and student members of minority groups comprise about 15 percent of the students. Some 45 percent of students receive some form of financial assistance. There are no fraternities or sororities, but a comprehensive program of student activities and campus life enhancement is offered.

Faculty There are 97 full-time faculty members and about 160 part-time adjunct faculty members. Twenty-eight percent of the faculty have earned their Ph.D degrees. The student-faculty ratio (with adjunct faculty included) is approximately 20:1.

Support Services The campus is fully accessible and offers a number of services and programs for disadvantaged and disabled students, including a nationally recognized bridging program for students with head injuries and brain damage.

Tuition: $1350 for area residents, $2250 for state residents, $3210 for nonresidents, per year (1996-97)

Contact: Director: W. Andrew Geoghegan, 500 Longview Road, Lee's Summit, Missouri 64081-2105; Telephone: 816-672-2258; Fax: 816-672-2078; E-mail: geoghega@longview.cc.mo.us

---

LONGWOOD COLLEGE

4 Pu G M Sc Tr

▼ Honors Program

Initiated in 1983, the Longwood Honors Program offers courses in a wide variety of majors to academically oriented students seeking intellectual challenge. Honors courses emphasize discussion and writing, regardless of discipline. The small classes (usually no more than 20 students) encourage teacher-student interaction and opportunities for hands-on learning. For example, the Honors section of Introduction to Anthropology includes a three-day dig, allowing students to apply the principles and terms learned in the classroom. Currently 155 full-time undergraduates participate in honors.

In addition to honors sections of general education courses, classes of general interest, (e.g., The Old South, Hitler and the Holocaust, Issues of Sex and Gender), and enhanced courses in a student's major are available.

Honors students are housed on two floors of a centrally located dorm that has a computer lounge exclusively for honors use. Other benefits include priority registration and opportunities for travel to regional and national honors conferences.

Participation Requirements: To graduate from the Honors Program, students complete eight honors courses (three at

the 300 level or above) with a 3.25 cumulative average in honors and overall. In addition, students fulfill the honors language requirement by taking two courses in the same modern language, two courses in American Sign Language, or two courses in computer languages. Students successfully completing the Honors Program are recognized at graduation and on their transcripts.

Admission Process: Incoming freshmen with cumulative high school GPAs of 3.25 and combined SAT I scores of at least 1140 are eligible for the Honors Program. Freshmen with a Longwood GPA of 3.25 after the first semester are also encouraged to apply. Transfer students with a cumulative 3.25 GPA are also eligible.

Scholarship Availability: Twenty merit-based renewable scholarships of $1000 each are available, five to each class. In addition, two Advanced Honors Program Scholarships of $3000 each are awarded annually, one to a rising junior and one to a rising senior. These are renewable and merit based.

The Campus Context: Longwood College is a residential coeducational comprehensive state college of 3,300 offering programs leading to both the bachelor's and master's degrees. Located in south-central Virginia in a town of 7,000, Longwood is 1 hour from Richmond, Charlottesville, and Lynchburg, and 3 hours from Tidewater and northern Virginia. Twenty-one undergraduate majors with eighty-nine minors and concentrations are offered.

Student Body Longwood enrolls 2,900 undergraduates, the majority from Virginia. Thirty-five percent are men and 65 percent are women. The ethnic distribution is 2 percent Asian, 9 percent African American, 1 percent Hispanic, 87 percent white, and 1 percent other. Sixty percent of students receive financial aid; work-study is widely available. The campus has eight national fraternities and thirteen national sororities. Longwood has 110 clubs and student organizations, including a campus radio station.

Faculty There are 190 faculty members, 69 percent with doctorates or other terminal degrees. The student-faculty ratio is 14:1.

Key Facilities The library houses 330,000 volumes and nearly 600,000 nonprint holdings.

Athletics Longwood has NCAA Division II membership in men's sports, including baseball, golf, basketball, soccer, tennis, and wrestling and in women's sports, including golf, field hockey, lacrosse, soccer, softball, tennis, and basketball. Club sports include riding, volleyball, men's and women's rugby, and synchronized swimming.

Study Abroad Longwood is affiliated with thirteen study-abroad programs for students in any major. Programs are located in England, France, Spain, Martinique, Venezuela, Austria, and Germany. Students may study for a summer, a semester, or a year and have credits earned apply to their Longwood degrees.

Tuition: $2684 for state residents, $8156 for nonresidents, per year (1996-97)

Room and Board: $4222

Mandatory Fees: $1686

Contact: Director: Susan Bagby, Learning Center, Farmville, Virginia 23909; Telephone: 804-395-2789; E-mail: sbagby@longwood.lwc.edu

LOUISIANA STATE UNIVERSITY AND A&M COLLEGE

| 4 Pu G L Sc |

▼ Honors College

The Louisiana State University Honors College provides opportunity and challenge for academically able and intellectually motivated undergraduate students. Honors students pursue a rigorous academic program that satisfies all requirements of their academic departments and colleges and goes beyond those requirements to provide the basis for outstanding achievement and appropriate recognition for that achievement. From small-enrollment interdisciplinary seminars in the freshman year to independent research activities in preparation for the senior honors thesis, honors students work closely with selected members of the faculty.

The 30-year-old program currently enrolls 778 students.

Participation Requirements: During the first two years of study, the Honors College offers students four interdisciplinary courses for a total of 20 credit hours. These courses in humanities and liberal arts form the core of the students' academic program. The classes are small and are usually presented in a seminar format that encourages interaction with the professors and the other students and are taught by a select group of professors. The faculty are chosen for their skills in teaching and in developing the intellectual curiosity and problem-solving abilities of students. Students who meet certain requirements for the number of honors hours taken and GPA achieved receive sophomore honors distinction.

Honors students in the junior and senior years usually become more focused on a particular academic discipline. Upper-division honors work is characterized by intense intellectual involvement, rigorous standards, and a high level of increasingly independent achievement. Upper-division honors work typically culminates in a senior honors thesis or senior honors project, under the direction of a faculty member from the student's major department.

Completion of an upper-division honors program leads to graduation with upper-division honors distinction. Students who achieve both the sophomore and upper-division honors awards graduate with College honors. As a coordinating college, the Honors College works with all of the University's academic units to foster the development of undergraduate students. Rigorous academic programs are tailored to students' individual capabilities and to the variety and depth of resources available at the state's largest university. Graduates of the program receive degrees in their major fields plus honors recognition that enhances their credentials for graduate school admission and financial support or for entry into the most attractive job markets.

The program confers a sophomore honors distinction certificate, an upper-division honors distinction certificate, and a College honors diploma citation.

Admission Process: Entering freshmen with certain minimum ACT or SAT I scores and a 3.0 high school GPA are invited to apply for admission to the Honors College. The recommended test scores are 28 composite and 28 English or 27 composite and 30 English on the ACT and 1240 combined and 630 verbal on the SAT I. Students who approach but do not attain these qualifications may also apply. Continuing students who have completed at least their first semester of college and have attained at least a 3.0 GPA are also invited to inquire about admission.

Students should apply by March 15 for priority consideration.

Scholarship Availability: Application for admission to LSU constitutes an application for scholarships.

The Campus Context: Louisiana State University at Baton Rouge is a campus of eleven colleges: the College of Agriculture, the College of Design, the College of Arts and Sciences, the College of Education, the College of Basic Sciences, the General College, the College of Business Administration, the Honors College, the College of Engineering, the School of Music, and the Manship School of Mass Communication. The University offers seventy-three bachelor's degree programs, seventy-seven master's degrees, and fifty-six Ph.D programs. The campus is distinguished by its prominent Center for Advanced Microstructures and Devices and the Center for Coastal, Energy, and Environmental Resources.

Student Body There are about 20,000 students; 49 percent are men and 51 percent are women. The ethnic distribution includes 1,757 African-American students (8.6 percent), 793 Asian students (3.9 percent), 489 Hispanic students (2.4 percent), and 92 Native American students (.45 percent). There are 620 international students. Sixty percent of students receive financial aid. There are twenty-three fraternities and fourteen sororities.

Faculty The total number of faculty is 1,291. Of the 1,204 full-time faculty members, 85 percent have terminal degrees. The student-faculty ratio is 18:1.

Key Facilities University libraries offer students and faculty members support for instruction and research through collections containing more than 2.4 million volumes, microform holdings of more than 3.5 million, and a manuscript collection of more than 12 million items.

LSU maintains one of the largest computing facilities in the country. The System Network Computer Center (SNCC) provides computing resources and services (24 hours per day) in support of instruction, research, and administrative data processing. Currect resources include an IBM 9672-R53 mainframe processor supporting a heavy academic and administrative workload. Additionally, the mainframe is augmented with a state-of-the-art high-performance UNIX computing cluster that includes an IBM scalable power-parallel system for student computing. These resources are integrated with the campuswide, fiber-optic backbone and are connected to the Internet, World Wide Web, and state networks. Extensive software is also maintained.

Athletics The Director of Athletics manages a broad spectrum of intercollegiate sports programs for men and women. Louisiana State University is a charter member (1932) of the Southeastern Conference. LSU meets teams from other major universities in NCAA Division IA competition in football, basketball (men's and women's), baseball, indoor and outdoor track and field (men's and women's), cross-country (men's and women's), golf (men's and women's), tennis (men's and women's), swimming (men's and women's), women's gymnastics, women's volleyball, women's soccer, and women's softball.

Study Abroad Through the Office of Academic Programs Abroad, students travel worldwide to study for a summer, semester, or academic year. Participating students earn credit toward their LSU degrees and return to the Baton Rouge campus to complete their curricula. Students select from a variety of options. Many join group programs led by LSU faculty members, such as summer schools in London and Paris. Others participate in exchange and junior year–abroad programs, which place students directly in overseas universities where they study with students in the host countries. A few students study in programs offered by other U.S. schools or enroll directly in a foreign university.

Support Services The Office of Services for Students with Disabilities assists students in identifying and developing accommodations and services to help overcome barriers to the achievement of personal and academic goals. The office provides services to students with temporary or permanent disabilities. Specialized support services are based on the individual student's disability-based need.

Job Opportunities Through the Federal Work-Study Program, jobs are provided to full-time students who show financial need. Students earn an hourly wage (beginning at minimum wage) and are paid every two weeks. Those students who want to work on campus but do not qualify on the basis of financial need may seek regular student employment by contacting various departments on campus.

Tuition: $2687 for state residents, $5987 for nonresidents, per year (1996-97)

Room and Board: $3570

Contact: Director: Dean Billy M. Seay, 201 LSU Honors Center, Baton Rouge, Louisiana 70803; Telephone: 504-388-8831; Fax: 504-388-8828; E-mail: hnseay@lsuvm.sncc.lsu.edu

LOYOLA COLLEGE

4 Pr G M Sc

▼ Honors Program

The Honors Program at Loyola brings together students and faculty members with various interests, aiming for academic achievement and intellectual challenge and growth. The program offers students who are serious about their intellectual growth a specially designed series of classes and activities in the humanities.

Because it is committed to the tradition of the liberal arts, the program places special emphasis upon ideas—specifically, those ideas that have shaped the world in which we live. Students in honors engage in a dialogue with the great thinkers of the Western world, both in order to see how essential questions of human existence have been asked over and over again and in order to learn to what extent we are all products of our own historical age.

Courses in the Honors Program enrich and complement the academic experience inherent in a Loyola education. All honors classes are small, and many are conducted as seminars. They contain a judicious combination of lecture, discussion, and student presentation, and, no matter the subject, they always emphasize effective speaking and writing.

The Honors Program offers a wide range of activities in addition to its academic curriculum. The program sponsors a variety of events on campus and makes numerous cultural experiences available off campus. All these activities are designed to demonstrate that the ideas honors students study in the classroom are alive in the culture at large.

The Honors Program has existed for thirteen years and currently serves 174 students; 54 are admitted each year.

Participation Requirements: The Honors curriculum replaces humanities requirements in the College-wide core. Students in honors are free to major in any department at the College. At the heart of the curriculum is a seven-course sequence. Students take two courses in the first semester of their freshman year, one in each of the following four semesters, and a seminar in their senior year. Four of these are interdisciplinary explorations of Western intellectual history, moving from the ancient, through the Medieval and Renaissance, to the modern world. The other three courses are seminars and have a more contemporary focus. The remaining courses in the honors curriculum are electives, taken from upper-division offerings in the departments of English, history, philosophy, and theology. At graduation, honors students are given certificates, and the notation Honors Program Participant appears on their transcripts.

Admission Process: Admission to the Honors Program is by invitation only, and students are invited to enroll as incoming freshmen. Prospective students should indicate their interest in honors by checking the appropriate box on the College's Application for Admission. They must have scored above 1300 on the Scholastic Assessment Test and maintained a high school GPA of at least 3.5 on a 4.0 scale They then are sent a separate application for admission to the Honors Program. Students are accepted into honors on a rolling basis. Admission is extremely selective, and neither acceptance by the College nor an award of an academic scholarship is a guarantee of admission to honors.

Scholarship Availability: Loyola offers an extensive merit scholarship program. Presidential Scholarship awards range from $3000 to full tuition. General guidelines for scholarship eligibility are a combined SAT I score of at least 1250 and a high school GPA of at least 3.7. Students admitted to the Honors Program are not automatically awarded an academic scholarship; however, more than 90 percent of the current students in the Honors Program have received scholarship awards.

The Campus Context: Loyola College in Maryland is composed of the College of Arts and Sciences and the Sellinger School of Business. The College offers thirty-two majors and five bachelor's degree programs (B.A., B.S., B.B.A., B.S.E.E., and B.S.E.S). Special facilities include an art gallery, the world's fifth-largest artificial turf athletic field, and multimedia classrooms.

Student Body Undergraduate enrollment is 45 percent men and 55 percent women. The ethnic distribution is 87 percent white, 5 percent African American, 2 percent Asian, 2 percent Hispanic, and 4 percent other. There are 70 international students. Seventy-five percent of the students are residents, 25 percent are commuters. Sixty-five percent of students receive financial aid. There are no fraternities or sororities.

Faculty Of the 427 faculty members, 221 are full-time. Eighty-nine percent have terminal degrees. The student-faculty ratio is 14:1.

Key Facilities There are 307,276 volumes in the Loyola/Notre Dame Library. Loyola has ten computer labs with IBM and Macintosh computers. On-campus housing is available.

Athletics The Loyola College Greyhounds compete at the NCAA Division I level. Four of Loyola's twelve teams compete in the Metro Atlantic Athletic Conference. Men's lacrosse plays an independent schedule, while the women's lacrosse program competes in the Colonial Athletic Association. Loyola fields teams for both men and women in basketball, cross-country, lacrosse, soccer, swimming and diving, and tennis, as well as men's golf and women's volleyball. Loyola also has an extensive club sports program, fielding teams in nine different sports for both men and women. The thriving intramural sports program offers an opportunity for friendly competition on campus. Among the many sports offered are flag football, basketball, softball, soccer, volleyball, tennis, racquetball, and squash. There are three fitness centers on campus equipped with weight training machines, Lifesteps, Lifecycles, NordicTracks, ergometers, and fitness testing equipment.

Study Abroad Loyola sponsors three different study-abroad programs. Loyola in Leuven, Belgium, is a one-year program of study at the University of Leuven. Leuven is one of the most prestigious universities in the low countries and is centrally located in the heart of Europe. Loyola in Bangkok, Thailand, is a summer-fall program of study at Bangkok's Business Administration College in Thailand. Loyola students attend classes with students from Thailand and numerous other countries. Loyola in New Castle, England, is a year-long program that offers a study-abroad experience in an English-speaking atmosphere. All three of Loyola's programs include extracurricular travel excursions.

Support Services Disability support services, adaptive computer equipment, and accessible facilities are available for students with disabilities. Campus work-study positions are available.

Tuition: $15,200 per year (1996-97)

Room and Board: $6280 minimum

Mandatory Fees: $510

Contact: Director: Dr. Ilona McGuiness, 4501 North Charles Street, Baltimore, Maryland 21210; Telephone: 410-617-5000; Fax: 410-617-2198; E-mail: honors@loyola.edu; Web site: http://www.loyola.edu

---

LOYOLA UNIVERSITY CHICAGO

4 Pr G M Sc

▼ Honors Program

Since 1936, the Honors Program has served the most intellectually talented and highly motivated students at Loyola University Chicago. In an atmosphere charged with challenging teaching methods and enthusiastic student participation, professors and students work together in small, stimulating honors classes, exploring critical issues in each discipline.

The intimate, collegial atmosphere helps develop a close working relationship among honors students and faculty members. The most motivated students capitalize on this relationship by becoming involved with independent faculty research projects and by attending a multitude of "brown bag" colloquia by resident and visiting scholars.

While honors students and faculty members come from all across the country and from all walks of life, they share a common bond—the search for truth and meaning through analysis, discussion, and research. Collaboration and individual attention are the hallmarks of the program. As a result, honors students experience a unique sense of community even within the context of the larger university community.

This sense of community is manifest outside the classroom as well. Honors students enjoy social and intellectual interaction in the honors common rooms. They plan social and cultural events as members of the Honors Student Association. Lively classroom discussion, close faculty-student working relationships, a strong sense of community, and intellectual rigor combine in the Honors Program to create the best atmosphere for students wanting to take full advantage of the educational opportunities at Loyola University Chicago.

There are 464 students in the program, which represents 10–15 percent of each class.

Participation Requirements: Designed for flexibility, the Honors Program curriculum provides an opportunity for in-depth exploration of critical issues within Loyola's Core Curriculum. No additional courses are required to earn the honors degree. Approximately one third (42 semester hours) of an honors student's courses must carry honors credit. Honors credits can be earned by taking special honors sections in core courses, by contracting with a professor in a regular course, or by taking graduate-level courses. Students who fulfill the course requirements of the Honors Program with a GPA of 3.3 receive the honors degree. This distinction is noted at graduation and is recorded on transcripts.

Admission Process: Honors applications are sent to highly qualified students who are identified after they apply to Loyola University Chicago. A completed Honors Program application includes the application form, a brief essay, and one faculty recommendation. The deadline for the Honors Program application is March 1.

Scholarship Availability: Most applicants to the Honors Program receive merit-based awards when they are admitted to Loyola University. All new freshmen admitted into the Honors Program are considered for one of three full-tuition Ignatian Honors Program Scholarships. Finalists are invited to campus for an interview. In addition, Loyola provides scholarships, grants, loans, work-study pay, and other forms of financial support.

The Campus Context: Loyola University's traditional undergraduate liberal arts campus is located on a 45-acre site of large trees and open green space along the shore of Lake Michigan on Chicago's far north side. Nearly 2,000 students reside in on-campus housing. The Lake Shore campus is also home to the Marcella Niehoff School of Nursing. In addition, Loyola University has Schools of Business, Social Work, Law, Education, and Medicine. Degree programs include the B.A., B.S., B.S.Ed., B.A. (Classics), B.B.A., and B.S.N.

Student Body There are approximately 1,100 freshmen and a total of 8,106 undergraduates. Students come from all fifty states and seventy-four other countries. Approximately 30 percent of the student body are African American, Asian-American, Latin American, or Native American. The student-faculty ratio is 13:1. Seventy-five percent of students receive financial aid.

Faculty Of the 421 full-time faculty members, 96 percent have terminal degrees. Of the 275 part-time faculty members, 49 percent have terminal degrees.

Key Facilities There are 1.3 million volumes in the combined university libraries and open computer labs on all campuses.

Athletics Loyola participates in NCAA Division I in eleven sports, as well as having many intramural team and individual sports. Large fitness and recreational sports facilities are available on several campuses.

Study Abroad Through Loyola's Rome Center Campus, students in all majors have the opportunity to earn Loyola credit while studying in Rome for a semester, a year, or a summer.

Tuition: $14,400 per year (1996-97)

Room and Board: $6210

Mandatory Fees: $420

Contact: Director: Dr. Joyce Wexler, 6525 North Sheridan, Chicago, Illinois 60626; Telephone: 312-508-2780

LOYOLA UNIVERSITY NEW ORLEANS

4 Pr G S Tr

▼ University Honors Program

The Loyola University Honors Program offers the opportunity for academically superior, highly motivated students to take challenging honors courses and to participate in special cultural and intellectual enrichment activities.

Honors students also participate together in such cultural activities as trips to the opera, theater, and art museums, and they attend special seminars and lectures. These supplemental activities are optional but are usually very popular and well-attended. Honors students also have the use of a University honors center as a place to study, relax, and discuss. In addition, students in the full University Honors Program have priority registration with seniors. An active student University Honors Association plans social activities and programming and works with the Honors Director and the University Honors Advisory Board on developing curriculum and policy for the program.

In addition to the University Honors Program and Honors Certificate Program, several departments at Loyola have departmental honors programs, which usually consist of special research projects in the senior year and require GPAs of 3.5 in the major. Students can participate in both the University Honors Program and the honors program of their major.

University Honors graduates wear a white stole at graduation, and their achievement is noted in the graduation program and on their diploma and transcript. Honors Certificate Students are so designated in the graduation program and on their transcripts. A University Honors Program Outstanding Student Award is presented annually to the graduating senior with the highest GPA in honors classes, and a University Honors Association Award is presented to the graduating senior who has the most outstanding record of community service to the Honors Program, Loyola University, and the larger community.

The 16-year-old program currently has an enrollment of 100. About 5–8 percent of the entering first-year students are in the Honors Program.

Participation Requirements:
The Honors Program is open to qualified students of all undergraduate colleges and majors. Students in the University Honors Program take a total of 48 credit hours of honors courses throughout the four undergraduate years. These honors courses replace the required common-curriculum courses and therefore do not add to the number of requirements for graduation. In addition to the full University Honors Program, qualified students may choose to participate in the Honors Certificate Program, which consists of 24 credit hours of honors courses. Honors certificate students complete their common-curriculum requirements from the regular nonhonors offerings. Students in the University Honors Program and the Honors Certificate Program are required to maintain a 3.3 overall GPA.

The Honors curriculum includes courses in literature, philosophy, history, religious studies, art, economics, political science, math, and sciences. In their senior year, honors students in the College of Arts and Sciences write a thesis based on original research and students in the Colleges of Business Administration and Music take specially designed honors courses in their major. The honors classes, which are taught by the most outstanding faculty members, are usually smaller than the regular classes, and emphasize active student participation, extensive readings in primary sources, and challenging writing assignments.

Admission Process:
Incoming freshmen with high SAT I or ACT scores and high school GPAs of 3.5 or better are invited to apply to the University Honors Program. The application consists of an essay and a teacher recommendation. The University Honors Advisory Board, consisting of faculty members and Honors students, evaluates the applications and selects the participants. In addition, students with outstanding academic records in their freshman year at Loyola, as well as qualified transfer students, are invited to apply to the Honors Program. If accepted, they are given Honors credit for previous work that was equivalent to the Loyola freshman honors courses. Qualified students who want to enter the Honors Program after the beginning of their sophomore year usually enter the Honors Certificate Program.

The deadline for applying to the program is March 10.

Scholarship Availability:
Although many students in the University Honors Program receive full or partial University scholarships, the scholarships are not tied to participation in the University Honors Program.

The Campus Context:
Loyola University New Orleans is a coeducational Jesuit university in historic uptown New Orleans. Founded by the Society of Jesus in 1912 as a Catholic and Jesuit institution, Loyola is committed to providing a rigorous value-centered liberal arts education to all qualified persons without regard to race, ethnicity, creed, age, or sex. Loyola is composed of five colleges: the College of Arts and Sciences, the College of Business Administration, the College of Music, the School of Law, and the City College for evening students.

Loyola University New Orleans has been listed among the top 10 regional colleges and universities in the South by *U.S. News & World Report* and has been rated as one of the nation's best opportunities for affordable quality education in *Barron's 300: Best Buys in College Education* and *America's 200 Best Buys in College Education*. The University offers ninety-five undergraduate, graduate, and law degree programs.

Student Body The undergraduate enrollment is 3,583—38 percent men and 62 percent women. The ethnic distribution is 3.4 percent Asian, 13 percent African American, 13 percent Hispanic, .6 percent Native American, 64 percent white, .5 percent other, and 5.5 percent unspecified. There are 233 international students. Thirty-four percent of the students are residents; 66 percent are commuters. Sixty-four percent of students receive financial aid. There are three fraternities and six sororities.

Faculty The faculty numbers 251 full-time and 171 part-time. Eighty-six percent have terminal degrees. The student-faculty ratio is 11.9:1.

Key Facilities Loyola University New Orleans has outstanding facilities for its nationally renowned College of Music, including a 600-seat performance hall with excellent acoustics, a music recording studio, and a computerized piano laboratory. The Department of Communications has one of the most highly equipped facilities in the South, with television and radio studios, graphic arts studios, an engineering shop, darkrooms, and a news bureau with national wire service. Writing labs are in all major buildings, equipped not only with computers but also with skilled writing tutors. Academic enrichment provides special facilities for students who need extra help with academic work. The University's library houses 300,433 volumes. There are eleven computer labs in instructional buildings, plus computer clusters in the three residence halls.

Athletics Intercollegiate sports (NAIA Division 1) include men's basketball, baseball, golf, tennis, and cross-country and women's basketball, golf, soccer, tennis, cross-country, and volleyball. In addition, students can join many intramural sports clubs. The Recreational Sports Complex includes an Olympic-size pool, handball courts, indoor tennis courts, a state-of-the-art weight room, an indoor track, and a basketball court.

Study Abroad The University Honors Program encourages students to participate in study-abroad programs. Loyola sponsors summer programs in Mexico, Italy, Belgium, Greece, and London. The program in Mexico is also available for a semester and a year. The College of Business Administration also sponsors various international internships.

Support Services The University is fully accessible to disabled students.

Job Opportunities Work-study is awarded through the financial aid process; student assistantships are available through each department and are not contingent on being eligible for financial aid. Positions are available in the residence halls as resident assistants and desk assistants. In addition, the Counseling and Career Development and Placement Center maintains listings of employment opportunities in the local community as well as nationally.

Tuition: $12,950 per year (1996-97)

Room and Board: $5830

Mandatory Fees: $316

Contact: Director: Dr. Ted Cotton, Monroe 537M, Box 75, 6363 St. Charles Avenue, New Orleans, Louisiana 70118; Telephone: 504-865-2708; Fax: 504-865-2709

MANHATTAN COLLEGE

4 Pr G M

▼ Honors Enrichment Program

The Manhattan College Honors Enrichment Program serves the School of Arts, the School of Science, and the School of Education. The program, initiated in 1993, is a cocurricular program that has as its aim the enrichment of campus life for honors students. The program is administered by the Honors Committee, a committee of faculty members and students. The program coordinator reports to the deans of the three schools served.

There are currently 130 students in the program.

Participation Requirements: At present, there are four components of the program. The first is the symposia. Each year, the Honors Committee selects a theme topic for the following school year (1993–94 was "The Mind", 1994–95 was "The City", 1995–96 was "Language", and 1996–97 was "Peace and Justice in the Modern World"). Three symposia are offered each semester; generally one is sponsored by each school. Student presenters discuss their recent research and scholarship, adapting the presentations to the year's theme, and then take questions from the student and faculty audience. In an effort to make the symposia more interactive, a talk-show format was adopted in 1996–97; a faculty member helps the presenter(s) interact with the audience. Students have indicated that they particularly enjoy presentations from schools other than their own.

The second component is Collegewide lectures. Students are asked to take advantage of the many lectures and presentations offered by faculty and guest speakers each semester. Professionals and academics from all over the country and the world speak at Manhattan College on a variety of topics, and honors students appreciate the wealth of offerings in the course of a single semester.

The third component is outside activities. New York City offers one of the broadest ranges of activities in the arts and sciences in the world. Students are encouraged to enjoy the offerings by attending at least one activity off campus; almost anything except movies is included in the list of possible activities. In order to receive transcript credit for participating in the program, a student must, in the course of each semester, attend one of the three activities listed above, plus any two others from the list. They write brief critiques of the programs and activities and attempt to apply the event to

the year's theme. The fourth and last component of the program is the honors seminar. In spring 1996, the program began an honors seminar for college credit. The year's offering was "Mozart and Revolution," a study of "Le Nozze di Figaro" and "Don Giovanni" in light of their revolutionary qualities. Two faculty members team-taught the seminar. The spring 1997 offering is "No More Bystanders: The Holocaust and Personal Responsibility."

Admission Process: Students who have a cumulative GPA of 3.5 or above are eligible for membership. Interested students with lower GPAs may be admitted if they have a letter of recommendation from a faculty member. Entering first-year students who have received Presidential Scholarships are invited into the program in the fall semester. In January of each year, first-year students with a 3.5 GPA are invited to join.

The Campus Context: Manhattan College, founded by the Brothers of the Christian Schools in 1853, is situated on a beautiful Federalist Revival campus in Riverdale, New York, and is about 45 minutes from downtown Manhattan. Fifty undergraduate majors are offered leading to the baccalaureate, including liberal arts, science, education, business, and engineering.

Student Body Undergraduates number 2,400. The ethnic breakdown of students is 5.2 percent black, .2 percent Native American/Alaskan, 7.9 percent Asian/Pacific Islander, 12.4 percent Hispanic/Latino, and 74.3 percent white. International students represent forty-two other countries.

Faculty There are 188 full-time faculty members (plus adjunct faculty members); 90 percent have doctorates. The student-faculty ratio is 15:1.

Key Facilities Manhattan College has a 195,000-volume library as well as 250 IBM and IBM-compatible computers.

Athletics Division I intercollegiate athletics include men's basketball, baseball, soccer, cross-country, track and field, lacrosse, tennis, and golf and women's basketball, soccer, swimming, cross-country, track and field, volleyball, lacrosse, softball, and tennis. Manhattan also offers intramural sports and club crew for men and women.

Study Abroad Study-abroad programs are available for all students in all majors, with opportunities around the world.

Support Services Facilities for differently abled students are available throughout the campus.

Job Opportunities Work opportunities for students include work-study and part-time employment.

Tuition: $13,800 minimum per year (1996-97)

Room and Board: $7150 minimum

Mandatory Fees: $130

Contact: Coordinator: Dr. Thomas S. Ferguson, Manhattan College Parkway, Riverdale, New York 10471; Telephone: 718-862-7137; Fax: 718-862-8016

MANKATO STATE UNIVERSITY

 4 Pu G M Sc Tr

▼ Honors Program

The Honors Program of Mankato State University is designed to replace the mainstream general education requirements with a more challenging and flexible program. The program provides top students with the opportunity to interact at least weekly with faculty members and facilitates personal interaction among students and faculty members.

The program consists of three main components. The first is seminars, meeting once weekly. These seminars are taken each quarter, with varied topics. Honors sections of general education courses are another component. These are sections of regular general education courses that are taken only by honors students. These classes are often much smaller than regular sections and offer students a chance to work more closely with faculty members. Topics courses are the third component. These consist of classes taught in a discussion/seminar format, offered through different disciplines. The topics courses are taken by upper-level students. The final requirement is a senior project. This is completed in conjunction with the student's major discipline, with an adviser through the major.

The Honors Program publishes a quarterly newsletter, *On Our Honors*. This newsletter offers information on upcoming courses, honors club activities, and welcomes student contributions. The honors club plans activities such as trips to the Twin Cities area for plays, pizza parties, and discussions on courses to be offered.

The flexible course requirements of the Honors Program at Mankato State University allow many students to more easily graduate with a double major or to graduate early. The combination of small classes and top students and faculty members allows students to actively learn and interact. The honors newsletter and honors club provide for social interaction for honors students. The combination of these features makes the Honors Program at Mankato State University a unique opportunity for students to get all that they can out of their college experience.

Upon graduation from the University, the Honors Program student is designated a University Scholar. This is noted upon the transcript and in a certificate presented to the student. Honors cords are worn by graduates at the graduation ceremonies.

Students in the program number approximately 250.

Participation Requirements: In order to graduate as part of the Honors Program, a student must maintain a 3.3 GPA and manifest high competency in communication skills. Those students pursuing a B.A. degree are also required to complete at least one year of a foreign language.

Admission Process: Students must first apply and be admitted to Mankato State University. If they meet the requirements, they may then apply for admission to the Honors Program. Qualifications for entering the program are graduation in the upper 10 percent of the high school class and a minimum composite score of 25 on the ACT test or its equivalent.

Scholarship Availability: No scholarships are offered strictly to Honors students. However, Mankato State University offers a variety of scholarships to both incoming freshmen and transfer students and students in their major disciplines. Students are urged to contact either their major department or the Admissions Office for further details on these scholarships.

The Campus Context: Mankato State University is located in Mankato, Minnesota, in the Minnesota River valley. The University was founded as a Normal School in 1868. In 1921 it became a state teachers college, and in 1957 broadened its mission and became Mankato State College. In the 1970s the College was granted university status and began moving to its current location on the hill overlooking Mankato. Mankato is located approximately 70 miles south of the Minneapolis/St. Paul metropolitan area. Programs are available leading to six baccalaureate degrees, six master's degrees, and a specialist degree.

Student Body Undergraduate enrollment is 11,000. Students from more than sixty countries make up an international student enrollment of 425. A wide variety of activities are available for students. The Student Development Programs and Activities Office coordinates many groups and provides on-campus movies, speakers, and other entertainment. Nine fraternities and five sororities involve many students in activities both on and off campus.

Faculty There are 600 full-time faculty members, supplemented by adjunct faculty members.

Key Facilities The Memorial Library has approximately 1 million volumes and 3,200 current periodicals. The library features an on-line catalog access system.

The Academic Computer Center (ACC) is a centralized computer lab available for students. Available equipment includes Macintosh and IBM computers; VAX, AS400, and AT&T minicomputers; and dot matrix and laser printers. The lab is open for all students to use. Students with their own personal computers and modems may access the campus computer network via telephone lines.

Three housing complexes on campus offer rooms for single, double, and triple occupancy. Choices available include quiet study floors, coed floors, intercultural floors, and others. The residential complexes house approximately 2,800 students each year.

Athletics Intramural sports are available in all seasons and students may sign up to play volleyball, softball, basketball, and floor hockey.

Study Abroad Students have the opportunity to study abroad. Mankato State University offers regularly scheduled programs in Mexico and France, various foreign study tours, and the opportunity to share other universities' study-abroad programs.

Job Opportunities Students are offered a range of work opportunities on campus, including assistantships, work study, and nonneed-based employment.

Tuition: $2517 for state residents, $5625 for nonresidents, per year (1996-97)

Room and Board: $2965

Mandatory Fees: $379

Contact: Director: Lee Cornell, MSU 226 P.O. Box 8400, Mankato, Minnesota 56002-8400; Telephone: 507-389-2968; Fax: 507-389-6376 E-mail: honors@vax1.mankato.msus.edu

MARICOPA COMMUNITY COLLEGES

2 Pu G L Sc Tr

▼ District Honors Program

The mission of the Honors Program at Maricopa Community Colleges is to foster a climate of excellence in the colleges and the surrounding communities, to recognize and reward the talent and motivation of outstanding community college students and faculty members, to promote a sense of scholarship and community among program participants and among the colleges, and to raise the awareness of the high quality and variety of educational opportunities and services offered by the Maricopa County Community College District.

The Honors Program of Maricopa Community Colleges was initiated in January 1981 as a Joint Council on Education Program (JCEP) Grant to Scottsdale Community College. JCEP was an internal grant program that allocated funds for innovative and exploratory projects.

The initial grant allowed a faculty committee to investigate the initiation of a community college honors program and to determine factors that were crucial to the design of such a program. The committee's six-month endeavor provided the basis for the district's current Honors Program. In June 1981, the Governing Board allocated funds for the development and implementation of honors programs at each of the campuses. The Office of the Vice Chancellor for Student and Educational Development was assigned to provide coordination of the colleges' programs. Since 1981, the Governing Board has approved funds each year to support the colleges' programs. The Honors Committee at each campus is free within district guidelines to administer these funds according to its needs.

The Honors Forum Lecture Series features nationally known speakers who address specific issues related to an annual theme. The theme is generally adapted from the annual study topic and materials developed by Phi Theta Kappa, the two-year college honorary society.

An Honors Forum course offered at the colleges explores in greater depth the theme and issues discussed throughout the year. The Forum activities provide the opportunity for all honors students throughout MCCCD to have common learning experiences based on the topic chosen for the year. Honors students may be required to attend the lecture and write a synopsis for the honors forum class.

Three times each fall and spring semester, a guest speaker visits two of the ten colleges for informal discussion and a question-and-answer period. A third college hosts dinner with the distinguished visitor. College faculty members and students are invited, as well as the Chancellor, Vice-Chancellors, and Governing Board members. All honors students, faculty members, staff, administrators, and Governing Board members are invited to "Applaud and Celebrate" the activities and accomplishments of the year at an annual convocation held in the spring. Students are recognized and rewarded with special scholarships. This is also an opportunity to recognize and reward faculty members who have taught honors courses for three, five, eight, and twelve years.

Approximately 2,250 students and 400 faculty members participate.

Participation Requirements: Students who are Honors Fee Waiver Scholars and President's Scholars must complete a minimum of 12 hours (100 level and above) of course work each semester. This includes the completion of one honors course each semester. A GPA of 3.25 must be maintained and students must remain in good standing at one of the colleges/centers.

Awards, certificates, and diploma citations conferred upon program completion are issued under the individual jurisdiction of the ten colleges which comprise Maricopa Community Colleges. These colleges include Chandler-Gilbert Community College, Estrella Mountain Community College Center, GateWay Community College, Glendale Community College, Mesa Community College, Paradise Valley Community College, Phoenix College, Rio Salado College, Scottsdale Community College, and South Mountain Community College.

Admission Process: In the President's Scholar category, a student must be graduated (within the top 15 percent of the class at the end of the sixth, seventh, or eighth semesters) from a North Central Accredited (NCA) high school in Maricopa County and apply within one academic year from high school graduation. Enrollment in MCCCD college/center must include at least one honors course per semester. The applicant may not be enrolled in another postsecondary institution, summer school excluded. College-preparatory schools are not included in this category as long as the student has not earned college credits. President's Scholars may enroll in the Honors Program at any MCCCD college/center. Enrollment must be for at least 12 credit hours per semester (fall/spring). The scholarship will not cover the cost of course work below 100 level and/or pass/fail classes (P/Z option). Remedial and/or pass/fail-option classes may be included in a student's schedule to meet the 12-credit-hour minimum requirement, but the award will be prorated for the semester.

Scholarship Availability: A number of scholarships are available to honors students, including the President's Scholarship ($500 per semester for up to four semesters), the Honors Fee Waiver (up to $100 per semester, not to exceed four semesters), the Betty Heiden Elsner Scholarship ($100 per semester for two semesters), Chancellor's Scholarship (full tuition and fees for one year plus $150 per semester for books/supplies), and the Foundation Scholarship ($1000 annually per college to be distributed at the discretion of the college).

Tuition: $720 for area residents, $4320 for state residents, $4470 for nonresidents, per year (1996-97). Residents of participating Arizona counties pay area-resident tuition rates.

Mandatory Fees: $300

Contact: Coordinator: Professor Loman B. Clark Jr., 2411 West 14th Street, Tempe, Arizona 85281-6941; Telephone: 602-731-8026; Fax: 602-731-8111; E-mail: clark@maricopa.edu

---

MARSHALL UNIVERSITY

    4 Pu G M Sc Tr

▼ Honors Program

The Honors Program at Marshall University, which is open to students of all majors, was established in the early 1960s to provide maximum educational opportunities for students of high ability. Honors students are encouraged to raise their expectations of themselves by pursuing enriched courses within and beyond the regular curriculum. The centerpiece of the program is the team-taught, interdisciplinary seminar that brings together outstanding, motivated students and stimulating professors, usually some of the best teachers on campus. The program typically offers three or four of these 4-hour seminars per semester; they are limited to 15 students.

The Honors Program is housed in the John R. Hall Center for Academic Excellence (CAE), which brings together all Honors and Scholarship Programs at Marshall. The facilities include a computer lab, scholarship library, reading room, student lounge, and two seminar classrooms. The CAE also contains the offices of the Executive Director of the CAE, the Chair of Honors, and two secretaries. In 1995, Honors students formed the Marshall University Honors Student Association (MUHSA), which is open to all eligible students. MUHSA sponsors academic and social events on campus and it advises the faculty committee that oversees Honors through its three seats on that committee, ensuring Honors students a voice in deciding the direction of the program.

The number of students in the program is approximately 150–180.

Participation Requirements: Students who wish to graduate with University Honors on their diplomas must complete 24 hours of honors classes, consisting of HON 101 (the freshman year orientation class), 4 hours of a 100-level seminar, 8 hours of upper-level seminars, and 11 hours of honors credit made up of departmental honors classes or independent study in honors. They must do this while maintaining a 3.3 GPA in all courses and a cumulative 3.3 GPA in honors courses. In the past, interdisciplinary seminars have included topics such as "Poetry and the Condition of Music," "War in the Twentieth Century," "Plagues and Epidemics," and "Primatology and Human Evolution." Honors students are advised by the Honors Director and by faculty members in the student's major field of study.

Admission Process: Students may begin honors work at any stage in their college careers, although many begin as freshmen. Entering freshmen with an ACT composite of 26 (or SAT I equivalent) and a 3.3 GPA can enroll in any honors course. Transfer students or students already enrolled with a minimum 3.3 GPA can enroll in any honors course.

Scholarship Availability: Superior high school or transfer students (3.5 GPA and minimum ACT composite of 27) can apply for academic scholarships or tuition waivers, the John Marshall Scholarship Program, the Erma Byrd Scholars Program, and the Society of Yeager Scholars Program. The Honors Program also offers an annual $1000 travel-abroad scholarship and a $500 award for domestic study.

The Campus Context: Marshall University is one of West Virginia's two state universities. Founded in 1837, it is located on a 65-acre urban campus that houses six different colleges—Business, Liberal Arts, Fine Arts, Science, Education, Community and Technical College—and three schools: Nursing, Medicine, and the Graduate School. Marshall University has forty different bachelor's degree programs and seventeen different associate degree programs.

The University has a 30,000-seat football stadium, 10,000-seat basketball stadium, and a state-of-the-art 543-seat theater facility with main stage and experimental stage. The University has also just begun construction on a $22-million library. Academic facilities include the Birke Art Gallery, H.E.L.P. Center for those with learning disabilities, Center for International Programs, Psychology Clinic, Speech and Hearing Clinic, and the WPBY-TV and WMUL-FM studios.

Student Body: Undergraduate enrollment is 10,210; 53 percent are women and 47 percent are men. The ethnic distribution is 94 percent white, 4.2 percent black, less than 1 percent Hispanic, 1 percent Asian, and less than 1 percent Native American. There are 51 international students. Sixty-nine percent of undergraduates receive financial aid. There are over 100 social organizations on campus, including ten national fraternities and eight national sororities.

Faculty: The total faculty is 619 (excluding the Community College, Medical School, and Library). Of the 410 full-time faculty members, 81 percent have terminal degrees. The student-faculty ratio is 22:1.

Key Facilities: The Library contains 423,000 bound volumes and the campus contains 450 Macintosh and DOS computers for student use in computer centers, labs, classrooms, and the library. Dorms also provide access to the main academic computer.

Athletics: The University is a member of the NCAA and participates in Division I athletics in men's football, men's and women's basketball, men's and women's track and field, men's and women's cross-country, men's golf, men's soccer, women's tennis, and women's volleyball. The University also has more than twenty intramural programs.

Study Abroad: Marshall University has various study-abroad programs, including formal exchange programs with two universities in England and programs in Spain and Mexico.

Support Services: All campus buildings are accessible for the mobility-impaired student, while two residence halls have been fully renovated and modified extensively for disabled students. Separate programs for learning-disabled students are also available.

Tuition: $2116 for state residents, $5878 for nonresidents, per year (1996-97) [For Kentucky residents of Boyd, Carter, Greenup, and Lawrence Counties, Ohio residents of Lawrence County: $3948 full-time per year, $164.75 part-time per semester hour]

Room and Board: $4240

Contact: Director: Dr. Richard Badenhausen, Chair, University Honors Council, Huntington, West Virginia 25755; Telephone: 304-696-6405; Fax: 304-696-3197; Web site: http://www.marshall.edu/cae/

MARYWOOD UNIVERSITY

4 Pr C M Sc Tr

▼ Honors Program

The honors program was inaugurated in 1981. Honors students come from all of the disciplines; they are campus leaders, volunteers, and tutors. Honors courses are available in religious studies, philosophy, mathematics, science, psychology, history, social science, world literature, modern foreign language, and fine arts. Honors students engage in independent research under the supervision of a faculty member as they complete their honors thesis, which may be submitted for publication in the honors journal.

There are 154 students in the program.

Participation Requirements: To graduate with an honors degree, students must complete a minimum of 21 honors credits; at least 15 credits must be in small, seminar-style honors courses or colloquia, and another three credits must be in the honors thesis in the student's major program. In addition, the student must graduate with an overall QPA of 3.25 or greater. Any student meeting the requirements may take honors courses, whether or not the honors degree is sought.

All honors courses and projects are designated by a special code that appears on a student's transcript, and honors courses and the honors degree are noted on all official transcripts. Honors students are assisted by the Marywood Committee on Scholarships.

Admission Process: Capable incoming freshmen are placed in honors courses that meet their liberal arts requirements. Beginning with the second semester of the freshman year, any student with a 3.0 or better average may select honors courses. At the end of the sophomore year, those students who have completed at least three honors courses (with a 3.0 or better average) may elect participation in the program leading to an honors degree.

Scholarship Availability: Marywood University offers full tuition Presidential Scholarships and partial tuition I.H.M. scholarships to applicants who have demonstrated academic excellence in high school.

The Campus Context: Housed on a 130-acre campus, Marywood is a comprehensive 2A College consisting of four schools: the Undergraduate School of Arts and Sciences, two excellent graduate schools, and the School of Continuing Education. A child-care facility, the Early Childhood Center, the Military Family Institute, a theater, radio and TV stations, and a post office are located on the campus. Marywood offers sixty undergraduate baccalaureate degree programs and majors.

Student Body Undergraduates number 1,434 full-time and 346 part-time. Seventy-six percent are women and 24 percent are men (the University became coeducational in 1990). Ninety-five percent of the student population is white, 3 percent are members of minority groups, and 2 percent are nonresident aliens. Thirty percent of the students are residents and 70 percent live off-campus. Eighty percent of students receive financial aid. There are no fraternities or sororities.

Faculty There are 128 full-time faculty members; 80.6 percent have terminal degrees. The student-faculty ratio is 12:1.

Key Facilities The University library contains a print collection of 459,177 items; students have access to 39,135 items in the media collection. Students also have access to the libraries of eight neighboring colleges. With 20 percent Macintosh and 30 percent DOS/Windows, 210 computers in twelve labs located in nine buildings are available for undergraduate use.

Athletics Women's sports include basketball, field hockey, softball, tennis, and volleyball. Men can enjoy baseball, basketball, cross-country, and tennis. The University also sponsors active programs in intramural and club sports, including lacrosse, skiing, and soccer.

Study Abroad Study abroad is encouraged by many departments, especially the art and foreign language departments.

Support Services Facilities are friendly to students with disabilities and many support services are readily available for them.

Job Opportunities Students are offered a wide range of work opportunities, including work-study, peer tutoring, and other campus employment.

Tuition: $12,640 per year (1996-97)

Room and Board: $5200

Mandatory Fees: $545

Contact: Director: Sister Dorothy A. Haney, IHM, PhD, Professor of Philosophy, Scranton, Pennsylvania 18509; Telephone: 717-348-6211 ext. 2302; Fax: 717-348-1817; E-mail: haney@ac. marywood.edu

---

McHenry County College

2 Pu G S Sc

▼ Honors Program

The Honors Program is devised to attract and retain academically talented students. Its curriculum is structured to help students develop a strong foundation in academic skills such as critical thinking, problem solving, reading, and writing within a small-class environment. Students in the program have an opportunity to participate in NCHC activities, including honors semesters. They are also supported in research projects through the Honors Council of the Illinois Region. Honors at McHenry provides students with local recognition of their academic achievement and then assists them in making a link to the honors programs at four-year/senior institutions through transcript notation and individual articulation.

Founded in 1987, the program currently enrolls 55 students per semester.

Participation Requirements: Honors Program members must maintain a 3.5 GPA. Students in the program complete 16 to 20 hours of honors courses, which are separate sections of existing courses and are identified on the transcript. At graduation, honors graduates have a special tassel to identify them and a special gold seal on their diplomas.

Admission Process: Students may gain admission to the Honors Program based on any two of the following criteria: a high school GPA of 3.5; a minimum composite ACT score of 24 or minimum combined SAT I score of 1000; college-transfer GPA of 3.5 for a minimum of 12 hours; MCC GPA of 3.5 for a minimum of 12 hours; membership in good standing of Phi Theta Kappa; two academic letters of recommendation; and a personal interview with the Honors Coordinator or appointed representative. Any student with a 3.2 GPA can enroll in an honors course.

Scholarship Availability: The Honors Program offers thirteen scholarships per semester. These generally are for tuition in honors courses, although they can be applied to books if the student already has other tuition scholarships.

The Campus Context: Located on a 110-acre campus in a suburban setting, McHenry County College offers three transfer degree programs: the Associate in General Education, the Associate in Science, and the Associate in Arts degrees.

Student Body Full-time enrollment is 2,321: 49 percent men and 51 percent women. Four percent of the student body are members of minority groups: 1 percent Asian, less than 1 percent African American, and the remainder Hispanic. Fifty-three percent of students receive some financial aid. All students commute to campus. While there are no social fraternities or sororities on campus, there is a chapter of Phi Theta Kappa.

Faculty Of the 232 faculty members, 72 are full-time and 7 hold doctorates. The student-faculty ratio is 10:1.

Key Facilities The library houses 39,089 volumes. Computer facilities include academic computing labs, classroom support labs, and approximately fourteen computer classrooms with a minimum of twenty-four computers per room.

Athletics In athletics, McHenry offers women's softball, basketball, and tennis and men's baseball, soccer, basketball, and tennis. The fitness center, open to students and the community, has multipurpose facilities for indoor and outdoor activities.

Study Abroad Study abroad is available with honors credit for participation in the Illinois Consortium for International Studies and Programs (ICISP) with sites in Canterbury, England, and Salzburg, Austria.

Support Services Disabled students will find an excellent special needs program to accommodate them.

Job Opportunities There are numerous opportunities for student employment on campus

Tuition: $1170 for area residents, $5342 for state residents, $6123 for nonresidents, per year (1996-97)

Mandatory Fees: $14

Contact: Directors: Dr. Carol E. Chandler and Dr. Dora M. Tippens, 8900 US Highway 14, Crystal Lake, Illinois 60012-2761; Telephone: 815-455-8691 or -8692; Fax: 815-455-3762; E-mail: cchandle@pobox.mchenry.cc.il.us

---

Mercy College

4 Pr D S Sc Tr

▼ Honors Program

The Honors Program at Mercy College is open to all motivated day students who have General Education requirements to fulfill or room in their programs for electives. Some major courses may also be taken as an honors option.

Honors classes are conducted as seminars that emphasize a spirit of inquiry in an atmosphere of collegiality between students and faculty members. The stimulating environment encourages students to raise their academic expectations while the supportive community offers opportunities to develop new leadership capacities. Trips, special events, and service projects provide cultural experiences outside of the classroom.

Students who have taken three or more honors courses and have maintained a GPA of 3.2 or greater receive a Certificate of Membership. Students who have taken nine of more honors classes receive the Christied Scholar Award. Awards are given for scholarship, academic development, and leadership. Outstanding student papers are presented in an annual symposium to which the entire campus is invited.

The 16-year-old program currently enrolls 85 students.

Participation Requirements: To be an official member of the Honors Program, a student must have taken at least three honors courses and must maintain a GPA of 3.2 or above. Members of the Honors Program are also expected to be active in the community life of the honors club. Community meetings are held at least bimonthly in the Honors Student Center.

Scholarship Availability: Mercy College offers many scholarships to exceptional students. Many students in the Honors Program take advantage of these scholarships.

The Campus Context: Mercy College is a comprehensive college offering both undergraduate and graduate degrees. Founded in 1950 by the Sisters of Mercy, the College became independent in 1969. Set on the spectacular Hudson River in Westchester County, just 35 minutes from the heart of New York City, Mercy College is one of the largest independent and coeducational four-year colleges in New York State. The main campus is located in Dobbs Ferry, with branch campuses situated in Yorktown Heights, White Plains, and the Bronx.

The College offers twenty-nine undergraduate majors leading to baccalaureate degrees and four graduate majors leading to master's degrees.

Student Body There are 6,355 undergraduate enrollees and 650 graduate students. Thirty-five percent of the population are men and 65 percent are women. The ethnic distribution is .16 percent Native American, 1.6 percent Asian, 7.8 percent black, 17.3 percent Hispanic, and .4 percent other. Two hundred students live in the Residence Hall. There are 189 international students.

Faculty Mercy has 157 full-time faculty members and 485 part-time adjunct faculty members, with more than 60 percent of the full-time faculty members holding doctorates. The student-faculty ratio is 17:1.

Key Facilities The library holds 293,000 volumes. There are more than 500 microcomputer systems available, both IBM-compatible and Macintosh.

Athletics Intercollegiate athletics in men's soccer, basketball, baseball, and tennis are offered, and women's intercollegiate athletics include volleyball, basketball, softball, and tennis. Golf and cross-country teams exist for both men and women.

Study Abroad Mercy College encourages students to enrich their educational experience by spending some time studying abroad in approved programs. Academic credit is given for satisfactory foreign study.

Job Opportunities Students are offered work opportunities on campus that include work-study and campus employment.

Tuition: $7200 per year (1996-97)

Room and Board: $6600 minimum

Contact: Director: Dr. Nancy A. Benson, 555 Broadway, Dobbs Ferry, New York 10522-1189; Telephone: 914-674-7432; Fax: 914-693-4133

MERCYHURST COLLEGE

4 Pr G M Sc Tr

▼ **Honors Program**

The Mercyhurst College Honors Program (MCHP) is a rich assortment of curricular and extracurricular opportunities for academically accomplished students who seek extraordinary intellectual and artistic stimulation. Each year the MCHP offers thirteen to fifteen courses in which 20 (or fewer) honors students join an outstanding member of the honors faculty to explore topics that frequently cross disciplinary boundaries. Each of these courses satisfies a Collegewide Liberal Studies Core requirement. Classes are lively, often featuring student-led discussions of provocative ideas discovered in primary sources. A host of specialty options are available ranging from floating 1- or 2-credit seminars to team-taught, two-term, super courses. Honors students may create courses in cooperation with interested faculty members and sometimes assist in teaching these courses.

Extracurricular activities are a major part of the MCHP experience. Honors students at Mercyhurst College create many of the events that define the intellectual and artistic life of the College. From performing arts presentations to debates on timely issues, MCHP students play a prominent role in national, regional, and Collegewide conferences, symposia, shows, and performances. Planning such events, as well as purely social activities, is enhanced by the MCHP residence option, which permits a limited number of honors students to live in the honors dormitory. Honors students at Mercyhurst have read papers at national professional meetings, been successful in major national scholarship competitions, had their papers published in a variety of journals, and had their work shown in regional exhibits. MCHP students study at some of the most prestigious graduate and professional schools upon leaving Mercyhurst.

Approximately 210 honors students are in the MCHP. This represents about 8 percent of the College student population.

Participation Requirements: Students who complete nine honors courses (or the equivalent) and maintain a 3.35 QPA graduate with Mercyhurst College Honors. Students may graduate as Mercyhurst College Honors Scholars after completing fourteen honors courses, achieving a 3.5 QPA, and satisfying numerous extracurricular requirements. Remaining in good standing in the MCHP requires only that honors students achieve a 3.2 QPA in the sophomore through senior years. There are no minimum course requirements.

Admission Process: Participating in the MCHP requires an invitation from the Director. Each year about 60 entering freshmen are invited to join the program. Invitations are based on SAT I or ACT scores, high school records, and recommendations. Transfer students are eligible to join the MCHP and invitations are based on former college or university performance. Students already at Mercyhurst who have a record of academic achievement are also encouraged to consider the MCHP, particularly if recommended by a faculty member.

Scholarship Availability: While the MCHP Director supervises the awarding of just one academic scholarship, many are available through the College's Office of Financial Aid.

The Campus Context: Mercyhurst College, in Erie, Pennsylvania, is located on 75 acres of orchards, lawns, and gardens overlooking Lake Erie. Erie, located in the rolling hills and vineyards of Pennsylvania, is the state's only port and home to the famous beaches and nature preserves of the Presque Isle peninsula. Founded in 1926 by the Sisters of Mercy, the College is a vibrant, coeducational institution of nearly 2,500 students, the majority of whom are campus residents. The B.A., B.S., and M.S. are offered in thirty-five different degree programs.

Numerous certificate programs are also available. Recent additions to the Mercyhurst College campus include a student union, an ice center, a performing arts center/opera house, an apartment complex, and a townhouse village. Other features include an observatory, a theater, a language laboratory, and a food lab/restaurant.

Student Body The student body of about 2,500 is composed of 54 percent women and 46 percent men, with 66 students from fifteen other countries. Eighty-three percent are campus residents and nearly 90 percent of students receive financial aid.

Faculty A faculty of 207 includes 107 full-time faculty members, 60 percent of whom have a Ph.D. or other terminal degree. The student-faculty ratio is 17:1.

Key Facilities The College library owns 160,000 volumes and uses CD-ROM and Internet access to utilize the world's great libraries and databases. There are 140 PCs available to students in several locations, including a sophisticated science computing center that offers four UNIX machines. Students may use e-mail and access the Internet in many computer centers.

Athletics The athletics program offers a multitude of fitness and sport activities to the Mercyhurst community. The College offers eighteen varsity intercollegiate sports, including men's and women's crew, volleyball, basketball, soccer, lacrosse, cross-country, tennis, women's softball, and men's baseball, football, and ice hockey. All sports are NCAA Division II affiliated, except lacrosse, which is NCAA Divison I. All participate in either the Great Lakes Intercollegiate Athletic Conference (GLIAC), the Eastern College Athletic Conference (ECAC), or both. Intramural sports include football, volleyball, golf, basketball, hockey, soccer, softball, badminton, bowling, and tennis.

Study Abroad Many study-abroad opportunities exist through the academic departments and the Honors Program.

Job Opportunities A wide variety of job opportunities exist in work-study and assistantship positions.

Tuition: $10,920 per year (1996-97)

Room and Board: $4464

Mandatory Fees: $699

Contact: Director: Dr. Ludlow L. Brown, 501 East 38th Street, Erie, Pennsylvania 16546; Telephone: 814-824-2356; Fax: 814-824-2438; E-mail: bbrown@paradise.mercy.edu; Web site: http://utopia.mercy.edu

MESA STATE COLLEGE

4 Pu G S Sc Tr

▼ **Honors Program**

The Honors Program at Mesa State College offers promising and motivated students enhanced opportunities for academic growth. All aspects of the program are focused on exciting learning experiences, an emphasis on developing intellectual skills rather than collecting facts, close relationships with the honors faculty members and with other honors students, and the assistance of the Honors Program Director in accessing the academic, administrative, and personal support that will allow students to make the most of their college careers.

Lower-division honors courses consist of specially designed sections of general education courses, taught by faculty members recruited for their expertise and teaching excellence. By varying the offerings from semester to semester, students are able to fulfill the general education requirement in small, discussion-based classes instead of large lecture classes. Upper-division honors courses are interdisciplinary, focused around themes or issues that can be illuminated from various perspectives.

Honors students also have the option of producing an honors thesis on some topic within their major. Under the guidance of an adviser they pursue a line of research/inquiry culminating in a written work that will be bound and included in the College library's holdings. Such projects are especially valuable in preparing students for graduate work, and the successful completion of an honors thesis is cited at graduation and on students' transcripts.

The program is still growing, having begun in 1993. It will be capped at approximately 125 students. There are currently 70 students enrolled in the program.

Participation Requirements: Students selected for enrollment must maintain a GPA of at least 3.0 and must take at least one honors course a year to be retained in the program. If students accumulate an average of at least 3.0 in 18 hours of honors courses, 6 of which are upper-division, they are cited at graduation and on their transcripts as having earned academic honors.

Admission Process: Students must submit an application to the Honors Program separate from the application to the College. The exact application package depends on whether the applicant is an incoming freshman or a current student at the College.

Entering freshmen should apply by May 1. Currently enrolled students may apply each semester.

Scholarship Availability: Mesa State College offers a large number of scholarships for exceptional students.

The Campus Context: Mesa State College is an architecturally pleasing, beautifully planted, 42-acre campus bordered by a residential neighborhood. The town of Grand Junction is located in the western part of the state of Colorado. Both the location of the College and its spreading reputation as providing a top-notch education at a public college price has made it the fastest-growing college in Colorado. Its twenty-five degree programs lead to the B.A., B.S., B.B.A., or B.S.N.

Student Body There are 4,700 undergraduates enrolled, 44 percent are men and 56 percent are women. These include 67 international students. Sixty-three percent of all students receive financial aid.

Faculty Of the 180 full-time faculty members, 85 percent have terminal degrees. The part-time faculty numbers 100. The student-faculty ratio is 21:1.

Key Facilities The library houses 205,000 volumes. Many Macintosh and DOS computer labs are located in the library and academic buildings. The Tutorial Learning Center provides learning support. A new science building will be completed in fall 1997.

Athletics Mesa State has NCAA Division II teams for men in baseball, basketball, tennis, and football and for women in soccer, softball, basketball, golf, cross-country, tennis, and

volleyball. In addition, there are many intramural sports. The campus has a new 32,000-square-foot Recreational Center.

Support Services All buildings are handicapped-accessible.

Tuition and Fees: $1500 for state residents, $5460 for nonresidents, per year (1996-97)

Room and Board: $4100

Mandatory Fees: $433

Contact: Director: Dr. Sally Matchett, P.O. Box 2647, Grand Junction, Colorado 81502; Telephone: 970-248-1646; Fax: 970-248-1199

MIAMI UNIVERSITY

4 Pu G L Tr

▼ Honors Program

As an integral part of Miami University, the University Honors Program offers students a learning community that consciously supports the University's goals for liberal education: thinking critically, understanding contexts, engaging with other learners, and reflecting and acting. The program's mission is to support and provide opportunities for individuals who are strongly motivated academically and who desire a highly challenging and intellectually enriched learning environment at Miami. The University Honors Program is committed to nurturing the growth and development of these students. In return for these opportunities, students are asked to take responsibility for their education and meet all Honors Program requirements.

The program empowers students to see themselves as generators of knowledge rather than as passive transmitters of wisdom; moves students toward greater self-reflexivity about pragmatic and value issues surrounding responsible participation in a community; increases student awareness of their relation to communities and issues beyond those in which they are immediately and locally involved; increases students' abilities to communicate with others, both verbally and in writing; increases student appreciation of the enriching visions of human possibility offered by artistic and aesthetic expression; enhances students' abilities to contextualize the events and milestones of their lives; and broadens students' abilities to learn from experience different from their own.

Upon completion of all requirements for the Honors Program, students will have the designation "Graduated with University Honors" entered in their transcripts.

The 12-year-old program enrolls approximately 750 students.

Admission Process: Students are notified by the Office of Admissions that they are eligible for the Honors Program;

following notification, they are able to enroll during summer orientation. Other students interested in entering the Honors Program are encouraged to complete an application during summer orientation. Shortly after orientation ends, applicants are notified about the selection committee's decision. Applications also are accepted by a specific date each semester. Once accepted into the Program, they are eligible to enroll in honors courses through the Honors Office.

Scholarship Availability: The Joanna Jackson Goldman Memorial Prize annually supports a graduating Miami senior for a year of independent scholarship or creative activity. The amount of the Prize is approximately $12,000. Eligibility for the award includes a student's outstanding academic record, demonstrated capacity for independent work and creative initiative in some field of scholarship or the arts. The application deadline is early December.

The Campus Context: The University is composed of the College of Arts and Science, the School of Applied Science, the Richard T. Farmer School of Business Administration, the School of Education and Allied Professions, the School of Fine Arts, and the School of Interdisciplinary Studies (Western College Program). There are 119 degree programs on campus.

Student Body There are 15,601 students; 46 percent are men and 54 percent are women. The ethnic distribution of students is 3 percent African American, 2 percent Asian, and 1 percent Hispanic. There are approximately 300 international students. Commuters account for 90.2 percent of the students. Forty percent of the undergraduates receive some form of financial aid. There are twenty-seven fraternities and twenty-one sororities on campus.

Faculty The total number of faculty is 766. Full-time faculty members number 713. Eighty-nine percent of the faculty have terminal degrees. The student-faculty ratio is 28:1.

Key Facilities Special facilities of importance to Honors students are two Research Scholar Rooms, which are available each year to upperclass students conducting research. Women should apply for the J. Belden Dennison Research Scholar Room and men for the Joseph F. Hogan Honors Scholar Room. Applications are available in the Honors Office.

All Miami University students are automatically assigned accounts on the University's centrally managed, multi-user computing sysems (Miami U, running the IBM VM/CMS operating system, and MiaVX1, running the Digital Open VMS operating systems). These accounts allow access to e-mail (including list server lists), NetNews, information browsing tools (including World Wide Web), Miami services (including the Career Planning and Placement Office, Miami University Campus Information, and MiamiLINK: Miami University Libraries' Information Network), and a variety of other network and computational tools. The libraries house 4.3 million volumes.

Athletics All athletics are Division I. They include men's and women's basketball, football, golf, ice hockey, soccer, men's wrestling, women's field hockey, precision skating, volleyball, and softball.

Study Abroad Miami University has a strong commitment to international study opportunities for students. Some of the

programs the University offers are Aarhus University Denmark (semester or academic year); American Collegiate Consortium for East-West Cultural and Academic Exchanges (academic year in the former Soviet Union); Conservatoire de Musique de la Ville de Luxembourg (semester only); Federal University of Parana, Brazil (academic year); International Student Exchange Program (academic year); Kansai University of Foreign Studies, Japan (academic year); University of East Anglia, United Kingdom (semester/academic year); University of the Americas—Pueblas, Mexico (semester/academic year); and Vienna University of Economic and Business Administration, Austria (semester/academic year).

Support Services For students with physical disabilities, the Office of Disability Resources ensures program accessibility and compliance relative to Section 504 of the Rehabilitation Act of 1973 and the Americans with Disabilities Act. Miami provides such aids as sound amplifiers, adapted computing equipment, reading machines, and services such as sign language interpreters as requested, closed-caption television on campus, and a network of telecommunication devices for the deaf throughout various University offices, as well as volunteer reading programs for students who require taped textbooks.

Job Opportunities The Office of Student Financial Aid coordinates all student employment on campus. Students who do not qualify for work-study jobs may seek paying jobs on campus. A brochure, *Working On Campus,* provides information about campus employers, job classifications, and wage rates.

Tuition: $4210 for state residents, $9966 for nonresidents, per year (1996-97)

Room and Board: $4440

Mandatory Fees: $962

Contact: Director: Dr. Susan Barnum, Bishop Hall, Oxford, Ohio 45056; Telephone: 513-529-3399; Fax: 513-529-4920; E-mail: honors@msmail.muohio.edu; Web site: http://www.muohio.edu/honors/

MIDDLE TENNESSEE STATE UNIVERSITY

4 Pu G M Tr

▼ Honors Program

The 22-year-old MTSU Honors Program is a 24-semester hour integrated enrichment program offering courses in all five of the University colleges.

The Honors Program's commitment to enrichment extends beyond the classroom. The Honors Student Association hosts faculty firesides, a special invitation to HSA members to a faculty member's home for an evening of informal discussion and social interaction. In addition, there are Honors Lyceum events—Poetry Slams, Song Slams, Celtic music, and Blues concerts—to showcase the talent of the

University and the community. Also offered is the Honors Lecture Series, an interdisciplinary approach to a single topic where faculty members, administrators, and guest speakers lecture from their discipline's perspective.

Outstanding class recognition, a 12-hour certificate after meeting the general studies requirement, and an Honors Medallion awarded to graduating seniors are several ways superior students are recognized. To graduate with University Honors, students must achieve a 3.25 GPA.

There are 425 students enrolled in the program.

Participation Requirements: The first 12 hours of the Honors curriculum consist of lower-division/general studies courses. Enrollment is limited to 20 or fewer students. The next 9 hours offer upper-division or University Honors interdisciplinary study. These courses are limited to 15 or fewer students. The final requirement for graduation with University Honors is an honors thesis/creative project. Each thesis writer is assigned an adviser and 3 committee members. After the thesis defense and public presentation, theses and creative projects are bound and become part of the permanent holdings of the MTSU library. The University is very proud of its emphasis on undergraduate research as it prepares seniors for advanced study.

Admission Process: Entering freshmen must have a minimum ACT composite score of 26 or a high school GPA of 3.0 on a 4.0 system. Returning students and transfers must have a 3.0. Students whose GPA falls below a 3.0 will be unable to register for honors classes.

Scholarship Availability: Scholarship opportunities exist for in-state entering freshmen and those who have achieved outstanding academic records while participating in the Honors Program. In particular, three academic achievement awards ($1000) are assigned by the Honors scholarship committee.

The Campus Context: Middle Tennessee State University is located in Murfreesboro, less than a mile from the exact geographic center of the state. Murfreesboro, a historic city of about 50,000, is 32 miles southeast of Nashville via I-24 and is easily accessible from any direction. MTSU students and personnel can enjoy the advantages of a metropolitan atmosphere without the impersonalization associated with a big city. The five academic colleges include Basic and Applied Science, Business, Education, Liberal Arts, and Mass Communication. The University offers a total of nine undergraduate degrees.

Student Body The total undergraduate enrollment is 17,424. Ethnic distribution is 15,011 white students, 1,769 African-American students, 184 Hispanic students, 334 Asian students, 5 Native American students, and 69 unclassified students. There are 223 international students. Students receiving financial aid number 10,500. There are twenty-six fraternities and fifteen sororities.

Faculty There are 689 faculty members, 71 percent have terminal degrees. The student-faculty ratio is 21:1.

Key Facilities The library holds more than 600,000 volumes. Computer facilities include more than forty computer labs on campus. All full-time faculty members have PCs in their offices. Fiber optics connect all buildings and departments.

Athletics The University is a member of the Ohio Valley Conference and National Collegiate Athletic Association. MTSU is represented annually in athletics by baseball, basketball, cross-country, football (moving to I-A), golf, and tennis, as well as a women's program that includes basketball, tennis, cross-country, softball, track, and volleyball.

Study Abroad The International Programs and Services Office (IPSO) is the clearinghouse for study-abroad and exchange program development and information for MTSU students and faculty members. IPSO facilitates study-abroad and exchange opportunities by advising students on study, travel, and work programs; advertising departmental programs; joining institutional study-abroad consortia; holding special events and presentations; and maintaining reference books, videos, and informational catalogs on study, travel, and work programs overseas.

Job Opportunities A work-study program is established on campus.

Tuition: $1714 for state residents, $6050 for nonresidents, per year (1996-97)

Room and Board: $2558

Mandatory Fees: $300

Contact: Director: Dr. John Paul Montgomery, 106 Peck Hall, Murfreesboro, Tennessee 37132; Telephone: 615-898-2152; Fax: 615-898-5455; E-mail: honors@frank.mtsu.edu; Web site: http://www.mtsu.edu/~honors

MIDLAND COLLEGE

2 Pu G S Sc Tr

▼ **Honors Program**

The Midland College Honors Program is designed to offer a set of stimulating courses to academically talented students. It was inaugurated in fall 1995 to give the College's highest achieving students a chance to challenge their abilities with more rigorous course requirements than those expected of the mainstream two-year college student. The program develops students' critical thinking, writing, and speaking skills through advanced projects and discussion groups that involve research as well as oral and written presentations. Students work closely with instructors to complete a series of independent-study assignments that require time and effort beyond the standard course criteria. These may include extended biology research projects, analytical theme reports, and small-group participatory sessions with other honors students.

Participation Requirements: Students take one honors course per semester throughout the two-year college curriculum to satisfy the 12-hour requirement for honors students. These are built around a core of two humanities courses. Additional honors credit is earned from among elective courses in such fields as biology, economics, or literature. Courses are offered for vocational-technical as well as academic credit.

Admission Process: First-time and transfer students are accepted into the program following an application process that involves completion of a 750-word essay (describing a student's reasons for pursuing honors courses) and an interview with a faculty panel. Students must meet at least one of the following admission criteria: inclusion in the top 20 percent of the high school graduating class, a combined score of 1050 or above on the SAT I or a composite score of 23 or above on ACT, a cumulative GPA of 3.2 for a minimum of 12 semester hours in college, or two letters of recommendation from high school or college faculty members, counselors, or employers. Each honors student is encouraged to work with an Honors Council faculty member as a mentor.

Scholarship Availability: Midland College offers a variety of privately funded sources of financial aid such as the Abell-Hanger and Fasken Scholarships, in addition to public sources of assistance.

The Campus Context: Midland College is a beautiful 115-acre campus with a series of easily accessible one- and two-story buildings designed with a southwestern appearance. The institution is a comprehensive two-year college offering students the resources of a privately funded endowment of more than $6 million. The College is located in Midland, which has a population of about 95,000 people who are primarily employed in white-collar jobs provided by the oil industry. The sister city of Odessa, 20 miles away, combines with Midland to offer a metropolitan statistical area of almost 250,000 residents.

The College is divided into six instructional divisions: Business Studies, Health Sciences, Technical Studies, Communications/Fine Arts, Math/Sciences, and Social/Behavioral Sciences. Midland offers five degrees at the associate level in forty-nine fields of study.

Student Body The student body consists of 4,000 credit students and 10,000 noncredit students; 41 percent are men, 59 percent are women. Ethnic distribution is 75 percent white, 17 percent Hispanic, 5 percent African American, and 3 percent other. There are 40 international students. All students commute except resident athletes who are housed in on-campus dorms. Forty-eight percent of students receive financial aid. There are twelve social and special interest clubs.

Faculty Eighty-seven faculty members are full-time; 26 instructors possess doctoral degrees and 59 possess master's degrees. There are 198 adjunct faculty members. The student-faculty ratio is 31:1.

Key Facilities The library houses 50,293 volumes. Computer facilities include eight computer labs, including a writing lab, a multipurpose lab, a journalism lab, a math lab, and an office studies and computer instruction lab.

Athletics In athletics, men's and women's varsity basketball and men's golf teams are active and available.

Study Abroad International study is available in individual course trips to such destinations as Central America, Europe, Asia, and the Middle East.

Support Services Disabled-student services include complete counseling and support for studies and job placement.

Job Opportunities Work-study is available on campus (15 hours a week) and part-time employment is available as well.

Tuition: $632 for area residents, $680 for state residents, $974 for nonresidents, per year (1996-97)

Contact: Director: Dr. William G. Morris, 141 Allison Fine Arts Building, 3600 North Garfield, Midland, Texas 79705; Telephone: 915-685-4641; Fax: 915-685-4769; E-mail: wmorris@ midland.cc.tx.us

MILLIKIN UNIVERSITY

4 Pr G S Sc Tr

▼ Honors Program

Begun in 1974, the Millikin University Honors Program, open to all students, consists of two parts: a freshman honors program (Freshman Honors Scholars or FHS) and a University honors program (James Millikin Scholars or JMS). Freshman Honors Scholars take one specially designed honors seminar each semester of their first year. These seminars, interdisciplinary courses in the humanities, are discussion-based and require considerable reading, writing, and oral presentations. During the second semester, Freshman Honors Scholars and other qualified first-year students may apply for admission into the James Millikin Scholars Program. Students selected for the program take an additional seminar each semester of their sophomore year, one in the social sciences and one in the natural sciences or mathematics. Again, these are interdisciplinary in nature and open only to honors students. During their last two years, students in the James Millikin Scholars program design and complete an undergraduate research project, usually in their major area.

Students who continue through the JMS program are allowed to substitute their honors seminars for all general education requirements, giving them considerable flexibility to explore diverse areas of interest outside of their major area. Freshman Honors Scholars may replace any two comparable general education requirements with the humanities seminars. Many James Millikin Scholars have two majors or a major and one or more minors.

Currently, 80–100 students enter as Freshman Honors Scholars. Approximately 35 James Millikin Scholars are chosen from each freshman class. Students who do not continue in the JMS program are still considered part of the honors program as long as they maintain the required GPA. These students may participate in honors-sponsored events and enroll in honors seminars on a space-available basis.

Participation Requirements: To remain in the honors program, FHS or JMS students must maintain a cumulative GPA of 3.4 and satisfactorily complete all required honors seminars. Successful completion of the JMS program is noted at graduation and is recorded on the student's transcript.

Admission Process: Students who achieve a combined score of 27 or better on the ACT and rank in the upper 10 percent of their high school classes are eligible for participation in FHS.

Scholarship Availability: Those students who are accepted to the FHS program receive a minimum scholarship of one third tuition if they are non-need scholars and a maximum amount equal to what they need up to tuition. The scholarship remains in effect as long as the student maintains a 3.4 GPA. No additional scholarships are awarded for students selected for the JMS program.

The Campus Context: Millikin University was founded in 1901 and is located in Decatur, Illinois, a city of about 85,000, in the heart of central Illinois. Millikin's 40-acre campus is located near one of Decatur's most attractive residential areas. It includes classroom buildings, Staley Library, Scovill Science Hall, Richards Treat University Center, and the Kirkland Fine Arts Center.

When Millikin was founded, it was considered unique for its time because the founder, James Millikin, required that the institution be one "where the scientific, the practical and the industrial shall have a place of equal importance, side by side, with the literary and classical." Fifty-four different undergraduate majors lead to a B.A. or B.S. degree in the College of Arts and Sciences, the College of Fine Arts, and the School of Nursing and the Tabor School of Business.

Student Body There are 1,850 full-time students, mostly from Illinois and neighboring states. Forty-two percent are men and 58 percent are women. The ethnic distribution is 5 percent African American, .2 percent Native American, 1 percent Asian American, 1 percent Hispanic, and 88 percent white. The 19 international students represent 1 percent of the population. Sixty-nine percent of the students are residential; 31 percent are commuters. Ninety-four percent of the students receive financial aid. The campus has five fraternities and three sororities.

Faculty There are 126 full-time faculty members and 80 part-time faculty members. Ninety-one percent have terminal degrees. The student-faculty ratio is 14:1.

Key Facilities The Staley Library contains 160,000 volumes. There are five computer labs (two Macintosh-based and three DOS-based) with approximately 100 computers. Additional small facilities are located in the Greek house and the

residence halls. Many students bring computers to campus and are connected to the Millikin network.

Athletics Intercollegiate athletic competition is governed by the College Conference of Illinois and Wisconsin and Division III of the NCAA. Men's programs include football, cross-country, wrestling, soccer, swimming, basketball, baseball, track, golf, and tennis. Women's programs include softball, basketball, tennis, track, swimming, cross-country, and volleyball. Intramural competition is provided for both men and women.

Study Abroad Millikin is affiliated with the Institute of European Studies/Institute of Asian Studies. This affiliation permits qualified students ordinarily in their junior year to study abroad for a year, a semester, or a summer. Locations include sites in Australia, Austria, China, England, France, Germany, Italy, Japan, Russia, Singapore, Spain, and Taiwan. Other opportunities are available for off-campus study within the U.S.

Support Services Seventy-five percent of the campus is accessible to physically disabled students.

Job Opportunities Students have numerous opportunities for campus work. Approximately 700 students work on campus in areas such dining services, physical plant, department offices, and the library. Many students also work with faculty. The University also provides tutoring services for which the student tutors are paid.

Tuition: $13,988 per year (1997-98 est.)

Room and Board: $5070

Mandatory Fees: $91

Contact: Director: Dr. Cheryl L. Cohn, 1184 West Main Street, Decatur, Illinois 62522; Telephone: 217-424-6293 or 217-424-6277; Fax: 217-424-3993; E-mail: ccohn@mail.millikin.edu

MINOT STATE UNIVERSITY
4 Pu G S Tr
▼ Program in Honors

The Program in Honors at Minot State University has been in existence for seven years and is intended to provide an opportunity for students who have a desire to reach beyond the normal bounds of their university curriculum and attain broader yet more intensive educational goals. Small classes and the development of individual analytical skills are emphasized throughout the honors classes. Students are drawn to the program from all majors available on campus and thus bring a variety of skills and insights to the honors experience. This is augmented by a strong representation of nontraditional students within the program. Outstanding teaching faculty at the University who desire to work with students seeking greater intellectual heights comprise the honors faculty and serve as honors advisers together with the Director and the students' major advisers.

The 43 students currently enrolled in the Honors Program not only have full access to all of the University's facilities, they are granted early registration, extended library privileges, and the use of a well-appointed Honors Center with its own bank of computers connected to the Internet.

Participation Requirements: The Honors curriculum consists of two freshman seminars, three underclass courses chosen from a broad range (one each from the areas of humanities/fine arts, natural sciences/mathematics, and social sciences) and at least one year of a foreign language. This is followed by two seminars during the junior year and a capstone project or essay.

Admission Process: Students are selected for the Honors Program in one of two ways. Incoming freshmen with a high school GPA of 3.7 and/or a minimum cumulative ACT score of 25 are invited to join the honors seminar and from there pass into the program. Transfer students and students who do not meet the initial requirements but who demonstrate the ability to do honors work based on their university performance are recruited for application.

The Campus Context: Minot State University was founded in 1913 as the North Dakota Normal School and became a state university in 1983. The campus is located in Minot, North Dakota, situated near the geographical center of North America, 50 miles south of the Canadian border. As a land-grant public institution, Minot State's mission is dedicated to the education of all inhabitants of the state and larger community. The University offers forty-seven undergraduate majors leading to baccalaureate degrees in arts and sciences, business, and education/social sciences.

Student Body Enrollment currently is approximately 3,700, including some 600 international students, principally from Canada. The majority of the student population is from North Dakota.

Faculty There are 235 full-time faculty members in addition to adjunct members. Sixty-five percent of full-time faculty members have terminal degrees. The student-faculty ratio is 16:1.

Key Facilities The campus library houses 350,000 volumes. There are two on-campus computer labs with Macintosh and DOS computers plus Internet connections for all faculty offices.

Athletics Men's athletics include football, basketball, track, tennis, and cross-country; women's athletics are available in basketball, track, tennis, cross-country, and volleyball.

Study Abroad Minot State University is a member of ISEP (International Student Exchange Program) providing its students with study-abroad opportunities around the world. Institutional exchange programs with Keele University in England and Kyushu University in Japan provide additional possibilities.

Support Services The North Dakota Center for Disabilities serves the upper Midwest in providing outreach programs and services in special education, communication disorders, and speech pathology.

Job Opportunities Work-study is available on campus in a variety of areas.

Tuition: $2044 for state residents, $2450 full-time for residents of Manitoba, Montana, Saskatchewan, and South Dakota, $5018 for nonresidents, per year (1996-97); $92.58 per semester hour part-time for residents of Manitoba, Montana, Saskatchewan, and South Dakota

Room and Board: $2049

Mandatory Fees: $180

Contact: Director: David C. Bradley, 208 Model Hall, MSU, Minot, North Dakota 58707; Tel: 701-858-3014; Fax: 701-839-6933; E-mail: bradleyd@warp6.cs.misu.nodak.edu

MISSISSIPPI STATE UNIVERSITY

4 Pu G L Sc Tr

▼ University Honors Program

The University Honors Program is a challenging variation of the standard curriculum, through which students in all academic majors enrich their undergraduate study. The University-wide program that relies on the Giles Distinguished Professors and the elected Honors Council as its faculty and student advisory groups serves departmental majors in all colleges and schools by tailoring programs for talented students.

Freshmen and sophomores meet institutional core curriculum requirements by choosing from among forty departmental courses in five colleges; juniors and seniors earn elective credits, conduct independent research, formulate special projects, adapt advanced courses for honors credit, or utilize internships, study-abroad, honors seminars, or thesis options. Credits offered through the Honors Program support a unique honors design sequence in the School of Architecture, the preparatory programs for Schillig, Hearin-Hess, Stennis, and Truman scholars, and the early admissions program of the College of Veterinary Medicine.

Individual small-enrollment courses taught by carefully selected outstanding members of the professorial teaching faculty are enhanced by field trips, guest lecturers, and innovative experimentation as expansions of challenging and interesting study that students elect to pursue without adding to degree requirements.

Honors Forum is an emblem of the focus of the program on expanded exposure and experience. The weekly session has consistently relied on co-sponsorship with such units as the Cultural Diversity Center, the Women's Study Program, the Center for International Security and Strategic Studies, and colleges, schools, and departments to host participants of international reputation in diverse fields.

Forum also coordinates instructive and analytical programming with the University performing arts and lecture series to ensure students' insight into formal presentations, performances, and exhibitions.

The UHP also provides access to experiential study programs, including a summer archaeological dig in LaHav, Israel, open to students in all disciplines, an interdisciplinary elective art/biology course on the Gulf coast and the Mississippi barrier islands, geology/geography study on San Salvador Island in the Caribbean, and core-level art courses in the Province of Umbria, Italy.

Confidence in the ability of capable students to select options that reflect their interests and concerns is central to the philosophy of a program that presents diverse options for an undergraduate experience. The MSU Honors Program does not impose requirements for particular courses; instead it attempts to present both breadth and depth of options for study and experience that will contribute equally to academic and personal development.

The University Honors Program will celebrate its thirtieth anniversary in 1997. The liberal arts Stephen D. Lee Honors Program established in 1967 was expanded into a University-wide program in 1982 and has grown to a 1996 enrollment of 995 students who have an average ACT composite of 28.8 and an average GPA of 3.7. Annual enrollments of 900 to 1,000 in forty rotated honors courses in five colleges/schools reflect a breadth of institutional commitment to the Honors Program as a named MSU priority for undergraduate education.

Participation Requirements: UHP students who complete 12 hours of graded honors course work and 2 pass/fail credits for Forum receive Phase I certification; those who complete a total of 24 hours of graded course work, including internship, independent research, and/or study-abroad credits, and 4 Forum credits receive Phase II certification and distinction as an Honors Scholar. The distinctions are noted on the official transcript and are recognized at an annual awards ceremony, at which students with 4.0 averages, selected outstanding students from each class, and elected outstanding honors faculty members are also identified.

Admission Process: Admission for entering freshmen is determined by two categories: unconditional admission with a minimum composite score of 28 on the ACT and/or a minimum combined score of 1230 on the SAT I, a ranking in the upper 20 percent of one's class, and correlative high school grades; and conditional admission for those who do not meet the primary standard directs advisement for specific courses based on standardized test subscores and evidence of academic strength in a subject matter area. After earning a minimum of 15 hours, at MSU or elsewhere, any student with a 3.4 cumulative average has full privileges, including priority preregistration. Transfer students may apply honors credits earned elsewhere to UHP requirements.

Scholarship Availability: Fifty competitive $800 Honors Program Scholarships for 1995 entering freshmen were awarded to recipients with an average ACT composite of 30; University Freshman Academic Scholarships range from $3000 (minimum composite score of 24 on the ACT or minimum combined score of 1090 on the SAT I) to $11,000 (minimum ACT composite score of 32 or minimum combined SAT I score of 1390). National Merit awards may be added with an MSU award for another $17,000. Recipients of the Schillig Leadership Scholarships ($28,000) and Hearin-Hess ($20,000) engineering awards are named Honors Scholars without additional MSU funding other than National Merit awards. All of these awards carry a waiver of out-of-state tuition; Eminent Scholar awards from the Mississippi Legislature may add from $4000 to $10,000 for Mississippi residents. College and departmental scholarships may be added after the freshman year.

The Campus Context: Mississippi State University, established in Starkville, Mississippi, under the auspices of the Morrill Act in 1878, is a comprehensive Research I land-grant institution. Its students and alumni define the excellence of its achievements in learning, research, and service, notably in the selection of 11 Truman Scholars in the last thirteen years and through alumni such as noted author John Grisham, past-president of Dow Chemical Hunter Henry, former editor of the *New York Times* Turner Catledge, gourmet Craig Claiborne, professional baseball star Will Clark, and Von Graham, CEO of Arthur Andersen.

There are eleven colleges/schools: Accountancy, Agriculture and Home Economics, Arts and Sciences, Architecture, Business and Industry, Continuing Education, Education, Engineering, Forest Resources, Veterinary Medicine, and the Graduate School. In addition, the Mississippi Agricultural and Forestry Experiment Station with ten branches and the Mississippi Cooperative Extension Service are located at MSU.

Degree programs offered include eighty-three bachelor's, sixty-four master's, one education specialist, twenty-eight doctoral, and one professional, including 113 majors at the B.A./B.S. level.

The grounds of the University comprise approximately 4,200 acres, including the central campus that typifies the geographical beauty of the South, in part because of academic emphasis of landscape architecture and horticulture. Among more than fifty academic buildings, the notable structures around an open central quadrangle include Lee Hall, Montgomery Hall (National Register), Colvard Union, and McCool Hall, a gift of the founder of Holiday Inn Corporation to house the College of Business. McComas Hall houses the University Theater and the University Gallery.

Former residences house special units such the Templeton Collection, a nationally recognized museum of ragtime music and period instruments, and the Honors Program, in a 3,500-square-foot 1898 home converted to create a library, computer laboratory, a student lounge, a student council office, and well-appointed reception rooms widely utilized by the entire University community. Honors students have access to photocopiers, monitors with VCRs, and personal computers in the Burke Computer Laboratory.

The current University bulletin lists forty-four special units supporting teaching, research, and service. The University Honors Program heads an entry that includes Army and Air Force military programs, the Institute for the Humanities, the Division of Business Research, one of eighteen National Science Foundation Engineering Research Centers, the Research Center of the John C. Stennis Space Center, the Raspet Flight Research Laboratory, the Center for Robotics, Automation, and Artificial Intelligence, the *Mississippi Quarterly* literary journal, the Social Science Research Center, the State Chemical Laboratory, the Center for International Security and Strategic Studies directed by the former chief diplomat of Hungary, and the Cobb Institute of Archaeology, housed in a teaching, research, and museum facility that focuses on both Middle Eastern and Native American concerns.

Student Body Mississippi State University, frequently having the largest enrollment in the state, has a current enrollment of 12,693 students, including an undergraduate enrollment of 10,232. Fifty-nine percent are men while 41 percent are women. The ethnic distribution is 16 percent African American, .2 percent Native American, 1 percent Asian-American, .6 percent Hispanic, and 82 percent white. The 200 international students represent 2 percent of the student population. There are 8,392 in-state residents (82 percent of the student body) and 1,840 out-of-state and international residents (18 percent of students). Approximately 80 percent of undergraduate students receive some form of financial aid. Mississippi State University has eighteen national social fraternities and ten national sororities, which have approximately 17 percent of the student body as members. MSU also has 250 registered organizations. *The Reflector* (newspaper) and *The Reveille* (yearbook), as well as a student-operated radio station WMSV, unite service and experiential learning.

Faculty MSU has a full-time instructional faculty of 775. Eighty-nine percent are in the tenure-track professorial rank, 8 percent are at the rank of instructor, and 3 percent are at the rank of lecturer. Ninety-three percent hold terminal degrees appropriate to their disciplines. Only professorial-rank faculty members teach honors courses, having been selected by agreement of the department, the Honors Program administrator, and the Honors Council, which conducts a separate student evaluation of all honors classes.

The undergraduate student-faculty ratio is 26:1, an interesting ratio in relation to usual enrollments of 10 to 20 in honors courses.

Key Facilities The University Libraries house 1.3 million volumes and more than 7,387 periodical subscriptions, including the collections of Mitchell Memorial Library, the School of Architecture Library, and the College of Veterinary Medicine Library, all of which offer on-line computer access. Special collections and archives include extensive Mississippiana and contributions of such notables as U.S. Senator John C. Stennis, U.S. Representative G. V. Montgomery, and Turner Catledge, former editor of the *New York Times*. A new central library of 235,000 square feet was completed in 1995 at a cost of $14.6 million.

Computing access is a priority at Mississippi State University, as represented in both implementation and plans for full on-line access in all residence halls, as well as through major computing centers and laboratories available to undergraduate students in Butler Hall, McCain Engineering, Hilbun Hall, and Mitchell Library, as well as large multiuser UNIX systems in Allen Hall. Academic and research computing is facilitated by a large, rapidly expanding campus network that links dozens of mainframe computer systems and departmental servers with thousands of workstations.

Network access to remote branches of the University, as well as to the Internet, is provided through high-speed wide-area connections through the campus network. Dialup access is provided to faculty members, students, and staff via a large modem pool, a medium for registration by telephone. In addition to the campus network, the Computing Center provides general-purpose computing facilities in support of the academic and research missions of the University.

Among twenty on-campus residence halls, Hightower and Duggar are designated as freshman and upper-division co-residential facilities to accommodate men and women honors students.

Athletics Intramural sports utilize four basketball courts, three volleyball courts, a fitness machine circuit, an outdoor swimming pool, a fitness/jogging trail, and playing fields for softball and flag football. Other organized programs having facilities include racquetball, tennis, and soccer. Plans for a new indoor facility to include a swimming pool and various courts have been approved and funded for 1997 construction.

Intercollegiate efforts under the auspices of the 12-member Southeastern Conference include football, basketball, baseball, cross-country, track, tennis, and golf for men and basketball, volleyball, tennis, golf, cross-country, track, and soccer for women. Campus facilities include Scott Field (41,200-person capacity), the M Club (400-person capacity), a multipurpose coliseum (9,200-person capacity), four practice football fields, a six-court tennis complex, Noble (Baseball) Field (6,700-person capacity), an all-weather running track, a soccer field, and a physical fitness complex. MSU gained recent recognition by being one of the "Final Four" in the NCAA national basketball competition.

Study Abroad Study abroad is advocated as one the institutional priorities for undergraduate education and supported through academic exchanges with institutions in Italy, England, Holland, Germany, Spain, Quebec, Mexico, Costa Rica, Japan, and Korea. The Honors Program has a ten-year-old study-travel program concentrated in northern Italy, where MSU faculty and Italian counterparts teach courses in art history and photography. The School of Architecture has the most active program with semester study options in England, Holland, and Spain. A growing program is the International Business Program that conjoins business and language study culminating in an internship while living with a host family.

Support Services Mississippi State University has gained national recognition for its commitment to accommodation of physically disadvantaged or learning-disabled students. Virtually all major classroom and laboratory buildings are accessible, but priority registration and focused advising ensure students' full advantage of every University function.

The Office of Student Support Services provides numerous services for special needs students, including orientation and academic advising for new students, financial aid advising, arrangement of classroom accommodations, special services of notetakers and readers, and special equipment and resources such as adapted examinations. Academic support is designed for those with learning disabilities; access to appropriate housing is ensured. Extensive handicapped parking and widespread sidewalk access distinguish the institutional commitment to accommodation.

Job Opportunities Work opportunities transcend the level of being simply sources of income. Work-study and wages employment opportunities exist in all divisions. Particularly valuable is the Cooperative Education Program, which combines practical experience with formal education in a five-year program of alternating semesters. Co-op students earn competitive salaries as reflected in the $6 million earned by 800 MSU students who were employed by major businesses in 1995.

Tuition: $1996 for state residents, $4816 for nonresidents, per year (1996-97)

Room and Board: $3215

Mandatory Fees: $595

Contact: Director: Dr. Jack H. White, Post Office Drawer EH, Mississippi State, Mississippi 39762; Telephone: 601-325-2522; Fax: 601-325-0086; E-mail: jhw1@ra.msstate.edu; Web site: http://www.msstate.edu/index2.html

---

MISSISSIPPI VALLEY STATE UNIVERSITY

4 Pu G S Tr

▼ Honors Program

Mississippi Valley State University's Honors Program enhances the University's academic offerings and fosters an intellectual campus climate. Honors Program goals are to provide educational opportunities and support activities to a core group of students capable of moving at an accelerated pace, to promote enhanced educational opportunities to students capable of excelling in particular disciplines of study, and to promote all-campus events and activities aimed at developing and maintaining an inviting and invigorating intellectual and cultural atmosphere.

The Honors Program at MVSU challenges high-potential students to do their best in the company of their peers. Honors sections of core curriculum courses motivate freshman and sophomore honors students to get a good start in their college careers. Honors courses throughout the University program provide a motivating atmosphere through a student's senior year.

Students enrolled in the Honors Program are given special opportunities, including easy access to computers, special dormitory accommodations, and diverse travel opportunities.

The 10-year-old program enrolls 80 students.

Participation Requirements: To remain active in the Honors Program, students are required to enroll in a minimum of 12 credit hours each semester. Students should maintain a cumulative GPA of 3.0 or better.

Admission Process: Freshman applicants must achieve a minimum ACT composite score of 20 (or the SAT I equivalent) with no subscore below 16 and meet the general admission requirements of the University. Graduating high school seniors with an ACT composite score of 20 or above are extended an invitation to join the program upon their acceptance into the University. An information sheet and application form are enclosed in the letter, and students are required to complete the application form and write an essay. Once the information is in the Honors Program's office and evaluated/documented, a letter of acceptance is sent to admitted students. Sophomore/transfer students whose cumulative GPA is at least 3.2 and whose candidacy for admission into the program is supported by recommendations from two college teachers will be considered for admission.

Scholarship Availability: Scholarships that are offered are mainly academic or athletic in nature.

The Campus Context: MVSU offers a choice of twenty-seven degree programs.

Student Body Ninety-eight percent of students receive some form of financial aid. There are a total of eight fraternities and sororities on campus.

Faculty The student-faculty ratio is about 25:1. There are 199 faculty members, 10 part-time and 189 full-time; 47 percent have terminal degrees.

Key Facilities The library holds 200,000 volumes. Internet accessibility is available there. Other departments also offer computer availability.

Athletics Athletics for men and women are offered; the University is a member of the Southwestern Athletic Conference.

Support Services Disabled students will find the buildings on campus accessible.

Job Opportunities Work opportunities include work/study and work aid.

Tuition: $2278 for state residents, $4780 for nonresidents, per year (1996-97)

Room and Board: $2384

Contact: Director: Barbara J. P. Washington, 14000 Highway 82 West, Itta Bena, Mississippi 38941; Telephone: 601-254-3642; Fax: 601-254-6704/3542

MONMOUTH UNIVERSITY

4 Pr G M Sc Tr

▼ Honors Program

The goal of the Honors program at Monmouth University is to present a curriculum with courses that provide a unique learning experience. Group identity materializes among those participating. From the outset of the freshman experience, students see themselves as contributors to an especially dynamic community. A sense of freedom of expression develops inside the classroom and is often carried on outside of class.

Courses in the Freshman Honors Program are clustered together, with faculty members developing common themes and assignments, enhancing the opportunity for students to make connections and to see issues from different points of view. Every course in each cluster is limited to 20 students, fostering a classroom environment of diversity, discussion, and debate. Honors students annually produce a journal, *Crossroads*, whose purpose is not only to involve the students in the creative process of a journal, but also to help them gain professional experience publishing their honors theses and projects.

Faculty members are selected for their breadth of learning and multidisciplinary expertise and are distinguished contributors in their respective fields. Students in the honors community are encouraged to develop a special rapport with their professors. Such rapport is important not only in the classroom, but also during extracurricular activities scheduled to enhance the material and theme of the program. These activities include free trips to some of the great Broadway shows, visits to New York museums, a film series, three annual honors parties, and a series of guest lectures.

The Honors Program at Monmouth was established in 1979 and was reconceptualized ten years later, with the cornerstone of the program being the Freshman Honors Cluster. Enrollment in the Honors Program is currently about 350 students, including 130 new freshmen. The four-year program at Monmouth is growing steadily, having tripled in size over the last five years.

Participation Requirements: Beyond the freshman year, a student can take one or more honors courses or pursue the entire Honors Program. Students in the program must complete the requirements of their major and maintain a GPA of 3.2. In addition, to graduate from the program and have the diploma so noted, a student must successfully complete 19 credits (if English 151H is taken) or 22 credits (if the English 101H-102H sequence is taken) as follows: English 151H, Writing and Research (3 credits) or English 101H-102H, College English I & II (6 credits); at least one honors seminar from humanities, social sciences, mathematics/natural sciences, or business (3 credits); HO 498H, Senior Honors Thesis Proposal (2 credits) and HO 499H, Senior Honors Thesis (2 credits). Students in the Honors Program are advised by specially designated honors advisers and the department in which the student's major is housed.

Admission Process: Students eligible for the Honors Program are those who enter the University on academic scholarship or are admitted to the University with a high school rank in the top 20 percent and a total combined SAT I score of 1100 or better, have a cumulative GPA of at least 3.2 after taking 12 credits at Monmouth University, or transfer to Monmouth University with at least 30 credits in an acceptable program and a cumulative average of at least 3.2 in all previous college-level work.

Scholarship Availability: Many students in the program hold academic scholarships from the University. The Honors Program promotes the Truman, Rhodes, Carnegie, Mellon, and Roosevelt scholarships and fellowships. The program also awards monetary prizes for the best scholarly paper, best scholarly group project, best non-paper project, and for the highest GPA. Graduates of the Honors Program have their transcripts and diplomas duly noted.

The University utilizes institutional resources (academic grants and scholarship programs) and is a participant in all major state and federal aid programs.

The Campus Context: The 138-acre Monmouth University campus is located in a quiet, residential area 2 miles from the Jersey Shore and about 90 minutes from both New York City and Philadelphia. The campus includes among its fifty buildings a pleasant blending of old and contemporary architectural styles. Monmouth University is an independent, comprehensive institution of higher learning comprising six schools: the School of Humanities and Social Sciences; the School of Science, Technology and Engineering; the School of Education; the School of Business Administration; the Edward G. Schlaefer School; and the Graduate School.

Student Body The total number of undergraduates at Monmouth is 3,880 (3,147 full-time and 733 part-time); 42 percent are men and 58 percent are women. The ethnic distribution of undergraduates is .2 percent Native American, 1.5 percent Asian-American, 4.5 percent African American, 4 percent Hispanic/Latino, and 77 percent white. There were 62 (1.7 percent) international students registered in fall 1995. Approximately 55 percent of undergraduate students receive financial aid. Monmouth University has eight fraternities and six sororities. There are also a number of Honors Societies on campus.

Faculty There are 179 full-time faculty members at the University, 71 percent of whom hold terminal degrees. Full-time faculty members are supplemented by adjuncts. The average institutional class size is 23 (the honors classes have a maximum capacity of 20).

Key Facilities The Guggenheim Memorial Library has 248,000 volumes on the shelves and subscribes to 1,300 periodicals. Extensive back files of periodicals are maintained in bound form and on microfilm. The Library's automated resources include GOALS (Guggenheim On-Line Automated Library Services), a public access catalog, and a circulation and library management system (which may be reached from public terminals within the building and across Monmouth's campus). GOALS may also be accessed from off-campus with a modem-equipped personal computer. The Library recently created an Information Commons of twelve networked computers capable of accessing all campus computer resources and the Internet.

The academic programs are supported by state-of-the-art computer hardware, software, and facilities. The major components include five UNIX and nine Novell server systems connected by a sophisticated campus Ethernet network spanning twenty-three buildings and encompassing more than 750 workstations campus-wide. More than 320 workstations distributed among seventeen laboratories are specifically dedicated to student use. The University provides each student with a personal account for electronic mail, production tools such as word processing, spreadsheet, database, and presentation software, World Wide Web browsing tools, and electronic access to the Library's catalog. The University maintains campus network connections in the residential halls.

About 34 percent of the undergraduates live in the eleven residence halls; the University opened a new residence hall in fall 1996, and further building is planned.

Athletics Athletics constitute an integral part of a Monmouth University education. The NCAA Division I athletic program offers excellent opportunities for qualified athletes who wish to participate. Both the men's and women's programs compete on the Division I level, and are members of the Northeast Conference. The athletics program fields men's varsity teams in baseball, basketball, cross-country, football, golf, indoor track, soccer, tennis, and outdoor track and field. Women's varsity teams participate in basketball, cross-country, indoor track, lacrosse, soccer, softball, tennis, and outdoor track and field. Women's field hockey begins in fall 1997.

Study Abroad Monmouth is a member of the College Consortium for International Studies, through which most students enroll in programs located in Spain, Ireland, France, and England. Monmouth is also a member of the Partnership for Service-Learning, an organization that combines academic study and community service in several countries including England, Jamaica, and the Philippines.

Support Services The Office of Students with Disabilities serves those students who have special needs, whether they are the result of a permanent disability or a temporary condition. It provides information, guidance, and referrals in working with students and faculty members in supporting academic needs. It also assists in locating interpreters, notetakers, readers, and writers, as well as coordinating housing accommodations and arranging for special parking. All buildings on campus have wheelchair access.

Job Opportunities The Federal Work-Study Program provides on-campus and off-campus employment in a variety of settings to eligible students. Currently, the University provides employment for more than 300 students in the program. There are also a number of part-time, on-campus jobs during the school year. In general, students in this non-need-based employment program are limited to a maximum of 20 hours per week.

Tuition: $13,270 per year (1996-97)

Room and Board: $5808

Mandatory Fees: $530

Contact: Director: Dr. Brian T. Garvey, West Long Branch, New Jersey 07764-1898; Telephone: 908-571-3620; Fax: 908-263-5293; E-mail: garvey@mondec.monmouth.edu; Web site: http://www.monmouth.edu/monmouth/academic/honors.html

MONTCLAIR STATE UNIVERSITY

4 Pu G M Sc Tr

▼ Honors Program

Conceived in 1985 by faculty who relish the stimulation of working with exceptional students, the Honors Program at Montclair State University has produced graduates who succeed in every field of endeavor. Some of its alumni have gone on to study for doctorates at Temple, Yale, Boston, and New York Universities, while others have graduated from medical school. It is worth noting that as of fall 1996, every one of its students who has applied to law school has been admitted. Among program graduates who have not yet gone on to advanced study are members of major accounting firms, artists, writers, musicians, social workers, business executives, researchers, and master teachers.

Throughout the undergraduate experience, the Honors Program emphasizes interdisciplinary study. It is the University's belief that new insights and understandings are gained outside the artificial boundaries imposed by subject areas. This approach creates a climate that fosters creativity and original thinking, for faculty members and students alike. For those admitted into the Honors Program, the undergraduate experience offers an opportunity to work intensively with a distinguished member of the faculty on advanced curricular, extracurricular, and individual projects. It means greater opportunities for achievement, recognition, and leadership, not only during undergraduate studies but in the years to follow.

There are currently 175 students in the program.

Participation Requirements: During the freshman year, honors students take two year-long seminars: Great Books and Ideas and Twentieth Century Civilization. Great Books and Ideas focuses on seminal thinkers from Plato to Nietzsche as they reveal themselves through their own writings. Twentieth Century Civilization concentrates on profound ideas and issues of our own time; in this interdisciplinary course, students explore twentieth-century revolutions that range from the political to the artistic. In the sophomore year, honors studies may include a year's seminar on interdisciplinary science, a semester on the foundations of the creative process, or a seminar on social analysis. Juniors prepare for advanced work as they immerse themselves in courses centered on ways of knowing and modes of inquiry.

Honors students take 8 to 10 honors courses during their first three years. Most of them can be applied toward fulfillment of the University's general education requirement.

Students who complete the honors sequence and maintain at least a 3.2 GPA receive an honors certificate, which is conferred at a special ceremony.

Admission Process: To be eligible for the Honors Program, students must meet at least two of the following criteria: a rank in the top 10 percent of their high school class, a score of at least 600 on either the verbal or the math sections of the SAT I, a combined SAT I score of at least 1200, and an unusual ability in the creative arts, exceptional leadership, or other extraordinary accomplishment. Those who qualify for consideration will be asked to complete an application that includes a brief essay. In addition, some students may be interviewed by a member of the Honors Program advisory board as part of the admission process.

Scholarship Availability: There are currently about 170 students in the Montclair State University Honors Program and to varying degrees all of them are supported by scholarships, ranging from the full tuition and fee waivers offered to all of New Jersey's Bloustein Scholars; to endowed Honors Program awards of $1250, $100, and $750 per year; and finally to book scholarships of up to $250 per year awarded to all students enrolled in honors seminars.

The Campus Context: Established in 1908, Montclair State University is a state-assisted, coeducational, comprehensive public teaching university with a wide range of undergraduate and graduate programs and a commitment to excellence in instruction and research. MSU is located on a beautiful 200-acre campus in a leafy suburb in northern New Jersey, 12 miles west of midtown Manhattan. The University offers forty-three undergraduate degree programs.

Student Body There are a total of 9,600 undergraduates, 6,702 are full-time. Sixty-two percent are women, 38 percent men. The ethnic distribution is 65.5 percent white, 14.3 percent Hispanic, 10.8 percent African American, 4.7 percent Asian/Pacific Islander, and .3 percent Native American. Seventy percent of the students are commuters, 30 percent are residents. Seventy-two percent of students receive financial aid. There are forty-one fraternities and sororities.

Faculty Of the 444 full-time faculty members, 84 percent hold terminal degrees. Including the supplementary adjunct faculty, the student-faculty ratio is 15:1.

Key Facilities The library houses 418,547 books, 3,800 periodical subscriptions, and more than 1 million nonprint items. The University has extensive and growing computer facilities, including computer laboratories, computer classrooms, and a campuswide microcomputer network. All students are provided the opportunity to maintain a user account on the central system.

Athletics The athletic program features a full range of intercollegiate sports for men and women, and a major athletic facilities program has been launched, with the completed construction of a new fieldhouse and baseball stadium. MSU's athletic program is in the New Jersey Athletic Conference, in NCAA Division III.

Study Abroad There is an active and comprehensive international study program; many students in the Honors Program have taken a semester abroad, and several have participated in the Oxford University International Summer School. Full transfer credit is available for approved study-abroad programs.

Job Opportunities Student assistantships and work-study opportunities exist widely, and there are active internships and cooperative education programs available to most majors.

Tuition: $2580 for state residents, $3930 for nonresidents, per year (1996-97)

Room and Board: $5334

Mandatory Fees: $674

Contact: Director: Dr. Tom Benediktsson, Upper Montclair, New Jersey 07043; Telephone: 201-655-7374; E-mail: benediktsson@saturn.montclair.edu

MONTGOMERY COLLEGE

| 2 Pu C M Sc Tr |

▼ Honors Program

The Honors Program at Montgomery College consists of several different categories of courses and tutorials designed to provide high-ability students with a stimulating course of study and a congenial academic environment. Class sizes are small, and the students work closely with faculty members. Interdisciplinary topics and independent study opportunities are available.

There are four kinds of honors offerings: regular honors courses printed in the College catalog with an HP prefix, honor modules or sections of existing courses with an II suffix, honors thread courses (EIP 101–104), and honors tutorials and seminars (HP 251, IIP 258, EIP 260, EIP 261, HP 266). Offerings are listed in the schedule of classes each semester. Honors Program courses are listed for each campus. The selection of courses varies from semester to semester and from campus to campus

Three different awards are presented by the Honors Committee each spring semester. The Honors Achievement Certificate is given to all honors students who complete 2 honors courses and who have a 3.4 GPA. The Honors Scholar Program Award is granted to all students who complete this structured program. The most prestigious award is the Outstanding Honors Student of the Year Award.

The program is more than 30 years old and currently enrolls 273 students.

Admission Process: Students who have completed at least 12 credits at Montgomery College and who have a 3.2 GPA are eligible to enroll in honors courses, Montgomery College students (especially first-semester students) who do not meet these requirements, or high school students in the Early Placement Program, may also apply for special permission to enroll in honors courses.

Scholarship Availability: The Montgomery College Foundation supports honors scholarships every year that range from $50 to $175. Application forms are available in late November from the Campus Honor Coordinators. In December, the College-wide Honor Committee reviews the applications and awards ten or more scholarships.

The Campus Context: Established in 1946, Montgomery College is an accredited, public two-year college with campuses at Takoma Park, Rockville, and Germantown, Maryland. Montgomery College is the oldest and largest community college in Maryland. The College offers an excellent array of career and technical education programs and more than 900 academic credit courses. Offerings include forty-six associate degree programs, thirty one-year certificate programs, as well as a variety of transfer programs for students ultimately seeking a baccalaureate degree. In addition, more than 100 career and enrichment programs are offered through Continuing Education.

Student Body There are approximately 22,940 credit students and 20,000 noncredit students. About 3,890 students attend the Germantown Campus. Of the total student body, 90.7 percent live in Montgomery County, 4.5 percent live in other Maryland counties, and 4 percent live out-of-state.

Tuition: $660 for area residents, $1710 for state residents, $2010 for nonresidents, per year (1996-97)

Mandatory Fees: $144

Contact: Director: David B. Kieffer, Germantown Campus, Observation Drive, Germantown, Maryland 20876; Telephone: 301-353-7791; Fax: 301-353-7719; E-mail: dkieffer@umd5.umd.edu

MOREHOUSE COLLEGE

4 Pr C D M Sc Tr

▼ **Honors Program**

Morehouse College offers a four-year, comprehensive Honors Program providing special learning opportunities for students of superior intellectual ability, high motivation and broad interests. Faculty members in the program nurture the student throughout his college life, in the areas of scholarly inquiry, independent and creative thinking, and exemplary scholarship. Honors Program students take special sections of regular Morehouse courses, taught by honors faculty members who are chosen on the basis of their reputations as outstanding teachers. Course enrollment is limited to 20 students. The program is open to all students in all academic disciplines.

The Honors Program Club, one of the College's chartered student groups, elects its officers and sponsors activities for HPC members and for the College community. Morehouse is actively involved in the state, regional, and national Honors organizations; Georgia State Honors Council affords students a chance to try out their leadership skills and to be elected to offices.

The Honors Program at Morehouse College was established in 1981 and restructured in 1987. It currently enrolls 210 students, 88 of whom are freshmen.

Participation Requirements: Students in lower-division honors (freshmen and sophomores) are enrolled in special sections of English, foreign languages, world history, mathematics, philosophy, political science, and sociology. Other freshman and sophomore courses are chosen by the student and are taken with members of the student body in the regular program. On the basis of his status as an Honors Program freshman and sophomore, a student is expected to earn honors on the departmental level as a junior and senior. In upper-division honors there are no Honors Program courses; rather, the student completes special course-related assignments, makes presentations, participates in seminars, and focuses on departmental research.

The honors senior thesis is a staple of honors programs across the country. Currently under study at Morehouse, the senior thesis (or project) component of the HP degree will provide excellent preparation for students desiring to do graduate or professional study or to enter high-level jobs upon graduation. Also being considered is a community service component that will enable talented, concerned students in the HP to help persons in Atlanta neighborhoods and to receive recognition for this kind of work.

Honors Program students must maintain a GPA of at least 3.0 during the freshman and sophomore years. The minimum for juniors and seniors is 3.25. Any student falling below the minimum has the next semester to raise his GPA and to resume his good standing in the program. If he does not attain the minimum, he will be dropped from the program. Students below the minimum 3.0 will have until May to improve their GPAs. No first-semester freshman below 2.7 is dropped from the program or put on probation unless he falls so low that he cannot reach the minimum cumulative GPA by May.

Admission Process: Admission to the Honors Program is based on SAT I scores and high school GPA. Second-semester freshmen and first-semester sophomores may apply to the program if they are not admitted as incoming freshmen, but the most desirable time to join is at the start of the freshman year. Generally, students with combined SAT I scores of at least 1100 or an ACT composite of 26 or above are eligible for the program. The deadline for applying to the program is April 18.

Scholarship Availability: The Morehouse Honors Program does not award scholarships to its students. More than 90 percent of HP students receive full or partial awards from the College's scholarship pool. Morehouse College Honors Program students have been recipients of the following national competitive scholarships: The Rhodes Scholarship

(1994), Marshall Scholarships (1994 and 1996), and the UNCF Mellon Scholarship (1991, 1994, and 1996).

The Campus Context:
Morehouse College offers three degree programs and is a men's school with a population of 2,926.

Student Body Eighty-five to 90 percent of students are African-American students. There are 91 international students. Approximately 55 percent of the students are residents, 45 percent commuters. Eighty percent of students receive financial aid.

Faculty Of the 231 faculty members, 167 are full-time and 70 percent hold terminal degrees. The student-faculty ratio is 16.7:1.

Key Facilities The library houses approximately 1.5 million volumes. Seven computer facilities on campus are located in the Academic Computing Center, Electronic Classroom, Mathematics Lab, Writing Skills Lab, Computer Science Labs, Biology Lab, and Business Department Lab. There are five fraternities.

Athletics The intercollegiate athletics program is recognized by the College as a valuable asset in developing campus spirit. Morehouse College athletic teams are known as the Maroon Tigers. College colors are maroon and white. Teams compete with those of similar-sized institutions in football, basketball, tennis, and track and field sports. Morehouse College is a member of the Southern Intercollegiate Athletic Conference (SIAC) composed of sixteen colleges and universities in five states, and the National Collegiate Athletic Association (NCAA), Division II. This affiliation permits all Morehouse College athletes to receive regional and national recognition for their accomplishments. The intercollegiate athletic program is under the direction of the Director of Athletics.

A member of an athletic team must maintain good academic and social standing and may not represent the College if he is on athletic, academic, or disciplinary probation. All students who meet association eligibility regulations may become candidates for athletic teams.

Study Abroad Study-abroad programs are available in every discipline, including the business programs of the renowned London School of Economics. There are also two Morehouse-based programs: the Summer Program in Oaxaca, Mexico, which has attracted Morehouse participants since the early 1980s, and the Summer Program for French students on the island of Martinique. Both programs begin immediately after final examinations and last four weeks. Each offers 6 hours of credit with optional internships. To facilitate study abroad, certain financial aid scholarships are available to students, including the Merrill Scholarship. All students who wish to study abroad for a semester or a year and receive Morehouse credit must submit appropriate applications to the Director of Study Abroad and International Exchanges.

Support Services International students who are admitted to Morehouse College are provided with various services at the Center for International Studies. These include nonacademic advising, immigration matters, host-family opportunities, and other services that help make their experience at Morehouse successful.

Job Opportunities Students can find employment through the work-study program, as well as mentoring and assignments/internships in scientific and computer laboratories.

Tuition: $7700 per year (1996-97)

Room and Board: $5976

Mandatory Fees: $1554 per year (full-time), $777 per semester (part-time)

Contact: Director: Jocelyn W. Jackson, 830 Westview Drive, SW, P.O. Box 140141, Atlanta, Georgia 30314; Telephone: 404-215-2679; Fax: 404-215-2679

MORGAN STATE UNIVERSITY

4 Pu G L Sc

▼ Honors Program

The Morgan State University Honors Program operates within the framework of the undergraduate General Education Program. Depending upon the major selected, there are extensions of the program in many academic departments. Course curricula of General Education, Honors Sections, and activities for the upper division and departmental majors provide additional experiences designed to stimulate learning, analyses, and productions.

Historically, Morgan has been among the top five universities producing African-American students who go on to earn doctoral and other terminal degrees. Of the honors program students that recently graduated, many are enrolled at Harvard, the University of Maryland at Baltimore, Massachusetts Institute of Technology, the University of Maryland College Park, Johns Hopkins University, Ohio State University, Rensselaer Polytechnic Institute, Cambridge University (England), the University of Baltimore, the University of North Carolina, Chapel Hill, Morgan State University, and in a growing number of other graduate and professional school programs.

Honors Program students are encouraged to seek business, science, industrial, and governmental internships, work-study, and other co-operative learning experiences. Academic departments, the University's career planning and placement office, and the honors program office work together to assist students to maximize opportunities for their growth and development.

Freshman honor students living on campus are strongly encouraged to select the honors dorms. Honors residence halls are among the featured units of the University's Residence Life Department. Harper-Tubman Houses (women) and Cummings House (men), recently renovated units, provide individual climate-controlled rooms that are fiber-optic-facilitated for computer and cable television use. These halls also house study rooms and computer laboratories.

The CBHP students are integral parts of the University community. They sharpen leadership skills in all clubs and organizations. Some participate in student government and on University athletic teams as well as University academic teams. CBHP students play in the marching band, sing in the University choir, act in plays, and dance in staged performances. They even engage in the occasional game of chess, "E" games, billiards, bid whist, or pinochle. Morgan State University Honors Program students are ordinary people who enjoy the challenge and exhilaration of achieving at extraordinary levels.

The 10-year-old program currently enrolls approximately 733 students.

Admission Process:
Each year approximately 200 students enter the University as first-time, full-time freshmen in the Honors Program. Many are recruited through the University's admissions office. Others apply as the result of their knowledge of the University or the Honors Program. Each year, between 700 and 800 students are enrolled in the curriculum-based honors program. Between 60 and 70 percent of the students are Maryland residents. The other students in the honors program represent thirty-four states; Washington, D.C.; and five other countries.

Admissions categories have the following requirements: to be an Honors Associate, state residents must have a 3.0 cumulative GPA and a minimum combined score of 1000 on the SAT I, out-of-state residents must have a 3.0 GPA and a minimum combined score of 1100 on the SAT I; to be a Regents Scholar, state residents must have a 3.2 cumulative GPA and a minimum combined score of 1100 on the SAT I and out-of-state residents must have a 3.2 GPA and a minimum combined score of 1200 on the SAT I.

Scholarship Availability:
CBHP Associates are eligible to receive scholarships for tuition and fees. Regents Scholars are eligible to receive scholarships that may include tuition, fees, room, board, books, and/or incentives. Other incentives may be available, depending upon GPA level and SAT/ACT scores earned.

A small number of incentives awards are made available each year to students who do not have the combination of credentials required for the Curriculum-Based Honors Program but do have strong credentials or unusual talents and skills. All scholarships and academic achievement awards require the maintenance of a cumulative 3.0 GPA and 12 credits per semester.

Scholarship award notifications are formally made on or near March 30, for the next fall semester. Earlier awards are given. Applications are received, reviewed, and responded to on a rolling basis.

Maintenance of Honors Program scholarships requires a minimum 3.0 cumulative GPA and the successful completion of 30 credit hours each year, during the four-year (eight-semester funding period). A ninth semester of funding is possible but very competitive and is based on considerations of critical need. Leaves-of-absence from the traditional funding period must be supported with documentation before the leave is taken. Internships are strongly encouraged.

Among particular awards available to students are Regents Scholars awards (providing tuition, fees, room, board, and books), Honor Associates awards (providing tuition and fees), and National Merit and Distinguished Scholar awards, which may carry incentives and additional designations as Thurgood Marshall Scholars.

The Campus Context: Morgan State University is composed of the following colleges and schools: the College of Arts and Sciences, the Earl Graves School of Business and Management, the School of Education and Urban Studies, the School of Engineering, and the School of Graduate Studies. The University offers fifty-nine degree-granting programs. Eighty percent of the campus has been renovated or constructed within the last ten years.

Student Body Undergraduate enrollment is 41 percent men and 59 percent women. The ethnic distribution is 94 percent African American, 1 percent Asian, 2 percent foreign, 1 percent Hispanic, 1 percent Native American, 2 percent European American, and 1 percent other. There are 104 international students. Thirty-two percent of students are residents, while 68 percent commute. Seventy-five percent of students receive financial aid. There are nine fraternities and sororities recognized by the Pan-Hellenic Council and another ten fraternities and sororities of the Council of Independent Organizations.

Faculty Of the 425 faculty members, 237 are permanent, 75 are full-time contractual, and 113 are part-time. Eighty-one percent hold terminal degrees. The student-faculty ratio is 15:1.

Key Facilities The library houses 350,000 volumes. Computer facilities include six major computer labs and a supercomputer.

Athletics Morgan provides an extensive NCAA Division I intercollegiate athletic program that includes football, men's and women's basketball, track and field, cross-country, and tennis and women's volleyball, softball, and bowling. The University is a member of the Mid-Eastern Athletic Conference, the Eastern Collegiate Athletic Conference, the National Collegiate Athletic Association, and the Inter-collegiate Association of Amateur Athletes of America. Athletic grants-in-aid are offered to qualified participants.

Support Services All student facilities that have been renovated or constructed since 1986 are handicapped-accessible and account for 80 percent of all facilities.

Job Opportunities Work-study and part-time employment are available to students on campus.

Tuition: $3412 for state residents, $7992 for nonresidents, per year (1997-98)

Room and Board: $5090

Contact: Director: Stanley T. Rich, Jenkins Building #105, 1700 Cold Spring Lane, Baltimore, Maryland 21251; Telephone: 410-319-3429; Fax: 410-319-3788; E-mail: honors@moac.morgan.edu; Web site: http://www.morgan.edu

MORRIS COLLEGE

4 Pr G S Sc

▼ Honors Program

The Morris College Honors Program provides an environment conducive to intellectual stimulation and growth through honors courses, seminars, and cocurricular experiences. Consistent with the institution's goal of promoting the intellectual and personal growth of all students, the Honors Program is designed to challenge, promote critical thinking, and to meet the needs of scholars who are academically well-prepared, intellectually gifted, and highly motivated. The Collegewide Honors Program, established in 1983, is open to students of all majors.

There are currently 30 students enrolled in the program.

Participation Requirements: During the freshman and sophomore years, students enroll in honors sections of the core curriculum for a total of at least 12 hours. Juniors and seniors must enroll in honors seminars for a total of 8 hours. A senior thesis is required. Students are admitted to the program during the second semester of their freshman year. A formal induction ceremony is held during the Academic Honors Day Convocation.

Students who are enrolled in the Honors Program automatically become RARE Scholars (Reinforcers, Achievers, and Representatives of Excellence), the official honors student organization. RARE scholars are committed to enhancing the intellectual environment through strong leadership, superior academic achievement, and other qualities portrayed by the exemplary Morris College student. RARE sponsors forums, debates, the Adopt-A-Freshman Program, and social activities. RARE scholars are active participants in the National Association of African American Honors Programs (NAAAHP) and the Southern Regional Honors Council (SRHS). Prior to graduation, a formal ceremony is held for honors graduates and their parents. Honors graduates wear honors stoles and medallions during Commencement.

Admission Process: Second-semester freshmen with 3.4 GPAs are invited to complete applications for admission to the program. References from two professors are required. An interview is conducted by honors students who make their recommendations to the Director.

Scholarship Availability: Morris College offers a number of Presidential, endowed, and United Negro College Fund scholarships. Ninety percent of students receiving these scholarships are in the Honors Program.

The Campus Context: Morris College, located in Sumter, South Carolina, was founded in 1908 by the Baptist Educational and Missionary Convention of South Carolina. In 1978, Morris College achieved the goal of accreditation by the Commission of the Southern Association of Colleges and Schools. On January 1, 1982, the College became the 42nd member of the United Negro College Fund, the nation's largest and most successful African American fundraiser. The College has embarked upon a new era of American higher education that has enabled it to render even better service to its students and to the community. The College offers twenty undergraduate majors and B.A., B.S., and B.F.A. degrees.

Student Body Undergraduate enrollment is 912 students: 65 percent women and 35 percent men. Ninety-four percent of students receive financial aid. The campus has eight fraternities and sororities.

Faculty There are 48 full-time faculty members; 60 percent have doctorates. There are also 17 adjunct faculty members. The student-faculty ratio is 16:1.

Key Facilities The library houses 95,819 volumes. There are four network computer facilities.

Athletics Athletics include intercollegiate basketball and cross-country for women and men. There are women's softball and men's baseball teams.

Job Opportunities Students are employed as tutors in the Student Support Services Program and in other programs, including work-study.

Tuition: $4990 per year (1996-97)

Room and Board: $2691

Mandatory Fees: $115

Contact: Director: Dr. Liz Bell, 100 West College Street, Sumter, South Carolina 29150; Telephone: 803-775-9371; Fax: 803-773-3687

MOUNT WACHUSETT COMMUNITY COLLEGE

2 Pu G S Sc Tr

▼ Honors Program

The Honors Program at Mount Wachusett Community College provides an intellectually challenging academic experience, emphasizing stimulating courses, a high degree of student-faculty interaction, and an interdisciplinary perspective. Consequently, students who have demonstrated substantial potential in prior high school or college-level study are exposed to a highly individualized experience. As a result of the program, honors graduates will be better prepared to continue their advanced studies at colleges and universities throughout the country and to bring their academic talents to the attention of future employers.

The College's Honors Program is seven years old, and has an enrollment of about 40 students, graduating 15 to 16 students per year.

Participation Requirements: Participation in the program requires a 3.3 GPA. Honors students whose GPA drops below the required 3.3 will be allowed on probationary semester to continue the program and raise their cumulative average. All honors students are required to participate in certain classes, including two English, a math, and a lab science, as well as two honors courses. These may be component courses based upon courses already required by a student's degree program or specially designed honors courses. A component course is any course already required by a student's degree program that has been deemed suitable as an honors component by the respective division. A component course is designed to require such additional activities as independent research, one-on-one tutorials, and/or a special project. Any particular component course is the result of a written agreement between a faculty member and a student that receives approval by the respective Division Dean. An Honors Colloquium is also required. Interdisciplinary in nature, past titles of these classes have been Gender Issues in American Society, Literature and Culture, Perspectives on Leadership, and Critical Thinking.

Students completing the Honors Program receive special recognition at graduation, and the program is designated on their official transcripts.

Scholarship Availability: Mount Wachusett Community College provides a tuition waiver to all honors students during their final semester, when they are completing both their honors and degree requirements with a minimum 3.3 average.

The Campus Context: Founded in 1963, Mount Wachusett Community College is located on a scenic 274-acre campus in north-central Massachusetts and is one of fifteen state-supported community colleges in Massachusetts. It has an enrollment of 1,800 students plus 1,400 in continuing education. There are twenty-five degree programs and sixteen certificate programs.

Student Body Sixty-four percent of enrollees are women, and 9 percent of the students belong to ethnic minority groups. Eight international students attend. All students commute, and 60 percent receive financial aid. Phi Theta Kappa and Alpha Beta Gamma are the two honor societies on campus.

Faculty There are 69 full-time faculty members supported by a large number of adjunct faculty members. Ten percent of full-time faculty members have doctoral degrees, and 87 percent have master's degrees.

Key Facilities The library contains 55,000 volumes and twelve IBM-compatible computers. The Apple Orchard contains twenty-three Macintosh computers, and there are an additional 140 IBM-compatible computers in computer labs.

Athletics The College does not have an intercollegiate sports program, but there is a fitness and wellness center located in a large athletic facility that is open to the community as well as the campus.

Study Abroad There is an International Education Committee that has initiated overseas excursions for college credit.

Support Services All facilities are fully wheelchair-accessible, and there is a disabilities counselor.

Job Opportunities The work-study program is available to all students.

Tuition: $3060 for state residents, $7860 for nonresidents, per year (1996-97)

Mandatory Fees: $100

Contact: Coordinator: Dr. Thomas Malloy, 444 Green Street, Gardner, Massachusetts 01440-1000; Telephone: 508-632-6600; Fax: 508-630-3211; Web site: http://www.mwcc.mass.edu

MURRAY STATE UNIVERSITY

4 Pu G M Sc Tr

▼ Honors Program

The Murray State University Honors Program is designed to enrich the educational experience of highly motivated students by increasing the opportunity for interacting with outstanding research faculty members, both in small class settings such as honors seminars and in ongoing research experiences.

The Honors Program seminars are courses specially designed to meet the needs of the most able students. Instruction takes various forms, but interactive learning is stressed. The honors seminars are distributed among the social sciences, fine arts, humanities, literature, natural sciences, and international affairs. Students typically enroll in one of these seminars throughout their college experience or until the honors sequence is completed.

There are approximately 180 to 200 students in the Honors Program out of a campus population of approximately 8,100 students.

Participation Requirements: Honors students may be enrolled in any undergraduate curriculum. To remain in good standing in the Honors Program, a student must maintain a GPA 3.2 (on a 4.0 scale). A student who successfully completes all the requirements of the Honors Program (course sequence, language and mathematics competencies, travel abroad, senior thesis) is awarded the honors medallion, which is worn at Commencement. The honors diploma is also awarded at graduation and a citation on the academic transcript indicates successful matriculation in the Honors Program.

Admission Process: The program accepts entering first-year students who are National Merit Semifinalists or have a composite ACT score of 26 or above and rank in the top 10 percent of their high school class.

Scholarship Availability: Twelve Presidential Scholarships are awarded annually to entering freshmen who generally have a composite ACT score of 28 or above and rank in the top 7 percent of their high school class. The award covers in-state tuition, fifteen meals per week, and a semiprivate dormitory room. Fifty University Scholarships are offered each year, which cover in-state tuition fees. Numerous departmental scholarships are also available.

Peterson's Honors Programs

The Campus Context: Murray State University was founded in 1922 and is located in the Jackson Purchase lake area of western Kentucky. The University's 232-acre main campus is in Murray, a city of 17,000, which has been highlighted as Kentucky's safest college town. The University is composed of six colleges: Business and Public Affairs, Education, Fine Arts and Communication, Humanistic Studies, Industry and Technology, and Science. Eighty-five undergraduate majors are offered, leading to a Bachelor of Arts or Bachelor of Science degree.

Murray State is the home of the National Boy Scout Museum with its fine collection of Norman Rockwell prints. It also houses a Center of Excellence for Reservoir Research and the Mid America Remote Sensing Center, which studies satellite-generated data for resource management. Murray State has consistently been ranked among the top 25 percent of southern regional and liberal arts colleges in *U.S. News & World Report's* annual issue of "America's Best Colleges".

Student Body About 8,100 undergraduates and graduates are enrolled, the majority from the mid-central states of Kentucky, Illinois, Tennessee, Indiana, and Missouri. The campus has nine fraternities and six sororities.

Faculty There are 350 full-time teaching faculty members; 80 percent hold doctoral or terminal degrees. The student-faculty ratio is 22:1.

Key Facilities The University libraries contain approximately 850,000 resource materials, including 460,000 bound volumes, and subscribe to approximately 3,000 periodical and serial titles annually. Computer labs and terminals are located in each of the college's buildings and libraries as well as in the residential hall areas.

Athletics Murray State is a charter member of the Ohio Valley Conference and is a Division I member of the National Collegiate Athletic Association. There are eight men's and seven women's sports. Riflery is sponsored as a coeducational sport. Sponsored sports for men include football, basketball, baseball, golf, cross-country, tennis, indoor track, riflery, and outdoor track and field. Competition is available for women in cross-country, tennis, basketball, riflery, softball, and indoor and outdoor track and field. The Murray State rifle team has won three national championships, and one of its members won a gold medal at the 1984 Olympic Games.

Study Abroad The mission of Murray State University includes as a priority the commitment to international education in order to prepare students to function in an increasingly interdependent world. Murray State is the headquarters for the Kentucky Institute for International Studies, offering programs during the academic year and each summer in Austria, Spain, France, Germany, Italy, Mexico, and Ecuador. It is a member of the Cooperative Center for Studies in Britain, offering programs in the English-speaking countries of the British Commonwealth.

Support Services The Services for Students with Disabilities Program is located in the Learning Center. Services include securing textbooks on cassette tapes, test proctoring, tutorial assistance, guidance, and counseling.

Job Opportunities The University offers a wide variety of financial aid programs. The Financial Aid Office handles all requests for student employment.

Tuition: $1354 for state residents, $3274 for nonresidents, per year (1996-97)

Room and Board: $2340

Contact: Director: Mark Malinauskas, P.O. Box 9, 310 N Applied Science, Murray, Kentucky 42071; Tel: 502-762-3166; Fax: 502-762-3405; E-mail: mjmalin@msumusik.mursuky.edu

---

NASSAU COMMUNITY COLLEGE

2 Pu G M Sc Tr

▼ Honors Program

Nassau's rigorous Honors Program, now in its fifteenth year, has about 250 students in the program. Students at the College who have GPAs of 3.4 or better are also invited to take some honors classes if seats are available, bringing the number of students taking honors to about 500. The program appeals to the many talented and highly motivated students who want to develop their potential more fully as they study for the associate degree. The transfer-oriented curriculum features at its core enriched work in English, history, calculus, foreign language, philosophy, computers, and the humanities and social sciences.

More than fifty sections of challenging honors classes are offered each term in addition to two special seminars of an interdisciplinary and/or multicultural nature. This umbrella program accommodates all majors at the College and enhances transferability. All students in the program are personally advised by the Coordinator of the Program who also writes all their letters of recommendation. In addition to the excellent honors faculty, consisting of almost all award-winning instructors for Excellence in Teaching, honors classes, because of their small size (no more than 22 students per class), allow for a great deal of personal interaction and discussion.

Over the years, as the program has continually grown and expanded, participants have the opportunity to supplement their academic work with honors-sponsored extracurricular activities such as the Adopt-A-Class Program, the Writing Literacy Project, the Selected Scholars Program, and the Honors Club and Journal, which provide creative outlets.

Another special feature of Nassau's Honors Program is its Honors Connection Program, an outreach vehicle to the high schools. The Connection Program provides a unique opportunity to highly motivated high school juniors and seniors to take college courses for credit on campus.

There are currently 471 students enrolled in the program.

Participation Requirements: To maintain membership in the program, students must keep up a 3.3 GPA each semester. The average GPA of each graduating class has been 3.6 or above. Students usually graduate with a minimum of 35 to 55 honors credits out of the mandatory 64 to 66 credits necessary for a degree. An H designation is noted on the transcript next to each honors course taken.

Admission Process: Freshmen are selected for the program based on their high school transcripts, which must reflect a 90 average in English, social studies, math, and science. Students already in attendance at Nassau can enter the program after their first semester if they have achieved a GPA of 3.5 or better and have been recommended by an instructor.

Scholarship Availability: For two graduating Honors Program participants, a scholarship, based on academic abilities and service to the program and community, is available. A special Honors and Awards Ceremony to honor graduates is held each May. At this time all honors graduates receive special certificates and the winners of the two Honors Program Scholarships are announced.

The Campus Context: Nassau is the largest of SUNY's thirty community colleges and enjoys a nationwide reputation for academic excellence and ease of transferability to four-year schools. Located in the heart of Nassau County, Garden City, the 225-acre campus is approximately 20 miles from New York City. The Commission on Higher Education of the Middle States Association of Colleges and Schools describes Nassau's faculty as "perhaps without rival across the community colleges of the nation." Nassau offers three degree programs: the A.A. in liberal arts; the A.S. in liberal arts and sciences, business and accounting, nursing, computers, and allied health science programs; and an A.A.S. degree in twenty-seven different areas. Also, Nassau offers fourteen different certificate programs.

Over the years the campus has expanded physically. In 1978, two new academic wings, a modern library, a physical education complex, and an administrative tower were added to the existing classroom and administrative buildings. To meet current demands, a third academic wing, including a new student center, theater, and art facilities, has been built.

Student Body Since Nassau opened its doors in 1960, its enrollment has increased from 632 to the current figure of 22,500. It still maintains an attractive student-faculty ratio of 21:1. Of the 22,500 students, approximately 55 percent are women and 45 percent are men. More than a quarter of the student population is over the age of 25. All students commute to campus. Nassau does not have a formal fraternity/sorority system. It does, however, have a full range of clubs and organizations.

Faculty There are more than 600 full-time faculty members, the majority of whom have doctorates or terminal degrees in their fields.

Key Facilities The library houses approximately 180,000 volumes. College facilities include a general-purpose facility that is available to all members of the academic community and a state-of-the-art Academic Computer Center in the library. In addition, there are a variety of learning or help centers to assist students in all curricula available.

Athletics Nassau has men's and women's teams in every sport. Expert coaching in some of the finest indoor and outdoor athletic facilities has made the men's and women's varsity teams dominant forces in the National Junior College Athletic Association. Individual athletes have gone on to prominence at senior colleges and universities, as well as in professional sports as coaches and physical education teachers.

Support Services A full range of services is available for disabled students, including full access to all classroom buildings, bus service, special counselors, and tutors.

Tuition: $1130 per semester (full-time) or $84 per credit (part-time) (1997-98)

Mandatory Fees: $25

Contact: Coordinator: Professor Carol Farber, 1 Education Drive, Garden City, New York 11530; Telephone: 516-572-7194

NEUMANN COLLEGE

4 Pr C S Sc Tr

▼ Honors Program

Founded in 1989, the Honors Program is two-tiered, including a Freshman Honors and a College Honors Program. There are 30 students currently enrolled in the program.

Freshman Honors consists of two 6-credit multidisciplinary seminars that are team-taught, one in the fall and the other in the spring semester. The seminars incorporate aspects from the disciplines of philosophy, history, political science, psychology, literature, and communication arts. In addition, there is an emphasis on the integration of computer skills during both seminars. College Honors consists of a series of three multidisciplinary seminars that are offered to sophomore, junior, and senior students. The seminar topics are selected primarily through student input.

The focus of the Honors Program is on innovative, experimental methodologies that seek new ways to develop critical thinking and communication skills. All honors seminars are discussion-oriented with small group work and in-class exercises devoted to critical thinking skill development. There are no lectures and no essay examinations, but rather students are evaluated on the development of strong oral and written communication and critical-thinking skills. The Director of Honors is also the adviser to honors students during their first year.

Participation Requirements: Completion of the College Honors Program requires an overall GPA of 3.6 or above in 9 credits of honors seminars. Those who successfully complete the program are awarded a certificate of completion at the Honors Convocation.

Admission Process: Freshman Honors usually consists of 15 students selected for their academic, extracurricular, and leadership achievements in high school; candidates must also be interviewed by the Director of Honors. While SAT I scores and class rank are considered, emphasis is given to those students who have demonstrated a potential for leadership and academic excellence. Entrance into College Honors requires an overall GPA of 3.4 or above and an interview with the Director of Honors. College honors seminars are limited to 15 students.

Scholarship Availability: Neumann College offers scholarships to students based on merit. All Honors students are on scholarship.

The Campus Context: Founded by the Sisters of St. Francis of Philadelphia, Neumann College is a small suburban campus in Delaware County, Pennsylvania, near Philadelphia and Wilmington. With a curriculum that balances the liberal arts and the professions, it now serves not only the community of the Delaware Valley but also a more diverse demographic population. Neumann offers the Bachelor of Arts degree, Bachelor of Science degree, and Liberal Studies degree.

Student Body Undergraduate enrollment is 1,040; 231 (22 percent) are men and 809 (78 percent) are women. While 901 students are white, diversity comes from the 3 American Indian/Alaskan, 18 Asian/Pacific Islander, 74 African American, and 13 Hispanic students. Fifteen percent of students are residents while 85 percent commute. Eighty-nine percent of students receive financial aid. There are no fraternities or sororities.

Faculty Of the 140 faculty members, 51 are full-time. Sixty percent of full-time faculty members hold terminal degrees. The student-faculty ratio is 8:1.

Key Facilities The library houses 90,000 volumes and 600 periodical subscriptions. Computer facilities include thirty-five PC and thirteen Macintosh computers. Neumann's most distinguished facility is the Life Center, which houses the 300-seat Meagher Theatre and Athletic Center as well as meeting rooms, multipurpose rooms, and kitchen facilities.

Athletics The Neumann College intercollegiate athletic program provides students with the opportunity to compete with other colleges in eastern Pennsylvania, New Jersey, Delaware, and Maryland. The level of competition falls within the framework of Division III of the National Association of Intercollegiate Athletics (NAIA) and the National Collegiate Athletic Association (NCAA). Varsity sports are offered to both men and women who compete in the Pennsylvania Athletic Conference.

Study Abroad Qualified students may study abroad by obtaining permission of the division chairperson to join a program

sponsored by a regionally accredited American college or university. Such programs are offered as summer institutes and academic year programs.

Support Services Disabled students will find all facilities handicapped-accessible.

Job Opportunities There is a federally funded work-study program and direct employment by units of the College.

Tuition: $12,400 per year (full-time), $295 to $495 per credit according to program (part-time) (1997-98)

Mandatory Fees: $470

Contact: Director: Robert P. Case, One Neumann Drive, Aston, Pennsylvania 19014-1298; Telephone: 610-558-5578; Fax: 610-459-1370; E-mail: bcase@smptgate.neumann.edu

---

NEWBERRY COLLEGE

4 Pr C S Sc Tr

▼ Summerland Honors Community Program

At Newberry College, students and faculty members walk together on the path of knowledge and along the way they bring to life a distinctive learning community. The Summerland Honors Program accentuates all that is best about living and studying at Newberry College, a place where people are willing to seek innovative and memorable educational opportunities and experiences by taking risks inside and outside of the classroom. The Summerland Honors Community is a perfect haven for students to search for understanding and to consider a myriad of questions old and new.

In many ways the human story has been and will continue to be a quest for identity. How have we understood what it means to be human? The Summerland Honors Community Program is structured upon the theme, Quest for Identity, and will afford opportunities to explore this essential question from a number of vantage points. Indeed, each of the three years of paired, interdisciplinary, and team-taught seminars focuses on a particular perspective concerning this quest for identity. Year one studies the question from the perspective of the arts and humanities. Year two examines the question through the lens of the natural sciences. The third year probes the quest for identity from the perspective of the social sciences.

In each of the six honors seminars, students will also participate in enrichment activities designed to engage them actively in their learning and to provide opportunities for them to apply their knowledge in service to the campus and the local community. Finally, an integrative capstone course in the senior year will ask students to reflect and build on the preceding three-year experience. Courses taken in the honors program will fulfill core requirements in the humanities, natural sciences and social sciences, as appropriate.

Members of the Summerland Honors Community learn to weave a tapestry of understanding around any topic and to layer insight upon insight thereby achieving a breadth and a depth of understanding. Participants become independent learners who take responsibility for leading and sustaining study and discussion on any topic. The service-learning component provides even greater opportunities for growth and rewards. Summerland Honors Community graduates are prepared and motivated for active citizenship, empowered and ready to assume positions of advocacy for social change as a way to make life more productive and meaningful.

An innovative curriculum and a spirited learning community enable participants to realize Newberry College's institutional goals. While educating the whole person, the Summerland Honors Community promotes the development of communication skills (oral and written), the development of critical-thinking skills, and emphasizes an awareness of ethical concerns.

Fall 1996 marks the inaugural year of the program, which will be limited each year to 20 participants. There are a total of 35–40 students currently enrolled in the program.

Participation Requirements: In order to graduate from the Honors Program, a student must hold a cumulative 3.25 GPA in the Honors Program and in the general curriculum. Six Summerland Honors Seminars are required to graduate from the program. Students must also complete the Senior Capstone Experience. Successful completion of the Honors Program requirements is noted at graduation, is recorded on the student's transcript, and is designated on the student's diploma.

Admission Process: Admission to the Summerland Honors Community is based on multidimensional criteria, including high school GPA, high school class rank, SAT I/ACT equivalent scores, and interviews with members of the Newberry College community. Applications are received from February to May.

Scholarship Availability: Most Summerland Honors students receive Founder Scholarships and Presidential Scholarships; however, they are eligible for other Newberry College scholarships.

The Campus Context: A private undergraduate liberal arts institution established in 1856, Newberry College is affiliated with the Evangelical Lutheran Church in America. With a mission focused on educating the whole person, Newberry epitomizes the typical small-college amenities of personal attention, easy rapport between students and faculty, and a supportive environment for academic, personal, and social development. Degree programs include the B.A. (fourteen majors), B.S. (twelve majors), B.M., and B.M.E.

Student Body There are 750 undergraduates enrolled; 48 percent are women and 52 percent are men. International students account for 2 percent of total undergraduates. Ninety percent of students receive some form of financial aid. There are three social sororities, six social fraternities, two academic sororities, and five academic fraternities.

Faculty There are 50 full-time faculty members (supplemented by adjunct faculty members); 65 percent have doctoral degrees. The student-faculty ratio is 11:1.

Key Facilities The library houses 100,000 volumes. The campus has one computer lab with thirty units that have Internet and e-mail access.

Athletics Intercollegiate athletics for men include baseball, basketball, football, golf, soccer, and tennis. Athletics for women include basketball, golf, softball, tennis, and volleyball. Newberry College also has intramural football, baseball, and softball.

Job Opportunities Students are also offered a variety of work-study opportunities on campus.

Tuition: $11,996 per year (1997-98)

Room and Board: $3218

Mandatory Fees: $330

Contact: Director: Dr. Jesse L. Scott, 2100 College Street, Newberry, South Carolina 29108; Telephone: 803-276-5010; Fax: 803-321-5627; E-mail: honors@newberry.edu; Web site: http://newberry.edu

NEWBURY COLLEGE

2+2 Pr G S Sc Tr

▼ Honors Program

The Newbury College Honors Program is open to the top 10 to 15 percent of students enrolled in the College, regardless of major. Admission to the program is available to entering students or students who have completed one semester at Newbury.

Students take one course per semester (3 or 4 credit hours) as an honors course, although they may elect to take more than one course per semester and a seminar in their final year. Honors sections are integrated into the regular course offerings, and, in addition to regular course work, students are expected to produce a significant report or presentation on a topic of their choice, growing out of the course work and prepared throughout the semester in close cooperation with the mentoring faculty member. The Honors Project must contain significant creative and critical aspects and, where appropriate, a self-reflective component.

The Honors Seminar is a multidisciplinary seminar with a different area of focus each session. Students may be required to undertake off-campus visits as part of the seminar, which culminates in a final project designed to incorporate all honors work done during the student's career at Newbury.

The emphasis of the program is on participation in a learning community of closely connected students and faculty members working together.

The first students were admitted for the fall 1996 semester. Currently, there are 25 students in the program. Expected enrollment is approximately 70 students (about 8 percent of the total full-time student enrollment).

Admission Process: Entering students are invited to join the program after a review of their admission application by the Honors Committee. Students who have completed a semester at Newbury may be recommended by a faculty member.

Scholarship Availability: Admission to the Honors Program results in a small scholarship award. Many honors students typically receive one or two additional and more substantial merit-based scholarships.

The Campus Context: Newbury College is located in Brookline, a largely residential suburb of Boston. It is within walking distance of mass transit service to Boston and also has a downtown residence hall connected to the campus by regular shuttle service. Newbury is a 2+2 college granting associate and bachelor's degrees.

Student Body Undergraduate day enrollment is 1,054: 54 percent women, 46 percent men. The ethnic distribution is 55 percent white, 23 percent international, 13 percent African American, 7 percent Hispanic, and 3 percent Asian-Pacific Islander.

Faculty There are 54 full-time and 57 part-time faculty members.

Key Facilities Four computer labs on campus offer both Mac- and IBM-based platforms. The Academic Resource Center provides learning support for all students on campus.

Tuition: $11,110 per year (1996-97)

Room and Board: $6600 minimum

Mandatory Fees: $525

Contact: Coordinator: Dr. Christopher Fauske, 129 Fisher Avenue, Brookline, Massachusetts 02146; Telephone: 617-730-7145; Fax: 617-730-7182

NEW HAMPSHIRE COLLEGE

4 Pr G S Sc Tr

▼ Honors Program

The New Hampshire College Honors Program seeks to encourage, communicate, and reward educational excellence. To that end, the program offers enhanced learning opportunities as well as scholarships to students who demonstrate a high level of interest, initiative, and ability. Honors students are encouraged to be actively involved in their own education.

The honors curriculum, comprising a minimum of 20 percent of the students' course work, consists of four kinds of experiences. The first is honors sections of courses required in students' curricula. Honors classes are limited to a maximum enrollment of 15 students per section. They encourage reading, discussion, experiential learning, and individual exploration. Honors sections are offered in the College Core (general education), the Liberal Arts Core, and the Business Core.

The second experience is honors modules. A student may gain honors experience credit in any course he or she is taking by creating one or more units of additional learning within its context. For example, an honors module in the context of an interdisciplinary humanities class might consist of attendance at an opera performance, plus attending several pre- and post-performance group meetings and writing a short paper. In a business administration class it might consist of a series of interviews conducted with business leaders about a selected topic, culminating in a report to the class about the experience.

The third kind of experience is a sophomore-level interdisciplinary honors seminar. Sophomore Honors Program students attend a year-long seminar whose specific topic changes annually. Students help choose both the topic and the instructor from proposals submitted by faculty members during the prior year. The class is limited to 15 students and meets once a week. Past topics have included Futurology, Democratization and International Investment, Changing Views of Humanity and the Environment, and Latin American Area Studies.

The fourth honors curriculum experience is a senior-year independent study on a topic and with a faculty mentor of the student's choice. Projects may consist of traditional research, experiential learning, case studies, creative work, or combinations of the above.

The Honors Program curriculum is thus adaptable to each student's individual needs and interests, and can be made to mesh well with virtually any undergraduate major or program offered at New Hampshire College. Honors students are also offered opportunities for trips, special programs, volunteerism, retreats, and other enriching activities.

Graduating Honors Program students are recognized at graduation honors ceremonies by receiving an Honors Program Medal, having their names listed in the graduation program, and receiving a notation on their transcripts.

There are approximately 45 students in the program, which was founded in 1992. Growth is expected to a maximum of 60. Fifteen entering freshmen are accepted each year.

Participation Requirements: Once accepted to the program, students must maintain a 3.0 in every semester, as well as grades of B in all honors experiences. Currently, students in all majors and programs are eligible, with the exception of the two-year culinary program.

Admission Process: Generally, applicants should have combined SAT I scores of at least 1000 (new scaling), high school GPAs of 3.2 or better, outstanding entrance essays, and evidence of initiative and interest in learning. Students usually enter the program at the beginning of their freshman year, but transfer students may also be accepted if they offer fewer than 60 transfer credits. Current New Hampshire College freshmen and sophomores are also accepted for entrance into the next year's honors class on a space-available basis.

Scholarship Availability: Currently, every student participating in the Honors Program receives an annual scholarship of $2000, which is in addition to any other merit or college scholarships that might be offered.

The Campus Context: New Hampshire College, founded in 1932, is a private, accredited, nonprofit, coeducational, professional college. The campus, on 200 wooded acres, is located along the Merrimack River in Manchester New Hampshire and is at the crossroads of northern New England. It is an hour's drive from the best skiing in the East, the beaches of New Hampshire and Maine, and the cultural activity of Boston. There are twenty-two majors leading to baccalaureates in business, liberal arts, and hospitality administration.

The College has embarked on an $8.5-million construction project to be completed during 1996–97. The project involves three new buildings on the campus: a 250-bed dormitory, a hospitality management/culinary arts facility, and the Graduate School of Business.

Student Body Undergraduate enrollment is 1,200: 55 percent men and 45 percent women. Ethnic distribution of the total undergraduate population is 1 percent African American, 1 percent Hispanic, 3 percent Asian American, and 35 percent unknown. There are approximately 220 international students. Seventy-five percent of students receive financial aid. There are four fraternities and four sororities.

Faculty The College has 70 full-time undergraduate faculty members, 22 full-time graduate faculty members, 99 total undergraduate faculty members, and 137 total graduate faculty members. Sixty-five percent of full-time faculty members have terminal degrees. The student-faculty ratio is 17:1.

Key Facilities In addition to the 76,269-volume library there are more than 350 IBM-compatible and Apple computers in the campus network.

Athletics New Hampshire College is a member of the National Collegiate Athletic Association, the Eastern College Athletic Association, and the New England Collegiate Conference. All intercollegiate teams compete at the Division II level. Men's teams include basketball, soccer, baseball, ice hockey, and lacrosse. Women's teams include basketball, soccer, vol-

leyball, and cross-country. Athletic scholarships are available for soccer and basketball for both men and women. A strong intramural program is also available.

Study Abroad Students have the opportunity to study abroad during the fall term at the University of North London in London and the University of Greenwich in Woolwich, England.

Support Services Disabled-student facilities include a Learning Center and tutoring services. Most of the campus is accessible for physically disabled students.

Job Opportunities Students are offered a wide range of work opportunities on campus that include work-study and campus payroll positions.

Tuition: $12,400 per year (1997-98)

Room and Board: $5756 minimum

Mandatory Fees: $580

Contact: Director: Dr. Robert R. Craven, 2500 North River Road, Manchester, New Hampshire 03106-1045; Telephone: 603-668-2211; Fax: 603-645-9665; E-mail: cravenro@nhc.edu; Web site: http://www.nhc.edu

---

NEW MEXICO STATE UNIVERSITY

4 Pu D L Tr

▼ University Honors Program

The University Honors Program provides motivated undergraduate students with opportunities to broaden and enrich their academic programs. In small classes taught by master teachers, honors students engage in lively discussion and collaborative investigation of interdisciplinary topics. By taking honors courses, students also work toward completing general education requirements and disciplinary requirements in their majors. Honors courses are challenging, but the individual attention students receive makes the honors experience worthwhile.

Approximately 1,000 students are enrolled in the program each year.

Participation Requirements: After completing the 18 required credits of honors work with an overall GPA between 3.5 and 3.74, students earn the right to graduate with University Honors. If students attain an overall average of 3.75 or better, including the required honors credits, students are eligible to graduate with Distinction in University Honors. Both forms of recognition are noted on diplomas and transcripts, as well as in Commencement programs. Each student is also awarded a certificate of distinction. Upon completion of two upper-division courses, students receive recognition on the Commencement program along with a certificate of distinction.

Admission Process: An entering freshman must have a minimum composite ACT score of 26 to qualify; other students need a 3.5 GPA to enroll. For new freshmen, continued participation is contingent on maintaining a GPA of 3.3; sophomores, juniors, and seniors must maintain a GPA of at least 3.5. Students who do not meet minimum eligibility requirements may petition the Honors Director for admission to the program. A student may enter the program from the first semester of freshman year until the beginning of the second semester of the sophomore year.

Scholarship Availability: New Mexico State University administers an extensive program of grants, scholarships, and loans. The awarding of grants and loans is based on need, while the awarding of scholarships is based mainly on academic ability and, in some cases, need.

The Campus Context: New Mexico State University is a campus of several colleges: Agriculture and Home Economics, Arts and Sciences, Business Administration and Economics, Education, Human and Community Services, and the Graduate School. A total of 146 degree programs are offered.

Student Body Of the 15,643 students, 7,847 are men and 7,796 are women. Diversity is demonstrated by the 4,901 Hispanic, 499 Native American, 327 African-American, and 145 Asian-American students. The University enrolls 743 international students. About 14 percent receive graduate assistantships; 20.2 percent of the students receive various grants; 18 percent receive scholarships, graduate fellowships, waivers, and childcare; 4.6 percent participate in work-study; and 7.2 percent engage in on-campus employment.

Faculty There are a total of 865 faculty members, making the student-faculty ratio 19.3:1.

Key Facilities The library houses 929,494 volumes. There are five computer facilities operating both DOS-based and Macintosh computers.

Tuition: $2196 for state residents, $7152 for nonresidents, per year (1997-98 est.)

Room and Board: $3288 minimum

Contact: Director: Dr. William Eamon, Las Cruces, New Mexico 88003; Telephone: 505-646-2005; Fax: 505-646-1755

NORFOLK STATE UNIVERSITY

4 Pu G M Sc Tr

▼ Honors Program

The Honors Program, now in its second decade, offers an enriched and challenging program of study for full-time students who show exceptional academic potential. All students taking special Honors (H) courses are considered part of the program, which is open to all majors. Students completing 15 or 30 hours of honors courses receive special diplomas inscribed "Parsons Vice-Presidential Scholar" and "Parsons Presidential Scholar," respectively.

Benefits of the program include the following: small enriched courses taught in-depth; the opportunity to work closely with top faculty members; seminars and lectures given by visiting scholars; opportunities to present original research at state, regional, and national collegiate honors council meetings; invitations to civic and cultural events, with opportunities to meet famous leaders and artists; recognition of work at the annual Honors Luncheon and the Awards Convocation; special housing and computer lab opportunities; and rewards in employment and graduate school.

Honors courses are not designed to be much more difficult than regular courses; they are designed to be different. They are generally taught seminar-style in the Parsons Honors Center. Most require more independent work from students and all offer participation in cocurricular and extracurricular trips and activities.

The 12-year-old program currently enrolls 180 students.

Participation Requirements: Most honors courses are core curriculum offerings required for all majors (e.g., English 101 H). There are also major courses in specific departments (e.g., Accounting 201 H) and interdisciplinary seminars (e.g., GST 345/346 H and 445/446 H), with topics that change each semester. Students graduating as Parsons Vice-Presidential Scholars (15 hours) or Parsons Presidential Scholars (30 hours) must take at least one such seminar and have a 3.0 GPA upon graduation (with no grade lower than a C on an honors course and a 3.0 GPA for all honors courses taken). Parsons Presidential Scholars are also required to participate in community service for academic credit. Parsons Vice-Presidential Scholar and Parsons Presidential Scholar are both diploma citations.

Admission Process: Students may be invited to enter the Honors Program in the following circumstances: upon admission as freshmen according to high school records (3.0 GPA minimum) and other indicators of academic proficiency (these students are expected to complete the 30-hour sequence of courses and required seminars) or as sophomores, juniors, or seniors having achieved a 3.5 or above GPA for all courses completed in the curriculum (or 3.0 by permission of the instructor).

Scholarship Availability: The Honors Program grants no scholarships directly, but students who participate in the program have an advantage in competing for regular University scholarships. Students accepting Presidential Scholarships or Board of Visitor Scholarships from the University are expected to participate in the Honors Program. For complete information, students should contact the Financial Aid Office directly.

The Campus Context: Norfolk State University (NSU) is composed of the following eight colleges: the School of Arts and Letters, the School of Business, the School of General and Continuing Education, the School of Education, the School of Health Related Professions and Natural Science, the School of Social Science, the School of Social Work, and the School of Technology. Sixty-eight degree programs are offered on campus. Among distinguished facilities are the L.

Douglas Wilder Performing Arts Center (a 1,900-seat state-of-the-art theater), the Center for Materials Research Lab, the Brambleton Community Outreach Center, and nationally ranked ROTC and NROTC programs and facilities.

Student Body Undergraduate enrollment is approximately 36 percent men and 64 percent women. The ethnic distribution is 83 percent black, 13 percent white, and 4 percent other. There are 52 international students. Residents make up 21 percent of the student population and commuters 79 percent. Eighty-two percent of the students receive financial aid. There are fourteen fraternities/sororities, sixteen honor societies, four literary societies, and three military societies.

Faculty Of the 616 faculty members, 412 are full-time, and 44 percent hold terminal degrees. The student-faculty ratio is 14:1.

Key Facilities The University computer system consists of an Ethernet Local Area Network (NSULAN) using DECNET and TCP/IP protocols with two Digital Equipment Corporation computers, a VAX 11/785 and a VAX 8350, both running the VMS operating system. There are approximately 180 access stations, of which 135 are accessible in six student laboratories on campus. There are also fourteen dial-in telephone access lines. All students, faculty members, and staff members are provided free and unrestricted access to all academic computing resources. The library houses 325,195 volumes.

Athletics The Department of Athletics is currently a member of the Central Intercollegiate Athletic Association but has applied for entry to Division I within the National Association of Intercollegiate Athletics, effective July 1997. There are varsity teams in baseball (men), basketball (men and women), football (men), wrestling (men), track and field (men and women), softball (women), volleyball (women), and tennis (men and women) and a wide variety of intramural sports activities.

Study Abroad The University's Office of International Studies and Programs is a member of the World Affairs Council of Greater Hampton Roads, the Virginia Council for International Educational Exchange, the African Studies Association, and GRITS: Study Abroad Administrators in Virginia, North Carolina, and South Carolina. For further information, students may contact the Office of International Studies and Programs.

Support Services Although the University does not have an actual student facility for the disabled, it provides services to disabled students on an as-needed basis. Some of the services currently provided are TDD's, readers, interpreters, and a hearing device (FM system). The University has also provided temporary use of such equipment as wheelchairs.

Job Opportunities Work study opportunities are available.

Tuition: $2865 for state residents, $6492 for nonresidents, per year (1996-97)

Room and Board: $4096

Contact: Director: Dr. Page R. Laws, 2401 Corprew Avenue, Norfolk, Virginia 23504; Telephone: 757-683-8208 or 757-683-2303; Fax: 757-683-2302; E-mail: honors@vger.nsu.edu; Web site: http://cyclops.nsu.edu/honors/homepage.htm

NORTH ARKANSAS COMMUNITY TECHNICAL COLLEGE

2 Pu G S Tr

▼ Honors Program

The Honors Program at North Arkansas Community Technical College (NACTC) offers interested students an opportunity to be actively involved in their learning. The College's basic philosophy holds that honors classes are to be different, not more difficult. The classes are part of the general education core curriculum; most degrees require these courses, and all of the classes transfer to four-year institutions. Only 15 students may enroll in an honors section of a class. Each semester, NACTC offers eight honors classes.

With the exceptions of Western Civilization and Critical Thought, the honors classes are different versions of regular classes. All honors classes emphasize discussion, hands-on learning, collaborative projects, and individual responsibility for learning; the classes are learner-centered. The Honors Western Civilization course is a two-semester, team-taught course. Each semester has fifteen seminars, with each seminar focusing on a great idea that has shaped Western culture. Students study such ideas as evolution, rationalism, individualism, and Roman rule and then try to identify the consequences and implications of those ideas. A different instructor leads each seminar; some of the seminar leaders are employed by NACTC, and some are from the community. Students do not take tests; instead, they write two-page papers, develop time lines, teach an idea, and do projects. Members of the community are invited to visit these sessions.

In Critical Thought, students study ways to survive in the information age. They study the structure of arguments, common fallacies, and semantics. Throughout the semester, they analyze newspapers, magazines, television shows, public speeches, and advertising. They develop definitions for words commonly tossed around in the media, such as right, liberty, liberal, conservative, victim, etc. Throughout the semester, they develop a notebook with examples of the topics of study. At the beginning of the semester, each student chooses two magazines with opposing viewpoints to monitor for three months. Students might choose one magazine for general readers and one for a specific audience (e.g., one liberal and one conservative or one financial and one social). The students try to determine how public opinion and their own personal opinions are shaped.

On campus, the students have a study room and kitchen area. The study room has computers with Internet access, a telephone for student use, cubicles for storage of student books and jackets, and dictionaries and handbooks. There are activities for the students, such as coke and chip days, cookie days, pizza for lunch, and final mania days. Students hold a reception for faculty members; they may choose to "roast" faculty members, pay tribute, or have a get-acquainted activity with faculty members and administrators. Students design and execute these activities.

There are between 90 and 100 students enrolled in honors classes each semester; an average of 3 students graduate from the program each year.

Participation Requirements:

To graduate from the program, a student must complete 18 hours of honors classes, 3 of which must be Critical Thought, and hold a 3.3 GPA. Students are advised to take only the classes that will fulfill degree requirements. Students who graduate from the program wear an honors cord at graduation and have a gold honors seal on their diplomas.

Participation in the Honors Program offers students opportunities that they would not otherwise have. Each spring, the honors art instructor takes the students enrolled in Honors Art Appreciation on a weekend field trip to a museum; the instructor of Shakespearean Studies takes a group to Stratford, Canada, for the Shakespearean Festival. Instructors in other classes bring in guest speakers and take the students on one-day field trips.

Admission Process:

The College invites a student to participate in the Honors Program based on his/her ACT scores or on his/her GPA after completing 12 college-level hours. A student who does not meet the criteria may take a particular class with permission from the instructor.

The Campus Context:

North Arkansas Community Technical College, located in the Ozark Mountains in north central Arkansas, has two campuses. One 20-acre campus primarily houses the technical programs, and the other 40-acre campus houses the transfer programs. Numerous recreational facilities are just 30 minutes away: Branson, with all its music shows to the north; Lake Taneycomo and Lake Bull Shoals, also north; Lake Norfork to the east; White River to the east; and Buffalo River to the south. The College offers A.A., A.S., and A.A.S. degrees and numerous certificates in technical fields; a well-developed college-preparatory program; an ABE-GED program; and a continuing education program.

Student Body The College serves students primarily from five counties. Of the 1,400 students enrolled, only 50 are from other states. The average age of students is 27. Forty-two percent of full-time students are men, and 58 percent are women. Sixty-five percent receive financial aid. The College also has several student organizations, including Phi Beta Lambda and Phi Theta Kappa.

Faculty The College employs 63 full-time faculty members.

Key Facilities The library has 22,675 volumes and subscribes to 379 periodicals. NACTC has four computer classrooms, all IBM compatible; in addition, computers are available in the library, the instructional support lab, and two mini labs.

Athletics In athletics, NACTC offers men's and women's basketball and men's baseball.

Support Services The campuses have ramps, door openers, and bathroom facilities for handicapped students.

Tuition: $36 for area residents, $44 for state residents, $88 for nonresidents, per hour (1997-98)

Mandatory Fees: $3 per credit hour, up to 12 hours

Contact: Director: Dr. Marty Terrill, Pioneer Ridge, Harrison, Arkansas 72601; Telephone: 501-743-3000; Fax: 501-743-3577; E-mail: terrill@nactc1.nactc.cc.ar.us; Web site: http://pioneer. nactc.cc.ar.us

NORTH CAROLINA STATE UNIVERSITY

4 Pu G L Sc*

▼ University Scholars Program

The University Scholars Program (USP) of North Carolina State University (NCSU) provides promising, academically talented students with a variety of mind-stretching and unique educational experiences, both in and outside of the classroom, to encourage these outstanding students to perform at the highest level of achievement of which they are capable. (Students should be aware that in addition to the USP, North Carolina State offers various upper-level departmental honors programs that are administered independently by the departments.)

Cosponsored by each of the undergraduate schools and colleges of NC State, the Office of the Provost, and the Department of University Housing in the Division of Student Affairs, the USP combines special academic offerings with a series of cocurricular and extracurricular opportunities.

In the freshman and sophomore years, students in the USP may enroll in special honors or scholars sections of basic courses in the humanities and social sciences, mathematics, and natural sciences. These sections are deliberately kept small and are taught by instructors known for their excellence in teaching. All of these classes fulfill requirements for graduation from NCSU; thus, students are not required to take additional courses in order to participate in the USP. To ensure that University Scholars are eligible to register for their required Scholars Forum, honors and scholars courses, and regular, nonscholars sections of courses, USP participants receive "Scholars Advanced Scheduling" privileges.

Academic work in the Scholars Program is complemented and enriched by a series of special events called the Scholars Forum. These weekly activities are intended to broaden each student's personal, professional, and cultural horizons. Forum events may include conversations with distinguished faculty members, addresses by major public figures, debates and discussions on significant public issues, and visits to museums and historic sites. They may also include introductions to cultural activities, the viewing of significant films, and explorations of opportunities open to students for personal growth and international study.

University Scholars are also expected to attend cultural events on the NC State campus and in the Raleigh community. Tickets for these events are provided as part of the program. Scholars are also provided the opportunity to attend a range of international films and events, both on campus and at the North Carolina Museum of Art. Additionally, the Scholars Council, a body made up of student representatives from each NCSU school and college, plans a variety of social activities and special trips for University Scholars and arranges for USP students to participate in worthwhile community service projects.

To encourage the development of close working relationships and friendships among participants in the USP, scholars are invited and encouraged to live in the same residence hall, Sullivan, located on West Campus. To assist and communicate effectively with these students, the USP office is also located in Sullivan Residence Hall. Scholars are guaranteed housing on campus as long as they remain active in the USP.

Finally, through the University Scholars Program, NCSU is a member and participates in the activities of the North Carolina Honors Association, the Southern Regional Honors Council, and the National Collegiate Honors Council.

The 16-year-old program has 800–1,000 active participants each year.

Participation Requirements: USP students must complete 21 hours of honors course work, register for three semesters of the Scholars Forum, and earn an minimum overall GPA of 3.2 and minimum honors GPA of 3.0. Honors courses are designated on the permanent transcript, and students in the program are recognized at an annual University Honors Convocation. Students who complete the program have an Honors designation in the Commencement program and are awarded a certificate.

Scholarship Availability: While there are no scholarships available through the program, all recipients of major University scholarships are expected to participate.

The Campus Context: North Carolina State University is composed of twelve colleges: the College of Agricultural and Life Sciences, the School of Design, the College of Education and Psychology, the College of Engineering, the College of Forest Resources, the College of Humanities and Social Sciences, the College of Management, the College of Physical and Mathematical Sciences, the College of Textiles, the First-Year College, the Graduate School, and the College of

Veterinary Medicine. On the undergraduate level, eighty-nine baccalaureate degrees are offered.

Student Body Undergraduate enrollment is approximately 18,500; 59 percent women and 41 percent men. The ethnic distribution is approximately 82 percent white, 10 percent African American, 5 percent Asian/Pacific Islander, 2 percent Hispanic, and 1 percent Native American. There are about 182 international students who make up 1 percent of the population. Approximately 40 percent of the students are residents; the remaining 60 percent are commuters. There are twenty-four fraternities and ten sororities.

Faculty Of the 2,623 faculty members, 2,382 are full-time, and 92 percent have terminal degrees.

Key Facilities The library houses approximately 2.3 million volumes, 3.7 million microform titles, 19,000 serial subscription, and eight on-line bibliographic services. Computer facilities are numerous. Most student residential rooms are linked to a campus network, and there is a Computer Purchase Plan available. There are 4,100 computers available for student use in the computer center, computer labs, research center, learning resources center, classrooms, library, student center, and dorms; all provide access to the main academic computer, off-campus computing facilities, e-mail, on-line services, and Internet. Staffed computer labs on campus are open 24 hours a day and provide training in the use of computers and software. Academic computer expenditures exceed $13.1 million per year.

Athletics In athletics, NCSU belongs to NCAA Division I (except football, which is I-A). There are eleven varsity sports for men, nine for women, and one that is coed. Men's varsity sports include soccer, cross-country, football, basketball, swimming, indoor track, wrestling, golf, tennis, track, and baseball. Varsity sports for women are soccer, cross-country, volleyball, basketball, indoor track, swimming, gymnastics, track, and tennis. A coed rifle team also competes. The University also maintains an extensive program of intramural-recreational sports administered by the Department of Physical Education; seventeen intramural sports and thirty sports clubs/activities are supported.

Study Abroad NC State sponsors a variety of study abroad programs, including Semester in Santander, Spain; Summer Programs in Oxford, London, Vienna, Mexico, and Lill; and Summer Design Programs in Prague, Berlin, and Santander. Additionally, NC State participates in ISEP and programs sponsored by other institutions.

Support Services The Office of Disability Services (DSS) provides assistance based on each student's particular needs and circumstances. Students may receive priority scheduling, tutors, priority housing, test accommodations, reader/taping services, van transportation, note takers, interpreters, taping of lectures, parking, and additional learning resources. The Student Organization for Disability Awareness meets periodically to provide mutual support and suggestions to the DSS office.

Job Opportunities Hundreds of work-study opportunities are available on campus; many academic departments provide paid research and other work opportunities to students and service units (University Housing, University Dining, Campus Student Center, etc.) provide hundreds of opportunities for on-campus work.

Tuition: $2200 for state residents, $10,732 for nonresidents, per year (1997-98 est.)

Room and Board: $3350

Contact: Director: N. Alexander Miller III, Campus Box 7316, Raleigh, North Carolina 27695; Telephone: 919-515-2353; Fax: 919-515-7168; E-mail: alex_miller@ncsu.edu; Web site: http://www2.ncsu.edu/ncsu/univ_scholars/

NORTH CENTRAL COLLEGE

4 Pr G M Sc Tr

▼ College Scholars Program

The College Scholars Program was created to attract students capable of superior work and to provide them with the opportunity to have a challenging and broadening intellectual experience. Course work emphasizes interdisciplinary study, individualized research, and other special projects. The five-course History of Ideas seminar series is of particular interest to freshmen and sophomores. The seminar format encourages lively discussion of intellectually engaging issues ranging from the classical era through the twentieth century. College Scholars are advised by specially selected honors advisers, usually in their major, and are encouraged to develop independent studies and take designated honors courses. Participants are encouraged to become involved in Wingspread Scholars (a regional conference program), the Richter Fellowship Program (funding for independent study work), and/or the Fulbright Program. Social activities throughout the academic year encourage contact with professors and other students to provide intellectual stimulation and support.

College Scholar is a title bestowed upon graduating students who have completed 9 honors credits, including at least one Honors Seminar at the 300 or 400 level, and a Senior Honors Thesis (which is hardcover-bound and shelved in the College library). College Scholars Participant is a title bestowed upon graduating students who have completed at least 5 honors credits, including one Honors Seminar at the 300 or 400 level. A grade of A or B must be earned for honors credit to be awarded. All honors course work is noted on the student's transcript.

The College Scholars Program at North Central College (NCC) was established in 1982. There are approximately 260 members.

Participation Requirements: To sustain membership in the program, a student must maintain a minimum GPA of 3.0.

Admission Process: Admission to the program is by invitation (entering freshmen) and by application (throughout the academic year). Acceptance of entering freshmen is based on the student's ACT/SAT score, high school record, NCC Admission Counselor's recommendation, and results of a personal interview. Other applicants are selected using demonstrated interest in the program, ACT/SAT scores, high school and/or college GPA, and a recommendation from an NCC professor.

Transfer students who participated in an honors program at another institution are admitted to the College Scholars Program upon submission of an application. They may bring honors credit to NCC from a similar program, provided they were in good standing at the institution from which they are transferring.

Scholarship Availability: Freshmen applying to North Central College may qualify for Presidential Scholarships (academic) in amounts from $2000–$11,500; transfer students may qualify for renewable academic scholarships of up to $7000 and/or one of ten Phi Theta Kappa (a community college honor society) scholarships of $2000 awarded each year. Performing arts scholarships are awarded in amounts up to $1500. Endowed departmental scholarships and scholarships for students preparing for allopathic or osteopathic medical careers are awarded yearly.

The Campus Context: Founded in 1861, North Central College is an independent, comprehensive college of the liberal arts and sciences known nationally for excellence in teaching and for the quality of its faculty and students. The 54-acre campus is located in a beautiful old residential area of Naperville, a city of more than 100,000. Naperville is located in the heart of the rapidly growing high-technology Illinois Research and Development Corridor that is bounded by Argonne National Laboratory on the east and Fermi National Accelerator Laboratory on the west and is 29 miles from downtown Chicago.

The College awards Bachelor of Arts and Bachelor of Science degrees in fifty-eight majors from twenty-two academic departments and offers preprofessional programs in engineering, law, and medicine in cooperation with major research universities. The College offers master's degrees in five areas.

Student Body North Central enrolls nearly 1,700 full-time undergraduates. About 800 live in College-owned housing, and about 900 live off-campus or commute. An additional 710 undergraduates are enrolled part-time in day, evening, or weekend classes. Of the undergraduate students, 45 percent are men and 55 percent are women; 12 percent are members of minority groups. There are 32 undergraduate (2 graduate) international students representing nineteen countries. More than 380 students are enrolled in graduate programs. Ninety-four percent of freshmen receive financial aid. North Central College does not have social fraternities or sororities; however, there are more than thirty-five student organizations and performing groups active on campus. NCC also maintains an award-winning student-staffed radio station and several student publications.

Faculty Eighty-four percent of the 93 full-time teaching faculty members have a doctorate or highest degree in their field, and faculty members also serve as the academic advisers to students. There are approximately 23 half-time faculty members, most of whom have a long-standing relationship with the College. The student-faculty ratio is 14:1.

Key Facilities Oesterle Library offers North Central students and faculty ready access to more than 28 million items at 800 Illinois libraries in addition to the 116,300 volumes in the stacks. Computers are also available for student use.

Students, faculty, and staff are on a voice, video, and data network and have full Internet access from their residence halls, classrooms, computer laboratories, and offices. There are fifty-eight 486 computers in the student computer labs, and all full-time faculty offices have Pentium 90 computers. The Science Division has an additional twelve special-purpose computers for graphical and numerical processing. North Central also has state-of-the-art language and market research laboratories. In the sciences, students can use a high-performance digital NMR spectrometer, gas and liquid chromatographs, ultraviolet visible and infrared spectro-photometers, a pulsed nitrogen laser, and an environmental chamber to pursue laboratory research.

Athletics North Central College is a member of the NCAA Division III and the College Conference of Illinois and Wisconsin (CCIW). Student athletes participate in eighteen intercollegiate sports. Men compete in baseball, basketball, cross-country, football, soccer, swimming, tennis, track and field, and wrestling; women compete in basketball, cross-country, soccer, softball, swimming, tennis, track and field, and volleyball.

Study Abroad International study is encouraged at North Central. Through its association with the Institute of International Education, the College maintains current information concerning at least 200 domestically accredited programs in more than sixty countries. Students are encouraged to apply for a Richter Fellowship—a distinctive program that grants up to $5000 for independent study projects of unusual merit and scope. Smaller grants are available for projects on or off campus.

Support Services North Central College has made and continues to make modifications to its facilities and programs so as to provide access for those individuals with disabilities.

Job Opportunities Students are employed on campus in a variety of areas: academic offices, business office, residence halls, food service, maintenance, activity center, library, etc.

Tuition: $13,074 per year (1996-97)

Room and Board: $4854

Mandatory Fees: $120

Contact: Director: Dr. Thomas F. Sawyer, 30 North Brainard Street, Naperville, Illinois 60566-7063; Telephone: 708-637-5330; Fax: 708-637-5121; E-mail: tfs@noctrl.edu

NORTH DAKOTA STATE UNIVERSITY

4 Pu G S Sc Tr

▼ Scholars Program

An interdisciplinary alternative for highly motivated students, the North Dakota State University (NDSU) Scholars Program provides an opportunity for the lively exchange of ideas within and outside the classroom. Scholars enroll in a colloquium (small discussion class) each of the first three years. Though the themes vary, the basic structure and format of the colloquia in all three years remain the same: discussion, reading, and writing focused on themes and ideas that can be explored through several different disciplines. During the fourth year, scholars complete an independent study project or senior thesis, usually in their major field, with the guidance of a faculty member in the discipline and a Scholars Program adviser.

Although the program is housed in the College of Humanities and Social Sciences, scholars have primary majors in the range of disciplines offered at North Dakota State, such as engineering, chemistry, computer science, pharmacy, and architecture. The program also has a Student Council that organizes a variety of cocurricular and social activities, including a series of lectures by faculty members outside the Scholars Program, trips to galleries and theatres, volunteer activities, and informal social activities.

Begun in 1969, the program currently has 60 active students.

Participation Requirements: Students must take one 3-credit colloquium each of the first six semesters of the program. A senior thesis is required in the fourth year.

Admission Process: First-year scholars are selected on the basis of high school grades, a writing sample, and/or recommendations and interviews. After the first semester, students from any college within the University may apply to join the program. The deadline for applying to the program is April 1.

Scholarship Availability: Two $1000 scholarships are available to scholars having majors within the College of Humanities and Social Sciences. Several annual awards ($300–$400), regardless of major, are granted based on academic performance.

The Campus Context: North Dakota State University is composed of seven colleges: Agriculture, Business Administration, Engineering and Architecture, Human Development and Education, Humanities and Social Sciences, Pharmacy, and Sciences and Mathematics. The University offers twenty-one doctoral programs, forty-eight master's programs, and eighty-one bachelor's programs. There are noteworthy research facilities in chemistry, biochemistry, pharmacy, psychology, and plant sciences. The Institute for Regional Studies is also well known.

Student Body The student population is 57 percent men and 43 percent women. International students constitute 4 percent of the total student body. Sixty-five percent of the students receive financial aid.

Faculty Of the 404 faculty members, 88 percent hold terminal degrees. The student-faculty ratio in undergraduate classes is 19:1.

Key Facilities The library houses 450,000 bound volumes and 3,450 serials. Information Technology Services provides a complete range of computer services (UNIX/DOS/Macintosh).

Athletics In athletics, North Dakota State University is in the NCAA Division II and also participates in the North Central Intercollegiate Athletic Conference. Men's sports include baseball, basketball, football, cross-country, gold wrestling, and indoor/outdoor track; women's sports are basketball, cross-country, indoor/outdoor track, softball, and volleyball.

Study Abroad Study abroad is available through direct exchange programs in Mexico, the Netherlands, and Australia. Many other arrangements are available through individual departments.

Tuition: $2110 for state residents, $5634 for nonresidents, per year (1996-97). Tuition for nonresidents eligible for the Western Undergraduate Exchange and Western Interstate Commission for Higher Education programs and residents of Manitoba, Montana, Saskatchewan, and South Dakota: $3166 per year full-time, $131.92 per credit part-time. Minnesota resident tuition: $2356 per year full-time, $98.17 per credit part-time.

Room and Board: $2968

Mandatory Fees: $300

Contact: Director: Paul Homan, P.O. Box 5075, Fargo, North Dakota 58105; Telephone: 701-231-8852; Fax: 701-231-1047; E-mail: phoman@plains.nodak.edu; Web site: http://www.acm.ndsu.nodak.edu/~nuschlrs/index.html

NORTHEASTERN OKLAHOMA A&M COLLEGE

2 Pu G M Sc Tr

▼ College Honors Program

The Honors Program at Northeastern Oklahoma (NEO) A&M College is intended to encourage academic excellence by providing special opportunities and challenges for exceptional students.

Expectations for performance in the program are high. Standards are set to challenge and motivate the students. Retention is based on GPA, and yet honors students are expected to strive against the standards established. They are not expected to compete with each other for grades. Through NEO A&M College's Honors Program, the challenge to perform at the top of a student's ability is matched by the opportunity to do so in an environment that is simultaneously fun, exciting, and intellectually challenging.

Participation Requirements: There are several elements of the Honors Program, and a student may elect to participate in all aspects of the program or may select one avenue of participation. The Colloquium and the maintenance of the 3.5 GPA are mandatory portions of the program. However, many students choose to take special sections of general education courses and earn honors credit and recognition on their transcript for such efforts. Students may also contract with individual instructors for honors credit in general education courses not in the schedule and, with the approval of both the instructor and the Honors Program Director, earn honors recognition for contract completion.

The Honors Faculty Advisory Committee has agreed to require honors students to enroll in one course each semester that may be categorized as an honors course in addition to enrolling the Scholar Leadership Colloquium. The availability of these courses varies by semester.

In addition to the above requirements, each student in the Honors Program must maintain a 3.5 GPA each semester and enroll in at least one honors course each semester. The enrollment requirement is met by the colloquium in semesters in which no other honors sections are available. Each student in the Honors Program must enroll every semester in the Scholar Leadership Colloquium.

Honors student housing is available for honors students upon completion of one semester of college credit with a minimum of a 3.5 GPA. Students apply for honors student housing in residence halls on campus, and the students vie for the privilege of living in these single occupancy rooms for the double occupancy rate. Other conditions for obtaining this housing are that the student must have no record of any disciplinary action and that the student must maintain at least a 3.0 GPA for the semester and a 3.5 cumulative GPA or a 3.5 GPA for that semester to remain eligible.

Admission Process: All students who wish to participate in the Honors Program must be admitted to Northeastern Oklahoma A&M College. A student may apply to the program and be accepted by meeting one of two criteria: earning a composite ACT score of 26 or higher or earning an ACT score of 26 or higher on one of the subtests and having a high school GPA of 3.5 or higher.

Tuition: $1125 for state residents, $2925 for nonresidents, per year (1996-97)

Room and Board: $2270 minimum

Contact: Director: Dr. Doris Snyder, 200 I Street NE, Miami, Oklahoma 74354-6497; Telephone: 918-540-6204; Fax: 918-542-9759

NORTHEAST STATE TECHNICAL COMMUNITY COLLEGE

2 Pu G S Sc Tr

▼ Honors Program

The Northeast State Technical Community College (NSTCC) Honors Program consists of honors sections of regular courses in biology, English, psychology, history, and math and four interdisciplinary foundation courses: Scientific Perspectives, Literary Perspectives, Artistic Perspectives, and Social Science Perspectives. These classes offer challenging, stimulating opportunities for increased knowledge and personal growth for students as they are small, discussion- and writing-based classes with a high level of teacher-student interaction.

Students must fulfill a requirement to attend and write about one Lyceum lecture per semester. These lectures, presented by both program faculty members and special guests, are designed to not only impart information but also generate critical thinking and discussion on campus about important issues. This year's topics have included the history of the Bosnian conflict and the Christian response to the Holocaust, among others.

The Honors Program was implemented in 1991–92 and has a current enrollment of 27 students.

Participation Requirements: To receive an honors diploma, students must complete 18 hours of honors courses, with 6 hours of foundation course work included. Successful completion of Honors Program requirements is noted on the student's diploma and transcript.

Admission Process: Students may enter the program in one of two ways: they may enter as first-semester freshmen with an ACT composite of 23 or better or an SAT combined score of 910 and an acceptable writing sample, or transfer/returning students may be enrolled after completion of 12 hours of college-level course work with a minimum 3.25 GPA, a faculty recommendation, and an acceptable writing sample.

Scholarship Availability: Beginning in fall 1996, there are two scholarship opportunities available to NSTCC honors students. Currently, there is the Don Bratcher Memorial Honors Scholarship, which is funded by Honors Program faculty members in varying amounts each semester contingent upon available funding. The scholarship awards are based on GPA and hours earned and on the essays submitted by the applicants. Beginning in fall 1996, there is another scholarship sponsored by the NSTCC Foundation. Fifty $200 book scholarships are awarded to honors students each semester. All students enrolled in the program full-time who meet the minimum GPA requirement and fulfill the Lyceum requirement are eligible to receive the scholarship until graduation.

The Campus Context: Northeast State Technical Community College is a two-year technical community college located in Blountville, Tennessee, about 2 hours' drive northeast of Knoxville, Tennessee. The school offers a University Parallel transfer curriculum and a variety of technical terminal degrees in such fields as drafting, electrical technology, emergency medical technician studies, and business. Northeast State is the home of the QUALITY FIRST program, a recognized leader in the quality and productivity movement. Now in its tenth year, the program has worked with more than 100 companies in assisting in change and improvement in all levels of the companies' operations. There are a total of sixteen different degree programs offered.

Student Body The enrollment in fall 1995 was 3,488: 1,830 men and 1,658 women. The approximate ethnic distribution is 96.5 percent white, 2 percent black, and 1.5 percent other. Sixty-five percent of the students receive financial aid.

Faculty There are 92 full-time faculty members. The student-faculty ratio is 17:1.

Key Facilities The library houses 25,025 volumes. There are two computer labs for writing students, with twenty-five Macintosh workstations for developmental writing classes and twenty-five IBM-compatible workstations for the composition students. Mathematics students also have a tutorial lab with Macintosh workstations. There are computers available for student use in the library and for computer programming and word processing courses in the classrooms.

Support Services Disabled students have access to all areas and all activities on campus. The campus community includes a sizable contingent of hearing impaired and physically challenged persons. A counselor/coordinator and several interpreters are assigned to assist these students.

Tuition: $1024 for state residents, $4096 for nonresidents, per year (1996-97)

Mandatory Fees: $44

Contact: Director: Rita Quillen, Associate Professor of English, P.O. Box 246, Blountville, Tennessee 37617-0246; Telephone: 423-323-3191; Fax: 423-323-3083; E-mail: rsquillen@nstcc.cc. tn.us

NORTHERN ARIZONA UNIVERSITY

4 Pu G M Sc Tr

▼ New Century Honors Program

The Northern Arizona University (NAU) New Century Honors Program consists of a core of courses designed to place top students with top faculty members in a joint effort to grow intellectually. Most courses are multidisciplinary, team-taught, and have enrollments of fewer than 20. Lively exchanges, informality, and zest are the rule. The Honors Student Advisory Board provides support, counsel, and merriment for the entire program. Honors students are advised by the Student Advisory Board and the Honors Director as first-year students and then coadvised in following years with advisers from the student's major field(s). There is a lot of interchange, beginning with a camping retreat the weekend before classes start and continuing through numerous pizza parties, field trips, and visits to museums, galleries, theaters, observatories, and the research centers that surround Flagstaff.

The program is the oldest honors program in Arizona, having begun in 1955, and currently includes approximately 400 students.

Participation Requirements:
The core courses include 32–34 semester hours, which substitute for the General Education/Liberal Studies requirements required of other students. AP courses with a score of 4 or 5 fulfill some honors requirements. Students may major in any of the sixty-four baccalaureate programs on campus. To graduate with honors, as noted at Commencement and on the transcript, students must graduate with a 3.5 (A=4.0) overall.

Admission Process:
Eligibility for the program is confined to those students whose high school rank and/or ACT or SAT scores place them in the top 5 percent of their graduation class (SAT 1290 or higher, ACT 29 or higher). Students should apply directly to the program for admission using a form that can be mailed or faxed.

Scholarship Availability:
Several dozen scholarships are available; awards range from several hundred to several thousand dollars. Awards are made on the basis of financial need, academic qualifications, and evidence of student involvement. Applications for scholarships are due in mid-February, with awards announced in mid-March of each year.

The Campus Context:
Northern Arizona is the smallest of three state-supported universities in Arizona and emphasizes excellence in undergraduate instruction. It was founded in 1899 and enrolls about 16,000 students on-campus, with another 4,000 enrolled through interactive television in distance education. NAU offers sixty-four undergraduate degrees, including all of the liberal arts and sciences and professional degrees in health sciences, nursing, business, forestry, hotel restaurant management, education, and engineering.

NAU is located in Flagstaff in north-central Arizona. Flagstaff is a city of about 50,000 whose elevation approximates 7,000 feet on the high Colorado Plateau. The area is surrounded by ponderosa pine forests. Six miles to the north, the extinct volcanoes of the San Francisco Peaks rise to nearly 13,000 feet; both downhill and cross-country skiing are excellent. The four-season climate is cool; the air is crisp, cool, and dry and meets EPA standards as "pristine" air.

The Grand Canyon is a 90-minute drive to the north, and six other national parks and monuments are within a similar radius. The area contains many geological, astronomical, and biological sites of interest: five major astronomic observatories are within a 15-minute drive, including Lowell, where the planet Pluto was discovered. Also nearby is the U.S. Geologic Survey's Center for Astrogeology.

Student Body Among the 16,000 students, the men/women ratio is nearly equal, and about 11 percent of students are members of ethnic minority groups, primarily Hispanic and Native American. International students comprise 4 percent of the student body. More than half of all students choose to live in residence halls on campus; all halls are fully wired for the electronic age and contain computer laboratories. There are about a dozen fraternity and sorority houses.

Faculty There are approximately 600 faculty members on campus, with more than 90 percent holding the earned doctorate or other terminal degrees. Graduate students rarely teach classes; there are about thirty master's programs and ten doctoral programs on campus. The student-faculty ratio is 22:1.

Key Facilities The library contains more than a 1.5 million volumes, largely computer indexed. It subscribes to about 6,000 current periodicals, including more than seventy local, national, and international newspapers.

Athletics The varsity athletic programs meet NCAA standards for gender equity and include all major and minor sports except baseball, golf, lacrosse, hockey, soccer, and tennis. There is a wide range of intramural sports, including most winter sports. Year-round active participation in outdoor sports of all kinds is common for both students and townspeople.

Study Abroad Through its international education program, NAU honors students typically spend a semester or two abroad in England, France, Spain, Portugal, Mexico, Japan, Germany, and other less well-known countries. Many of these programs allow the student to pay regular NAU tuition in place of the tuition at the host university.

Job Opportunities More than half of all honors students currently work part-time; there is a wide range of both on-campus and off-campus work, co-op, and internship opportunities, including work-study and other federal and state programs. There are also specialized programs for members of the Navajo, Apache, and Hopi tribes and students with disabilities. All campus buildings are handicapped-accessible.

Tuition:
$2010 for state residents, $7526 for nonresidents, per year (1996-97)

Room and Board: $3390

Mandatory Fees: $70

Contact:
Director: Dr. Charles W. Barnes, Box 5689, Flagstaff, Arizona 86011; Telephone: 520-523-3334; Fax: 520-523-6558; E-mail: chuck.barnes@nau.edu; Web site: http://www.nau.edu/honors

NORTHERN KENTUCKY UNIVERSITY
4 Pu G C Sc Tr

▼ Honors Program

At the core of the honors experience, the seminars emphasize discussion and discovery of ideas, almost always with an interdisciplinary emphasis. Seminars are organized on a topical basis, fulfilling the overall framework of four general areas: Humanity and Nature, Humanity and Society, Humanity and the Imagination, and Humanity and the Machine. In addition to an interdisciplinary focus, seminars are also available in a World Cities/World Cultures series, designating specific cities and regions for intensive study. Students may also substitute or use designated international study opportunities for honors credit. A number of seminars are cross-listed with disciplines when appropriate (e.g., a World Cities course in Paris is cross-listed with the French major). Faculty members noted for their excellence in teaching are recruited from all University departments to participate in the program.

All students must complete a Senior Honors Thesis (often but not necessarily in their majors), which gives them the opportunity to research and write about topics of significance, conduct original research, or develop creative projects. The thesis may be completed in written form or it may document a creative project (such as a photography exhibition).

In addition, cocurricular activities sponsored by both the program and the student Honors Club are available. These include campus events, lecture series, field trips, and other activities that integrate learning and experience. Students may choose to be active in state, regional, and national associations of honors students.

The 13-year-old program currently enrolls 100 students.

Participation Requirements: The Northern Kentucky University Honors Program provides qualified students with 15 semester hours of seminars, each having a maximum enrollment of 15 students, and 6 hours of Senior Honors Thesis credit. Those students who successfully complete the 21 hours become designated "University Honors Scholars" and fulfill the requirement of a minor towards graduation.

Admission Process: Entering freshmen with a composite ACT score of 26 (or significant achievement in high school), already enrolled students with a minimum GPA of 3.0, and transfer students from other honors programs are eligible for the program.

Scholarship Availability: Scholarships are offered for the outstanding junior honors student and the outstanding honors student majoring in business; students who do individual research projects or international study are eligible for Zalla Fellowship monies.

The Campus Context: Northern Kentucky University is composed of three colleges: the College of Arts and Sciences, the College of Business, and the College of Professional Studies. Among the distinguished facilities on campus is the collection of public sculptures by internationally recognized artists such as Red Grooms and Donald Judd and the historic Kentucky one-room log schoolhouse.

Student Body Undergraduate enrollment is 11,500: 42 percent men and 58 percent women. Three percent of the student body is African American. There are 160 international students. Ninety-three percent of the students are commuters, and 7 percent are residents. Forty-five percent of the students receive financial aid. There are seven fraternities and six sororities.

Faculty Of the 764 faculty members, 373 are full-time; 82 percent hold terminal degrees. The student-faculty ratio is 17:1.

Key Facilities The library houses 285,000 volumes. Computer facilities include dual platform (Apple and IBM) computer labs in all major buildings.

Athletics The NKU Norse play NCAA Division II games in the Great Lakes Valley Conference. On the varsity level, there are six men's sports (baseball, basketball, cross-country, golf, soccer, and tennis) and five women's sports (basketball, cross-country, fastpitch softball, tennis, and volleyball).

Study Abroad Study abroad for honors students is offered summers (in odd-numbered years) in London; other study-abroad opportunities are available in Europe, Latin America, and Australia.

Support Services Disabled students find the entire campus wheelchair-accessible.

Job Opportunities Work opportunities on campus exist as federal and other work-study opportunities.

Tuition: $2020 for state residents, $5500 for nonresidents, per year (1997-98)

Room and Board: $3164 minimum

Contact: Director: Tom Zaniello, Landrum 429, Highland Heights, Kentucky 41099; Telephone: 606-572-5400; Fax: 606-572-6093; E-mail: tzaniello@nku.edu; Web site: http://www.nku.edu

NORTHERN STATE UNIVERSITY

4 Pu G S Sc Tr

▼ Honors Program/Honors Society

Northern State University (NSU) has developed two tracks in its approach to honors education. The first is the traditional, small-college approach: a requirement of 18 credit hours of honors classes, including an honors project or thesis supervised by a faculty committee. This is called the Honors Program. The second track is the Honors Society, which is separate yet interwoven with the Honors Program. These two tracks allow students maximum involvement in intellectual experiences and also the ability to choose how deeply to become involved with the honors concept.

Courses available to students in the Honors Program include English Composition, Literature, The Physics of Music, Environmental Photography, and an honors seminar for first-year students. Courses are developed by interested faculty members and cover a wide range of topics. Additionally, students are encouraged to contract for honors credit with individual members of the faculty. Thus any regularly scheduled class can be taken as an honors course with the student, professor, and honors director fashioning the requirements.

The honors thesis or project is begun in the junior year and completed (ideally) in the first semester of the senior year. The student is responsible for forming a faculty committee and proposing the project to the committee. The student then prepares and defends the thesis or project under the supervision of the committee. There are no alternatives to the thesis or project. Approximately 25 students are active in the program.

The Honors Society is a student-run and student-funded organization that is deeply involved in the intellectual life of NSU. The society publishes *Shelterbelt,* an anthology of student literature and art in full color. Over the years the society has purchased a collection of international films, both modern and classic. These films are available to all members and are also shown as part of a film discussion series. The society sponsors a Quiz Bowl for high school students attending the Northern South Dakota Science Fair that is held annually on campus. Teams of faculty members, administrators, and students test their wits and reflexes in a campuswide quiz show produced by the society. Other programs have included food collection for the local food pantry and a "shadowing" program for high school students. The society has a lounge area with a TV, a VCR, and two computers. Approximately 100 students are active in the society.

Participation Requirements: Students in the Honors Program must maintain a 3.25 GPA. Students who successfully complete the Honors Program graduate in their chosen majors, but their degree is designated *In Honoribus,* this being the highest academic honor granted by NSU. The diploma itself is oversized, and the honors graduates are singled out at Commencement and are awarded their diplomas before all other undergraduate degrees. The first *In Honoribus* degree was awarded by NSU in 1988.

Admission Process: Invitations to join the Honors Program are determined by ACT scores and high school class rankings, but self-nominations are accepted.

In contrast to the selectivity of the Honors Program, the NSU Honors Society is open to all students and is funded primarily by general activity fees. There is a high correlation of membership between the Honors Program and the Honors Society, as might be expected, but many students enjoy membership in the society without being members of the Honors Program.

Scholarship Availability: Students interested in the Honors Program/Honors Society should apply to the Office of Financial Assistance to be considered for a range of scholarships. The recommended deadlines are important and should be carefully followed.

The Campus Context: Northern State University, located in northeastern South Dakota, began life as the Northern Normal and Industrial School in 1901 and continues as a regional (South Dakota, North Dakota, Minnesota) university of 2,600 students. The compact campus of large trees and well-maintained buildings is located in South Dakota's third-largest city, Aberdeen (population 25,000). The nearest metropolitan area is the twin-city area of Minneapolis and Saint Paul, about a 5-hour drive. Airline connections are frequent. NSU plays a major role in the life of the community and enjoys widespread support from fans of athletics and the arts. The campus has five art galleries, a performing arts center, and a multiuse sports center.

NSU comprises the College of Arts and Sciences, the School of Business, the School of Education, and the School of Fine Arts. In support of both NSU and the state business community are the Small Business Institute and the South Dakota International Development Institute (SDIDI). An English as a second language program is provided by the SDIDI. There are forty-nine majors and forty-one minors available.

Student Body Fifty-seven percent of the students are women. Ninety-six percent are white, 3 percent are foreign nationals, 2 percent are American Indian, and 1 percent is black. Thirty-seven percent of the students live on campus, and 10 percent commute. Eighty percent receive financial assistance. There are no social fraternities and sororities, but there are numerous departmental and honorary organizations.

Faculty The faculty numbers 136, of whom 120 are full-time. Eighty percent have terminal degrees. The student-faculty ratio is 19:1.

Key Facilities The library has just undergone a major building project, doubling in physical size. Holdings are about 225,000 volumes, plus considerable electronic capability. More than 500 personal computers, both Mac and DOS, are available in twenty-three labs on campus. Student labs have access to the Internet and the World Wide Web.

Athletics NSU is now affiliated with the NCAA Division II, having transferred from the NAIA in 1995, and is the only South Dakota school in the Northern Sun Intercollegiate Conference, which otherwise comprises Minnesota state universities. NSU competes in men's and women's basketball, golf, cross-country, indoor track and field, outdoor track and field, and tennis; men's football, baseball, and wrestling; and women's softball and volleyball.

Study Abroad Study abroad opportunities include formal arrangements with the University of Warsaw (Poland), the University of Sichuan (China), Fachhochschule Magdeburg (Germany), and the National Student Exchange, as well as short trips organized by individual faculty members to various European countries.

Support Services The campus is being converted, with additional ramps and elevators, to full access for the physically disabled.

Job Opportunities More than 400 work-study positions are funded each year through the Office of Financial Assistance, and many departments also have budgets for direct payment for student labor.

Tuition: $1646 for state residents (and residents of Minnesota), $4832 for nonresidents, per year (1996-97) $2469 per year full-time and $77.18 per credit part-time for nonresidents eligible for the Western Undergraduate Exchange.

Room and Board: $2672

Mandatory Fees: $844

Contact: Director: R. James Krueger, 12th Avenue and South Jay Street, Aberdeen, South Dakota 57401; Telephone: 605-626-7728; Fax: 605-626-3022; E-mail: kruegerj@wolf.northern.edu or honors@wolf.northern.edu; Web site: http://www.northern.edu

NORTHWESTERN STATE UNIVERSITY OF LOUISIANA

4 Pu C M Sc Tr

▼ Louisiana Scholars' College

Established as Louisiana's designated honors college by the Board of Regents in 1987, the Louisiana Scholars' College offers a comprehensive program of honors study in the liberal arts tradition. Highly motivated undergraduates benefit not only from the guidance of a knowledgeable and committed faculty, but also the encouragement to excel that comes from working closely with other outstanding students. Faculty members are carefully chosen in an intensive search process. They come from such prestigious institutions as Hendrix College, Purdue University, Tulane University, Tufts University, Middlebury College, and the University of North Carolina at Chapel Hill. The romance language professor studied at the University of Sorbonne in Paris, and the German professor received his doctoral degree from Tubingen in Germany.

Students work closely with faculty members, often in small, seminar-style classes. Students develop a core of knowledge that they hold in common with one another. All participate in "great books" seminars, sharing their experience of Homer, Plato, Dante, Shakespeare, Jefferson, Mozart, Darwin, Woolf, and other major figures. Students pursue a discipline-centered major or a multidisciplinary concentration that includes a senior thesis—a work that can take the form of a scientific study, a critical essay, or a project in the arts.

One of the benefits of housing an honors college on the University's campus is the multitude of choices that are open to the students. Scholars' College students have served as editor-in-chief of Northwestern's newspaper, manager of the radio station, and president of the Student Government Association. Many participate in the marching band (the state's largest), choral and dance ensembles, and theatrical performances and in the arts. Students play soccer, join the rowing team, run track, and are involved in a broad spectrum of intramural and intercollegiate sports. Within the College, students have established a film society, volunteered as tutors in the local schools, organized a book-swapping network, and held musical performances.

The College also has an honors dorm. Located near the center of campus, the dorm contains suites consisting of two rooms and a bathroom. Several lounges are the setting for occasional seminars, study sessions, and student forum meetings. More than a dormitory, it offers students in the College an environment in which to become a close-knit community.

Opened in 1987, the College currently enrolls 250 students.

Participation Requirements: Students are required to complete their core curriculum in the College and strive to maintain a 3.0 or better GPA. A 3.0 or better GPA is required for graduation from the Honors College. Also, students complete a senior thesis—a work that can take the form of scientific study, a critical essay, or a project in the arts. Graduation from Louisiana Scholar's College includes a State Certificate of Excellence.

Admission Process: Admission to the College is on a competitive basis, with consideration given to achievement, extracurricular involvement, and a letter of recommendation.

Scholarship Availability: Generous scholarships are available. Scholarships are awarded to more than 90 percent of the incoming freshmen. These include academic, sports, theater, and band scholarships; out-of-state fee waivers; and many more. Louisiana Scholars' College and Northwestern combine their scholarships to offer the best awards possible to the honors students. Academic-performance–based scholarships are also available to top students during their four years of study. Students in the College have won prestigious Younger Scholars Awards from the National Endowment for the Humanities. Others have held the Rotary International Fellowship for study abroad.

The Campus Context: Northwestern State University of Louisiana houses the following departments: Department of Business, Department of Creative and Performing Arts, Department of Education, Department of Family and Consumer Sciences, Department of General Studies, Department of Health and Human Services, Department of Journalism, Department of Language and Communication, Department of Mathematics and Sciences, Department of Military Science, Department of Nursing, Department of Psychology, Department of Social Sciences, and the Louisiana Scholars' College, which is considered a separate department. There are more than ninety areas of study incorporated into fifty-two degree programs leading to Bachelor of Arts or Bachelor of Science degrees.

Northwestern has much to offer students. The Louisiana Folklife Center was established in 1976 at Northwestern to identify, document, and present Louisiana's traditional arts. The Williamson Museum, founded in 1921, specializes in the anthropology and geography of Louisiana and adjacent areas. The Center for History of Louisiana Education contains a comprehensive collection of books, journals, theses, dissertations, manuscripts, tapes, and other materials available to researchers. As Louisiana's first "Normal" school, Northwestern was a natural choice for this honor. The most recent addition to the campus is the National Center for Preservation Training and Technology.

Student Body The student population is 40 percent men and 60 percent women. The ethnic distribution is 71 percent white, 20 percent black, and 8.5 percent other. Seventy percent of the students on campus receive some form of financial aid. Students have more than 130 clubs and activities, including thirteen fraternities and sororities, to choose from.

Faculty The faculty at Northwestern includes 262 professors, 73 percent with terminal degrees. Fourteen faculty members are dedicated to the Scholars' College, and all have terminal degrees. The student-faculty ratio 33:1. For the Scholars' College, it is 17:1.

Key Facilities Library resources include about 310,000 books and bound periodicals, more than 2,500 serial titles, a large U.S. Government documents collection, about 700,000 microforms, and more than 6,000 audiovisual items. Computer labs, either Mac or PC, are found in every department. Most are connected to the VAX, allowing students access to the Internet and mainframe programs. The journalism lab, a Mac lab, includes scanners. The Scholars' College has its own computer lab, complete with e-mail and World Wide Web access. The library has on-line searches via modem and a room with computers dedicated to the Internet.

Athletics Athletics are an important part of many students' college years. Students can become involved in football, basketball (both men's and women's), baseball, softball, women's soccer, women's tennis, track and cross-country (both men's and women's), and/or women's volleyball. The teams have won numerous championships over the years. Six GTE Academic All-American Awards have been given since 1989. All the teams are NCAA Division I, except football, which is NCAA Division IAA. Also available are club sports, such as the rowing team, intercollegiate flag football, and more. For those interested in staying on campus to compete, there is a full range of intramural sports to choose from.

Study Abroad Study-abroad opportunities are spearheaded by the International Programs Office. Northwestern is a member of the International Student Exchange Program (ISEP), a network of 150 institutions of higher education. More than twenty-five countries are on the list of possible places to study, including Asia, Africa, Canada, Europe, Australia, and Latin America. ISEP students pay regular tuition and fees, including room and board, at Northwestern prices. Also available are course offerings at international study sites, usually during the summer, by Northwestern and Scholars' College faculty members. Past sites have included Italy, Greece, and major corporations across the northern part of Europe.

Support Services The campus is handicapped-accessible and includes Student Support Services, an office set aside to assist the disabled with all of their needs.

Job Opportunities The campus has a student employment office that tracks job opportunities, gathers information on interested students, and makes matches between the two.

Tuition: $2067 for state residents, $4497 for nonresidents, per year (1996-97)

Room and Board: $2216 minimum

Mandatory Fees: $187

Contact: Director, Honors Program, Natchitoches, Louisiana 71497; Telephone: 800-838-2208 (toll-free); Fax: 318-357-5908; E-mail: lscrecruits@alpha.nsula.edu; Web site: http://www.nsula.edu/departments/scholars/

OAKLAND UNIVERSITY

$\boxed{\text{4 Pu C M Sc Tr}}$

▼ Honors College

The Honors College at Oakland University was established for highly motivated students seeking an unusually challenging undergraduate education. It offers a specially designed general education and additional requirements, in conjunction with a departmental major from the College of Arts and Sciences or one of the professional schools.

Students who apply to, and are admitted by, the Honors College are typically high achievers who want to notice, question, and think about what they are achieving. They choose small classes (10–20 students), which allow interaction with the professor and other students, rather than the anonymity of large lecture courses. Students take at least half of their required eight general education courses in Honors College core courses—courses that permit and encourage independence of thought.

Moreover, the Honors College students commit themselves to achieving a second-year-foreign language competency and to the creation of an original Independent Project. Finally, the graduating seniors take a Senior Colloquium together.

The Honors College is a place sought out by those students who want to challenge themselves and who want to learn intellectual and academic cooperation as well as independence. There are currently 250 students enrolled in the program.

Admission Process: Students are invited and chosen to be members of the Honors College program based on their high school average and ACT scores. College averages are considered for those already attending a university who wish to apply.

Scholarship Availability: The Honors College awards six nonrenewable scholarships and a $2000 per-year renewable scholarship to incoming students.

The Campus Context: Oakland University was created in 1957, on what was then the Wilson estate, from 1,500 undeveloped acres, located in suburban Oakland County, about 40 miles north of Detroit. Originally a branch of Michigan State University, it gained its autonomy in 1970.

Student Body Currently, there are 13,000 students, 1,200 of whom live on campus.

Faculty There are more than 350 faculty members at Oakland.

Tuition: $3448 minimum for state residents, $10,160 minimum for nonresidents, per year (1996-97). Part-time tuition ranges from $107.75 to $118.50 per credit for state residents and from $317.50 to $342 per credit for nonresidents.

Room and Board: $4250

Mandatory Fees: $254

Contact: Director: Dr. Brian Murphy, Rochester, Michigan 48309; Telephone: 810-370-4450; Fax: 810-370-4203; E-mail: bmurphy@oakland.edu

---

OAKTON COMMUNITY COLLEGE

2 Pu G M Sc Tr

▼ Honors at Oakton

Honors at Oakton offers academically talented students all the advantages of a traditional liberal arts college education: small classes, distinguished faculty members, and challenging courses. It is a program designed for students who have the ability to succeed anywhere but who choose to remain close to home and obtain a high-quality education at an affordable cost. Through participation in the student-centered, writing-intensive program, students are prepared to face the challenges of further education and competitive career markets.

Honors students themselves are the best advocates of Honors at Oakton. These comments are typical of those found on students' evaluations of their courses: "There is a closeness established among a smaller group, and I felt more at ease." "Honors students were really excited about the class and challenges. They were trying to achieve something extra for themselves, which impressed me." Honors classes feature discussions and student involvement and independent and collaborative work. One student wrote: "We were guided into an understanding of the whys rather than just bone dry facts."

Honors at Oakton features interdisciplinary, team-taught seminars, honors sections of general education courses, and the opportunity to pursue honors contract work in regular courses. Honors classes are usually composed of about 15 students, and they are taught by the best faculty members in the College. Oakton honors students have won a Truman Fellowship and a place on the Phi Theta Kappa All-American team; they have given papers at the National Undergraduate Research Conference, the annual conference of the National Collegiate Honors Council (NCHC), and the conference of the Society for Ecological Restoration.

Honors at Oakton sponsors a student organization and a variety of out-of-classroom activities, including trips to the theatre, symphony, and Chicago area museums; such guest speakers as Scott Turow, Tim O'Brien, Leon Lederman, and Frances Fitzgerald; an off-campus leadership workshop; and an annual banquet. Personalized counseling assists students at every step with academic choices, and when the time comes to transfer, students are able to attend workshops on choosing a transfer institution, finding and applying for financial aid, and completing the application. An annual luncheon brings transfer admission directors from Northwestern University, the University of Chicago, Loyola University, DePaul University, and other Chicago-area colleges and universities to campus to meet with honors students. Oakton honors students have transferred successfully to such institutions as these, as well as Cornell University, Oberlin College, Grinnell College, the University of Notre Dame, and many other outstanding colleges.

Honors at Oakton enrolls between 150 and 200 students every year.

Participation Requirements: Students must take 18 hours of honors courses to graduate as an Honors Program Scholar, but many students take fewer than 18 hours, and some take many more. All honors courses are specially designated on the transcript. To graduate as an Honors Scholar, students must maintain a 3.25 GPA, and honors program graduates are specially noted at graduation.

Admission Process: To be admitted to Honors at Oakton, a student must have an ACT of 25 or an SAT of 1150 and be in the top 20 percent of the high school class. Students are also admitted to Honors at Oakton based on a 3.5 GPA at Oakton or a transfer school or a GED score of 300. Students with a bachelor's degree or higher are automatically eligible for Honors at Oakton. Students must maintain a 3.25 GPA to continue in the program.

The Campus Context: Oakton Community College has two campuses, one in Des Plaines and the other in Skokie, Illinois. Among special services, a modern child-care center is available for children of students, staff, and faculty. Tutoring is available for all subjects, as are support services for students with physical and learning disabilities. Other features include media-based courses, adult student services, and international student services. The College offers three baccalaureate degrees and thirty-five vocational degrees and certificates.

Student Body The total enrollment at Oakton is 10,400: 44 percent men and 56 percent women. All are commuter students, with an average age of 30. Approximately 6 percent of students receive financial aid.

Faculty Of the 600 faculty members, 152 are full-time and 448 are part-time. The student-faculty ratio is 17:1.

Key Facilities The library houses 70,000 volumes and has immediate access to material from Illinois libraries. There are fourteen computer labs housing 600 computers. A full array of constantly updated courses is available in computer science, applications, and technology.

Athletics Oakton has ten intercollegiate athletic teams competing in the Skyway Conference: golf, cross-country, women's volleyball, and tennis; men's soccer in the fall; men's and women's basketball in the winter; and baseball, women's softball, and men's tennis in the spring.

Study Abroad Students have opportunities for study abroad in Canterbury, England; Salzburg, Austria; San Jose, Costa Rica; and Diemen and Hertogenbosch, the Netherlands. There are also study-abroad and NCHC-sponsored semesters for honors students.

Job Opportunities Students find opportunities for employment on campus as 15-hour-per-week student aides.

Tuition: $1050 for area residents, $3840 for state residents, $4590 for nonresidents, per year (1996-97)

Mandatory Fees: $48

Contact: Director: Dr. Rinda West, 1600 East Golf Road, Des Plaines, Illinois 60016; Telephone: 847-635-1914; Fax: 847-635-1764; E-mail: rinda@oakton.edu

---

OHIO DOMINICAN COLLEGE

4 Pr G S Sc Tr

▼ Honors Program

The Ohio Dominican College Honors Program is designed for creative and intellectually curious and academically able students who are willing to explore new ideas or new applications in various theoretical or practical fields.

The Honors Program at Ohio Dominican College has existed continuously since 1960.

Participation Requirements: To complete the program, the student must earn 16 credits in Honors Option courses, usually during the first four semesters for those who enter as freshmen. Special arrangements are made for transfer students. A major project, undertaken through independent study during the junior and senior years, is the capstone of the program. On the completion of this project, the student gives a public presentation.

A student-planned curriculum that allows students to combine offerings from a variety of departments in a pattern suited to their personal gifts, talents, and individual educational goals is a possible option within the Honors Program. The program also conducts public forums on significant public issues, usually under the auspice of the National Issues Forum, sponsored by the Kettering Foundation.

Students completing the Honors Program receive a gold cord, which is worn over the academic gown at Commencement. Courses completed for honors credit are noted on the transcript. Students of the College are eligible for membership in three national honor societies: Delta Epsilon Sigma, Kappa Gamma Pi, and Psi Chi. Membership is determined by faculty vote.

In a given academic year, approximately 60 students and 20 faculty members participate in the Honors Program. Faculty members participate in the Honors Program not only by offering Honors Option courses, but also by presenting to the College Community Honors Colloquia on topics reflecting their personal research interests or travel experiences. The Director of the Honors Program is assisted and advised by the Honors Committee, which consists of 4 teaching faculty members and 3 honors students.

Admission Process: Entrance to the program is possible after a high school student has been accepted and given a scholarship award. Enrolled students with a 3.2 GPA or special recommendation by a professor are also eligible. An interview with the Director should be arranged as early as possible. All courses in the curriculum are available for the Honors Option, which is designed through a special agreement between the professor and student.

The Campus Context: Ohio Dominican College is a Catholic liberal arts college with a Dominican tradition, guided in its educational mission by the Dominican motto to contemplate truth and to share with others the fruits of that contemplation. The College offers the Bachelor of Arts, Bachelor of Science in Education, Bachelor of Science, Associate of Arts, and Associate of Science degrees. Thirty-three majors, twenty-seven minors, and a variety of certificate programs are available.

Ohio Dominican offers students a high-quality, career-oriented liberal arts education in an intimate attractive setting conducive to intellectual exchange, personal growth, and the development of enduring values. Ohio Dominican is pleased that its campus family includes students of varying ages from different backgrounds and cultures who experience varying life circumstances. The services and policies of the College are intended to address this diversity.

Ohio Dominican's 80-acre campus is located on the northeastern edge of Columbus, the state capital. The city population is approximately 643,000. Columbus is at the center of a six-county metropolitan area with a population of 1,472,000.

Student Body Enrollment in fall 1995 was 1,736: 35 percent men and 65 percent women. The ethnic distribution is as follows: 74.3 percent white, 15 percent black, 1.8 percent Hispanic, 1.2 percent other American minorities, and 1.1 percent Asian or Pacific Islander.

International students represent 6.3 percent of the student population. Approximately 85 percent of the students receive some form of financial aid. College scholarships involve a community service component.

Faculty Of the 104 total faculty members, 58 are full-time; 78 percent of those hold terminal degrees. There are 27 adjunct faculty members. The student-faculty ratio is 16:1.

Key Facilities The Spangler Learning Center is an outstanding college resource containing 154,000 volumes with CD-ROM and microform resources, more than 500 continuing periodical subscriptions, daily and weekly newspapers, and a professional staff for personal and group reference service.

Computer facilities are available in the Academic Center, Computing Services, library, and Multimedia Center. The Computer Services facilities consist of PC microcomputers utilizing the Microsoft Professional Office suite (the college standard) of software products, including Word, Excel, Access, and Power Point. Other standardized and discipline-specific software is available.

In January 1996, the campus was connected to the Dominican Learning Network, utilizing Microsoft's NT operating system and Windows applications. The Internet is available to students at several locations on campus, including three state-of-the-art computer classrooms and open-area student computer workstations. The Multimedia Center has a student worksite consisting of a multimedia computer, flatbed scanner, and color printer. For advanced special projects, a 35-mm slide scanner and CD-ROM writer are available.

Athletics Students participate in six intercollegiate sports, including men's soccer, basketball, and baseball and women's volleyball, basketball, and softball. There are intramural sport and recreation programs, including leagues, tournaments, contests, lessons, classes, and outings.

Study Abroad Individualized study abroad programs are arranged through the International Office.

Support Services Campus Ministry programs include pastoral care of students, liturgical and ecumenical worship experiences, and educational experiences, including days of reflection, weekend retreats, inquiry classes, lectures, and marriage preparation.

Campus buildings and facilities are accessible for persons with disabilities. The Director of the Academic Center works with students to ensure that their special needs for educational services are met.

Job Opportunities Work-study job opportunities, funded by the federal government or the College, are available. The Columbus metropolitan area offers job opportunities with local employers. Work hours can usually be arranged according to class schedules.

Tuition: $8910 per year (1996-97)

Room and Board: $4570

Contact: Director: Sister Thomas Albert Corbett, OP, Columbus, Ohio 43219; Telephone: 614-251-4612; Fax: 614-252-0776; E-mail: corbett@odc.edu; Web site: http://www.odc.edu/

THE OHIO STATE UNIVERSITY

4 Pu C L Sc Tr

▼ University Honors Program

Within the context of a major research university, the Ohio State University Honors Program offers outstanding students a variety of exciting learning opportunities, including more than 150 honors classes each year. Honors classes have an average size of 18 students, are taught by members of the faculty with a strong commitment to undergraduate education, and can only be taken by honors students.

Honors students have many opportunities for research and scholarship under the guidance of a faculty member. Typically, this culminates in a senior honors thesis and graduation with distinction. Grants and scholarships are available on a competitive basis to students involved in their own research projects. Each spring selected students present their research at an Undergraduate Research Recognition Event.

Three honors living centers provide on-campus housing for honors students. They provide rooms in a variety of sizes and configurations, comfortably furnished study areas, a fully equipped kitchen, game areas, and television lounges. Personal computer centers are located within or near all three honors residence halls.

An active program of cocurricular activities is associated with the University Honors Program, including the Honors Peer Mentor Program, which matches first-quarter honors students with upperclass honors students, and the Honors Program Board, which plans and stages a variety of cultural and educational programs, service projects, and student-faculty events.

The 12-year-old program currently enrolls 3,600 students.

Participation Requirements: To maintain honors eligibility, students must maintain a minimum GPA and in the Colleges of Arts and Sciences follow an approved honors contract.

In addition to Summa, Magna, and Cum Laude recognition awarded to students graduating in the top 10 percent of the class, graduation with honors is awarded to students completing an honors contract. Graduation with distinction is given to students successfully completing a thesis project.

Admission Process: To join the program, students must have graduated in the top 10 percent of their high school class and have either an ACT score of 30 or above or a SAT score of 1300 or above. Outstanding students who do not meet these criteria are encouraged to submit an essay with their applications.

Scholarship Availability: The Ohio State University offers a competitive merit aid program, with scholarships awarded based upon a student's high school record, ACT or SAT scores, and the results of an on-campus scholarship program. These scholarships include University Scholarships, $1200 per year awards for four years; Tradition Scholarships, half in-state tuition for four years; Medalist Scholarships, full in-state tuition for four years; and Presidential Scholarships, which provide full in-state tuition, room and board, book allowance, and miscellaneous expenses for four years.

National Merit and National Achievement Scholarships are awarded to National Merit/Achievement finalists who designate Ohio State as their first-choice institution of attendance by February 15. Such students may also receive a Distinguished Scholarship. Taken together, these scholarships cover full in-state tuition plus $3000 per year for 4 years.

Other financial assistance, including scholarships, research support, grants, loans, and part-time employment, is available to qualified students at the Ohio State University.

The Campus Context: There are nineteen colleges at the Ohio State University: Arts; Biological Sciences; Business; Dentistry; Education; Engineering; Food, Agricultural, and Environmental Sciences; Human Ecology; Humanities; Law; Math and Physical Sciences; Medicine and Nursing; Optometry; Pharmacy; Social and Behavioral Sciences; Social Work; University College; and Veterinary Medicine. Students may enroll in 215 majors in 104 academic departments. Distinguished facilities on campus include the Ohio Supercomputer Center, Wexner Center for the Arts, and the James Cancer Research Center and Hospital.

Student Body Undergraduate enrollment is 40,993: 21,320 men and 19,673 women. The ethnic distribution is 87 percent white, 6.7 percent African American, 4.4 percent Asian-American, 1.6 percent Hispanic, and 0.3 percent Native American. There are 3,827 international students. About 18 percent of students live on campus, and another 21.6 percent live in the area adjacent to campus. There are thirty fraternities and twenty sororities.

Faculty Of the 4,310 faculty members, 3,909 are full-time, 95 percent of whom have terminal degrees. The student-faculty ratio is 14:1.

Key Facilities The library houses 4.7 million volumes. Extensive computer facilities include two Cray supercomputers.

Athletics In athletics, Ohio State has thirty-two Division I intercollegiate varsity teams, seventy sports clubs, and sixty-two intramural sports programs.

Study Abroad Study-abroad opportunities are coordinated through the Office of International Education.

Support Services Disabled-student facilities include accessible buildings and special services.

Job Opportunities A wide array of work opportunities are available both on and off campus.

Tuition: $3468 for state residents, $10,335 for nonresidents, per year (1996-97)

Room and Board: $4907

Contact: Director: Dr. David Hothersall, Kuhn Honors House, 220 West Twelfth Avenue, Columbus, Ohio 43210; Telephone: 614-292-3135; Fax: 614-292-6135; E-mail: osuhons@osu.edu; Web site: www.osu.edu/units/honors/honors.html

OHIO UNIVERSITY

4 Pu C M Sc Tr

▼ Honors Tutorial College

Ohio University's Honors Tutorial College is based on the tutorial model of collaborative learning found at Oxford and Cambridge Universities, in which each student meets in individual sessions to discuss and explore content assigned, researched, and examined.

The College was founded in 1973 after nearly ten years of departmentally based honors programs. The Honors Tutorial College is a full degree-granting college in twenty-five academic disciplines ranging from biological sciences to physics and journalism to dance. A Secondary Education Certificate is also available for Honors Tutorial students. These programs are separate and distinct from the traditional undergraduate degrees, although the honors student's curriculum may include traditional course work as well as tutorials.

Each program has a core curriculum, and students enroll in at least one tutorial each term. Additional collateral course work is selected with the help of an adviser in a fashion that permits tailoring of each student's total college curriculum. There is no hour minimum for graduation; students must demonstrate competencies through high-quality writing, thinking, and a research thesis or project that is defended before graduation.

Honors Tutorial students are the only students not responsible for the University's General Education requirements, save Freshman English and Junior Composition, which may be waived. Most programs are three years in duration, and students often remain a fourth year and complete the requirements for the master's degree in their discipline.

Approximately 200 faculty members participate as tutors each year, giving service, in most cases, to the College in addition to their normal academic loads. Tutors are full faculty members with outstanding teaching and research credentials.

Admission Process: Students are selected on the basis of SAT I and ACT scores, rank in high school class, achievement, academic discipline, a written essay, and personal interview by both the Dean's Office and the Director of Studies in the academic program of choice. Although some programs require higher scores and indications of achievement, the minimums for consideration (not admission) are 1240 SAT, 30 ACT, and rank in the top 10 percent of the student's high school class. Significant scholarly, literary, artistic, and community experiences are also considered in the determination of the student's application. A very limited number of openings are available for transfer students from both within and outside the University.

The College currently has a ceiling of 225 students. Each year the College receives more than 400 applications, from which it selects approximately one third for on-site personal interviews and traditionally admits 100 for a yield of 55-65.

Applications for the following fall semester are due by December 15.

Scholarship Availability: Scholarships and grants are available from full tuition, room, and board to smaller grants and awards. Research apprenticeship programs provide, on a competitive basis, salary for student researchers to work with faculty members on significant projects.

The Campus Context: Ohio University, a "Research II" university, is the oldest university in the Northwest Territory, having been founded in 1804. It offers academic programs on five regional campuses in addition to the main campus at Athens. The Honors Tutorial College programs are only available on the Athens campus. The University is located on a residential campus in southeast Ohio.

There are ten colleges on campus: Honors Tutorial, Arts and Sciences, Communication, Engineering, Fine Arts, Osteopathic Medicine, Health and Human Services, University College, Education, and Business. In addition, the University offers certificate programs in many areas, most notably women's studies and international studies. Students are enrolled in 311 baccalaureate, fifty-eight master's, fifty-six doctoral (including osteopathic medicine), and twenty-four associate degree programs.

The University has excellent science laboratories, including an accelerator facility, and state-of-the-art electronic media facilities, including public television and radio stations, film facilities, and digital photojournalism labs.

Student Body Of the approximately 19,500 students enrolled at the Athens campus, about 54 percent are women and 46 percent are men. Minority distribution is 5.4 percent, and there are more than 1,200 international students from more than 100 countries. Last year 5,352 students received scholarship assistance. There are thirty sororities and fraternities on the Athens campus with strong student support.

Faculty There are more than 800 full-time faculty members on the Athens campus, nearly all with appropriate terminal degrees. The ratio of students to faculty in nontutorial classes is 17:1.

Key Facilities The University library has ARL (Association of Research Libraries) status and contains more than 2 million volumes. The library system is part of OhioLink, a computer network of university libraries. The University has many mainframes and specialty mini-mainframes for specific departments and research. Each student is given an e-mail address and is able to access University, library, and Internet facilities from the dormitory room. The Honors Tutorial College supports an excellent computer laboratory in the Honors Dorm, a dorm in which most honors students live.

Athletics The 13,000-seat Convocation Center is the site of sporting events, and the new Ping Recreation Center is one of the finest multipurpose facilities in the nation. The University offers a full range of athletics, with MAC-level finalists in basketball.

Study Abroad The University has a full-time Study Abroad Office, helping students take advantage of programs at more than 100 universities around the world. In addition, the Honors Tutorial College has special exchange agreements with a number of universities abroad, and students are encouraged to participate.

Support Services The University is in full compliance with the Americans with Disabilities Act (ADA) and has available administrative, instructional, and other appropriate support, including specialty technologies, for students needing such assistance.

Job Opportunities The University offers work-study programs and an advanced career exploration work program. In addition, the Athens business community offers a number of work opportunities for students.

Tuition: $4080 for state residents, $8574 for nonresidents, per year (1996-97)

Room and Board: $4473

Contact: Dean: Dr. Joseph H. Berman, 35 Park Place, Athens, Ohio 45701; Telephone: 614-593-2723; Fax: 614-593-9521; E-mail: berman@ohiou.edu

OKLAHOMA CITY UNIVERSITY

4 Pr G M Tr

▼ University Honors Program

Oklahoma City University (OCU) established the University Honors Program in 1990 to meet the special interests and needs of intellectually gifted students. Open to qualified undergraduates of all majors, the University Honors Program offers honors sections of Foundation Curriculum (general education) courses. Honors students may choose from a wide variety of these courses, which include psychology, computers and artificial intelligence, literature and philosophy, history, and many others. During their first semester in the Honors Program, all new students enroll in the 1-hour Honors Colloquium, a course designed to help each class of honors students become better acquainted with each other and the Honors Program. The capstone honors course is the Junior-Senior seminar, which is offered with varying topics each semester.

At Oklahoma City University, an honors course generally covers the same material as a traditional course, but honors sections are smaller and more often use a seminar format. The requirements differ from those of regular classes, not so much in the amount of work demanded as in the type of work. Honors classes typically involve extensive class participation, and written work is often in the form of essays or individual research projects.

In addition to the academic advantages of the University Honors Program, OCU honors students enjoy other benefits as well. Honors students have the benefit of priority semester enrollment and an additional .25 added to each credit hour of honors courses. Honors students have opportunities to meet with visiting scholars and attend special events, both social and academic. As part of a network of the National Collegiate Honors Council, OCU honors students may present papers at regional and national conferences and participate in exciting summer and semester programs.

There are 120 students in the program.

Participation Requirements: In order to be a University Honors Program graduate, students must complete 25 hours in honors sections of Foundation Curriculum courses while maintaining at least a 3.5 cumulative university GPA and a 3.25 cumulative GPA in honors courses.

Two courses, the Honors Colloquium and the Junior-Senior Seminar, are required for all students in the program. Students may select from a variety of courses, including independent research, to complete the balance of the 25-hour requirement. Upon successful completion of the requirements, honors students receive special recognition upon graduation, a gold stole to wear at the Commencement ceremony with their cap and gown, and a special designation on their diplomas.

Admission Process: The University Honors Program welcomes applications during the fall semester from all interested OCU first-year and sophomore students. To be eligible, a student must have a 3.5 GPA in a minimum of 12 OCU hours. The application process includes documentation of previous University midterm grades, written recommendations from 2 OCU faculty members, and a brief essay describing why the student wishes to join the program.

Currently enrolled students should apply no later than October 15.

Scholarship Availability: OCU offers a wide variety of scholarships, both academic and need-based, to students of exceptional ability and promise.

The Campus Context: Oklahoma City University is a campus of six colleges and schools: Petree College of Arts and Sciences; Margaret E. Petree School of Music and Performing Arts; Kramer School of Nursing; Meinders School of Business; Wimberley School of Religion; and the Law School. Nine bachelor's degrees with seventy-one majors and eleven master's degrees with forty-one majors are offered on campus.

Distinguished campus facilities include the Petree College of Arts and Sciences Building, a two-story structure featuring classrooms, offices, a learning center, seminar and meeting rooms, and a mass communication center that houses the campus newspaper and OCU-TV2 station. OCU-TV2 is a wireless cable television station that provides students with hands-on production experience and access to a professionally designed studio and two control rooms. The Sarkeys Law Center, opened in spring 1994, houses classrooms, seminar rooms, moot courtrooms, the Native American Legal Resource Center, administrative offices, and student organization offices. The Gold Star Building, renovated in 1996, which houses the law library, faculty offices, and the offices of the OCU Law Review, contains four floors of library space and offices and is crowned by a tower that has become an Oklahoma City landmark. The Kramer School of Nursing building is a state-of-the-art newly constructed facility. The Noble Center for

Competitive Enterprise building houses the Meinders School of Business, the B.D. Eddie Business Research and Consulting Center, the Jack Conn School of Community Banking, offices, and classrooms.

The Kirkpatrick Fine Arts Center, which houses the Margaret E. Petree School of Music and Performing Arts, offices, classrooms, and practice rooms, contains the Kirkpatrick Theater, a 1,119-seat facility with a fully equipped proscenium stage; Burg Theater, a 255-seat auditorium with a three-quarter round stage used for dramatic productions, lectures, and other special presentations; dance studios; costume and scene shops; dressing rooms; and the recently constructed 500-seat Petree Recital Hall, which is designed to offer the finest facilities for large and small instrumental and vocal ensembles and solo recitals and audio and television recording of performances and is equipped with two 9-foot Steinway Concert Grand pianos.

The Bishop W. Angie Smith Chapel is home to the Wimberly School of Religion and Church Vocations, classrooms, and offices. In this building, designed by Pietro Bulluschi, the main chapel seats 650 and features four large German stained glass windows depicting the seasons. The Norick Art Center, designed to be as functional, comfortable, and safe for students as possible, contains the Hulsey Gallery, designed by specifications from the Smithsonian Institute.

Student Body Undergraduate enrollment is 2,400: 45 percent men and 55 percent women. The ethnic distribution is as follows: white, 81 percent; Asian/Pacific Islander, 6 percent; black, 6 percent; American Indian, 5 percent; and Hispanic, 2 percent. There are 717 international students. Eighty percent of the students are commuters, while the other 20 percent are campus residents. Sixty-four percent of all undergraduates receive financial aid, and 88 percent of all domestic undergraduate students receive financial aid. There are three social fraternities and three social sororities.

Faculty Of the 367 faculty members, 161 are full-time. Sixty-nine percent of full-time faculty members have terminal degrees. The student-faculty ratio is 14:1.

Key Facilities The Dulaney-Browne Library houses 292,651 volumes, 230,966 government documents, 4,180 current serials, 577,525 microforms, 10,738 sound recordings, and 785 films and videos. Library resources also include archives for the Oklahoma Conference of the United Methodist Church, the University Archives, the Foundation Center collection, the Shirk History Center, the Rapp Language Laboratory, the Listening Library, the children's literature collection, and the reference collection. The campus has 130 computers, ten in each residence hall and the others located in four labs.

Athletics OCU is a member of the Sooner Athletic Conference and National Association of Intercollegiate Athletics (NAIA), offering nine men's and women's sports. Men's sports include basketball, baseball, soccer, golf, and tennis. Women's sports include basketball, softball, soccer, and tennis. Men's basketball has won four national championships, women's basketball has won one national championship, softball has won three National Championships, and a member of the men's tennis team has won the national singles championship. All teams have been participants in post-season championship competition, and individual members of the various teams have been named All-Americans and Academic All-Americans.

Study Abroad OCU is a member of the Council on International Education, offering opportunities for students to study and do internships in Europe, Russia, Latin America, and Asia. OCU has existing relationships with various colleges and universities throughout the world. Academic departments offer a range of international study opportunities each year, and the University sponsors overseas trips for performing arts majors.

Support Services The Office for Disability Concerns meets each semester to review requests for special accommodations and make recommendations as to what services are appropriate and available. Ninety-nine percent of the campus is accessible to the physically disabled.

Job Opportunities Numerous work opportunities for students are available through the Federal Work-Study Program, University Work Studies Program, and contract labor.

Tuition: $8050 per year (1996-97)

Room and Board: $3990

Mandatory Fees: $85

Contact: Director: Dr. Virginia McCombs, 2501 North Blackwelder, Oklahoma City, Oklahoma 73106; Telephone: 405-521-5457; Fax: 405-521-5447; E-mail: vmccombs@frodo.okcu.edu; Web site: http://frodo.okcu.edu/www/departments/honors/honors.html

OKLAHOMA STATE UNIVERSITY

| 4 Pu G C D L Tr |

▼ University Honors Program

The University Honors Program provides many opportunities and challenges for outstanding undergraduate students in a supportive learning environment. Special honors sections of general education courses, interdisciplinary honors courses, and special honors projects allow students to enhance their learning experience. Classes are small (typically 20–22 students, but frequently smaller), and a wide range of honors courses is offered each semester. Honors courses are taught by members of the faculty who are experienced and known for excellence in the classroom and in their academic fields. Frequent interaction with other honors students and faculty members helps honors students develop a "feeling of belonging" in the small-college atmosphere of the Honors Program while being able to take advantage of the opportunities offered by a comprehensive research university.

Active participants in the Honors Program (6 honors credit hours per semester during the freshman and sophomore years, 3 hours per semester thereafter) earn use of the Honors Program Study Lounge and computer lab in the Edmon Low Library, priority enrollment for the following semester, and extended semester-long library checkout privileges. They also have the option to live in Parker Honors Hall on a space-available basis.

Special honors advising is provided by Honors Advisors, who themselves have earned honors program degrees.

Honors Program students regularly participate in conferences of the Great Plains Honors Council and the National Collegiate Honors Council, as do members of the faculty and professional honors staff. Opportunities for community service are available, as are research opportunities with faculty members that lead to the senior honors thesis or senior honors report.

Approximately two thirds of Honors Program degree students continue their education in graduate and professional schools, including some of the most prestigious in the nation, while others seek immediate entry into their chosen career fields.

In the 1995 decennial accreditation review of Oklahoma State University by the North Central Association of Colleges and Schools, the University Honors Program was found to be one of the major strengths of the university. The OSU Honors Director is Vice President of the National Collegiate Honors Council.

The Honors Program has been in existence since 1965 in the College of Arts and Sciences and since 1989 on a University-wide basis. There are currently 608 active participants.

Participation Requirements: The Honors Program degree is the highest distinction that may be earned by an undergraduate student at Oklahoma State University (OSU). Requirements include completion of the General Honors Award (21 honors credit hours with a distribution requirement over four of six broad subject-matter areas and including a minimum of two honors seminars or special interdisciplinary honors courses), completion of the Departmental or College Honors Award (12 upper-division honors credit hours, including a senior honors thesis or senior honors project), a total of 39 honors credit hours, and an OSU cumulative GPA of at least 3.5. Transfer students may count up to 15 transfer honors credit hours toward the General Honors Award. The honors hood is conferred on Honors Program degree recipients at Commencement, along with a special Honors Program degree diploma.

Admission Process: Freshmen are eligible for admission to the University Honors Program on the basis of ACT composite scores of 27–29 (SAT 1200–1310), with a high school GPA of 3.75 or higher; or an ACT score of 30 or higher (SAT 1320 or higher), with a high school GPA of 3.5 or higher. Continuing students are eligible according to the following OSU and cumulative GPAs: 0–59 credit hours, 3.25; 60–93 credit hours, 3.37; 94 or more credit hours, 3.5.

Scholarship Availability: The University Honors Program does not award scholarships. For information about scholarships, interested students should contact the Director of University Scholarships at OSU.

The Campus Context: Oklahoma State University is a campus of nine colleges: Agricultural Sciences and Natural Resources; Arts and Sciences; Business Administration; Education; Engineering, Architecture, and Technology; Human Environmental Sciences; Graduate College; Osteopathic Medicine (in Tulsa); and Veterinary Medicine. There are eighty-six bachelor's, sixty-five master's, one specialist, and forty-five doctoral degree programs offered. Among the unique facilities on campus are an Advanced Technology Center, a Center for International Trade Development, a Food Processing Center, the Noble Research Center, the Old Central (Oklahoma Museum of Higher Education), the Seretean Center for the Performing Arts, the OSU Telecommunications Center, and the Center for Laser Technology.

Student Body Undergraduate enrollment is 14,564: 54.1 percent men and 45.9 percent women. The ethnic distribution of students is Caucasian, 79.6 percent; international, 7.3 percent (1,063); Native American, 7.2 percent; black, 2.5 percent; Hispanic, 1.7 percent; and Asian, 1.7 percent. Almost 74 percent of the students receive financial aid. There are twenty-three fraternities and thirteen sororities on campus.

Faculty The faculty totals 972. Of the 960 full-time faculty members, 81 percent have terminal degrees. The student-faculty ratio is 14:1.

Key Facilities The OSU library houses 1.7 million volumes. In addition to the University mainframe computer, there are computer labs maintained by Computing and Information Services in the following locations: Bennett Hall (fifty systems), Wilham Hall (ninety systems), Student Union (sixty systems), Classroom Building (twenty-six systems), Poultry (twenty-three systems), and the College of Business Administration (eighty systems). Some individual colleges and departments also have computer laboratories. All students automatically receive an e-mail address. The Edmon Low Library is computerized, and the Honors Program Study Lounge and computer facility are now located in the Library.

Athletics OSU is a member of the new Big 12 Conference, one of the most competitive NCAA conferences in the nation.

Study Abroad Study-abroad opportunities are handled by the OSU Office of International Programs, which should be contacted directly. Bailey Family Memorial Trust scholarships for study abroad are frequently received by Honors Program students.

Support Services Facilities for disabled students include computer labs with adaptive technology. A list of full services is available from the Student Disabilities Services Office.

Job Opportunities There is a campus work-study program and employment with various campus units.

Tuition: Full-time: $1248 minimum for state residents, $4020 minimum for nonresidents, per year (1996-97); part-time: $52 minimum for state residents, $167.50 minimum for nonresidents, per credit hour.

Room and Board: $4160 minimum

Mandatory Fees: Full-time: $460 minimum per year; part-time: $28.76 minimum per semester

Contact: Director: Robert L. Spurrier Jr., 509 Edmon Low Library, Stillwater, Oklahoma 74078-1073; Telephone: 405-744-6799; Fax: 405-744-7074; E-mail: rls0108@okway.okstate.edu; Web site: http://www.okstate.edu/honors

OLD DOMINION UNIVERSITY

4 Pu G L Sc Tr

▼ Honors College

Established in 1986, the Academic Honors Program was renamed the Honors College in 1996. It administers the Undergraduate Research Program, the award-winning President's Lecture Series, degrees with honors for the academic departments, and a program of study for honors students. This four-year program offers specially designed, low-enrollment courses exclusively to honors students. In the first two years, the majority of these courses is used to fulfill the University's lower division General Education requirements. To complete the course of study in the Honors College, students must take a minimum of six general education honors courses, two upper-division courses as honors, a junior tutorial, and a senior colloquium. Academic degrees are earned in any of the six colleges of the University.

With an emphasis on teaching, innovation, and small classes, the Honors College offers the experience of a small liberal arts college within the framework of a large university. After four years of such an experience, students are better equipped to structure their lives and careers to meet their individual needs and strengths. A program that offers the best of both a small college and a large university naturally promotes greater sensitivity to self and society.

There are approximately 525 students in the Honors College.

Participation Requirements: Currently enrolled students and transfer students who have completed their lower-division general education requirements may participate in the honors experience by taking upper-division courses as honors (open to any student with a GPA of 3.25), earning a degree with honors in their major, or competing for a $1000 undergraduate research grant (open to all juniors and seniors with minimum GPAs of 3.4). Students must maintain an overall GPA of 3.0. Each spring at the Honors College awards banquet, graduates receive a certificate, a medal to wear on their gown, and a silver tassel for their mortar board. Their names are listed separately in the graduation program, and note of their accomplishment is made on their student transcripts.

Admission Process: Criteria used to select the 150 first-year students admitted annually include high school GPA and curriculum, SAT scores, class rank, and a written personal statement. Other students are admitted on the basis of a 3.5 college GPA, completion of at least four remaining general education courses as honors courses, and two letters of recommendation from University faculty members.

Scholarship Availability: All Honors College students receive an annual $500 stipend. The College also has an endowed scholarship, the Cranmer/Skinner Scholarship, which provides two awards each year. The Claire Nesson Academic Honors Scholarship funds an additional 2 honors students each year. Students who opt for the dual-degree program between the College of Arts and Letters and the College of Engineering and Technology are eligible to apply for the endowed Sumitoma Scholarship. This scholarship also requires that the student study Japanese and do an internship at the Sumitoma Corporation in Japan (expenses paid).

The Campus Context: Old Dominion University had its formal beginning in 1930 as the Norfolk Division of the College of William and Mary. It gained its independence in 1962. Currently, the University has seven colleges: the College of Arts and Letters, the College of Business and Public Administration, the Darden College of Education, the College of Engineering and Technology, the College of Health Sciences, the Honors College, and the College of Sciences. Old Dominion University has sixty-five baccalaureate programs, sixty master's programs, two certificates of advanced study, and twenty-one doctoral programs.

Student Body Of the 17,400 students, 54 percent are women, 15 percent are African American, 5 percent are Asian American, and 3 percent are Native Americans and Hispanics. About 80 percent of the entering freshmen come from Virginia. At present, 850 international students from more than 100 countries are in residence. About 2,500 students live on campus in residence halls, while another 3,500 live adjacent to the campus in a variety of private apartments and a number of special houses. There are seventeen fraternities and ten sororities on campus.

Faculty The full-time faculty numbers 623. All tenured and tenure-track faculty members must hold the doctorate or the terminal degree in their field. The student-faculty ratio is 15:1.

Key Facilities The library holds 1.8 million items. The University has an IBM 3090 mainframe and UNIX platform and four public networked labs; the dorms and campus buildings are also networked. In all, there are 1,600 computer workstations.

Distinguished facilities include TELETECHNET—in partnership with several community colleges, military installations, and private corporations, Old Dominion delivers upper-division undergraduate courses to place-bound students throughout the Commonwealth of Virginia. Other facilities of note include the Child Study Center, the Applied Marine Research Facility, and the close research connections with NASA (Langley) and the Continuous Electron Beam Accelerator Facility in Hampton, Virginia.

Athletics The athletic teams have won twenty national championships since 1975, including three in women's basketball, seven in field hockey, eight in sailing, and a Division II men's basketball crown in 1975. Teams have competed on the Division I level within the NCAA since 1976 and currently belong to the Colonial Athletic Association. The University sponsors sixteen intercollegiate sports, including eight men's sports (soccer, wrestling, basketball, swimming, tennis, baseball, golf, and sailing) and eight women's sports (soccer, basketball, cross-country, field hockey, swimming, tennis, lacrosse, and sailing).

Study Abroad Study abroad is available in every discipline and ranges in length from short summer group programs to individual exchanges lasting for a semester or a full academic year. Currently, study abroad is offered at eighty universities worldwide, including direct exchanges with England and Australia.

Job Opportunities A substantial number of jobs are available for students on campus, including work-study opportunities.

Tuition: $4020 for state residents, $10,380 for nonresidents, per year (1996-97)

Room and Board: $4770

Mandatory Fees: $96

Contact: Dean: Dr. Louis H. Henry, 2228 Webb Center, Norfolk, Virginia 23529-0076; Telephone: 757-683-4865; Fax: 757-683-4970; E-mail: lhh100f@redwood.webb.odu.edu

ONONDAGA COMMUNITY COLLEGE

2 Pu G S Sc Tr

▼ **Honors Program**

The Honors Program is currently being developed. It will be open to qualified students from all curricula. Unofficial piloting of Individual Honors Enrichment Contracts was done in spring 1996. Official piloting of this type of offering began in fall 1996. Official piloting of honors sections began in spring 1997. The development of Honors Seminars and/or other specialized courses should follow. The final stage should be the determination of the criteria for an Honors Diploma or Honors Concentration to be awarded to students.

Participation Requirements: Requirements and conditions for participation in the program will be developed as the offerings run. It is anticipated that those participating initially will be students who are currently enrolled. However, those new and prospective students interested in participating can request further information by contacting the coordinator.

The Campus Context: Onondaga Community College (OCC), located in Syracuse, New York, is part of the sixty-four-campus network of the State University of New York. OCC was established in 1961 by Onondaga County. The College's flexibility and adaptability to community needs is the primary mission of the institution. OCC offers small classes and thus individualized attention to its students.

Situated in the geographical center of Onondaga County, OCC occupies a 181-acre campus on Onondaga Hill, 4 miles from downtown Syracuse, overlooking the hills and valleys of central New York. The seven buildings, all of contemporary design, house one of upstate New York's most modern and complete educational facilities in a picturesque, wooded setting. OCC offers the A.A., A.S., and A.A.S. degrees and certificates in approximately fifty programs of study.

Student Body Accredited by the Middle States Association of Colleges and Schools, the College had a total enrollment in credit courses for fall 1995 of 7,447 students (full- and part-time); 43 percent were men, and 57 percent were women. The ethnic distribution of students is as follows: white: 88.5 percent; African American, 7 percent; Native American, 1.4 percent; Asian/Pacific Islander, 1.3 percent; Hispanic/Latino, 1.2 percent; and nonresident/alien, 0.4 percent. All of the students commute to campus. Fifty-five percent receive financial aid. A nonresidential campus, OCC has a chapter of Phi Theta Kappa, a national two-year college honor society, and a large number of campus clubs organized through OSSA (Onondaga Student Services Association).

Faculty OCC has 195 full-time faculty members. Twenty-seven percent hold earned doctorates. In addition, almost 300 adjunct instructors teach one or more courses on a part-time basis. The student-faculty ratio is 17.5:1.

Key Facilities The College's library holds more than 95,000 books, 400 periodical titles, 9,000 media programs, 1,000 pamphlet subject files, CD-ROM periodical indexes, and access to on-line databases through the Internet. In addition to an open-access computer lab, OCC has many fully equipped departmental laboratories.

Athletics The College sponsors a successful intercollegiate program for men in baseball, cross-country, basketball, lacrosse, and tennis. Women's teams include softball, cross-country, volleyball, and tennis. In recent years, OCC's teams have successfully competed and won on the regional level, allowing participation in the NJCAA National Championships.

Study Abroad As a member of the College Consortium on International Studies, OCC is able to offer students the opportunity to participate in many programs of study abroad.

Support Services The Office of Services for Students with Special Needs works to assist in the educational and social aspects of college life for students who are disabled. The campus is almost completely handicapped-accessible.

Job Opportunities An active Cooperative Education Office, OCC CARES, a service organization, and work-study programs for those meeting financial aid requirements provide many opportunities for OCC students.

Tuition: $2450 for area residents, $4900 for state residents, $7350 for nonresidents, per year (1996-97)

Mandatory Fees: $96

Contact: Coordinator: Dr. Hal Kugelmass, Syracuse, New York 13215; Telephone: 315-469-2640; Fax: 315-469-2597

OREGON STATE UNIVERSITY

4 Pu G M Sc Tr

▼ University Honors College

The University Honors College (UHC) is a campuswide degree-granting college, one of eleven at Oregon State University (OSU). It awards the Honors Baccalaureate of Science or Arts in the academic discipline, designating one of two tracks within the UHC. Students may major in any academic discipline and complete either the 30-credit "Honors Scholar" or the 15-credit "Honors Associate" track. The goal of the UHC is to provide a small college environment within a larger university and to stress education that focuses on relationships rather than subjects or disciplines. UHC classes are limited to 20 at the lower division and 12 at the upper division, and a writing-intensive skills requirement is included in the "Honors Scholar" track.

UHC courses are denoted by a departmental prefix and an H suffix or HC prefix. All courses are proposed by interested faculty members or by other nomination and are screened by the UHC Council. UHC courses are not automatically renewed and are assumed to be taught on a basis that requires a renewal application. UHC courses may be regular quarter-length classes or offered in a compressed, weekend, or evening-course format. About three quarters of UHC offerings parallel the general education requirement of the institution; the remainder are UHC colloquia designed especially for UHC students. A study-abroad option is available, either independently or as part of OSU's unique concurrent degree requirements for an International Degree.

The University Honors College at OSU currently has nearly 350 students (80 percent are from Oregon, 22 percent are members of minority groups, and 2 percent are international students) and is designed to enroll approximately 400 students.

Participation Requirements: Once admitted, UHC students must maintain a 3.25 GPA to remain in good standing. Subpar performance results in up to a two-quarter window to improve academic performance prior to dismissal from the UHC portion of OSU.

Admission Process: Applicants to the UHC must be admitted or applying to OSU. An application form is available upon request from the UHC. The deadlines are as follows: fall term admission, February 1; winter term admission, November 15. Admission criteria are flexible and include an opportunity to "write-in" thorough responses to a series of three essay questions. Transfer students (also students participating in the National Student Exchange) from a recognized honors program may be automatically admitted upon request.

Scholarship Availability:
UHC students are supported by scholarships from their academic colleges or by Presidential, Oregon, and Out-of-State Laurels (merit-based) Scholarships. Additional scholarship support is being developed.

The Campus Context:
The main OSU campus comprises 264 buildings spread across 420 wooded, sylvan acres in the mid-Willamette Valley on the banks of the Willamette River, about 85 miles south of metropolitan Portland and equidistant from the Pacific Ocean and the Cascade Mountains (1-hour driving time). Among the "off-site" holdings are the Hatfield Marine Science Center, a Portland Center, the McDonald/Dunn Forests, and a number of distant learning sites.

Oregon State University is a member of the PAC 10 Conference and is one of eighty-eight Carnegie Research I institutions in the country. In addition to the UHC, OSU has eleven undergraduate degree-granting colleges. There are eighty bachelor's programs, seventy-nine master's programs, fifty-seven doctoral programs, and twenty-one professional degree programs.

Student Body With nearly 14,500 students (44 percent women), OSU enrolls students from every state in the country and 100 other countries (more than 1,300 students). Members of American minority groups comprise approximately 12.9 percent of the overall student body. UHC students have the option of living in the UHC Residence Hall (McNary Hall) or any other campus facility. The majority of the students live on or near campus. There are fifteen sororities and twenty-five fraternities.

Faculty The student-faculty ratio is 16.4:1.

Key Facilities The library houses approximately 1.3 million volumes. OSU is known for extensive student access computing facilities, including five general student access areas with 341 machines and 1,764 other machines, including a ten-station UHC student access lab/instructional facility. All students are given Internet addresses upon enrolling at OSU, and all residence halls have computer jacks in student rooms. UHC uses weekly e-mail messages to share information with and communicate with its students.

Athletics Athletics includes fifteen sports recognized at NCAA Division I and plentiful intramural and informal opportunities.

Study Abroad Coordinated by the Office of International Education, OSU offers fifty-eight programs in thirty countries and includes a concurrent International Degree option to be awarded in conjunction with another baccalaureate degree.

Support Services Coordinated by Services for Students with Disabilities, services for disabled students include note takers, sign language interpreters, books on tape, alternative testing, etc.

Job Opportunities Through Student Employment Services, various employment opportunities exist on campus, including work-study and study employment.

Tuition:
$2694 for state residents, $10,332 for nonresidents, per year (1996-97)

Room and Board:
$4587

Mandatory Fees:
$753

Contact:
Director: Dr. Jon Hendricks, 229 Strand Hall, Corvallis, Oregon 13126; Telephone: 541-737-6400; Fax: 541-737-6401; E-mail: honors@ccmail.orst.edu

---

PACE UNIVERSITY (NEW YORK)

4 Pr G M Tr

▼ University Honors Program

One of the major curricular aims of the Honors Program is to equip students with a solid foundation in the academic disciplines while making them aware that most critical thinking crosses disciplinary boundaries and is interdisciplinary in scope. For this reason, freshman-year honors courses in English, speech, philosophy, and history are clustered. A freshman lecture series reinforces this by bringing faculty members from all divisions of the University to speak with students about the nature and social context of intellectual inquiry. Upperclass students later apply these skills and methods of inquiry in the writing of an honors thesis.

Honors Program students also have the opportunity to participate in international travel sponsored by the program. International travel is usually offered in conjunction with a University course. Students may travel either for academic credit or personal enrichment.

The Honors Program at the New York City campus of Pace University was established in 1983. Currently, there are 240 students in the program, almost all of whom receive partial or full scholarship aid.

Participation Requirements:
Depending upon the number of credits a student has when entering the program, he or she completes five, six, or eight honors courses in the Honors Humanities core. This is one of the two requirements for graduation from the program. The other is the completion of an honors thesis in the junior or senior year, which may (but does not have to) be in the student's major area of study. Students entering with AP or college credit for courses in the honors core are allowed credit for those courses if they so choose but are also encouraged to apply that credit to elective courses. A 3.3 GPA is required for graduation from the program. An honors medal is awarded at graduation to all students successfully completing the program. Students' transcripts also indicate all honors course work and record the writing of the honors thesis. Honors students with junior standing and a 3.5 GPA are offered membership in Alpha Chi, the National Honors Society.

The New York Honors Program also strives to make the cultural richness of New York City available to its students. Opera, ballet, jazz, film, theater, and museums are all a part of the cultural programming regularly put into place each semester for the program's students. Freshmen are required to attend at least five events a semester; upperclassmen must choose at least two.

Admission Process: Most students enter the program as freshmen. Freshmen are selected each spring on the basis of high school average, SAT I scores, and a personal interview. Current students with fewer than 66 credits are required to have a 3.3 GPA and must provide faculty recommendations. Transfer students with fewer than 66 credits are also eligible. Only in exceptional circumstances are students with more than 66 credits admitted to the program.

The Campus Context: The New York City campus of Pace University is located just north of the Wall Street financial district. It abuts the Brooklyn Bridge, looks out upon City Hall, and is a short walk from the World Financial Center, the SoHo branch of the Guggenheim, and Greenwich Village. Students may major in all areas of arts and sciences, business, education, nursing, and computer science.

Student Body The 8,400 undergraduates come from all fifty states and eighty other countries; 62 percent are women and 38 percent are men. The ethnic distribution of undergraduate students is 39 percent white, 18 percent black, 18 percent Asian, 13 percent Hispanic, and 12 percent not listed. There are 340 international students.

Faculty Of the 447 full-time faculty members, 85 percent hold terminal degrees. The student-faculty ratio is 15:1.

Key Facilities University libraries hold 750,000 volumes and 675,000 microfilm titles. There are 425 computers in the University computer center.

Athletics Pace New York is NCAA Division II, except men's basketball. Athletic opportunities includes men's and women's basketball, tennis, cross-country running, and track and field; men's football and lacrosse; and women's softball and volleyball.

Job Opportunities The University has an outstanding co-op program that arranges paid employment for eligible students beginning at the end of their freshman year. Because of Pace's prime location in New York, employment opportunities and internships are readily available with major corporations and leading cultural institutions and government agencies.

Tuition: $12,710 per year (1996-97)

Room and Board: $5340

Mandatory Fees: $320

Contact: Director: Dr. Harold Brown, One Pace Plaza, New York, New York 10038; Telephone: 212-346-1697; Fax: 212-346-1217; E-mail: hbrown@pacevm.dac.pace.edu

PACIFIC LUTHERAN UNIVERSITY

4 Pr G S

▼ Honors Program

Now in its fourth year, the Honors Program at Pacific Lutheran University (PLU) centers on the theme "Taking Responsibility: Matters of the Mind, Matters of the Heart." It integrates academic and experiential learning opportunities with the objective of preparing participants for lives of service and servant leadership. The program, a total of 26 credits, emphasizes the importance of student-directed learning and culminates in an experiential project that students design, implement, and evaluate (with faculty support). All but 8 of the total Honors Program credits fulfill other University requirements.

Participation Requirements: Students must complete PLU with a minimum 3.5 GPA. All entering freshman honors students take the Freshman Honors Experience: A. Honors Core sequence: "Identity, Community, Legacy, and Faith" and B. Honors Critical Conversation: "Experience and Knowledge."

During the sophomore and junior years, students take four 1-credit Virtue Seminars (HONOR 301–308), preferably one each semester (or multiples in a semester to accommodate study abroad or other scheduling conflicts). Continuing on the focus on "Taking Responsibility," the seminars focus on those qualities necessary to responsible leadership. Using different "virtues" as a centering theme, students consider each virtue from several perspectives, including classical, contemporary, and nonwestern perspectives. These seminars provide students with a weekly opportunity to interact with their intellectual peers around a unifying theme and readings.

Participation in J-Term study abroad/off-campus courses, some offered as honors sections, are strongly encouraged but not required. Most participants of the honors J-Term abroad are sophomores or juniors, but freshmen and seniors may go as well.

Honors students take two 4-credit honors courses (usually) during the sophomore and/or junior years. They may take Honors-by-Contract courses, in which "added dimensions" to convert them to honors are agreed upon in a contract between professor and student by the following means: taking a regularly scheduled course which, by contract, explores the topic through greater depth or breadth, or doing an independent study or research project (the student may do only one of these) whose finished product is of potentially publishable quality.

Seniors take the HONR 490: Honors Challenge Experience (4 credits), offered in either fall or spring. This seminar, including academic analysis and an experiential component, brings a sense of closure to the program theme of responsibility and is called "Responsibility in Action."

Admission Process: Each fall, 35 freshmen are selected to participate in the program. Honors students are selected on the basis of grades and scores (high school GPA of 3.8 or 1200 SAT) and recommendations.

Scholarship Availability: Pacific Lutheran University offers several non-need-based awards for undergraduate students. These include Regents' and President's Scholarships, which are awarded in recognition of outstanding academic achievement, leadership, and service.

The Campus Context: Pacific Lutheran University was founded in 1890 and is owned by the Evangelical Lutheran Church in America. The 160-acre campus is an hour's drive from Mt. Rainier in one direction and downtown Seattle in another. PLU offers an insightful and challenging liberal arts foundation (with more than sixty majors and minors) complemented by five professional schools (arts, business, education, nursing, and physical education). Campus facilities include a 6-acre wilderness preserve, two gymnasiums, a computer user lab, an auditorium seating 1,200, a student center with media complex and games room, a Science Center, a Music Building with 534-seat concert hall, and Nursing Building. The academic calendar is 4-1-4.

Student Body Total enrollment is 3,581.

Faculty The University has a student-faculty ratio of 15:1.

Key Facilities The library houses 434,900 volumes. In addition to voice mail and Internet access in every residence hall room, there are eight computerized classrooms and many more with computer and big-screen display; specialized computer laboratories are established for computer science, business, mathematics education, chemistry, engineering, and journalism. The fully automated Mortvedt Library includes on-line information access technologies.

Athletics Sports include baseball, basketball, cross-country, football, golf, soccer, softball, swimming, tennis, track and field, volleyball, and wrestling. Club sports include crew, lacrosse, rugby, skiing, and volleyball. Facilities include a fitness center, a 9-hole golf course, lighted tennis courts, a track, and soccer, baseball, and softball fields.

Study Abroad PLU offers study-abroad opportunities on six continents. Popular choices include Australia, Austria, Baltic States, Caribbean, China, Costa Rica, Denmark, Ecuador, England, France, Germany, India, Jamaica, Japan, Mexico, Norway, Singapore, Spain, Tanzania, and Trinidad. Study abroad is open to any major, and most PLU financial aid can apply to the student's international experience. Back on campus, international students hail from nearly two dozen countries, from Africa and South America to Europe and the Middle East.

Support Services Disabled students find the campus totally handicapped-accessible.

Job Opportunities College work-study and state work-study are available for at least part-time students.

Tuition: $15,136 per year (1997-98)

Room and Board: $4814

Contact: Chair: Dr. Beth Kraig, Tacoma, Washington 98447-0003; Telephone: 206-535-7296; E-mail: kraigbm@plu.edu; Web site: http://www.plu.edu

PACIFIC UNIVERSITY

4 Pr G S Tr

▼ University Honors Program

The University Honors Program at Pacific University is dedicated to challenging excellent students to explore and develop their gifts as thinkers, researchers, and leaders. The program seeks to mentor students as they prepare for careers, graduate school, and service to their communities, honoring intellect and character as well as talent and achievement.

Students admitted to the program participate in interdisciplinary seminars designed to encourage them to reflect upon the relationship between education, experience, and culture and to examine the relationships among various approaches to understanding the world. Taken in the first two years, these seminars provide a foundation for pursuing inter-, multi-, and extradisciplinary work and afford students the opportunity to develop skills for collaborative work. These seminars fulfill various core requirements for the College of Arts and Sciences.

In the third year of the program, students translate this knowledge into action: drawing on the skills they have developed in the seminars, they design, coordinate, and present a miniconference to the University community. Students choose the topic for this conference in the fall and invite Pacific faculty members and outside lecturers to present models of research appropriate to completing their project. In the spring, students prepare and present this collaborative research project, developing the research model and skills they investigated in the fall as they ready their own presentations for the keynote speaker, organize the conference, and prepare to facilitate community-wide discussion. By offering this miniconference to the community, students put into practice the value of service that describes the University's mission and gain firsthand experience of ambitious collaborative and interdisciplinary work.

In their senior year, honors students concentrate on their own projects, working with a faculty mentor and the Director of the Honors Program. Students design and realize a creative project that may involve literature research, experimentation, interviews, studio art work, performance, or a combination of these approaches. Seniors also mentor the juniors as they prepare the annual miniconference and attend that conference as active participants. Throughout the year, seniors participate in student-directed seminars as they develop their research projects. Responsible for educating an audience of their peers, students select readings and facilitate seminar discussion in order to establish a common foundational understanding of the principles, concepts, and methods that describe the student's approach to his or her project. As members of an informed audience, students serve one another as constructively critical readers and listeners and explore another model of collaboration. This program gives students the choice to pursue for their honors thesis either a fully collaborative project (modeled after the type of collaboration that characterized the junior miniconference) or individual research. Though senior projects are often based in a discipline, the program supports students interested in continuing to explore inter-, multi-, or extradisciplinary approaches. All honors theses and projects are presented to the community. The 33-year-old program currently enrolls 40–45 students.

Participation Requirements: In the first and second years, students take Honors 100 (First-Year Honors Seminar I), an interdisciplinary seminar that explores the relationship between education, experience, and culture; Honors 200 (Spring Honors Seminar), an interdisciplinary seminar that introduces students to methods of intellectual investigation and discourse through a sequence of readings, discussion, and written assignments centered around a new topic each year (this seminar may be taken twice for credit); and Honors 250 (Sophomore Honors Seminar I), a coordinated program of readings, films, discussion, and creative writing assignments designed to guide students in their exploration of questions of intellectual importance.

In the third year, students take Honors 300 (Junior Honors Seminar I and II). These seminars support students as they design, organize, and present a multidisciplinary miniconference. In the fourth year, students perform honors research under the guidance of a faculty mentor and the Director of the Honors Program. The conclusion is a public presentation. Students who complete the program get a University Honors Citation on their diploma.

In order to remain in the program, students should maintain a cumulative GPA of 3.5. First-year students may continue with a 3.2 or better, but must achieve a 3.5 cumulative GPA by the end of the sophomore year.

Admission Process: Prospective students are invited to apply to the University Honors Program when they apply for admission to the College of Arts and Sciences. University Honors admission decisions are based on GPA, SAT or ACT scores, and an essay that reveals the student's background, interests, and motivations. University Honors students entering Pacific generally have a high school GPA of 3.7, SAT scores of 1200, or ACT scores of 26, but applications from other interested students are considered. Transfer students with a cumulative GPA of 3.5 or higher are also invited to apply for admission to the program when they apply for admission to the College of Arts and Sciences. All qualified and interested transfer students are invited to interview with the Honors Committee.

Currently enrolled students should apply to the program by February 15.

Scholarship Availability: No particular scholarships are reserved for honors students, although many receive residential awards.

The Campus Context: Pacific University is composed of six colleges and schools: College of Arts and Sciences, College of Optometry, School of Occupational Therapy, School of Physical Therapy, School of Professional Psychology, and School of Education. There are twenty-six undergraduate degree programs.

Among the noteworthy facilities on campus are the Strain Science Center, the Taylor-Meade Performing Arts Center, and suite-living.

Student Body The undergraduate enrollment is 40 percent men and 60 percent women. The ethnic distribution of minority students is 13 percent Asian, 3 percent Hispanic, 1 percent black, and 1 percent American Indian/Alaska Native. There are 62 international students, including students in the English Language Institute. Sixty-five percent of the students are residents on campus. Ninety-two percent of students receive institutional aid. There are three fraternities and three sororities on campus.

Faculty Of the 128 full-time faculty members, 85 percent have terminal degrees. The student-faculty ratio is 13:1.

Key Facilities The library houses 140,260 catalogued volumes, 28,708 periodical volumes, and 84,993 government documents. The University has 800 computers, including open-access labs with both PC-compatible and Apple Power Macintosh computers. Each residence hall is fully network-ready.

Athletics In athletics, Pacific University is a member of the Northwest Conference of Independent Colleges (NCIC). Membership is limited to northwest independent, private, four-year colleges/universities and is intended to provide a broad base of athletic competition for men and women. Each conference member must participate in a minimum of six conference sports for men and six for women. The sporting events at Pacific University include baseball, men's and women's basketball, men's and women's cross-country, men's and women's golf, men's and women's soccer, softball, men's and women's tennis, men's and women's track and field, volleyball, and wrestling.

Intramural activities include flag football, a golf tournament, volleyball, 3-on-3 basketball, and a racquetball tournament in the first semester and 5-on-5 basketball, softball, soccer, a tennis tournament, and sand volleyball in the second semester. Pacific offers a degree in exercise science that is designed for students in the physical therapy, occupational therapy, exercise physiology, biomechanics, education, and sports medicine programs.

Study Abroad All students at Pacific are encouraged to consider overseas study as an educational experience. Pacific offers a variety of international study programs that incorporate most academic disciplines. Depending on the particular program, students may study abroad for either a semester or full academic year and do not necessarily need foreign language competency. Financial aid and other scholarship awards are applicable to overseas study. For Pacific's Modern Language and International Studies majors, study abroad is a requirement. Pacific has twenty-eight different programs in twelve countries, including Austria, China, Ecuador, England, France, Germany, Japan, Mexico, the Netherlands, Scotland, Spain, and Wales.

Support Services The Office of Services for Students with Disabilities exists to serve students who qualify for special services under federal law. Pacific University provides the same educational opportunities for students with disabilities that it provides for all students, unless undue burden would result. The University maintains academic standards that apply to all students.

Students with disabilities may require additional or specialized services to meet academic standards. If it is determined that a student does fit the criteria for having a learning disability, the following accommodations may be available: tutoring, special classroom and housing accommodations, permission to tape lectures and/or discussions, books on tape, note takers, advance copies of syllabi and lecture notes, access to voice activation and speech synthesis software, extra time for exams, space with minimal distraction for exams, reduced class load, and resource materials.

Job Opportunities Work opportunities are available on campus as teaching and research assistants, clerical workers, groundskeepers and recyclers, statisticians, team managers, field crew helpers, and community service-related jobs.

Tuition: $15,368 per year (1996-97)

Room and Board: $4067 minimum

Mandatory Fees: $286

Contact: Director: Dr. Diane Young, 2043 College Way, Forest Grove, Oregon 97116; Telephone: 503-359-2802; Fax: 503-359-2242; E-mail: youngde@pacificu.edu; Web site: http://www/pacificu.edu

---

PARADISE VALLEY COMMUNITY COLLEGE

2 Pu G S Sc

▼ Honors Program

At Paradise Valley Community College (PVCC), honors courses are offered as single courses, as concurrent sections with regular sections, and as project courses. With the latter two, honors students are expected to do additional, in-depth work that will enhance their classroom experiences.

Honors students participate in several programs designed during the school year to build a learning community among Maricopa Community College District (MCCD) honors students. They may attend special programs, concerts, theater events, and guest lectures each semester. The Maricopa district brings six nationally prominent guest speakers for the honors program each year; they visit with students at several of the campuses during their stay. All honors students from the ten MCCD colleges also have the opportunity to take an annual honors trip to a different site each year. In addition, honors students are recognized each spring at a district-wide Honors Convocation and receive special recognition at graduation. Honors course work receives an honors designation on college transcripts.

The 8-year-old program currently enrolls 75 students.

Participation Requirements: In order to remain eligible for this program, students must enroll in a minimum of 12 hours per semester and maintain a 3.25 GPA. Students must also enroll in and complete at least one honors course each semester.

Admission Process: The Paradise Valley Community College Honors Program is open to all students who graduate in the top 15 percent of a Maricopa County high school class or who have earned a 3.25 GPA in at least 12 credit hours from any of the Maricopa Community Colleges. All students who apply and who qualify are accepted.

Scholarship Availability: The Presidents' Scholarship program is open to all Maricopa County high school graduates who are in the top 15 percent of their high school classes. Students may apply as early as the end of their junior year and remain eligible for two semesters following graduation, provided they do not attend any other college or university during that time. The scholarship is renewable for up to four consecutive semesters, provided students continue to meet the requirements of the Honors Program. This portion of the program is designed to attract top area high school students to Maricopa colleges.

Returning students may be eligible for the fee waiver portion of the program if they have earned a 3.25 GPA in at least 12 credit hours at any of the Maricopa Community Colleges. Fee waivers are awarded depending on the number of credits students are taking. There is no time limit on the number of semesters of eligibility, within reason, as long as students maintain a 3.25 GPA and take one honors course per semester.

The Campus Context: The PVCC story began in the late 1970s amid the rapid growth of the Greater Paradise Valley area. As the population north of the Phoenix Mountains expanded, community advocacy for a higher educational facility to serve the area grew as well. In 1983, following a request by the Paradise Valley Community Council, the Maricopa Community College District Governing Board created the Northeast Valley Task Force to study the feasibility of such a facility. Funding for the first phase of this new facility was provided by a countywide bond election in September 1984. In early 1985, Dr. John A. Córdova, then Dean of Instruction at Phoenix College, was selected Provost of the Northeast Valley Education Center (NVEC), as the facility was then named. NVEC began operations as an extension of Scottsdale Community College in offices on Bell Road.

On December 5, 1985, a "groundlifting" ceremony for the new campus was held at its present location. In November 1986, the Governing Board changed the name to Paradise Valley Community College Center in anticipation of opening the new campus. PVCC was dedicated on May 2, 1987, and classes at the new campus began that fall with more than 4,000 students. Paradise Valley Community College began offering classes from temporary offices near 30th Street and Bell Road in northeast Phoenix in the fall of 1985. In the fall of 1986 the College moved to its present campus on the southeast corner of 32nd Street and Union Hills Drive.

Today, enrollment totals more than 5,500 full- and part-time students. An additional 1,000 students are enrolled in noncredit community education programs that include the PVCC Chamber Orchestra, Flute Choir, and Women's Chorus and watercolor, drawing, and money management classes. PVCC's students come primarily from the north Phoenix, Scottsdale, Cave Creek, Carefree, and Paradise Valley areas and represent the diversity of the College's service area. Students include recent high school graduates, working adults, and active senior citizens. The average age is around 30.

Paradise Valley Community College is one of Arizona's newest community colleges, receiving its first accreditation in 1990 from the North Central Association of Colleges and Schools. Following full accreditation in 1990, the Governing Board designated PVCC an independent college within the Maricopa Community College District.

The curriculum focuses on transfer to four-year institutions and offers a range of undergraduate courses in fall, spring, and summer terms. New offerings include degree and certificate programs in international business and hazardous materials technology.

Today, Paradise Valley Community College enjoys an international reputation for excellence led by President Raúl Cárdenas. The College was recently named a Regional Center for Asian Studies by the East-West Center of Honolulu, Hawaii. PVCC is a member of the World Trade Center of Arizona. The College is proud of its 1,000-piece Buxton Collection of American Indian and Western Arts and Crafts, which was dedicated during PVCC's tenth anniversary celebration. The Buxton collection contains religious or quasi-religious art from the American Southwest as well as from Spain, Mexico, and Central and South America. The pieces were acquired at art shows and sales conducted by the Heard Museum, the Friends of Mexican Art, various art galleries, and, in many cases, from the artists themselves.

In 1995, PVCC received a ten-year reaccreditation from the North Central Association, which called the College a "premier" institution. It offers the associate degrees in arts, general studies, applied science, and business.

Student Body Of the 5,500 undergraduates enrolled, the majority are from the southwest; 37 percent are men and 63 percent are women. The ethnic distribution of students is Caucasian, 85.33 percent; Hispanic, 5.64 percent; other, 4.68 percent; Asian, 2 percent; American Indian, 1.24 percent; and African American, 1.11 percent. There are approximately 50 international students. All students are commuters. Twenty-one percent of the students receive financial aid.

Faculty There are 59 full-time faculty members and 201 part-time faculty members. More than 30 percent of full-time faculty members have their doctorates or other terminal degrees. The student-faculty ratio is 21:1.

Key Facilities The library houses 24,000 volumes. Computer facilities include an IBM Lab and Macintosh Apple Lab. Other facilities include 175,000 square feet of classrooms, laboratories, offices, public meeting rooms, and a state-of-the art Fitness Center on a 90-acre site. The Student and Community Services Center building houses the Phoenix office of Northern Arizona University, which offers classes on the PVCC campus.

Athletics Paradise Valley Community College is currently participating in its first year of competition in intercollegiate athletics. Cross-country is offered for both men and women as a fall sport, while men's and women's tennis and men's golf are offered as spring sports. As one of the colleges in the Maricopa Community College District, PVCC is a Region 1 member of the NJCAA. Athletic teams at PVCC compete in tennis and cross-country at the Division II level, while golf is a Division I sport. Any student interested in athletics at PVCC should contact Cindy Shoenhair, Assistant Athletic Director, for more information.

Study Abroad Paradise Valley Community College does not offer study abroad at this time. However, it does offer an International Internship, which is a 3-credit course (IBS122).

Support Services For disabled students, the Paradise Valley Community College Special Services Office provides reasonable accommodations, classroom accessibility, resources, support services, and auxiliary aids to assist students in a successful college career.

Job Opportunities Students can find a variety of work on campus. Work-study jobs are available to students who show financial need. Tutoring opportunities are available through the Learning Assistance Center.

Tuition: $1020 for area residents, $4620 for state residents, $4770 for nonresidents, per year (1996-97)

Mandatory Fees: $10

Contact: Director: Dr. Linda Knoblock, 18401 North 32nd Street, Phoenix, Arizona 85032; Telephone: 602-493-2814; Fax: 602-493-2981; Web site: http://www.pvc.maricopa.edu/

PELLISSIPPI STATE TECHNICAL COMMUNITY COLLEGE

2 Pu G S Sc Tr

▼ **Honors Program**

Pellissippi State Technical Community College instituted an honors program in fall 1995 to offer academically able and highly motivated students the opportunity to participate in courses designed to provide an enhanced college experience.

There are currently 50 students enrolled in the program.

Participation Requirements: Students may participate in honors by taking one course or by taking several. Honors Program students take the same number of hours for graduation as other students. Enriched sections of the general university parallel courses are offered in such subjects as Western Civilization and General Biology. The courses are open to any student who meets the entry-level criteria for the particular course. Thirty-five students enrolled in four courses during the inaugural term. All graduating students who complete 12 hours of honors courses and maintain a 3.0 GPA are given special recognition on their diploma.

Scholarship Availability: Designed for students who meet certain criteria and participate in the Honors Program, up to twenty scholarships are available for Pellissippi Scholars. In order to apply for the scholarship, a student must have a 25 or higher composite ACT score and a minimum 3.5 GPA in high school or previous college work. The student must complete an application and write an essay. Recommendations are required for students who do not have an ACT score. A committee then evaluates the applications and selects the recipients.

Pellissippi Scholars are required to take at least one honors course each semester, maintain a 3.0 GPA, and complete 12 hours of honors courses by the time they graduate.

The Campus Context: Pellissippi State Technical Community College was founded as State Technical Institute at Knoxville, Tennessee, and became a community college offering university-parallel courses in 1988 while still maintaining its emphasis on technology. A Tennessee Board of Regents institution, the College serves Tennessee's third-largest metropolitan area. Pellissippi State grants A.A. and A.S. degrees for university-parallel students; the A.A.S degree in seventeen technical career programs such as chemical and environmental engineering technology, communications graphics technology, and video production technology; and five certificate programs.

The College recently completed a new 500-seat performing arts center and an Educational Resources Center that contains the library, study areas, computer classrooms, and a Learning Center for tutoring in math and English. In fall 1996 the College developed Weekend College, a series of classes that allows students to complete certain degrees in four years by attending classes on the weekends.

Student Body There are 7,468 students enrolled, including 79 international students; 45.1 percent are men and 54.9 percent are women. Almost 32 percent receive financial aid.

Faculty Of the 435 total faculty members, 146 are full-time, approximately one fourth of whom have doctorates or other terminal degrees. The student-faculty ratio is 19:1.

Key Facilities The library houses 31,600 volumes. About 540 IBM-compatible computers are located in twenty-four labs on three campuses, and fifty-seven Macs are located in three Macintosh labs on the main campus. All students have computer accounts with access to the Internet.

Job Opportunities A small number of work-study positions are available on campus.

Tuition: $1098 for state residents, $4096 for nonresidents, per year (1996-97)

Mandatory Fees: $74

Contact: Director: Dr. Carol Luther, 10915 Hardin Valley Road, P.O. Box 22990, Knoxville, Tennessee 37933-0990; Telephone: 423-694-6439; E-mail: cluther@pstcc.cc.tn.us

PHILADELPHIA COLLEGE OF TEXTILES AND SCIENCE

4 Pr G S Sc Tr

▼ Honors Program

The Honors Program at the Philadelphia College of Textiles and Science (PCT&S) was established in 1985 to bring together highly motivated students and dedicated faculty members in a program that is both challenging and supportive. Overall, the program aims to reach beyond professional or specialized training and to inspire students to a full lifetime of broad and intellectual curiosity, self-sustained inquiry, and personal growth. It attempts to develop critical thinking and leadership skills and widen awareness of global issues.

The program is a combination of accelerated, enriched courses and cocurricular activities designed to challenge selected students at the College. The program's core of 22 credits is composed of honors work in both College Studies and career-specific courses. There are an optional community service learning component and opportunities for honors credit for seniors taking graduate-level courses. Honors credit is available during study abroad and through co-op and internship programs.

Participating faculty members from across campus often teach enriched sections of existing courses or supervise independent study or research projects. These faculty members are dedicated teachers and scholars respected for their effectiveness in the classroom and for original contributions to their field of specialty. The Honors Program not only challenges students, but also demands an extension of faculty roles beyond customary professional expectations. These are the roles of the catalyst and mentor as well as of one who perceives and understands shifting pressures on students and student energies as the term progresses.

The 10-year-old program enrolls approximately 100 active students.

Participation Requirements: Students are expected to maintain a B/B+ average and enroll in at least one honors course per year. Students are recognized at graduation if they have maintained a 3.0 GPA and taken at least three honors courses.

Students receive the full honors awards if they have a 3.3 or better GPA and have completed the required 22 honors credits.

Transfer students who enter the College with more than 45 credits may waive all or some of the lower-division honors requirements and satisfy all of the required 22 honors credits with upper-division honors courses. Transfer students who have participated in an honors program at another institution may transfer lower-division honors credits.

Any student enrolled at the College may enroll in honors courses as a non-certificate honors student if their overall GPA is above 3.0. Honors courses are noted on student transcripts, and completion of the program is cited on the diploma at Commencement.

Admission Process: The program is offered each year, by invitation, to a select number of qualified students. Admission to the Honors Program is based upon proof of a student's potential for high academic achievement. A majority of honors students are identified by their high school performance. The College may evaluate the student's GPA, class rank, SAT/ACT scores, and extracurricular activities. All entering freshmen and/or transfer students may apply for admission to the Honors Program. Although there is an attempt to identify eligible students before admission to the College, students who have demonstrated academic excellence during their first and second term may also be invited to join the program.

A student may be admitted to the Honors Program at one of the following times in their baccalaureate experience: prior to matriculation as either a freshman or a transfer student, if admission criteria for the Honors Program have been met (based on high school rank, standard test scores, interviews, etc.) or after one term of work at PCT&S, with a faculty recommendation and GPA above 3.1.

Scholarship Availability: The College offers a number of faculty grants and scholarships to freshmen and transfer students, based on academic merit. Many students receiving these scholarships and grants are also in the Honors Program.

The Campus Context: The Philadelphia College of Textiles and Science is composed of four schools: the School of Architecture and Design, the School of Business Administration, the School of Science and Health, and the School of Textiles and Materials Technology. Thirty-six undergraduate and seven graduate programs are offered on campus. The College is well known for the Paley Design Center.

Student Body There are 1,850 full-time undergraduates: 39 percent men and 61 percent women. The ethnic distribution is Caucasian, 76 percent; African/American, 11 percent; Native American, 7 percent; Asian American, 4 percent; and Hispanic, 2 percent. There are 123 international students. Of the total student population, 60 percent are resident and 40 percent are commuters. Ninety percent of freshmen and 70 percent of continuing students receive financial aid. There are four fraternities and two sororities.

Faculty The total number of faculty members is 446; 87 percent are full-time, and 63 percent have terminal degrees. The student-faculty ratio is 20:1.

Key Facilities There are 85,000 volumes in the library. The campus has 120 computers, Macintosh and IBM. There are multiple labs in the computer center, library, learning center, and architecture and design center (CAD lab/studios).

Athletics The College has NCAA Division II teams in women's basketball, field hockey, lacrosse, soccer, softball, and tennis. For men, the College has an NCAA Division I soccer team and Division II teams in basketball, baseball, golf, and tennis.

Study Abroad Study-abroad options are available in Austria, Australia, England, France, Germany, Ireland, Italy, Mexico, Scotland, and Spain.

Support Services For disabled students, the campus has wheelchair ramps, elevators, special parking, special class scheduling, and lowered telephones.

Job Opportunities A variety of work opportunities is available on campus in administrative and academic offices and labs.

Tuition: $12,716 minimum per year full-time, $395 to $432 per credit part-time (1996-97)

Room and Board: $5874

Contact: Director: Dr. Abigail Lee Miller, School House Lane and Henry Avenue, Philadelphia, Pennsylvania 19144-5497; Telephone: 215-951-2818; Fax: 215-951-2652; E-mail: miller@hardy.texsci.edu

---

PIMA COUNTY COMMUNITY COLLEGE

2 Pu G M Sc Tr

▼ Honors Program

The Pima County Community College (PCCC) Honors Program began in 1973 and is open to students of all majors. It consists of a core of two honors courses, with four principal criteria distinguishing them: they embody learning strategies and teaching techniques (such as those used in seminar classes) that challenge and engage the abilities of honors students, they provide academic content intensity, they place emphasis upon the development of verbal and written skills, and they engage the students in the exercise of problem-solving techniques. All Honors Program students must complete the two core courses: HON 201-Introductory Honors Course or HON 204 Occupational Honors Seminar and HON 203-Honors Seminar in Research Techniques.

HON 201 is an introduction to the Honors Program, with the emphasis on the evolution of higher education from Plato's academy to the modern trade school. Course methodology includes the extensive application of seminar skills, with special emphasis on problem-solving strategies. HON 204 is an introduction to the Honors Program, with the emphasis on creative and critical thinking techniques, problem-solving strategies, and research exploration. This course also includes extensive analysis developed through student projects and presentations. HON 201 is for students anticipating transfer to senior institutions in academic fields, while HON 204 is for students enrolled in technical fields.

Also required of all Honors Program students is HON 203, Honors Seminar in Research Techniques. It is strongly advised that each student enrolled in HON 201 or HON 204 also enroll in HON 203 during the same semester.

In addition to the core courses, Honors Program students are advised to enroll in honors core curriculum courses. These are regular courses that correlate with the College's general education requirements and are designated as Honors Program courses. They may be offered in English composition, humanities and fine arts, physical and biological sciences, mathematics, and social and behavioral sciences.

In addition, the Honors Program may offer a number of honors enrichment courses. These are regular sections infused with course modules that are designed to enable Honors Program students to explore more fully course content not available in honors core curriculum courses. Students considering enrollment in an enrichment section must first consult with an Honors Program Campus Coordinator. There are 1,495 active students (taking at least one Honors Program course per semester).

Participation Requirements: To graduate from the Honors Program, students are required to complete 9 units in honors core curriculum courses, maintain a GPA of 3.5, and have met the College's minimum reading requirement. In order to meet Honors Program requirements within two years, students should complete at least one Honors Program course per semester. Successful completion of the Honors Program requirements is evidenced on the student's transcript.

Admission Process: Students may apply to the Honors Program if they meet one of the following criteria: new students must show evidence of PCCC assessment scores that qualify them for WRT 101 or MTH 130 and must have met the College's minimum reading requirements; continuing PCCC students must have completed at least 9 hours of college-level courses numbered 100 or above with a GPA of 3.5 and must have met the College's minimum reading requirements; and transferring college students must have completed at least 9 credit hours of college-level courses numbered 100 or above with a GPA of 3.5 and must have met Pima County Community College's minimum reading requirements.

Students wishing to apply for admission to the Honors Program must submit a completed application by the end of the Drop/Add period of the semester they wish to begin honors studies. Students who do not meet the Drop/Add deadline are considered for admission to the program for the next regular semester.

Scholarship Availability: Every year the PCCC Honors Program offers ten one-time $200 scholar awards to fully

accepted Honors Program students. The criteria for selection of recipients of the award include: completion of HON 201 or HON 204 and HON 203, completion of greatest number of Honors Program courses, and description of participation in community-service learning projects.

The Campus Context: The Pima County Community College District was established in 1966 and built its first permanent facilities in January 1971. The College is composed of five campuses, a District Central Office, and a District Support Services Center, with a total of seventy-two buildings on 412 acres across the Tucson metropolitan area. The Community Campus of PCCC houses the College's interactive classroom system hub, with broadcast-quality production facilities and the telecourse distribution center. This campus also provides space for Northern Arizona University's interactive classroom and the distribution control center for their distance learning operations in the southern part of the state.

The Desert Vista Campus is also the home of the nonprofit vocational program, the Center for Training and Development (CTD). The CTD cooperates with community-based organizations and agencies to provide training to persons with disabilities and to those who are educationally or economically disadvantaged. In 1994–95 PCCC served more than 53,600 students in credit and noncredit courses, offering forty-six university transfer associate degree programs and forty-nine occupational associate degree programs.

Student Body The ratio of men to women continues to be stable from prior years, with men accounting for 45 percent of the credit enrollment and women accounting for 55 percent of the credit enrollment. Minority credit enrollment is 13,378, which equals 36 percent of the total enrollment. The ethnic distribution of the total enrollment is as follows: 23,723 (64 percent), Anglo/Other; 9,368 (25 percent), Hispanics; 1,457 (4 percent), African Americans; 1,590 (4 percent), Asian Americans; and 963 (3 percent), Native Americans. In 1994, more than twenty-four countries were represented in a total population of 616 (2 percent) international students. All PCCC students are commuter students. About 20 percent of the students receive some form of federal financial aid.

Faculty The total faculty of PCCC numbers 1,567. Of this total number, 319 (20 percent) are full-time and the rest are adjunct faculty members. A total of 56 (18 percent) full-time faculty members have doctoral degrees. The student-faculty ratio is 23:1.

Key Facilities Four of the PCCC campuses have library buildings that house 211,3222 volumes. Each campus has a computer laboratory with personal computers available for student use. The total number of MS-DOS computers is 148, and the total number of Macintosh computers is 64.

Tuition: $930 for state residents, $4500 for nonresidents, per year (1996-97)

Mandatory Fees: $10

Contact: Director: Ms. Eva Cota, Office of Minority and Interdisciplinary Education, 4905-B East Broadway Boulevard,

Tucson, Arizona 85709-1010; Telephone: 520-748-4932; Fax: 520-748-4788; E-mail: ecota@pimacc.pima.edu

PITTSBURG STATE UNIVERSITY

4 Pu G & D M Sc Tr

▼ Honors College and Departmental Honors Program

Pittsburg State University offers two types of honors programs: The Honors College and the Departmental Honors Program.

The primary mission of the Honors College is to provide a more meaningful educational experience for select superior students. The Honors College curriculum at the freshman-sophomore level offers intellectually stimulating general education courses. The junior-senior level Honors College students become integrated into the Departmental Honors Program.

Established in 1986, the Honors College currently enrolls approximately 140 students.

Participation Requirements: To graduate from the Honors College program, entering freshmen must complete a minimum of 12 hours of general education honors courses and honors orientation. A minimum 3.4 GPA must also be maintained. Presidential and transfer scholars must also complete the Departmental Honors Program with a minimum of 9 credit hours. Departmental Honors offers the opportunity for mentored research above normal requirements for designated upper-level course work. Other Honors College scholars are also encouraged to complete Departmental Honors. A 3.5 GPA is required to enter Departmental Honors course work, which is open to any qualified campus student.

Admission Process: Honors College members are a carefully screened and select group of scholarship recipients. Most enter the program their freshman year after formal application and acceptance. A small number of junior-level transfer students, screened international students, and high-achieving freshmen are also admitted. To be eligible, freshmen must have a 28 composite ACT, a minimum 3.7 high school GPA (on a 4.0 scale), and/or provide proof of adding multicultural diversity to the honors program. Transfer scholars must have completed 40 semester hours with a minimum GPA of 3.75 on a 4.0 scale. A transcript verifying class standing and course preparation, a letter of activities and awards, and recommendations comprise the application package. The deadline for high school applicants is March 1 and for transfers is April 1.

Scholarship Availability: The Honors College has 12 Presidential Scholars, 20 University Scholars, 6 Transfer Scholars, and an additional group of select scholars admitted annually. Presidential Scholars receive fall and spring tuition, room and board, and a book allowance. University and Transfer Scholars receive fall and spring in-state tuition and are eligible for other awards.

The Campus Context: Pittsburg State University is one of six Kansas Regents institutions. It is located 120 miles south of Kansas City. Honors College students can enroll in any of more than 100 majors in the College of Arts and Sciences, the School of Business, the School of Education, and the School of Technology.

Student Body University enrollment is approximately 7,000.

Key Facilities Library, computer, and other academic resources are readily available.

Athletics Pittsburg State is in the NCAA Division II, with a long tradition of "Gorilla" pride in the sports programs, most notably football. Other sports include men's and women's basketball, track, and cross-country; men's baseball and golf; and women's volleyball and softball.

Tuition: $1876 for state residents, $5976 for nonresidents, per year (1996-97)

Room and Board: $3188

Contact: Director: Dr. Robert S. Hilt, 320 Russ Hall, Pittsburg, Kansas 66762; Telephone: 316-235-4329

PORTLAND STATE UNIVERSITY

4 Pu G M Sc Tr

▼ University Honors Program

The Honors Program at Portland State University (PSU) is a small, degree-granting program primarily meant for students who intend to go on to graduate or professional school. It is therefore the faculty's intent to shape an environment and culture like that of a small liberal arts college within the larger university. Once admitted to the program, students in honors are excused from general University requirements and instead work toward the undergraduate degree by means of a combination of courses within the honors college and work within the departmental major. Students may choose any of the departmental majors offered at Portland State.

Students in honors at Portland State come from a diverse range of backgrounds and pursue a wide variety of majors. While most (better than 80 percent) of students come directly from high school, honors at Portland State also admits a number of "returning" students and transfers (although applications are generally not accepted from students with more than about 60 quarter hours of credit). What students in the honors college share is a commitment to learning and an equal commitment to excellence, which is reflected in their achievements. They are active in a wide variety of campus and extracurricular activities. In one recent year, program students were chairing the student senate, serving as editors of the newspaper and literary magazine, and chairing not only the history and business, but also the foreign language honor societies.

Students from the program share, as well, a record of achievement. The program is extremely proud of the level of success of the graduates: a recent survey indicated that better than 80 percent of Honors Program graduates had gone on to one or more advanced degrees, whether a professional degree (e.g., M.D., J.D., or M.B.A.) or one of the academic degrees (e.g., Ph.D.). The program was begun in 1969, and enrollment is limited to 200. There are currently 150 students enrolled in the program.

Participation Requirements: After the core courses of the first and second years, course work in the honors college falls into one of two kinds: courses in the "middle tier" and the upper-division seminars (called colloquia) connected with the Visiting Scholars' Project. The middle tier and colloquia courses are generally small—never more than 15 students—and interdisciplinary in nature.

Each year the program brings to campus a number of noted American and international scholars to work with program students in the upper-division seminars. Visiting lecturers (numbering at this point nearly 200) have included the noted French historian, member of the College de France, and Director of the Bibliotheque Nationale, Emmanuel Le Roy Ladurie; Nobel laureates Sir Peter Medawar and Gunther Stent; feminist philosopher, playwright, and novelist Helene Cixous; and economist Robert Heilbroner.

In 1985, the University Honors Program began a unique internship program for its students in Washington, D.C. That project began with one student working for an academic quarter in the Smithsonian's Archives; since that beginning the project has grown substantially, both in number of students and in their success. Sixteen to 20 students each year are now placed in internships covering a wide range of possibilities: the entire array of Smithsonian-associated institutions, carefully selected nongovernmental organizations such as Common Cause, many federal offices and agencies in the capital, and, for premedical students, valuable internships in the National Institutes of Health and the National Institute of Mental Health. Students completing the program receive an honors diploma.

The deadline for applying is April 30.

Scholarship Availability: Some limited tuition-remission scholarships are available.

The Campus Context: There are seven major academic units: the College of Liberal Arts and Sciences, the School of Business Administration, the School of Education, the School of Engineering and Applied Science, the School of Fine and Performing Arts, the School of Urban and Public Affairs, and the Graduate School of Social Work. Thirty-three bachelor's, thirty-eight master's, and seven doctoral programs are offered.

Student Body Total enrollment, including graduate level, is 14,348. Forty-seven percent of the population is men and 53 percent is women. Ethnic distribution is as follows: 68.1 percent white, 8.6 percent Asian/Pacific Islander, 5.3 percent international students, 2.9 percent Hispanic, 2.8 percent black, 1.2 percent Native American, and 11 percent other/no

response. Almost 45 percent of the students receive some form of financial aid. The campus has five fraternities and six sororities.

Faculty There are 501 full-time faculty members.

Key Facilities The library houses more than 1 million volumes. There are ten computer labs, including a special Honors Program computer lab.

Athletics PSU sponsors sixteen intercollegiate varsity sports. Men's sports are football, basketball, cross-country, golf, outdoor and indoor track (Big Sky Conference), baseball, and wrestling (PAC 10). Women's sports are cross-country, basketball, soccer, tennis, outdoor and indoor track, volleyball (Big Sky Conference), and softball. Admission to athletic events is free with a valid University ID card. A wide range of intramural and club sports for men and women is also offered. Recreational hours for the gymnasium, handball court, swimming pool, and weight rooms are available.

Study Abroad The Office of International Education Services sponsors a wide variety of study-abroad programs year-round, including opportunities in Europe, Eastern Europe, Russia, China, Southeast Asia, Australia, Africa, South America, and Central America. Residence credit and home campus registration are offered, as is financial aid.

Support Services Disabled Services for Students offers a wide range of services and assistance, including note takers, test readers/writers, sign-language interpreters, priority registration, adapted computers, and classroom equipment. Most buildings are fully accessible.

Job Opportunities PSU participates in the Federal Work-Study Program for students demonstrating a need for part-time employment to pursue a college education. The Student Employment Office manages other student employment opportunities.

Tuition: $2694 for state residents, $9960 for nonresidents, per year (1996-97)

Room and Board: $4500

Mandatory Fees: $486

Contact: Director: Professor Lawrence P. Wheeler, P.O. Box 751, Portland, Oregon 97207; Telephone: 503-725-4928; Fax: 503-725-5363; E-mail: wheelerl@pdx.edu; Web site: http://www-adm.pdx.edu/user/hon

PRAIRIE VIEW A&M UNIVERSITY

4 Pu C M Tr

▼ Benjamin Banneker Honors College

The Benjamin Banneker Honors College responds to the national need for undergraduate colleges to produce more graduate- and professional-level researchers, practitioners, and faculty members in certain scientific and technical fields. Students are specifically selected for their outstanding academic achievement in high school and are primed to pursue, upon graduation, study at highly competitive academic institutions. The College contributes toward their desired end by undergirding intensive training in the students' areas of specialization with an innovative honors curriculum in the liberal arts.

The core of the Benjamin Banneker Honors College concept is to provide excellent training in scientific and technical fields. In these areas, separate class sections are designed to move faster and explore more material than the corresponding regular sections. Small classes and intimate associations with fellow students and faculty members characterize instruction in the College. An integral part of the curriculum involves an emphasis on discourse as a learning catalyst. Students engaged in this process are encouraged to remain open-minded about new ideas, to develop a questioning attitude, to avoid common fallacies and reasoning, and to express themselves in an articulate and concise manner.

Students in the College receive the Banneker Pin for completion of honors core requirements, a certificate for completion of the program, and a seal on the diploma.

The 12-year-old Honors College currently enrolls 450 students.

Admission Process: Students are required to have the following high school qualifications in order to be eligible to participate: a minimum 3.0 GPA on a 4.0 scale; a SAT I score of at least 1010 or an ACT score of 21; a strong college-preparatory background in mathematics, science, and English; recommendations from high school teachers, including rating of academic performance, motivation, and self-discipline; and rank in the upper 25 percent of their high school graduating class. Transfer students with a college GPA of 3.0 are also eligible.

The Campus Context: Prairie View A&M University (a division of Texas A&M) is composed of eight colleges and schools: the College of Agriculture and Human Sciences; the College of Arts and Sciences; the Benjamin Banneker Honors College; the College of Business; the College of Education; the College of Engineering and Architecture; the College of Nursing; and the Graduate School. Seventy-six degree programs are offered on campus.

Student Body The undergraduate enrollment is approximately 6,000: 46 percent men and 54 percent women. The ethnic distribution is 86 percent black, 8 percent white, 3 percent international, 2 percent Hispanic, and 1 percent Asian or Pacific Islander. The resident population is 47 percent, while the other 53 percent commutes. Sixty-two percent of the students receive financial aid.

Faculty Of the 329 faculty members, 248 are full-time.

Key Facilities The library houses 305,436 volumes.

Job Opportunities There are several kinds of employment opportunities available to students: work-study funded by the

state and federal government; hourly employment funded by departments from grants, etc.; and teaching and research assistantships.

Tuition: $900 for state residents, $6660 for nonresidents, per year (1996-97)

Room and Board: $3620

Mandatory Fees: $1000

Contact: Dean: Jewel L. Prestage, P.O. Box 125, Prairie View, Texas 77446-0125; Telephone: 409-857-4116 or 4117; Fax: 409-857-2519

QUEENS COLLEGE OF THE CITY UNIVERSITY OF NEW YORK

4 Pu G M Sc Tr

▼ Scholars Program

The Queens College Scholars Program has primarily been a scholarship effort to attract strong freshmen to Queens College. A complete honors curriculum (including special courses and programming) is currently in the process of being developed.

The first program, Honors in the Western Tradition, is an 18-credit honors minor with a planned sequence of courses. The program is intended for students who wish to gain an understanding of the fundamental works of literature, religion, and philosophy that have shaped the Western tradition. Honors in Mathematics and Natural Sciences is a program intended for students who have demonstrated exceptional ability in mathematics and sciences at the high school level and plan to continue these studies at Queens College. The program is designed to provide research skills, enrich the academic life of participants, and encourage interaction among students who have similar interests.

The Business and Liberal Arts (BALA) program is a rigorous, interdisciplinary minor that connects liberal arts students to the world of business. BALA offers a series of courses designed to bridge study in the traditional liberal arts with a business career. Some departments also offer honors concentrations; for example, "Honors in Financial Economics" is offered through the College's Department of Economics. In some instances, participation in these honors programs is indicated on a student's transcript.

Admission Process: Students interested in the Scholars Program are encouraged to contact the Admissions Office for application deadlines.

Scholarship Availability: For more than fifteen years, the Queens College Scholars Program has awarded a small group of academically outstanding incoming freshmen four-year scholarships. Scholarships are based on the student's high school record, letters of recommendation, SAT I scores, and a personal essay. Approximately thirty-five 4-year full-tuition scholarships are awarded to incoming freshmen. Approximately 40 incoming freshmen are awarded partial two-year scholarships. As of fall 1996, the College is awarding ten scholarships to academically strong incoming transfer students who hold an associate degree.

Renewal of scholarships is contingent on a student's maintenance of a high standard of academic performance. Queens College scholars are required to participate in a fall-semester freshman seminar to introduce them to college life. The College's outstanding faculty and the various courses of student and honors sequences are available at the College. In addition, special sections of LASAR (Liberal Arts and Sciences Area Requirement) courses are designated as scholar sections.

Currently no awards, certificates, diplomas, or citations are associated with the program. There are other honors programs at Queens College that are more discipline-oriented and specialized.

The Campus Context: Queens College is one of the senior colleges of the City University of New York (CUNY) system, and like the CUNY campuses, Queens is a commuter school. Queens College was cited by the *New York Times Selective Guide to Colleges* as the strongest college within the CUNY system. Funded by the state of New York, Queens College serves all the people of the state, but most of the College's students live in New York City's five boroughs or the counties of Nassau, Suffolk, or Westchester. The campus is located off the Long Island Expressway in the urban/suburban area of Flushing, Queens.

The College has four academic divisions: Arts and Humanities, Mathematics and Natural Sciences, Social Sciences, and the School of Education. There are fifty-six undergraduate majors leading to the baccalaureate, which includes the Bachelor of Arts, Bachelor of Science, Bachelor of Fine Arts, and Bachelor of Music.

Student Body The student population is diverse and achievement oriented—sixty-seven native languages are spoken here, providing an extraordinary environment.

There are close to 14,150 undergraduate students enrolled in all divisions. Thirty-nine percent are men, and 61 percent are women. The ethnic distribution of the total undergraduate population is 54.4 percent white, 16.5 percent Asian-Pacific Islander, 15.5 percent Hispanic, 8.8 percent African American, and 4.8 percent other. More than 40 percent of the students receive financial aid. In addition to various academic honor societies, including Phi Beta Kappa, there are three social fraternities and two social sororities on campus.

Faculty Of the 987 total day and evening faculty members, including adjuncts, 541 are full-time, including 80 percent with terminal degrees. The student-faculty ratio is 17:1.

Key Facilities Among the College's facilities is the Aaron Copland School of Music, which, in addition to its academic programs, provides the College community with the oppor-

tunity to attend musical and performing arts events by students and distinguished faculty members. The 490-seat LeFrak Concert Hall is noted for its tracker organ. The campus also has a 2,143-seat Golden Center auditorium.

The landmark Chaney-Goodman-Schwerner clock tower at the Rosenthal Library is dedicated to the memory of three civil rights workers who were murdered in Mississippi during the Freedom Summer of 1964. One of them, Andrew Goodman, was a Queens College student.

The library contains print and nonprint material, including more than 700,000 books, 2,500 current periodicals, and an extensive collection of microform material. In addition, the library is a selected depository for many United States government publications. The College's library also provides Internet access through computer labs and public access workstations and has twenty databases available to students through its on-line catalog.

In addition to courses offered by the Department of Computer Science, students are provided access to the College's computer systems. Students, faculty, and staff members use the College facilities that provide more than 200 IBM and compatible PCs plus Apple microcomputers for classroom and open laboratory use.

Athletics The intercollegiate program competes on the varsity level and includes basketball, baseball, cross-country, lacrosse, swimming, tennis, track, volleyball, and water polo. The recreational program is made up of two components: organized intramural activities and informal open recreation.

Study Abroad Students are invited to participate in study-abroad programs, which include semester and yearlong programs to China, Denmark, Ecuador, Greece, Italy, and Paris. Students are able to participate in programs offered by any of the CUNY campuses. Queens College sponsors the New York/Paris exchange program.

Support Services Disabled students find most of the academic and administrative buildings accessible, including the library, dining hall, and student union. Special parking is available. Only restrooms in the newer buildings on campus are handicapped-equipped and have lowered drinking fountains. Some of the buildings have been equipped with automatic doors. The Office of Special Services provides a full range of services to enhance educational and vocational opportunities for students at Queens College with disabilities.

Job Opportunities Students eligible for federal financial aid may elect on- or off-campus work-study. In addition, the College hires a limited number of college aides to assist in department and administrative offices and in the library.

Tuition: $3200 for state residents, $6800 for nonresidents, per year (1996-97)

Mandatory Fees: $187

Contact: Director: Professor Elizabeth A. Roistacher, Office of Honors and Scholarships, Powdermaker Hall, Room 19, 65-30 Kissena Boulevard, Flushing, New York 11365; Telephone: 718-997-5502; Fax: 718-997-5508

RADFORD UNIVERSITY

| 4 Pu G M Tr |

▼ Honors Program

The Radford University Honors Program is an academic enrichment program whose overarching mission is to enhance the academic culture of the institution by providing a range of curricular and educationally oriented extracurricular opportunities for all members of the Radford University community. Within the context of this broad mission, the Honors Program functions as both a student development program and a faculty development program. As a student development effort, the mission of the Honors Program is to provide motivated and academically outstanding students with unique educational opportunities and a challenging personalized curriculum. As a faculty development effort, the mission of the Honors Program is to provide motivated faculty members with the opportunity to pursue specialized and interdisciplinary scholarly interests through the development of new courses and the opportunity to engage in pedagogical experimentation and reflection on their teaching methods. There are 100 students in the program, with approximately 600 taking honors courses each semester.

Participation Requirements: The Honors Program houses two distinct programs: one program provides a series of courses (limited to 20 students) open to all students who have a 2.0 GPA or written permission from the faculty member teaching the course. All students wishing to enroll in an honors course must receive permission of the Honors Program Director. It also offers a wide range of academic and cultural events activities that are open to the entire University and area communities. The highlight of these activities is a semester-long symposium offered each spring on a topic of importance. This symposium's focus is often the focus of many of the honors courses being offered that semester and culminates in Honors Week.

The other program is the Highlander Scholar Program. This program is for students who wish to graduate either from the Honors Program or from the Honors Program with honors in their major. One of the conditions placed on a successful applicant is the commitment to meet program requirements, consisting of 27–28 hours of work in honors, a 3.5 GPA, and meeting all Honors Program objectives. To apply for admission to this program, students must have completed one semester at Radford University with a minimum 3.0 GPA and 15–32 hours, a minimum 3.2 GPA and 33–64 hours, and a minimum 3.4 and 65 hours and above. Highlander Scholars are expected to serve on a committee and run the Honors Program, including all events sponsored by the program, including the symposium. The Student Assistant Director (a paid position) and the Student Executive Board (composed of four members elected from each class) oversee the work of the committees. They are expected to mentor incoming students who take honors courses.

Scholarship Availability: The University's foundation offers several four-year scholarships. Students who earn these are encouraged to be a part of the Honors Program.

The Campus Context: The Honors Program falls under the Office of the Vice President for Academic Affairs, specifically under the Associate Vice President for Academic Enrichment with other enrichment programs.

Radford University, founded in 1910, is located in a small city in the New River Valley of southwest Virginia between the Appalachian and Blue Ridge Mountains, 40 miles south of Roanoke on Interstate 81. In addition to its 175-acre campus, the University owns a 376-acre tract of land known as the Selu Conservancy.

Radford University is a coeducational, comprehensive public university with highly diverse curricula for undergraduates and selected graduate programs. It has five undergraduate colleges: Arts and Sciences, Business and Economics, Education and Human Development, Nursing and Health Services, and Visual and Performing Arts. Within these undergraduate colleges, 112 undergraduate programs are offered. Special facilities include a speech and hearing clinic and the English Language Institute. Special programs include freshman connections, a collaborative academic and residential life program, writing across the curriculum, an oral communication program, and an undergraduate forum.

Student Body There are 8,300 undergraduates enrolled; 85 percent are from Virginia, and the remaining 15 percent come from forty-one states and sixty countries. Fifty-five percent of the students receive financial aid. There are twenty-three fraternities and sororities.

Faculty The full-time faculty totals 395 (70 percent with doctorates); the part-time faculty totals 180. The student-faculty ratio is 18:1.

Key Facilities The library holds 293,000 volumes. The college maintains 200 microcomputers.

Athletics The campus has eight intercollegiate sports for men (basketball, soccer, tennis, baseball, cross-country, gymnastics, lacrosse, and golf) and nine for women (basketball, volleyball, tennis, gymnastics, field hockey, golf, cross-country, soccer, and softball). All compete in the Big South Conference, NCAA Division I. The University also offers numerous intramural athletic programs.

Study Abroad Study abroad is available through exchange programs with Antwerp, Nottingham, and London. Other opportunities are available through departments and other organizations affiliated with the National Collegiate Honors Council (NCHC).

Support Services Disabled-student services are provided for all students with disabilities. Thirteen of fifteen residence halls are accessible, and 80 percent of academic buildings are accessible.

Job Opportunities Internships, work-study, and work scholarship programs are provided through the Financial Aid Office. Career placement services are provided by the Career Services Center.

Tuition: $3180 for state residents, $7952 for nonresidents, per year (1997-98)

Room and Board: $4416

Mandatory Fees: $1164

Contact: Director: Earl B. Brown Jr., Box 6971 RUS, Radford, Virginia 24142; Telephone: 703-831-6100; E-mail: ebrown@ ruacad.ac.runet.edu

RAMAPO COLLEGE OF NEW JERSEY

4 Pu C S Tr

▼ College Honors Program

The Ramapo College Honors Program is designed for students who desire a scholarly environment and an opportunity to interact with challenging faculty members and like-minded students. The Honors Program provides expanded opportunities for learning and reflection. Graduation from the College Honors Program is one indicator of a highly motivated, highly skilled, self-initiating individual.

There are currently 20 students enrolled in the program.

Participation Requirements: All students enrolled in the College Honors Program are urged to participate in a 3-credit seminar on research and ways of knowing given during the spring semester of the first year in which they enter the program. College honors students are required to participate in a 3-credit seminar during the fall semester of their senior year that will prepare them for the task of creating a senior thesis. Students must complete a 3-credit senior thesis or project that demonstrates considerable artistic/intellectual achievement; screenplays, installations, and research monographs are acceptable options in the fulfillment of this requirement. Each student is required to take three H-option courses in areas related to their major.

H-Option courses are those in which students, in consultation with their instructors, do additional, in-depth work. The H-Option is not simply an add-on to the given course requirements; it requires students to perform more extensively and more intensively. The number of H-Option courses required for graduation with College Honors varies from two (for students who transfer into honors courses) to three (for all other students). Each H-Option course must be at the 200, 300, or 400 level and carry at least 3 credits. Students are encouraged to make experiential education (co-op, service-learning, fieldwork) a component of one of their H-Option courses.

During the first four weeks of the semester, the student designates one or two of the courses in which he or she is registered as an "H-Option" course. This designation is accomplished by completing the H-Option contract form with the course instructor and filing that form with the Director of the Honors Program in the Office of Academic Affairs. At the end of the semester, if the student successfully completes

the honors work and attains a grade of A- or A in the course, he or she is awarded an H or an H+ grade. In the event that the student does not successfully complete the honors work or does not earn a grade of at least A- in the course, he or she receives only a letter grade; no honors credit is earned. One 3- or 4-credit course at the 200 level and two 3- or 4-credit courses at the 300 level or higher can be taken for an H-Option as long as the faculty member and the student are in agreement about the contract.

The H-Option contract provides explicit provision for periodic consultation between the student and instructor for both project design and implementation, the description of work to be completed, and the description of the evaluation procedure.

The Honors Project is the culmination of the student's honors work at the College. The project is proposed and approved in the junior year and undertaken in the senior year as an independent study under the guidance of a faculty member. Students earn 3 credits for the completion of the proposal and an additional 3 credits for the completion of the project. Projects may result in research monographs, screenplays, performances, and installations. Students must receive a grade of A- or better for the proposal and the project in order to earn honors credits.

The benefits of the Honors Program are numerous. Graduate and professional schools regard enrollment in honors as one indicator of excellence. Students are encouraged to take part in nationwide conferences and are eligible for financial support so that they may attend. Successful completion of the Honors Program is indicated on the student's official transcript. Students are recognized for their accomplishments at the annual Honors Convocation.

Admission Process: Students are encouraged to apply to the Honors Program during their first semester at the College. Admission is based on the following criteria: grade point index, SAT I scores, extracurricular/leadership activities, and recommendations. Transfer students are also invited to seek admission to the program. Students who were enrolled in an honors program at another institution may receive honors transfer credits. Evaluation is made on a case-by-case basis.

The Campus Context: Established in 1969, Ramapo College is a four-year state college of liberal arts, sciences, and professional studies offering twenty-six academic majors. The 300-acre campus is only 25 miles from New York City. More than 600 courses are offered days, evenings, and Saturdays each semester. The Bachelor of Arts, Bachelor of Science, Bachelor of Social Work, and Master of Arts in Liberal Studies degrees are offered. Joint programs offered are the Bachelor of Science in Nursing with the University of Medicine and Dentistry of New Jersey and the Master of Science in Management with the New Jersey Institute of Technology.

The campus is built around four academic buildings, a student center, a library, a gymnasium, playing fields, an administration building, and the International Telecommunications Center. The Angelica and Russ Berrie Center for Performing and Visual Arts will be constructed in the near future.

Student Body There are 2,608 full-time and 1,935 part-time students from all the state's counties, other states, and other countries. About 1,200 students are housed on campus.

Faculty Of the 156 full-time faculty members, 90 percent have the doctorate or other terminal degree. The faculty is supplemented by adjunct specialists and other visiting scholars.

Key Facilities There are 170,000 volumes in the library.

Support Services The barrier-free campus is accessible to disabled students.

Tuition: $3752 for state residents, $5496 for nonresidents, per year (1996-97)

Room and Board: $5678

Contact: Director: Dr. Martha Ecker, 505 Ramapo Valley Road, Mahwah, New Jersey 07430; Telephone: 201-529-7530; Fax: 201-529-7508

RANDOLPH–MACON COLLEGE

4 Pr G S

▼ Honors Program

The Randolph–Macon Honors Program, established in 1982, is designed to challenge and stimulate superior students by allowing them to substitute for regular collegiate requirements special courses, specifically designed for the program, that are unique, low-enrollment, and high-participation and developed and taught by excellent teachers. Honors students are expected to take at least four of these courses during their first three years at the College.

In addition, the program requires an honors student to complete at least two departmental honors units. These may take the form of a senior thesis, independent study or research, or an individualized honors contract in a regular course offering. Students normally take these units in their major or minor department during their junior and senior years.

Honors students also have the advantage of the use of a former faculty home that was dedicated to the use of the program. It contains a seminar room; a library; a living room area for meetings, programs, and sociability; a fully equipped kitchen; several personal computers; study space; and a room where two honors students may live.

The Student Honors Association provides programming for the cultural and social events and publishes a monthly *Gazette* to provide information to students about upcoming activities and an opportunity for students to publish articles they have written.

There are currently about 90 students in the program.

Participation Requirements: Students must maintain a cumulative GPA of 3.25 (3.0 for freshmen) and make no grade lower than B- in an honors course to continue as members of the program.

Admission Process: Students gain entrance to the program by invitation before they enroll at the College if specific criteria are met (top decile of graduating class and 1200 or better on combined SAT I verbal-math scores) and by academic performance during their first year in residence at the College.

The Campus Context: Randolph–Macon College is a coeducational, liberal arts, undergraduate institution located in Ashland, Virginia, a town of about 7,000 located 15 miles north of Richmond, Virginia.

The January term (students normally enroll in one 4-week course) provides opportunities for courses off campus and allows nearly 100 students to enroll for credit in academic internships in a variety of departments. The College offers Bachelor of Arts and Bachelor of Science degrees. There are twenty-nine majors available.

Student Body Total enrollment is 1,050, currently evenly divided between men and women. Financial aid is primarily awarded on the basis of need. More than half of the student body receives financial aid. Interested students should contact the Admissions Office. A variety of extracurricular activities exist, ranging from publications to drama to service organizations. Ninety percent of students live on campus. There are six chapters of national fraternities and four chapters of national sororities on campus.

Faculty The faculty includes 90 full-time faculty members plus 15 full-time–equivalent instructors. Most full-time faculty members have terminal degrees.

Key Facilities Computer facilities are available to students in three large laboratories. In addition, dormitories are wired so that students, using their own PCs, have access to e-mail and the World Wide Web.

Athletics The College participates in NCAA Division III athletics and fields eight teams for men and six for women. In addition, an extensive intramural program is available. A new athletic complex is scheduled to open in 1997.

Study Abroad The Study Abroad Program offers opportunities to enroll in courses in colleges and universities in the United Kingdom, France, Spain, Germany, Italy, Greece, Japan, and South Korea.

Tuition: $15,255 per year (1996-97)

Room and Board: $3895

Mandatory Fees: $375

Contact: Co-Director: Dr. Kristen Klaaren, Telephone: 804-752-7332, E-mail: klaaren@rmc.edu; Co-Director: Dr. Bruce Torrence, Telephone: 804-752-7331, E-mail: torrenc@rmc.edu; Fax: 804-752-7231; Ashland, Virginia 23005; Web site: http://www.rmc.edu

REDLANDS COMMUNITY COLLEGE

2 Pu C S Tr

▼ Honors Program

The Redlands Community College (RCC) Honors Program consists of course work that offers academically talented students stimulating class experiences and interaction with other exceptional students. The benefits that the students receive are recognition by faculty members and administrators of their academic abilities and achievements, enhanced opportunities for acceptance in honors programs at four-year institutions, participation in a challenging and enriching curriculum, interaction with other honor students, and special recognition at their graduation ceremonies.

The designated honors courses, the interdisciplinary seminars, and the contracted courses are taught by faculty members who have exhibited excellence in teaching and who have shown a distinct interest in working with honors students. The honors faculty and the Honors Directors are available to the students to aid them in their research and presentations at the Great Plains NCHC Regional Conference and the University of Oklahoma Undergraduate Research Day.

Because Redlands Community College is a small school, honors students have access to all campus facilities and an honors study room with a reference library, a multimedia computer, and access to the Internet. Students graduating with honors must have a 3.25 GPA. In addition to being recognized at their graduation ceremonies, honors students have their accomplishment noted on their transcripts.

In existence for twelve years, the program currently enrolls 30 students.

Participation Requirements: After acceptance, honors students must successfully complete 11 credit hours of honors work to graduate with honors. Nine of the hours may be completed through a contract with an individual instructor or by taking designated honors courses. Two credit hours must be earned through interdisciplinary honors seminars. Honors students are also encouraged to participate in the Great Plains NCHC Regional Honors Conference. In order to get honors credit for a contracted course, honors students must complete an honors project and receive at least a B in the course. The honors project does not affect the student's grade in a contracted course. Students who graduate with honors are given special recognition at the graduation ceremony and receive a medallion at an honors dinner.

Admission Process: Students applying to the RCC Honors Program for the first time as freshmen must meet requirements based on ACT scores and high school GPAs. Other students may rely on their college GPAs and a successful interview with an Honors Director.

Scholarship Availability: Scholarships are available through various departments in the College but are not designated honors scholarships.

The Campus Context: Redlands Community College offers forty-seven degree programs.

Student Body The College has an undergraduate enrollment of 778 men and 1,159 women. The ethnic distribution of students is 83 percent white, 6 percent American Indian, 4.5 percent black, 3 percent nonresident alien, 2 percent Asian, and 2 percent Hispanic. All of the students are commuters. Seventy-one percent receive financial aid.

Faculty Of the 112 faculty members, 24 are full-time. Ten percent have terminal degrees. The student-faculty ratio is 24:1.

Key Facilities There are five computer facilities in classrooms and the student commons. Among other special facilities are the Multimedia Building, Equine Center, the Cultural Center, and the Olympic-size pool.

Athletics RCC sponsors three intercollegiate athletic teams, which compete in women's basketball, men's basketball, and men's baseball. Each team is a member of the National Junior College Athletic Association Division II and a member of the Bi-State Conference. Books, tuition, and fee scholarships are available in each of the intercollegiate sports. As a member of the NJCAA Division II, RCC may award no housing assistance. Each team at RCC has had the enviable opportunity to compete in its respective national tournaments many times.

Support Services All buildings meet the requirements for accessibility. In addition, there are special services and equipment for the deaf and blind.

Job Opportunities There are twenty work-study positions, and approximately 40 students are working on E&G money.

Tuition: $1208 for state residents, $3008 for nonresidents, per year (1996-97)

Contact: Director: Linda Hasley, 1300 South Country Club Road, El Reno, Oklahoma 73036; Telephone: 405-262-2552 ext. 2308; Fax: 405-422-1200

RICKS COLLEGE

2 Pr G M Sc

▼ Honors Program

Established in 1969, the Ricks College Honors Program is designed to help students with high academic ability and a positive attitude toward learning derive maximum benefit from their college experience. To do this the program offers both honors sections of classes available to the general student body and classes available only to students admitted to the Honors Program. The approximately fifteen offerings each semester include major, general education, and elective classes in a variety of disciplines but principally from the humanities. Classes are limited in size to 20 students. In addition to classes, the program furnishes a lounge for study and conversation, several retreats a year, and other opportunities for fellowship. Approximately 300 students enroll in honors classes each semester. A higher number is admitted to the program.

Participation Requirements: Participants are required to take 12 credits in the Honors Program, including at least one class of a Western Civilization type, and have a cumulative GPA of at least 3.5. Honors Program graduates have their name listed separately in the graduation program, wear a distinctive gold cord at graduation, and have their graduation with honors noted on their transcript.

Admission Process: To be admitted, a student must have a cumulative GPA of at least 3.3.

Scholarship Availability: In addition to scholarships available through the general College Scholarship Office, the Honors Program pays $50 each semester to a student who is in an honors class, pays a $5 fee, and has a 3.5 GPA. In addition, having complied with the same conditions, a student may take overload classes without paying the charge that would otherwise be assessed.

The Campus Context: Ricks College is located in Rexburg, a city of some 15,000 people in rural southeastern Idaho, 85 miles south of Yellowstone National Park and 50 miles west of the Teton Mountains. Airlines service Idaho Falls, which is 30 miles to the south.

Ricks College is sponsored by the Church of Jesus Christ of Latter-Day Saints (LDS) and has a comprehensive liberal arts, vocational, and scientific curriculum consisting of approximately 1,000 courses, 150 majors, and forty career programs. The College offers eighty-six associate degree programs in arts and science, forty associate degrees in specialized disciplines, seven 1- or 2-year certificate programs, a three-year interior design program, a baccalaureate degree in nursing, and an Army ROTC program. Ricks College is accredited by the Commission on Colleges of the Northwest Association of Schools and Colleges.

Student Body The College has an enrollment of approximately 8,400, which makes it the largest private two-year college in the nation. Students come principally from Idaho and the surrounding states but also from all fifty states and forty countries. Students participate in more than eighty clubs and organizations, intramurals sports, and other recreational programs. Much of the campus maintenance work is done by student employees. Weekly devotionals and frequent forums provide spiritual and intellectual stimulation. Some forty-seven LDS ward congregations serve students, and other religious congregations are available in the community.

Faculty Ninety-two percent of the 335 full-time faculty members have either master's degrees or doctorates.

Key Facilities The beautifully landscaped campus of 400 acres, 75 percent of which is farmland, has eighteen major buildings and eight dormitory complexes. The College also operates a 120-acre Livestock Center with an adjacent astronomy observatory and an Outdoor Learning Center at the foot of the Teton Mountains. Numerous computers are available for student use in the library and in labs throughout the campus. Two auditoriums seat 4,200 and 960 patrons each, and a superb fine arts building contains a 700-seat acoustically renowned concert hall, a 540-seat drama theater, and three recital and performance facilities of 200 seats each. The College supports a public FM radio station and a student-operated AM station.

Athletics Ricks College fields ten competitive teams in seven sports and consistently places high in national rankings. Football is played in 5,000-seat Viking Stadium and basketball in 3,590-seat Hart Gymnasium.

Study Abroad A number of off-campus and overseas study tours are available during the summer and the regular academic year.

Tuition: $1870 minimum per year for full-time church members, $3648 per year for full-time non-church members, $114 per semester hour for part-time non-church members (1996-97)

Room and Board: $2300 minimum

Contact: Director: Richard L. Davis, 294 Smith Building, Rexburg, Idaho 83460-0835; Telephone: 208-356-1253; Fax: 208-356-2390; E-mail: davisr@ricks.edu

ROCHESTER COMMUNITY AND TECHNICAL COLLEGE

2 Pu G S Sc Tr

▼ Honors Program

Honors at Rochester Community and Technical College (RCTC) offers challenge, recognition, and a myriad of other opportunities through several avenues.

First, the Honors Program curriculum offers special honors courses to provide students with a strong grounding in primary texts and critical thinking.

Second, the Honors Program offers mentoring and help in transferring. Students work closely with the RCTC Honors Program Coordinator, who serves as a personal academic mentor, often with the help of a faculty member in the major field. Working with the Coordinator on schedule set-up also earns them the right to priority registration. In addition, to help take the mystique out of the transfer process, Honors Program students are able to participate in "Bridging the Transfer Gap," a workshop designed specifically to address the transfer needs of highly motivated Honors Program students. The Coordinator also writes recommendations and calls transfer institutions.

Third, the RCTC Honors Program offers camaraderie and activities meant to stimulate the intellect. Students can attend special Honors Program SALON sessions throughout the year, have the option of working with GATE (Gifted and Talented) children in the Rochester Public Schools, develop special events for the University Center-Rochester (UC–R) campus, have a "big brother" or "big sister" to help them with various aspects of college life, and have the opportunity to attend conferences with other honors program students from the state, Midwest, and/or nation.

Fourth, students who qualify can also become a member of Phi Theta Kappa (PTK), an international two-year college academic honor society that provides educational and cultural programs and scholarships. The 3-year-old program currently enrolls 60 students (PTK membership is not included in that number).

Participation Requirements: To earn an Honors Diploma, students must apply to the program, be accepted, take a total of 20 honors credits, and maintain a GPA of 3.25 or above. At graduation, students who have at least a 3.3 GPA and who have completed at least 20 credits of honors credits receive a certificate, receive and wear a golden medallion at the graduation ceremony, are identified on the graduation program, and are named as Honors Program graduates as they walk across the stage. The transcript also clearly identifies honors credits.

Admission Process: Interested individuals may apply anytime during the year by filling out an application form. Honors Program students are selected on the basis of GPA, school and/or community experiences, and other life experiences. For the English Honors sequence, the students must also score above 90 percent on the college writing placement test.

Scholarship Availability: Presidential Scholarships are available to all entering freshmen in the top 5 percent of their high school graduating class. RCTC offers a number of other scholarships for both incoming, returning, and outgoing students, and many students who receive scholarships are also in the Honors Program.

The Campus Context: The 4,000 members of the diverse student body of Rochester Community and Technical College, founded in 1915, can choose from sixty-four areas of study, including both transfer and technical majors. Students can attend RCTC full-time, part-time, days, evenings, or weekends, and RCTC offers some classes via computer modem and television.

The campus (University Center–Rochester) also houses students at the University of Minnesota–Rochester Center (UMN–RC) and Winona State University–Rochester Center (WSU–RC), institutions that collaborate with RCTC to offer four-year and graduate degrees to approximately 6,000 students. For example, the University Center at Rochester has more than a dozen "2 plus 2" programs with Winona State University–Rochester Center that allow students to take the first two years of a four-year degree at RCTC and then transfer to WSU–RC for the final two years.

There are also twenty-four master's-level programs available in Rochester, more than half of which are offered by WSU–RC and the UMN–RC. The UMN–RC now also offers a Bachelor of Arts degree in English.

Student Body The student profile includes 60 percent women; 43 percent of students are 25 and older. About half of the students are from Rochester, while 40 percent come from elsewhere in Minnesota.

Faculty There are 100 full-time RCC faculty members who are supplemented by adjunct faculty members.

Key Facilities The Goddard Library houses 65,000 books, 650 periodical titles, and a variety of microforms, CD-ROMs, and electronic databases. The library catalog (PALS) is computerized. The campus has numerous computer and ITV labs. All students have access to e-mail addresses.

Athletics Diverse offerings are available, including intramurals.

Support Services Facilities for disabled students are available.

Job Opportunities Work-study is available.

Tuition: $1997 for state residents, $3994 for nonresidents, per year (1996-97)

Mandatory Fees: $209

Contact: Coordinator: Dr. Julie Rodakowski, 851 30th Avenue SE, Rochester, Minnesota 55904-4999; Telephone: 507-285-7165; Fax: 507-285-7496; E-mail: julie.rodakowski@roch.edu; Web site: http://www.roch.edu/RCTC/honorsprogram

ROSE STATE COLLEGE

2 Pu C S Sc Tr

▼ Honors Program

The Honors Program at Rose State College (RSC) offers all students an opportunity to experience an intellectual and cultural enrichment of the college environment. Students may elect to be involved in any part of the Honors Program. Each semester, honors-designated sections or regular courses, primarily those that satisfy General Education degree requirements, are offered, along with special topics and interdisciplinary courses in most semesters. A third option is the contract for honors credit, which students may arrange on an individual basis with mentoring professors. Students admitted to the Honors Program become eligible to apply for Honors Scholarships.

There are currently 35 students enrolled in the program.

Participation Requirements: To graduate from the program, students must meet all requirements for a two-year degree with a 3.5 or higher GPA; earn at least 12 honors credit hours at RSC; earn A's or B's in all classes taken for honors credit; and submit an annotated résumé of all honors work to the Honors Committee. Those who successfully complete the Honors Program receive appropriate notations on diplomas and transcripts.

Admission Process: Although any RSC student may take offered honors classes, those who wish to enter the Honors Program must have a 3.5 GPA in high school and an ACT score of 27 or above, complete two RSC honors classes with an A or B, or demonstrate a special skill or talent to the Honors Committee.

The RSC Honors Program completed its first year with 7 students admitted as honors students and 30 students completing honors classes or honors contracts. Students and professors alike praised the quality of the honors experience, citing the increased student/mentor interaction and opportunities for pursuit of individual interests in particular.

The Campus Context: Rose State College is a two-year college located on 100 acres in Midwest City, Oklahoma, a suburb of Oklahoma City. Forty-six degree programs are offered leading to the Associate in Arts, Associate in Science, and Associate in Applied Science degrees.

Student Body Approximately 8,500 students enroll in the fall and spring semesters, 41 percent men and 59 percent women. Sixty-six percent of the student body is full-time; the remaining 34 percent is part-time.

Faculty There are 152 full-time faculty members (supplemented with adjunct faculty), 24 percent with doctorates or other terminal degrees. The student-faculty ratio is 21:1.

Key Facilities The library houses 80,000 volumes. There are eight computer labs with PCs.

Support Services Disabled students have access to all buildings (with electronic doors) and special tables/chairs in classrooms.

Tuition: $868 for state residents, $2728 for nonresidents, per year (1996-97)

Mandatory Fees: $341

Contact: Director: Claudia Buckmaster, Humanities 113, Midwest City, Oklahoma 73110-2799; Telephone: 405-733-7506; Fax: 405-736-0370; E-mail: cbuckmaster@ms.rose.cc.ok.us

ROWAN UNIVERSITY

| 4 Pu C S Sc Tr |

▼ **School of Liberal Arts and Sciences Honors Program**

The Rowan University Interdisciplinary Honors Program is open to students in every academic major. Emphasis is placed on interdisciplinary study and active learning. The program's smaller classes nurture development of student writing, speaking, and critical-thinking skills. Connections among ideas and disciplines are enriched by encouraging students to question, study, and analyze primary texts.

Students take the initiative in their own learning and work in collaboration with peers. They join in selecting texts, nominating faculty members for the program, and creating curriculum. The concentration provides the space for students to take up different points of view outside any single discipline. Students think critically about the interplay between liberal learning and career preparation within and beyond academic fields.

Participation Requirements: Students must complete three-lower level and three upper-level courses in the concentration. All students must enroll in a capstone seminar or complete an interdisciplinary independent honors project. All honors courses fulfill general education requirements. They are also applicable to writing intensive and multicultural–global requirements. A minimum of 18 credit hours in interdisciplinary studies and a 3.5 GPA are required for completion of the concentration.

Admission Process: Applications for admission are reviewed by faculty members and students. Criteria for acceptance rest on a combination of scores on standardized tests (AP exam scores and 1200 on the SAT I), letters of recommendation, and high school rank. Students with a 3.5 GPA at the end of their first year are invited to apply for admission to the program. Exceptional students can submit an application essay and request peer and faculty interviews to gain admission.

Scholarship Availability: More than 70 percent of Rowan University students receive financial aid through an assortment of grants, scholarships, loans, and part-time employment. Last year's grant and loan programs totaled more than $8 million. Each year, alumni, private groups, and individuals also provide more than $120,000 in scholarships to incoming students.

The Campus Context: After 70 years as Glassboro State College, a $100-million gift from Henry and Betty Rowan provided the means to transform the College. The Rowan University vision is to become a regional university that emphasizes undergraduate programs. A new $18-million library, funded by the state, opened in spring 1995. The 200-acre campus is only 30 minutes from Philadelphia and 55 minutes from Atlantic City.

Five schools form the University: Liberal Arts and Sciences, Education and Related Professional Services, Business Administration, Fine and Performing Arts, and Engineering.

Student Body About 5,000 undergraduates enroll in thirty-one undergraduate degree programs. Rowan University has more than 150 chartered student organizations. Clubs, honor societies, fraternities, and sororities work in the framework of an elected Student Government Association. Homecoming, Family Weekend, and Project Santa offer community-wide activities. The Glassboro Center for the Arts and the Annual Jazz Festival provide part of the wide range of cocurricular cultural activities available to enrich student life.

Faculty Of the 324 full-time faculty members (supplemented by an adjunct faculty), 80 percent have doctorates or appropriate terminal degrees. The student-faculty ratio is 17:1, and the average class size is 23.

Key Facilities The 300,000-volume library is networked to computer labs. There are six residence halls and three apartment complexes. Fourteen IBM and Macintosh labs are located in academic buildings.

Athletics Rowan has had ten NCAA Division III championships in basketball, baseball, soccer, and track and field, and more than 100 All-American athletes have attended Rowan. The intramural program is extensive and complements the intercollegiate competition. The Recreational Center and Student Center offer a full range of activities.

Study Abroad Qualified undergraduates earn 15–30 credits in overseas programs in Europe, Latin America, Australia, Asia, and Africa. Programs are coordinated with all academic majors as integral components of the degree models.

Job Opportunities Federal Work-Study (no more than 20 hours per week) is available to students who qualify for federal financial aid. Institutional Work-Study offers opportunities for students who are not eligible for need-based financial aid.

Tuition: $2740 for state residents, $5480 for nonresidents, per year (1996-97)

Room and Board: $4768

Mandatory Fees: $1011

Contact: Director: David R. Applebaum, Ph.D., History Suite-Robinson Hall, Glassboro, New Jersey 08028-1701; Telephone: 609-256-4500 ext. 3988; Fax: 609-256-4921; E-mail: applebaum@mars.rowan.edu; Web site: http://www.rowan.edu

RUSSELL SAGE COLLEGE

4 Pr C S Tr

▼ Honors Program: "Honoring Women's Voices"

The Honors Program at Russell Sage College (RSC) is an 18-credit academic program that honors women's voices in all fields and endeavors, offers sustained opportunities for cross-disciplinary study through multidisciplinary approaches, supports students in directing their own learning, provides opportunities for independent projects, provides experience in knowledge acquisition in diverse ways, and is open to all students who desire an intellectual challenge.

In addition to course work, the Honors Program includes a junior-year internship or community field placement and a senior seminar during which the student completes her honors project. Class size is limited to 18, and all classes are taught by full-time faculty members. Faculty members are encouraged to address both the content and pedagogical issues that are indicated by the theme. This involves efforts at including scholarship about and by women. Furthermore, faculty members are encouraged to conduct their courses in such a way as to promote self-discovery and cooperative learning.

Begun in fall semester 1996, the program comprises approximately 30 first-year students, members of the Class of 2000.

Admission Process: First-year students entering RSC with a high school GPA of 3.3 or better may be provisionally accepted into the Honors Program during their first year. Following completion of 6 honors credits (with a grade of B or better and an overall GPA of 3.3 or better), students may apply for acceptance. The application process includes an essay, a letter of recommendation, and a transcript review. Transfer students currently enrolled in an honors program are accepted into the program upon completion of the essay, interview, and letter of recommendation. They must meet the GPA requirements listed above.

Scholarship Availability: There are no honors scholarships at this time.

The Campus Context: Russell Sage College is open to women only, while Sage Evening College, Sage Graduate School, and the affiliated Junior College of Albany are coeducational. RSC offers thirty-five degree programs. Among special facilities on campus are the Allies Center for the Study of Difference and Conflict, the Allies Center for Conflict Mediation Information and Education, the Center for Citizenship, the Center for the Exploration of International Issues, a First-year Mentoring Program, the Helen M. Upton Center for Women's Studies, and the Social Policy Research Center.

Student Body Undergraduate enrollment is 100 percent women and includes 12 percent historically underrepresented groups and 2 international students. Forty-nine percent of students reside on campus. RSC has no sororities.

Faculty Of the 160 faculty members, 120 are full-time. Eighty-five percent have terminal degrees. The student-faculty ratio is 9:1.

Key Facilities The library houses 230,000 volumes. Computer facilities include five classrooms, with two more in development. The Computing Center has multiple Sun SPARCserver 1000s.

Athletics In athletics, the College is NCAA Division III in basketball, tennis, soccer, volleyball, and softball.

Study Abroad Study abroad is available at Oxford University and Shanghai Institute, as are programs in Puerto Rico, Spain, and the Bahamas.

Support Services Many of the buildings are handicapped-accessible.

Job Opportunities Work-study grants are available.

Tuition: $13,400 per year (1996-97)

Room and Board: $5560 minimum

Mandatory Fees: $270

Contact: Director: Prof. Lisa A. Callahan, Troy, New York 12180; Telephone: 518-270-2278; Fax: 518-475-0030; E-mail: callal@sage.edu

SACRED HEART UNIVERSITY

4 Pr G S Sc Tr

▼ Honors Program

The Honors Program at Sacred Heart University (SCU) is interdisciplinary and open to all students who qualify. In keeping with the mission of Sacred Heart University, "...to prepare men and women to live in and make their contribution to the human community," Sacred Heart University offers an Honors Program that serves the special needs of students who have excelled in academic work. The program provides an intellectually challenging experience for the student who demonstrates high potential for interdisciplinary learning in a small classroom setting that encourages critical and independent thinking and that gives students direct access to honors faculty members. Upon graduation, the student receives a certificate of completion in the Honors Program in addition to a notation on the University transcript.

Sacred Heart University's Honors Program must meet curriculum requirements and has distinctive features. The honors curriculum consists of a number of courses designed specifically for the Honors Program. They are interdisciplinary in nature and team-taught by professors from different disciplines. This approach allows students to deepen and expand their view of a given topic and also fosters an appreciation for the elegance of interdisciplinary learning and understanding. These courses fulfill academic core requirements for the baccalaureate degree. Completion of 18 credits in specifically designed honors courses earns the student an honors minor. The transcript informs other academic institutions and prospective employers of the student's accomplishments.

Throughout the course of the academic year, the Honors Program invites speakers to address students and faculty members on topics outside the usual honors curriculum. The Cum Laude Society, an extracurricular group open to all students, coordinates discussion groups and organizes activities that respond to the University's commitment to "combining education for life with preparation for professional excellence." The Honors Program at Sacred Heart was initiated in 1973. For each entering class, 40 students are invited to participate in the Honors Program. Therefore, maximum enrollment in any year is 160. Currently, 88 students are actively pursuing the honors minor.

Participation Requirements: During the freshman year, honors students enroll in the English Honors Seminar, a two-semester program, and the Freshman Seminar. Successful completion of Honors English with a grade of A or B results in the student having Effective Communication waived. A minimum grade of C is required to receive credit. During the sophomore year, interdisciplinary courses offered by honors faculty members focus on the humanities and social and behavioral sciences.

Courses emphasizing humanities and the natural and physical sciences are offered during the junior year. Senior-year offerings include individualized instruction with an honors faculty member in a discipline chosen by the student. This should include a service learning component. Successful completion of 18 credits in honors courses results in the honors minor.

Admission Process: Students are eligible for the Honors Program during the first year based upon the following criteria: SAT I recentered scores totaling 1100, with at least 620 on the verbal; high scores on University placement exams; a high school GPA of at least 3.2 on a 4.0 scale and/or graduation in the top 10 percent of the high school class; and an interview with the Honors Director.

Students are eligible for honors courses and the Honors Program after their first year based upon recommendations from faculty members, a college minimum cumulative GPA of 3.2, completion of Freshman English and Effective Communication, and an interview with the Honors Director.

Scholarship Availability: The University offers an academic scholarship program that is available to qualified students. These students must meet two of the following criteria: a 3.2 cumulative high school GPA in English, math, science, social studies, and foreign language; a high school ranking within the top 20 percent of the class; and/or SAT I scores of 1100 or better. The scholarship is awarded on a sliding scale, with points being given according to GPA rank and SAT I scores. The amount of the scholarship, which is based solely on academic merit, ranges from $3000 to $6000 a year. There is no separate application procedure necessary. The student is recommended for the scholarship through the admission process. The scholarship committee notifies in writing students who have received this scholarship. Students who apply for another scholarship, the University's Scholars, must meet the same qualifications as above, but must also be valedictorian or salutatorian of their high school graduating class. This scholarship is worth $9000.

The Campus Context: Sacred Heart University is a coeducational, independent, comprehensive Catholic university offering twenty-five undergraduate degree programs, with combined undergraduate/graduate degrees in business, chemistry, computer science, and physical and occupational therapy. Certification programs in education, preprofessional health and law advising programs, and NATA-accredited athletic training internships are available.

Founded in 1963, the University has experienced unprecedented growth over the past six years, making it the third-largest Catholic university in New England. Recent improvements to the suburban 56-acre campus have included new academic and student life programs and six new residence halls and new athletic fields. During summer 1996, construction began on the William H. Pitt Health and Recreation Complex, which is scheduled for completion in late 1997. Committed to technology, the University was the first in New England to require entering students to have a computer.

Student Body There is a full-time undergraduate enrollment of 2,200 and a part-time undergraduate enrollment of 2,000.

There are 1,600 graduate students. Together, these students represent eighteen states and fifty-five countries. Twenty-four percent are from multicultural backgrounds. Sixty-five percent of the population lives in residence halls on campus. Eighty-five percent of the students receive financial assistance.

Faculty There are 130 full-time faculty members and 220 adjunct members, making the student-faculty ratio 14:1. Eighty-one percent of the faculty members have terminal degrees.

Key Facilities The library houses 177,000 volumes. The University's computer network includes five computer classrooms, a multipurpose lab, and more than 120 IBM-compatible and Macintosh computers. All incoming students are required to purchase University-approved laptop computers. Six residence halls were built between 1992 and 1994. Other new construction includes a $1.2-million synthetic-surfaced multipurpose athletic field and extensive renovations to the main academic buildings, including state-of-the-art science labs, faculty offices, and renovations to existing classrooms and the dining hall.

Study Abroad Sacred Heart is a member of two consortia of colleges (CCIS and IES/IAS) that sponsor more than forty study-abroad sites. Students have studied in Ecuador, England, Mexico, Spain, Belize, Germany, and Italy. Nonconsortia programs include sites in Australia, Ireland, Central America, and Egypt. One out of every 3 students who studied abroad received merit scholarships from outside the University. The University also has a campus in Luxembourg that specializes in an M.B.A. program.

Support Services The University's facilities are accessible to all students.

Job Opportunities Students are offered a range of work-study positions. Some non-work-study positions are also available.

Tuition: $12,212 per year (full-time); $265-$400 per credit, according to course load (part-time) (1996-97)

Room and Board: $6380

Mandatory Fees: $500

Contact: Director: Dr. Carol Batt, 5151 Park Avenue, Fairfield, Connecticut 06432; Telephone: 203-365-7506; Fax: 203-365-7542; E-mail: battc@sacredheart.edu

---

St. Cloud State University

4 Pu G M Sc Tr

▼ University Honors Program

The St. Cloud State Honors Program is an unique alternative to the University's general education program. Established thirty-one years ago, the program has a feeling of community fostered among the students that is part of what makes the program so successful. The program begins by accepting about 100 students each year. These diverse students from a variety of backgrounds are pursu-

ing a wide range of academic interests. These students are active participants in small classes of fewer than 25 students. Most classes are topical, so new course titles are offered every quarter and seldom repeated unless popularity necessitates offering it more than once. There are currently 350 students enrolled in the program.

The Honors Program also offers two honors residence halls to further create an atmosphere of community. W. W. Holes Hall is generally reserved for incoming freshmen and offers traditional residence hall living. Benton Hall, however, offers apartment-style living for upperclassmen and honors students returning to the halls.

In addition, the opportunity to become involved in the Honors Club allows the students to have a direct voice in how the program is run and any changes that are made. A student committee reviews applications and selects new, incoming students; they also determine scholarship recipients and program policy. They also select course topics and recruit the professors to teach those classes. Committees meet to discuss any changes in the program. The students also have the opportunity to represent the program at the regional and national conventions. In addition, students become actively involved with each other while enjoying a multitude of social events and by volunteering in the community.

Honors students don't just limit themselves to the honors community, though; they become leaders in all of their disciplines and actively participate in a multitude of clubs, programs, and organizations. As a matter of fact, one third of the thirty Excellence in Leadership awards given out across campus this year were given to honors students, even though honors students make up only 3 percent of the seniors on campus.

In addition to the unique variety of innovative courses, there are many benefits from being in the program. Honors students are given priority registration, beginning with the first quarter of their second year. Students are given honors class listings a year in advance, making it easier to plan their schedules. They also have the opportunity to take advantage of the many international studies programs that St. Cloud State offers, and they have the special opportunity to study at Oxford University in England. At graduation, students are given honors distinction in addition to it being indicated on their diploma and transcript.

Participation Requirements: Students must complete 60 credits of honors to fulfill their general education requirements. The required core includes four orientation and integration courses, English Composition and Research and Speech Communication. Also required are three quarters of a foreign language. Twenty-two credits are then divided between literature and fine arts, philosophy, social sciences, natural science, technology, and mathematics. These courses are topical so that new topics are offered each quarter and students can wait and take the ones that interest them the most. An additional 14 credits of electives can be taken any time to complete the 60 credits. In fall 1998 St. Cloud State University is transferring to a semester system. However, the current honors system has been designed to offer a smooth transition for students. Students must maintain an overall GPA of 3.0 to graduate in the Honors Program.

Admission Process: Students can apply at the end of the junior year in high school in order to ensure admission to the honors program in their freshman year of college. High school students living near SCSU or staying in a residence hall can take honors courses in the PSEOA (Post-Secondary Enrollment Options) program in order to experience honors prior to college enrollment.

Applying to Honors and applying to the University are separate processes and can be done in either order—neither is automatic. Students must submit ACT scores in order to be admitted to the University. Honors applications are reviewed weekly or biweekly. The University accepts some credits from general education, transfer, and AP, CLEP, and IB tests.

Scholarship Availability: Honors students are eligible for several honors scholarships in addition to the many general University freshman scholarships. General University scholarships range from $500 to full tuition. Additional honors scholarships tend to be a standard $1200 divided over four years. Honors students have the opportunity to have their Honors Program application double as their scholarship application simply by checking a box on the program application. This saves time and paperwork. Several smaller scholarships are available each year for students actively involved in the Honors Club.

The Campus Context: St. Cloud State University has been in existence for more than 125 years. The University was founded originally as a teaching school, and superior education has been its priority in all disciplines ever since. St. Cloud State University is composed of five colleges: the College of Social Science, the College of Fine Arts and Humanities, the College of Business, the College of Education, and the College of Science and Technology. A total of 130 degree programs are offered on campus.

Student Body Undergraduate enrollment is approximately 13,000; graduate enrollment is approximately 1,200. Women make up 54 percent of the enrollment, and men 46 percent. Of the total population, about 91 percent are Minnesota residents.

The ethnic distribution of students is 77.3 percent white, 15.8 percent not listed, 3.5 percent nonresident alien, 1.6 percent Asian, 0.8 percent Hispanic, 0.4 percent American Indian, and 0.4 percent black. There are 484 international students. Eighty-five percent of the students are residents; the remaining 15 percent commute. Sixty-eight percent of the students receive financial aid.

Faculty Of the 678 faculty members, 599 are full-time; 76 percent have terminal degrees. The student-faculty ratio is 22:1.

Key Facilities The Learning Resource Center houses 704,922 volumes in print, with more than 2 million print and nonprint items (film, microfiche, audiovisual, etc.). Student computer labs abound in all departments on campus, relieving students of the need for a personal computer. The Beehive, as with all the labs on campus, offers students a wide variety of computer programs with both Macintosh and IBM computers. The Beehive also offers flexible hours, allowing students to work until 1 a.m. on school nights. Internet, e-mail, and World Wide Web access is available from all computers.

Athletics St. Cloud University participates in eighteen sports for men and women, all NCAA Division II, except hockey, which is Division I.

Study Abroad St. Cloud State encourages students to enhance their education by taking advantage of one of the many study-abroad programs offered through the University. Aside from airfare cost, these overseas programs are usually offered at the same cost of tuition as St. Cloud State. During their time abroad, students have the opportunity to live and study in another culture while completing many of their general and major requirements.

Students are also given ample time for independent travel and exploration. One of the most popular destinations is St. Cloud State's campus in Anwick, England, where students live and study in the Duke of Northumberland's castle. Other campuses include China, Costa Rica, France, Germany, Denmark, and the new campus in the Czech Republic. Honors students have the special opportunity of studying abroad at Oxford University in England.

Support Services The Office of Student Disability Services offers a wide range of assistance, including priority registration, sign language and oral interpretation, note taking, alternative testing, referrals to support services, etc.

Job Opportunities Work-study is available in most of the offices and departments on campus for the many students who qualify for financial aid. In addition, non-work-study positions on campus can be acquired by many students who do not qualify for financial aid.

Tuition: $2526 for state residents, $5470 for nonresidents, per year (1996-97)

Room and Board: $3027

Mandatory Fees: $378

Contact: Director: Dr. David Boyer, 420 7th Avenue S, Administrative Services 210, St. Cloud, Minnesota 56301; Telephone: 320-255-4945; E-mail: honorprg@tigger.stcloud. msus.edu; Web site: http://condor.stcloud.msus.edu/~honors

SAINT FRANCIS COLLEGE (PENNSYLVANIA)

4 Pr G S Tr

▼ **Honors Program**

The Saint Francis College (SFC) Honors Program is designed to challenge highly motivated students. It offers innovative course work, extensive faculty-student interaction, individualized honors advising, and additional opportunities for tutorial and independent study. The Honors Program curriculum affords many choices so that honors students may design a personal program of study.

One clear differentiation between this program and virtually all others is the Semester of Service. All SFC Honors Program students are required to undertake a service project to benefit specifically the College or the local community. The reason for requiring the service semester is simple: the truly well educated student shares his or her talents. The Semester of Service project reflects the Franciscan ideal of concern for others above self and the Honors Program's commitment to that ideal. Founded in 1984, the program currently enrolls 100 students.

Participation Requirements: All courses completed for honors credit are duly designated on the student's transcript. Those who complete all honors curricular requirements and who have achieved at least a 3.25 cumulative GPA receive the Honors Program diploma—a large, hand-lettered parchment diploma presented in traditional rolled fashion at Commencement. Honors Program graduates receive special velvet diploma bags during the annual awards convocation hosted by the President. The notation "Honors Program Graduate" appears on the transcript and in the Commencement program.

Admission Process: Enrollment is by invitation only. First quintile, 3.25 GPA (or 90 percent), recommendations, extracurricular activities, and SAT I average are commensurate with scholarship requirements.

Scholarship Availability: Although there are no scholarships tied directly to the Honors Program, because eligibility guidelines are similar, all Honors Program members are scholarship recipients. Most scholarships awarded by the College are based on academic accomplishment, not on financial need. Some are based on service to the College or on other criteria determined by the donors.

The Campus Context: Saint Francis College is the oldest Franciscan college in the country. Located on 600 wooded acres, the mountain-top campus is 1/2-hour from the cities of Altoona and Johnstown and less than a 2-hour drive from Pittsburgh.

In addition to twenty-six majors—seven in the health sciences—the College also offers an innovative general education program designed to cultivate the knowledge, skills, and values that students will use and live by the rest of their lives. It includes interdisciplinary freshman seminars, linked courses, thematic minors and clusters, a convocation program, a special freshman advising program, senior capstones, service learning, a summer reading program for freshmen, and emphasis courses in values and ethics, multiculturalism and global awareness, communications, creative and critical thinking, and primary source materials.

The College is justly proud of its academic reputation. Students have won prestigious academic All-American honors,

graduate fellowships, and numerous other national awards. The campus is also distinguished by the Southern Alleghenies Museum of Art, Dorothy Day Center for Social Justice, Center for Global Competitiveness, Center of Excellence for Remote and Medically Underserved Areas (CERMUSA), and Mount Assisi Monastery and Gardens.

Student Body Equally divided among men and women, the 1,200 undergraduates enrolled at Saint Francis come primarily from the Northeast. There are two national sororities, one local sorority, and two national fraternities.

Faculty A 15:1 student-faculty ratio ensures personal attention from 78 full-time professors, nearly 75 percent of whom hold doctoral or terminal degrees.

Key Facilities Three fully equipped computer labs provide Internet and e-mail access for all students. A state-of-the-art electronic/multimedia classroom and a distance learning/teleconferencing studio provide interactive learning opportunities.

Athletics The College sponsors a nineteen-sport NCAA Division I program for both men and women and a full student-directed intramural program for all students. The Maurice Stokes Athletics Center features an indoor swimming pool, racquetball courts, indoor tennis and volleyball courts, a suspended running track, a weight room, and a 3,500-seat basketball arena. Other facilities include a nine-hole golf course, outdoor tennis courts, and soccer and softball fields.

Study Abroad Study abroad is encouraged for all honors students. A semester (or more) of study abroad may substitute for a required upper-level honors colloquium. In recent years, Honors Program students have studied at Oxford University, the University of Heidelberg, the University of Cork, and Richmond College in London.

Job Opportunities Both internships and work-study are available for qualified students.

Tuition: $12,288 per year (1996-97)

Room and Board: $5650

Mandatory Fees: $950

Contact: Director: Donna M. Menis, 305 Scotus Hall, Loretto, Pennsylvania 15940; Telephone: 814-472-3065; Fax: 814-472-3044; E-mail: dmmfa2@scotus.sfcpa.edu; Web site: http://www.sfcpa.edu

SAINT JOSEPH'S UNIVERSITY

4 Pr G M Sc Tr

▼ Honors Program

The Saint Joseph's University (SJU) Honors Program seeks to produce well-educated, articulate citizens who exemplify the highest standards of academic, professional, and personal achievement. It offers an enriched general education curriculum that broadens cultural interests, integrates knowledge, sharpens writing skills, and encourages student involvement in the learning process.

The curriculum is composed of intellectually rigorous courses that satisfy both general education and major requirements. The honors core consists of a group of yearlong, interdisciplinary, team-taught courses in arts, sciences, and business that appear in a regular cycle. These sequence courses are complemented by freshman seminars in English, philosophy, and theology and one-semester courses in a wide range of disciplines at various levels of entry.

There are distinctive benefits attached to belonging to the Saint Joseph's Honors Program. Team-taught courses allow distinguished faculty members to share their knowledge and expertise with students in a challenging academic environment. Individual honors courses stress a detailed and thoroughly scholarly exploration of different fields of knowledge. The student-faculty ratio in the Honors Program is 10:1. Honors students are assigned an individual adviser who guides them through the registration process and assists them in shaping their future career plans. Honors students register ahead of other students.

Honors suites in the residence halls allow like-minded students to live together, even as freshmen. Honors students are provided with free tickets and transportation to concerts and performances by world-renowned institutions such as the Arden Theater Company, the Curtis Institute of Music, the Philadelphia Orchestra, the Pennsylvania Ballet, the Academy of Vocal Arts, the Philadelphia Museum of Art, and the Franklin Science Institute. Receptions, concerts, and lectures are regularly sponsored by the Honors Program for honors students.

A student advisory committee reports to the program directors about social activities, class work, registration, and other student concerns. Students have access to Claver House, a quiet retreat where honors students can study, work with personal computers, and attend receptions. Students have opportunities to present research and creative work at national conferences and seminars; they are also kept informed about scholarship and funding opportunities for graduate and professional work.

Participation Requirements: Students may enroll in General Honors, which is awarded upon successful completion of eight courses in the honors core. Because all honors courses fulfill other curricular requirements of the University, the Honors Program imposes no courses over and above those required of non-honors students. Students are required to maintain a cumulative average of 3.5 or better in order to graduate with the General Honors Certificate.

Students may also participate in Departmental Honors, which is awarded upon successful completion of the general curriculum and a two-semester research project in their senior year. Students of exceptional caliber may apply for the University Scholar designation. Those who qualify are freed

from four to ten of their senior-year course requirements in order to complete an independent project of unusual breadth, depth, and originality.

General Honors Certificate is noted on the student's permanent record and is awarded upon successful completion of General Honors. An Honors Degree, noted on the permanent record and acknowledged on a distinctive diploma, is awarded to students who have completed General Honors and the Departmental Honors project. University Honors, noted on the permanent record and acknowledged on a distinctive diploma, is awarded to students who have completed General Honors and the University Scholar research project.

Admission Process: Incoming students are invited into the Honors Program if their SAT I combined score is above 1350 and they rank in the top 3 percent of their graduating high school class. Freshmen who achieve a GPA of 3.5 or better in their first semester at SJU are also invited to join the Honors Program.

Scholarship Availability: Each year, Saint Joseph's University awards merit-based scholarships to freshman candidates who have outstanding academic and achievement records. Students are selected by a scholarship committee. A formal application is not required for merit-based scholarships; however, for any additional assistance, candidates must apply. Instructions are given in detail at the time of the candidate's application. Students who are awarded these scholarships are automatically invited to join the Honors Program. Board of Trustees' Scholarships are awarded to freshman recipients who have superior academic records. Candidates typically rank at or near the top of their high school class, have an "A" GPA, and SAT I scores in the 1400 and above range. These scholars must maintain a 3.2 GPA in order to retain their scholarship each year.

Presidential Scholarships are awarded to candidates who achieve significant results in their high school class and have SAT I scores of 1300 and above. The value of this scholarship ranges from one-half to three-quarter tuition. These scholars must maintain a 3.2 GPA in order to retain their scholarship each year.

University Scholarships are awarded to incoming freshmen who rank in the top 10 percent of their high school graduating class and have SAT I scores in the 1200 and above range. The value of this scholarship ranges from one-fourth to one-half tuition. The Anthony and Blanche Calabro Scholarship Fund, founded by Anthony D. Calabro, assists students in the Honors Program.

The Campus Context: The University offers forty degree programs.

Student Body Saint Joseph's University has a full-time undergraduate enrollment of 2,867: 45 percent men and 55 percent women. The ethnic distribution of students is 83 percent white, 9 percent black, 3 percent Hispanic, and 2 percent Asian/Pacific Islander. There are 83 international students. Fifty-four percent of the students are residents; the remaining 46 percent commute. Eighty-five percent of the students receive financial aid.

Faculty Of the 405 faculty members, 179 are full-time; 95 percent hold terminal degrees. The student-faculty ratio is 17:1.

Athletics Saint Joseph's University is a member of NCAA Division I in the following sports: men's baseball, basketball, cross-country, golf, lacrosse, soccer, tennis, and track and field (indoor and outdoor) and women's basketball, cross-country, lacrosse, soccer, tennis, track and field, field hockey, and softball.

Support Services In accordance with the Americans with Disabilities Act (ADA) guidelines, students with disabilities are ensured equal educational opportunities, counseling services, and access to facilities and programs.

Job Opportunities Saint Joseph's University participates in the Federal Work-Study program. Students may work up to 8 hours per week. The number of jobs is contingent upon government allocations.

Tuition: $14,400 minimum per year (1996-97)

Room and Board: $6450

Mandatory Fees: $300

Contact: Director: Dr. Agnes Rash, 5600 City Avenue, Philadelphia, Pennsylvania 19103; Associate Director: Dr. David R. Sorensen, Telephone: 610-660-1795; Fax: 610-660-2160 (Dr. Sorensen); E-mail: arash@sju.edu or dsorense@sju.edu; Web site: http://www.sju.edu

ST. LOUIS COMMUNITY COLLEGE AT FLORISSANT VALLEY

2 Pu M Sc

▼ Honors Program

The Honors Program at St. Louis Community College at Florissant Valley encourages students to work up to their capacity. This allows them to be recognized as achievers by both employers and educational institutions. This program has been serving honors students for more than eleven years. Honors credit gives students an edge in the job market and in scholarship awards. Honors students are often eligible to receive full and partial scholarships both at this college and transfer institutions. Florissant Valley is fully accredited by the North Central Association of Colleges and Universities. With few exceptions, honors courses are transferable to other colleges and universities.

The program emphasizes small classes and lively discussion in the classroom. Students are expected to complete honors-quality work and are given one-on-one attention from their honors instructors and the honors office staff. Upon successful completion of honors classes, students are given certificates of recognition. In addition to regular honors courses, selected seminars are also offered for honors credit. A seminar is a course focused on a particular theme or topic. It has a limited enrollment and usually two faculty members or several guest speakers. It requires participation, close attention to detail, solid research, and a love of discussion. The atmosphere is exciting as students and faculty members learn from each other. The fall 1996 seminar was entitled "The Arts: Landscape of Our Times." This seminar was produced on this campus in cooperation with the National Collegiate Honors Council and broadcast via satellite to more than sixty colleges nationally.

The Honors Program currently enrolls 200 students per semester.

Admission Process: In order to qualify, students must have a score of 1100 or above on the SAT I, a composite score of 25 on the ACT, scores on the Florissant Valley Assessment Tests that correlate with the above, graduate with a cumulative high school GPA of 3.5 or above on a 4.0 scale, or have completed at least 12 college credits in courses numbered 100 and above with a cumulative GPA of 3.5 on a 4.0 scale.

The Campus Context: St. Louis Community College at Florissant Valley awards the Associate in Arts, Associate in Applied Science, and General Transfer Study degrees as well as Certificates of Specialization and Certificates of Proficiency. One of the distinguished facilities on campus is the Child Development Center, a lab school for the child development program that serves students and other people in the community. This program also serves four-year colleges. State and national accreditation are expected within the year.

Student Body The College has an undergraduate enrollment of more than 7,000 students. The student body is diversified, consisting of 37 percent men and 63 percent women. Sixty percent are white, 31 percent are African American, and 9 percent are other nationalities, including American Indian, Asian, and Hispanic, among others. Eighty-nine percent of the students are local residents, and the remaining 11 percent are commuters. Twenty-eight percent of students receive financial aid. There is an active chapter of the Phi Theta Kappa honor society on campus that serves students, the campus, and the community in a variety of ways. Currently, there are 373 members.

Faculty With more than 385 part-time and 142 full-time faculty members, students benefit from a student-faculty ratio of 13:1. Terminal degrees for faculty members include twenty-three Ph.D.s, three Ed.D.s, and five M.F.A.s.

Key Facilities There are more than 87,000 volumes in the campus library. There are computer labs at five different locations on this campus.

Athletics Florissant Valley offers more than forty-five activities through its physical education department. Professional (pre-teaching) courses and continuing education courses are also offered. The nine fitness/wellness-related courses, centering in the Fitness Center, are the most popular. An athletic scholarship fund benefits approximately 100 team members each year.

Study Abroad Throughout the year, various study-abroad opportunities are offered in several locations around the world, including Canterbury, England.

Support Services The College recognizes that some students have special needs and has an office that provides services for students with documented disabilities.

Job Opportunities Students often have the opportunity to work on this campus through the work-study program and other occasional jobs.

Tuition: $1344 for area residents, $1696 for state residents, $2144 for nonresidents, per year (1996-97)

Contact: Director: Dr. K. Ann Dempsey, 3400 Pershall Road, St. Louis, Missouri 63135; Telephone: 314-595-4461; Fax: 314-595-4544; Web site: http://www.stlcc.cc.mo.us/fv/honors

SAINT LOUIS UNIVERSITY

4 Pr G M Sc Tr

▼ University Honors Program

The Saint Louis University Honors Program was founded in 1938, making it one of the oldest honors programs in the nation. The Honors Program is open to undergraduates from all schools within the University. Honors students range from those students contemplating entering medical or law school who desire a humanities emphasis to business and computer science majors. Others include nursing, physical therapy, biology, and humanities majors, such as English and philosophy. Many students participating in the Medical Scholars and the Pre-Law Scholars Programs also belong to the Honors Program.

Honors students enroll in discussion-oriented classes with limited enrollments. Much of the University's core requirement can be fulfilled through special honors sections. The Honors Program is in the process of revising its curriculum to emphasize interdisciplinary courses that integrate the humanities and social science disciplines represented in the core curriculum. The goal is to make students aware of the connectedness of the different areas in the core, while allowing them to complete the requirements of their majors and preprofessional programs. Students are encouraged to engage in independent projects that enable them to pursue a particular subject in greater depth.

The Honors Program Office advises and registers honors students, offering individual curriculum advice to students each semester. It also sponsors a number of academic and social extracurricular activities each year, including an evening at the internationally renowned Saint Louis Symphony Orchestra in the spring. Students are invited to participate in book discussion groups or attend the theater. They may also take part in other activities sponsored by the Honors Student Association, an organization made up of students in the Honors Program. There are currently 280 students in the program.

Participation Requirements: To graduate with an honors bachelor's degree, a student must complete at least 24 credit hours of honors work and maintain at least a 3.3 cumulative GPA.

Admission Process: Beginning honors students are chosen on the basis of their interest in the program and on the basis of their previous academic achievement as revealed by ACT or SAT I scores, rank in their high school class, and other evidence of intellectual curiosity.

Scholarship Availability: Saint Louis University offers a number of scholarships to first-time freshmen based on academic achievement in high school or special categories such as specific majors, minority status, or leadership abilities.

The Campus Context: Saint Louis University is a Jesuit institution founded in 1818. It has two campuses located in midtown St. Louis, Missouri, and one in Madrid, Spain. The St. Louis campuses are Frost and Health Sciences, which are located in an area containing prominent theaters and Powell Symphony Hall. The Frost Campus is a mix of Gothic and modern architecture, tree-lined walkways, and colorful gardens. It is home to the College of Arts and Sciences, the School of Business and Administration, the College of Philosophy and Letters, Parks College of Engineering and Aviation, the School of Social Service, the Graduate School, and the School of Law. The Health Sciences Campus encompasses one of the world's largest Catholic medical centers, with the Schools of Allied Health Professions, Nursing, Medicine, and Public Health.

Among distinguished facilities is the historic Cupples House, containing the McNamee Art Gallery, the Museum of Contemporary Religious Art, the Center for Medieval and Renaissance Studies, the Centre for the Study of Communication and Culture, and the Simon Recreation Center. Also on this campus is the Saint Louis University Hospital complex and research center.

The University offers seventy-three programs in the College of Arts and Sciences, eleven programs in the School of Business and Administration, sixteen programs in the School of Allied Health Professions, eighteen programs in Parks College of Engineering and Aviation, and programs in the School of Medicine, the School of Nursing, the School of Social Service, the School of Law, the College of Philosophy and Letters, the School of Public Health, and the Graduate School.

Student Body Total enrollment is 11,300: 48 percent men and 52 percent women. The ethnic distribution is 69.3 percent white, 10 percent international, 8 percent African American, 7.2 percent nonspecified. 4.1 percent Asian, 1.9 percent nonresident/alien, and 0.2 percent American/Alaskan native. Seventy-eight percent of the students receive financial aid. There are five sororities and ten fraternities.

Faculty Of the 1,100 full-time faculty members, 98 percent hold the highest degrees in their field. The student-faculty ratio in undergraduate programs is 15:1.

Key Facilities Library holdings include 1.4 million volumes, 12,800 serial subscriptions, 1.1 million microforms, and 200,000 government documents combined in the Pius XII Memorial Library, Omer Poos Law Library, Health Science Center Library, and Parks College Library. Computing facilities are available on each campus to support instructional, research, and administrative activities. Services include microcomputing labs, large-scale computing, software, international e-mail networks, and consulting assistance. Microcomputing facilities are also located in individual departments.

Athletics As a member of Conference USA, the Saint Louis University Billikens compete in NCAA Division I against such schools as the University of Cincinnati, DePaul University, the University of Louisville, Marquette University, Memphis State University, and Tulane University in basketball, baseball, cross-country, field hockey, golf, soccer, softball, swimming, rifle, tennis, and volleyball. More than twenty intramural sports run the gamut from flag football to water polo.

Study Abroad Programs are offered in France at Lyon or in Germany at Baden–Wurttenberg for one year of work in language and cultural study and/or regular university courses. Students also have the opportunity to study at the Madrid campus in Spain.

Support Services Most facilities on campus are handicapped-accessible. A disabilities coordinator is available to help students with learning and/or physical disabilities obtain accommodations or services needed for academic classes.

Tuition: $13,900 per year (1996-97)

Room and Board: $5150

Mandatory Fees: $110

Contact: Director: Dr. Sylvia Neely, Xavier Hall 328, St. Louis, Missouri 63103; Telephone: 314-977-3951; Fax: 314-977-7296; E-mail: neelys@sluvca.slu.edu; Web site: http://www.slu.edu/organizations/honors

ST. MARY'S COLLEGE OF MARYLAND

4 Pu G S Sc Tr

▼ Honors Program

The St. Mary's College of Maryland Honors Program was created in 1979 as part of a legislative initiative to retain Maryland's most talented students in-state for their undergraduate education. The General Assembly granted St. Mary's special merit funds in the form of Margaret Brent–Leonard Calvert Fellowships and encouraged the College to offer curricular and extracurricular enrichment opportunities for high-ability students with the maturity, motivation, and intellectual capacity to benefit the most from them.

The current form of the Honors Program has remained true to this tradition but has evolved with the changing needs and context of the College environment. Fellowships are now available for non-Maryland residents, and the program is attracting an increasingly diverse pool of students. All honors students are exempt from the General Education curriculum and instead complete an alternative curriculum that focuses on multidisciplinary, frequently team-taught seminars, intensive in their requirements for reading, writing, and discussion.

Seminars vary from semester to semester and represent different specialty fields. Recent offerings have included "Global Change," "Freud and His Legacy," "Cognition and Communication," and "Social Problems and Economic Realities." In addition to the seminars, the Honors Program has requirements in composition, mathematics, and foreign language. Moreover, in the senior year, each honors student completes an 8-credit original project, guided by a committee of 3 faculty members expert in the subject matter of the project.

In addition to the special curriculum, merit scholarship support, and individualized attention from honors administrators and faculty members, the Honors Program also sponsors extracurricular events, both on and off campus, for honors students. These events frequently take advantage of the College's proximity to Washington, D.C., and Baltimore and the extraordinary cultural events that these cities offer.

Participation Requirements: Once a student joins the Honors Program, maintenance of a target GPA on a specified number of credits is required to stay in good standing and to maintain the Brent–Calvert or France–Russell Fellowships. This target begins at 3.0 in the first year and rises to a 3.5 by junior year. Successful completion of the Honors Program is noted at graduation, as is one of four categories of Honors Program success. Special certificates are awarded at an Honors Forum and Banquet at the end of the senior year.

Admission Process: Most students in the Honors Program are selected directly from high school, based on their cumulative GPA, the rigor of their course work, their combined SAT scores, letters of recommendation, an application essay, and special talents and activities. However, approximately 25 percent of the students who graduate from the program enter it after they have completed at least a semester of college work, either at St. Mary's or elsewhere. Most of these students join the program during their freshman year or at the beginning of their sophomore year. The size of the program ranges from 60–80 students, with between 15 and 20 entering and graduating each year.

Applications must be submitted by January 15.

The Campus Context: St. Mary's College of Maryland is a state-supported, undergraduate, coeducational, residential college located in southern Maryland, 68 miles southeast of Washington, D.C., on beautiful Chesapeake Bay waters. The campus of 275 acres consists of rolling meadow, lawn, and woodland along the shores of the St. Mary's River. Founded in 1840 as a women's seminary, St. Mary's has evolved into a four-year institution that in 1991 was designated by the state of Maryland as its public honors college. It is described by many of the college guides as a public Ivy and a best buy. It offers nineteen majors, including an independent, student-designed major.

Student Body There are approximately 1,600 students enrolled.

Faculty There are 111 full-time faculty members, 87 percent with doctorates or other terminal degrees, supplemented by more than 50 part-time faculty members. The student-faculty ratio is 13:1.

Key Facilities There are 146,126 bound-volume equivalents in the library with extensive interlibrary loan and on-line services available. The College has two mainframes and 486 microcomputers.

Athletics Athletics include fifteen intercollegiate sports, six club sports, and a diverse intramural athletic program; sailing teams receive national rankings.

Study Abroad Many study-abroad options exist; in recent years, honors students have studied in Chile, China, Costa Rica, Czechoslovakia, Ecuador, England, France, Germany, Russia, and Spain.

Tuition: $5500 for state residents, $9300 for nonresidents, per year (1997-98)

Room and Board: $5480

Mandatory Fees: $1075

Contact: Director: Dr. Laraine M. Glidden, P.O. Box 236, St. Mary's City, Maryland 20686; Telephone: 301-862-0348; Fax: 301-862-0436; E-mail: lmglidden@osprey.smcm.edu

ST. MARY'S UNIVERSITY OF SAN ANTONIO

4 Pr G S Sc

▼ Honors Program

The St. Mary's University Honors Program is a special course of study designed to challenge some of the most academically gifted undergraduates. The program's curriculum ("the academic marathon") is a sequence of eight enriched courses, commencing with philosophy and culminating in a senior thesis in the student's major field. Honors courses normally meet general core curriculum requirements, and participation in the program is compatible with all majors.

In addition to the academic curriculum, the program offers a rich variety of social and cultural opportunities ranging from concerts and theater performances to campouts and community service projects. Through the curricular and cocurricular offerings, the program seeks to nurture the intellectual, moral, and cultural talents of the students as they prepare for lives of leadership and service to their communities. Successful completion of Honors Program requirements is announced at graduation and is indicated on the student's transcript. Graduates typically go on to pursue graduate and professional studies in medicine, law, and a host of other disciplines. An estimated half of the graduates eventually go on to earn doctoral degrees. Founded in 1985, the program currently serves 90 students.

Participation Requirements: Students must maintain a 3.25 (B+) to remain in the program.

Admission Process: Although admission is selective, the program actively seeks a community of students who are diverse in their backgrounds and interests. From among more than 100 students invited to apply each year, the program enrolls approximately 25. Students are normally recruited directly from high school and usually rank in the top 5 percent of their classes, with commensurate scores on their college admission exams (currently an average SAT I score of 1280 and an average ACT score of 28). Students may join the program in their sophomore year if they have earned a 3.8 or above GPA in their first year at St. Mary's.

Applications must be submitted by March 15.

Scholarship Availability: While there are no honors scholarships per se, students admitted to the program who remain in good standing are guaranteed not less than $5000 per year in scholarship or grant support administered through the University. Students who would otherwise have received less than $5000 are automatically raised to this level. Members are also guaranteed the option of a campus work-study position, either federal or institutional, if they desire it. Engineering majors may qualify for a fifth year of guaranteed support.

The Campus Context: St. Mary's University, founded in 1852 by Marianist brothers and priests, is the oldest university in San Antonio and the oldest and largest Catholic university in Texas and the Southwest. A historic and culturally diverse city of more than 1 million residents, San Antonio is an important gateway to Latin America and a major center of international trade and commerce. St. Mary's University encompasses three undergraduate schools offering more than forty degree programs, a graduate school, and a school of law.

Student Body The total enrollment exceeds 4,200 students, including 2,600 undergraduates. Undergraduate enrollment is 57 percent women. With respect to ethnic distribution, 63 percent of undergraduates identify themselves as Hispanic, 26 percent as Anglo, 3 percent as African American, 2 percent as Asian or Pacific Islander, and fewer than 1 percent as Native American. International students number 115. About 87 percent of undergraduates receive financial aid. More than 40 percent live on campus. More than seventy student organizations offer opportunities for campus involvement, including twenty-nine academic and professional organizations, five honors societies, four service organizations, nine social fraternities and sororities, and a variety of religious, political, cultural, and special interest organizations.

Faculty A faculty of more than 300 includes 176 full-time members. Nearly 90 percent of full-time faculty members hold the doctoral degree or its equivalent in their fields. The student-faculty ratio is 14:1.

Key Facilities Library resources include more than 200,000 books, more than 1,000 periodical titles, a media center, and a government documents depository containing more than 185,000 items. Computer facilities include four computer labs (academic library, biology, mathematics, and engineering) as well as tutoring computers in the Learning Assistance Center. Selected classrooms are enhanced with computer and multimedia facilities.

Athletics In athletics, St. Mary's now competes in the NCAA Division II, having previously captured national championships in NAIA women's softball and men's basketball. Men's and women's teams compete in ten varsity sports. In addition to its intramural programs, the University sponsors an active intramural program.

Study Abroad The University actively encourages study abroad, operating its own programs in London, Puebla (Mexico), and Innsbruck (Austria).

Support Services Virtually all facilities on campus are accessible to disabled students.

Job Opportunities Work opportunities on campus include not only Federal Work-Study but also a special Honors Work-Study option for those who qualify.

Tuition: $10,380 per year (1997-98)

Room and Board: $4308

Mandatory Fees: $228

Contact: Director: Dr. Daniel Rigney, Reinbolt 302/Box 47, One Camino Santa Maria, San Antonio, Texas 78228; Telephone: 210-436-3201; Fax: 210-436-3500; E-mail: drigney@stmarytx.edu

---

ST. PHILIP'S COLLEGE

2 Pu G S Sc

▼ GIVE Honors Program

The St. Philip's College GIVE (Great Ideas, Visions and Experiences) Honors Program, open to students of all majors, offers challenging and rewarding opportunities for academically exceptional students. The program provides an exciting learning experience for students who like the challenge of small, discussion-based classes and who look forward to the stimulation of teacher-student interaction. Unlike traditional courses, which present material from a single field of study, Honors Program courses draw ideas and information from many fields, addressing concerns common to all disciplines and recognizing that there are no boundaries to thought and inquiry. Honors Program courses examine the historical and intellectual origins, the growth, and the development of today's issues, the connections among them, and their consequences for tomorrow. Throughout the courses, the Honors Colloquia are designed to refine skills in critical thinking, writing, and public speaking. Honors Program students are advised by the Honors Director and by faculty members in the student's major field of study. Students enjoy a close relationship with honors faculty members and with each other in a network of academic and personal support.

Honors Program students have access to all of the resources at St. Philip's College, San Antonio College, Palo Alto College, and the University of Texas at San Antonio. While students enjoy the advantage of a small, challenging program, they have access to all the resources of four community colleges and a major university, including an internationally respected faculty, fully equipped computer labs, access to four libraries with well over a million holdings, and a wide range of student services.

Participation Requirements: Students in the GIVE Honors Program are required to take the same number of credits for graduation as every other St. Philip's College student. Honors Program students take the Interdisciplinary Honors Seminar [Humanities I & II (HUMA 1301 & HUMA 1302), Western Civilization I & II (HIST 2311 & HIST 2312), World Civilization I & II (HIST 2321 & HIST 2322), and Interdisciplinary Studies I & II (IDST 2372 & IDST 2373)] and courses in foreign language, lab science, English, and mathematics.

Admission Process: To apply for the Honors Program, students must first be enrolled at St. Philip's College and then apply to the GIVE Honors Program. The application process includes a formal application, two letters of reference from instructors, and a statement written by the student describing his or her interests, academic goals, and future plans. In addition, students must supply a certified copy of their college transcripts, showing a cumulative GPA of at least 3.25 (on a 4.0 scale) and proof that they passed (or are exempt from) the TASP (Texas Academic Skills Program) exam.

Scholarship Availability: Accepted students are awarded a full scholarship that pays all fees and tuition to St. Philip's College. They also receive a voucher for books and supplies for each semester that they are in the Honors Program.

The Campus Context: St. Philip's College is located on the east side of San Antonio, 2 miles from the center of town and easily accessible from all parts of San Antonio and its surrounding areas. St. Philip's College, founded in 1898, is a comprehensive, public community college whose mission is to provide a high-quality educational environment that stimulates leadership, personal growth, and a lifelong appreciation for learning. As a historically black college, St. Philip's College strives to be an important force in the community, responsive to the needs of a population rich in its ethnic, cultural, and socioeconomic diversity.

St. Philip's College seeks to create an environment fostering excellence in academic and technical achievement while expanding its commitment to opportunity and access. The College takes pride in its individual attention to students in a flexible and sensitive environment. As a dynamic and innovative institution, St. Philip's College values the role of creative and critical thought in preparing its students, campus, and community to meet the challenges of a rapidly changing world.

The College offers seventy-two associate majors, including liberal arts and sciences, business, and education.

Student Body Undergraduate enrollment is 8,000.

Faculty There are 179 full-time faculty members (supplemented by 343 adjunct faculty members), 30 percent with doctorates or other terminal degrees. The student-faculty ratio is 15:1.

Key Facilities The library houses 104,349 volumes. There are four computer labs located in the library and academic buildings.

Job Opportunities Students are offered a wide range of work opportunities on campus, including assistantships and work-study.

Tuition: $734 for area residents, $1262 for state residents, $2366 for nonresidents, per year (1996-97)

Contact: Director: Dr. J. Paul De Vierville, 1801 Martin Luther King Drive, San Antonio, Texas 78235; Telephone: 210-531-3491; Fax: 210-531-4760; E-mail: jdevierv@accd.edu

SALISBURY STATE UNIVERSITY

4 Pu G M Sc Tr

▼ Thomas E. Bellavance Honors Program

The Thomas E. Bellavance Honors Program at Salisbury State University (SSU) is designed to bring together superior students and dedicated faculty members in a small University environment within the diversity of opportunity of the larger University community. It offers motivated students who are serious about their intellectual growth a variety of special classes enhanced by many cultural events and activities. The program fosters close individual contact between students and faculty members and brings together talented students with many interests.

Honors courses and extracurricular activities are intended to enrich and complement other educational opportunities and programs available to Salisbury State students. The overarching goal of the Honors Program is to give high-achieving students intense and exciting educational experiences to enhance their development as independent thinkers and learners who are able and eager to take an active role in their own intellectual development. Real learning involves exploration and discovery, and the Honors Program gives students the opportunity and encouragement to be Columbuses of the intellectual life.

There are currently 175 students enrolled in the program.

Participation Requirements: To begin their intellectual journey, Honors Program students are required to take a sequence of four honors core courses: "Critical Thinking and Writing," "Western Intellectual Tradition I," "Western Intellectual Tradition II," and "Scientific Knowledge." These are designed to give students in the Honors Program a shared intellectual experience in the arts and sciences in order to develop a community of learners and to encourage a spirit of collegiality in pursuit of knowledge, a spirit that is essential for intellectual growth and personal fulfillment.

Students who complete the core are awarded a Certificate of Completion, which goes into their academic record. Core courses and honors electives also satisfy both general education and honors requirements so that students need not take these courses in addition to those required for graduation in their majors.

Those students who finish the four-course sequence with a 3.0 GPA in the core and in their courses overall are also invited to graduate with honors by taking two additional honors courses and writing an honors thesis in their major. The additional honors courses are in a variety of disciplines that are designed to augment the core experience, covering topics such as non-Western cultures, mathematical reasoning, art and music histories, and many more.

The honors thesis is the capstone intellectual experience for students in the Honors Program and is a valuable opportunity to do independent research with a faculty mentor on a topic of personal interest in one's major field. Clearly, the thesis experience is excellent preparation for graduate or professional school. Students who fulfill these requirements and receive an overall GPA of 3.35 are recognized on their transcript and diploma as having graduated with University Honors.

Tangible benefits of the Honors Program include small, stimulating classes taught by creative, supportive faculty members; recognition on transcripts and diplomas of participation in the Honors Program; use of the Honors Center, a lovely nine-room house adjacent to campus with lounges, a computer room, study areas, a kitchen, and a recreation room; participation in a variety of cultural, social, and public-service activities; and scholarships and small monetary awards to recognize outstanding scholars in the program. But even more important are the intangible benefits the students have received. As one honors graduate stated, "The Honors Program provided me with a nurturing environment in which to develop a higher level of thinking skills which I will use throughout college and throughout my life."

Admission Process: Incoming freshmen with superior academic records (minimum 3.25 GPA/combined SAT I scores of 1250) are invited to join the program prior to arriving at Salisbury. Current undergraduates with University GPAs of 3.25 or better are also invited to apply for admission.

The Campus Context: Founded in 1925, Salisbury State University is a nationally accredited, four-year comprehensive university offering thirty-five distinct undergraduate and graduate degree programs in a friendly atmosphere that encourages close relationships between faculty members and students. Salisbury State is also a member of the University of Maryland

System, which is comprised of eleven campuses, about seventy centers and institutes, and three other research and public service institutes.

The University is located on U.S. Route 13 at the southern edge of Salisbury, Maryland, which has a metropolitan population of 70,000 and lies 30 miles west of Ocean City, Maryland; 115 miles southeast of Washington, D.C.; and 125 miles south of Philadelphia, Pennsylvania. SSU is cited in the *1996 Guide to 101 of the Best Values in America's Colleges and Universities,* receiving an "A+" rating. Salisbury State has been described by the *Baltimore Sun* as "one of the most attractive campuses in Maryland," with its designation as a national arboretum and a $47-million investment in buildings and grounds. It is one of the state's highest-endowed public universities, providing more than $750,000 in scholarships each fall.

Student Body There are 4,400 full-time undergraduates enrolled from twenty-nine states and twenty countries. There are four national sororities and six national fraternities.

Faculty Of the 200 full-time tenure-track faculty members, 84.5 percent have terminal degrees. Distinguished faculty members include National Endowment for the Humanities scholars and Fulbright professors. The student-faculty ratio is 17:1.

Key Facilities The campus has a 430,000-volume library with intracampus borrowing privileges from the University of Maryland System. Computer facilities include 185 Macintosh and DOS computers, eighteen VAX terminals, and two UNIX workstations located in student computer labs.

Athletics Salisbury State is in NCAA Division III, with nine men's and ten women's intercollegiate teams. Intercollegiate athletics for men include cross-country, football, soccer, basketball, swimming, baseball, lacrosse, tennis, and track and field. Women's intercollegiate sports are include cross-country, field hockey, soccer, volleyball, basketball, swimming, lacrosse, softball, tennis, and track and field. There are also twenty-two intramural sports teams and eighteen sports clubs.

Study Abroad Salisbury State University encourages students' participation in study-abroad programs in a country of their choice. Faculty advisers provide information about programs, courses, and requirements. Students electing to study abroad in a University-approved program during their senior year may also apply up to 30 semester hours of approved transfer credits toward the final 30-hour residency requirement for graduation.

Job Opportunities Salisbury State University students are offered a range of work opportunities on campus, including hourly and work-study employment. The Center for Career Services and Professional Development also coordinates internships in a variety of government, service, and business organizations.

Tuition: $2746 for state residents, $6498 for nonresidents, per year (1997-98)

Room and Board: $5060

Mandatory Fees: $1096

Contact: Director: Dr. Raymond A. Whall, University Honors Center, Salisbury, Maryland 21802; Telephone: 410-546-6902; Fax: 410-543-6068; E-mail: rawhall@ssu.edu; Assistant Director: Anna Marie Roos; Telephone: 410-546-6943; E-mail: amroos@ssu.edu; Web site: http://www.ssu.edu/schools/honors.html

SAN DIEGO STATE UNIVERSITY

4 Pu G M

▼ University Honors Program

The University Honors Program at San Diego State University (SDSU) has been established to serve the needs of students whose academic potential has already been demonstrated and who wish to challenge that potential in special classes and through other opportunities designed for very capable students.

Students are encouraged to contribute and develop in an active way and to get to know the instructors personally. To ensure this, honors classes are smaller than the average, and the course work is developed to appeal to the superior student. Classes emphasize uniqueness in organization, method, and approach; they do not simply demand greater quantity of work. Lower-division classes provide 4, rather than the usual 3, units to acknowledge special readings and projects to permit individual response to the subject matter of the course.

Because of the general nature of the program, students in all majors are encouraged to apply. One of the strengths of the program is the opportunity to be in an intellectual peer group involving students from a wide variety of backgrounds who express a diversity of points of view and perspectives shaped by their different fields of study. Students apply to the Honors Program because they value intellectual growth. They enjoy learning and like to grapple with ideas, understanding that definitive answers or resolutions to problems are often elusive.

In addition to the opportunities in conjunction with the classes, honors students are encouraged to develop original projects and research inspired by their personal interests. The work may culminate in a senior thesis during the final year, and it provides valuable preparation for careers in many fields, both academic and nonacademic. Projects may involve students in off-campus internships if they so desire.

The Honors Director meets personally with each student to help in identifying special interests and talents and in defining the student's future plans.

Honors students receive privileges in registration to facilitate choice of classes and are encouraged to seek satisfaction of some basic course requirements through waivers, challenge exams, and advanced placement.

There are currently 250 students enrolled in the program.

Admission Process: Entering freshmen should have an SAT I score of 1100 or above (minimum ACT score of 26), a GPA of 3.5 or above, or a successful record of advanced classes in high school. The selection committee is guided in its decision by the student's motivation and interest in the program and by high school records, test scores, and other evidence of a commitment to learning.

Students may also apply before the start of their third semester in college if their SDSU GPA is 3.5 or above. Upperclass students should write a letter describing in detail their general academic and related interests (including possible choice of major) and their plans, however tentative, for a future career. A transcript and a sample of the student's work must accompany the application. Any original or photocopied (not retyped) essay written within the past year, whatever the subject, is acceptable. Generally, receipt of applications is required the semester prior to admission.

The Campus Context: San Diego State University encompasses 4.5-million square feet in forty-four academic buildings. It offers bachelor's degrees in seventy-six areas, master's in fifty-five, and doctorates in nine.

Student Body Enrollment is roughly 41,000, divided almost equally between men and women. Ethnic distribution is 53 percent white, 12 percent Mexican-American, 5 percent black, 5 percent Filipino, 4 percent other Hispanic, 3 percent Southeast Asian, 1 percent Pacific Islander, 1 percent American Indian, 2 percent nonresident, and 10 percent other/not listed. There are thirty-one fraternities and sororities on campus.

Faculty The total number of faculty members is 2,953, of whom 1,216 are full-time.

Key Facilities The library houses more than 1 million volumes.

Support Services Disabled Student Services offers accessibility information, orientation for students, reader services, and assistance with books on tape, etc.

Tuition: None for state residents, $7380 for nonresidents, per year (1996-97)

Room and Board: $6192

Mandatory Fees: $1902

Contact: Director: Dr. Thomas J. Cox, 5500 Campanile Drive, San Diego, California 92182-1623; Telephone: 619-594-1261; Fax: 619-594-7934; E-mail: tjcox@mail.sdsu.edu

SAN FRANCISCO STATE UNIVERSITY

4 Pu G S Sc

▼ **Presidential Scholars Program**

The San Francisco State University (SFSU) Presidential Scholars Program is available to a select group of approximately 25 new freshmen each fall following an application process that takes place in February and March. Those selected for the Presidential Scholarship receive automatic payment of registration fees for the freshman year, renewable for as many as three additional years if renewal criteria are met. Scholars take an orientation seminar and a general education course as a group and share in periodic cocurricular, cultural, and social events.

The Presidential Scholars Program was initiated in 1995–96. It is expected to include approximately 100 students once four classes of freshmen have been admitted. Currently, there are 75 students enrolled in the program.

Participation Requirements: In order to continue in the program, students must complete at least 24 units per year, take no more than 3 units per year on a credit/no-credit basis, maintain a cumulative GPA of at least 3.25, and participate in all required activities, including the scholars orientation and seminar plus one or two meetings and one or two special events per semester.

Admission Process: Applicants for the Presidential Scholarship must have applied and been accepted as first-time freshmen for the fall semester, have a high school GPA of at least 3.8, and complete an application showing evidence of academic and personal achievement, extracurricular contributions to school and/or community, and the ability to express oneself effectively.

The Campus Context: San Francisco State University is located in the city of San Francisco, the hub of the San Francisco Bay Area. Founded in 1899, SFSU is now a comprehensive university, one of twenty-two campuses of the California State University (CSU) system. SFSU's eight colleges include Behavioral and Social Sciences, Business, Creative Arts, Education, Ethnic Studies, Health and Human Services, Humanities, and Science and Engineering. SFSU offers 112 bachelor's and ninety-four master's degree programs.

Student Body Undergraduate enrollment is approximately 20,500 students: 58.6 percent women and 41.4 percent men. The ethnic distribution includes 35.5 percent non-Hispanic white, 28.8 percent Asian, 13.4 percent Hispanic, 9 percent Filipino, 7.7 percent African American, .9 percent American Indian, .6 percent Pacific Islander, and 4.1 percent other/not specified. There are 825 international students. About 1,350 students are campus residents. Forty-nine percent of students receive financial aid. SFSU has sixteen fraternities and eleven sororities.

Faculty SFSU has 1,486 faculty members, 751 of whom are tenured or on tenure track.

Key Facilities The Library holds more than 3.5 million books, periodicals, microform, and CD-ROM materials. Internet accounts are available free of charge to all faculty members, staff members, and students. All permanent faculty members have Internet-capable computing equipment. All rooms in the residence halls are wired for Internet access. In addition to one 24-hour computer lab in the residence halls, the

University has two central computer labs, college-housed computer labs in each of the eight colleges, a faculty and staff computer training center, and multimedia computing equipment and training through the Center for the Enhancement of Teaching.

Athletics SFSU is a member of the Northern California Athletic Conference, the only nonscholarship Division II conference in the NCAA. The Athletics Program offers fourteen varsity teams. Men's teams include baseball, basketball, cross-country, soccer, swimming, track and field, and wrestling. Women's teams include basketball, cross-country, soccer, softball, swimming, track and field, and volleyball. Athletic facilities include two gymnasiums, an indoor pool, a weight room, a conditioning center, a wrestling room, a 6,500-seat stadium, an all-weather track, a softball field, a baseball field, and fourteen tennis courts.

Study Abroad California State University International Programs provide numerous opportunities for students to earn residence credit at their home CSU campus while pursuing full-time study at a host university or special study center abroad. CSU International Programs serve the needs of students in more than 100 designated academic majors and are affiliated with thirty-six recognized universities and institutions of higher education in sixteen countries, offering a wide selection of study locales and learning environments. Additional study-abroad opportunities are available for study in each of seven foreign languages.

Support Services With few exceptions, the campus is completely accessible to persons with disabilities. Additionally, the Disability Resource Center provides support services for a broad range of students with disabilities. Services include registration assistance and priority registration, classroom accommodations, mobility services, deaf services, print access, and learning disability services.

Job Opportunities Numerous student assistantships and work-study opportunities are available through the Career Center.

Tuition: None for state residents, $7380 for nonresidents, per year (1996-97)

Room and Board: $5600

Mandatory Fees: $1982

Contact: Director: Dr. Gail Whitaker, ADM 447, 1600 Holloway Avenue, San Francisco, California 94132; Telephone: 415-338-2789; Fax: 415-338-1814; E-mail: whitaker@sfsu.edu; Web site: http://www.sfsu.edu

SCOTTSDALE COMMUNITY COLLEGE

2 Pu G M Sc Tr

▼ College Honors Program

The Honors Program at Scottsdale Community College (SCC) provides general education for students who seek challenges in learning, who are curious, who question, and who are eager to test assumptions. The program offers a series of specially designed courses for transfer and two-year students. The purpose of the Honors Program is to foster greater depth of thought in reading, writing, and discussion with faculty members and guest lecturers that will better prepare honors students to complete baccalaureate degrees or begin their careers.

The 15-year-old program enrolls 125 students.

Participation Requirements: Honors students are expected to register as full-time students, enroll in at least one honors course each semester, and maintain a GPA of 3.25.

Admission Process: Recent high school graduates must rank in the top 15 percent of their graduating class; continuing or transfer students must have completed 12 credit hours of college classes with a 3.5 or better. Applications are due each August and January.

Scholarship Availability: Scottsdale Community College offers a variety of stipends for honors students in addition to scholarships that are available to all students. The Chancellor's, Maricopa Foundation, and Betty Elsner Scholarships are Maricopa College District awards for continuing honors students. For recent Maricopa County high school graduates in the upper 15 percent of their graduating class, Presidents' Scholarships are available from the District. Partial fee waivers are awarded to all honors students who do not receive any of the above awards.

The Campus Context: Scottsdale Community College is one of ten colleges in the Maricopa Community College District. It was founded in 1971 and is located on the Pima/Salt River Reservation just east of the city of Scottsdale, Arizona. There are three degree programs at the College, the Associate of Arts degree for transfer students, the Associate of Applied Science degree for students in occupational programs, and an Associate of General Studies degree for students whose educational goals require flexibility. Several of the occupational programs are unique: the School offers certificate programs in tribal management, equine science, interior design, and hotel and restaurant management in addition to the usual programs.

Student Body Spring enrollments for the College were 9,649 total. The breakdown is 87 percent first-year and 56 percent women. The ethnic distribution is as follows: 81 percent Caucasian, 4.1 percent American Indian, 5.5 percent Hispanic, 1.5 percent African American, 2.7 percent Asian, and 4.8 percent international. Thirty-one percent are between the ages of 20 and 25. While there are no sororities or fraternities, there are twenty-eight officially recognized clubs and organizations for students interested in the arts, environment, ethnic groups, and communication, in addition to a community garden.

Faculty There are 135 full-time and 319 part-time faculty members, with a student-faculty ratio of 17:1. Sixty-eight percent of the faculty members have terminal degrees, and 26 percent have doctorates.

Key Facilities The library at SCC has 46,000 volumes; however, students have ready access to the more than 500,000 volumes available in all of the Maricopa College libraries. Computers are available to all students in the library, the computer lab, the Writing Center, and the Independent Study Lab in the Social and Behavioral Sciences Division.

Athletics The athletic program has a strong intramural program emphasizing lifelong sports (golf, handball, jogging) and intercollegiate competition in baseball, basketball, cross-country, football, golf, soccer, tennis, and track and field. Students in the intercollegiate program must conform to the eligibility rules established and maintained by the National Junior College Athletic Association.

Support Services The Office of Disability Resources and Services assists all students with disabilities through a variety of social and academic services. All buildings are in compliance with the Americans with Disabilities Act, and special parking permits are available.

Tuition: $1088 for area residents, $3584 for state residents, $4000 for nonresidents, per year (1996-97)

Mandatory Fees: $10

Contact: Coordinators: Kathy Schwarz and Kimb Williamson, 9000 East Chaparral Road, Scottsdale, Arizona 85250; Telephone: 602-423-6525; Fax: 602-423-6298 or 602-423-6365; E-mail: schwarz@sc.maricopa.edu or williams@sc.maricopa.edu; Web site: http://www.sc.maricopa.edu

SEMINOLE COMMUNITY COLLEGE

2 Pu G S Sc Tr

▼ Honors Program

Seminole Community College's (SCC) Honors Program allows academically talented students to substitute 22 hours of interdisciplinary studies for more traditional Associate in Arts degree requirements. Honors Program courses make the most of team teaching, so the perspective to which honors students are exposed is varied and demonstrates there are no bounds to thought. Parallel courses (i.e., Honors English II and Honors Humanities I) are available for honors students who have taken one of the 3-credit–hour courses that is a component of the honors core course Revolutions in Thought: Renaissance to the Present. The 9-year-old program currently enrolls 52 students.

Participation Requirements: Honors Program students take 22 hours in the Honors Core (Honors English I, Civilization and Its Discontents: The Roots, Science and Today's Society, and Revolutions in Thought: Renaissance to the Present or Honors English II and Honors Humanities I, Civilization and Its Discontents: The Future). Honors students are expected to attend two seminars per month, planned especially for

them, to strengthen the sense of a strong academic camaraderie with other honors students and honors faculty members (e.g., guest lectures by faculty members and visiting artists and special demonstrations at the planetarium). In order for students to receive an honors diploma, they must have earned 18 hours in honors courses and have a 3.0 GPA.

Honors students are also given the opportunity to participate in a newly organized student leadership program initiated by Dr. E. Ann McGee, SCC President. This program gives students the opportunity to interact on an individual basis with leaders at Seminole Community College and culminates with students traveling to Tallahassee, Florida, with Dr. McGee to lobby state legislators for SCC.

Students in the Honors Program have the opportunity to work closely with members of the honors faculty in classroom and mentor situations. Honors faculty members typically help students select courses that ensure their eligibility for an honors diploma from the College.

Admission Process: Students are identified at registration as potential Honors Program participants. The minimum criteria (two of three) used are an ACT score of 25 or a combined SAT score of 1100, a cumulative high school GPA of 3.4, or demonstration of special talents or abilities. Those students identified for active recruitment into the Honors Program must have an interview with the Program Coordinator and/or honors faculty members and have a letter of application describing their reasons for wanting to join the Honors Program.

Scholarship Availability: Honors students who express a need and meet the criteria can receive scholarships funded by the Academic Improvement Trust Fund established by the State Legislature. These merit scholarships were created to provide money for academically talented students and to expand the diversity among community college graduates. Each year, Seminole hosts a Dream Auction whose proceeds are matched from the state. Honors students must have demonstrated serious scholarship in previous honors classes or in high school. Those having higher GPAs are likely to receive more scholarship funds. Currently, approximately 42 percent of Honors Program participants receive full or partial scholarships for a total of $11,025 for Term I Honors Diploma.

The Campus Context: Seminole Community College has been providing high-quality programs in central Florida for thirty years. It was established in 1965 when the legislature authorized a state-supported junior college in Seminole County. The main campus, which lies near several growing business and residential areas, has maintained the natural beauty of Florida. The Hunt Club Center is housed in the western part of Seminole County. The area surrounding the main campus is dotted with lakes and wooded sanctuaries and is perhaps one of the most attractive locations in Florida. As a comprehensive community college, SCC offers instruction in three distinct educational areas: college credit, vocational noncredit, and adult and continuing education. The College grants one Associate of Arts degree and twenty-eight Associate of Science degrees.

Student Body Undergraduate enrollment is 43 percent men and 57 percent women. The ethnic distribution is 75.8 percent white, 9.5 percent black, 8.7 percent Hispanic, 4.3 percent Asian, 1 percent American Indian, and .7 percent other. All students commute to campus. Although there are no traditional fraternities or sororities, there is a chapter of the National Community College Honor Society, Phi Theta Kappa.

Faculty Of the 559 faculty members, 143 are full-time and 16 percent have terminal degrees. The student-faculty ratio is 19:1.

Key Facilities The library houses 77,000 books and periodicals. There are twelve computer facilities on campus.

Athletics Seminole Community College is a member of the Florida Community College Activities Association, which is the governing body for intercollegiate sports competition for junior college participation within the state. SCC teams compete in basketball, baseball, and softball.

Study Abroad Students have the opportunity, through ENL 2950 Travel Study in British Literature, Summer Semester in Cambridge and ANT 2950 Travel Study in Anthropology, to combine preparation on campus, international travel, and study abroad in the respective disciplines. Content varies depending on the program in which students enroll. Students must be 18 years of age on or before departure. Permission of instructors or the department chair is required. Destinations vary dependent on the content to be covered.

Support Services Disabled Student Services provides grant-funded support services and auxiliary aids to students with documented physical or mental disabilities. Through this office, qualified students with disabilities may request course substitutions; special support services such as interpreters, note takers, and tutors; and testing accommodations. Disabled Student Services administers state auxiliary aid funds, coordinates support services with area agencies and College departments, and conducts workshops to help faculty members and students create a positive learning environment for students with disabilities.

Job Opportunities Students are offered a range of work opportunities on campus, including tutoring and work-study.

Tuition: $973 for state residents, $3890 for nonresidents, per year (1996-97)

Mandatory Fees: $176 for state residents, $236 for nonresidents

Contact: Director of Honors Program, 100 Weldon Boulevard, Sanford, Florida 32773-6199; Telephone: 407-328-2052; Fax: 407-328-2201; E-mail: jcockerham@ipo.seminole.cc.fl.us; Web site: http://www.seminole.cc.fl.us

SHAWNEE STATE UNIVERSITY

4 Pu G S Sc Tr

▼ Honors Program

The Shawnee State University Honors Program, open to students of all majors, offers honors classes, honors academic advisement, and various social activities and receptions. The five-year-old program has 55 student members. Membership in the Shawnee State University Honors Program is by invitation only.

Participation Requirements: Honors students who graduate with a 3.8 cumulative GPA and successfully complete at least 24 credit hours of honors courses receive a special certification on their transcripts.

Admission Process: The Honors Program Committee, composed of 7 faculty members and 1 honors student, selects the top 3 percent of students based on ACT scores and cumulative GPAs. Letters of invitation are sent during fall quarter.

Scholarship Availability: The Financial Aid Office offers a number of scholarships for students who demonstrate a high degree of academic ability or special talent.

The Campus Context: Located on the Ohio River in downtown Portsmouth, Shawnee State University is currently in the midst of a massive campus expansion plan that, by the year 2000, will have brought more than $100 million to the University for new buildings, landscaping, land acquisition, and parking. Shawnee State University is composed of five colleges offering thirty different degree programs: Arts and Sciences, Education, Business, Health Sciences, and Engineering Technologies.

Student Body Undergraduate enrollment is 3,185: 41 percent men, 59 percent women. The ethnic distribution is 83 percent white, 4 percent African American, 1 percent Hispanic, 1 percent Native American, 1 percent international. Most students commute. Eighty percent of the students receive financial aid. There are five fraternities and sororities.

Faculty There are 239 faculty members; 119 are full-time, and 50 percent have terminal degrees. The student-faculty ratio is 13:1.

Key Facilities The library houses 110,000 volumes. The Shawnee State University Library is also a charter member of OhioLINK, a consortium of university libraries. Circulating items in other OhioLINK libraries can be obtained within 72 hours. When materials are not accessible via OhioLINK, conventional interlibrary loans are available. Two hundred computers are available for student use in computer labs, the learning resource center, classrooms, and the library. A staffed computer lab on campus provides training.

Athletics Athletic policies at Shawnee State conform to those of the National Association of Intercollegiate Athletics (NAIA). At the present time, Shawnee State fields teams in men's and women's basketball; men's soccer, golf, and baseball; and women's volleyball, softball, and tennis. The University's intercollegiate athletic teams are affiliated with the Mid-Ohio Conference.

Study Abroad Study opportunities are available for students in China, Russia, Germany, Mexico, and other locations.

Support Services A full range of equipment and services is available. An individual plan is developed for each disabled student.

Job Opportunities Regular employment is available to all University students, regardless of financial need, on the basis of current openings. The Federal Work-Study Program is available to students who can demonstrate financial need.

Tuition: $2445 for state residents, $3264 full-time and $91 (per quarter hour part-time) for Kentucky residents of Boyd, Greenup, Lewis, and Mason Counties and West Virginia residents of Cabell and Wayne Counties, $4620 for nonresidents, per year (1996-97)

Room and Board: $3945

Mandatory Fees: $531

Contact: Coordinator: Dr. Mark L. Mirabello, Office of the Provost, 940 Second Street, Portsmouth, Ohio 45662; Telephone: 614-355-2351; Fax: 614-355-2351; E-mail: mmirabello@shawnee.edu

---

SHEPHERD COLLEGE

4 Pu G S Sc Tr

▼ Honors Program

The mission of the Honors Program at Shepherd College is to create an academic environment in which gifted students can experience education in a dynamic and interactive way. Through seminars that promote active engagement in the subject area, independent research, a student-centered curriculum, and innovative teaching techniques, students in the Honors Program have the opportunity to become more self-directed in their learning. In the Honors Program, education does not simply take place in the classroom or through texts. Students become directly involved in the area of study through international and domestic travel, field trips, one-to-one interaction with professors and classmates, and a variety of activities outside the classroom that enhance the learning experience.

In addition to expanding the students' academic horizons, the Honors Program encourages student leadership and service to the community. The aim is to create graduates who are independent thinkers, insatiable learners, and responsible, socially conscious citizens. Honors students will leave Shepherd equipped to attend the finest graduate schools in the country and to be successful as solid contributors in their chosen professional careers. Graduates of the Honors Program are given recognition at graduating ceremonies.

The Honors Center at Shepherd College is located on the first floor of the Thacher Hall residence building. The Center includes the Office of the Director, the newly redecorated study lounge, and a computer lab. The Honors Residence Wing is also located on the first floor, allowing students to take full advantage of these facilities.

The 5-year-old program currently enrolls 100 students.

Participation Requirements: During the freshman year, honors students must participate in the honors core: Honors Written English and Honors History of Civilization. This two-semester, team-taught seminar introduces freshman honors students to major types of expository and critical writing in conjunction with the study of Western civilization. Topics focus on philosophical thought throughout history with emphasis on changes in government, economics, arts, science, and literature.

After completing the freshman core seminar, honors students may choose an honors course in a specific discipline or a special topics course. Special topics courses are team-taught seminars that cover interdisciplinary studies. In the past, these courses have included analysis of environmental issues; an exploration of the arts through theater, fine art, music, and dance; and the study of the history and culture of regions both within the United States and on an international level.

During their junior year, honors students begin research toward a major thesis to be completed as a graduation requirement. Each student chooses a mentor from the faculty and begins to formulate a reading list that would contribute to a thesis proposal. In collaboration with his/her thesis director, the student develops an original idea about the chosen topic and then analyzes the information using research to substantiate this idea.

Scholarship Availability: The Shepherd College Presidential Scholarship is awarded to freshman students who have demonstrated outstanding academic potential based on both their high school grades in a college-preparatory program and their scores on either the American College Test or the Scholastic Assessment Test. The quality of high school courses as well as extracurricular activities both within and outside the high school will also be considered.

Scholarships also may be awarded to transfer students who have demonstrated outstanding academic progress based on their previous college course work and grades. The staff of the Office of Admissions will select the students to receive this scholarship. Up to fifty Presidential Scholarships of $1000 each may be awarded annually without regard to the state of residence of the student.

The Rubye Clyde Scholarship has been set up by the Shepherd College Foundation in recognition of Rubye Clyde McCormick and is designed for outstanding West Virginia students with solid academic credentials. Full tuition and fees as well as room and board for one year (about $5000) are provided through the scholarship. This scholarship is renewable if the student meets academic criteria established by the Shepherd College Foundation. In order to renew the scholarship, the student must have a 3.5 GPA or above with a course load of 15 credit hours per semester. This scholarship is open to a student in any major or field of study.

The Hearst Foundation, Inc., was founded in 1945 by publisher and philanthropist William Randolph Hearst. In 1948, Mr. Hearst established the California Charities Foundation. Soon after Mr. Hearst's death in 1951, the name was changed to the William Randolph Hearst Foundation. Both foundations are independent private philanthropies operating separately from the Hearst Corporation. The charitable goals of the two foundations are essentially the same, reflecting the philanthropic interests of William Randolph Hearst—education, health, human services, and culture. Any student applying to the Honors Program is eligible for an award from these foundations. Potential recipients are judged on leadership, community service, and a superior academic record.

The Campus Context: Shepherd College is an institution offering thirty-six degree programs. Among its notable facilities are the Civil War Center and the Sara Cree Wellness Center.

Student Body The Shepherd College student population consists of approximately 40 percent men and 60 percent women. The minority ethnic distribution is about 5.5 percent, with about 3 percent black students and less than 1 percent Hispanic, Asian American, American Indian, and international students. There are eleven professional fraternities, five social fraternities, and four sororities.

At Shepherd College over 90 percent of financial aid is awarded to students who have, through application, shown that they need additional money to meet college expenses.

Faculty There are 247 faculty members; of the 120 full-time faculty members, 66 percent hold terminal degrees. The student-faculty ratio is 18:1.

Key Facilities The library houses 160,000 volumes and 330,000 total items and is a Selective Federal Depository. There are a number of computer facilities on campus, including microclassrooms with forty-six computers running DOS/Windows 3.1 and twenty-five computers running Windows 95; computer labs with twenty-one computers running DOS/Windows 3.1 or Windows 95, and a VAX system providing access to a mainframe through WVNET. Laser printers and scanners are available for student use. Internet access is available in the library and White Hall, with dial-in access available in the residence halls.

Athletics Shepherd College is a member of the National Collegiate Athletic Association (NCAA) and the West Virginia Intercollegiate Athletic Conference (WVIAC). Varsity sports for men are soccer, football, basketball, baseball, tennis, golf, and cross-country; varsity sports for women are volleyball, basketball, tennis, softball, and cross-country.

Study Abroad Study-abroad opportunities at Shepherd College can take two forms. Through classes, student trips have included travel to Hungary and Senegal. Independent travel is also encouraged and arrangements can be made with the director.

Support Services The College counselor has been designated as the staff member to assist students with disabilities.

Job Opportunities Work-study is available to students who qualify for financial aid. For those who do not qualify, individual departments do budget money for student assistants. The Residence Life Office offers positions as Resident Assistants and Hall Security.

Tuition: $2160 for state residents, $5098 for nonresidents, per year (1996-97)

Room and Board: $3970

Contact: Director: Dr. Patricia Dwyer, 199 Thacher Hall, Shepherdstown, West Virginia 25443; Telephone: 304-876-5244; Fax: 304-876-3101; E-mail: pdwyer@intrepid.net

SHIPPENSBURG UNIVERSITY OF PENNSYLVANIA

4 Pu C M Tr

▼ Honors Program

The Honors Program is designed for academically motivated students who thrive in an atmosphere of creative learning and intellectual exploration. The program, which is open to all majors, offers courses within the general education curriculum. Honors courses differ from regular offerings by their small enrollment and emphasis on student participation. First semester students generally enter the program through groups of two or three courses which might include World History I, Honors English, and a social science course such as world geography or cultural anthropology. Second semester students might take World History II, Basic Oral Communication, and a humanities course in music or literature.

At the sophomore and junior levels, there are course offerings such as Great Books and Chemistry in the Modern World. Other honors elective courses often develop around topics that encourage in-depth examination of a central theme or concept. Program participants are also encouraged to write a thesis or do an independent study in their major.

Honors students also receive special advising and priority scheduling to ensure them access to appropriate courses and professors. To broaden professional experiences, many honors students volunteer time to Admissions, Shipshape, or World Care. Some honors students organize a Saturday school for middle school children. Honors students have the opportunity to meet in small discussion groups with internationally known figures. The state system also offers a 6-credit honors summer program with a thematic focus. Shippensburg University provides 2 students with a full scholarship to participate in this special, intensive program.

The program began in 1984 and currently enrolls 140 students.

Participation Requirements: To graduate from the Honors Program, students must complete 24 credit hours of honors general education courses. Students are expected to maintain a minimum 3.25 overall QPA and a 3.25 QPA in honors courses. Graduation from the Honors Program requires 24 hours of honors credits. Successful completion of the Honors Program is noted at graduation and is recorded on the student's transcript. Students also receive a Certificate of Graduation from the Honors Program.

Admission Process: Shippensburg University's Honors Program accepts 40 students for each entering class from those who formally apply. Entering University students should have a minimum SAT I score of 1100 (28 on the ACT), be in the upper-fifth of their high school class, and have participated in a variety of extracurricular activities. If an entering freshman is not admitted to the program because of limited space, but obtains a QPA of 3.25 the first semester, the student is encouraged to reapply for acceptance. The Director of Honors interviews interested, currently enrolled students to determine if they meet the criteria for admission and are able to complete 24 credits of general education honors courses. Interested high school seniors, transfer students, and undergraduates enrolled at Shippensburg University may obtain an application form from the Honors Program.

Applications must be submitted by March 1.

Scholarship Availability: The University does not offer scholarships designated specifically for honors students. However, it does offer a number of scholarships for qualified students.

The Campus Context: Founded in 1871, Shippensburg University is a member of the Pennsylvania State System of Higher Education. It is a comprehensive, regional university offering both undergraduate and graduate programs. The University is conveniently located in the Chamberland Valley of south central Pennsylvania, approximately 3 hours from Philadelphia, 2 hours from Washington, D.C., and 1 hour from Harrisburg. The beautiful 200-acre campus blends traditional and modern architecture, providing students with a comfortable and progressive environment.

Shippensburg is a small university with a faculty dedicated to teaching. The emphasis on academic excellence has helped graduates to be recruited by businesses, government agencies, and educational institutions. Shippensburg graduates are regularly selected for admission to the finest graduate and professional programs. Small classes and a friendly campus make it easy to make friends, get involved, and receive the most from a university education. Visitors to the campus can see why a small university with a broad curriculum and diverse activities can start them on their way to success.

Fifty undergraduate programs are offered in the College of Arts and Sciences, the John L. Grove College of Business, and the College of Education and Human Services. A Division of Undeclared Majors offers students undecided about their majors a chance to earn credits.

Twenty-three graduate degree programs are also offered. Special or distinguishing facilities on campus include fashion archives; an art gallery; a vertebrate museum; an on-campus elementary school; public service centers in arts/humanities, government, and management; a planetarium; and the Women's Center.

Student Body Undergraduate enrollment is 5,576: 46.5 percent men, 53.5 percent women. There are 59 international students on campus. Of the total student population, 42.1 percent live on campus, 33.1 percent live in apartments in town, and 24.8 percent commute from home. Sixty-six percent of the freshmen receive financial assistance. Students belong to one local fraternity, twelve national fraternities, three local sororities, and eight national sororities.

Faculty Of the 376 total faculty members, 330 are full-time, and 80 percent have doctorates or terminal degrees. The student-faculty ratio is 20:1.

Key Facilities The library houses a 853,866-volume collection. There are twelve microcomputer laboratories on campus. A modem pool of forty 28,800-baud modems connected to a terminal server gives students the ability to connect to the campus network from off campus and from residence halls.

Athletics Shippensburg competes in Division II of the NCAA, offering eight men's and nine women's sports. Twenty-nine intramural activities are also offered. Intercollegiate sports include men's baseball, basketball, cross-country, football, soccer, swimming, track and field, and wrestling, and women's basketball, cross-country, field hockey, lacrosse, soccer, softball, swimming, tennis, track and field, and volleyball. Intramural sports include men's basketball, bowling, cross-country, golf, pool, racquetball, softball, street hockey, swimming, table tennis, tennis, track, volleyball, and wrestling, and women's aerobics, basketball, racquetball, softball, tennis, two-on-two basketball foul shooting contest, volleyball, and water aerobics. Coed sports include aerobics, basketball, bike hiking, softball, ultimate Frisbee, volleyball, and water aerobics.

Study Abroad Shippensburg University encourages students in all majors to study in another country and provides a foreign study adviser for advice in the choice of country, program, and length of time. Programs are available that range from three weeks to an academic year. Because of its membership in the Pennsylvania Consortium for International Education, Shippensburg participates in and offers credit for programs in Great Britain, France, Germany, Austria, and Spain.

Support Services Learning and/or physically disabled students attend regular classes and receive scheduling preferences if registered with the Office of Social Equity. Most buildings are completely or partially accessible. Accommodations such as note takers, audio-aids, readers, and tutors can be obtained through the Office of Social Equity. Specialized equipment includes a Xerox Kurweil personal reader, a Comtek Telecaption 4000 closed caption decoder, VTEK viewing machines to magnify print, and phones with a TDD for the hearing impaired.

Job Opportunities There are opportunities for part-time employment on the campus through federal and commonwealth work programs. Students with demonstrated financial need are given priority in job placement, but an effort is made to place as many students as possible who have desired work skills. These positions include work in administrative and faculty offices, the library, classes, residence halls, and on the campus grounds. Students may also apply directly for jobs available through the food service and Student Association organizations on campus.

Tuition: $3368 for state residents, $8566 for nonresidents, per year (1996-97)

Room and Board: $3700

Mandatory Fees: $862

Contact: Director: Dr. John E. Rogers Jr., 1871 Old Main Drive, Shippensburg, Pennsylvania 17257; Telephone: 717-532-1604; Fax: 717-532-1273; E-mail: jeroge@ark.ship.edu; Web site: http://www.ship.edu

SOUTHEASTERN LOUISIANA UNIVERSITY

4 Pu G L Sc Tr

▼ Honors Program

The Southeastern Louisiana University Honors Program is dedicated to the promotion of scholarly excellence through exciting instruction, stimulating reading, careful observation, problem-solving analysis, sharpening of written expression, and lively discussion. The Honors curriculum is designed to measure up to the real meaning of education that is "liberal": a process of learning that properly frees the mind and spirit.

Honors students are encouraged to engage in critical analysis in preparation for a lifetime of self-education. Through reading primary writings by the most influential philosophers, literary artists, and scientists, students will learn how and what the greatest minds have thought. Small classes allow for exchange of ideas and intense debate with other students and professors. Emphasis is consistently placed on analysis, discovery, and synthesis—on learning how to think.

Southeastern's Honors Alternative Core Curriculum offers to students of all majors a choice among three integrated sequences of core courses that will engage them in systematic inquiry and, in the process, develop their ability to think creatively and critically. Two Honors Core Curriculum options require special sequences of honors courses; one does not. Most honors courses in these core curricula are enhanced versions of, or substitutes for, courses that students already must take, regardless of their major.

Students who satisfy the academic requirements by completing the courses that make up one of the three alternate core curriculum options are eligible to receive the following: Core A—the Certificate of Excellence, Core B—the Honors Diploma, and Core C—the Honors Diploma in Liberal Studies. Students who complete Core B or Core C also complete Core A as a matter of course and thus earn the Certificate of Excellence in addition to an Honors Diploma.

Fringe benefits of the SLU Honors Program include small honors classes, a close advisory relationship with faculty members who teach honors courses, early priority registration, the option to earn an Honors Diploma or Honors in Liberal Studies Diploma, and the opportunity to attend state, regional, and national conventions for university honors students. On campus there are special honors social and academic functions, and honors students are eligible to live in Cardinal Newman, the honors residence hall. Students in the program are also eligible for academic scholarships and receive the Certificate of Excellence Award if they complete the four-year program.

The SLU Honors Program is 16 years old, and was revised to its current standards in 1989. There are currently 550 students in the program.

Admission Process: Any student who has the requisite academic credentials may join the Honors Program. A composite score of 21 on the ACT qualifies an entering freshman, and a minimum cumulative GPA of 3.0 qualifies a student with 12 or more university hours to join the Honors Program. Traditional and nontraditional students in every major are encouraged to join.

Scholarship Availability: The Southeastern Louisiana University Honors Program offers two scholarships to its members. Numerous Board of Trustees Scholarships and Presidential Honors Scholarships are awarded on a competitive basis. Information regarding other available scholarships may be obtained from the Honors Program office.

The Campus Context: Southeastern Louisiana University was founded as a junior college in 1925, and in 1928 was established as a four-year curricula college. In 1946 SLU became an accredited university and now consists of five colleges: College of Arts and Sciences, College of Basic Studies, College of Business, College of Education, and School of Nursing. Southeastern has sixty-six degree options available on the associate, bachelor's, and master's level in business, education, nursing, and liberal arts and sciences.

Student Body There are approximately 14,500 students enrolled at Southeastern; about 13,050 are undergraduates. Of the undergraduates, approximately 40 percent are men, 60 percent women. The undergraduate population has an ethnic make-up of 89 percent white and 11 percent minority students. There are about 50 international students. The majority of students enrolled are commuters. The nine fraternities/sororities on Southeastern's campus have more than 560 student members.

Faculty Of the 606 faculty members, 435 are full-time (63 percent with a doctorate) and 171 part-time.

Key Facilities There are approximately 330,000 bound volumes in Sims Memorial Library along with over 3,700 titles on microfilm, 2,300 periodical subscriptions, and national on-line catalog utilities. There are approximately 400 computers on campus available for general student use with access to the main academic computer, off-campus computing facilities, and the Internet.

Athletics In athletics Southeastern is a member of the Southland Conference, offering men's golf; women's soccer and volleyball; and baseball, basketball, cross-country, tennis, and track and field for both men and women.

Study Abroad Students may enroll for credit in study-abroad courses in Mexico and Canada.

Support Services The Office of Student Life will work with students with disabilities to help them adjust to campus life.

Job Opportunities A work-study program is available.

Tuition: $1930 for state residents, $4162 for nonresidents, per year (1996–97)

Room and Board: $2320 minimum

Mandatory Fees: $120

Contact: Dr. Jim Walter, Director, SLU Honors Program, 11 North Pine, P.O. Box 489, Hammond, Louisiana 70402; Telephone: 504-549-2135; Fax: 504-549-3478; E-mail: xhon2293@selu.edu

---

SOUTHERN UNIVERSITY AND A&M COLLEGE

| 4 Pu C L Sc Tr |

▼ Honors College

The Honors College at Southern University in Baton Rouge provides an enhanced educational experience for students who have a history of strong academic achievement and motivation and who have shown exceptional creativity and talent. Innovative pedagogy, flexible and competitive curricula, and mentoring relationships with distinguished faculty members and scholars are focal points of the program. The College also provides cultural and intellectual opportunities designed to motivate students to perform at the highest level of excellence that they are capable of and through which they may become knowledgeable and effective leaders. The 10-year-old College currently enrolls 600 students.

Participation Requirements: The core curriculum consists of honors colloquia and designated honors courses in the general curriculum and the student's major area of study. Students pursue Honors Contract courses and courses from the general curriculum and the student's major area of study to complete the requirements for the honors degree. The College grants several awards, including the Straight "A" Student Award, an award for the graduating senior with the highest average in the College; The Chancellor's Scholar's Award; and the Honors Medallion.

Admission Process: Participation in the Honors College is voluntary. However, students must apply for admission to the College, which falls into two classification types: General Honors and University Honors. Students applying for General Honors must have a minimum ACT composite score of 23 or SAT I composite score of 1040; a minimum high school GPA of 3.3; an assessment of cocurricular activities; two letters of

recommendation from the high school principal, counselor, or instructor; and an essay on a designated topic or a recently corrected writing activity 3–5 pages in length. Students applying as University Scholars must have a minimum ACT composite score of 25 or SAT I composite score of 1140; a minimum high school GPA of 3.5; an assessment of cocurricular activities; two letters of recommendation from the high school principal, counselor, or instructor; and an essay on a designated topic or a recently corrected writing activity 3–5 pages in length.

Students in college may apply to the Honors College based on a minimum GPA of 3.5, two letters of recommendation, and an interview.

Scholarship Availability: Scholarships are available in two categories. Tier I, a maximum, full scholarship available to incoming freshmen, includes tuition with out-of-state fees, room and board, and books and supplies in variable amounts. Applicants must have a minimum cumulative GPA of 3.6, a minimum ACT score of 28 or SAT I score of 1260, thirteen college-preparatory courses, and 15 credit hours pursued.

Transfer students may apply for Tier I scholarships based on a minimum GPA of 3.6 and 30 credit hours, which may not include developmental education courses. Tier I scholarship retention is based on a cumulative 3.3 GPA with 15 credits earned the previous semester. Tier II partial scholarships offering tuition or room and board are available to incoming freshmen who have a minimum cumulative GPA of 3.2 and a minimum ACT score of 21 or minimum SAT I score of 990 with thirteen college-preparatory classes and 15 credit hours pursued. Alternative criteria are a high school graduation rank of 1 or 2, National Achievers, and National Merit Scholars. Transfer students with a minimum cumulative GPA of 3.5 and 30 credit hours, which may not include developmental education courses, are also eligible. Tier II scholarship retention is based on a cumulative GPA of 3.0 with 15 credit hours earned the previous semester.

Other available scholarships include the Formosa Plastic Scholarship, the Thurgood Marshall Scholarship, and the Union Pacific Railroad Scholarship.

The Campus Context: Southern University and A&M College is composed of eleven colleges and schools: College of Agricultural, Family and Consumer Sciences; School of Architecture; College of Arts and Humanities; College of Business; College of Education; Honors College; Junior Division/General Studies; School of Nursing; School of Public Policy and Urban Affairs; and College of Sciences. The institution offers sixty-six degree programs. Among special campus features are an important sculpture acknowledging the founding of Baton Rouge, the Louisiana basketball arena and dome, and a student union building with a food court and picnic facilities.

Student Body Of the 8,768 students, 42.5 percent are men and 57.5 percent are women. Ninety-six percent of the students receive financial aid. There are eight fraternities and sororities.

Faculty Of the 590 faculty members, 499 are full-time; 53 percent hold terminal degrees.

Key Facilities The library houses 483,955 volumes. Computer facilities include a computer technology center and nine labs in the colleges, five labs in the dormitories, and five labs in the computer science departments. There is one computer for every 3 faculty members on campus.

Athletics Southern University has an athletic history that is steeped in the tradition of excellence and continues to grow. The Department of Athletics has produced and continues to produce individuals who have made enormous contributions to the sports world and the world as a whole. The Department of Athletics offers competition in sixteen sports, including baseball, men's and women's golf, softball, men's and women's tennis, men's and women's track and field, and volleyball. It operates under the jurisdiction of the National Collegiate Athletic Association (NCAA) and the Southwestern Athletic Department (SWAC). Recently, the Southern University Department of Athletics was certified without any restrictions by the NCAA. Athletic facilities include the A. W. Mumford Stadium (football), the F. G. Clark Activity Center (basketball), the Lee-Hines Field (baseball), and tennis courts. Construction is under way for a softball field.

Study Abroad Study-abroad opportunities are available through various departments and colleges. In addition, opportunities are also coordinated by the System Office of International Affairs and Development. The University has articulation agreements with the University of Ghana (Honors College) and the Universidad del Valle de Orizaba, Mexico (community service).

Support Services Disabled students find the campus accessible and facilities available to them.

Job Opportunities There are student work opportunities on campus.

Tuition: $2028 for state residents, $4808 for nonresidents, per year (1996-97)

Room and Board: $3022

Contact: Dean: Dr. Beverly D. Wade, P.O. Box 9413, Baton Rouge, Louisiana 70813; Telephone: 504-771-4845; Fax: 504-771-4848; E-mail: beverlingd@aol.com; Web site: http://www.subr.edu

SOUTH MOUNTAIN COMMUNITY COLLEGE

| 2 Pu G S Sc Tr |

▼ Honors Program

The philosophy of the Honors Program at South Mountain Community College is consistent with that of the Maricopa Community College District: to provide education for the diverse interests, needs, and capacities of the students it serves. The Honors Program exists to enhance the academic preparation of exceptional students in their initial college years. The aim of the Honors Program is to promote a sense of scholarship and community among its participants.

The Honors Program is designed to enhance students' intellectual growth by offering challenging courses and increased contact with other honors students. The program includes honors sections of general education classes, honors contract options, faculty mentors, special activities, and forum presentations that permit students to hear and talk with prominent lecturers. Each year the Maricopa District Honors Program presents an Honors Forum Series based on an honors study topic selected in conjunction with Phi Theta Kappa, the international honor society for two-year colleges. The Honors Forum course (HUM 190) is offered to prepare students for concepts discussed at the lectures. Finally, each honors course is designated HONORS on the student's official transcript.

Honors students enjoy a sense of community, an environment of excellence, and greater depth in their academic experience under the guidance of faculty mentors. In addition to honors sections of general education courses, special seminars, and the contract option, students are able to participate in honors-sponsored cultural, social, and educational events, including opportunities for travel to honors conferences and Phi Theta Kappa activities. The program, which began in 1981, currently enrolls 50 students per academic year.

Participation Requirements: To graduate as a South Mountain Community College Honors Program scholar a student must complete a total of 15 credits in course work designated as Honors. The course work must include 3 credits of HUM 190 (Honors Forum) and 12 credits selected from at least three different course prefixes. Students who complete the above distribution of courses with grades of A or B and an overall GPA of 3.2 or higher will receive special designation as Honors Program Graduates at the annual College award program and on the graduation program. The Honors designation indicates excellence and commitment both to prospective employers and to the admissions offices at other colleges and universities.

Admission Process: Any student may enroll in a specific honors section with the instructor's approval. Recent high school graduates who are in the top 15 percent of their high school class from a Maricopa County high school should apply for the President's Scholarship, which will also give them standing in the Honors Program. Continuing students should submit an Honors Program application to the Honors Coordinator.

Scholarship Availability: Honors Program students have several opportunities for scholarships and fee waivers. Graduates of a Maricopa County high school who have ranked in the top 15 percent at the end of the sixth, seventh, or eighth semester and who have not attended another college or university are eligible for the President's Scholarship. Continuing students who have completed 12 or more credits of college-level work at SMCC or another college or university with a cumulative GPA of at least 3.25 are eligible to apply for fee waiver status. All continuing members of the SMCC Honors

Program who plan to return for the following academic year are considered by the Honors Committee for the Chancellor's Scholarship, Honors Foundation Scholarship, and the Betty Hedin Elsner Scholarship. In addition, applications for the All-USA Academic Team and the Guistewhite Scholarship are available through the Honors Office.

The Campus Context: South Mountain Community College, a member of the Maricopa County Community College District, was founded in 1979. The College is located in the shadow of South Mountain Park, the largest municipal park in the United States. Near both downtown Phoenix and Tempe, just minutes from the I-10 and Superstition freeways and Arizona State University, South Mountain Community College is served by the Phoenix Transit Bus System. Known as the "College with the Personal Touch," South Mountain is one of the smaller of the Maricopa colleges. The College offers three degrees—Associate of Arts, Associate of General Studies, and Associate of Applied Science—as well as several certificate programs. Among the campus facilities is a child-care center licensed by the Arizona Department of Health Services and Department of Economic Security.

Student Body Of the 2,500 enrolled students, the majority are from the Phoenix area. All students commute to campus.

Faculty There are 40 full-time faculty members, 28 percent with doctorates.

Key Facilities The Learning Resource Center includes the MCCCD Online Public Access Catalog, Eureka, InfoTrac, and EVIN, in addition to standard library materials. Computer facilities house Macintosh, IBM, and Digital computers.

Athletics Men's sports are basketball, baseball, soccer, and cross-country; women's sports are softball, volleyball, basketball, soccer, and cross-country.

Support Services The campus is handicapped-accessible.

Job Opportunities Opportunities for work-study jobs exist in most departments.

Tuition: $992 for area residents, $4309 for state residents, $4867 for nonresidents, per year (1996-97)

Mandatory Fees: $10

Contact: Coordinator: Helen J. Smith, 7050 South 24th Street, Phoenix, Arizona 85040; Telephone: 602-243-8122; Fax: 602-243-8329; E-mail: smith_h@smc.maricopa.edu; Web site: http://www.smc.maricopa.edu (under construction)

SOUTHWEST STATE UNIVERSITY

4 Pu G M Sc Tr

▼ Honors Program

The Honors Program provides a way for qualified students to design their own general studies requirements by selecting specific courses from the catalog and/or designing specific projects that complement their particular strengths.

Honors students are allowed to enroll in classes that are full at the time of registration and may take any class for an extra honors credit. Upon completion of their work, honors students are given special recognition at Commencement and acknowledgment on their transcripts. The program sponsors an Honors Club, which sanctions social events and trips.

The Honors Program was initiated in 1971 and currently enrolls 130 students.

Admission Process: Students wishing to enter the program must have achieved a composite ACT score of at least 26 and must provide a letter of reference from a high school counselor or principal.

Scholarship Availability: Scholarships are awarded on a competitive basis to currently enrolled honors students. Incoming and transfer students are awarded scholarships, when qualified, by the Admissions Office working in conjunction with the President's Office.

The Campus Context: Southwest State University (SSU), one of seven institutions in the Minnesota state university system, opened its doors in 1967 and graduated its first class in 1971.

Southwest State's academic program is administered through the Division of Academic Affairs. The University offers forty-three baccalaureate majors, four associate degree majors, and thirty-three minors. In addition, two master's degree programs and six certifications are offered. Students can enter a four-year bachelor's program (Bachelor of Arts, Bachelor of Science, or Bachelor of Applied Technology), opt for a two-year associate degree (Associate in Science), or enter one of sixteen preprofessional programs.

SSU is fully accredited by the North Central Association of Colleges and Schools. Individual departments hold accreditation from the American Chemical Society, the National Board of Teaching, and the National Association of Schools of Music.

Southwest State's modern campus covers 216 acres and includes twenty-four buildings that incorporate barrier-free architecture to provide maximum accessibility for the University's physically disabled students. All academic buildings are connected by enclosed skywalks and hallways and have ramps and elevators.

Student Body Today the University enrolls over 2,800 students. Sixty-five percent of SSU's students come from the nineteen-county service area in southwestern Minnesota, while the remainder come primarily from other parts of Minnesota and the Upper Midwest.

Faculty The University has 125 faculty members. Two thirds of the full-time faculty members have earned the highest degree in their discipline.

Tuition: $2496 for state residents, $5624 for nonresidents, per year (1996-97)

Room and Board: $2900

Mandatory Fees: $484

Contact: Director: Dr. Hugh M. Curtler, Marshall, Minnesota 56258; Telephone: 507-537-7141; Fax: 507-537-7154; E-mail: curtler@ssu.southwest.msus.edu.

SOUTHWEST TEXAS STATE UNIVERSITY

4 Pu G M Sc Tr

▼ Honors Program

The Southwest Texas State University Honors Program provides challenges and opportunities for talented students through a curriculum designed to enhance traditional courses of studies. In small, seminar-type classes, honors students discuss ideas and raise questions stimulated by readings, field trips, and presentations. Dedicated faculty members provide an atmosphere that promotes curiosity, creativity, and a lifetime love of learning. Although specific topics vary, each course crosses traditional disciplinary boundaries and offers students an opportunity to pursue knowledge in an exciting and distinctive atmosphere. Recent course offerings have included Comedy and the Human Predicament; Astronomy in Art, History, and Literature; and Baseball and the American Experience.

The Honors Program was established in 1967 by Dr. Emmie Craddock, a professor of history at SWT. Initially the program offered only one course per semester. Today, up to ten courses are offered each long semester. There are approximately 275 students in the program.

Participation Requirements: To graduate in the Honors Program, students must complete at least five honors courses (15 hours), including Thesis Research Methods and the Honors Thesis. The honors courses can be taken at any time and can be chosen from the offerings each semester. Most honors courses substitute for certain General Studies and/or individual school requirements and thus become integral parts of the degree program. To remain in the Honors Program, a student must maintain a minimum GPA of 3.25.

The Freshman Honors Cohort for entering freshmen allows up to 25 freshmen to take one honors course and the Freshman Seminar together. The Freshman Cohort provides entering honors students an introduction to the University as well as to the SWT Honors Program. To apply for the Cohort, the general honors applications must be received by the spring prior to the fall semester in which the student enters SWT.

Participation in the SWT Honors Program is like joining a family. Honors students have access to two seminar rooms, a lounge, and a computer lab with Internet capabilities. Students are eligible to register early if they sign up for an honors course. Many students have presented their honors research at national conferences and have published work in regional and national publications.

Admission Process: Entering freshmen with a composite ACT score of 27 or SAT score of 1180 or who are in the top 10 percent of their class are eligible to apply for admission to the program. Currently enrolled and transfer students with a GPA of at least 3.25 are also eligible. Students can submit applications at any time during their college education and can withdraw from the program at any time without penalty.

Scholarship Availability: All freshman and transfer applicants and currently enrolled students who have completed at least one honors course may apply for the Emmie Craddock Scholarship if, as freshman applicants, they have a minimum ACT score of 27 or SAT score of 1150 or, as transfer or continuing students, they have a GPA of 3.5 or above. Currently enrolled students who have completed 60 hours and at least one honors course are eligible to apply for the James and Elizabeth Camp Scholarship if they have a GPA of 3.3 or above. Applications are available only through the Honors Program office and are due in January.

The Campus Context: Southwest Texas State University was founded in 1899 as the Southwest Texas Normal School. Located along the springs of the San Marcos River in San Marcos, Texas, SWT is approximately midway between Austin and San Antonio. Set along the edge of the Texas hill country, SWT offers recreation and beauty. Southwest Texas State is a mid-sized university that offers small-school advantages, such as one-on-one interaction between students and faculty members. The campus is home to seven colleges (Liberal Arts, Education, Science, Business, Applied Arts and Technology, Fine Arts and Communication, and Health Professions) with 130 different degree plans.

Student Body Undergraduate enrollment is 21,000: 44.6 percent men, 55.4 percent women. The minority ethnic distribution of the total undergraduate populations is 18 percent Hispanic, 5.4 percent African American, and 1.6 percent Asian American. Almost half of the students receive financial aid. Fifty-four percent of students are commuters.

Faculty Of the 916 faculty members, 687 are full-time. The student-faculty ratio is 20.3:1.

Key Facilities The library houses 2.8 million volumes. There are thirty-three fraternities and sororities on campus.

Athletics The Bobcats compete in the Southland Conference in NCAA Division I (I-AA in football). SWT fields teams for NCAA competition in baseball, basketball (men's and women's), cross-country (men's and women's), football, men's golf, softball, tennis (men's and women's), track and field (men's and women's), and women's volleyball. These are official NCAA teams that recruit most of their athletes, but anyone can walk on for a tryout. The "unofficial" teams are everywhere—on a sunny day, they are found in any space big enough to resemble a field. Some teams play in organized intramural leagues, while others fill a free afternoon.

Job Opportunities Students are offered a wide range of work opportunities throughout campus, including work-study opportunities.

Tuition: $960 for state residents, $7380 for nonresidents, per year (1996-97)

Room and Board: $3787

Mandatory Fees: $1196

Contact: Director: Dr. Eugene Bourgeois II, San Marcos, Texas 78666; Telephone: 512-245-2266; Fax: 512-245-3847; E-mail: eb04@swt.edu

SPELMAN COLLEGE

4 Pr G S Tr

▼ Ethel Waddell Githii Honors Program

Working with all the academic departments and programs, the Ethel Waddell Githii Honors Program of Spelman College seeks to amplify the intellectual opportunities for the students and faculty members of the entire Spelman community. The program identifies students who have a love of learning and equips them to become lifelong learners by granting them the opportunity to participate actively in their intellectual and personal development from the early stages of their college careers. Students are invited to choose from among the more challenging and innovative courses within a wide variety of disciplines, select courses which have been specially designed for the program, and suggest new courses to meet their intellectual curiosity. The Honors Program also sponsors special events, makes arrangements for the students to attend cultural activities in Atlanta, and promotes community service opportunities in keeping with the student's academic explorations.

Participation Requirements: Honors students may major in any traditional department or develop their own major. Honors students take the same number of credits for graduation as all other Spelman students. Honors students take a core curriculum of honors math, honors freshman composition, honors philosophy, and two honors electives. If a student has received AP credits for one of these courses, she may be exempted from the corresponding course. All of the courses may be used to fulfill the College's core curriculum. In addition, all students in the Honors Program write an honors thesis in their major. The thesis might include—for example, in the case of an art student—a portfolio or performance.

To remain in the program, freshmen and sophomores must maintain a 3.1 GPA. Juniors and seniors must maintain a 3.2 GPA. Successful completion of the Honors Program is noted on the transcript and on the graduation program.

Admission Process: Freshmen are selected each April for the Honors Program on the basis of their high school average and SAT scores, as well as by an application process that includes the writing of essays. Application deadlines are January 12 and April 12.

Scholarship Availability: There are no scholarships given for participation in the Honors Program; however, Honors Program students are encouraged to apply for regular scholarships given by the College.

The Campus Context: An outstanding historically black college for women, Spelman strives for academic excellence in liberal education. The College is a member of the Atlanta University Center consortium, and Spelman students have the opportunity to take classes on all of the other members' campuses. The College is located very close to the center of Atlanta, Georgia, on a beautiful 32-acre campus graced with historic nineteenth-century buildings as well as the recently completed, state-of-the-art Cosby Building for the Humanities. Plans are under way for a new science building that should be completed by 1998. The College has, for the last several years, been regularly listed by *Money* magazine as one of the ten best buys in American higher education.

Student Body Undergraduate enrollment is 1,961. Sixty percent of the students are residents on campus.

Faculty There are 134 full-time faculty members, 83 percent with doctorates or other terminal degrees. The student-faculty ratio is 14:1.

Key Facilities The library houses 1.4 million volumes. Computer facilities include sixty IBM-compatible computers located in dormitories and academic buildings.

Study Abroad Spelman students are encouraged to spend their junior year on either domestic or international exchange. The College participates in a wide range of exchange programs and offers some scholarships to students who take advantage of these opportunities.

Job Opportunities Students are offered a range of work opportunities on campus, including work-study and general work programs.

Tuition: $8150 per year (1996-97)

Room and Board: $6130

Mandatory Fees: $1350

Contact: Director: Dr. James J. Winchester, 350 Spelman Lane, SW, Box 1395, Atlanta, Georgia 30314; Telephone: 404-223-7556; Fax: 404-215-7863; E-mail: jwinches@spelman.edu

STATE UNIVERSITY OF NEW YORK AT BUFFALO

4 Pu G M Sc Tr

▼ University Honors Program

The University Honors Program at the State University of New York at Buffalo provides academically talented students with the opportunity to pursue a rigorous and challenging intellectual experience within their undergraduate studies. In bringing to UB some of the brightest high school students in the United States, the Honors Program creates a small-college atmosphere within a large university setting. Here, each Honors Scholar has the opportunity to create a program of study that fits his or her unique interests.

Honors Scholars receive merit-based scholarships, participate in small honors seminars, are provided with a faculty mentor upon entrance to UB, attend evening with faculty programs, and work on major research projects early in their college careers.

The University Honors Program encompasses all undergraduate divisions. Approximately 120 students are admitted each year. The general Honors Program admits 90 to 100 freshman students for the fall semester of each year. Included in this number are 10 students who enter as Performing and Creative Arts Scholars who major in art, dance, media study, music, and theater. Approximately 20 current University students are admitted to the Honors Program each year. A Transfer Honors Program allows for the admission of 20 transfer students for the fall semester.

The 15-year-old program currently enrolls 400 students.

Participation Requirements:
To maintain their status in the University Honors Program, entering freshman Honors Scholars participate in the Freshman Honors Colloquium for their first semester. In addition, they complete four honors seminars within their first two years of study at UB. Students entering as transfer Honors Scholars or current UB students complete two honors seminars in their junior year. Freshmen must maintain a minimum GPA of 3.2. Sophomore, junior, and senior Honors Scholars must maintain a 3.5 GPA each semester and cumulatively to graduate as Honors Scholars. Students in the program receive the following transcript notation: University Honors Scholar, University Honors Program.

Admission Process:
Freshmen entering the Honors Program are selected on the basis on their high school average and SAT scores. Applications are due by the end of January.

Scholarship Availability:
Students who qualify for the Honors Program receive one of three scholarships: the Distinguished Honors Scholarship, which covers the entire cost of attending UB for four years (including tuition, room, board, fees, and expenses), a $3000-a-year scholarship for four years, or a $1000-a-year scholarship for two years. Students selected for the Performing and Creative Arts Program receive $2000 per year for four years. Transfer and current Honors Scholars receive a scholarship of $1000 each year for two years. Performing and Creative Arts applicants must submit a separate application to the program; auditions, portfolios, and a personal interview are required. Transfer and current students are selected on the basis of their college performance (minimum GPA 3.8), a written personal statement, and letters of recommendation from their professors.

The Campus Context:
The State University of New York at Buffalo is composed of many schools and faculties offering ninety-three undergraduate majors and sixty-four minors: the School of Architecture, Faculty of Arts and Letters, Faculty of Natural Sciences and Mathematics, Faculty of Social Sciences, School of Engineering and Applied Sciences, School of Health Related Professions, School of Management, School of Medicine and Biomedical Sciences, School of Nursing, and School of Pharmacy. Those with graduate programs only are the School of Dental Medicine, Graduate School of Education, School of Information and Library Studies, School of Law, and School of Social Work.

The University at Buffalo is the largest of SUNY's sixty-four units and the largest public university in the Northeast. It is a member of the Association of American Universities, the most prestigious academic organization in the country. The University is located on two campuses. UB's original campus, located in the northeast corner of Buffalo, houses the schools of Dentistry and Medicine and Biomedical Sciences. Three miles away in the town of Amherst is the 1,200-acre North Campus. Highlights of this campus include the new Center for the Arts, which contains three theaters, two dance studios, a University Gallery and Art Department Gallery, and the National Center for Earthquake Engineering Research.

Student Body Undergraduate enrollment is 16,150: 54.89 percent men and 45.11 percent women. The ethnic distribution of students includes 22.9 percent minority students (7.3 percent African American, 3.5 percent Hispanic, 11.6 percent Asian American, and 0.5 percent Native American). There are 312 international students. Twenty-one percent of the students live on campus. Sixty percent of the students receive financial aid. There are thirteen fraternities and eight sororities. In addition, there are nine culturally based chapters of national fraternities and sororities.

Faculty Of the 2,137 faculty members, 1,323 are full-time; 95 percent hold terminal degrees. The student-faculty ratio is 12:1.

Key Facilities The campus has ten libraries containing 2.9 million volumes and 23,600 serials. There are twelve public computing sites on campus, all with laser printing available. Ten of these sites are staffed by computer consultants. The University contains over 700 mainframe terminals and over 700 microcomputers for student, faculty, and staff use. All students are issued computer accounts at orientation. The University supports IBM and Macintosh computers and uses UNIX and VAX systems.

Athletics UB participates in NCAA Division I varsity athletics. Varsity athletics for men include basketball, cross-country, football, soccer, swimming, diving, tennis, track and field, and wrestling. Varsity athletics for women include basketball, cross-country, soccer, swimming, diving, tennis, track and field and volleyball. UB also offers a wide range of intramural activities in team and individual competition, as well as co-recreation and club teams.

Study Abroad Students are able to take any study abroad program offered through UB, the SUNY System, or any other accredited school in the United States.

Support Services The Office of Disability Services provides and coordinates services for persons with disabilities. It helps to support the educational and social objectives and goals of individuals with disabilities at the University.

Job Opportunities Students on Federal Work-Study can often find part-time jobs in offices and laboratories on campus. Students can also work for the libraries, computing services, food service, or in the Commons.

Tuition: $3400 for state residents, $8300 for nonresidents, per year (1996-97)

Room and Board: $5455

Mandatory Fees: $790

Contact: Academic Director: Dr. Clyde Herreid, Professor of Biology, 214 Talbert Hall, Buffalo, New York 14260; Telephone: 716-645-3020; Fax: 716-645-6143; Web site: http://wings.buffalo.edu/provost/honors/

STATE UNIVERSITY OF NEW YORK COLLEGE AT ONEONTA

| 4 Pu G S Sc Tr |

▼ Oneonta Scholars Program

The Oneonta Scholars Program is a four-year, 27-credit program designed for students who wish to seek out challenging academic experiences and want to contribute to the intellectual and cultural life of the academic community. Freshman and sophomore course work emphasizes skill development and interdisciplinary perspectives while junior and senior course work emphasizes discipline-based experiences. The courses are designed to fit into the student's program of study. Scholars take the same number of credits as other students and courses taken during the freshman and sophomore years satisfy general education requirements.

The Oneonta Scholars Program is designed to develop and foster the qualities found in an Oneonta Scholar: inquisitive, creative, independent, and critical thinking; strong academic ability; and a high capacity for independent work. Students who participate in the Scholars Program have the opportunity to enjoy exciting and challenging course work in a small-class setting, to develop close working relationships with Oneonta's best faculty members, and to become part of a network of similarly motivated students.

The four-year Oneonta Scholars Program was implemented in the fall of 1996. It is a direct outgrowth of the pilot Freshmen Scholars Program, which was initiated in 1994. There are currently 17 students involved in the new program.

Participation Requirements: During the freshman year, students take 9 core credits. In the fall, students take the Freshman Scholars Seminar and Fundamentals of Information Literacy. The Freshman Scholars Seminar is designed to build critical-thinking, reading, writing, speaking, and listening skills. Fundamentals of Information Literacy helps students to understand issues related to literacy in the information age while building skills that allow the student to identify, retrieve, and evaluate information in print, microform, and electronic formats. During the spring, the student takes Philosophy of Science, which examines the philosophical methods, structure, theories, and presuppositions of modern science. Philosophy of Science provides the intellectual foundation from which students can undertake future scholarly study.

During the sophomore year, students take two Sophomore Scholars Seminars (one each semester). These seminars take an interdisciplinary perspective by identifying controversies and current issues that have implications for or can be examined through other disciplines. Topics will vary from semester to semester.

The junior and senior year course work allows the student to specialize in his or her major. Students take Ethical Dilemmas in Professional Life, attend a junior/senior symposium, and, working with a faculty mentor, complete at least 3 credits of independent work in an area of the student's own choosing. The independent work can take the form of an internship, field experience, thesis, research project, or creative work. Students also have the opportunity to take 3 credits in a discipline-based Advanced Seminar.

Once accepted into the program, the student must maintain a minimum overall GPA of 3.3 and receive no less than a grade of B in any Scholars course in order to maintain eligibility. Successful completion of the program is noted on the student's transcript.

Admission Process: The eligibility process is flexible to ensure that all qualified students have the opportunity to apply. Students may enter the program up to the first semester of their junior year. Entering freshmen are invited to participate based on SAT I scores, high school class rank, and high school GPA. Returning students and transfer students may initiate the application process.

Scholarship Availability: The College at Oneonta has recently established the Mildred Haight Memorial Scholarships. Beginning in 1997, 20 incoming freshmen receive $500 grants each to purchase books and other educational supplies at the College Bookstore. The awards are being made to accepted students early in the admission cycle, and the primary criterion is high school GPA.

The Campus Context: The State University of New York College at Oneonta, a state-supported, comprehensive, coeducational college of the liberal arts, was founded in 1889 and was incorporated into the State University of New York system in 1948. Oneonta State is located in Oneonta, New York (population 15,000), about halfway between Albany and Binghamton, just off Interstate 88 near the western foothills of the Catskill Mountains. In a comprehensive study of academic quality and cost, *Money* magazine's *1996 Money Guide: Your Best College Buy Now* ranked Oneonta seventy-ninth among some 2,000 public and private four-year colleges and universities nationwide, and fifteenth among schools in the Northeast. The College at Oneonta has sixty-five undergraduate degree programs and twenty master's degree programs.

Outstanding facilities include Milne Library, with the largest collection of library materials among all the SUNY colleges, and the nationally recognized Physics and Chemistry Multimedia Laboratory. The campus also features the Goodrich Theatre in the Fine Arts Building, the Hunt College Union, the Electronic Classroom in the Instructional Resources Center, and the Morris Conference Center. In addition, the College owns and maintains a facility on Otsego Lake in Cooperstown, which houses the Biological Field Station and the Cooperstown Graduate Program in History Museum Studies.

Student Body The College at Oneonta enrolls 5,200 full- and part-time students. The student population is as follows: 40 percent men, 60 percent women; 7.6 percent minority enrollment; 0.4 percent international student enrollment; 45 percent residential, 55 percent commuter. Eighty percent of students receive financial aid. There are eight sororities and no fraternities.

Faculty The College at Oneonta has 350 faculty members, 240 of whom are full-time. Seventy-four percent of the faculty members have a terminal degree. The student-faculty ratio is 20:1.

Key Facilities Milne Library houses 537,832 volumes, the largest collection of library materials among all the SUNY colleges. The College at Oneonta has more than 300 PCs for student use, many networked to a central VAX cluster; unlimited campuswide access to the Internet; eighteen computer labs (nine open seven days a week); and eleven specialized labs for computer graphics, geographic mapping, economics and business, and other disciplines. The Chemistry and Physics Multimedia Lab is nationally known.

Construction has begun on the new 91,000-square-foot SUNY-Oneonta Field House. The main area will seat 3,000 people for basketball games and 4,500 people for events that permit seating on the floor, such as lectures or debates. The new Field House will also house a dance studio, two racquetball courts, an indoor track, a weight training/fitness center, and other administrative and support spaces.

Athletics The College at Oneonta competes in the NCAA, ECAC, NYSAIAW, and SUNY Athletic Conference, fielding intercollegiate teams for men in baseball, basketball, cross-country, lacrosse, soccer, tennis, and wrestling, and for women in basketball, cross-country, field hockey, lacrosse, soccer, softball, swimming, tennis, and volleyball. Men's soccer is in NCAA Division I; all other intercollegiate athletic teams compete in NCAA Division III.

Study Abroad Study-abroad programs (some for a full year, some for a semester, and some for the summer) are offered in Japan, Germany, England, Canada, and India. Oneonta students also participate in the hundreds of other study-abroad programs available each year through other SUNY colleges and universities. The Office of International Education assists students who wish to pursue opportunities for education abroad.

Support Services Through the Office of Services for Students with Disabilities, Oneonta provides a range of educational accommodations unique to individual students. Such provisions include special testing accommodations and classroom services for students with documented need of them. Other available services include placement-testing accommodations during orientation, housing accommodations, assistance with access problems, advisement about particular disability issues, assistance with funding coordinates, and referrals to appropriate resources.

Job Opportunities The College has a professionally staffed Student Employment Service providing students with on-campus and off-campus employment opportunities.

Tuition: $3400 for state residents, $8300 for nonresidents, per year (1996-97)

Room and Board: $5590

Mandatory Fees: $358 to $484

Contact: Coordinator: Lynne A. Sessions, 332C Netzer Administration Building, Oneonta, New York 13820; Telephone: 607-436-3184; Fax: 607-436-2719; E-mail: sessiola@oneonta.edu

STATE UNIVERSITY OF NEW YORK COLLEGE AT OSWEGO

| 4 Pu G S Sc Tr |

▼ College Honors Program

The SUNY Oswego Honors Program consists of a core of courses designed to stimulate students' intellectual growth and develop their analytical abilities. Unlike traditional courses, which present material from a single field of study, Honors Program courses draw ideas and information from many fields, addressing concerns common to all disciplines and recognizing that there are no boundaries to thought and inquiry. Honors Program courses examine the historical and intellectual origins, growth, and development of today's issues, the connections among them, and their consequences for tomorrow. The program emphasizes small classes—about 20 students—and the lively exchange of ideas in the classroom. The Honors Program seeks out faculty members who have demonstrated excellence in teaching, who are especially skilled in their fields, who are interested in thinking across disciplines, and who are committed to working with students in a variety of formal and informal settings. Honors Program students are advised by the Honors Director and by faculty members in the student's major field of study. Students enjoy a close relationship with honors faculty members and with each other in a network of academic and personal support.

Honors Program students have access to all of SUNY Oswego's facilities. This is one of the great benefits of the

Honors Program; while students enjoy the advantages of a small, challenging program, they have access to all the resources of a major university, including an internationally respected faculty, a library with over one million holdings, fully equipped computer labs, and a wide range of student services.

Participation Requirements: Students in the Honors Program can major in any area the College offers and take the same number of credits for graduation as every other SUNY Oswego student. Honors Program students take 18 hours in the Honors Core (Intellectual Traditions I and II, The Social Sciences, Literature and the Arts, Science in the Human Context, and The Search for Meaning), as well as courses in a language, lab science, English, and math. (If an Advanced Placement course covers the same material as an Honors Program course, the AP course will fulfill the honors requirement. For example, a student with AP credit in calculus or a lab science already will have met those particular requirements.) In addition, students in the Honors Program explore a subject of their choice in depth with a faculty adviser—usually within their major—by writing a senior thesis.

To graduate from the Honors Program, students must have a 3.0 GPA overall, a 3.3 GPA in their major, and a 3.3 in the Honors Core (Honors 140, 141, 200, 201, 300, and 301). Successful completion of the Honors Program requirements is noted at graduation and is recorded on the student's transcript.

Admission Process: Freshmen are selected each May for the Honors Program on the basis of their high school average and their SAT I scores. Sophomores and first-year students who are not selected may also apply for admission.

The Campus Context: The State University of New York, College at Oswego was founded in 1861 as the Oswego Normal School, and became a SUNY college in 1962. SUNY Oswego is located in Oswego, New York, about 50 miles northwest of Syracuse, and occupies 700 acres right on the shore of Lake Ontario. Oswego offers sixty undergraduate majors leading to the baccalaureate, including liberal arts and sciences, business, and education. In the past decade a number of highly respected national publications, including *U.S. News & World Report, Barron's,* and *Money Magazine,* have rated SUNY Oswego's education as outstanding, an "Ivy league education at a state university price."

Student Body There are 6,000 undergraduates enrolled; the majority are from the Northeast.

Faculty Of the 300 full-time faculty members, 75 percent have doctorates or other terminal degrees. There are also adjunct faculty members. The student-faculty ratio is 22:1.

Key Facilities The library houses 400,000 volumes. There are 300 Macintosh and DOS computers, located in the library, dormitories, and academic buildings.

Athletics Intercollegiate athletics for men include baseball, basketball, cross-country, diving, golf, hockey, lacrosse, soccer, swimming, tennis, and volleyball. SUNY Oswego also offers a wide range of intramural sports and club teams, including crew (rowing) for both men and women.

Study Abroad Through its International Education Program, SUNY Oswego students in all majors have the opportunity to study overseas in England, France, Spain, Mexico, Italy, Germany, Puerto Rico, Australia, Hungary, and Japan. Students may study abroad for a summer, for a semester, or for a year. Credits earned in this way apply to the student's SUNY Oswego degree requirements.

Job Opportunities Students are offered a range of work opportunities on campus, including assistantships and work-study.

Tuition: $3400 for state residents, $8300 for nonresidents, per year (1996-97)

Room and Board: $5460

Mandatory Fees: $487

Contact: Director: Dr. Norman L. Weiner, 105A Mahar Hall, Oswego, New York 13126; Telephone: 315-341-2190; Fax: 315-341-5406; E-mail: weiner@oswego.oswego.edu; Web site: http://www.oswego.edu/acad-dept/honors.html

---

STATE UNIVERSITY OF NEW YORK COLLEGE AT PLATTSBURGH

4 Pu C M Sc Tr

▼ Honors Program

Honors Seminars, Learning Communities, Honors Tutorials, mentoring programs, and research opportunities are just a few of the special teaching/learning relationships that distinguish SUNY Plattsburgh's Honors Program. All of these relationships are energized by interactions between bright, active, and motivated students and committed teacher/scholars. Intellectual and academic challenges in a supportive and developmental context encourage students to self-discovery and accomplishment beyond what they may believe they can do.

The organization of the Honors Program is fairly simple. It is a four-year program divided between General Honors (primarily for freshmen and sophomores) and Advanced Honors (for juniors and seniors). In the General Honors portion of the Honors Program, students are expected to complete four Honors Seminars. Honors Seminars are highly interactive classes limited to 15 students. Seminar topics change every semester, though all seminars satisfy part of the College's General Education Program. At least one Learning Community is also offered each semester to General Honors students. The Advanced Honors part of the program allows students to undertake research projects of their own design under the guidance of a faculty mentor. Students are expected to make a public presentation of the honors thesis, which is the normal outcome of the research project. Advanced honors students also can pursue Honors Tutorials dealing with a wide range of topics.

The Honors Program at SUNY Plattsburgh is housed in the Redcay Honors Center. Facilities include a large study/lounge, two specially designed seminar rooms, a library, and a computer lab. On the administrative side of the Honors Center is a reception/secretarial space, the Director's office, and an office for visiting scholars. Students in the Honors Program have direct access to visiting scholars. The distinguished roster of visiting scholars includes a number of Nobel Laureates, such as Joseph Brodsky, Eugene Wigner, and Derek Walcott.

The success rate of students who complete the Honors Program and apply to graduate and professional schools is nearly 100 percent. Honors Program alumni have distinguished themselves in many fields and maintain close contact with currently enrolled students.

The Honors Program is fully integrated into the rest of the College. Virtually every academic program at the College is represented among students in the Honors Program. The Honors Program is a supplement to rather than a substitute for other high-quality academic programs on campus.

The Honors Program was established in 1984. There are currently about 250 students in the program.

Admission Process: Entering freshmen whose high school average is 92 or above and whose SAT I scores are 1200 or above are automatically admitted into the Honors Program. Others may be admitted on the basis of an interview. Currently enrolled students with a 3.5 or higher GPA are automatically admitted.

Scholarship Availability: The College awards a number of full-tuition, four-year renewable Presidential Scholarships through the Honors Program each year to incoming freshmen. Additional Sophomore Presidential Scholarships are usually awarded. The Honors Program itself also awards a number of Redcay Honors Scholarships and Redcay Advanced Honors Scholarships.

The Campus Context: SUNY Plattsburgh is a campus of three schools: the School of Arts and Sciences, the School of Professional Studies, and the School of Business and Economics. Fifty-six undergraduate majors are offered on campus. Among the distinguished facilities are the SUNY Plattsburgh Art Museum including the Winkel Sculpture Garden, Rockwell Kent Gallery, Burke Fine Arts Gallery, and Museum Without Walls. The campus is proud of its Health/Fitness Center, Valcour Conference Center on Lake Champlain, Twin Valleys Outdoor Education/Recreation Center in the Adirondacks, and Miner Center for In Vitro Cell Biology Research.

Student Body Undergraduate enrollment is approximately 5,200: 40 percent men, 60 percent women. International students on campus number about 200.

Faculty There are 270 full-time faculty members, 90 percent with a Ph.D. or other terminal degree. The student-faculty ratio is 21:1.

Key Facilities The Feinberg Library houses more than 350,000 volumes, with computerized indexing and access. There are VAX minicomputers (academically dedicated) and hundreds of microcomputers widely distributed on campus, along with a campuswide optical fiber network with complete Internet access.

Athletics SUNY Plattsburgh offers a full range of intercollegiate athletics. The College is committed to the principles of Division III of the NCAA in all intercollegiate athletics. Club sports include rugby, volleyball, and skiing. The College has hosted the World University Games and was the staging site for the U.S. Olympic Team for the 1976 Montreal Olympics, resulting in world-class athletic facilities.

Study Abroad Students will find unlimited opportunities for study in Canada, including placement in Canadian universities, private corporations, and government agencies, through its nationally prominent Center for the Study of Canada. Similar opportunities abound in Central and South America through the College's Southern Cone Program. Opportunities for study abroad in more than 140 countries exist through SUNY. The Honors Program supports and encourages its students to take advantage of these opportunities and many do so.

Support Services The campus is fully handicapped-accessible.

Job Opportunities There are many employment opportunities for students on campus. These include assistantships, work-study and temporary service positions, research positions, and positions with various College services.

Tuition: $3400 for state residents, $8300 for nonresidents, per year (1996-97)

Room and Board: $4250

Mandatory Fees: $437

Contact: Director: Dr. David N. Mowry, 121-123 Hawkins Hall, Plattsburgh, New York 12901; Telephone: 518-564-3075; Fax: 518-564-3932; E-mail: mowrydn@splava.cc.plattsburgh.edu

SUFFOLK COUNTY COMMUNITY COLLEGE

2 Pu C L Sc Tr

▼ Honors Program

The Honors Program at Suffolk County Community College is designed to provide a special challenge to academically talented and highly motivated students. It combines small classes, gifted faculty members, enthusiastic students, and rigorous course work to create an environment that nurtures intellectual growth.

The program challenges its students to fulfill their true potential and provides them with an enhanced college experience. Offering both day and evening classes to full-time and part-time students, the program has consistently attracted a mix of recent high school graduates and returning adult students whose diverse experiences enrich classroom discussions and expand the opportunities for learning.

Honors alumni consistently report that the program has prepared them superbly for the demands of baccalaureate and graduate studies. The program offers special transfer advising assistance; graduates have been admitted to some of the nation's most prestigious colleges and universities.

As a comprehensive community college, Suffolk strives to provide a full spectrum of learning opportunities, reflecting the varied needs of county residents. The Honors Program is an important element of that continuum and exemplifies the College's commitment to academic excellence. Students are encouraged to explore the challenges and rewards of honors classes at Suffolk's three campuses.

The Honors Program at Suffolk County Community College has been in existence for ten years; there are approximately 750 students currently enrolled in the program.

Participation Requirements: A minimum of 16 credits in interdisciplinary honors courses and 6 credits in supplementary honors courses satisfies the diverse requirements for the Honors Diploma.

Alternatively, qualified students may enroll in the Honors Certificate of Recognition Sequence as part of their chosen curriculum. High school graduates with a B+ average or better are encouraged to apply. The Honors Recognition Sequence is accomplished by successfully completing a minimum of 12 credits of interdisciplinary honors courses or 8 credits of interdisciplinary courses and 6 credits of supplementary courses.

Students enrolled in the Honors Program are expected to maintain a GPA of at least 3.2 each semester. If a student receives a grade lower than B in an honors course, his/her participation in the program is subject to review. Suffolk County Community College students must maintain a 3.2 GPA to graduate from the program.

Admission Process: Qualified students may enroll in the Honors Diploma Sequence while engaged in a curriculum of their choice. High school graduates with a B+ average or better are encouraged to apply.

Scholarship Availability: The scholarship program is administered under the auspices of the Suffolk County Community College Foundation. Scholarships are made possible through the generosity of various individuals, student organizations, College faculty and staff members, local and community groups, business firms, and by fundraising activities of the Suffolk County Community College Foundation.

Scholarships are available to full-time and part-time freshmen and transfer students in virtually all academic career programs. Awards are based primarily on academic merit, service to the community, and recommendations from teachers, employers, and community leaders. The amounts of the awards range from the cost of books to the cost of full tuition.

To maintain full-time scholarship eligibility for four semesters, recipients must remain enrolled as full-time Honors Program students in good academic standing and maintain a 3.2 GPA. To continue part-time scholarship eligibility for four semesters, recipients must enroll in honors courses three of the four semesters and maintain a 3.2 GPA and good academic standing.

The Campus Context: The Ammerman Campus at Selden encompasses 156 acres and has twelve academic, administrative, and auxiliary buildings. The Western Campus at Brentwood occupies a 207-acre site with eleven academic, administrative, and auxiliary buildings, including a 95,000-square-foot building that houses classrooms, laboratories, the library, and a theater. The Eastern Campus is located on a 192-acre site near Riverhead and contains three academic and two auxiliary buildings. In 1985, the College opened a satellite facility called the TechniCenter, located at 205 Oser Avenue in the Hauppauge Industrial Park. The TechniCenter brings the College to the student. Designed specifically for business and industrial training, it offers many options for both management and labor: credit courses, noncredit courses, and specifically tailored technical training. Degree programs offered include A.A. (five majors), A.A.S. (thirty-eight majors), A.S. (nine majors), and fourteen one-year certificate programs.

Student Body Undergraduate enrollment is 20,745: 40.7 percent men, 59.3 percent women. The minority ethnic distribution of the total undergraduate population is 4 percent African American, 6 percent Hispanic, 1.6 percent Asian American. Sixty-five percent of full-time students and 50 percent of all students (by head count) receive financial aid.

Faculty There are 401 full-time faculty members and 977 adjuncts.

Key Facilities There are 208,000 volumes in the library. The campus has 250 IBMs and fifty Macs available for student use. Special facilities include the Academic Skills Center, ESL Resource Center, Language Lab, Math Learning Center, Reading Center, and Writing Center.

Athletics Intercollegiate athletic programs are offered at the Ammerman and Western campuses. Eastern Campus students may participate at the campus of their choice. At the Ammerman Campus, men may compete in baseball, basketball, bowling, cross-country, golf, lacrosse, soccer, tennis, track and field, and volleyball (club). Women may compete in basketball, bowling, cheerleading, cross-country, equestrian, softball, tennis, track and field, and volleyball. The Western Campus offers athletic competition for men in baseball, basketball, bowling, golf, and soccer, while women may compete in bowling and softball.

Support Services The College is committed to maximizing educational opportunities for students with disabilities by minimizing physical, psychological, and learning barriers. Special counseling is available on each campus to help students achieve academic success through the provision of special services, auxiliary aids, and reasonable program modifications. Examples of services/accommodations include registration and scheduling assistance, use of tape recorders, sign language interpreters, special testing conditions, notetakers, reader services, taped texts, and specialized library equipment.

Tuition: $2180 for state residents, $4360 for nonresidents, per year (1996-97)

Mandatory Fees: $106

Contact: Assistant Dean: M. Cecile Forte, Office of Academic Affairs, 533 College Road, Selden, New York 11784; Telephone: 516-451-4098; Fax: 516-451-4681; E-mail: fortec@sunysuffolk.edu; Web site: http://www.sunysuffolk.edu/

SUSQUEHANNA UNIVERSITY

4 Pr G M Sc* Tr

▼ University Honors Program

The Honors Program at Susquehanna University offers a challenging program of study for the exceptional student interested in a more independent and interdisciplinary approach than that usually offered to an undergraduate. The program is especially well suited to the aggressively curious, active learner who values breadth of study, multiple perspectives, and answers that go beyond the superficial. It has been recognized as a model for other honors programs throughout the country.

Limited to 50 students in each entering class, the program includes a series of special courses and projects throughout all four undergraduate years. Discussion groups, lectures, off-campus visits, and residential programs complement Honors Program courses.

The University's Scholars' House, a small, comfortable residence for students involved in academically challenging projects, serves as the center of many Honors Program activities, including fireside chats, a film series, and practice sessions for the University's College Bowl team. Most, but not all, of the Scholars' House residents are members of the Honors Program. Some of their projects include the establishment of a campus jazz society, the development of a World Wide Web connection for the Scholars' House, an economic and ecological study of the tradeoffs facing the logging industry in Maine, a comparison of Christianity and Buddhism, and a children's book.

As a member of the National Collegiate Honors Council, Susquehanna regularly participates in or hosts special events for honors program students from throughout the Northeast and other regions. Honors students also have access to a variety of special off-campus projects at locations ranging from the Woods Hole Oceanographic Institution in Massachusetts and the United Nations in New York to Pueblo Indian sites in New Mexico.

The first honors class enrolled in 1982. Approximately 150 students are currently enrolled.

Participation Requirements: Participating students take an honors course during three of their first four semesters. The first course, "Thought," focuses on ideas and their expression. "Thought and the Social Sciences" or "Thought and the Natural Sciences" are cross-disciplinary views of the social and natural sciences. "Thought and Civilization" is an interdisciplinary look at literature and cultures. These Thought courses replace required Core courses.

In the sophomore year, honors students write a research-supported essay developing a topic of their choice. This experience offers students an opportunity to work one-on-one with faculty members early in their undergraduate studies.

As juniors and seniors, honors students select 8 semester hours from a series of 300-level interdisciplinary honors seminars that also fulfill the University's Core requirements or that serve as especially interesting and challenging electives. As seniors they also engage in a senior honors seminar that fulfills the Core requirement for a "Futures" course and a senior research project.

Students normally must maintain a cumulative GPA of 3.0 or higher at the end of each semester to remain in the Honors Program. Candidates who successfully complete all the requirements of the Honors Program graduate with University Honors.

Scholarship Availability: Scholarships are held by many students in the University Honors Program, but are not tied to the program in any way. Honors Program enrollees typically qualify for one of the top scholarships awarded by Susquehanna. A description of these scholarships and their value during the 1996-97 academic year follows.

University Assistantships, Susquehanna's most prestigious academic scholarships, are awards of $9000 that include a professional work experience (about 10 hours a week on average) with a member of the University faculty or administrative staff. Recipients typically rank in the top 5 percent of their high school classes and score in the top 10 percent nationally on standardized tests.

The other five scholarships are valued at $7500 annually. Recipients of these scholarships typically rank in the top 10 percent of their high school classes and rank in the top 15 percent nationally on standardized tests. Valedictorian/Salutatorian Scholarships are given to students who rank first or second in their high school classes in a demanding academic program. Degenstein Scholarships, funded by the Charles B. Degenstein Scholars Program, are given to exceptionally able students with preference to those intending to major or minor in programs within Susquehanna's Sigmund Weis School of Business. The Lawrence M. and Louise Kresge Isaacs Endowment for Music provides an award to an outstanding music major on the basis of an audition with the music faculty and high academic achievement. Scholarships for Distinguished Achievement in Science and Mathematics are awarded to students planning majors in the sciences, computer science, or mathematics; recipients are chosen on the basis of outstanding academic achievement. Presidential Scholarships are awarded on a competitive basis to new students who have demonstrated superior academic achievement and personal promise.

The Campus Context: Susquehanna University is organized into three schools: the School of Arts and Sciences, School of Fine Arts and Communications, and Sigmund Weis School of Business. Bachelor of Arts, Bachelor of Science, and Bachelor of Music degrees are offered.

Special care has been taken to maintain the architectural integrity of the campus, especially during recent years of renovation and expansion projects including construction in 1995 of three new residence halls—Shobert Hall, Roberts House, and Isaacs House. The new housing provides a combination of townhouse and apartment-like living spaces for 87 students. Susquehanna is also very proud of its new Broadway-caliber Degenstein Center Theater and museum-quality art gallery. Fisher Science Hall has been featured as a model facility for undergraduate science education by Project Kaleidoscope, a national effort to strengthen undergraduate science and mathematics education supported in part by the National Science Foundation.

The Scholar's House was opened in 1994 for members of the Honors Program and other interested students. Adjacent to the Charles B. Degenstein Campus Center, the newly remodeled residence for 24 students has become a stimulating environment for intellectual camaraderie. In 1996, Susquehanna students celebrated the twentieth anniversary of the nationally recognized Project House System, in which groups of volunteers organized and approved as "project houses" live and work together.

Student Body Undergraduate enrollment is 1,568 full-time, 11 part-time; 47 percent men, 53 percent women. The ethnic distribution is 84 percent white, 2 percent African American, 2 percent Hispanic, 1 percent Asian American, 1 percent other, 10 percent unknown. Approximately 4 percent of students receive merit-based financial aid; approximately 70 percent of the student body receive need-based financial aid. There are four sororities and four fraternities.

Faculty There are a total of 145 faculty members, 105 full-time. Of the 90 percent with terminal degrees, 87 percent have the Ph.D. The student-faculty ratio is about 14:1.

Key Facilities The library houses 229,000 volumes. There are 110 microcomputers available in four computer laboratories. The majority of lab computers are IBM-type, but there is also a small lab with Macs. Thanks to connections in every residence hall room, students have access to the World Wide Web and other Internet functions using Netscape and other browsing software. Students also have access to e-mail both on and off campus and to the library on-line catalog, including First Search, a service that provides access to more than fifty databases on a wide variety of subjects.

Athletics Susquehanna is an NCAA Division III school and a member of the Middle Atlantic Conference. There are twenty-one varsity sports for men and women. Men's teams include baseball, basketball, cross-country, football, golf, indoor track, soccer, swimming, tennis, and track. Women's teams include basketball, cross-country, field hockey, indoor track, lacrosse, soccer, softball, swimming, tennis, track, and volleyball. Rowing, for men and women, is a club sport with a full-time

coach. Other club sports include conditioning, cycling, rugby, indoor soccer, and men's volleyball. Susquehanna also sponsors an active intramural sports program.

Study Abroad Susquehanna strongly encourages students to consider study abroad. There are eleven direct exchange programs including the University of Konstanz (Germany), the University of Copenhagen (Denmark), Senshu University (Japan), and many others available through national clearinghouses. Susquehanna also sponsors a semester in London exclusively for junior business majors. Courses are taught by faculty members from the University's Sigmund Weis School of Business and faculty members from leading London universities. There are also a number of opportunities for internships abroad.

Support Services Disabled students will find that all of Susquehanna's classroom buildings, administration buildings, library, chapel/auditorium, campus center, and gymnasium are wheelchair-accessible, as are several of the residence halls.

Job Opportunities Students are offered a range of work opportunities on campus including work-study, assistantships, and cash jobs. A graduated pay scale rewards increased responsibility for second-, third-, and fourth-year students who return to their previous positions.

Tuition: $17,400 per year (1996-97)

Room and Board: $5080

Mandatory Fees: $290

Contact: Director: Dr. James Sodt, 514 University Avenue, Selinsgrove, Pennsylvania 17870-1001; Telephone: 717-372-4435; Fax: 717-372-2722 (Admissions/Financial Aid); E-mail: sodtj@susqu.edu; Web site: http://www.susqu.edu

Syracuse University

4 Pr G L

▼ Honors Program

The Honors Program is divided into two 2-year sections: General University Honors for students entering the program as freshmen or sophomores and Thesis Project Honors for juniors and seniors. Students may participate in either section or both. A total of 900 students are currently enrolled in the program, which began in 1965.

Participation Requirements: General University Honors provides an exciting start to a student's college career. It enriches the student's education and provides an instant introduction to students who share the desire for a rigorous intellectual experience. Honors students take four special courses in addition to one orientation seminar and two other lower-division seminars over a period of four semesters. The freshman honors seminar is an ongoing orientation to Syracuse University that introduces students to the world of ideas and the many educational opportunities available on campus and in the community at large. This is a course designed to ease the transition from high school to higher education. Students are assigned to a small group that meets weekly with a faculty member to discuss a few time-tested ideas, explore new ways of thinking, examine unorthodox views, and reflect on the purpose and goals of a quality undergraduate education. The seminar provides students with a preview of what the college experience is all about.

Specially designed honors courses are offered in a wide variety of disciplines. Generally, they can be used to satisfy a basic requirement in the student's home college. These courses are quite different from those offered in the regular curriculum. They are smaller, use different texts, and have different assignments. Discussions are usually spirited and the level of student participation is expected to be high.

Two lower-division seminars, usually taken in the sophomore year, are intended to expose students to cultural and civic life in the wider community so that they will have a more informed basis for participation in life. In one semester, students attend the opera, the Syracuse Symphony, the Equity Theater at Syracuse State, and the exhibitions at the Everson Museum of Art. Through background discussions before each event, students understand what they are going to see, and an extensive review afterward heightens their appreciation of the event. The other seminar offers the same experience-based approach to the study of civic life in the local community. Students may explore distinct political practices that are deeply rooted in the unique subcultures within the larger community of Syracuse, such as Hmong refugees, Native Americans, Latino communities, and the Islamic community. In other seminars, classroom discussion of political values combined with volunteer work in community agencies help students focus on the tension between democratic ideals and public realities.

Thesis Project Honors has as its central feature an undergraduate honors thesis project, which allows students opportunities to work intensively with faculty members on original research. Students focus on a single aspect of the major or explore a related issue. The thesis project may be presented in any appropriate form—prose, performance, or multimedia—but must include a written analysis and/or critique. Thesis project research is complemented by advanced, enhanced, and graduate-level course work. Junior and senior honors seminars serve as forums for developing and presenting the honors thesis project. The junior seminars assist students in defining a research design and strategy. The senior honors seminar assists students in refining focus, gathering resources, and completing the research plan as well as preparing for graduate school or job applications and interviews.

A student completing requirements for general University Honors receives a certificate and a notation is recorded on the transcript. Upon fulfillment of the requirements for Thesis Project Honors, honors in the major area is awarded on the diploma.

Admission Process: The average total SAT I score of entering freshmen is approximately 1350 and the high school average is 93 percent. Students entering general University Honors their second or third semesters must have at least a 3.5 GPA. Students must also have a 3.5 GPA to be admitted to Thesis Project Honors.

May 1 is the deadline for applying to the program.

Scholarship Availability: There are no scholarships associated directly with the Honors Program. However, Syracuse University provides a generous merit scholarship program for all qualified students regardless of financial need.

The Campus Context: Syracuse University has eleven undergraduate colleges on campus, including the School of Architecture, the College of Arts and Sciences, the School of Education, the College of Engineering and Computer Science, the College for Human Development, the School of Information Studies, the School of Management, the College of Nursing, the Newhouse School of Public Communications, the School of Social Work, and the College of Visual and Performing Arts. More than 200 degree programs are offered on campus.

Distinguished facilities on campus include the Holden Observatory; the Carrier Dome, the only multipurpose domed stadium on a college campus in the U.S.; the Crouse College Auditorium with a 3,823 pipe Holtcamp organ; the Institute for Sensory Research; Newhouse II, which contains two full-sized television studios, newsroom teaching studio, class studios, and editing and mixing suites; the Arthur Storch Theatre, a 200-seat house for drama; the Schine Student Center; the Bird Laboratory; the Gebbie Clinic with clinical and laboratory suites for hearing and speech pathology; the Science and Technology Center, which is affiliated with the Northeast Parallel Architecture Center; dozens of scientific laboratories containing state-of-the-art equipment, including one of the finest laser spectroscopy laboratories in the world; and the Joe and Emily Lowe Art Gallery.

Student Body Undergraduate enrollment is 10,289; graduate enrollment is 4,430. The student population is 52 percent women. Approximately 19 percent of the students are of ethnic minority groups, and 4 percent are international students. Eighty-two percent of the students receive financial aid. There are twenty-three fraternities and nineteen sororities.

Faculty Of the 1,378 faculty members, 807 are full-time. Eighty-seven percent of full-time faculty members hold terminal degrees. The student-faculty ratio is 12:1.

Key Facilities The library's collections include 2.7 million volumes, 16,400 periodicals and serials, and 3.5 million microforms. Computer facilities include sixteen public computer clusters with 450 machines (50/50 IBM-Macintosh); 750 more computers are available through colleges and departments (70 percent are Macintosh).

Athletics In athletics, all women's and men's varsity teams are NCAA Division I, and many are nationally ranked. Men's sports include basketball, crew, cross-country, football, gymnastics, lacrosse, soccer, swimming and diving, indoor track and field, outdoor track and field, and wrestling. Women's sports are basketball, cross-country, field hockey, lacrosse, crew, soccer, swimming and diving, indoor track and field, outdoor track and field, and volleyball. A member of the Big East Conference, Syracuse University teams are known as the Orangemen and Orangewomen. Sports at Syracuse are not just for the varsity athlete. The campus recreation program, one of the largest in the country, sponsors more than fifty sports on both the intramural and club levels.

Study Abroad Syracuse University Abroad (DIPA, for Division of International Programs Abroad) maintains international sites in Spain, France, Italy, England, Hong Kong, and Zimbabwe. Tuition per semester for Syracuse students studying abroad is the same as on-campus study. Individual financial aid packages pertain to international study, and students may apply for special study-abroad grants.

Support Services Physically disabled students find the campus accessible, and a coordinator of resources is available in the Office of Student Assistance. Learning-disabled students can apply for assistance in the Center for Academic Achievement.

Job Opportunities Between 2,500 and 3,000 students qualify for and receive work-study employment on campus. About the same number of students find non-work-study positions around campus. Many students find part-time jobs in local businesses.

Tuition: $16,710 per year (1996-97)

Room and Board: $7440

Mandatory Fees: $432

Contact: Director: Professor D. Bruce Carter, 306 Bowne Hall, Syracuse, New York 13244-1200; Telephone: 315-443-2759; Fax: 315-443-3235; E-mail: bcarter@psych.syr.edu; Web site: http://sumweb.syr.edu/honors/index/htm

TARLETON STATE UNIVERSITY

4 Pu G S

▼ Honors Degree Program, Presidential Honors Program

The Honors Degree Program offers honors sections of most core curriculum subjects, including English, history, government, chemistry, biology, and speech. Honors classes present students with intellectually challenging material, innovative approaches to subjects, increased opportunities for honing critical-thinking and writing skills, and the opportunity to interact closely with similarly motivated students. Honors classes—depending on the subject—emphasize discussion and student participation, primary sources and monographs over textbooks, textbooks that emphasize critical thinking over textbooks that emphasize feedback of information, special lab equipment that would not be available to most science students until graduate school, student projects and research, and essay exams over multiple choice tests.

In addition to taking honors sections of the core curriculum courses, students who have completed at least four of these basic honors courses may, with the permission of the department head and the director of the Honors Degree Program, take one upper-level special problems course for honors credit. Plans are in progress for additional honors classes in several areas, as well as an upper-level departmental component.

The 7-year-old program currently enrolls 80 to 100 students each semester in honors classes.

The Presidential Honors Program at Tarleton State University is made up of a select group of students chosen as entering freshmen on the basis of demonstrated excellence in academics as well as leadership, service, and a capacity for intellectual inquiry. The program looks for highly motivated students with a wide range of interests who have a strong desire to further their education—not only toward the end of job security or professional advancement, but with the goals of increasing their knowledge and benefiting their society. Presidential Honors Scholars participate in intellectual and creative activities, both directed and independent.

The 15-year-old program currently enrolls approximately 30 students, with 10 admitted each fall.

Participation Requirements (Honors Degree Program): All Tarleton students who have a GPA of at least 3.0 are eligible for honors classes. Students with a lower GPA may register for an honors class with the permission of the instructor. Any student who completes 18 or more hours of such classes with a minimum 3.0 GPA in honors classes and overall will receive recognition as an Honors Degree Program graduate. Graduation from the Honors Degree Program is indicated on the student's transcript.

Participation Requirements (Presidential Honors Program): In the first two years, students take an annual Honors Seminar, a specially designed course open only to them. Seminar topics have focused recently on a variety of subjects—Issues in Education; Political Leadership; the Development of Scientific Thought; and Philosophy, Sophistry and Democracy. Students also enroll in at least 9 hours of Tarleton's regularly scheduled honors classes offered in the Honors Degree Program, and they must complete a 3-hour senior independent research project. Presidential Honors Scholars must have at least a 3.4 cumulative GPA and must complete a minimum of 15 hours of solid academic courses every semester. PHP students have the opportunity to attend a professional conference in their major field of study. They also provide leadership and service to the University and the community. Graduation from the program is indicated on the student's diploma.

Scholarship Availability: While there is no scholarship directly associated with the Honors Degree Program, students interested in scholarships should pursue the Presidential Honors Program described above.

Students admitted to the Presidential Honors Program receive an annual scholarship of $2500 and priority in dormitory assignments, registration, and other areas of campus life. Presidential Honors Scholars are free to pursue any major course of study offered at Tarleton. The scholarship is renewable for four years, as long as the student meets required standards. Recipients are required to participate in the Honors Degree Program (see above) and maintain a 3.4 GPA in each long semester and an 3.0 overall GPA.

The Campus Context: Tarleton State University is composed of several colleges: Arts and Sciences, Agriculture and Technology, Education and Fine Arts, Business Administration, and Graduate Studies.

Student Body The undergraduate enrollment is 6,369: 47.48 percent men and 52.52 percent women. The ethnic distribution of students is 0.71 percent American Indian/Native Alaskan, 0.57 percent Asian/Pacific Islander, 2.81 percent black, 4.55 percent Mexican American, 91.21 percent white. There are 10 international students. Seventy percent of the students receive some form of financial aid. Students participate in five sororities and six fraternities.

Faculty There are more than 220 faculty members and the student-faculty ratio is 20:1.

Key Facilities The library houses 285,000 volumes. There are numerous computer labs on the campus.

Athletics In athletics, Tarleton State is in NCAA Division II, Lonestar Conference.

Study Abroad Some study abroad opportunities are available.

Support Services Disabled students will find wheelchair access to all buildings, a Teaching and Learning Center with special facilities and programs for disabled students, and an in-house training and research facility for exercise physiology for individuals with neurological disabilities. The Disabilities Certification Officer is the Associate Vice President for Academic Affairs.

Job Opportunities Work opportunities on campus include work-study, regular student employment, and graduate assistantships.

Tuition: $960 for state residents, $7380 for nonresidents, per year (1996-97)

Room and Board: $2324 minimum

Mandatory Fees: $978

Contact: Director: Dr. Craig Clifford, Box 0545, Stephenville, Texas 76402; Telephone: 817-968-9423; E-mail: cliffor@vms.tarleton.edu

TEMPLE UNIVERSITY

4 Pu G M Sc Tr

▼ **Temple University Honors Program**

The Temple University Honors Program began as the College of Arts and Sciences Honors Program in 1967. In 1986, the program was expanded to include outstanding students enrolled in all thirteen schools and colleges at the University. The honors program offers these academically talented, motivated, and interested students a place of their own in the context of a major research university.

The heart of the program is a set of courses open only to honors students and typically taught by specially selected, full-time faculty members, many of whom have won the Temple University Great Teacher Award. The program features small classes of about 20 students and encourages a lively, seminar-style classroom atmosphere. Students (representing nearly every major in the university) usually complete university CORE requirements through their honors courses. In addition, they take honors lower- and upper-level electives, some created specifically for the program. They may also participate in departmental honors programs. University honors students enrolled in the School of Business Management participate concurrently in SBM Honors, a four-year program.

The University Honors Program, in collaboration with the Honors Student Council, arranges special lectures, poetry readings, political panels, career talks, and field trips. The students publish a newsletter, manage a Web site, own an honors listserv, and spend time in the honors lounge, where computers and companionship are available. They are eligible to live on the honors floor in the residence halls, where an honors student is the resident assistant.

The program is jointly administered by a physics professor and a religionist who serve as academic advisers for honors students. Working closely with departmental advisers, they help students with course selection, decisions about majors, career choices, scholarship and graduate school applications, and job opportunities and internships. The staff also includes 2 graduate students and 2 undergraduate honors students.

Participation Requirements: Honors students receive an Honors Certificate after having passed eight honors courses (six for transfer students), usually after about two years. Students are encouraged to continue taking appropriate honors courses throughout their undergraduate studies. They must maintain a 3.0 GPA overall. Successful completion of the Honors Program is recorded on the student's transcript.

Admission Process: During the normal application process to the University, all students are screened for honors; no separate application is required. Selection criteria include high school credentials, application essay, recommendations, and SAT I scores. About 200 freshmen annually are accepted; most are offered financial aid based on merit and/or need. Transfer students and freshmen or sophomores already at Temple may also be admitted if their college performance is excellent.

The Campus Context: Temple University was founded in 1884 by Russell Conwell, whose mission was to bring higher education to the poor. Temple has grown into a major Research I university. Its main campus is situated on 76 acres in Philadelphia, Pennsylvania. More than 100 undergraduate degree programs are offered in the College of Allied Health Professions; the Tyler School of Art; the College of Arts and Sciences; the School of Business and Management; the School of Communications and Theater; the College of Education; the College of Engineering; the College of Health, Physical Education, Recreation and Dance; the Esther Boyer College of Music; the School of Pharmacy; the School of Social Administration; the Architecture Program; and the Department of Landscape Architecture and Horticulture. There are 107 undergraduate programs of study, eighty-seven master's programs, and forty-nine doctoral programs.

Student Body Temple's enrollment is 27,000, including 18,000 undergraduates of great ethnic diversity; 52 percent are women, 81 percent are state residents, and 2 percent are international students.

Faculty Of the 2,650 faculty members, 1,650 are full-time; 86 percent have terminal degrees. The undergraduate student-faculty ratio is 13:1.

Key Facilities The library houses 2.1 million volumes, 15,600 periodicals, and 70 CD-ROMs. There are 2,000 computers for student use.

Athletics In athletics, Temple is a member of NCAA Division I in all sports except men's football (Division I-A). Intercollegiate sports are men's baseball, football, golf, and tennis; women's fencing, field hockey, lacrosse, softball, and volleyball; and basketball, crew, gymnastics, soccer, and track and field for both men and women. Intramural sports are basketball, bowling, football, rugby, soccer, softball, tennis, and volleyball.

Study Abroad Study abroad is available at Temple's campuses in Rome and Tokyo; there are also exchange programs with several universities in Germany, Britain, France, and Puerto Rico.

Support Services The University has excellent facilities for disabled students.

Job Opportunities There are 610 part-time jobs available on campus.

Tuition: $5628 for state residents, $10,510 for nonresidents, per year (1996-97)

Room and Board: $5712

Mandatory Fees: $220

Contact: Directors: Dr. Dieter Forster and Dr. Ruth Tonner Ost, 1301 Cecil B. Moore Avenue, Philadelphia, Pennsylvania 19122-6091; Telephone: 215-204-7573; Fax: 215-204-6356; E-mail: dieter@vm.temple.edu or rost@vm.temple.edu; Web site: http://www.temple.edu/honors

TENNESSEE TECHNOLOGICAL UNIVERSITY

4 Pu G M Sc Tr

▼ Honors Program

One of the prime purposes of the Honors Program is to stimulate a joy of learning in gifted scholars that requires attention to individual needs, problems, and interests. To enable the program to fulfill this purpose, the University has undertaken a commitment to fund the Honors Program on a basis other than the production of student credit hours. Therefore, honors sections will be smaller than most corresponding regular sections of the same courses. This should facilitate greater exchange between faculty and students and among students, thus encouraging a more thorough understanding of the subject matter and greater attention to the individual student.

Since the classes are smaller and most of the students have a background in the material, professors are able to cover more material than in the regular sections or can go into more depth and detail on the same material. A major reason for participation in honors work from the point of view of the student is the challenge and excitement of being in an academic situation with others of similar ability. This interchange among students is at least as important as the classroom experiences provided. Peer group pressures influence to a large extent whether an individual student will strive to do his or her best and gain all he or she can from an undergraduate education, and honors classes create a highly motivated peer group.

In addition to the academic services provided to the University, the HP sponsors various events that are open both to the campus and the surrounding community. Honors students often find close friends within their courses and engage in fun extracurricular activities such as hiking in the many nearby natural areas. When classes get hectic, there is always the Friday night jam session in the Honors Center or the Tuesday Trip to Subway for blowing off some steam. There are 253 full members of the program. According to the Honors Charter, membership cannot exceed 5 percent of the full-time enrollment at Tennessee Tech.

Participation Requirements: There are three categories of membership in the Honors Program. A full member has a 3.5 cumulative QPA (except first-semester members who may drop to a 3.1) and is making progress toward graduation with honors. An associate member is one who has formally been admitted to the Honors Program but whose QPA is temporarily lower than 3.5 but remains at least 3.1. He or she must continue to be an active participant in the program and continue to take honors courses. An affiliate member is a student who enrolls in one or more honors courses but who has not been admitted to full membership.

Honors 101, a one-semester-hour honors seminar, is required of all students who are admitted as full members of the program. The purpose of the course is to create a sense of appreciation for the contributions an honors education can give to students willing to work at an honors level and to give better guidance to these students in their academic programs as they relate to the general honors requirements.

Nondepartmental courses designated as Honors Colloquia (Honors 401) have been established, with at least one such colloquium offered each semester during the regular academic year. These courses, under the direction of members of the honors faculty, investigate topics chosen by the Honors Council to appeal to honors students from a wide variety of interests and majors, and frequently involve faculty from many different departments. While not necessarily interdisciplinary, all colloquium topics are approached from a broad viewpoint rather than being highly specialized studies in a particular field. In no case does the subject matter of a colloquium exactly duplicate that of a course already taught elsewhere in the University. The colloquium presents an opportunity to explore new fields and new relationships as the interests of the honors students require.

An independent studies course designated Honors 402 is offered by the Honors Program to allow a student in collaboration with a faculty member to explore an area of interest not ordinarily covered in regular classes. The student and the professor who consents to direct the project will jointly submit a proposal for the independent study to the Honors Director for approval.

In addition to all relevant University, college, and departmental requirements of the student's chosen curriculum, to graduate *in cursu honorum* the student must complete the following requirements: 1) successful completion of Honors 101 (1 semester hour); 2) successful completion of at least two honors colloquia (Honors 401), or one colloquium and one independent studies (Honors 402); 3) successful completion of at least 15 additional semester hours in honors courses in at least three different disciplines; and 4) achievement of a minimum cumulative QPA of 3.5.

Admission Process: Incoming freshmen must have an ACT composite 26 or higher or the SAT I equivalent of 1170. These students fill out an application and become full members upon the approval of the Honors Director. As full members, they receive priority registration and a Big Sibling (an established honors student) who serves as their mentor. Transfer students, or students enrolled at Tech more than one semester, may enter the Honors Program by completing one honors course with a cumulative QPA of 3.5 or higher.

Scholarship Availability: The TTU Honors Program does not provide actual funds to students as scholarships. However, due to an agreement with the Tennessee Board of Regents, the Honors Program provides Enrichment Options to students in place of the work requirements attached to all scholarships given through the University. In place of the 75 hours of work Financial Aid attaches to each scholarship, full members of the Honors Program can substitute other activities such as the Little Sibling Program, where freshmen and established students work and play with one another; service activities; work with a mentoring professor on research or a special project; presentations (both attending and giving); workshops; attending state, regional, and national honors conferences (TTU routinely sends a large delegation); participating in campus clubs and/or interest groups; playing intramural sports; and many other intellectual and social activities.

The Campus Context: The 235-acre main campus of Tennessee Technological University is located on Interstate 40,

approximately 75 and 100 miles from Nashville and Knoxville, respectively. Cookeville has a population of more than 25,000 and is located on Tennessee's Highland Rim. Because of its strategic location, there are many parks and nature areas within short driving distance. The campus is compact, and everything is within easy walking distance. Students and faculty members enjoy the second-lowest crime rate among the state's major colleges and universities.

TTU, part of the Tennessee Board of Regents, is a four-year public coeducational university consisting of the following schools and colleges: Colleges of Agriculture and Home Economics (5 percent of enrollment), Arts and Sciences (21 percent), Business Administration (16 percent), Education (20 percent), Engineering (25 percent), the School of Nursing (4 percent), and the School of Graduate Studies. Tech is accredited by nine agencies, including the Southern Association of Colleges and Schools. Thirty-eight undergraduate majors are offered, with fifty-four options leading to the B.S. degree and three leading to the B.A. degree. Eight graduate programs lead to the M.S., seventeen to the M.A., one to the M.B.A, sixteen to the Ed.S., and one to the Ph.D. in engineering.

TTU is the only state institution with three engineering-related Centers of Excellence: the Center for Electric Power; the Center for the Management, Utilization and Protection of Water Resources; and the Center for Manufacturing Research and Technology Utilization.

TTU has two Chairs of Excellence in the College of Business Administration: the J.E. Owen Chair of Management Information Systems and the William Eugene Mayberry Chair of Production and Operations Management.

Noteworthy facilities include the Counseling Center, Career Services, Women's Center, University Recreation & Fitness Center, and the Joe L. Evins Craft Center.

Student Body The total enrollment is 8,228, with full-time students numbering 7,357. The population comes from ninety-four of Tennessee's ninety-five counties, forty-one other states, and forty-five other countries. Fifty-three percent are men, 47 percent women; 93 percent are white, 3 percent African American, and 2 percent Asian American or Pacific Islander. Sixty-six percent of the students receive financial aid (approximately $22 million is administered annually). There are six sororities, sixteen social fraternities, and chapters of Omega Phi Alpha and Alpha Phi Omega.

Faculty There are 379 faculty members, 77 percent with doctoral degrees. The student-faculty ratio is 12:1 in Honors, 25:1 campuswide.

Key Facilities The 521,900-volume library houses 288,500 books, 102,000 periodicals, and 131,000 U.S. government publications. There are 160 computers located in labs and VAX terminals in dormitories.

Athletics TTU is a member of NCAA Division I and the Ohio Valley Conference. It has thirteen intercollegiate teams, including football, basketball, baseball, and rugby (both men's and women's). The women's basketball team has won 7 OVC championships, including the All Sports Trophy—second place in 1993, first in 1990.

Job Opportunities Students will find work on campus in the Computer Center Helpdesk, Food Services, Campus Bookstore, and the Centers of Excellence; many other campus departments look to the student body for employees.

Tuition: None for state residents, $4336 for nonresidents, per year (1996-97)

Room and Board: $3720

Mandatory Fees: $1920

Contact: Director: Dr. Connie Hood, Box 5124, TJ Farr 204, Cookeville, Tennessee 38505; Associate Director: Dr. Mary Pashley; Telephone: 615-372-3797; E-mail: honors@tntech.edu

TEXAS A&M UNIVERSITY

4 Pu G C D L Sc Tr

▼ University Honors Programs

The University Honors Program at Texas A&M University offers special opportunities for high-achieving students to pursue academic work that challenges their interests and abilities. The program is campuswide, encompassing all undergraduate colleges within the University. As a result, honors students have access to the entire spectrum of educational resources available at Texas A&M. Honors courses and individualized research programs bring together outstanding students and faculty members in an environment designed to encourage initiative, creativity, and independent thinking.

Taught by some of the University's most distinguished faculty members, honors classes are kept small. Honors students have the opportunity to work one-on-one with leading professors and to receive individual attention and special services typically available only on smaller campuses. At the same time, students enjoy the resources of one of the nation's major research universities, including state-of-the-art laboratory, library, and computing facilities. It is no surprise that in 1996 *U.S. News & World Report* ranked Texas A&M University as second in terms of educational value in the nation among public institutions.

Honors students at Texas A&M pursue regular majors in any one of the 150 degree plans available to undergraduates through the College of Liberal Arts, Geosciences and Maritime Studies, Agriculture and Life Sciences, Architecture, Education, Veterinary Medicine, the College and Graduate School of Business, and Look College of Engineering. Students customize their honors curriculum by choosing from the over 300 honors course sections a year, selecting honors studies in their core curriculum requirements and/or within their disciplines. With the help of honors advisers, they are encouraged to pursue honors sequences that may be departmental, college-level, or University-level.

The University Honors Program, in conjunction with its scholarship program, attracts successful, confident, and motivated students from across the nation. Texas A&M is among the top five institutions enrolling National Merit Scholars and among the top twenty in the enrollment of National Achievement Scholars. Scholarships are for students with a proven academic record who also show promise of leadership. Scholarship winners have the option to be placed in the Freshman Honors Hall, a leadership laboratory that trains bright young people to become active participants in the University community. The Honors Hall often receives the distinction of Hall of the Year for its strong commitment to the University community, and its residents emerge consistently as student leaders across the campus.

Honors students receive multiple services from the Honors Program Office: a special newsletter, freshman college night gatherings, advising on national scholarship competitions, and help in accessing the resources of the University and beyond.

There are currently 3,000 students enrolled in the program.

Participation Requirements: While participation is flexible, students may only receive University-level honors graduation designation on the transcript by completing the following requirements: 36 honors hours over a defined distribution requirement for University Honors; 22 honors hours across the core curriculum for Foundation Honors; or 9 honors hours and a senior thesis for University Undergraduate Research Fellows distinction. Students completing departmental or collegiate honors tracks receive an Honors Certificate from the corresponding unit.

Admission Process: No application is necessary to participate in the Honors Program. Incoming freshmen with a minimum 1250 on the SAT (28 ACT) and who graduated in the top 10 percent of the class are automatically admitted to honors study if they wish. Thereafter, any student who maintains a 3.4 cumulative GPA may take honors courses. Transfer students are admitted on a case by case basis, usually with a 3.5 GPA. Students are free to take as few or as many honors courses as they wish.

Scholarship Availability: The Office of Honors Programs and Academic Scholarships also is responsible for the selection and administration of all the major four-year academic scholarships. Each spring the office makes about a thousand award offers to students with exemplary academic records and a proven record of leadership and community involvement. The average SAT I score of students receiving the top scholarship award is 1430. The Texas A&M Scholarships are for $2500 or $3000 a year and are renewable for four years by meeting specific renewal criteria. Texas A&M University also sponsors any National Merit Finalist with a scholarship through the National Merit Corporation. There are also scholarships for currently enrolled honors students. To encourage study abroad among the honors community, a $1000 award is offered to students who wish to take part in a Texas A&M-sponsored study abroad program. An additional incentive scholarship program rewards scholarship students after their freshman year to become University Scholars. As ambassadors of the University, University Scholars will have distinguished themselves on campus during their first year with their academic and leadership record. Currently enrolled students who are not on scholarship may compete for one-year scholarship awards of $1000.

The Campus Context: The 5,000-acre campus of Texas A&M University is located in the Bryan/College Station area, a couple of hours' drive from Dallas, Houston, San Antonio, and Austin. Texas A&M University is a land-grant, sea-grant, and space-grant university and is the flagship of the Texas A&M University System. Ten colleges make up the main campus at College Station: Liberal Arts, Geosciences and Maritime Studies, Agriculture and Life Sciences, Architecture, Education, Medicine, Veterinary Medicine, the College and Graduate School of Business, and Look College of Engineering. The University offers 151 undergraduate degree programs.

Among distinguished facilities on campus are the George Bush School of Government and Public Policy, the George Bush Presidential Library, the World Shakespeare Bibliography, a cyclotron, the Texas Transportation Institute, the Nautical Archaeology Program, and the Institute of Biosciences and Technology.

Student Body Approximately 33,000 undergraduates comprise 80 percent of the total enrollment at the University. The ethnic makeup is approximately 3 percent Asian American, 5 percent African American, 15 percent Hispanic, and 76 percent white. The student body is typically of traditional college age with 1 percent nontraditional students and is evenly divided between men and women. Ninety-two percent are full-time students. Half of the students enrolled ranked in the top 10 percent of their high school graduating class, and the mean composite SAT I score was 1174. TAMU has the fifth-largest endowment per student in the nation among public institutions. Over 60 percent of the freshman class usually receives some type of financial aid.

Faculty There are 2,410 full time faculty members, 98 percent with terminal degrees. The student-faculty ratio is 20:1.

Key Facilities The library houses 2.1 million volumes and 3.6 million microforms. There are 15,000 computers connected to the campus network.

Athletics Texas A&M University is a member of the new Big 12 Conference. Within that alliance approximately 475 TAMU student-athletes carry the Aggie banner into competition in ten sports, all at the NCAA Division I level. For the academic year of 1995–96, Texas A&M ranked sixteenth nationally in the Sears Cup ratings, the annual review of successful intercollegiate athletic programs sponsored by *USA Today* and Sears, Roebuck Corporation. Highlights of the Aggie athletic facilities are 72,000-seat Kyle Field, a new student recreation center that includes a state-of-the-art natatorium, and the soon-to-

be-completed 12,500-seat Reed Arena. While athletic endeavors and facilities are the primary focus of most of the Department of Athletics, Texas A&M's Center for Athletic Academic Affairs has been recognized as providing one of the most comprehensive and successful academic support programs in the country.

Study Abroad There are multiple semester and summer study abroad programs available to students in all majors. Each summer alone, there are ten to fifteen programs that take Aggies around the world, with special concentration in Texas A&M's areas of geographic priority: Mexico and Latin America, Europe, and Pacific Asia. Texas A&M has two study-abroad centers, one in Castiglion Fiorentino, Italy, and one in Mexico City.

Tuition: $1024 for state residents, $7872 for nonresidents, per year (1996-97)

Room and Board: $2496

Mandatory Fees: $1464

Contact: Interim Executive Director: Dr. Susanna Finnell, 101 Academic Building, College Station, Texas 77843-4233; Telephone: 409-845-6774; Fax: 409-845-0300; E-mail: sfinnell@tamu.edu; Web site: http://http.tamu.edu:8000/~honors/

TEXAS CHRISTIAN UNIVERSITY

4 Pr G M Tr

▼ Honors Program

At the present time, the Honors Program membership numbers approximately 370 from an undergraduate student body of 5,900.

The Honors Council is the Honors Program's primary governing body. It develops program goals and philosophies and approves new honors courses. The council is an official University committee consisting of both faculty members and honors students. The Honors Week Committee is also a University committee consisting of both professors and students. It plans and supervises the activities of Honors Week. The Honors Cabinet is the student governing body of the Honors Program. It serves as an advisory body to the Director by addressing student concerns about program policy, classes, and activities.

One of the Cabinet's primary goals is to build a sense of community in the Honors Program. Cabinet members plan both academic and social extracurricular activities such as the Fall Escape, firesides, trips to museums and plays, and dinners, as well as other activities designed to provide opportunities for students and professors to get to know one another. Cabinet members elect the Cabinet Chair, Vice-Chair, and Secretary at their first meeting in January. The Chair is an ex officio member of the Honors Council and the Honors Week Committee and also serves on Intercom, a committee of TCU student leaders.

Participation Requirements: Students in the Honors Program must remain in good academic standing by meeting certain grade requirements and fulfilling honors curriculum requirements. Freshmen and sophomores are expected to participate in at least one honors class each semester until they have fulfilled the Lower Division honors requirements. They must, however, complete these requirements no later than the end of their sophomore year. Continuance in the program past the freshman year requires a cumulative TCU GPA of 3.0; to continue past the sophomore year requires a cumulative TCU GPA of 3.4. After completing the Lower Division honors requirements, juniors and seniors are eligible to engage in Departmental and University Honors courses. Honors degrees are conferred upon Honors Program graduates who complete the Lower Division requirements, meet the specific Departmental and/or University Honors criteria, achieve an overall TCU and cumulative GPA of 3.5 or higher, and complete at least 60 credit hours at TCU exclusive of credit by examination.

During their freshman and sophomore years, honors students must complete either the Honors Intellectual Traditions Track or the Honors Sections Track to fulfill the Lower Division requirements. Both tracks emphasize the history of Western civilization and are comprised of 15 credit hours.

The Honors Intellectual Traditions Track requires an Honors Freshman Seminar (or another 3-hour honors class) in the first semester of the freshman year, three semesters (9 hours) of Honors Intellectual Traditions (HHIT 1113, 2123, 2133), and an additional honors class (3 hours) of the student's choice. The HHIT sequence explores interrelationships among history, religion, literature, philosophy, and art from the ancient Greek, Hebrew, and Roman worlds through the twentieth century. The Honors Sections Track requires 15 hours of courses, consisting of 6 hours of History of Civilization (HIST 2003, 2013) plus 9 hours of honors classes. The 9 hours of honors classes are chosen from specially designated honors sections of UCR courses offered each semester.

Students who complete the Lower Division honors curriculum requirements and achieve a cumulative GPA of 3.4 by the end of their sophomore year are invited to begin work toward one or both tracks for graduation with honors. The distinctions of University Honors and Departmental Honors are an official part of the student's degree and are listed on the student's academic transcript. University Honors are awarded to students who complete four Honors Colloquia (The Nature of Society, On Human Nature, The Nature of Values, and The Nature of the Universe or Origins). Additionally, students must show evidence of proficiency in a foreign language at the sophomore level either through completion of 6 hours of 2000-level foreign language courses or through credit by examination.

Departmental Honors are awarded to students who engage in honors courses involving significant research in their major. Requirements typically consist of a junior-level seminar and a Senior Honors Project. Since these are research courses, their descriptions are intentionally broad. Although the form of a project is not restricted, and may include compositions, exhibits, or performances, the project must culminate in a document that is housed in the Special Collections Department of the Mary Couts Burnett Library, with its 1.7 million volumes.

Admission Process: Admission to the TCU Honors Program, founded in 1962, is by invitation and is separate from admission to the University. Entering freshmen are invited to join on the basis of criteria set each year by the Director and the Honors Council. Generally speaking, these include both SAT I/ACT scores and graduating rank in class. The goal of the invitational criteria is to produce a program membership of the top 10 to 12 percent of the students entering TCU each fall. Since intellectual motivation is a significant factor in determining academic success, those who fall slightly short of test score criteria, but who wish to undertake the challenge, may be admitted at the discretion of the Honors Program Director. Additionally, freshmen achieving at least a 3.4 GPA at the end of the fall semester are eligible to join the program.

Scholarship Availability: Merit-based scholarships range in value from $1500 per semester to forty-two full-tuition scholarships.

The Campus Context: Texas Christian University, founded in 1873 as AddRan Male and Female College, has five undergraduate colleges, including the AddRan College of Arts and Sciences, Harris College of Nursing, the College of Fine Arts and Communications, the School of Education, and the M. J. Neeley School of Business.

Student Body There are approximately 5,900 students currently enrolled, 41 percent men and 59 percent women. The ethnic distribution of the student body is as follows: African American, 4.5 percent; American Indian, 0.5 percent; Asian American, 2.3 percent; Hispanic, 5.8 percent; Anglo American, 78.5 percent; and unknown, 4.1 percent. There are more than 300 international students enrolled. Of the TCU student body, 52.2 percent live on campus while 47.8 percent prefer to live off campus. Fifty-five percent of the student body receives some type of financial aid. TCU houses nine social fraternities and nine social sororities, as well as numerous service fraternities and honorary societies, including Phi Beta Kappa, Mortar Board, Golden Key National Honor Society, and Alpha Lambda Delta.

Faculty The student-faculty ratio is 15:1, with a faculty of 350, including 338 full-time professors, 93 percent of whom have terminal degrees.

Key Facilities Honors housing is currently available on campus.

Job Opportunities There is a wide range of work opportunities on campus.

Tuition: $9420 per year (1996-97)

Room and Board: $3800

Mandatory Fees: $1090

Contact: Director: Dr. Kathryne S. McDorman, TCU Box 297022, Fort Worth, Texas 76129; Telephone: 817-921-7125; Fax: 817-921-7333; E-mail: atrinkle@gamma.is.tcu.edu; Web site: http://www.tcu.edu

TEXAS LUTHERAN UNIVERSITY

4 Pr G S Sc Tr

▼ Scholars Program

To become a member of the Texas Lutheran Scholars Program is to become a part of a group of about 60 TLU students who have been selected because of their superior academic achievement (GPA above 3.4). Students are chosen at the end of their freshman or sophomore year, have new opportunities for liberal learning beyond the general requirements of students, and are permitted greater flexibility in curriculum planning. Academic requirements for Scholars are meant to encourage breadth as well as depth of study, interdisciplinary understanding, and the challenge appropriate to high academic standing.

Scholar seminars and the directed readings course provide Scholars the opportunity to work closely with their professors and with students who are their intellectual peers. Scholars have the option of a senior honors thesis or performance project to fulfill their honors course requirement; this may be coordinated with one's departmental senior seminar. Scholars can even write their own curriculum if they choose to. Additional benefits of Scholars Program membership include reductions in costs of tickets to cultural events on campus and in the surrounding region. The Scholars Study Grant program provides research and special project funds for Scholars involved in independent study courses or other research. Informal forums for discussion of student/academic issues or for talking with special guest speakers enhance lunch or supper get-togethers.

In existence for more than twenty years, the program now enrolls 71 students.

Participation Requirements: Scholars at Texas Lutheran University must fulfill the University's 124-credit hour requirement for graduation as well as the associated 30 upper-division hour requirement. In addition, Scholars must complete the general education core courses, GEC 131-132 and GEC 134, or be exempted from the former by advanced placement examination. Scholars applicants are expected to have completed this requirement by the time of application to the program.

Unique to Scholars is the requirement of 12 upper-division hours in the subject areas, although Scholars are required to take fewer total hours here. Except for theology (where the 6-hour requirement still holds), Scholars need take only a minimum of 3 hours in each of the other seven subject areas, but four courses must be taken at the junior or senior level.

The honors courses are designed especially for Texas Lutheran University Scholars and only Scholars can register for them. These courses were created to provide Scholars with the kind of intellectual discussions appropriate to their level of academic ability; the seminars are generally interdisciplinary in nature. All Scholars must fulfill 4 to 6 hours of honors course work to graduate as Scholars. Courses include a senior-level directed readings course and a sophomore-level course that focuses on arts and ideas.

Scholars must maintain a 3.0 GPA. The deadline for applying to the program is April 1.

The Campus Context: Texas Lutheran University is located in Seguin, Texas; the campus is 160 acres and is roughly 35 miles from San Antonio. Texas Lutheran has celebrated its 104th year of service to higher education. Texas Lutheran gained college status in 1932; as of August 1996 Texas Lutheran College became Texas Lutheran University. Texas Lutheran is affiliated with the Evangelical Lutheran Church in America. The University offers twenty-seven majors and nine preprofessional programs. Bachelor of Arts, Bachelor of Science, and Bachelor of Business Administration degrees are conferred. In the center of the campus is the Chapel of the Abiding Presence.

In addition, Jackson Auditorium, which seats 1,100 people, is an exciting center for cultural events, and Hein dining hall provides both indoor and outdoor ambiance for all meals. There is also the Alumni Student Center (ASC), which is the home of many of the organizations on campus, as well as mailboxes, a bookstore, and a snack bar. Other focal points on campus are the Jesse H. Jones Physical Education Center, home to the Texas Lutheran Bulldogs, and the Johnson Health Center. Moody Science has been renovated and a new section of the Krost Building was added in the spring of 1996.

Student Body The student population is 1,248, including the 241 students at Randolph Air Force Base and 16 students enrolled at Guadalupe Valley Hospital. Gender distribution is 38 percent men, 62 percent women. Ethnic distribution is 75.2 percent white, 14.0 percent Hispanic, 4.5 percent international, 2.9 percent African American, 1.7 percent Asian American, 0.6 percent Native American. Sixty-six percent of full-time students live in College housing.

Ninety percent of students receive financial aid. No student pays the full cost of his/her education. Earnings from a substantial endowment coupled with generous gifts help reduce the expenses so that charges assessed to students represent only about 75 percent of the cost of their schooling. There are four social fraternities and four social sororities, one service fraternity and one service sorority, and one honor fraternity and one honor sorority.

Faculty The total number of faculty members is 94; 63 are full-time. Sixty-eight percent of the faculty members have terminal degrees. The student-faculty ratio is 14:1, and the average freshman class size is 30 students.

Key Facilities The library houses 141,000 volumes. In addition, an on-line search system and resources of over 200,000 volumes in the Council of Research are available. Texas Lutheran has a computer lab open to all students throughout the week, complete with 386, 486, and Pentium IBM-compatible PCs as well as Macintosh computers.

Athletics Intercollegiate athletics for men include soccer, tennis, basketball, golf, and baseball. Intercollegiate athletics for women include soccer, tennis, volleyball, basketball, and fast-pitch softball. Texas Lutheran is a member of the National

Association of Intercollegiate Athletics (NAIA) and the Heart of Texas Conference. The campus also has intramural softball, football, basketball, and volleyball, all of which are coed.

Support Services Texas Lutheran provides a limited number of reserved parking spaces throughout the campus for handicapped students. Most classroom buildings, residence halls, and administrative buildings, as well as the library, have access ramps, and some have elevators.

Job Opportunities Part-time campus jobs are available to students who are in good academic standing. Preference is given to students with financial need, but particular job skills and departmental referral occasionally take precedence. Normally students work 6 to 10 hours per week.

Tuition: $10,300 per year (1997-98)

Room and Board: $3772

Mandatory Fees: $70

Contact: Director: Dr. Annette Citzler, Seguin, Texas 78155; Telephone: 210-372-6072; Fax: 210-372-8096

TEXAS TECH UNIVERSITY

4 Pu G M Sc Tr

▼ Honors Program

Plato wrote, "The unexamined life is not worth living." The Texas Tech Honors Program is dedicated to examining life and society in a search for truth through unusual classes, challenging reading, and stimulating instruction. Emphasis is placed on discovery and analysis: *on learning to think.* In small classes, students exchange views with each other and their professors. In reading primary sources, students encounter the great minds of the past and present. Students are encouraged to think for themselves and to prepare themselves for a lifetime of self-education.

One of the unique features of the Texas Tech Honors Program is its extensive student involvement. Students sit on committees, engage in recruiting, help make decisions on course content and textbooks, and evaluate their faculty members. Honors students are members of their own student organization, Eta Omicron Nu, which publishes *Elysium,* a literary and artistic journal. Members of Eta Omicron Nu contribute to *HON,* a newsletter, and sponsor an annual awards banquet as a part of their activities. Honors students also represent the University at national and regional honors conventions.

Most entering freshmen choose honors courses that fulfill University general education requirements in such areas as English, American history, and political science. Honors also offers a variety of courses that satisfy college and departmental requirements.

The seminars examine, in great detail, a variety of subjects. Seminars are both theoretical and practical, crossing the boundaries that often divide areas of specialization. Seminars seek to help one think conceptually and imaginatively. Honors seminars are offered in humanities, fine arts, the sciences, and social science on a rotating basis. The topics and instructors for these seminars are selected in a process that features student involvement. Classes of this kind are offered in most of the University's colleges.

With the approval of the Director of Honors, students may elect to write a senior honors thesis or complete a project under the supervision of a faculty specialist. A completed senior project earns 6 hours of senior-level honors credit. A student who successfully completes such a project in addition to the regular honors requirements will graduate with the distinction of "Highest Honors."

Individual Studies offers a junior- or senior-level honors student an opportunity for private reading and research in a one-to-one relationship with a faculty member. In effect, the student enrolled in Individual Studies is the only member of the class.

With the approval of the Director of Honors and the concerned faculty member, contract courses are offered to students so that they may undertake honors-level work in a nonhonors course. An opportunity of this nature enriches the student's academic experiences, earns honors credit, and brings the student into closer contact with a variety of professors. There are approximately 500 students in the program.

Participation Requirements: Students who complete 24 hours of honors courses, including two honors seminars, and who have maintained a GPA of 3.25 overall are designated as having graduated with honors. This designation is noted on the transcript and is in addition to any distinction, such as magna cum laude, that the student may also have earned.

Admission Process: There are several different routes to admission into the Honors Program, but in the final analysis students must be formally accepted before they can take advantage of the various benefits and advantages that the program offers. The minimum requirement for admission to the Honors Program consists of one or more of the following: 1) a cumulative SAT I score of 1200 or a cumulative ACT score of 28; 2) graduation within the top 10 percent of the high school class; 3) submission of a written essay (in addition to the essay required by the application) in which compelling reasons are provided for why either of the above criteria has not been met, and an explanation of why the student thinks that he or she would especially benefit by belonging to the Honors Program; or 4) a 3.25 GPA as a continuing Tech student or transfer student. Other factors that will be considered in the admission process will be the nature and extent of extracurricular activities, grades in college-preparatory high school classes, and a written essay.

Because there are limits on the number of students that can be admitted, students must apply to Honors as soon as they are reasonably sure that they will be attending Texas Tech. Applications will be considered beginning on March 1. Students will be admitted on a rolling basis as applications are received between March 1 and June 15. Applicants cannot be admitted outside of these enrollment dates unless there are exceptional circumstances that hindered the student from applying at that time.

Scholarship Availability: A few modest scholarships are available.

The Campus Context: Texas Tech University has historically offered excellent educational opportunities combined with the advantages of being a major research institution. The University is an attractive and remarkably congenial school with a well-deserved reputation for innovative programs designed to assist the undergraduate student. Set in Lubbock, the principal metropolitan area of the South Plains, the citizens of Tech enjoy a pleasant year-round climate and immediate access to some of North America's best recreational areas.

Tuition: $960 for state residents, $7380 for nonresidents, per year (1996-97)

Room and Board: $4084

Mandatory Fees: $1366

Contact: Director: Dr. Gary Bell, Box 41017, Lubbock, Texas 79409-1017; Coordinator: Dr. Danielle Roth-Johnson; Telephone: 806-742-1828; Fax: 806-742-1331; E-mail: algmb@ttuvml.ttu.edu

TOWSON STATE UNIVERSITY

4 Pu D C S Sc

▼ University Honors Programs

Honors programs at Towson State University (TSU) include the Honors College, the Departmental Honors Program, and the Student Grants Program.

The Honors College program is based upon a group of courses that are open only to those who have qualified for the Honors College. All of these courses fulfill general education requirements. While many of them are honors sections of general education courses, there are some that are unique to the Honors College experience. Every attempt is made to encourage collegiality among Honors College students and faculty members with the goal of forming a true community of scholars.

Honors College classes are small, usually 12–19 students, and are taught in seminar style in order to facilitate discussion and collaborative learning. Honors College courses do not require extraordinary amounts of work

compared to nonhonors courses, but they do require active participation. The Honors College is in the process of developing several interdisciplinary seminars in order to maintain the interdisciplinary emphasis the University has announced in its strategic plan. The Honors College chooses its faculty members because of their ability to encourage students to become actively involved in the learning process. The Honors College faculty members view themselves as facilitators and guides rather than lecturers.

One of the centers of honors activities at Towson State University is the Lieberman Room of the Honors College. The combination lounge, conference room, and art gallery is used by honors students and faculty members and is often the site of Honors College courses. The room contains an extraordinary collection of contemporary art that was donated to the University by Dr. and Mrs. Sidney Lieberman, both alumni of the class of 1932.

The Departmental Honors Program is a separate but complementary part of the University Honors Programs. Departmental Honors experiences are designed for juniors and seniors who have completed the lower-level requirements in their majors and are now ready to focus on specific areas of their discipline. Departmental Honors is recommended for students who are considering attending graduate school or a related professional program.

A student begins the Departmental Honors experience by developing the necessary background for his or her topic. This may be the result of an upper-level elective course or an independent-study program with a faculty member. Working with a faculty mentor, the student develops a specific thesis topic and submits a proposal to the University Honors Board. Upon approval of the proposal, the student begins the research or creative activity described in the proposal. The results of this effort are presented as a thesis in a format appropriate for the student's discipline. Students receive 6–9 academic credits for their efforts, and graduate with honors in their major.

The Student Grants Program is available for the qualified student who is interested in independent research (not part of a course) on a special project such as making a film, field studies, or research requiring travel or special materials. The program offers funding for travel, books, laboratory equipment, and materials. The student must submit a proposal and a budget in the format required by the Student Grants Committee. The Student Grants Program will be revised during the 1997–99 period.

The Departmental Honors program, which admits 8–10 students a year, began in the mid-1960s. The Honors College, with 15-20 graduates per year and 200 students taking courses in any given semester, was instituted in 1982, as was the Student Grants Program, which offers research funds to 10–20 students per year.

Participation Requirements: Honors-eligible students may take as many or as few Honors College courses as they wish. However, students must complete at least five Honors College courses with a minimum GPA of 3.2 in order to be designated as graduates of the Honors College. Transfer students may use a maximum of two honors-designated courses from their previous institution in completing these requirements.

Students who complete five or more Honors College courses with at least a 3.2 GPA can receive designation as graduates of the Honors College. This designation appears on the transcript and on the diploma. Transfer students may use a maximum of two honors-designated courses from their previous institution in completing these requirements. Honors College participation requirements are currently under review and may change during the next two years.

To be eligible for Departmental Honors, a student must have a current minimum overall GPA of 3.25 and a GPA of at least 3.5 in those courses required for the major. It is expected that the student will maintain this level of achievement throughout the program. In order to graduate with honors in the major, the student must complete and successfully defend a thesis or creative project. Students who complete and successfully defend an honors thesis, which can be a research thesis or a creative project, depending on the major, and who maintain a 3.25 overall average and a 3.5 average in required courses in the major, receive departmental honors, a citation which appears on the transcript and diploma.

To be eligible for the Student Grants Program, the student must be either a junior or senior with a minimum GPA of 3.0, have a faculty adviser for the project, and submit a proposal to the Student Grants Committee.

Admission Process: Students are invited to participate in the Honors College program if they meet one or more of the following criteria: a minimum combined SAT I score of 1180 and a high school GPA of 3.25, placement in the top 10 percent of their high school graduating class, or special permission of the honors program director after review of the student's academic record. Students transferring from another college or university, or students enrolled at Towson before entering the Honors College, must have a minimum GPA of 3.2 in order to be eligible to participate in the Honors College Program.

Scholarship Availability: Towson State University awards a limited number of academic scholarships to qualified incoming freshmen and transfer students each fall. Candidates are selected as admissions applications are received from academically gifted high school seniors and from Maryland community college transfer students with an A.A. degree (and no subsequent course work attempted), without regard to financial need. Priority is granted to the earliest admission applicants. No separate application for these scholarships is needed, but an admission application, transcripts, and test results should be filed and completed by December 1. However, applications may be considered after the December 1 deadline if scholarships remain available. Each merit scholarship can only be applied toward educational expenses at the University.

Towson Scholars are those entering freshmen whose SAT scores and high school averages entitle them to annual tuition, fee, room, and board. Strongest consideration is given to those with 3.75 or higher GPAs and 1270 or higher SAT I scores. The scholarship is awarded for four years if the student maintains a 3.25 cumulative GPA each semester and full-time status at the University. Recipients are asked to render special services to the University community.

Presidential Scholarships vary in amounts up to full tuition and fees. A minimum 3.5 cumulative GPA and minimum 1270 combined SAT I score is required for scholarship consideration. The Honors College Scholarship, a supplementary award for select Presidential Scholars chosen by the Honors College Selection Committee, provides annual campus housing in addition to the tuition and fees provided by the Presidential Scholarship.

University Scholarships vary in amounts up to full tuition. They are awarded to freshmen who have cumulative GPAs of 3.5 or higher and combined SAT I scores of 1180 or higher, who are in the top 10 percent of the TSU entering class, who have demonstrated ability in a visual or performing art, or who have demonstrated academic leadership qualities.

Provost's Scholarship awards range from $500 to $3000. Provost's Scholarships are awarded to entering freshmen according to SAT scores or GPAs for students specifically recruited to assist the University in meeting goals of talent, leadership, academic potential, citizenship, or diversity.

The Campus Context: Towson State University consists of seven colleges: the College of Business and Economics, the College of Education, the College of Fine Arts and Communication, the College of Health Professions, the College of Liberal Arts, the College of Natural and Mathematical Sciences, and the College of Graduate and Extended Education. Students may choose among forty undergraduate and twenty-four graduate degree programs.

Towson State University is located on a beautiful rolling campus in the northern suburbs of Baltimore. It is convenient to the amenities of both the Baltimore and Washington metropolitan areas. Because of its location, Towson is able to place students in internships in many state and federal government agencies.

The general education curriculum at Towson stresses contexts for learning that include the impact of science and technology on all dimensions of experience; American social, political, economic, and cultural history and how it shapes choices for the future; cultural legacies from the Western Heritage and how they predicate, advance, or impede contemporary understanding and choices; and global awareness and recognition of the role of human diversity in a rapidly evolving world order. The general education curriculum also stresses the development of skills for gathering and evaluating information, analyzing and interpreting, weighing alternatives, forming and expressing opinions and conclusions, appreciating diverse points of view, and moving comfortably in the realm of ideas and values.

Student Body Undergraduate enrollment is 13,063, with 10,080 full-time and 2,983 part-time and nondegree students. Fifty-nine percent of the students are women. The ethnic distribution of the student body is 9 percent African American, 1 percent American Indian, 3 percent Asian, 2 percent Hispanic,

82 percent Caucasian, and 3 percent international. Resident students make up 32 percent of full-time undergraduates. Seventy-two percent of students receive financial aid. There are nine fraternities and eight sororities.

Faculty Of the 1,021 total faculty members, 480 are full-time. More than 84 percent of full-time faculty members hold terminal degrees. The student-faculty ratio is 17:1.

Key Facilities The library houses 550,000 volumes. The on-line catalog of the library is integrated with those of the other ten institutions in the University of Maryland System. A cooperative borrowing and delivery agreement with the other UMS institutions gives students access to the resources of those other libraries. In addition, other bibliographic computer networks provide access to state and national databases.

Towson has thirty-five to forty computer labs dispersed around the campus. Some are maintained centrally as general purpose labs, but most are equipped to meet the specific needs of students in the departments that maintain them. For instance, the sociology/anthropology/political science computer lab includes networked software for simulating an archaeological dig, statistical software for complex analysis, and communication software for an interinstitutional course in international negotiation.

Athletics With the motto "Athletic Excellence with Integrity," Towson State University is committed to a growing comprehensive intercollegiate athletic program as an integral part of the student's total educational experience. The program is a member of the National Collegiate Athletic Association's (NCAA) Division I. In addition, TSU enjoys membership in the Eastern College Athletic Conference (ECAC) and North Atlantic Conference. The Tigers field men's varsity teams in baseball, basketball, cross-country, football, lacrosse, golf, soccer, swimming and diving, tennis, and outdoor track.

Women's teams are fielded in basketball, cross-country, field hockey, gymnastics, lacrosse, soccer, softball, swimming and diving, tennis, outdoor track, and volleyball. Both men and women compete for state, regional, and national honors under the guidance of an outstanding coaching staff. The athletic department is proud that its athletes are students first and foremost. Towson is among the top ten universities nationally in the parity of its graduation rates of athletes and nonathletes.

Study Abroad Towson maintains twenty-five exchange programs with partner institutions in twelve countries, including Germany, the United Kingdom, France, Spain, Russia, Japan, China, and Korea. In addition, full-time degree candidates may enroll in one of the cooperative University of Maryland System programs abroad (Mexico City or Florence), in the International Student Exchange Program (ISEP), in a program sponsored by an American college or university, or directly enroll in a foreign university and petition for transfer of the credits. Towson also cooperates with the University of Maryland College Park and the University of Maryland Baltimore County to offer a three-week summer study-abroad program specifically for students enrolled in the honors programs of the three universities.

Support Services Towson State University is in full compliance with Section 504 of the Rehabilitation Act of 1973 and the Americans with Disabilities Act of 1990. All University programs and activities are accessible to individuals with disabilities. Students with disabilities should register with the Office for Students with Disabilities immediately after admission to ensure the timely provision of required support services. Accommodations are provided according to individual need. Services include readers; writers; interpreters; notetakers; arrangements to help remove or circumvent architectural, social, or procedural barriers; and information on special equipment available at TSU.

Job Opportunities Towson State University employs thousands of undergraduate students in on-campus jobs. Examples include clerical/office work, tutoring, ushering at sports events, managing recreation facilities, graphics production, monitoring computer labs, and technical work. Hourly pay rates depend on the nature of the job; all student workers are paid at least minimum wage.

Tuition: $3080 for state residents, $8158 for nonresidents, per year (1997-98)

Room and Board: $4830

Mandatory Fees: $1040

Contact: Dr. Annette Chappell, Associate Vice President for Academic Affairs, 8000 York Road, Towson, Maryland 21252; Telephone: 410-830-2028; Fax: 410-830-3129; E-mail: chappell-a@towson.edu

---

TULSA COMMUNITY COLLEGE

2 Pu C S Sc Tr

▼ Honors Program

The TCC Honors Program offers honors courses to curious and self-motivated students who wish to grow personally and academically. The goal of the program is to provide students with an enriched academic environment through more direct involvement in their own learning experience. Classes are smaller, interaction with peers and professors is lively, and opportunities for independent study are provided. The Honors Program was developed eleven years ago. TCC currently has 30 Honors Scholars.

Admission Process: All students are welcome to take honors courses; however, a 3.0 GPA is recommended. In order to become an Honors Scholar, the student must meet two of the following criteria: combined score of 1100 on the SAT I or composite ACT score of 25 or above; high school GPA of 3.5, ranking in the upper 10 percent of the high school graduating class, or membership in high school honor society; 3.5 GPA on a minimum of 12 credit hours; demonstration of special abilities or awards in writing or other significant projects; completion of two honors credit courses at TCC with a grade of B or A. Students must also receive a letter or recommendation from a qualified instructor and must be approved by all honors coordinators.

Scholarship Availability: Many Scholars qualify for the TCC Regents Fee-Waiver; Tulsa University also offers partial scholarships to TCC Honors Scholar graduates. Also, the TCC Honors Program awards "Talentships" each year to Honors students— honors faculty members recommend students for the award.

The Campus Context: Tulsa Community College is composed of four campuses: Metro, Northeast, Southeast, and West. Among the distinguished facilities available to students are international language labs, a Disabled Student Center, a Center for the Hearing Impaired, nurseries for horticulture, a performing arts center, a Computer Integrated Manufacturing Center, specialized medical labs, and Career Assessment Centers.

Student Body The student population is 40 percent men and 60 percent women. The ethnic distribution of students is 82 percent white, 8 percent black, 2 percent Asian American, 5 percent Native American, 2 percent Hispanic, 1 percent other. There are 126 international students from forty-eight different countries.

Faculty Of the 1,015 faculty members, 240 are full-time. Fourteen percent of the full-time faculty members hold doctorates. The student-faculty ratio is 21:1.

Key Facilities Library holdings include 114,602 volumes. The Computer Instructional Labs are designed to provide many services to students. These services include microcomputers to support courses where microcomputer technology is used, computer- aided instruction packages to supplement classroom work for certain courses, program construction for computer language courses, instructional assistance for equipment and software usage, and a centralized workspace for students. The labs are staffed with personnel to assist in these areas.

Study Abroad Study abroad is encouraged. The International Campus allows students to earn credit for TCC course work taught in another country by TCC faculty members.

Support Services Disabled students will find computer and adaptive equipment, tape recorders and tapes, academic counseling, extended test time, reserved classroom seating, accessible bathrooms, and reserved parking.

Job Opportunities There is a Federal Work-Study program offering approximately 100 positions at minimum wage, with a 20-hour work week.

Tuition: $1140 for state residents, $2978 for nonresidents, per year (1996-97)

Contact: Director: Earnie Montgomery, 909 South Boston MC510, Tulsa, Oklahoma 74119-2095; Telephone: 918-595-7378; Fax: 918-595-7298; E-mail: sking@vm.tulsa.cc.uk.us

UNION COUNTY COLLEGE

2 Pu C S Sc Tr

▼ **Honors Program**

The Union County College Honors Program now consists of an Honors option to the Liberal Arts Program. Students take a series of four HRS courses and complete three honors contracts. The first two HRS courses examine aspects of world culture from the perspectives of philosophy, religion, science, and the arts under the rubric of "Knowing and Being." These two courses are team taught by faculty from the disciplines of writing and literature, art history, and physics. Guest lecturers from nearby four-year colleges and from the faculty at large bring their specialties to students in the program. The third HRS course, Leadership Development through the Classics, is modeled on the PTK Leadership Development Program and is team taught by the Honors Program Director and the Faculty Advisor to the College's PTK chapter. The fourth HRS course, independent study, allows students to work with a faculty mentor and the Honors Program Director to study a subject of their choice in depth. In addition, students complete honors contracts in three non-honors courses.

The program is being revised to allow students to complete the Honors Program in other programs as well as the Liberal Arts/Honors option. By Fall '97, students will be able to select from a number of honors sections in key courses throughout most programs (life and physical sciences, philosophy, English, and psychology, for example) to complete the program. The requirement for a total of seven honors courses will probably remain the same, but as yet no decision has been made as to what core courses will be required.

The program was established in 1987 and has enrolled as many as 60 students. Classes are small, usually between 15 and 20 students.

Participation Requirements: To maintain scholarships and to graduate with Honors Program distinction, students must maintain a 3.2 GPA.

Admission Process: For entrance into the program, students must have a 3.5 GPA, 1050 SATs, rank in the top quarter of high school class, or special talents.

Scholarship Availability: Honors Program students compete favorably for the many scholarships available at the College, and the Honors Program Director has a substantial scholarship pool for Honors Program students. Scholarship deadline is May 15.

The Campus Context: Union County College, founded in 1934 as a junior college, has three campuses and is located in north-central New Jersey, with convenient commuting to most of the New York metropolitan area. The Elizabeth Campus is an urban campus located on the eastern edge of the county.

The Plainfield Campus is located in a small-town environment on the western edge of the county. The main campus is centrally located in the residential area of Cranford and the Honors Program is located on this campus.

A total of sixty-two degree programs (A.A., A.S., A.A.S., diploma, and certificate) are offered.

Student Profile Enrollment is approximately 10,000: 36 percent men, 64 percent women; 23 percent African American, 7 percent Asian, 16 percent Hispanic, 54 percent white. Three thousand students receive financial aid (43 percent of the 7,000 full-time-equivalent students, 30 percent of the total 10,000 students). Since there are no dorms, all students commute. The many student organizations include chapters of Phi Theta Kappa (national honor) and honors chapters for psychology, engineering, and mathematics, a newspaper, and a literary magazine.

Faculty There are 436 faculty members, 175 full-time, and 40 percent with terminal degrees. The student-faculty ratio is about 23:1.

Key Facilities The library holds 115,723 volumes, with many subscriptions and an active program for acquiring books. Computer labs on the Cranford campus total eight now (7 PCs and 1 Mac) with two more to be added soon. The Elizabeth campus has twelve labs (all PCs, one dedicated to Engineering/Physics). And the Plainfield campus has four labs (three PCs, one NOVELL), but one will be moved to the Cranford campus in the near future.

Athletics Athletic opportunities include golf (Division III), men's soccer, baseball, and basketball (Division III), women's softball (Division III), and women's basketball (Division II).

Support Services The College provides a special counselor for students with disabilities who makes appropriate academic adjustments for students with learning disabilities. Technological support includes Reading Edge, Optelec Enlarging Machine, and Dec Talk for word processing. In addition, the College has sound-enhancement equipment, calculators with speech and big print, Franklin Spelling Ace, NCR notebooks, Speaking Language Master, tape recorders, and lab stations for people who use wheelchairs.

Job Opportunities The College offers many work-study opportunities as part of financial aid; in addition, the Academic Learning Center employs about 50 tutors and paraprofessionals.

Tuition: $2112 for area residents, $4224 for state residents, $8448 for nonresidents, per year (1996-97)

Mandatory Fees: $370

Contact: Director: Dr. Karl E. Oelke, Cranford, NJ 07016; Telephone: 908-709-7680; Fax: 908-709-4076; E-mail: oelke@ hawk.ucc.edu

THE UNIVERSITY OF ALABAMA

4 Pu G S Sc Tr

▼ Computer-Based Honors Program

Whether one wants to be an English professor, a marketing executive, or an electrical engineer, not being able to apply computer technology to one's career field is a lot like not being able to read. The Computer-Based Honors Program, a department of New College at the University of Alabama, is looking for 20 students who want to approach their fields of study, whatever they may be, with the best tools the Information Age has to offer. The CBHP, cited by the National Institute of Education as one of the six most intriguing honors programs in the United States, gives students opportunities to learn how to use computing technology in their major field of study. The program also gives 6 members of each entering class the chance to earn while they learn—six fellowships of $2500 per year, renewable for four years, are awarded on a competitive basis to CBHP students. (Out-of-state tuition is waived.)

At the beginning of the freshman year, students take a highly accelerated course to introduce them to basic concepts of computing, to at least two computer languages, and to practical uses of the computer in problem solving. Although this course advances rapidly, it does not require any prior experience with computers.

When students are proficient in using the computer, they work as computer-oriented research assistants with faculty members or industry associates whose interests coincide with theirs. Projects in which CBHP students are involved usually entail researching a particular subject or experimenting with the computer as an instructional tool. The student participates in planning the project, in preparing the computer programs needed to complete the project, and in interpreting the results.

During the sophomore, junior, and senior years, students meet with other CBHP students in a weekly seminar with the program director. This systematic, long-term contact with students whose abilities are comparable to their own provides students with a forum for satisfying social and intellectual exchanges not readily available anywhere else.

The Computer-Based Honors Program was founded in 1968 with a National Science Foundation grant. There are a maximum of 80 students in the program.

Participation Requirements and Scholarships: The average ACT score is 32; the average SAT I score is 1300 to 1340. The average high school GPA is 3.9 to 4.0. The application, transcript, and essay are due by January 15. Twenty students are admitted based on their applications and are invited for a two-day visit to the campus. Six scholarships are awarded. Twenty-five total scholarships are awarded at $2500 per year, renewable based on continued superior performance. The Computer-Based Honors Program serves as a minor. "Computer-Based Honors Program" appears on the diploma and transcript.

The Campus Context: The University of Alabama consists of fourteen colleges and schools: Arts and Sciences, Commerce and Business Administration, Communication, Community Health Sciences, Continuing Studies, Education, Engineering, Graduate School, Human Environmental Sciences, Law, Library and Information Studies, New College, Nursing, and Social Work. The University offers 275 degrees in more than 150 fields of study, providing its students a wide range of choices, and offers courses of study at the bachelor's, master's, specialist, and doctoral levels.

Student Body Of the roughly 15,000 undergraduate students on campus 48 percent are men, 52 percent women; 83 percent are white, 12 percent African American, 1 percent Hispanic, and 3 percent international; 61 percent receive financial aid. There are forty-eight fraternities and sororities and more than 300 student organizations.

Faculty Of the 995 faculty members, 805 are full-time, with 97 percent holding terminal degrees. The student-faculty ratio is 19:1.

Key Facilities There are more than 2 million volumes in the libraries and state-of-the-art computing facilities in every major building.

Athletics The Crimson Tide sponsors eleven women's and nine men's sports, competing at the NCAA Division I level as a participant in the twelve-school Southeastern Conference. The University of Alabama is home to twelve national football championships, three gymnastics championships, and a host of national and SEC individual champions in other sports.

Study Abroad The Capstone International Program Center offers a large number of study abroad opportunities.

Support Services The campus provides unrestricted access for disabled students.

Job Opportunities Nineteen percent of the students work part-time on campus with average annual earnings of $2000.

Tuition: $2470 for state residents, $6268 for nonresidents, per year (1996-97)

Room and Board: $3680

Contact: Director: Dr. Cathy Randall, Maxwell Hall, P.O. Box 870352, Tuscaloosa, Alabama 35487; Telephone: 205-348-5029; Fax: 205-348-2247; E-mail: cbhp@ua1vm.ua.edu; Web site: http://www.ua.edu/~cbhp

THE UNIVERSITY OF ALABAMA

4 Pu G L Sc Tr

▼ University Honors Program

Qualified students seeking a special academic challenge in their undergraduate work can find it in the University Honors Program. More than 700 students from all schools and colleges in the University participate in the program. The University Honors Program gives outstanding students the opportunity to work with their peers and with outstanding faculty members in an enriched academic environment. It also offers students the opportunity to combine some of the benefits of a small-college experience with the advantages of a major research university.

Honors courses have limited enrollment in order to facilitate interaction between students and faculty members. Honors courses often parallel regular University courses, but they offer enriched content and provide for more student input and creative writing. The University Honors Program fulfills core curriculum and other requirements, allowing students to pursue their own specific degree and study objectives within the honors framework. Students in the program do not take a full schedule of honors courses. Most students take perhaps two honors courses each semester. However, all students are expected to take at least one honors course during each academic year of their first two years of the program in order to retain the privilege of priority registration. The evaluation of student work in honors courses neither penalizes nor unduly rewards students for their honors course work. Most students perform well in classes they find to be interesting and challenging.

Founded in 1987, the program now enrolls 710 students.

Participation Requirements: Students may choose one of two options in the University Honors Program. In the Honors Division, each student takes a 3-hour General Honors Survey and 15 additional hours of honors courses. With the approval of the director of the University Honors Program, a student may in exceptional cases substitute an honors thesis for one of these courses. In the Special Honors Division, each student either takes two 3-hour General Honors surveys and 15 additional hours of honors courses and completes a 3-hour thesis; or takes one 3-hour General Honors Survey and 15 additional hours of honors courses and completes a 6-hour thesis. Funds may be available to support research for the honors thesis.

The official transcript will identify honors courses, thereby enhancing an honors student's position in competing for employment or admission to professional schools. The University diploma will indicate an Honors Division or Special Honors Division status, with that distinction noted at graduation ceremonies. Each year the Honors Program Student Association, a body of students who are also members of the Honors Program, gives the Outstanding Honors Program Graduate Award to a senior who has served the honors community faithfully and well over his or her undergraduate career at the University.

Admission Process: National Merit Finalists, National Achievement Finalists, U.S. Presidential Scholars, and Alumni Honors Scholars are automatically admissible to the program. Other students with an ACT of at least 28 or an SAT I score of at least 1290 may also apply to the program after they have earned a GPA of 3.3 or higher for a semester's work at the University of Alabama. All participants must maintain at least a 3.3 GPA and give evidence of actively pursuing an honors degree to remain a member in good standing of the program.

Scholarship Availability: The Jo Nell Usrey Honors Scholarship is available to an entering freshman student who is participating in the University Honors Program. This scholarship is available to a student who is receiving no other financial aid from the University. The scholarship is renewable if the student maintains a 3.3 GPA and continues to participate in the University Honors Program.

The Campus Context: The University of Alabama at Tuscaloosa consists of fourteen colleges and schools: Arts and Sciences, Commerce and Business Administration, Communication, Community Health Sciences, Continuing Studies, Education, Engineering, Graduate School, Human Environmental Sciences, Law, Library and Information Studies, New College, Nursing, and Social Work. The University offers 275 degrees in more than 150 fields of study, giving students a wide range of choices at the bachelor's, master's, specialist, and doctoral levels.

Student Body Of the total student body, 48 percent are men and 52 percent women. The ethnic distribution of minority students is 12 percent African American; 1 percent Hispanic-American; and 3 percent international. There are forty-eight fraternities and sororities as well as more than 300 student organizations on campus.

Faculty Of the 995 faculty members, 805 are full-time, with 97 percent holding terminal degrees. The student-faculty ratio is 19:1.

Key Facilities There are more than 2 million volumes in the libraries and state-of-the-art computing facilities in every major building.

Athletics The Crimson Tide sponsors eleven women's and nine men's sports, competing at the NCAA's Division I level as a participant in the twelve-school Southeastern Conference. The University of Alabama is home to twelve national football championships and three national gymnastics championships. The University is also the home of many other national and SEC individual champions in other sports.

Study Abroad The Capstone International Program Center offers a large number of study abroad opportunities.

Support Services The campus provides unrestricted access for disabled students.

Job Opportunities Nineteen percent of the students work part-time on campus with average annual earnings of $2000.

Tuition: $2470 for state residents, $6268 for nonresidents, per year (1996-97)

Room and Board: $3680

Contact: Director: Dr. Ralph Bogardus, Box 870169, Tuscaloosa, Alabama 35487-0169; Telephone: 205-348-5500; Fax: 205-348-5501; E-mail: uhp@ualvm.ua.edu; Web site: http://www.ua.edu/honors.html

THE UNIVERSITY OF ALABAMA AT BIRMINGHAM

| 4 Pu G M Sc Tr |

▼ University Honors Program

Combining cultural diversity with high academic standards, the UAB Honors Program provides an innovative, interdisciplinary curriculum designed for bright, motivated students of all disciplines, backgrounds, and ages. The 33-hour honors core curriculum, which replaces the general degree requirements at UAB, is interdisciplinary, with courses team-taught by scholar/teachers in disciplines as diverse as engineering, English, theology, biochemistry, business, and psychology; the study of a single subject—such as the environment—from these multiple perspectives generates critical thinking, mutual understanding, and teamwork. In addition, the curriculum is perpetually innovative, with no course offered more than once, so that students are introduced to the latest in information, methodologies, social trends, and technologies.

The intensive extracurricular focus of the Honors Program extends the undergraduate experience beyond the course work to a way of life. The faculty members, students, and staff of the Honors Program comprise a close community of active teachers and learners who share their energy and commitment not only with each other but with the larger community, where honors students provide services to local public school students, homeless women and children, and the elderly.

The Honors House, a magnificent old church on the UAB campus that was built in 1902, houses a number of computers that are linked to the Ethernet. All entering students receive an e-mail account, and computer workshops familiarize students with the newest technologies. All the honors course work takes place in the Honors House, as do over fifty lectures, films, social gatherings, and discussion groups each year. The Honors House is available to honors students at all times, and the facilities include a kitchen, a pool table, computers, a copy machine, a stereo, a television, and lots of space for studying and relaxing.

During the past fourteen years, hundreds of students in the Honors Program have attended state, national, and regional honors conferences, given formal academic presentations, served in regional and national elected offices, and/or attended honors semesters in the Czech Republic, New York, or El Paso. UAB has hosted a regional conference and two state conferences, and it has also sponsored numerous field trips for its students, from ski trips to museum visits.

The 14-year-old program currently enrolls 200 students.

Participation Requirements: In order to remain in the program, students must maintain a GPA in their honors course work of at least 3.0. During each year of participation in the program, honors students are included in the University Honors Convocation and receive the notation "University Honors Program" on their transcripts. Students who complete the program graduate "With University Honors" and—in addition to being acknowledged in the Commencement program—are honored at a special graduation ceremony for honors students.

Admission Process: Students are selected for the program on the basis of national test scores, GPA, two letters of recommendation, an essay, a personal interview, and any special evidence a student chooses to submit. There are no numerical minimums for scores or GPAs, but the program seeks students with academic ability, creativity, intellectual promise, and competence in basic skills.

The deadline for applying to the program is August 1.

Scholarship Availability: While most honors students are awarded scholarships by the University, the program awards twelve scholarships of four kinds: 1) five University Scholarships (full tuition and fees plus $1000 per year for four years) for students with a minimum 28 ACT and 3.5 GPA; 2) three (sometimes four) Hess-Abroms Honors Scholarships ($2500 per year for four years) for students who best meet the general program criteria indicated above; 3) three Juliet Nunn Pearson Scholarships ($1000 each) for promising incoming students; and 4) two Frank Barber Memorial Scholarships ($1500 each) for students already in the program, on the basis of need and merit.

The Campus Context: The University of Alabama at Birmingham is composed of twelve schools (undergraduate enrollment in parentheses): Arts and Humanities (796), Natural Sciences and Mathematics (1,387), Social and Behavioral Sciences (1,621), Education (1,092), Engineering (588), Business (1,465), Medicine, Nursing (445), Optometry, Dentistry (9), Health-Related Professions (377), and Public Health. Special features include a major academic health center; Reynolds Historical Library; and Alabama Museum of Health Sciences. The University offers 139 degree programs.

Student Body Undergraduate enrollment is 10,805; 55 percent are women; 20 percent are African American, 74 percent white, and 6 percent other. There are 514 international students; 9 percent resident. Forty-five percent of undergraduates receive financial aid. There are ten fraternities and six sororities.

Faculty The faculty members total 2,047, with 1,885 full-time and 89 percent with terminal degrees. The student-faculty ratio is 19:1.

Key Facilities The library houses 1.5 million volumes. More than 600 computers are available to students, including IBM, Macintosh, and IBM-compatible computers.

Athletics In athletics, the University is NCAA Division I in men's and women's basketball, soccer, golf, tennis, rifle, cross-country and track; men's football and baseball; and women's volleyball.

Study Abroad Study abroad programs are available in Mexico, France, the Bahamas, Israel, and Scotland (two programs); a combined business program is available in Austria, Belgium, Germany, and the Netherlands; and there are five additional UAB exchange programs.

Support Services There is a Disability Support Services Program.

Job Opportunities Work opportunities include work-study, co-op, and numerous research and lab positions.

Tuition: $2400 for state residents, $4800 for nonresidents, per year (1996–97)

Room and Board: $6384

Mandatory Fees: $300

Contact: Director: Dr. Ada Long, 1190 10th Avenue South, Birmingham, Alabama 35294-4450; Telephone: 205-934-3228; Fax: 205-975-5493; E-mail: humc009@uabdpo.dpo.uab.edu; Web site: http://bmewww.eng.uab.edu/hu/

THE UNIVERSITY OF ALABAMA IN HUNTSVILLE

4 Pu G M Tr

▼ University Honors Program

The Honors Program at the University of Alabama in Huntsville enhances the opportunity for academic excellence. It offers study of the scientific and humanistic accomplishments of the past and present in order to increase knowledge of the self and of the world. It provides academically talented undergraduate students with opportunities to develop their special talents and skills within an expanded and enriched version of the curriculum. Students in the Honors Program participate in structured enrichment activities that include honors course work parallel to regular offerings, special interdisciplinary seminars, field trips, and the option of independent study and research. First- and second-year students take Honors Forum, a course designed to introduce the multidisciplinary focus of the honors education. Seniors complete an Honors Senior Project directed by an adviser in their major and formally present their research findings in a public forum. In all of these specially designed classes and activities, students are assured an exciting academic career that will also nurture their special talents. The Honors Program offers personalized academic guidance and counseling for all honors students, but especially for first- and second-year participants. The UAH Honors Program provides a path to a unique education.

The Honors Program is housed in a small complex that includes the director's and assistant's office and two comfortably outfitted study and lounge rooms. These rooms also include computers, basic reference books, and selected journals, newspapers, and other print media. This setting provides the opportunity for academic and social interaction among students, special campus guests, the director, and honors faculty members.

The 7-year-old program currently enrolls 170 students.

Participation Requirements: An honors student is required to maintain a cumulative GPA of 3.3 or above. Graduation from the program requires 28 hours of honors course work. Graduating honors students are awarded University Honors recognition at Honors Convocation and at Commencement. The title of the senior project is printed in the Commencement booklet and "University Honors" is printed on the diploma.

Admission Process: All academically eligible students are urged to participate in the Honors Program. The minimum requirement for first-year students is a high school GPA of 3.5. Minimum test scores for admission are as follows: ACT composite, 28: English 29; math 26. SAT I composite, 1200: verbal 610, math 590. Enrolled UAH students who complete 12 hours of course work with a GPA of 3.3 or higher may be invited to join the program based on outstanding performance.

Scholarship Availability: Scholarships are handled through the Financial Aid Office. Although no funds are designated specifically for honors students, many of them receive scholarships based on academic merit.

The Campus Context: The University of Alabama at Huntsville offers a considerable number and variety of degree programs: thirty-eight bachelor's degrees (B.A., B.S., B.S.B.A., B.S.E., B.S.N.), fifteen master's degrees (M.A., M.S., M.S.E., M.S.N.), and ten doctorates (Ph.D). UAH is home to the following research and development centers: Aerophysics Research Center, Center for Applied Optics, Center for Automation and Robotics, Center for Management and Economic Research, Center for the Management of Science and Technology, Center for Microgravity and Materials Research, Center for Space Plasma and Aeronomic Research, Consortium for Materials Development in Space, Earth Systems Science Laboratory, Information Technology and Systems Laboratory, Johnson Research Center, Propulsion Research Center, and the Research Institute.

Student Body Undergraduate enrollment is 51 percent men and 49 percent women. The ethnic distribution is: 79 percent white (non-Hispanic); 11 percent black (non-Hispanic); 2 percent Hispanic; 3 percent Asian/Pacific Islander; 1 percent American Indian/Alaskan Native; 4 percent nonresident aliens. Forty-five percent of undergraduates receive financial aid. There are six fraternities and five sororities on campus.

Faculty The total number of instructional faculty members is 469; 283 are full-time and 93 percent have terminal degrees. The student-faculty ratio is 10:1.

Key Facilities In addition to the 426,344 books, serial backfiles and government documents, the library houses 413,909 titles on microfilm, 3,105 current serial subscriptions, and 1,835 sound recordings. Approximately 250 personal computers are available for student use. They are located in the computer center, the student center, the library, and computer labs. Students have access to the campus mainframe computer (DEC 7000/910), the Alabama Super Computer (CRAY X-MP 24), and the Internet.

Athletics UAH is a member of the NCAA and the Gulf South Athletic Conference and offers the following Division II intercollegiate sports: men's baseball, ice hockey, and soccer; women's softball and volleyball; and basketball, cross-country,

and tennis for both men and women. The men's hockey team won the Division II National Championship for 1996 and all 6 starters were All-Americans. UAH finished the season with a record of 26-0-3. UAH offers the following intramural sports: basketball, bowling, crew, flag football, golf, racquetball, softball, swimming, table tennis, volleyball, and weightlifting.

Study Abroad Study-abroad opportunities exist.

Support Services All University buildings are accessible for the physically disabled. Note-taking and reader services are available. The following services are available for learning-disabled students: note-taking, readers, remedial courses, study skills courses, tutors, tape recorders, and oral and untimed tests.

Job Opportunities UAH offers part-time on-campus student employment and Federal Work-Study.

Tuition: $2698 for state residents, $5656 for nonresidents, per year (1996-97)

Room and Board: $3645

Contact: Director: Dr. Richard F. Modlin, Honors Program, Huntsville, Alabama 35899; Telephone: 205-895-6450; Fax: 205-890-7339; Web site: http://www.uah.edu

UNIVERSITY OF ALASKA FAIRBANKS
4 Pu G M Sc Tr
▼ Honors Program

The University of Alaska Fairbanks Honors Program is open to students in all majors. The program features the personalized attention of small classes with top professors within a larger research university. Specially selected faculty advisers guide honors students through their years as undergraduates.

The Honors Program offers an enriched core curriculum for approximately 100 talented students. Honors courses are offered in all disciplines with the availability of honors contract work in standard University courses. Many of these courses are designed specifically for the Honors Program and are frequently interdisciplinary. Honors students take at least one honors course per semester toward completion of the 27 credits of honors course work required for graduation in the program. Students may also earn honors credit for study abroad and internships.

The program emphasizes undergraduate research. In their senior research projects, all honors students have the opportunity to work directly with faculty members. All honors students must complete a senior honors thesis in their major discipline.

The Honors Student Advisory Committee organizes social events and fundraising activities that contribute to a sense of community within the University.

Currently, there are 102 students in the program.

Admission Process: Students apply first to the University, then make application to the Honors Program. Students from other recognized college and university honors programs are welcomed as transfer students. There is no formal deadline.

Scholarship Availability: The Donald R. Theophilus Fund for Scholars and the Howard and Enid Cutler Scholarship are designated for honors students. Many general University scholarships are awarded to honors students ranging from $250 to $1000.

The Campus Context: The University of Alaska Fairbanks offers a once-in-a-lifetime opportunity to experience the adventure of Alaska at the nation's farthest-north university. Situated in the Tanana Valley, between the Alaska Range to the south and the Brooks Range to the north, there are many opportunities for outdoor activities and observation of wildlife and scenic beauty. UAF is a four-year university that is home to the University of Alaska Museum and the Geophysical Institute. UAF is the national leader in National Science Foundation-funded arctic research. The University offers degrees in seventy-five majors.

Student Body The undergraduate enrollment is 8,976 (this figure includes the rural campuses); 55 percent are women, 45 percent men. Eighty-six percent are Alaska residents, 11 percent are from other states, and 3 percent are from other countries. Ethnic minorities comprise approximately 21 percent of the total student body. Ninety-one percent are undergraduates, 9 percent are graduate students. The average age is 30.

Faculty There are approximately 600 full-time faculty members. The student-faculty ratio is approximately 13:1.

Key Facilities The University's Rasmuson Library houses approximately 800,000 volumes, not counting government documents and materials on microfilm and microfiche. It has the world's most extensive arctic and circumpolar archives. IBM and Mac computers are available in the Honors House.

Athletics The University of Alaska Fairbanks offers intercollegiate athletics in several sports, including skiing, volleyball, hockey, basketball, and marksmanship.

Study Abroad The University is affiliated with several study abroad and student exchange programs. UAF students may enroll at one of 115 NSE colleges and universities throughout the U.S. and pay the in-state tuition rate. UAF also has student exchanges or study abroad programs with universities in Canada, Denmark, England, France, Germany, Italy, Japan, Mexico, Norway, Russia, Sweden, and Venezuela. Honors students are encouraged to participate in such programs.

Support Services Almost all academic buildings are accessible to disabled students. Special parking, equipped restrooms, and lowered drinking fountains are also available throughout campus.

Tuition: $2100 for state residents, $6300 for nonresidents, per year (1996-97)

Room and Board: $3790

Mandatory Fees: $330

Contact: Director: Dr. John S. Whitehead, Fairbanks, Alaska 99775; Telephone: 907-474-6612; Fax: 907-474-5817; Web site: http://zorba.uafadm.alaska.ecu/honors

THE UNIVERSITY OF ARIZONA

4 Pu G L Sc Tr

▼ **Honors Center**

The Honors Center at the University of Arizona is a community of scholars. The program draws on the resources of one of the top fifteen public universities in the country and adds the benefits of an innovative, personal, and challenging learning community. It is no wonder that more than 600 new students (including more than 50 National Merit Scholars) decide to join the ranks each year.

UA Honors students have the option of enrolling in University-wide offerings of more than 200 honors courses each semester. The average class size is 15 students. There are no required honors courses; students work with their adviser to decide which honors course opportunities are most appropriate for their curriculum. Honors courses emphasize the development of written and verbal skills, as well as research and problem-solving techniques. The atmosphere in the courses is one of interaction and challenge, but not competition.

The UA Honors Center offers a full complement of benefits to round out students' educational experiences. There are four honors residence halls, each equipped with a computer lab, to house 700 students. Students may apply for $40,000 in research grants awarded annually. They may wish to attend one of the monthly Forum Luncheons, where they can meet other honors students and faculty members in an informal setting. There is a network of more than 100 honors advisers throughout the campus to assist students in reaching their personal and academic goals. Finally, many students appreciate the extended library privileges and early registration opportunities that are a part of the program. The Honors Center was founded in 1962 and currently has 2,670 students actively participating in the program.

Participation Requirements: To graduate with honors, students complete between 18 and 30 units of honors course work, including a senior thesis in their major area of study. Students who complete the requirements for graduation with honors (unit requirement, senior thesis, and maintenance of a cumulative GPA of 3.5 or higher) have that distinction indicated on their diploma. The degree would read, for example, "Bachelor of Arts with Honors" or "Bachelor of Science with Honors". All students who graduate with honors receive a gold cord to wear with their graduation cap and gown. Those honors students who complete requirements and maintain a 4.0 GPA receive a silver bowl inscribed with their name, "Academic Award of Excellence," and their year of graduation. Students are also eligible to qualify for academic distinction (cum laude, magna cum laude, summa cum laude) based on their cumulative GPA.

Honors graduates go on to win national awards, such as the Truman, Marshall, and Rhodes scholarships. UA honors students are placed into medical and law school at twice the national average, and they receive fellowships and grants to continue their education at top-ranked graduate programs throughout the U.S.

Admission Process: Honors admission is offered to a select group of students each year. To be considered, the University of Arizona's general application for admission must be completed. Strength of curriculum, test scores, GPA, and class rank are all part of the consideration process. To remain active members of the Honors Center, students must maintain a cumulative GPA of 3.5 or greater.

Scholarship Availability: The University of Arizona awards over $16 million in scholarships each year. One of the strongest programs, for National Merit Finalists, provides scholarships of at least $4300 for Arizona residents and $6500 for nonresidents. The Honors Center works with the Office of Scholarships and Financial Aid to identify and target outstanding students for University awards. The best advice for those students who are interested in receiving scholarship assistance is to apply early. The University begins making scholarship offers in the winter before a student's anticipated enrollment (i.e., December for August enrollment).

The Campus Context: The University of Arizona, founded in 1888, is located in Tucson and offers a top-ranked education on a 343-acre, resort-like campus. The University has been designated by the Carnegie Commission as a Research I institution, the highest ranking, since 1976. With 133 different degree programs, the University is also one of fifty-eight institutional members of the Association of American Universities. The UA is ranked thirteenth among public universities in research and development, and undergraduate students benefit from funding brought in by research grants. The faculty members, technology, and equipment available, in all disciplines, are simply among the best in the country. Special facilities on the campus include the Center for Creative Photography, the Arizona Cancer Center, the Arizona State Museum, the Udall Center for Studies in Public Policy, and the Optical Sciences Center. Independent sources consistently rank UA among the nation's top schools: *U.S. News & World Report* listed UA in the top 5 up-and-coming U.S. universities, UA was named in the 1994 edition of *The Guide to 101 of the Best Values in American Colleges and Universities*, and Barron's lists UA among its recommended colleges.

Student Body Undergraduate enrollment is 51 percent men, 49 percent women; 12 percent Hispanic, 4 percent Asian, 2 percent African American, 2 percent Native American, and 70 percent Anglo. There are just under 1,000 international undergraduate students. Sixty-eight percent of freshmen live on campus (4,836 total spaces in the residence hall system).

Just over two thirds of the students receive $170 million in financial aid each year. The campus has nineteen sororities and twenty-seven fraternities.

Faculty There are 1,469 faculty members, 97 percent with doctoral degrees. The student-faculty ratio is 20:1.

Key Facilities The library holds 4 million volumes. There are seven open-access computer labs and many departmental specialty labs. Labs contain a combination of Windows/DOS, Macintosh, and UNIX-based machines. Each residence hall room provides a free direct link to UAInfo, the World Wide Web, and the Internet for students bringing personal computers to campus.

Athletics UA participates in NCAA Division I, Pac-10 athletics. The University maintains the nation's fourth-ranked all-around sports program, with six teams ranked in the top 10 nationally. The women's softball team has won the national championship twice in the last three years. Eight sports are available to men (baseball, basketball, football, tennis, golf, swimming/diving, cross-country, and track and field) and ten sports are available to women (basketball, golf, tennis, softball, volleyball, swimming/diving, cross-country, track and field, gymnastics, and soccer). Students also participate in intramural and club sports, which attract more than 20,000 students annually. On a day-to-day basis, students pursue their personal best in the Student Recreation Center, an $11-million building, created in response to student requests, that has won national awards for design and program quality.

Study Abroad The UA's Study Abroad Office has information about hundreds of program opportunities throughout the world. Students may choose to participate in UA-sponsored programs in Mexico, Europe, the Mediterranean, Russia, and Taiwan, or join another university program as a transfer student for a summer, semester, or academic year. Study-abroad scholarships are available to help support program costs.

Support Services The Center for Disability Related Resources assists students with physical, developmental, and learning disabilities.

Job Opportunities Students are offered a range of work opportunities on campus, including assistantships and 2,313 work-study positions.

Tuition: $1940 for state residents, $8308 for nonresidents, per year (1996-97)

Room and Board: $4410

Mandatory Fees: $69

Contact: Director: Dr. Patricia MacCorquodale, Slonaker House, Room 107, Tucson, Arizona 85721-0006; Telephone: 520-621-6901; Fax: 520-621-8655; E-mail: xilo@ccit.arizona.edu; Web site: http://www.honors.arizona.edu/honors.html

UNIVERSITY OF ARKANSAS

4 Pu C L Sc Tr

▼ Fulbright College of Arts and Sciences Honors Studies Program

The Fulbright College Honors Studies Program was created in 1956. Initially, though many core honors courses were offered, the focus was mainly departmental. In 1986, a four-year honors core was developed. Now students are able to participate in honors studies in one of two ways—The Four-Year Scholars Program or the Departmental Honors Program. Both programs are designed to provide bright, energetic students with a deeper understanding of their fields and to place that understanding in the context of a broad liberal arts education.

Participation Requirements: The Four-Year Scholars program offers an honors core curriculum as an alternative to the regular core. An NEH-sponsored four-semester humanities course has been designed to combine world literature, world civilization, and fine arts requirements. Students also have the opportunity to choose among a wide variety of colloquia. Departmental honors students must complete 12 hours of honors classes. Both groups complete an honors research or terminal project in the field of study.

Students who successfully complete required honors course work and a research project in their field of study will graduate with honors. Cum laude, magna cum laude, summa cum laude—depending on the quality of the work completed—will be noted on transcripts and diplomas. Students graduating with honors wear stoles and medals at graduation marking their outstanding accomplishments.

Admission Process: Students are admitted on several criteria: high school records, class rank, ACT or SAT I scores, academic awards and prizes, and participation in special programs or institutes. Students entering the Four-Year Scholars Program usually have a high school GPA of 3.5 or better and a score of 28 on the ACT (1240 on the SAT I) or higher. Students entering the Departmental Honors Program usually have a current college GPA of 3.25 and must be recommended by a member of the student's department. These guidelines are flexible. A student who does not meet the basic requirements should schedule an interview with the director.

Scholarship Availability: The University of Arkansas awards numerous academic scholarships. Most of the students participating in Honors Studies have been awarded one of these scholarships. Only the Sturgis Fellowships are directly awarded by the Honors Studies Office. The Sturgis Endowment for Academic Excellence funds eleven fellowships ($43,000 for four years) each year. In addition to room, board, and tuition, Sturgis Fellowships can be used to pay for travel abroad or for equipment, such as computers and musical instruments.

The Campus Context: The University of Arkansas (Fayetteville) is comprised of seven colleges: Fulbright College of Arts and Sciences, School of Architecture, College of Business Administration, Dale Bumpers College of Agriculture and Food and Life Sciences, College of Education, and College of Engineering.

Student Body The undergraduate enrollment totals 11,973. Forty-seven percent are women, 53 percent men. African Americans make up 6.02 percent of the population, Asians 2.5 percent, Hispanics .9 percent, and Native Americans 1.82 percent. Eighty percent of the students live off campus. There are 285 international undergraduate students at the University of Arkansas.

Study Abroad The Fulbright Institute at the University of Arkansas houses the Study Abroad Program. Many campus scholarships (up to $8000 each) specifically for study abroad are available. The University has a variety of exchange programs.

Tuition: $2224 for state residents, $5786 for nonresidents, per year (1996-97)

Room and Board: $3780 minimum

Fees: $186

Contact: Professor Elizabeth Payne, Old Main 517, Fayetteville, Arkansas 72701; Telephone: 501-575-2509; Fax: 501-575-2642; E-mail: epayne@comp.uark.edu

UNIVERSITY OF ARKANSAS AT MONTICELLO

4 Pu G S Sc Tr

▼ Honors Program

The UAM honors curriculum consists of four core colloquia for freshman and sophomore students and independent work at the junior and senior levels, leading to a senior thesis. The core courses are interdisciplinary and are unique in the University curriculum. Colloquia topics vary and are related closely to the annual theme around which cocurricular and extracurricular activities are designed. These four courses may substitute for general education requirements in the humanities, social science, and math or science. Class size is limited to facilitate discussion.

Faculty members are invited to participate in the Honors Program, both as colloquia instructors and as mentors for the upper-level students working toward theses. Preferred faculty members are engaged actively in research and have a demonstrated interest in sharing enthusiasm for intellectual inquiry.

Cocurricular and extracurricular activities are vital elements in the program. From the informal Brown Bag Friday talks in the Honors Center each week to Sunday in the City, a monthly excursion to Little Rock for events such as symphony performances, IMAX films, and traveling exhibits at the Design Museum to satellite programming through NCHC and travel to research conferences, UAM

Honors Program students are offered a rich variety of intellectual stimulation. In addition, students have exclusive, 24-hour access to the Honors Center, which includes multiple computers with Internet access, a full kitchen, activity room, and study lounge.

The 2-year-old program has 55 participants.

Participation Requirements: Graduation as a University Honors Scholar requires completion of 18 hours of honors courses and two Honors Options courses in the major, maintenance of a minimum 3.0 GPA, and completion of a senior thesis.

Admission Process: High school students with ACT composite scores of 24 and above are recruited directly for the program. Students must apply to the program, providing transcripts and letters of recommendation, and are invited to the campus for an interview that includes attending a Brown Bag Friday presentation; writing a brief, extemporaneous essay; meeting faculty members in an interview setting; and touring campus facilities. Rising sophomores and transfer students may apply for fall admission to the program when vacancies are available and all admission criteria are met.

Scholarship Availability: The Honors Program includes full-tuition, four-year scholarships for entering freshmen with a book credit of $150 per semester. Entering sophomores are offered three years of full tuition and the book allowance.

The Campus Context: The University of Arkansas at Monticello is situated in the pine forests of southeast Arkansas on the edge of the rich Mississippi Delta and is the home of the state's only school of forestry. UAM was established in 1909 as the Fourth District Agricultural School, and 300 acres of University land are still devoted to agricultural teaching and research. The campus is located 100 miles southeast of Little Rock and became part of the University of Arkansas system in 1971.

Student Body There are 2,370 undergraduates, primarily from southeast Arkansas: 41 percent men, 59 percent women. The ethnic distribution is 85 percent Caucasian and 15 percent African American. Eighty-five percent of the students are commuters.

Support Services Some facilities are accessible for the disabled on the lower floors. The Office of Special Student Services coordinates the needs of disabled students.

Tuition: $1906 for state residents, $4114 for nonresidents, per year (1996-97)

Room and Board: $2400 minimum

Contact: Director: Dr. Linda J. Webster, Monticello, Arkansas 71656; Telephone: 501-460-1232; Fax: 301-696-3810; E-mail: webster@uamont.edu; Web site: http://cotton.uamont.edu/~webster/webster.html

UNIVERSITY OF CALIFORNIA, DAVIS

4 Pu G M

▼ Davis Honors Challenge

The Davis Honors Challenge (DHC) is a new, one-year honors program designed for 240 highly motivated first- and second-year students who want to enhance their education through special courses, closer contacts with faculty members, and dynamic interaction with academic peers. Essay applications are screened without reference to national exam scores or high school/university GPA.

The goals of the DHC are to foster students' critical thinking and analytic interpretation skills, to improve their communication and research skills, to provide them experience in group dynamics and collaborative exploration of problems, and to develop their familiarity with electronic communication and visual presentation methods.

Integrated Studies (IS) is an invitational, residential honors program for 70 first-year students. Its goals are to help students integrate ideas from humanities, natural sciences, and social sciences and correlate information from self-contained disciplines through interdisciplinary or multidisciplinary approaches to learning; to provide excellent teaching for first-year students in small, highly personalized situations; to provide an academic residential community, similar to the best small-college communities, within a large research university; to provide students with challenging, participatory approaches to learning, incorporating recent technological advances such as electronic communication; to provide "hands-on" exposure to contemporary scholarly methodology; to encourage student participation in undergraduate research; to encourage student-faculty interactions on a more personal level than that realized in the large classroom situation common to public research universities; and to provide effective, personalized advising on academic matters.

Integrated Studies faculty members are specialists with proven excellence in teaching who have a particular interest in how their research and discipline are related to other disciplines, to contemporary society, and to philosophical issues of the day.

The Davis Honors Challenge is a year old and currently enrolls 400 students. The Integrated Studies program is 27 years old and currently enrolls 70 students. The deadline for applying to the program is June 15 for the fall semester.

Participation Requirements: Davis Honors Challenge students are required to take three honors courses during the academic year. They may choose two from a list of honors courses offered by departments ("H courses") or courses with DHC discussion sections. The third required course is a 3-unit, problem-oriented, interdisciplinary DHC seminar. Integrated Studies students are required to take three specially designed

IS courses and two 1-unit IS seminars during the academic year. All students who complete either program will receive transcript notation.

Scholarship Availability: Regents Scholars, selected by an independent faculty committee, are guaranteed places in Integrated Studies. Neither DHC nor IS controls any scholarship funding or the scholarship selection process.

The Campus Context: The University of California began in 1868; classes began the following year at the College of California in Oakland. The first buildings on the Berkeley campus were completed in 1873. Today the University is one of the largest and most renowned centers of higher education in the world. Its nine campuses span the state, from Davis in the north to San Diego in the south. In between are the Berkeley, San Francisco, Santa Cruz, Santa Barbara, Riverside, Irvine, and Los Angeles campuses. All UC campuses adhere to the same admission guidelines and high academic standards, yet each has its own distinct character, atmosphere, and academic individuality. Together, the nine campuses have an enrollment of more than 163,000 students, 90 percent of them California residents.

Founded in 1905 as the University Farm and designated as a general campus in 1959, UC Davis offers a full range of undergraduate and graduate programs, as well as professional programs in law, management, medicine, and veterinary medicine. With 5,200 acres, UC Davis is the largest of the nine University of California campuses and third in budget, total expenditures, and enrollment. UC Davis stands twenty-second in research funding among universities in the United States, according to recent information from the National Science Foundation. In 1996, *U.S. News & World Report* ranked UC Davis among the top 10 public universities nationally, just four years after the magazine identified the campus as one of the five "up-and-coming" national universities. The campus' unusual resources include a 150-acre arboretum, seven natural reserves, more than twenty research institutes or centers, five museums, and three galleries.

The University's reputation for excellence has attracted a distinguished faculty of scholars and scientists in all fields of scholarship. UC Davis faculty members rank sixteenth in quality among comprehensive public universities nationwide, according to a multiyear study of U.S. doctoral programs reported in 1995 by the National Research Council. Creative teaching and academic innovation are encouraged by several programs, including the $30,000 Prize for Teaching and Scholarly Achievement, believed to be the largest award of its kind in the country.

Ecologically aware and socially innovative, Davis has a small-town friendliness and spirit of volunteerism that distinguishes it from cities of similar size. Residents are active in local, national, and international political causes, in the arts, and in community organizations. Students compose a large portion of the city's population of 53,000, making Davis one of the state's few remaining "college towns."

UC Davis has three colleges: Letters and Science, Agricultural and Environmental Sciences, and Engineering. The biological sciences program is administered through the intercollegiate Division of Biological Sciences. In addition, UC Davis has four professional schools: Law, Management, Medicine, and Veterinary Medicine. Altogether, 100 undergraduate majors and seventy-five graduate degree programs are offered.

Student Body Undergraduate enrollment is 18,819: 48.6 percent men, 51.4 percent women. The ethnic distribution is 45.2 percent Caucasian, 1.2 percent American Indian/Alaskan Native, 3.5 percent black/African American, 6.9 percent Chicano/Mexican American, 3.8 percent Latino/other Spanish American, 3.7 percent Filipino/Philipino, 13.6 percent Chinese/Chinese American, 1.9 percent Japanese/Japanese American, 2.5 percent Korean/Korean American, 0.5 percent Polynesian, 9.6 percent other Asian, 2.2 percent East Indian/Pakistani, 5.5 percent other or no data, and 3 percent international students. Most of the students are residents. There are twenty-five fraternities and eighteen sororities.

Faculty Of the 1,598 faculty members, 1,331 are full time; 98 percent hold terminal degrees. The student-faculty ratio is 18.7:1.

Key Facilities The UC Davis Library System contains more than 2.8 million volumes and receives 47,000 periodical and journal titles annually. The thirteen on-campus computer labs include six Macintosh and five PC facilities, as well as a media distribution facility and new media laboratory.

Athletics UC Davis has recently been awarded the Sears Directors Cup for its successful participation in nonscholarship Division II intercollegiate athletics. Intramural sports programs serve 13,000 of the 18,000 undergraduates.

Study Abroad Through the Education Abroad Program, the University offers study in cooperation with more than 100 institutions in thirty different countries.

Support Services The Disability Resource Center offers students full services and accommodations.

Job Opportunities The Student Employment Center assists students and student spouses to obtain on-campus positions.

Tuition: None for state residents, $8394 for nonresidents, per year (1996-97)

Room and Board: $5468

Mandatory Fees: $4230

Contact: Director (DHC) Kenneth L. Verosub; Director (IS) Nora A. McGuinness, Integrated Studies, 162 Kerr Hall, Davis, California 95616-8518; Telephone: 916-754-4098 (DHC), 916-752-9906 (IS); Fax: 916-754-8311 (DHC), 916-754-8311 (IS); E-mail: verosub@honors.ucdavis.edu (DHC), namcguinness@ucdavis.edu (IS)

UNIVERSITY OF CALIFORNIA, IRVINE

4 Pu G M Sc Tr

▼ **Campuswide Honors Program**

Located on 1,500 acres of beautiful coastal foothills 5 miles from the Pacific Ocean, the University of California,

Irvine (UCI), offers its most talented students the opportunities of the Campuswide Honors Program. UCI, known for research and teaching excellence, has a lively student body with an international background and a casual lifestyle. The Campuswide Honors Program is dedicated to promoting high standards of scholastic excellence and personal growth by combining the best of an excellent liberal arts college with the broad range of opportunities offered by a major research university.

One of the Honors Program's major features is its curriculum, a series of interdisciplinary and discipline-based classes designed to challenge and introduce talented students to important topics, issues, and methods of inquiry. Honors students gain from the same dynamic and creative spirit that this past year led to 2 of its faculty members' receiving the Nobel Prize in different disciplines (physics and chemistry). At UCI students can engage in research as undergraduates, working with faculty members and their research teams.

The Campuswide Honors Program enrolls approximately 400 students from the freshman through senior years (about 3 percent of the undergraduates) and represents every major on campus.

Honors advising by faculty members, professional staff, and peers provides students with assistance in planning their course of study and applying for scholarships, graduate and professional school, internships, and education abroad programs.

One hundred Campuswide Honors students live in honors houses on campus; honors students also have the privilege of special reading rooms in the libraries and are invited to participate in many social and cultural activities, including weekly coffee hours, beach bonfires, poetry readings, visits and informal lectures in faculty members' and students' homes, and annual camping retreats to places such as the Anza-Borrego Desert State Park.

Participation Requirements To graduate from the Campuswide Honors Program, students complete sequences of honors classes, finish a research thesis project, and achieve a minimum GPA of 3.2 (most honors students have GPAs above 3.5). Successful completion of the Campuswide Honors Program is noted at the Honors Convocation and appears on the diploma and final transcript.

Ninety percent of Campuswide Honors graduates pursue graduate or professional degrees within two years of graduation from UCI. Recent graduates benefiting from the Campuswide Honors Program are attending Harvard, Princeton, Cornell, Stanford, Berkeley, UC San Diego, UCLA, the Universities of Chicago and London, and other excellent schools.

Admission Process: Admission is competitive, with most students invited while in high school. About half of the incoming freshmen last year had SAT scores over 1400 and high school GPAs over 4.2 (honors courses weighted).

Scholarship Availability: A majority of Campuswide Honors Program students are awarded Regents' Scholarships, the most prestigious University of California award. Regents' Scholars are selected for outstanding scholastic achievement and leadership potential and in recent years have received the equivalent of full in-state fees for four years.

The Campus Context: Founded in 1965, UCI is the youngest of the University of California campuses and ranks among the leading research universities in the United States. UCI offers forty-seven bachelor's degree programs, forty-one master's degree programs, thirty-six Ph.D. programs, an M.D. program, and teacher credential programs.

Student Body There are 13,833 undergraduates enrolled: 47 percent men, 53 percent women. The ethnic distribution of undergraduates is 2.6 percent African American; 53.3 percent Asian American and Pacific Islander; 9.4 percent Chicano; 4 percent Latino; 6 percent Native American; 25 percent white/Caucasian; 5.2 percent unlisted. There are 448 international students. Approximately 33 percent of UCI undergraduates reside on campus. In addition, about 10 percent live in apartments across the street from the campus. Sixty percent receive some form of financial aid. There are 275 student organizations registered on campus, with a combined membership exceeding 14,000 students. This includes twenty-nine sororities and fraternities.

Faculty Of the 1,428 faculty members, 998 are full-time equivalent; 98 percent have terminal degrees (Ph.D., M.D.). The student-faculty ratio is 19:1.

Key Facilities The UCI libraries house 1.5 million volumes. Extensive computer resources are available to students, including twelve computer laboratories, with others in the developmental stage. Hardware within these labs includes IBM PCs, Macs, X-terminals, and UNIX workstations. Several of the labs are open 24 hours a day. All residence halls are connected to the UCI computer network through the Ethernet.

Athletics UCI's intercollegiate athletic program features nineteen sports. UCI's men's and women's teams compete in NCAA Division I and the Big West Conference. The men's teams include basketball, cross-country, track and field, golf, swimming, diving, and tennis. Men's soccer, volleyball, and water polo teams compete in the Mountain Pacific Sports Federation; the sailing team competes in the Intercollegiate Yacht Racing Association; and crew in the Pacific Coast Championships. UCI women's teams compete in basketball, crew, cross-country, soccer, swimming, diving, tennis, track and field, and volleyball.

Study Abroad Students may participate in the Education Abroad Program (EAP) of the University of California, which operates in cooperation with about 100 host universities and colleges in thirty countries throughout the world. UCI's International Opportunities Program helps students take advantage of worldwide opportunities for study, work, internship, volunteering, research, and noncredential teaching.

Support Services Disabled students receive assistance from admission through graduation from the Disability Services Office. Specialized services and equipment include assistance in the classroom, a computing lab for disabled students providing special computer technology and training, and a van that can be used for off-campus transportation for medically and academically related purposes.

Job Opportunities Students are assisted in finding jobs on campus and in the community by the Career and Life Planning Center.

Tuition: None for state residents, $8394 for nonresidents, per year (1997-98)

Room and Board: $5565 minimum

Mandatory Fees: $4050

Contact: Director: Dr. Roger McWilliams, Division of Undergraduate Education, 204 Engineering Tower, Irvine, California 92697-5680; Telephone: 714-824-5461; Fax: 714-824-2092; E-mail: honors@uci.edu; Web site: http://www.honors.uci.edu/~honors

UNIVERSITY OF CALIFORNIA, RIVERSIDE

4 Pu G M

▼ University Honors Program

In the innovative University Honors Program (UHP), students are invited to participate in seminars, courses, and a wide variety of projects intended to enhance their total university experience.

The University Honors Program was established eight years ago with a major grant from the Ford Foundation. The UHP is divided into two components: the Lower Division Program and the Upper Division Program. In the Lower Division Program, students take a minimum of four honors seminars (or honors sections of courses). Additionally, students participate in the Freshman Colloquium, which includes a set of workshops on research skills and a series of lectures by some of the most distinguished and stimulating UCR faculty members. These workshops and lectures give a challenging and exciting introduction to university research. In the sophomore year, special internships are available providing hands-on experience in many contexts both at UCR and in the Riverside community.

The Upper Division program culminates in a senior thesis (or portfolio or performance). This is a major intellectual or artistic accomplishment, which is guided carefully by a faculty supervisor.

In addition to the faculty supervisor, a second "reader" also gives comments, and must approve the project. The senior theses are presented at a conference in the spring, and are bound and kept in the University Honors Program office. The experience of working carefully and closely

with faculty mentors on a significant project is profound and deeply rewarding. The bond between student and faculty member can be very close and the basis of a lifelong friendship.

The University Honors Program provides a framework within which intellectual development is encouraged and fostered. One of the goals is to stimulate students to pursue serious research and perhaps academic careers in the future. Students with these interests often find it rewarding to live and to socialize with others with similar orientations. UCR seeks to provide not only intellectual stimulation, but also a set of social activities and opportunities to get involved in community service.

The program currently enrolls 250 students. Students who participate receive Lower Division and Upper Division notation on their transcripts. Many are also eligible for the Golden Key National Honor Society as well as other honorary scholastic societies, including Phi Beta Kappa.

Admission Process: Participation in Lower Division Honors is by application. Students are invited to apply or may call and request an application from the UHP office. Admission requires that an incoming freshman have a cumulative GPA of 3.5 or above, an SAT I of at least 1350, and an excellent high school record of both scholarship and service. Transfer students must have a cumulative GPA of 3.5.

Students who have achieved Lower Division honors at UCR may apply for participation in Upper Division honors. Students who have not participated in Lower Division honors at UCR may also apply or be nominated by a faculty member for Upper Division honors. The following materials must be submitted: 1) a statement of goals describing, in general terms, the project the student wishes to pursue; 2) two letters of recommendation from faculty members or other individuals who can refer to the student's abilities as a student and a scholar; and 3) a student information sheet.

Verification of the student's transcript is also required; transfer students may be required to submit copies of their transcripts from previous institutions. Admission to the program is based upon these materials. Most students have a 3.4 overall GPA when they are admitted to the Upper Division UHP.

Scholarship Availability: There are several different scholarship programs offering assistance to students.

Residential Fellowship Program UHP students are eligible to apply for a UHP Residential Fellowship. UHP Fellows live together in the Aberdeen and Inverness Residential Hall where they are responsible for a wide range of activities and events that enrich both dorm living and the honors experience. The fellowship represents a significant reduction in the cost of room and board and is awarded in a competitive process. Applications are available in the Winter Quarter and are based on academic merit and involvement in service and/or campus activities. Preference will be given to incoming freshmen and transfer students.

American Honda Foundation/UHP Research Grant This grant funds research expenses (i.e., materials, books, some travel) for honors projects in the natural and social sciences. All women and underrepresented minority Upper Division students are encouraged to seek out this opportunity. Typical awards are between $100 and $500.

UC Education Abroad Program (EAP) The Education Abroad Program offers a unique time- and cost-effective opportunity for UCR students. EAP places UC students in regular courses at top international host institutions with the host country students, in thirty-three countries nationwide, offering both short-term and year-long program options at a cost comparable to UCR's while earning UC credit. Fellowships for UHP students to participate in EAP are available.

The Campus Context: The University of California, Riverside, is composed of the College of Humanities, Arts, and Social Sciences; College of Natural and Agricultural Sciences; and The Marlan and Rosemary Bourns College of Engineering. There are 164 degree programs offered in eighty-two disciplines.

Special campus facilities include the Center for Entrepreneurial Studies, Agricultural Experiment Station, Air Pollution Research Laboratory, Archaeological Research Unit, Archaeometry Laboratory, Center for Bibliographic Studies and Research, Natural Reserves/Research Centers, California Educational Research Co-op, Center for Ideas and Society, Center for Environmental Research and Technology, Center for Social and Behavioral Science and Research, Comprehensive Teacher Education Institute, Dry Lands Research Institute, Institute of Geophysics and Planetary Physics, California Museum of Photography, Presley Center for Crime and Justice Studies, and the USDA Salinity Laboratory.

Student Body Undergraduate enrollment is 48 percent men, 52 percent women. The ethnic distribution is 6 percent African American, 0.7 percent Native American, 15.3 percent Chicano, 4.2 percent Latino, 39.1 percent Asian-Pacific Islander, 30.3 percent white, 2.1 percent other, with 2.3 percent unknown. There are 268 international students. Approximately 30 percent live in campus housing; approximately 55 percent receive financial aid. There are thirty fraternities/sororities.

Faculty The faculty is composed of 430 budgeted FTE (full-time equivalent) members. Ninety-seven percent have terminal degrees. The student-faculty ratio is 18:1.

Key Facilities There are 1.8 million volumes in the library. Computer facilities include three computer labs and approximately 400 computers (Intel PC, Apple/Macintosh, Power PC, and UNIX); students get e-mail accounts.

Athletics UCR's 175 student-athletes compete on eleven National Collegiate Athletic Association (NCAA) Division II sports teams in the California Collegiate Athletic Association. UCR offers five teams for men interested in participating on the collegiate level: basketball, baseball, cross-country, tennis, and track and field. Women's sports are basketball, cross-country, softball, tennis, track and field, and volleyball. Athletic programs are supported by student fees and by private gifts developed through the work of the UCR Athletic Association.

Study Abroad UCR encourages students to include an international experience as part of a degree objective. The Inter-

national Services Center coordinates the application process. Students interested in language, literature, science, art, culture, history, government, or social institutions of the EAP countries have the opportunity to gain substantially from firsthand academic experiences. Opportunities are available at each class level, with the year abroad traditionally taken in the junior year. Short-term options are available in selected countries and in targeted academic fields. ISC advisers are available to discuss academic expectations, cultural adjustment, and re-entry.

Support Services Disabled students will find disability related counseling, mobility services, testing arrangements, and adaptive equipment.

Job Opportunities Work opportunities on campus include the Federal Work-Study Program.

Tuition: None for state residents, $8394 for nonresidents, per year (1996-97)

Room and Board: $5870

Mandatory Fees: $4105

Contact: Director: Dr. John M. Fischer, Professor of Philosophy, 3154 Library South, Riverside, California 92521-0157; Telephone: 909-787-5323; Fax: 909-787-5320; E-mail: honors@ucrac1.ucr.edu; Web site: http://members.tripod.com/~UHP/UHP.htm

UNIVERSITY OF CENTRAL ARKANSAS

4 Pu G M Sc Tr*

▼ Honors College

The University of Central Arkansas Honors College has offered a minor in honors interdisciplinary studies for students in all majors for fourteen years. UCA established the Honors College to heighten the educational experience for intellectually gifted students with demonstrated records of achievement. It provides a structured setting within which the student is encouraged to test varied skills by subjecting them to the give and take of dialogue with other students and faculty members.

The program is divided into two parts: the Honors Program for freshmen and sophomores and the Honors College for juniors and seniors. The Honors Program consists of a two-semester Freshman Honors Seminar and a two-semester Sophomore Honors Seminar. This four-course sequence is entitled "The Human Search." The Honors College consists of interdisciplinary seminars, an Oxford Tutorial, and the completion of an honors thesis project. This 30-hour curriculum stresses the arts of inquiry, conversation, and collaboration. Dr. Terrel Bell, former U.S. Secretary of Education, called the program "an Ivy League education at a bargain basement price." UCA has been cited by Warren Martin of the Carnegie Foundation for having a "creative and innovative program."

Students who graduate from the Honors College receive a hand-crafted medallion worn at Commencement, a special certificate (which includes printing of the thesis title) and acknowledgment of honors category on the diploma. There are currently 230 students in the program.

Participation Requirements: Students enrolled in the Honors Program must maintain a 3.25 GPA. To be admitted into the Honors College, the student must have completed at least one course in the Honors Program and must have an overall GPA of 3.4. While in the Honors College, students must maintain an overall GPA of 3.4. Sophomores deliver a Sophomore Lecture as part of the College application process, and seniors give an oral presentation of their honors thesis project.

Scholarship Availability: Nearly all students in the program receive University scholarships. Supplemental honors scholarships are available, ranging in value from $250 to $5000 a year, and are awarded based on merit and need. Funds are also awarded on a competitive basis to students who submit proposals for travel abroad and for undergraduate research or internship programs.

Transfer students are accepted if space allows. The requirements vary, depending on the student's year in school, credits earned, and so on.

The Campus Context: The University of Central Arkansas is located in Conway, Arkansas, just 30 minutes from Little Rock, and includes the College of Business Administration, College of Education, College of Fine Arts, College of Health and Applied Sciences, College of Humanities and Social Sciences, and College of Natural Sciences and Mathematics.

Student Body Undergraduate enrollment is 7,878: 39 percent men, 61 percent women. The ethnic distribution is 78.4 percent Caucasian, 11.6 percent black; 1 percent American Indian; 1 percent Asian American; 1 percent Hispanic; 7 percent other. There are 315 international students. Of the total population, 1,540 students are residents and 6,338 are commuters. Seventy-two percent of the students receive financial aid. There are ten fraternities and nine sororities.

Faculty Of the 398 full-time faculty members, 75 percent have terminal degrees. There are an additional 146 part-time faculty members. The student-faculty ratio is 18:1.

Key Facilities The library houses about 1 million items, including 350,000 monographs and 2,500 bound periodicals. UCA's Data Processing Department offers its students and staff access to the Internet and facilities such as e-mail through the various computer labs located across the campus. Individual departments have created PC labs for students studying in that specialty. The Honors College has its own PC lab located in the Honors Center in McAlister Hall. It is generally open from 8 a.m. to midnight while classes are in session.

Athletics The athletic program at the University of Central Arkansas has been one of the most successful in the state over the past 30 years. UCA teams dominated the Arkansas Intercollegiate Conference for much of the 1970s and all of the 1980s, and have been just as successful since moving into the prestigious NCAA Division II and Gulf South Conference in 1993. UCA currently fields intercollegiate teams in ten sports, five for men and five for women. The women's sports include volleyball, basketball, tennis, softball, and cross-country. The men's sports include football, basketball, baseball, soccer, and golf. The teams compete in the sixteen-team Gulf South Conference, the largest Division II conference in the country and one of the most highly respected athletically.

The UCA women's program finished second overall in 1995–96 for the GSC All-Sports Award, which goes to the school that finishes the highest in the final standings in its combined sports. The UCA football team, the winningest in Arkansas over the last two decades, won nine straight AIC titles and three NAIA national championships from 1983–91. The men's basketball team reached the nationally televised NAIA championship game in Kansas City, Missouri, twice in the early 1990s. UCA is also the alma mater of six-time NBA All-Star and two-time Olympian Scottie Pippen, who was an All-American in 1985–87. UCA placed 35 student-athletes on the GSC Honor Roll in 1995–96, with senior football player Brian Barnett receiving a prestigious NCAA Postgraduate Scholarship for $5000 for his classroom work. Barnett had a 3.93 GPA in physical therapy.

Study Abroad UCA offers several three- to five-week, credit-bearing study abroad opportunities during the summer months. All of the programs are coordinated by specific academic departments in conjunction with the Office of International Programs. Students may participate in a three-week field experience in Honduras and earn credit in either sociology or health science. The course is designed to provide participants with firsthand knowledge of the public health problems facing a developing nation and includes visits to a variety of urban and rural health facilities and programs. Visits to Mayan ruins and the coast are featured as well. UCA students may choose to participate in a five-week Spanish language and culture program at the University of Guadalajara to earn credit in Spanish. Language training is offered at beginning, intermediate, and advanced levels. To more fully experience Mexico, participants live with local families. In addition to the academic program, creative workshops and guided excursions are also available.

Interested students may travel to England for three weeks every other summer as part of a study trip sponsored by the Department of English. Participants visit London, Stratford-on-Avon, the Lake Country, and other places of literary, theatrical, and historical interest. Credit in English may be awarded.

In addition to opportunities available through the UCA International Programs Office, Honors College students are eligible for grants for study abroad. The Travel Abroad Grants (TAG) program has sent students to India, Southeast Asia, Great Britain, Honduras, France, and Africa, just to name a few destinations. These students did everything from attending universities in these countries to traveling, working in internships, and assisting in local medical care for remote villages.

Support Services All classroom buildings and facilities are handicapped-accessible. All facilities comply with Arkansas state law concerning handicapped accessibility.

Job Opportunities Work opportunities exist for undergraduates in two programs: the UCA Student Help Program and the Federal Work-Study Program, which is federally funded. Besides work-study opportunities, Honors Scholars are eligible to apply for Undergraduate Research Grants for Education (URGE). These grants give honors students the chance to participate in research for their honors theses, departmental theses, internships, and major areas of study. Some examples of recent URGEs are dolphin communication, cancer research, art history, environmental ethics, and foreign language instruction in elementary schools.

Tuition: $1682 minimum for state residents, $3507 minimum for nonresidents, per year (1996-97)

Room and Board: $2710 minimum

Mandatory Fees: $410-$574

Contact: Director: Dr. Norbert O. Schedler, P.O. Box 5024/ McAlister 306, 201 Donaghey Avenue, Conway, Arkansas 72035; Telephone: 501-450-3198; Fax: 501-450-5958; E-mail: barbarar@ cc1.uca.edu; Web site: under construction

UNIVERSITY OF CENTRAL FLORIDA

4 Pu G L Sc Tr

▼ University Honors Program

The Honors Program at the University of Central Florida is the center of academic excellence at the University. Its purpose is to enhance and broaden the education of the most able undergraduate students attending UCF. The program includes intensified course work within the General Education Program (GEP), as well as interdisciplinary seminars, lectures, and activities beyond the classroom.

Honors classes are the program's main attraction. Honors GEP classes are smaller than regular sections and are taught by select faculty members. Seminar and lecture classes are proposed by faculty members and involve innovative, cutting-edge knowledge in their fields. Since the Honors Program draws students from all five colleges on campus, it must maintain strong academic programs tailored to the needs of each student. The Honors Program values diversity of education and is as responsive to the demands of the psychology major as it is to the demands of the engineer.

Social acclimation of students to the University is an important issue. UCF believes that if students are not comfortable socially, their academic work will suffer. Social acclimation for the honors students begins in the honors symposium, which is required for every entering student but open to all honors students. Meeting once a week, the symposium is used to showcase scholarly activity by UCF

and visiting professors and to carry out program business. In order to make contacts the students need meeting places, and honors gives them two options. The honors lounge is a center of social activity where students can play chess or checkers or have lunch. The study lounge gives them a quieter environment in which to study individually or in groups and is equipped with state-of-the-art computers. Cultural events are also part of the social support that honors provides. There are day trips to museums, reduced tickets to local cultural events, and program-sponsored speakers at informal lunches and dinners that students are encouraged to attend.

Student participation in the management of the Honors Program is integral to its success. The Student Honors Advisory Council participates in class selection, discusses program policy, and informs students of upcoming honors events in a newsletter. The Advisory Council is also responsible for coordinating and encouraging student participation in national and regional meetings of professional organizations such as the National Collegiate Honors Council.

The Honors Program always strives to meet the changing needs of its current students as well as protecting the interests of those to come. In the past two years, it has instituted a system whereby current students act as program representatives. Honors Ambassadors give high school and open-house presentations to high school students seeking a college or university, while Peer Advisors counsel new students during orientation sessions. The Einstein Circle is a club that honors and nonhonors students created for social interaction.

The Honors Program is committed to quality—its graduates have attended institutions such as Harvard, UCLA, Duke, and Penn State. Since its origin in 1989, the program's enrollment has grown to about 500 students. The Honors Program is a premier program in terms of academic integrity and student support, one that relishes future challenges and changes.

The deadline for applying is March 1.

Participation Requirements: To graduate from the Honors Program, students must maintain both a 3.2 overall GPA and a 3.0 GPA in honors courses, take 22 credit hours of General Education course work in honors as well as Symposium I and II, one upper division lecture, and two seminars. Students are only required to take 11 credits outside of their major field of study, which gives them a more rounded education without compromising their major. All honors course work is undertaken in small classes limited to 20 students (with a 17:1 student-faculty ratio) where close faculty-student interaction is essential. Students may also select Honors in the Major, involving original research and a senior thesis in consultation with Honors faculty.

Successful completion of the Honors Program requirements is recorded on the student's transcript and noted at graduation.

The Campus Context: The University of Central Florida is located in east central Florida, a region with a population of about 2 million. Known principally for its tourist attractions, the area is one of the fastest-growing regions in the nation. East central Florida is noted for its many lakes. Atlantic beaches are an easy hour's drive from the main campus. The area offers Broadway productions, pop and classical music headliners, art festivals, a Shakespeare festival of UCF origin, and the National Basketball Association's Orlando Magic.

UCF is a 1,442-acre campus comprised of fifty-one permanent buildings—valued at more than $130 million—radiating outward from an academic core, where UCF's colleges, classrooms, and library are located. UCF houses five colleges—College of Arts and Sciences, College of Business, College of Education, College of Engineering, and College of Health and Public Affairs. The College of Health and Public Affairs offers master's programs. Each of the other four colleges offers both master's and doctoral programs. More than $22 million in construction, including a $14-million communications building, is planned over the next three years.

New facilities recently completed or now under construction include a 700-bed residence hall, an $11-million student union, and an $11-million building to house the Center for Research and Education in Optics and Lasers. Other distinguished facilities on campus include the Institute for Simulation and Training, the Space Education and Research Center (SERC), the Center for Applied Human Factors in Aviation (CAHFA), the Florida Solar Energy Center (FSEC), the Florida-Canada Institute, the Small Business Development Center (SBDC), and the Department of Aerospace Studies (Air Force ROTC).

Key Facilities The University Library, housed in a 200,000-square-foot facility, has a collection of over 960,000 volumes (books, journals, and government documents) with approximately 5,000 subscriptions (journals, newspapers, and other serials) and over 7,500 media titles. The library is a partial depository for U.S. and Florida documents and U.S. patents. LUIS, the library's on-line catalog, is accessed through terminals in the library, at other campus locations, or from off-campus computers. Through LUIS, library users are able to determine whether the UCF library owns a particular item and the location and availability of the item. LUIS also provides on-line access to catalogs of all state university libraries in Florida and to ERIC, IAC, and other indexes.

Computer Services and Telecommunications provides central support services for administrative data processing, instruction and research computing, telecommunication networks, e-mail, telephony, information technology, training, user help, and microcomputer technology retail to the University. Central instruction and research computing is provided primarily by computers located on the main campus as follows: Novell LAN fileservers, IBM RS/6000 model 580, IBM ES/9000 mode 170, and other Internet and campus facilities. There are four public-access IBM PC labs located in the Computer Center and the Engineering, Education, and Business buildings. UNIX, PowerMac, and Macintosh equipment is also available at various labs. Voice response systems are available for dial-up registration, grades, and financial aid information. Access to the Internet and campus information servers is available to all students.

Athletics The University of Central Florida is a member of the National Collegiate Athletic Association (NCAA) Division I and competes in the Trans America Athletic Conference. UCF's current intercollegiate sports for men include baseball, basketball, cross-country, golf, football, soccer, and tennis. Women's sports include basketball, cross-country, golf, soccer, track, tennis, and volleyball. Crew and waterskiing are intercollegiate club sports for both men and women. UCF recreational facilities include lighted tennis and racquetball courts, an outdoor swimming pool, golf driving range, volleyball and basketball courts, and ball fields.

Study Abroad The UCF study-abroad programs are designed and administered by UCF faculty members. Students have a choice of programs that last one year, one semester, or six weeks. Some programs require proficiency in a foreign language, others do not. Prerequisites, length of stay, and academic requirements vary by program. UCF has summer programs in Canada, Germany, Italy, Spain, and Russia. UCF faculty members and students also participate in State University System programs in London, England, and Florence, Italy.

Support Services Student Disability Services provides information and orientation to campus facilities and services, assistance with classroom accommodations, assistance with course registration, disabled parking decals, counseling, and referral to campus and community services for students with disabilities. Services are available to students whose disabilities include, but are not limited to, hearing impairment, manual dexterity impairment, mobility impairment, specific learning disability (such as dyslexia), speech impairment, visual impairment, or other disabilities that require administrative or academic adjustments.

Tuition: $1830 for state residents, $7074 for nonresidents, per year (1996-97)

Room and Board: $4240

Mandatory Fees: $95

Contact: Director: Dr. Allyn MacLean Stearman, Orlando, Florida 32816-1800; Telephone: 407-823-2076; Fax: 407-823-6583; Web site: pegasus.cc.ucf.edu/honors/

UNIVERSITY OF CONNECTICUT

4 Pu G D L Sc Tr

▼ Honors Scholars Program

The Honors Scholars Program at the Storrs campus (the main campus) of the University of Connecticut is for enthusiastic and energetic students who enjoy small classes, extensive discussions with professors, and the challenge of articulating and refining their own ideas in an original thesis. The program is open to undergraduate students in all schools and colleges. Each student designs his or her program of study with the help of a permanently assigned faculty adviser in the student's area of interest.

First-year and sophomore Honors Scholars normally take two honors courses per term, but they may take more or fewer courses each term depending on their other academic and extracurricular activities. Each term, the University offers thirty to forty honors courses for first-year and sophomore students. The courses cover a wide range of topics and disciplines, including calculus, genetics, ancient history, moral philosophy, and public speaking. The average size of first- and second-year honors classes is 16 students. The Storrs Honors Scholars Program also offers three interdisciplinary seminars each term for sophomores. Two faculty members from different disciplines jointly teach each seminar. The seminars' design enables students to think about a topic or problem from multiple theoretical perspectives. A recent example is "Incest, Rape, and the Gallows: Family Violence and Community Justice in New England, 1805-1806," which was team-taught by professors from the School of Family Studies and the history department.

During their junior and senior years of study, Honors Scholars take their honors courses primarily within their major. All seniors must complete a thesis, which is not merely an accurate report of some findings but an original interpretation of observations that reveal the student's thoughtfulness and analytic rigor. Some departments, such as Biology, ask students to present and defend their theses at a meeting of department faculty and upper-division students. All senior Honors Scholars are eligible to apply for scholarship funds to help with the collection of data and the presentation of theses at professional conferences.

The Honors Scholars Program sponsors a monthly lecture series on current events and on intellectual debates within different disciplines. It also administers a Washington Internship Program for upper-division students who would like to work one semester for a member of Congress. Social amenities of the Honors Scholars Program include a student-run literary magazine, an ad hoc music group and film club, picnics and parties each term, and a nineteenth-century house that provides rooms for studying, practicing music, chatting, and holding classes.

A student organization, the Honors Program Coordinating Council, allows students to plan Honors Scholars activities at the Storrs campus and has representatives who sit at faculty meetings. Honors Scholars also have the option of living in designated honors floors in a residence hall.

The Honors Scholars Program is diverse in terms of students' ethnic and racial backgrounds. Approximately 25 percent of the students are from populations historically underrepresented at the University. An Honors Program for upper-division students in the humanities and social sciences is available at the Stamford regional campus. The Stamford Honors Program features interdisciplinary seminars, an evening lecture series, and a senior-year thesis component.

The 34-year-old Honors Scholars Program currently enrolls 850 students.

Participation Requirements: To remain in good standing in the Honors Scholars Program, students must take at least one honors course per academic year. In addition, first-year students must earn a total GPA of at least 3.0 and sophomores and juniors a total GPA of at least 3.1. To graduate with the title "Honors Scholar" on one's official transcript and diploma, a student at minimum must complete 12 hours of upper-division honors course work, complete a senior thesis, and have a total GPA of 3.2. Departments sometimes add further requirements for the Honors Scholar designation.

The Honors Program also offers a Sophomore Honors Certificate to students who have been unusually active in the Honors Scholars Program during their first two years of study. Although the Honors Scholars Program is the core of the honors program, the University offers two additional programs for highly motivated students.

A Degree with Distinction is awarded to students who have completed an academic program in which they demonstrate that they have mastered a discipline in depth, even though they may not have had the time or schedule flexibility to complete an honors thesis. To receive a "with Distinction" designation on a diploma, a student must attain an overall GPA of at least 3.2 and a GPA in the major of at least 3.5, and complete a creative project in a format the student's major department defines. Typically, students in the Degree with Distinction Program are part-time students, students in highly structured professional schools, or students with time-consuming extracurricular commitments, such as community service, varsity athletics, or jobs.

Finally, the Honors Program offers a University Scholar Program that enables highly talented juniors to design a plan of study for their last two years that is geared toward special interests. University Scholar candidates are able to take classes in all colleges on campus, have access to graduate courses, and may in some cases have normal University distribution requirements waived. Graduation as a "University Scholar," which appears on a student's diploma, is the highest academic honor that the University bestows on undergraduate students.

Admission Process: High school seniors should have a combined SAT I score of at least 1320 and be in the top 8 percent of their graduating class. Case-by-case decisions are made for students who have overcome unusual challenges or who have demonstrated outstanding ability in particular fields of study. Transfer students must have earned, at their previous institution, a total GPA of at least 3.4. Any first-year student or sophomore at the University of Connecticut who earns a total GPA of 3.2 while at the University is eligible to join the program, regardless of high school record or SAT scores.

Scholarship Availability: The University's Undergraduate Admissions Office awards approximately 80 four-year merit-based scholarships to incoming students. These scholarships are renewable for up to four years, provided that students meet the minimum grade requirement (normally a 3.2 overall average). The Admissions Office awards these scholarships according to a mixture of the following criteria: class rank, high school GPA, rigor of curriculum, extracurricular activities, and SAT I scores. In addition, the Honors Program Office offers about a half dozen 1-year awards (worth approximately $500-$800) to incoming Honors Scholars who have not received merit scholarships from the Admissions Office. Private donors have funded the Honors Program scholarships and have specified criteria for the awarding of each scholarship. Typical selection criteria include students' majors, hometowns, and SAT scores.

The Campus Context: The University of Connecticut has nine schools and colleges offering ninety-three degree programs on the Storrs campus: School of Allied Health Professions, School of Business Administration, School of Education, School of Engineering, School of Family Studies, School of Fine Arts, College of Liberal Arts and Sciences, School of Nursing, and School of Pharmacy. Distinguished facilities on campus include the William Benton Museum of Art, the Museum of Natural History, Thomas J. Dodd Research Center, Harry A. Gampel Pavilion, and the Jorgensen Auditorium.

Student Body There are 11,336 students on the Storrs campus with an equal balance of men and women. The ethnic distribution is 4 percent African American, 6 percent Asian American, 4 percent Latino American, 84 percent Caucasian, 1 percent international (about 200 students). Residents make up 68 percent of the student population, commuters 32 percent. Seventy percent of the students receive financial aid. There are thirteen fraternities and five sororities.

Faculty Of the 1,148 faculty members, 1,106 are full-time; 93 percent have terminal degrees. The student-faculty ratio is 14:1.

Key Facilities The library houses 2 million volumes. Computer facilities include more than 1,800 terminals on campus located in the Computer Center, the Babbidge Library, various schools and colleges, and some residence halls. The mainframe is an IBM ES 9000.

Athletics In varsity athletics, Division I sports at the University of Connecticut are baseball, men's and women's basketball, men's and women's cross-country and track, women's field hockey, men's golf, men's ice hockey, women's lacrosse, men's and women's soccer, men's and women's tennis, and women's volleyball. Football is a Division II sport. A wide variety of intramural sports is also available.

Study Abroad The University of Connecticut is in the forefront of study abroad programs; not only transfer credit but also grades earned abroad can be applied to degree programs. Through the Study Abroad Office, there are opportunities for study in virtually all countries, and there are extensive offerings for students in all colleges.

Support Services Disabled students are assisted by the Center for Students with Disabilities; students with documented learning disabilities are assisted by the University Program for College Students with Learning Disabilities.

Job Opportunities Students interested in employment will find work-study opportunities, numerous internship opportunities, and a Student Employment Office on campus.

Tuition: $4158 for state residents, $12,676 for nonresidents, per year (1997-98 est.)

Room and Board: $5461

Mandatory Fees: $938

Contact: Director: Cyrus Ernesto Zirakzadeh, 113 Wood Hall, 241 Glenbrook Road, U-147, Storrs, Connecticut 06269-2147; Assistant Director: Patricial Szarek, Telephone: 860-486-4223; Fax: 860-486-0222; E-mail: adhon1@uconnvm.uconn.edu

UNIVERSITY OF DAYTON

4 Pr G L Sc

▼ Honors and Scholars Program

The University of Dayton has a University-wide Honors Program restricted to 40 entering first-year University Scholars each year. Only students admitted to the University as beginning University Scholars are eligible to apply to the Honors Program. Honors students are entitled to all the benefits awarded to University Scholars.

The University Honors Program began in 1979 and graduated its first full class of students completing the program in 1983. It currently enrolls 150 honors and approximately 1,700 scholars.

The University of Dayton admits selected beginning and transfer undergraduate students to the University as University Scholars. Students who do not matriculate at the University as Scholars but subsequently earn a cumulative GPA of 3.5 or higher at the end of an academic year are added to the roster of University Scholars. Scholars whose GPA falls below a cumulative 3.0 at the end of an academic year are dropped from the roster of University Scholars.

The only automatic curricular impact of being named a University Scholar is the halving of the usual full-year first-year English composition requirement to a special one-semester course. Connected with this course is the visit to campus of the annual Scholars Author, one of whose books the first-year students will have studied in their Scholars English class.

In addition, University Scholars are given automatic permission to enroll in an extensive variety of specially designed Scholars sections of regularly offered courses. Many of these classes satisfy University-wide general education requirements. Registration in Scholars sections is not required of University Scholars, but all Scholars classes are given special designation on University transcripts. Moreover, funding to Scholars for conducting or presenting research is limited to Scholars who have taken two or more Scholars courses.

The Scholars Program also sponsors an annual Scholars Symposium, an annual Scholars Speaker in the Distinguished Speakers Series, an annual Scholars Artist Residency connected with the University Arts Series, and deeply discounted tickets to selected cultural events.

Special Scholars sections of University residence halls are available to limited numbers of first-, second- and third-year students.

The program began in 1979-80; its annual enrollment is 1,200 to 1,300 students, or approximately the top 20 percent of the undergraduate student body.

Participation Requirements:
Honors Program students take a series of five semester-long Honors Program Seminars during their first five semesters at the University. Currently in English, history, sociology, philosophy, and engineering systems design, these seminars satisfy University-wide general education requirements. In the final seminar, the entire junior Honors Program class works as a team on a complex project using a systems approach. Students must then complete an acceptable honors thesis and graduate with a 3.0 or higher GPA to be awarded an Honors Program degree. Students graduating from the honors program are recognized at University Commencement.

Admission Process:
All prospective Honors students and Scholars should apply no later than April 1.

Scholarship Availability:
Many Honors Program students are awarded scholarships as University Scholars. Supplementary scholarships are available to Honors Program students who are not already receiving full-tuition scholarships but are doing commendable academic work and making important contributions to the life of the University community. Honors Program students are also eligible for substantial funding for the required independent research (thesis) project, the culminating stage in the Honors Program degree.

The Campus Context:
Founded in 1850 by the Society of Mary, the University of Dayton is a private, coeducational school directed by the Marianists, a Roman Catholic teaching order. It is among the nation's largest Catholic institutions of higher learning. The main campus of more than 100 landscaped acres is on a hill overlooking the city of Dayton, Ohio. Among special facilities are the Language Learning Center, Diverse Student Population Services for African American and Latino students, and the University of Dayton Research Institute.

The University's major academic units are the College of Arts and Sciences, the School of Business Administration, the School of Education, the School of Engineering, and the School of Law. There are more than seventy degree programs on campus.

Student Body Undergraduate enrollment is 6,000: 52 percent women and 48 percent men. The population includes 2.5 percent African American and 1 percent Hispanic students as well as 65 international students. First- and second- year students are 96 percent residents, with only 4 percent commuting to campus. Ninety percent of the students receive some form of financial aid plus nonrepayable grants, scholarships, educational loans, and part-time employment. There are ten sororities and fifteen fraternities.

Faculty Of the 781 faculty members, 404 are full-time; 85 percent have terminal degrees. The student-faculty ratio is 15:1.

Key Facilities The library houses 1.3 million volumes, 701,937 microforms, 3,095 periodical subscriptions, and 1,000 records and tapes, as well as access to on-line bibliographic retrieval services. Computing facilities include access to CRAY-YMP at the Ohio Supercomputer Center, Columbus; PC networks; and access to the Internet.

Athletics In athletics, the University of Dayton is a member of the Atlantic 10 Conference; the football team plays in the Division I-AA Pioneer League. There are seven men's intercollegiate sports: football, soccer, cross-country, basketball, baseball, golf, and tennis. There are nine women's intercollegiate sports: volleyball, soccer, cross-country, basketball, indoor track, softball, golf, tennis, and outdoor track.

Study Abroad The International Education Programs Office can help students find opportunities to study, work, or do service abroad. Students can earn up to a full semester of credit abroad in cities such as Madrid, Dublin, London, Vienna, and Lille. The Department of Languages offers opportunities to earn up to 6 credit hours in Segovia, Spain; Mexico; Marburg, Germany; Quebec; and Paris. The School of Business offers study abroad programs in Augsburg, Germany.

Support Services Disabled Student Services provides assistance and counseling for prospective and enrolled students with physical or learning disabilities. It assists with the identification of special needs and the coordination of special services and related aspects of campus adjustment.

Job Opportunities The Federal Work-Study Program provides on-campus employment opportunities for full-time and three-quarter-time students who demonstrate financial need. University employment opportunities for students who do not qualify for the Federal Work-Study Program are available through the Student Employment Office. Cooperative Educations ("the co-op system") allows students to alternate terms of on-campus study with terms of off-campus work at jobs related to their academic concentration.

Tuition: $13,170 per year (1996-97)

Room and Board: $4430

Mandatory Fees: $470

Contact: Director: Dr. R. Alan Kimbrough, 125 Alumni Hall, Dayton, Ohio 45469-0311; Telephone: 513-229-4615; Fax: 513-229-4298; E-mail: kimbroug@trinity.udayton.edu

University of Delaware

 4 Pu G M Sc Tr

▼ University Honors Program

The University of Delaware Honors Program, begun in 1976, consists of a great many honors courses available in nearly all academic fields, honors residence hall living (required of first-year students and optional for upperclass students) and extracurricular activities, and an exemplary undergraduate research program. Small classes with other honors students and very close relationships with advisers are the norm.

Participation Requirements: First Year Honors admits are advised into a program of studies that can qualify them for the First Year Honors Certificate (requirements: at least 15 honors credits out of the 30 or more credits taken in the first year, a 3.0 or higher grade average, and living in the first-year honors residence hall complex). These credits must include an Honors Colloquium course, which involves extensive writing experiences in conjunction with a trained peer tutor. First- year students typically take other honors credits in major or general education courses of their choice.

Upperclass students can, if they choose, work toward other forms of recognition: the Advanced Honors Certificate, the Honors Foreign Language Certificate, the International Honors Certificate, the Degree with Distinction, and the Honors Degree (the latter two require independent research and a senior thesis). Many honors topics are available in upper-division courses to enable students to qualify for these forms of honors recognition. There are special seminars and tutorials, mainly for and required of honors degree candidates. Each honors course taken and each honors form of recognition earned is recorded on the student's transcript. Students do not graduate "from the Honors Program"; they graduate with whatever forms of honors recognition they may have chosen and have succeeded in earning.

The University offers a very extensive array of extracurricular activities for honors students, based in the Honors Center and the honors residence halls. These include trips (such as concerts, plays, and museums), faculty-led discussions, and recreational and social activities of all sorts. Many honors students participate in community service projects, although it is not a requirement to do so. These vital aspects of the program create a strong sense of community among the honors students.

The Undergraduate Research Program is a nationally respected model for involving students in real research collaboration with faculty mentors. Students learn how to apply for research support; small grants are available for supplies and expenses and large stipends ($2500) for full-time summer research. Often student researchers are coauthors of their faculty mentors' published articles.

Admission Process: First-year students must apply for admission to honors when they apply for admission to the University. Other University of Delaware students may begin participating in honors courses and opportunities any time after they have achieved a 3.0 (B) or higher grade average in courses taken at the University. Entering first-year honors contingents have numbered 300 to 400 students in recent years—about 10 percent of the entire freshman class. The boundaries are fluid. Once honors-coded, a student retains that status regardless of changing degrees of honors participation, for the students are completely free to decide for themselves the extent of their honors involvement. At present there are approximately 1,450 students enrolled in the program.

The deadline for applying is March 1.

Scholarship Availability: Honors students compete for and receive the lion's share of the University's general pool of merit scholarships. A few awards are restricted to the Honors Program and are based on competitive examinations given in February. A small number of these scholarship recipients who are exceptionally strong in the humanities or social sciences are designated as Alison Scholars and are given special opportunities for development of their abilities. The university has active chapters of Phi Beta Kappa, Phi Kappa Phi, Alpha Lambda Delta, Phi Sigma Pi, and many other academic honor societies; honors students are leaders in them.

The Campus Context: The University of Delaware serves as the state's public university, and is a Research II land-grant, sea-grant, and space-grant institution. Chartered by the state of Delaware in 1833 (but with origins traceable to 1743), its main campus, consisting of seven colleges, is located in Newark, Delaware, a suburban community of 30,000 midway between Philadelphia and Baltimore. There are 114 undergraduate majors available.

Student Body There are 15,000 full time undergraduates: 57 percent women, 43 percent men. Eleven percent are minority students.

Faculty Of the 915 full-time faculty members, 87 percent have the doctorate or terminal degree. The student-faculty ratio is 17:1.

Key Facilities The library houses 2.2 million volumes; there are thirty student computing sites. Many student musical performance and theatrical groups exist on campus.

Athletics There are twenty-two varsity sports (eleven for men, eleven for women; North Atlantic Conference, Division I; football-Yankee Conference, I-AA) and innumerable intramural and fitness opportunities.

Study Abroad UD has extensive study-abroad programs in Europe, Asia, Latin America, and Africa.

Tuition: $3990 for state residents, $11,250 for nonresidents, per year (1996-97)

Room and Board: $4590 minimum

Mandatory Fees: $440

Contact: Director: Dr. Robert F. Brown, Newark, Delaware 19716; Telephone: 302-831-2340; Fax: 302-831-4194; E-mail: robert.brown@mvs.udel.edu; Web site: http://www.udel.edu/admissions/page28.html

UNIVERSITY OF DENVER

| 4 Pr G M Tr |

▼ University Honors Program

The Honors Program at the University of Denver serves students of high ability and demonstrated academic achievement. The goal of nurturing a community of scholars who value and are committed to intellectual pursuit involves providing both challenging classroom experiences and enriching extracurricular activities through the residential honors floors and the Honors Student Association.

During the first two years, students are given the opportunity to complete their Core Curriculum requirements with specially designed honors classes in the Divisions of Arts and Humanities, Social Sciences, and Math/Natural Sciences/Engineering. Many departments also offer honors sections of introductory classes such as calculus, engineering, and psychology. Approximately half of the first-year honors students elect to take the three-quarter Coordinated Humanities sequence, which combines the Freshman English and Arts and Humanities requirement. Co-Hum is structured chronologically from antiquity through the twentieth century. Each quarter students take courses on the history and literature of a given time period and choose to supplement their study with a coordinated seminar on art, music, philosophy, or religious studies.

Two 2-credit honors seminars taken during the sophomore and junior years keep students in touch with the program and with other honors students and add breadth to their studies. Topics offered in recent years include Computers and Consciousness, Colonizing Mars?, Sherlock Holmes, The Technology of Music, Theater in Denver, and The Archaeology of Gender.

During the senior year, students—with the exception of business majors who follow a series of three business honors seminars—do a senior project in their major area. This can be graduate-level research, a thesis, an art exhibit, a concert, etc. The senior project culminates in an end-of-the-year Honors Symposium at which students present the results of their work to the University community.

There are 400 students in the program.

Participation Requirements: Students must take at least 10 credits of honors courses during their first two years and two honors seminars during the second and third years and complete either an senior honors project or 6 credits of business honors seminars.

Admission Process: First-year students are selected each spring by the University Honors Committee primarily on the basis of high school GPA, test scores, and class rank. Any student of high motivation and high achievement may also apply for admission to the program.

Scholarship Availability: The University of Denver offers extensive merit aid based on academic quality rather than need. Merit scholarships range from $2000 through full tuition each year. Scholarships are renewable and require that students remain in good academic standing. Almost all students admitted to the honors program have received one of these awards. Eighty percent of undergraduate students receive financial aid; 66 percent of aid distributed to undergraduate students is in the form of scholarships or grants, 29 percent is in student loans, and 5 percent of aid is work-study.

The Campus Context: The University of Denver, the oldest independent university in the Rocky Mountain region, enrolls more than 8,500 students in its undergraduate, graduate, professional, and nontraditional programs. The University was founded in 1864 by John Evans while he was governor of the Colorado Territory. Earlier, Evans had established Northwestern University in Evanston, Illinois.

The University offers thirteen bachelor's degrees in more than 100 areas representing a full range of disciplines in the arts, humanities, social sciences, natural sciences, business, and the professions. For qualified students there are five-year integrated degree programs leading to the baccalaureate degree and the Master of Business Administration or Master of International Management, and a Bachelor of Science along with a Master of Business Administration.

Student Body The total enrollment is 8,515. Undergraduate enrollment is 2,825; graduate enrollment is 2,984, and nontraditional enrollment is 2,706. Among the undergraduates there are 372 minority students (15.08 percent) and 333 international students (11.79 percent). The student population is 49 percent men, 51 percent women. Forty-two percent are Colorado residents, 58 percent non-Colorado (all fifty states). There are approximately eighty student groups on campus, including department, honorary, minority, and religious organizations, social fraternities and sororities, and hobby, interest, and service groups.

Faculty DU employs 387 full-time appointed faculty members; 89 percent hold the highest degrees offered in their fields. The student-faculty ratio is 13:1.

Key Facilities The library houses 2.7 million items, including 4,796 journals and periodicals. It is linked by computer with all major libraries in the region. It is open 100 hours per week, offering reference services, computerized bibliographic search services, and access to the University's central computers.

Computer facilities are available in every residence hall 24 hours a day. Student access labs have been established at several different central locations on campus. Many departments have their own labs. All students are given e-mail addresses and access to the World Wide Web upon matriculation.

Athletics DU's Division of Athletics, Recreation and Wellness sponsors eighteen varsity sports, eleven club sports, eleven intramural sports, and seven sponsored special activities.

Study Abroad The University of Denver encourages undergraduate study abroad and offers a wide range of opportunities in Europe, Africa, Asia, Australia, Canada, and Latin America. Students may go abroad for part of their studies and spend a summer, quarter, semester, or year studying in another country. Programs overseas can include courses in any of the major fields offered at the University of Denver and represent a variety of program types, from direct exchanges that integrate students into the host university to study centers set up for English-speaking students. Financial aid that a student receives can, in many cases, be used to finance overseas study as well.

Support Services Services for students with physical disabilities are coordinated through the Office of Disabled Persons' Resources. Examples of accommodations include readers, peer note-takers, interpreters, testing adaptations, adaptive technology, and advocacy.

Job Opportunities Students are offered a range of work opportunities on campus, including assistantships and work-study. Off-campus jobs are plentiful and varied due to the University's urban location.

Tuition: $21,274 per year (1996-97)

Room and Board: $5538

Mandatory Fees: $348

Contact: Co-Directors: Dr. Susan Stakel and Dr. Paul Strom, Office of Undergraduate Studies, Denver, Colorado 80208; Telephone: 303-871-2601; Fax: 303-871-4783; E-mail: sstakel@du.edu or pstrom @du.edu

---

UNIVERSITY OF EVANSVILLE

4 Pr G M

▼ Honors Program

The University of Evansville Honors Program admits bright, talented students who have the desire to excel scholastically in a stimulating academic environment. The program challenges students to maximize their potential in all areas of study and offers an enhanced curriculum with the opportunity to share ideas and viewpoints with other outstanding students. The program attracts students from all majors and fosters independent thinking. All honors students seek a significant challenge from their professors as well as from each other. Participation in the Honors Program provides students with a rewarding college experience both in and out of the classroom.

Honors classes are interdisciplinary and are taught across the curriculum. Students in the Honors Program are able to enroll in any honors class regardless of major. The senior project is intended to serve as the capstone of the program and is presented at the University of Evansville, at a regional conference, or at the National Conference for Undergraduate Research.

Currently, 130 students are participating in the program.

Participation Requirements: Honors students are required to complete five honors classes during their tenure at the University. In the senior year, each student completes a research project or performance and presents the project in a public forum.

Admission Process: Freshmen are selected each May on the basis of an Honors Program application, which includes such information as class rank, test scores, extracurricular activities, leadership roles, and one or more short essays. Applications submitted during the first semester of the freshman year are also considered. Applications are accepted in March each year.

Scholarship Availability: Academic scholarships ranging from $2000 to $8000 are available, although they are not restricted to Honors Program participants.

The Campus Context: The University of Evansville is a fully accredited, independent, comprehensive, liberal arts- and sciences-centered university with several professional schools. Founded in 1854, the University is affiliated with the United Methodist Church. UE is committed to a broad-based education for its undergraduate students. *U.S. News & World Report* ranks the University of Evansville as one of "America's Best Colleges in The Midwest." Located in southwestern Indiana, Evansville is situated within 150 miles of Louisville, Nashville, St. Louis, and Indianapolis. Evansville has a population of approximately 125,000 with a metropolitan-area population of about 279,000. The scenic 80-acre campus includes twenty-eight major buildings, sensibly arranged for the convenience of students. There are seventy-five degree programs on campus.

Student Body Approximately 2,775 undergraduate students from across the nation and more than forty countries attend the University. The student body is 55 percent women, with an ethnic distribution of 84 percent white, 2.6 percent black, 0.8 percent Hispanic, 1 percent Asian, 5 percent international, and 6.6 percent unknown. Ninety-two percent of the students receive some form of financial aid. There are five fraternities and four sororities on campus.

Faculty There are 193 faculty members, 182 of whom are full-time. Eighty-seven percent hold terminal degrees. The student-faculty ratio is 13:1.

Key Facilities Library holdings total 244,500 volumes. Campus computer laboratories consist of seven labs (six PC and one Mac) with a total of 132 computers housed in academic buildings. An additional eighteen computers are installed in residential buildings.

Athletics A member of the NCAA, the University of Evansville competes at the Division I level in all fifteen sports. UE sponsors varsity teams for men in football, basketball, cross-country, golf, tennis, soccer, and swimming and diving; and for women in soccer, softball, basketball, volleyball, swimming and diving, cross-country, and tennis. Women's golf will become a varsity sport in 1997. UE is a member of the Missouri Valley Conference in fourteen sports. The football team competes in the Pioneer Football League.

Study Abroad Study abroad at the University of Evansville enjoys a high profile, with the Offices of Academic Advising, Financial Aid, and Residence Life joining forces to encourage students to study either at the University's own Victorian manor house in England or in one of the other 125 approved study-abroad sites. Virtually all majors can study abroad at UE with most of their financial aid intact. UE's Victorian manor house, Harlaxton College, has over 100 rooms, offering not only UE course credit but also a Meet-a-Family program, optional field trips, and competitive sports against locals. Twenty-five percent of the 1996 graduating class studied at Harlaxton.

Support Services All campus buildings are handicapped-accessible.

Job Opportunities About 600 students are employed on campus. Work-study positions are available through a federally funded program for students who demonstrate financial need according to the Free Application for Federal Student Aid (FAFSA). The average job represents 7 to 8 hours of work per week at the current minimum wage for academic-year earnings of $1000 to $1200.

Tuition: $12,990 per year (1996-97)

Room and Board: $4080 minimum

Mandatory Fees: $280

Contact: Director: Professor James A. Reising, 1800 Lincoln Avenue, Evansville, Indiana 47722; Telephone: 812-479-2358; Fax: 812-479-2009; E-mail: reising@evansville.edu

THE UNIVERSITY OF FINDLAY

4 Pr G M Sc Tr

▼ Honors Program

The University of Findlay Honors Program provides a challenging educational experience that enriches and accelerates a student's academic growth. The program encourages and stimulates students beyond general academic excellence by providing opportunities for independent research, individual guidance, and specially designed courses and seminars. Students design their own honors curriculum by virtue of the projects they develop and the honors classes they choose.

Admission to the Honors Program requires a certain GPA for semester hours earned. Freshmen, however, may be admitted to the program during the first semester on the basis of their high school GPA and ACT score. Students must also obtain the recommendations of 2 faculty members for admission to the program.

Students who choose to develop their own projects do so through either a 1-hour contract or an independent research project. Both options allow students to pursue individual academic interests in conjunction with a professor who works with the student on the project. The projects are approved by the Honors Advisory Board on the basis of academic scope and depth and creativity. Students may also enroll in Honors Seminars that are developed by faculty members and are offered each semester on a one-time basis. These seminars are intense courses challenging the highest level of academic excellence within various fields of the liberal arts curriculum, offering honors students the opportunity to study beyond the regular curriculum.

Since its beginning in 1984, the Honors Program has enjoyed continuous growth and currently enrolls 150 students. In March of 1995 the faculty adopted new goals for the program. Whereas previous goals emphasized independent study, new goals now include more freshman participation, more opportunities that challenge the highest level of academic excellence, more opportunities for faculty development and collaborative faculty/student research, and an environment that will encourage the aspirations and the achievement of superior students.

Participation Requirements: In order to graduate as an Honors Scholar in a particular field, a student must have accumulated 16 hours of honors credits, 4 of which are a senior major independent research project, with grades of B or above in all honors endeavors. The student must also have accumulated a 3.5 or higher GPA. Honors Scholars are recognized by designation in the graduation program, the University of Findlay bachelor's hood, and a special diploma from the Honors Program.

Scholarship Availability: The University of Findlay offers numerous scholarships to students of exceptional ability.

The Campus Context: The University of Findlay was founded as Findlay College in 1882 by the Churches of God, General Conference (formerly Churches of God in North America) and the citizens of the city of Findlay. The institution is the only university affiliated with the Churches of God and it acknowledges, preserves, and honors its Judeo-Christian heritage. Its four colleges are the College of Liberal Arts, College of Professional Studies, College of Sciences, and College of Graduate Studies. Nine degree programs are offered on campus. There are several distinguished facilities: the Mazza Gallery, a one-of-a-kind collection of illustrator art of children's books; English and Western equestrian farms; a preveterinary facility; and the Environmental Management facility.

Student Body Undergraduate enrollment is 2,785: 43 percent men, 57 percent women. The ethnic distribution is 74 percent Caucasian; 5 percent African American; 5 percent Hispanic/Latino; 1 percent Asian/Pacific Islander; 1 percent Native American, and 14 percent international (270 students). The resident-commuter ratio is 1:2. Eighty-five percent of the students receive financial aid. There are four fraternities and two sororities.

Faculty There are 116 full-time faculty members, 45 percent with terminal degrees. The student-faculty ratio is 18:1.

Key Facilities The library houses 122,617 volumes. Several million dollars have been designated for upgrading equipment and the wiring of the entire campus. The capital improvement has included the installation of fiber optics throughout all the buildings. Computer labs are available and accessible to students for both classroom and individual use. Beginning in the fall of 1996, students will be afforded the opportunity to access the computer system for academic purposes from their individual residence hall rooms. All students have the option of opening an e-mail account.

Athletics The University of Findlay is affiliated with both the National Collegiate Athletic Association (NCAA) Division II and the National Association of Intercollegiate Athletics (NAIA) Division II. The University also competes in the Mid-Ohio Conference and the Mid-States Football Association. Varsity teams include men's baseball, basketball, cross-country, football, golf, soccer, swimming and diving, tennis, track and field, and wrestling. Women's varsity sports include basketball, cross-country, golf, soccer, softball, swimming and diving, tennis, track and field, and volleyball. Equestrian teams, hockey, and water polo are club sports.

Study Abroad Students may participate in study-abroad programs and experience international living in the International Honors House on campus.

Support Services Individuals who need auxiliary aids for effective communication in programs and services of the University of Findlay are invited to make their needs and preferences known to the ADA Compliance Coordinator.

Job Opportunities Students may apply for many work opportunities and assistantships on campus.

Tuition: $13,000 per year (1996-97)

Room and Board: $5210

Mandatory Fees: $112

Contact: Director: Marjorie M. Schott, 1000 North Main Street, Findlay, Ohio 45840; Telephone: 419-424-4821; Fax: 419-424-4822; E-mail: schott@lucy.findlay.edu; Web site: http://packy.findlay.edu

UNIVERSITY OF HOUSTON

4 Pu C L Sc Tr

▼ Honors College

Created to serve the intellectual needs of gifted students in more than 100 fields of study, the Honors College provides the careful guidance, flexibility, and personal instruction that nurture individual excellence. Members are encour-

aged to sharpen special skills in pursuit of their personal academic goals. At the same time, they devote a significant portion of their formal course work to a collective examination of the system of values and achievements that form the Western cultural heritage, a knowledge of which has traditionally defined the educated individual.

For the 300 students who join each fall, the Honors College offers all the advantages of a small college without sacrificing the wealth of resources and rich diversity of a large university. The faculty members and staff of the Honors College believe that a university education should offer more than the acquisition of career skills. The Honors College challenges the University's best students to develop the attributes of mind and character that enhance all facets of life.

The Honors College offers a full array of services, including scholarships, tuition waivers, residence halls, and internships.

The University Honors Program was founded in 1959 and by 1993 had grown to become the Honors College at the University of Houston. Currently, the Honors College enrolls about 950 students.

Participation Requirements: Honors students are expected to take at least one honors course each semester and to maintain a cumulative GPA of 3.25.

Scholarship Availability: The Honors College has its own scholarships that are awarded each semester to students who are excelling in their honors courses. In addition, the University of Houston has a generous scholarship program for new students. The application for scholarships is the same as the application for the Honors College.

Financial aid is available through federal aid and academic scholarships. All-expense scholarships are available to National Merit and National Achievement finalists. Waivers of nonresident tuition are available to qualified students.

The Campus Context: The University of Houston campus is home to fourteen colleges: College of Architecture; College of Business Administration; College of Education; Cullen College of Engineering; Conrad N. Hilton College of Hotel and Restaurant Management; College of Humanities, Fine Arts, and Communications; College of Natural Sciences and Mathematics; College of Optometry; College of Pharmacy; College of Social Sciences; College of Technology; Law Center; Honors College; and Graduate School of Social Work. Within the University of Houston there are 114 bachelor's degree programs, 125 master's degree programs, and sixty-two doctoral degree programs.

Student Body There is a large diversity of students at the University of Houston consisting of 56 percent white, 14 percent Asian/Pacific Islander, 14 percent Hispanic, 9 percent African American, and 7 percent international students from around the globe. There are 2,291 students who live on campus in the University dorms and apartments, and about 22,000 who live off campus. There are more than 280 student organizations on campus, including seventeen national fraternities, ten national sororities, and many other professional and honor societies.

Faculty With a student population of 30,757 and faculty members numbering 1,326, the student-faculty ratio is 23:1.

Key Facilities There are many special facilities on campus, such as the new Alumni Center, the Moores School of Music, the Texas Center for Superconductivity, the University Hilton, KUHF (Houston Public Radio), KUHT (Houston Public Television), and the Sarah Blaffer Gallery.

Three libraries house 1.75 million volumes, 3.1 million microfilms, and 15,000 journals. Around the campus, there are various computer labs consisting of 4,000 workstations with both Mac and IBM computers.

Athletics Cougar athletics are on the rise with the new Alumni Center and Athletic Facility, which includes an indoor arena for football, tennis, volleyball, and much more. Students may attend home football and baseball games free of charge. There is an extensive intramural program, and the University's gyms, pools, and other sports facilities are open year-round.

Study Abroad There are many different study abroad options at the University, including programs in France, Italy, Germany, Spain, Israel, and Mexico.

Support Services The Center for Disabilities at the University of Houston provides academic support services to students with health impairments, learning disabilities, psychiatric disorders, or physical handicaps. The campus is accessible via ramps, curb cuts, free inner-campus handicapped parking, Braille signs, and so on. Care services are also available through the University Housing Department.

Job Opportunities Work-study and regular employment opportunities are readily available on campus.

Tuition: $960 for state residents, $7300 for nonresidents, per year (1996-97)

Room and Board: $4405

Mandatory Fees: $766

Contact: Director: Dr. Ted Estess, Houston, Texas 77204-2090; Telephone: 713-743-9010; Fax: 713-743-9015; Web site: http://www.dc.uh.ed/honors

UNIVERSITY OF IDAHO

4 Pu G M Sc Tr

▼ **University Honors Program**

Established in 1982, the University Honors Program invites dynamic students to join their peers and distinguished professors in exploring a diverse and challenging curriculum of liberal arts studies. Members of the Honors Program receive many opportunities to develop their initiative, creativity, and critical-thinking skills. By seizing such opportunities, afforded by interaction with other honors

students and participation in honors courses, members receive a rich educational experience at the University of Idaho.

The 360 students currently involved in the Honors Program represent nearly every major, ranging from engineering to English. Many are leaders on campus and in their living groups, and each year members of the Honors Program elect representatives to serve on the Honors Student Advisory Board. Through such activities as the annual spring trip, fall "raft and read" excursion, concerts, plays, and films, Honors Program members can forge strong friendships with one another, as well as benefit intellectually from exposure to others' diverse perspectives on life and learning.

Participation Requirements: A member in good standing of the University Honors Program must be registered at UI, take at least one honors course every third semester, and maintain a minimum overall 3.0 cumulative GPA. Students who do not maintain at least a 3.0 cumulative GPA will have permission to enroll in honors courses for one additional semester. To earn an honors certificate at graduation, students must complete 30 specified honors credits with a minimum GPA of 3.0 in those credits. These credits must be completed as follows: history, literature, and philosophy, 10-11 credits; sciences, 4 credits; fine arts, 3 credits; economics, 3 credits; math, 3 credits; seminars, 6 credits. Eighteen credits out of the 30 required for an honors certificate also satisfy general University core requirements that all students must complete to graduate. Although members in good standing are not required to complete all Honors Certificate requirements, they are urged to work toward the certificate.

Admission Process: Students entering from high school are invited to apply for admission to the program if they have one of the following: a 28 ACT composite score, a 1200 SAT I combined verbal and math score, or a 3.7 high school GPA. Admission is selective. Each student applying must respond, in writing, to two essay questions that will be sent to those who fill out and return a postcard application. Responses are examined by the director and associate director to determine admission. Students with special talents and interests are encouraged to apply. Interested students who do not meet the GPA or test-score criteria listed above may write the honors director explaining their reasons for seeking admission. In these cases, in addition to the required written responses, 2 former teachers must also send letters of recommendation to the director.

First-semester University students who have demonstrated superior performance may apply for admission to the program. Transfer students are considered on a case-by-case basis; students in good standing in an honors program at their previous school are automatically admitted.

Scholarship Availability: Each year a small number of scholarships are offered to students entering the Honors Program. They cover the full cost of resident fees and are awarded based on academic merit, as well as on the entrance essays. No additional application form is required. Financial need is not a factor. Likewise, a small number of Honors Program out-of-state tuition waivers are offered to non-Idaho residents. The waivers may be held independently of or in conjunction with other scholarships. Both scholarships and tuition waivers are awarded for up to eight semesters for freshmen, six semesters for sophomores, and so on. They are contingent on a student's satisfactory progress toward an honors certificate (averaging one honors course a semester) while maintaining an overall GPA of 3.3.

The Campus Context: The University of Idaho is the state's comprehensive land-grant institution with primary responsibility statewide for doctoral degrees, research programs, and professional public service. There are 118 on-campus programs leading to the baccalaureate. As the state's premier institution of higher education, UI has a nationally recognized program of general education and ranks nationally as a research university. On campus are the Colleges of Agriculture; Art and Architecture; Business and Economics; Education; Engineering; Forestry, Wildlife, and Range Sciences; Law; Letters and Science; and Mines and Earth Resources.

Student Body Undergraduate enrollment is 13,043: 54 percent men, 46 percent women. Four percent of the students have an ethnic background other than Caucasian; 191 international students represent seventy-four countries. Ten percent of the students receive work-study; 27.5 percent are scholarship recipients; 60 percent receive assistance from long-term or short-term loans. The twenty fraternities and eight sororities serve 1,715 students.

Faculty There are 1,102 faculty members; 844 are full-time. The student-faculty ratio is 16:1.

Key Facilities The library houses more than 2 million volumes. The campus has several PC and Mac student computer labs, with a wide variety of general-use, state-of-the-art software provided to all networked computer labs and classrooms. A new computer backbone with extensive and expanding availability of computer access has recently been installed. There are nineteen student general-use computer lab facilities, with a total of 550 computers available to students. UI's goal is to have a student to computer ratio of 15:1. More than 9,000 students have computing accounts.

Athletics A strong intercollegiate athletic program is available for both men and women. Men's programs include football, basketball, cross-country, indoor and outdoor track, tennis, and golf. The women's programs consist of basketball, volleyball, cross-country, indoor and outdoor track, tennis, and golf. Teams compete in the Big West Athletic Conference.

Study Abroad Students may participate in the following study abroad programs: International Student Exchange Program (ISEP), Council on International Education Exchange (CIEE), University Studies Abroad Consortium (USAC), and Cooperative Center for Study in Britain (CCSB). Students may also participate in UI's direct exchange programs with universities in Ecuador, Spain, France, Germany, Sweden, Denmark, and the United Kingdom.

Support Services The services for students with disabilities provide support for students with temporary or permanent disabilities, in accordance with the Rehabilitation Act of 1973

as amended in 1992, and the Americans with Disabilities Act of 1990. Buildings on campus continue to be brought to code to be handicapped-accessible.

Job Opportunities A student employment program was initiated in fall 1995 and provides student employment in positions covering all aspects of University functions ranging from trainee levels to coordinator and technical levels. Students gain job experience, references, and additional financial resources while pursuing an academic degree.

Tuition: None for state residents, $7420 for nonresidents, per year (1996-97)

Room and Board: $3600

Mandatory Fees: $1768

Contact: Director: Daniel K. Zirker, Psychology Building, #102, Moscow, Idaho 83844-3044; Telephone: 208-885-6147; Fax: 208-885-7710; E-mail: zirker@uidaho.edu or sflores@uidaho.edu; Web site: http://www.uidaho.edu/honors_program

THE UNIVERSITY OF ILLINOIS AT CHICAGO

4 Pu C L Sc Tr

▼ Honors College

Started in 1982, the Honors College at the University of Illinois at Chicago offers an enhanced academic experience to well-prepared undergraduates through a wide range of honors programs and activities. All Honors College students complete some type of honors work each term. Freshmen enroll in at least one honors course each semester, either a year-long interdisciplinary honors core course or a departmental honors offering such as accelerated chemistry or honors calculus. Beyond the freshman year, students choose from a variety of honors options, including honors courses, 1-credit-hour honors seminars in a broad range of disciplines, independent research projects, the College's Undergraduate Research Assistantship Program, tutoring in the College peer tutoring program, completion of an honors project in a regular course, and departmental honors courses and senior theses. All these activities are monitored through an advising/mentoring system that is one of the College's strengths.

At the end of the first year, students are assigned to an Honors College fellow, a faculty mentor in the student's major department. The fellows are faculty members interested in working with honors students and include many of UIC's outstanding scholars. They act as advisers for the students' honors work and as resources for advice and guidance on major, curriculum, preparation for graduate school, and careers. The Honors College fellow mentoring process puts students into close and continuing contact with faculty members at an early stage in their college experience.

UIC honors students who opt to live on campus may take advantage of the Honors House program. The Honors House occupies a separate wing of the Student Residence and Commons. In addition to sharing living space with other Honors College students, students in the program participate in educational and social activities designed to create a special living/learning environment and a sense of an honors residential community.

In addition, the College offers all its students facilities such as a computer lab featuring a personal computer network and laser printer, typewriters, social and study lounges, photocopying facilities, and activities such as student-faculty luncheons, annual dinner dances, the college newsletter, and the student literary journal, *Still in Spin*. Honors College students also receive extended library privileges and priority registration each term. Honors College membership status will be noted annually on students' transcripts and at the Honors Day ceremony held each spring.

There are approximately 1,200 students enrolled in the Honors College.

Participation Requirements: All students in the Honors College are expected to fulfill the following requirements to ensure continued membership: 1) Students must successfully complete an honors activity each term, except summer. 2) Students must maintain a minimum cumulative GPA of 4.25.

Admission Process: Student members of the Honors College are undergraduates selected from all UIC colleges and departments on the basis of their academic achievement. Entering freshmen who have a minimum ACT score of 26 and who rank in the upper 15 percent of their high school graduating class are invited to become members of the Honors College. Transfer students with at least a 4.25 cumulative GPA (A=5.0) are also encouraged to apply.

Scholarship Availability: The Honors College provides merit-based scholarship opportunities for beginning freshmen: the University Scholar Awards, which cover full tuition and fees for up to four years, and the Lebus Scholarship, covering tuition and fees for the freshman year.

The Campus Context: Located in the heart of Chicago, within walking distance of the Loop, the University of Illinois at Chicago is a vital part of the educational, technological, and cultural fabric of the Chicago metropolitan area. UIC is the largest university in the Chicago area and one of the eighty-eight leading research universities in the nation. It has ninety buildings on 216 acres. Many of its faculty members have national reputations in fields as diverse as virtual reality, X-ray laser technology, urban affairs, medicinal plants, and neurosurgery. UIC offers bachelor's degrees in ninety-two academic areas, master's degrees in eighty-eight disciplines, and doctorates in fifty-one specializations.

UIC's academic organization consists of the Colleges of Architecture and the Arts, Associated Health Professions, Business Administration, Dentistry, Education, Engineering, Liberal Arts and Sciences, Medicine, Nursing, Pharmacy, and Urban Planning and Public Affairs; the Jane Addams College of Social Work, the School of Public Health, the Graduate College, the Honors College, and the UIC Medical Center.

Student Body The total enrollment is 24,589 (1995 figure); 16,142 are undergraduates. Forty-seven percent are men, 53 percent women. The minority ethnic distribution is 11 percent African American, 17 percent Hispanic, and 19 percent Asian. There are 324 international students (2 percent). Ten percent of undergraduates live in campus housing. Seventy-two percent of the students receive financial aid.

Faculty Full-time faculty members number 2,136; 90 percent of the faculty hold Ph.D.s; the student-faculty ratio is 11:1.

Key Facilities The library houses 1.8 million volumes. There are twelve public computer labs on campus, with 486/66 PCs and PowerMac computers. In addition, the Honors College has a reserved lab for its students with eight Pentium PCs.

Athletics UIC fields fifteen teams in NCAA Division I intercollegiate athletics. Home for UIC Flames basketball is the UIC Pavilion. In addition, many intramural and recreational activities are provided for students, faculty members, staff, and alumni.

Study Abroad UIC offers a broad range of options for international study that meet both the needs and interests of students. Students can study abroad for a summer, a semester, or a year from a selection of programs located in thirty-seven countries. Credit earned through these programs applies to the student's degree as approved by the college.

Job Opportunities Many work opportunities are available on campus. Twenty percent of the students hold jobs on campus, earning an average of $2000 per year.

Tuition: Full-time: $2870 minimum for state residents, $8610 minimum for nonresidents, per year; part-time: $478 minimum for state residents, $1435 minimum for nonresidents, per semester (1996-97)

Room and Board: $5188

Mandatory Fees: $906

Contact: Dean: Lansine Kaba, 851 South Morgan Street (M/C 204), Chicago, Illinois 60607-7044; Telephone: 312-413-2260; Fax: 312-413-1266; E-mail: lkaba@uic.edu; Web site: http://www.hc.uic.edu

UNIVERSITY OF LA VERNE

4 Pr G S Sc Tr

▼ **University Honors Program**

The University of La Verne Honors Program is open to students majoring in all fields of study. For those who demonstrate exceptional academic achievement and motivation, the ULV Honors Program offers increased opportunities for intellectual and personal growth through an interdisciplinary curriculum that emphasizes critical thinking skills and the integration of knowledge from various disciplines. Honors students participate in specially designed seminars and colloquia, receive individualized attention from faculty mentors, and take part in community outreach activities and cultural programs.

There are approximately 60 students in the program.

Participation Requirements: Students receive the designation "Honors Program Graduates" on their diplomas and final transcripts by completing four interdisciplinary seminars (topics vary), a minimum of three colloquia, and a senior capstone seminar that integrates their major field of study with a broadly focused theme. Honors Program participants complete at least 10 semester hours of honors course work, including representative seminars and colloquia. Honors Program graduates and participants are recognized at the Honors Commencement Breakfast, when their graduation medallions and certificates are presented by the Honors Director, the President, and other academic officers.

Honors Program students are given preferential registration schedules, receive individual academic advisement from the Honors Director, and enroll in a special Honors section of University 100, the college orientation course for first-year students.

Admission Process: Candidates must have a combined SAT score of 1050 or above/ACT of 25 and a minimum 3.5 cumulative high school average. Transfer students need a minimum 3.3 cumulative college GPA. Students are encouraged to apply by March 1 for fall admission and by December 1 for spring admission. Candidates for admission after these dates will be considered on a space-available basis. The University of La Verne subscribes to the Candidate's Reply Date of May 1 (for fall semester) and does not require advance payment or confirmation or intent to enroll prior to this date.

Scholarship Availability: Honors students may be eligible for various scholarships, including (but not limited to): the President's Scholarship (3.8 GPA required), the Dean's Scholarship (3.6 GPA required), and the Honors at Entrance Scholarship (3.5 high school GPA required).

The Campus Context: The University of La Verne is a comprehensive university offering bachelor's, master's, and doctoral degrees to approximately 6,000 students. Major divisions include the College of Arts and Sciences, the School of Business and Economics, the College of Law, the School of Organizational Management, and the School of Continuing Education. Central campus enrollment is approximately 1,050, while the remainder of the student population studies at centers located throughout California, in Alaska, and in Athens, Greece. An independent, nonsectarian institution of higher learning founded more than 100 years ago by members of the Church of the Brethren, the University of La Verne offers a strong liberal arts curriculum as well as education in

selected professional fields for undergraduate students. ULV is located in the San Gabriel Valley, about 30 miles east of Los Angeles. ULV is accredited by the Western Association of Schools and Colleges and is a member of the Association of Independent California Colleges and Universities, the Independent Colleges of Southern California, and the American Assembly of Collegiate Schools of Business. There are forty-six undergraduate, sixteen master's, and three doctoral degree programs. Special facilities include the Dailey Theater for the Performing Arts; the Child Development Center; and the unique Supertents, housing the Student Center, Minority Resource Center, and theater.

Student Body The undergraduate enrollment is 1,050 (46 percent men, 54 percent women). Ethnic distribution is 44 percent Caucasian, 29 percent Hispanic, 12 percent international, 6 percent Asian/Pacific Islander, 5 percent African American, 1 percent Native American, 2 percent other. The 140 international students represent thirty-two countries. Seventy-five percent of students receive financial aid. There are six fraternities and sororities and over twenty clubs and organizations.

Faculty There are 123 total full-time faculty, 70 percent with doctorates or other terminal degrees. The University-wide student-faculty ratio is 18:1.

Key Facilities Library holdings total 396,000 volumes: 175,000 volumes in Wilson Library, 221,000 volumes College of Law. Computing facilities include 150 microcomputers of various models and operating systems, high-power graphics workstations, mainframe access, full Internet access, and consultation services.

Athletics In athletics ULV offers eight NCAA Division III intercollegiate sports for men: baseball, cross-country, football, golf, soccer, tennis, and track; one non-conference men's sport (volleyball); and seven NCAA Division III intercollegiate sports for women: basketball, cross-country, soccer, softball, tennis, track, and volleyball.

Study Abroad Study abroad is available through Brethren Colleges Abroad consortium in China, Ecuador, England, France, Germany, Greece, Japan, Mexico and Spain; ULV semester abroad opportunities in China/Hong Kong and Mexico; and travel studies through departments, especially during January Interterm.

Support Services Disabled Student Services are coordinated through the Health Center and Office of Student Services. Special parking permits, elevator keys, and other support services are available.

Job Opportunities Student employment is widely available through work-study as well as other opportunities. The Career Development Center provides guidance and assistance in finding employment. Placement services and internships are available through many academic departments.

Tuition: $14,605 per year (1996-97)

Room and Board: $4330 minimum

Mandatory Fees: $60

Contact: Director: Dr. Andrea Labinger, 1950 Third Street, La Verne, California 91750; Telephone: 909-593-3511 ext. 4357; Fax: 909-596-9111

UNIVERSITY OF LOUISVILLE

4 Pu C L Sc Tr

▼ Arts and Sciences Honors Program

The University of Louisville has a comprehensive Honors Program for students who have shown promise of sustained, advanced intellectual achievement. Established in 1982, the Honors Program provides the opportunity for students to study in small classes and engage in an intensive and challenging educational experience. Honors classes promote discussion, personalized study, in-depth research, and reading, as well as close relationships with faculty members and peers.

Eligible freshmen are invited to enroll for Honors Campus Culture, an orientation to campus life for new students, presented in a weekend format before the fall semester begins. Honors sections of general education courses are offered each semester. These classes provide a strong foundation for upper-level study and meet requirements across colleges. College Scholar Seminars are interdisciplinary courses open to sophomores, juniors, and seniors. Often team-taught, these seminars tend to focus on topics of immediate interest to students. Some recent courses have been "AIDS in Society," "The Holocaust and the Western Imagination," "Religion and Mass Media," "Politics of Identity," and "Science and Environmental Policy." Additionally, the Overseers' International Seminars combine semester-long, in-depth study with substantially subsidized travel to locations outside the United States. Recently established, the first two seminars explore the rainforests of the Amazon and the Mayan sites of Mexico. Seminar topics change annually, and specific descriptions are mailed to all eligible students each semester.

The Honors Building is a renovated, 100-year-old townhouse typical of Victorian Louisville. The second-oldest building on campus, it is now home to a classroom, seminar room, library, computer center, and the administrative offices of the Honors Program. Situated close to commuter parking and residence halls and equipped with kitchen facilities, the Honors Building is a convenient place for honors students to study, relax, and meet for meals. Throughout the year, the Honors Building is also the site of many presentation, reception, and social events open to honors students.

Redefined in 1985, the Honors Program has been enrolling and tracking increasing numbers of students. Approximately 750 students are currently involved in honors work, a number which represents about one third of all University of Louisville students who are eligible.

Participation Requirements: Honors students may major in any undergraduate program in the University and fulfill the same requirements as all students. Although there is no required minimum level of participation in honors, eligible students are advised by the Honors Program staff and are encouraged to take at least 15 hours of honors-designated course work during their academic careers. Additionally, active honors students choose to be involved in many of the extracurricular offerings of the Honors Program, such as peer mentoring, community service projects, career mentoring with experienced professionals in the local area, attendance at regional and national honors conferences, and undergraduate research related to senior honors projects.

All honors course work is noted on a student's transcript, and college honors are awarded on the basis of GPA and other factors determined by each undergraduate unit.

Admission Process: New students are eligible to take courses in the Honors Program if they have an ACT composite score of 26 or the equivalent SAT I composite score of 1180. Belated admission to or continuation in the program requires a college GPA of 3.35 or higher. Transfer students are eligible to participate if their transferred GPA is 3.35 or higher. Registration in honors courses requires permission acquired during advising with an Honors Program staff member.

Scholarship Availability: While no scholarships are awarded through the Honors Program, many full tuition scholarships are awarded to honors-eligible students through the Office of Admissions. Continuing students may apply for annual scholarships that are awarded solely on the basis of academic performance.

The Campus Context: The University of Louisville is a state-supported, urban university located in Kentucky's largest metropolitan area. The University has three campuses encompassing thirteen graduate and undergraduate colleges, schools, and divisions. These include Arts and Sciences, Business and Public Administration, Music, the Speed School of Engineering, Nursing, and Health and Social Sciences. Nationally recognized graduate programs are offered in dentistry, education, law, and medicine. The University offers a total of 164 degree programs.

Among the distinguished facilities are the J.B. Speed Art Museum, the Computer-Aided Engineering Lab with Robotics Laboratory, and the Rapid Prototype Facility.

Student Body Undergraduate enrollment is approximately 15,200; 47 percent are men and 53 percent women. Minority students represent more than 17 percent of the undergraduate population; international students make up another 1.5 percent. Ninety-two percent of undergraduates commute to campus; 8 percent live in residence halls. Sixty-two percent of students receive some form of financial aid. Students may participate in sixteen fraternities and ten sororities.

Faculty Of the 1,757 faculty members, 1,208 are full-time, 89 percent with doctorates or other terminal degrees. The student-faculty ratio is 12:1.

Key Facilities The University libraries house a total of 1.3 million volumes. Computer facilities include a campuswide network with more than 1,000 PCs and terminals and dormitory and Internet access. There are many student computer labs.

Athletics The University fields an outstanding athletics program, providing intercollegiate competition for men and women in seventeen varsity sports.

Study Abroad The International Center organizes study-abroad programs, led by University of Louisville faculty members, to many different countries. The center supports the American International Relations Club, a student organization that encourages interaction among Americans and international students. Many opportunities are available to work or study in Montpellier, France, or Mainz, Germany, through the Sister City program. New initiatives are combining course work at the University with extended overseas experiences.

Support Services The Disability Resource Center provides specialized services to meet the needs of disabled students. Buildings and classrooms are required to be accessible to all students.

Job Opportunities There are many opportunities to work on campus through work-study programs, undergraduate research grants, assistantships, and cooperative education.

Tuition: $2570 for state residents, $7250 for nonresidents, per year (1996-97)

Room and Board: $3330

Contact: Director: Dr. John H. Flodstrom, Honors Building, Louisville, Kentucky 40292; Telephone: 508-852-6293; Fax: 508-852-0459; E-mail: jhflodo1@ulkyvm.louisville.edu; Web site: http://www.louisville.edu

UNIVERSITY OF MAINE

4 Pu G M Tr

▼ Honors Program

First-year students of marked academic ability are invited to apply for admission to the University Honors Program. The work of the first and second years, under the direction of staff members drawn from all colleges of the University, provides the stimulus and guidance that should enable a superior student to begin building a balanced view of the liberal arts and sciences today and the foundation for the more specialized work that is to come. The Honors Program reaches its peak in a project that is written during the senior year and considers some special area within the students's major field.

Students may be admitted at any stage of the Honors Program up to the opening of the junior year. Several honors courses are taken in common with students of all colleges within the University. These courses constitute the core of the Honors Program. Formal recognition is conferred following a successful completion of the Honors Program in the form of three grades: honors, high honors, and highest honors.

The Honors Committee of each college consists of faculty members currently teaching in the program, as well as departmental representatives selected by the chairs and ratified by the dean. The principal duties of this committee are to serve on Senior Thesis Examinations and to serve as a liaison between departments and the Honors Program. Each college has its own honors secretary.

The more than 60-year-old program currently enrolls 250 students.

The Campus Context: The University of Maine at Orono, which offers eighty-one degree programs, is composed of the Colleges of Business Administration; Education; Engineering; Natural Resources, Forestry, and Agriculture Sciences; and Social and Behavioral Sciences. Among special facilities on campus are the Maine Center for the Arts, including the Hudson Museum and the Hutchins Concert Hall; The Maine Folklife Center; the Margaret Chase Smith Center for Public Policy; and the Maynard F. Jordon Planetarium and Observatory.

Student Body Of the 7,333 undergraduate students enrolled, 48 percent are women. Students from minority groups represent 4 percent of the student population and international students represent less than 1 percent. Seventy-three percent of the students receive financial aid. There are seventeen fraternities and ten sororities on campus.

Faculty Of the 634 faculty members at the University, 486 are full-time and 82 percent hold terminal degrees. The student-faculty ratio is 13:1.

Key Facilities The library houses 870,000 volumes. Computer facilities include the Computing & Data Processing Service and the Computing & Instructional Technology Center. There are seventeen fraternities and ten sororities on campus.

Athletics Through the Department of Athletics and Recreation, the University offers programs in recreation and competitive intramural and intercollegiate sports. Because these activities are recognized as an integral part of the educational process, the University supports them with a professional staff, equipment, and facilities. These programs are to promote educational leadership, physical fitness, an opportunity for recreational pursuit, and athletic excellence through competition. Students are offered an equal opportunity for participation and achievement.

Study Abroad The University of Maine supports a number of study-abroad opportunities throughout the world. Several of these programs are direct one-to-one exchanges with universities in Canada, Europe, Australia, Asia, and South America. English-speaking programs are widely available, even in countries where English is not the native language. There are many opportunities for language immersion programs in French, German, Russian, Spanish, and other languages. Through reciprocal student-exchange programs, students pay tuition, fees, and sometimes room and board to the University of Maine as they would while enrolled at UMaine. They pay no regular fees at the host institution. Financial aid and scholarships may be used as appropriate. Applicants must have a minimum GPA of 2.75. For information, contact the Office of International Programs.

Support Services The Onward Program assists disabled students with academic, physical, and advocacy needs.

Job Opportunities Student employment is available through Federal Work-Study, regular jobs, and the Work Merit Program.

Tuition: $3570 for state residents, $10,110 for nonresidents, $5355 for nonresidents eligible for the New England Regional Student Program, per year (1996-97)

Room and Board: $4842

Mandatory Fees: $569

Contact: Director: Ruth Nadelhaft, 5777 Robert B. Thomson Honors Center, Orono, Maine 04469-5777; Telephone: 207-581-3262; Fax: 207-581-3265; E-mail: ruthn@maine.maine.edu

UNIVERSITY OF MAINE AT AUGUSTA
4 Pu G S Tr

▼ Honors Program

The Honors Program at the University of Maine at Augusta offers those students who have demonstrated intellectual potential and personal commitment an enriched academic experience. Not only will studies at UMA be enhanced socially and intellectually, but the honors student will be better prepared to continue his or her advanced studies and bring academic talents and abilities to the attention of prospective employers.

The Honors Program is not a separate degree program, but is designed to augment the course work required for a degree. In most cases, honors courses can be substituted for required or elective credits.

Any student, upon the recommendation of the Director of the Honors Program, may register for an honors course without being formally admitted into the program. However, to graduate from the program with honors designation, a student must meet the specific requirements of the Honors Program.

There are currently 80 students enrolled in the program.

Participation Requirements: The requirements of the Honors Program are flexible to meet the needs of students—whether part-time, full-time, traditional, or nontraditional.

UMA offers two honors options, one for associate degree students and another for bachelor's degree students. For those students in the Associate Degree Honors Program, 15 credit hours of honors courses are required, and for those in the Bachelor's Degree Honors Program, 21 to 24 hours are required. All Honors Program participants are required to take a foundation course in critical thinking and writing, an interdisciplinary topical seminar (honors colloquium), and a capstone seminar with thesis. The remaining credits may include other topical seminar courses, honors independent studies, or nonhonors courses contracted for honors credit.

In addition, an Honors Program student has the option of completing 45 hours of community service in lieu of an honors elective. Also, upon completion of the associate degree honors requirements, a student may continue in the bachelor's degree honors program. In addition to the requirements for the associate degree program, the continuing student is required to complete 6 additional hours of honors electives and a senior honors thesis.

It is also possible for students at a distance to participate in the UMA Honors Program since at least one honors course per year is offered over the Educational Network of Maine interactive television system.

The UMA Honors Program began offering courses in the spring semester of 1986, with 24 students. All students admitted to the program automatically become members of the Honors Program Student Association. Upon completion of the Honors Program requirements, the student receives a Certificate of Completion and a medallion to be worn at graduation.

Admission Process: To enter the Honors Program, an interview with the Program Director is scheduled, and the student must submit an application form and three letters of recommendation for consideration by the Honors Council. To continue in the program, the student must maintain a GPA of 3.2 and earn a minimum grade of B in honors courses.

Tuition: $2820 for state residents, $6870 for nonresidents, $4230 for nonresidents eligible for the New England Regional Student Program, per year (1996-97)

Mandatory Fees: $135

Contact: Director: Jon A. Schlenker, 46 University Drive, Augusta, Maine 04330; Telephone: 207-621-3262; Fax: 207-621-3293; E-mail: schlenj@access.enm.maine.edu; Web site: http://www.uma.maine.edu

UNIVERSITY OF MAINE AT FORT KENT
4 Pu C S Sc Tr

▼ Honors Program

The University of Maine at Fort Kent Honors Program offers qualified students the opportunity to participate in a series of upper-level seminars exploring a different interdisciplinary topic each semester. Honors seminars extend students' possibilities for individual research, public presentation and publication of papers, and for participation in University of Maine Systemwide Honors events.

The seminar format guarantees small class size and active interaction among seminar participants.

Honors seminars may be led by faculty members from any academic discipline who propose seminar topics to the Honors Committee, which selects the seminar to be offered each semester.

In addition to participation in the seminars, honors students are invited to a University of Maine Systemwide Honors Conference held each spring on a different campus. Also in the spring, the UMFK Honors Program hosts an Honors Academy and Banquet to celebrate the year's accomplishments.

The Honors Program also offers an honors section of English Composition II, designed to prepare first-year students for participation in a seminar-type course. Admission to the Honors section of English Composition II is dependent upon performance in English Composition I.

There are currently 10 students enrolled in the program.

Participation Requirements: Those who complete four honors seminars with a grade of B or higher earn the designation of Honors Scholar upon graduation. Honors Program seminars automatically count for upper-level elective credit. By special arrangement with the appropriate academic division, honors seminar work may be counted as upper-level credit toward a particular major.

Admission Process: Students with a GPA of 3.0 or better are encouraged to enter the Honors Program. Admission to the Honors Program is by application to the Honors Committee for individual seminars.

The Campus Context: The University of Maine at Fort Kent, an integral and cooperating member of the seven-campus University of Maine System, was founded as the Madawaska Training School in 1878 to prepare bilingual teachers to serve the French-speaking people of Northern Aroostook County. It has evolved into a modern, liberal arts-based, regional university offering associate degree programs as well as fourteen undergraduate majors leading to the baccalaureate; these include French, environmental studies, business, nursing, and teacher education.

The University is located in one of Maine's most northerly towns, Fort Kent, which is separated from Canada only by the St. John River and is the terminus of U.S. Route 1, which originates in Key West, Florida. It also serves as a meeting place for people completing a canoe trip on the Allagash waterways.

The University of Maine at Fort Kent has an exchange agreement with the College St. Louis Maillet in Edmundston, New Brunswick, Canada, through which students may study French in a French-speaking institution.

Faculty The 570 undergraduates are taught by 30 full-time faculty members, supplemented by adjunct faculty members. The student-faculty ratio is 16:1.

Key Facilities The campus has a 60,000-volume library with computer links to UM System libraries. Computers are located in dormitories, the library, and academic buildings. The University of Maine at Fort Kent also houses a site for statewide interactive television.

Athletics In athletics, there are facilities for racquetball, handball, badminton, basketball, volleyball, and weightlifting. There is intercollegiate competition in soccer, skiing, and basketball. Intramural opportunities are available in basketball, softball, volleyball, and individual sports. Fitness and wellness classes are also available.

Job Opportunities Students are offered a range of work opportunities on campus through work-study.

Tuition and Fees: $2820 for state residents, $6870 for nonresidents, $4230 for nonresidents eligible for the New England Regional Student Program, per year (1996-97)

Room and Board: $3600

Mandatory Fees: $220

Contact: Director: Professor Wendy Kindred, Haenssler Honors House, 16 Pleasant Street, Fort Kent, Maine 04743; Telephone: 207-834-7591; Fax: 207-834-7503; E-mail: kindred@ maine.maine.edu

UNIVERSITY OF MARYLAND BALTIMORE COUNTY

4 Pu G M Sc Tr

▼ Honors College

UMBC's Honors College seeks to develop the talented and curious individual's faculties of analysis and exposition through an enhanced liberal arts experience, to foster a sense of membership in an intellectual community, and to instill learning as a way of life. The College frequently notes that the English word "school" derives ultimately from the Greek term schole, meaning "leisure", and that the word "liberal" in the phrase "liberal arts" refers to the freedom associated with free time, i.e., time away from survival needs and available for intellectual development.

Among the advantages offered by a medium-sized research university, the UMBC Honors College provides the atmosphere of a small community of learning and energetically sponsors a variety of programs and activities that often intentionally blur the distinction between the curricular and extracurricular. Toward that end, every year the College sponsors a variety of special courses—whether honors versions of regular courses or specially commissioned interdisciplinary honors seminars (such as Methods and Materials of Research, Knowledge and Responsibility, Professional Issues and Decision Making, The Sixteenth Century, and Medicine in Literature)—and encourages participation in activities ranging from its Visiting Scholar Program (through which College members attend a seminar and dine with such individuals as Robert Coles, Jonathan Kozol, Noam Chomsky, Lani Guinier, and Marge Piercy), community service projects (such as Project Discover, which addresses the needs and outlook of fourth- and fifth-grade students in the inner city), and cultural events (e.g., trips to New York to see Tom Stoppard's *Arcadia* at Lincoln Center or the Greek National Theater production of Sophocles' *Electra*) to study/travel programs abroad (among which the College itself has conducted sessions in England and Greece).

By special contract with an instructor, a member of the College may receive honors credit for a regular course. Small classes—maximum 25, average about 17—encourage collaborative learning through dialogue between student and instructor and the involvement of students in research. The motto of the College is "Learning for living, not only for making a living."

On completion of six honors courses with a minimum grade of B in each, members receive the Certificate of General Honors at an annual ceremony. A notation of the award appears on the student's transcript.

Initiated as the Honors Program in 1982, the Honors College was given its present coherence and designation in 1988. At any given time, there are 500 members of the Honors College.

Admission Process: A separate application for admission to the College must be submitted in addition to that submitted for admission to UMBC; the Honors College application requires a composition, answers to background and interest questions, and a letter of reference. Although a personal interview is not required, it is invited. While the chief criterion for membership in the College is an abiding curiosity and a will and energy during the university years to learn how to satisfy that curiosity, generally a minimum combined SAT I score of 1200 (recentered) and a minimum cumulative high school GPA of 3.5 will be sufficient for admission as a freshman to the Honors College. In fall 1995, the profile of the Honors College freshmen consisted of an average unrecentered SAT I score of 1250 and a high school GPA of 3.77.

Transfer students or UMBC students who did not apply as freshmen are expected to have established a minimum cumulative college GPA of 3.25. Members maintain their eligibility by taking at least one honors course per academic semester and establishing and keeping a 3.25 cumulative GPA.

Scholarship Availability: The Honors College offers scholarships for both the regular academic year and the summer. All prospective freshmen who submit applications by March 1 are considered for academic-year scholarships that are highly competitive and are awarded on the basis of the SAT I verbal score, high school GPA, analytical and expository ability as demonstrated in the application composition, and breadth of intellectual outlook as demonstrated in the answers to the interest questions on the application. Approximately 15 percent of the freshmen entering the College receive such scholarships, which may be added to other awards from UMBC and/or sources outside the University. Each spring, all members of the College are invited to apply for summer scholarships; proposals involving independent research and/or study abroad are particularly encouraged for summer awards.

Research and scholarship opportunities, as well as educational enrichment for outstanding undergraduate students, are offered through the Meyerhoff Scholarship Program for Science and the Humanities Scholars and Artists Scholars programs.

The Campus Context: The University of Maryland Baltimore County opened in 1966 and has grown to become a flourishing mid-sized research university of approximately 10,000 students (graduate and undergraduate). A highly selective university in the eleven-campus University of Maryland System, UMBC is situated on 500 acres southwest of the city of Baltimore and affords immediate access both to that city's cultural, social, and commercial benefits (such as the Walters Art Gallery, the Baltimore Museum of Art, the Inner Harbor, Oriole Park at Camden Yards, the Meyerhoff Symphony Hall) and to those of Washington, D.C. Philadelphia is 2 hours and New York 3½ hours away. There are twenty-seven undergraduate (B.A./B.S.) degree programs, twenty-two M.A./M.S./M.F.A./M.P.S. programs, and nineteen Ph.D. programs offered on campus.

In addition to an Arts and Sciences Program affording the opportunity to major in twenty-five different areas, there is the College of Engineering. Students obtaining certification in education must also complete the requirements for one of the academic majors.

Special facilities of particular significance to undergraduates include the Shriver Center, which places students in co-ops and internships in the immediate area and around the world, manages community service projects that bring the resources of the University to the public, and connects students to a wide range of social service projects. Among its special programs are the Student Literacy Corps, a tutoring program for children and adults in Baltimore, and the Shriver Peaceworker Program for returning Peace Corps volunteers. The Howard Hughes Medical Laboratory offers undergraduate students extensive research opportunities in the biomedical field. UMBC also has an imaging resource center, a molecular biology laboratory, and an art gallery.

Student Body A total of 8,899 undergraduates are enrolled at UMBC, distributed according to the following categories: women 4,576 (51.5 percent); men 4,323 (48.5 percent). The ethnic distribution is African American, 1,350 (15.2 percent); American Indian, 46 (0.5 percent); Asian American, 1,025 (11.5 percent); Hispanic, 190 (2.1 percent); white, 6,033 (67.8 percent); other, 51 (0.57 percent). There are 204 international students representing sixty-three countries. About 24 percent of students are residents, 76 percent commuters. Forty-nine percent of students who applied for aid received some form of financial aid. There are 108 registered organizations on campus, including twelve fraternities and eight sororities.

Faculty Full-time faculty members number 427, 88.6 percent with terminal degrees. Part-time faculty number 329, 48.3 percent with terminal degrees. The total number of faculty members is 756, 71 percent with terminal degrees. The student-faculty ratio is 14.4:1.

Key Facilities The UMBC library contains more than 600,000 volumes and more than 4,000 periodicals; electronic resources including on-line catalog, bibliographic and full text databases, Internet and World Wide Web access; special collections including photography (more than 1.5 million photographs), scientific archives (such as those of the American Society for Microbiology), science fiction, Marylandia, English graphic satire, and utopian literature. UMBC students have access to 400 microcomputers, either Intel-based PCs or Macintosh Apples, through which they may access the Internet.

Athletics There are eleven men's and eleven women's NCAA Division I sports available on campus. UMBC belongs to the Big South and East Coast Athletic Conferences and supports a number of intramural and club sports.

Study Abroad UMBC maintains study abroad programs in Mexico, Germany, Italy, and the United Kingdom. Students may also receive credit for participation in programs sponsored by other universities. The Honors College, in cooperation with relevant departments, sponsors yearly travel/study programs. Locations have included England, Greece, and China.

Support Services The UMBC campus is 93 percent handicapped-accessible and a Director of Support Services is available to coordinate student requests for assistance.

Job Opportunities Twenty-six percent of undergraduates work on campus during the academic year.

Tuition: $3400 for state residents, $8192 for nonresidents, per year (1996-97)

Room and Board: $4746

Mandatory Fees: $736

Contact: Director: Dr. Jay M. Freyman, Associate Professor of Ancient Studies, 1000 Hilltop Circle, Baltimore, Maryland 21250; Associate Director: Dr. Katherine Z. Keller, Affiliate Faculty in English; Telephone: 410-455-3720; Fax: 410-455-1063; E-mail: freyman@umbc2.umbc.edu

---

UNIVERSITY OF MARYLAND COLLEGE PARK

| 4 Pu G L Sc Tr |

▼ University Honors Program

The University Honors Program is the long-established program for the most talented students on campus in their first two years. It offers the opportunity to become part of a close-knit community of faculty members and intellectually gifted undergraduates committed to acquiring a broad and balanced education.

University Honors combines the best of a major research institution—preparing the student for up-to-date, productive careers—with the best of a wide-ranging undergraduate program, developing the intellectual breadth necessary for a long, responsible life in a complex, fast-changing world. The Honors Program challenges the student to explore the full range of the academic and social diversity of the College Park campus and to seek ways to serve the needs of the larger world off campus.

Through an exciting array of small classes taught by experienced faculty and through contact with other like-minded undergraduates, honors will provide an intellectual home for the curious, adventuresome, and enthusiastic student. Pleasure in dialogue and debate, involvement in the world of ideas and opinions, and a willingness to experiment with unfamiliar concepts characterize the students involved in the program.

The first two years of honors emphasize broadening intellectual horizons through a mix of honors seminars—mostly lively interdisciplinary courses—and "honors-version" courses offered in various departments (these are smaller and more focused versions of regular departmental offerings). In small class settings, faculty members and students explore the major issues, universal themes, and intellectual concepts that enable the various disciplines to do their share of the work of the mind. These courses will allow the student to explore or test a commitment to a possible major while meeting the University's distribution requirements—and they will open broad new intellectual vistas unavailable in high school.

All honors students take either HONR 100 or 200. HONR 100, "The Responsibilities of a Liberally Educated Person," is a first-semester colloquium that encourages beginning students to think broadly about the personal and social value of education and about what it means to be an educated person. Carefully selected readings, community service projects, and cross-cultural activities are shared with 15 other honors students during the first semester. HONR 200 introduces students to the world of research. Conversations with selected faculty members in a variety of academic areas, as well as visits to their labs, studios, or field stations, give students insight into the issues of disciplinary method, personal commitment, ethics, and funding of university research and other creative projects.

Honors seminars, of which students take at least three over five semesters, choosing from scores of different courses, form the heart of the program. They are limited to 15-20 students and emphasize individual responsibility and lively intellectual exchange. Faculty members are chosen not only for their knowledge and interest in their subject but also for their commitment to undergraduate honors education. HONR 169Z, "Knowledge and Its Human Consequences," is a wildly interdisciplinary course aimed at second-semester students: it will allow the student to study six "texts" from six different disciplines to see how knowledge is constructed and what the human consequences of different kinds of knowledge are.

Approximately 2,000 students are currently enrolled in the program.

Participation Requirements: The 600 most talented students are admitted each year (about 15 percent). Students normally complete their Honors Citation in four or five semesters and then may pass on into departmental honors work. Students may continue to take honors seminars and stay involved with the program by teaching in HONR 100 or 200, serving on committees, and so on. To earn the Citation, 16 credits of honors work (1 credit for HONR 100 or 200 plus five 3-credit honors courses of which three must be seminars) and a GPA of at least 3.2 are required.

Scholarship Availability: Most merit scholarships are independent of participation in honors, though most major scholarship winners are automatically admitted to honors. There are small scholarships for students in good standing in the program for their second and third years.

The Campus Context: The University of Maryland at College Park is the flagship campus of the University of Maryland system and is located on a traditional campus of Georgian buildings in suburban College Park between Washington, D.C., and Baltimore, Maryland. The exceptional resources of the Washington-Baltimore area provide students with extensive research and internship opportunities to enhance the quality education they receive at UMCP.

Student Body In fall 1995 the undergraduate enrollment was 24,373: 52 percent men, 48 percent women. Ethnic distribution was Caucasian, 66.3 percent; African American, 13.9 percent; Asian, 15.1 percent; Hispanic, 4.4 percent; and Native American, .3 percent. International students numbered 802. Thirty-five percent of students are residential, 65 percent commute. Forty-three percent of students receive financial aid.

Faculty The total number of faculty members is 3,061; 2,420 are full-time and 88 percent hold doctorates or other terminal degrees.

Key Facilities The University libraries hold more than 2.4 million volumes. There are approximately 1,700 computers for students (IBM, Mac, and UNIX) available in computer laboratories throughout the campus, many of them open 24 hours a day.

Study Abroad Through the Study Abroad Office, students may participate in a wide range of overseas study programs, including programs in Brazil, Denmark, Great Britain, France, Germany, Israel, and Mexico.

Support Services There is an office of support services for disabled students. The campus is 80 percent accessible.

Job Opportunities There is an extensive college work-study program on campus.

Tuition: $3494 for state residents, $9553 nonresidents, per year (1996-97)

Room and Board: $5442

Mandatory Fees: $675

Contact: Director: Dr. Maynard Mack Jr., Anne Arundel Hall, College Park, Maryland 20742; Telephone: 301-405-6771; Fax: 301-405-6723; E-mail: mmack@deans.umd.edu; Web site: http://www.inform.umd.edu/honors

UNIVERSITY OF MASSACHUSETTS AMHERST

4 Pu G L Sc Tr

▼ Honors Program

The Honors Program at the University of Massachusetts Amherst offers academically talented students the advantages of a small college and the wide-ranging opportunities of a nationally recognized major research institution. Honors students participate in small classes and colloquia, receive individual counseling, and have outstanding opportunities to conduct significant research while working closely with faculty members. The Honors Program is a comprehensive, four-year program with a full range of offerings and resources available to students at every level of their undergraduate studies.

Honors students have a wide variety of academic and social interests but share a desire to explore and excel. The Honors Program offers several categories of courses—entirely enriched honors courses, colloquia, interdisciplinary seminars, independent study, and an honors thesis, project or activity. Honors courses limit enrollment to 20 and stress dialogue between leaders and learners. In addition, many junior and senior honors students take graduate-level courses and obtain honors credit. Courses taken through the Five College Consortium (Amherst College, Hampshire College, Mount Holyoke College, and Smith College in cooperation with the University of Massachusetts Amherst) may be petitioned for substitution as honors courses. Students are also encouraged to incorporate international study, internships, and cooperative education into their honors experience. Portions of this work may be approved as substitutions to fulfill honors course requirements.

First-year students are formally inducted into the program at a banquet to which their families and other special guests are invited. Each student receives a certificate of membership during the ceremony.

All incoming honors students take Honors 191A, "Meet UMass." This 1-credit course gives first-year students an introduction to the varied resources available at the University of Massachusetts and through the Honors Program and the Five College Consortium. Students meet other honors students and become involved with the University community at large. Special interest seminars, community service projects, and social and cultural activities are shared with the 14 other honors students in the 191A class. Students also participate in Pizza and Prof Night seminars where they have the opportunity to meet faculty members from various departments and talk with them in an informal setting.

The Honors Program offers honors housing through preferential placement in the Orchard Hill Residential Area where honors and nonhonors students live. Honors students may elect this option during the new students' summer orientation. Living together, honors students share learning and living experiences.

The Honors Program encourages students to undertake research and supports their efforts by helping to identify faculty mentors, teaching thesis workshops, offering research fellowships for financial assistance, co-sponsoring a University systemwide conference on undergraduate research, and publishing a professional-quality journal of student research, *The Commonwealth Undergraduate Review.* A variety of resources and services are available to students through the Honors Program. The advising component is both comprehensive and integrative with individual counseling from faculty, professional, and peer advisers. The computer laboratory located in the honors office has twenty networked Macs and PCs with laser printers, optical scanners, a variety of software, and connection to the campus fiber-optic system for access to the libraries of the Five College Consortium and to the Internet. The program also publishes a newsletter, sponsors service projects and student gatherings, and administers a competitive awards program. Graduating honors students may request a dean's letter of recommendation for prospective employers and graduate schools.

Established in 1961, the program now has a total membership of 1,600.

Participation Requirements: To graduate with Commonwealth Scholar honors, students must take a minimum of 48 graded credits in residence; complete at least six honors courses, including three at the 300 level or higher, with a grade of B or better; and attain a cumulative 3.2 GPA. Honors students who seek greater challenge can pursue individualized research culminating in an honors thesis or project. Membership in the Honors Program and successful completion of research as part of a departmental or interdisciplinary honors track is necessary to achieve the higher honors of magna cum laude with a minimum 3.5 GPA and summa cum laude with a minimum 3.8 GPA. Students who complete a minimum of 48 graded credits in residence and graduate from the Honors Program receive one or more of the following types of honors noted on their diplomas and transcripts, depending on their honors track and GPA: Commonwealth Scholar Honors; Departmental Honors or Interdisciplinary Honors; and cum laude, magna cum laude, or summa cum laude.

Admission Process: Entering first-year students are admitted to the program by invitation. Each student's application to the University is evaluated on the basis of academic achievement in high school, test scores, and an essay by the student. Average first-year honors students rank in the top 8 percent of their high school class, attain a 3.5 high school GPA in their academic course work, and score 1310 on the SAT I. Entering transfer students may be admitted either by invitation or by applying to the program during the first month of their entering semester if they have a 3.2 GPA or higher from their previous institution. Others may apply based on their academic record at the University if they have a 3.2 GPA or higher.

Scholarship Availability: The University of Massachusetts Amherst has a variety of merit scholarships available for incoming first-year and transfer students. Selections, which are administered by the Admissions Office, are made during the admission process.

In addition, the Honors Program has an endowed scholarship fund and several research fellowships. The recipient of the David J. Snyder Memorial Scholarship is selected annually from among Honors Program members to receive a one-time grant that is applied directly toward the student's tuition. Selection is based on a combination of financial need and academic achievement at the University.

Each spring, up to ten Honors Research Fellowships are awarded on a competitive basis to junior-year students. The fellowships cover up to $1000 of expenses directly related to each student's research culminating in a senior-year thesis or project. Also, 2 honors alumni fund additional honors research fellowships. For the Peter DiGiammarino '75 Honors Research Fellowship in BDIC, an Honors Program student in the Bachelor's Degree with Individual Concentration program is selected annually to receive financial support of up to $1000 for materials and/or activities directly related to his/her senior-year research culminating in a thesis or project. For the Melvin Howard '57 Honors Research Fellowship in Management, an Honors Program student in the School of Management is selected annually to receive financial support of up to $1000 for materials and/or activities directly related to his/her senior-year research culminating in a thesis or project.

The Honors Program also administers a competitive awards program. The deadline for applications is in the spring, generally mid-March. Recipients are announced at the honors graduation and awards banquet where they receive a special certificate. For the Honors Director's Awards, ten annual awards of $500 each are made to senior Honors Program students based on the excellence of their thesis or project. For the Class of 1941 Humanitarian Award, depending on endowment earnings, one or two awards of at least $1000 are made annually. Recipients are chosen from among junior and/or senior Honors Program students in good standing who provide documentation of their community service and submit a written essay.

The Robert G. Cooke Award, in memory of Robert Cooke, Class of 1925, carries a cash prize of approximately $1000. Selection is made from among senior Honors Program students who have shown outstanding academic achievement, including successful completion of research in the student's major, and have demonstrated significant University or community service. The Howard H. Quint Memorial Prize in Honors was established in memory of Professor Howard Quint, former history department chair and a founder of the Honors Program. The prize of approximately $400 is awarded jointly by the history department and the Honors Program to a senior student enrolled in the Honors Program, based on the student's academic record through the junior year.

Entering first-year honors students receive a certificate of membership at the Honors Induction ceremony held in October of their first semester.

The Campus Context: The University of Massachusetts Amherst is composed of ten colleges: Humanities and Fine Arts, Natural Sciences and Mathematics, Social and Behavioral Sciences, Arts and Sciences, Interdisciplinary and Other Programs, Education, Engineering, Food and Natural Resources, Management, Nursing, and Public Health and Health Sciences. Degree programs on campus include six associate, eighty-eight baccalaureate, seventy-two master's, and fifty-two doctoral degrees.

Among special facilities are the Fine Arts Center, art galleries, an on-campus elementary school, and the Learning Resources Center. Through the Five College Consortium, students at the University of Massachusetts Amherst also have direct access to the wide range of courses and faculty at Amherst College, Hampshire College, Mt. Holyoke College, and Smith College. Course registration is easy. No fee is involved. Coordinated academic calendars, open library borrowing, and fare-free buses linking the campuses contribute to a strong sense of community among the schools. Lectures, films, concerts, and other events at all five campuses create an exciting and intellectually rich environment.

Student Body Undergraduate enrollment is 52 percent men, 48 percent women. The ethnic distribution is 6 percent Asian, 5 percent black, 5 percent Hispanic, and 84 percent white. There are 408 international students. Fifty-seven percent of the students live on campus, 43 percent commute. Sixty percent of students receive financial aid. There are twenty-two fraternities and thirteen sororities.

Faculty Of the 1,273 instructional faculty members, 1,146 are full-time; 92 percent hold terminal degrees. The student-faculty ratio is 18.5:1.

Key Facilities The library houses 2.7 million volumes. Computer facilities are available in the Graduate Research Center, the W.E.B. DuBois Library, selected dormitories, and in numerous department-supervised computer rooms. Facilities are available to all students for $20 per semester. Modems are provided in the residence halls, and computers are available at the University Store at a student discount. The Honors Computer Lab is available at no fee to members of the Honors Program.

Athletics Amherst is a member of NCAA Division I and the Atlantic 10 Conference. It offers twenty-seven intercollegiate sports and twenty intramural sports programs. Outdoor facilities include 120 acres of multipurpose fields and twenty-three tennis courts. In addition, the University has an ice rink, three swimming pools, five handball/squash courts, seven racquetball courts, weight rooms, a fitness center, basketball/volleyball/badminton courts, and indoor/outdoor tracks.

Study Abroad The University has ninety international exchanges with thirty-one countries. The International Programs Office (IPO) offers assistance to students interested in arranging a semester or year abroad. IPO keeps on file, by country and subject/major, information on programs available at other institutions. Students are encouraged to meet with a specific resource person regarding the program of interest. In addition, they are encouraged to meet with their faculty adviser to be sure the selected study abroad program fits well with the curriculum requirements of their individual major. The study abroad programs are designed to provide international study at a cost comparable to that of the University. Any financial aid, scholarships, or loans that a student receives to attend the University apply while the student participates in an approved study abroad program.

Support Services Disability Services works to provide accommodations to qualified disabled students, ensuring that the University offers an environment that is accessible and equitable to all students. Accommodations include preferential scheduling, special transportation, orientation programs, housing assistance, a reader's directory for the blind, classroom interpreters for the deaf, and counseling services.

Job Opportunities The Office of Financial Aid Services provides current listings of on- and off-campus temporary, part-time, and seasonal job opportunities that can be used to defray educational costs. In addition, the University offers a need-based Federal Work-Study program that provides part-time employment to students in a variety of on-campus departments and off-campus agencies.

Tuition: $2109 for state residents, $8842 for nonresidents, per year (1996-97)

Room and Board: $4228

Mandatory Fees: $3304 minimum

Contact: Director: Dr. Linda Nolan, 504 Goodell Building, Box 33295, Amherst, Massachusetts 01002-3295; Telephone: 413-545-2483; Fax: 413-545-4469; E-mail: honorspg@acad.umass.edu; Web site: http://www.umass.edu/honorspg

UNIVERSITY OF MASSACHUSETTS BOSTON

| 4 Pu C M Sc Tr |

▼ **Honors Program, College of Arts and Sciences**

The Honors Program offers, in part, an accelerated, enhanced, and more rigorous version of the College's General Education program. At its heart is an array of 200-level courses, of which students select six. These courses—unique to the program and not honors sections of standard courses—are multidisciplinary and involve special enrichments such as assignments at Boston's

Museum of Fine Arts, computerized experiments, and presentations by visiting scholars. Recent offerings include "Shapers of the 17th Century," "Art and Society in Latin America," "Austen and Byron," and "The History of Eugenics." Typically honors students take only one semester of honors composition (instead of the two semesters required of other students), and only one skill-intensive Honors Core course (instead of three). They are required to study math and foreign language and must meet a higher standard in these fields than students generally do.

The emphasis at the advanced levels of the four-year program falls on independent projects and research. All honors students take a semester of Junior Colloquium, a unique course in the College that attempts to socialize them to the role of the researcher. Under a faculty leader and with the assistance of visiting scholars, the group explores a common topic while each student defines an individual research project. Recent topics include "Media and Cultural Change," "Plagues and People," and "Humor: Its Many Meanings." All program students are required to complete a senior-year thesis or project in the major. Honors students are also urged to participate in the annual Conference on Undergraduate Research, co-sponsored by the Honors Programs of the four undergraduate campuses of the University of Massachusetts System: Amherst, Boston, Dartmouth, and Lowell.

Honors students enjoy their own lounge. New students are welcomed and introduced at special events: an Honors Reception in the fall and a Family Night in the spring, which features a lecture by an honors faculty member.

The 20-year-old program currently enrolls 115 students.

Participation Requirements: A student who takes the full program completes 27 credits in honors sections, in addition to the requirements in math and language and the senior thesis. Transfer students and late-admitted students take a modified version of the program. Enrollment in honors classes is limited to 20 students; the Junior Colloquium is limited to 15. Students in the program must maintain a minimum 3.0 GPA. The program awards the Robert H. Spaethling Prize to the one or two students who complete the first two years of the program with the highest distinction. Successful completion of the entire program is recognized at the College's Spring Honors Convocation and is recorded on the student's transcript.

Admission Process: Freshmen and new transfer students for fall term are selected mainly during the summer orientation periods; for spring term during the January orientation periods. Continuing students are selected during preregistration periods in November and April. The program chooses students according to ability, motivation, and excellence of preparation, as evidenced by high school and college records, test scores, and special accomplishments. A personal statement and an interview with the Director are required.

Scholarship Availability: The campus offers thirty Chancellor's Scholarships and four Commonwealth Scholarships to incoming students each year; many of these full-tuition grants are awarded to members of the Honors Program. Continuing students with 30 graduation credits may apply for a variety of merit scholarships.

The Campus Context: The Boston campus of the University of Massachusetts was founded in 1964. To the original Liberal Arts College were later added four others: Management, Community and Public Service, Nursing, and Education. Degree programs include the B.A. and B.S., with sixty-one major programs and sixty-five minors, concentrations, and undergraduate certificate programs; twenty-five programs and six additional graduate certificates leading to the M.A.; and seven Ph.D. programs.

Among the special facilities is WUMB-FM, a public radio station staffed in part by students. A new campus center will open in 2001. The Office of Student Life and the Student Senate sponsor about fifty organizations as well as the student newspaper, *The Mass Media*; the literary magazine, *The Watermark*; the Harbor Art Gallery; and the Wit's End Cafe.

The campus is situated 3 miles from downtown Boston on a peninsula reaching into Boston Harbor. It shares this site with the John F. Kennedy Presidential Library and the Massachusetts State Archives and Museum. The University is conveniently located at an exit of the main North-South Expressway, and free shuttle buses connect it to the local subway stop. City buses also serve the campus. UMass-Boston is a commuter campus; its Housing Referral Service assists students in finding accommodations and roommates in Boston and its environs.

Student Body Undergraduate enrollment is 8,997. The median age of students is 26; 46 percent are men, 54 percent women. Thirty-one percent of the students are members of ethnic minorities; the distribution is .5 percent Native American, 9.9 percent Asian American, 14.4 percent African American, 5.6 percent Hispanic, 1 percent Cape Verdean. International students make up 2.8 pecent of the undergraduate population.

Faculty The faculty members include winners of more than forty National Science Foundation grants, thirty-five Fulbright Fellowships, sixteen fellowships from the National Endowment for the Humanities and five from the National Endowment for the Arts, five Ford Foundation Fellowships, eight Guggenheim Fellowships, a special merit grant from the National Institutes of Health, and a Pulitzer Prize. Of the 835 faculty members, 464 are full-time and 89 percent of the full-time faculty members hold terminal degrees. The student-faculty ratio is 16:1.

Key Facilities The Healey Library holds more than 550,000 volumes and subscribes to more than 3,000 periodicals. The University's membership in several library consortia gives students access to other major collections in the Boston area. Computing Services operates three Macintosh labs, five PC labs, and one VAZ lab. In addition to serving as a resource used by students who are learning computer languages, various labs offer World Wide Web access, word processing, and accounting software. All labs are staffed by computer consultants.

Athletics The Clark Athletic Center includes a gymnasium, skating rink, and six-lane, T-shaped pool. A new Fitness Center has recently opened, and special rooms on campus accommodate dance, wrestling, and other contact sports. Other facilities include an eight-lane, 400-meter track, eight tennis courts, twenty-four sailboats, and football, soccer, and softball fields. There are eighteen varsity teams. UMass-Boston participates in Division II in hockey and Division III in other competitive sports.

Study Abroad There are diverse study abroad opportunities. The University has exchange agreements with about forty international universities. Special programs include a winter session program in Cuernavaca and a summer program in Ireland.

Support Services The Lillian Semper Ross Center provides a full range of services to students with physical, emotional, and learning disabilities, including an Adaptive Computer Laboratory. The campus is fully accessible to disabled students.

Job Opportunities The Student Employment Office assists students with placement in work-study and non-work-study positions on campus. The Office also maintains listings of nearby off-campus companies and organizations interested in employing students.

Tuition: $2109 for state residents, $8842 for nonresidents, per year (1996-97)

Mandatory Fees: $2239

Contact: Director: Dr. Monica McAlpine, McCormack Hall 4-425, 100 Morrissey Boulevard, Boston, Massachusetts 02125-3393; Telephone: 617-287-5520; Fax: 617-287-6511; E-mail: mcalpine@umbsky.cc.umb.edu

UNIVERSITY OF MASSACHUSETTS LOWELL

4 Pu G S Sc Tr

▼ Honors Program

The University of Massachusetts-Lowell Honors Program was recently established as a University-wide, comprehensive enrichment program of undergraduate studies, including research as a basic component, for outstanding students in all majors. Although departmental honors programs have existed since the start of the 1970s, the consolidation into a full-fledged University Honors Program (which still allows purely departmental honors projects) was undertaken in 1995 with the establishment of a 24-member Honors Council under the aegis of the University College.

The mission of the Honors Program is "to provide enriched academic opportunities to meet the educational needs of exceptionally talented students and to foster the pursuit of scholarly excellence in undergraduate higher education. By fostering interactions among outstanding, motivated students and outstanding, dedicated faculty, the Honors Program is directed toward the recruitment, development,

guidance, retention and professional growth of gifted students in activities designed to enhance their critical, cognitive and creative potential."

Normally, all freshman honors students are placed in special sections of the College Writing two-semester course taught by the English department, and all sophomore honors students are enrolled in the two-semester Honors Colloquium conducted by the Honors Director. Over and above this, they are also free to take additional departmental courses, including core and general education courses, for honors credit as either designated honors courses or "Contract Honors" courses. Many of these are given in seminar format; thus honors students enjoy the benefits of small class size and individualized attention. Any student who attains a GPA of at least 3.5 after the first semester is eligible for initiation into the Freshman Honors Society, the Lowell Chapter of Alpha Lambda Delta.

In general, the program emphasizes personalized advising and guidance, encourages students to use the excellent library facilities and multimedia, and offers a wide range of special services, including an especially attractive, secure, and elegant honors residence accommodation for students who wish to live on campus. For all participants, field trips, distinguished guest speakers, cultural events, and undergraduate research opportunities are central features of the honors experience. Trips, conferences, receptions, and informal pizza parties promote close contact with honors faculty members and with the Honors Council, which administers the program under the auspices of the University College.

Among the students, there is a strong sense of community; study groups and peer counseling are encouraged as elements of daily life in the "Honors family." Honors students feature prominently in community service projects and are often approached specifically by local employers or institutions as exemplifying the best of the University's undergraduate scholar resources.

Inaugurated in 1995 with a seed group of freshmen and sophomores, the program expanded the following year to admit juniors and offer about forty courses. With an enrollment of approximately 100, it is still in its initial stages. When fully developed, it will cater to 400-500 outstanding students imbued with a lifelong love of learning and dedication to excellence.

Participation Requirements: Students enrolled in the Honors Program in their freshman year must complete at least 24 credits of honors course work. Students admitted as sophomores complete at least 18 honors credits; students admitted as juniors (only under special circumstances in their first semester) complete at least 15 honors credits. All Honors Program credits must be completed at a satisfactory level with a grade of B or better. In each of the above participation categories, at least 3 of the total required credits must be obtained from satisfactory completion of an honors thesis or project entailing original research or scholarly activity. This is normally undertaken in one or both semesters of the senior year.

All students' academic transcripts show the honors courses taken by that student for honors credits, regardless of whether the above requirements have been met. Students who graduate with a cumulative GPA of at least 3.25 and the requisite number of honors credits will, in addition to the conventional baccalaureate degree (which may be awarded, where appropriate, at the cum laude, magna cum laude, or summa cum laude level) in their major discipline, have an Honors Diploma conferred upon them at Commencement.

Admission Process:
To be eligible for admission to the Honors Program, applicants must have achieved a score of at least 1200 combined on the new SAT I scale or at least 26 on the ACT; and/or have graduated in the top 15 percent of their high school class; and/or must submit at least two detailed letters of recommendation for honors work from principals, teachers, or guidance counselors. Transfer students must have an overall cumulative GPA of at least 3.25 from an acceptable accredited academic institution of higher learning.

Scholarship Availability:
Membership in the Honors Program does not entail any additional fees. On the contrary, many of the available Commonwealth of Massachusetts or University scholarships (as well as those from business, industry, and private donations) are awarded to Honors scholars.

The Campus Context:
The University of Massachusetts-Lowell was constituted in 1991 as one of the five campuses comprising the UMass system (along with Amherst, Boston, Dartmouth, and the Medical School at Worcester). The campus is situated in the Merrimack Valley, approximately 25 miles northwest of Boston. Its antecedent institutions of higher learning were Lowell State College and Lowell Technological Institute, established respectively in 1894 and 1895. Their merger in 1973 marked the formation of the University of Lowell, conferring baccalaureate and higher degrees. The Lowell campus itself is made up of three campuses (North, South, and West Campus), together with ancillary facilities at, for example, the Wannalancit Mill in central Lowell. Special facilities on campus include Centers for Learning (on the North and South Campus), an Adaptive Computing Laboratory, and a Counseling Center.

At present, the Lowell campus is comprised of six undergraduate colleges—Arts and Sciences, Engineering, Fine Arts, Health Professions, Management, and University College, offering courses at the bachelor's, master's, and doctoral level—as well as one college, Education, that offers graduate degrees only. There are twenty-nine bachelor's degree programs and ten Bachelor in Continuing Education programs available on the Lowell campus.

Student Body The undergraduate population is composed of 6,336 full-time day students and 3,900 continuing education students. Sixty-one percent are men and 39 percent women. The ethnic distribution of students is 80 percent white, 6.8 percent Asian, 3.5 percent Hispanic, 2.9 percent black, and 0.3 percent Native American, with an additional 4.6 percent

unknown. The 121 international students make up 1.9 percent of the population. Ninety-one percent of the students are in-state, 9 percent out-of-state. Twenty-nine percent live on campus, 71 percent are commuters. Approximately 75 percent of the students receive financial aid. Although there are no fraternities or sororities recognized by the University, at least two have been independently organized.

Faculty All 445 faculty members are full-time; more than 90 percent hold terminal degrees. The student-faculty ratio is 16:3 (222 credit hours per faculty member).

Key Facilities The campus has two libraries with an operating budget of approximately $2.7 million. Computer facilities include more than fourteen locations on the North Campus and seven on the South Campus that offer extensive opportunities for computation, word processing, spreadsheets, graphic design, multimedia, tutorials, computer-assisted design, e-mail, and network processing, The libraries and dormitories house some computer facilities and an effort is currently under way to create a separate, special facility for honors students.

Athletics A broad-based program of athletic and recreational opportunities is fostered by the University to promote the general health, welfare, and development of all participants. The Recreational Sports Office provides a comprehensive program for the entire community, including intramural sports, informal recreation, sports clubs, and instructional programs. There are more than thirty intramural sports offered in individual and team formats in a variety of lifetime/leisure sports such as tennis, badminton, and racquetball.

Team sports include soccer, volleyball, basketball, and ice hockey. Sports clubs include bowling, dance, equestrian, cheerleading, karate, lacrosse, outing, rugby, volleyball, skiing, shooting, and swimming. The Department of Athletics currently offers a program of twenty varsity sports. The school is a member of the NCAA and competes primarily at the Division II level (ice hockey is Division I and football is Division III). A gymnasium (including Nautilus facilities and a 25-yard, six-lane swimming pool, together with a wrestling/aerobics room and squash, basketball, volleyball, and racquetball courts) is on the North Campus, adjacent to athletic fields, tennis courts, and a running path. The South Campus also has extensive facilities, and the Tully Forum offers ice hockey and recreational ice skating.

Study Abroad Study-abroad opportunities are available to those undergraduate students in their sophomore or later years who have a cumulative GPA of 2.5 or better and faculty recommendations. Through the coordinator of the Study Abroad Office, students can find programs in twenty-two countries, with financial aid if needed.

Support Services The Office of Disability Services offers extensive assistance, counseling, and coordination facilities for disabled students. The following list gives an indication of the scope of such services: adaptations, classroom procedures, housing, individual accommodations, interpreters, note-taking, parking/transportation, personal care attendants, preferential registration, readers/aides/scribes, specialized equipment, adaptive technologies, oral exams, taped books, the Adaptive Computing Lab, the American Sign Language Club, enlarged print literature, and Braille.

Job Opportunities Work-study opportunities for qualified students are manifold and encouraged.

Tuition: $1700 for state residents, $7347 for nonresidents, $5322 for students eligible for the New England Regional Student Program, per year (1997-98)

Room and Board: $4165 minimum

Mandatory Fees: $2722

Contact: Director: Dr. Eugene Mellican, 1 University Avenue, Lowell, Massachusetts 01854-2881; Telephone: 508-934-2527 (Department of Philosophy); Web site: http://www.uml.edu/www/honors/umhonpg.html/

THE UNIVERSITY OF MEMPHIS

4 Pu GD L Sc Tr

▼ University Honors Program

The University of Memphis' University Honors Program, founded in 1975, provides exceptional educational opportunities for highly motivated and able students. The program enables students to take advantage of the more intimate learning environment offered by small classes. Honors faculty members promote active learning and provide excellent teaching, including individualized support and attention.

The program offers special curricular options and the opportunity to earn honors distinction. Classes within the program span the entire range of the University. A general education curriculum is available for freshmen and sophomores, while juniors and seniors may pursue interdisciplinary or departmental honors or may even design their own honors curriculum.

Lower-division students are expected to pursue the Honors Certificate, which is bestowed on any honors student who completes a minimum of 12 hours of honors course work (usually general education courses) with a grade of A or B and the 1-credit-hour Honors Forum. Honors sections at the lower-division level are academically challenging, and efforts are made to keep their size considerably smaller than regular sections.

Upper-division students may choose from three tracks leading to graduation with honors. Departmental, Interdisciplinary Liberal Arts, or Individualized Thematic Honors are conferred upon students at graduation who attain overall GPAs or 3.25 or higher and who complete the program requirements.

The extensive cocurriculum program combines out-of-classroom experiences, such as cultural events or discus-

sions with visiting scholars, with an active social environment in which to meet other honors students, thereby creating an honors community atmosphere.

There are currently 565 students enrolled in the program.

Admission Process: Incoming freshmen who score at least 27 on the ACT or 1200 on the SAT I are invited to participate in lower-division courses. Transfer students or students previously or currently enrolled at the University of Memphis are eligible for the program if they have overall GPAs of 3.0 for freshmen and sophomores and 3.25 for juniors and seniors.

Scholarship Availability: The University of Memphis provides more than $3 million in scholarships to high-ability students. Many students who receive scholarships are members of the University Honors Program.

The Campus Context: Located on a beautifully landscaped campus in a quiet residential area, the University of Memphis is the largest institution in the Tennessee Board of Regents system. Since its founding in 1912, the University of Memphis has evolved into a distinguished urban university with nationally recognized academic, research, and athletic programs.

Thirty different degrees are offered in 119 majors through the nine colleges of the University.

Student Body A total enrollment of about 20,000 students includes graduate students, law students, and almost 16,000 undergraduates. Approximately 2,500 students live on campus. The student population represents every state and seventy-four other countries. Approximately 40 percent of students are between ages 18 and 22, with minority students accounting for 20 percent of the total enrollment. Fifty-five percent of the students are women.

Faculty The 993 full-time faculty members provide a student-faculty ratio of 20:1; 75 percent of the faculty members have doctorates or other terminal degrees.

Key Facilities The new McWherter Library houses 1 million volumes and 2.9 million cataloged microformat pieces.

Athletics The University of Memphis sponsors teams representing the University in nine intercollegiate sports for men and seven intercollegiate sports for women. The University of Memphis is a member of the National Collegiate Athletic Association (NCAA) Division I-A and the Conference USA, newly formed in 1995-96.

Study Abroad The University of Memphis offers a British Studies program each summer in London, England. The University is also a member of the International Student Exchange Program, and as such has sent students to universities in Spain, Argentina, and Canada. Scholarships are available for both programs.

Support Services Student Disability Services provides information, guidance, and specialized support services that enable students with disabilities to take full advantage of the educational opportunities at the University. Services include pre-enrollment planning, early registration, coordination of academic accommodations with faculty members, alternative testing service, campus shuttle service, and coordination of adapted campus housing.

Job Opportunities Students are offered a range of work opportunities on campus, including assistantships and work-study.

Tuition: $2112 for state residents, $6448 for nonresidents, per year (1996-97)

Mandatory Fees: $68

Contact: Director: Dr. David Patterson, 115 Old Brister Library, Memphis, Tennessee 38152; Telephone: 901-678-2690; Fax: 901-678-5367

UNIVERSITY OF MIAMI

4 Pr G L Tr

▼ Honors Program

In 1957, the faculty of the University of Miami established the General Honors Program to provide an academically challenging course of study for outstanding students. The program was later expanded by the addition of departmental honors. Students who satisfactorily complete the requirements for general and/or departmental honors are graduated with General Honors and/or Departmental Honors; the award is noted on the graduate's diploma and official transcript.

The program now offers approximately 200 courses and sections each semester at the introductory through advanced levels, in a wide variety of fields, in all colleges and schools of the University. In general, honors courses are small classes taught as seminars with emphasis on interactive learning and discussion.

Invitations to General Honors are extended to approximately 15 percent of the entering freshman class on the basis of their outstanding scholastic achievement in high school and their high scores on college entrance examinations. A student of any undergraduate school or college is eligible for consideration as a member of the Honors Program. The program currently enrolls 1,438 students.

Participation Requirements: To remain in the Honors Program, a student must maintain an overall academic average of 3.0 and complete at least two honors courses per academic year. To graduate with General Honors, a student must complete at least 24 credits in General Honors courses and have an overall GPA of 3.0. Twelve of the 24 credits must be in courses at the 200 level or above. No more than 12 credits in the student's major may be counted toward the 24 credits in General Honors.

Admission Process: Freshmen and sophomores may be admitted to the Honors Program if they have achieved a 3.3 or

higher cumulative GPA in their college courses. Transfer students may apply if they have a 3.3 or higher cumulative GPA and have earned no more than 60 credits toward graduation. Inquiries should be made directly to the Honors Program office. All applicants should note that admission to the University of Miami must precede admission to the Honors Program.

Students may withdraw from the program at any time at their discretion. They should notify the Honors Office in writing of their intention to withdraw. Honors students' GPA and general performance are reviewed each academic year. Any student who fails to maintain the required cumulative GPA or fails to take the required number of honors credits will be excused from the program. Student may re-enter the program when their GPA has been raised to a 3.0; however, students must inform the Honors Office of the improved average and of their interest in re-entering the program.

The Campus Context: The University of Miami has four campuses: Coral Gables, Medical Campus, Rosenstiel School Campus, and South Campus. They incorporate 149 University-owned buildings totaling approximately 4.6 million square feet on more than 400 acres of land. The University offers twenty-three bachelor's programs, twenty-five master's programs, and nine doctoral programs.

Student Body Undergraduate enrollment is 8,289 (48.7 percent men, 51.3 percent women). The ethnic distribution is 53.9 percent white, 25.7 percent Hispanic, 7.9 percent Asian, 12.3 percent black, and 0.2 percent American Indian. International students constitute 9.9 percent of degree undergraduates. Twenty-five percent of the students are residents, 75 percent commuters. Seventy-five percent to 80 percent of the students receive financial aid (University and federal funds). There are fifteen fraternities on campus.

Faculty Faculty members total 11,403 (7,481 full-time), 97 percent with terminal degrees. The student-faculty ratio is approximately 13:1.

Key Facilities The library houses 2 million UM publications and 497,607 government publications. The Ungar Computing Center (the central facility) is equipped with an IBM ES9021 Model 580, DEC VAX cluster with two VAX 4000-600 systems, two VAX 3000, and numerous DEC workstations. There are over forty computer labs located in the residential colleges, libraries, schools, and colleges. The University has a campus network with a gateway to national and international networks.

Athletics The Hurricanes compete in Division I of the NCAA with nine men's and eight women's sports. In 1991, UM became a member of the Big East Conference. Men's competition includes baseball, basketball, crew, cross-country, football, swimming and diving, tennis, indoor track and field, and track and field. Women's competition includes basketball, crew, cross-country, golf, swimming and diving, tennis, and track and field.

Study Abroad The University of Miami Study Abroad Program offers an extensive array of overseas programs in more than twenty countries. Half of the programs offer course work taught in English. Many departments at UM encourage study abroad options as part of their basic curriculum. Studying abroad is open to sophomores, juniors, and seniors for a semester, a full academic year, or during the summer. Full University credit is awarded for approved courses.

Support Services The Office of Student Disability Services (ODS) is the primary University office responsible for coordination of services and accommodations for students and employees with disabilities. ODS functions as a clearinghouse for information, as a coordinator of services, and as an advocate.

Job Opportunities Through the Federal Work-Study Program, the University offers on-campus jobs to undergraduate students demonstrating financial need.

Tuition: $19,140 per year (1997-98 est.)

Room and Board: $7352

Mandatory Fees: $373

Contact: Director: Dr. Perri Lee Roberts, P.O. Box 248106, Coral Gables, Florida 33124-5595; Telephone: 305-284-5384; Fax: 305-284-5241; E-mail: proberts@umiamivm.ir.miami.edu; Web site: www.miami.edu/honors/document/home.htm

UNIVERSITY OF MINNESOTA

> 4 Pu C L Sc Tr

▼ College of Liberal Arts Honors Division

The College of Liberal Arts (CLA) Honors Division was created nearly three decades ago to serve the academic and intellectual needs of high-ability students. CLA honors students are eligible for honors courses, honors advising, honors housing, special cocurricular programs, scholarships, and recognition at graduation. Most important, CLA Honors offers students the opportunity to take courses from some of the University's best and most distinguished teachers in small classes that promote discussion and active learning. CLA Honors can provide students with the best of both worlds: the resources of a world-class research university and the sense of community that is usually associated with much smaller colleges.

Approximately 1,500 students are enrolled in the CLA Honors Division, which comprises about 12 percent of the student enrollment in the College of Liberal Arts. Students in the program may choose from a wide variety of courses. These courses range from honors sections of introductory courses in most disciplines to advanced honors courses in the student's major. In addition, the program offers small, discussion-oriented, special-topic Honors Seminars at the freshman-sophomore and junior-senior levels.

Participation Requirements: Honors students who take at least four honors courses and achieve A in at least half their

credits during their first two years of study earn the freshman-sophomore Honors Certificate, which is also noted on their transcript. Upperclass students who take four more honors courses, achieve A in at least half their advanced classes, and meet departmental honors requirements may graduate with an honors degree.

Admission Process: New freshmen are admitted by application in the year prior to their arrival on campus. Generally these new freshmen are in the top 10 percent of their high school classes and have a composite score of at least 28 on the ACT or 1260 (verbal and math combined) on the SAT I. The University's Office of Admissions publishes a booklet, "Academic Scholarships & Honors Programs," which contains an application for all freshman scholarships and honors programs on the campus. Transfer students may enter the CLA Honors Division if they have received grades of A in at least 60 percent of their college credits and if they will declare a CLA major. Waller Scholarships for $1500 are available through CLA Honors to transfer students intending to graduate with CLA majors.

The Campus Context: The University of Minnesota, Twin Cities Campus, has one of the largest campuses in the U.S. Undergraduates may study in the College of Liberal Arts (offering more than sixty majors), the Institute of Technology, the College of Human Ecology, the Carlson School of Management, the College of Agriculture, the College of Natural Resources, and the College of Biological Sciences.

Student Body Undergraduate enrollment is approximately 25,000 students, equally divided between men and women.

Key Facilities The Twin Cities Campus libraries contain some 5 million volumes.

Tuition: $3620 minimum for state residents, $10,327 minimum for nonresidents, per year (1996-97)

Room and Board: $4056

Mandatory Fees: $470

Contact: Director: Professor Gordon Hirsch, 115 Johnston Hall, Minneapolis, Minnesota 55455; Telephone: 612-624-5522; Fax: 612-624-6839; E-mail: hirsc002@maroon.tc.umn.edu

THE UNIVERSITY OF MISSISSIPPI

> 4 Pu C M Sc Tr

▼ The McDonnell-Barksdale Honors College

The McDonnell-Barksdale Honors College offers an enriched program of study designed to stimulate the intellectual growth of undergraduate students while providing them with an entire honors college experience. The program originated in 1953 as the Faulkner Scholars Program and existed as an honors program until fall 1997. The College is open to students of all majors. The

College, along with the building that houses it, is named for two Ole Miss alumni: Netscape Corporation President James L. Barksdale and his wife, Sally McDonnell Barksdale, who made the largest private gift ever to the University of Mississippi to fund this unique institution. It brings together selected students and distinguished faculty members in an atmosphere that reveals both the nature of an inquiring mind and the role of the faculty in the discovery of knowledge. Because of the exceptional quality of the students and professors, the interdisciplinary approach to learning on the lower-division level, the emphasis on discussion, the depth of research on the upper-division level, and close faculty-student relations, there is assurance of a high intellectual level in honors courses.

The honors curriculum begins with core courses, one taken each semester through the spring semester of the sophomore year. Honors courses taught in all majors by the University's most outstanding faculty members are available to complete the honors academic curriculum. Honors courses stress both writing and oral communication skills.

When a student is accepted into the Honors College, a faculty member with a special interest in the program and the student's major field will be assigned as adviser to the honors student. The adviser will be available to the student throughout completion of the program.

Honors College students receive the benefits of small classes; camaraderie with other exceptional students; easy and unlimited access to computers, research, teaching, rigorous academic oversight, colloquia and forums, study abroad, and intern and service opportunities; priority floors in residence halls; and special activities at the Honors College's new building, located in the center of the Oxford campus.

Students who take honors courses will receive a special "H" designation on their transcripts for each course satisfactorily completed. All students who successfully fulfill all Honors College requirements will graduate with special recognition and will receive a special distinction on their diplomas.

Approximately 75 first-year students are in the Honors College. Transfer students may apply.

Admission Process: The Honors College selects its students based on evidence of distinguished academic performance, significant achievement in scholastic and extracurricular activities, and the promise of substantial contribution to the University community throughout their college careers. The profile for the 1996 entering class reveals an average ACT score of 29 and an average high school GPA of 3.85. Among the diverse group of students admitted to the College are 26 valedictorians and salutatorians as well as 21 National Merit Finalists and Semifinalists. Their collective involvement in extracurricular enterprises, such as student government, the creative and performing arts, academic competitions, athletics, and community service, is noteworthy.

Scholarship Availability: The University of Mississippi offers a number of scholarships to students of exceptional ability. Two special scholarship opportunities are available only to students enrolled in the Honors College. Barksdale Scholarships, four annual awards valued at $6000 per year, are limited to Mississippi residents. The Honors Scholarships, five annual awards valued at $2000 per year, are open to all applicants.

The Campus Context: Home is a place where one can feel secure, accepted, and part of a family. That's just what students find at the University of Mississippi. Known around the world as Ole Miss, the University is located in the beautiful and delightfully southern town of Oxford, Mississippi. There are several distinguishing facilities on campus, including the Center for Wireless Communication, Mississippi Center for Supercomputing Research, Research Institute for Pharmaceutical Sciences, National Center for the Development of Natural Products, National Center for Physical Acoustics, National Food Service Management Institute, Center for the Study of Southern Culture, and Rowan Oak (William Faulkner's home).

Ole Miss offers more than 100 majors and special programs for undergraduates in seven academic divisions: College of Liberal Arts, School of Education, School of Accountancy, School of Engineering, School of Business Administration, School of Pharmacy, and the Law Center. Of the degree programs on campus, there are sixty-eight bachelor's, forty-two master's, twenty-six doctorates, three specialists, and two first professionals.

Student Body Founded in 1844, Ole Miss currently serves 8,117 undergraduate students. Of these students, 47.5 percent are men and 52.5 percent are women. The ethnic distribution of total undergraduates is as follows: 84.4 percent white, 10.1 percent black, 1.3 percent Asian/Pacific Islander, .7 percent Hispanic, .2 percent American Indian/Alaskan, and 2.5 percent non–U.S. citizen. Currently there are 198 international students. The University participates in a full range of federal and state financial aid programs. Help is available to 80 percent of students through scholarships, grants, loans, and part-time employment from both government programs and University funds. The University has thirty-two nationally recognized social fraternities and sororities. With nearly 200 academic and special interest clubs and honoraries, almost every major field of study has its own professional society.

Faculty The total number of faculty members at Ole Miss is 525. Of those, 455 are full-time faculty members, with 83 percent holding terminal degrees. The student-faculty ratio is 17:1.

Key Facilities The John Davis Williams Library, which contains the main collections of books, periodicals, microforms, manuscripts, audiovisual materials, and maps for use by the University community, currently houses 821,965 volumes. The University also has four branch libraries on campus: the Blues Archive, the Music Library, the Department of Chemistry Library, and the School of Pharmacy Library. Two autonomous libraries, the James O. Eastland Law Library and the Public

Policy Research Center Library, complement the resources contained in the Williams Library and its branches.

The University maintains three walk-in microcomputer sites, a microcomputer teaching lab, and two rooms of terminals for e-mail access. In addition, there are smaller departmental computing sites. The University operates an ISM mainframe and a Silicon Graphics academic server, and the faculty and students have free access to the Mississippi Center for Supercomputing Research, which includes two CRAY computers and a high-performance SGI workstation. The campus is completely networked, including residence halls, and there is a fiber-optic campus backbone with T1 connection to the Internet.

Athletics Ole Miss offers some of the best action in the Southeastern Conference, including football, basketball, tennis, baseball, track, softball, volleyball, soccer, and golf, which infuse the campus with excitement throughout the year. Intramural sports for both men and women allow students to grow in mind, spirit, and body. More than forty competitive events are held throughout the school year.

Study Abroad Ole Miss offers study-abroad opportunities to qualified students during the academic year and the summer. Students of all classifications can choose from more than forty countries. Many of the programs are exchange programs that charge the school tuition and apply the student's school scholarships to the cost.

Support Services The University has made numerous changes in the physical environment of the campus to accommodate students with physical disabilities. It continues to work with students on an individual basis to provide reasonable accommodations within the campus environment.

Job Opportunities Students are offered a range of work opportunities on campus as well as off campus, including assistantships and work study.

Tuition: $1996 for state residents, $4816 for nonresidents, per year (1996-97)

Mandatory Fees: $635 per year (full-time), $295 per semester (part-time)

Contact: Director: Dr. Gay B. Hatfield (Interim Director), University, Mississippi 38677; Telephone: 601-232-7294; Fax: 601-232-7739; E-mail: honors@olemiss.edu; Web site: http://www.olemiss.edu

UNIVERSITY OF MISSOURI–COLUMBIA

4 Pu G L Tr

▼ Honors College

The MU Honors College is a campuswide program designed to provide talented students with appropriate academic challenges and special opportunities. The Honors College does not offer academic degrees; rather, it serves outstanding students from all of MU's undergraduate colleges by providing a more personalized education and individual attention and support. Honors courses are of two types: honors sections of regularly offered courses and special honors colloquia that are limited to 20 honors students (e.g., Italian Cinema, The Old Order Amish, and Medical Ethics).

The academic centerpiece of the Honors College, the four-semester Humanities Sequence, provides an interdisciplinary introduction to Western culture and intellectual history from ancient to contemporary times. A staff of outstanding instructors combines lectures and small discussion groups in this study of the artistic, literary, religious, and philosophical expressions of Western civilization. The Humanities Sequence follows a great books tradition. Students are asked to read original works, in translation, from Plato to Sartre in philosophy and from Homer to Toni Morrison in literature. The Humanities Sequence includes the following courses: the Ancient World, the Middle Ages and the Renaissance, the Early Modern World, and the Modern Era.

In spring 1997, the Honors College introduced a Social Science Sequence as a companion to the Humanities Sequence. An Honors Science Sequence for nonscience majors is scheduled to begin in fall 1997.

The Honors College Community Involvement Program (HCCIP) is a nationally recognized outreach program that pairs honors students with at-risk youth from local secondary schools. HCCIP encourages MU's brightest and most energetic students to improve the lives of those around them. As mentors, pals, and tutors, the honors students not only make a difference in the lives of the young people, they also develop leadership and public service skills for themselves as well as a sense of social responsibility.

Primarily designed for first- and second-year students, the Honors College accepts approximately 650 new students each year or about 15 percent of the incoming freshman class.

Participation Requirements: Honors College students must maintain a 3.0 or higher GPA to remain Honors eligible. However, students may take as many or as few honors courses per semester as they like. Honors classes receive a "GH" (General Honors) designation on their transcript. If a student takes 20 hours of honors course work and graduates with a 3.3 cumulative GPA or better, he or she can earn an Honors Certificate, which is also noted on the transcript.

Admission Process: Currently, students are automatically eligible for the program out of high school if they have a minimum ACT score of 28 (or its equivalent on the SAT) and rank among the top 10 percent of their graduating class. Students who are not automatically eligible but who believe they would profit from enrolling in honors courses are encouraged to petition the College by including an essay with their applications. Honors-eligible students will be sent an application to the College shortly after being accepted to MU. Other students may write to the Honors College and request an application. Transfer students and students already attending MU are eligible if they have a 3.5 cumulative GPA and at least 30 college credit hours.

Scholarship Availability: Other than administering the National Merit Program, the Honors College does not offer scholarships to incoming freshmen.

The Campus Context: The University of Missouri–Columbia, established in 1839, is the first public university in the area of the former Louisiana Territory. Rated among the nation's very best by the *Fisk Guide to Colleges* and the *Insider's Guide to Colleges,* Missouri is often called a "public ivy"—academically rigorous, pleasantly affordable, and friendly. Missouri is a place where honors undergraduates can find a comfortable home and combine the advantages of a small college with the resources of an acclaimed research institution. MU offers more than 200 undergraduate and graduate degree programs from the Colleges of Agriculture, Arts and Science, Business and Public Administration, Education, Engineering, Human Environmental Science, Journalism, Natural Resources, Nursing, and Social Work and the School of Health Related Professions. Distinguished campus facilities include a research reactor; the postbaccalaureate Schools of Law, Medicine, and Veterinary Medicine; and the world's first School of Journalism.

Student Body Undergraduate enrollment is 18,000; graduate is 4,000. The total enrollment includes 48 percent men and 52 percent women. The ethnic distribution is 4 percent Native American, 2.3 percent Asian American, 5.3 percent African American, 1.3 percent Hispanic American, and 6.4 percent international students. Approximately 75 percent of students receive financial aid. There are thirty-four fraternities and twenty sororities, to which approximately 25 percent of the students belong.

Faculty Of the 1,599 faculty members, 1,538 are full-time. Eighty-seven percent hold a Ph.D. or professional degree. The student-faculty ratio is 14:1.

Key Facilities MU's library consists of seven branches containing more than 10 million bibliographic sources for research, including 2.7 million volumes.

Athletics MU sports include Big 12 basketball, baseball, and football along with diving, golf, gymnastics, softball, swimming, tennis, track and field, volleyball, and wrestling. The campus also has an extensive range of intramural and club sports.

Study Abroad Through agreements with universities around the world, MU students can study abroad during the summer, for a semester, or for an entire year. Missouri sponsors study-abroad opportunities in Australia, China, Costa Rica, Denmark, France, Germany, Italy, Japan, Mexico, the Netherlands, Romania, Russia, Spain, Taiwan, and the United Kingdom.

Support Services Services for disabled students include alternative testing arrangement, classroom accommodations, and on-campus transportation.

Tuition: $3389 for state residents, $10,129 for nonresidents, per year (1996-97)

Room and Board: $4172

Mandatory Fees: $479

Contact: Director: Dr. Stuart B. Palonsky, 211 Lowry Hall, Columbia, Missouri 65211; Telephone: 573-882-3893; Fax: 573-884-5700; E-mail: honorssp@showme.missouri.edu; Web site: http://www.missouri.edu/~honorwww/

THE UNIVERSITY OF MONTANA–MISSOULA

4 Pu G M Sc Tr

▼ The Davidson Honors College

The Davidson Honors College is a campuswide association of faculty and students united by a common concern for academic and personal excellence. Its mission is to foster intellectual and civic values and to support the best possible teaching and learning circumstances for participating faculty and students.

The College offers an academic and social home to motivated and talented students as they pursue their undergraduate education. Students from all major areas in the College of Arts and Sciences and the professional schools are welcome, as are students undecided about a major. Honors is not a major in itself but an enhanced approach to fulfilling General Education requirements. It is compatible with all undergraduate majors.

The Davidson Honors College building is located at the center of the UM campus. It provides honors students with a large, comfortable lounge area; kitchen space; a multimedia computer lab; and quiet study rooms in addition to classrooms and office space.

The Honors Students' Association sponsors a variety of social activities and community service projects throughout the year. A special honors/international dormitory floor is available. The Davidson Honors College also sponsors the University of Montana Volunteer Action Services, an office coordinating local service agencies with campus resources and supporting the integration of community service experience into the academic curriculum.

There are 422 students in the College.

Participation Requirements: Davidson Honors College students are required to complete a minimum of seven honors courses, including one cluster of lower-division courses, one honors seminar, and an honors thesis or project.

Graduation through the Davidson Honors College requires a cumulative GPA of 3.0 or higher and 3.4 or higher in the major field. Upon completion of the requirements, students receive their bachelor's degrees as University Scholars in their respective majors and have this noted on their diplomas.

Admission Process: Students must apply separately to the Davidson Honors College. Selection is made by the faculty adviser. The priority deadline is February 1.

Scholarship Availability: The Davidson Honors College administers the Presidential Leadership Scholarships, UM's premier academic scholarship program for incoming freshmen. The Davidson Honors College also administers other campus-based scholarship programs for juniors and seniors, as well as several national competitions.

The Campus Context: The University of Montana has provided a high-quality, well-rounded education to students and a wide range of services to Montanans since it was chartered in 1893. UM is the center of liberal arts education in Montana, balancing that core commitment with intensive programs of professional preparation. The University is a major source of research, continuing education, economic development, and fine arts and entertainment, as well as a driving force in strengthening Montana's ties with countries throughout the world.

UM's Missoula campus comprises the College of Arts and Sciences, the Graduate School, the Davidson Honors College, the College of Technology, and seven professional schools, including business administration, education, fine arts, forestry, journalism, law, and pharmacy and allied health sciences. In addition to Missoula, UM includes three affiliated campuses: Western Montana College of the University of Montana, Dillon; Montana Tech of the University of Montana, Butte; and College of Technology of the University of Montana, Helena. The variety and number of degree programs offered are bachelor's, fifty-two; master's, forty-five; doctorate, nine; Associate of Applied Science, thirteen; and Certificate of Completion, fifteen.

Student Body Undergraduate enrollment is 10,088; graduate enrollment is 1,665. Of the total, 49 percent are men and 51 percent are women. Fifty percent of undergraduates receive financial aid. There are 390 international students from fifty-seven countries. UM has ten national fraternities and four national sororities. Most maintain chapter houses near campus.

Faculty Of the 477 full-time faculty members, 84 percent hold doctoral or terminal degrees.

Key Facilities The library houses 673,852 volumes. There are six computer labs housing 130 computers: twenty-five Macintosh and 105 DOS or Windows-based.

Athletics In intercollegiate athletics, UM is NCAA Division I and a member of the Big Sky Conference. Men's sports include football (I-AA), basketball, cross-country, tennis, and indoor/outdoor track. Women's sports include basketball, cross-country, golf, soccer, tennis, indoor/outdoor track, and volleyball.

Study Abroad The Office of Foreign Languages and Literatures acts as an information and referral center for foreign study opportunities in a wide variety of countries.

Support Services Disability Services for Students guarantees equal access to the University of Montana–Missoula academic programs by students with disabilities. This is accomplished through the coordination and provision of adjunct services

and through responsible advocacy designed to promote a hospitable and accessible learning environment.

Job Opportunities Students are offered a range of work opportunities on campus, including assistantships and work-study.

Tuition: $2484 for state residents, $6733 for nonresidents, per year (1996-97)

Room and Board: $3962

Contact: Dean: John Madden, Missoula, Montana 59812; Telephone: 406-243-2541; E-mail: dhc@selway.umt.edu

UNIVERSITY OF NEBRASKA AT OMAHA

`4 Pu G M Sc Tr`

▼ University Honors Program

The Honors Program at the University of Nebraska at Omaha is for students who want to get the most out of their efforts and who enjoy stimulating experiences. The Honors Program consists of the University's most talented, involved, and exciting students, along with highly qualified and dedicated faculty members.

Honors students participate in special limited enrollment sections of core requirement courses, taught at a level and pace appropriate for honors students. Interdisciplinary colloquia are the core of the Honors curriculum and allow students to see the interaction between disciplines while offering an alternative way of fulfilling University requirements. An important advantage of honors classes is the stimulation able, motivated students offer each other.

Outside of the classroom the Honors Program Student Advisory Board provides social and cultural activities, including guest speakers, tours, weekend trips, and an annual banquet. During Honors Week, senior honors students offer colloquia for the entire University community on their senior theses/projects. Honors students have their own lounge and study room in the Honors Office where they can visit, share ideas with friends, study, or just relax. A real sense of community exists.

There are many opportunities available to Honors Program participants. Honors students interested in medical careers can apply for early admission to the University of Nebraska Medical Center through the UNO Medical Scholars Program. Internships and experiential learning opportunities are also available for students. UNO honors students have been recipients of Truman Scholarships and Rotary Scholarships.

All honors courses are noted on the student's transcript. If a student completes the Honors Program and meets all of the criteria, he or she is recognized at graduation, receives recognition in the Commencement Program, has an appropriate notation made on the diploma, and receives personal letters of recommendation from the Chancellor. The 17-year-old program currently enrolls 100 students.

Participation Requirements: Students meet the requirements of the University Honors Program by successfully completing 30 hours of credit in honors courses and by meeting their college's GPA requirements of 3.25–3.50 for the Honors Program. The 30 hours are part of a student's overall program, not additional hours. The 30 hours of honors credit are usually met in the following manner: 12–15 hours of honors sections of general education requirements; 6 hours of interdisciplinary colloquia; 3–6 hours of senior thesis or project; and 3–6 hours of special seminars, internships, electives, or experiential classes.

Admission Process: Students are admitted to the Honors Program as entering freshmen if they have minimum ACT scores of 26 or minimum SAT I scores of 1200 or by special recommendation from high school principals or counselors. Students already enrolled are admitted to the Honors Program if their overall GPA ranges from 3.25 to 3.5, depending upon their respective colleges. Transfer students from other Honors Programs will be eligible if they were members in good standing in their previous programs and complete the Honors Program requirements.

Scholarship Availability: The Honors Program offers four scholarships designed specifically for honors students. They are the Distinguished Scholarship, World Herald Scholarship, Scottish Rite Scholarship, and Nebraska Banker's Association Honors Scholarship. In order to receive any of these scholarships a student must participate in the Distinguished Scholarship Competition.

The Campus Context: The University of Nebraska at Omaha is a campus of nine colleges, including the College of Arts and Sciences, College of Business Administration, College of Public Administration and Community Service, College of Continuing Studies, College of Education, College of Information Science and Technology, College of Fine Arts, College of Human Resources and Family Sciences, and College of Public Affairs and Community Service. The type and number of degree programs offered are Bachelor of Arts (twenty-nine majors); Bachelor of Science (fifty-eight majors); Bachelor of Fine Arts (three majors); Bachelor of Music (three majors); M.A., M.S., and M.B.A. (fifty-six concentrations); and Ph.D. (five programs, three of which are jointly administered with University of Nebraska at Lincoln).

Student Body The total undergraduate enrollment is 12,446: 48 percent men and 52 percent women. The ethnic distribution of students is 82.7 percent white, 6 percent black, 2.4 percent Hispanic, 1.9 percent Asian/Pacific Islander, .5 percent American Indian/Alaskan, and 1 percent nonresident alien. There are 221 international students on campus. All students are commuters. Fifty-five percent of the students receive financial aid. There are sixteen fraternities and sororities.

Faculty The total number of faculty members is 423, of whom 156 are full-time. More than 81 percent of the faculty members have terminal degrees. The student-faculty ratio is 30:1.

Key Facilities The library houses 698,161 volumes. There are ten computer labs on campus, each with thirty to fifty computers. Students have access to word processors and the Internet through the computer labs.

Athletics The University of Nebraska at Omaha has a complete intercollegiate athletic program that includes sports for men and women. The University is a member of the NCAA Division II and competes in the North Central Conference. The men's and women's teams have won several NCC championships. In addition, Campus Recreation offers a wide variety of recreational and sports activities to UNO students, faculty, staff, and their families. Major programs include informal recreation, intramural sports, sport clubs, aquatic activities, outdoor recreation, noncredit instruction, and other special events.

Study Abroad Study-abroad opportunities are offered through the Honors Program and through the Office of International Studies.

Support Services The Office of Services for Students with Disabilities, known as SSD, has a professional special needs counselor available to assist students in determining eligibility and reasonable accommodations. The Disabled Students Agency's (DSA) purpose is to support students with temporary or permanent disabilities and to assist disabled students to assimilate into the University population by providing special resources.

Job Opportunities Help in finding on- and off-campus employment is available in Student Employment Services, located in the Career Planning and Placement Services Office. Job postings are listed in the Campus Wide Information System. Internships are posted in specific categories. Weekly employment lists are available in the Career Planning and Placement Office.

Tuition: $2124 for state residents, $5735 for nonresidents, per year (1996-97)

Mandatory Fees: $204

Contact: Rosalie C. Saltzman, Omaha, Nebraska 68182-0218; Telephone: 402-554-2696; Fax: 402-554-3781; E-mail: saltzman@ unocdc.unomaha.edu

UNIVERSITY OF NEVADA, LAS VEGAS

4 Pu G L Sc Tr

▼ **Honors College**

The Honors College (HC) provides a dynamic, diverse, and inclusive learning community for all qualified high school, transfer, and continuing students who choose to participate. This community is built around a shared commitment to academic excellence that manifests itself in rigorous traditional courses, innovative interdisciplinary seminars, opportunities for research and internships, and other special educational activities that form the nucleus of the honors experience at UNLV.

The HC, by collaborating with UNLV's outstanding faculty and utilizing resources found in the vibrant city of Las Vegas, creates educational opportunities and encourages unique curricular development; this allows students from disparate majors to challenge themselves and enhance their academic and personal growth by working together or independently in traditional and nontraditional formats. Consequently, the HC, in concert with departments, faculty, and students, is determined to be a locus of quality undergraduate education and to augment UNLV's quest to become a premier urban university.

The College offers students two ways to enhance and enrich their undergraduate experience: University Honors (UH) and Department Honors (DH). Both programs are available to all undergraduates regardless of their major. Twenty-six percent of graduates have earned degrees in liberal arts, 21 percent in business and economics, 17 percent in science and mathematics, and 12 percent in engineering. The remaining 24 percent have graduated from other colleges on campus. These statistics demonstrate one of the great strengths of Honors at UNLV—the disciplinary diversity of the students who participate. The first class of 38 students entered the HC in fall 1985. The College now admits approximately 80 freshmen a year and has a total enrollment of 300 students.

Participation Requirements: *University Honors:* Students participating in UH are required to complete a minimum of 30 credits of honors courses graded with conventional letter grades (A,B,C,D,F). Students joining UH directly from high school ordinarily use honors courses to satisfy most of UNLV's general education core requirements. Students joining UH after enrolling at UNLV or who transfer to UNLV may apply some of their regular courses toward the honors core but will still be required to meet the 30-credit minimum and the specific curricular requirements of the honors core.

Participants in UH typically take between one fourth and one third of their courses through the HC; the majority of courses are concentrated in the student's major and related areas.

Department Honors: DH is a two-year program and has two focal points: a senior thesis/project, usually done in the student's major field, and four 400-level honors seminars. Students join this program before the start of their junior year. Students can graduate with UH, DH, or both. DH combines the broadening experience of four upper-division honors seminars with a 6-credit senior thesis/project that functions as the capstone of the undergraduate experience. The honors seminars count as generic core courses and can be used to satisfy the fine arts, humanities, or social science core requirements.

The honors experience provides a small-college atmosphere within the larger university. Students share a common core of classes and have the opportunity of studying together in the Lloyd Katz Honors Lounge, living in honors clusters in the residence halls, and attending special events together. These opportunities are designed to help students reach their academic potential.

Students who complete all curriculum requirements for UH or DH with a UNLV cumulative GPA of 3.3 or higher and a cumulative honors GPA of 3.0 or higher will receive an HC Medallion at graduation and have their successful participation denoted on their final UNLV transcript. Students graduating with honors can also earn the Latin designations cum laude, magna cum laude, or summa cum laude if they satisfy the appropriate HC requirements.

Admission Process: Students can join UH directly from high school, after one or more semesters at UNLV, or when transferring to UNLV from another college or university. High school students in the top 5 percent of their high school class, with an ACT composite score of at least 28, or with a combined Scholastic Assessment Test (SAT I) score of at least 1250 are encouraged to apply. Current UNLV students or transfer students with a 3.5 or higher college GPA are also encouraged to apply. The criteria listed above are guidelines; each student applying for admission to UH will have his or her application carefully reviewed by the Honors College Admission Committee.

To be eligible to participate in DH, students must have a cumulative GPA of 3.5 or higher or be students in good standing in the UH Program.

Scholarship Availability: The HC has approximately $150,000 of scholarship money that is awarded to freshmen and continuing students.

The Campus Context: UNLV is located in the exciting and dynamic city of Las Vegas and is surrounded by picturesque mountains and desert. Its beautifully landscaped 335-acre campus is home to 20,000 students who are enrolled in more than 139 undergraduate, master's, and doctoral degree programs. UNLV has nine academic colleges not including Honors: business, education, engineering, fine arts, health sciences, hotel administration, liberal arts, sciences, and urban affairs.

Student Body Fifty-four percent of the students are women and approximately 15,000 are undergraduates. Almost half of the undergraduates receive some form of financial assistance. About 24 percent of the students are evenly divided among the following four categories: international students, black non-Hispanic, Hispanic, and Asian/Pacific Islander. More than 1,000 students live on campus; the remainder of the students either commute or live in one of the apartment complexes near the University.

Faculty UNLV has 590 full-time faculty members. Ninety-two percent have terminal degrees. The student-faculty ratio is 22:1.

Key Facilities The James R. Dickinson Library has more than 700,000 volumes and is home to the HC. The HC space in the library includes the Lloyd Katz Honors Lounge, which has nine computers for student use and a quiet study area. The University has a CRAY Supercomputer and many other computer laboratories and facilities.

Athletics UNLV is a member of the NCAA and Western Athletic Conference and competes in fourteen intercollegiate Division I sports. Men's sports include baseball, basketball, football, golf, soccer, swimming and diving, and tennis, and women's sports include basketball, cross-country, indoor and outdoor track, softball, swimming and diving, tennis, and volleyball.

Study Abroad The Office of International Programs offers a wide variety of study-abroad programs. Most programs allow students to remain registered at UNLV while studying abroad. Programs are currently available in Australia, Chile, Costa Rica, England, France, Germany, Italy, Mexico, Spain, Switzerland, and Thailand. UNLV also participates in the National Student Exchange (NSE). Scholarships and financial aid are available.

Support Services The Disability Resource Center provides academic accommodations for students with qualified disabilities.

Job Opportunities Employment opportunities exist for students whether or not they qualify for financial aid.

Tuition: $1995 for state residents, $3092 for nonresidents eligible for Western Undergraduate Exchange, $7430 for nonresidents, per year (1997-98)

Room and Board: $5300

Mandatory Fees: $50

Contact: Director: Len Zane, Box 457003, 4505 Maryland Parkway, Las Vegas, Nevada 89154-7003; Telephone: 702-895-3537; Fax: 702-895-4193; E-mail: lenz@ccmail.nevada.edu; Web site: http://www.nevada.edu/~honors

UNIVERSITY OF NEVADA, RENO

4 Pu G D M Sc Tr

▼ Honors Program/112

The Honors Program of the University of Nevada, Reno, is designed for students who are eager to learn in the environment of intellectual exchange and interaction, who are self-motivated, who are determined to test values and discuss ideas with professors and peers, and who possess strong academic records. The program is open to students in all majors. The program features instruction by carefully selected outstanding faculty members, small classes, honors residences, an honors center, and an active Honors Student Association.

Scholarships, undergraduate research grants, and study-abroad opportunities are available. All students are provided free accounts on the Internet. The program takes particular pride in the success of its graduates in postgraduate fellowship competitions and in admission to graduate/

professional schools. The program is rated as one of the nation's best in *Ivy League Programs at State School Prices: The 55 Best Honors Programs at State Universities Nationwide.*

The current program began in fall 1989 and now enrolls 288 students.

Participation Requirements: Thirty academic credits are required to complete an honors degree. Honors degrees are assigned traditional Latin designations of achievement according to GPA at graduation. Honors classes are available in the University's core curriculum, in the student's major, and as electives. Students have a wide choice of courses and have latitude in choosing courses to take for honors. The only required course is the Honors Senior Thesis/Project, which is completed in the student's major. The program is designed to fit within a student's educational program without the need for additional time or credits. A 3.25 GPA is required to continue in the program. In addition to course work, a variety of activities are available to students, including the program's Pizza Seminars, in which current topics and issues of general interest (e.g., gender communication, world religions, diversity) are discussed in an informal atmosphere.

Completion of the Honors Program is the only way to graduate with Latin distinction at the University of Nevada, Reno. Distinctions are: summa cum laude (with highest praise), 3.9 or higher; magna cum laude (with great praise), 3.7–3.89; and cum laude (with praise), 3.5–3.69. Students who complete the Honors Program but have a GPA lower than 3.5 graduate with honors recognition.

Admission Process: Participation in the program is by direct application to the Honors Program. The Admission Committee reviews considerable information about the applicant, including the academic record, activities, work experience, teacher recommendations, and an admission essay. Students are encouraged to apply if they meet one of the following criteria: 3.65 GPA (unweighted), 28 ACT or equivalent SAT I score, or top 10 percent of graduation class. Achievement of one or more of these numerical criteria does not itself guarantee admission because the entire application is carefully reviewed. Students should be advised that average and mean scores of admitted students are well above the minimum scores stated in the application criteria. Transfer students are welcome. The Honors Program application deadline is March 1.

Scholarship Availability: Scholarships are available by application to the Scholarship Office. Scholarships are primarily based on academic achievement.

The Campus Context: The University of Nevada, Reno, is a campus of ten colleges: Agriculture, Arts and Sciences, Business Administration, Education, Engineering, Human and Community Sciences, Mackay School of Mines, Reynolds School of Journalism, Graduate School, and the University of Nevada School of Medicine. Seventy-four undergraduate and sixty-one graduate degree programs are offered on campus.

The University is home to the unique Basque Studies Program and is headquarters for the University Studies Abroad Consortium.

Student Profile The student population is 47 percent men and 53 percent women. The ethnic distribution is white, 78.6 percent; international, 5.2 percent; Asian/Pacific Islander, 5.1 percent; Hispanic, 4 percent; black, 1.6 percent; American Indian, 1.2 percent; and not listed, 4.3 percent. Twelve percent are resident students; the 88 percent of commuter students includes students living in neighborhoods near the University. Approximately 50 percent of the students receive financial aid. The campus has ten fraternities and four sororities.

Faculty There are 810 faculty members; 696 are full-time and 77 percent have terminal degrees. The student-faculty ratio is 19:1.

Key Facilities The library holds 880,000 volumes. There are twenty-two computer labs with PCs/Macs and full Internet access.

Athletics The University is NCAA Division I and a member of the Big Western Conference. Men's programs are maintained in baseball, basketball, football, golf, and tennis. Women's programs are in basketball, swimming, track, volleyball, and tennis. Extensive intramural sports are available to all students.

Study Abroad The headquarters for the University Studies Abroad Consortium (USAC) is located on campus. USAC currently has programs in Australia, Chile, Costa Rica, England, France, Germany, Italy, Spain, and Thailand. Other opportunities exist through department and college affiliations. The University is a member of the National Student Exchange. Honors credit is available for study abroad.

Support Services Disabled students find the campus totally accessible. Academic support services are available.

Job Opportunities Support services are also available for both on-campus and off-campus student employment. Job lists are maintained at both offices. Work-study is encouraged for eligible students.

Tuition: $1920 for state residents, $7020 for nonresidents, per year (1996-97)

Room and Board: $4695

Mandatory Fees: $114

Contact: Director: Francis X. Hartigan, Reno, Nevada 89557; Telephone: 702-784-1455; Fax: 702-784-1756; E-mail: honors@honors.unr.edu; Web site: http://www.honors.unr.edu

THE UNIVERSITY OF NEW MEXICO
4 Pu G L Tr
▼ General Honors Program

The General Honors Program (GHP) at the University of New Mexico (UNM) originated in 1957 with a group of 30 students. The GHP continues to offer high-achieving students many of the personal advantages of a small liberal arts college within the diversity of a large research university. At the heart of the GHP are small interdisciplinary seminars taught by selected faculty members who are committed to exploring significant ideas while encouraging active student participation. The emphasis in the seminars is on intensive reading and writing and active student participation. The GHP is open to students of all majors. The seminars are specifically designed for honors—all are interdisciplinary and many are team-taught.

The GHP is housed in the Dudley Wynn Honors Center, named after its founder. In addition to housing four classrooms, the center provides a place for informal discussions, student activities, and various group projects. In a warm, friendly atmosphere, GHP students meet to study together, continue seminar discussions, or just relax between classes. The large central area, affectionately known as the Forum, is also used for more formal lectures and receptions.

There are currently 1,112 students participating in the General Honors Program.

Participation Requirements: Admission is by application only, and students must take a minimum of 18 credit hours (six seminars) in the GHP, with a minimum of one seminar at each level (100–400). They are required to maintain a minimum cumulative GPA of 3.2. Some colleges require that students file a petition for permission to count the seminar toward graduation. Students may enter the GHP at any point, provided they can complete the requirements. Transfer students may be able to transfer up to 9 hours of comparable work.

Two 100-level seminars, Ancient and Modern Legacies, offer a common opportunity for students. They not only learn about significant ideas and traditions beginning with the Greco-Roman and Judeo-Christian, but also learn the process of seminar learning and honors education. Several 200-level seminars examine other legacies and world views: women, Africa, the Far East, the Americas, and medieval Europe and the origins of mathematics, science, and technology. The 300-level seminars are interdisciplinary explorations of specific topics designed to demonstrate the interconnectedness of academic disciplines. Recent seminars have focused on the significance of biomedical ethics, the nature and politics of nuclear energy, the origins of prejudice, arts across cultures, and creative leadership. At the 400 level, seniors are offered a capstone seminar that includes a service-learning component. They may also choose to be student teachers, a unique opportunity for undergraduates, or to research and write a thesis.

In addition to the curriculum, the GHP affords students a variety of other learning opportunities, including field-based language and cultural programs, international and national exchange opportunities, leadership in student organizations, and the opportunity to staff Scribendi: The Western Regional Honors Review, an outstanding literary magazine.

Students who fulfill the requirements of the program become candidates for graduation with an honors designation.

Honors distinctions used at UNM are cum laude, magna cum laude, and summa cum laude. Graduation with an honors designation is not automatic. Honors levels are determined by the General Honors Council. Aside from the minimum requirements of the GHP, students are expected to have a reasonably broad liberal arts education. Students should attempt to take course work in the humanities, languages, social sciences, mathematics, physical sciences, and life sciences insofar as it is possible to do so within the restrictions of their majors and minors.

The Campus Context: Founded in 1889, the University of New Mexico occupies a 700-acre campus along the old Route 66 axis of Albuquerque. Albuquerque is defined by the Rio Grande, a river that has supported the life-giving land along its gentle banks since prehistory. The second defining natural monument is the Sandia Mountains, the southernmost shield of the Rockies. The protective wall of the Sandias and the Rio Grande create an inspirational urban setting of great beauty of livability. As the epicenter of one of America's most ethnically diverse populations, UNM serves a broad cross-section of people with different needs, goals, and perceptions. This fact has made UNM a model of the contemporary multicultural institution—a true University for the Americas. The campus is composed of thirteen colleges and schools: Anderson Schools of Management; Architecture and Planning; Arts and Sciences; Education; Engineering; Fine Arts; Graduate Studies; Health Sciences; Law; Medicine; Nursing; Pharmacy; and University Studies. Students may earn bachelor's degrees in ninety-eight majors and master's and doctoral degrees in sixty-nine concentrations.

There are five museums, housing collections from art to natural history, and nine libraries among the more than 170 buildings. Other distinguished facilities include the Learning Resource Center, Planetarium, radio station, TV station, Robotics Laboratory, Microcomputer Laboratories, Photohistory Collection, and a Lithography Institute. Additionally, there are UNM extension campuses located in Los Alamos, Santa Fe, Taos, Gallup, and Valencia County. Faculty members and students number about 40,000 on all campuses. Altogether, the University employs nearly 15,000 people. It functions as the state's largest institution of higher learning and offers more than 170 accredited areas of study.

Student Body There are 24,431 students enrolled (undergraduate enrollment is 15,516): 43.1 percent men and 56.9 percent women. The ethnic distribution is 58.6 percent white, 28.1 percent Hispanic, 5.2 percent Native American, 2.65 percent African American, 3.1 percent Asian, and 1.1 percent international (505). Commuters make up 92 percent of the student population and residents the remaining 8 percent. Eighty-five percent of the students receive financial aid. Two percent of the men belong to ten national fraternities. One percent of the women belong to the four national sororities.

Faculty The total number of faculty members is 2,257. Of the 1,461 full-time faculty members, 92 percent have terminal degrees. Benchmark accomplishments among the UNM faculty include the development of an entirely new field, high-energy atomic physics, by Professor Howard Bryant. His pioneering work led to the development of the Quantum Theory and the Big Bang Theory. UNM's nationally ranked mathematics department attained worldwide stature when a UNM professor helped provide the solution to a longstanding problem known as the Atiyah-Jones Conjecture. The student-faculty ratio is 13:1.

Key Facilities There are nine libraries containing 1.8 million volumes, 5 million microform items, and 320,034 audiovisual forms and subscriptions to 18,230 periodicals. The campus has seven computer pods and four classrooms in various locations on campus. Computers in use include IBM and compatible microcomputers, Apple Macintosh microcomputers, and X-terminals.

Athletics There are thirteen intercollegiate sports for men and eleven for women. There are also thirty-two intramural sports for men and twenty-six for women.

Study Abroad National Student Exchange offers students an opportunity for educational travel and study at 112 participating schools across the U.S. The International Programs provides services for students to travel abroad to England, France, Spain, Mexico, Italy, Germany, and many other countries.

Support Services Ninety-five percent of the campus is accessible to disabled students.

Job Opportunities Students are offered a wide range of scholarship and employment opportunities, including assistantships and work-study.

Tuition: $2071 for state residents, $7822 for nonresidents, per year (1996-1997)

Room and Board: $3968

Contact: Director: Dr. Rosalie C. Otero, 114 Humanities Building, Albuquerque, New Mexico 87131-1566; Telephone: 505-277-4211; Fax: 505-277-4271; E-mail: otero@unm.edu and ghp@unm.edu; Web site: http://www.unm.edu/~ghp

UNIVERSITY OF NORTH CAROLINA AT ASHEVILLE

4 Pu D M Sc Tr

▼ University Honors Program

The University Honors Program offers special educational opportunities to academically talented and motivated students. The college-wide program welcomes freshmen, transfers, and continuing students from all academic departments.

The Honors Program offers courses as well as cocurricular activities designed to extend learning beyond the classroom. Courses include special sections of many general education requirements, such as freshman composition and humanities, and challenging junior and senior honors seminars. The Honors Program emphasizes both breadth and depth in liberal education. The breadth comes through special emphasis on interdisciplinary courses. Depth, or excellence in a particular field, is encouraged through undergraduate research with a faculty mentor in the academic major. Additional educational opportunities include independent study and internships.

The Honors Program also offers a range of extracurricular activities designed to foster community and leadership among participants. Honors students have the option of living with other honors students in special group housing.

The 10-year-old program currently enrolls 300 students.

Participation Requirements: Students who complete requirements of the Honors Program graduate with Distinction as a University Scholar. Those requirements include completion of 15 hours of honors credit (including the Senior Honors Colloquium and an honors special topics course) with a 3.5 GPA, a 3.5 GPA in the last 60 hours of credit, and completion of a research or creative project.

Admission Process: Freshmen apply to the Honors Program as part of their application to the University of North Carolina at Asheville (UNCA). Additional materials from Honors Program applicants include an essay and list of cocurricular activities. Participants are chosen on the basis of SAT I scores, rank in class, essay, and leadership activities. Transfer students may also apply for admission, provided they have earned a 3.5 GPA on all transfer hours. Continuing UNCA students may apply if they have earned a 3.0 GPA. Students must maintain a 3.0 GPA and must complete at least one 3-hour honors course during their first four semesters in order to remain a member of the Honors Program.

Scholarship Availability: The Honors Program itself does not offer scholarships but cooperates closely with the University Laurels Academic Merit Scholarship Program. Students interested in those academic scholarships apply as part of the UNCA application process. Students identified as merit scholarship candidates are invited to the campus for Interview Day, usually scheduled in February. Many candidates for the University Laurels Academic Merit Scholarships are also considered for admission to the University Honors Program.

The Campus Context: The University of North Carolina at Asheville is the "Public Liberal Arts University" in the state's widely respected system of higher education. As such, UNCA is a place where students, faculty members, and staff members know and interact with each other across departmental and disciplinary lines, where the focus is always upon undergraduates, and where the curriculum teaches students to become their own best and lifelong teachers. Located in the mountains of western Northern Carolina, UNCA offers undergraduate degree programs in the arts and humanities, the natural and social sciences, and selected preprofessional programs firmly grounded in the liberal arts. A total of thirty-seven degree programs are offered on campus.

The University has earned national recognition for its Humanities Program, a four-course sequence of history and world culture that is the core of UNCA's liberal arts curriculum and, according to the National Endowment for the Humanities and the Association of American Colleges, a "model" for other institutions of higher education.

UNCA's Undergraduate Research Program, which provides funding and faculty support for student research projects, trips to conferences, and publication opportunities in all disciplines, has received widespread attention and national acclaim. The National Conference on Undergraduate Research, a multidisciplinary forum founded and hosted by UNCA in 1987, continues to draw thousands of faculty and student participants from around the country every year.

The University's 265-acre hilltop campus, located 1 mile from downtown Asheville, is named one of America's "most livable cities" in Rand McNally's *Places Rated Almanac* and one of the nation's top ten cities in *Outdoor* magazine. The region has the largest concentration of national forest on the East Coast, and the surrounding Blue Ridge and Great Smoky Mountains are the ideal setting for any outdoor enthusiast.

Student Profile The undergraduate enrollment is 3,176: 44 percent men and 56 percent women. The ethnic distribution is 92.2 percent white, 1.6 percent Asian, 1.4 percent black, 1.4 percent Hispanic, and .4 percent American Indian. There are 36 international students. The resident/commuter ratio is 3:7. Forty-four percent of students receive financial aid. UNCA has three fraternities and three sororities.

Faculty The total number of faculty members is 263; 153 are full-time, and 82.4 percent have terminal degrees. The student-faculty ratio is 12:1.

Key Facilities The library houses 231,645 volumes. Computer facilities include a VAX 4000, a Digital 2100 AXP Server, more than 600 PCs, a campus-wide LAN, and Internet access. There is a Teleconference Center on campus.

Athletics The Justice Health and Fitness Center houses an indoor swimming pool, basketball court, dance studio, and fully equipped weight room. Outdoor athletic facilities include the recently completed Greenwood Fields (for soccer, baseball, and softball), tennis courts, and a track. A new multimillion-dollar addition to the complex, opened in 1996, adds three indoor courts, an elevated track, racquetball courts, and an extensive weight facility. UNCA is a member of the NCAA's Big South Conference. Division I intercollegiate sports include men's basketball, baseball, cross-country, golf, soccer, tennis, and track and women's basketball, cross-country, soccer, tennis, track, and volleyball.

Study Abroad There are numerous study-abroad opportunities. Students may take part in summer programs sponsored by UNCA at Oxford and Cambridge; study for a semester in Santander, Spain; study at the Universidad del Azuay, a university in Cuenca, Ecuador, with which UNCA has an exchange relationship; and take advantage of summer and academic-year programs abroad at sites ranging from Costa Rica to Poland offered by the North Carolina Consortium for Study Abroad.

Support Services UNCA complies with laws that are designed to protect the rights of disabled persons, including the Americans with Disabilities Act (ADA) of 1990 and Section 504 of the Rehabilitation Act of 1973. UNCA focuses on the students as individuals and works toward equal opportunity, full integration into the campus environment, physical accessibility, and the provision of reasonable accommodations, auxiliary aids, and services to students.

Job Opportunities   Work opportunities on campus include federal and institutional work-study.

Tuition: $730 for state residents, $7046 for nonresidents, per year (1996-97)

Room and Board: $3650

Mandatory Fees: $1043

Contact: Director: Dr. Phyllis Lang, 141 Karpen Hall, Asheville, North Carolina 28804; Telephone: 704-251-6227; Fax: 704-251-6614; E-mail:plang@unca.edu; Web site: http://www.unca.edu/factsheets/honors_fact.html/

UNIVERSITY OF NORTH CAROLINA AT CHARLOTTE

4 Pu G M Sc Tr

▼ University Honors Program

The University Honors Program at the University of North Carolina at Charlotte offers a curriculum of study that is creative, imaginative, and challenging. The program's innovative course work focuses on global issues, including war and peace, economics and the international community, science and values, and human rights. Enrichment seminars introduce students to the arts and diverse cultural activities of the Charlotte metropolitan area and the world through an Honors Study Abroad experience.

Beyond the classroom, honors students volunteer in a variety of service projects ranging from delivering food to a soup kitchen in Charlotte to working with children in Scotland. Many honors students choose to live in Poplar Hall, a unique coed, apartment-style residence hall considered to be the most desirable on campus. Features of Poplar Hall include a computer lab devoted exclusively to honors students as well as spacious common areas where students attend lectures, discussion groups, and honors meetings. Other highlights of the Honors Program include an annual retreat to Sunset Beach.

The University Honors Program is more than just rigorous classes. Its goals are to foster creativity, stimulate the imagination, and encourage students to be active in improving the human condition.

The Honors Program has received local and national recognition for its academic excellence and community service. For example, the student-initiated project of delivering leftover cafeteria food to the uptown soup kitchen has been featured in national publications such as *USA Today* and *Ecodemia*.

Honors students have also received National Merit Scholarship awards such as the Phi Kappa Phi Graduate Fellowship.

The University Honors Program at UNCC began thirteen years ago and currently enrolls 180 students.

Participation Requirements: To graduate with University Honors, students must complete a four-course sequence of honors courses, 4 credit hours of enrichment seminars, a 40-clock-hour community service laboratory, and a senior project. Graduates must maintain a 3.0 GPA overall and 3.2 GPA in University Honors courses.

Admission Process: UNCC actively recruits the upper 2–3 percent of entering students into the Honors Program as they apply to the University. The admission criteria are based on high school rank and SAT scores, which results in a predicted GPA. All applicants must submit an essay along with their application. Upper-division students with a GPA above 3.5 are also encouraged to apply to University Honors.

Scholarship Availability: Approximately 40 percent of the full-merit scholars who are enrolled at UNCC participate in the University Honors Program. Although the program actively recruits them, their participation is by their election. The Honors Program also awards small study-abroad scholarships to all active honors students who choose to study abroad.

The Campus Context: As the fourth-largest member of the University of North Carolina system, UNC Charlotte combines state-of-the-art facilities with 1,000 acres of landscaped grounds, forests, and streams. Located in the leading urban center of the Carolinas, the campus is easily accessible from major interstates and highways. The University, neighboring University Research Park, and new residential communities make up the rapidly growing University City area of north Charlotte.

UNC Charlotte offers its almost 16,000 students eighty-one undergraduate and graduate degree programs. In addition, the city of Charlotte, located in the Southern Piedmont of North Carolina, is one of the fastest-growing urban centers in the nation and offers a diversity of cultural and educational opportunities.

Student Body   Undergraduate enrollment is 49 percent men and 51 percent women. The ethnic distribution includes 13.9 percent African Americans and 3.1 percent international students. Twenty-seven percent of the population are out-of-state students; 27 percent of students live on campus. Approximately 6,400 students received financial aid in 1995–96. There are twenty-three fraternities and sororities and a new student center for campuswide activities.

Faculty   The total number of full-time faculty members is 640. Faculty members hold their highest degrees from U.S. graduate schools and thirty international universities. The student-faculty ratio is 16:1, and the average class size is 33.

Key Facilities   The library houses 577,386 bound volumes and more than 1 million units in microform. There are more than 200 computers, including Gateway 2000 and Macintosh machines, available in student labs on campus. Internet access is provided.

Athletics UNC Charlotte offers fourteen intercollegiate sports for men and women on the varsity level, including baseball, basketball, cross-country, golf, softball, soccer, tennis, track, and volleyball.

Study Abroad Numerous study-abroad opportunities exist, ranging from ten-day trips to various countries around the world to full academic years spent abroad.

Support Services Disability Services assists students with academic and physical accommodations based on documentation of disability. Services include, but are not limited to, priority registration assistance; orientation to available services; development of individualized educational plans; special testing accommodations; taped textbooks, Braille, and/or large print services for visually impaired students; assistive technology loans; referrals to tutoring and other campus support services; interpreting services for students who are deaf; individual counseling and advising; and referrals to human services agencies.

Job Opportunities Work opportunities on campus are available, ranging from cooperative education with multinational corporations to working in the campus bookstore, library, or an academic department. UNC Charlotte has its own Student Employment Office to aid interested students in finding a job.

Tuition: $874 for state residents, $8028 for nonresidents, per year (1996-97)

Room and Board: $3120 minimum

Mandatory Fees: $844

Contact: Director: Dr. Al Maisto, Maple Hall, 9201 University City Boulevard, Charlotte, North Carolina 28223-0001; Telephone: 704-547-4824; Fax: 704-547-3116; E-mail: amaisto@email.uncc.edu

UNIVERSITY OF NORTH CAROLINA AT GREENSBORO

| 4 Pu G M Tr |

▼ Honors Program

The UNCG Honors Program offers highly qualified students a blend of specially created honors seminars and designated honors sections in various fields of study. Honors classes are small and are designed to promote discussion and critical thinking. A close association with faculty members and other students is one aspect of the program that provides special opportunities for honors students to grow intellectually through contact with the honors community. This particular feature of the Honors Program assures students that the personal attention typically associated with a small, private liberal arts college is available while attending a comprehensive state university.

There are currently 150 students in the UNCG Honors Program.

Participation Requirements: Students in the Honors Program also complete the requirements for one of the academic or professional majors offered at the University. In order to complete the program, students are required to take 18 hours of courses. Three credit hours must be used to satisfy the Senior Honors Thesis. Six of the credit hours must be obtained in Honors Core Seminars. These seminars cover topics and explore areas of study that lie off the beaten track. Recent offerings have included gender and science, the structure of poetry, and current issues in the law. The remaining 9 hours may include any other combination of honors courses, including core seminars, honors sections of freshman seminars, honors sections of regularly scheduled courses, or honors independent studies. Having an Honors Program allows the University's talented faculty to teach classes in specific areas to students who wish to explore interesting and unusual topics.

Admission Process: Any student who has a GPA of 3.3 or better may apply to join the Honors Program at UNCG. Admission is granted on a rolling basis; admission for entering freshmen is based on high school grades and SAT scores. All Merit Award Program Scholarship recipients and Superintendents' Award recipients are invited to join the program.

The Campus Context: UNCG is located amidst a thriving metropolitan area. Greensboro boasts the luxuries and amenities of a larger city while still affording the charm and comfort of a small-town atmosphere. The campus itself is located near the bustling downtown area, yet its immediate surroundings include a neighborhood of student and faculty homes, quaint apartment houses, and Tate Street, which is lined with a wide variety of shops, restaurants, and coffee houses. UNCG possesses the unique blend of a state university education and resources with a college-town feel. Academic programs are offered in the College of Arts and Sciences as well as the Schools of Business and Economics, Education, Health and Human Performance, Human Environmental Sciences, Music, and Nursing.

Student Body With more than 12,000 students, the UNCG student body is diverse in its interests and backgrounds. Of the total University population, 35.6 percent are men and 64.4 percent are women. The ethnic distribution of the total UNCG population includes 81.1 percent white, 13.5 percent African American, and 1.9 percent Asian.

Faculty Of the approximately 500 full-time faculty members, 93 percent hold terminal degrees in their disciplines. The student-faculty ratio is 14.9:1.

Key Facilities Jackson Library has more than 850,000 volumes as well as access to numerous electronic information resources, local and remote.

Athletics UNCG competes in fourteen intercollegiate sports and became a member of the NCAA Division I in 1991. In 1996, the men's basketball team advanced to the NCAA Tournament, playing its part in the NCAA's "March Madness."

UNCG also offers a wide range of intramural sports and club sports as well as a new recreation center that offers a full range of recreational services to the campus.

Tuition: $986 for state residents, $9304 for nonresidents, per year (1996-97)

Room and Board: $3505

Mandatory Fees: $957

Contact: Director: Bruce Caldwell, 200 Foust Building, Greensboro, North Carolina 27412; Telephone: 910-334-5673; E-mail: caldwell@iago.uncg.edu

UNIVERSITY OF NORTH CAROLINA AT WILMINGTON

4 Pu G/D M Sc Tr

▼ Honors Scholars Program

The Honors Scholars Program at UNCW seeks to provide academically talented students with a variety of innovative and challenging educational experiences both in and out of the classroom. The goal is to encourage curiosity, critical thinking, and independent work skills by offering exciting academic and cultural activities as well as the opportunity for close working and social relationships with the faculty. The program includes academics, cocurricular activities, and the opportunity to reside in a designated honors residence. The four-year program began at UNCW in fall 1994.

In fall 1996 there were a total of 210 students in the program, including 80 freshmen, 60 sophomores, and 70 juniors and seniors.

Participation Requirements: Honors students take a 3-credit freshman interdisciplinary honors seminar in their first semester and a 3-credit honors topical seminar in their sophomore year. In addition, students take 2 credits of honors enrichment seminars and 12 hours of honors sections of basic studies in their first two years. Honors classes are small—usually 20 students or fewer—to encourage discussion and independent work. If eligible, students may achieve departmental honors in their major in their last two years, culminating in a 6-credit senior project. University honors requires the full four-year participation with honors in a discipline.

Admission Process: Students may enter the program as incoming freshmen (by invitation based on high school grades, SAT scores, and class rank) or as sophomores based on earned GPA. Students enter departmental honors based on an earned GPA of 3.2 or better.

Scholarship Availability: A limited number of merit scholarships are available on a competitive basis for students accepted into the Honors Scholars Program. In addition, several academic departments have scholarship funds for majors in their disciplines.

The Campus Context: The University of North Carolina at Wilmington is one of the sixteen autonomous campuses of the University of North Carolina. It is composed of the College of Arts and Sciences and three schools—the Cameron School of Business Administration, the Watson School of Education, and the School of Nursing. Forty-six undergraduate and eighteen graduate degrees are offered. UNCW is located on a beautiful 650-acre campus in the historic city of Wilmington. The internationally ranked marine biology program has the advantage of the University's location, which is only 5 miles from the Atlantic Ocean and the town of Wrightsville Beach.

Student Body Undergraduate enrollment is 8,107. The student population is 6.3 percent African American, 91 percent white, and 2.6 percent other ethnic groups. There are a total of 150 international students, 66 of whom are degree-seeking. There are 22.7 percent on-campus residents and 25 percent nontraditional students. Forty-five percent of the students receive financial aid. There are twelve fraternities and eleven sororities with no on-campus chapter housing.

Faculty Of the 457 faculty members, 365 are full-time. Eighty-nine percent have terminal degrees. The student-faculty ratio is 16:1.

Key Facilities The library houses 400,000 bound volumes and 480,000 government documents. The six computer labs provide a ratio of 40 students per computer; there is an additional 24-hour computer lab for exclusive use of honors students living in an honors residence.

Athletics UNCW holds Division I membership in the Colonial Athletic Association and fields seventeen varsity teams, including men's and women's programs in basketball, cross-country, golf, soccer, swimming and diving, tennis, and track and field. Other varsity programs include baseball, volleyball, and softball. Seahawk athletic facilities include the modern 6,000-seat Trask Coliseum, an Olympic-size swimming pool with diving well, a 1,200-seat baseball stadium, a new soccer field, and a state-of-the-art track and field complex. A year-round offering of club and intramural sports (including basketball, football, tennis, and volleyball) is available to all students. The University's Ultimate frisbee club has won the national championship. The emphasis on athletics is balanced by an attention to academics—UNCW has the highest graduation rate of varsity athletes in the entire UNC system.

Study Abroad The Honors Scholars Program encourages students to broaden their horizons by studying abroad. The Office of International Programs offers many opportunities for students to participate in global study. There are UNCW study-abroad programs to England, Ecuador, and Paris; summer study-abroad programs (recently to Australia, Barbados, France, Great Britain, Portugal, and Sweden); and bilateral exchange linkages with about thirty universities worldwide. The University is a member of ISEP (International Student

Exchange Program). The Honors Program ran an honors course in spring 1996 that included a spring break study trip to London.

Support Services The Office of Disabled Student Services assists in adapting general University programs and offering necessary services, including tutoring, testing assistance, readers, note-takers, and services such as assistance with class registration.

Job Opportunities Campus work opportunities include Federal Work-Study, work assistant, recreational facilities, and computer lab jobs.

Tuition: $874 for state residents, $8028 for nonresidents, per year (1996-97)

Room and Board: $3900 minimum

Mandatory Fees: $874

Contact: Director: Dr. Diane E. Levy, Wilmington, North Carolina 28403-3297; Associate Director: Dr. Patricia Turrisi; Telephone: 910-962-4181; Fax: 910-962-7020; E-mail: levyd@uncwil.edu; Web site: http://cte.uncwil.edu/honors/

UNIVERSITY OF NORTHERN COLORADO

| 4 Pu G M Sc Tr |

▼ Honors Program

The UNC Honors Program was established in 1958 with the intent of aiding the University's most highly motivated undergraduate students in research and writing a thesis. It became a full four-year program linked to Life of the Mind, an NEH-funded general education program, in 1985. Since then, the Honors Program has grown dramatically to its current membership of 300 students and faculty coordinators in every college. In 1992, Honors and Life of the Mind were recognized by CCHE as co-Programs of Excellence in Colorado. UNC Honors has three principal dimensions: enrichment in general education, enrichment in the major field, and the Student Honors Council.

To satisfy the enrichment in general education dimension, each student in the Honors Program is required to take at least three Life of the Mind courses as enrichment in his or her general education curriculum. These highly interactive and interdisciplinary courses are open to all students and are taught by UNC faculty members who have demonstrated excellence in teaching. In addition, Honors students are required to take a connection seminar during their sophomore year. These team-taught seminars bring together some of UNC's best professors with the intent of connecting disciplines, cultures, and times. The seminars focus on interdisciplinary topics such as science and ethics, the art of film, art and technology, urban development and alternative communities, and issues in multiculturalism.

The enrichment in the major field component of the program allows each UNC honors student to research and write a thesis under the mentorship of a faculty adviser in his or her field. The thesis is the academic capstone of each honors student's college career. Beyond the assistance given to them by their adviser, each honors student is provided with several other opportunities and aids through the Honors Program. Students are given the opportunity to present their theses at Research Day during Academic Excellence Week at UNC and at the National Conference on Undergraduate Research.

Chartered in 1985, the Student Honors Council (SHC) is one of UNC's most active student organizations on campus and in the Greeley community. It comprises 11 elected officers and seeks the involvement of all honors students. Throughout the academic year, the council organizes and coordinates several academic and social activities on campus and in the community. The International Film Series and Fall Film Festival are run by the council. Academic pizza seminars are offered by the council with the intent of gathering students to discuss controversial issues and/or to meet and learn more about a UNC faculty member. SHC also offers an After School Enrichment Program for two of the elementary schools in Greeley. It cosponsors events such as poetry readings with the UNC English Department and academic forums and film discussions with several of the cultural centers on campus. Finally, the council produces and publishes five newsletters a year that are sent to students, faculty, and alumni of the Honors Program.

Admission Process: Students are selected for the Honors Program on the basis of their GPA (3.5 high school, 3.25 college), class rank (top 10 percent), ACT score (composite of 27), a letter of introduction, and letters of recommendation. They may apply for the program as incoming freshmen, transfers, or at any time throughout their University career (as long as they are still able and willing to meet all program requirements before graduation).

Scholarship Availability: Honors students are given the opportunity to apply for a grant for up to $500 from the CCHE Mind/Honors Programs of Excellence fund for research expenses.

The Campus Context: University of Northern Colorado has undergraduate enrollment in six colleges: Arts and Sciences, Education (including a laboratory school with grades K–12), Health and Human Sciences, Business Administration, Performing and Visual Arts, and Continuing Education. There are 107 undergraduate degree programs offered.

Student Body The student population is 8,569 (41 percent men and 59 percent women). The ethnic distribution is 1 percent Native American, 3 percent African American, 4 percent Asian American, 8 percent Hispanic, and 84 percent white. There are 93 international students. Thirty-two percent of the students live on campus. Sixty-seven percent of all undergraduates receive financial aid. There are nine fraternities and five sororities.

Faculty   Of the 552 faculty members, 425 are full-time and 127 part-time. Seventy-eight percent of the faculty members have terminal degrees. The student-faculty ratio is 21:1.

Key Facilities   The library houses 901,042 volumes. Computer facilities include ten PC labs, four Mac labs, and an IBM mainframe.

Athletics   In athletics, University of Northern Colorado is NCAA Division II. Men's varsity sports include basketball, football, golf, tennis, track, and wrestling, and women's varsity sports include basketball, golf, soccer, swimming, tennis, track, and volleyball.

Support Services   Disabled students are assisted by the Disability Access Center.

Tuition: $1914 for state residents, $8416 for nonresidents, per year (1996-97)

Room and Board: $4270 minimum

Mandatory Fees: $464

Contact: Director: Dr. Ron Edgerton, 1905 10th Avenue, Greeley, Colorado 80639; Telephone: 970-351-2940; Fax: 970-351-2947; E-mail: rkedger@bentley.univnorthco.edu

---

UNIVERSITY OF NORTH TEXAS

 4 Pu G M Sc Tr

▼ University Honors Program

The University Honors Program of the University of North Texas (UNT), is designed for talented and motivated undergraduates who want to build an excellent broad-based education and intellectual foundation. The honors program is open to any qualified undergraduate student in any major at UNT.

Honors students have the opportunity to take their University core requirements in the honors environment of small classes taught by professors with strong commitments to undergraduate education. Honors courses are specially designed to provide challenging and exciting course material. Courses are offered in a wide variety of disciplines, including the sciences, mathematics, social sciences, humanities, and fine arts. Honors faculty members are encouraged to use innovative and thought-provoking teaching techniques to challenge the intellect of honors students.

In addition to general education courses, the University Honors Program offers two specially designed courses to enrich the honors student's curriculum. Freshmen enroll in the Honors Freshman Seminar, a 1-semester-credit-hour,

interdisciplinary course that is built around exploration of a common topic across disciplinary boundaries. Themes for past seminars include the environment, human rights, and the acquisition of knowledge. Seniors are required to take the Capstone Seminar, a 3-semester-credit-hour, interdisciplinary course that explores the fundamentals of international understanding, including both cooperation and conflict. The Capstone Seminar is periodically offered as a study-abroad opportunity in Europe.

All honors courses are designated with the letter H on student transcripts. Students completing the full program (36 hours) receive the designation of University Honors Scholar on their transcripts. All honors graduates are awarded a medallion to wear with their regalia at Commencement.

Honors students are encouraged to participate in a variety of activities, including the Cross Fire/Last Lecture series, which is housed within Academic Core Programs. During each academic year, honors students edit and produce their own literary magazine entitled PROCESS. Individual academic advising and on-line schedule changes are available to honors students through the Office of Academic Core Programs. Honors students are encouraged to take advantage of the Humanities Reading Room, which is part of the honors complex.

The University Honors Program was created in fall 1994 and currently has an enrollment of approximately 325 students.

Participation Requirements: There are two tracks available to students interested in honors participation. The University Honors Program requires 36 hours in honors courses, including completion of the Freshman and Capstone Seminars. The Honors Option requires 18 hours of honors courses, including the Capstone Seminar; 6 hours in addition to the Capstone must be upper-division courses. All students in the University Honors Program must maintain a 3.0 cumulative GPA.

Admission Process: Students may contact the Office of Academic Core Programs to request an application form or may request one through the Web site. A high school transcript and two letters of recommendation should accompany the application. Successful applicants usually have an SAT I score of at least 1150 or an ACT score of at least 27.

Scholarship Availability: Honors students are eligible for many scholarships that are awarded by application to the University Scholarship Office. Beginning in fall 1997, a number of honors scholarships will be awarded directly by the Office of Academic Core Programs.

The Campus Context: The University of North Texas is located in Denton, Texas, a small college community that is 35 miles north of Dallas and Fort Worth, a metropolitan area of 4 million people. With more than 25,000 students, UNT is the largest university in the region and the fourth-largest university in Texas. There are nine colleges and schools on campus: College of Arts and Sciences, College of Business Administration, School of Community Service, College of Education, School of Library and Information Sciences, School of Merchandising and Hospitality Management, College of Music, School of the Visual Arts, and the Toulouse School of Graduate Studies. Eighty-one undergraduate programs are offered.

Student Body The total student enrollment is 25,114, comprising 18,654 undergraduates and 6,460 graduates. The ethnic distribution is 79.1 percent white, 6.7 percent African American, 6.2 percent Hispanic, 2.9 percent Asian/Pacific Islander, .8 percent American Indian, and 4.3 percent nonresident alien. Gender distribution is 52.5 percent women and 47.5 percent men. More than 9,000 students receive financial aid.

Faculty The full-time faculty numbers 813. The student-faculty ratio is 17:1.

Key Facilities Library holdings include more than 1.5 million cataloged items in four separate facilities on campus. Computing facilities offer fourteen general access labs in ten buildings on campus supporting PC, Macintosh, and PowerMac platforms.

Athletics UNT competes in Division I-A of the National Collegiate Athletic Association in seven men's sports: football, cross-country, basketball, golf, tennis, indoor track, and outdoor track. Women also compete in NCAA Division I-A in volleyball, basketball, tennis, golf, cross-country, indoor track, and outdoor track. In addition, Recreational Sports offer opportunities for participation in intramural sports, fitness classes, or sports clubs and access to exercise facilities.

Study Abroad The Study Abroad Center offers exchange programs in thirty-seven countries; additional opportunities are available through faculty-led, affiliated, and nonaffiliated programs. The National Student Exchange program provides students with the opportunity to study at any of 140 universities in the United States or its territories at in-state tuition rates. Both programs allow exchanges for either a semester or a year, and financial assistance is available.

Support Services The Office of Disability Accommodation furnishes assistance with registration, scheduling, academic access, and certain educational auxiliary aids for students whose disabilities necessitate special accommodations for equality of educational opportunity.

Job Opportunities The Student Employment Service provides a variety of employment opportunities on and off campus to currently enrolled students in order to help them offset their college expenses and develop good work records.

Tuition: $960 for state residents, $7380 for nonresidents, per year (1996-97)

Room and Board: $3767

Mandatory Fees: $1084

Contact: Director: Dr. Gloria C. Cox, Office of Academic Core Programs, General Academic Building 302, P.O. Box 5187, Denton, Texas 76203; Telephone: 817-565-3305; Fax: 817-565-4517; E-mail: cox@cas.unt.edu; Web site: http://www.cas.unt.edu/acadcore

University of Oklahoma

4 Pu G L Tr

▼ Honors College

The Honors College incorporates a curricular program dedicated to providing academically talented students with the opportunity to develop their intellectual potential to the fullest. The Honors College utilizes the best research and teaching faculty members from all undergraduate colleges of the University to offer special honors courses at both the upper-division and lower-division levels. The courses are limited to approximately 22 students, with enrollment restricted to members of the Honors College. This gives each honors course a rich environment of academically talented students. The lower-division honors courses include courses that fulfill the OU general education requirements. The upper-division courses include special-topic seminars, team-taught colloquia, and independent study and research with faculty members in the student's major discipline. Students in the Honors College may elect to enroll in up to 6 credit hours of honors courses each semester. Honors students must complete a minimum of 20 hours of honors-designated course work, including 12 credit hours outside their major, 5 hours of honors reading and research, and a 3-credit–hour honors colloquium.

The program began in 1962 and went through a major reorganization in 1987 and became an Honors College in 1997. There are approximately 1,440 students currently enrolled.

Participation Requirements: Continued membership in the Honors College requires both maintaining an OU cumulative GPA of 3.4 and exhibiting continued progress toward completion of the curricular requirements of an honors degree. Progress is defined as completing at least one honors course during every 30 credit hours earned at the University, or approximately one honors course per academic year for full-time students. Most honors students take two or three honors courses per year.

Students successfully completing the Honors Curriculum with a 3.4 GPA have a cum laude designation on their diploma, with a 3.61–3.79 GPA a magna cum laude designation, or with a 3.8 GPA or higher a summa cum laude designation.

Admission Process: Freshmen entering the University of Oklahoma are eligible to apply to the Honors College if they have a composite ACT score of 29 or higher or a recentered SAT I total of 1230 or higher (1150 on old SAT I) and they rank in the top 10 percent of graduates in their high school class or they have a high school GPA of 3.75. Transfer students who come to the University of Oklahoma with 15 or more college credit hours and a transfer GPA of 3.4 or higher are eligible to apply. OU students who have earned 15 or more hours of OU credit and have maintained a cumulative GPA of 3.4 or higher are eligible to apply. Final admission into the Honors College is determined by the director's evaluation of the Honors College application form, which includes a written essay of 400–500 words.

The Campus Context: The University of Oklahoma, established in 1890, is composed of nine colleges: Architecture, Arts and Sciences, Business Administration, Education, Engineering, Fine Arts, Geosciences, Law, and Liberal Studies. There are 110 undergraduate degree programs offered on campus. When finished, the Sam Noble Oklahoma Museum of Natural History at OU will be the largest University-based museum in the United States, housing more than 5 million natural history artifacts.

Student Profile Undergraduate enrollment is 15,527: 52 percent men and 48 percent women. There are 1,718 international students. Sixty-two percent of students receive financial aid. There are twenty-two fraternities and fifteen sororities.

Faculty Of the 989 faculty members, 834 are full-time.

Key Facilities The campus is equipped with PC and Macintosh computer labs in the library, classroom buildings, and some of the dorms.

Study Abroad Study abroad is available through reciprocal exchange with sixty programs worldwide. Honors credit is given for study abroad.

Support Services The Office of Disabled Student Services provides support services to students with disabilities. The office is committed to the goal of achieving equal educational opportunity and full participation for students with disabilities. OU has adopted the Americans with Disabilities Act Accessibility Guidelines.

Tuition: $1940 minimum for state residents, $5405 minimum for nonresidents, per year (1996-97)

Room and Board: $3904

Mandatory Fees: $186

Contact: Interim Director: Dr. Carolyn Morgan, 1300 Asp Avenue, Norman, Oklahoma 73019; Telephone: 405-325-5291; Fax: 405-325-7109; E-mail: cmorgan@uoknor.edu; Web site: http://www.uoknor.edu/honors/honhome.htm

UNIVERSITY OF OREGON

4 Pu C M Sc Tr

▼ Robert D. Clark Honors College

The Robert D. Clark Honors College, located within the University of Oregon, offers the advantages of a small, liberal arts college as well as the University's rich resources and curriculum. The Clark Honors College brings together excellent students and selected faculty members in a program that is both challenging and supportive.

The Honors College provides an extensive curriculum of liberal arts courses, which complements students' work in their chosen majors. The curriculum is a balance of interrelated courses in the humanities, social sciences, natural sciences, and mathematics. This core accounts for about one third of students' credits toward graduation. The Honors College grants the Bachelor of Arts degree.

The Honors College emphasizes the development of fundamental rhetorical skills: writing, reading, speaking, and listening. Enrollment in any course rarely exceeds 25 students, and many classes are seminars where each student is encouraged to play an active role in discussion.

One of the most challenging and rewarding experiences in the Honors College is the honors thesis. In their senior year, students prepare an advanced research or creative project and present it orally before a faculty committee. In preparation for the honors thesis, students work individually with professors from their major field. As the culminating experience of their undergraduate career, the senior thesis and oral presentation give students an opportunity to demonstrate both the breadth of learning attained in the Honors College and the specialized knowledge gained from their major.

Close advising is an important aspect of the Honors College, from summer or fall orientation preceding the first year to faculty supervision of the honors thesis in the senior year. The Honors College aims to reach beyond professional or specialized training to inspire students to a full lifetime of broad intellectual curiosity and personal growth.

The Robert D. Clark Honors College was established in 1960. About 500 students are currently enrolled, representing interests in all scholarly disciplines. Students come from all over the nation and world. Every year the student body increases in ethnic and geographical diversity.

Admission Process: High school seniors who have demonstrated academic excellence are encouraged to apply to the Honors College. A small number of transfer students are also accepted each year. Students must apply both to the University for general admission as well as to the Honors College. A complete Honors College application consists of an application form, two teacher recommendations, transcripts, SAT or ACT scores, and an essay, all of which must be sent in one packet directly to the Honors College. Application materials are contained in the Honors College brochure, which is available by contacting the Honors College office.

The early admission deadline is November 1; regular application deadline is February 1. Students who complete their application by November 1 or February 1 are guaranteed full consideration by the Honors College admissions committee, which notifies students of a decision by April 1. A second but much smaller round of admissions decisions for applications completed by May 1 is expected. Those students will be notified by mid-June.

Scholarship Availability: Scholarships are awarded through the University, academic departments, and private sources. Oregon Presidential Scholarships are designated for promising students from Oregon. The University of Oregon is the only public institution in Oregon to sponsor National Merit Scholarships. The general University scholarship application is due February 1. The Honors College awards a small number of merit scholarships. All students who complete their Honors College application by November 1 or February 1 are eligible for these awards.

The Campus Context: Located at the southern end of the beautiful Willamette Valley, the University of Oregon in Eugene lies between the Pacific Ocean to the west and the Cascade Mountains to the east. Eugene, a city of more than 117,000, is small enough to be friendly and casual and large enough to offer many cultural opportunities. The city is known for its parks, bike and running paths, outdoor craft and food markets, and performing arts.

Students can spend their weekends immersed in the stacks of the UO library system—the largest in the state—or enjoying the white water of the McKenzie River, which flows out of the Cascades northeast of town.

Students can participate in more than 270 clubs on campus, including political and environmental groups, professional organizations, cultural heritage organizations, religious groups, and service programs.

More than 250 concerts and recitals are presented annually by visiting artists, faculty members, and advanced students. Three theaters on campus offer a full range of plays produced both by faculty members and qualified students.

Athletics Intercollegiate competition, club sports, and intramurals offer several levels of athletic participation. The University is a member of the Pac-10 Conference (NCAA Division I) and sponsors seven women's teams (basketball, cross-country, golf, softball, tennis, track and field, and volleyball) and seven men's teams (basketball, cross-country, football, golf, tennis, track and field, and wrestling).

Study Abroad Students can also take advantage of the many study-abroad programs offered by the University on every continent. Programs last from one quarter to one full year.

Tuition: $2694 for state residents, $10,818 for nonresidents, per year (1996-97)

Room and Board: $4342

Mandatory Fees: $846

Contact: Director: David Jacobs, 1293 University of Oregon, Eugene, Oregon 97403-1293; Telephone: 541-346-5414; E-mail: hcadmit@honors.uoregon.edu; Web site: http://www.uoregon.edu/

UNIVERSITY OF PORTLAND

4 Pr G S Sc Tr

▼ Honors Program

The Honors Program was designed for students of exceptional ability who seek an intellectually challenging academic experience. It is open to students with superior high school records who are highly motivated to learn through exposure to stimulating ideas.

Honors students may concentrate their studies in any major field at the University; the honors curriculum fills a portion of the University core requirements for graduation in all majors. Through a combination of seminars and small classes of 10 to 20 students, the program provides an opportunity for in-depth study in the core curriculum. The Honors Program professors are among the best at the University, and they are specifically selected to be part of the program. The students and faculty form a community that facilitates learning in and out of the classroom.

Freshmen take a one-week early course just prior to their fall semester. This is both an academic course and an introduction to the program. Freshmen and sophomore honors students choose one course each semester from among the honors courses offered that term. In the junior year, honors students participate in a junior seminar. Seniors complete an independent research project or thesis under the supervision of a faculty member in the area of the student's major. Each student who completes all Honors Program requirements has a designation entered on their transcript, wears a bachelor's degree hood during the graduation ceremony, and receives a medallion with their name, year of graduation, and University of Portland Honors Program engraved.

Approximately 25 entering freshmen are accepted each year (about 5 percent of the total entering freshmen) as are 3 or 4 sophomores or transfer students. There are currently 105 students in the program.

Participation Requirements: In addition to the orientation course, four regular honors classes, a junior seminar, and a thesis or project in their major, students are expected to participate in some of the cocurricular activities offered each year, which include trips to plays, symphony, ballet, opera, weekend retreats, and barbecues. In order to continue in good standing in the program, freshmen must earn a minimum GPA of 3.0, sophomores a 3.1, juniors a 3.2, and seniors a 3.3.

Admission Process: Students accepted to the University of Portland may apply for admission to the Honors Program. The Honors Program Advisory Committee composed of students and faculty review these applications and make recommendations on acceptance to the director. The deadline for application is April 13, 1998.

The Campus Context: The University of Portland is situated on 120 acres in a quiet residential neighborhood on a bluff overlooking the Willamette River. The campus is 15 minutes from downtown Portland, 90 miles from the Oregon Coast, and 60 miles from the Cascade Mountains. There are six colleges and schools on campus, including the College of Arts and Sciences, Multnomah School of Engineering, School of Business Administration, School of Education, School of Nursing, and the Graduate School. Fifty-five degree programs are available.

Student Body Undergraduate enrollment is 2,100; 57 percent are men and 43 percent are women. Ten percent of the students are international students, 45 percent are campus residents, and 82 percent of students receive financial aid.

Faculty There are 198 faculty members, 138 of whom are full-time. Ninety-three percent have terminal degrees. The student-faculty ratio is 16:1.

Key Facilities The Wilson W. Clark Memorial Library shelves nearly 350,000 bound volumes of books and journals. The campus has six computer labs and four computer classrooms.

Athletics The University provides a strong intramural and recreational athletic program for students. The intercollegiate program competes at the NCAA Division I level. The men's and women's programs compete in the West Coast Conference in basketball, cross-country, soccer, and tennis. The men's program also offers golf, baseball, and track (the track program competes as an independent). The women's program also offers volleyball.

Study Abroad The University provides an academic-year program in Salzburg, Austria, and two summer-study programs in London and Tokyo. The University is also a member of the Independent Liberal Arts Colleges Abroad consortium, which offers three additional study-abroad opportunities: a spring semester at Watford, England; a fall or spring semester in London; and a spring semester in Granada, Spain. In conjunction with the Institute of European Studies, the University offers a one- or two- semester program in Paris or Nantes, France, for students interested in advanced studies in the French language.

Tuition: $14,300 per year (1996-97)

Room and Board: $4380 minimum

Mandatory Fees: $100

Contact: Director: Dr. James G. Stemler, N. Willamette Boulevard, Portland, Oregon 97203; Telephone: 503-283-7221; Fax: 503-283-7399; E-mail: stemler@uofport.edu

---

UNIVERSITY OF ST. THOMAS

4 Pr G S Sc

▼ Honors Program

The purpose of the Honors Program at the University of St. Thomas is the creation of virtuous professionals, makers and preservers of a culture not hostile to the virtuous life. This requires two distinct but related educational activities: the tradition or the handing over of artifacts and archetypes of Western culture to students and an apprenticeship in the redeployment of these cultural instruments in the contemporary world, which ideally will result in their reform and transformation. Established in 1989, the program currently enrolls 50 to 60 students.

Participation Requirements: The program begins with four interdisciplinary, team-taught seminars that have a two-fold purpose: to connect the study of Western culture with the problem of living one's life and to provide structural principles for understanding culture itself and, therefore, of facilitating understanding of non-Western cultures. Team-teaching both furthers the interdisciplinary nature of the courses and encourages collaboration in learning among students and faculty.

These four courses are the necessary prologue to a course in reflective practical action. This course combines reading and discussion with individual service projects. In this way, students learn how values become incarnate in the world through work and how self-development is connected with service to others.

An undergraduate research project, which culminates in the presentation of results in a University forum, is designed to foster professional creativity and responsibility as well as collaboration with a faculty mentor.

A final team-taught seminar undertakes an interdisciplinary approach to the analysis and solution of some contemporary problem. As they prepare to leave the University, students discover that their education, liberal and professional, has given them the power to understand and transform contemporary society in the light of their values.

Successful completion of the Honors Program is noted on the student's transcript. Graduates of the Honors Program receive a certificate and medallion at Commencement, and Honors Program is printed on their diploma.

Admission Process: Students who wish to be members of the Honors Program must be in the top 10 percent of their graduating class, attain a score of at least 1180 on the SAT I, and be interviewed by the director.

Scholarship Availability: All members of the UST Honors Program receive scholarships. These include the President's Scholarship, a four-year, full-tuition scholarship awarded to students graduating in the top 10 percent of their high school class with an SAT I score of at least 1190 (or 26 on the ACT) and who have strong recommendations from their principal or senior counselor; the St. Thomas Aquinas Scholarship, a four-year, half-tuition scholarship awarded to the first 75 students accepted for admission by March 1 who are in the top 25 percent of their graduating class and have an SAT I score of at least 1140 (or 25 on the ACT); and Scholarships for Excellence, four-year, full-tuition scholarships for students in the top 25 percent of their graduating class who have been recognized as National Merit Scholarship Semifinalists, National Hispanic Award Winners, or Outstanding Black Scholars.

The Campus Context: The University of St. Thomas is composed of the School of Arts and Sciences, School of Education, Cameron School of Business, and School of Theology. Among the distinguished facilities are a genetic research facility in the Biology Department. Thirty-two degree programs are offered on campus.

Student Body Undergraduate enrollment is 1,479, with 34 percent men and 66 percent women. The student population is 57 percent white, 19 percent Hispanic, 6 percent African American, 7 percent Asian Pacific, 1 percent Native American, and 2 percent unknown. The 205 international students represent 8 percent of the student body.

Key Facilities The library houses 200,000 volumes. There is a computer facility with forty computers and a writing laboratory with thirteen computers and six portables.

Athletics The John D. Jerabeck Activity and Athletic Center has a basketball/volleyball arena with bleacher seating capacity of more than 800, four racquetball/handball courts, locker rooms for men and women, a weight room, a dance/cardiovascular exercise studio, a sauna, and six large classrooms. Outdoor facilities at the JAAC include two tennis courts, a swimming pool, and a basketball area.

Tuition: $10,962 per year (1997-98)

Room and Board: $4250 minimum

Mandatory Fees: $108

Contact: Director: Dr. Mary C. Sommers, 3800 Montrose Boulevard, Houston, Texas 77006; Telephone: 713-525-3148; Fax: 713-525-2125; E-mail: sommers@basil.suthom.edu

UNIVERSITY OF SOUTH CAROLINA

4 Pu G L Sc Tr

▼ South Carolina Honors College

South Carolina Honors College represents the University of South Carolina's tangible commitment to providing its finest undergraduates with a superlative education consonant with their abilities and potential. The College serves as a visible and vital academic unit intended to attract the best high school students in the state and provide them with a firm foundation for their future achievements.

Over the past three decades, the administrations of five University presidents created and sustained the Honors Program and its successor College. Their efforts resulted in an Honors College offering a peerless academic experience unifying the benefits of a small liberal arts college with the opportunities of a comprehensive university. It fuses these qualities in a unique synthesis, offering complementary combinations and counteracting the potential negatives of each academic environment. Everything that is done reflects the integration, not separation, of these educational alternatives.

As in a fine liberal arts college, Honors College classes are limited in size, populated by talented students, and taught by faculty members dedicated to designing courses that involve these students more actively in their own education. Honors students, however, are not set apart from the University but are a part of it. This simple change in preposition makes a world of difference for the students; it opens to them the world of the comprehensive University, with its research resources, diverse programs and curriculum, and rich campus culture.

The goals of the College are best represented by the type of student it hopes to attract and fulfill: leaders who are scholars; young men and women with a love of learning and faith in the role of reason; students who combine those elements common to all educated people, namely, the ability to use language with clarity and grace; appreciation of experimental sciences and scientific method; and insight into their own and other cultures through history, literature, and the arts, as well as the social sciences.

The Honors College sets high standards for its students and, therefore, for itself. Success is measured not only by the quality of the students attracted to the College but by the quality of the academic program the College offers them. Graduation with Honors from the South Carolina Honors College involves more than earning good grades; it stands for a substantive experience that challenges the students across the breadth of their academic endeavors.

Each semester, the Honors College offers between 90 and 100 courses across the undergraduate curriculum. In addition, the graduate schools of law, medicine, and public health also offer honors courses. In the lower division, the College provides courses that may be used to fulfill the general education requirements of all the undergraduate colleges in the University. In addition, upper-division courses are offered in areas with sufficient majors or general interest. Honors courses consist of honors sections of existing University courses or special classes developed especially for and existing only in the Honors College.

The Honors College office is located on the historic Horseshoe, the antebellum campus of the University. Honors facilities include classrooms, student lounges, and honors housing for up to 400 students in the Horseshoe area. The 20-year-old College has approximately 850 students.

Participation Requirements: Students who wish to earn honors from South Carolina Honors College must complete 45 credits of honors course work, including a 29–30 credit core and a 3–15 credit senior thesis. Honors core requirements consist of 6 credits of English, 8 of science, 6 of history of civilization, 6 of humanities/social sciences, and at least 3 credits of math/analytical.

Graduation with Honors from South Carolina Honors College is an official University honor that appears on the diploma and the transcript of each student who fulfills the requirements. In addition to formal recognition at each University Commencement, the Honors College holds its own ceremony to recognize those students completing all the requirements.

The College also offers its own interdisciplinary degree, the Baccalaureus Artium et Scientiae. In order to be admitted, applicants must be fourth-semester Honors College students with a minimum GPA of 3.6. They must develop a program of study approved by a panel consisting of the Associate Dean and Dean of the Honors College and 2 faculty advisers. They must take the maximum general education requirements of both the College of Science and Math and the College of Liberal Arts; complete an advanced foreign language course; take at least 69 credits of honors course work, including at least a 9-credit senior thesis; and maintain a minimum 3.5 GPA.

Admission Process: Entering freshmen generally score over 1300 on the SAT I and rank in the top 5 percent of their high school class. They are selected on the basis of an application that includes both academic and extracurricular criteria. Students who have completed at least one semester of college (at USC or elsewhere) may also apply. To remain in the Honors College, students must maintain a minimum GPA that is set at 3.0 their first semester and rises to 3.3 by their senior year. The deadline for applying is February 1.

Scholarship Availability: Two scholarships, the South Carolina Honors College Scholarship and the William A. Mould Scholarship, are administered through the Honors College. The South Carolina Honors College Scholarship is awarded to out-of-state honors students with no other scholarship support. The Mould Scholarship is awarded to a deserving student on the basis of need. Recipients are selected based on their enrollment in the Honors College.

The vast majority of honors students hold scholarships granted by the University of South Carolina. Students complete the same application for the University's major merit scholarships as for the Honors College.

The Campus Context: There are eighteen colleges and schools within the University of South Carolina. They are the College of Applied Professional Sciences, College of Business Administration, College of Criminal Justice, College of Education, College of Engineering, School of the Environment, College of Journalism and Mass Communications, Law School, College of Liberal Arts, College of Library and Information Science, School of Medicine, School of Music, College of Nursing, College of Pharmacy, School of Public Health, College of Science and Mathematics, College of Social Work, and South Carolina Honors College. More than 400 degree programs, including 80 bachelor's degrees, are offered on the Columbia campus.

The University of South Carolina is home to several distinguished facilities, including McKissick Museum, accredited by the American Association of Museums, and the University of South Carolina Press. The Koger Center for the Arts hosts University, local, national, and international performances. In addition, the University has a number of research bureaus and institutes, including Belle W. Baruch Institute for Marine Biology and Coastal Research; Center for Electrochemical Engineering; Center for Mechanics of Materials and Nondestructive Evaluation; Center for Industrial Research; Center for Industry Policy and Strategy; Center for Information Intelligence Technology; Center for Outcomes Research and Evaluation; Center for Retailing; Center for Science Education; Center for the Study of Suicide and Life Threatening Behavior; Division of Research, College of Business Administration; Earth Sciences and Resources Institute; Electron Microscopy Center; Institute for Families in Society; Richard L. Walker Institute of International Studies; Institute of Public Affairs; Institute for Southern Studies; Institute for Tourism Research; the National Resource Center for the Freshman Year Experience and Students in Transition; the Riegel and Emory Human Resource Research Center; South Carolina Institute of Archaeology and Anthropology; Southeast Manufacturing Technology Center; and TRIO Programs.

Student Body Undergraduate enrollment is 15,915 and comprises 41 percent men and 59 percent women. The ethnic distribution among the student population is 17.8 percent African American, 3 percent Asian/Pacific Islander, 1.3 percent Hispanic, .2 percent Native American, 75.3 percent white, and 2 percent nonresident alien. There are 329 international students. The student body is made up of 39 percent residents and 61 percent commuters. Approximately 55 percent of students receive financial aid. There are twenty-one fraternities and fifteen sororities.

Faculty Of the 1,379 total faculty members, 1,155 are full-time and 90 percent have terminal degrees. The student-faculty ratio is 17:1.

Key Facilities The library houses more than 7 million items, including 2.6 million volumes and more than 4 million units in microform. The Computer Services Division (CSD) offers free mainframe and microcomputer application classes. CSD provides a public microlab with laser printing and text/graphics scanning support and a reference room of computer periodicals. CSD also sponsors a public microlab located at the Thomas Cooper Library. Departmental computer labs are located throughout campus, and students, faculty, and staff can access the University mainframe via modem and emulation software.

Athletics The University sponsors an extensive program in intercollegiate sports that includes nine sports for men and ten sports for women. Baseball, basketball, cross-country, football, golf, soccer, softball, swimming, tennis, track, and volleyball are offered. The University of South Carolina is a member of the Southeastern Conference, and its athletic teams regularly play teams of that conference as well as those of other institutions across the nation. Among the facilities for athletics at the University are Williams-Brice Stadium, with a seating capacity of 80,250; the Coliseum, which seats more than 12,400; and an all-weather track with stands for 2,500. The baseball stadium seats 4,000, and stands with a capacity of 2,000 are located at the Sam Daniel Tennis Center. The University Club provides USC golfers with an excellent course for matches as well as practice. The George Terry Spring Sports Center and an indoor facility, including dressing rooms and a weight room located at Williams-Brice Stadium, provide complete, modern facilities for varsity athletes.

The Sol Blatt Physical Education Center provides extensive indoor space for student sports, including an Olympic-sized swimming pool. New women's basketball locker rooms were completed in 1994, and improvements to the overall women's athletic facilities have been made. Construction has been completed on a basketball practice facility and volleyball competition site adjacent to the Coliseum as well as to new boxes, club seating, a press box, and a football office complex with a departmental video studio at Williams-Brice Stadium.

Study Abroad Study Abroad Programs offers a great variety of study-abroad and exchange opportunities for students who wish to study in another country. Overseas study programs are available for both undergraduate and graduate students. The Honors College in particular has special exchange relationships with the Universities of Kent, Hull, and Leeds in England. The length of the study-abroad program may be the academic year, one semester, or a short-term program during the summer. The International Programs Office provides guidance to students considering study abroad and maintains a resource library with information about program offerings and financial aid.

Support Services Disability Services provides assistance to disabled students by operating a transportation service, providing microphones to instructors teaching hearing-impaired students, and serving as a liaison between students and faculty in providing services to accommodate disabled students who meet ADA guidelines.

Job Opportunities The Federal Work-Study Program provides part-time employment for students to meet their educational expenses. To be eligible for employment under this federal program, a student must be enrolled in the University or fully accepted for admission and demonstrate financial need. Students who are enrolled at least half-time work an average of 15 to 20 hours per week. During vacation periods it is sometimes possible to work up to 40 hours per week. Pay rates vary with the job assignment. The Student Employment Office is a source of information about part-time job opportunities in the city of Columbia. Many students also locate employment in one of the academic departments of the University.

Tuition: $3362 for state residents, $8574 for nonresidents, per year (1996-97)

Room and Board: $3692 minimum

Contact: Dean: Dr. Peter C. Sederberg, Harper College, Columbia, South Carolina 29208; Telephone: 803-777-8102; Fax: 803-777-2214; E-mail: peters@ss1.csd.sc.edu; Web site: http://web.csd.sc.edu/honors/index.html

UNIVERSITY OF SOUTHERN COLORADO

4 Pu G S Sc Tr

▼ Honors Program

The objective of the University of Southern Colorado Honors Program is to promote the intellectual curiosity of the University's most capable students, enabling them to confront complex issues. To accomplish this objective, the program offers small classes designed to develop critical thinking skills, expand the scope of investigation of a topic, and explore issues in greater depth than can be done in conventional classes. The program also features interdisciplinary courses that encourage students to make connections among diverse areas of learning.

There are currently 70 students enrolled in the program.

Participation Requirements: Students may graduate with honors after completing 16 hours in the Honors Program. To receive a minor in honors, students must complete 22 hours of general education and upper-division courses in honors. To graduate from the Honors Program, students must maintain an overall GPA of 3.5 and an Honors GPA of 3.0. Successful completion of the Honors Program requirements is noted at graduation and is recorded on the student's transcript.

Admission Process: Freshmen are selected prior to the fall semester on the basis of their high school GPA and their ACT score (minimum 3.5 and 25, respectively). Sophomores and first-year students who are not selected may also apply for admission, as may transfer students and continuing USC students.

The Campus Context: USC's campus, spanning more than 275 acres, is located at the north end of Pueblo, a historically and culturally rich city of 100,000 located near the Greenhorn Mountains in the colorful Pikes Peak region of southern Colorado. Campus enrollment exceeds 4,000, with students from throughout southeastern Colorado, the entire state, the nation, and several other countries, representing a diversity of age groups and backgrounds, both rural and urban.

Student Body Undergraduate enrollment is 47 percent men and 53 percent women. Twenty-nine percent of students are members of minority groups (25 percent Hispanic). The majority of students commute to campus. Seventy-two percent receive financial aid.

Faculty The total number of faculty members is 220, 98 percent of whom have advanced degrees. The student-faculty ratio is 21:1.

Key Facilities The campus has a 250,000-volume library. There are five computer labs on campus.

Study Abroad Through the University's International Education Program, students in all disciplines have the opportunity to study overseas. Students may apply to study abroad for a summer or a regular semester.

Support Services The USC campus is accessible to disabled persons, and the residence hall provides adequate living facilities for handicapped students. Individualized support services such as readers, tutors, note-takers, and interpreters are available for qualified students. All persons with disabilities, including those who are learning disabled, are eligible for support.

Job Opportunities The Federal Work-Study Program is designed to provide jobs to students who, without the earnings from the employment, could not attend the University. The program is funded by the federal government and the Colorado General Assembly. The University annually employs approximately 700 students in the work-study program. USC offers both full-time work-study and no-need work-study.

Tuition: $1682 for state residents, $7412 for nonresidents, $2522 for students eligible for the Western Undergraduate Exchange, per year (1996-97)

Room and Board: $4180

Mandatory Fees: $410

Contact: Director: Dr. Gayle K. Berardi, 2200 Bonforte Avenue, Pueblo, Colorado 81001; Telephone: 719-549-2342; Fax: 719-549-2705; E-mail: berardi@uscolo.edu

---

UNIVERSITY OF SOUTHERN MAINE

4 Pu G S Sc Tr

▼ University Honors Program

Honors at USM is a community-style program in which all students take the same series of courses. These begin with four 4-credit colloquia, taken one per semester, and include Wisdom Stories From Four Worlds, which investigates justice and the relationship of the individual to social institutions in ancient Greece, Rome, the Judaic world, and early Christianity; Piety, Politics, and Holy War, which focuses on the relationship of religion and political power and the development of the mystical tradition in Christianity and Islam into the later Catholic Church and the Islamic Empire; Scientific Revolutions and Critiques, which traces the structure of science from Aristotle to the modern environmental movement, with particular emphasis on the relationships between science, religion, and magic in Renaissance and Reformation times; and Progress, Process, or Permanence, which deals with alienation and uncertainty, particularly as exemplified in nineteenth- and twentieth-century literature and philosophy. All of the colloquia emphasize readings from original materials, extensive writing, and a discussion format. Classes are limited to 15 students.

Honors faculty members are from departments in various colleges and schools at USM. They are chosen for their excellent teaching records and their desire to teach in an interdisciplinary environment.

The University of Southern Maine enrolls many nontraditional students, and this diversity is reflected in those taking honors courses. An honors class usually includes traditional students just out of high school, part-time students who also work, and older students who are returning to school. Students with many different majors are found in the program.

All honors courses are taught at Honors House, a converted residential building adjacent to the Portland campus. The building contains offices, seminar rooms, a kitchen, and a student lounge with computer facilities. It is also the editorial headquarters for *The Maine Scholar*, a refereed journal supported by all the Honors Programs in the University of Maine System. The *Scholar* accepts works from students, faculty, and independent writers that are directed toward its yearly theme. Recent thematic issues include the environment, childhood, and death and dying.

There is an active Honors Student Association that sponsors social and cultural events on campus and coordinates volunteer work by members of the program. Student representatives are voting members of the Honors Faculty Board, which governs program operations.

The program was developed in the early 1980s with the help of funding from the National Endowment for the Humanities and accepted its first students in 1986. About 38 students each year are now accepted. The total enrollment is fewer than 100, or approximately 1 percent of the USM undergraduate student body.

Participation Requirements: Honors students must also take a 3-credit honors seminar; seminars are offered each semester on a different topic. Under the direction of a faculty committee, all students do a senior thesis project to complete their honors work, beginning with a thesis workshop. Elective honors courses are available in writing and in directed research or reading. Completion of the colloquium sequence excuses the student from 15 credits of USM core courses; completion of the sequence plus the seminar and thesis allows students to graduate with University Honors.

Admission Process: Students must apply by May 1 to start the program the following fall. There is no GPA requirement for applicants. The application portfolio includes a completed application form, two recommendations, a personal essay, and academic transcripts; the program arranges an interview for the applicant with one of the honors faculty members when the written application materials are complete. Open houses for applicants and their families are held two or three times during the spring, when they can talk to current honors faculty members and students. Applications are accepted from individuals entering the University for the first time or from those who have attended previously. Completion of program requirements normally requires three years, although it is possible to complete them in two.

Scholarship Availability: Honors currently awards seven scholarships per year, in amounts from $1000 to $2000, to students in the program. Students must have completed at least one honors course before they can apply. Both academic performance and financial need are considered in scholarship awards. Small grants are also available to assist with thesis expenses. Honors students are usually very successful at competing for University-wide scholarships as well.

The Campus Context: The University of Southern Maine is the second-largest of the seven universities in the Maine public university system. USM has two principal campuses: a city location in downtown Portland and a traditional New England campus in the small town of Gorham, 10 miles inland. Many classes are taught at both campuses, which are connected by free shuttle buses. The school offers approximately forty undergraduate majors and seventeen graduate programs in the College of Arts and Sciences and the Schools of Business, Applied Science, Nursing, Education and Human Development, and Law. Self-designed undergraduate majors are available, and a number of honors students have pursued these.

Student Body USM enrolls about 9,500 students, about 7,800 of whom are in undergraduate degree programs. Approximately 1,000 students are dorm residents. The undergraduate population is 41 percent men and 59 percent women; 2.6 percent are members of minority groups, and 6 percent are international students. Ninety-four percent of students are Maine residents, and 65 percent receive financial aid, the average award totaling about $4300.

Faculty The University currently has 321 full-time faculty members, supplemented with adjuncts.

Key Facilities The USM library has about 400,000 volumes, with another 200,000 in the law library. There are more than 1 million microform units as well. All Maine system universities participate in an interlibrary loan program. Computer labs, with both IBM and Mac computers and Internet access, are available on both campuses. Internet connections and access to the campus local area network are also available in residence halls.

Athletics USM participates in athletics at the NCAA Division III level and offers fourteen intercollegiate athletic programs, including a baseball team that has won the national championship (1991). There are also extensive intramural activities and clubs for off-campus sports such as skiing and sailing.

Study Abroad The University encourages students to spend a semester or more at a foreign university; students can study in Austria, Canada, England, Ireland, Latvia, the Netherlands, or Ukraine. Scholarships and financial aid are available. In addition, USM is a member of the National Student Exchange program, in which degree students can spend up to a year at one of 120 participating universities in the United States while paying only in-state tuition. Five colleges and universities in the Portland region also participate in the Greater Portland Alliance, allowing students to take courses at other schools that are not offered at USM.

Tuition: $3330 for state residents, $9420 for nonresidents, $4995 for nonresidents eligible for the New England Regional Student Program, per year (1996-97)

Room and Board: $4554

Mandatory Fees: $380

Contact: Director: Dr. Bill Hayes, 96 Falmouth Street, P.O. Box 9300, Portland, Maine 04104; Telephone: 207-780-4330; Fax: 207-780-4933; E-mail: hayes@usm.maine.edu; Web site: http://macweb.acs.usm.maine.edu/honors/HonorsHome.html

UNIVERSITY OF SOUTHERN MISSISSIPPI
4 Pu C M Sc Tr
▼ Honors College

The University of Southern Mississippi's Honors College is a comprehensive four-year program that aims to identify, encourage, and reward academic excellence in all fields and to serve students who desire a broadly based undergraduate education. The honors curriculum is designed for students who have intellectual curiosity and the ambition and discipline to master a comprehensive liberal education, whatever major field of study they choose. Students may pursue any undergraduate degree program offered by the University while they are members of the Honors College.

Each year, the Honors College sponsors a lecture series that honors students attend to earn credits. Recent speakers include Supreme Court Justice Antonin Scalia, editor James Fallows, and evolutionary theorist Stephen Jay Gould.

The Honors College at USM was founded as an honors program in 1957; it was organized as a separate college in 1976, making it the sixth-oldest Honors College in the nation. There are approximately 350 students in the program.

Participation Requirements: The program is divided into two parts: General Honors (freshman and sophomore years) and Senior Honors (junior and senior years). The cornerstone of the General Honors program is a four-semester humanities survey entitled World Thought and Culture, better known as colloquium, which substitutes for the general core requirements in history, literature, and philosophy. These classes are taught by a team of humanities professors who provide an overview of human endeavor from the beginnings of civilization through the twentieth century. The other component of the General Honors program is the departmental honors sections of general education requirements. Each of the honors courses requires more reading, writing, and classroom participation than typically might be required in a lower-division course, and they are usually smaller in size than non-honors courses as well. Students in the Honors College are required to complete 26 hours of honors course work in

General Honors as well as maintain a 3.0 GPA in all course work; a GPA of 3.25 is required to continue into Senior Honors.

In Senior Honors, students continue with honors course work, but they emphasize independent study and scholarship leading to an honors thesis in their major. During the junior year, students enroll in two honors seminars taught by professors from a wide variety of disciplines; at least six different seminars are presented each year. Prospectus Writing, a course taken during the junior year, helps students plan and prepare the bibliography for the senior thesis. During the senior year, honors students undertake the senior thesis, a substantial undergraduate study carried out under the direction of a research adviser from the department of the student's major. Students must also pass a special comprehensive examination in the major taken in their final semester.

Students completing Senior Honors receive on their diplomas a Latin designation for graduation with honors and wear the distinctive honors medallion with the academic robe at Commencement.

Admission Process: Students are admitted to the Honors College based on ACT or SAT scores, high school GPA, teacher recommendations, and an essay. The Honors College also accepts transfer students and rising juniors into the Senior Honors program provided they have a 3.5 GPA in 40 or more hours of course work.

The application deadline is March 15.

Scholarship Availability: The University offers several Presidential Scholarships each year to entering honors freshmen on a competitive basis; these scholarships cover the costs of tuition, room, board, and fees. Other scholarships offered exclusively to Honors College students are the George R. Olliphant Scholarships and Honors College Scholarships. The Honors College also encourages participation in USM's study-abroad program and offers scholarship support for students studying abroad in the summer.

The Campus Context: The main campus of the University of Southern Mississippi is located in Hattiesburg, Mississippi; often called "the Hub City," Hattiesburg is located 90 miles south of the state capital of Jackson, 75 miles north of the Gulf Coast, and 105 miles northeast of New Orleans, Louisiana. There are six academic colleges: the Arts, Business Administration, Education and Psychology, Health and Human Sciences, Liberal Arts, and Science and Technology. There are also the Honors College and International and Continuing Education. The campus offers eighty-nine undergraduate majors culminating in B.A., B.S., B.S.B.A., B.F.A., B.M., B.M. E., B.S.N., or B.S.W. degrees. Distinguished facilities on campus include the Polymer Science Research Center, one of only seven polymer science programs in the nation, and the Payne Center, a new world-class fitness facility that is home to recreational sports and fitness programs that serve alumni, students, faculty, and staff.

Student Body Undergraduate enrollment for the Hattiesburg campus is 12,113 (43 percent men and 57 percent women). The ethnic distribution among students on campus is 78 percent Caucasian, 2 percent Asian, 18 percent African American, 1 percent Native American, and 1 percent Hispanic. International students from more than sixty countries number 310. Seventy-two percent of the students on the Hattiesburg campus receive financial aid. There are thirteen residence halls housing 3,400 students. Honors housing is available for students; there are floors designated for this purpose in four dorms on campus. Residence in honors housing is not required, but many students take advantage of this special opportunity to live with other honors scholars. There are thirteen fraternities and twelve sororities.

Faculty The total number of faculty members is 675, of whom 580 are full-time. A total of 528 faculty members have terminal degrees. The student-faculty ratio is 18:1.

Key Facilities The library houses 1.8 million volumes. There are approximately 500 computer terminals available for student use, including Macintosh/IBM (DOS, Windows 3.1, and Novell), thirty Linux workstations, and fifteen UNIX/ VMS multiuser systems. Full Internet access is free to all students.

Athletics The University of Southern Mississippi is a member of the NCAA Division I-A and Conference USA; fifteen intercollegiate sports, including baseball, basketball, cross-country, football, golf, tennis, and track, are offered.

Study Abroad USM began its credit-abroad programs in 1976 with the creation of the British Studies Program. Since 1986, more than 3,000 students have participated in these programs that now include study in Australia, Austria, Canada, the Caribbean, France, Germany, Ireland, Mexico, New Zealand, Scotland, Spain, and Wales.

Support Services All buildings are physically accessible to disabled students, and there is adequate handicapped parking available on campus. Disabled Student Services helps disabled students obtain the modifications they need in order to attend the University.

Job Opportunities Work study, assistantships, and a variety of student employment opportunities are offered on campus.

Tuition: $2518 for state residents, $5338 for nonresidents, per year (1996-97)

Room and Board: $2505

Contact: Director: Dr. Maureen Ryan, Box 5162, Hattiesburg, Mississippi 39406-5162; Telephone: 601-266-4533; Fax: 601-266-4534; E-mail: mryan@whale.st.usm.edu, ahewitt@ocean. st.usm.edu

UNIVERSITY OF SOUTH FLORIDA

4 Pu G,D L Sc Tr

▼ University Honors Program

The University of South Florida (USF) Honors Program is designed for the academically superior student who wishes to go the extra mile, who embraces challenge, who wants to enhance the University experience, and who is intrigued by alternative approaches to learning. USF offers a four-year honors program for incoming freshmen and a two-year program for qualified transfer students. Honors is for motivated students regardless of major. Honors students develop a strong sense of community.

The Honors Program seeks to attract students of superior academic ability and provide them with intellectual challenges and enrichment. The student-centered, student-oriented Honors Program assists students in developing and refining critical skills in thinking, reasoning, analysis, and writing. Program goals are achieved by providing opportunities for students and faculty members to interact closely in a series of liberal arts–oriented, mainly team-taught, interdisciplinary classes of limited size and then by having students work independently on a senior thesis/project under the close supervision of faculty mentors.

The first part of the program emphasizes the development of thinking, reasoning, analytical, and writing skills. Then, these problem-solving and research abilities are applied to an individual research project or original creative work. These skills prove invaluable as students pursue graduate or professional school and career choices and challenges.

Honors students are afforded special services within a highly individualized and nurturing environment. This environment fosters a sense of belonging and provides both an academic and social home throughout the USF years. USF Honors is an exciting experience that combines the advantage of a small, highly personalized college with the resources of a major state university. It is a place where students can reach out, learn, and grow. Students in the program receive special recognition at the University's graduation ceremony, and their honors status is noted on the transcript and the diploma.

The program began in 1983 and currently enrolls 600 students.

Participation Requirements: The Four-Year Track (28 credits that substitute for the University's liberal arts requirements) encompasses a student's entire college career; the Two-Year Track (13 credits that substitute for an equal number of liberal arts requirements) is for the junior and senior years. Small, intimate classes encourage interaction among students and faculty members.

Admission Process: Students in the Four-Year Track typically have weighted high school GPAs of 3.5 and SAT I scores in the range of 1300 or ACT scores in the range of 29. Two-Year Track students typically have 3.5 transfer GPAs and SAT I scores or ACT scores in the same range as Four-Year Track students. Students with these credentials are admitted to honors if they so desire.

Scholarship Availability: Every student in the Honors Program who is enrolled in an Honors Program course and who maintains the required Honors Program GPA is awarded a scholarship each semester. Scholarships range from $800 to $1500 per year. Non-Florida residents receive scholarships in the form of out-of-state tuition waivers that average about $3000 per year.

The Campus Context: University of South Florida is composed of six undergraduate colleges: Arts and Sciences, Business, Education, Engineering, Fine Arts, and Nursing. There are two professional schools: Medicine and Public Health. All colleges are located on the Tampa campus, with some degree programs offered at the regional campuses in St. Petersburg, Lakeland, and Sarasota. The University offers seventy-nine undergraduate degree programs and 116 graduate degree programs (including master's, specialty, doctoral, and M.D. degrees).

The College of Fine Arts is home to the internationally known Graphicstudio, the only university art program in the country to have its collections archived at the National Gallery of Art in Washington, D.C. The College of Public Health is the only one in the state of Florida. The College of Education, which has a new facility opening in fall 1997, is the largest urban college of education in the country with 130 faculty members and more than 23,000 alumni. The College of Engineering, which developed the country's first carport for electric vehicles, hosts the annual Engineering Expo, the largest and oldest exhibition in the country (6,000 participants last year). USF presented about 17,000 student credit hours via distance learning technology last year and supports more than 125 remote distance learning affiliate sites.

Among distinguished facilities is the Sun Dome, an 11,000-seat multipurpose facility; Martin Luther King Plaza, an area at the center of campus dedicated to Martin Luther King that provides students and faculty members with space to gather at events, study, and enjoy the Florida sunshine; and the Phyllis P. Marshall Center, home to many student services. There are more than 300 registered student organizations.

Student Body The student population is 58 percent women and 42 percent men. The ethnic distribution is 78.2 percent Caucasian, 8.7 percent African American, 8.4 percent Hispanic, 4.4 percent Asian/Pacific Islander, and .3 percent American Indian. There are 894 international students. Nine percent of the students reside on campus. Fifty-eight percent of undergraduate students receive financial aid. There are eighteen national fraternities and twelve national sororities.

Faculty There are about 2,000 total faculty members, of whom 1,481 are full-time, 85.4 percent with terminal degrees. Among the faculty members are 73 Fulbright Scholars and 42 endowed chairs. The student-faculty ratio is 22:1. Eighty-four percent of the classes have fewer than 40 students; 2 percent have more than 100 students. Approximately 2,800 classes are offered each semester.

Key Facilities The library houses 1.5 million volumes, 9,937 periodical subscriptions, 4 million microforms, and 112,461 audiovisuals. Students have 34,000 seat hours per week of open computing facilities. Eight individual facilities include IBM and Macintosh computers in addition to printing capabilities. Residence halls are wired for direct access to the mainframe, and all students have e-mail addresses, Internet access, and help-desk support upon request.

Athletics USF sponsors eighteen intercollegiate sports that compete at the NCAA Division I level, and the Bulls are a charter member of Conference USA. Men and women athletes participate in baseball, basketball, cross-country/track, golf, soccer, softball, tennis, and volleyball. Fall 1997 has the first season of Bulls football. Students can also choose to participate in a wide range of intramural and club sports. All recreational facilities, including six football and soccer fields, twenty-two tennis courts, eight basketball and volleyball courts, a 1.4-mile fitness trail, four pools, twelve racquetball courts, and 6,500 square feet of free weight and cardiovascular equipment, are free to students with their student ID. In addition, USF has a Riverfront Park for canoe rental and picnics and offers many exciting outdoor adventure trips throughout the year.

Study Abroad USF offers the world as a classroom. Most study-abroad programs run four to eight weeks, usually during the summer. Shorter tours are also available. Programs include visits to England, Spain, France, Normandy, Germany, Greece, Italy, Mexico, Russia, Trinidad, and more. There is also an International Student Exchange Program, which allows students to go on exchange for a term or year to schools in any of ten countries at a cost comparable to those USF.

Support Services Student Disability Services provides resources to students with documented disabilities. In 1996, 560 students received assistance. Some exceptions can be made for students who do not meet the University's admission requirements.

Job Opportunities Students have the ability to work on campus through the Federal Work-Study Program or for an hourly rate in many different departments. Job listings of on- and off-campus employers are posted in the Career Resource Center.

Tuition: $1961 for state residents, $7206 for nonresidents, per year (1996-97)

Room and Board: $4598

Contact: Director: Dr. Stuart Silverman, 4204 East Fowler Avenue-CPR 107, Tampa, Florida 33620; Telephone: 813-974-3087; Fax: 813-974-5801; E-mail: ssilvern@chuma.cas.usf.edu

---

THE UNIVERSITY OF TENNESSEE AT CHATTANOOGA

4 Pu G & D M Sc Tr

▼ University Honors Program

The University Honors (UHON) program at UTC is a four-year interdisciplinary program that stresses the importance of a global perspective and encourages development of intellectual and leadership skills. The UHON seminars are designed especially for UHON students and typically have about 15 students in each class.

UHON Program members have special benefits, including intensive, personal academic advisement; priority registration for classes; 24-hour access to the UHON Reading Room and adjacent computer lab; stipend for local symphony, opera, and theater performances; and partial funding for spring UHON-sponsored cultural trips, with domestic designations in even years and foreign destinations in odd years. The UHON Program began as the University Scholars in 1977, became the Brock Scholars Program in 1979, and took its current form as the University Honors Program in 1986 through a grant from the National Endowment for the Humanities. The program is currently made up of about 140 exceptional students, slightly less than 2 percent of the total undergraduate enrollment.

Participation Requirements: The required UHON curriculum consists of 33 semester hours (Humanities I and II; Classical and Medieval Historical and Political Thought; Development of Scientific Thought; Origins of Social Science; Contemporary Social Science; one course from Chinese and Japanese Traditions, Traditions of India, or African Traditions; two courses from music, art, or theater history and aesthetics.) During the senior year, each UHON student carries out an independent departmental honors project under the guidance of a faculty member in the major. The project carries 4 hours of academic credit and usually results in a research paper of substantial length and quality, which must be defended before a committee from the major department.

Students must maintain a 3.5 cumulative GPA for all college course work, complete at least 24 hours toward graduation each academic year, complete the sequence of UHON core seminar courses including the departmental honors project, and, at the end of the junior year and thereafter, maintain a 3.5 GPA in the major. UHON students are expected to participate fully in the social, cultural, and service life of the University.

UHON students receive designations on their diplomas and in the Commencement program as William E. Brock Jr. Scholars, Honors Fellows or Associate Honors Fellows, as appropriate, and Honors or Highest Honors, as appropriate, in the subject area of the departmental honors project.

Admission Process: Applicants must request and complete a separate application to the UHON Program by December 15 of the senior year of high school. Final selections are completed by March 1 of the senior year. Transfer students and students not entering as freshmen may be admitted as Associate Honors Fellows if they have completed at least 36 hours of course work with a 3.5 cumulative GPA or better; they are eligible for all benefits of the UHON Program except the William E. Brock Jr. Scholarships.

Scholarship Availability: About twenty new William E. Brock Jr. Scholarships are awarded each year to freshmen selected for the UHON Program. Those students not receiving Brock Scholarships are considered for all other merit-based awards offered by the University. The University typically awards more than $1.5 million in financial awards annually. In addition, all UHON students in good standing receive a waiver of out-of-state tuition, if appropriate.

The Campus Context: The University of Tennessee at Chattanooga began in 1897 as a private liberal arts college, the University of Chattanooga, and joined the University of Tennessee in 1970. In September 1996, *U.S. News & World Report* ranked UTC third in the "Best Value" category among regional universities in the South, and the School of Engineering received a top 30 ranking among national engineering undergraduate programs that do not offer Ph.D. degrees.

The University is composed of the College of Arts and Sciences, the College of Education and Applied Professional Studies, the College of Engineering and Computer Science, the School of Business Administration, and the College of Health and Human Services, which includes the School of Nursing and the School of Social and Community Services. Degree programs include Bachelor of Arts, Bachelor of Fine Arts, Bachelor of Music, and Bachelor of Science in forty-six undergraduate majors with ninety-one program concentrations. Master's degrees are offered in sixteen majors with forty-eight program concentrations.

There are a number of special facilities. The Smart Classroom with interactive video network capability transmits credit courses statewide. The Challenger Space Center is the first in the nation housed on a university campus and the first to incorporate a university teaching mission as part of its basic purpose. The physical therapy program, one of two such programs in the state, has one of the country's few high-tech gait analysis laboratories. WUTC FM 88.1, a 30,00-watt public radio station, is a program service member of National Public Radio and American Public Radio.

Student Body Undergraduate enrollment is 8,331 (45 percent men and 55 percent women). The student population is 82.1 percent white, 12.8 percent black, 1.2 percent Hispanic, 3.5 percent Asian/Pacific Islander, and .4 percent American Indian. There are 185 international students. Residents living in campus housing make up 16.4 percent of the population, and commuters, 83.6 percent. Sixty-five percent of students receive financial aid. There are seven fraternities and eight sororities.

Faculty Of the 551 faculty members, 321 are full-time. Eighty-one percent hold terminal degrees. The student-faculty ratio is 17:1.

Key Facilities The library houses 442,741 books and 1.1 million microforms. Computer facilities include IBMs and Macs in three large general purpose labs and twenty-three departmental labs. The number of computers changes constantly as new facilities are added. E-mail accounts and Internet and World Wide Web access are available. There is an on-line library catalog and on-line class registration facility.

Athletics In athletics, UTC is NCAA Division I. Men's sports are basketball, cross-country, football (I-AA), golf, indoor and outdoor track, tennis, and wrestling. Women's sports are basketball, cross-country, indoor and outdoor track, soccer, softball, tennis, and volleyball. Club sports include men's and women's crew (rowing) and men's soccer and rugby. UTC's recreational facilities include an indoor racquet center; natatorium; and a 12,000-seat arena with specialized areas for dance, gymnastics, and wrestling. A new football stadium is projected for completion by fall 1997.

Study Abroad UTC sponsors bilateral exchange programs to Masaryk University in Brno, Czech Republic, and Haifa University in Israel and participates in the Cooperative Center for Study in Great Britain. ISEP programs are available in several locations. International exchange students are honorary members of the UHON while at UTC.

Support Services Disabled students will find UTC committed to providing equal opportunity for all students. Most buildings are wheelchair accessible, and many projects are under way to enhance accessibility.

Job Opportunities Work opportunities on campus include laboratory and research assistantships for undergraduates, tutoring and work-study programs, and jobs in the bookstore and food service areas.

Tuition: $2064 for state residents, $6400 for nonresidents, per year (1996-97)

Contact: Director: Robert C. Fulton III, 615 McCallie Avenue, Chattanooga, Tennessee 37403; Telephone: 423-755-4128; Fax: 423-785-2128; E-mail: robert-fulton@utc.edu; Web site: http://www.utc.edu:80/univhon/index.html

---

THE UNIVERSITY OF TENNESSEE AT MARTIN

    4 Pu G M Sc Tr

▼ Honors Programs

Honors Programs at the University of Tennessee at Martin comprise the University Scholars Program and the Honors Seminar Program. Together these programs involve approximately 360 students annually in honors courses, seminars with visiting speakers, independent research and creative projects, cultural activities, and service projects.

The University Scholars Program, founded in 1981, is a sequence of courses and extracurricular activities for a select group of talented and motivated students. The major goal is to provide special academic opportunities that will help these students to perform with distinction in their careers and as citizens. Interdisciplinary inquiry and independent study and research characterize this program. The program currently is limited to 60 undergraduate students at all levels in the University. Scholars students enroll every semester in one University Scholars course, accumulating a four-year total of 10 hours toward graduation with the designation University Scholar.

The Honors Seminar Program, founded in 1984, brings together students and distinguished campus visitors (scholars, leaders, or artists) in seminars to discuss and examine issues and ideas. Approximately 300 students are currently active in the program. Honors Seminar students attend a series of public presentations by visiting speakers. They select one speaker with whom to study in more depth in two special seminars. Up to 4 hours of elective credit toward the degree may be earned.

Admission Process: Students with a minimum ACT composite score of 28 and high school GPA of 3.5 may apply for University Scholars Program admission prior to their freshman year. A few students with outstanding freshman college records at UTM or who are transferring from another institution may also be invited to apply. A 3.3 GPA is required for good standing. Students qualify for the Honors Seminar Program by having an ACT composite score of 25 or higher and a high school GPA of 3.5 or higher. Students apply for the program by completing the regular applications for admission and financial aid at UTM. A 3.2 GPA is required for good standing.

Scholarship Availability: Students invited into the University Scholars Program are assured of a scholarship package totaling $3200 for each year of their participation. Honors Seminar students are assured of a scholarship package of at least $1500 for the freshman year. Honors Seminar students with a minimum ACT composite of 28 receive the Chancellor's Award, which guarantees a freshman scholarship of at least $2500. Students whose performance is satisfactory are eligible for workships earning $1500 in their sophomore, junior, and senior years. Chancellor's Award holders receive a $1000 scholarship for their sophomore, junior, and senior years in addition to the workship option. A limited number of out-of-state honors students are selected for tuition scholarships.

The Campus Context: The University of Tennessee at Martin, located in northwest Tennessee, is a primary campus of the University of Tennessee system. UT Martin offers undergraduate degree programs in more than eighty specialized fields of study through the Schools of Agriculture and Human Environment, Arts and Sciences, Business Administration, Education, Engineering Technology and Engineering and in the Division of Fine and Performing Arts.

The University community enjoys a 250-acre campus that features forty-six academic and support buildings. Residence halls house more than half of the student body. The campus is a registered botanical garden and has received the Professional Grounds Maintenance Society's Grand Award for school and university grounds. Honors Programs are housed in the Holland McCombs Center on the quadrangle. The Honors Center portion of McCombs consists of an office, the Tennessee Room, a seminar room, and Honors Study.

Student Body Of the 5,498 undergraduates, 56 percent are women and 44 percent are men. The ethnic distribution includes 14 percent African American and 1.3 percent Asian.

Faculty There are 260 full-time faculty members, 62 percent of whom have terminal degrees. The student-faculty ratio is 21:1.

Key Facilities Paul Meek Library, which was recently expanded from 65,000 to 120,000 square feet, has more than 300,000 volumes. The campus is wired with fiber-optic cables connecting academic, administrative, and residential buildings.

Athletics UT Martin is a NCAA Division I institution and a member of the Ohio Valley Conference. Intercollegiate athlet-

ics include basketball, cross-country, indoor and outdoor track, softball, tennis, and volleyball for women and baseball, basketball, cross-country, football, golf, riflery, and tennis for men. There are also several recreational activities and sports for men and women.

Study Abroad Honors Program students are encouraged to study abroad through tours associated with courses and led by University professors. Semester and academic-year fellowships abroad are encouraged.

Tuition: $2014 for state residents, $6350 for nonresidents, per year (1996-97)

Room and Board: $2990 minimum

Contact: Director: Dr. Ernest W. Blythe Jr., 19 Holland McCombs Center, Martin, Tennessee 38238; Associate Director: Dr. William H. Zachry, Telephone: 901-587-7436; Fax: 901-587-7841; E-mail: eblythe@utm.edu; Web site: http://www.utm.edu/departments/acadpro/honors/honors.htm

THE UNIVERSITY OF TENNESSEE, KNOXVILLE

4 Pu G M Sc Tr

▼ University Honors Program

The University Honors Program at the University of Tennessee, Knoxville, is a campuswide program open to students pursuing any of 107 academic majors in ten colleges. Admission is available only to entering students who are recipients of one of the following four-year academic scholarships: Whittle, Tennessee, African American Achiever, Bicentennial, Bonham, Haslam, Holt, Neyland, and Roddy Merit. Other students on campus may be eligible to take honors courses or to join departmental honors programs. Waivers of out-of-state tuition are available to selected qualified students.

Entering students are assigned a peer mentor and select a faculty mentor to provide advice on academic issues, career opportunities, and the senior project. Honors students receive priority in course selection and residence hall selection each term and in orientation before their first year. During the academic year, students have unlimited access to the honors lounges, including their computer facilities and study areas. Honors dinners are held on a regular basis each year, and afternoon receptions are held to feature both academic and extracurricular opportunities.

The goals of the University Honors Program are to provide enhanced academic opportunities and to promote campus and community involvement to students that are appropriate to their diverse interests.

The 12-year-old program currently enrolls 450 students.

Participation Requirements: University Honors students typically take a 1-credit honors seminar each semester and honors courses during the first two years, and they complete a senior project under the supervision of a faculty mentor. Students are also eligible to participate in one of the many departmental honors programs on campus. A 3.25 GPA is required to maintain full standing in the program. Honors courses are indicated on transcripts.

Scholarship Availability: Whittle Scholars and Tennessee Scholars are selected by a committee of the University Honors Program and require a separate application. Haslam Scholars require a separate application to the College of Arts and Sciences or the College of Business Administration. The remaining honors scholarships do not require a separate application and are awarded based upon certified grades and scores (African American Achiever and Bicentennial) and school and community activities (Bonham, Holt, Neyland, and Roddy Merit) reported in the application for admission.

All honors students must first be awarded one of the four-year (two-year for transfer students) honors scholarships. There are nine different scholarships. Approximately 200 scholarships are awarded each year covering a minimum of tuition. Out-of-state recipients in the University Honors Program do not pay out-of-state tuition.

The deadline for completed applications for scholarships and for admission (submit application at least three weeks prior) is February 1. There are no residency requirements for scholarships, with the exception of Bicentennial Scholars, who must be Tennessee residents. Tennessee Scholars is the only program available to entering transfer students.

The Campus Context: The University of Tennessee, Knoxville, is composed of eleven colleges (ten offering undergraduate degrees): Agriculture and Natural Resources, Architecture and Planning, Arts and Sciences, Business, Communications, Education, Engineering, Human Ecology, Law, Nursing, and Social Work. There are 107 undergraduate and 156 graduate/professional degree programs offered on campus.

Among the facilities available to all students are the University Center (study, cultural events, speakers, and cafeterias), Clarence Brown Theatre and Carousel Theatre (campus and professional theatrical productions), Music Hall (faculty, student, and visiting musical productions), International House (cultural programs and study and conference areas), and Center for International Education (study-abroad programs and international students).

Student Body Undergraduate enrollment is 18,735, equally divided between men and women. The ethnic distribution among students is 90 percent white, 5 percent African American, 1 percent Hispanic, and 3 percent Asian. There are 900 international students. Thirty-five percent of the students are residents, and 60 percent of students receive financial aid. There are twenty-five fraternities and sixteen sororities.

Faculty Of the 1,304 faculty members, 1,100 are full-time. Eighty-seven percent have terminal degrees. The student-faculty ratio is 17:1 (includes graduate students).

Key Facilities The library houses more than 2 million volumes. Computer facilities include a UNIX system and remote labs (PC and Mac) in residence halls, five classroom buildings, and the main library. Most academic departments have computing labs for majors. University Honors has three rooms (two are reservable) with PCs and Macs.

Athletics The University of Tennessee, Knoxville, is an NCAA Division I school and a member of the Southeastern Conference. Men's varsity sports are baseball, basketball, football, golf, swimming and diving, tennis, and track and cross-country. Women's varsity sports are basketball, crew, golf, soccer, softball, swimming and diving, tennis, track and cross-country, and volleyball. Sports clubs (intramurals) accommodate participants in twenty-two men's and twenty-three women's sports.

Study Abroad The University is a participating institution in ISEP (International Student Exchange Program) and maintains information on numerous academic exchange and study-abroad programs. Two regularly offered programs at UTK are Normandy Scholars (intensive study during spring semester, study at Caen during the summer) and Semester in Wales (at Swansea during each fall semester).

Support Services The Office of Disability Services coordinates support for students who need assistance, including transportation on campus, handicapped parking facilities, audio taping, and compliance with access to facilities mandated by the Americans with Disabilities Act.

Job Opportunities The Office of Financial Aid maintains listings of employment opportunities for students and coordinates the Federal Work-Study Program. Students also may be employed on research contracts and grants through academic departments.

Tuition: $2060 for state residents, $6416 for nonresidents, per year (1996-97)

Room and Board: $3620

Mandatory Fees: $140

Contact: Director: Dr. Thomas W. Broadhead, Knoxville, Tennessee 37996-1410; Telephone: 423-974-7875; Fax: 423-974-4784; E-mail: twbroadhead@utk.edu; Web site: http://honors.asa.utk.edu

THE UNIVERSITY OF TEXAS AT ARLINGTON

4 Pu G M Sc Tr

▼ UTA Honors Program

The Honors Program at the University of Texas at Arlington is a community of exceptionally able and highly motivated students who want the excitement and stimulation of a major urban university and the individual attention available at a smaller college. Having as its purpose the promotion of a general spirit of inquiry among students and faculty, the Honors Program sets the standard of academic excellence for the University.

Honors scholars study together in interdisciplinary team-taught courses, honors sections of lower-division requirements, advanced honors courses in disciplinary majors, and honors seminars and colloquia. Sameness and Difference, the Role of the Outsider, Innocence and Experience, Gods and Heroes in Western and Non-Western Cultures, Origins: Scientific and Mythological Constructions, Rituals and Symbols of Power, and Women, Men, and the Family are recent examples. Two new interdisciplinary courses will expand offerings to include science and technology: a two-course sequence in writing, technology, and design and an integrated sciences course. The honors thesis is the culmination of work in the major and draws on experiences from the Honors Program. The program is compatible with any major, and all honors course offerings fulfill core, departmental, and/or college requirements.

The honors curriculum is designed to offer a special interdisciplinary emphasis at each level of the student's academic career. Through an ancient/modern/postmodern world studies sequence, the freshman core sequence explores world cultures from a variety of disciplinary perspectives and critical methodologies across topics and themes of current and enduring interest.

Integrated Sciences is a team-taught, multidisciplinary science course offering study in the methodologies, scope, and interrelatedness of the sciences in their respective searches for knowledge. This course meets a non–lab science requirement for nonscience majors and an elective science requirement for science majors. Honors freshmen may also choose from honors sections of science courses in mathematics, biology, chemistry, geology, and physics.

During the sophomore year, honors students follow an American studies sequence and study American history, literature, politics, and culture in a series of courses organized in a cohort configuration with special guest lectures and small group discussions. The sequence fulfills department, college, and University requirements in history, literature, and political science.

During the junior year, students take the junior research colloquium, which is a research methods course that initiates the thesis/project. Students work collaboratively to choose thesis topics, select thesis advisers, and complete abstracts and annotated bibliographies. Heavy emphasis is placed on group critiques and on the use of technology to locate and develop source material.

The honors senior thesis/project is the culmination of the student's University career. It draws on the student's work in the major discipline and on the interdisciplinary experiences in the Honors Program. Hypermedia theses/projects are encouraged, and students are urged to submit projects for publication.

The final course in the Honors Program is the senior seminar, which is designed around an issue or issues of current significance. Honors students are expected to contribute to the seminar from their experiences in the program and from their in-depth research.

In addition to a challenging curriculum, the Honors Program regularly schedules a variety of social and intellectual activities that extend learning experiences beyond the classroom, including informal gatherings, lecture series, and artistic performances. The Honors Student Advisory Council (HSAC), elected from the honors student body, the Honors Faculty Advisory Council (HFAC), and the director are responsible for the ongoing operation of the Honors Program.

Created in 1978 with approximately 30 students, the UTA Honors Program enrollment is currently 450 students or 2.5 percent of the undergraduate student population. The University's goal is to increase enrollment in the Honors Program to 5–10 percent over the next three years.

Participation Requirements: UTA does not offer honors degrees; degrees are awarded by the major departments of the University's colleges and schools. To graduate as an Honors Scholar with a bachelor's degree, honors students must complete the degree requirements in a disciplinary major to include at least 24 hours of honors course work overall, at least one honors core course (3 hours), the honors junior colloquium (recommended, 3 hours), the honors senior seminar (recommended, 3 hours), the honors senior thesis (3 hours), and at least 9 hours of advanced honors course work in the major. Students must maintain an overall GPA of 3.0. Continuing UTA students who join the Honors Program and transfer honors students are not required to complete the core course.

Admission Process: The Honors Program seeks students with broad interests, varied talents, and diverse cultural backgrounds. Admission is competitive. Entering freshman honors candidates must have a combined SAT I score of 1180 or an ACT score of 27 and be in the upper 25 percent of their high school graduating class. Continuing and transfer honors candidates must have a minimum 3.0 GPA. Admission, however, is not based solely on grades or scores; the Admissions Committee considers faculty recommendations and student statements of purpose in the selection of candidates.

Scholarship Availability: The Honors Program, in conjunction with the UTA Scholarship Office, awards a number of Honors Presidential Scholarships each year. Departmental and organizational scholarships and financial aid are also available.

The Campus Context: Located in the heart of the Dallas/Fort Worth metropolitan area, one of the fastest-growing areas in the nation, the University of Texas at Arlington has emerged as a comprehensive educational and research university organized into nine units: College of Business Administration, College of Engineering, College of Liberal Arts, College of Science, School of Architecture, School of Nursing, School of Social Work, School of Urban and Public Affairs, and Center for Professional Teacher Education.

UTA ranks among the nation's top fifty schools in the graduation of engineering professionals, the University's Energy Systems Research Center is consistently rated as one of the nation's top ten, and UTA was chosen as one of NASA's three sites for research in hypersonic aircraft. Eighty-seven percent of the University's applicants are accepted into medical schools. The wheelchair basketball team, the Movin' Mavs, holds ten current world records, and the University's wheelchair athletes have won more than 150 gold medals in international track competitions. The *Shorthorn*, the school newspaper, was named best college newspaper by the Rocky Mountain Collegiate Press Association. Out of ninety-three M.S.W. programs nationwide, the School of Social Work was ranked ninth in faculty productivity/publications, and the School of Urban and Public Affairs was rated the fourth-best program of its kind in the nation.

Student Body The second-largest component of the University of Texas system, UTA enrolls about 21,000 students, of whom approximately 16,000 are undergraduate. Fifty-one percent of the student body are women. Sixty-seven percent are Anglo, 9.9 percent are African American, 10 percent are Asian American, 8.5 percent are Mexican American, and .5 percent are Native American. The international student population is 1,355. Approximately 10 percent of UTA's students live on campus; 90 percent are commuters. About 30 percent receive financial aid. UTA is home to thirty honor societies in addition to fourteen national fraternities and eight national sororities.

Faculty UTA employs 1,668 faculty members, of whom 642 are full-time. Of the full-time faculty members, 78.9 percent hold terminal degrees. More than 12 percent of part-time faculty members hold terminal degrees. Excluding graduate teaching assistants, the student-faculty ratio is 27:1; including GTAs the ratio is 17:1. Faculty members teach in fifty-five undergraduate, fifty-eight master's, and nineteen doctoral programs.

Key Facilities The library contains more than 1.7 million books, microforms, government documents, maps, and technical reports and subscribes to more than 5,500 current journals and serials. It holds one of the nation's most extensive Texas and Gulf Coast cartography collections and was designated as the depository for more than 1 million U.S. Nuclear Regulatory Commission documents and photos.

Athletics All men's and women's intercollegiate teams are members of the Southland Conference. All teams compete in Division I of the National Collegiate Athletic Association. Teams are fielded in men's baseball, basketball, cross-country, golf, tennis, track and field, and wheelchair basketball and in women's basketball, cross-country, softball, tennis, track and field, and volleyball.

Study Abroad UTA offers twenty study-abroad and student exchange programs located in ten different countries worldwide.

Support Services The Office for Students with Disabilities ensures equal opportunity and access to all programs and activities on campus and offers specially designed services for specific disabilities.

Job Opportunities The Offices of Student Employment Services and Human Resources make available to all students current job listings, including work-study and non–work-study positions, internships, and teaching and research assistantships. Through these offices at least 1,200 work-study and non–work-study students are employed on campus, and approximately 3,425 students are employed off campus.

Tuition: $960 for state residents, $7380 for nonresidents, per year (1996-97)

Room and Board: $2900

Mandatory Fees: $1261

Contact: Director: Carolyn A. Barros, Box 19419, Arlington, Texas 76019; Telephone: 817-272-2338; Fax: 817-272-3156; E-mail: honors@uta.edu; Web site: http://www.uta.edu/hons/

THE UNIVERSITY OF TEXAS AT AUSTIN

4 Pu C M Sc Tr

▼ Business Honors Program

The Business Honors Program (BHP) is an innovative degree program providing intellectual challenge and professional development for a select group of outstanding students in the College of Business (CBA). The program offers an intense educational experience to enhance the student's academic and leadership potential.

The core of the BHP consists of twelve courses taught at an advanced level by experienced professors. In addition to excellent academic credentials, these professors bring a wealth of business experience to the classroom. Modeled after graduate business courses, the curriculum emphasizes discussion, case-study, and research of actual business situations. Students are exposed to leading-edge theories and examples of the best business practices. This hands-on approach utilizes team projects with written proposals and oral and multimedia presentations. Students also have opportunities to represent the University at national conferences and international case competitions. While course size is limited to enhance interaction and cohesiveness, the program has recently grown and currently consists of about 100 students in each of the four classes.

Established in 1964, the Business Honors Program has consistently broadened students' academic experiences while providing preparation for immediate entry into challenging business careers or graduate study. The select nature and size of the BHP provides students with many advantages of a smaller college while utilizing the outstanding faculty and resources of a world-class university. BHP students are able to double major in the CBA. The second major could include accounting, engineering route to business, finance, international business, management, management information systems, marketing, or the professional program in accounting (a five-year concurrent B.B.A./M.B.A. program). They may also combine Business Honors with another major outside the CBA, such as economics, government, history, or the Plan II Honors program in the College of Liberal Arts.

The BHP is coordinated by a faculty director, a program administrator, and specially appointed counselors to advise students about degree planning, course scheduling, career opportunities, summer internships, résumé writing, and interviewing principles. Students benefit from a growing international network of alumni who hold important positions in areas such as investment banking, management consulting, public accounting, and law.

Admission Process: Freshman admission is based upon high school ranking, SAT scores, leadership in organizations, and extracurricular events. A business résumé, essay, and current recommendations are required to complete the admission packet. Successful applicants will demonstrate the ability to balance outstanding academics with the leadership skills necessary in business. Emphasis shifts to earned GPA, rigor of course work, and leadership for those applying at the end of the first year in college. Transfer admission is very limited and only for students entering as sophomores.

The deadline for admission for freshmen is February 1 and May 1 for internal transfers (sophomore).

The Campus Context: Founded in 1883, the University of Texas at Austin has grown into a campus of 350 acres with a student body of 38,000 undergraduate students and 12,000 graduate students. Undergraduates may choose courses from more than 160 fields of study, supported by extensive computer facilities and one of the largest academic libraries in the nation. The city of Austin, with a population of about 500,000, is a green and cosmopolitan setting for the University. Students benefit from both the local communities in arts—dance, music, theater, and the visual arts—and the numerous recreational activities made possible by the temperate climate of the hill country of central Texas.

Tuition: $960 for state residents, $7380 for nonresidents, per year (1996-97)

Room and Board: $4550

Mandatory Fees: $1652

Contact: Director: Dr. Eli Cox III, GSB 3.142, Austin, Texas 78712; E-mail: epciii@ccwf.cc.utexas.edu; Administrator: Wm. Kyle Villyard; E-mail: kyle.v@mail.utexas.edu, Telephone: 512-475-6325; Fax: 512-471-2388

THE UNIVERSITY OF TEXAS AT AUSTIN

4 Pu C M Sc Tr

▼ The Dean's Scholars Program

The Dean's Scholars Program is founded on the principle that the challenge of education is to understand nature and humanity's part in it. As such, the investigation of nature must be the common quest for students and faculty alike. Science is one of the most important intellectual achievements of human history; it is also a central determiner of human development. The Dean's Scholars Program desires students interested in individual discovery and in acquiring a broad view of how science fits into the community—the broad view necessary for assuming important scientific careers and, eventually, leadership positions in the scientific community.

The Dean's Scholars Honors Program offers exceptional science and mathematics majors a unique opportunity to enrich their undergraduate education in the College of Natural Sciences at the University of Texas at Austin. Since 1983, the program has challenged talented and highly motivated undergraduates by introducing them to cutting-edge research and placing them into contact with superior students with similar aptitudes and interests. Dean's Scholars experience the dual advantage of involving themselves in a smaller group of select students while enjoying the opportunities of a large institution. The Dean's Scholars Program is thirteen years old and currently has 125 students participating.

Participation Requirements: Each student is required to attend a weekly seminar and maintain a 3.3 GPA. Eventually all students engage in research activities.

Participation in the Dean's Scholars Program, which continues throughout an undergraduate's career at UT, offers a number of important advantages. Specifically, students work directly with faculty members involved at the forefront of scientific research. Students pursue their own research projects under the direction of distinguished faculty members and pursue any of the more than thirty majors offered by departments within the College of Natural Sciences. Some students are also enrolled in the Plan II Honors Program, where they gain an important research perspective. Dean's Scholars view science as dynamic: the living, changing exploration of nature.

Perhaps the most rewarding aspect of the program is the opportunity for superior students representing diverse majors to interact with each other through academic pursuits and frequent informal social activities. In weekly seminars, Dean's Scholars explore contemporary issues and ideas in science and are introduced to the research activities of the faculty. These seminars are supplemented by weekly, informal lunches attended by faculty members from throughout the University community. Weekend field trips traditionally include visits to the McDonald Observatory in the Davis Mountains and to the Marine Science Institute at Port Aransas. Through these and other special activities, Dean's Scholars gain an appreciation for the research of their fellow students and more fully recognize how their own individual research fits into the entire scientific enterprise.

Recent graduates of the Dean's Scholars Program have entered Ph.D. programs in scientific disciplines at leading institutions worldwide. Some have entered M.D./Ph.D. programs. In addition, Dean's Scholars have won some of the most prestigious and competitive graduate fellowships, including Marshall Scholarships for study at Cambridge University and National Science Foundation Fellowships.

Admission Process: The Dean's Scholars Program is highly selective, admitting about 30 freshmen each year as well as a small number of upperclass students. Dean's Scholars seek the intellectual challenge and stimulation of an interdisciplinary program emphasizing scientific research. Although Dean's Scholars typically achieve high SAT scores and class ranking, admission is not based solely on these criteria, but more important, on evidence of a student's interest in science, research, and individual discovery. As Dean's Scholars, students are oriented toward research, encouraged through their work to perceive the world as presenting questions that can be answered through experimentation.

Applications must be submitted by February 15.

The Campus Context: Founded in 1883, the University of Texas at Austin has grown into a campus of 350 acres with a student body of 38,000 undergraduates and 12,000 graduates. Undergraduates may choose courses from more than 160 fields of study, supported by extensive computer facilities and one of the largest academic libraries in the nation. The city of Austin, with a population of about 500,000, is a green and cosmopolitan setting for the University. Students benefit from both the local communities in arts—dance, music, theater, and the visual arts—and the numerous recreational activities made possible by the temperate climate of the hill country of central Texas.

Tuition: $960 for state residents, $7380 for nonresidents, per year (1996-97)

Room and Board: $4550

Mandatory Fees: $1652

Contact: Directors: Dr. Alan Kaylor Cline and Dr. David Bruton Jr., The College of Natural Sciences, Austin, Texas 78712; Telephone: 512-471-4536; Fax: 512-471-4998; E-mail: cline@cs.utexas.edu; Web site: http://www.cs.utexas.edu/users/cline/dsbrochure.html

THE UNIVERSITY OF TEXAS AT AUSTIN

4 Pu C L Sc Tr

▼ Engineering Honors Program

The Engineering Honors Program at the University of Texas at Austin presents an opportunity for exceptional high school students who have excelled in science and mathematics to apply for admission to the Freshman Engineering Honors Program. They may continue beyond the first year through the Engineering Honors Program if they exhibit high academic performance and meet other criteria established by the Engineering Honors Committee. Approximately 1,000 students are currently enrolled in the program.

Participation Requirements: After the first year, a limited number of sophomore through senior engineering students who demonstrate exceptional academic ability participate in the Engineering Honors Program. The Engineering Honors Committee selects students who are then encouraged to pursue guided independent study and research. To be eligible, a student must be in the top 10 percent of his or her classification and degree plan and must meet other criteria established by the Engineering Honors Committee. To remain in the program, a student must continuously meet the academic standards established by the committee. A student must maintain an overall GPA after each long semester that ranks in the top 10 percent of his or her degree plan class with the following exception: If a student's overall GPA falls below the 10 percent requirement, but is 3.5 or greater, the student will have one long semester to reestablish his or her GPA in the top 10 percent. If after one long semester the student's GPA is still below the required 10 percent, he or she will not be allowed to participate in the program; if at the end of a long semester a student's overall GPA falls below 3.5 and he or she is not in the top 10 percent of the degree plan class, he or she will not be allowed to participate in the program.

The Engineering Honors Program provides special academic advising for each honors student. Each department appoints a faculty adviser to provide individual guidance to honors students. Faculty advisers help students explore educational opportunities and develop their intellectual potential in the College of Engineering.

A limited number of students whose high school class standing and admission test scores indicate strong academic potential and motivation may pursue both a B.S. in engineering and a B.A. through the Liberal Arts Plan II Honors Program. This dual-degree option, offered jointly by the College of Engineering and the College of Liberal Arts, provides a student with challenging liberal arts courses while he or she pursues a professional degree in engineering. Admission to this program requires three separate applications: one to UT Austin, one to the Plan II Honors Program, and one to the College of Engineering. Students interested in this dual-degree plan option should contact both the College of Engineering Office of Student Affairs and the Liberal Arts Plan II Honors Program Office for more information on applications and early deadlines.

Honors students may enroll in special sections of calculus, English, physics, and engineering classes taught by eminent faculty members renowned for teaching excellence and empathy for students. Course material covered in honors sections is generally identical to that in regular sections. However, honors sections provide subject enrichment opportunities not available in regular sections, including supervised independent study and participation in research activities.

The Department of Chemical Engineering offers a four-year honors curriculum with honors sections of selected courses offered once a year. Chemical engineering students who complete the Freshman Engineering Honors Program and maintain a GPA of at least 3.5 may participate in the honors curriculum. Other chemical engineering students who achieve outstanding scholastic records at UT Austin are also eligible. Honors sections of selected chemical engineering courses are offered each year. These sections cover the same material as regular sections, but provide a stimulating environment conducive to higher-level discussion.

Admission Process: The College of Engineering accepts up to 10 percent of the entering freshman class into the Freshman Engineering Honors Program. This first-year honors program recognizes students whose high school records and scores in college entrance examinations indicate they have an excellent chance of becoming engineering scholars. Although all students follow the same basic curriculum, special sections taught by outstanding teachers are arranged for students in the program.

Eligibility for the program is determined by the applicant's scholastic rank in high school, SAT or ACT score, scores on the College Board SAT II: Subject Tests in Mathematics Level I (or Level II) and in Writing, and written comments submitted by high school teachers. Preferential consideration is given to applicants enrolled in Advanced Placement calculus, valedictorians or salutatorians, and/or National Merit Scholars. Students with SAT I scores of 1350 and above are encouraged to apply for this program. Applicants of exceptional merit will be considered for early admission. Approximately 10 percent (100 students) of the entering freshman class are admitted to the Freshman Engineering Honors Program.

Transfer students may participate in the program after they have completed 24 semester hours of UT Austin course work applicable to their degrees. Transfer students must be in the top 10 percent of their classification and degree plan. To continue in the program, a student must maintain the academic standards established by the Engineering Honors Committee.

Scholarship Availability: The College of Engineering offers financial assistance for a substantial number of its students through an extensive scholarship program. The majority of the scholarships granted by the College are awarded on a competitive basis. The majority of the scholarships are awarded based on standardized test scores, high school class rank, high school curriculum, and extracurricular activities. Some scholarships have other specific criteria that are determined by the company funding the scholarship. The value of the scholarships ranges from $500 to $9000 per year, with the majority in the $2000 range. Most of the scholarships are renewable for up to four years as long as academic standards are maintained. Academic standards vary depending on the size of the scholarship and/or the source of funds. The College of Engineering uses the UT Freshman Scholarship Application. If the applicant lists engineering as the major, the scholarship application is forwarded to the College for

consideration. February 15 is the priority deadline. Applications will be accepted after this date; however, they will not be considered until all other previous applications have been considered.

Engineering honor societies recognize students who maintain outstanding scholastic records and demonstrate desirable character and personality traits. Honor societies frequently support projects that aid students and benefit the College of Engineering. Embracing all branches of engineering is the Texas Alpha Chapter of Tau Beta Pi, which was organized at UT Austin in 1916. Only students in the upper fifth of the senior class or the upper eighth of the junior class, as well as a few graduate students, qualify scholastically for membership. Character and personality traits are also considered in selecting new members. The chapter generally elects fewer members than the number of eligible students. Engineering students are also eligible for membership in Phi Kappa Phi, a national academic honor society that elects its membership from the top few percent of the entire student body, and in the Golden Key National Honor Society. Each branch of engineering belongs to a chapter of a national honor society.

The Campus Context: Founded in 1883, the University of Texas at Austin has grown into a campus of 350 acres with a student body of 38,000 undergraduates and 12,000 graduates. Undergraduates may choose courses from more than 160 fields of study, supported by extensive computer facilities and one of the largest academic libraries in the nation. The city of Austin, with a population of about 500,000, is a green and cosmopolitan setting for the University. Students benefit from both the local communities in arts—dance, music, theater, and the visual arts—and the numerous recreational activities made possible by the temperate climate of the hill country of central Texas.

Tuition: $960 for state residents, $7380 for nonresidents, per year (1996-97)

Room and Board: $4550

Mandatory Fees: $1652

Contact: Director: Dr. Alvin H. Meyer, College of Engineering, Ernest Cockrell Jr. Hall 2.200, Austin, Texas 78712-1080; Telephone: 512-471-4321; Fax: 512-475-6893; E-mail: engrsao@mail.utexas.edu

---

THE UNIVERSITY OF TEXAS AT AUSTIN

    4 Pu C S Sc Tr

▼ Humanities Honors Program

The Humanities Program offers able and highly motivated students the opportunity to design an independent course of study dedicated to a theme, topic, culture, period, or question that cannot be adequately pursued through a single departmental major. In consultation with the humanities staff, those accepted into this honors program plan a major tailored to their unique intellectual interests that consists of 43 hours beyond the basic education requirement of the University.

A premedical student, for example, might focus on medical ethics and create a major with courses in philosophy, zoology, nursing, sociology, and anthropology. A student interested in the history of ideas might compose a major from courses in history, religious studies, philosophy, English literature, and art history. Someone who anticipates a career in foreign service might focus on relations between cultures and combine courses in government with Middle Eastern studies, foreign languages, journalism, and anthropology. Humanities students often study abroad for one or two semesters, integrating international course work into their contracts in the program. The possibilities are as broad as one's abilities, interests, and imagination.

Founded in 1975, the program currently enrolls approximately 60 students.

Admission Process: Humanities majors normally apply to the program during the sophomore year, but freshmen are particularly encouraged to initiate the consultations that precede admission. Humanities ordinarily expects a minimum 3.35 GPA for admission. In addition to the GPA requirement, a student composes a four-page letter to the director defining the objectives, general plan of study, and central subject areas of the proposed degree program. This letter, essentially an intellectual autobiography and an exposition of interests, goals, items of personal curiosity, and related readings, is the foundation for all subsequent planning. Several revisions of this document may be required to bring the student's intentions, assumptions, and interests into focus. Successful applicants devise a contract degree plan with the Director that is grounded in their definition and successful explanation of intellectual goals and motivations. It is not necessary or even desirable to list courses or plan a curriculum in advance. Proposals for the senior thesis are not made until the senior year.

This is an interdisciplinary program in which students pursue goals that would be difficult or impossible in standard majors.

Scholarship Availability: Partial tuition scholarships and work opportunities are available.

The Campus Context: Founded in 1883, the University of Texas at Austin has grown into a campus of 350 acres with a student body of 38,000 undergraduates and 12,000 graduates. Undergraduates may choose courses from more than 160 fields of study, supported by extensive computer facilities and one of the largest academic libraries in the nation. The city of Austin, with a population of about 500,000, is a green and cosmopolitan setting for the University. Students benefit from both the local communities in arts—dance, music, theater, and the visual arts—and the numerous recreational activities made possible by the temperate climate of the hill country of central Texas.

Tuition: $960 for state residents, $7380 for nonresidents, per year (1996-97)

Room and Board: $4550

Mandatory Fees: $1652

Contact: Director: Dr. Norman Farmer, College of Liberal Arts, West Mall Building 3.114, Austin, Texas 78712; Telephone: 512-475-6747; Fax: 512-471-5393; E-mail: nfarmer@mail.utexas. edu; Web site: http://www.dla.utexas.edu/depts/humanities/

THE UNIVERSITY OF TEXAS AT AUSTIN

4 Pu C M Sc

▼ College of Pharmacy

Some undergraduate pharmacy students look for educational stimulation and challenge beyond the traditional undergraduate curriculum. To enrich the educational experience of these outstanding students, the College offers an undergraduate honors program. This selective program is designed to challenge the participants, introduce them to new ideas, and place them into close contact with others who have similar aptitudes and interests. A special feature of the Honors Program is the completion of a two-semester research project under the direct supervision of a faculty member of the student's choice concluding with a seminar presentation.

The College of Pharmacy is one of thirteen colleges at the University of Texas at Austin. One hundred twenty-five students enroll per year. A five-year B.S. degree program and a six-year Pharm.D. program are offered. In addition, M.S. and Ph.D. degrees are offered in five subdisciplines within pharmacy.

The program began six years ago and admits 10 to 15 students each year.

Participation Requirements: A 1-semester-credit-hour honors course is offered by each of the five divisions within the College of Pharmacy. In order to complete the core honors course requirements, the honors student must select at least two of the five courses. In addition, the honors student must complete at least two honors elective courses. Students also must enroll in the Honors Tutorial, a two-semester sequence of courses that includes conducting a research project and presenting the completed work during the Honors Seminar. Although the honors students are expected to attend the Honors Seminar each semester that they participate in the program, they will receive credit during the semester in which they present their research project.

Honors students graduate with Special Honors, a distinction that appears on their transcript.

Scholarship Availability: Honors students are encouraged to apply for professional and government-sponsored undergraduate research fellowships as well as scholarships available through the College of Pharmacy.

The Campus Context: Founded in 1883, the University of Texas at Austin has grown into a campus of 350 acres with a student body of 38,000 undergraduates and 12,000 graduates. Undergraduates may choose courses from more than 160 fields of study, supported by extensive computer facilities and one of the largest academic libraries in the nation. The city of Austin, with a population of about 500,000, is a green and cosmopolitan setting for the University. Students benefit from both the local communities in arts—dance, music, theater, and the visual arts—and the numerous recreational activities made possible by the temperate climate of the hill country of central Texas.

Tuition: $960 for state residents, $7380 for nonresidents, per year (1996-97)

Room and Board: $4550

Mandatory Fees: $1652

Contact: Director: Joanne Richards, Undergraduate Honors Program, Austin, Texas 78712-1074; Telephone: 512-471-1737; Fax: 512-471-8783; E-mail: joanne-r@uts.cc.utexas.edu

---

THE UNIVERSITY OF TEXAS AT AUSTIN

4 Pu C M Tr

▼ Plan I Liberal Arts Honors Program

Plan I Honors comprises all the various honors opportunities in the College of Liberal Arts available to Plan I students. These include honors courses from the freshman to the senior year, the Liberal Arts Honors Program, and departmental honors programs. Students are encouraged to begin their honors work in the freshman year, though they may wait until the end of the sophomore or beginning of the junior year. Upper-division students who are eligible for the Liberal Arts Honors Program will be notified at the end of their sophomore year and begin taking courses in the junior year.

Plan I Honors is designed for students who desire flexibility and choice in their honors work and who want to pursue an honors degree in a particular discipline. During the freshman and sophomore years, students have the opportunity to enroll in special 1-hour classes, have access to supplemental academic advising, and may take honors sections of the basic educational requirement courses. This freshman and sophomore year experience prepares students for honors work in the Liberal Arts Honors Program or one of the College's departmental honors programs.

A key component of Plan I Honors is academic advising. Freshmen and sophomores in Plan I Honors are provided with the consistent and caring advising they need to plan for the upper-division work that will lead to their honors certification.

Plan I Honors provides two introductory courses for prospective honors majors, taken in the first semester of the freshman year and the first semester of the sophomore year. Both courses cultivate students for upper-division honors work. The Idea of the Liberal Arts, taken in the freshman year, features weekly lectures by some of the College's best teachers; they discuss what it means to study their disciplines, what is new in their fields, and what career opportunities open up to those who pursue their particular major. The Nature of Inquiry allows students to extend their contact with the College faculty and examine more closely how scholars in the liberal arts pursue their research.

Students in Plan I Honors have the opportunity to enroll in honors sections of the basic educational requirement courses such as English, social sciences, foreign languages, and humanities. These sections are identified in the course schedule each semester.

The Liberal Arts Honors Program (LAH) is a series of upper-division interdisciplinary courses taught by award-winning faculty members and designed to provide students with a capstone experience in which they enrich their majors and relate them to other disciplines.

Each department within the College also has its own honors program and honors adviser. These programs afford students with upper-division standing the opportunity to take tutorial courses, write a senior thesis supervised by a faculty mentor, and in many departments, enroll in seminar courses. Many departments offer their honors students a variety of opportunities to meet with faculty members and other honors majors, as well as assistance with applications for fellowships and study abroad, field trips, and seminars. Plan I Honors began six years ago, and approximately 175 students will be admitted for the fall. The program currently enrolls 500 students.

Admission Process: Admission to the freshman/sophomore program is by application, and eligibility to apply is based on high school record and SAT scores. Applications may be obtained from the Liberal Arts Honors Plan I office.

For the LAH Certification Program for juniors and seniors, there is no application process. Liberal Arts Plan I majors with a minimum 3.35 GPA and 60 or more hours in residence are eligible to register for the LAH courses using the telephone registration system. Liberal Arts Honors are awarded upon graduation to students who have earned a B or better in at least three of the LAH courses and who have maintained a 3.5 overall GPA at the University.

Departmental honors generally requires a minimum 3.0 overall GPA and a departmental GPA of 3.5 or better for admission. Students who excel in their course work, senior thesis, and senior examination are awarded special honors in their major upon graduation.

Scholarship Availability: There are no scholarships affiliated with the program, but many of the participating students are holders of University scholarships.

Awards: The director, faculty, and staff have all received awards pertaining to their specific roles. The program has been nominated for a Templeton Honor Roll Award through the Intercollegiate Studies Institute.

Mission Statement: The Honors Programs in the College of Liberal Arts afford students many and varied opportunities to enrich their academic experience. Each serves different student needs and approaches intellectual frontiers by different routes, but both encourage independent creative study, individual work with faculty members, and freedom to pursue one's academic adventure wherever it may lead. Some of these opportunities consist of specially designed courses, some allow students to follow a special major, and still others complement existing majors. This diverse program is specifically designed to allow as many as possible of the bright, highly motivated students who attend this large research university to engage in an enhanced course of study.

The Campus Context: Founded in 1883, the University of Texas at Austin has grown into a campus of 350 acres with a student body of 38,000 undergraduates and 12,000 graduates. Undergraduates may choose courses from more than 160 fields of study, supported by extensive computer facilities and one of the largest academic libraries in the nation. The city of Austin, with a population of about 500,000, is a green and cosmopolitan setting for the University. Students benefit from both the local communities in arts—dance, music, theater, and the visual arts—and the numerous recreational activities made possible by the temperate climate of the hill country of central Texas.

Tuition: $960 for state residents, $7380 for nonresidents, per year (1996-97)

Room and Board: $4550

Mandatory Fees: $1652

Contact: Director: Bob Abzug, Professor, College of Liberal Arts, WMB 3.120, Austin, Texas 78712-1105; Telephone: 512-471-3458; Fax: 512-471-5393; E-mail: declerck@mail.utexas.edu; Web site: http://www.dla.utexas.edu/courses/special/lah/

THE UNIVERSITY OF TEXAS AT AUSTIN

4 Pu G L Sc Tr

▼ Plan II Honors Program

The Plan II Honors Program, established sixty years ago at the University of Texas at Austin, is a challenging interdisciplinary curriculum leading to the Bachelor of Arts degree. Plan II differs from most honors programs in that its core curriculum is itself a major consisting of courses especially designed for Plan II students in the humanities, sciences, and social sciences. The courses constitute about a third of a Plan II students' course work. Students take the remainder of their general requirements and their electives from the regular list of University courses.

The flexibility of the Plan II curriculum allows students to complete the equivalent of a second major in a particular subject area if they so choose. Many students complete a premedical curriculum or prelaw curriculum in conjunction with their Plan II major or take courses in business or communication as preparation for careers in those areas. Some Plan II students actually earn a second degree in areas such as engineering, architecture, or business by using electives to fulfill the requirements.

Plan II attracts students seeking the advantages of a small liberal arts college and the resources and diversity of a large university. Plan II prides itself on having top-notch professors teaching first-year courses. Plan II students get to know their professors and each other in small classes, especially in the world literature class and the interdisciplinary seminars. Two full-time academic advisers are available throughout the semester to help students with selecting courses, determining areas of concentration, setting long-term academic or career goals, or simply adjusting to college life. The director, associate director, and other professors are active as faculty advisers. Peer advisers are also on duty daily to assist students with routine matters.

Students often talk about the sense of community they feel in Plan II. The office is a home-base for students who come in to use the computers or typewriters, check out the latest announcements on the bulletin boards, or simply chat with each other or a staff member. The Plan II Students Association sponsors coffees and book discussion groups with faculty members, monthly newsletters, a theater group, a freshman retreat to a Texas hill country ranch, and occasional picnics and parties.

There are 750 students enrolled in the program.

Admission Process: Admission to Plan II is competitive and is separate from admission to UT Austin. All applicants must write essays and provide information about their academic and extracurricular accomplishments. This year more than 1,100 applications were received for the 175 places in the Plan II freshman class. The average SAT I score of the incoming class is in the mid-1400s, and nearly 80 percent graduated in the top fifth of their high school class. However, admission to Plan II is not based on scores and grades alone; other criteria include a lively spirit of intellectual adventure, strong writing skills, or exceptional analytic or imaginative abilities.

The program admits a small number of transfer students in the spring of the freshman year and fall of the sophomore year.

The deadline for applying is January 20.

Scholarship Availability: Plan II has a limited number of scholarships, which it awards on a need/merit basis to continuing students. Many students in the program receive National Merit scholarships from the University.

The Campus Context: Founded in 1883, the University of Texas at Austin has grown into a campus of 350 acres with a student body of 38,000 undergraduates and 12,000 graduates. Undergraduates may choose courses from more than 160 fields of study, supported by extensive computer facilities and one of the largest academic libraries in the nation. The city of Austin, with a population of about 500,000, is a green and cosmopolitan setting for the University. Students benefit from both the local communities in arts—dance, music, theater, and the visual arts—and the numerous recreational activities made possible by the temperate climate of the hill country of central Texas.

Tuition: $960 for state residents, $7380 for nonresidents, per year (1996-97)

Room and Board: $4550

Mandatory Fees: $1652

Contact: Director: Dr. Paul Woodruff, College of Liberal Arts, W. C. Hogg Building, Suite 4.104, Austin, Texas 78712-1105; Telephone: 512-471-1442; Fax: 512-471-7449; E-mail: planii@ utxvms.cc.utexas.edu; Assistant Director: Karen Bordelon, kjb@ mail.utexas.edu; Web site: http://www.dla.utexas.edu/~plan2/

THE UNIVERSITY OF TEXAS AT AUSTIN

4 Pu C M

▼ Senior Fellows Program

The Senior Fellows Program is a College-wide honors program that is a broad, interdisciplinary supplement to the various departmental majors in the College of Communication. The program is designed for students with the talent and interest to go beyond the usual undergraduate experience. Senior Fellows enroll in four seminars taught by specially chosen members of the faculty in the College of Communication. These courses differ from traditional undergraduate classes in several ways: Only Senior Fellows are allowed to enroll in the seminars; enrollment for a given seminar is limited to 15–20 students; the seminars are discussion oriented; they cross the usual department boundaries; they treat subjects normally not encountered in the undergraduate curriculum; and they emphasize original thinking, interesting reading, and intensive interaction with members of the faculty. Senior Fellows do carry a regular major in one of the depart-

ments of the College; Senior Fellows courses in most cases substitute for upper-division requirements.

The program began nine years ago, and 30 students per year are admitted for a one-year or two-year sequence. Current enrollment is 450. During graduation ceremonies, graduating Senior Fellows receive a medallion of honor.

Admission Process: Junior or senior standing is required. To be selected for the program, juniors must have a GPA of at least 3.3 and have completed 45 hours of course work at the University at the time of application (spring) and 60 hours at the time of enrollment (fall). Those who begin the program as seniors must have completed 75 hours of course work at the time of application (spring) and 90 hours at the time of enrollment (fall) and have achieved a GPA of at least 3.3 in their course work at the University.

March 6 is the deadline for applying.

Scholarship Availability: There are no scholarships for the Senior Fellows Program at this time.

The Campus Context: Founded in 1883, the University of Texas at Austin has grown into a campus of 350 acres with a student body of 38,000 undergraduates and 12,000 graduates. Undergraduates may choose courses from more than 160 fields of study, supported by extensive computer facilities and one of the largest academic libraries in the nation. The city of Austin, with a population of about 500,000, is a green and cosmopolitan setting for the University. Students benefit from both the local communities in arts—dance, music, theater, and the visual arts—and the numerous recreational activities made possible by the temperate climate of the hill country of central Texas.

Tuition: $960 for state residents, $7380 for nonresidents, per year (1996-97)

Room and Board: $4550

Mandatory Fees: $1652

Contact: Director: Janet Staiger, Professor, College of Communication, Austin, Texas 78712; Telephone: 512-471-6653; Fax: 512-471-4077; E-mail: jstaiger@uts.cc.utexas.edu

UNIVERSITY OF TEXAS AT EL PASO

4 Pu G M Sc Tr

▼ University Honors Program

The UTEP Honors Program, open to students of all majors, is designed for the academically motivated student who seeks an intellectual challenge and a more personal focus in his or her education. The program provides an environment conducive to intellectual growth through honors courses, group activities, and interaction in the Honors Lounge, which is available for study, conversation with other honors students, and Honors Council meetings. The Honors Lounge is a home for honors students and facilitates a sense of community among students and faculty.

Honors classes are small, theoretically oriented, and taught by outstanding faculty members in a personalized classroom environment. Creative thinking, writing, verbal, and reading skills are emphasized. During the first two years, honors classes encourage students to broaden their academic horizons, while the last two years emphasize depth. For some students, this depth will culminate in an honors senior thesis, a year-long research project that is bound and placed in the library as a permanent record of the student's achievement. Students graduating with the University Honors Certificate, University Honors Degree, and/or a cumulative GPA of 4.0 receive a certificate(s) designating their respective honor or honors. Students who join the Honors Council participate in an induction ceremony and receive a certificate of membership.

Each semester, a variety of honors sections are offered at the lower- and upper-division levels. These courses can be used to meet requirements for the bachelor's degree as well as the University Honors Degree (e.g., English, history, accounting, or biology). Departments offering courses include accounting, anthropology, biological sciences, chemistry, English, finance, geological sciences, history, languages and linguistics, philosophy, physics, political science, sociology, and theater arts. Well before registration, the Honors Program publishes descriptions of honors courses and biographical data on honors faculty for the students' information. Students may also contract for honors credit in non-honors courses. All honors courses completed are designated with honors on the student's academic transcript. Students must apply to participate in the program. The program is 15 years old and currently enrolls 320 students.

Participation Requirements: The Honors Program offers two options: the University Honors Degree and the University Honors Certificate. The Honors Degree requires the student to complete a minimum of 30 hours of honors courses and have a minimum GPA of 3.3 upon graduation. These include honors courses in all basic education areas and 6 hours of upper-division honors hours and/or 6 hours of honors thesis. The graduate will have University Honors Degree on the diploma and on the permanent academic transcript. The Honors Certificate requires 18 hours of honors courses, 6 hours of which must be upper-division, and a minimum cumulative 3.3 GPA upon graduation. Such students will have University Honors Certificate recorded on their diploma and permanent transcript. A University Honors Certificate will also be awarded.

All students who satisfactorily complete the Honors Program requirements graduate with special recognition. Graduating with honors adds a special distinction to transcripts and diplomas and, therefore, to graduate and/or professional school applications. In addition, honors graduates are publicly recognized at the annual Honors Convocation and at Commencement ceremonies.

The Honors Program hosts faculty and campus visitors to speak on topics of interest to honors students. Such speakers have included judicial persona as well as mayoral and city council candidates.

Honors students are invited to join the Honors Council and, thereby, interact with other honors students and assist in the planning of honors activities according to their interests. Students who join the Honors Council participate in an induction ceremony and receive a certificate of membership.

Admission Process: Freshman students may apply to the program if they have a superior score on the SAT or ACT or rank in the top 15 percent of their high school graduation class. A cumulative GPA of 3.3 is required for admission of current or transfer students. Once admitted to the program, students must maintain a 3.3 GPA.

Scholarship Availability: UTEP offers many scholarships to students of exceptional ability. There are 116 Honors Program members holding scholarships ranging in amounts from $150 to $4000.

The Campus Context: The University of Texas at El Paso is composed of six colleges, including Business Administration, Education, Engineering, Liberal Arts, Nursing and Allied Health Sciences, and Science. The University offers fifty-nine bachelor's degree programs, fifty-six master's degree programs, and five doctoral degree programs.

The campus has several distinguished facilities. The Sun Bowl, which is the second-oldest college bowl in the U.S., seats 52,000. The Special Events Center, which is used for graduations, basketball games, and concerts, seats 12,222. The UTEP Dinner Theatre is a very successful theater that produced the American premier of Timothy Rice's *Blondel*. In 1989, the Union Dinner Theatre was selected from more than 800 colleges and universities to perform its production of the musical *Chess* at the Kennedy Center for the Performing Arts in Washington, D.C. Over the past eleven years, the Union Theatre has grown to become one of the most successful arts organizations in El Paso.

Student Body Undergraduate enrollment is 13,915. Fifty-four percent of the students are women. The student body is 18.5 percent white, 2.7 percent black, 68 percent Hispanic, 1.5 percent Asian American, .3 percent Native American, and 7.9 percent Mexican. Commuters comprise 84.7 percent of the students; 41 percent of students receive financial aid. There are eight fraternities and six sororities.

Faculty Of the 819 total faculty members, 496 are full-time. Eighty-three percent have terminal degrees. The student-faculty ratio is 20:1.

Key Facilities The library houses 667,400 books, 160,075 bound journals, and 219,218 documents. Computer facilities include five to six labs with PCs and Macs. An additional twelve labs, featuring personal computers, are located in various colleges and departments.

Athletics The UTEP Miners have a rich sports tradition that includes the 1966 National Basketball Championship, seven

Western Athletic Conference basketball championships, twenty national championships in track and field, numerous bowl bids in football, nationally ranked men's and women's tennis teams, a second-place finish in the NCAA Golf Championships, and a rifle team that has become a perennial top 10 squad.

Study Abroad As a member of the Texas Consortium for Study Abroad, UTEP is able to offer qualified students the possibility of an academic year, semester, or summer session at universities in Australia, Austria, Britain, Czech Republic, France, Hong Kong, Italy, Japan, Mexico, Russia, and Spain. Internships are also available in Britain.

Support Services The Disabled Student Services Office provides support and advocate services to help mainstream both physically and learning disabled students into the campus community. The office also extends services to students who become temporarily disabled due to injury or recent surgery and to women with at-risk pregnancies. A wide array of support services are available free of charge to assist disabled students in their college career. These services include note-taking, sign language interpreters, a telecommunication device for the deaf, special test accommodations, equipment loan programs, and arranging to have classes moved from inaccessible to accessible locations.

Job Opportunities Part-time job opportunities are posted on the bulletin board outside the Career Services Center Services Office. After filling out the proper application card, students are referred to the board to check on jobs and obtain a referral from the secretary. The requirements for consideration for part-time campus employment are met with an application along with proof of enrollment.

Tuition: $960 for state residents, $7380 for nonresidents, per year (1996-97)

Mandatory Fees: $1096

Contact: Director: Dr. Lillian F. Mayberry, Honors House, El Paso, Texas 79968-0607; Telephone: 915-747-5858; Fax: 915-747-5841; E-mail: mayberry@utep.edu; Web site: http://www.utep.edu/honors/

THE UNIVERSITY OF TOLEDO

4 Pu G L Sc Tr

▼ University Honors Program

The Honors Program at the University of Toledo provides an academically stimulating environment that encourages students to make the most of their University education. Students meet other students with similar interests, become involved in research or creative projects, work with honors faculty members, attend conferences, and receive help in preparing for future career or professional goals.

The University Honors Program is available across all colleges and in all majors, including interdepartmental

programs such as Africana studies and women's studies. Honors courses are offered within various departments as well as in the Honors Program itself, providing a wide range of selections for students in the program.

Among the many advantages of honors participation is the option of taking courses designed with honors students in mind. These courses are smaller in size, focus on student-faculty interaction, may be set up as interdisciplinary seminars, and give students an opportunity to get to know their peers and their professors. Honors seminars cover a range of disciplines and issues; recent examples include Native American Spirituality, Mars: A Scientific and Popular History, and California.

In addition to a range of stimulating courses, honors students have the chance to meet other honors students through priority housing in the Academic House and International House Residence Halls, participation in the Student Honors Organization at UT (SHOUT), attendance at student Brown Bag Presentations, and participation in the Honors Colloquium, as well as through many other intellectual, social, and community events.

The Honors Program also encourages student participation at regional and national research conferences. Many students present their research, read or perform creative work, or exhibit artwork and other projects to academic audiences. Students also receive help and advice in applying for various scholarships, internships, or travel-abroad programs.

Honors students have priority advanced registration when enrolling in their courses, and the honors staff and departmental advisers provide personal attention in academic advising, including advice about overall educational and personal objectives, assistance in graduate and professional school selection, and the preparation of letters of recommendation.

Students graduating from the Honors Program receive a citation on their diplomas. In addition, students are awarded an Honors Medallion upon graduation.

The 33-year-old program currently enrolls about 700 students.

Admission Process: Admission to the Honors Program is based on high school GPA, ACT or SAT scores, an extracurricular résumé, and references. Students entering directly from high school with a 3.75 GPA or higher and an ACT composite of 28 or higher (or SAT combined score of 1240 or higher) are encouraged to apply. Highly motivated students with at least a 3.5 GPA and an ACT composite of at least 25 (or minimum SAT combined score of 1140) are also considered for admission to the program.

Scholarship Availability: Many honors students receive University-sponsored scholarships such as the National Merit, Achievement, and Hispanic Scholars Programs. The minimal application standards for many other scholarships are the same as for the Honors Program. The Huebner Scholarship, available through the Honors Program, offers short-term aid to honors students in need.

The Campus Context: The University of Toledo is a nationally recognized comprehensive public university with a broad range of undergraduate and graduate programs serving students from almost every county in Ohio, all fifty states, and ninety-eight countries. The University of Toledo enrolls more than 21,000 students and is located in a suburban setting within the metropolitan Toledo area that is home to 600,000 people.

The nine colleges on campus include Arts and Sciences, Business Administration, Community and Technical, Education and Allied Professions, Engineering, Graduate School, Law, Pharmacy, and University College. The University offers 157 undergraduate majors.

Distinguished features of the campus include the Academic Center complex, which consists of the Honors Center office and classroom building, the Academic House Residence Hall, and the all-suite International House Residence Hall. The three-building Engineering Complex, completed in 1995, houses the Polymer Institute, National Center for Tooling and Precision Components, and the Edison System Facility. The Lake Erie Research Center, located at Maumee Bay State Park, is a cutting-edge soil and water research and education facility. The Art Department is located in the award-winning Center for the Visual Arts designed by Frank Gehry.

Student Body The student body is 53.5 percent women. More than 12 percent of the students are African American, .7 percent are American Indian/Alaska Native, 1.8 percent are Asian/Pacific Islander, 2.3 percent are Hispanic, and 75.5 percent are white. There are 749 international students. Nearly 84 percent of the students are commuters; 54.7 percent of the students receive some form of financial aid. There are fifteen fraternities and thirteen sororities at the University of Toledo.

Faculty The total number of faculty members is 1,355, of whom 988 are full-time. Seventy-nine percent of the faculty members have terminal degrees. The student-faculty ratio is 18:1.

Key Facilities The library houses 1.5 million volumes. Computer facilities include 2,750 computers and terminals.

Athletics Intercollegiate athletic teams for men consist of baseball, basketball, cross-county, football, golf, swimming, tennis, and track and field. Women's teams consist of basketball, cross-country, golf, soccer, softball, swimming, tennis, track and field, and volleyball. The state-of-the-art Student Recreation Center has been recognized as one of the best in the country.

Study Abroad The Salford study-abroad program is available for majors in biology, chemistry, and physics. Study-abroad opportunities include Costa Rica, France, Germany, Ireland, Japan, Mexico, Malaysia/Singapore, Scotland, and Spain.

Support Services The Office of Accessibility provides a variety of services for disabled students, including note-taking, tutoring, counseling, an adaptive computer room, and intercampus transportation.

Job Opportunities In addition to many work-study opportunities, the Career Services office coordinates and posts information about a variety of part-time jobs and provides students a chance to participate in a career mentor (job-shadowing) program.

Tuition: $2997 for state residents, $8282 for nonresidents, per year (1996-97)

Room and Board: $4092

Mandatory Fees: $781

Contact: Director: David Hoch, Honors Academic Center, Toledo, Ohio 43606-3390; Telephone: 419-530-6030; Fax: 419-530-6032; E-mail: honors@uoft02.utoledo.edu; Web site: http://www.utoledo.edu/www/honors

THE UNIVERSITY OF WEST ALABAMA

4 Pu G S Tr

▼ Honors Program

The University of West Alabama Honors Program provides academically talented undergraduates with an option in education that gives enhanced academic preparation for four years. The primary goals of the program are to provide the superior student with a more stimulating and challenging curriculum, enriched classes, and closer contacts with outstanding faculty and to allow individuals to follow their own intellectual interests more independently. The program design combines academic study with participation in social and cultural activities, and it provides the option of honors housing, thus giving participants frequent opportunities for interaction with like-minded peers. In the honors community, students share a commitment to scholarship and to each other.

Participation Requirements: Honors students pursue their own major within the honors framework, usually taking one to two honors courses per year. The program curriculum for freshmen includes honors versions of basic curriculum courses (English composition and literature, history, and biology) and a freshman-level University honors course, Honors Forum. This class combines class work, field trips, and attendance at special lectures and dinners. The sophomore-level interdisciplinary course, Honors Special Topics, brings to class faculty members from diverse disciplines to discuss with students a fundamental issue or theme or a historical period. The junior- and senior-level honors courses, Mentored Studies and Honors Thesis, provide opportunities to work independently in an area of special interest under the supervision of a major-field professor.

Students who meet all the requirements of the Honors Program graduate with the designation Honors Scholar, which is noted on official transcripts and diplomas. Participation in honors courses is noted on official transcripts.

Admission Process: The University of West Alabama Honors Program accepted students for the first time in the fall quarter 1996. This expanded four-year program replaces the Freshman Honors Program. The program is open to entering freshmen with an ACT composite score of 22 or higher and an area score of 24 or higher in biology, English, or history. Transfer students who are interested should apply to the Director of the Honors Program for admission.

The Campus Context: The University of West Alabama is located in Livingston, Alabama, the county seat of Sumter County. It is 116 miles southwest of Birmingham, 130 miles west of Montgomery, and 37 miles east of Meridian, Mississippi. As a regional institution, the University's foremost commitment is to meeting the educational needs of the state and particularly of the West Alabama area. The University offers associate degrees in nursing, industrial maintenance, and allied health; thirty undergraduate majors lead to the baccalaureate degree in the Colleges of Liberal Arts, Natural Sciences and Mathematics, Business, and Education; and the degrees of Master of Education, Master of Arts in Teaching, and Master of Science in Continuing Education are also offered.

Student Body The undergraduate enrollment is 1,974; 56.8 percent are women. The ethnic distribution of the total student body is 64.9 percent Caucasian, 33 percent African American, and 2.1 percent other. There are 16 international students. Thirty-two percent of the total undergraduate population are commuters, 42 percent are campus residents, and 26 percent live locally off campus. Seventy percent of the students receive financial aid. There are seven fraternities and five sororities.

Faculty There are 96 full-time faculty (supplemented by adjunct faculty), 60 percent of whom have doctorates. The student-faculty ratio is 18:1.

Key Facilities There are 242,913 volumes in the library. There are 250 Macintosh and DOS computers located throughout campus in the Student Union Building, library, and academic buildings.

Athletics The University, as a member of the National Collegiate Athletic Association, competes in the Gulf South Conference in varsity athletics for men in baseball, basketball, football, and tennis. UWA also sponsors a program of varsity athletics for women in basketball, softball, tennis, and volleyball. Intramural competition in major and minor sports is provided for the recreation and development of the students. Tournaments are organized and conducted in various sports.

Study Abroad Students are encouraged to study abroad, and those who do so for a quarter can fulfill the requirements of the Departmental Honors Project. As an institutional member of the Alabama Council for International Programs, the University offers students ready access to information about opportunities for studying overseas.

Support Services It is the policy of the University of West Alabama to provide reasonable accommodation for environmental and program accessibility for persons defined as handicapped under Section 504 of the Rehabilitation Act of 1973 and the Americans with Disabilities Act of 1990. The Office of Student Life serves the special needs of students with permanent disabilities.

Job Opportunities The Federal Work-Study Program provides jobs for undergraduate students who need financial assistance in order to pay part of their educational expenses.

Tuition: $2400 per year (1996-97)

Room and Board: $2634 minimum

Mandatory Fees: $384

Contact: Director: Ms. Mary Pagliero, Station #23, Livingston, Alabama 35470; Telephone: 205-652-3765; Fax: 205-652-3717; E-mail: livmp01@uwamail.westal.edu

UNIVERSITY OF WISCONSIN-EAU CLAIRE

4 Pu G M Sc Tr

▼ University Honors Program

The University Honors Program provides an extra measure of challenge and enrichment for students in any of the colleges at the University of Wisconsin–Eau Claire campus. It strives to enhance their critical thinking and communication skills, capacity for independent learning as well as working in teams, and leadership abilities. Courses are limited to a maximum of 20 students and are highly interactive. Students receive individual attention by faculty members in ways that cannot be done in larger courses. Almost all honors courses apply to credits needed for general education and provide a special means of meeting graduation requirements. The program does not increase the number of courses students are required to take as an undergraduate.

Colloquia courses change from semester to semester, and some are team-taught. They are usually offered during several semesters, but new ones are added each year and some are dropped. Departmental courses are predictably scheduled each semester and include basic courses in accounting, art, biology, chemistry, communications, economics, history, mathematics, music, philosophy, physics, political science, psychology, religious studies, and sociology. The first-year seminar is team-taught by honors seniors who enroll in Mentoring in Honors and are supervised by the director. The course provides an introduction to the baccalaureate degree, the purpose of a liberal education, and the nature of academic disciplines. The senior honors seminar is a retrospective, integrative experience. Most departments offer students the opportunity to earn departmental honors in their majors. Students may pursue departmental honors without being participants in the University Honors Program. Admissions to departmental programs generally require a 3.5 GPA in the major and in total credits.

The physical location of the program provides a classroom; a student study area with computers, a refrigerator, and a microwave; a conference room; a reception area; and the director's office. A student organization arranges trips to museums, theaters, and concerts as well as a variety of social activities. Outside of classes there are weekly Breakfasts with a Profess, monthly Pizzas with a Professor, special speakers, and support for attending state, regional, and national honors conferences.

The University Honors Council establishes policies for the program, approves honors courses, and selects honors faculty. This council consists of faculty representatives from each of the colleges as well as student representatives. More than 110 faculty members have taught honors courses.

The 14-year-old University Honors Program currently enrolls 350 students.

Participation Requirements: To earn University Honors, students must complete at least the following: a 1-credit first-year honors seminar, 12 credits of interdisciplinary honors colloquia (or 9 credits of colloquia if a senior 1-credit Mentoring in Honors is completed), 12 credits of departmental courses limited to honors program students, and a 1-credit senior-level honors seminar. They must have at least a 3.5 GPA at graduation. This totals 24–26 credits of honors courses out of the 120 needed for graduation.

Students completing the requirements for University Honors receive special recognition during the Commencement ceremonies. They wear an honors medallion on a gold ribbon along with gold cord, and they stand to be recognized. Their achievement is noted on their permanent records and transcripts. They each receive a special certificate.

Admission Process: Students are invited to participate in the honors program in several ways. Most are recruited as incoming first-year students based on two criteria: they must be in the top 5 percent of their high school graduating class and they must have an ACT composite of at least 28 or an SAT I score of at least 1280. Because these criteria miss a number of outstanding students, some are invited based on faculty recommendations and placement test scores. Finally, students are invited after they have completed 15 credits if they have a 3.67 GPA or better. Transfer students who have been participating in honors programs at other college or universities are admitted and given credit for previous honors courses toward meeting the program's requirements for graduation with University Honors.

Scholarship Availability: Students eligible to participate in the University Honors Program are awarded at least a $500 freshman honors scholarship. Larger scholarships are also available and awarded competitively.

The Campus Context: UWEC is a comprehensive university within the UW System and emphasizes its mission as a liberal arts institution. The University composes the Colleges of Arts and Sciences, Business, and Professional Studies. The College of Professional Studies includes the Schools of Education, Nursing, and Health and Human Services. There are a total of seventy-seven degree programs offered.

Special facilities on campus include the Goodner Collections and Owens Collection of Native American Materials, the S. W. Casey Observatory, the L. E. Phillips Planetarium, and the James Newman Clark Bird Museum.

Student Body Undergraduate enrollment is 60 percent women. The ethnic distribution of students that are members of minority groups is .5 percent black, .8 percent American Indian, 1.8 percent Asian, and .8 percent Hispanic. There are 167 international students. Thirty-six percent of the students live in residence halls, and 60 percent of students receive financial aid. There are twelve fraternities and sororities.

Faculty Of the 515 faculty members, 417 are full-time and 91 percent hold terminal degrees. The student-faculty ratio is 19:1.

Key Facilities The library houses 527,412 volumes. There are eighteen general computer labs with Apple Macintosh and PC systems available for students and faculty. The student-to-computer ratio is 11:1.

Athletics The athletic program for women consists of varsity teams in basketball, cross-country, golf, gymnastics, soccer, softball, swimming and diving, tennis, track and field, and volleyball. The men's program consists of varsity teams in basketball, cross-country, football, golf, hockey, swimming and diving, tennis, track and field, and wrestling. Both the men and women compete on the national level as members of the National Collegiate Athletic Association (NCAA) Division III.

Study Abroad The University academic community strongly encourages students to live and study overseas. Students must be in good academic standing to participate and are required to carry a minimum credit load of 12 hours. Programs are offered on a regular basis in Australia, Austria, China, Denmark, France, Germany, Great Britain, Japan, Latvia, Mexico, Poland, Spain, and Sweden. Two percent of students participate in international study programs.

Support Services Services are available to students with disabilities and handicap conditions, including diagnosed learning disabilities. All academic buildings are handicapped-accessible, and students have a choice of accessible residence halls on both upper and lower campus.

Job Opportunities Work opportunities on campus include federal and non-federal work-study.

Tuition: $2572 for state residents, $8036 for nonresidents, per year (1996-97)

Room and Board: $2904 minimum

Mandatory Fees: $2

Contact: Director: Dr. Ronald E. Mickel, 209 Schneider Hall, Eau Claire, Wisconsin 54702-4004; Telephone: 715-836-3621; Fax: 715-836-2380; E-mail: mickelre@uwec.edu; Web site: http://www.uwec.edu/Admin/Honors/honors.htm

UNIVERSITY OF WISCONSIN–MILWAUKEE

| 4 Pu G M Sc Tr |

▼ University Honors Program

Established in 1960 within the College of Letters and Science, the University Honors Program became University-wide in 1982. It brings together outstanding students and faculty from all UWM schools and colleges. Committed to the importance of the liberal arts, the program offers small discussion seminar classes that provide many of the benefits of a small liberal arts college at a large metropolitan university. It attracts some of the most talented students from the University's various schools and colleges.

Honors classes differ from regular classes at UWM in that they are small interactive seminars. With a maximum of about 15 students each, honors seminars are conducted in an atmosphere of openness and intellectual exchange. Exploring fundamental works in the humanities, arts, natural sciences, and social sciences, the seminars generate lively discussion of major issues and problems. No examinations are given. Instead, students are encouraged to think critically about important questions and to explore these questions through writing. Grades are based on the quality of each student's written and oral work.

In 1991, the Honors Program received a Bradley Foundation grant funding 3 visiting assistant professors to teach exclusively in the program for three-year terms. The Bradley Professors have strengthened a strong undergraduate teaching program by providing continuity for the curriculum and personal attention to students. In addition to the Bradley Professors, some of UWM's best teachers and scholars teach regularly in the program, offering undergraduates the opportunity to work with faculty members often available only to graduate students. The Honors Program seeks to bring to a public institution the same level of excellence in liberal arts that is associated with the country's best private colleges.

The Honors Program was established in the College of Letters and Science in 1960. Approximately 400 students are currently participating in the program.

Participation Requirements: The honors curriculum comprises introductory humanities seminars with variable topics (e.g., The Shaping of the Modern Mind); honors calculus; upper-level seminars in humanities, social and natural sciences, and

the arts; independent study; research; study abroad; and an optional senior thesis or project. Students can major in any area. Honors students fulfill many of their general education requirements (GER) through honors seminars. They can also use upper-level honors credits to fulfill major requirements. Students may remain in the program as long as they maintain at least a 3.0 GPA. In order to graduate with an honors degree, students must have a 3.5 GPA overall at time of graduation and complete 21 honors credits. Students who successfully complete the program receive an honors degree, graduation distinction, and special notation on their transcripts.

All students successfully completing the Honors Program receive an honors certificate from the Dean of Letters and Science at a formal honors graduation reception. Students in the College of Letters and Science, School of Fine Arts, and School of Education receive an honors degree, a special diploma with honors distinction. Students from all schools and colleges receive a special honors distinction on their transcripts.

Admission Process: Freshmen entering the program must rank in the top 20 percent of their high school class, have an ACT composite score of 26 or above, and score well on UWM's English Placement Test. Continuing and transfer students must have at least a 3.4 GPA for at least 12 credits of college work to be admitted. Because UWM is a commuter campus, many honors students are returning students who work full- or part-time while carrying challenging academic loads. Others are top students from local high schools. This diversity is part of the program's strength.

Scholarship Availability: For the past three years, an anonymous donor has provided an Honors Scholarship ($1500–$2000) for an honors senior. The William F. Halloran Scholarship, instituted this year, offers $500 to a second-semester freshman in the College of Letters and Science. The Milwaukee Braves/Fred Miller Scholarship offers four-year support of $1100 per semester to an honors student. The Herman Weil Prize (variable amounts) is offered for research expenses to students writing senior theses.

The Campus Context: The University of Wisconsin–Milwaukee is a campus of eleven schools and colleges: School of Allied Health Professions, School of Architecture and Urban Planning, School of Business Administration, School of Education, College of Engineering and Applied Science, School of Fine Arts, College of Letters and Science, School of Library and Information Science, School of Nursing, School of Social Welfare, and Graduate School. Eighty undergraduate majors, forty-six master's programs, and seventeen Ph.D. programs are offered on campus. UWM is the only school in Wisconsin to offer a nationally accredited professional degree in architecture and one of only fifteen schools in North America to offer the Ph.D. program in architecture.

Among distinguished facilities on campus are the new School of Business Administration (1995), considered the most technologically advanced building in the UW System; Center for Business Competitiveness; Institute of Chamber Music; Center for Great Lakes Studies; Professional Theatre Training Program; Laboratory for Surface Studies; Center for Teacher Education; Center for Twentieth Century Studies; and the Women's Studies Consortium.

The campus is home to the Greene Museum, which contains the mineral and fossil collection of Thomas A. Greene, a Milwaukee pioneer wholesale druggist. The collection includes more than 20,000 minerals and 70,000 fossils. UWM has four art museums on campus displaying the permanent University collection as well as student artwork.

Student Body Undergraduate enrollment is approximately 17,700 and is 54 percent women. The ethnic distribution of students is 9 percent black, 1.9 percent Asian, .95 percent Indian, 3.6 percent Hispanic, 1.3 percent Southeast Asian, and 81.5 percent white. There are 269 international students (1.5 percent of the population). Of the total number of students, 89.6 percent are commuters, and 48 percent receive financial aid. The campus has nine fraternities and five sororities.

Faculty Of the 1,354 faculty and instructional staff members, 825 are full-time. Eighty-seven percent of full-time faculty members hold the terminal degree in their field. The student-faculty ratio is 17:1.

Key Facilities The library contains nearly 5 million bibliographical listings, more than 1 million book titles, and 1.2 million volumes. The Golda Meir Library is the second-largest academic library in Wisconsin and houses the American Geographical Society Collection, the largest privately owned geographical research collection in the Western Hemisphere.

Computer facilities include four general access labs open for student use as well as computer labs within individual schools and colleges with approximately 800 student workstations. The labs provide IBM, IBM-compatible, and Macintosh computers. The Sandburg Residence Hall rooms are in the process of being wired for network access. Campus computers are linked to WiscNet, a statewide higher education network that includes other campuses of the UW System; CICNet, which includes the Big-10 institutions; and the Internet and the National Information Infrastructure.

Athletics UWM students are eligible to participate in sixteen intercollegiate sports, or they can get their exercise in numerous intramural and club sports. UWM is a member of the Midwestern Collegiate Conference, one of the top NCAA Division I athletic conferences in the country. UWM competes in basketball, cross-country, soccer, swimming, track, and volleyball for men and women and in men's baseball and women's tennis.

Study Abroad Students have the opportunity to participate in study-abroad programs coordinated through the Office of International Studies and Programs. Architecture and urban planning students may attend a spring semester program in Paris or a summer program in Oxford, England. Fine arts students can take drawing and painting during the spring semester in Paris and study in Florence or Paris in the summer. The College of Letters and Science offers semester programs in Chile, England, France, Germany, Israel, Japan, and Spain and summer programs in China, Ireland, Mexico, Morocco, and Poland.

Support Services The Student Accessibility Center (SAC) promotes access to educational programming for UWM students with disabilities. Services are made available according to the student's individual needs. Students with disabilities are encouraged to contact SAC upon acceptance to UWM. To ensure that appropriate accommodations are provided, SAC relies on the medical and diagnostic reports that students provide.

Job Opportunities There are more than 1,500 student employment positions on campus.

Tuition: $3102 for state residents, $9965 for nonresidents (1996-97)

Room and Board: $2912 minimum

Mandatory Fees: $2

Contact: Director: Professor Lawrence Baldassaro, 224 Garland Hall, P.O. Box 413, Milwaukee, Wisconsin 53201; Telephone: 414-229-4658 or 414-229-4636; Fax: 414-229-6070; E-mail: larryb@csd.uwm.edu; Web site: http://www:uwm.edu:80/Dept/Honors

UNIVERSITY OF WISCONSIN–OSHKOSH

4 Pu G M Tr

▼ University Scholars Program

The University Scholars Program is the honors program of the University of Wisconsin–Oshkosh. It offers a challenging and enriched education experience to undergraduate students who have clearly demonstrated their commitment to academic excellence. The curriculum of the Scholars Program has a 19-credit requirement built around several interdisciplinary courses and specially selected general education courses.

Courses in the University Scholars Program are limited to 25 students and average about half that number. About twelve honors courses are offered each semester to University Scholars, who have early registration privileges. Special orientation and registration workshops are held for all University Scholars, and a collegiate Peer Advising Program, initiated by students, is now in effect to offer continuing peer-to-peer advice and mentoring in the various colleges of the University.

Scholars courses and the faculty members who teach them are selected by the University Scholars Program Committee, composed of faculty representatives from all colleges and the University Scholars Student Association (USSA). All University Scholars must also attend a cultural activity and file an activities report each semester they are in the program.

In addition to this curriculum, the University Scholars Program emphasizes participation in the broader life of the University. The University Scholars Student Association organizes recreational programs, a lecture series

(Pizza with Professors) and field trips to cultural sites in the region. Students in the program are actively encouraged to participate in the Upper Midwest Honors Conference, held each spring, and the new Wisconsin Collegiate Honors Council Conference, held each fall.

The program has been in operation since 1981. There are currently 300 students in the program and the number is increasing. The University limits the number of Scholars to no more than 5 percent of the undergraduate student enrollment or about 425 students.

Participation Requirements: All Scholars enroll in the following courses for a total of 7 academic credits: honors seminar (3 credits), a topical seminar for new Scholars; Culture Connection (1 credit), a cultural activities course; and a Scholars senior thesis (3 credits), a thesis or project unique to the Scholars Program but earning credit in a student's departmental field of study, or a Scholars senior seminar (3 credits), an interdisciplinary, topical capstone seminar. The remaining 12 academic credits are earned in sections of general education courses that are exclusively designated for University Scholars.

University Scholars must maintain a minimum GPA to remain in the program: freshmen, 3.2; sophomores, 3.3; juniors and seniors, 3.4; and 3.5 to graduate as a University Scholar.

For each semester of their participation in good standing, the term University Scholar appears on the student's official transcript. Graduating Scholars present their senior thesis project at a special Senior Scholars Symposium. At a special awards ceremony held each semester prior to University graduation, they also receive a University Scholars Medallion, which they wear at graduation ceremonies. This medallion is presented to each Scholar by the Chancellor of the University in the presence of the student's family and friends. The designation Graduated as a University Scholar appears on the graduate's official transcript.

Admission Process: All students who are in the top 10 percent of their high school graduating class and who have an ACT composite score 26 or better are automatically eligible for admission, as are all high school valedictorians and National Merit Scholars. Entering students who meet only one of these criteria may send a letter to the director seeking admission to the program explaining why special consideration is warranted in their case. Second-semester students who meet specific GPA requirements after their first semester are invited to participate in the Scholars Program without regard to high school standing or ACT score. Approximately 75 students per year enter the program in their first semester; about 40–50 enter each year in their second semester having met the grade point requirements.

Scholarship Availability: There are no scholarships or fellowships specifically set aside for University Scholars, though University Scholars receive a wide range of scholarships available on the basis of academic achievement.

The Campus Context: The University of Wisconsin–Oshkosh is a campus of four colleges, including the Colleges of Letters and Science, Education and Human Services, Business Administration, and Nursing. Fifty degree programs are offered.

Student Body The student body is 59 percent women. European-Americans constitute 95 percent of enrolled students; the remaining 5 percent are mostly Asian. About 80–100 international students are enrolled annually. About 65 percent of the students are residents, and approximately 85 percent of University students receive some form of financial aid. There are thirteen fraternities and sororities.

Faculty Of the 529 faculty members, 401 are full-time. Seventy-nine percent of full-time faculty members have terminal degrees. The student-faculty ratio is 19:1.

Key Facilities The library houses 372,767 volumes and 17,090 periodicals. Many computer facilities are available. Four buildings contain IBM computer labs (with more than thirty computers) and five Macintosh labs (differing sizes). Each residence hall has a small computer lab with IBMs and a few Macs; faculty and staff have a development computer lab. The English department has a teaching computer lab, and the library has computers for Web and Internet reference and finding holdings of the University's library and other libraries in the state.

Athletics For spectators and competitors, the nineteen-sport intercollegiate athletic program offers a wide variety of opportunities to University students. The athletic program is a member of the National Collegiate Athletic Association (NCAA) Division III. The men's and women's sports programs are members of the Wisconsin Intercollegiate Athletic Conference. Men's sports include baseball, basketball, cross-country, football, soccer, swimming and diving, tennis, track and field (indoor and outdoor), and wrestling. Women's sports include basketball, cross-country, golf, gymnastics, soccer, softball, swimming and diving, tennis, track and field (indoor and outdoor), and volleyball.

Study Abroad There are no official University study-abroad programs.

Support Services Disabled students will find that the campus is generally handicapped-accessible. Some residence halls and all classrooms are designed to be accessible. Buildings have a designated entrance with buttons for accessibility. Bathrooms are near classrooms. A lounge with computers is specially designated for handicapped students.

Job Opportunities Every department is allocated money for student assistants and work study. The University is the largest employer of students in the area. The number of jobs available on campus consistently outnumbers the students available for work.

Tuition: $2417 for state residents, $7881 for nonresidents, $2747 for Minnesota residents, per year (1996-97)

Room and Board: $2511

Mandatory Fees: $2

Contact: Director: Dr. Jerry A. Stark, University Scholars Program, Polk 8, 899 Algoma Boulevard, Oshkosh, Wisconsin 54901-8601; Assistant Director: Ms. Kathleen Propp, Telephone:

414-424-1303; Fax: 414-424-7317; E-mail: stark@vaxa.cis.uwosh.edu, propp@vaxa.cis.uwosh.edu

UNIVERSITY OF WYOMING

4 Pu G M Sc Tr

▼ University Honors Program

For students with an enthusiasm for learning, the University of Wyoming Honors Program offers a sequence of challenging core courses, extracurricular activities, and the experience of independent research within the major. Additional benefits include the opportunity to compete for a Scholar's Stipend, the option to live in a residence hall section reserved for honors students, and special recognition on the transcript and at graduation ceremonies.

Honors core courses are small, taught by some of the University's best faculty members, and designed to bring together talented students from all majors and colleges across campus. Courses are innovative and interdisciplinary, set up to encourage a sense of close community among the participants. Like other UW students, a student in the Honors Program follows a course of study leading to a degree in one of the UW colleges, with a major in one area of specialization. The honors core courses count toward graduation requirements in all colleges.

The honors research project, initiated in the junior year and developed through the senior year, involves a topic chosen by the student and supervised by a faculty specialist. By becoming familiar with research methods and developing an expertise on a particular topic, the student gives his or her educational program a highly individual stamp. The research project often leads directly into graduate studies or a special career path.

Honors courses are taught by faculty members selected each year on the basis of competitive applications invited from all colleges in the University. Those selected are chosen on the basis of their course proposal and their demonstrated interest in innovative and effective teaching. The 12-year-old program currently enrolls 480 students.

Participation Requirements: Honors Program students take a total of 15 credits hours: Freshman Colloquium (6 credits) involves the student in the works and history of Western culture, with a particular emphasis on analytical reading, writing, and class discussion; Non-Western Perspectives in the sophomore year looks at issues central to human experiences from the perspectives of African, Asian, Middle Eastern, or Native American peoples; Modes of Understanding in the junior year challenges the students to examine the nature, limits, and validity of knowledge in selected areas of academic thought; and the Senior Honor Seminar asks students to confront a complex social issue, examine it from several perspectives, and take a stance on some aspect of the issue. Students who successfully maintain a 3.25 GPA and complete the program requirements receive a certificate, recognition at Commencement ceremonies, and Honors Program designation on their transcript.

Extracurricular activities, such as cultural trips to Denver and service projects, are arranged by a student organization. Students are encouraged to consider opportunities for spending one year at a foreign university, and the Honors Program Office cooperates with the UW study abroad staff to make arrangements. Offices of the program director and the program assistant are located in the Honors Center in Merica Hall. The center also includes a classroom, where many honors classes meet, an office for faculty-student conferences, a student computer room, and a student lounge.

Admission Process: Freshmen are selected for admission to the Honors Program on the basis of their high school GPA or their SAT/ACT scores. Continuing or transfer students with a minimum GPA of 3.25 are accepted into the program up to the beginning of their junior year.

Scholarship Availability: Scholars' Stipends in the amount of resident tuition and fees for four years are awarded to 18 incoming freshmen. Selection is made on the basis of academic courses, grades, SAT/ACT scores, two letters of recommendation, and an essay written by the student. A limited number of scholarships for upperclass students are also awarded on the basis of academic achievement and financial need. The Boyd Special Academic Opportunities scholarships are awarded to assist students who are studying in another setting, such as study abroad, internships, or coops.

A recent scholarship addition is the Dr. Scholl Foundation Honors Scholarship for students in the UW Honors Program with preference to nonresident or nontraditional students.

The Campus Context: The University of Wyoming, a land-grant university and the only four-year school in the state, was founded in 1886. The 785-acre campus in Laramie, a town of 27,000, lies at 7,200 feet in southeastern Wyoming. Located between two mountain ranges and within 2 hours of Denver, Colorado, students are within easy driving distance of outdoor activities and cultural opportunities. The University comprises six undergraduate colleges: Agriculture, Arts and Sciences, Business, Education, Engineering, and Health Sciences. Students may pursue master's and Ph.D. degrees in all colleges through the Graduate School or the J.D. in the College of Law. The University offers eighty-eight undergraduate degrees, seventy graduate degrees, and one preprofessional degree.

Student Body Undergraduate enrollment is 8,737; 51 percent are women. The student body's ethnic distribution is 84 percent Caucasian, 5 percent Hispanic, 1 percent African American, 1 percent American Indian, 1 percent Asian American, and 3 percent other. International students (4 percent) come from sixty-two countries. Ninety-nine percent of the students are residents of the campus. Fifty-two percent of freshmen and 68 percent of continuing students receive financial aid.

Faculty There are 626 full-time instructional faculty members; 84 percent have the terminal doctorate, 2 percent the J.D., and 14 percent the master's or other appropriate degree. The student-faculty ratio is 15:1.

Key Facilities The library houses more than 1 million books and 11,000 periodicals. There is also access to 21 million volumes through CARL (Colorado Alliance of Research Libraries). Computer facilities include an academic mainframe: DEC 7620 AXP. Several Novell and Windows NT file servers are available for student use. Students can use 154 computers in six computer labs. Residence hall rooms have campus data network connections.

Athletics The University is NCAA Division I in intercollegiate sports: for men, basketball, cross-country, football, golf, swimming and diving, track and field–indoor, track and field–outdoor, and wrestling and for women, basketball, cross-country, golf, soccer, swimming and diving, track and field–indoor, track and field–outdoor, and volleyball. There are more than twenty club and intramural sports.

Study Abroad Through the International Student Services Office, the University sponsors and participates in a number of study-abroad and student exchange programs worldwide. UW students with sophomore status or above and with a minimum GPA of 2.7 can study for a semester or academic year at one of hundreds of available exchange sites. In addition, domestic exchange opportunities are available through the National Student Exchange program.

Support Services Disability Support Services provides special programs and academic support services to students with physical handicaps or learning disabilities, including readers, note-takers, interpreters, classroom and testing accommodations, assistance with parking and housing, counseling and referral services, access to computers, and tutoring.

Job Opportunities Approximately 2,000 students are employed on campus in all departments, colleges, and support units. Part-time jobs are also available in the community.

Tuition and Fees: $1944 for state residents, $7032 for nonresidents, per year (1997–98)

Room and Board: $4245

Mandatory Fees: $382

Contact: Director: Duncan Harris, 102 Merica Hall, Laramie, Wyoming 82071; Telephone: 307-766-4110; Fax: 307-766-2255; E-mail: dharris@uwyo.edu; Web site: http://www.uwyo.edu

---

UTAH STATE UNIVERSITY

| 4 Pu G L Sc Tr |

▼ **Honors Program**

Utah State University's Honors Program, established in 1965, provides a distinctive academic environment for highly motivated undergraduates. Honors is not organized as a separate college or department; its members do not take on additional general education requirements; and students do not major in honors. At Utah State, honors is a program woven through the University's colleges and departments that allows students to do enhanced class work in a portion of their general education and upper-division courses.

Honors students work in smaller classes; they pursue their studies in greater depth; and they enjoy closer contact with professors. Members of the program may take intensive seminars, experimental classes, and interdisciplinary courses. They gain honors credit on their transcripts and work toward one of three honors degrees options (suited to entering freshmen, upper-division students, transfer students, or re-entry students).

Honors courses feature the University's leading professors, active student participation, and diverse class experiences. The courses emphasize the development of a student's skills in writing, speaking, and critical thinking. Students earn honors credits in honors-dedicated courses, which are composed entirely of honors students and feature small class size, with every class meeting offering accelerated course material; and honors complement courses, which are an additional component to a regular USU course in which a small group of honors students meets separately with the professor to examine course material in greater depth. Enrollment for these classes is limited to honors students and honors-eligible students. Upper-division honors students enrolled in a department honors plan may also use honors contracts to earn honors credit in course work leading to an honors degree.

The Honors Program serves students who work hard, who raise questions, and who seek answers. It is designed for those who want to go beyond minimum requirements and narrow specialties. The program benefits students who want to make the most of their University experience. Its members form a community of scholars whose curiosity, creativity, and enthusiasm for learning foster educational achievement and personal growth.

Where students start in the Honors Program depends largely on the status of their general education course requirements. Students who need to complete general education course work begin with the orientation course (1 credit, pass/fail, fall or winter quarter), which provides the information students need to start working in honors. Students who have completed their general education course work begin by applying for admission to a department honors plan (in which students will complete a portion of their upper-division course work for honors credit).

The program is 31 years old and currently enrolls 600 students.

Participation Requirements: Students may work toward one of three honors degree options. These are University Honors with Department Honors, which requires 40 total honors credits in lower-division courses selected from the honors course list and upper-division courses within an official department honors plan and includes the creation and presentation of a senior thesis/project and seminar; Department Honors, which requires 20 total honors credits in upper-division courses within an official department honors plan and includes the creation and presentation of a senior thesis/project and seminar; and University Honors, which requires 40 total honors credits in lower-division courses selected from the honors course list and an individually designed upper-division plan and includes the creation and presentation of a senior thesis/project and seminar.

Admission Process:

Honors is open to all incoming freshmen (those who have no university transcripts), regardless of high school GPA or ACT scores. Students with university transcripts (transfer or re-entry students or students with concurrent enrollment credit) must have a minimum cumulative GPA of 3.3 to join the program. There are no extra fees to pay. Once in the program, honors students must maintain a minimum GPA of 3.3.

Scholarship Availability:

The Morse Honors Scholarship, named in honor of the former director of the USU Honors program and the former provost of USU, is a $600 scholarship available to Honors Program students with a minimum 3.5 cumulative GPA who have been accepted into a department honors plan (or an individually designed plan for University Honors). The key criterion is the promise of outstanding academic achievement (as indicated by record in honors courses, proposed honors senior project, and GPA). Financial need is also considered. The application includes a statement of academic objectives, honors program activities, senior project proposal, postgraduation plans, and other scholarship and/or financial aid information. The deadline is mid-April.

The Campus Context:

Utah State University was founded in 1888 as the state's land-grant college. The 400-acre campus, with 100 buildings, is located a magnificent valley of northern Utah, in the city of Logan, the county seat of Cache County. USU is made up of a School of Graduate Studies and eight colleges: Agriculture, Business, Education, Engineering, Family Life, Humanities, Arts, and Social Sciences, Natural Resources, and Science. Undergraduates may choose from more than forty-five department majors.

USU sponsors a wide range of cultural activities appealing to the community, including the Performing Arts professional concert series; Arts and Lectures Series; Festival of the American West and Great West Fair; Irving Wassermann Festival; Ronald V. Jensen Living Historical Farm; Nora Eccles Harrison Museum of Art; Old Lyric Repertory Theatre; USU Theatre; department recitals, concerts, and exhibits in art, dance and music; and Utah Festival Opera.

Student Body Enrollment is approximately 19,900 students. Students are from every county in Utah, all other states, Puerto Rico, and sixty-nine other countries. Eighty-six percent of students are Utah residents. More than 120 organizations offer special interest and social activities and a sense of belonging for USU students, such as preprofessional and honorary societies, residence halls, and eleven fraternities and sororities.

Faculty There are 809 faculty members at USU, creating a 25:1 student-faculty ratio.

Key Facilities Libraries house more than 1.9 million bound volumes and subscribe to 6,200 periodicals. In addition, the libraries have cooperative agreements with all universities and colleges in Utah. Access to information worldwide is available via electronic technology with delivery available through interlibrary loan.

The campus has eleven computer centers for undergraduate use, with 472 DOS units, 158 Mac units, and twenty-four DEC 5000 workstations.

Student Services, located in the Taggart Student Center, provides a hub for programs and agencies facilitating academic support services, admissions, career services, Children's House, counseling center, Disability Resource Center, financial aid, high school/college relations, housing, International Student Office, multicultural affairs, parking, Personal Development Center, programs and entertainment, Student Health Services, Student Support Services, substance abuse prevention/education, and Women's Center/Re-entry Center.

Athletics USU is a member of the Big West Athletic Conference, where men's teams have competed since 1978 and women's teams since 1990 in all major sports. USU has won ten conference championships, including 1995–96 titles in men's cross-country and basketball and men's and women's track and field. Utah State athletic teams participate at the NCAA Division I-A level in football, women's volleyball and soccer, and men's and women's cross-country, tennis, softball, and track and field. Athletic facilities on campus include the Romney Stadium (30,257); the Dee Glen Smith Spectrum (10,270); the Nelson Recreation Fieldhouse; the Health, Physical Education and Recreation Building; and the Western Surgery Center. A new, multipurpose, indoor practice facility is under construction.

Study Abroad The USU Study Abroad Program offers exchange opportunities in China, Germany, Japan, Korea, and Mexico.

Support Services The Disability Resource Center of Utah State offers campus orientation, building access, registration assistance, technical equipment (such as computers, voice synthesizers, closed captioned decoders, scanners, and enlarged output devices), referral information, taped texts, telephone services, counseling, tutors, interpreters, and readers.

Job Opportunities Students have a number of work opportunities to choose from on campus, including assistantships, work-study, and a Cooperative Education Internship Program.

Tuition: $1584 for state residents, $5568 for nonresidents, per year (1996-97)

Room and Board: $3639

Mandatory Fees: $387

Contact: Director: Dr. Daniel J. McInerney, 374 Merrill Library, Logan, Utah 84322-3015; Telephone: 801-797-2715; Fax: 801-

797-3941; E-mail: honors@cc.usu.edu; Web site: http://www. usu.edu/~honors/index.html

UTAH VALLEY STATE COLLEGE

2/4 Pu G M Sc

▼ Honors Program

The Honors Program at Utah Valley State College is designed to challenge motivated students. Students who enter honors are deeply committed to realizing their academic, professional, and human potential. Honors courses facilitate this goal by providing small classes (no more than 20 students) that encourage an intimate, intensive, and stimulating learning experience. Students interact with each other and distinguished faculty members who have been carefully selected on the basis of scholarship, teaching ability, and rapport with students. The emphasis is on the development of reading, writing, and discussion skills that lead to productive analysis in all areas of the human experience. There are approximately 250 honors students currently enrolled.

Participation Requirements: Honors graduates complete honors courses that fulfill general education requirements and write a thesis. They must maintain a 3.5 GPA. Upon graduation, an honors seal is placed on the diploma and the transcript.

Admission Process: To enter the honors program, a candidate must meet GPA and ACT or SAT requirements and be interviewed by the honors director.

Scholarship Availability: Graduates have preferred transfer and access to scholarships at all Utah universities.

The Campus Context: Utah Valley State College is a beautiful campus surrounded by the Rocky Mountains and situated 40 miles south of Salt Lake City in Orem, Utah. A state college, it is composed of two interdependent divisions. Students are the primary focus and first priority at Utah Valley State College. The lower division embraces and preserves the philosophy and mission of a comprehensive community college, while the upper division consists of selected programs leading to baccalaureate degrees in areas of high community demand and interest. The two-fold mission sets Utah Valley State College apart from other colleges. Students can earn a marketable associate degree and then pursue a bachelor's degree in classes that are scheduled with the working professional in mind. Most students are commuters. The mean age of students is 22.

Student Body The student enrollment is currently 14,200 and rapidly growing. Two percent of students are international (most are Hispanic, Asian, Polynesian, and American Indian), and the rest represent all fifty states. All major financial aid programs and a broad variety of scholarships are available. More than 60 percent of students receive financial aid.

Faculty There are 325 contract faculty members and approximately 260 adjuncts.

Key Facilities Computer labs and on-line services are widely available and provide general or specialized (e.g., math, English) services.

Athletics Utah Valley Sate is a member of the Scenic West Athletic Conference of the NCAA.

Study Abroad There are many study-abroad opportunities available, including Western Europe, Russia, and Asia.

Support Services The campus offers full access to challenged individuals and a comprehensive range of student services.

Tuition: $1194 for state residents, $4329 for nonresidents, per year (1996-97)

Mandatory Fees: $280

Contact: Director: JaNae Brown Haas, AD 203, 185, 800 West 1200 Street, Orem, Utah 84604; Telephone: 801-222-8067; Fax: 801-226-5207; E-mail: haasja@cc.uvsc.edu; Web site: http://www.uvsc.edu

VALDOSTA STATE UNIVERSITY

4 Pu G M Sc Tr

▼ University Honors Program

The Honors Program at Valdosta State University provides special classes and activities for students who have demonstrated their commitment to academic achievement and who are looking for experiences that will enrich them beyond the scope of the average. Honors courses are not more difficult than non-honors courses, just more enjoyable and rewarding, designed to encourage students to think creatively, foster in them a love of learning, and provide the best possible foundation for their academic careers and personal lives.

The Honors Program offers special sections of classes in a wide variety of disciplines, including the humanities, the sciences, mathematics, fine arts, and the social sciences. Each course satisfies core curriculum requirements while at the same time counting toward completion of the Honors Program. Enrollment is limited to 15 students per section, with each course offering a unique blend of solid content and stimulating format in an enriched environment.

Honors seminars are a special feature of the Honors Program. These seminars are interdisciplinary and discussion based, focused each year on a different timely and interesting topic. Entering students enroll in the Honors Introductory Seminar during their first year. After having completed the requisite number of honors courses, students then finish their honors experience with the Honors Capstone Seminar. These seminars—Myth and Ritual in Modern Society, the Question of Evil, Native American

Religions, Cosmology, Modern and Contemporary Views of Human Nature, Society and the Sexes, the Individual and Society, Moving Beyond Hatred, Developing Ethical Decision Making Skills, Geology and Mythology in the Mediterranean, Issues in Science and Religion, the American View of Nature, Women in the Arts, and the Role and Function of a University—are designed to give all students in the Honors Program a shared intellectual experience in order to develop a community of learners and encourage a spirit of collegiality in the pursuit of knowledge, a spirit that is essential for intellectual growth and personal fulfillment.

The Honors Option allows students to continue honors work during their junior and senior years. Through the Honors Option, students may receive honors credit while enrolled in regular course sections by extending class work into new areas or pursuing it in greater depth.

Honors students may also become members of the Honors Student Association and enjoy a variety of special activities and social events. Through participation in the Honors Forum, a series of lectures and discussions led by VSU faculty, visiting scholars, and members of the community, honors students have the opportunity to discuss new ideas and exciting research in a relaxed yet challenging atmosphere. Honors students also engage in public and community service projects, such as delivering the *New York Times* to professors in order to raise money to meet the educational needs of disadvantaged middle school students. Finally, through its membership in the National Collegiate Honors Council, the Southern Regional Honors Council, and the Georgia Honors Council, the VSU Honors Program opens the door to numerous conventions, symposia, trips, and study abroad and offers many opportunities to meet and work with other honors students from all parts of the nation and the world.

There are 300 students in the 21-year-old program.

Participation Requirements: To complete the program, students must accrue 24 hours of honors course credit, including two honors seminars, and participate in some form of community service. Students who complete the Honors Program receive an Honors Program diploma, transcript notation, and a gold seal on their University diploma. Students also receive public recognition at the University's annual Honors Day ceremony.

Admission Process: Students with a high school GPA of 3.0 and a verbal or math SAT I score of 550 receive invitations to join the Honors Program. Other students who demonstrate qualities of the superior student are encouraged to apply. Students already enrolled in a university should have at least a 3.0 GPA to seek admittance.

Scholarship Availability: The Honors Program does not offer scholarships itself; however, the University offers a large number of scholarships. Residents of Georgia who have the Hope Scholarship have most of their tuition paid for them.

The Campus Context: Noted for its Spanish Mission architecture, Valdosta State University is composed of five colleges (Arts and Sciences, Business Administration, Fine Arts, Nursing, and Education). The University offers ninety-four degree programs with forty-nine undergraduate majors leading to the B.A. or B.S., ranging from astronomy to sports medicine, including a pre-engineering tandem program with Georgia Tech.

Student Body The University has 8,000 undergraduates are enrolled; 59 percent are women. Twenty percent of the student body are African American and 60 percent are Caucasian. Ten percent are from out of state. The campus has twenty-one fraternities and sororities.

Faculty There are 400 full-time faculty members (not including a considerable number of adjunct faculty), 73 percent of whom hold doctorates or other terminal degrees. The student-faculty ratio is 23:1.

Key Facilities The library houses 1.2 million volumes. There are fifteen computer labs scattered across campus housing a total of 1,700 PCs.

Athletics VSU has an NCAA Division II athletic program, consisting of baseball, basketball, cross-country, football, golf, and tennis for men and basketball, cross-country, softball, tennis, and volleyball for women. The football team has been especially strong in Division II, coming in second for two years in the national championships.

Study Abroad Numerous study-abroad opportunities exist through the Office of International Programs.

Support Services Much of the campus is accessible to disabled students, and the Special Services Office of the University has a strong presence on campus, ensuring that all special-needs students find adequate support.

Job Opportunities Numerous work opportunities exist through the Work Study Program Office.

Tuition: $2043 for state residents, $5922 for nonresidents, per year (1996-97)

Room and Board: $3300

Contact: Director: Dr. Brian Adler, 101 West Hall, Valdosta, Georgia 31698; Telephone: 912-249-4894; Fax: 912-333-7389; E-mail: badler@grits.valdosta.peachnet.edu; Web site: http://www.valdosta.peachnet.edu/vsu/dept/cas/honors/honors.html

VALENCIA COMMUNITY COLLEGE

2 Pu G L Sc

▼ Honors Program

To better fulfill its mission to provide quality educational opportunities to a diverse student population, Valencia

Community College inaugurated its Honors Program in January 1990. The Honors Program now serves more than 1,000 students on four campuses. The program annually attracts dozens of students with SAT I scores in excess of 1400 and ACT scores in excess of 32. There are a number of valedictorians and salutatorians from twenty-two local high schools, and students from several other states and countries have been attracted to Valencia because of its Honors Program. The program offers students a choice of more than forty different honors courses across the curriculum. In addition, it offers a four-semester sequence of Interdisciplinary Studies (IDS). Students may choose to take only honors courses or only IDS or to mix and match the two approaches to honors. The Honors Program emphasizes small classes (average size is 15) and participative learning. Most classes are seminar style and seek to help the student become an independent learner. The Honors Program faculty is made up of master teachers, many of whom are noted authors and scholars in their disciplines. There is a close mentoring relationship between honors faculty members and students. Students are advised by 5 special honors counselors and receive preferential early registration for classes.

For the past five years, 100 percent of Honors Program graduates have transferred as full juniors to upper-division colleges and universities, two thirds of them on scholarships and many of those to prestigious institutions. The Honors Program currently has more than fifty transfer scholarships to eighteen different colleges and universities where Valencia's honors director is permitted to select students who will receive the scholarships.

One of the hallmarks of the Honors Program is its holistic approach to developing honors students. This approach seeks to develop students' social and leadership skills in addition to intellectual and academic abilities. Toward this end, the program sponsors numerous field trips, a speakers series, social events, leadership training, and trips to state, regional, and national honors conferences (all at program expense). In addition, the program provides an annual spring break trip to a foreign country. While this trip is not paid for entirely by the program, it is heavily subsidized so that students pay only a fraction of the cost.

In addition to the resources offered by Valencia and the Orlando area, students in the Honors Program have full check-out privileges at the libraries of Rollins College and the University of Central Florida. Each of Valencia's campuses also offers an Honors Resource Center where honors students have access to computers, group study areas, and other resource materials in addition to a comfortable and well-appointed room in which to just relax or carry on a conversation.

Participation Requirements: Students in the program may elect to take as many or as few honors courses as they wish. If students have 12 hours of honors course work (out of 60 hours required for an Associate of Arts degrees) and a 3.0 overall GPA at graduation, they will receive an Honors Certificate. Students with 24 hours of honors course work and a 3.25 overall GPA at graduation will receive an Honors Degree. Both Honors Certificate and Honors Degrees graduates and their guests participate in a special buffet dinner/graduation ceremony. In addition, they are distinguished at the regular College Commencement ceremony by the wearing of honors stoles and honors medallions as well as having a special section in the Commencement program.

Honors Degree graduates also have their transcripts marked with the designation Graduated With an Honors Degree.

Admission Process: To be admitted to the Honors Program, students must meet one of the following requirements: be in the top 10 percent of their high school graduating class; have a cumulative high school GPA of 3.5 on a 4.0 scale or 4.3 on a 5.0 scale; have a minimum combined SAT I score of 1170; have a minimum composite ACT score of 26; have a CPT score of 100 or above in writing and 97 or above in reading or an 83 or above in elementary algebra and 44 or above in college-level mathematics; or have a cumulative Valencia GPA of 3.25 or higher with a minimum of 12 hours of college-level course work completed.

The Campus Context: Valencia Community College was founded in 1967 as Valencia Junior College. The name was changed to Valencia Community College in 1971. Valencia is located in Orlando, Florida, and has three campuses ranging from 99 to 180 acres each, as well as two satellite centers and a downtown center housing administrative offices. Valencia is the fourth-largest of twenty-eight community colleges in the Florida higher education system. However, Valencia is now the second-largest producer of Associate of Arts degrees in the United States. Valencia also has the fourth-largest community college foundation in the nation. Its Honors Program has produced a number of award-winning students, including several Academic All-American first- and second-team winners, more first- and second-place Florida Collegiate Honors Council writing contest winners than any other college or university in the state, and a winner of the coveted Portz Award given by the National Collegiate Honors Council. Valencia is fully accredited by the Southern Association of Colleges and Schools.

Student Body Valencia enrolls approximately 28,000 credit-seeking students; 88 percent are enrolled in Associate of Arts degree programs and 12 percent are enrolled in Associate of Science degree programs. Valencia has nearly 500 international students, which is unusual for a community college. Thirty-eight percent of all students receive financial aid.

Faculty Of the total faculty members, 63 percent are full-time and 37 percent are adjuncts.

Key Facilities Computer facilities include more than 2,000 DOS and Macintosh computers located in labs, libraries, and academic buildings.

Athletics Intercollegiate athletics for men include baseball and basketball and for women, softball and basketball. In addition, Valencia offers club soccer and a wide range of intramural sports for both men and women.

Study Abroad Through its international education program, Valencia students have an opportunity to study abroad for a summer, semester, or year. Credits earned in this way apply toward the student's Valencia degree requirements.

Job Opportunities Students are offered a range of work opportunities on campus, including both Federal and Valencia Work-Study opportunities.

Tuition: $1178 for state residents, $4156 for nonresidents, per year (1996–97)

Contact: Director: Ronald G. Brandolini, 1800 South Kirkman Road, Orlando, Florida 32811; Telephone: 407-299-5000 Ext. 1729; Fax: 407-299-5000 1 1912; E-mail: rbrando@valencia. sundial.net; Web site: http://www.gate.net/~valencia/honors/honors2.html

VILLANOVA UNIVERSITY

4 Pr G M Sc Tr

▼ Honors Program

The Villanova University Honors Program is a distinctive academic community comprised of students and faculty members who particularly enjoy the experience of intellectual growth. The program is designed to provide exceptional opportunities for critical and independent thinking, for the creative exchange of ideas, and for the synthesis of intellectual insights into lived experiences. Honors enhances the academic life central to a Villanova education by bringing together talented students and faculty members in challenging seminars, individual research projects, and cocurricular activities. Members of the program enjoy the benefits of a small college environment, while taking full advantage of the many resources of the broader University community.

Honors students receive excellent academic advisement throughout their college careers in course and major selection, in preparing for summer and postgraduate opportunities, and in learning to identify and develop their own intellectual voices. Villanova Honors Program graduates are frequently elected to Phi Beta Kappa and other prestigious honor societies, often receive the medallions awarded for academic excellence at graduation, and are highly successful in their pursuit of prestigious fellowships, graduate and professional school acceptances, and career opportunities.

Students can major, minor, or take individual courses in the Honors Program. An academic division within the College of Arts and Sciences, the program currently offers courses in the humanities, social sciences, and natural sciences, which are required areas of study for all of the University's majors. Honors courses are taught by faculty members who have distinguished themselves as dynamic teachers and scholars. These small seminars emphasize interdisciplinary approaches, extensive reading and writing, and the development of critical skills of judgment and analysis in a climate of mutual respect and cooperation. Innovative courses in the program include team-taught seminars and seminars given by visiting professors. All honors courses are enriched by a variety of lectures, cultural events, and social activities.

Faculty members and students meet outside of class individually, as a class, and as part of larger program events. The student-run Honors Events Committee invites speakers and organizes trips to cultural events in New York and Washington, D.C. Local Philadelphia highlights like the Philadelphia Orchestra, Independence Hall, and South Street are a short train ride away, with a regional rail-line stop on campus. Students present their own research in the informal atmosphere of Friday Colloquia and share their musical and artistic talents in recitals and exhibitions. All students are invited to contribute to *The Polis*, the program's literary magazine. In addition, students participate equally with faculty members in setting policy and selecting new courses for the program. Every year is different depending on the special interests and initiatives of students themselves.

Honors students participate actively in all aspects of the Villanova community; honors is only one aspect of their campus life. Averaging two to three courses (the standard courseload is five) in the program per semester, honors students bring to the program their own diversity of talents, interests, and experiences. They often hold leadership positions in student government, campus publications, musical and theatrical performance groups, and volunteer service projects, both on and off campus.

Founded more than 35 years ago, the Villanova Honors Program has grown from a core of interdisciplinary humanities seminars into a four-year curriculum, which serves approximately 500 students from all of the University's colleges: Liberal Arts and Sciences, Commerce and Finance, Engineering, and Nursing. Currently, 484 students are registered with the Honors Program. There are a total of 120 majors and sixty minors across the four years (approximately thirty majors and fifteen minors in each graduating class).

Participation Requirements: To remain active in the program, honors students must earn a minimum GPA of 3.25. Students who complete the program requirements may graduate with a Bachelor of Arts, Honors Program (B.A.H.) or Bachelor of Science, Honors Program (B.S.H.). Both the B.A.H. and the B.S.H. degrees may be combined with a second major in another discipline. Each of these four-year comprehensive majors culminates in a year-long senior thesis project. The Honors Program Sequence in Liberal Studies (Honors Minor) is another option. All Honors Program certifications require a minimum GPA of 3.25.

Admission Process: Incoming students are invited to apply to the program in the June immediately prior to their enrollment at Villanova based on their SAT scores (1300), high school record (rank in the top 10 percent), and/or a previously expressed interest in the program. Current undergraduate students apply upon the recommendation of a faculty member or through their own initiative.

Scholarship Availability: Villanova University offers a number of merit-based scholarships to members of each incoming class. Designed to recognize distinctive achievement and to attract superior students to the University, these scholarships include the four-year full tuition Presidential Scholarship administered by the Honors Program, sizable partial-tuition Villanova Scholar Awards, Commuting Scholar Awards, Augustinian Scholarships, and college-specific scholarships that are administered through the University Office of Admission.

All of the students who receive scholarships to Villanova are invited to participate in the courses and activities of the Honors Program.

The Campus Context: Villanova University is composed of four colleges: the College of Liberal Arts and Sciences, the College of Commerce and Finance, the College of Engineering, and the College of Nursing. Students can choose from forty undergraduate majors and thirty graduate programs. Special facilities on campus include the St. Augustine Center for the Liberal Arts, an observatory, and the new engineering laboratory building that is to be completed in spring 1998.

Student Body Undergraduate enrollment is currently 6,771. The student body is equally divided between men and women. The ethnic distribution of the students is 2 percent African American, 3 percent Native American, 2 percent Hispanic, 3 percent Asian, and 90 percent Caucasian. The population includes 2 percent international students. Resident students comprise 61 percent of the student population. Forty-nine percent of the students receive financial aid. There are thirteen fraternities and eight sororities.

Faculty Of the 707 faculty members, 454 are full-time and 90 percent hold terminal degrees. The student-faculty ratio is 13:1.

Key Facilities The library houses 677,163 volumes. There are 400 computers available on campus for general student use. Most computers are IBM or IBM-compatible. There are some Macs on campus. Students have access to the Internet, World Wide Web, and e-mail.

Athletics Most sports are Division I except ice hockey and water polo, which are Division III, and football, which is Division I-AA. Women's sports are basketball, field hockey, softball, track, cross-country, volleyball, swimming and diving, crew, soccer, and tennis. Men's sports are basketball, football, baseball, track, cross-country, ice hockey, swimming and diving, water polo, soccer, and tennis.

Study Abroad Villanova sponsors study-abroad programs in Chile, England, France, Ireland, Israel, Italy, Spain, and Palestine. Students also can enroll for credit in study-abroad programs at other institutions. Approximately 8 percent of Villanova students participate in study-abroad opportunities.

Support Services Disabled students find an office on campus to work with students' individual needs.

Job Opportunities Work-study positions are available as part of financial assistance packages. Other non-work-study jobs are available in offices, laboratories, libraries, and food services.

Tuition: $17,530 minimum per year (1996–97)

Room and Board: $7470

Mandatory Fees: $260

Contact: Director: Dr. Edwin L. Goff, 800 Lancaster Avenue, Villanova, Pennsylvania 19085; Coordinator: Nancy F. Hensler, B.A.H., Telephone: 610-519-4650; Fax: 610-519-7249; E-mail: egoff@email.vill.edu

VIRGINIA COMMONWEALTH UNIVERSITY

4 Pu G L Sc Tr

▼ Honors Program

The VCU Honors Program is designed to meet the needs of academically talented undergraduate students through a challenging and exciting program with high academic standards. The University Honors Program offers students an opportunity to exchange ideas, ask questions, participate in research, and explore values with fellow students and teachers who have been carefully selected for their scholarship and teaching excellence. The University Honors Program offers the opportunity for students to expand their creative and intellectual horizons and to benefit from small classes in which there is greater interaction between students and faculty and among students themselves. Some honors courses are special sections of regular classes open only to honors students. Class size is limited (usually to 20 or fewer students) to maximize student participation and interaction with the instructor. In these special sections, subjects are discussed in-depth, and discussions often continue after class.

Other courses are unique to the Honors Program. Of particular interest among these are the modules. These are single-focus courses that occupy only one third of a semester. The modules are often interdisciplinary and strive to connect the student's studies. Honors students receive personal and careful advising from both the Honors Program faculty and faculty members in their major field of study. This allows them to devise courses of study that meet academic requirements while allowing for the development of individual educational objectives.

Honors students, while benefiting from their association with a smaller unit within the University, also have the benefit of the resources of a major research university. Virginia Commonwealth University is located on two Richmond campuses: the Academic Campus and the Medical College of Virginia Campus. The University offers a wide range of academic opportunities and is committed to its mission of excellence in teaching as well as to the expansion of knowledge through research.

The Honors Program offers a variety of intellectual, cultural, and social activities as important supplements to classroom study. Among these are weekly brown bag lunches, honors seminars, an outstanding lecture series, and the Honors Idea Exchange, which is a registered student campus organization composed of honors students. The center of activities and community for the University Honors Program is Valentine House, a Victorian brownstone house in the heart of the Academic Campus. In the house, students have meeting rooms, quiet study rooms, a computer laboratory, a copy machine, and recreation areas. Valentine House is open during the day and at night for study.

The Honors Program is committed to enriching the student's academic and personal endeavors. Since those in the Honors Program are serious students, special privileges are provided beyond the vast resources available to all VCU students. These privileges include access to early registration the week before the rest of the student body, graduate student library privileges, and honors housing in specific wings of the residence halls. Guaranteed admission programs with professional-level health sciences programs and graduate programs in basic health sciences, business, education, and others represent other opportunities for qualified honors students.

The Honors Program at Virginia Commonwealth University began in 1983 and has grown over the years to currently serve more than 1,000 students.

Participation Requirements:

Successful completion of the Honors Program leads to graduation with University Honors, an accomplishment that is documented on official transcripts and diplomas. Graduation requirements for completing the Honors Program differ according to school or major. In addition to completing at least six module courses and maintaining a minimum cumulative GPA of 3.5 and a minimum 3.2 GPA in honors courses, honors students present a dossier documenting how they have met the University's expectations for an honors education.

Admission Process:

The Honors Program is open to entering freshmen with SAT I scores of 1270 or higher who rank in the upper 15 percent of their graduating class and to transfer students and continuing students with an overall GPA of 3.5 or higher with 30 college semester hours. Students may also be admitted on an individual basis with evidence of sufficient personal commitment to do honors-level work.

Scholarship Availability:

In addition to a significant number of merit-based scholarships awarded by the University, the Honors Program recognizes continuing VCU students who demonstrate academic achievement in the Honors Program. Honors Program Scholarships are awarded by the Honor Council, an advisory board to the Honors Program. Thirty-five scholarships of $550 or more are awarded each semester to students active in the Honors Program. The Honors Program scholarships may be received for as many as seven semesters. Scholarships are open to continuing honors students in all majors.

The Campus Context:

Virginia Commonwealth University is a state-aided institution with undergraduate, graduate, and health professions programs located on its two campuses in Richmond, Virginia. The Medical College of Virginia Campus is located near the financial, governmental, and shopping areas of downtown Richmond; the Academic Campus is 2 miles west in Richmond's historic Fan District, a residential area that dates from the nineteenth century. Currently, VCU operates a College of Humanities and Sciences, the School of Graduate Studies, and eleven schools, including Allied Health Professions, Art, Business, Dentistry, Education, Engineering, Mass Communications, Medicine, Nursing, Pharmacy, and Social Work. VCU offers fifty-five baccalaureate, sixty-three master's, twenty doctoral, and three first-professional degrees, along with eighteen postbaccalaureate certificate programs.

Student Body VCU enrolls approximately 21,000 students in undergraduate and graduate programs on the two campuses. More than 12,000 VCU students are undergraduates. Of these undergraduates, approximately 60 percent are women. The student body is 72 percent white and 17 percent black. VCU enrolls nearly 500 international students each year. Some 85 percent of VCU students are commuter students, and roughly 70 percent of students receive financial aid. There are twenty-one social fraternities and sororities that serve students.

Faculty The full-time faculty at VCU numbers 1,550; approximately 1,000 adjunct faculty members supplement the full-time faculty. Of the full-time faculty members, 88 percent hold terminal degrees. The student-faculty ratio is 13:1.

Key Facilities The University libraries house in excess of 1.1 million volumes in the two campus libraries. VCU students, faculty, and staff have access to a wide variety of computing resources, such as electronic library holdings, electronic mail, and special databases and programs. These facilities also allow connection to the Internet, including the World Wide Web, the University fiber-optic backbone network, and local area networks on both the Academic and MCV campuses. Local dial-up access is also available to the University network and associated computer resources. Public laboratories with a wide array of hardware and software are located in many locations around the campuses.

Athletics More than 250 student athletes participate in the sixteen athletic programs sponsored by the University. Athletic teams for men include baseball, basketball, cross-country, golf, soccer, tennis, and indoor and outdoor track and field. Women's teams include basketball, cross-country, field hockey, soccer, tennis, volleyball, and indoor and outdoor track and field. VCU also offers a wide range of intramural sports for men and women.

Study Abroad VCU students may extend their educational horizons by studying abroad. The Center for International Programs cooperates annually with the Department of Foreign Languages to offer summer study programs in Austria, France, Italy, Russia, and Spain or Guatemala. In addition, it has coordinated topics courses in Brazil, Indonesia, Mexico, and the United Kingdom. The Department of Foreign Languages, in an agreement with EUROCENTRES, offers short-term, semester-long, or year-long culture and language immersion programs in France, Germany, Italy, Japan, Russia, and Spain. VCU students may also participate in the International Student Exchange Program, which allows enrollment in member institutions worldwide.

Support Services The Program of Services for Students with Disabilities provides information and assistance in academic planning and advising to VCU students identified as having a disability.

Job Opportunities Students have access to a variety of work opportunities on campus, including assistantships and work-study.

Tuition: $3125 for state residents, $11,050 for nonresidents, per year (1996–97)

Room and Board: $4352

Mandatory Fees: $946

Contact: Director: Dr. John Berglund, 920 West Franklin Street, P.O. Box 843010, Richmond, Virginia 23284-3010; Telephone: 804-828-1803; Fax: 804-828-1355; E-mail: jberglun@ atlas.vcu.edu; Web site: http://www.vcu.edu/honors

VIRGINIA POLYTECHNIC INSTITUTE AND STATE UNIVERSITY

4 Pu G L Sc Tr

▼ University Honors Program

While the University Honors Program offers a significant complement of honors core curriculum courses, a colloquia series, and research opportunities, the major focus for the program is to encourage each student to seek a superior education consisting of the following elements: significant accomplishment in the instructional arena, participation in intellectual life beyond the instructional level, leadership/ service activity, and extensive interaction with members of the faculty.

To these ends, such activities as a summer reading program leading to student-faculty conversation groups, special classes taught by senior faculty members, special classes concerning research methodologies, participation in co-op education, working with faculty members in research,

participation in major scholarship competitions, and seeking one of two honors degrees become tools students use. Because of the high quality of entering students, freshman honors courses are designed to assist students with Advanced Placement, International Baccalaureate, and other earned college credits link to the broader curriculum of the University. A personal statement and curriculum vita project assists students in preparing to use the curriculum to their advantage. Honors students are encouraged to seek diversity, and, as a result, many choose multiple majors and minors, often across college boundaries. The Honors Program and Graduate School maintain a five-year bachelor's/master's program.

The staff consists of a director and two associate directors. The faculty members participating in the program are drawn from the University at large, but the Academy of Teaching Excellence (made up of about 80 faculty members who have won major teaching awards) oversees the program. Faculty participation is both high (typically 200 faculty members participate in some aspect of the program) and enthusiastic. Working with the faculty, honors students have participated in research that has led to participation in professional meetings and publication in academic journals.

Honors provides access to the major facilities of the University, including some (such as graduate library privileges) not open to other undergraduate students. The Honors Program offers special lectures, faculty teas, and special leadership seminars in a not-for-credit environment. These activities are all integral to the education of the whole person.

The University Honors Program is more than 25 years old. The last six have been under the direction of the Academy of Teaching Excellence. There are about 1,500 students in the program.

Admission Process: Entering students must score 1300 or higher on the SAT I (620 verbal, 600 math) and must be in the top 10 percent of their graduating high school class. If the school does not rank, students must have a 3.75 GPA or better for automatic qualification. Students not meeting these criteria are invited to apply upon demonstration of special talent.

Scholarship Availability: The Honors Program offers merit-based scholarships as well as others that are both need- and merit-based. Scholarships range from $1000 to $3000. The honors application serves as the application for these scholarships.

The Campus Context: The seven colleges within the University are the Colleges of Agriculture and Life Sciences, Architecture, Arts and Sciences, Forestry and Wildlife, Human Resources and Education, and Veterinary Medicine and the Pamplin College of Business. Virginia Tech offers 103 degree programs.

Student Body The University enrolls more than 19,000 students. The student body is 42 percent women. There are more than 1,300 international students. Virginia Tech is a residential campus.

Faculty There are more than 1,600 faculty members, 1,430 of whom are full-time. The student-faculty ratio is 17:1.

Key Facilities The library holds more than 1.8 million volumes. Virginia Tech is a national leader in providing students access to the latest in computing facilities. Every dorm room is connected to the World Wide Web through Eudora (hardwired). There are computer labs in several dorms and academic buildings. The environment is very conducive to both DOS and Mac users. Special computer facilities include a multimedia lab, scientific visualization lab, and a new information building. Many departments are experimenting with computerized learning environments.

Athletics Most athletics are NCAA Division I. Virginia Tech is football's Sugar Bowl champion and has a renowned basketball team.

Study Abroad Virginia Tech owns a villa in Riva St. Vatale, Switzerland. Each semester, 2 faculty members take 25 students for a semester's study. Many other opportunities for study abroad are available in the various colleges.

Support Services Handicapped-accessible facilities are extensive and managed by a special office on campus.

Job Opportunities Work-study and other campus jobs are available. Many other off-campus opportunities exist. Honors students often participate in the co-op program.

Tuition: $4131 for state residents, $10,783 for nonresidents, per year (1996-97)

Room and Board: $2910 minimum

Contact: Director: Charles J. Dudley, 1 Hillcrest Hall, Blacksburg, Virginia 24061-0427; Telephone: 540-231-4951; Fax: 540-231-4522; E-mail: honors@vt.edu; Web site: http://www.vt.edu:10021/univhonors/

WAGNER COLLEGE

4 Pr G M Sc Tr

▼ Honors Program

The Wagner College Honors Program offers students in all majors an opportunity for academic enrichment, both inside the classroom and out.

All honors courses at Wagner fulfill the College-wide distribution requirements, and they are designed to provide the College's best students with a challenging, interactive learning environment that will enhance their overall academic experience at the College. The classes are small and taught by Wagner's finest faculty members.

The honors experience at Wagner extends beyond the classroom to a variety of cocurricular activities organized for honors students, ranging from a speaker series, pretheater dinners, and other events on campus to trips into Manhattan to visit galleries and museums and attend plays and concerts. This creates a close-knit learning community for honors students that provides them with stimulation, friendship, and support. Many of Wagner's finest honors students also play an important leadership role on campus in student government, athletics, music, and theater. The Honors Program at Wagner is now in its fifth year and has become an important feature of the College's academic program.

There are 275 students in the program.

Participation Requirements: Students are expected to complete ten honors courses (30 hours), usually two each semester during the freshman and sophomore years and two courses in their major during the junior and senior years. The final honors course is a senior honors project, which gives advanced students an opportunity to work independently with a faculty mentor. Students who complete the program and maintain a minimum GPA of 3.0 receive an Honors Certificate upon graduation.

Admission Process: Students apply first to Wagner, and the Admissions Office decides who will be invited to join the Honors Program. Transfer students who wish to join may apply to the program director at the end of the freshman year or the beginning of the sophomore year. February 15 is the priority deadline.

Scholarship Availability: Wagner awards Presidential or Dean's Merit Scholarships to the best incoming freshmen, who are also invited to join the Honors Program. Scholarship recipients are not required to join the program, however, and students who have not received these prestigious scholarships are permitted to apply for admission to the Honors Program.

The Campus Context: Wagner College is a competitive, four-year private college founded in 1883. It is located on a lovely 105-acre, wooded campus on a hill overlooking New York harbor, only a ferry ride away from Manhattan. Twenty-two degree programs are offered on campus.

Student Body Undergraduate enrollment is 1,500; 58 percent are women. The ethnic distribution includes a minority population of 17 percent and 44 international students. Sixty-five percent of students are residential, and 70 percent receive some form of financial aid. There are five fraternities and five sororities.

Faculty The faculty numbers 182, of whom 78 are full-time; 82 percent hold terminal degrees. The student-faculty ratio is 18:1.

Key Facilities There are 285,000 volumes in the library. Other facilities include a mainframe computer and 150 IBM PC terminal environments, two electron microscopes, an art gallery, and a planetarium.

Athletics Wagner is NCAA Division I-A in all intercollegiate athletics except football, which is Division I-AA. Wagner is one of the five founders of the NIT at Madison Square

Garden, and it has a tradition of excellence in baseball, basketball, and football. There is a well-equipped fitness center in the Student Union.

Study Abroad Wagner offers extensive opportunities for study abroad in Asia and Europe as well as other parts of the world. In association with the prestigious Institute for European and Asian Studies, Wagner students may study for a semester or summer in London, Madrid, Paris, Rome, Tokyo, and Vienna, among other locations.

Support Services The campus is partially accessible to disabled students and makes readers available for blind students.

Job Opportunities Work opportunities on campus include Federal Work-Study and non–work-study positions available in most administrative offices, residence halls, and academic departments.

Tuition: $16,000 per year (1997-98)

Room and Board: $6000

Contact: Director: Dr. Alison A. Smith, Staten Island, New York 10301; Telephone: 718-390-3253; Fax: 718-390-3467; E-mail: aasmith@wagner.edu; Web site: http://www.wagner.edu

---

WALDORF COLLEGE

2/3 Pr C S Sc Tr

▼ Honors College

The Honors College at Waldorf provides a rewarding learning environment for highly capable students. The program is distinguished by its select faculty, interdisciplinary courses and seminars, independent projects, and a culminating world trip.

In addition to special course offerings and the world trip, Honors College students may choose to go on regional cultural trips, usually at no cost, to attend plays, concerts, lectures, and conferences.

There are 60 students currently enrolled in the program.

Participation Requirements: Whether students attend Waldorf for their A.A. degree or for the accelerated three-year B.A. degree, they may remain Honors College students as long as they meet the 3.2 GPA eligibility requirement. Each semester students may take honors sections of general education courses, honors courses, and/or independent projects in their majors. Honors College students with at least a 3.5 GPA who also take several prescribed courses, undertake a special research project in their major, and give a presentation at Waldorf's annual academic conference are eligible for Waldorf Scholar status. Waldorf Scholars travel for two or three weeks to a global destination with 2 faculty members. Students pay a nominal fee for the trip; the College subsidizes about 85 percent of the cost in honor of its Scholars.

Entering students take a two-semester freshman seminar that replaces the first-year English requirement, and they may elect to take honors sections of other required courses. Sophomores typically take a philosophy course that is team-taught by selected faculty members, administrators (including the president of the College), and outside resource persons from the community. Honors colloquia, which focus on controversial issues in a seminar setting, are offered each semester.

The Campus Context: Waldorf College is a distinctive two- and three-year residential college affiliated with the Evangelical Lutheran Church of America. It occupies 50 acres and fourteen buildings in Forest City, Iowa, to which it attracts a student body of about 550 students from the region and from twenty states and twenty nations of the world. The College offers a variety of A.A. degrees as well as B.A. degrees in business and communications. All entering students are equipped with IBM Thinkpads, and the campus is fully networked. Computer facilities and student access to high-end technology at Waldorf exceed the capabilities of most other institutions in the region. The Honors College, another special offering at Waldorf, is an expansion of the very successful Honors Program that has been a feature at Waldorf for ten years.

Student Body Of the 555 students, 44 percent are women. Four percent represent ethnic minorities. There are 77 international students. Ninety-five percent of the students receive financial aid.

Faculty The faculty totals 50, of whom 31 are full-time and 22 percent have Ph.D. or terminal degrees.

Key Facilities The library houses 40,000 volumes. All students are provided IBM Thinkpad laptops; also available are a fourteen-station multimedia lab and two computer labs. Waldorf's business and communications programs offer work in the new multimedia lab that has fourteen PowerMacs. The AVID digital video editing suite is also available to students.

Athletics Waldorf has a very successful program of intercollegiate athletics, competing in Region XI of the National Junior College Athletic Association. Sports include baseball, basketball, football, golf, soccer, and wrestling for men and basketball, golf, softball, and volleyball for women.

Study Abroad Business and communications B.A. students can spend a winter term studying in Oxford, England; Honors College students may participate in the world trip, a guided study trip abroad.

Support Services The campus is accessible to the physically disabled; support personnel and programs are available to the learning disabled.

Job Opportunities Waldorf offers work-study and other work opportunities on campus.

Tuition: $11,050 per year (1997-98)

Room and Board: $4200

Mandatory Fees: $200

Contact: Director: Dr. Nicholas Preus, 106 South 6th Street, Forest City, Iowa 50436; Telephone: 515-582-8225; Fax: 515-582-8194; E-mail: preusn@thor.waldorf.edu

WALSH UNIVERSITY

4 Pr G S Sc Tr

▼ General Honors Program

The Walsh University Honors Program offers motivated and capable undergraduate students the opportunity to broaden and deepen their academic experience. Students participate in an intellectually challenging and innovative curriculum emphasizing interdisciplinary and independent studies. Outside of the classroom, honors students have the advantage of enriching cultural and social activities planned especially for them. As members of the Walsh University Honors Society, honors students join with faculty, administrators, and peers in fostering a community of learners with a shared sense of purpose in the pursuit of academic excellence.

The program began in 1993–94. There are currently 45 students in the program, which can accommodate up to 20 students in each of the freshman, sophomore, junior, and senior classes.

Participation Requirements: In both semesters of their freshman year, students in the General Honors Program take special sections of history and English. In their sophomore year, they take an interdisciplinary course (Honors 200) organized around a significant theme or historical movement; the topic changes from year to year and the class is normally team-taught. Past courses have included one on the environment taught by a philosopher and mathematician and one on issues of aging taught by a sociologist and a member of the nursing faculty. Each year, faculty members who wish to teach the interdisciplinary course submit proposals to the Honors Committee. Qualified transfer and second-year students can join the Honors Program under the Track II option with Honors 200.

In their junior year, honors students take a team-taught, interdisciplinary course with rotating topics and complete a junior honors project in one of their regularly scheduled upper-division courses, usually in their major.

The capstone of the honors program is the senior honors thesis, an independent research project of either 3 or 6 credits that allows students to investigate issues of significance while working closely with a supportive faculty mentor. Honors projects are modeled on the types of research, writing, and creativity typical of graduate schools and are meant to serve as preparation for such study. The project includes an oral presentation in a final celebration with faculty members and peers in fulfilling the final requirements of the program.

All honors courses except the senior thesis fulfill either core or major requirements. Students completing the General Honors Program graduate with 24–27 credit hours of honors courses. Track II students graduate with 12–15 credit hours.

Admission Process: To be eligible to apply for the General Honors Program, students must meet any two of the following three criteria: a high school GPA of 3.5 or above, a minimum ACT score of 27 or a minimum SAT I score of 1200, and graduation in the top 10 percent of one's high school class. Track II candidates must have completed at least 30 credit hours of undergraduate work with at least a 3.3 GPA. Students remain in good standing in the Honors Program with a 3.3 cumulative GPA and at least a grade of B in all honors courses.

Scholarship Availability: The University offers a limited number of full tuition Presidential Scholarships to incoming freshmen. Presidential Scholars are automatically part of the Honors Program. To apply for a Presidential Scholarship a student must meet two of the following three criteria: 4.0 GPA, rank in the upper 1 percent of the graduating class, and a minimum score of 31 on the ACT or 1230 on the SAT I. All other students accepted into the Honors Program receive an Honors Program Scholarship. For the 1996-97 school year this scholarship was $1300 per year, with periodic increases as tuition rises. Honors Program scholarships are renewable each year a student remains eligible for the program.

The Campus Context: Walsh University is an independent, coeducational, Catholic liberal arts institution. Founded by the Brothers of Christian Instruction, Walsh University is dedicated to a values-based education with an international perspective in the Judeo-Christian tradition. Walsh University is located in North Canton, 5 miles north of Canton in northeastern Ohio. Akron is 20 miles away, and both Cleveland and Youngstown are within an hour's drive. Walsh University has nine major buildings on its 60-acre suburban campus. More than forty degree programs are offered.

Among distinguished campus facilities is the Hannon Child Development Center, which provides specialized educational facilities for special-needs and at-risk children ages 2–10 and their families. It has teaching stations for teacher preparation students, a motor development room for physical activities, classrooms for University and early education students, and a computer classroom. The Science Center was recently renovated extensively in support of the University's proposed physical therapy program. The University currently offers a pre–physical therapy program and is seeking approval from the Ohio Board of Regents and the American Physical Therapy Association for its own five-year bachelor's degree in physical therapy. Renovations have included the creation of a mini-clinic, academic laboratory, conference room, and offices.

Student Body Undergraduate enrollment is approximately 1,300. Fifty-nine percent are women. The ethnic distribution is .1 percent American Indian/Alaskan Native, 5 percent black/African American, .3 percent Asian American, and 80 percent white. There are 47 international students. Resident students make up 30 percent of the population, and approximately 80 percent of the students receive financial aid.

Faculty There are a total of 125 faculty members, 65 of whom are full-time. Fifty-nine percent hold terminal degrees. The student-faculty ratio is 19:1.

Key Facilities The library houses 130,000 volumes, 750 current periodical subscriptions on paper, and 400 current periodical subscriptions with full text on CD-ROM. There are seventy-five computers on campus available to students, including Macs and PCs. There are large computer labs in the Lemmon residence hall and the Hannon Child Development Center. Computers in other buildings are also available to students. Campus computers are networked with Internet access. Computer hookups with Internet access are located in each residence hall room (student must provide computer).

Athletics Walsh University has eight men's and eight women's intercollegiate athletic teams, which are members of the Mid-Ohio Conference (MOC), National Association of Intercollegiate Athletics (Division II) and the Mid States Football Association. Men's sports include baseball, basketball, cross-country, football, golf, soccer, tennis, and track. Women's sports include basketball, cross-country, soccer, softball, synchronized swimming, tennis, track, and volleyball. In 1995–96, Walsh won the MOC All-Sports Award, becoming the first school to win the award three times.

Support Services Facilities for disabled students include the Lemmon residence hall, which is particularly suited for special-needs students. Most of the campus is accessible to disabled students, and Walsh offers assistance for disabled students on an individual basis.

Job Opportunities With the exception of the summer sessions, work opportunities on campus are offered through the Federal Work-Study Program.

Tuition: $9900 per year (1996-97)

Room and Board: $4760

Mandatory Fees: $300

Contact: Director: Dr. David J. Baxter, 2020 Easton N.W., North Canton, Ohio 44720; Telephone: 330-490-7045; Fax: 330-499-8518

Washington State University

 4 Pu G L Sc Tr

▼ University Honors Program

The University Honors Program (UHP) at Washington State University is one of the oldest (founded in 1960) and best-known honors programs in the nation. A free-standing academic unit, the UHP offers highly motivated and talented students an alternative curriculum in place of general education requirements. The UHP has as its primary goal the fostering of genuine intellectual curiosity and the encouragement of lifelong learning among its students. The UHP aims to support the best possible teach-

ing and learning opportunities for participating faculty and students. Honors courses are small and are taught by faculty members who have a commitment to teaching undergraduate students. The UHP has a tradition of encouraging students to study a foreign language and to study abroad. Approximately half of the honors students complete a foreign language through the intermediate level or study abroad on one of the University's special Honors Exchanges or education abroad programs.

Several special programs are available to WSU honors students. These include the Honors/Veterinary Medicine program that enables eligible students to complete a B.S./D.V.M. in six years rather than eight; the 4 & 1 program that allows students to obtain a B.A. in a liberal arts major and an M.B.A. in five years rather than six; special Honors Exchanges to Wales and Denmark; and the opportunity to live in WSU's Scholars Residence Hall (opening in 1997).

Approximately 950 students are enrolled in the UHP. Honors students major in every department and college at WSU.

Participation Requirements: The honors curriculum is a four-year program that requires the same number of credits as the general education program. To graduate from the UHP, students must have a minimum 3.2 overall GPA. Each spring, the UHP honors its graduates with a banquet the night before Commencement when certificates, awards, and special honors medallions are distributed. Completion of the UHP also is noted on students' transcripts.

Admission Process: Admission of first-year students to the UHP is by invitation. After students have applied and been admitted to WSU, Honors Program faculty members review their files and identify prospective honors students based upon their high school grades, test scores (SAT or ACT), and (if available) recommendations from high school faculty members or counselors. Transfer and international students are admitted on an individual basis after eligibility has been determined. Students already at WSU may seek admission to the UHP if their GPA is 3.4 or better.

Within WSU guidelines, the UHP accepts Advanced Placement and Running Start credits to fulfill honors requirements.

Scholarship Availability: The Honors Program administers two scholarship programs, the Bornander Scholarships and the Johnson Scholarships. In addition, WSU has many merit scholarship programs at the departmental, college, and University level. Honors students are among the most frequent recipients of these awards.

The Campus Context: Washington State University was founded in 1890 as the state's land-grant university. There are ninety-six degree programs offered in the eight colleges, which include the Colleges of Pharmacy, Liberal Arts, Veterinary Medicine, Agriculture and Home Economics, Business and Economics, Engineering and Architecture, Sciences, and Education. The main campus in Pullman is located in the rolling farmlands of southeast Washington. WSU is one of the largest residential campuses west of the Mississippi River. WSU's branch campuses were established in 1989 and are located in major urban areas in the state: Spokane, the Tri-Cities, and Vancouver.

At this time, honors is available only on the Pullman campus. The UHP is housed in Bryan Hall, one of the oldest buildings on campus. Within the Honors Center are faculty and staff offices, a library, and a student lounge. Other special or distinguishing campus facilities include Stevens Hall, on the Historic Register, the oldest and most continuously in-use residence hall West of the Mississippi River; the new Veterinary Teaching Hospital; a new main library; Beasley Performing Arts Coliseum; and art, anthropology, and science museums.

Student Body Undergraduate enrollment is 14,654; 48 percent of the students are women. The minority ethnic distribution is 1.7 percent Native American, 5.5 percent Asian American, 2.3 percent African American, and 3.2 percent Hispanic. There are 898 international students. Forty-two percent of students live on campus, and 55 percent of WSU undergraduate students receive financial aid. The campus has twenty-five fraternities and fourteen sororities.

Faculty Instructional faculty members number 1,206. Seventy-eight percent have terminal degrees. The student-faculty ratio is 16:1.

Key Facilities WSU libraries house more than 1.7 million volumes. There are seven University-operated computer labs; many other computer labs are located in departments and colleges.

Athletics WSU is a member of the NCAA's PAC 10, and facilities are available for all major sports, including baseball, basketball, crew, football, golf, swimming, tennis, and track and field. WSU has one of the largest University-sponsored intramural programs in the nation.

Study Abroad Through WSU's Education Abroad Office, students can participate in exchanges, study-abroad programs, internships, and service-learning opportunities in most countries around the world. The Honors Program has special exchanges to Wales and Denmark.

Support Services Eighty percent of the campus is accessible to physically disabled students.

Job Opportunities Work opportunities are available on and off campus.

Tuition: $3142 for state residents, $9758 for nonresidents, per year (1996-97)

Room and Board: $4150

Mandatory Fees: $128

Contact: Director: Dr. Jane Fiori Lawrence, Bryan Hall, Room 206, Pullman, Washington 99164-5120; Telephone: 509-335-4505; Fax: 509-335-3784; E-mail: lawrencj@wsuvm1.csc.wsu.edu

WEBER STATE UNIVERSITY

4 Pu G M Sc Tr

▼ Honors Program

The Honors Program is designed to offer students of superior ability and motivation opportunities to broaden and enrich their academic program and accelerate their preparation for graduate work. The Honors Program provides a separate curriculum including courses that fulfill part of a student's general education requirements. In addition to general education classes, workshops, seminars, upper-division classes, tutorials, and independent student and research classes are offered. University students write a senior thesis as a capstone experience.

Honors Program classes are limited to a maximum of 20 students and are taught by a select faculty. Honors faculty members are distinguished by their commitment to academic excellence and for their ability to work and communicate with highly motivated undergraduates. The University's teaching method emphasizes reading original sources, writing essays, and Socratic dialogue. The Honors Program also creates a learning community of students and faculty members through extracurricular social and cultural activities, guest speakers, study groups, participation in national and regional conferences, and travel-abroad opportunities.

There are two honors designations in the Weber Honors Program: University Honors and Departmental Honors. University Honors are available to all Honors Program students graduating with a bachelor's degree. Departmental Honors are available to students majoring in departments with designated Departmental Honors options. The new honors student begins taking University Honors classes to satisfy their general education requirements starting with an introductory honors education class. Established in 1969, the program currently enrolls 380 students (101 seniors, 87 juniors, 97 sophomores, and 95 freshmen).

Participation Requirements: To graduate with University Honors, a student must complete a minimum of 40 University Honors credits, including 20 honors core credits, and can include 10 credit hours of classes with an honors component in their major. The Honors Core classes include Perspectives in the Applied Arts and Sciences: Introduction to Honors Education (4 credits), choice of at least one West and one East, Intellectual Traditions: Great Ideas of the West in the Classical and Medieval Eras (4 credits), Intellectual Traditions: Great Ideas of the Modern Era (4 credits), Intellectual Traditions: Great Ideas of the East (4 credits), Great Books (3 credits) or Directed Readings, Oxbridge Tutorial Method (3 credits), Honors Colloquium (2–4 credits), and Honors Senior Project (2–8 credits, taken over a two-quarter period normally during the last two quarters of the senior year).

The requirements for graduation with Departmental Honors vary depending on the student's departmental major.

Most departments require students graduating with Departmental Honors to complete 10 credit hours of University Honors classes, 20 hours of upper-division classes in their major with an honors component, and maintain a cumulative 3.5 GPA.

Students are expected to take an honors class every quarter until general education requirements are completed, after which they are expected to take at least one course every other quarter. No grades below B will be acceptable for credit toward graduation with University or Departmental Honors. Student progress is reviewed quarterly. An honors student having apparent difficulty in maintaining these standards will be offered counseling and assistance from the honors professional staff.

Official recognition is given for the completion of University Honors or Departmental Honors. Notation of these achievements is made on the graduating Honors student's transcript and diploma and entered into Commencement programs.

Admission Process: A student may apply for entrance into the Honors Program anytime after formal acceptance by the Weber State Admissions Office. However, to take advantage of the many options available, early entrance is recommended. An application form is available in the honors office. The applicant is asked to provide evidence of a cumulative GPA of at least 3.5 or an ACT score of 26 or SAT I score of 1150; provide a recommendation from a university professor, a high school teacher or counselor, or another professional educator; give the honors director a writing sample; attend an honors orientation with a member of the Honors Program staff; and register for the honors introductory class. Incoming first-year students may elect to participate in the Honors Bridge Program.

The Campus Context: Weber State University, established 1889, is a four-year institution of higher education in Ogden, Utah. WSU offers 153 separate degrees and is the largest and most comprehensive undergraduate program in the state of Utah. It has a student body of 14,000 drawn predominantly from the Wasatch Front but also including students from thirty-eight states and forty-one other countries. Its forty-one buildings house abundant classrooms and laboratories, excellent student computing facilities, outstanding performing arts auditoriums, a spacious library, and a well-equipped health and fitness center. There are six colleges on campus: Applied Science and Technology, Arts and Humanities, Business and Economics, Education, Health Professions, and Science and Social and Behavioral Sciences.

WSU is large and complex enough to offer a stimulating educational challenge but small enough to be concerned about the welfare of individual students. WSU works closely as partners-in-learning with communities and organizations.

Student Body Undergraduate enrollment is 13,996; 53 percent are women. Ethnic distribution of the total undergraduate population is 1 percent African American, .8 percent Native American, 2.1 percent Asian/Pacific Islander, and 2.7 percent Hispanic. About 55 percent of the students receive financial aid.

Faculty There are 441 full-time faculty members, 68 percent of whom have doctorates or other terminal degrees. The student-faculty ratio is 19:1.

Key Facilities The library houses 352,000 bound volumes; 2,068 periodical subscriptions; 429,309 titles on microform; 24,114 audio, video, and computer titles; and 58,603 maps.

Student computer labs are distributed around the campus and are under the charge of various departments. In addition, academic computing manages fifty-two PC workstations in natural science and nine PC and three Mac workstations in the library. The Honors Centre is on the second floor of the library; there are five PC/Windows computers available for student use. There are twenty-five PC and two Mac workstations in the Wattis Lab, fifty-two PC workstations and a classroom with thirty workstations in social science, and forty-three Mac workstations in education.

Support Services WSU is a fully accessible campus for disabled students. Service programs include reading, note-taking, interpreting, scribe service, and campus transportation.

Job Opportunities Cooperative education, internship programs, and on-campus job opportunities, including work-study, are available through the Career Services Office.

Tuition: $1461 for state residents, $5148 for nonresidents, per year (1996-97)

Room and Board: $3270

Mandatory Fees: $402

Contact: Director: Dr. Ronald L. Holt, 2904 University Circle, Ogden, Utah 84408-2904; Telephone: 301-626-6230; Fax: 301-626-7568; E-mail: rholt2@weber.edu

---

WESTERN KENTUCKY UNIVERSITY

 4 Pu G M Sc Tr

▼ University Honors Program

The University Honors Program, begun in 1963, offers special classes, colloquia, and seminars designed to meet the educational abilities and needs of Western's highest-achieving students. Completing the Honors Program is very beneficial when students apply to competitive graduate and professional schools and compete for prestigious fellowships and scholarships.

The program is designed to encourage students to expand their intellectual curiosity, acquire a broad understanding of the world, and develop their abilities to read with insight, think logically and creatively, write with precision, and engage in original scholarly research.

Since all honors work except for the 1-hour course entitled Opportunities in Honors and the two 1½-hour colloquia or seminars fulfill either the general education requirements or count toward one's major, a student can in most cases complete any baccalaureate program and the Honors Program without increasing the number of hours needed for graduation.

Honors classes are kept small, and participation is limited to honors-eligible students. For these reasons, honors courses allow deeper presentation of course material and freer discussion than are possible in most classes. As appropriate for each course, honors sections often include a greater focus upon original sources, research methods, complex issues, and analytical writing. Honors classes are also more likely to include classroom debates, student-led classes, and group research projects. Most honors courses offer general education credit.

Other advantages of membership in the program include participation in intercollegiate honors organizations such as Kentucky Honors Roundtable, Southern Regional Honors Council, National Collegiate Honors Council, and National Conference on Undergraduate Research; opportunities to serve as a student representative on the Honors Committee, which oversees program policies, curriculum revisions, budget allocations, and student concerns; the opportunity to be elected student representative (one in each academic class) by the honors students to serve a one-year term; honors priority registration, in which honors students who are registering for at least one honors course may register at the same time as seniors; honors housing on designated floors of a coeducational residence hall; honors forums and cultural events; the Student Honors Research Bulletin, in which are published the best student papers nominated by faculty each year; and honors scholarships.

The 33-year-old program currently enrolls approximately 400 students.

Participation Requirements:
Participants must maintain a college GPA of at least 3.2. However, a one-semester grace period is usually provided for those whose GPA falls below 3.2.

Students recognized as Honors Program graduates must have a final GPA of 3.4 or higher. The designation Graduate of the University Honors Program is added to each graduate's final transcript, as is the title of the student's senior honors thesis. Graduates also receive an Honors Program certificate in recognition of completion of the program.

Admission Process:
Students starting the Honors Program as entering freshmen should have a minimum 3.5 high school GPA and a score of at least 25 on the ACT or 1150 on the recentered SAT I. However, those with very strong grades or aptitude scores who do not meet the other standards are considered individually. Students with at least 16 hours of college work are admitted with a minimum 3.2 college GPA.

Scholarship Availability:
The Honors Program awards about twenty-five $250 scholarships to entering honors freshmen each year. These scholarships may be added to any other scholarship a student receives to attend Western. Honors students who do not receive this scholarship as freshmen may apply for later years. The honors scholarship is increased to $400 for students in their junior and senior years. Honors scholarships are awarded on a competitive basis. For entering freshmen, high school GPA and aptitude test scores are considered most strongly. For returning students, college GPA and progress toward completion of the honors curriculum are considered most strongly, with some consideration of financial need. Honors scholarships are automatically renewed for up to four years for students making regular progress toward the completion of the honors curriculum and maintaining a 3.2 GPA or better. For continuation in the second semester of their junior year, students must file an undergraduate degree program approved by the honors director the fall semester of the junior year.

The Campus Context: Western Kentucky University is composed of five colleges: Potter College of Arts, Humanities and Social Sciences; College of Business Administration; College of Education and Behavioral Sciences; College of Science, Technology and Health; and Community College. Sixteen degree programs are offered on campus. Special facilities include the Kentucky Library and Museum and the Hardin Planetarium.

Student Body Undergraduate enrollment is approximately 58 percent women. The ethnic distribution of students is 6.6 percent African American, .9 percent Asian, .6 percent Hispanic, .3 percent American Indian, and 91.4 percent white. There are 78 international students. Thirty-two percent of the students are residents. Sixty percent of the students receive financial aid. There are fifteen fraternities and ten sororities.

Faculty Of the 859 faculty members, 542 are full-time; 70 percent hold terminal degrees. The student-faculty ratio is 19:1.

Key Facilities The library houses more than 500,000 volumes. The entire campus is networked. More than 660 computers are available in the library, classroom buildings, and student center.

Athletics Western has intercollegiate athletics teams in baseball, basketball, cross-country, football, golf, soccer, swimming, tennis, track and field, and volleyball. The University is a member of and adheres to the regulations of the Sun Belt Conference and the National Collegiate Athletic Association. The intramural-recreational sports program exists to provide all students, faculty, and staff a setting for constructive participation in recreational activities. It consists of men's and women's competitive sports, coed sports, faculty/staff activities, recreational free-play, instructional programs, organized fitness classes, and sports club activities.

Study Abroad Among study-abroad options are the Western in France Program in Montpelier, France, and Study Tour Programs in Britain, including the Ireland Program, Celtic Program, and King's College Program. Also available are summer terms, special-interest Christmas vacation tours, and Semester in Cambridge. The Kentucky Institute for International Studies offers summer study programs in Austria,

Ecuador, France, Germany, Italy, Mexico, and Spain. Study-travel programs are also offered by various University departments.

Support Services The Student Support Services Program provides comprehensive, continuing academic assistance for undergraduate students with academic potential who meet financial guidelines, are from families where neither parent holds a bachelor's degree, or are physically disabled. In coordination with the Office of the Dean of Student Life, the project offers individual assistance to qualified students with disabilities (including learning disabilities) in need of accommodation. Tape recorders, alternative testing procedures, and a support group are available as needed. All services are free of charge to qualified students.

The Office for Disability Services helps students with disabilities experience an adequate academic and social environment while attending the University. The office coordinates its activities through many other campus offices as well as public agencies. Students with disabilities receive priority in academic advising and class selection with particular attention to locations of accessible classes.

Job Opportunities Employment for students is available through the Federal Work-Study Program (FWS), Institutional Work Program, full-time summer employment opportunities, and referral service for off-campus job placement.

Tuition: $1740 for state residents, $5220 for nonresidents, per year (1996–97)

Room and Board: $2666

Mandatory Fees: $290

Contact: Director: Dr. Sam McFarland, Garrett Conference Center 105, 1 Big Red Way, Bowling Green, Kentucky 42101-3576; Telephone: 502-745-2081; Fax: 502-745-2081 *51; E-mail: sam.mcfarland@wku.edu, lisa.beaty@wku.edu; Web site: http://wkuweb1.wku.edu/Dept/Special/Honors/index.htm

WESTERN WASHINGTON UNIVERSITY

4 Pu G M Sc Tr

▼ University Honors Program

The Western Washington University Honors Program was created in 1962 to offer selected students of high academic achievement the opportunity to participate in a challenging intellectual enterprise. Since then, honors has grown to offer a wide variety of courses in general education, more specialized seminars, and the opportunity to work one-on-one with a faculty member in the completion of a senior project.

Honors courses are rigorous and stress active participation, writing, and independent thinking. Honors faculty members come from programs and departments throughout the University and are known campuswide for their excellence as classroom teachers.

Honors students come from every college in the University, but the largest number major in the natural sciences, including programs such as premedicine and environmental science. Students in honors must fulfill all the requirements set forth in the University's *General Catalogue*, including those for general education and the major. Students with AP credit, work in the International Baccalaureate program, or other forms of credit that award them advanced standing may be able to count that work toward completion of the requirements for the program.

The program admits up to 50 freshmen each year and has a total enrollment of about 160.

Graduation through honors is a mark of distinction, and students are recognized at Commencement and receive notations on their transcripts indicating they have completed the program.

Participation Requirements: Students who enter the program as freshmen complete a year-long sequence of courses that introduces them to the Western cultural tradition and other general education courses and specialized seminars. Seminar topics change annually and cover all the major disciplinary areas (e.g., natural sciences, humanities, and social sciences). Honors classes are always small and open only to honors students. Sections of the freshman sequence and other general education courses have enrollments of not more than 25 to 30, while seminars enroll 12 or fewer. All students who graduate through the program must complete a senior project, where they work individually with a professor or, in some instances, more than one professor. The project is usually in the major, but in some cases it may be in an auxiliary area. Students are encouraged to think creatively about the project, and while many elect to write a traditional thesis, recitals, shows, and other creative works have all been offered to fulfill this requirement. To graduate through honors, students must maintain a minimum 3.5 GPA for the last 90 graded credits of academic work and fulfill specific departmental requirements where they exist. Students in the program have gone on to graduate and professional programs at the finest institutions in the nation.

Admission Process: Admission to the program is competitive. Entering freshmen, transfer students, and already enrolled Western students may apply directly or answer an invitation from the program. Honors does not use set formulas for admission. Rather, candidates are evaluated according to a number of factors in order to determine the likelihood of their success in the program. When reviewing an applicant, the program considers previous academic achievement, including GPA and class rank; a detailed letter of recommendation; scores on appropriate tests; the applicant's writing; and when possible, an interview. In considering students for admission, the program regards a demonstrated commitment to serious academic work to be at least as important as aptitude. Applications must be received by March 15.

The Campus Context: Western Washington University was founded in 1893 as the one of the state's normal schools. It became a college of education in 1937, a state college in 1961, and a university in 1977. The University is located in Bellingham, a community of 50,000 on Puget Sound, about 90 miles north of Seattle, Washington. The 190-acre campus is located on a hill high above Bellingham Bay, an arm of Puget Sound, and in the words of one publication "is a stunning blend of art and nature." Its outdoor sculpture collection is internationally renowned. Almost 200 undergraduate majors are offered leading to baccalaureate degrees in the humanities, social sciences, natural sciences, and many applied and professional programs; students may also design their own majors. Western has been mentioned numerous times in *U.S. News & World Report, Barron's,* and *Money* magazines as an outstanding educational value. Its Honors Program has been cited in *Money* magazine as one of the twenty-five best in the nation. Outdoor activities are easily accessible and include skiing, boating, and hiking.

Student Body The total enrollment is 10,250, more than 90 percent of whom are undergraduates. Students come primarily from the state of Washington. Women outnumber men by approximately 55 to 45 percent. Members of minority groups constitute approximately 15 percent of enrollment, with those of Asian descent most common. Approximately 50 percent of students receive financial aid. Western does not have fraternities or sororities.

Faculty There are more than 425 full-time faculty members and in excess of 100 adjunct faculty members. Almost all hold doctorates or other terminal degrees. The student-faculty ratio is 24:1.

Key Facilities The Wilson Library holds more than 500,000 volumes and an additional 500,000 microform titles. There are networked microcomputing labs across campus available to students with general purpose software for both Macintosh and IBM computers. Students regard computer facilities as easily accessible, but many students bring their own.

Fourteen residence halls house approximately 4,000 students. The campus has a residential character, and most students live within walking or easy driving distance.

Athletics The University offers broadly based intercollegiate sports programs for men and women. Western competes in the National Association of Intercollegiate Athletics Division II. Approximately two thirds of students participate in intramural sports.

Study Abroad Western students may study abroad through ISEP or other international programs. Study abroad is compatible with most majors, and many honors students elect the option to do academic work in another country.

Job Opportunities A wide variety of on-campus employment opportunities is available.

Tuition: $2433 for state residents, $8616 for nonresidents, per year (1996-97)

Room and Board: $4478

Mandatory Fees: $180

Contact: Director: Dr. George Mariz, 228 Miller Hall, Bellingham, Washington 98225-9089; Telephone: 360-650-3446; Fax: 360-650-4837; E-mail: gmariz@mail2.admcs.wwu.edu

WEST VIRGINIA UNIVERSITY

4 Pu G L Sc Tr

▼ University Honors Program

The Honors Program incorporates a style of learning and living at West Virginia University tailored to the highly motivated, excelling student's special requirements. Honors courses, designed to stimulate creativity and provoke in-depth discussion, are offered in classes with 20 or fewer students. First-rate faculty members noted for their scholarly achievement and outstanding instruction teach the honors classes. These same teachers and other faculty members serve as honors advisers, guiding students through their individual academic programs.

Upon graduation, the students' diplomas and transcripts indicate the degree earned and the designation University Honors Scholar. In addition, 2 graduating seniors are chosen each year for the Joginder and Charlotte Nath Award, which is geared toward students doing research. The Dennis O'Brian Award recognizes 2 outstanding seniors who have exemplified service, toward both the community and the Honors Program.

Begun in 1981, the Honors Program has graduated 622 students. Currently, there are 700 students in the program. Generally, the Honors Program accepts the top 5 percent of WVU students.

Participation Requirements: To graduate as a University Honors Scholar (UHS), students must complete a minimum of 24 credit hours of designated honors courses. There are two tracks that a student may follow. One is the regular track, which requires a minimum of 18 hours of honors classes plus a 3-credit senior seminar and 3–6 credit hours in a summer guided reading or research study for a minimum total of 24–27 hours. The other is the thesis track, in which students take a minimum of 18 hours of honors classes plus 6–12 hours of independent research. Switching between these two tracks is flexible. In order to remain in the program, the student must maintain a minimum 3.2 GPA during the freshman year and a 3.3 during the sophomore and junior years. A student must achieve a 3.4 GPA or better during the senior year in order to graduate UHS.

All entering freshmen are required to take a 1-credit honors orientation class, which is taught by upper-class honors students, and to live in the honors section of Dadisman Hall if they are living on campus. Trips to Washington, D.C., and Pittsburgh are planned throughout the year, as well as ski trips and other social and cultural events through the local community.

Admission Process: Entering freshmen are considered for admission to the program on the basis of their ACT or SAT composite standard scores and their high school GPAs or their status as National Merit Semifinalists. WVU students with fewer than 34 credit hours and at least a 3.7 GPA with no grades of I or W may also apply. There is no deadline for application to the program. Transfer students who have accrued 34 or fewer college credit hours and have maintained an overall GPA of 3.7 or better with no grades of I or W from an accredited institution may be accepted as a WVU honors student. In addition, honors students with college GPAs that meet WVU standards for regularly admitted honors students will be accepted if the honors admissions standards at the University from which a student is transferring are similar to those at WVU.

Scholarship Availability: Most scholarships are offered through the Scholars Program and vary in amount. Many students in the Scholars Program are also in the Honors Program, although acceptance into the Scholars Program does not automatically qualify a student for the Honors Program, or vice versa. If students have no other aid of any kind (scholarships, grants, or loans), the Honors Program does offer a small stipend for full-time honors students.

The Campus Context: West Virginia University Agricultural College, officially founded in February 1867, was renamed West Virginia University in 1868, and the land-grant mission has shaped the University's overall curriculum ever since. WVU is located in Morgantown, West Virginia, about 70 miles south of Pittsburgh and 200 miles west of Washington, D.C. WVU is a member of the North Central Association of Colleges and Schools and has three branch campuses: Potomac State College in Keyser, West Virginia; WVU–Parkersburg in Parkersburg, West Virginia; and WVU Institute of Technology in Montgomery, West Virginia.

The Morgantown campus contains 158 buildings on 673 acres. Eleven campus buildings are listed on the National Register of Historic Places. WVU operates eight experimental farms and four forests throughout the state. More than $350 million has been invested in new facilities for the Colleges of Engineering and Mineral Resources and Business and Economics, Engineering Research Center, National Research Center for Coal and Energy, Ruby Memorial Hospital, and the WVU/NASA Independent Verification and Validation Facility. In addition, the Personal Rapid Transit (PrT) moves students from one end of campus to the other in only a matter of minutes. Built by the U.S. Department of Transportation as a national research project, the PrT consists of computer-directed, electric-powered cars that operate on a concrete and steel guideway.

WVU is composed of seven colleges and seven schools. The Colleges are Agriculture and Forestry, Eberly College of Arts and Sciences, Business and Economics, Creative Arts, Engineering and Mineral Resources, Human Resources and Education, and Law. The Schools are Dentistry, Journalism, Medicine, Nursing, Pharmacy, Physical Education, and Social Work. The University offers a total of 164 degree programs.

Student Body Undergraduate enrollment is 51 percent women. The ethnic distribution of undergraduates is 91.4 percent white; 3.5 percent black, 2 percent Asian or Pacific Islander, .9 percent Hispanic, and .2 percent American Indian/Alaskan

native. There are 286 international undergraduate students. Approximately 60 percent of the students at WVU receive some form of financial aid. There are nineteen fraternities and thirteen sororities on campus.

Faculty Of the 1,617 total faculty members, 1,417 are full time; 85 percent of the full-time faculty members hold doctorates or the highest degree offered in their field. The student-faculty ratio is 17:1.

Key Facilities The University libraries include ten facilities containing 1.7 million volumes and 2 million microforms and microfilms. The University's Master Plan includes a large, state-of-the-art addition to the Charles Wise Library.

Mainframe computing resources are available to students via public computer sites maintained by WVU Computing Services. Student sites are located in the Evansdale Library and the Mountainlair (student union). Additional computer sites are located in almost all residence halls. Many academic departments also provide microcomputer and mainframe access in computer labs throughout the campus.

Athletics As a member of the NCAA, WVU competes on the Division I level. Men's intercollegiate athletics include baseball, basketball, cross-country, diving, football, riflery, soccer, swimming, tennis, track, and wrestling. Women's intercollegiate athletics include basketball, cross-country, gymnastics, riflery, soccer, swimming, tennis, track, and volleyball. WVU also offers intramural sports and sports clubs, including everything from frisbee to crew.

Study Abroad Various opportunities for study abroad are available through WVU. The Honors Program has a special relationship with the University of Leeds in England. Many students work through ISEP, although other programs are available as well.

Support Services All buildings on campus are handicapped-accessible, and special facilities can be found across the campus. Disability Services is a resource center that provides services for individuals with a wide range of disabilities, including those with mobility, sight, or hearing impairments, as well as those with hidden disabilities such as diabetes, cardiovascular problems, learning disorders, asthma, allergies, or epilepsy.

Job Opportunities Students can apply for work-study through the Financial Aid Office. Other work opportunities can be found through the student union or by contacting specific departments within the University, including the Student Services Center.

Tuition: $2262 for state residents, $7124 for nonresidents, per year (1996-97)

Room and Board: $4584

Contact: Director: Dr. William E. Collins, 248 Stalnaker Hall, P.O. Box 6635, Morgantown, West Virginia 26506-6635; Telephone: 304-293-2100; Fax: 304-293-7569; E-mail: honors@wvnvaxa.wvnet.edu; Web site: http://wvnvaxa.wvnet.edu/~HONORS

WICHITA STATE UNIVERSITY

4 Pu G M Tr

▼ Emory Lindquist Honors Program

The Emory Lindquist Honors Program serves students in all six degree-granting colleges of the University. In 1996, the program inaugurated a new honors curriculum in which students pursue an honors track through the University's general education requirements and complete a senior project in their major field. Additional nonrequired honors courses are also available.

The honors program provides academic advising services and faculty mentoring, actively supports students seeking national postgraduate scholarships and fellowships, and encourages participation in regional and national honors organizations.

The program maintains a popular student lounge and computer room and expects to open an honors residence facility within two years. The student-led Honors Society sponsors a continuing series of lectures, discussions, field trips, and social occasions.

In addition to recognition awarded by the University to all students achieving outstanding academic records, Honors Program graduates are eligible for additional recognition. Students who satisfy honors graduation requirements receive the notation Honors Program Graduate on their transcripts and are recognized at Commencement. The highest-ranked honors program graduates each year are named Emory Lindquist Scholars and are recognized at Commencement. With departmental approval, Honors Program participants completing a senior project earn departmental honors at graduation.

The program is 33 years old and currently enrolls 250 students.

Participation Requirements: The honors track in general education begins with a sequence of three freshman/sophomore seminars. Enrollment in these seminars is limited to 15 students. Seminar topics range widely, but are consistent with the general education program's focus on the traditional liberal arts and sciences. Honors seminars are also designed to develop a student's learning skills by emphasizing writing, oral communication, library research, and mathematics. After completing the seminar sequence, honors students are required to take two upper-division honors Issues and Perspectives courses. Finally, students (along with their department major adviser) design a two-course senior project, typically involving independent research, a senior thesis, and a community project.

Admission Process: Generally, freshmen are admitted to the program if their composite score on the American College Testing's ACT is 26 or higher or if their high school GPA is 3.5 or higher as certified by the University. Transfer and continuing students may enter the program if they have achieved a minimum GPA of 3.25 in university-level studies and if they satisfy the minimum GPA requirements. Those who are not members of the program may enroll in honors courses if they have the permission of the honors director. To be admitted to the program, a student must submit an honors program application and meet with a program representative.

Scholarship Availability: No scholarships are reserved for honors program members. However, many participants hold major University scholarships, most of which are awarded through the annual Distinguished Scholarship Invitational. Approximately $3.4 million is awarded annually.

The Campus Context: Wichita State University is composed of six colleges: Barton School of Business, College of Education, College of Engineering, College of Fine Arts, College of Health Professions, and Fairmount College of Liberal Arts and Sciences. There are 113 degree programs on campus. Among distinguished facilities are the National Institute of Aviation Research, Weidemann Hall (Markusson Organ), and the Outdoor Sculpture Collection.

Student Body Undergraduate enrollment is 14,250; 54 percent are women. Members of minority groups make up 15 percent of students, and there are 9 percent international students. Eighty percent of students commute to campus. There are ten fraternities and eight sororities.

Faculty Of the 461 full-time faculty members, 87 percent have terminal degrees. The student-faculty ratio is 18:1.

Key Facilities The library houses 1 million volumes. University Computing provides mainframe computer and PC labs with individual workstations.

Athletics Wichita State University is a Division I member of the NCAA, competing in eleven intercollegiate sports (seven men's, eight women's), including men's and women's basketball, baseball, bowling, cross-country, golf, rowing, softball, tennis, track, and volleyball. Both men's and women's bowling teams hold multiple national championships in the past decade; the baseball team is a frequent participant in the College World Series.

Study Abroad The University participates in many cooperative study-abroad programs.

Support Services Wichita State University has one of the most handicapped-accessible campuses in the region. A campus office provides signing services, on-campus transportation, and other enabling assistance to disabled students.

Job Opportunities Special work-study opportunities and many other on-campus jobs are available.

Tuition: $1845 for state residents, $7965 for nonresidents, per year (1997-98 est.)

Room and Board: $3639 minimum

Mandatory Fees: $644

Contact: Director: Almer J. Mandt, III, 1845 Fairmount, Wichita, Kansas 67260-0102; Telephone: 316-978-3375; Fax: 316-978-3234

WIDENER UNIVERSITY

| 4 Pr G S Sc Tr |

▼ Honors Program

Guided by the principle that serious students create opportunities to learn from one another as well as from faculty, Widener's honors classes are limited to a maximum of 15 students and are conducted as seminars. Faculty members encourage student involvement in setting the direction of courses. Participants in Widener's Honors Program also attend a minimum of eight outside-of-class events including performances, lectures, and art museum receptions on campus; cultural events in Philadelphia and Wilmington; presentations at nearby schools and cultural centers; and various social events. Students in the Honors Program find that they have joined a community of mutual support and friendship in which the educational experience is exceptional.

Each year in March, Widener celebrates Honors Week. The purpose of Honors week is threefold: to recognize the members of the eighteen academic honor societies, to foster the spirit of academic achievement, and to engage the campus community in a series of academic lectures and student presentations culminating in an Honors Convocation on Friday evening.

Honors courses are not necessarily more demanding than regular classes in terms of the amount of work required. Rather, they are structured to allow for spirited discussion and interaction. A sampling of the courses that have been offered include the Renaissance, the Psychology of Hypnosis, Impressionism, Race and Ethnicity in American Society, Communism in Theory and Practice, and Children at Risk. Students may also elect to purse an independent study honors course. The usual course distribution is a freshman honors seminar, freshman honors English, one junior honors colloquium, and at least two other honors courses. However, students are encouraged to take as many additional honors courses as they wish. Honors courses are taught by faculty members selected for their ability to stimulate and challenge inquisitive students.

All honors courses count toward the University's general education requirements, which must be met by all students for graduation. Thus, students enrolled in any of Widener's undergraduate majors may participate in the program. Now in its ninth year, the Honors Program in General Education currently has 100 student participants.

Participation Requirements: In order to continue in the Honors Program, each participant must maintain a minimum overall GPA of 3.0 and a minimum GPA of 3.0 in all honors courses taken. A Certificate of Honors in General Education is awarded at graduation to students who successfully complete at least five honors courses. Those who also complete a second junior honors colloquium or an honors independent study earn a Certificate of Advanced Honors in General Education.

Admission Process: High school students who apply to Widener are invited to participate in the Honors Program based on SAT scores and high school records. Traditionally, students who are in the top 10 percent of their graduating classes and have SAT I scores of 1200 or higher are invited to participate. Applicants selected for the Honors Program are given priority consideration for Widener's Presidential Scholarships. After the first and second semesters of the freshman year, other students displaying excellence in college work may apply for admission to the program.

The Campus Context: Widener University is composed of three campuses and eight schools and colleges, including the College of Arts and Sciences, School of Engineering, School of Management, School of Nursing, School of Law, School of Hotel and Restaurant Management, School of Human Service Professions, and University College. All full-time undergraduate programs are offered on the main campus in Chester, Pennsylvania.

Of the 124 degree programs leading to the associate, bachelor's, master's, or doctoral degree, fifty-one are baccalaureate programs for full-time students.

Student Body Within the total enrollment on all three campuses of 8,500 students, 2,300 are full-time undergraduates and, thus, eligible for consideration for the Honors Program. Of the 2,300 undergraduates, 48 percent are women and 61 percent are residential students. The diversified student body includes 11.2 percent African Americans, 3.4 percent Asian Americans, 77.7 percent Caucasians, 2.2 percent Latin Americans, and .5 percent Native Americans. The 3 percent international students come from forty-five other countries. Approximately 66 percent of the full-time undergraduates receive financial aid. Widener offers an active social life and a full range of cocurricular and extracurricular activities. In addition to eight social fraternities and four sororities, all nationally affiliated, there are eighty student clubs and organizations.

Faculty Widener's excellent faculty numbers 692, of whom 283 are full-time. Ninety-two percent hold the doctorate or terminal degree in their field. The student-faculty ratio is 12:1.

Key Facilities The University's library holds 228,000 volumes and numerous computer laboratories with hardware and software appropriate to the courses of study. Academic facilities supporting the courses include the television studio and graphics labs for the communication studies program; kitchens and front-desk labs for the hotel and restaurant management majors; and field-specific laboratories for electrical, mechanical, and chemical engineering for each of the science majors and for nursing, languages, and pre–physical therapy majors.

While neither art nor music are offered as majors, there are excellent facilities for those who wish to pursue these interests. The Widener Art Museum houses a permanent collection of eighteenth- and nineteenth-century American and European art and presents five exhibitions by contemporary artists and a juried student art show each year. The music studio offers lessons by professional musicians and both musicians and engineering students produce compact disks in the state-of-the-art recording studio. Honors students and students not in the program populate the Writing Center, the Academic Skills Center, and the Math Center, where faculty members and outstanding students offer one-on-one assistance with homework, term papers, and research.

Athletics With a brand-new stadium and full athletic complex, Widener also offers twenty-four NCAA Division III varsity sports for men and women, a cheerleading squad, ROTC rifle and pistol team, and a full range of intramurals.

Support Services Disabled students will find ready access to most buildings and a willingness to accommodate for special needs, coordinated by an on-campus specialist.

Job Opportunities Work-study opportunities and internships are also available.

Tuition: $13,560 minimum per year (1996-97)

Room and Board: $5910

Contact: Director: Dr. Elnora Rigik, One University Place, Chester, Pennsylvania 19013; Telephone: 610-499-4108; Fax: 610-876-9751; E-mail: honors.program@widener.edu

WILLIAM RAINEY HARPER COLLEGE

2 Pu G M Sc Tr

▼ Honors Program

The Harper College Honors Program offers a variety of general education courses to all students who have been accepted into the program. Students choose those courses that fit their academic and career needs. Honors courses differ from traditional courses in ways determined by the instructors in consultation with the institutional Honors Committee; in general, students are given greater responsibility for designing projects, taking on leadership roles in class discussions, and planning classroom activities. On occasion, interdisciplinary courses are offered. Small classes are the norm: they usually have between 8 and 15 students. Honors instructors are selected for their demonstrated excellence in teaching and for expertise in their chosen disciplines. Honors students are advised by the Honors Coordinator, honors faculty, and college counselors.

English 101, English 102, and Speech 101 (the communications core) are offered every semester during the regular academic year. A journalism independent study is also offered for those students interested in working on the honors newsletter, *The Challenger.* Other courses in business/social science, the humanities, and mathematics/science are also regularly offered. Summer honors courses are also available.

In addition, honors students at Harper automatically become members of the Honors Society, the social arm of the program. The Honors Society elects its own officers and meets weekly to discuss program plans and conduct wide-ranging, open discussions on topics of current interest. Cultural, social, and community service events are planned and carried forward by members of the society.

Honors students are encouraged to attend and actively participate in honors conferences and conventions.

The Harper College Honors Program has been active since 1989 and currently enrolls 200 students.

Participation Requirements: Honors students must successfully complete four honors courses and maintain a minimum 3.0 GPA in order to graduate from the Harper College Honors Program. Students who take three or fewer honors courses will have the honors course designation indicated on transcripts but will not qualify for honors graduation. The number and type of honors courses taken is at discretion of the student. Each Honors Program graduate receives a citation on the diploma as well as an Honors Program pin, which is awarded at the annual Honors Convocation.

Scholarship Availability: Students who qualify with a 3.5 or better GPA are encouraged to join Phi Theta Kappa. There are a number of scholarships available only to PTK members.

The Campus Context: William Rainey Harper College in Palatine, Illinois, is a public community college and part of the Illinois system of higher education. The College, established in 1965 by voter referendum, is governed by an elected Board of Trustees. Harper serves high school districts 211 (Palatine and Schaumburg Townships), 214 (Elk Grove and Wheeling Townships), and Barrington United School District 220. The Harper College district covers an area of about 200 square miles. Academic programs are administered primarily through seven divisions: Liberal Arts; Business and Social Science; Life Science and Human Services; Academic Enrichment and Language Studies; Wellness and Human Performance; Technology, Mathematics, and Physical Science; and Student Development. Fifty-five degree programs are offered on campus.

Student Body There are 15,000 undergraduates enrolled (7,600 full-time equivalent); 58 percent are women. The ethnic distribution is 10.3 percent Asian, .3 percent Native American, 3 percent African American, 6.7 percent Hispanic, and 74 percent white; there are 109 international students. About 13–15 percent of students receive financial aid. All students commute to campus.

Faculty Of the 821 faculty members, 221 are full-time. The student-faculty ratio is 18:1.

Key Facilities The library houses more than 100,000 books, 126,000 media items, and 850 magazine titles. There are more than fifty computer labs on campus with more than 850 computers.

Athletics Harper offers varsity baseball, basketball, football, golf, soccer, softball, tennis, track and field, and wrestling, plus a variety of intramural athletic programs. Honors students are counseled and encouraged to participate in competitive sports.

Study Abroad Harper's International Program regularly offers study-abroad opportunities to places such as Canterbury, England; Salzburg, Austria; the Netherlands; Costa Rica; and Mexico. Students who study abroad may have one of the four courses required for Honors Program graduation waived.

Support Services Buildings on campus are disabled-accessible. In addition, Harper offers instructional support services, learning disability testing, tutoring services, testing accommodation, reader and scribe services, TTY (telephones for the deaf), and academic advising. A recent Honors Program graduate is dyslexic; the program welcomes students who face such challenges.

Job Opportunities Students are offered a range of work-study opportunities on campus. The Honors Program student aide is a work-study participant.

Tuition: $1260 for area residents, $5686 for state residents, $6547 for nonresidents, per year (1996-97)

Mandatory Fees: $50

Contact: Coordinator: Dr. Trygve Thoreson, Liberal Arts Division, Palatine, Illinois 60067; Telephone: 847-925-6489; Fax: 847-925-6039; E-mail: tthoreso@harper.cc.il.us

---

WRIGHT STATE UNIVERSITY

 4 Pu G M Sc Tr

▼ University Honors Program

The Wright State University Honors Program was created in 1972 to meet the needs of the University's brightest, most ambitious students. It is open to students of all majors and provides a varied curriculum consisting of honors sections of general education courses; a service-learning sequence; interdisciplinary core courses in the humanities, social sciences, and natural sciences; and broadly interdisciplinary topical senior seminars. Departments are also free to propose honors sections of regular courses both at the introductory and advanced level. First-year students are able to participate in learning communities of linked courses in which the same 20 students enroll. Most majors offer students the opportunity for intense honors work in the major during the senior year. Students may choose from three honors designations, which are noted on the transcript and in the Commencement program: University Honors Scholar, General Studies Honors, and Departmental Honors.

The primary mission of the Honors Program is to produce a body of graduates who are well educated, socially conscious, and capable of assuming leadership roles in society. The Honors Program is responsible for providing

undergraduates with all the tools and with every opportunity to create a stimulating, well-rounded, solidly grounded, and socially responsible education. The program currently has approximately 800 alumni, disproportionately distributed in the medical, legal, and academic professions, where many of them are beginning to move into leadership roles. Alumni surveys indicate that the program is fulfilling its mission.

The Honors Program encourages diversity in its student body, its faculty, and course content and extracurricular activities. Transfer students and nontraditional students are particularly welcome additions to the student mix. Students who complete honors work at another NCHC institution receive honors credit at Wright State for those courses.

Honors classes are small, with either 15 or 20 students. Faculty members are encouraged to try innovative, student-centered teaching styles. Honors classes usually feature discussion, collaboration, creative projects, or extensive research papers. Most honors courses are writing intensive. Ongoing assessment indicates that students are happy with their honors courses, often citing them as the only undergraduate courses that challenged them to think analytically. To recognize and encourage outstanding teaching, the students select a faculty member as Honors Teacher of the Year.

About 10 percent (175 members) of each incoming class enter the University as honors students. The overall number of active participants averages about 600. Honors students may elect to live in the Honors House, Maple Hall.

Participation Requirements: To remain active, students must maintain a minimum 3.0 GPA and make progress toward graduation with honors. Approximately 75 students complete one of the honors degree options each year. To meet their requirements, students choose from sixty to seventy courses each year. Students who complete University Honors take a minimum of eight honors courses plus a departmental program. General Studies Honors requires eight courses and a minimum cumulative GPA of 3.4. Many departmental programs also require students to complete at least one University Honors seminar.

Admission Process: Students are admitted to the program based on high school or college performance.

Scholarship Availability: Honors students are supported by a comprehensive scholarship program. Fifteen to 20 incoming students receive substantial Honors Scholarships that commit them to four years of participation in the Honors Program. Continuing students compete for awards of varying amounts. Several modest awards are usually offered each quarter. Upper-division honors students are recognized with Distinguished Senior Awards, Research Grants, and the Heritage and Salsburg Scholarships. A small fund exists that helps students with limited travel to conferences.

The Campus Context: Wright State is a comprehensive metropolitan university located 12 miles northeast of Dayton, Ohio. The 557-acre main campus includes twenty major buildings and a 200-acre biological preserve.

Student Body Approximately 16,000 students pursue a variety of degrees: more than 100 undergraduate majors and forty graduate or professional programs, including the M.D., Psy. D., Ph.D., and Ed.S. Most students are Ohio residents, with a fairly small international component (1.7 percent). Eleven percent of students are classified as members of minority groups (mostly African American), and 55 percent are women. Fraternity and sorority life is growing, but still represents a relatively small presence on campus. While Wright State is primarily a commuter school, approximately 2,000 students live on campus.

Faculty On the main campus, excluding the medical school, Wright State has a total of 520 full-time faculty members. At the assistant professor rank and above, 89 percent hold earned doctorates in their field.

Key Facilities The Paul Lawrence Dunbar houses more than 520,000 volumes, the Fordham Health Sciences Library, and a music library. Through OhioLINK, students may search all academic libraries in the state. All students are eligible to receive an account for access to a variety of computer systems, thus enabling access to Internet resources. The campus is in the process of becoming networked.

Athletics Playing in NCAA Division I athletics, Wright State emphasizes women's and men's basketball and baseball and women's volleyball and fields competitive teams in other sports. Wright State competes in the Midwestern Collegiate Conference.

Study Abroad Students may choose from a variety of study-abroad opportunities. No programs currently require such an experience. Approximately 35 students per year participate.

Support Services Wright State is especially noted for its services to students with disabilities.

Tuition: $3600 for state residents, $7200 for nonresidents, per year (1996-97)

Room and Board: $4005

Contact: Director: Dr. Anna Bellisari, 179 Millett Hall, Dayton, Ohio 45435; Telephone: 513-873-2660; E-mail: honors@desire.wright.edu

---

YOUNGSTOWN STATE UNIVERSITY

4 Pu G M Sc Tr

▼ University Scholars and Honors Programs

The Honors Degree Program is designed to create a continuing community of intellectual excellence. Exceptional students brought together from diverse disciplines and challenged with extraordinary courses and learning experiences outside the classroom can find in the program opportunities to develop their full cultural and intellectual potential, with their unique academic achievements being recognized with an honors degree. Intended to foster interdisciplinary interaction, self-expression, experimentation, leadership, and academic excellence, the Honors Degree Program serves as a tangible emblem of Youngstown State University's commitment to education, teaching innovation, and cultural enrichment.

The 23-year-old program currently enrolls 360 students.

Participation Requirements: To graduate from the Honors Program, students must have a minimum 3.4 GPA overall and have completed 36 credit hours of honors courses, with 12 hours outside their major, three courses related by department, two courses at the 700-800 level as honors or nonhonors, and a senior thesis. Students wear an honors medal at Commencement, and, upon graduation, students are distinguished by a diploma recognizing their honors degree.

Admission Process: First-quarter students either in the top 15 percent of their high school graduating class or with a minimum ACT score of 26 (or minimum combined SAT I score of 1140) as well as other interested students may apply. University Scholars who have an ACT score of at least 28 or an SAT I score of at least 1260 are automatically enrolled in the program. Students who have completed at least 12 hours with a minimum GPA of 3.4 are also encouraged to join the Honors Degree Program.

Scholarship Availability: The University Scholarship is YSU's most prestigious scholarship. These are awarded to first-year students who have graduated from high school in the same year that they will enroll at YSU as full-time students. Candidates must have, as minimum criteria for award consideration, a score of 28 or better on the ACT or 1220 or better on the SAT I and be recognized as National Merit or Achievement Semifinalist or rank in the upper 15 percent of high school class pursuing a college-preparatory curriculum. The value of the scholarship (estimated at $8000) includes all fees and tuition for up to 58 hours per year (20 quarter hours for two quarters and 18 quarter hours for one quarter), plus campus room and board fees and a $360 academic-year book allowance. If renewed for four years of study, the estimated value of the scholarship is $34,000.

Forty new University scholarships (full cost) are awarded annually for a total of 160.

The Campus Context: Youngstown State University had its beginning in 1908 as the School of Law of the Youngstown Association School. It underwent many changes until 1967, when it joined the Ohio system of higher education and became known as Youngstown State University. The current colleges that are part of the Youngstown State include College of Arts and Science; the Warren P. Williamson, Jr. College of Business Administration; the College of Education; the College of Engineering and Technology; the College of Fine and Performing Arts; and the College of Health and Human Services. There are eighty-one degree programs on campus, some with more than one track or concentration.

Among distinguished facilities are the McDonough Museum, Veterans Memorial, and Butler Institute of American Art.

Student Body Undergraduate enrollment is 12,102; 5,702 are men and 6,400 are women. Approximately 9,800 students receive financial aid. There are five sororities and eight fraternities.

Faculty Of the 742 faculty members, 392 are full-time. Seventy-seven percent of faculty members hold terminal degrees. The student-faculty ratio is 18.6:1.

Key Facilities The library contains 629,590 volumes, more than 1 million microforms, and 201,996 government documents. The library is part of the Online Computer Library Center, which provides reference and interlibrary loan services. It is also a member of OhioLINK, a statewide library and information network linking university, college, and community college libraries as well as the State Library of Ohio.

Computer labs are available in several buildings on campus and contain IBM and Macintosh computers. The personal computers are located in Meshel Hall, and the honors residence halls are also connected to the campus Ethernet network. Network personal computers allow access to local software as well as to other facilities on campus such as Maag Library and Internet sites worldwide. The honors residence hall is also equipped to allow students to hook up their computers in their rooms to the network with the purchase of an Ethernet card.

Athletics Participation in athletics is open to any student who qualifies under the YSU, NCAA, and conference eligibility regulations. Men's teams compete in intercollegiate baseball, basketball, cross-country, football, golf, tennis, and track and field. Women's intercollegiate teams compete in basketball, cross-country, softball, soccer, tennis, track and field, and volleyball.

Study Abroad Various departments offer study-abroad opportunities for credit. Students interested in international study consult with their major departments and the study-abroad adviser.

Support Services Facilities for disabled students include a lounge, adapted rooms in housing, Archenstone reading machine in the library, a computer for voice input and output at end of year, and a campus escort service.

Job Opportunities There are many opportunities for students to work on campus, including positions in parking services, the library, or computer labs and as resident assistants, peer assistants, research assistants, and office assistants.

Tuition: $2718 for state residents, $4338 for nonresidents within a 100-mile radius, $6354 for nonresidents outside a 100 mile-radius, minimum per year (1996-97)

Room and Board: $4200

Mandatory Fees: $648

Contact: Director: Dr. Nathan P. Ritchey, One University Plaza, Youngstown, Ohio 44555; Telephone: 330-742-2772; Fax: 330-742-4743; E-mail: nate@math.ysu.edu, alcossen@cc.ysu.edu; Web site: http://www.ysu.edu/honors/index.htm

GEOGRAPHIC INDEX

▲

Notes

Notes

Note

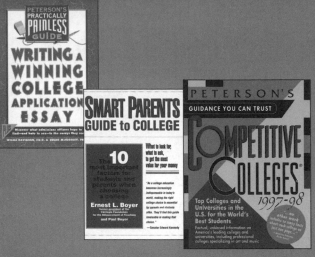
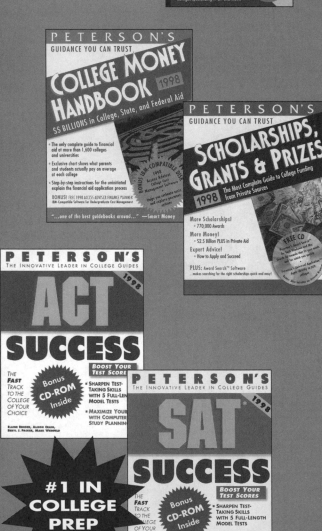